1705

NELSON'S

New Illustrated Bible Manners & Customs

NELSON'S
New Illustrated
Bible Manners
& Customs

How the People of the Bible Really Lived

Howard F. Vos

THOMAS NELSON PUBLISHERS
Nashville

Published in Nashville, Tennessee, by Thomas Nelson, Inc.

Book text designed by BookSetters, White House, Tennessee

Library of Congress Cataloging-in-Publication Data

Vos, Howard Frederic, 1925–
    Nelson's new illustrated Bible manners & customs : how the people of the Bible really lived / Howard F. Vos.
      p.   cm.
    Includes bibliographical references and indexes.
    ISBN 0-7852-1194-2
    1. Bible —History of biblical events. 2. Bible—Social scientific criticism. I. Title.
    BS635.2.V67   1999
    220.9'5—dc21   99-12227
                                                        CIP

Printed in the United States of America

    4 5 6 7 — 04 03 02 01

CONTENTS

Color Insert B

Discovering How Bible Peoples Really Lived

Stories of Bible people are part of the heritage of most Americans. We have heard stories of Joseph and his "Technicolor Dreamcoat" and his rule over Egypt during a great famine. Of Moses who grew up in Pharaoh's court and led his people out of Egypt in the great Exodus. Of David the shepherd boy who became a king and built an empire. Of Solomon and his glorious reign. Of Esther who saved her people from destruction in the days of King Xerxes of Persia. Of Jesus who came to show the world a new and better way to relate to God. Of the apostle Paul who charged across the Roman world with a message of good news, but endured beatings, stoning, and a shipwreck along the way. And stories of Noah and Daniel and more.

We have heard of all this even if we didn't grow up in Sunday school or never darkened the door of a church or a synagogue. Films, videos, musicals, novels, dramas, and art images have told us the stories—either in fictionalized or faithful accounts.

And now we wonder how much of these stories may be true or plausible. Or what life was like in Bible times. Or how Bible people really lived. How did they dress? What did they eat? What kinds of houses did they live in? How did they make a living? What was their family life like? Can we discover anything about their government? Or their religion? These and many other questions may fill our minds.

In an effort to answer these questions, numerous books on Bible customs have been written. But they have tended to deal with life in Old or New Testament times in a general way, without noting differences in time and place. And they often have proceeded on the assumption that the customs of a rural Egypt, Palestine, Jordan, or Iraq in modern times will provide clues to what life was like in Bible times. The result has been a very limited idea of ancient life and sometimes a very wrong idea of what actually happened.

We have to come to grips with the fact that life differed greatly in the various Bible lands—in Mesopotamia, Palestine, Egypt, Phoenicia, Syria, Iran, Cyprus, Asia Minor, Greece, Malta, and Italy. And we need to recognize that life changed considerably with the passage of time. So it seemed to me that the only way to deal adequately and accurately with the whole subject of Bible customs was to slice the biblical narrative into twenty segments and look at the customs during each time period and in each of the Bible lands involved.

The Goal of This Book

This book, then, will tell the story of God's people from Abraham (about 2000 B.C.) to the end of the New Testament (about A.D. 100) in twenty historical segments. But it is not a history book. There is a historical thread, but the emphasis is on the lives and customs of the people: their environment (the places they lived), government, religion, warfare, houses and furniture, diet and foodstuffs (agriculture), clothing, family relationships and daily life (including education), their work, travel and commerce, and more. These topics appear in the same order in each of the chapters. That makes it easy to trace a specific topic through the whole sweep of Bible times.

Too often accounts of the past have centered on the rulers, on the powerful and the wealthy. Our effort here is to describe what it was like for the various peoples of the Bible to live all of life. In short, the goal is to make the Bible come alive again as we watch individuals, great and small, meet their individual and corporate challenges.

How We Know About the Lives of the Biblical Peoples

Explorers and archaeologists have been poking around in the dust heaps of the Bible lands for some 200 years. These mounds we now usually call by their Arabic names—tells. And in time investigators discovered that they encased "layer cake" civilizations. That is, they revealed layers of occupation, cities built one on top of another. But more of that later.

The early explorers were treasure hunters who looked for museum pieces and art objects to fill private and museum collections. As they burrowed into the tells, often wreaking terrible destruction, they did make some wonderful discoveries. For example, they found the Black Obelisk of Shalmaneser III (ruler of Assyria 859–825 B.C.). This black limestone pillar has pictures around its four sides with descriptive captions. One of them shows King Jehu of Israel (841–814) paying tribute to Shalmaneser. Jehu's claim to fame was that he put an end to the wicked reign of Ahab and Jezebel.

Then the Monolith Inscription of Shalmaneser tells of that Assyrian king's fight with a coalition of kings which included Ahab of Israel, who furnished 10,000 men and 2,000 chariots for the contest.

Another important discovery was the Cyrus Cylinder found at Babylon. The

The Black Obelisk of Shalmaneser
In the second register King Jehu bows before Shalmaneser and brings tribute.
(Photo by Gustav Jeeninga)

inscription on this clay cylinder tells us that King Cyrus of Persia permitted various peoples to go back to their homes and rebuild their temples after he took Babylon in the days of Belshazzar (Daniel 5). Here we have the Persian version of the Hebrew record of their return from captivity (Ezra 1).

Thousands of other objects came to light in this way—some with a direct biblical connection and others providing information about life in Bible times. But many of these had a limited value because they were torn out of the context in which they belonged. Often we haven't known what they were used for or when they should be dated.

Gradually archaeology has become a science. Now we strip away the soil of the tells layer by layer or stratum by stratum in what is called stratigraphic excavation. As the name implies (literally meaning writing or recording of the strata or layers), we seek to record carefully every aspect of our finds. The work is meticulous, involving larger or smaller picks and hoes, brushes of various kinds, baskets, and wheelbarrows. Underwater excavation follows procedures just as exacting as those

The Cyrus Cylinder, in which King Cyrus gives the order permitting captive peoples to return home
(British Museum)

used on land. No longer is it a hunt for buried treasure or specialized antiques.

Not only is archaeology a science in its own right today, but it also gets help from other sciences, and so it is proper to call it a composite science. It draws on the expertise of anthropologists, sociologists, geologists, zoologists, engineers, linguists, climatologists, computer programmers, statisticians. The list goes on. Emerging technologies also help archaeologists do their work: ground-penetrating radar, infrared aerial photography, sonar, underwater exploration techniques, and computer reconstruction of everything from tiny figurines to entire cities.

Of course the material remains of the world of the Bible would be of only limited value to us if we couldn't read the inscriptions accompanying them or the literature those peoples produced. Fortunately, ancient Egyptian, Persian, Assyro-Babylonian, Hittite, and other languages have been deciphered. And whole libraries have been found, such as the Dead Sea Scrolls, the Assyrian library of Ashurbanipal (668–627 B.C.), Hittite palace archives, and caches of records in private homes. It is now possible to get a Ph.D. in Egyptian, Hittite, Assyro-Babylonian (Akkadian), and most other ancient Near Eastern languages.

Nor would all this archaeological work be very useful if there were no way of dating it effectively. Fairly exact chronologies now exist for ancient Egypt, Mesopotamia, Palestine, Turkey, Greece, Rome, and other Mediterranean lands.

In this flurry of exploration and excavation, we have uncovered a wealth of knowledge from the ruins of cities throughout the Middle East: Jericho, Jerusalem, Babylon, Corinth, Ephesus, Athens, Caesarea, Nineveh, Ur, Pergamum, Sardis, among dozens of others.

Archaeologists have made numerous exciting discoveries at some of these biblical cities. They have found the walls that Nehemiah built at Jerusalem (Nehemiah 6), the temple of Diana at Ephesus (Acts 19), an inscription mentioning Pontius Pilate in the theater at Caesarea, the throne room of Nebuchadnezzar at Babylon, remains of the synagogue of Jesus' day at Capernaum, the judgment seat or administrative podium at Corinth where Paul stood before the Roman governor Gallio (Acts 18:12–16), and the palace of the Assyrian king

Tools used for excavation—brushes, trowels, picks, oversized hoe, rubber buckets, and wheelbarrow

Walls that Nehemiah built in Jerusalem

Sennacherib (704–681 B.C.). On a couple of walls the king pictured his destruction of Lachish just prior to the attack on Jerusalem in 701 B.C. (see Isaiah 36—37). Then there is the ongoing excavation of Pompeii, which shows what life was like in a Roman town of New Testament times.

And the day of diminishing returns has not yet set in. In 1993 a stone engraved with the words "The House of David" and "King of Israel" was excavated in northern Israel. Dating to the days of David some 3,000 years ago, this find helps to confirm the existence of this bigger-than-life Hebrew hero.

Important new discoveries connect with Jesus' ministry too. Excavations at Sepphoris, the Roman capital of Galilee during part of Jesus' lifetime, tell us of a bustling pagan city of some 30,000, located only an hour by foot from Nazareth. Possibly Jesus' "city set on a hill" (Matthew 5:14), it shows that Jesus was not just a small town boy who grew up in a provincial Jewish context.

Then there is the discovery of a fishing boat under the waters of the Sea of Galilee (1986). Dating to New Testament times, it has now been raised, reconditioned, and put on display for tourists. About 26 feet long, it could have been sailed or rowed by a crew consisting of four oarsmen and a helmsman. We can imagine some of Jesus' disciples caught in a storm while rowing across the sea in a boat like this (Mark 6:48).

In 1990 a limestone burial box was found in a previously unknown burial cave beneath Jerusalem. Ornately sculpted, it was engraved with the name of Caiaphas, the Jewish high priest who tried Jesus. With

it were found eleven other burial boxes. This is now commonly believed to be the family tomb of *the* Caiaphas.

As a result of all this research and discovery, books, journal articles, and monographs on every conceivable aspect of life in the lands of the Bible appear in increasing and almost bewildering volume. I have sought to use this incredible richness of information, plus endless study of material remains in the museums of the Middle East, Europe, and America and on-the-spot observations at almost all the biblical sites, to paint in these pages a picture of life as the people of Bible times lived it.

A first-century bakery at Pompeii, showing an oven (left) and mills for grinding wheat into flour (right)

Thousands of books, magazine articles, and encyclopedia articles have been used in writing this book. Brief, fairly specialized bibliographies appear at the end of each chapter. Then at the end of the book appear lists of general works (encyclopedias, atlases, journals) and books that relate to several of the chapters of the book. Extended indexes also will point the reader to other subjects of interest.

Model of a first century fishing boat found in the Sea of Galilee (Photo by Frederick C. Veit)

Chapter 2

LIFE IN ABRAHAM'S HOMETOWN

UR OF MESOPOTAMIA

(Genesis 11—12)

"The God of glory appeared to our father Abraham when he was in Mesopotamia, before he dwelt in Haran [while in Ur, Genesis 11:31], and said to him, 'Get out of your country and from your relatives, and come to a land that I will show you.'" (Acts 7:2–3 NKJV)

The apostle Paul mentions him in the New Testament as an exemplary man of faith, but how much do you really know about Abraham? Almost everyone in Western civilization and the Middle East knows *something* about him. He is revered as the ancestor of the Jews and Arabs alike. His traditional tomb at Hebron in Palestine is a flash point of controversy between the two peoples. Sometimes on the evening news, scenes of demonstrations there erupt before our eyes. For their part, Christians look upon Abraham as the ancestor of Jesus Christ and as the father of the faithful. So he is held in high esteem by followers of all three great monotheistic religions. Throughout much of our classical and even popular literature, art, and music we find references to him.

Yet most people know only sketchy details about him. If we are to gain an understanding of this remarkable and pivotal Old Testament figure, we must dig rather deeply into his background, his culture, and his actions. What shaped this man before he responded to God's call, before he risked all to travel to an unknown country? At least a partial answer comes to us from an analysis of the first 75 years of his life.

The drama of the people descended from Abraham began in a remarkable period of history. As we try to understand that history we shall begin to appreciate the special way God called Abraham and led him from Ur to start a new life of following God by faith (Genesis 11:31; 12; Acts 7:2–3).

Abraham embarked on a truly unusual move when he left Ur of the Chaldees for a territory known variously as Canaan, Palestine and, later on, as Israel. Consider that God commanded it in a personal appearance to Abraham in a pagan society where people worshiped many gods. Then, too, God didn't tell Abraham where He was sending him or what he should do when he got there. We make adequate and sometimes elaborate preparations when we move. We have chosen a town, bought or rented a house, landed a job, and arranged for a moving van. Not Abraham—he had no idea where God would take him when he pulled up stakes and left Ur.

Further, this move was important because eventually Abraham and his descendants (the Israelites) would be given the land where he would settle—the land of Canaan (Genesis 13:14–17).

Finally, for his faithfulness in making this move Abraham was to become the father of a great nation—the Jewish people (Genesis 12:2–3). And through him, in God's time, all the peoples of the earth would be blessed (Genesis 12:3b). The blessing ultimately would come through his descendant Jesus Christ. We should also not forget that in a moment of weakness Abraham became the ancestor of the Arabs through his slave girl Hagar. All this was connected with the culture he came from before the great move!

Ancient Sumerian Ur: Important and Prosperous

So what is the significance of the move, you ask. For us today, Ur is not an important place, nor is it located in one of the more progressive regions on earth. Conditions were quite different then, however. Instead of being situated in a cultural and political backwater, Ur was at the forefront of developments. If we have our chronology straight (see later discussion) Ur controlled a powerful empire and was perhaps the greatest city-state in the world at the time. The only possible exception was the Harappan culture of the Indus Valley, to be seen at such cities as Harappa and Mohenjodaro. Those cities were on the wane by 2000 B.C., however, and seem never to have been as advanced as the Mesopotamian cities.

Not only was Ur an important and prosperous place in Abraham's day, but it also stood in the general area where civilization began. The usual view is that civilization involves such developments as writing, the wheel—for pottery making and transportation—monumental architecture, the decorative arts, and metallurgy. All of these things appeared first in southern Mesopotamia, and the people who get credit for those many achievements were the Sumerians, who lived at the northern end of the Persian Gulf and who controlled Ur in Abraham's day.

The earliest monumental architecture (three large temples) was found at Obeid (4 miles northwest of Ur) dating from about 4000 B.C. At Uruk (biblical Erech,

Genesis 10:10), another 35 miles up the Euphrates from Obeid, civilization really began. Pottery was produced on a spinning potter's wheel and four-wheeled chariots with solid wheels were built by 3500 B.C. Soon after 3500 the inhabitants were writing on clay tablets in crude pictograms and by 3000 were using wedge-shaped cuneiform. We might well imagine Abraham learning to write on a clay tablet.

At Uruk, too, archaeologists uncovered monumental architecture in the form of large temples, the first ziggurat or stage-tower, and city walls. Fairly sophisticated artistic production appeared in the decoration of the temples and the cylinder seals of the period. Cylinder seals were small stone cylinders one to three inches long and incised with artwork. These could be rolled across wet clay and serve as a signet or evidence of ownership. An irrigation system was also developed in the Uruk period. If Ur was the leading city of the world in Abraham's day, and if it was located in an area that stood at the forefront of cultural advancement, Abraham's decision to leave Ur and follow God's call takes on new significance.

The Land of Mesopotamia

Mesopotamia is roughly 600 miles long (northwest to southeast) and 300 miles wide at its greatest extent in the north and some 100–150 miles wide in the south. To give some idea of distances, Ur is about 150 miles north of the head of the Persian Gulf and 220 miles south of modern Baghdad.

Northern Mesopotamia was known generally in ancient times as Assyria and southern Mesopotamia as Babylonia. Babylonia was subdivided into Sumer (in the south next to the Persian Gulf) and Akkad (in the north where the two rivers come closest together). In Abraham's day, rulers of Ur called themselves kings of Sumer and Akkad.

CUNEIFORM WRITING PREDATES ABRAHAM

Cuneiform [kyu NAY uh form] is a script in which numerous ancient languages were written. The term simply means "wedge-shaped." The Sumerians developed it by about 3000 B.C., gradually evolving it from pictographs. They usually wrote it on wet clay tablets with a stylus that had a triangular end and sharp edges. Thus it was possible to create combinations of wedges and tailings (as one used the end or the edge of the stylus) to represent the many syllables of ancient Mesopotamian or other Near Eastern languages. The tablets were then either sundried or baked. Cuneiform also could be chiseled in stone when public monuments or inscriptions were erected.

The Persian cuneiform was deciphered first, in the 1830s and 1840s, as a result of the work of Georg Grotefend, Edward Hincks, and Henry Rawlinson especially. Then other cuneiform languages were deciphered—Assyro-Babylonian, Elamite, Sumerian, and Hittite, among others. Major work on Assyrian, Sumerian, and Hittite dictionaries is now in progress, with the Assyrian project at the University of Chicago largely finished.

Cuneiform as it was written during the Ur III period

Languages in cuneiform are syllabic in form, so the student had to learn hundreds of signs (200 in Hammurabi's day, c. 1792-1750 B.C.) standing for individual syllables, instead of the 22 letters of the Hebrew alphabet. Modern Old Testament students who struggle with their studies in Hebrew can be very glad that the Old Testament was written in alphabetic Hebrew instead of a syllabic language of the ancient Near East!

Ancient cuneiform characters were impressed on soft clay tablets with a pointed stylus. These tablets were then generally baked to form a piece of writing that was virtually indestructible. Sometimes tablets were merely sundried.

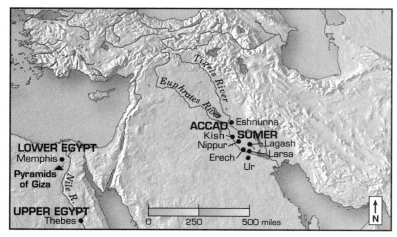

Ancient Near East

The Land

Where Abraham Lived

To get some idea of what Abraham's life was like, it is useful to also look first at the region where he lived. The area is called *Mesopotamia*, which means "land between the rivers." Apparently Jewish scholars of Alexandria, Egypt, coined the term when they translated the Old Testament into Greek during the third century B.C. (see Genesis 24:10). The rivers between which this land lies are the Tigris on the east and the Euphrates on the west—both referred to often in the Bible, especially prophetic writing. Both rivers originate only a few miles apart in the mountains of Armenia and flow closest together (c. 25 miles) in the area of modern Baghdad. Finally they join about a hundred miles north of the Persian Gulf and flow as a single stream into the Gulf. These rivers overflowed every spring while the crops were standing on the soil, requiring levees (dikes)to protect the farmland.

Mesopotamia today has little rainfall, and evidently the situation has not changed much since ancient times. The region south of Baghdad receives less than ten inches per year, sometimes as little as two inches. In the hills of Assyria the average is about twenty inches per year. Because there is so little rainfall in the south, irrigation was necessary and vast networks of irrigation canals were con-

structed. These canals required a lot of people to construct and maintain them, as well as to man the levees to protect against the annual floods. These geographical factors encouraged an urban way of life, in southern Mesopotamia at least. And urban life required governmental organization and preparation for defense and led to a division of labor and social stratification. Abraham's family may well have been active in the business and political community of that era.

The lower half of Mesopotamia, in which Ur was located, was alluvial soil, built up over the millennia by deposits from the Tigris and Euphrates—quite different from the region to which God would take Abraham. There was no stone. There were no great timbered hillsides, as in Canaan, or mineral resources. The people who lived there learned to make everything from the soil they irrigated. They grew their food on the soil and exchanged the surplus for metals, timber, and other things they could not produce. They made their clothing primarily from wool, but also from flax (linen). Though the temperature in southern Mesopotamia is excessive during the summer (sometimes over 120 in Babylon in August), wool with a coarse weave does "breathe."

They built their homes, temples, and public buildings from clay brick (baked and sundried) and fashioned their dishes from clay. When they developed their writing, they made clay tablets on which they wrote wedge-shaped characters (cuneiform) with a small wood stylus. It is not inconceivable that Abraham knew how to write in cuneiform before he left Ur.

(For more on this topic, go to p. 29.)

Government

Ur and Her Empire

As I understand the chronology, Ur was in control of an empire in the days of

Population in the Region

How many lived in this region has produced educated guesses that are quite striking. By 2000 B.C., there were fifteen to twenty cities in Sumer, with most of them having a population of perhaps 10,000–20,000. Uruk may have had 50,000 and Ur as many as 200,000. In the whole area of Sumer—cities and rural dependencies—there were probably more than half a million people.

Abraham and was enjoying one of the most brilliant periods in the history of Mesopotamia. The great Ur-Nammu, governor of Ur, had wrenched power from the hands of his overlord Utuhegal of Uruk (biblical Erech) and quickly founded the powerful and prosperous Third Dynasty of Ur. (The First Dynasty had dated about 2500 B.C. and the Second about 2300.) And this golden age lasted a little over a century.

If we accept 2166 B.C. as the date of Abraham's birth at Ur (see sidebar, "Date of Abraham"), we wonder how this squares with the political chronology of the Ur III period. The period began about 2112 according to the French scholar Georges Roux,[1] 2135 according to Carl Roebuck of Northwestern University,[2] or 2200 according to McGuire Gibson of the University of Chicago.[3]

We are not sure how old Abraham was chronologically when he left Ur for Haran; but he could have left during the Third Dynasty of Ur, at the height of her glory, whether we begin the period with the chronology of Roux, Roebuck, Gibson, or a slightly different date of another scholar. The position I am taking in this chapter is that Abraham knew Ur during her golden age and that all the following discussion about life in the city furnishes a context for the patriarch's early life. There was no earthly reason why he should have wanted to leave Ur!

The empire Ur-Nammu carved out probably roughly approximated the area of modern Iraq. At its heart was the territory of Sumer (north of the Persian Gulf) and Akkad (area where the Tigris and Euphrates come close together). In this whole area, the former city-states (e.g., Uruk, Larsa, Kish, Eridu) were now treated as provinces. And in place of their kings, the king of Ur appointed administrators to keep order, administer justice, enforce laws, build public works, and collect taxes. Then there were the conquered territories, also divided into provinces and ruled by civilian or military governors. These included Susa and most of northern Mesopotamia. Finally, there were outlying regions, independent states, such as Elam, that were tied to Ur by marriage and other kinds of alliances. Later Abraham was to organize such alliances in Canaan for security purposes.

The provinces directly under the control of Ur were supervised by means of a network of roads with stations a day's walk apart, where officials accompanied by soldiers received supplies. Royal messengers and inspectors periodically circulated at the command of the king to make sure that local administrations worked smoothly. At the head of the whole administrative pyramid stood the king as absolute ruler, worshiped as a god during this golden age. Previously the king had commonly been viewed as merely a representative of the gods.

During the Ur III period the economic machine seemed to work smoothly. Though in earlier times the temples controlled

Tigris at Baghdad with a modern Iraqi in a boat made of reeds and covered with pitch.

much of the land, now the palace owned a much larger share. The state also operated huge factories employing hundreds or even thousands of workers producing such commodities as leather, textiles, flour, bread, or beer. The state also seems to have controlled the international trade.[4] The majority of the so-called merchants were in fact civil servants. The records tell us in some detail about the temple and palace sectors of the economy, but we do not know as much about the private sector. There were private merchants and businessmen involved in the domestic economy, and metalwork seems to have been in the hands of private artisans.

Imagine Abraham and his extended family actively engaged in agriculture and commerce during this period. He had clearly accumulated significant economic resources, large enough to finance moving parts of his extended family from Ur to Haran.

(For more on this topic, go to p. 31.)

Religion

"And Joshua said to all the people, 'Thus says the LORD God of Israel: "Your fathers, including Terah, the father of Abraham and the father of Nahor, dwelt on the other side of the River in old times; and they served other gods."'"

(Joshua 24:2 NKJV)

We've set Abraham in his geographic, political and economic environment up to now. But what was the religious worship in his home like? Where was he spiritually when God spoke to him? Joshua gives us a clue when he addressed the Israelites at the end of his life, observing that their ancestors, notably Terah, had served "other gods" "beyond the Euphrates" (Joshua 24:2 RSV and NRSV).

What that means may be illustrated by the sacred enclosure of the moon god Nanna, located in the northwestern part of Ur. This enclosure measured about 400 yards long and 200 yards wide. Inside this enclosure rose the great brick ziggurat or stage-tower of Nanna, measuring about 200 feet in length, 150 feet in width, and 70 feet in height. Each of the three stages of the tower was smaller than the one below, and on the topmost level stood the temple of the god. Gardens beautified the terraces.

The ziggurat at Ur was only one of several that Ur-Nammu built in the cities of Sumer. Whether he was particularly devout, or a good politician who sought to placate the priesthood for royal infringement on their power and landholding, must remain an open question.

Nanna's special functions were to light up the night, to measure time (Sumer observed a lunar calendar), and to provide fertility. Nanna was expected to give general prosperity: fish in rivers, plants on land, long life in the palace, abundance of cattle and dairy products to cow herders, as well as human fertility. We know that in some places and at some times in Mesopotamian history, fertility rites involved the "sacred marriage," in which the king slept with the high priestess of Nanna. But how often they took place, whether they were annual or took place after his coronation or on some special occasion, we cannot tell. We simply do not have any records that reveal the details of some of the customs of the Ur III period.

In line with the phases of the moon, festivals were

The Empire of Ur during the Ur III period

DATE OF ABRAHAM

If we follow the chronological references in the Old Testament literally, we can arrive at a specific date for Abraham. Of course it is necessary to work backward. A good place to begin is with the dedication of the temple. First Kings 6:1 puts that event in the fourth year of Solomon's reign (966) and says that the Exodus took place 480 years earlier. Thus we arrive at a date of about 1446 for the Exodus. (Discussion of the date of the Exodus appears in chapter 4.) Then Exodus 12:40-41 puts the entrance of Jacob and his sons into Egypt 430 years earlier, and we are now back to about 1876.

Next we look at the specifics of the patriarchal period. From Genesis 12:4; 21:5; 25:26; and 47:9 we learn that Abraham entered Canaan when he was 75 and was 100 when Isaac was born. Isaac was 60 at Jacob's birth, and Jacob was 130 when he stood before Pharaoh at the time of the Hebrew migration to Egypt. If we add 25, 60, and 130 we arrive at 215 for the total time that the patriarchs lived in Canaan. If we add 215 to 1876, we arrive at the date of 2091 for Abraham's entrance into Canaan. Since he was 75 at the time, we add 75 to 2091 and arrive at 2166 for the date of his birth in Ur.

celebrated on the first, seventh and fifteenth days of the month during the Third Dynasty of Ur. On the day the moon was invisible and thought to be dead, special offerings were made; these seem to have been in charge of the reigning queen. The people believed that on that day Nanna went to the underworld to judge and make administrative decisions. That done, the god reappeared in the night skies as the new moon.

During the festivals people must have come from considerable distances, and there must have been feasts, processions or parades, music and dance events, and markets or fairs. But we do not have detailed statements from scribes describing such events.

In addition to the state cult or the city cult, the populace worshiped personal gods. In some of the houses rooms were set aside as shrines; often reception rooms doubled as shrines. Commonly these shrines had an altar in the corner, standing about waist high. Here one might worship a family or a personal god, but nothing is known of beliefs or practices of private cults of that sort. Passing references to personal deities do appear in letters of citizens of Ur found on clay tablets dating to the period.

That was the religious environment in which Abraham grew up and did his business. Joshua makes it clear that Abraham's father at least worshiped idols—and Abraham may have done so as well for many years.

(For more on this topic, go to p. 31.)

Warfare

Warfare in the Golden Age

By force of arms, Ur-Nammu quickly brought all of Mesopotamia under his control. The military machine by which he achieved this is not described in detail in the archaeological sources, but they provide some educated observations or suppositions. The infantry wore metal helmets, even

The ziggurat of Ur as partially restored

(Photo by Gustav Jeeninga)

though all metal had to be imported. At least some of the soldiers wore heavy cloaks, possibly leather and metal-studded for body protection.

The front ranks of infantry apparently were protected by large rectangular shields, but judging from pictorial representations of the period, most of the soldiers do not seem to have carried shields. Rather, they wielded a spear in one hand for thrusting and a battle-ax in the other for slashing and probably had a dagger at their waists for protection if they lost one of the other weapons. A shield would have reduced their offensive capability. Though they used the sling and bow and arrow, those do not seem to have figured prominently in the pitched battles commonly fought by heavy infantry. Archers served as support troops and officers rode in clumsy four-wheeled battle wagons.[5]

In Genesis 14 we read of an attack on Sodom and Gomorrah that involved the capture of Lot and his family and their removal as captives—and Abraham's quick strike response force that recaptured Lot and his family. Where did he learn the tactics of warfare? Probably while still living in Ur of Chaldees.

(For more on this topic, go to p. 32.)

Housing and Furniture

Plan of the City

The city-state of Ur was a prosperous industrial, commercial, and agricultural center with a population of some 360,000, according to estimates of the excavator, C. Leonard Woolley,[6] though some scholars would now reduce the figure to about 200,000. The city center was enclosed by a wall about two and one-half miles in circumference and seventy-seven feet thick. The thickness of the wall was not so much an indication of the need for formidable fortifications as a reminder that the area had no stone so it was necessary to erect an earthen rampart or embankment. Inside the wall lived about 25,000 people.

Dominating the northwest part of Ur stood the sacred enclosure of the moon god Nanna (discussed earlier). There were north and west harbors, where riverboats

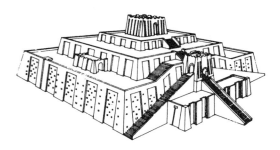

Artist's depiction of the ziggurat at Ur

A war scene on the so-called "Standard of Ur" shows clumsy battle wagons of the period 2500 B.C.

and ocean-going vessels could dock. Apparently the open waters of the Persian Gulf were more accessible about 2000 B.C. than they are now; the silting action of the rivers had not yet created the solid landfill visible in the area today.

Streets of the City

Now let's walk the streets of Ur during the time of Abraham and stop at a few houses. The streets are winding and narrow. In fact, we can frequently touch the buildings on either side with outstretched arms. Under such circumstances wheeled vehicles are prohibited from operating in town. It is a tight squeeze when two individuals pass carrying large bundles or when a loaded donkey and a pedestrian meet. To prevent people from getting hurt on sharp edges, sharp corners of buildings are rounded off at intersections. There are no yards with grass and no trees anywhere in sight.

The streets are windowless. Only doors open into houses that are constructed around a central courtyard open to the sky. At least the lower courses of exterior walls are of burnt brick. At the doorways there are often brick sills or thresholds to keep rain water from draining into the house. Because garbage is thrown into the street, the street level constantly rises and gradually becomes higher than that of the house floor. Sometimes a brick stair leads from the street down into the house. Eventually it

may be necessary to rebuild the house at a higher level.

Houses and Furniture

The houses of the middle class commonly measured forty by fifty feet or more and had ten to twenty rooms. They were normally two stories during the Third Dynasty of Ur, demonstrating a

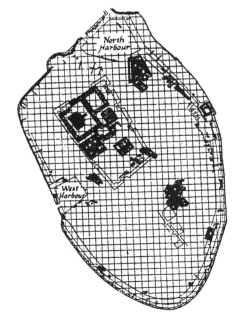

Plan of Ur

A street scene in Ur with house walls dating to Abraham's time. The presence of Iraqi workers shows how narrow the streets were.

greater sophistication than the one-story houses of earlier periods or later construction in Babylonian times. On the first floor they had a kitchen for cooking, an eating area, guest room, lavatory, servants' quarters and storage; on the second floor family bedrooms were located. These were reached by means of a brick stairway that led up to a wooden balcony about three feet wide that ran around the courtyard.[7] Small houses for the poorer classes commonly had an open courtyard with a couple of rooms at the back of the courtyard.

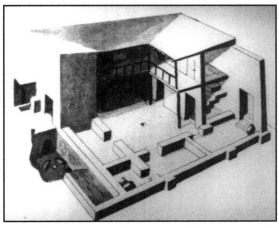

Half-section of a private house at Ur in Abraham's day. The main entrance is on the right. On the extreme left, the domestic chapel and family burial ground.

Cooking or baking of bread took place in the courtyard.

How many individuals may have lived in these houses is still debated. Essentially, though, they were one-family dwellings. Sons and daughters lived there until they established homes of their own, and aged parents may have lived with the family. But homes for an extended family were not common in the city. Since houses were already stacked one against another, there was little if any room for additions to an existing structure if family units were added. The situation was different in the countryside, where there was opportunity to add to houses and where there are some indications in existing records of joint ownership and joint working of land.

Furniture was sparse, as in many places in the Orient today. People might simply sit on a rug or a small cushion on the floor. There were some folding chairs (generally without a back) and tables. Oil lamps, saucers with a flax wick stuck in the oil, provided light at night. In the bedroom or guest room one might simply unfold a bedroll and sleep on the floor. But there were some brick benches on which mattresses could be unrolled; during the day such benches could serve as "sofas." Some rooms had alcoves in which bedrolls were piled. Wood and wicker chests provided storage. Imagine Sarah keeping house in such an environment before Abraham took her on her first journey to Haran.

(For more on this topic, go to p. 33.)

Diet and Foodstuffs

Agriculture

So what did Sarah serve Abraham for dinner while they were still living in Ur? We can make an educated guess from what was produced on farms outside the city, where there lay vast tracts of farmland and small agricultural villages. One could walk down a relatively straight road with fields carefully marked out on both sides by means of fairly accurate surveying techniques. Farmers were using stone or copper hoes and wooden plows drawn by oxen and cultivating barley, wheat, and vegetables. Sheep and cattle grazed here and there and groves of date palms and fruit trees studded the landscape.

Here and there irrigation canals appeared. At first irrigation canals were simple ditches and levees were simple dikes. And some parts of the system were always that. But by Abraham's day, when kings ruled city-states, they dug and regularly dredged canals that provided both for irrigation and transport. So produce could be shipped to the town markets on these canals from one part of the state to another. Boats with sails could be seen plying the canals of the irrigation system.

Though fairly primitive tools and back-breaking toil pervaded the atmosphere, there was one invention that made the Sumerian agricultural program look quite modern: the seeder or machine planter. The way this machine worked is clearly illustrated in the accompanying illustration from about 1500 B.C. A yoke of oxen draw a seeder, with their driver beside them. Behind the seeder follows a farmer holding it by two handles. The pointed instrument makes a shallow trench in the soil. Rising from the frame of the seeder is a tube, on the top of which is a funnel. A third man walks beside the seeder and drops grain into this funnel with one hand, while holding a sack of grain over his shoulder with the other. The grain

A plow with a seeder attachment, from a Kassite seal, second millennium B.C. A man drives the team of oxen while a farmer holds the plow and opens a furrow. An attendant drops seed into the funnel, through which it drops into the ground.

drops through the tube and falls into the trench made by the seeder.[8] Seeders are known in ancient Mesopotamia before 2500 B.C. and were still in use after 1500 B.C.[9] The only known parallel to this apparatus comes from the Far East.[10]

Bible students generally think of the sower scattering seed by hand in Bible times (e.g., Matthew 13), and moderns credit Jethro Tull with invention of the seed drill in 1701 in England, but Mesopotamians in Abraham's day had roughly the equivalent of Tull's ingenious machine.

Sumerian Diet

The diet of the Sumerians during the period when Abraham lived in Ur was quite varied. Cereals included barley—the most important—wheat, millet, and emmer (a variety of wheat). Among the vegetables grown were chick-peas, lentils and vetches (vegetables of the family of legumes—beans, peas), onions, garlic, lettuce, turnips, leeks (along with onions, a garden herb of the lily family), mustard, cabbage, radishes, and a variety of cucumbers. A large number of herbs and spices was produced as well. Mustard, cumin, and coriander, along with salt, provided flavoring for food. The most important fruits were the apple, pomegranate, and fig. The main sweetener was the date palm, from the sap of which a substance known as *lal* or honey was extracted.

Animal husbandry was also basic to the food supply and the economy. Bulls, cows, and calves were important for their meat and skin. Numerous varieties of sheep (that cannot as yet be related to modern strains) provided meat and wool. Goats and kids were also numerous. Pigs were raised in quantity and provided meat, fat, and skin. Sumerians especially enjoyed pork. The donkey and the horse provided transportation, and the ox was the main draft animal.

The meat of domesticated animals was supplemented by hunting. At that period of time there were still plenty of deer, wild boars and gazelles in the countryside, as well as a great variety of birds. Though the varieties of fish had declined in number by the Ur III period, fishermen still caught a dozen varieties by nets, traps, and fishing lines.

(For more on this topic, go to p. 35.)

Dress

The people of Sumer in Abraham's day wore woolen clothes, which would seem to be terribly uncomfortable in the high temperatures of the region. The coarse weave of the fabric, however, probably made the experience tolerable. Moreover, garments were loose-fitting, so air could circulate around the body.

Women wore a shawl-like garment draped over one shoulder, usually the left, with the other shoulder exposed. It extended from the neck to well below the knees and sometimes to the ankles. Almost always they wore their hair long and woven into a pigtail, which they then wound around their heads.

Men frequently wore a flounced skirt or kilt and sometimes a felt cloak draped around the upper body. Alternatively, they chose a long "chiton" or shirt extending to the knees and carried a big shawl with fringed edges, draped over the left shoulder and under the right one. Normally they were bearded and wore their hair long and parted in the middle, though some were clean shaven (using copper razors). Fortunately abundant pictorial representations, supplemented by written materials of the period, enable us to know how these people dressed.

No doubt Abraham's family dressed in the style of the period.

(For more on this topic, go to p. 36.)

Beer, the Most Popular Beverage

The most popular beverage was beer, made from barley. To brew it, the barley was soaked until it germinated and sprouted. Then it was spread out to dry. Next the malted grain was crushed and flavored with herbs or spices or dates and either eaten or made into cakes (beer-bread) for storage or transport. Then the beer-bread and hulled grain were mixed together and warmed in a slow oven, and the mash was spread on a large mat to cool. The next step involved addition of a sugary substance to aid fermentation and dumping of the mash with water into the brewing vat. This had a perforated base with a filter, through which the beer dripped into another vessel below. Although we cannot be sure of the alcoholic content of the beer, we know from the contemporary drinking songs that it "makes the liver happy" and "rejoices the heart."

Family Life

We do not have as much information as we would like on family life during the golden age of Ur, so we do not know if Abraham's family was typical of that period. Certainly it was greatly affected by the virtual "state socialism" of the period. Temple and palace supervised the population and made heavy demands upon it—there was little time for rest or recreation. Only some of the upper class boys went to school. Of the other classes, most went to work on the farm or in one of the shops in town as soon as they were able.

Some of the poorest people were forced to hire out their children and sometimes their wives as servants until they were free of debt. There were few slaves, which were normally taken as prisoners of war. Interestingly, the large state factories with their thousands of workers, referred to earlier, employed a large percentage of

A Sumerian priest with a flounced skirt
(Pergamon Museum, Berlin)

women.[11] This means that large numbers of women were out of the house and unable to shoulder their household tasks.

Marriage was as much a link between families as between individuals. Families negotiated marriages for their children. Betrothal or the engagement was a contract normally entered into by the fathers of the prospective bride and groom. During the Ur III period this involved a legal oath taken in the name of the king and commonly included a feast. Either at this point or later the bride and groom evidently exchanged words a little like modern wedding vows. They said to each other words approximating, "You are my wife and I am your husband," and vice versa.

Bethrothal was reinforced by gifts from the groom's side and a dowry provided by the bride's side. Later there was the physical move of the girl to the father-in-law's house. The marriage might be consummated at that time with co-habitation, but there are cases where the bride moved in with the future in-laws before she was old enough for mar-

riage. A father was supposed to provide each daughter with a dowry; and if he had not done so before his death, his sons were expected to set aside sufficient funds from his estate to meet this need.

Though Scripture does not say anything about the marriage of Abraham and Sarai (Sarah), it must have included all the elements we have just identified.

The special purpose of marriage was to secure sons to perpetuate the male line. In the event that the wife was barren, she could supply a slave girl to her husband to be a substitute for her and bear her children. This action is clearly reflected in Genesis 16:1–4, where barren Sarai gives a slave girl (Hagar) to Abraham to bear him a son. Interestingly, this practice seems to have been common in Mesopotamia, and it is provided for specifically in the later Code of Hammurabi (see sidebar on following page). Polygamy seems to have been uncommon during the Ur III period; but as noted, a wife might provide a concubine for her husband if she were barren. And sometimes he himself owned slave girls.

Slaves were procured by war, plunder, purchase from abroad, reduction to debt slavery, or birth in the household to slave parents. They were not numerous in most households during this period, and probate accounts normally mentioned only a couple per family. Release of slaves was common and the process is described in the laws of the period.

There are numerous texts from the Ur III period dealing with the division of estates after the death of the head of the family. Usually the eldest son received an extra portion of the estate and this commonly involved receiving the family house. The latter was probably granted in part because the family burial plot was normally under the shrine in the house (of the upper classes at least), and it was the son's responsibility to care for it and to make offerings to the family gods.[12]

Education

If you have thought of Abraham as a farmer who lived in a tent, you know by now that he quite probably started life as an upper class family member in a reasonably spacious permanent home in town. That also means that he could well have received a good education, for education seems to have been fairly widespread at Ur during the Third Dynasty. A substantial percentage of the upper class boys went to school. The social positions of fathers of hundreds of the students are known and include governors, ambassadors, temple administrators, accountants, tax officials, and others. Students paid tuition and presumably the teachers' salary came from that source. Originally the goal of these schools was to train scribes for temple and palace and later to meet business needs. The curriculum included botanical, zoological, mineralogical, geographical and theological texts, along with Sumerian grammar and mathematics. Students were able to extract square and cube roots and to do exercises in practical geometry.[13]

The head of the Sumerian school was the professor or "school father," and the pupil was called the "school son." There was an assistant professor known as "big brother," who wrote new tablets for the pupils to copy. These included mathematical tables, mathematical problems, grammar exercises, lists of names of trees, animals, stones and minerals, villages, and cities. Then there were literary compositions, proverbs, fables and essays, to name a few. He also checked the copies made by the pupils and heard them recite. In addition, there was a man in charge of Sumerian, one in charge of drawing, and one in charge of the whip. Discipline was stern. In some instances there may have been as many as 25-30 in a classroom. Probably the number was more commonly about 15, but we don't know much about class size.

Large numbers of the tablets of Sumerian schoolboys, ranging from beginners' first attempts to copies of advanced students have been recovered from the excavations. So we know what the pupils studied and the level of their proficiency, but the "lectures" of the professors are forever lost to us. Thus we shall never know about the philosophy of education or pedagogical methods.

A Son for Abraham

"Sarai, Abram's wife, had borne him no children. . . . So Sarai said to Abram. . . . Please, go in to my maid; perhaps I shall obtain children by her."
(Genesis 16:1–2 NKJV)

Paralleling this event are laws 145 and 146 from the Code of Hammurabi: "If a man takes a [wife] and she does not present him with children and he sets his face to take a concubine, that man may take a concubine and bring her into his house. . . . If a man takes a [wife] and she gives to her husband a maidservant and she bears children, and afterward that maidservant would take rank with her mistress; because she has borne children her mistress may not sell her for money, but she may reduce her to bondage and count her among the female slaves." See development of the parallel later in Genesis 16 and in chapter 21. Abraham and Sarah were definitely children of their culture.

In the schools the boys apparently sat on brick benches and studied for many years. We know nothing about summer vacations.

(For more on this topic, go to p. 38.)

Work, Travel, and Commerce

As we walk the streets of Ur, some doors open into houses of business. There we see piles of clay tablets that prove to be bills of lading, invoices, letters of credit, court cases, and tax records. Over in the corner an accountant is engaging in double-entry bookkeeping.[14] That is, accountants did not simply make lists of sales or expenditures, but tried to balance inflow against outflow, to demonstrate profit and loss. As noted, Ur was a great commercial and industrial center with north and west harbors. And business houses of the city had their agents working all over the Euphrates and Tigris valleys to the north and along the Persian Gulf to the south.

Also, as noted, there were great state factories, as well as temple factories. The state maintained a network of roads to facilitate administrative and military control and the safe movement of raw materials into and manufactured goods out of the state industrial centers. The volume of agricultural production, industry, trade and administrative activity certainly indicates a high level of prosperity. Chief exports included textiles and wool, leather, sesame oil and barley, and numerous items manufactured from copper and silver, as well as jewelry. Metals, especially copper from the mineral rich hills of Oman, woods and luxury goods (e.g., fragrances) ranked high among imports.

Travel—Transportation

Travel or transport of goods commonly took place on land. Individual men using a headstrap or in pairs carrying sacks or vessels suspended from poles moved all sorts of goods from place to place. The ass was the pack animal of choice, however. It could carry a load of up to 130 pounds in two half-packs (one on each side), at a rate of about 2.5 m.p.h. for six hours (for a total of 15 miles a day). A mule on the other hand, an ass-horse hybrid, could carry a load of 160 pounds at a rate of 3 to 4 m.p.h., for a total of 20–25 miles a day.[17]

Scripture also mentions the use of camels in Abraham's day (Genesis 12:16) and later in Rebekah's day in northern Mesopotamia (Genesis 24:64; cf. Isaac, Genesis 24:10). Critics used to doubt the use of camels so early, especially in Egypt. But Joseph P. Free marshaled considerable evidence for their presence in Egypt and elsewhere in the East. And K. A. Kitchen has collected some of the available information on the domestication and use of the camel in Mesopotamia and Syria during the patriarchal period.[18] Thus the evidence shows the authenticity of the record concerning Abraham and the patriarchs. But some are unfamiliar with the evidence and critics are still reticent to accept any extensive use of the camel in the Near East before about 1000 B.C.

Water Transport

Bulky and heavy commodities (grain, metals, stones, timber, etc.) were in all places and at all times moved by water. Of course Mesopotamia had the Tigris and Euphrates and their tributaries and an increasing network of canals. Boats on the canals or rivers were often reed or boat rafts and sometimes canoes with upturned ends. They might float downstream with the current or be drawn along canals or rivers by animal or even human power. Commonly they were buoyed by inflated sheepskins with the necks tied with hemp or liquorice fiber. A raft with 200 skins supported five tons; one with 800 skins took a load of some 36 tons.[19] Square sails were used on boats in the Persian Gulf and on some stretches of the rivers or even canals, but we don't know much about the ocean-going vessels of the time. Goods were usually packaged in leather, fabric, or wood. But large pottery jars were produced by the Ur III period.[20]

Work—Industry

Of course we want to know what sorts of goods were transported across Mesopotamia by land or by water or were sent abroad, as

Camels in a market in Beersheba

A Better Way to Go

A one-humped camel could carry double the load of a mule at a stretch of 20–25 miles, could go ten to fourteen days without water, and move about 3 m.p.h. It could also ford rivers with relative ease.[21] Two-humped camels had also appeared by Abraham's day.

well as what industry was capable of producing at the time. What might Abraham been involved in before he left Ur? Something has already been said about commodities traded, but now we look in a little more detail at goods produced for domestic or foreign consumption.

Agriculture

Agriculture fed the population, provided surpluses for internal exchange and long distance commerce. It was basic to the ancient Mesopotamian economy. But we now know that the commonly-held view that ancient Sumer had a temple-state economy is wrong. That is, temples did not own all the land that was worked for the god of the city-state. Rather, while temples owned large tracts of land, so did the king and the nobility. And large numbers of ordinary citizens also owned and worked small tracts of land for themselves.[22]

Below them in the social stratification substantial numbers of farmers worked as "sharecroppers," giving a share of the crop for the use of the land. Slaves stood at the bottom of the social scale. Some of these were prisoners taken in war with a nearby city-state or a foreign power; others were individuals reduced to slavery for a crime committed or an unpaid debt. In the latter case, they remained in servitude only until the debt was paid.

Probably the small, private farms were engaged in subsistence agriculture. Surplus in quantity seems to have come from the large farms of temple and nobility. Wheat, barley, figs, dates, wool, and leather were the common exports provided by the farms of Sumer.

Brickmaking

Brickmaking was something that almost all farmers did when they needed a few bricks for construction. But there were men in the building trades who produced them in quantity. The preferred period for brickmaking was May-June, when after the spring rains there was water for manufacture and the summer ahead for drying. July-August was then especially a time of building. But as a matter of fact, bricks might be made any time of the year. Chopped straw or dung was commonly used as a bonding material. The bricks were made in wooden molds, open at the top and bottom, so the brickmaker could simply fill his mold, lift it, and put it down again and repeat the process. Often, as in Egypt, brickmaking took place alongside a cultivated field next to a canal or river, because there plenty of water was available.

How many bricks one made in a day is hard to estimate. But one archaeologist reported that his brickmaker could produce 3,000 a day.[23] Such a person was not ordinary, however. He was trying to make and maintain a record, and he was reasonably well-fed and well-paid. Certainly ancient workers did not often work at top speed.

Kiln-fired bricks were very expensive because fuel was costly and they were therefore not often used in public or private construction. Thresholds, door sockets, and courtyards especially required baked brick. We do not know much about the ovens used for baking bricks.

A liquid form of the same mixture used for brickmaking served for mortar and wall plaster. Decoration often consisted of colored clay cones pressed into wet plaster in such a way as to form geometric patterns. Painted plaster was more common in both public buildings and residences than is often thought. It is hard to know much about this subject because most of the wall plaster has crumbled away. In ziggurats open channels were regularly left in the core, where layers of sundried brick alternated with layers of reeds to create a ventilation system and prevent trapped humidity from destroying the structure.

Bricks of Various Sizes

The size of bricks also varied. Measurements taken in one excavation recorded bricks about 12″ x 7″ x 3″, at another 15″ x 7″ x 3″, at yet another about 8″ x 3″ x 2″ and at a fourth, 23″ x 10″ x 3″. Bricks that we use in building today commonly measure about 8″ x 4″ x 2″.

Woodworking

Because Sumer was an area essentially without forests, it may seem strange to discuss woodworking here. Yet there were many employed in that activity during the Ur III period. Though construction was essentially in brick, wood was used for interior finishing of temples, palaces, homes of the wealthy, and even those of moderate means. Good timber (oak, pine, and other woods) was imported from the Zagros mountain areas to the east and the mountains and hills of the north. But trees were grown locally in the south. In fact, during Ur III there was planned and organized exploitation of the riverine thickets of what is now southern Iraq.[24] And trees regarded as foreign were successfully cultivated in groves.

Especially to be found in the south were palm, poplar, tamarisk, willow, and some fir. Palm was used for supports and roof beams; poplar for structural and roofing purposes, some furniture, and the production of charcoal; tamarisk and willow for roof structures; fir for general construction and especially for boats. In a timber and fuel starved area, nothing was wasted. Branches, foliage, and grasses were collected for roof construction (when mixed with clay) and for fuel.

Workers were engaged in felling trees, turning them into timber and simple tools, and collecting branches and foliage. They prepared logs, roof beams, pegs, rungs, posts, planks, hoes, sickle handles, plowshares, furniture, and more. Each kind of activity presented its own special challenge, with skills to be learned. Generally boys learned from their fathers, and younger workers from the more experienced—on the job.

Metalworking

There were no gold deposits in Mesopotamia. Any gold circulating there probably came from western Iran and the upper reaches of the Tigris and Euphrates in modern Turkey. In its native state, gold was always alloyed with silver in what is called electrum—a mixture of gold and silver, containing anywhere from twenty to fifty percent silver. Whatever gold and silver Abraham possessed (Genesis 13:2 and 24:35) must have been obtained through commerce.

Because gold and silver were constantly recycled and constantly plundered when cities were sacked in warfare or when later political administrations took over, we do not have the number of examples of workmanship that we desire. Commonly what we do have comes from tombs, where it was buried with royalty or persons of high position. It was especially used in gold jewelry as beads, pendants, gold bands, hairpins, earrings, and gold foil for sewing on clothing. Gold objects from Ur I graves (c. 2500 B.C.) included a ceremonial helmet, daggers and vases in gold. No goldsmith's workplace has yet been discovered in Mesopotamia. Cast gold was confined to objects in royal or temple service or to small pieces of jewelry, which Abraham and Sarah may have used.

Silver was commonly found combined with gold in electrum or present in lead ores. The source of Mesopotamian silver was primarily the lead ore of Iran or Turkey, or perhaps the Indus Valley. It was used principally for bowls or dishes, for personal adornment, for plating wood, for small statues (especially of the gods), and for currency (passing by weight). Abraham paid four hundred shekels of silver for a burial cave for Sarah (see Genesis 23:15–16). Because silver was so soft, it was usually alloyed with copper to make commodities comparable to modern sterling silver.

Copper was the most widely used of metals during the third–second millennia B.C., and especially the Ur III period. The source of supply for Sumer at the time under discussion here (about 2000 B.C.) seems to have been almost exclusively Oman, at the southeast tip of the Arabian Peninsula. In the ancient Near East copper ores, the oxides,

The so-called "Treasury" of Ur was probably the Hall of Justice. The use of brick, the buttress and recess style of architecture in the facade, and the arch as a weight-carrying device are all evident here.

appeared in weathered surfaces and were identified by their greens, blues, and bluish-green outcroppings. Thus copper was relatively easy to extract; it did not have to be dug from deep in the earth.

Tin does not seem to have been naturally combined with copper in the Near East (to make bronze), nor was tin readily available there. Therefore it was necessary to bring in tin and to deliberately combine it with copper. Early on it was used as a solder for silver or copper. Where tin came from is a question not easily answered. It appears that some was found in Turkey. Some came by land through Iran, or by sea up the Gulf, most likely from Afghanistan.[25]

Copper was partially smelted on location and then circulated as ingots (in various forms), to be finished off by local smiths. Some rings of copper, earlier identified as rings, bracelets, or armbands, are now thought to be ingots. Copper/bronze was used for metal vessels, chisels, razors, platters and spoons, spearheads, daggers or short swords, ax heads, and a variety of small tools, including agricultural tools (sickles, hoes, adzes).

Pottery making

Ancient contemporary comments on Mesopotamian pottery making and pictures of manufacture in progress are quite rare. Moreover, few pottery making installations have been discovered. Manufacture seems to have taken place in rural areas where raw materials and water were available and where kiln firing did not create a social nuisance. By the Ur III period it appears that palace and temple organized and controlled most pottery making.[26] Pottery was made on a potter's wheel or molded by hand and was generally undecorated or unpainted. Glazes were not applied to pottery until centuries after Abraham's day. And the accompanying craft of producing glass vessels did not come until about the middle of the second millennium B.C.[27] though a few glass beads were made as early as Abraham's day or before.[28] Until very recently archaeologists were interested almost exclusively in the finished products of ancient Mesopotamian pottery works and the dating of them, rather than in production processes. Therefore our knowledge of manufacture is extremely limited.

(For more on this topic, go to p. 42.)

Who Was Abraham?

Who was Abraham? How did he fit into the commerce and industry of Ur? Or did he? I have taken the position in this chapter that

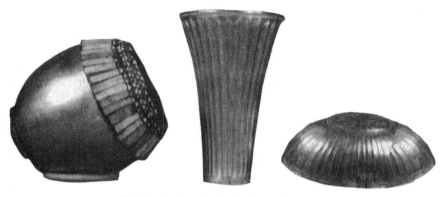

Gold bowls from Ur, dating from about 2500 B.C.

Abraham knew Ur during its golden age, the Ur III period. And we have looked at what life was like then. The city was powerful, wealthy, and sophisticated, an urban center surrounded by sedentary farmers. It was not a place where nomadic chieftains and their followers wandered about, living in tents. Certainly, too, Abraham was not an ignorant Arab sheik living in a migratory state and for whom it meant nothing to move from Ur to Haran and then on to Palestine. But then who or what was he? Several scholars, not known for an evangelical persuasion, have wrestled with this question.

Cyrus Gordon's View

Cyrus Gordon, formerly of Brandeis University, advanced the view that Abraham was not merely a powerful patriarch but a merchant prince. He came to this conclusion on the basis of his interpretation of certain textual materials discovered at Ras Shamra in Syria. He put the patriarchs in the context of the middle of the second millennium B.C. and believed that Abraham was part of the merchant movement referred to in the literature of Ras Shamra. Briefly put, Gordon became intrigued with complaints of the king of Ras Shamra to the Hittite king about activities at Ras Shamra of Hittite merchants from Ura (in Hittite territory). He identified this northern Ura as the biblical Ur and thought Abraham may have been part of the merchant group there.

He noted several biblical references that indicate that the patriarchs were merchants. First, Joseph told his brothers that if they could prove their honest intentions, they would be permitted to trade in the land (Genesis 42:34). Second, the Shechemites gave permission to Jacob's household to "dwell and trade" and "acquire real estate" in their territory (Genesis 34:10). Third, in Genesis 23 Abraham was permitted to buy land from Ephron the Hittite for 400 shekels of silver—called "current money with the merchant" (v. 16 KJV). Moreover, besides this reference, Genesis 13:2 and 24:35 mention that Abraham was rich in gold and silver.[29]

Gordon concluded that "the patriarchal narratives, far from reflecting Bedouin life, are highly international in their milieu, in a setting where a world order enabled men to travel far and wide for business enterprise. . . . Abraham comes from beyond the Euphrates, plies his trade in Canaan, visits Egypt, deals with Hittites, makes treaties with Philistines, forms military alliances with Amorites, fights kinglets from as far off as Elam, marries the Egyptian Hagar, etc."[30]

While the Bible student may not be prepared to accept the idea that Abraham was part of the merchant movement described in the literature of Ras Shamra, or that Abraham lived so late, he will at least agree that Gordon has portrayed Abraham to be much more than the Bedouin nomad scholars a generation ago thought him to be.

William F. Albright's Thesis

Taking a very different approach from that of Gordon, William F. Albright, formerly professor at Johns Hopkins University, came

A contemporary desert caravan

to a similar conclusion about Abraham. Albright preferred to place Abraham in the twentieth or nineteenth century B.C. instead of the middle of the second millennium and therefore did not connect him with any Ras Shamra developments, as Gordon had. Albright pointed to the work of Nelson Glueck, Yohanan Aharoni, and Beno Rothenberg, who in the 1950s traced the twentieth–nineteenth century B.C. caravan routes through the Negev and desert of north-central Sinai.

Albright noted the discovery of literally hundreds of currently unoccupied sites along the old caravan route from Suez through the wilderness of north-central Sinai to Kadesh-Barnea and Gerar. Thence the routes made their way to Hebron, Jerusalem, Bethel, Shechem, Damascus, Aleppo, and other Syrian cities, to Mesopotamia and Asia Minor.

Then Albright noted that Abraham came from the great commercial city of Ur and lived in the important commercial center of Haran, which means "caravan city." He spent time on the main trade route in Damascus, Shechem, Bethel, Hebron, Beersheba, and Gerar, and especially between Kadesh and Shur while he was a "foreign resident" in Gerar. It is to be remembered that during the latter period (Genesis 20:1) Abraham had a very large entourage. For the battle recorded in Genesis 14 he had been able to field 318 armed "retainers," who with their families would have constituted a community of at least a thousand.

Albright argued that Abraham could not have survived in this virtually rainless desert unless he had been engaged in the rather extensive and lucrative caravan trade between Palestine and Egypt. And Albright noted the specific indication of Genesis 13:3, which he translated: "And his caravan journeyed by stages from the south (Negev) to Bethel."

He also observed that Egyptian texts speak of donkey caravans numbering 500, 600, and even 1,000 operating in the Sinai and the Sudan during the twentieth–nineteenth centuries B.C. So Albright pointed to the great wealth of Abraham, his extensive community, and his commercial activities. He argued that though Abraham was semi-nomadic, he was not merely a nomad wandering where he wished in search of pasture and water supply.[31] He was something of a merchant prince.

David Noel Freedman's Position

Using different data from those of Gordon or Albright, David Noel Freedman of the University of California viewed Abraham as a "warrior-chieftain" and a "merchant prince" who belonged to "urban culture and civilization." Moreover, he believed that if Abraham could not read and write, he probably made use of professional scribes available to the leaders of society in his day to help keep records of business transactions and to prepare communications. In such a way information could have survived for later generations.[32]

But who was Abraham?

All of these scholars give new perspectives on Abraham, but they do not yet tell us who Abraham was. Should we classify him as a private merchant or businessman engaged primarily in domestic commerce and possibly going with Terah to Haran, another great commercial center, to pursue business interests? Or was he a civil servant engaged in international trade that seems to have been monopolized by the state?

It is to be remembered that Abraham paid silver "current with the merchant" for the burial place for Sarah at Hebron (Genesis 23:16). The French Assyriologist Roux observes that silver, "used as a standard for exchanges," was "hoarded by high officials and did not circulate unless authorized by the Palace."[33] Did Abraham get his hands on a quantity of silver as an official in the employ of the government of Ur? Was he possibly a favorite of the court?

In any case, most people were not free to leave Ur or the territory of Sumer during the Third Dynasty of Ur. Certainly slaves or serfs tied to the soil were not. Neither were soldiers in "uniform," workers in the state factories, most religious functionaries, and members of the bureaucracy at most levels. None of them could move about at will. Abraham and Terah must have been free merchants or possibly high officials in the government involved in international trade, who could gain permission to go elsewhere or arrange a "transfer" to Haran. Evidently they were members of the upper class and could find a way to leave Ur. Evidently, too, it cost them a great deal to leave, for the region from which they came was perhaps the most culturally advanced and the most prosperous in the world at the time, and any other place would seem inferior.

God's Blessing on Abraham

But as Abraham went, God blessed him, and his possessions increased rapidly. Soon after entering Canaan, he and Lot had so many flocks and herds that they had to separate (Genesis 13:5–9). And as noted, at an early date Abraham had 318 armed retainers in his camp (Genesis 14:14), and he must have been the head of a community that numbered well in excess of a thousand.

Moreover, as a wealthy and powerful leader, and with the widespread availability of education at Ur in Abraham's day, there is no reason on the face of it why he could not have known how to read and write. Or at least, as a wealthy man, he could have employed scribes. This fact changes completely our view of the early chapters of the Old Testament. Abraham or his scribes could have written the accounts of such famous events as the visit of the angels to predict the birth of Isaac (Genesis 18:1–15), the sacrifice of Isaac (Genesis 22:1–19), or the destruction of Sodom and Gomorrah (Genesis 18:16—19:38).

It is unnecessary to believe that the early stories of Genesis were passed down by word of mouth and therefore subjected to the possibility of extensive corruption (as some believe), protected only by miraculous preservation through the centuries. Nor is it necessary to claim that God dictated those stories to Moses, thus guaranteeing accuracy. Abraham's originals or early copies could have been passed on to Moses, who included them in the book of Genesis.

Now we move on to see what life was like for Abraham and his descendants, the Patriarchs, as he left for Canaan and as they lived there during the next couple of centuries.

Notes:

[1]Georges Roux, *Ancient Iraq*, 3rd ed. (New York: Penguin Books, 1992), 162.

[2]Carl Roebuck, *The World of Ancient Times* (New York: Scribner's, 1966), 33.

[3]McGuire Gibson, *The Oriental Institute 1981–82 Annual Report*, 41.

[4]Roux, 172–73.

[5]John Hackett, ed., *Warfare in the Ancient World* (New York: Facts on File, 1989), 23–26.

[6]C. L. Woolley, *History of Mankind*, vol. 1 (New York: New American Library, 1967), 2:123–33.

[7]C. L. Woolley, *Abraham* (New York: Scribner's, 1936), 111–15.

[8]Jacquetta Hawkes, *The First Great Civilizations* (New York: Alfred A. Knopf, 1973), 96.

[9]Harriet Crawford, *Sumer and the Sumerians* (Cambridge: Cambridge University Press, 1991), 44.

[10]A. Leo Oppenheim, *Ancient Mesopotamia*, Rev. ed. (Chicago: University of Chicago Press, 1977), 314.

[11]Roux, 173.

[12]J. N. Postgate, *Early Mesopotamia* (New York: Routledge, 1992), 99.

[13]Woolley, *Abraham*, 118–33.

[14]Woolley, *Abraham*, 118–33.

[15]Samuel N. Kramer, *History Begins at Sumer* (Philadelphia: University of Pennsylvania, 3rd rev. ed., 1991), 3–9, 351.

[16]P. R. S. Moorey, *Ancient Mesopotamian Materials and Industries* (Oxford: The Clarendon Press, 1994), 12.

[18]Joseph P. Free, "Abraham's Camels," *Journal of Near Eastern Studies* (July 1944), 187–93; K. A. Kitchen, *Ancient Orient and Old Testament* (Chicago: InterVarsity Press, 1966), 79–80; Kitchen, *Illustrated Bible Dictionary* (Downers Grove, Ill: InterVarsity, 1980), 1:228–30.

[19]Moorey, 10.

[20]Ibid., 11.

[21]Ibid., 13.

[22]Samuel N. Kramer, *The Sumerians* (Chicago: University of Chicago Press, 1963), 76–77.

[23]Moorey, 305.

[24]Ibid., 349.

[25]Ibid., 301.

[26]Ibid., 141.

[27]A. Leo Oppenheim in *Glass and Glassmaking in Ancient Mesopotamia* (Corning, N.Y.: The Corning Museum of Glass Press, 1970), 16.

[28]See discussion in Moorey, 190–192.

[29]Cyrus Gordon, "Abraham and the Merchants of Ura," *Journal of Near Eastern Studies* (January, 1958), 28–30.

[30]Ibid., 30.

[31]William F. Albright, *Yahweh and the Gods of Canaan* (Garden City, N.Y.: Doubleday, 1968), 51, 62–73.

[32]David N. Freedman, "The Real Story of the Ebla Tablets," *Biblical Archaeologist* (December, 1978), 158.

[33]Roux, 173.

Bibliography:

Bottero, Jean, *Mesopotamia*. Chicago: University of Chicago Press, 1992.

Crawford, Harriet. *Sumer and the Sumerians*. Cambridge: Cambridge University Press, 1991.

Hawkes, Jacquetta. *The First Great Civilizations*. New York: Alfred A. Knopf, 1973.

Jacobsen, Thorkild. *The Treasures of Darkness*. New Haven, Conn: Yale University Press, 1976.

Kramer, Samuel N. *History Begins at Sumer*. Philadelphia: University of Pennsylvania Press, 3rd ed., 1981.

Kramer, Samuel N. *The Sumerians*. Chicago: University of Chicago Press, 1963.

Lloyd, Seton. *The Archaeology of Mesopotamia*. London: Thames & Hudson, 1978.

Lloyd, Seton. *Foundations in the Dust*. London: Thames & Hudson, rev. ed., 1980.

Moorey, P.R.S. *Ancient Mesopotamian Materials and Industries*. Oxford: At the Clarendon Press, 1994.

Oppenheim, A. Leo. *Ancient Mesopotamia*. Chicago: University of Chicago Press, rev. ed., 1977.

Oppenheim, A. Leo, and others. *Glass and Glassmaking in Ancient Mesopotamia*. Corning, N.Y.: The Corning Museum of Glass Press, 1970.

Postgate, J.N. *Early Mesopotamia*. New York: Routledge, 1992.

Roux, George. *Ancient Iraq*. New York: Penguin Books, 3rd ed., 1992.

Schenck, Helen, ed., "The World of Ur," *Expedition*, Vol. 40, No. 2, 1998

Van DeMieroop, Marc. *The Ancient Mesopotamian City*. New York: Oxford University Press, 1998.

Whitehouse, Ruth. *The First Cities*. Oxford: Phaidon, 1977.

Woolley, C. Leonard. *The Sumerians*. New York: W.W. Norton, 1965.

Woolley, C. Leonard. *Ur 'of the Chaldees'*. Rev. by P.R.S. Moorey. London: the Herbert Press, 1982.

LIFE IN CANAAN DURING THE DAYS OF THE PATRIARCHS

Chapter 3

(Genesis 13—46)

"Then Abram took Sarai his wife and Lot his brother's son, and all their posses-sions that they had gathered, and the people whom they had acquired in Haran, and they departed to go to the land of Canaan." (Genesis 12:5 NKJV)

When Abraham moved into Canaan (c. 2090 B.C.), he entered what was for him a quite differ-ent world—a life fundamentally different from what he had known in the cities of Ur and Haran in Mesopotamia. As Abraham left highly urbanized Mesopotamia and wandered around in Canaan, Scripture implies that he found the land in a rather rural state—few urban centers stood in his path. It might be compared to a resident of Manhattan, New York, moving to Montana.

Abraham also found himself in a land quite different from what the Hebrews were to discover half a millennium later in the days of Moses. When Moses sent in spies to explore Palestine in preparation for the Hebrew conquest (c. 1440 B.C.), they reported that "the cities are walled, and very great" (Numbers 13:28 KJV), and "the cities are great and walled up to heaven" (Deuteronomy 1:28 KJV). It is easy to see why the spies would have been impressed with Canaanite fortifications, for those cities were perched on impressive, defensi-ble hills. And on days when low-hanging clouds filled the sky, they would seem to be walled to heaven.

But where were these walled cities in Abraham's day? Current scholarship in-dicates that there was general de-urbaniza-tion throughout Palestine by about 2200 B.C. This abandonment of towns resulted from a significant weather shift to drier conditions, combined with a greatly weakened econ-omy and the disruption of trade systems.[1] That explains why Abraham could so read-ily roam about without seeming to conflict with local peoples; almost no significant cities or organized city-states would have confronted him and his large retinue.

New cities were gradually built up in Palestine during the period of 2000-1900 B.C. and re-urbanization was completed during the following century. This means that towns and cities began to reappear during the days of Isaac and Jacob. They could well have caused these Hebrew fam-ilies problems if the Hebrews had remained in the land after about 1875. Instead, Jacob and his extended family were brought to Egypt by Joseph. It is noteworthy, how-ever, that the central and southern hill country of Palestine, where many of the patriarchal activities occurred, continued to be rather thinly settled even after the land re-urbanized.

The Land

Where the Patriarchs Lived

"And the LORD said to Abram. . . : 'Lift your eyes now and look from the place where you are—northward, southward, eastward, and westward; for all the land which you see I give to you and your descendants forever. And I will make your descendants as the dust of the earth; so that if a man could number the dust of the earth, then your descendants also could be numbered. Arise, walk in the land through its length and its width, for I give it to you.'" (Genesis 13:14–17 NKJV)

As we follow the movements of Abraham, Isaac, and Jacob in Palestine or Canaan, we may get the impression that they lived in a large, wide open land and traveled great distances. Yet this was not the wide open spaces of Montana. The Old Testament generally considers the eastern boundary of Canaan to be the Jordan River and the western boundary the Mediterranean Sea. The width of the country at the Sea of Galilee is only 25–30 miles; at the northern end of the Dead Sea, about

55 miles; and at the southern end of the Dead Sea, about 85 miles. Northern and southern limits were commonly placed at Dan (north) and Beersheba (south; see Judges 20:1 and 1 Samuel 3:20). The distance between Dan and Beersheba is just under 150 miles. This area totals some 6,000 to 7,000 square miles and would be about

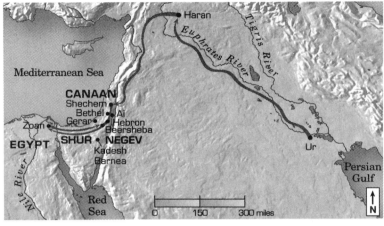

Journeys of Abraham

the size of Connecticut and Delaware combined. The distance between Jerusalem and Bethlehem is only about 5 to 6 miles; between Jerusalem and Hebron, 23 miles; and between Jerusalem and the later city of Samaria, 30 miles.

This small area has a surprisingly varied landscape and climate, which was probably even more pronounced in Abraham's day. The land divides into four divisions lengthwise and two regions laterally. The coastal plain (3 to 24 miles wide, sea level to about 500 feet in altitude) extends along the Mediterranean Sea. East of that rises the Piedmont or Shephelah or foothills (about 40 miles long from north to south, 8 miles from east to west, and 500 to 1,000 feet in altitude). Apparently plentiful forests blanketed the hills of the Shephelah in Abraham's day and later (1 Kings 10:24). The Western Plateau or Western Mountain Ridge ranges in altitude from 2,000 to 4,000 feet and divided into Galilee in the north, Samaria in the center, and Judea in the south. Galilee and Samaria evidently also had considerable forest cover in Old Testament times.

The Sea, or Lake, of Galilee, at the point where the Jordan River flows into the northern end of the lake
(Photo by Willem A. VanGemeren)

THE ANCIENT FORESTS OF PALESTINE

"Only the trees which you know are not trees for food you may destroy and cut down, to build siegeworks against the city that makes war with you."

(Deuteronomy 20:20)

The Law of Moses prohibited the indiscriminate cutting of trees (Deuteronomy 20:19–20), but that did not prevent the destruction of the forests that once covered much of Palestine. The demands for shipbuilding, siegeworks in time of war, smelting of metals, and cooking of food, to name the more obvious uses, ultimately resulted in destruction of the great old forests of the land.

At the north once stood the famous forest of Lebanon, with its cedars and pine and myrtle trees. Farther south, trees covered the Carmel Range and much of the Sharon Plain. Inland stood the forests of Galilee and Ephraim, home of wild animals (2 Kings 2:24; 1 Samuel 17:35). The forest of Hereth in Judah, that stretched to the edge of the Plain of Philistia, provided cover for David in flight (1 Samuel 22:5). The Zor was a dense thicket along the lower course of the Jordan, above where it emptied into the Dead Sea. Transjordan had its forests too, especially in Bashan in the north. Oaks, terebinths, and Aleppo pines were especially plentiful in these stands of timber.

But over the millennia the trees were gradually felled. Especially when the Assyrians, Babylonians, and Romans fought in the land, they used them for siegeworks. Soil erosion and more erratic rainfall followed the stripping of the land. Israeli and Jordanian reforestation efforts in recent decades are only beginning to make a difference.

The fourth longitudinal division of Canaan is the Jordan Rift, which extends some 300 miles from Mount Hermon to the Red Sea. This deep depression has an average width of ten miles and descends to a depth of about 1,300 feet at the shore of the Dead Sea, the lowest spot on earth. Towering over the northern end of the Jordan Valley is Mount Hermon, 9,232 feet above sea level. From its slopes flows most of the water for the Jordan.

About sixty miles north of Jerusalem the Jordan flows through the Sea of Galilee. That pear-shaped body is about thirteen miles long and seven miles wide. Its surface lies at about 700 feet below sea level and its greatest depth is 150 feet. Almost due east of Jerusalem the Jordan flows into the Dead Sea, about 50 miles long and 11 miles wide and 1300 feet deep at its lowest point. Among the other fairly substantial rivers of Palestine is the Jabbok, which flows into the Jordan from the hills to the east about 24 miles north of the Dead Sea. Along its banks Jacob wrestled with the angel on his way back from Mesopotamia (Genesis 32:22–29). Though that river was a fairly important stream then, its waters now are almost completely captured for irrigation.

The lateral regions of Canaan include Esdraelon in the north and the Negev in the south. Esdraelon extends northwest and southeast and is about 24 miles in length from Mount Carmel to Mount Gilboa. The Kishon (on the south bank of

Aerial view of the twisting Jordan River. Its bed measures some 200 miles in the 60-mile distance between the Sea of Galilee and the Dead Sea.

A Changeable Climate

As noted in this chapter, a dry cycle hit Palestine before and during Abraham's day. This resulted in a decline of village life and an abandonment of many villages. In the days of Isaac and Jacob there apparently was a shift toward increased precipitation and renewed town life.

Then beginning around 300 B.C. and continuing into the New Testament period, the climate of the whole Mediterranean basin turned colder and more humid than today. The level of the Dead Sea was many feet higher than it is now. And southern Judea and the Negev produced myrrh, frankincense, and quality wines under Nabatean cultivation.[2]

If we can document two periods when climate differed considerably from today, possibly there were also other times when this happened.

which Elijah executed the priests of Baal, 1 Kings 18:40) flows through the plain of Esdraelon, which was much more marshy in Old Testament times than now; modern drainage projects have improved its agricultural usefulness.

The Negev in the south is roughly a triangle, with its base at the southern edge of the Judean hills and its apex on the Gulf of Aqaba. Its total area is about 4,600 square miles, the size of Connecticut. In Abraham's day and subsequently there was a considerable number of settlements in this now virtually desert and uninhabited region. Clearly the climate has changed over the years (see sidebar) and the ancients apparently knew better than more recent inhabitants how to utilize water resources. They were very careful with water management, maintaining water reservoirs or cisterns everywhere. We see them in the remains of their villages. Beersheba (especially the home of the Patriarchs, Genesis 21, 22, 26, 28, 46) stands in the northern Negev.

(For more on this topic, go to p. 8 or p. 45.)

Government

Patriarchal Rule

In a land and at a time when urban life had largely disappeared, the government that really mattered, as far as Scripture is concerned, was that of the patriarch over his extended family. *Patriarch* means literally "rule of the father." And his rule was absolute; he controlled the political, economic, military, religious, and social affairs of his clan. He even had the power of life and death over them, as is clear from Abraham's sacrifice of his son Isaac (Genesis 22).

(For more on this topic, go to p. 8 or p. 48.)

Religion

The Patriarchs and their Altars

"And he [Abraham] moved from there to the mountain east of Bethel . . . there he built an

altar to the LORD and called on the name of the LORD." (Genesis 12:8 NKJV)

And Their House

Just as Abraham led his family in worship and influenced his whole community of a thousand or more to worship and follow God, so in our time we hear of people groups in which tribal leaders have influenced their whole tribes to trust in God. We are so accustomed to the extreme individualism of Western society and the emphasis on individual conversion that we need to be reminded how God sometimes works in other societies. Occasionally in tribal societies first the tribal leaders and then the whole tribe or extended family turns to God.

Because the patriarchs' extended families were the people of God in their day, the patriarchs had the responsibility of leading them in worship, or at least acquainting them with the ways of God. But we need to be careful not to assume too much. Scripture does not speak of regular or periodic events, like weekly services, with Hebrew leaders officiating at a sacrifice or urging their households to follow God, until we get to the time of the Exodus. Abraham, Isaac and Jacob had very private meetings with God. For example, Abraham built an altar to God near Shechem (Genesis 12:7) after God had appeared to him there. Subsequently he built altars at Bethel (12:8) and at Mamre near Hebron (13:18).

Though Abraham called on the Lord in those places, there is no mention of sacrifice or of an audience being present. Having been erected after God's promise to give the land to Abraham and his descendants, those altars may be regarded as symbolic of God's gift of the land—a kind of symbolic staking out of territory. It may be assumed, however, that Abraham's "calling" on the Lord at those altars (Genesis 12:8; 13:8) involved some witnesses. Interestingly, Luther in his German Bible translated this verb "preached" instead of "calling." That Abraham must have offered sacrifices in the presence of family

members is indicated by the familiarity that Isaac had with the practice when Abraham proceeded to offer him in Genesis 22.

Without reading too much into the patriarchal practices, we may possibly assume that religious belief and experience then was much the same as in primitive or less sophisticated societies ever since. Servants, slaves, or subordinate groups tend to accept religiously what their masters believe and expect them to believe. Also, the dependents seem to derive a certain religious security from association with the dominant figure and even to feel that they gain a certain amount of holiness from association with him. This was certainly true of the Manicheism of the third century A.D., in which lay members participated in the holiness of their leaders, and often has been true in certain Roman Catholic or Eastern Orthodox or even evangelical Protestant groups.

(For more on this topic, go to p. 10 or p. 54.)

Warfare

Abraham to the Rescue

"Now when Abram heard that his brother [Lot] was taken captive, he armed his three hundred and eighteen trained servants who were born in his own house, and went in pursuit."
(Genesis 14:14 NKJV)

A pagan Canaanite altar from Megiddo, dating before Abraham's day. Though the Mosaic Law prohibited steps that put the priest above the heads of the people, we cannot be sure of the height of altars in the patriarchal period.

(Photo by Gustav Jeeninga)

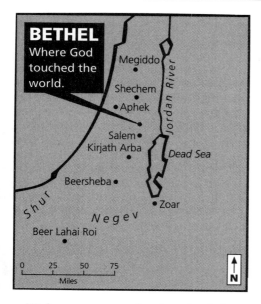

BETHEL
Where God
touched the
world.

Megiddo

Shechem

Aphek

Jordan River

Salem
Kirjath Arba

Dead Sea

Beersheba

Shur

Zoar

Negev

Beer Lahai Roi

0   25   50   75
Miles

N

We have one example of patriarchal warfare—in Genesis 14. Five kings of the area of Sodom fought with four invading kings of the East and lost heavily. The invaders carried off much plunder and many captives, including Lot. Abraham immediately activated his force of 318 "trained servants," which we might call his quick response strike force, and went off in hot pursuit (Genesis 14:14). Presumably they were equipped with the weapons Abraham would have known as a member of the bureaucracy of Ur. If so, they wielded a spear in one hand and a battle-ax in the other and probably had a dagger at the waist for extra protection. Since they attacked under cover of darkness (v. 15), they probably did not use slings or bows or arrows.

Dividing into companies to give the impression of greater numbers, and attacking the rear guard and the baggage train under cover of darkness, Abraham's mini-army was immensely successful and returned with the captives and the booty. To assess this foray, it is important to remember that it was a surprise attack at night on the supply/baggage train—not a frontal attack by day. Also, the spotlight in the story focuses on Abraham, but three other men (possibly with personal armies) also joined his force (v. 24).

(For more on this topic, go to p. 11 or p. 57.)

Tents and Furniture

"So Abram moved his tents and went to live near the great trees of Mamre at Hebron."
(Genesis 13:18 NIV)

Scripture presents the patriarchs as essentially nomadic dwellers in tents. Put yourself in the place of Sarah, who had known the rather sophisticated lifestyle of the cities of Ur and Haran. No close neighbors to discuss events of the day. No markets nearby to shop in on a daily basis. No thick walls to keep rooms cool. But don't equate that nomadic lifestyle with tenting in a national park.

The tents, made of goatskins during this period, were long and almost flat, but slightly higher in the center so the rain would run off. They were portable; the skins and poles could be bundled up and taken elsewhere quite easily. To afford privacy, families could hang curtains to create separate rooms. Frequently there was a private section for the women and small children. A raised tent flap could provide a sort of reception area where guests were welcomed. Or, as in the case of Abraham's entertaining the heavenly visitors, the shelter of an adjacent terebinth tree served as a kind of reception area (Genesis 18:4).

Abraham's well at the ancient city of Beersheba

(Levant Photo Service)

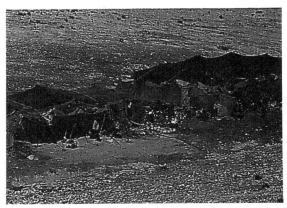

Tents used by modern Arab bedouins probably are similar to those of the patriarchs. Made of goat hair, they had flaps that could be lowered at night and had divider flaps that compartmentalized them into rooms.

(Photo by Gustav Jeeninga)

If a man practiced polygamy, there might be separate tents for his wives and concubines. In Jacob's family, Rachel and Leah had separate tents, and the concubines Bilhah and Zilpah shared a third (Genesis 31:33). Such an arrangement must have been common to avoid the family squabbles that otherwise might occur.

The patriarchs had fairly large establishments. As noted in the last chapter, Abraham had a thousand or more in his entourage. Lot also had quite an extended household, and the two of them found it necessary to separate because the land could not support them (see Genesis 13). How many there were in Isaac's company we do not know, but there were so many that they required a tent city. In fact, there were so many tents that his son Jacob could live and work among them (Genesis 25:27). Later, Jacob seems to have had a tent city of his own, and he bought a piece of land near Shechem on which to pitch it (Genesis 33:19).

There seems to have been little or no furniture in the tents. As in Ur, a bed was a mat or bedroll that was unrolled on the ground at night. Commonly, a table was a skin or mat that was spread on the ground, and people sat on mats or rugs around the "table" to eat their meals. A cushion stuffed with goat hair or sheep's wool would pro-

vide some comfort for a person who had to sit for a long time.

Dishes were made of baked clay, and the most common was a saucer or bowl from which one could either eat or drink. Fingers served as the most effective utensils, and sauces or juices could be sopped up with bread or drunk from the side of a bowl when it was tipped up. Clay cups and wooden spoons were also available. Large clay pots provided storage for grains, wine, olive oil, or milk; and moderate sized ones were used to bring water from a well or spring and to keep water until it was consumed. Clay jars have a remarkable capability of keeping water cool, even on a fairly hot day.

Clay Pots for Home and Business

"[Rebekah] went down to the spring, filled her jar, and came up." (Genesis 24:16 RSV)

Everyone used clay jars or pots in the ancient Near East—and they have been widely used even in recent times. Large jars buried in the ground served as a sort of silo where grain could be stored in vermin-proof containers. They also provided storage for oil and wine, and made for easy transport aboard ships. Salted fish and meats could be stored or shipped in them.

Because pottery styles and decor changed periodically, a science of dating and study of places of origin has been worked out. Thus we get help in developing a chronology and patterns of commerce for ancient times.

People of that time also used clay jars to draw water from wells (see Genesis 24:13–20; John 4:7, 11, 28). And when drinking water was brought back home, it was commonly poured into clay jars and covered. There it would be kept relatively cool all day. On my first trip to Palestine, in 1960, I was a guest in a stone house that had several large clay jars in a pantry to keep drinking water cool. We could always count on a refreshing drink on a hot Palestinian day.

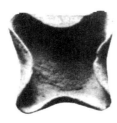

A Palestinian lamp of the patriarchal period

Goatskins also served as wine or water bottles (note: new wine in new wineskins, Matthew 9:17). Lamps were made of clay and in the patriarchal period looked a little like a square saucer with corners pinched to hold wicks, normally made of flax or linen. One of my Palestinian lamps dating to the patriarchal period measures five inches across. The fuel in these lamps was olive oil.

Cooking usually occurred in the open, but on a rainy day it might be done under a raised tent flap. A whole sheep or goat or a cut of meat or a fowl could be roasted on a spit. Vegetables or stew were cooked over an open fire in a copper or bronze kettle. Bread, which was formed into flat cakes like pancakes, only thinner, was baked in an oven.

How did Abraham and Sarah and their servants prepare the elaborate meal for the men that appeared while Abraham was at Mamre (Genesis 18)? They probably prepared some of the food with an outdoor oven. Though they changed slightly in form over the centuries, at this time an oven probably was merely a pit in the ground. This was some three feet deep and two to three feet in diameter and shaped in the form of a large jar. It had walls plastered with clay and a bed of pebbles on which a fire was built.

When used for baking, the oven was heated to the desired intensity with a quick fire of grass, thorns, dry twigs, or dung mixed with straw (cf. Matthew 6:30; Luke 12:38; 1 Kings 17:12; Malachi 4:1; though these refer to a later time, the kindling of the fire was much the same over the centuries). When the oven was heated, the inner surface was quickly wiped and the bread placed on the inner wall of the oven. The hardly more than paper-thin bread baked almost instantaneously. Alternatively, the ashes could be swept from the pebbles on which the fire had burned and the bread baked on the hot stones.

There is, no doubt, a reference to these pit ovens in Genesis 19:28, where the smoke of Sodom and the other ruined cities of the plain is compared to the smoke of an "oven" or "furnace" or "kiln" (depending on the version used) in the process of being heated. *(For more on this topic, go to p. 12 or p. 59.)*

Diet and Foodstuffs

"So Abraham hurried into the tent to Sarah and said, 'Quickly, make ready three measures of fine meal; knead it and make cakes.' And Abraham ran to the herd, took a tender and good calf, gave it to a young man, and he hastened to prepare it. So he took butter and milk and the calf which he had prepared, and set it before them." (Genesis 18:6–8 NKJV)

Fresh Bread Daily

Prior to baking, the bread dough of wheat or barley had been prepared in a wooden kneading-trough and allowed to rise for a few hours. A small lump of leavened dough had been preserved from the previous day's baking to provide leaven for the current batch of dough. And even before the dough could be prepared, barley or wheat had to be ground into meal, either with a mortar and pestle or between two flat stones, and mixed with water and salt to make a dough.

The mention of baking bread raises the question of what people ate during the patriarchal period. The meal set before the heavenly guests (angels) who visited Abraham with the announcement of the birth of an heir is some clue (see Genesis

A painting from the tomb of Knum-hotep at Beni Hasan (about halfway between Cairo and Aswan) showing the arrival of Semitic tribesmen in Egypt shortly after 2000 B.C. It illustrates clothing and arms of the period and possibly Joseph's "coat of many colors."

18:5-8, noted above). The menu consisted of bread, butter, milk and the meat of a calf.

Meat was reserved for special occasions. Animals were too valuable as sources of wool or milk to slaughter in quantity. Milk, cheese, and butter came from cows or goats. Wheat or barley could have been raised by the patriarchal community; they were not always wandering. Or they could have purchased it from local inhabitants. Honey provided sweetening and olive oil furnished cooking oil. There were, of course, wild fruits in season. Stews made of beans, lentils and peas probably furnished the most common family meal. Bread was baked daily. Figs were prized for their sweetness in a society that knew no sugar, and grapes were also plentiful. The variety of foods available to the Israelites after the Conquest of Joshua and settlement in the land was, however, greater than during the patriarchal period.

That is not to say that food was at all limited in quantity or quality. An Egyptian noble, Sinuhe, living in Palestine in exile about 1960 B.C., bragged about how good the land was—with plentiful grapes (and wine), honey, olives, every kind of fruit, barley, wheat, various kinds of cattle (and abundance of milk) and plenty of wild game and fowl.[2]

(For more on this topic, go to p. 15 or p. 63.)

Dress

"Then Jacob tore his clothes, put on sackcloth and mourned for his son many days."
(Genesis 37:34 NIV)

Biblical writers would not make it with *People* magazine. When describing what might be considered the "rich and famous" of their day, they completely leave out what kind of clothes they wore, how they did their hair. Biblical writers were concerned with attitudes and actions.

As a result the Bible provides us with almost no help in describing how an average Israelite or foreign personality dressed during the time of Abraham. The Hebrew words for clothing may be translated "coat" or "cloak" or "garment" and leave us with a vagueness of understanding. Fortunately we have Egyptian, Assyrian, Roman and

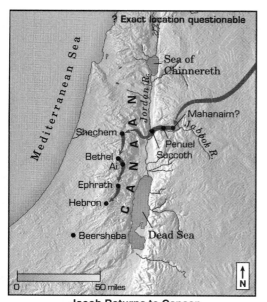

Jacob Returns to Canaan
After 20 years in northern Mesopotamia, Jacob returned to Canaan. He encountered the angels of God at Mahanaim and wrestled with a messenger of God at Penuel.

other pictures that add to our knowledge of Hebrew dress. And fortunately we have a fairly large group picture in color that dates to the patriarchal period. It comes from the tomb of the noble Khnum-hotep at Beni Hasan in Middle Egypt and dates to about 1892 B.C.,[3] approximately when the caravan brought Joseph as a slave to Egypt.

The picture portrays thirty-seven Asiatics who came from Palestine to engage in trade in Egypt. The group of men, women and children included armed warriors (with bows, spears, and throw-sticks), who traveled with them for their protection. Most of the men and women wore the almost universal sleeveless tunic, which had a shoulder strap over one shoulder, leaving the other shoulder bare. It extended to below the knees or to mid-calf. But some of the men wore only a kilt that extended below the knees. Other styles of tunics of the period had short or long sleeves. The fabric was wool or sackcloth (a coarse cloth of goat or camel's hair). The clothing in the Egyptian scene was brightly dyed with red and blue and black vertical stripes. Probably their everyday clothing was white or off-white, however,

because dyed fabric was much more expensive. Almost certainly these were "dress-up" tunics worn to impress the Egyptians that they were prosperous merchants who expected good prices for their wares.

Normally the tunic was held in at the waist by a girdle or belt of folded wool cloth, in which men kept their money and other valuables and in which soldiers carried their swords. When engaged in manual labor on a hot day, men normally wore only a kilt or a loincloth. Usually neither men nor women wore underwear and slept in the same clothes they wore during the day. Pajamas are unknown. In this picture, men were bearded (as Semites normally were) and had their hair cropped moderately back of the neck, while the hair of women extended down on their shoulders. On their feet both men and women wore sandals.

Joseph's "Coat of Many Colors."

"Now Israel loved Joseph more than all his children, because he was the son of his old age: and he made him a coat of many colours."
(Genesis 37:3 KJV)

Any discussion of dress in the patriarchal period raises the question of what Joseph's "coat of many colors" (Genesis 37:3 KJV) looked like. Certainly it was ostentatious and was designed to be a status robe. A similar robe was worn by princesses in 2 Samuel 13:8. Perhaps influenced by the 2 Samuel reference, the New Revised Standard Version and the Revised English Bible translations render the Hebrew "long robe with sleeves." The New Jerusalem Bible translates it "decorated tunic." The New American Standard Bible calls it a "varicolored tunic," essentially the same as the King James Version. And perhaps that is all that the text intends. On the assumption that the average man wore an undyed tunic on almost any occasion, one richly dyed in the fashion of the Asiatics who came to Egypt in the twentieth century B.C. would have been much more expensive and probably would have excited the envy that Joseph's brothers displayed.

(For more on this topic, go to p. 16 or p. 65.)

Impact of the Nuzi Tablets

Supplementing the Code of Hammurabi are the Nuzi tablets (found 1925–31 at Nuzi, about 10 miles southwest of modern Kirkuk in northeastern Iraq). These Hurrian texts included about 5,000 tablets from family archives and date to 1500 B.C. or slightly later. In the late 1960s additional Nuzi-type texts were unearthed elsewhere in northern Mesopotamia. Scholars initially found closer parallels between the Nuzi texts and the patriarchal narrative than are now accepted.[4] And subsequently, as additional Nuzi-type materials have come to light elsewhere and more study of the texts themselves has occurred, there is some modification of the earlier views.[5]

The subsequent discussion follows current thinking in the field and does not usually include initial interpretations. Incidentally, though the Nuzi texts date long after the days of the patriarchs, in some instances they reflect views and practices followed for centuries. Of course the law codes and the Nuzi tablets are now supplemented by a host of other less extensive collections uncovered in various places in Mesopotamia and Syria.

Family Life

Family Relationships and Mesopotamian Parallels

Ever since the beginning of the twentieth century, Bible scholars have been finding parallels to and supposed confirmations of numerous patriarchal family relationships and practices in Mesopotamian literature. This exercise began with the discovery of the Code of Hammurabi at biblical Shushan (Susa) in Iran in 1901. Hammurabi is variously dated, but the two most commonly accepted chronologies today are 1792–1750 and 1728–1686 B.C. (During the early decades of this century Hammurabi was dated closer to 2000 B.C.) The oldest of the various earlier Mesopotamian codes discovered since World War II is that of Ur-Nammu, dating to the Ur III period and thus to the time of Abraham (see last chapter). Though these earlier codes have many similarities to Hammurabi's, they are not as extensive or as well preserved and most of the laws paralleling patriarchal customs do not exist in them.

Finding a Wife

"So Abraham said to the oldest servant of his house, . . . 'Swear by the LORD, the God of heaven and the God of the earth, that you will not take a wife for my son from the daughters of the Canaanites, among whom I dwell; but you shall go to my country and to my family, and take a wife for my son Isaac.'" (Genesis 24:2-4 NKJV)

In the ancient Near East, and certainly in the patriarchal period, marriages were arranged by the families involved. The father usually instituted plans for marriage on behalf of his son. The prospective bride was a more or less passive participant in the negotiations. Thus, Abraham sent his servant to find a wife for his son Isaac from among his kindred (Genesis 24:4). Laban gave his daughters to Jacob (Genesis 29:23, 28).

Marriages involved financial agreements or arrangements between the parties involved. Among the Hebrews, as well as at Nuzi and elsewhere, the groom's side would give a gift and the father of the bride would equip his daughter with a dowry, which would then pass to the groom with his bride. The dowry was a sort of share of the family estate, which would later pass to the sons in the family. The giving of gifts to the bride's family is clearly stated in the procurement of Rebekah to be Isaac's bride (Genesis 24:53). Jacob did not have any gift to offer, so he pledged his labor as a sort of indentured servant (Genesis 29:18ff.). There are plenty of Mesopotamian marriage contracts from the second millennium B.C. that put the patriarchal narrative in context.

Apparently the practice of making a gift to the bride's family or performing an act to please them in lieu of payment continued through later Hebrew history. Examples

THE URBAN DEVELOPMENT IN
MESOPOTAMIA IN THE BRONZE AGE

Cartography Hallwag Berne

At Nuzi (top center) in northern Mesopotamia
about 10 miles southwest of modern Kirkuk were
found about 4,000 clay tablets, mostly in private
family archives, with social customs parallel to the
patriarchal narratives.

that illustrate this point appear in Exodus 22:16-17; 1 Samuel 18:25; and Joshua 15:16 (cf. Judges 1:12), where the newer versions generally refer to the "bride-price." It confuses the sense of what is going on for some versions (e.g., NASB) to continue to translate "dowry" in such passages. A dowry should be provided by the bride's family, not by the groom.

The Jacob-Laban narrative comes into sharper focus when viewed in the context of the practices of the time. Jacob had paid his "bride-price," fourteen years of labor, for his wives Leah and Rachel, and thus demanded that the marriage agreement be concluded by giving him his wives (Genesis 29:21; 30:26). Laban kept engaging in delaying tactics so he would not have to complete the marriage agreement and did not provide dowries for his daughters. Leah and Rachel complained that their father had sold them and then saw his assets dwindle so there would not be a dowry or inheritance for them (Genesis 31:14–15).

As Laban's flocks declined in number and Jacob's increased, the sisters concluded, "all the wealth which God has taken away from our father belongs to us and our children" (31:16 NASB). So they decided that the dowry issue had been resolved; they believed themselves equipped with a proper dowry by God. With the bride-price fully paid by twenty years of Jacob's labor and the dowry provided from Laban's property, Jacob and

his wives decided to leave Haran. It was sheep shearing time in the spring (Genesis 31:19), and labor contracts for the year had been fulfilled. Nothing should legally stand in the way of their going. (See discussion on labor contracts below.)

Producing an Heir

"But Abram said, 'Lord GOD, what will You give me, seeing I go childless, and the heir of my house is Eliezer of Damascus? . . . indeed one born in my house is my heir!'"
(Genesis 15:2–3 NKJV)

"So Sarai said to Abram, 'See now, the LORD has restrained me from bearing children. Please, go in to my maid; perhaps I shall obtain children by her.' And Abram heeded the voice of Sarai."
(Genesis 16:2 NKJV)

Children were of special concern to ancient Near Eastern families and to the patriarchal families in particular. Having a son was significant socially because it meant perpetuation of the family line and a certain prestige in the community. Economically, it meant securing an heir to whom one could leave property and who could manage the family affairs. Personally, it meant care for one in old age and someone who could arrange for proper burial, in a day when there were no social security benefits or homes for the aged.

Ideally, an heir should be born to a man and his wife, but that did not happen any more certainly in ancient society than in contemporary life. So men resorted to various alternatives. One was adoption. This would assure one of an heir and care in old age, but it did not provide for perpetuation of one's line. Thus a man might take a concubine or his wife could provide a slave girl to her husband for purposes of procreation. In rare cases, when the wife contracted a disease that prevented her from child-bearing, a man might take a second wife (see Code of Hammurabi, #148). Actually, all of these courses of action were pursued.

Abraham had all the usual reasons for wanting an heir, but in his case he also enjoyed the promise of the Abrahamic Covenant, which assured him that in him "all the families of the earth shall be blessed" (Genesis 12:3 NKJV), and that "one who will

come *from your own body*" would be his heir
(Genesis 15:4 NKJV). Very possibly Abraham,
like men of Nuzi and elsewhere in the early
Near East, had adopted an heir. He mentions
Eliezer of Damascus as the "heir of my
house" (Genesis 15:2). Having taken things
into his own hands, he at least had someone
to care for him in his old age and to inherit
and administer his properties.

Time dragged on and there was still no
natural heir, so now Sarah suggested
another stratagem: she would give her
slave girl Hagar to Abraham for purposes
of procreation (Genesis 16:2–4). Evidently
this practice would protect the wife because
the Code of Hammurabi (#145) specifically
states that the concubine would not rank
with the wife. Also, if such a slave bore a
child and then created an impossible situation for the wife, she could be appropriately disciplined (Code of Hammurabi
#146). Of course this happened in the case
of Hagar and Ishmael (see Genesis 16, 21).
Old Assyrian and Nuzi marriage contracts
somewhat parallel the Code of Hammurabi
and show that using a slave to produce an
heir was an accepted practice in the early
Near East. Later barren Rachel (Genesis
30:3) gave her maid Bilhah to Jacob; and
Leah, who had stopped bearing, gave her
maid Zilpah to Jacob to increase her offspring (Genesis 30:9). Interestingly, God did
not honor these human solutions. He
stepped in to provide the child of promise,
Isaac, as a son of Abraham *and Sarah*. And
He chose to move forward the line of Christ
through Judah, who was a son of Jacob *and
Leah* (Matthew 1:2), not her slave girl.

Bartering Away an Inheritance

*"Now Jacob cooked a stew; and Esau came in
from the field, and he was weary. And Esau said
to Jacob, 'Please feed me with that same red stew,
for I am weary.'. . . But Jacob said, 'Sell me your
birthright as of this day.' And Esau said, 'Look, I
am about to die; so what is this birthright to me?'
Then Jacob said, 'Swear to me as of this day.' So
he swore to him, and sold his birthright to Jacob."*
(Genesis 25:29–33 NKJV)

The sale of Esau's birthright to Jacob is
one of the most familiar accounts of the Old
Testament. As the story goes (Genesis

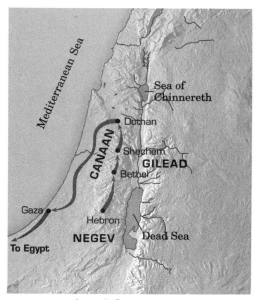

Joseph Goes to Egypt
Joseph searched for his brothers, eventually finding them at Dothan. His brothers sold him to a caravan of Midianites passing by en route from Gilead
to Egypt.

25:27-34), once when Esau returned from
hunting, he was utterly famished as he came
upon Jacob cooking a lentil stew, probably
mixed with onions and garlic. Esau was
seized with an almost uncontrollable desire
to have some. Taking advantage of the situation, Jacob demanded that Esau sell his
birthright for the lentil stew. In patriarchal
society, possession of the birthright involved
headship of the family, priestly function in
the family, inheritance of property, and possession of the covenant promises.

It is not the purpose of the present discussion to evaluate the conduct of Jacob and
Esau and to point out the aspects of their sin.
The only question at the moment is whether
the sale of the birthright is known from the
Nuzi texts. In the past other examples of the
sale of the birthright in patriarchal society
have been identified in the Nuzi tablets, but
those interpretations are questioned now.
The best that can be said is that there are several examples of part of an inheritance being
transferred from one brother to another, but
not between the eldest and a younger
brother. Such actions are a far cry from the
Jacob-Esau transfer. Unlike the parallels

A Cycle Tied to Shearing

Shearing time in the spring was the focal point of the herding cycle. At that time accounts were settled and new contracts drawn up. Then, after shearing, herdsmen took their flocks back to pasture. The six-year period of Jacob's service for the flocks is close to the six and one-half-year turnover time of the Nuzi flocks. That is, within that period of time the original flock belonging to Laban could have died off and been replaced by the colored livestock belonging to Jacob. Finally, Jacob left when Laban was at the shearing, at the end of the contract period, so he could leave honorably with his obligations fulfilled for the year just past and before the assumption of new responsibilities.[7]

between other patriarchal actions and the customs of the ancient Near East, in this case commentators do not find a known case of an eldest son who, like Esau, sold his inheritance or his inheritance rights. Such similarities that do exist come from late Babylonian or Persian texts of the first millennium B.C., rather than from this early period.

Fussing Over Contracts

"Thus I have been in your house twenty years; I served you fourteen years for your two daughters, and six years for your flock, and you have changed my wages ten times." (Genesis 31:41 NKJV)

As Jacob and Laban traded charges and countercharges when Laban caught up with the fleeing Jacob, Jacob complained that Laban had "changed my wages ten times" (Genesis 31:41). And Jacob proceeded to imply provisions of contracts and his fulfillment of them. After all, he had not eaten the rams of Laban's flocks; he had taken care that ewes and female goats did not miscarry; he had personally borne the loss of animals stolen or killed by wild animals; he had been vigilant in looking after the herds day and night (Genesis 31:38–40).

Martha A. Morrison has rendered a very useful service in showing how the Jacob-Laban narrative bears strong resemblance to Old Babylonian herding contracts, which are supplemented by the Code of Hammurabi and the Nuzi tablets.[6] Jacob as a free herdsman agreed with Laban, a livestock owner, to tend his flocks and herds in return for predetermined wages and gave a good account at the end of the period of service.

Stealing Household Gods

"Now Laban had gone to shear his sheep, and Rachel had stolen the household idols that were her father's." (Genesis 31:19 NKJV)

As Jacob and his extended family fled from Laban, Rachel made off with the family gods or *teraphim* (Genesis 31:19). The view held for some decades was that the family gods or house gods in Nuzi served as symbols or tokens or titles of inheritance rights and that possession of them would have given family headship to Jacob instead of the natural sons of Laban. It is now generally held, however, that the Nuzi information has been wrongly understood and that possession of the *teraphim* did not confer legal status on Jacob as the principal heir.[8] Each new household normally made new house-god images.

Not only must the old interpretation of Nuzi materials be abandoned, but it also appears that neither Jacob nor Rachel had any desire to inherit Laban's estate or to stay in Mesopotamia and manage it. We are left only with suppositions. Perhaps Rachel, who was now leaving the only home she had known, wished to take some symbol of family connections with her. Or possibly she was not yet as fully weaned from the old paganism as Bible students would like to believe. The fertility and good fortune of the family were the responsibility of the family gods.

Making a Will

"Let peoples serve you, and nations bow down to you. Be master over your brethren, and let your mother's sons bow down to you. Cursed be everyone who curses you, and blessed be those who bless you!" (Genesis 27:29 NKJV)

To Each His Portion

The right of inheritance is assumed and vigorously defended throughout the Old Testament period. Whether or not the practice was followed during the patriarchal period, under the Law of Moses the firstborn received a double portion of his father's possessions given to the other sons (Deuteronomy 21:15–17). But there were considerations other than mere primacy of birth. Reuben was Jacob's firstborn, but he had been guilty of incest·and his birthright was given to the sons of Joseph (see Genesis 49:4 and 1 Chronicles 5:1).

When Isaac (Genesis 27) and Jacob (Genesis 48) came to the end of their lives, they bestowed blessings which some have interpreted as oral wills, uttered in a patriarchal society that did not employ writing. And this practice of making an oral will with legal validity was reflected in the Nuzi texts. To be specific, Nuzi tablet PS56 described a situation in which a man on his deathbed had given a certain woman as wife to his unmarried son. After the father's death the son claimed the validity of the grant. But commentators now observe that the son won his case because of the testimony of witnesses and not because of any intrinsic legality of the oral statement. Moreover, current writers note that the older view confused an unchangeable patriarchal blessing with the tangible benefits of inheritance. Isaac and Jacob conferred social benefits or standing (apparently with divine prophetic enablement), not possession of property. Their blessing was the wish of a dying father and did not primarily involve inheritance rights.

In another connection, it appears that the right of inheritance was not affected by the status of the mother. This is implied in Genesis and clearly stated in the Code of Hammurabi. After the birth of Ishmael to the slave girl Hagar, Sarah took special action to prevent Ishmael from having inheritance rights along with Isaac and certainly not as the firstborn (see Genesis 21:10). The Code of Hammurabi (Law 170) states that if a slave girl bears children to the master of the house and he accepts them as his children, they are to share equally with the children of the wife in their father's estate. But if the father fails to acknowledge such children as his own, they would have no claim on his estate. In such an event, they shall be set free (Law 171).

Education

In their statements about oral wills during the patriarchal period, commentators seem to assume that there was no formal education at this time and the patriarchs could not read or write. This may have been true, especially of Isaac and Jacob, but as wealthy merchants they, like Abraham, may have had literate scribes to "keep their books." The leadership in Israel would be in an entirely different position in the days of Joseph and Moses, when they had access to the learning of the Egyptian court.

(For more on this topic, go to p. 16 or p. 68.)

Work, Travel, and Commerce

The patriarchal narrative indicates plenty of comings and goings during the days of Abraham, Isaac and Jacob. Abraham himself migrated from Mesopotamia to Palestine and then temporarily went to Egypt during a famine (Genesis 12) and moved about in Palestine itself. As noted in the last chapter, Albright held that Abraham was a caravaneer, plying his trade in central and southern Palestine. And he may have been. Moreover, he chased the kings from the East northward, recaptured Lot and the other prisoners taken, and recovered the booty the invaders had plundered (Genesis 14). Isaac did not move around as much as Abraham had, but Jacob lived for twenty years in northern Mesopotamia near Haran, later moved about somewhat in Palestine, and in response to an invitation from Joseph and the Egyptian Pharaoh, settled in Egypt and ended his days there.

The most extensive travel expedition reported in the patriarchal narrative occurs in Genesis 14, where four kings from Elam, Mesopotamia and other points East invaded Palestine and defeated the kings of

The mound of Dothan (center), the Old Testament city where Joseph's brothers threw him into a pit and later sold him to slave traders (Genesis 37:17–28).

Sodom and Gomorrah and three other kings of adjacent city-states. Critics used to assert that travel was not so extensive in the patriarchal period as indicated in this chapter and that military control of Palestine by Mesopotamian kings did not exist at this time.

The expedition of kings of Elam and Babylonia appears in a very different light when we learn, for instance, that as early as 2300 B.C. Sargon of Akkad (near Babylon) made raids on the Amorites of Syria and Palestine. Of particular significance for the present study is the fact that prior to Hammurabi's rule in Babylon, Kudur-Mabug, an Elamite king of Larsa (north of Ur), claimed to be "prince of the land of Amurru," which may have included Palestine and Syria.[9] Furthermore, a wagon contract found at Mari in the Middle Euphrates region and dating to the patriarchal period gives as one of the conditions of rental that the wagon shall not be driven to the Mediterranean coastlands, hundreds of miles away.[10] This prohibition implies extensive travel during the period under consideration. Prohibitions are rarely stipulated unless the forbidden act has some likelihood of occurring.

In addition, for the twentieth and nineteenth centuries B.C., we have a substantial amount of information from Egypt about the operation of donkey caravans in the Sinai and Sudan. These number 500, 600 and even 1,000 donkeys. Records from Mari in northwestern Mesopotamia describe donkey caravans traveling between Cappadocia in eastern Asia Minor and Armenia and Mesopotamia. The largest of these involves 3,000 donkeys in a single caravan.[11]

To this general period dates the Ishmaelite caravan that bought Joseph and carried him to Egypt. And now we have an accumulation of evidence that the Hyksos (an ethnic mixture with a Semitic preponderance) began to infiltrate the eastern delta of Egypt by around 1900 B.C. and took over the government about 1730 B.C. They furnish us with an ancient example of illegal aliens. In this context the Hebrews came in 1876 B.C., but as legal aliens, as invited guests. All this flurry of commercial and ethnic goings-on provides a context for patriarchal movement, commercial activity, and ultimate settlement of the Hebrews in Egypt.

In summary, Abraham came from an advanced civilization as a reasonably wealthy and possibly literate person. He was able to move about freely in Canaan because there were few cities. Because the climate at the time resulted in more rainfall, his herds prospered and he became a wealthy man. He may well have carried on an active trade with the caravans going through Canaan between Egypt and Assyrian and Mesopotamian countries. His family relationships may well have been broadly governed by practices growing out of or reflected in the Code of Hammurabi. Despite having a vital relationship with God, he probably did not express his faith in as many public observances as is commonly assumed.
(For more on this topic, go to p. 18 or p. 75.)

NOTES:

*A large deciduous tree with great straggly boughs, which when leafless resembles an oak.

[1] See Suzanne Richard, "Toward a Consensus of Opinion on the End of the Early Bronze Age in Palestine-Transjordan," *Bulletin of the American Schools of Oriental Research* (Winter 1980), 5-34.

[2] Arie S. Issar and Dan Yakir, "The Roman Period's Colder Climate," *Biblical Archaeologist*, June 1997, 101-06.

[3] James B. Pritchard, ed., *The Ancient Near East; An Anthology of Text and Pictures* (Princeton: Princeton University Press, 1958) 1, 7.

[4] Pritchard, 1, fig. 2.

[5] See, for example, Cyrus H. Gordon, "Biblical Customs and the Nuzi Tablets," *Biblical Archaeologist,* February, 1940, 2-12.

[6] See, for example, M. J. Selman, "Comparative Customs and the Patriarchal Age," in *Essays on the Patriarchal Narratives* (Winona Lake, Ind: Eisenbrauns, 1980), 91-140.

[7] Martha A. Morrison, "The Jacob and Laban Narrative in Light of Near Eastern Sources," *Biblical Archaeologist*, Summer 1983, 155-164.

[8] Ibid., 156-58.

[9] John VanSeters, *Abraham in History and Tradition* (New Haven: Yale University Press, 1975), 93.

[10] A. T. Clay, *Light on the Old Testament from Babel,* 2nd ed. (Philadelphia: Sunday School Times, 1907), 137.

[11] A translation of this wagon contract may be found in George A. Barton, *Archaeology and the Bible,* 7th ed. (Philadelphia: American Sunday-School Union, 1937), 346-47.

[12] William F. Albright, *Yahweh and the Gods of Canaan* (Garden City, N.Y.: Doubleday, 1968), 71-72.

BIBLIOGRAPHY:

Aharoni, Yohanan. *The Land of the Bible: A Historical Geography*. London: Burns & Oates, 1967.

Baly, Denis. *The Geography of the Bible*. New York: Harper & Brothers, 1957.

Millard, A.R., and D. J. Wiseman, eds. *Essays on the Patriarchal Narratives*. Winona Lake, Ind: Eisenbrauns, 1983.

Orni, Efraim, and Elisha Efrat. *Geography of Israel*. Jerusalem: Israel Universities Press, 3rd ed., 1971.

Van Seters, John. *Abraham in History and Tradition*. New Haven: Yale University Press, 1975.

Walton, John H., and Victor H. Matthews. *The IVP Bible Background Commentary: Genesis—Deuteronomy*. Downers Grove, Ill: InterVarsity Press, 1997.

Wood, Leon J. *A Survey of Israel's History*. Rev. by David O'Brien. Grand Rapids: Zondervan, 1970.

LIFE IN EGYPT DURING THE SOJOURN AND BONDAGE OF ISRAEL

(Genesis 39—50; Exodus 1—12)

T alk about culture shock! Any Canaan resident who moved to Egypt during the patriarchal period experienced the wrenching differences between a basically agrarian culture and an advanced civilization. So consider what Abraham faced when he briefly visited Egypt (Genesis 12). Yes, he had come from a rather sophisticated environment in Ur, but Egypt's royal household was culturally altogether different—and Abraham was not prepared for that.

By the time the slave traders marketed Joseph in Egypt (Genesis 37, 39), not much had changed. But Joseph was young and unattached and quickly adapted to his new environment. Sometime later he brought his father Jacob and his whole family in. Joseph assigned them to the land of Goshen (Genesis 46), where they would be less subject to the influence of idolatrous Egyptian culture.

They still had to adapt to a very different way of life. Instead of a place where farmers tilled their soil watered by rain and heavy dew, they had come to a region where it almost never rained and where the soil had to be irrigated. Instead of scenery dominated by hills and valleys and stands of trees, the great wide river, the Nile, functioned as the center of all of life. Instead of a decentralized and de-urbanized Palestine, they came to an Egypt with a central government that exercised at least moderate control over the whole stretch of the Nile Valley from the Mediterranean to Aswan— a distance of about 725 miles.

The Land

Egypt During the Israelite Sojourn and Bondage

"Then Jacob arose from Beersheba; and the sons of Israel carried their father Jacob, their little ones, and their wives, in the carts which Pharaoh had sent to carry him. So they took their livestock and their goods, which they had acquired in the land of Canaan, and went to Egypt, Jacob and all his descendants with him." (Genesis 46:5–6 NKJV)

It is often said that the Egypt to which the Hebrews had come *is* the Nile, or that Egypt is the gift of the Nile. That is very true because, as noted above, there is almost no rainfall in the country. Along the Mediterranean at Alexandria, rainfall totals up to about 8 inches per year; at Cairo it is 1½ to 2 inches; and south of Cairo it is less than an inch. Therefore, without the Nile there would be no Egypt.

The Nile provides water for irrigation of crops and water for drinking and for daily needs. Moreover, its annual flood* has deposited a layer of silt over the whole valley from earliest times. Without this won-

A boat sails south on the Nile, against the current.

derful topsoil the sands of Egypt would be relatively sterile. The water-laid soil of Egypt is so productive that until the last few years (when the population has greatly multiplied), Egypt has always had vast quantities of food to export all over the Mediterranean world.

The Nile also serves as the main highway of Egypt. This is true because boats and barges can float north with the current. And then, because there is a constant southerly wind and the current is very weak, it is possible to hoist a sail and move south against the current.

The Nile met other needs too. Along its banks lay plenty of good clay that could be made into bricks to build houses and into pottery to serve as dishes. Along its banks also grew papyrus reeds, used for making sheets of writing material (our word *paper* comes from papyrus), and flax, from which linen cloth was made. So the Nile provided for almost all the needs of a non-industrial society.

Lower Egypt

Egypt consists of two lands: the trough of upper Egypt in the south and the spreading delta of lower Egypt in the north. The delta is a pie-shaped region formed by silt deposits of the Nile over the millennia. Roughly the equivalent of lower Egypt, it is about 125 miles from north to south and about 115 miles from east to west. In ancient times the Nile had seven branches in the delta, but these gradually silted up. Today two branches remain: the western is known as the Rosetta, and the eastern as the Damietta. In the days of the pharaohs, Egyptians did not live in the northern delta in very large

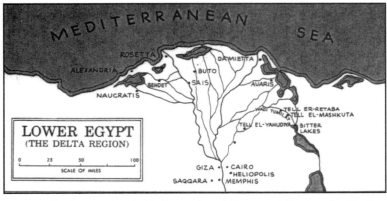

Goshen was located in the eastern delta, especially along the Wadi Tumilat.

numbers. There were no important towns along the coast.

At the eastern edge of the delta the Egyptians built defenses against Asiatic invaders—tribal peoples of Palestine and even Assyrians and Babylonians. In the vicinity of these fortresses they established store cities or granaries with sufficient supplies for the Egyptian garrisons. During the years that the Egyptians enslaved the Israelites, they forced them to build store cities in this area—Pithom and Ramses (Exodus 1:11). The land of Goshen (Genesis 46:28—47:31) was located in the eastern delta in the area around the Wadi Tumilat, a valley about 40 miles long connecting the Damietta branch of the Nile with Lake Timsah, now a part of the Suez Canal system. Some of the richest fields in Egypt lie to the north of the Wadi Tumilat.

The Nile Valley

The Nile valley (or Upper Egypt, higher in altitude than the delta) represents a tube, shut in on either side by cliffs and corked up at the southern end by the cataracts. Egypt proper extended north from the first cataract* at Aswan. From Aswan to Cairo at the base of the delta is approximately 600 miles, and from Cairo to the Mediterranean is another 125 miles, making the country approximately 725 miles long. If one includes the valley south to the fourth cataract, which Egypt ultimately conquered, the length of the country was about 1,100 miles. The part of the valley between the first and sixth cataracts is known as Nubia.

From cliff to cliff the Nile valley ranges from about 10 to 31 miles in width between Cairo and Aswan. But the cultivated area stretches only about 6 to 10 miles wide along that stretch of the river and narrows to 1 or 2 miles in width around Aswan, a mere 5,000 square miles. If one adds the most heavily populated southern part of the delta, ancient Egypt would approximate 10,000 square miles, roughly equal to the state of Maryland or a little less than the area of the country of Belgium. Thus the inhabited part of Egypt long has been one of the most densely populated spots on the face of the earth.

The cliffs of the Libyan tableland, which rise to approximately 1,000 feet, flank the valley on the west. Beyond that rolls the Libyan desert, part of the great Sahara. West of the Nile extends a chain of oases, the largest of which is the Fayum, about 55 miles southwest of Cairo. In the center of the Fayum is Lake Qarun, Egypt's only large inland lake, which today covers 90 square miles and is about 17 feet deep. Surrounded by slightly less than a half million acres of good farmland, that area received special attention during the Middle Kingdom (c. 2000–1775 B.C.) and under the Ptolemies (305–30 B.C.). To the east of the Nile, between the river and the Red Sea, rise granite mountains (to a height of 6,500 feet) with gold-bearing quartz veins and deposits of alabaster and semiprecious stones.

The first cataract at Aswan, now largely obliterated by the Aswan Dam. Cataracts are places where the river fails to cut a clear channel, leaving rocks piled in irregular masses in the streambed.

The ancient Egyptians lived in comparative isolation and peace in their valley home. The cataracts on the south, the deserts on the east and west, and the harborless coast of the Mediterranean protected them from invasion and left them free to develop a native culture. Chiefly at the two northern corners of the delta, outside influences could sift in. Semitic incursions from the east and Libyans, possibly of European origin, from the west threatened stability, so defenses were erected to protect against both.

The security of their valley home and the regular provision of the sun and the Nile gave the Egyptians a sense of confidence and well-being that was not the lot of other

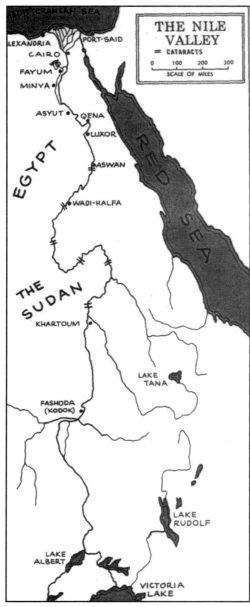

The Nile Valley south of Cairo, about ten miles wide

Period (c. 1580–1100 B.C.), "when Egypt ruled the East" and when the Hebrews were in bondage there.

(For more on this topic, go to p. 29 or p. 84.)

Government

Governmental Structure and Philosophy

The Hebrews entered Egypt in 1876 B.C. if we accept the chronology of the Old Testament based on the Hebrew text (see sidebar in chapter 2). At that time Egypt was in her Middle Kingdom (c. 2000–1775 B.C.). The pharaohs had lost their absolute power over the land at the collapse of the Old Kingdom (c. 2200 B.C.) and now a feudal style regime ruled. The nomarchs (rulers of the forty-two regions or nomes of the land) and other nobles checkmated the king. Unable to rule by simply issuing commands, the kings tried to win over the populace by presenting themselves as leaders who had the best interests of the people at heart. Thus, they talked a lot about *ma'at*, or social justice, and claimed that if people could not get justice in the courts of the nobles, they could in the royal courts.

Instead of spending a large part of the state revenues on building their pyramids, the pharaohs sought instead to launch projects that had some public benefit, such as canals or land reclamation. They often passed on to prospective rulers the admonition: "Build thy memorial in the love of thee," instead of in great palaces and pyramids.

peoples of the ancient Near East. They built their great capitals at Memphis (biblical Noph, near modern Cairo) and at Thebes (biblical No or No-Amon, 440 miles south of Cairo, at modern Luxor) and had no great upset of their way of life by external forces until the Hyksos domination about 1730 B.C. (see p. 52). Though life was not destined to be quite the same thereafter, they gained a new sense of power and importance during the Empire

The pharaohs still built pyramids, but those of the Middle Kingdom were not the large, expensive structures like those of the Old Kingdom. Usually they were made of mud-brick and covered with a limestone facing. As these pyramids have been used as "quarries" over the millennia and facings have been removed, they have greatly deteriorated.

Rulers of this period also tried to demonstrate their interest in the masses by artistic expression. Busts or statues of the kings emphasize the heavy burden of kingship and portray the king as a watchful shepherd who looked after the nation. Responsibility lined the faces of the pharaohs; they had deep creases at the corners of the mouths and hollows under the eyes.

The Pharaoh of Joseph's Day

"Then Pharaoh sent and called Joseph, and they brought him quickly out of the dungeon. . . . And Pharaoh said to Joseph, 'I have had a dream, and there is no one who can interpret it. But I have heard it said of you that you can understand a dream, to interpret it.'" (Genesis 41:14–15 NKJV)

This part of the story shows Joseph going from obscurity to power. Why? Because he could interpret the dream, which predicted seven years of plenty in Egypt followed by seven years of famine. Further it urged the king to appoint an administrator who could store up food-stuffs during the years of plenty to prepare for the lean years to follow. Amazingly, the pharaoh gave Joseph the job—and the power to enforce his commands.

If Jacob and the rest of his extended family entered Egypt in 1876 B.C. under the guidance of Joseph, we are curious to know who was ruling at the time. Most Egyptologists conclude that Sesostris III (also spelled Sen-Usert or Senwosret) ruled from 1878 to 1841 or 1840. If we accept that chronology, Sesostris III was the pharaoh of the great famine and his father Sesostris II (1896–1878) was the pharaoh during the years of plenty and the one involved in the Scripture quoted above.

A lintel from a gate (now in the Louvre in Paris) showing Sesostris II making an offering to the god Mentou. Sesostris may have been the pharaoh in Joseph's day.

Though there is no indication in the biblical narrative that there was a change of rulers at the end of the years of plenty, that is very possible and does not present a problem for us. The policy of the father well may have been continued during the reign of the son, who would have been crown prince during the years of plenty. An alternate chronology, followed by some of the scholars at the Louvre Museum in Paris, puts the reign of Sesostris III at 1887–1850. Acceptance of those dates would mean that he was ruler during both the seven years of plenty and the seven years of famine.

Joseph as Prime Minister

"'See, I have set you over all the land of Egypt.' Then Pharaoh took his signet ring off his hand and put it on Joseph's hand; and he clothed him in garments of fine linen and put a gold chain around his neck. And he had him ride in the second chariot which he had; and they cried out before him, 'Bow the knee!' So he set him over all the land of Egypt. Pharaoh also said to Joseph, 'I am Pharaoh, and without your consent no man may lift his hand or foot in all the land of Egypt.'" (Genesis 41:41–44 NKJV)

After Joseph interpreted Pharaoh's dream, the king decided to appoint him to an administrative position so he could implement plans for dealing with the anticipated famine. Evidently Pharaoh appointed Joseph vizier of the realm, a position we might equate with prime minister. The Scripture quoted above quite comprehensively describes his duties.

Interestingly, the Genesis account intimates the position and duties of the vizier as generally understood. That officer served in a position second only to the king in the administration of government. All government documents had to have his seal to be considered authentic and binding (the "signet ring" which could be pressed into a wax seal on a document). He served as chief justice of the Egyptian courts,[1] controlled the reservoirs and food supply, supervised industries and conservation programs, maintained a census of cattle and herds, kept agricultural statistics—including tax records, storehouse receipts, and crop assessments—and conducted censuses of the population. The vizier saw the king on a daily or at least a frequent basis, depending on how close he was to the palace as he performed his duties.

Head of Sesostris III

Joseph's symbols of office, in addition to his signet ring, included an official chariot in which to ride, preceded by a herald who would announce his coming, and a gold collar or chain around his neck. Most of the English versions say that Pharaoh gave Joseph a "gold chain," and that may be what happened. The Septuagint (Greek) translation calls it a "necklace of gold," and the Hebrew uses a word that can be translated "collar" or "chain." The pharaohs of the period are sometimes pictured as wearing a gold chain around the neck with an amulet in the center. But often they wear a large gold collar, usually inlaid with precious or semi-precious stones, that covers the shoulders and upper chest. Genesis says that Pharaoh set Joseph over "all the land of Egypt" (41:41).

The Administration of Sesostris III

Yet does the administration of Sesostris III reveal anything about an involvement with Joseph or with a famine?

1. In the first place, Sesostris III continued the expansion of cultivation in the area of the Fayum that his father, Sesostris II, had undertaken. Was that an effort to provide more food in preparation for the famine years? Wilson notes that the Middle Kingdom pharaohs added an estimated 27,000 acres to the arable land in and near the Fayum.[2]

2. Second, while the Middle Kingdom pharaohs in general tried to restore the absolute control over the land that Old Kingdom rulers had enjoyed, Sesostris III effectively reduced the power of the nomarchs and brought them and the land in general under control of the crown. Was he able to do so because the famine bit deep

The Fayum region where Sesostris II and III greatly expanded the cultivated area

and this forced the people to capitulate to the king in order to get food and stay alive? Genesis 47:14–26 tells how the desperate Egyptians progressively fell under the control of Pharaoh. After their money ran out, they sold their livestock, their land, and even themselves into service to the crown.

3. Third, there is a question about whether or when there could have been a famine in Egypt, with an ever-flowing river available for irrigation and a flooding Nile to fill reservoirs and to deposit a new layer of rich silt annually. As a matter of fact, the rains of East Africa have not always been dependable, and there were "low Niles." Famine did occur. For example, there was one in the days of King Zoser, builder of the Step Pyramid, about 2700 B.C.[3] Then, during the Middle Kingdom, one occurred during the reign of Sesostris I, about 1970 B.C.[4] Another occurred during the Hyksos period, in the reign of Apepi III (or Apophis III), about 1600 B.C.[5] Yet another took place about a century later (c. 1500), during the Egyptian Empire period.[6]

These references confirm the existence of famines in ancient Egypt, though none of

State chariot of Tutankhamen
(Cairo Museum; Lehnert & Landrock)

them has anything to do with Joseph, if we follow the chronology adopted earlier. A cryptic statement may be pertinent, however. Early in the third year of Sesostris III (1876 B.C., the year Jacob and his extended family settled in Goshen, according to the chronology followed in this book), an Egyptian patrol at the southern border of Egypt interviewed a group of five Sudanese who reported, "The desert is dying from hunger."[7] While there is no elaboration about dry or famine conditions, the inference is there. Also, that same group said, "We have come to serve the palace!" That is, they had come to join the royal army. And Wilson observes that this marked the beginning of Egyptian dependence on foreign mercenary troops for both warfare and police duty at home.[8] Presumably this initial group of mercenaries arrived willing to join the Egyptian army because drought had stripped them of livelihood at home, as has been the case with so many in recent droughts in Africa.

4. Finally, in relating the Joseph narrative to Sesostris III, something further must be said about the office of vizier. The king was unusually tall (over six feet six inches)[9] among a people who were generally fairly short, and he was very successful on the battlefield. He advanced the border of Egypt on the south to the second cataract, 214 miles south of Aswan, as well as controlling his enemies internally. Eventually, Clayton claims, he divided the country into

This ancient Nilometer, used for measuring the flood stages of the Nile River, was located at Elephantine Island at Aswan, Egypt.

three administrative zones: the north, the south, and the Nubian region, each with a vizier.[10] But presumably Joseph was the only vizier in his day at the beginning of Sesostris' reign; what Sesostris did later to reorganize the country does not preclude Joseph's single overlordship. The normal responsibility of the vizier to look after the food supply and the irrigation system and to levy taxes certainly fits with the king's concern for regulating the land during the years of plenty and the years of famine.

Hebrew Settlement in Goshen

Joseph sent a message to his father Jacob: *"You shall dwell in the land of Goshen, and you shall be near to me, you and your children, your children's children, your flocks and your herds, and all that you have. There I will provide for you, lest you and your household, and all that you have, come to poverty; for there are still five years of famine."* (Genesis 45:10–11 NKJV)

We all know stories of political figures helping their sons get ahead. In this story a politically powerful son helped his father and family survive. When the famine in the region was about to do Joseph's family in, Joseph exercised his authority as vizier of Egypt. He invited his father and brothers and the extended family of the Hebrews to settle in Goshen (Genesis 45:9–11; 46:31—47:6). Evidently Joseph could have made this decision on his own (Genesis 45:10), but he referred the matter to Pharaoh for confirmation of his arrangements (Genesis 47:6). The decision was a wise one because:

1. The grasslands of the area provided pastureland for the sheep of the Hebrews;

2. The area was sparsely occupied and there was room for Hebrew expansion;

3. As shepherds, the Hebrews would be an irritant to Egyptian cattlemen and should be settled on the frontier where friction with the Egyptians would be reduced (46:34). Shepherds and cattlemen have never gotten on well anywhere in the world.

4. Additionally, they would be sufficiently "near" to Joseph for him to look after their interests (Genesis 45:10–11).

The text does not reveal that settlement in Goshen would preserve their distinctiveness as a people. If the Hebrews did not come in contact with many Egyptians, they would not intermarry with them or be greatly influenced by their idolatry. Moreover, settlement of the Hebrews in the eastern delta would make it easier for them to leave when the time came for them to return to Canaan. As a matter of fact, any fear that the Egyptians may have had about being saddled with provision for the Hebrews on a continuing basis should have been allayed. When Joseph's brothers appeared before Pharaoh, they said, "We have come to sojourn" (Genesis 47:4 NKJV), not to settle.

They put down their roots in Goshen, evidently in the eastern delta and evidently a part of Egypt, not merely on the border of it. The "land of Rameses" (47:11) was another name later given to the district. We get some help in locating Goshen from the Exodus narrative. As the Hebrews left Goshen, they went from Rameses through the Wadi Tumilat (a valley connecting the Nile and the Bitter Lakes region, now a part of the Suez Canal system) to Succoth (perhaps Tell el-Maskhutah; see Exodus 12:37). Rameses was probably a later name of an urban complex including the old Hyksos capital of Avaris. Rameses was built to the north of Avaris, adjoined it, and may be viewed as engulfing its southern suburb of Avaris.

A King Who Knew Not Joseph

"Now there arose a new king over Egypt, who did not know Joseph" (Exodus 1:8 NKJV), and he proceeded to oppress the Hebrews severely and to put them to hard labor. Scripture gives us no hint as to who this Pharaoh may have been, but a brief review of history subsequent to Joseph's day throws some light on the situation. Beginning as early as about 1900 B.C., Asiatics (known in historical literature as Hyksos, commonly called *Aamu* by the Egyptians) began to enter the eastern delta region.

Some Asiatics came as leaders of trading caravans, others as veterans of units of Egypt's border police (established early in the Middle Kingdom), but most as captives of war or immigrants seeking employment. Eventually they became so numerous that with little military effort they gained control of the eastern delta. By about 1730–1720 they were able to dominate the northern part of the country. Only the princes of Thebes stood up to them, but often even they capitulated to the Hyksos. Finally, about 1570 B.C., the Thebans successfully fought a war of liberation and subjugated the Hyksos, or expelled them and founded the Egyptian Empire.

Thutmose III is often identified as the Pharaoh of the Great Oppression.

(Lehnert & Landrock; Cairo)

The fear of the Hebrews grew gradually. During the Middle Kingdom Egyptians had no reason to resent the small community of Hebrews. During the period of Hyksos domination that followed, the Hyksos had no reason to oppress fellow Asiatics. But after establishment of the Empire, or New Kingdom, the native Egyptians determined not to allow the rapidly-increasing Hebrew population to become so numerous among them that a group of Asiatics, i.e. Hebrews, might again threaten their sovereignty.

So the meaning of Exodus 1:8 probably is that there arose an Egyptian king of a native Egyptian dynasty who knew not Joseph in the sense that he had no good will toward Joseph's people. Presumably, not long after the native Egyptians began their New

"Foreigners"

In the United States we know something about dealing with immigrant populations who retain a different language, have strong contacts with their homeland, and have large families. Politicians and labor leaders are constantly agitating to either send them home or apply melting pot pressure, like reducing bilingual education or keeping them from getting welfare benefits. For the same reasons the native Egyptians oppressed Asiatics living in the delta—and that included the Hebrews. Though the Hebrews had never been part of the Hyksos movement, they were ethnically related to them and therefore incurred the wrath, or at least excited the fear, of the native Egyptians.

Kingdom about 1570, they enslaved the Hebrews and began to force them to work on construction projects in the delta. Then around 1528–27 the Egyptians became so concerned about Hebrew population growth that they issued the edict calling for the killing of male babies and thus threatened the life of Moses (Exodus 1:16). The pharaoh who may have begun to enslave or oppress the Hebrews could have been Ahmose I (1570–1545), and the one who issued the order for execution of male infants was possibly Amenhotep I (1545–1525).

Pharaoh of the Exodus

Scripture is no more specific in naming the pharaoh of the plagues and the Exodus than in identifying the pharaoh of Joseph's day or the later pharaoh who did not know Joseph. If we compute the date of the Exodus from 1 Kings 6:1, it would be about 1446 B.C. According to the 1 Kings reference, construction of the temple began in the fourth year of Solomon's reign or 966, and the Exodus occurred 480 years earlier, or in 1446. We cannot be dogmatic about who was ruling at the time. One group of Egyptologists puts the rule of Thutmose III at c. 1468–1436 and his successor Amenhotep II at 1439–1413. Another group dates Thutmose III 1483–1450 and Amenhotep II, 1453/2–1425.

Amenhotep II is often thought to be the pharaoh of the Exodus.

If we follow the chronology of the first group, the date of the Exodus would fall during the reign of Thutmose III, and according to the second group, during the reign of Amenhotep II. More recent writers seem to prefer the chronology that dates Amenhotep 1453/2–1425; he reigned for two or three years in a co-regency with his father Thutmose III. Not only have I followed this chronology, but I also have long felt that Thutmose III (often called the Napoleon of ancient Egypt) must have been a great oppressor who brought the Hebrews to the point of desperation.

Thutmose conducted seventeen military campaigns up into Palestine and Syria to build the Egyptian Empire there. As he did so, he must have put very heavy demands on the Hebrews in the eastern delta to help him ready his attacks. The less intense reign of Amenhotep II, with less activity along the Sinai frontier, would seem to furnish a better context for the Exodus.

If the Exodus occurred about 1440, the conquest should have taken place forty years later, after the wilderness wandering. The Jericho excavations show that the town

"It Never Happened!"

Parenthetically, it should be noted that none of the Egyptian records mention plagues or an Exodus. And we should not expect them to do so; ancient Egyptians recorded only successes. After all, the pharaoh was supposed to be divine, and gods do not suffer defeat. If a king was not always successful on the battlefield, his scribes had to put a good face on a bad situation. Only once do the Egyptian inscriptions mention the Hebrews. After the Hebrew conquest and settlement in Canaan, Pharaoh Merneptah (1224–1214; alternatively 1212–1202) recorded a successful invasion of Palestine (evidently in the days of the Judges) and later reported: "Israel is laid waste, his seed is not."[11] This inscription is in the Cairo Museum.

fell about 1400 B.C. (see discussion in chapter 6). Also, Amarna evidence supports an invasion about 1400; and by that time Egyptian control in Canaan, which Thutmose III had fought so hard to establish, had slipped; and it would have been possible for the Hebrews to conquer the land (see later discussion under The Conquest, chapter 6).

(For more on this topic, go to p. 31 or p. 88.)

Religion

Moses, Pharaoh, and the Gods of Egypt

Like many other people, ancient and modern, the Egyptians personalized the forces of nature. And they thought of themselves as living in relation with them. Scholars sometimes speak of primitive human beings as living in an "I-Thou" relation to nature. That compares with the "I-It" relationship of modern Western civilization, in which we think of nature in an impersonal, material sense. Hence the Egyptians thought of the Nile, the sun, the moon, the earth and other elements of nature as personal forces to be reckoned with. Furthermore, the Egyptians considered the pharaoh or king divine throughout recorded Egyptian history, and that fact colors the biblical narrative.

Everywhere you went in Egypt you saw temples to a wide variety of gods. The ordinary person was not, however, allowed to take part in the daily ritual of the state gods—that was for the entrenched priesthood. During religious festivals, however, the common people did get involved in the processions, for then the statue of a deity was carried about and celebrations occurred.

The populace did get to worship the gods directly at shrines here and there. Though the villagers might have afforded the support of priests, they acted as their own priests as a way of achieving closer contact with their gods. They could drop in and say their own prayers and make an offering at the shrines. There they might worship Amon, the sun god; Ptah, patron of craftsmen; Khnum, the deity that controlled the annual inundation of the Nile; Hathor, goddess of love and beauty; Mertseger, the goddess who represented the great mountain of the West Bank (at Thebes) known as El-Qurn; or other deities.

In Moses' struggle with Pharaoh to spring his people loose from bondage in Egypt, he took on virtually the whole religious establishment. Each of the ten plagues constituted an attack on specific Egyptian gods.[12] At least he showed God's superiority to the many gods of Egypt and managed to repudiate them.

Plague 1: "And all the waters that were in the river were turned to blood" (Exodus 7:20 NKJV).

The Nile was the source of life of the Egyptians, and they worshiped it as a god, even composing an ancient hymn to it. Though they especially worshiped the Nile inundation as Hapi, various other gods were associated with the river. Turning the Nile to blood was not only an attack on their theology but also a threat to their very existence (Exodus 7:14–25).

Plague 2: "And the frogs came up and covered the land of Egypt" (Exodus 8:6).

The plague of frogs (Exodus 8:1–15) represented a nuisance and a health hazard, but

The Nile, source of Egyptian life, became a plague to them.

it also repudiated the frog-goddess Heket. She was supposed to be the defender of the home and the protectress of women during advanced stages of pregnancy.

Plague 3: "Then the LORD said to Moses, 'Tell Aaron, "Stretch out your staff and strike the dust of the ground," and throughout the land of Egypt the dust will become gnats"'" (Exodus 8:16 NIV).

The plague of almost invisible gnats (Exodus 8:16–19) with their painful sting does not specifically relate to the theology of Egypt, but the gnats certainly would have greatly irritated the divine king, the royal family, and the priesthood and therefore would have affected the national religion in that way.

Plague 4: "And the LORD did this. Dense swarms of flies poured into Pharaoh's palace and into the houses of his officials, and throughout Egypt the land was ruined by the flies" (Exodus 8:24 NIV).

The Hebrew text describing the fourth plague, swarms (Exodus 8:20–32), does not identify the insects, but they are often considered to be flies. The translation of the Septuagint (the Pentateuch portion produced in Egypt about 250 B.C.) identified them as the blood-sucking dogfly, which again would have greatly annoyed Pharaoh and the priesthood, along with everyone else and all the livestock. With this plague there is separation between the Israelites in Goshen and the Egyptians in the rest of the land.

Plague 5: ". . . the hand of the LORD will bring a terrible plague on your livestock in the field. . . And the next day the LORD did it: All the livestock of the Egyptians died, but not one animal belonging to the Israelites died" (Exodus 9:3, 6 NIV).

The fifth plague involved some sort of affliction of cattle and other domestic animals (Exodus 9:1–7). The judgment resulted in a widespread loss of personal property, including animals used for agriculture, warfare, and members of the bovine family that the Egyptians worshiped. They, for example, considered several bulls and cows sacred. The Apis bull was the sacred animal of the god Ptah. Hathor, goddess of love, beauty and joy, was represented by the cow. Commonly she appeared in human form, wearing on her head the sun-disc flanked by a cow's horns. This goddess is often portrayed as a cow suckling the king and giving him divine nourishment. Mnevis, a sacred bull worshiped at Heliopolis, was associated with the sun god Re. It appeared with the solar disc and the sacred uraeus serpent between its horns.

Plague 6: "So they took soot from the kiln, and stood before Pharaoh, and Moses threw it in the air, and it caused festering boils on humans and animals" (Exodus 9:10 NRSV).

Hathor, goddess of love and beauty, wearing on her head the sun-disc flanked by cow horns

In this plague (Exodus 9:8–11) Moses threw soot (or ashes) into the air in the sight of Pharaoh, and it caused a terrible plague of boils that apparently became open and running sores. The magicians were infected and could not stand before Pharaoh, either to duplicate or stop the miracle. Presumably the priesthood were afflicted along with the rest of the populace, and the Egyptian gods of healing, such as Sekhmet (represented as a lioness or a woman with a lion's head), could not protect the Egyptians.

Plague 7: "So there was hail, and fire mingled with the hail, so very heavy that there was none like it in all the land of Egypt since it became a nation. And the hail struck throughout the whole land of Egypt, all that was in the field, both man and beast; and the hail struck every herb of the field and broke every tree of the field" (Exodus 9:24–25 NKJV).

Likewise during the seventh plague, when fire and hail destroyed crops (flax and barley) and cattle (Exodus 9:13–35), the gods believed to protect the crops did not do so. In particular, the sky-goddess Nut failed to help—or became a plague to them.

Plague 8: "And the locusts went up over all the land of Egypt . . . they covered the face of the whole earth, so that the land was darkened; and they ate every herb of the land and all the fruit of the trees which the hail had left" (Exodus 10:14–15 NKJV).

The plague of locusts (Exodus 10:1–20) brought terrible suffering on the mass of Egyptians, destroying their farm income and bringing many to the verge of starvation with the loss of their food supply. The gods of agriculture failed to protect the crops. By this time the patience of the Egyptians was wearing thin, and some even dared to question Pharaoh's wisdom in dealing with the Hebrews (10:7).

Plague 9: "So Moses stretched out his hand toward heaven, and there was thick darkness in all the land of Egypt three days" (Exodus 10:22 NKJV).

The ninth plague especially discredited the gods of Egypt (Exodus 10:21–29)—three days of darkness so thick it could be "felt" (10:21). We might say, "The darkness was so thick it could be cut with a knife." One day of darkness might have been manageable, but three days of darkness became intolerable. With no public lighting, and little oil available for oil lamps, most people had to tough it out. The intense darkness meant that they could not stir from their homes to work or even to fill their water jugs.

Egyptians highly revered the sun, since it almost always shone brightly. Along with the Nile, the sun was recognized as the source of all life. Egyptians especially worshiped the sun as Amon-Re (the god of empire during the Eighteenth Dynasty, when the plagues took place) and as Aton (the sun disc), the deity of the Amarna Age. Of course deities connected with worship of the moon and stars also lost face in the ninth plague. After this catastrophe Pharaoh told Moses to leave his presence forever and to return only on pain of death (10:28).

Plague 10: "And it came to pass at midnight that the LORD struck all the firstborn in the land of Egypt, from the firstborn of Pharaoh who sat on his throne to the firstborn of the captive who was in the dungeon, and all the firstborn of livestock" (Exodus 12:29 NKJV).

The sun was worshiped as Amon, Aton, Re, Amon-Re. Here is the god Re.

The tenth plague (Exodus 12:29–36) involved the death of the firstborn of the Egyptians, including the divine Pharaoh (v. 29) and all the priests of the land, and of the livestock. This judgment humiliated the "divine" Pharaoh and demonstrated that the various gods of Egypt could not protect their priests or their people. With this plague God achieved the release of His people after 430 years in Egypt (Exodus 12:40). *(For more on this topic, go to p. 31 or p. 90.)*

Warfare

Warfare in Ancient Egypt

It's one thing to get rid of a security threat. It's quite another thing to lose a large reservoir of cheap labor. After the Hebrews left, led by Moses, second thoughts set in among the Egyptians. "So the Egyptians pursued them, all the horses and chariots of Pharaoh, his horsemen and his army" (Exodus 14:9 NKJV).

Dressed for Battle

Wooden models of Egyptian soldiers of the Middle Kingdom period show men dressed only in short white kilts with no body armor (though in battle they sometimes wore leather shirts and kilts). They carry lances with bronze blades upright in their right hands and shields on their left arms. These are square at the bottom and rounded to a point at the top and cover the body from the top of the shoulder to mid-thigh. The men are smooth shaven and have moderately-cropped hair. These were the Egyptian "regulars"; a second contingent, composed of Nubians, held four arrows with flint tips in their right hands and had curved bows in their left. From early times soldiers also had battle axes.

Who were the "horses and chariots of Pharaoh"? What sort of army did Sesostris III command when he subdued the Sudan in the days of Joseph, or Thutmose III when he built the Egyptian Empire, or Amenhotep II when he pursued the Hebrews after the Exodus.

These six-inch high wooden models of an Egyptian infantry unit were discovered in an Egyptian tomb that dated to about 1800 B.C.

During the Middle Kingdom professional officers led a permanent royal army. Sesostris III built a chain of mighty forts south of Aswan. These have been excavated but now are covered by the waters of Lake Nasser, the huge reservoir that has collected behind the Aswan Dam. The forts had huge rounded bastion towers complete with arrow slits providing angles of fire across a wide ditch.

From the beginning of the Empire or New Kingdom period (when the Hebrews were in bondage in Egypt) the Egyptians maintained a regular standing national or royal army, with its effectiveness greatly enhanced by the adoption of new weapons from the Hyksos. Most important of these was the horse-drawn chariot, new types of sword and dagger, and the composite bow (built up of layers of wood, sinew, and horn), with its greater striking distance than the earlier simple Egyptian bow. Men now frequently wore body armor, consisting of small bronze plates riveted to leather or linen jerkins.

In the early days of the Empire Period 5,000 men constituted the army's basic unit, a division, and that is essentially what Thutmose III had to work with in his empire-building activities. Such an army was a formidable force, however, because the small city-states of

Palestine and Syria could not muster large armies. Thutmose marched his men along the coast and sailed his navy offshore as supply vessels. He began his fighting season at harvesttime in Palestine (early summer, so he could live off the land). The Egyptian harvest had already been gathered and reservists could march off to war.

Before 1300 B.C. a second division had been added, and the Egyptian army grew to four divisions by the time Rameses II sought to rebuild the Egyptian Empire about 1275 B.C. By that time the division had been divided into 20 companies of 250 men, and each of these into five platoons of 50. The companies and platoons had officers equivalent to a modern gradation of officers. The army maintained its own ships for patrol and transport, and its own support units and cavalry. In the support units the civilian hierarchy consisted of scribes, quartermasters, stablemasters, etc. Each division had at least fifty chariots and each chariot had a crew of two: the bowman-warrior and driver-shield bearer. The chariots were built largely of wood, with large amounts of leather employed in covering the body of the vehicle and serving as tires. The wheels usually had six spokes and were about a yard in diameter. Two horses typically drew a chariot.

The heart of the army consisted largely of a volunteer force, with its ranks filled by second and third sons not in line to take over their father's profession. They chose

Thutmose IV in battle with the Syrians
(From his chariot in the Cairo Museum)

this means of securing a career, a livelihood and advancement. The army during the Empire Period also consisted of conscripts and foreign mercenary auxiliary units from Nubia, Libya, southern Canaan, and elsewhere.[13]

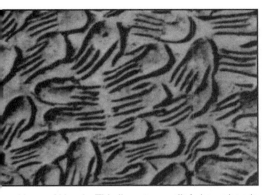

Heap of Hands. This limestone relief shows hands that were severed by the soldiers of Rameses III in their victory over the Libyans (c. 1190 B.C.). This was a common practice among the Egyptians, who used the hands to tally the number of enemy dead.

As far as weapons are concerned, Middle Kingdom soldiers carried axes, clubs, daggers and spears or lances; and Nubian auxiliaries their bows and arrows. The soldiers carried small individual shields and had large ones shared by two or three men. Sometimes they also had a wheeled siege tower. Men of the Empire Period had essentially the same weapons, with the addition of the chariot and other weapons adopted from the Hyksos, as noted above.

Incidentally, Egyptian victory scenes show numbers of severed hands, heads, or uncircumcised genitals of the slain foe, leading to two observations. First, the Egyptians practiced circumcision; boys were circumcised at about age fourteen, and Egyptians in this way made it clear that the casualties were foreigners.[14] Second, many peoples of the ancient Near East did not seem to have had much compunction about bodily mutilation and appear to have been rather cruel at times. Normally we think of the Assyrians as the outstandingly cruel people of the Near East (see discussion under Assyria, chapter 10), but the

Gore in Israel Too

Lest we think of the Hebrews as a cut above their enemies, we need to remember that for the hand of his daughter Michal Saul demanded of David the genitals of one hundred Philistines. David did not seem to bat an eye but went out and got two hundred genitals to show his prowess and worthiness to be the king's son-in-law (1 Samuel 18:25, 27). The rather matter-of-fact way that this report appears in the biblical text implies that the Hebrews must have done things like this on other occasions. Note, for example, Jehu's demand that the officials of Samaria behead the seventy sons of Ahab, and Jehu then had the heads piled in heaps outside the gate of the city (2 Kings 10:6–8).

Egyptian battle scenes can be rather gory too.

(For more on this topic, go to p. 32 or p. 100.)

Housing and Furniture

Joseph in Potiphar's House

"So Joseph found favor in his [Potiphar's] sight, and served him. Then he made him overseer of his house, and all that he had he put under his authority." (Genesis 39:4 NKJV)

Let's backtrack a bit to examine Egyptian houses and furniture. Joseph became head steward in the house of Potiphar not long after his arrival in Egypt as a slave (Genesis 39). As he served there, Potiphar's wife sought to seduce him, without success. A contemporary Bible student might wonder what Joseph was doing in the vicinity of Potiphar's wife's bedroom. Why did he continue to put himself at such risk? Excavated Egyptian houses of the Amarna period (about 1400 B.C.) may offer a clue. Even though they date later, presumably the general house plans of the wealthy did not change much over the centuries. In Amarna houses of the aristocracy, the apartments of the women were located near the front of the house, while storage areas and servants' quarters were at the back. So in fulfilling his duties Joseph would have had to pass his mistress's rooms daily.[15]

To begin with, it is important to note that mudbrick constituted the main construction material for Egyptian houses. To be sure, Egypt had plenty of stone, but quarrying and dressing stone proved to be very expensive, laborious, and time-consuming. Hence the Egyptians generally reserved stone masonry for the Old Kingdom pyramids, casings of Middle Kingdom pyramids, and temples. In some instances, foundations of palaces or houses of the very wealthy were laid in stone, but the superstructure was generally of brick. Though some Hebrews probably were forced to work on stone masonry, by and large they must have been involved in brickmaking. Dieter Arnold describes Egyptian stone construction in *Building In Egypt: Pharaonic Stone Masonry* (New York: Oxford, 1991).

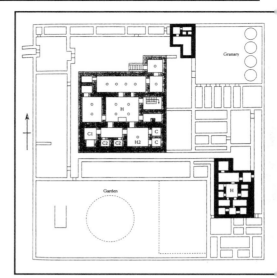

House of an Egyptian general at Amarna. The light gray is the house proper. The central hall (H) has a high ceiling carried by four wooden columns to a point higher than the rest of the house in a clerestory arrangement. In the hall there was a dais for the chair of the master of the house. This hall was used for public functions. A second hall (H2) was a private hall for the household. It was surrounded by rooms with clearly defined functions: bedrooms, bathrooms, storerooms. The black area housed secondary apartments of dependents. There was a garden filled with trees and plants and a granary and workshops and kitchens.

(Courtesy F. Arnold)

Archaeological Housing Shortage

In exploring the subject of Egyptian house design in Joseph's or Moses' day or the period of the Hebrew sojourn in general, we need to make a few generalizations. First, very few residential facilities in ancient Egypt have been excavated. Second, few houses can be excavated because they were located under modern occupation. Third, the Hebrews lived in the eastern delta, where remains were subjected to greater humidity and a higher water table than elsewhere in Egypt and thus would have decayed. Fourth, almost all residential structures, including the palaces, were made of mudbrick and therefore did not leave such durable or definitive remains as would have been the case if they were built of other materials. But there have been some excavations; models of houses have been found in tombs, and pictures of houses have been discovered in tombs.

For making bricks, workers moistened clay, mixed in chopped straw, worked the mixture with a hoe, and then poured it into wooden forms. These could be of various sizes but commonly were about 15 x 7 x 4 1/2 inches. The brick makers lifted the wooden forms when full and put them down alongside the brick just made. Eventually a whole field of wet bricks drying in the sun could be seen. Quality bricks could be produced by soaking a clay and straw mix in water for several days, during which time the straw would decompose and a gummy slime be created, ensuring greater coherence when the bricks dried.

Interestingly, we have from ancient Thebes a pictorial representation with an accompanying inscription from the tomb of Rekhmire, vizier of Thutmose III, of slaves making bricks. Among them are "Asiatic foreigners." This is the very time of the oppression and Exodus. Exodus 1:14 says,

"And they [the Egyptians] made their lives bitter with hard bondage—in mortar, in brick, and in all manner of service in the field. All their service in which they made them serve was with rigor" (NKJV). Later, during the Oppression, Pharaoh intensified the pressure on the Hebrews by making them go out and gather the straw for brickmaking and still maintain the production quota demanded (Exodus 5:7-14). In the Rekhmire scene, the taskmaster reminds the bricklayers, "The rod is in my hand; be not idle."[16]

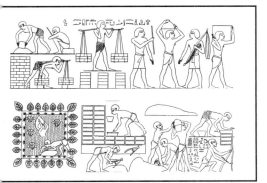

Semitic slaves making bricks, as pictured in the tomb of Rekhmire, vizier of Thutmose III, possibly Pharaoh of the Oppression.

The brickmakers' and bricklayers' task may not appear to be too rough. But think of the conditions. They worked out in the hot Egyptian sun all day (often in temperatures over 100°), driven to optimum production by taskmasters. They had no hats to protect their heads and wore nothing but a brief kilt or apron on their bodies. Because they soon looked like mud wrestlers, they often tossed the mud-caked kilt and worked only in penis sheaths.

Those who have ever gone to Masada and have seen signs everywhere about the necessity for frequent intake of water, or those who fought in the Gulf War (1991), will remember the instructions to the troops about frequent consumption of liquid; or those who have engaged in track and cross country events and obeyed training rules about salt and liquid intake; or those who have worked out of doors on construction in hot climates or in the hot summer months anywhere will appreciate the punishment the body takes from heat and sun.

In one of the illustrations on a stele, a wealthy ancient Egyptian father talked with his son about the condition of their bricklayers. He observed that their "kidneys suffer because they are out in the sun. . . with no clothes on." Their hands are "torn to ribbons by the cruel work." And they have to "knead all sorts of muck."[17] Certainly no one stood by to give the workers a drink every few minutes. It does not take much imagination to conclude that the severe "rigor" imposed on the Hebrews resulted in many of them dying of dehydration, heat prostration, heatstroke and the like.

As the Egyptians built brick walls, they did not lay courses as we do. Rather, they alternated a row of bricks laid on their long side with a row stood on their narrow side. They bonded the bricks together with a mortar composed of clay mixed with sand, chaff, and straw. Then they spread a plaster of similar mixture on the wall surfaces. Finally, the walls were whitewashed inside and out. Floors usually consisted of pressed clay or possibly of brick paving tiles. Windows were positioned high in the wall to keep the sun from beating directly on living areas, and windows and doors were placed in the north side if possible, to take advantage of winds blowing from the north. Ceilings or roofs consisted of trunks of date-palms (split or whole) and covered with palm branches, papyrus, matting and/or pressed clay. Cooking took place in a roofless kitchen or in the courtyard.

Houses had little furniture. The living room contained an earthenware bench or

Making bricks in modern Egypt

table around which the family squatted. Wooden chests or wall niches provided storage. Built-in platforms covered with matting served as a bed for most, but the wealthy had wooden beds with a wicker support for a mattress. The wealthy also had wooden chairs and stools.

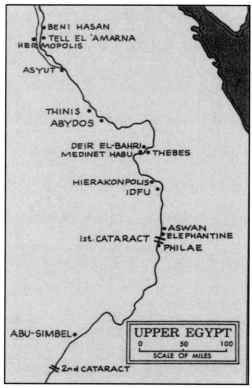

BENI HASAN
TELL EL 'AMARNA
HERMOPOLIS

ASYUT

THINIS
ABYDOS

DEIR EL-BAHRI
MEDINET HABU — THEBES

HIERAKONPOLIS
IDFU

ASWAN
1st. CATARACT ELEPHANTINE
PHILAE

ABU-SIMBEL

UPPER EGYPT
0   50   100
SCALE OF MILES

2nd CATARACT

Upper Egypt, showing Amarna (capital of Amenhotep IV) and Thebes (Middle Kingdom capital). At Thebes, especially in the tombs of the nobles, appear many scenes of everyday life.

A typical house of a family of the artisan class (we might call them middle class homes) at about the time of the Exodus contained four rooms on the first floor. A low wall divided the front room into two parts, the first serving as a hall and the second as a work area, where, for instance, flour might be ground. The middle room contained the living area proper, with a clay dais running around two sides of it and serving as something of a sofa or before which the family could squat to eat. The use of the two small rear rooms was clear. One had a clay dais on which they

placed a bed (a matting), and the other had a stairway to the second floor (under which was storage). The room above the bedroom, open to the sky, was a kitchen, with its typical cylindrical clay bread-oven. The adjacent two upper rooms served as family rooms.

Houses of poorer people might be one story, again of four rooms: the first a reception room, the second a living room, and the two rear rooms serving as a kitchen (open to the sky) and a bedroom, with a clay bunk covered with a mat. The roof was used for storage or sleeping on hot nights. These houses commonly measured some 15–16 by 48–50 feet, with the short side facing the street.[18] The very poor lived in one or two-room houses. Sometimes groups of small houses clustered around courtyards, often with shared facilities.

Most houses classified as single-hall houses. That is, one room served as a reception room for guests or a meeting place for the family. The houses of the more well-to-do or public officials might have two or more halls. The main hall in these houses served more as a reception area and the second hall as a living room for the family, with bedrooms opening off that. If houses had a third hall, this might serve as an office for the master of the house.

An external wall surrounded the houses and villas of the wealthy. The entrance led into a garden, usually with a fish pool, at the end of which lay a raised platform on which stood the house proper, which might consist of twenty to

Typical stools (or chairs) of the period of Hebrew bondage in Egypt

Wooden bed covered with sheet gold. From the tomb of Tutankhamen
(Lehnert & Landrock; Cairo)

thirty rooms. Villas included quarters for servants, a granary, and a variety of storage or work rooms.

(For more on this topic, go to p. 33 or p. 101.)

Diet and Foodstuffs

The Israelites complained to Moses while living on the bland and monotonous diet of manna in the Sinai wilderness, saying, "We remember the fish which we ate freely in Egypt, the cucumbers, the melons, the leeks, the onions, and the garlic" (Numbers 11:5 NKJV). The Egyptians indeed had a lot of variety in their diet at the time of the Exodus. But

The Baking of Bread

We don't know in what proportions the Egyptians grew wheat and barley. In fact, in the early days they used only one word for grain; they did not differentiate between wheat and barley. During the latter half of the Hebrew sojourn in Egypt, public bakeries became common and home production declined. By that time, too, some three to four dozen different kinds of bread had become available—varying according to form and content. For example, some bread looked like a modern pancake, some like a modern dinner roll, and some was hollow in the middle for filling with vegetables, like modern pita bread. Egyptians could also purchase breads seasoned with a variety of spices or honey or fruit, with no clear borderline between bread and pastry.

bread, whether of wheat or barley, served as the staple for all classes.

Plowing and sowing of grain took place at the same time. The farmer frequently broadcast the seed by hand in the path of the team (cows, not oxen) engaged in plowing. So the plow planted the crop instead of merely tilling the soil in preparation for planting. The harvesters cut the stems just below the ears and left the straw for brick-making, domestic fuel, and other purposes.

They then carried the grain in baskets to the threshing floor, where cattle or donkeys walked round and round on it to trample it and separate the grain from the husks. Winnowers then threw the grain into the air with wooden scoops to let the wind blow away the chaff.

Hoeing of the soil, plowing, and reaping with the sickle. From a tomb painting at Thebes.

Grain was crushed in a limestone mortar, then milled on a sloping stone with the use of a rubbing stone. When ground, the grain passed through sieves made of rushes to remove impurities and partly crushed grain. To make the bread they mixed the flour with a little salt and probably with sourdough that would act as yeast. Egyptians knew a pure form of yeast at least by 1500 B.C.

They sometimes baked bread on a flat stone placed over the fire, sometimes slapped on the outside of a cylindrical pottery oven open at the top, and sometimes in a mold placed over an open fire. Other methods existed.

Egyptians drank beer, the beverage of choice of the masses; only the rich drank wine. Women made the beer from barley, which they formed into loaves and then partially baked so as to make the yeast active but not to kill it. Then the loaves were crumbled and mixed with malted barley and water. They fermented the mash for several days and then strained it through a sieve into a large vat, from which it was poured into smaller jars. They added spices

Brewing beer from bread. From the tomb of Khentika at Saqqara.

and dates and other seasonings—hops were unknown. Tomb paintings illustrate various stages in the production.

In addition to bread and beer, the people consumed numerous vegetables, fruit, and fish. They ate a lot of legumes—beans, chick peas, and green peas. In addition, they consumed garlic, onions, leeks, Egyptian lettuce (which grew some three feet tall), and cucumbers. Dates were a favorite fruit and provided the main source of sugar for the poor; the wealthy used honey for sweetening. Archaeologists found evidence of bee-keeping in the early third millennium B.C. Finally, the spices used for seasoning included cinnamon, dill, mustard, and coriander.

Though the wealthy ate a considerable amount of meat, the lower classes could afford it only on special occasions. Numerous scenes of slaughtering and preparation of beef appear in tomb paintings, and sometimes we see wild game being prepared. The common people ate sheep, goats and pigs but apparently not the upper classes. All classes, especially the poor, ate poultry and wild birds. All classes enjoyed ducks and geese. Numerous kinds of fish provided important nourishment for the poor and some variety for the menus of the rich. Farmers added milk (from cows) and dairy products to their diets.

The serving of meals did not have the finesse to which we are accustomed. Poor families squatted around a low table, perhaps made of bricks, taking their food from common bowls with their hands or chunks of bread. The wealthy sat on mats or stools with little round tables in front of them. Servants brought the food which the wealthy ate from their own dishes, but again with their fingers or bread. Musicians and dancing girls entertained them while they ate. All classes apparently washed their hands before and after eating.

(For more on this topic, go to p. 35 or p. 101.)

Painting from a fifteenth century B.C. tomb at Thebes, showing the process of Egyptian wine-making. To the right, two men gather grapes from an arbor. To the left, five men tread out the grapes. The juice flows out of the vat to be stored in stopper jars.

Dress

Joseph and Potiphar's Wife (Genesis 39:12–18)

How did the Egyptians dress during the period of Hebrew sojourn in Egypt—and how did the Hebrews dress during that period? We get a hint at how little clothing a male might wear when we examine Joseph's experience in Potiphar's house.

As Joseph discharged his duties in Potiphar's house, Potiphar's wife "cast longing eyes" (Genesis 39:7 NKJV) on this handsome hunk (to use the vernacular; "well-built and handsome," Genesis 39:6 NIV) and tried to seduce him. As he escaped from her, she grabbed his "garment" (v. 12 NKJV) and held it for evidence against him. As noted in the last chapter, words describing clothing generally are unspecific in Scripture, except in prescribing the official clothing of the Hebrew priests or high priests. The Hebrew word used here is a general term meaning "covering" or "garment." The Septuagint (Greek) translates with a word meaning "clothes." The NIV renders the word "cloak," implying that something simply fell from Joseph's shoulders.

The Revised English Bible translates the Hebrew as "loincloth," and that is possibly closer to the truth, for men in all stations of life, including the king, wore a short kilt or apron for almost all activities. That kind of attire could explain what happened to Joseph.

Men's Clothing

The baking sun and high temperatures of the Nile Valley forced the Egyptians to wear light, airy clothing. They chose linen (made from flax) as their fabric of choice. Fibers from a young flax plant produced fine thread; those from a ripe plant were used for heavy fabric and rope. Egyptians used almost no wool; cotton did not come in until about the third century B.C. Tools of the garment makers from Joseph's time (the Middle Kingdom) consisted of knives or scissors and needles of bronze. Thread consisted of linen yarn. Egyptians did not use colored or patterned cloth because they did not have the technology for dyeing linen.

From earliest times men wore a belt from which hung a penis sheath or a short kilt. The kilt consisted of a rectangular piece of cloth wrapped around the buttocks, with the two ends crossed over in front and tucked in under the belt or tied at the waist or fastened with a buckle. Among the poor this remained very short for thousands of years, but among the more well-to-do it gradually lengthened.

As in modern times, styles changed from generation to generation and varied as a result of personal taste and class distinction. During the Middle Kingdom, in

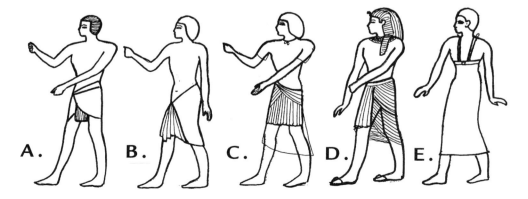

Men's clothing: (a) basic simple kilt (see other pictures in this chapter); (b) elaborate kilt with pleated front panel; (c) elaborately pleated kilt with sheer long shirt, worn by nobles; (d) crown and short kilt worn by pharaohs under a sheer overskirt; (e) garment worn by vizier when engaged in official duties (Joseph's clothing).

Joseph's day, a "maxi-kilt" became fashionable, extending to the calf. This was worn over the short kilt and was frequently pleated. Clothing for the upper part of the body also appears at this time. This consisted of a baggy tunic or shirt, a yard or more long. They simply sewed a rectangular piece of cloth up at the sides, with holes left for the arms and a hole cut in the center for the head. Some men also wore a fringed cloak wrapped around their body. Presumably the cloak and tunic were saved for dress-up occasions and could not have been worn when men were very active.

Joseph, as the head steward of Potiphar's house and a member of the lower aristocracy, probably owned a tunic and a cloak but did not wear them in carrying on his daily tasks. I believe that what Potiphar's wife grabbed was Joseph's longer "maxi-kilt" and ripped it off, leaving him in the shorter under-kilt.

During the Empire Period (the time of the Exodus) styles for wealthier men became more elaborate. Usually they wore a longer kilt over the short under-kilt. The longer kilt was usually pleated and was outfitted with a fringed sash. The tunic commonly had pleated sleeves. A light shawl, frequently fringed, was often thrown over the shoulder. All of this was of course for show. One could not work in such garb. In addition it was extremely expensive—much too expensive for lower class individuals.

We can only conjecture what Moses wore when he appeared before Pharaoh. Presumably he wore the longer kilt and a tunic, but whether it had sleeves is an open question. It is unlikely he sported the pleats and fringes of the upper aristocracy of Egypt.

Lower class men continued to wear a short kilt during the Middle Kingdom and Empire. And field hands commonly wore a simple apron, consisting of a triangle of material with the point hanging down behind and tied in front. Those who worked in the water—fisherman, boatmen, and papyrus gatherers—wore nothing at all. But villagers donned more conventional kilts when bringing produce to market and carrying on business in town.

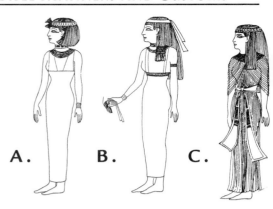

A.   B.   C.

Women's clothing: (a) simple long skirt and short hairstyle; (b) typical gown with shoulder straps and wig or natural hair; (c) cape covering shoulders, cape and dress pleated or crimped, embroidered sash.

Women's Clothing

Women during the Middle Kingdom and Empire periods commonly wore a long, white close-fitting dress (a sheath) held up with wide shoulder straps and extending to the ankles. Sometimes they covered their breasts and sometimes they did not. Surviving dresses show that the dresses were more baggy than the artists portray them. During the Empire the sheath dress became an undergarment. Over this, women wore a pleated, fringed robe consisting of a single piece of cloth, gathered around the waist and with the two top corners pulled over the shoulders and knotted under the breasts. Within this generalization, individuality was achieved with distinctive lines, embroidery, lace, and other decoration.

Servant girls usually wore only a skirt or apron while working. Dancing girls, musicians, singers and young waitresses commonly wore nothing but some jewelry.

Other Adornment

Most women and men went barefoot, but upper class people wore woven papyrus or leather sandals. Men and women wore adornment of various kinds from earliest times. With the Middle Kingdom came the introduction of bronze cloisonné inlaid with semi-precious gems and colored glass. The jewelry of the Middle Kingdom displays an almost microscopic quality of execution. During the Hyksos period earrings became fashionable in Egypt and pierced earrings became common during the Empire Period. Upper class men and women might wear armbands and bracelets.

Papyrus sandals from the tomb of Tutankhamen
(Lehnert & Landrock; Cairo)

As to other matters of appearance, in all periods men preferred their hair cut short, leaving their ears free. They used bronze razors from the Middle Kingdom on to create the smooth shaven look. The pharaoh wore a ceremonial beard, symbolizing divinity. Women wore their hair long and divided into three parts, one part hanging over the left side, a second part hanging down the right side, and a third part hanging down the back. Many Egyptians cropped their hair short, however, and donned wigs on special occasions. Some wore wigs over their full head of hair. Those who dispensed with wigs and retained a full head of hair kept it elaborately dressed. Wig-making and hairdressing kept many people occupied in ancient Egypt. Much could also be said about the cosmetic industry—about eye paint, rouge, lipstick, and body oils.

Hebrew Dress

Asiatic women also wore their hair long but undivided. Presumably that is how the Hebrew women in Egypt wore theirs.

Hebrew men in Egypt probably wore their hair longer than the Egyptians and were bearded. How the Hebrews dressed in Egypt is something about which we cannot be sure. Certainly Joseph and Moses while at the court dressed the way the Egyptians did. Certainly, too, as sheepherders, the Hebrews would have made some of their fabric from wool rather than linen. And they could have died the wool if they had wished. On the whole, Hebrew men probably did not look very different from the Egyptians. The Asiatics pictured in kilts in Khnumhotep's tomb (as noted in the last chapter) did not look markedly different from Egyptians of the period, except that the kilts were a little longer and they were bearded. But Egyptian women do seem to have worn narrower skirts than their Hebrew counterparts. Perhaps the Hebrews preferred to keep their style

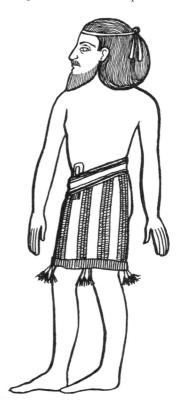

A captive Asiatic, pictured on a tomb wall of Seti I (c. 1300). A Hebrew or Hyksos man may have dressed this way.

because it gave them freer movement for physical activity.

(For more on this topic, go to p. 36 or p. 103.)

Family Life

Children

Children in ancient Egypt during the time of Joseph and up to Moses had a rather shaky beginning. Poor hygiene resulted in a high infant mortality rate. Ignorant of the germ theory of disease, the Egyptians sought to lay the responsibility at the feet of Seshat, the goddess of writing and arithmetic, who supposedly fixed the length of life at the moment of birth.[19] In the event of infant death, rich families had their little ones embalmed and placed in their own coffins. The poor buried theirs in linen wrappings or palm frond mats. In spite of infant mortality, families were usually large. Children were suckled openly without embarrassment; breast feeding normally continued for three years, longer than elsewhere.[20]

Soon after the birth of their children, poor women went back to work. This was possible because they carried their infants in a sling worn in front or in a fold of their clothes over the shoulder or left hip. That left both hands free and the mother could work unencumbered. Royal women normally did not bring up their own children but assigned them to a wet nurse.

As they grew up, children roamed about naked, even out of doors. Up to the age of ten or beyond they wore a long tress of hair hanging over the right ear while the rest was cropped short. Sometimes the long tress was braided. As the years went by, childish pastimes gave way to imitations of grown-up behavior. Children increasingly lent a hand with the easier adult tasks. The child's world was not so separated from the adult's as in contemporary Western society.

Normally boys were circumcised at about fourteen. Priests performed this seemingly religious ritual, which appears to have been a stepping-stone to adult life. In part it involved proof of manliness by ability to withstand pain.[21]

Marriage and Procreation

The Bible reports that Joseph married the daughter of a priest of On (Genesis 41:45). Why was he permitted to marry into an Egyptian family? There was no obstacle to marriage between people of different racial backgrounds in Egypt. An Egyptian man or woman could marry a Libyan, an Asiatic, a Negro from Nubia or someone else without any social stigma. Thus Joseph's marriage to an Egyptian was not unusual.

Because of what he had experienced, Joseph married at about age 30 (Genesis 41:45). This was old by Egyptian standards, since most males were still only boys when they married. Yet it is clear that a boy had to be not only sexually mature but also able to provide for his wife and thus settled in his occupation before he married. Girls seem to have married between about twelve and fourteen. They did not have to wait until established in a career. Some royal marriages, occurring for dynastic or other political reasons, took place when the individuals were very young. For example, Tutankhamen died at the age of eighteen or nineteen after a nine-year reign and marriage, so he must have been nine or ten when married.

How much intermarriage there may have been between Hebrews and Egyptians during the long period of Hebrew sojourn in Egypt is unclear. The fact that the Hebrews

King Tutankhamen and his wife. From his throne in the Cairo Museum.

(Lehnert & Landrock)

lived largely segregated in Goshen militated against ethnic fusion, but certainly there must have been some intermarriage. The meaning of the "mixed multitude" (Exodus 12:38 NKJV) that accompanied the Israelites in the wilderness is not spelled out in Scripture. Perhaps it refers to half breeds that were almost more Egyptian than Israelite. Or it may apply to Egyptians who, like "God fearers" or "proselytes" of New Testament times, were impressed with the superiority of the Hebrew monotheistic faith and the ability of God to work miracles (e.g., the plagues). That "mixed multitude" may have contributed to the calf worship at Mount Sinai. The whole bovine family was worshiped in Egypt, as noted earlier.

In order to arrange a marriage, a man would go to his prospective bride's father to ask for her hand. The mother seems to have been involved too, but the girl's consent does not seem to have been required. In the case of Joseph, the pharaoh, probably Sesostris II, arranged the marriage. We do not know the desires of the couple involved. For Pharaoh this was a good move because it established an alliance between the crown and an important priesthood and advanced the power of the crown, struggling as it was to reverse the feudalistic political conditions in the realm. The crown commonly arranged royal marriages, often when children were very young. And noble families also often must have arranged marriages to suit their purposes.

Marriages between kin frequently occurred among the common people, between cousins, stepbrothers and stepsisters, uncles and nieces, and others. Partners usually came from the same social stratum; marriage to a slave was treated only as concubinage. Though kings might have harems, commoners normally had only one wife, not because there was a law against it but because they could not afford more than one.

We have no information about a period of engagement. The wedding itself served as a social occasion, not a legal act as with us. It consisted of a series of activities, such as feasting, music, and dance. Then the bride almost always moved to the husband's own house. At times they moved in with the in-laws, but that usually did not work out very well. During the Middle and early New Kingdom periods in view in this chapter, they did not yet enter into marriage contracts recording material rights of a wife and her children when born.

The chief role of women was to provide their husbands with a male heir. If they failed to do so, they might present their husbands with a slave as a concubine; and then the couple could adopt the son or other children born to that union. Or the couple might adopt an orphan. The wife ruled the household and especially supervised bringing up the children. The wife of a poor farmer might also share the tasks of the field—plowing, sowing, and harvesting. On the whole husbands seem to have treated their wives decently, and Egyptian women of the ancient period fared better than women in other ancient Near Eastern countries.[22] Divorce, like marriage, was not a legal act but a private transaction by which one partner released the other. And divorce agreements, like marriage contracts, are known from the later periods.

Vacations; Recreation

Though life was hard, Egyptians did not spend all their time working. Royal craftsmen had one day off in ten. They observed numerous official holidays. Harvest festivals lasted several days, and they celebrated special holidays for each major divinity. Since the calendar was lunar, with only 360 days in the year, the Egyptians celebrated the extra five days at the end of the year as a holiday period.[23]

Dancing accompanied celebrations, feasts and religious services, and is frequently pictured on tomb walls. Dancing is depicted as active relaxation, with no clear borderline between dancing and acrobatic or gymnastic performances. Nor do we see dancing in male-female pairs as we know it; men and women always danced separately.

Dancing went along with music and song. In the New Kingdom the singer accompanied him or herself. A variety of instruments appears in the artistic representations: harp, flute, clarinet, trumpet, oboe, lute or mandolin, bone or ivory clappers,

Acrobatic dancers. From a tomb at Sakkara.
(Lehnert & Landrock; Cairo)

sistrum (a hand rattle with free moving metal strips strung on a series of horizontal wires), tambourine, and drums struck with fingers or open palms. A trumpet was used for signaling and became part of military equipment.

A musical entertainment. From a tomb at Sakkara.

Amusements for young men, particularly nobles and princes, included sports and drill and physical training for army recruits. Favorite male sports included wrestling, boxing, fencing with sticks (while wearing leather helmets), swimming, boat racing, gymnastic exercises, racing in a two-wheeled chariot, archery, and shooting a bow at a target while riding in a chariot.

Depictions show board games played by two or more people and informal entertainment at inns or beer houses, where boys and girls sat next to each other, and merrymaking proceeded without constraint and sometimes got out of hand.

Miriam and Her Timbrel: Music in Egypt

After the Hebrews had successfully crossed the Red Sea and escaped from the Egyptian army, the Hebrews celebrated: "Then Miriam the prophetess, the sister of Aaron, took the timbrel in her hand; and all the women went out after her with timbrels and with dances" (Exodus 15:20 NKJV).

The instrument, the Hebrew toph, had a skin stretched over a wooden hoop about ten or eleven inches in diameter. Thus it was a shallow hand drum, a little like a snare drum. The translation "tambourine," appearing in some versions, is misleading. Egyptian pictorial representations of the period do not show metal jingles around the edge of it, as found on the modern instrument.

The timbrel that Miriam played after the Red Sea crossing (Exodus 15:20). It is a wooden hoop with a skin stretched over it. The women would have engaged in a rhythmical beating of their timbrels, accompanied by a rhythmical body movement. From a tomb painting at Dendera.

The Egyptians enjoyed a rather well-developed level of music. The palace featured a director of musical entertainment. Playing musical instruments and singing formed part of the temple worship. Musicians participated in public ceremonies and played at many private banquets and other events. Instrumentalists and vocalists often appear on tomb paintings and during the Empire or New Kingdom are frequently named. During both the Middle Kingdom and Empire, musicians from abroad performed in Egypt and Egyptian musicians performed in other lands.[24] Should we look for a play-bill advertising the performance of the Byblos (Lebanon) String Quartet in Thebes?

How much the Hebrews played the horns, stringed instruments, woodwinds, and percussion that the Egyptians knew is open to question. If they carried those various instruments with them into the Sinai, it is questionable that that musical tradition survived through the long period of the Judges and into the monarchy. Presumably the later Hebrew development occurred because of a combination of Canaanite influence in Palestine, later contacts with Egypt and Mesopotamia, and native Hebrew achievement. (For a discussion of music in Israel, see under the United Monarchy.)

Moses and the Learning of Egypt: Egyptian Education

"And Moses was learned in all the wisdom of the Egyptians, and was mighty in words and deeds." (Acts 7:22 NKJV)

When adopted by Pharaoh's daughter (cf. Hebrews 11:24), Moses gained access to the best education Egypt had to offer. That education certainly included medical knowledge, though of course Moses did not train to be a doctor. How advanced Egypt was in this field is reflected in the Ebers, Smith, and Hearst papyri. The Ebers Papyrus, dating to the reign of Amenhotep I (1525–1504), the very years when Moses came to maturity, is sixty-five feet long and summarizes much of the medical knowledge then known in Egypt. It contains more than 700 diagnoses and prescriptions concerning digestive diseases, worm infestations, eye ailments, skin problems, burns, fractures, rheumatism, and discussions of the treatment of tumors and abcesses.

The Edwin Smith Papyrus text dates to about 1700 B.C. but is a copy of a work that originated in the Old Kingdom, before 2600 B.C. It contains forty-eight sections that discuss symptoms of diseases, diagnostic tra-

ditions and treatment. A third medical text, the Hearst Papyrus, dates to about 1600 B.C. and parallels much of what appears in the Ebers Papyrus but adds other diseases and medical conditions.

Village elders in the estate office, showing scribes with records and styluses. From tomb of Mereruka, Sakkara.

(Lehnert & Landrock)

In all of these the Egyptians mixed a certain amount of magic or superstition with solid medical information. They describe diagnosis and treatment, the setting of bones and even brain surgery. Even the modern reader must be impressed.

In treating bone fractures, the Egyptians used wooden splints and stiffened linen. They inserted wooden tubes into the mouths of those with jaw injuries in order to provide them with nourishment. Brick supports and body casts kept patients still and upright. The medical papyri carefully stipulated the dispensing of medicine, with specific instructions as to exact dosage and the manner in which it was to be taken. As was true of other professions, doctors had their hierarchy. At the top of the heap presided the "Chief of Physicians of South and the North," a kind of minister of health.

The Rhind Papyrus, dating to the late Hyksos period (c. 1600 B.C.) reveals the mathematical knowledge of the era. It discusses fractions, calculus and other aspects of mathematics.

In the field of religion, Moses would have become familiar with the various myths concerning the origins and working of the universe and the origin of human beings, and especially the *Book of the Dead*.

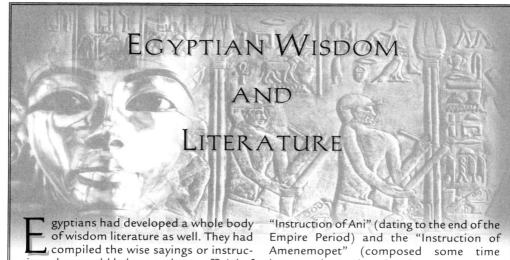

EGYPTIAN WISDOM AND LITERATURE

Egyptians had developed a whole body of wisdom literature as well. They had compiled the wise sayings or instructions that would help to make an official of the state successful; they usually were addressed to the official's son. In some respects this material parallels the Old Testament book of Proverbs. The oldest of these Instructions is "The instruction of the Vizier Ptah-Hotep," dating to the reign of Izezi (throne name Djedkare, 2414–2375 B.C.). Then about 2100 B.C. a pharaoh left for his son "The Instruction for King Merikare." Amenemhet I (1991–1962) penned an "Instruction for his son Sesostris I." All of these would have been known to Moses, and the practice of producing such literature continued, as is evident from the "Instruction of Ani" (dating to the end of the Empire Period) and the "Instruction of Amenemopet" (composed some time between the tenth and sixth centuries B.C.).

Typical of this literature are the following sayings of Ptah-Hotep: "Let not thy heart be puffed-up because of thy knowledge; be not confident because thou art a wise man. Take counsel with the ignorant as well as the wise." "If thou art a man of standing, thou shouldst found thy household and love thy wife at home as is fitting." "If thou art one to whom petition is made, be calm as thou listenest to the petitioner's speech. Do not rebuff him before he has . . . said that for which he came. A petitioner likes attention to his words better than the fulfilling of that for which he came."[25]

This instructed the deceased on how to overcome the dangers of the afterlife and consisted of spells and passwords put in the tombs.

He also undoubtedly became familiar with the entertainment literature, such as the *Eloquent Peasant* (a Middle Kingdom work that portrayed a peasant who suffered harsh treatment at the hands of officials but received honor and justice at the court of the king) or "Sinuhe" or the "Tale of the Shipwrecked Sailor."

How did Moses—or anyone else—become become familiar with the knowledge of the Egyptians? They had special tutors for the royal children, who taught writing, grammar, style, literature and mathematics. Princesses joined in, as did children of the highest-ranking courtiers. They developed a sort of "palace school."[26]

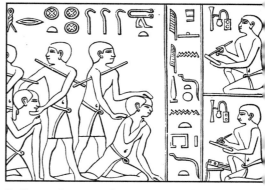

Scribes make a record as an overseer is brought in for reckoning. From a tomb wall.

They also had a few schools for scribes. Additionally, all major departments of government and the army took care of training as many scribes as they needed for themselves, and the teachers came from their own staffs. The temples operated in the same way. "Houses of Life" were associated with the major temples and focused on academic training for the priesthood, but some of their outstanding pupils became government functionaries.[27] Boys might start "school" between about five and ten and study for several years, depending on the requirements of their professions.

Stephen in Acts 7:22 described Moses as "mighty in words and deeds." We would expect him to have had the best education available, since he was being raised by a princess at the royal court. For princes and major public officials this included elegant and effective speech and wisdom and fair dealing.[28] Yet when Moses received his call to lead the Israelites, he demurred, saying that he could not communicate effectively (Exodus 4:10). Either he discovered this deficiency while "in school," or he had lost his proficiency during his years of herding sheep while in exile. In any case, he knew that the king, trained to speak eloquently, would expect a competing leader to be eloquent too. And he would not be impressed by anything less.

How did the Egyptians make some of their measurements? Here a group measures a field of wheat with a rope. From the tomb of Djesertkaresonb at Thebes.

As far as Egyptian education in general is concerned, fathers usually trained their sons to follow in their footsteps and mothers trained their daughters. This was true of scribes as well. Few sons of scribes went to an existing school. And few in the general populace learned how to read and write. Very few girls in any social class could read or write. During the New Kingdom, when Egypt built an empire, the schools surprisingly did not teach languages. Normally foreigners had to carry on Egyptian correspondence with foreign nations or subject peoples in the provinces.

How Egyptians Made Mummies; the Embalming of Jacob and Joseph

"Joseph directed the physicians in his service to embalm his father Israel [Jacob]. So the physicians embalmed him, taking a full forty days, for that was the time required for embalming. . . . Joseph died at the age of a hundred and ten. And after they embalmed him, he was placed in a coffin in Egypt. (Genesis 50:2–3, 26 NIV)

Throughout history people have been interested in preserving the body for future use after death—possibly resurrection. In today's world that might mean quick-freezing and storing the body for new advances in science that might give the person another opportunity at life. For the Egyptians of Joseph's day, the recourse was mummification.

Genesis reports that mummification took more than a month. We might think that the Egyptians were a rather morbid people to have spent so long preparing a body for burial, but just the opposite was true. Egyptians enjoyed life, at least a great many of the upper classes did. And they tried to defy death or extinction and to extend the good life that they knew here into the hereafter. They sought continued existence through preservation of the body. And they thought they could further guarantee that existence by erecting statues of themselves and splashing their names around in prominent places.

Joseph's reason for mummification was far different. If he was going to make the long trek back to Canaan with the body of Jacob, he had to preserve it somehow. It would decompose rapidly in the hot climate of Egypt and the Sinai. Moreover, he wanted his own body to be returned to Canaan—the Promised Land—when the Hebrews left Egypt (Genesis 50:25; cf. Exodus 13:19; Joshua 24:32). If that were to happen, it would have to be embalmed. He had no idea that they would not leave for over 400 years (Exodus 12:40)! Of course the Hebrews did not believe that their continued existence depended on preservation of the body.

Need for Mummification

In the earliest days Egyptians did not practice mummification because they did not need to. The sands beyond the area of cultivation were so dry and preservative in most of the land, that bodies are found still in a good state of preservation. In some instances it is possible to determine what a person buried in 3000 B.C. had for his last meal. But then during the Old Kingdom (2700–2200 B.C.) tombs became increasingly elaborate. The bodies removed from contact with the soil decayed rapidly. So mummification began to be practiced and continued throughout ancient Egyptian history down into the early Christian era.

For many centuries only members of the royal family, nobles, priests, high officials and the wealthy could afford to be embalmed. The poor continued to bury their dead much as they had from time immemorial, and they continued to benefit from the preservative nature of the desert sands.

Anubis, god of the dead and of embalming, takes care of the mummy. From the tomb of Amen Nakht.
(Lehnert & Landrock)

Beginnings of Mummification

During the some 3,000 years when Egyptians practiced mummification, the methods of embalmers varied quite a bit. And of course it took time to perfect their art. We need not look at the whole history of mummification but focus here on early developments and what went on in the days of Jacob and Joseph. By the time of the Fourth Dynasty, about 2600 B.C., Egyptians made their first attempts to inhibit decomposition by removal of internal organs. These organs were then wrapped in linen immersed in a solution of natron and put in a special recess in the burial chamber. Within a hundred years or so it was standard practice to put them in four limestone jars called canopic jars. Here are the steps in the mummification of the pharaoh and the most wealthy in Jacob's day.

Steps in the Mummification Process

First, immediately after death the Egyptians thoroughly cleansed the body using water containing the purifying agent natron. They then removed the internal organs through an incision in the left side. They took out the lungs, liver, stomach, and intestines. These were washed with palm wine laced with a variety of herbs and spices, wrapped in resin-soaked linen, and put in canopic jars. In patriarchal times

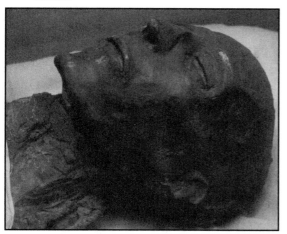

Mummified head of Seti I, c. 1300 B.C.
(Lehnert & Landrock; Cairo Museum)

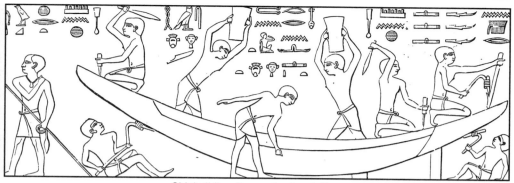

Shipbuilding. From a tomb painting.

these limestone jars had simple rounded lids; stoppers with the heads of gods came later. The evidence we currently have does not indicate that natron was used in treating the viscera. The kidneys and heart remained in the body—the heart was thought to be the seat of wisdom or intelligence. They did not remove the brain until the Empire Period.

Meanwhile, embalmers washed the body cavity with palm wine and spices and possibly a natron bath and temporarily packed it with absorbent material such as linen and with natron. Natron, an antiseptic that also absorbed moisture, was a natural salt consisting of baking soda and other salts found in the Natron Valley, some forty miles northwest of Cairo.

Now the body was ready for treatment— for the drying process. With the body about 75 percent liquid, the object was to remove that fluid and so to preserve the body. They laid the body on a bed that sloped toward the foot, where a basin caught anything draining from the body. Then they covered the corpse with piles of chalky white natron, and the drying action—which took place on the inside and outside of the body—proceeded for days. Meanwhile embalmers had to fend off rats and dogs that might try to carry away body parts. Genesis 50:3 indicates that the embalming-drying process took forty days in Jacob's case. There is independent information that after forty days the body would be totally dehydrated and virtually beyond all further natural decay. Apparently that was the normal time period for mummification, though sometimes it took much longer.

When the body had been dried out, embalmers washed it in a natron solution and packed it with resin-soaked linen to preserve its shape. Externally they wrapped it with linen strips totaling some 400 square yards or more. This they soaked with hot tree resin and then modeled the features of the face and body. The mummified person was thus protected against decay and insects and rats. And the body was put in a wooden mummiform coffin, which as early as Jacob's day had the painted facial features of the deceased along with other decorations.

It was in this condition—as mummies[29]—that Jacob and Joseph were carried to the Promised Land.

(For more on this topic, go to p. 38 or p. 103.)

Work, Travel, and Commerce

Egyptians maintained extensive and far-flung commercial relations all during her ancient history. To begin with, as noted, the Nile provided an all-weather highway, making possible local commerce. Even before Egypt became a united nation about 3000 B.C., she had trading relations with Phoenicia.[30] These continued during the Old Kingdom, Middle Kingdom, and Empire; that is, all the while that the Hebrews were in Egypt. The Phoenician trading capital during this early period was Gebal (Greek Byblos), twenty-five miles north of Beirut. It sent wine, oils used in the mummification process, and cedarwood for ships, coffins, and choice furniture.

Papyrus growing in a pool in front of the Cairo Museum

In exchange, the Egyptians sent gold, fine metalwork, and especially papyrus. In fact, so large was the volume of papyrus that flowed into Gebal that its Greek name "Byblos" came to be synonymous with papyrus, or book; our word *Bible* ("the Book") perpetuates the name of the ancient port.

While Egyptian ships hugged the coast of Palestine as they sailed north to Phoenicia, other Egyptian ships made their way across four hundred miles of open water to Crete to trade with the Minoans. Egyptian pottery and stone vases of the pyramid age (c. 2500 B.C.) have been found in Crete, and pottery of Cretan manufacture in Egypt. While Joseph served as vizier of Egypt, Cretans

Making Papyrus

Because of the importance of papyrus to Bible studies, let's examine its manufacture. First the Egyptians cut the pith of the papyrus stalk into thin strips. They laid these side by side in perpendicular fashion and covered them with a solution of resin from the plant. Then they placed a second layer of papyrus strips into place horizontally, and pressed the two layers together to form a sheet and allowed it to dry. The side on which the fibers ran horizontally (the recto) was preferred for writing. Sheets commonly measured about 10 by 5 inches but could be joined together in rolls a hundred feet or more in length.

were selling some of their famous pottery to the Egyptians, as witnessed by finds in the Fayum. And pictures of Cretans with various goods have been found painted on the walls of several tombs of high Egyptian officials during the Empire Period, especially during the days of Thutmose III.[31]

Relations with Nubia to the south were not so much commercial as exploitive, as Egypt exacted tribute in gold from the region.

Actually, the arts and crafts of Egypt had progressed to the point that she could have produced quality goods for export all during the Middle and New Kingdoms, when the Hebrews were there. The royal family and the nobility seemed to be the primary consumers of many commodities. And, of course, they wanted to have representations

The papyrus plant

Women weaving and washing, with their overseers. From a tomb painting.

Metalworkers. From the tomb of Mereruka,
Saqqara.

(Lehnert & Landrock)

of these items for use in the next life; so they stashed them away in their tombs. We don't know whether the craftsmen could have produced enough of their creations in mass quantity for export. Tomb paintings, especially of the nobility, picture all sorts of craftsmen at work, painstakingly making beds, chairs, wooden boats, chariots, leather goods, pottery, coffins, various kinds of metal objects, jewelry, and more.

The Egyptians developed the factory system during the pyramid age. That is, a number of craftsmen worked together in production centers as employees of the crown, the temples, or the nobility; and each workman carried out his part of the job.[32] This arrangement continued through the Middle and New Kingdoms, and there were state monopolies for production and export in the Ptolemaic period (c. 300–30 B.C.). Craftsmen normally trained their sons to carry on their line of work; and if they had no son, occasionally they would train someone else's son. There does not seem to

have been an apprentice system, however, and the Egyptians maintained no schools of a manual training sort.

No doubt sons of the Hebrews learned the various production processes developed by the Egyptians, and they seemed to know how to make fabrics, quality metal goods in bronze, and other materials for the tabernacle in the wilderness. But without continued

Ptah was the god of craftsmen and the
creator god.

practice during the wilderness wanderings, and with the dying off of the whole trained generation that left Egypt at the time of the Exodus, they entered Canaan with little expertise in the crafts. Moreover, the Hebrews lived largely to themselves in Goshen and primarily were involved in animal husbandry and agriculture.

(For more on this topic, go to p. 42 or p. 106.)

Stone carvers achieved some stunning work. Here is an especially fine piece of translucent alabaster from the tomb of Tutankhamen.

(Cairo Museum; Lehnert & Landrock)

Tombs Tell of Craftsmanship

Examples of Egyptian workmanship in the crafts come from many tombs of nobles, queens, and kings. But pride of place goes to the almost unrifled tomb of the young king Tutankhamen, who ruled Egypt from 1366 to 1357 B.C. and does not seem to have been twenty when he died. Howard Carter, working under the patronage of Lord Carnarvon, opened the tomb in November of 1922. There are now 1703 objects from the tomb in the Cairo Museum catalog, and some in Egypt have privately expressed to me the opinion that there may have been as many as 5,000 objects in the tomb when it was opened. As an example of how some of them may have been spirited away, over 300 objects from the tomb came to light in Lord Carnarvon's castle, when a retired butler revealed their hiding place in 1988.[33] The jewelry, alabaster vases and jars, chairs, beds, and the proliferation of gold in the young king's tomb excite the imagination as to what may have been put in the tombs of kings who ruled for decades. This tomb is important to ancient art history and to our knowledge of craftsmanship in Egypt soon after the time of the Exodus. Moreover, the contents give some idea of the "treasures of Egypt" (Hebrews 11:26) on which Moses turned his back when he chose to identify himself with the people of God.

The death mask of Tutankhamen
(Cairo Museum; Lehnert & Landrock)

NOTES:

*The flood began predictably between July 15 and 20 and attained its greatest height in October, after which the waters gradually fell.

*Cataracts are places (six in number) where the river has failed to cut a clear channel and rocks are piled in irregular masses in the streambed, presenting serious impediments to navigation. How serious is clear from the fact that while the first cataract is only two miles long, the second is 124 miles long and the fifth 100 miles long.

[1] But written codes of law apparently did not exist until the Twenty-fourth Dynasty, after about 700 B.C. John A. Wilson, *The Burden of Egypt* (Chicago: University of Chicago Press, 1951), 172.

[2] Ibid., 133.

[3] George A. Barton, *Archaeology and the Bible*, 7th ed. (Philadelphia: American Sunday School Union, 1937), 370.

[4] Stephen L. Caiger, *Bible and Spade* (London: Oxford University Press, 1947), 61.

[5] Ibid., 62.

[6] Barton, 371.

[7] Wilson, 137.

[8] Ibid., 138.

[9] Peter A. Clayton, *Chronicle of the Pharaohs* (New York: Thames & Hudson, 1994), 84.

[10] Ibid., 85.

[11] James B. Pritchard, *Ancient Near Eastern Texts*, 2nd ed. (Princeton: Princeton University Press, 1955), 378.

[12] Of special interest to this topic are John J. Davis, *Moses and the Gods of Egypt* (Grand Rapids: Baker, 1971); George Hart, *A Dictionary of Egyptian Gods and Goddesses* (London: Routledge & Kegan Paul, 1986); Manfred Lurker, *The Gods and Symbols of Ancient Egypt* (London: Thames and Hudson, 1980).

[13] Eugen Strouhal, *Life of the Ancient Egyptians* (Norman, Okla.: University of Oklahoma Press, 1992), 202–204.

[14] Ibid., 28, 29.

[15] See Adolf Erman, *Life in Ancient Egypt*, trans. by H. M. Tirard (New York: Dover Publications, 1971), 179–80. See further discussion on this episode in this chapter under "Dress."

[16] James H. Breasted, *Ancient Records of Egypt* (New York: Russell & Russell, 1962), 2, 293.

[17] Strouhal, 70.

[18] Ibid., 67–69.

[19] Ibid., 21.

[20] Ibid., 23.

[21] Ibid., 28–39.

[22] Ibid., 58.

[23] Ibid., 40, 41.

[24] Lise Manniche, *Music and Musicians in Ancient Egypt* (London: British Museum Press, 1991), 125. Manniche gives a very excellent discussion of music in ancient Egypt.

[25] Pritchard, 412–13.

[26] Strouhal, 35.

[27] Ibid., 235.

[28] Ibid., 32–33.

[29] One of the most valuable studies on mummification is by A. Lucas, former director of the Chemical Department of Egypt and Honorary Consulting Chemist of the Department of Antiquities of Egypt. See A. Lucas, "Mummification," in his *Ancient Egyptian Materials and Industries*, 3rd ed. (London: Edward Arnold, 1948), 307–90. See also James E. Harris and Kent R. Weeks, *X-Raying the Pharaohs* (New York: Charles Scribner's, 1973); Christine El Mahdy, *Mummies, Myth and Magic in Ancient Egypt* (London: Thames and Hudson, 1989); A. J. Spencer, *Death in Ancient Egypt* (New York: Penguin Books, 1982); and especially Salima Ikram and Aidan Dodson, *The Mummy and Ancient Egypt* (New York: Thames and Hudson, 1998).

[30] S. R. K. Glanville, ed., *The Legacy of Egypt* (Oxford: The Clarendon Press, 1942), 6.

[31] Sinclair Hood, *The Minoans* (New York: Praeger, 1971), 46–48.

[32] Strouhal, 137.

[33] *U.S. News & World Report*, March 21, 1988, 10.

BIBLIOGRAPHY:

Aldred, Cyril. *Akhenaten Pharaoh of Egypt.* New York: McGraw Hill, 1968

Aldred, Cyril. *Egyptian Art.* London: Thames & Hudson, 1980.

Aldred, Cyril. *The Egyptians.* London: Thames & Hudson, rev. ed., 1984

Aling, Charles F. *Egypt and Bible History.* Grand Rapids: Baker, 1981.

Allen, James P. and Others. *Religion and Philosophy in Ancient Egypt.* New Haven, Conn.: Yale University Press, 1989.

Andrews, Carol. *The Rosetta Stone.* London: British Museum Press, 1981.

Arnold, Dieter. *Building in Egypt.* Oxford: Oxford University Press, 1991.

Barocas, Claudio. *Monuments of Civilization: Egypt.* New York: Grosset and Dunlap, 1972.

Baines, John and Jaromir Malek. *Atlas of Ancient Egypt.* New York: Facts on File, 1980.

Bierbrier, Morris. *The Tomb-Builders of the Pharaohs.* New York: Charles Scribner's, 1984.

Bietak, Manfred. *Avaris, The Capital of the Hyksos.* London: British Museum Press, 1996.

Breasted, James H. *Ancient Records of Egypt.* New York: Russell & Russell, 5 vols., 1962.

Breasted, James H. *The Dawn of Conscience.* New York: Charles Scribner's, 1933.

Breasted, James H. *Development of Religion and Thought in Ancient Egypt.* Philadelphia: University of Pennsylvania Press, 1986.

Breasted, James H. *A History of Egypt.* New York: Charles Scribner's, 1946.

Brier, Bob. *The Murder of Tutankhamen.* New York: G. P. Putnam, 1998.

Bunson, Margaret. *The Encyclopedia of Ancient Egypt.* New York: Facts on File, 1991.

Carter, Howard. *The Tomb of Tutankhamen.* London: Sphere Books, 1972.

Clayton, Peter A. *Chronicle of the Pharaohs.* New York: Thames & Hudson, 1994.

Collier, Joy. *The Heretic Pharaoh.* New York: Dorset Press, 1970.

Currid, John D. *Ancient Egypt and the Old Testament.* Grand Rapids: Baker, 1997.

David, Rosalie. *The Pyramid Builders of Ancient Egypt.* London: Routledge, 1986.

Davis, John J. *Moses and the Gods of Egypt.* Grand Rapids: Baker, 1971.

Delia, Robert D. *A Study of the Reign of Senwosret III.* Ann Arbor: University of Michigan Microfilms, 1990.

Desroches-Noblecourt, Christiane. *Tutankhamen.* New York: New York Graphic Society, 1963.

Dodson, Aidan. *Monarchs of the Nile.* London: Rubicon, 1995.

Edwards, I. E. S. *The Pyramids of Egypt.* New York: Viking Penguin, rev. ed., 1985.

El Mahdy, Christine. *Mummies, Myth and Magic.* New York: Thames & Hudson 1989.

Emery, Walter B. *Egypt in Nubia.* London: Hutchinson & Co., 1965.

Erman, Adolf. *Life in Ancient Egypt.* Trans. by H.M. Tirard. New York: Dover Publications, 1971.

Fairservis, Walter A. *The Ancient Kingdoms of the Nile.* New York: New American Library, 1962.

Fakhry, Ahmed. *The Pyramids.* Chicago: University of Chicago Press, 1961.

Faulkner, Raymond O. *The Ancient Egyptian Book of the Dead.* Austin, Tex.: University of Texas Press, rev. ed., 1985.

Frankfort, Henri. *Ancient Egyptian Religion.* New York: Columbia University Press, 1948.

Gardiner, Alan. *Egypt of the Pharaohs.* London: Oxford University Press, 1961.

Grimal, Nicolas. *A History of Ancient Egypt.* New York: Barnes & Noble, 1997.

Harris, James E. and Kent R. Weeks. *X-Raying the Pharaohs.* New York: Charles Scribner's, 1984.

Hart, George. *A Dictionary of Egyptian Gods and Goddesses.* London: Routledge & Kegan Paul, 1986.

Hart, George. *Pharaohs and Pyramids.* London: Herbert Press, 1991.

Hobson, Christina. *The World of the Pharaohs.* London: Thames & Hudson, 1987.

Hoffmeier, James K. *Israel in Egypt*. New York: Oxford University Press, 1997.

Hoving, Thomas. *Tutankhamun, The Untold Story*. New York: Simon & Schuster, 1978.

Ikram, Salima and Aidan Dodson, *The Mummy and Ancient Egypt* (New York: Thames and Hudson, 1998).

Jack, J. W. *The Date of the Exodus*. Edinburgh: T. & T. Clark, 1925.

James, T. G. H. *Ancient Egypt, The Land and Its Legacy*. Austin: University of Texas Press, 1988.

James, T. G. H. *An Introduction to Ancient Egypt*. London: British Museum Press, 1979.

James, T. G. H. *Pharaoh's People*. London: The Bodley Head, 1984.

Janssen, Rosalind and Jac. *Growing up in Ancient Egypt*. London: The Rubicon Press, 1990.

Johnson, Janet. H., ed. *Life in a Multi-Cultural Society, Egypt from Cambyses to Constantine*. Chicago: Oriental Institute, 1992.

Jordan, Paul. *Egypt the Black Land*. New York: E. P. Dutton, 1976.

Kamil, Jill. *Luxor*. New York: Longmans, 2nd ed., 1976.

Kamil, Jill. *Sakkara*. New York: Longmans, 1978.

Kaster, Joseph, ed. *Wings of the Falcon*. New York: Holt, Rinehart, and Winston, 1968.

Kees, Hermann. *Ancient Egypt*. Chicago: University of Chicago Press, 1961.

Kemp, Barry. *Ancient Egypt*. New York: Routledge, 1989.

Lefkowitz, Mary. *Not Out of Africa*. New York: Basic Books, 1996.

Lehner, Mark. *The Complete Pyramids*. New York: Thames & Hudson, 1997.

Lichtheim, Miriam. *Ancient Egyptian Literature*. Los Angeles: University of California Press, 3 vols., 1973.

Lucas, A. *Ancient Egyptian Materials and Industries*. London: Edward Arnold, 3rd ed., 1948.

Lurker, Manfred. *The Gods and Symbols of Ancient Egypt*. London: Thames and Hudson, 1980.

McDonald, John K. *House of Eternity; The Tomb of Nefertari*. Los Angeles: J. Paul Getty Museum, 1996.

Manniche, Lise. *City of the Dead; Thebes in Egypt*. Chicago: University of Chicago Press, 1987.

Manniche, Lise. *Music and Musicians in Ancient Egypt*. London: British Museum Press, 1991.

Martin, Geoffrey T. *The Hidden Tombs of Memphis*. New York: Thames & Hudson, 1991.

Michalowski, Kazimierz. *Art of Ancient Egypt*. New York: Henry N. Abrams, n.d.

Michalowski, Kazimierz. *Karnak*. New York: Praeger, 1969.

Montet, Pierre. *Eternal Egypt*. New York: New American Library, 1964.

Montet, Pierre. *Everyday Life in Egypt*. London: Edward Arnold, 1958.

Morenz, Siegfried. *Egyptian Religion*. Ithaca, N.Y.: Cornell University Press, 1973.

Murnane, William J. *The Penguin Guide to Ancient Egypt*. New York: Penguin Books, 1983.

Murray, Margaret A. *The Splendor That Was Egypt*. New York: Frederick A. Praeger, 1969.

Nibbi, Alessandra. *The Sea Peoples and Egypt*. Park Ridge, N.J.: Noyes Press, 1975.

Nims, Charles F. *Thebes of the Pharaohs*. London: Elek Books, 1965.

Parkinson, Richard and Stephen Quirke. *Papyrus*. London: British Museum Press, 1995.

Partridge, Robert B. *Faces of the Pharaohs*. London: The Rubicon Press, 1994.

Pfeiffer, Charles F. *Tell El-Amarna and the Bible*. Grand Rapids: Baker, 1963.

Redford, Donald B. *Akhenaten the Heretic King*. Princeton: Princeton University Press, 1984.

Reeves, Nicholas. *The Complete Tutankhamun*. London: Thames & Hudson, 1990.

Reeves, Nicholas and Richard H. Wilkinson. *The Complete Valley of the Kings*. London: Thames & Hudson, 1996.

Rice, Michael. *Egypt's Making*. New York: Routledge, 1990.

Robins, Gay. *The Art of Ancient Egypt*. Cambridge, Mass.: Harvard University Press, 1997.

Robins, Gay. *Women in Ancient Egypt.* Cambridge, Mass.: Harvard University Press, 1993.

Robins, Gay, and Charles Shute. *The Rhind Mathematical Papyrus.* London: British Museum Press, 1987.

Rohl, David M. *Pharaohs and Kings, a Biblical Quest.* New York: Crown Publishers, 1995.

Romer, John. *Ancient Lives.* New York: Holt, Rinehart & Winston, 1984.

Romer, John. *People of the Nile.* New York: Crown Publishers, 1982.

Romer, John. *Valley of the Kings.* New York: William Morrow, 1981.

Romer, John and Elizabeth. *The Rape of Tutankhamun.* New York: Barnes & Noble, 1994.

Sandars, Nancy K. *The Sea Peoples.* London: Thames & Hudson, 1978.

Sauneron, Serge. *The Priests of Ancient Egypt.* New York: Grove Press, 1969.

Save-Soderbergh, Torgny. *Pharaohs and Mortals.* New York: Barnes & Noble, 1996.

Shafer, Byron E., ed. *Religion in Ancient Egypt.* Ithaca, N.Y.: Cornell University Press, 1991.

Shaw, Ian and Paul Nicholson. *The Dictionary of Ancient Egypt.* New York: Henry N. Abrams, 1995.

Shorter, Alan W. *The Egyptian Gods.* London: Kegan Paul, 1937.

Siliotti, Alberto. *Guide to the Valley of the Kings.* New York: Barnes & Noble, 1997.

Silverman, David P., ed. *Ancient Egypt.* New York: Oxford University Press, 1997.

Smith, Wilbur M. *Egypt in Biblical Prophecy.* Grand Rapids: Baker, 1957.

Spalinger, Anthony J. *Aspects of the Military Documents of the Ancient Egyptians.* New Haven, Conn.: Yale University Press, 1982.

Spencer, Alan J. *Death in Ancient Egypt.* New York: Penguin, 1982.

Stead, Miriam. *Egyptian Life.* London: British Museum Press, 1986.

Steindorff, G. and Keith C. Seele. *When Egypt Ruled the East.* Chicago: University of Chicago Press, rev. ed., 1957.

Strouhal, Eugen. *Life of the Ancient Egyptians.* Norman, Okla.: University of Oklahoma Press, 1992.

Trigger, B. G. and Others. *Ancient Egypt, a Social History.* Cambridge: Cambridge University Press, 1983.

Time-Life. *What Life Was Like on the Banks of the Nile.* Alexandria, Va., 1997.

Tyldesley, Joyce. *Hatchepsut.* New York: Viking, 1996.

Van Seters, John. *The Hyksos.* New Haven, Conn.: Yale University Press, 1996.

Watterson, Barbara. *The Egyptians.* Oxford: Blackwell, 1997.

Welsby, Derek A. *The Kingdom of Kush.* London: British Museum Press, 1996.

Wilkinson, J. Gardiner. *The Ancient Egyptians.* New York: Crown Publishers, 1989.

Wilson, Hilary. *Egyptian Food and Drink.* Aylesbury, Bucks, UK: Shire Publications, 1988.

Wilson, Ian. *Exodus.* San Francisco: Harper & Row, 1985.

Wilson, John A. *The Burden of Egypt.* Chicago: University of Chicago Press, 1951.

THE PEOPLE OF GOD WANDERING IN THE WILDERNESS

Chapter 5

(Exodus 13—40; Leviticus; Numbers; Deuteronomy)

It's really incredible! A horde of Israelites just released from slavery in Egypt strike out across the Sinai wilderness toward Canaan. That's probably close to three million men, women, and children crossing a genuine desert. Imagine what it was like to be in that crowd. For the sake of this chapter, put yourself in that crowd and join them for the journey of their life.

The Bible says that they traveled "by faith" (Hebrews 11:29), though it is hard to decide whether the faith of the Israelites or of Moses their leader was greater. The people trusted God and Moses to provide for them—with a blind faith. They didn't know how slim were the resources of the area—both in food and water.

Remember, it's been more than 400 years since the descendants of Abraham had the skills or equipment of a nomadic people. For 400 plus years they had been living in permanent houses in villages. And most of them started out with only the few things they could carry. We are not sure whether all of them even had tents.

But possibly they did because they had asked permission to go out into the wilderness on a three-day journey to sacrifice to their God (Exodus 8:27). The book of Exodus says nothing about how much they may have suffered until they were able to equip themselves for an extended journey.

Some of the Israelites surely had a vague idea of what they were up against, for they had lived in Goshen in the eastern delta, through which travelers and traders moved from Canaan and the Sinai. Their big advantage was that Moses had wandered in

The Wilderness of Sinai was a rugged, barren region (Exodus 19:1–2).
(Photo by Ben Chapman)

the Sinai and adjacent wilderness regions for forty years and knew first-hand how meager the resources were in the area through which they would be passing.

And it did take great faith. When we move a family, we make plans for a long time in advance, carefully select a moving company, and rent or buy a house or apartment before moving. Moreover, we either have a job before we leave our present homes or have some idea of how we shall support ourselves temporarily. If we are single, we might load our belongings into a car or van and strike out, but usually even then we have some idea of where we are going and how we shall proceed to meet our needs.

This was not a minor undertaking either. If we take literally the census figures in the Old Testament, the wilderness wandering involved millions of people. We read in Exodus 38:26 that a census taken in the third or fourth month after the Exodus reported 603,550 men twenty years old and above. Confirming that indication, a census taken about forty years later reported a total of 601,730 men twenty years and older (Numbers 26:31). We expect the later total to be smaller because God had severely judged the disobedient Israelites in the meantime. Before the first census was taken, a round figure of 600,000 men was said to have left in the Exodus (Exodus 12:37).

Six hundred thousand adult males would project to a total population of two and one-half to three million. Critics often talk about the problem of transcription of numbers in the Bible and drastically reduce the total involved here. Moreover, they are bothered by the extent of miracle required to support such a large number in a desert area. But if we depart from fixed indications in the Old Testament, our conclusions turn into wild guesses. And support for large numbers appears periodically in the biblical text and subsequent discussion.

If we stick with the traditional figure, it is as if the entire population of Chicago proper struck out across the American Southwest with its mountains and deserts, not knowing where they were going or how they would support themselves.

Significance of the Period

Bible students often treat the forty years of wilderness wandering as an insignificant parenthesis between the dramatic events of the bondage in Egypt and the plagues on the one hand and the conquest of Canaan under Joshua's leadership on the other. But this was a very important period. During these years God was molding this rag-tag bunch of slaves into a nation—into His covenant people. And He gave them their law, priesthood, sacrificial system, and the tabernacle, which provided a pattern for Solomon's temple later on. So all the basic religious institutions of Israel appeared during this desert experience.

Moreover, through miracle after miracle, God demonstrated His mighty power and prepared His people for the challenge of the conquest and settlement of Canaan. And if we accept the early date of the Exodus (c. 1440 B.C.), the period of wandering (c. 1440–1400) extended long enough for the Egyptian control of Canaan to slip so badly (during the Amarna Age) that the Israelites would not be forced to do battle with their former masters during the conquest.

The Land

The Sinai Peninsula

"They came to the Wilderness of Sinai." (Exodus 19:1)

Marah, where the bitter water was made sweet (Exodus 15:23), is thought to be 'Ain Hawara, about seven miles from the Red Sea.

Shaped like a wedge driven between Africa and Arabia (in Asia), the Sinai juts down into the Red Sea. The Gulf of Suez separates it from the African mainland, and the Gulf of Aqaba divides it from Arabia. Its northern shore fronts on the Mediterranean, and at the northeast it abuts on the land of Canaan. The peninsula is about 240 miles long and 120 miles wide.

Water in the Desert

For the last decade or so the Egyptian government has been pushing a plan to increase the population of the Sinai to one million by the year 2000. But the total probably will not exceed 400,000, approximately double the number of inhabitants in 1980.

Lack of water plagues the region, with most of the soil marginal in quality. Rainfall averages only about 1.6" per year, slightly less than that of modern Cairo. The Egyptian government faces daunting obstacles in trying to establish water pipelines from the Nile, with underground supplies offering more promise.

In recent years evidence has accumulated that there is a vast aquifer under the Sinai and the Negev. This holds 200 billion cubic meters of non-renewable fossil water that was deposited some 30,000 years ago, 70 billion cubic meters of which is under the Negev. At present over 25 million cubic meters of the water under the Negev is being used annually for industrial and agricultural purposes in Israel.[1]

A rugged, waste region, the Sinai peninsula features a landscape of wild beauty and grandeur. The barren mountain ranges of red and gray granite and gneiss often have colorful veins of stone that look almost unreal. Flaming orange and red indicate the presence of iron, black the presence of manganese, and bluish-green of copper. The peninsula consists of three main regions: the high mountains of the

south, the a-Tih Plateau in the center (about 60 percent of the total), and the northern plain along the Mediterranean—consisting mostly of gravel or shifting sand dunes. The few oases support little settled population even today. Only a fraction of one percent of the peninsula is currently under cultivation, probably no more than that was farmed in ancient times. Grazing grounds have always been sparse.

Scarcity of water raises the question of how the Israelites could survive in the Sinai. The biblical text mentions springs and wells that they found in their travels, but wouldn't a large number of Israelites exhaust the meager supplies of such an arid region? The answer may lie in a vast aquifer under the Sinai and the Negev.

An oasis in the Wadi Gharandel, the traditional site of the oasis of Elim, a stop between Marah and the Wilderness of Sin (Exodus 15:22—16:1)

The Location of Mount Sinai

Traditionally Mount Sinai, where Moses received the law, is identified with Jebul Musa (mountain of Moses). This 7,519-foot peak is one of three major peaks that dominate a region of mountains at the southern tip of Sinai. There is an adjacent plain or valley (er-Raha), about two miles long and seven miles wide, where the Israelites could have camped and where Bedouin today obtain water by digging shallow wells.

Numerous scholars and popularizers have suggested alternate sites for Mount Sinai, but not very convincingly. The technical discussion concerning them is quite

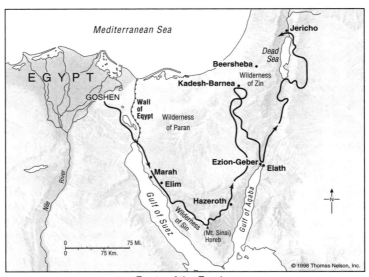

Route of the Exodus

beyond the purposes of this book. While we cannot be dogmatic about the location of the holy mountain, many scholars believe that the traditional site remains the most satisfactory. That a plain lies nearby able to accommodate the Israelites during Moses' reception of the law favors it. This is not true of other candidates for Mount Sinai.

Route of the Exodus and Wilderness Wandering

"God did not lead them by way of the land of the Philistines, although that was near; for God said, 'Lest perhaps the people change their minds when they see war, and return to Egypt.'" (Exodus 13:17 NKJV)

The question immediately arises as to where the Hebrews went as they left Egypt and marched out into the Sinai. They could have gone the short way, along the Mediterranean. Conquerors had taken this path from time immemorial as they sallied forth from Egypt to build empires and as they invaded Egypt from the north. And whether we take the early date of the Exodus (c. 1440) or the late date (c. 1275), Egyptian army contingents were stationed along that route in force and would have violently opposed Israelite movements. As

noted above, God Himself pointed out the futility of going in that direction.

A second route would have taken them across the central Sinai. That would have been a difficult march for so large a number, and water resources were minimal there. Instead God led them south along the Gulf of Suez past springs that were fed by the aquifer under the Sinai. The terrain was easier there too.

Red Sea vs. Reed Sea

"So God led the people around by way of the wilderness of the Red Sea. And the children of Israel went up in orderly ranks out of the land of Egypt." (Exodus 13:8 NKJV)

Exactly where the Hebrews went as they traveled east from Goshen remains a matter of considerable debate. Part of the problem relates to the meaning of the term *yam sûph* (translated "Red Sea" in the King James and other versions) and part of it is the difficulty or impossibility of identifying several of the sites connected with the Exodus narrative (for example, the three place names of Exodus 14:2 cannot be identified with any degree of certainty). Some have argued that *yam sûph* (based on the Egyptian) should be translated "Sea of Reeds" and have sought

A rocky shore along the Red Sea, at a point near where the Israelites crossed during the Exodus (Exodus 14).

to identify it as a lake or lakes now part of the Suez Canal system, where there are reeds. They observe that there are no reeds in or around the Red Sea and so it could not be the "Sea of Reeds." A Bitter Lakes route cannot be effectively supported, however, for several reasons.

1. The Greek translation of the Old Testament (the Septuagint), Acts 7:36, and Hebrews 11:29 understand *yam sûph* to refer to the Red Sea.

2. Exodus 14:27 and 15:5, 8, 10 seem to require something more than one of the lakes of the Suez region. While admittedly Exodus 15 is poetic language, "sank like lead in the mighty waters" (v. 10, various versions) does not seem to refer to a lake scene.

3. *Yam sûph* in Exodus 10:19, which refers to drowning of locusts of the eighth plague, would seemingly have to be more than marshy lakes of the Suez region. The Gulf of Suez is large enough to destroy the hordes of locusts and is properly placed for a northwest wind to blow the locusts into its waters.

4. Certainly in Numbers 14:25 *yam sûph* is the Red Sea.

5. A wide canal ran from the Mediterranean to Lake Timsah in the Bitter Lakes region. It was dug not for irrigation purposes but as a defense against Asiatics and for containment of runaway slaves. Well over 200 feet wide at the water level, it served as an effective deterrent and would

have kept the Israelites from going eastward into the Sinai.[2]

Offering a solution to the problem, Bernard F. Batto[3] and John Currid[4] conclude that *sûph* comes not from an Egyptian word meaning "reeds" but from the Hebrew word *sôph*, literally meaning "sea of the end," and referring to waters to the south, at the end of the land, i. e., the Red Sea. Batto notes that the Greeks applied the name Red Sea to the Red Sea, the Indian Ocean, and even to the Persian Gulf, "the sea at the end of the world." And he observes that the Dead Sea Scrolls *Genesis Apocryphon* and the Jewish historian Josephus included in the designation "Red Sea" (*yam sûph*) the Persian Gulf and everything to the south.[5] That is, for Greeks and Jews it included the extensive waters to the south and east that formed a continuous sea, beginning with the Red Sea.

On the basis of the foregoing argumentation, I subscribe to the old traditional view and conclude that the Hebrews journeyed southward to the west of the present canal system and crossed the Red Sea just south of the modern port of Suez.

Plausibility of the Red Sea Crossing

"But lift up your rod, and stretch out your hand over the sea and divide it. And the children of Israel shall go on dry ground through the midst of the sea." (Exodus 14:16 NKJV)

In making the assumption that the Hebrews crossed the Red Sea itself, our inquiring minds wonder how likely it was that they could have done so. Recently Doron Nof, professor of oceanography at Florida State University, and Nathan Paldor, an expert in atmospheric sciences at Hebrew University in Jerusalem, have produced a study that shows how strong winds in the region of the north end of the Red Sea (see Exodus 14:21) could have allowed the Israelites to cross. They also identify an undersea ridge that may have lowered the water level and provided a bridge for the Israelites to pass over.[6] These scholars were not trying to "prove" the accuracy of the Exodus narrative but merely sought to discover whether this crossing was scientifically plausible.

It should be pointed out that whether the Hebrews crossed large lakes in the Suez Canal region or the Red Sea itself, they needed a miracle to pass over on dry ground.

And whatever they crossed, they then went south along the west coast of the peninsula to Mount Sinai. From there they moved northeast to Kadesh Barnea at the southern edge of Canaan, where the spies brought back a report of great difficulty in taking the Promised Land. When the people then refused to go forward in faith, God condemned them to wander in the wilderness for about thirty-eight years.

(For more on this topic, go to p. 45 or p. 108.)

Government

"And the Lord went before them by day in a pillar of cloud to lead the way, and by night in a pillar of fire to give them light, so as to go by day and night." (Exodus 13:21 NKJV) *"Now the Lord spoke to Moses, saying: 'Speak to the children of Israel.'"* (Exodus 14:1–2 NKJV) *"These are the words which you shall speak to the children of Israel."* (Exodus 19:6 NKJV)

The Wilderness of Sin, an uninhabited region through which the Israelites passed between Elim and Mt. Sinai (Exodus 16:1)

Government during the period of wilderness wandering resembled a pure theocracy as closely as the world has ever known. A dictionary definition of theocracy is a government of a state by immediate divine guidance or by officials who are regarded as divinely guided.

As noted in Exodus 13:21 above, God directed the movements of the Israelites in the wilderness. They were to follow where and when the pillar of cloud or fire led them. When it stopped they were to stop.

God frequently told Moses exactly what to do and say. When the people strayed from that leadership they got into trouble. When they forcefully opposed it, they incurred God's judgment. In fact, Moses claimed divine inspiration in his leadership. When the people opposed him, Moses said, "Your murmurings are not against us but against the Lord" (Exodus 16:8 NKJV).

When Korah, Dathan, and Abiram rejected the leadership of Moses and Aaron, God caused the earth to open and swallow them up along with their households (Numbers 16:32). Subsequently he sent a fire to consume 250 rebellious priests (v. 35). Then when the Israelites turned ugly over this judgment, God sent a plague among them. It killed 14,700 (v. 49) before Aaron could make atonement for them.

On another occasion God expressly commanded Moses to send twelve spies into the land of Canaan, which God planned to give to the Israelites (Numbers 13:1). When ten of the spies gave a negative report and the people refused to move forward, God judged the whole people. He declared that all those over twenty (except the two spies making a positive report, Joshua and Caleb) would die in a wilderness wandering of about forty years (Numbers 14:29–35). God killed the ten rebellious spies instantly with a plague (v. 37).

Rebellion against Moses as God's appointed leader infected even his family. His sister Miriam in jealousy opposed Moses and received some temporary support from Aaron. Said Miriam, "Has the Lord spoken only through Moses? Has he not spoken through us also?" (Numbers 12:2 NKJV). God quickly brought her and Aaron into line and in punishment briefly smote her with leprosy.

Even Moses ran afoul of God's absolute control in the theocracy. Losing his patience with the Israelites at one of their many murmurings, he failed merely to speak to the rock to produce water for them, as God had commanded. Instead he struck the rock twice and assuming an authority that was not his, said, "Must *we* bring forth water?" (Numbers 20:10). In so asking, he had presumptuously put himself in God's place. In punishment God denied him the privilege of leading His people into the Promised Land, and Moses later died and God buried him somewhere in the vicinity of Mount Nebo (Deuteronomy 34:1–7).

Of course Moses' leadership involved legal or judicial administration. Early in the period of wandering Moses sat all day on some days to judge cases the people brought before him (Exodus 18:13). When Moses' father-in-law, Jethro, asked him why he was doing this, he responded in the spirit of the theocracy: "Because the people come to me to inquire of God" (Exodus 18:15 NKJV); "I make known the statutes of God and His laws" (v. 16 NKJV). Jethro then counseled Moses to establish a legal system in which there would be a hierarchy of courts and Moses would be the supreme court (Exodus 18:20–26). Moses listened to Jethro as one who brought God's counsel and relieved himself of hearing the multitude of petty grievances that continually arose.

Government also involves military affairs. Moses occasionally assumed the role of commander-in-chief of the army. Apparently at least part of the time he appointed Joshua to command forces in the field (e. g., Exodus 17:9). The theocratic nature of administration comes clear because God directly commanded Moses to take a military census of Israel, of all males twenty years old and above (Numbers 1:1–3). God also specified the names of commanders of main contingents of the forces. Comments on warfare appear subsequently.

Of course a theocracy involves governmental institution, direction, and control of religion in society. This is developed in the next section.

Religion and theocracy also include implications for social control and family affairs. That too appears in greater detail later on.

We must be careful not to view the theocracy as severe or judgmental and constantly forcing people to do what they found distasteful. God had to be firm with this motley

Jebel Musa, the mountain traditionally identified as Sinai, where Moses received the Law from God
(Matson Photo Collection)

horde of people. As He engaged in nation building, He had to teach them to respect authority. Moreover, if the Israelites were to be the people of God, they had to be a holy people. That is, they had to be set apart unto God and distinguished from their neighbors by a markedly different lifestyle. But theocratic rule was full of the grace and the goodness of God, as later comments on food and clothing and their salvation make clear.

(For more on this topic, go to p. 48 or p. 111.)

Religion

The Valley (er-Raha) where the Israelites may have camped while Moses was on Mt. Sinai

In the Wilderness Period

In a theocracy (direct rule of God), God promotes holiness of life among the people as a whole and provides for their eternal salvation. God met these two objectives through the giving of the law with its directives for living, the provision of festivals and feasts as means of corporate worship, the building of a tabernacle as a place where God especially dwelt among them and where the people could meet Him, and the institution of a priesthood that could represent the people to God and offer prescribed and acceptable sacrifices on their behalf to atone for their sins. Though most of the law had immediate relevance for their lives in the wilderness, some of it made sense only after they were in the land.

The Law—Directives for Living

"And the Lord came down upon Mount Sinai, on the top of the mountain" (Exodus 19:20). "And God spoke all these words" (Exodus 20:1 NKJV). "And they said, 'All that the Lord has said will we do, and be obedient.'" (Exodus 24:7 NKJV)

Soon after the Hebrews arrived at Mount Sinai, God proceeded to give them the Law, commonly called the Mosaic Law. This He did audibly to Moses, accompanied by repeated trumpet blasts, flashes of lightning, thunder, and the smoking of the mountain. God Himself was enveloped in a thick cloud or a ball of fire on the top of the mountain (Exodus 19:18–20; 20:18; 24:17–18). All this was to demonstrate that the words Moses

passed on to the Hebrews were indeed the words of God.

First God gave them the Ten Commandments (Exodus 20:1–17). Then He communicated the ordinances (Exodus 21:1–23:33), which especially had to do with social life, and after that directives for Israel's worship, especially the building of the tabernacle and the clothing of the priests (Exodus 25:1–31:18). This was a long process, with Moses staying on the mountain forty days and forty nights (Exodus 24:18). The book of Leviticus is also full of commandments that God gave to Moses for the children of Israel on Mount Sinai (Leviticus 27:34). The people committed themselves to obey the covenant (Exodus 19:8; 24:7).

Why the Law?

God did not give the Mosaic Law to the "called out" people as a way to gain spiritual life, but as a means by which they would become a "peculiar treasure" and a "kingdom of priests" (Exodus 19:5–6). That is, the Law served as a divinely instituted rule of life governing God's covenant people.

What the Law Tells Us

The laws of any society do not necessarily describe how that people lived. They only indicate how a dominant group in that society wanted it to behave. In this case the Mosaic laws describe how God wanted the Hebrews to conduct themselves. The laws tell about the real nature of Hebrew society only as we can discover the degree to which the Hebrews obeyed them. The greatest degree of compliance clearly came during this period of wandering when Moses and Aaron and the priesthood had the most direct control of society and when the distractions of life were comparatively minimal.

Adrift from God's Plan

During the days of the Conquest the people had other things than the laws of God on their minds as they were increasingly spread over a large chunk of land. During the long period of the Judges there was no central government and "every man did that which was right in his own eyes" (Judges 17:6). In the period of the monarchy Israel had to live through two royal administrations (those of Saul and David) before Solomon built the temple and a central sanctuary was firmly established.

Then after only about three decades the kingdom split. Apostasy increasingly infected the kingdom of Judah, while it was universal in Israel because a false religious system was established by royal decree. Next came the destruction of the temple and the Babylonian captivity, when living under the Law became impossible. And though the temple was eventually rebuilt during the restoration, the Jews lived under foreign domination, with only partial compliance possible— often on only an individual level. A more detailed understanding of the religious condition of Israel will become evident in subsequent chapters of this book.

The Ten Commandments

As God began to impart the law, He first gave Moses the Ten Commandments (Exodus 20:1–17). Moses repeats them with only slight variations in Deuteronomy 5:7–21. And all of them are repeated in principle under grace teachings in the New Testament—except the fourth, which enjoins observance of the Sabbath. After the resurrection of Jesus Christ on Sunday, Christians gave special significance to the first day of the week. They assembled themselves for worship on that day and frequently "broke bread" (took communion), but there never was any divine instruction as to how the day was to be spent.

A paraphrase and summary of the Ten Commandments follows.

The first prohibits worshiping anything before God.

The second declares God's spirituality and forbids making any material likeness of God.

The third safeguards God's name and deity.

The fourth demands that the Sabbath be observed as a day set apart unto God.

The fifth obligates children to honor their parents as they do God and to assume responsibility for them.

The sixth forbids murder and should be translated, "You shall not murder," rather than, "You shall not kill." Scripture authorizes capital punishment in such passages as Exodus 21; and while it encourages peace, it does not outlaw warfare.

The seventh requires sexual purity. While designed to protect the sanctity of marriage, it was applied by Jesus to all sexual immorality—thought as well as deed (Matthew 5:27–28).

The eighth stands for the rights of property.

The ninth prohibits lying and unfounded evidence in general.

The tenth forbids harboring evil desire for that which belongs to one's neighbor.

After enunciating the principles of the Decalogue, God proceeded to deal with relations between masters and servants, injuries to persons, property rights, crimes against humanity, the land and the Sabbath, the institution of the feasts of unleavened bread and harvest and firstfruits, the building of the tabernacle, regulations for the priesthood, and more. These are dealt with in the following discussion.

Special Days, Festivals and Feasts—Corporate Worship

Among the divinely appointed institutions described or alluded to in Leviticus

Feast	Month of Sacred Year	Day	Corresponding Month
Passover	1 (Abib)	14	Mar.-Apr.
Ex. 12:1–14; Lev. 23:5; Num. 9:1–14; 28:16; Deut. 16:1–7			
*Unleavened Bread	1 (Abib)	15–21	Mar.-Apr.
Ex. 12:15–20; 13:3–10; Lev. 23:6–8; Num. 28:17–25; Deut. 16:3, 4, 8			
Firstfruits	1 (Abib) and	16	Mar.-Apr.
	3 (Sivan)	6	May-June
Lev. 23:9–14; Num. 28:26			
*Weeks	3 (Sivan)	6 (50 days after	May-June
(Harvest or Pentecost)		barley harvest)	
Ex. 23:16; 34:22; Lev. 23:15–21; Num. 28:26–31; Deut. 16:9–12			
Trumpets	7 (Tishri)	1	Sept.-Oct.
Rosh Hashanah			
Lev. 23:23–25; Num. 29:1–6			
Day of Atonement	7 (Tishri)	10	Sept.-Oct.
Yom Kippur			
Lev. 16; 23:26–32; Num. 29:7–11			
*Tabernacles	7 (Tishri)	15–22	Sept.-Oct.
(Booths or Ingathering)			
Ex. 23:16; 34:22; Lev. 23:33–36, 39–43; Num. 29:12–38; Deut. 16:13–15			
*The three major feasts for which all males of Israel were required to travel to the temple in Jerusalem (Ex. 23:14–19).			

are several special days or feasts or seasons. These may be found primarily in chapters 16 and 23 through 26. Though the full implementation of some of them would have to wait until settlement in the land, others could be observed in the wilderness.

1. The Sabbath—the seventh day, a day of rest and one devoted to God. While individuals were to observe it at home and everywhere else, it was "a day of sacred assembly" (Leviticus 23:3).

2. The Feast of Passover and unleavened bread—the fourteenth day of the first month of the religious year (approximately April), reminded the Israelites of God's miraculous intervention in redeeming them from bondage in Egypt. It was followed on the fifteenth and twenty-first by days of holy convocation. During the week between those days, the Israelites were to eat unleavened bread (Feast of Unleavened Bread). The lamb slain on Passover looked forward to "Christ our passover, sacrificed for us" (1 Corinthians 5:7).

3. Harvest or firstfruits—probably the day after the first day of the Feast of Unleavened Bread and thus the sixteenth day of the month. The offering of the firstfruits of the land (from barley harvest) was to be brought to the priest. This prefigures

the resurrection of Christ as firstfruits from the dead (1 Corinthians 15:23; Romans 8:29).

4. Pentecost or Feast of Weeks—fifty days after the feast of firstfruits and thus after the wheat harvest. A day of rest, with a special meal offering presented, it perhaps signified that daily food came from the hand of God. It looked forward to the formation of the church on Pentecost (Acts 2) fifty days after the resurrection.

5. Feast of Trumpets—first day of the seventh month (approximately October), ushering in the civil year. It was a day of rest and holy convocation with special offerings being made to God.

6. Day of Atonement—tenth day of the seventh month, the most solemn day in the whole year. It was a day of fasting and holy convocation, when the high priest entered the most holy place to make atonement for the sins of the nation. It looked forward to the once-for-all sacrifice of Christ (Hebrews 9:12).

7. Feast of Tabernacles—a seven-day period at the end of the harvest season (fifteenth day of Tishri, approximately October) when the Israelites lived in tents. Daily burnt offerings were to be made, and the first and eighth days (day after its conclusion) were days of rest and holy convocation.

The Tabernacle—the House of God (Exodus 25–27; 30–31; 35–40)

"And let them make Me a sanctuary, that I may dwell among them."
(Exodus 25:8 NKJV)

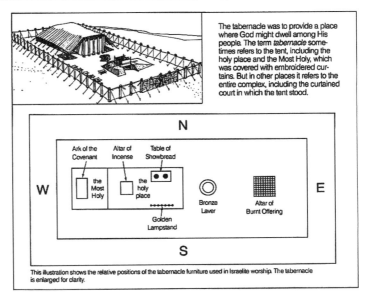

The tabernacle was to provide a place where God might dwell among His people. The term *tabernacle* sometimes refers to the tent, including the holy place and the Most Holy, which was covered with embroidered curtains. But in other places it refers to the entire complex, including the curtained court in which the tent stood.

This illustration shows the relative positions of the tabernacle furniture used in Israelite worship. The tabernacle is enlarged for clarity.

Not only does the Exodus narrative declare that God communicated instructions to Moses concerning building the tabernacle, but Acts 7:44 and Hebrews 8:5 supply New Testament confirmation of the fact. The tabernacle or tent was to be a sanctuary where God would especially dwell (Exodus 25:8). This does not mean, of course, that God ceased to be everywhere present; it signifies only that people might especially meet Him there.

Measurements connected with the tabernacle are given in cubits, approximately eighteen inches in length. Surrounding the tabernacle was a court with a 450-foot perimeter (150 feet by 75 feet), delimited by a linen curtain hung on bronze pillars (7½ feet high, spaced 7½ feet apart) with silver hooks. This court could be entered only on the east. The eastern half of the court was for the worshipers; in it stood the bronze altar (7½ feet square and 4½ feet high) made of acacia and shittim wood covered with bronze. Beyond the altar stood a bronze laver in which the priests washed in preparation for ministry at the altar or tabernacle.

In the western half of the court stood the tabernacle, 45 feet long and 15 feet wide. It was divided into two parts; the holy place on the east (30 feet long) could be entered by the priests, but the most holy place (15 by 15 feet) was accessible only to the high priest on the Day of Atonement. The tabernacle was made of forty-eight planks (20 on a side and 8 on the west end) of acacia wood covered with gold and held together with bars inserted into silver sockets. The structure was covered with a curtain of linen in blue, purple, and scarlet. Protecting this was first a covering of goats' hair, another of rams' skins, and a third of goatskins. Linen veils closed the entrances into the holy place and the most holy place.

Three pieces of furniture stood in the holy place: the table for the bread of the Presence on the north side, the golden lampstand on the south side, and the altar of incense before the veil that separated the holy place from the most holy place. The table (about 36 inches long by 18 inches wide by 27 inches high) was made of acacia wood and covered with gold, and had on it

Model of the tabernacle as it might have looked soon after it was built in the wilderness

twelve cakes of unleavened bread, representing the twelve tribes of Israel. The golden lampstand was made of pure gold and had seven branches. Its seven lamps the priests were to fill with oil each evening. The altar of incense was made of acacia wood covered with gold and was three feet high and one and one-half feet square.

Gifted Men for a Divine Project

"See, the Lord has called by name Bezaleel . . . and He has filled him with the Spirit of God, in wisdom and understanding . . . and all manner of workmanship, to design artistic works, . . . in cutting jewels . . . And he has put in his heart the ability to teach, in him and Aholiab." (Exodus 35:30-34 NKJV)

God chose to dwell among His people in a special way and in a special place: the tabernacle. In preparing His tabernacle, God left nothing to chance. First, He gave very specific instructions for building it. Then He recruited artisans to do the work. Again He left nothing to chance but "filled them with the Spirit of God." That is, the Holy Spirit controlled them and enabled them and taught them to do this specific work in the most elegant way possible. Bezaleel and Aholiab had the oversight and the gift of teaching to lead the whole company of artisans. And God "filled them [all] with skill" to bring the project to completion.

So there was the filling of the Spirit in the Old Testament and the giving of spiritual gifts for specific purposes. This anticipated the New Testament bestowal of gifts for accomplishment of the work of God (see, for example, Ephesians 4:11; 1 Corinthians 12).

inches long, with a depth and breadth of two feet, three inches, it contained the two tablets on which the Ten Commandments were written, a pot of manna, and Aaron's rod that budded. Its cover was called the mercy seat and represented the presence of God. Two cherubim of gold stood on the lid facing each other, with wings outstretched above the mercy seat. The priests could carry the furniture by the staves going through rings attached to it.

The tremendous amount of gold, silver, copper, and fabric required to build the tabernacle, and generously contributed by the Hebrews (Exodus 35:21–36:7), gives some indication of the wealth they had been able to amass while in captivity or had received from the Egyptians as they left.

The Priesthood—Intercessors with God (Exodus 28–29)

"Now take Aaron your brother, and his sons with him . . . that he may minister to Me as priest." (Exodus 28:1 NKJV)

For orderly ministration and worship, God now established a priesthood, with

The ark of the covenant dominated the most holy place. Covered with gold inside and out and measuring three feet, nine

Aaron in the distinctive dress of the high priest, including the ephod with twelve precious stones representing the tribes of Israel (Numbers 17)

Survival of the Hebrew Faith

The Bible student may well wonder how much of the faith of Abraham, Isaac, and Jacob survived during the four hundred years of bondage in Egypt. How did the approximately 70 Hebrews who entered Egypt (Genesis 46:27) keep from being absorbed by the mass of Egyptians? A key reason is that Joseph settled them in the land of Goshen, where almost no Egyptians lived and where the influence of Egyptian polytheism would be minimal.

The primary way for the Hebrew faith to be preserved during the centuries that followed was through the faithful leadership of the fathers of extended families. They must have acted as priests, as had Abraham, Isaac, and Jacob, presumably offering occasional sacrifices. Yet how much true faith remained among the Covenant People remains questionable.

No doubt God designed the ten plagues and the crossing of the Red Sea as much to impress the Hebrews as the Egyptians, for clearly Egyptian polytheism had made an extensive impact upon them. At Sinai they easily took up calf worship (Exodus 32:1-6), a universal practice among Egyptians. Remarkably Aaron, after he had been God's powerful instrument in smiting the Egyptians, led the way in instituting that worship. The period of wilderness wandering thus provided the Hebrews with basic religious institutions (tabernacle, priesthood, sacrificial system, and the Law) and the time for God to mold them into an instructed and obedient Covenant People.

which served the function of temporarily meeting God's righteous demands of sacrifice for sin. (Such repeated sacrifices looked forward to the perfect and complete sacrifice of Christ on the cross, Hebrews 7:27; 9:11–28.) They also had the responsibility of instructing the laity in the Law of God and the job of caring for the tabernacle.

The priests wore a long white linen coat with a girdle or belt that had blue, purple, and scarlet worked into it. They wore a plain cap and linen breeches under the coat.

The high priest's garments consisted of a robe, a coat, an ephod, a girdle, a breastplate, and a mitre. Over a white linen coat he wore a blue robe extending below the knees. Around the bottom of that were attached decorative pomegranates and golden bells. Over the robe he wore an ephod, consisting of two pieces of linen cloth joined with shoulder straps, on each of which was engraved the names of six tribes of Israel. A belt held it together around the waist. The breastplate was suspended by gold chains from the shoulder straps of the ephod and was tied to the waistband with blue lace. The breastplate was a pouch nine inches square, on which were mounted twelve precious stones engraved with names of the twelve tribes. The urim and thummim (meaning "lights" and "perfections") were kept inside the breastplate. Exactly what they were or how they were used in determining God's will is not spelled out. Attached to the headdress or turban (mitre) of the high priest a gold plate inscribed with the words "Holiness to the Lord" served as a reminder of the absolute purity of God's nature.

The Sacrifices or Offerings—Covering for Sins (Leviticus 1:1–7:38)

"This is the law of the burnt offering, the grain offering, the sin offering, the trespass offering, the consecrations, and the sacrifice of the peace offering, which the Lord commanded Moses on Mount Sinai, on the day when He commanded the children of Israel to offer their offerings to the Lord in the Wilderness of Sinai. (Leviticus 7:37–38 NKJV)

Aaron as high priest and his sons assisting him. He established their primary function that of representing the people before a holy God. They especially officiated in making the prescribed offerings to God,

If you are a casual reader of Leviticus you may be turned off by the immense

THE DAY OF ATONEMENT AND THE SINS OF ISRAEL

(LEVITICUS 16)

(Repeated annually on the tenth day of the seventh month: Tishri=October-November)

The Day of Atonement became the Hebrews' national day of contrition and confession of sin. The whole people fasted and observed a Sabbath of rest. The ritual for the Day of Atonement emphasized that sin is a serious, resulting in death. Yet God provided a miraculous atonement for sin by providing the sacrificial system, in which another can die in one's place. The comprehensiveness of the sins atoned for by the Day of Atonement ritual is staggering.

Because the high priest was sinful like his people, he had to offer sacrifice for his sin. He offered a bull for himself and his household (v. 11) and then took blood into the most holy place and sprinkled it on "the front of" and "before the mercy seat" (v. 14). He had to be cleansed from the pollution of sin before he could function as a mediator to offer "the sin offering for the people" (v. 15). He entered into the most holy place with a censer full of burning coals from the altar of burnt offerings on which he was burning incense. Presumably this averted divine wrath by creating a smoke screen to keep him from looking at the Shekinah glory, which represented God's presence.

The sin offering of the people consisted of two male goats. One was slaughtered and its blood sprinkled within the most holy place, before the altar of incense, and on the horns of the altar. This act made atonement not only for the sins of the high priest and his people but also for the tabernacle and the altar (vv. 16, 20), cleansing the place of God's dwelling from the pollution of the people's sins.

After all that the high priest brought forward the live goat, on whose head he placed both hands and confessed over it all the sins of the Israelites, thereby symbolically putting them on the goat's head. Then he sent the goat into the wilderness to make atonement for the sins of the Israelites (vv. 20-22). As the "scapegoat" it symbolized complete destruction of or entire removal of the sins of the people.

The ceremony of the Day of Atonement was meaningful for the Israelites and temporarily met God's requirements for dealing with sin. But the Book of Hebrews makes it clear that all this was typical, pointing to the sinless High Priest, who in His death on the cross provided not an annual but a once-for-all sacrifice for sins (Hebrews 9:11-12, 24-26).

amount of detail concerning feasts and sacrifices and regulations of life in ancient Israel. But when it comes to Scripture, it is important to stop just casually looking and start to "see." True sight or perception will sometimes involve the use of a pencil and even some tabulation. It soon becomes evident that the key word of Leviticus is "holy," which appears at least 87 times;

and the second key word is "atonement," which occurs at least 45 times. It seems clear, then, that what Leviticus teaches is that sinful human beings can approach the infinitely holy God of the universe only on the basis of sacrifice through shedding of blood.

Leviticus thus becomes a book for the people of God, showing how God is to be approached and worshiped. The book insists on holiness of body as well as soul. It makes clear that there is to be order and dignity in the worship of God, for He is a majestic, sovereign, and infinitely holy being. Since He is sovereign and holy and unapproachable by sinful human beings, God must take the initiative in establishing any kind of contact with them; and He has the right to prescribe the nature of that contact. Not surprisingly, no other book in the Bible contains so many direct messages from God as Leviticus. "The Lord spoke," "said," or "commanded" occurs 56 times; "I am the Lord," 21 times; "I am the Lord your God," 21 times.

The modern believer looking for Old Testament applications can easily neglect the basic meaning the Old Testament had for worshipers of the pre-Christian era. The sacrificial system (Leviticus 1:1–7:38) provided a way to approach God. Since the system was God-given, they could come to God by this means with the assurance that they would be received.

The system of offerings involved numerous significant principles: offerings were commonly substitutionary, in one's stead (e. g., Leviticus 1:4; 3:2; 4:4); offerings were to be of highest quality—the best one had to offer (e. g., Leviticus 1:3; 2:1); sacrifices were to be accompanied by a true penitence and uprightness of life (see Isaiah 1:11–24).

Of course the whole sacrificial system only provided a temporary covering of sin, a temporary dealing with the sin problem. It looked forward to the perfect sacrifice of Christ that made all other sacrifices obsolete. We rejoice in the inspired words of John the Baptist, "Behold! The Lamb of God who takes away the sin of the world!" (John 1:29 NKJV).

The prescribed offerings:

1. *The burnt offering* (Leviticus 1) was so called because it was to be wholly consumed and to rise in smoke toward heaven. It symbolized the entire surrender or consecration to God of the individual or of the people as a whole. This offering did not secure forgiveness of specific sins; one guilty of such sins had to make a sin offering for reconciliation before being eligible to make a burnt offering. But it did cover defects and imperfections. When individuals made a burnt offering, they laid hands on the animal to be sacrificed, indicating it

Model of a priest offering a sacrifice in the tabernacle in the wilderness
(Amsterdam Bible Museum Photo)

would be accepted on their behalf. Sacrifices related to one's financial status and might be a bull, a sheep, goat, or turtledove or pigeon. As an expression of the religious disposition of all true Israelites in covenant relationship with God, it had to be offered daily in the morning and evening, on the Sabbath, new moon, during the great festivals, and on the Day of Atonement.

2. *Grain offering* (Leviticus 2). The grain offering could be of fine flour or cakes baked without leaven, seasoned with salt and sprinkled with oil and incense. Some of it was to be burned and the rest was for the use of the priests. Various suggestions try to explain the significance of this offering. Some believe that it recognized the sovereignty of Yahweh and His generosity in the giving of earthly blessings through the dedication to Him of the best of His gifts. Grain offerings made in conjunction with burnt or peace offerings were either public or private. The law prescribed three public grain offerings: the twelve loaves of the bread of the Presence, the sheaf of wheat on the second day of Passover, and the two wave loaves at Pentecost.

3. *Peace offering* (Leviticus 3). Leviticus prescribes three Peace offerings: thank offering (Leviticus 7:12); votive—a sacrifice of a vow (Numbers 6:2); and a freewill offering (Leviticus 7:16). One might be genuinely thankful for some blessing received, might vow to make an offering to secure a blessing, or thank God for His blessings in general. Peace offerings became part of public occasions, such as an inauguration of a king, successful conclusion of certain enterprises, or during the great festivals. As with other sacrifices, the offerer placed his hand on the animal to indicate his identification with the sacrificial act and its substitutionary nature. In this case, part of the animal was to be burnt, part to be set aside for the use of the priests and part for the use of the offerer in a sacrificial feast. The sacrificial feasts celebrated the blessing of being part of the family of Yahweh (see Deuteronomy 12:12, 18).

4. *Sin offering* (Leviticus 4:1–5:13). The sin offering became necessary when a person or the whole congregation sinned unintentionally as a result of carelessness, igno-

rance or weakness of the flesh—not for one guilty of willful sin in open defiance against God and His commandments.

God offered to forgive sin with this offering (Leviticus 4:20, 26, 31, 35). The offerer, in the case of an individual, or the elders (in the case of the whole congregation), laid hands on the sacrifice before it was killed, symbolizing that the sin was now being transferred to the sacrifice. According to the offense or station in life, the sacrifice might be a bull, a male goat, a female goat, a ewe, or a turtledove or young pigeon. In the case of the poverty-stricken, fine flour was permitted as a substitute (Leviticus 5:11). Sin offerings were made for the whole congregation at the new moon, Passover, Pentecost, on the feasts of Trumpets and Tabernacles, and on the Day of Atonement. In the latter case the high priest was to take blood of the sacrifice within the most holy place and sprinkle it on the mercy seat of the ark (Leviticus 16:14–15).

5. *Guilt or Trespass offering* (Leviticus 5:14–6:7; 7:1–10). The sin offering, a ram or a lamb, symbolized general redemption, while the guilt offering atoned for some special offense. Because the sacrifice was for a special sin it was not offered during the great festivals or feasts. A guilt offering might be made if one had withheld firstfruits or tithes from Yahweh (Leviticus 5:15), had transgressed a prohibition of the Law (5:17), had been guilty of perjury or fraud against a neighbor (6:1–6), had raped a betrothed slave (Leviticus 19:20–22), or had been guilty of other specified wrongs. In addition to the sacrifice, some cases called for punishment and/or compensation.

The Law of Moses and Mesopotamian Law

The charge is often made that the Law of Moses was not divinely communicated but that it borrowed heavily from the Code of Hammurabi, or at least from the Mesopotamian context. The Mesopotamian materials were then supposedly purified of polytheistic elements and put in the Old Testament.

As a basis for our thinking, we need to note that the Code of Hammurabi was discovered in Susa (the biblical Shushan).

Found December 1901 and January 1902, it was broken in three pieces. When combined, the pieces revealed a code on a black diorite shaft almost eight feet high and six feet in circumference, with 3600 lines of cuneiform text arranged in 44 columns. A total of 282 laws, written in Akkadian, appear in the text. The top front of the shaft features a low relief of Hammurabi standing before the sun god Shamash, the god of justice, and presumably receiving the text of the code from him.

Hammurabi receives the laws in his famous code from Shamash, god of justice.
(From the top of his code, now in the Louvre, Paris)

Originally set up in the great Temple to Marduk in Babylon during the second year of Hammurabi's reign, the code was carted of by the Elamites to Susa about 1200 B.C. The code today sits on display in the Louvre Museum in Paris. If we accept the low chronology, Hammurabi is to be dated 1728–1686. Most scholars date him a little earlier, 1792–1750.

Now we know that Hammurabi's claim to originality was just idle boasting. In 1947, a Sumerian code of Lipit-Ishtar surfaced at Isin, in southern Mesopotamia. Dating before 1850 B.C. it had laws that were similar to Hammurabi's and showed that Hammurabi did not concoct all of his laws.

Some took the position that he was bringing up to date the common law of Mesopotamia. Then in the very next year (1948) at Eshnunna (modern Tell Asmar), also in southern Mesopotamia, an Akkadian code of King Bilalama came to light. This dated some seventy years earlier than Lipit-Ishtar's. Four years later, in 1952, archaeologists found the Sumerian code of Ur-Nammu at Ur, dating perhaps 2100–2050 B.C. Of course no one can predict whether other earlier codes are still to be found in Mesopotamia.

Scholars soon began to notice some similarities between the Code of Hammurabi and the Mosaic laws in the Old Testament. Many professed to find a dependence of Moses on the earlier code. But on more sober reflection, direct dependence or borrowing cannot be defended, for the attitude of the two codes is very different. Hammurabi's code is polytheistic, civil, and commercial, and punishments are geared to class distinctions. Moreover, though Hammurabi appears to pay lip service to the god of justice as the originator of the code, he clearly claims in the preamble and the epilogue of the code to be the wise law-giver who composed his code.

The Mosaic code, on the other hand, is monotheistic, civil, and religious, and does not recognize class distinctions in meting out punishments. Moses claims no credit for formulating his code; this was God's set of requirements for His people. Similarities between the codes may rise from their Semitic antecedents and the fact that to be called a law code at all or to meet the basic requirements of society, certain similar items would have to be included; e. g., control of murder, theft, and false testimony in the courts.

Because of some repetition of laws or legal principles in these ancient Mesopotamian codes and the Old Testament, we may assume that they to some degree reflect the common law or common customs of ancient Mesopotamia, perhaps analogous to some of the Anglo-Saxon common law that grew up in England in the late Middle Ages.[7] In evaluating the whole question of the degree of originality in the Mosaic code, we should not so much be

Lipit-Ishtar of Isin in southern Iraq (nineteenth century B.C.) composed a law code that dated earlier than Hammurabi's. (University Museum of Philadelphia)

looking for similarities between the Mosaic code and the ancient Near Eastern context as to be looking for distinctives. Remember that God's goal was to create a unique people that would glorify His name, that He wanted them to conform to a standard of His own specification. He shut up these people to Himself for a whole generation in the wilderness. So we should concentrate on distinctives rather than similarities.

(For more on this topic, go to p. 54 or p. 113.)

Warfare

"Now Amalek came and fought with Israel in Rephidim." (Exodus 17:8 NKJV)

The Hebrews had been on the march for only a few days when they faced their first foe at Rephidim, in the southwest of the Sinai peninsula, north of Mount Sinai. The skirmish may have been over water, since Rephidim was one of the few places where water supplies were available. The Amalekites were fierce, determined, and experienced fighters—used to defending themselves in the wild and dangerous wilderness.

Moses commissioned Joshua to organize some forces and go out to fight the Amalekites (Exodus 17:9). The Hebrews had overwhelming numerical superiority but no experience in fighting, though presumably some Hebrews had fought as mercenaries in the Egyptian army and knew the ways of warfare. They may even have carried swords, javelins and shields with them in the Exodus. Others, as sheepherders, may have been forced to defend their flocks against wild animals as David did later. Thus they may have become effective slingers and may have owned powerful clubs or even attack axes.

A Comparison of the Code of Hammurabi and the Mosaic Code

	Code of Hammurabi	Mosaic Code
Source:	Hammurabi claims credit for the laws; he established justice in the land	God is the source; Moses is only the instrument through which the legislation was given
View of God:	Polytheistic	Strictly monotheistic
Character:	Civil and commercial	Civil and religious
View of Society:	Punishments geared to class distinctions	All on an equal plane before God
Geographical Orientation:	Geared to a land of rivers, an irrigation culture	Intended for a dry land like Palestine

No doubt the Hebrews had some physical prowess, but the victory came primarily from divine intervention. Symbolic of God's power coming down on the side of the Hebrews, Moses stood on a hill overlooking the battle scene and held his hands high for hours, supported by Aaron and Hur (Exodus 17:12). The fact that Joshua's men defeated Amalek "with the edge of the sword" (v. 13) indicates that some Hebrews did have weapons.

To prepare for future conflicts, God Himself commanded Moses and Aaron to take a military census of all Israel a few weeks later, at Sinai. When they numbered all males twenty years and older, they came up with a total of 603,550 (Numbers 1:46). This represented a citizen army with considerable power and prevented absolutism, even in the heyday of the monarchy. Tribal heads probably became leaders in peace as well as in war. Presumably the political leaders Moses chose earlier became officers in the military. At least the way Exodus 18:25 reads leads us in that direction: "And Moses chose able men out of all Israel, and made them heads over the people: rulers of thousands, rulers of hundreds, rulers of fifties, and rulers of tens" (NKJV).[8] It is also interesting to see that each tribe had a tribal standard or banner under which to fight (Numbers 1:52).

Later, while Moses was still the leader of Israel and Joshua commander of the forces, Israel fought major contests east of the Jordan: against the Canaanites (Numbers 21:1–3); the Amorites (Numbers 21:21–26); and Bashan (Numbers 21:33–35). In each case those attacked were virtually wiped out and Israel took their land. Presumably in defeating each foe they captured enough war materiel to make them increasingly powerful. Scripture offers no detail about these fierce struggles in Transjordan. There is not even a hint of casualties.

(For more on this topic, go to p. 57 or p. 118.)

Housing and Furniture

During the period of wilderness wandering the people lived only in tents. In most instances they had to carry the tents themselves because they did not have draft animals such as mules to transport them. Therefore the tents must have been much smaller than the substantial tents of the days of Abraham, Isaac, and Jacob. Made of goat hair, they could be folded and carried by two or more by using the tent poles as handles. A little clothing or bed mats or rugs might also be folded into the package.

Under the circumstances we would not expect any furniture to be transported. People sat on the ground or on a spread or an animal skin. There were no tables; a mat or cloth was unrolled and laid on the ground and food spread on it. A few wooden or clay bowls served as dishes. Mats or bedrolls were opened up at bedtime.

(For more on this topic, go to p. 59 or p. 32.)

Diet and Foodstuffs

"And when the layer of dew lifted, there, on the surface of the wilderness, was a small round substance, as fine as frost on the ground. So when the children of Israel saw it, they said to one another, 'What is it?'" (Exodus 16:14–15 NKJV)

Manna. Before the children of Israel fled from Egypt they had packed food for the journey. But within a few days it was all gone and they grew desperate. God promised to rain bread from heaven to feed them (Exodus 16:4). By morning a small round substance as fine as frost covered the ground all around the camp. They had never seen anything like it before and they asked each other, "What is it?" The Hebrew for that question is *manna*, and our English word is only a transliteration of the Hebrew. So this divine bread was a "whatdyacallit," and they never seem to have found a name for it. But it continued to appear during the night every night for the entire forty years of the wilderness wandering and ceased abruptly as they entered Canaan and had access to the grain of the land (Joshua 5:12).

The Israelites were commanded to gather an omer (about a half peck) per person each morning before the sun got too hot and melted it. If their lack of faith persuaded them to pick up enough for another day, what was left over quickly spoiled and began to stink. For the Sabbath they were invited to gather a double amount because the manna appeared only six days a week, and that left over amount did not spoil. Manna was always regarded as a miraculous gift directly from God and not as a product of nature. All efforts to explain it as

Manna

The Hebrews asked, "What is it?" and ever since Bible students have been asking the same question. It was small like frost (Exodus 16:14) or coriander seed (Numbers 11:7), perhaps as much as 1/8 inch in diameter. Pale amber in color, it resembled bdellium (Numbers 11:7) and tasted like honey-wafers (Exodus 16:31). But what was it? And what produced it?

Some have thought it was a kind of fungus or lichen, but that is only a guess and has satisfied almost no one.

Others have linked it with the tamarisk tree, which secretes small, sweet, yellowish-white balls that melt in the sun. But this product appears for only three to six weeks a year, beginning in June. And manna first appeared in May and continued to be available daily for forty years. Alternatively, this secretion is thought to be produced by two species of insects, cicadas, that feed on the tamarisk tree. But if so, the short duration of its availability still holds.

The Jewish historian Josephus in the first century claimed that in his day manna was still coming down in that region in the rain (Antiquities III. 1.7).

None of these or other naturalistic explanations of the production of manna identifies the product. It appeared six mornings a week, all year long, for forty years in sufficient quantity to feed millions of people. No known commodity fills the bill. Clearly, manna was a miraculous food.

some natural commodity have failed. Psalms calls it "angels' food" (Psalm 78:25).

Manna was usually ground on millstones or beaten in a mortar before being made into cakes and cooked or baked (Numbers 11:8). It tasted like "wafers made with honey" (Exodus 16:31) or pastry baked with olive oil (Numbers 11:8). Extremely nutritious, it must have been in fact what the modern cereal *Total* claims to be—a provider of basic vitamins and minerals. But the Israelites were very human, and instead of being thankful for the supply they grumbled because of the lack of variety. They longed for the fish, cucumbers, melons, leeks, onions, and garlic of Egypt (Numbers 11:5).

How did they prepare their food? The biblical record leaves out that detail. We can only assume that part of the time they used dried animal dung from the flocks they had with them.

"So it was that quails came up at evening and covered the camp." (Exodus 16:13)

Quail. Even before God sent manna, He dumped a whole flock of quails on the Hebrew camp (Exodus 16:13). Quails are sandy-colored, heavy-bodied birds of the same general classification as pheasants and partridges, though smaller. They winter in the Sudan and migrate north in vast flocks in the spring (usually March) on their way to Egypt and Palestine. They fly up along the shore of the Red Sea and then up the Gulf of Suez or the Gulf of Aqaba. Their flight at night with the wind is exhausting, so when they alight they may be easily caught, even with bare hands.

Later, after the Israelites had become totally bored with eating manna day after day, they got very testy with God. He obliged with another deluge of quails. With an east wind (Psalm 78:26–28) He blew flocks of quail flying along the Gulf of Aqaba off course and into the Hebrew camp. They were fluttering helplessly "three feet above the surface of the ground" (Numbers 11:31, see NKJV and NIV and Hebrew original) and could easily be captured by hand. They were not piled three feet deep on the ground as the NRSV, CEV and some other versions indicate. Quails could be preserved by drying in the sun (Numbers 11:32), but apparently the Hebrews did not do a proper job on this occasion and many died from bacterial infection (salmonella poisoning?). This was described as an act of divine judgment on their grumbling.

Other foods. Scripture specifically mentions only manna and quails in connection with the wilderness wandering. But we have already seen that there were some sacrificial feasts following peace offerings. On such occasions at least a few people ate meat. And previous statements about the sacrifices at the Tabernacle presuppose the raising of substantial numbers of oxen, cattle, goats, rams, and lambs. It is not inconceivable that a family or an extended family did butcher an animal and share its meat on a special occasion. Also, there seems no reason on the face of it why the Hebrews could not have consumed the milk of cows or goats and butter or cheese made from that milk. Beyond that we cannot go. Certainly the meager rainfall did not permit raising any fruits or vegetables.

(For more on this topic, go to p. 63 or p. 133.)

Dress

"Your clothes have not worn out on you, and your sandals have not worn out on your feet." (Deuteronomy 29:5 NKJV)

God's care of the clothing of the Israelites remains just as incredible as His supply of food. Not only didn't the Hebrews have opportunity to raise food or buy it, they also did not have much opportunity to provide new clothing. Even if they had the thread, they did not have looms for weaving fabric. The assertion that their clothes did not wear out during that forty-year period implies also that their clothes grew with their bodies. After all, the people Moses was addressing on this occasion were all below twenty when they entered the Sinai, and some of them were babes in arms. How clothing was provided for the new generation born in the wilderness is not explained, unless the children inherited their parents' clothing.

The statement above also says something about fabrics and styles. Nearly all clothing worn in Egypt was linen, made from flax. That meant that the clothing brought into the Sinai was essentially made from linen. And we know that the Israelites brought quantities of worked linen with them. The clothing of the newly-constituted priesthood and much of the fabric used in the tabernacle was linen. Certainly the linen contributed for the tabernacle was only a small fraction of what existed among the people. The Hebrews did, however, have a lot of sheep with them in the Sinai. Thus they had a source of wool for making some cloth.

As to styles, all we know for certain is the clothing of the priests and the high priest, as described above. The rest of the people would have dressed much as they did while in Egypt. In fact, as noted, they came from Egypt in Egyptian garb. What appears on the subject in the last chapter should be reviewed. Since it is very hot in the Sinai during the day, presumably men often wore only linen kilts and women full-length, light weight, loose-fitting dresses. But it gets cold in the Sinai at night and the people needed something to keep them warm. Therefore it may be assumed that men and women owned long cloaks to wear at night or in high altitudes or to use as a blanket. Cloaks served as blankets at night even in New Testament Palestine.

(For more on this topic, go to p. 65 or p. 136.)

Family Life

Family Affairs

Through marriage the Hebrews found personal fulfillment. Through bearing children they kept the Hebrews from extinction among the nations and fulfilled a responsibility to the family to raise up an inheritance. In this context the Mosaic Law sought to guard the home, protect parents, control children, regularize marriage relationships, set limits on sexual activity and spell out laws of inheritance. What began during the generation of wandering clearly continued after entrance into Canaan.

God commanded that children honor their parents and assume responsibility for them (Exodus 20:12). For excessive physical violence against parents (perhaps with an intent to kill, Exodus 21:15) or for curses against father or mother (in various kinds of violence and disobedience, Exodus 21:17; Leviticus 20:9) children might be executed. Likewise, a totally rebellious and dissolute son might be executed (Deuteronomy 21:18).

Numerous controls regulated marriage and divorce. A man could not marry and subsequently tire of his wife and bring accusation against her to achieve a divorce without just cause (Deuteronomy 22:13–21). A man who became enamored with a captive of war had to give her time to mourn her lot and then marry her properly (Deuteronomy 21:10ff.). If a man committed adultery with a married woman, both of them were to be executed (Deuteronomy 22:22). In the event that a man raped a single woman, he was to pay the bride-price and marry her (Exodus 22:16–17). In a more positive vein, a newly married man was excused from military duty or other civic responsibilities for one year so he could properly cement his marriage (Deuteronomy 24:5). Polygamy, which occurred early in Israel's history, was recognized under the law (Exodus 21:10; Deuteronomy 21:15). Divorce could only be undertaken with a written certificate of divorce (Deuteronomy 24:1).

Men and women could practice sex only in the marriage relationship. God did not countenance adultery, homosexuality, mating with beasts, and various sexual liaisons within the family or with near relatives (Leviticus 20:10–21; cf. Exodus 22:19, 22). In the first three instances punishment was by execution. In cases of incest, lesser punishments were administered. Cross dressing was also proscribed (Deuteronomy 22:5).

Inheritance laws specified that the firstborn son received a double portion from his father's estate (Deuteronomy 21:15–17). Then the other sons got lesser amounts. Daughters received dowries when they married and grooms paid a bride-price to the family of the bride (Exodus 22:17). If a man died without leaving a son as heir, his daughters could inherit the estate (Numbers 27:8).

God also made provision for levirate marriage (from the Latin *levir,* a husband's brother), in which a single brother was expected to marry the widow of a man who died without leaving a son. The firstborn son of that union would then carry on the name and family of the dead man. Sons born later carried forward the name and estate of the second brother (Deuteronomy 25:5–10). A man who did not want to fulfill that obligation could get out of it—with difficulty.

Other Social Issues

Slavery

The law spoke to a number of other social issues with conditions that especially looked forward to settlement in the land. Though debt slavery was recognized, Hebrew slaves were to be freed after six years of service. But if the master had given the slave a wife who had borne him children, he could choose to remain in the household to live with them. In that event he was taken to the doorpost, where his ear was pierced and he would remain in perpetual servitude (Exodus 21:1–6). Persons freed were not to be sent away empty handed but given livestock, food and wine (Deuteronomy 15:12–18). A woman sold into slavery who was later married either to the master or his son was not given her freedom (Exodus 21:7). Individuals found kidnapping other Israelites and using them as slaves or selling them into slavery were to be executed (Exodus 21:16; Deuteronomy 24:7).

Manslaughter and Injury

For premeditated manslaughter the killer was to be executed, but in the case of accidental death he might flee to a place of refuge (Exodus 21:12–14). If one injured another in a fight, he had to compensate the injured man for his loss of time (Exodus 21:18–19). If anyone beat his servant and he died, the slave owner was to be punished (Exodus 21:20). If a man injured a pregnant woman so that she gave birth prematurely, he was to be punished if there was no lasting harm, but executed in the event that the child died (Exodus 21:22–23).

The principle of *lex talionis* or retaliation operated; that is, an eye for an eye and tooth for tooth, in all sorts of other personal injury cases. That was also true if one's ox injured or killed another (Exodus 21:22–32). Compensation should be made to one whose ox or donkey died through the carelessness of another (Exodus 21:33–36).

Theft and Damages

If a man stole livestock, the law prescribed restoration of two to five times the value of what was taken, depending on the circumstances. If he was killed while breaking in, no charges were to be made against the owner. The law provided for dealing with damage to objects that had been borrowed or damage to crops in the field (Exodus 22:1–15). God urged the appointment of just judges who were impartial and would not accept bribes (Deuteronomy 16:18–19).

Treatment of the Helpless

God forbade the oppression of strangers, widows and orphans, as He did charging of interest on loans made to the poor. God Himself would judge the guilty (Exodus 22:21–25; 23:9).

Education

"Then the Lord said to Moses, 'Write this for a memorial in the book and recount it in the hearing of Joshua.'" (Exodus 17:14)

When most of us think about education we have in mind formal education in such things as reading, writing, literature, history, and more. No doubt that level of education existed in the wilderness generation. Moses was to write in a book (scroll), as noted above, assuming that there were such things as books (scrolls) and that at least some people could read what had been written. As God gave the law, Moses "wrote all the words of the Lord" (Exodus 24:4), presupposing a readership. There was an engraving on the turban of the high priest, "Holiness to the Lord" (Exodus 28:36; 38:30), assuming that at least a great many of the priests around him could read it.

In Numbers 5:23 we find a reference to the priest's writing some curses, again with the assumption that the priest could

write and some could read the curses. Moreover, a man who divorced his wife had to give her a written certificate of divorce (Deuteronomy 24:1, 3). Either he had to know how to write or a priest had to write it for him. Then the people as a whole had been commanded to write certain words of the Law on the doorposts of their houses (evidently after settlement in the land), again with the assumption that they could do so and that passersby could read them (see Deuteronomy 6:9; 11:20). Finally, "Moses wrote this law and delivered it to the priests . . . and to all the elders of Israel" (Deuteronomy 31:9). Most of them should have been able to read it.

The Wilderness of Zin, a desert region south of Beersheba, through which the Israelites passed on their journey to the Promised Land (Numbers 13:21)
(Photo by Willem A. VanGemeren)

Moses and, without doubt, many other leaders in Israel, had learned to read and write in Egypt. The fact that God had imparted a law in written form meant that the ability to read and write had to be passed on to the new generation growing up in the wilderness. Though there may have been no priestly schools as such, it would have been natural for the older priests to teach some under their supervision.

Practice in a skill, trade, or profession is a second aspect of education. That kind of education was difficult to maintain in the wilderness. Metal workers, wood workers, engravers, jewelry makers, carpenters, and host of others had learned their trades well in Egyptian shops, but they lost their skills when deprived of materials with which to work. And they could not apprentice a new generation.

But a third kind of education—following a third dictionary definition—did go forward during the wilderness wandering: "to persuade or condition to feel, believe, or act in a desired way." God asked Moses to teach the commandments of God (Exodus 24:12) and he did so (Deuteronomy 4:11). Similarly, Aaron the high priest and his sons were to teach the statutes of the Lord (Leviticus 10:11). The people generally were to teach their children and grandchildren (Deuteronomy 4:9–10; 11:19). In fact, they were to teach the commandments, all the Divine instructions for living, "diligently to your children, and talk of them when you sit in your house, when you walk by the way" (Deuteronomy 6:7 NKJV), "precept upon precept, Line upon line, Here a little, there a little" (Isaiah 28:10 NKJV). Religious education was to be a constant concern of the people of God.

(For more on this topic, go to p.68 or p. 137.)

Work, Travel, and Commerce

God uprooted the children of Israel from the normal way of life of a settled society during the wilderness wandering, preventing the vast majority of people from pursuing the usual farming activities. Nor could members of the business community travel locally or abroad to pursue their fortunes. In fact, people could not move about as they wished because the divine cloud or pillar directed them when to advance or stop. But all this did not mean that no one had regular work or occupations.

The priests and Levites had to supervise the sacrifices and other worship activities of the people including finding fuel to burn the offerings. Moreover, they dismantled the tabernacle, packed it for transport, transported it, and set it up again every time the people moved. And, as just noted, they had a teaching responsibility.

For some months at least a considerable number of men were busy building the tabernacle. Those who knew how to cast bronze, gold, and silver, and to work with fabrics served under the expert direction of Bezaleel of the tribe of Judah and Aholiab of the tribe of Dan to build the sanctuary. All of these men had learned much in the workshops of Egypt, and Bezaleel and Aholiab received a special gift from God to produce quality workmanship (see Exodus 35:30–35; 36:1–8; 37:1–38:31). Gifted artisans made Aaron's garments (Exodus 28:3). The fact that the people could contribute so much metal and fabric indicated how much they had been able to amass while in Egypt or to receive as gifts when they left.

Then scattered references in Exodus—Deuteronomy indicate that fairly large numbers of oxen, cattle, goats, rams, and sheep accompanied the Hebrews as they left Egypt in the Exodus, while others were born in the wilderness. This required a substantial number to be engaged in animal husbandry. In fact, when God judged the people for refusal to enter the land of Canaan, He said, "Your sons shall be shepherds in the wilderness forty years" (Numbers 14:33). It must have taxed their abilities to find food for large flocks in such an arid place.

So the Israelites wandered in the wilderness for forty years. Rather than viewing this period as a wasted time, we need to see it as a time when God was busy forming the Hebrews into a nation and teaching them His ways. That process involved the giving of the Law, establishment of the tabernacle as a worship center, institution of a priesthood to manage it, and a sacrificial system to govern their relationship to Him. Moreover, God worked miracle after miracle on behalf of the Israelites to impress the people of Canaan and to melt the hearts of many of them with fear and soften them up for the Conquest. Said Rahab in Jericho, "the terror of you has fallen on us" (Joshua 2:9 NKJV). We turn now to that conquest.

(For more on this topic, go to p. 75 or p. 140.)

NOTES:

[1] Arie Issar, "Fossil Water under the Sinai-Negev Peninsula," *Scientific American*, July, 1985, 104–110.

[2] John D. Currid, *Ancient Egypt and the Old Testament* (Grand Rapids: Baker, 1997), p. 131; and James K. Hoffmeier, *Israel in Egypt* (New York: Oxford University Press, 1997), 172, 175.

[3] Bernard F. Batto, "Red Sea or Reed Sea?" *Biblical Archaeology Review,* July/August, 1984, 59.

[4] Currid, 135.

[5] Batto, 59–60.

[6] John N. Wilford, "Oceanographers Say Winds May Have Parted the Waters," *New York Times,* March 15, 1992, 12; Doron Nof and Nathan Paldor, "Are There Oceanographic Explanations for the Israelites' Crossing of the Red Sea?" *Bulletin of the American Meteorological Society,* March, 1992, 305–14.

[7] The texts of the Lipit-Ishtar, Eshnunna, and Hammurabi codes appear in James B. Pritchard, ed., *Ancient Near Eastern Texts,* 2nd ed. (Princeton, NJ: Princeton University Press, 1955), 159–180. For a useful comparison of the Hammurabi and Mosaic codes and translation of the Hammurabi code, see George A. Barton, *Archaeology and the Bible,* 7th ed. (Philadelphia: American Sunday School Union, 1937), 378–406.

[8] See Chaim Herzog and Mordechai Gihon, *Battles of the Bible* (Jerusalem: Steinmatzky, 1978), 20–21.

BIBLIOGRAPHY:

Adams, J. McKee. Revised by Joseph A. Callaway. *Biblical Backgrounds.* Nashville: Breadman Press, 1965.

Anati, Emmanuel. *The Mountain of God.* New York: Rizzoli, 1986.

Hobbs, Joseph J. *Mount Sinai.* Austin, Tex.: University of Texas Press, 1995.

Kaiser, Walter C. Jr. *A History of Israel.* Nashville: Broadman & Holman, 1998.

Merrill, Eugene M. *Kingdom of Priests: A History of Old Testament Israel.* Grand Rapids: Baker, 1987.

Pearlman, Moshe. *In the Footsteps of Moses.* Jerusalem: Steimatzky's Agency, 1973.

Walton, John H. and Victor H. Matthews. *The IVP Bible Background Commentary: Genesis-Deuteronomy.* Downers Grove, Ill.: InterVarsity Press, 1997.

SETTLING IN THE PROMISED LAND

Chapter 6

(Joshua; Judges; Ruth)

For forty years the Hebrews lived as nomads in tents in various areas of the Sinai. They defeated their attackers the few times they had been engaged in battle. Now they were regrouping for an assault on the fortresses and armed cities of a region vastly different from the days of Abraham, Isaac, and Jacob. One day Abraham roamed at will, seemingly, throughout Canaan, but now the region contained kingdoms with well-defined territories. They had established leagues of cities ready to join together to repel an invader, the Hebrews, that must have appeared like an overwhelming group of people.

You will remember that by the time Joshua and the Hebrews approached the Jordan River, they had already defeated "Sihon and Og" and had driven fear into many inhabitants of Canaan (Joshua 2: 9-10). Yet who were Sihon and Og—and who else would they face as they attempted to conquer the land of Canaan?

The Land

Canaan at the Time of the Conquest

East of the Jordan—Transjordan

At the southern edge of Transjordan (south of the Dead Sea and the Zered River)

lived the Edomites, descended from Esau and thus with blood ties to the Hebrews. At this time they seem to have lived in

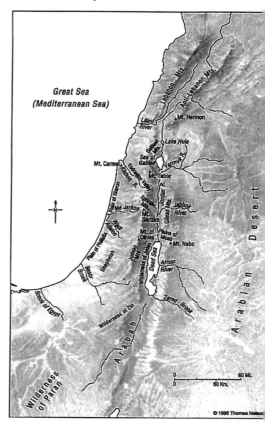

The Land of Canaan

semi-nomadic groups. A fierce, wild people, they represented a powerful barrier to the Hebrew advance. They weren't about to give permission for the Hebrews to cross their territory even peacefully.

North of the Edomites, on the Transjordanian plateau east of the Dead Sea, lay the kingdom of Moab. Its heartland was bounded on the south by the Zered River and on the north by the Arnon River, a distance of some thirty miles. But part of the time it controlled territory as far north as Heshbon, for a total of about sixty miles. Its sedentary population lived in a narrow strip of approximately fifteen miles between the Dead Sea and the Syrian Desert.

North of the Moabites, between the Arnon and Jabbok rivers (a distance of about fifty miles), lay the Ammonite kingdom along the Syrian desert frontier. Their capital was called Rabbah-ammon or Amman, now the capital of Jordan. West of the Ammonites, between the Arnon and Jabbok, an Amorite king by the name of Sihon had established himself. He ruled a territory some fifteen to twenty miles east and west.

Finally, north of the Yarmuk (which flows into the Jordan south of the Sea of Galilee) extended the kingdom of Og, who ruled the territory of Bashan, another Amorite kingdom. This principality stretched approximately from the Yarmuk in the south to Mount Hermon in the north. Most of Bashan consisted of a tableland some 2,000 feet in height that was quite fruitful and especially produced wheat and cattle.

West of the Jordan

"The. . . Amorites live in the hill country; and the Canaanites live by the sea, and along the Jordan." (Numbers 13:29 NRSV)

During the second millennium B.C. Egyptians used the name Canaan to describe the whole area from the Brook of Egypt northward along the coast to Lebanon, then inland to the Syrian Desert to include Bashan, then down the Yarmuk to the Jordan valley and south to the Dead Sea, and from there back to the Brook of Egypt.

Canaanites seem to have migrated from northern Arabia, perhaps as early as 3,000

B.C., but some scholars would put their entrance much later. The growth of cities in Canaan occurred during the period 2900-2700. Those cities seem to have largely disappeared between 2,300 and 2,000. Amorites from Syria entered Canaan sometime after 2,000 and probably were responsible for renewed city-building.

Scripture refers to several peoples living in Canaan at the time of the conquest: Hittites, Girgashites, Amorites, Canaanites, Perizzites, Hivites, and Jebusites (Deuteronomy 7:1). At the present stage of archaeological or historical investigation it is not possible to identify or differentiate them all. In fact, the Bible itself sometimes uses the terms Canaanite and Amorite interchangeably. Schoville has suggested that some of these population groups may be clans rather than different ethnic groups.[1]

For our present purposes it is not necessary to distinguish between these peoples. It is important to note, however, that a single culture dominated in the land, and we call it Canaanite; all these groups seem to have bought into it. Some elements of that culture surface in later discussion. Keep in mind that God condemned these pagan peoples and their corrupting ways and ordered that they be exterminated (Deuteronomy 7:2).

From a political perspective, existing kingdoms or leagues posed significant obstacles to the Israelites. As already noted, Sihon and Og, who ruled east of the Jordan, are called Amorite kings. West of the Jordan five Amorite kings joined a confederacy: Jerusalem, Hebron, Jarmuth, Lachish, and Eglon (Joshua 10:1-43). And Jabin, the Canaanite king of Hazor, led a powerful north Palestinian confederacy against the Israelites (Joshua 11:1-5). In this case it is said that Amorites, Hittites, Perizzites, Jebusites, and Hivites all joined battle against Joshua's army.

Canaan after the Conquest

"Now therefore, divide this land as an inheritance to the nine tribes and half the tribe of Manasseh. With the other half tribe [of Manasseh] the Reubenites and the Gadites received their inheritance, which Moses had

given them, beyond the Jordan eastward."
(Joshua 13:7-8 NKJV)

After the conquest and all during the days of the judges Canaan consisted of a mosaic of twelve tracts of land assigned to the tribes of Israel, plus pockets of pagan holdouts that the Israelites had failed to conquer. The verses noted above record the command to divide the land, and Joshua 13—21 spell out the allotments and boundaries of the tribes. These chapters present a real challenge to the Bible student because they are full of strange names of towns and districts.

What these descriptions boil down to is this. Reuben, Gad, and the half tribe of

Land allocated to the tribes of Israel

Manasseh got the territory east of the Jordan, and Moses parceled it out (Numbers 32). The half tribe of Manasseh settled in Bashan in

the north. Roughly, its boundaries extended between Mount Hermon on the north and the Jarmuk River on the south, with the Sea of Galilee and the upper Jordan forming the western border, and the Syrian Desert as the eastern border. Gad occupied the land between the Sea of Galilee and the Dead Sea and the Jordan River and the Syrian Desert. Reuben received the land east of the Dead Sea and north of the Arnon River.

The other nine and a half tribes received tracts west of the Jordan. Simeon occupied territory west of the southern end of the Dead Sea in the northern Negev and the southern Judean highlands. Judah got the rest of the Judean highlands west of the Dead Sea. The northern border of Judah lay approximately on a line extending west from the northern shore of the Dead Sea. Just above that Benjamin occupied a tract extending from the Jordan into central Palestine, and Dan's territory lay just west of Benjamin's. Ephraim had the southern part of Samaria; and the half tribe of Manasseh, the northern part.

From the southwest corner of the Sea of Galilee extended the territory of Issachar, and west of that lay the land of Zebulun. To the west and north of the Sea of Galilee up to the foothills of Mount Hermon, Naphtali had its holdings, and west of them Asher occupied the Carmel range and points north. Because of Amorite pressures on the western part of the territory of Dan, some Danites later migrated north and established themselves at the northern border of Canaan, conquering and renaming the town of Laish as Dan (Judges 18). The Levites did not have a separate allotment of land but held towns and districts scattered throughout all the rest of the tribes. This was designed to distribute a spiritual impact throughout Israel.

We discover from the books of Joshua and Judges that the Hebrews initially did not conquer the land assigned to these tribes. In fact, they did not get control of it all until the reign of David. In the days of the judges they did not control the coastal plain and were shut up to the hill country of Judea, Samaria, and Galilee west of the Jordan and the hill country east of the

Israel controlled only the hills east and west of the Jordan. The Canaanites continued to hold the lowlands and Jerusalem.

Jordan between the Arnon River on the south and just north of the Yarmuk River on the north. During the period of the judges a powerful Philistine league of five cities controlled the coastal plain: Gezer, Ashkelon, Ashdod, Ekron, and Gath.

(For more on this topic, go to p. 84 or p. 146.)

Government

During the Period of the Conquest

"Israel served the Lord all the days of Joshua, and all the days of the elders who outlived Joshua, who had known all the works of the Lord which He had done for Israel." (Joshua 24:31 NKJV)

The Philistine Threat

During the period of the judges the Philistines appear to have been at the height of their power. Their five cities or city-states controlled the coastal plain from the southern end of what is now the Gaza Strip to the northern outskirts of modern Tel Aviv. They oppressed the Hebrews for forty years, denying them access to iron so they could not manufacture weapons or make or maintain agricultural implements. Samson struggled with them with little real effect. And at the beginning of the monarchy Saul met defeat and death at their hands. After David's defeat of Goliath and the later rise of his kingdom, Philistine power began to decline.

They, however, remained strong during the days of Solomon and the subsequent kingdom of Judah. For a few years they paid tribute to Judah but then became independent. Later the Assyrians fought them effectively and wrought great destruction in the Philistine cities. Finally, when Nebuchadnezzar destroyed the kingdom of Judah and deported much of the population (597-586), he also destroyed the Philistine cities and carried off their people.

The questions of the origin of the Philistines, their early history, and the nature of their culture go far beyond the scope of this book. It is enough to say that excavations in Philistine land are beginning to bring to life this dead civilization. Of special importance among the newer literature are: Trude and Moshe Dothan, *People of the Sea: The Search for the Philistines* (1992); Trude Dothan, *The Philistines and Their Material Culture* (1982); and Robert Drews, *The End of the Bronze Age* (1993).

Government during the period of the conquest remained very much a theocracy. While Moses continued in the saddle, God led in the conquest of Transjordan (Numbers

At the renewal of the covenant, the people on Mount Ebal responded to the reading of the curses with a loud amen, so this came to be known as the Mount of Cursing.

21:1-3, 21-26, 33-35; Deuteronomy 2—3). And Moses approved the request of the tribes of Reuben and Gad and the half tribe of Manasseh to settle east of the Jordan, on condition that their fighting men would join the others in crossing the Jordan and conquering the land (Numbers 32).

Moreover, God directed Moses in the choice of those who would officiate in the division of Canaan after the conquest (Numbers 34:16-29). Furthermore, God commanded that all Israelites marry within their tribes to preserve their inheritances (Numbers 36).

The question may arise as to why the tribes east of the Jordan would be willing to send off their fighting men to join with the rest of the Israelites and leave their wives and children defenseless. There are at least two reasons. The enemies of Israel were so thoroughly defeated that they posed little if any threat. And the men who had to join Joshua were twenty years old and above. Men seventeen to nineteen could have provided defense of families and property.

In further continuation of the theocracy, God directed Moses to bring Joshua to the tabernacle and appoint him leader there (Numbers 27;15-23; Deuteronomy 32:14). Joshua led as Moses had led, following divine commands explicitly. These especially had to do with how to cross the Jordan, circumcision of the military force, the attack on Jericho, and the pursuit of other military goals. When about to pass off this earthly scene, Joshua led the people in renewing the covenant with God (Joshua 24:16-25).

As Joshua 24:31, quoted above, states, the theocracy held firm during the days of Joshua and the strong, committed elders of his generation. But during the period of the judges the political stability began to unravel because of the lack of a central government.

During the Days of the Judges

"In those days there was no king in Israel; everyone did what was right in his own eyes." (Judges 17:6; 21:25 NKJV)

Theocracy remained the ideal during the period of the judges. God continued to make His presence felt, but without a central government there was no united action. From a human standpoint, public and private affairs became very unpredictable. The book of Judges pictures a series of recurring cycles: apostasy from God, punishment in the form of oppression by neighboring tribes, cry to God for relief, redemption or release from bondage, and a period of rest from oppression. A cycle like that implies theocracy; God punishes for waywardness and brings prosperity when the people repent and call to Him for help. Moreover, He sovereignly called leaders (judges) to bring relief and to exercise executive and judicial functions in society. For example, it is said of Othniel (as well as others), "The Lord raised up a deliverer. . . . The Spirit of the Lord came upon him" (Judges 3:9-10 NKJV).

Though as divinely enlisted leaders the judges ruled over Israel, they almost never attained control over all twelve tribes. For example, Samson's area of activity was in the southwest, and he dealt essentially with the Philistines. Deborah and Barak fought in the north against Canaanites under the leadership of a second king Jabin of Hazor. Jephthah led his followers against the Ammonites on the eastern frontier. The judges were at the same time judges, civil functionaries, and military leaders.

Most of the judges figured especially as leaders of armies that rescued their people from oppression. Accounts of their warfare occurs in a later discussion. Samuel must be considered the exception, for he clearly became more than a general. In fact, 1 Samuel 7 does not indicate that Samuel led the forces, but it does not say who did. The chronicler calls Samuel a prophet (1 Samuel 3:20); he acted as a priest (1 Samuel 9:12-13; 13:8-13); and he functioned as a judge (1 Samuel 7:15-17). He established a circuit court in Bethel, Gilgal, and Mizpah, and regularly held court at his home in Ramah. There he also built an altar to the Lord.

Samuel also functioned as a transitional figure between the period of the judges and the kingship. In Samuel's later days the people demanded a king, and Samuel took the request as a sort of vote of no confidence—as a lack of appreciation for all his hard work. But God made it clear that the opponents really objected to the divine plan for a theocracy. God granted the Hebrews' wish but warned them of the disadvantages of a kingship (1 Samuel 8:9-21).

God had already introduced Israel to the concept of a king. It had been hinted at in Genesis 49:10 and Numbers 24:17, and Moses made some very clear statements about it in Deuteronomy 17:14-20. Samuel went on to anoint Saul and then David as king. But that is a story for a later chapter.

(For more on this topic, go to p. 88 or p. 148.)

Chronology of the Judges

We cannot establish an exact chronology of the judges. If we add up all the years of oppression and rest recorded in the book we get a total of 410 years. The book of Acts gives a total of 450 years for the period from Joshua to Samuel (Acts 13:20). Apparently that difference is to be accounted for by the forty years of Eli's ministry (1 Samuel 4:18). There is not room for 450 years, plus 30 for Joshua's leadership, 40 years for wandering in the wilderness, and some decades for Samuel's ministry between the time when Saul became king (c. 1050) and an early date for the Exodus (c. 1440). The usual conclusion is that some of the judges were contemporary (e. g., Samson in the southwest and Jephthah in the east) and that the period of the judges lasted some 300 years.[2]

Religion

In the Days of the Conquest

"This Book of the Law shall not depart from your mouth, but you shall meditate in it day and night, that you may observe to do according to all that is written in it." (Joshua 1:8 NKJV)

So said God to Joshua as he took over leadership of the Israelites. During the days of the conquest the word of God provided the marching orders for Joshua and the people of Israel. And the people obeyed it. They obeyed in crossing the Jordan (Joshua 3—4); the men from the two and one half tribes east of the Jordan fought alongside the other Israelites; the fighting men subjected themselves to circumcision as a sign of the covenant (Joshua 5:2-9); Israel kept the Passover on the plains of Jericho (Joshua

At the renewal of the covenant, the people on Mount Gerizim responded to the reading of the blessings with a loud amen, so this came to be known as the Mount of Blessing.

5:10); the Israelite forces followed divine instructions for battle in the conquest. The whole of Israel gathered between Mounts Ebal and Gerizim in Samaria to offer sacrifice and hear the reading of the law (Joshua 8:30-35). Subsequently they set up the tabernacle at Shiloh, nineteen miles north of Jerusalem (Joshua 18:1).

As Joshua neared the end of his life, he gathered the leaders of the tribes of Israel to Shechem, between Ebal and Gerizim, for a renewal of the covenant with God. The people pledged, "The Lord our God we will serve, and His voice we will obey" (Joshua 24:24). As noted above, Israel was faithful to God all the days of Joshua and the elders who outlived him, "who had known all the works of the Lord which He had done for Israel" (Joshua 24:31). In other words, those who had seen God work miraculously on their behalf in the Sinai, in the crossing of the Jordan, and in the conquest, held firm. They had experienced too much of the power of God to turn against Him. Moreover, they had also experienced God's tight control over the Israelites when they were gathered in one place under the leadership of Moses and Joshua.

The story changed with subsequent generations of Hebrews. Scattered all over Canaan without firm control, they had a fading memory of the supernatural working of God on their behalf. We need to remember that there had been a tendency to idolatry among the Hebrews all during the years since the Exodus. It was one thing to get the Hebrews out of Egypt and quite another to get Egypt out of the Hebrews.

During the Days of the Judges

"Another generation arose. . . who did not know the Lord nor the work which He had done for Israel. . . and they forsook the Lord God of their fathers." (Judges 2:10, 12 NKJV)

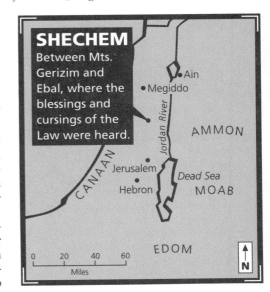

SHECHEM

Between Mts. Gerizim and Ebal, where the blessings and cursings of the Law were heard.

Ain
Megiddo
Jordan River
AMMON
CANAAN
Jerusalem
Hebron
Dead Sea
MOAB
EDOM

0   20   40   60
Miles

N

A NATURAL AMPHITHEATER

e valley between Mount Gerizim and Mount Ebal
med a natural amphitheater. A speaker's voice could
heard on both hillsides. Likewise, the shouts of a
wd on Gerizim could be heard on Ebal, and vice versa.
ese acoustics made Shechem, located in the valley, an
al site for the nation to ratify the covenant.

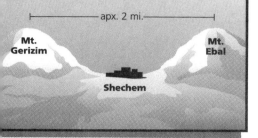

Idolatry among the Hebrews

The Hebrews found the visual representation of the many false gods of Egypt very difficult to shake. Moreover, the peoples in the Near East universally practiced the figural representation of their gods. The First and Second Commandments, which forbade such representation, definitely put the Hebrews in a minority position.

They had worshiped the gods of the Egyptians while in Egypt (Joshua 24:14). They made and worshiped a golden calf at Sinai after the giving of the Law (Exodus 32). They worshiped the Baal of Peor in Moab (Numbers 25). And there were images of foreign gods among them when Joshua renewed the covenant with them at the end of his life (Joshua 24:23).

Religiously, conditions changed during the days of the judges from what they had been for two generations: the generations of the conquest and of the wilderness wandering. No single dynamic figure called the people to serve God. Now scattered all over Canaan, the people had not systematically

Bronze idol of Baal, pagan god of war and fertility. Idols such as this were frequently plated with gold (Isaiah 40:19).

destroyed the pagan altars and images along with the cursed people themselves (Deuteronomy 7:1-6). All sorts of pagan influences remained among them.

Furthermore, though the central sanctuary continued to function at Shiloh, with its priesthood and sacrificial system, it seems to have had little influence. The Bible contains no record of annual celebrations of the Passover or the great feasts of Firstfruits, Pentecost, Trumpets, or Tabernacles, or of the observance of the Day of Atonement. This resulted in a downward spiral of religion and moral conditions.

The generalization that describes Israelite conduct during the period is that "they followed other gods from among the gods of the people who were all around them, and they bowed down to them. . . . They forsook the Lord and served Baal and the Ashtoreths [Canaanite goddesses]" (Judges 2:12-13 NKJV). Joshua had warned that the pagan peoples who were not destroyed would be "snares and traps" to them (Joshua 23:13). Serving Baal and the Canaanite goddesses undoubtedly involved religious

Canaanite Religious Practices

What predominated in the religion of the Canaanites was in fact a fertility cult. This involved human effort to enlist the gods in supplying the primary needs of humanity: the provision of their daily food and the propagation of the race. By imitative magic they sought in rite and myth to predispose the gods in their favor—to bless the fruitfulness of their crops, the health and increase of their herds, and the birth of children.

It is easy to see how both male and female ritual prostitutes played a part in their religious ceremonies. The prominence of the goddesses Ashera, Anat, and Astarte in the nude with sexual features emphasized clearly enhanced this facet of their religious practices. We may consider the worship of the fertility cult immoral. They considered it largely an amoral worship.

Of course there was a lot more to religion than that. Their belief in the kingship of Baal represented faith in the power of Order over Chaos. And their worship of Baal as a young warrior fully armed portrayed him, among other things, as the defender of his people. And there were other gods. They revered El as the senior god of the Canaanite pantheon and the creator of created things. They worshiped Reshef as the god who destroyed men in mass by war or plague. But we are not concerned with producing a grocery list of the gods here.

As in Israel, they offered whole burnt offerings of animals to the gods, as well as communion offerings in which they offered internal organs to the gods, with the rest divided among the worshipers in a sacrificial meal.

shrines to promote the fertility of the land or fertility in general and to symbolize the primary function of the nature god Baal and his consort Asherah. It is an open question whether the sons of the priest Eli were aping the practices of the Canaanites at the sanctuary at Shiloh or whether they were just guilty of sexual looseness (1 Samuel 2:22).

Gideon's father worshiped at an altar to Baal. God commanded Gideon to destroy it (Judges 6:25). And after Gideon's great victory he set up a shrine in his home town. "And all Israel played the harlot with it there. It became a snare to Gideon and to his house" (Judges 8:27 NKJV).

Though there were periodic revivals, from this time on idolatry became the national sin. During the reign of Solomon each of his foreign wives brought with her the gods of her own nation. After the division of the kingdom, the northern kingdom remained officially idolatrous throughout its history, and the southern kingdom continued heavily infected with this sin. Finally both kingdoms went into captivity because of this failure. In warning, God had foretold through Moses that such captivity in a foreign land would be their punishment for idolatry (Deuteronomy 29:24-28; cf. 1 Kings 14:15).

But the book of Judges is not just a book of gloom. Of the 410 years referred to in the

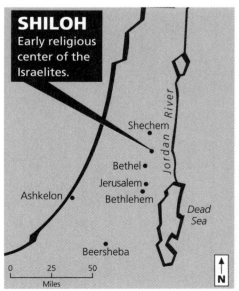

SHILOH
Early religious center of the Israelites.

Shechem

Jordan River

Bethel

Jerusalem

Ashkelon

Bethlehem

Dead Sea

Beersheba

0   25   50
Miles

N

prostitution because Canaanite worship was heavily laced with fertility deities and cultic fertility rites. Male and female prostitutes engaged in sexual activity at the cult

HUMAN SACRIFICE IN ISRAEL?

Did the spiritual decline during the days of the judges involve human sacrifice, an issue raised by Jephthah's vow (Judges 11:30-40)? Before Jephthah went into battle against the Ammonites, he vowed to God that if victorious, he would offer as a burnt offering whatever came forth from the doors of his house to meet him upon his return. After the victory his only child, a daughter, rushed out to meet him as he came back home. There has been endless discussion in biblical literature over this ill-considered vow.

Some argue that Jephthah was a rather wild man, living on the fringes of Israelite religious influence in an area where human sacrifice would have been practiced by pagans. He had made a vow, and one would expect him to keep it. Others argue just as cogently that human sacrifice was an abomination to God,

and it is inconceivable that any God-fearing person could have committed such a crime. They say his daughter was allowed two months to bewail her virginity, not her loss of life (Judges 11:37-38); and the implication is that she became a virgin devoted to the service of God at the central sanctuary (cf. Exodus 38:8; 1 Samuel 2:22; Luke 2:36-37). The real pain for Jephthah, then, was termination of his line.

Leon Wood observes that if he did literally sacrifice his daughter, the place of sacrifice would have been the tabernacle, and no priest would have been willing to officiate. He also notes that the latter part of Judges 11:31 may be translated "shall surely be the Lord's or I will offer it up for a burnt offering"—the first part indicating what Jephthah would have done if a human being had met him and the latter if an animal.[3]

book, during only about one hundred years are the people said to have been in sin. So Judges becomes also a book of faithfulness to God, a book of God's grace in watchcare and restoration.

An example of renewal came in the days of Samuel, when he called representatives of all Israel to Mizpah. In response to his call to get rid of their foreign gods, the people responded with confession of sin and action in putting away their idols. Then God gave them a military victory over the Philistines (1 Samuel 7).

In connection with Israelite renewal, Samuel offered sacrifice on an altar at Mizpah. This points up the fact that Shiloh had not become the indispensable center of

worship during the days of the judges. Legitimate altars could be and were built at other places. For example, Gideon built an altar (Judges 6:24), as did Samson's father Manoah (Judges 13:19) and some men of Israel (Judges 21:4).

In fact, God had prescribed how proper altars should be constructed. They might be of earth. Or if they were made of stone, they should be natural, unworked stone. And there should not be steps up to the altar. Thus the priests would not be elevated above the heads of the people and be indecently exposed as people looked up under their robes while they were officiating (Exodus 20:24-26; cf. Deuteronomy 27:5-6; Joshua 8:31).

False Worship at Dan (Judges 17—18)

A worship center that certainly did not meet God's standards stood in the mountains of Ephraim. There a man named Micah made household idols and set up a shrine in his house, consecrating one of his sons as priest. Later he got a Levite from Bethlehem in Judah to be his priest.

Meanwhile, many men of the tribe of Dan became increasingly desperate because they had not been able to dislodge the Canaanites from much of their allotted territory along the Mediterranean coast. So they decided to take matters into their own hands and strike out for a new home not provided for in the division of the land. On their way through Ephraim they kidnapped Micah's priest and carried off the idols from his shrine. Then, when they got to Laish, north of the Sea of Galilee, they conquered it, killed the inhabitants, took the city for themselves and renamed it Dan. They then set up Micah's gods in their own worship center, which remained active until the Assyrians took the northern part of Israel captive in 732 B.C. (Judges 18:30; cf. 2 Kings 15:29). Certainly this false worship helped prepare for Jeroboam's calf worship at Dan in 931 B.C. In other words, idolatrous worship persisted at Dan from the time of the judges until the Assyrian conquest.

(For more on this topic, go to p. 90 or p. 174.)

Warfare

The Conquest of Canaan

"When you have crossed the Jordan into the land of Canaan, then you shall drive out all the inhabitants of the land from before you, destroy all their engraved stones, destroy all their molded images, and demolish all their high places; you shall dispossess the inhabitants of the land and dwell in it, for I have given you the land to possess." (Numbers 33:51-53 NKJV)

God commanded the Israelites not only to march into Canaan and dispossess the existing inhabitants, but to kill them all (Deuteronomy 7:1-5). In fact, God warned the Israelites that if they did not drive out the inhabitants, "I will do to you as I thought to do to them" (Numbers 33:56). His wise plan: "I will not drive them out from before you in one year, lest the land become desolate. Little by little I will drive them out from before you, until you have increased, and you inherit the land" (Exodus 23:29-30 NKJV).

Rationale for God's Action

Critical scholars and well-meaning contemporary commentators frequently condemn God for these orders and the Hebrews for carrying them out. In a day when we read of the horrors of ethnic cleansing in Rwanda, Bosnia, and elsewhere, what can we say to defend such a course of action? God Himself said that if the Israelites did not remove these people and their idolatry from the land, they would become infected and suffer a like fate (Deuteronomy 7:4). Moreover, a study of Canaanite religion reveals that base sex worship prevailed among them and religious prostitution thrived. Presumably in time society would become so depraved and sexually transmitted diseases so widespread that the Canaanites would almost self-destruct.

Furthermore, in the counsels of divine justice, there seems to be a quota of iniquity that God permits before He punishes a people either in a minor way or by obliteration. And it seems that God will deal with a nation when it has reached such a place. This is not pure speculation. In Genesis 15 God was having a conversation with Abraham that concerned His promise to give Palestine to Abraham's descendants in perpetuity. In the process, He said that the promise did not mean that the Hebrews would always inhabit the land. In fact, they would be out of the land and held in bondage in a strange land (Egypt) for four hundred years (v. 13).

Finally, at the end of that time, the Hebrews would return to Palestine, "for the sin of the Amorites has not yet reached its full measure" (v. 16 NIV). After the four hundred years of bondage in Egypt, the Hebrews left in the Exodus and entered Canaan. Then, God commanded them to exterminate the Amorites (Deuteronomy 20:17). Evidently by that time the sin of the Amorites had reached "full measure."

God will clearly judge the sin of the nations when they are "ripe for punishment" (Genesis 15:16 REVISED ENGLISH BIBLE). We may wonder out loud whether Sodom and Gomorrah had reached their quota of iniquity when destroyed by divine judgment (Genesis 19), or whether Pompeii and the other cities at the foot of Mount Vesuvius had reached that point in A.D. 79. When we learn from the excavations about the degree to which Pompeii was given over to sexual preoccupation, we may conclude that life in the city was very base. We may also wonder about the iniquity quotas of modern cities and countries.

The Conquest as Holy War

"Truly the Lord has delivered all the land into our hands." (Joshua 2:24 NKJV)

So said the spies whom Joshua had sent to Jericho and its environs after they escaped from Jericho with Rahab's help. In part they believed this because the hearts of many Canaanites melted when they heard about God's miraculous working on their behalf in the wilderness and in conquests east of the Jordan (Joshua 2:9-11).

In connection with their covenant relationship with Him, God had commanded the Hebrews to conquer the land and eradicate the pagan shrines and pagan practices. Therefore they could be convinced that they were doing God's business as they marched forward. The spirit of holy war comes especially clear from David's spirited boast as he went out to meet Goliath: "This uncircumcised Philistine will be like one of them [lions and bears he had killed defending sheep], seeing he has defied the armies of the living God" (1 Samuel 17:36 NKJV).

The certainty that the Hebrews had done what God wanted them to do and that God had given them victory in battle appears on numerous occasions. For example, God said to Joshua, "See! I have given Jericho into your hand" (Joshua 6:2). Again He said, "Stretch out the spear. . . toward Ai, for I will give it into your hand" (Joshua 8:18). Later He told Barak, "I will deliver him [Sisera] into your hand" (Judges 4:7 NKJV). And later yet He promised Gideon, "I have

delivered it [the Midianite camp] into your hand" (Judges 7:9 NKJV).

The psychological value of all these promises should be self-evident. But in addition, God often specifically encouraged leader and army alike. For example, He said to Joshua at Ai, "Do not be afraid, nor be dismayed" (Joshua 8:1). And Joshua, having received divine encouragement, said to the troops at Gibeon, "Do not be afraid, nor be dismayed; be strong and of good courage, for thus the Lord will do to all your enemies against whom you fight" (Joshua 10:25).

So again and again they marched forward as God's people to do the will of God in the power of God.

Crossing of the Jordan (Joshua 3)

"The waters which came down from upstream stood still, and rose in a heap. . . . And all Israel crossed over on dry ground." (Joshua 3:16-17 NKJV)

Closely connected with the conquest of Canaan, and as a prelude to it, came the crossing of the Jordan. Of course the Israelites had to cross the Jordan to get to the other side. But the miraculous crossing of the Jordan was to demonstrate "that the living God is among you" and that He would drive out the seven peoples slated for expulsion and extermination (Joshua 3:10). As a matter of fact, the Jordan was normally a deep (at least 10-12 feet) and wide river (a hundred feet or more) in those days and an even greater river at harvest time. No more, for Syria, Jordan, and Israel using the river water for various purposes. But the volume of water in the river in Joshua's day made it an effective barrier to Israel's advance—and they had no boats or pontoons.

As the Joshua account tells it, when the feet of the priests who bore the ark touched the water's edge, the river dried up—all the way to Adam (modern Damieh) and Zaretan. Damieh is some sixteen miles north of Jericho, and Jericho a few miles north of the Dead Sea. Thus the Jordan bed was dry for twenty miles or more, and even a large number of people and animals could cross quickly.

Landslides have occurred at Damieh in more recent times. For example, on December 8, 1267, a bank collapsed into the Jordan there and dammed it up for sixteen hours. Something similar occurred in 1906. And during the earthquakes of 1927 a 150-foot embankment fell into the river, stopping the flow for twenty-one and a half hours.[4] It appears that the stopping of the Jordan in Joshua's day occurred as a result of an earthquake, for Psalm 114:3 says that on this occasion "The mountains skipped like rams, the little hills like lambs" (NKJV). But though the phenomenon may have been natural, the timing was supernatural "as. . . the feet of the priests who bore the ark dipped in the edge of the water" (Joshua 3:15).

The Fall of Jericho (Joshua 6)

"The wall fell down flat" (v. 20). "But they burned the city and all that was in it with fire" (v. 24). "And Joshua spared Rahab the harlot, her father's household, and all that she had." (v. 25 NKJV)

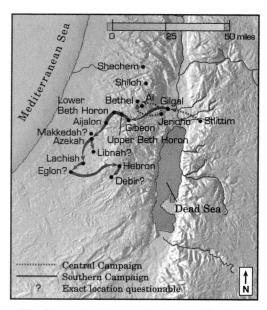

The Conquest of Canaan (Central and Southern Campaigns). From the camp at Gilgal, Joshua launched two campaigns. Jericho fell in the central campaign, which continued with an ambush of Bethel and Ai. Joshua launched the southern campaign against the Amorites assembled near Gibeon, and continued the assault all the way to Debir.

Throughout the period of the conquest and the judges God as the master strategist gave the victory. But we may ask how a ragtag bunch of Hebrews, without military training, and poorly supplied with war materiel accomplished what they did.

There are answers. One of the most important was morale. As we saw earlier, God often told the Israelites that He had given them the victory or Joshua and the judges assured their men that God had given them the victory. Thus the forces advanced with an incredible optimism, an uncrushable morale. Often in the pre-gun era men with high morale and brute strength have won battles. Certainly a good part of the success of the Muslim forces in the seventh century came from the belief that they went forth in the name of Allah and in his strength to conquer the world. And while a modern army may look to its weapons, morale is more important than many civilians realize.

Second, military strategy, stratagems, or psychological warfare contributed. A modern reader of the attack on Jericho may think it rather quaint or a little stupid for the Israelites to be marching around the walls of the city. But the people of Jericho got over the first terror of the Israelite host filing around the walls and gradually relaxed. Then on the seventh day the peaceful procession suddenly turned into a frenzied assault and caught the defenders off guard.

Third, as the Israelites conquered peoples east of the Jordan and took their weapons they overcame their lack of war materiel.

Fourth, we should not impose on the ancients of Canaan a contemporary view of modern standing armies instilled with military discipline and the power to maintain ranks under assault. By and large there were no standing armies with extensive training in those days. When a crisis arose, men laid down their plowshares and picked up their swords and battle-axes. The Canaanites had not really trained for warfare any more than the Hebrews, but they might have become a little more adept at it through experience as the city-states scrapped with one another. And they may have owned more weapons.

Fifth, God at times intervened through a natural phenomenon. In the case of Jericho, many have suggested that an earthquake caused the walls to fall. And it may be that earthquake action and aftershocks connected with the crossing of the Jordan so weakened the walls that they did collapse. If so, the miraculous element was the timing, as with the crossing of the Jordan: the walls fell just as the Hebrews attacked.

God gave specific instructions for the attack on Jericho. The Israelites were to march around the city once each day for six days and on the seventh day to march around it seven times. The armed men were to provide the vanguard, followed by seven priests bearing seven trumpets of rams' horns, and followed in turn by the ark and the people of Israel. For six days they should all walk silently around the city. As they encircled the city on the seventh day the priests were to blow a long blast on the trumpets, the people were to shout, and the wall of the city would fall down flat. Then the armed men would rush up over the debris and destroy every living thing and burn the city with fire.

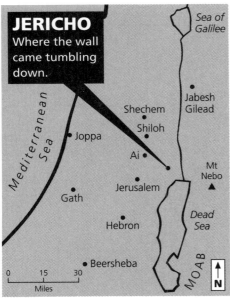

JERICHO
Where the wall came tumbling down.

Metals taken in the attack were to be put in the treasury of the house of the Lord, and Rahab and her family were to be rescued. According to the Joshua account, all happened as God had commanded and the people followed His directives to the letter. Well, almost! But before we look at the fiasco at Ai and punishment for disobedience, we need to review the debate over archaeological discoveries at Jericho.

Debate over the Fall of Jericho

Did events transpire as the biblical account states? The first extensive excavation at the site was a German Oriental Society dig led by Ernst Sellin and Carl Watzinger in 1907 to 1909. They found that the city covered only about eight and one-half acres. The Israelites could easily march around it once a day or even seven times in a day. Though Jericho seems important in the Old Testament narrative, it was not large like Babylon or Nineveh. Some scholars had doubted the Joshua narrative because they assumed Jericho was larger than it actually was. Since chronological systems were poorly understood at the time, the excavators were limited in arriving at further conclusions.

John Garstang, an Englishman, led the second archaeological expedition at Jericho from 1930 to 1936. Garstang identified the wall of Joshua's day as a double wall on top of the mound on which the city was built. He commented that the outer wall fell down the slope of the mound, and the inner wall collapsed into the space between the walls. Traces of intense fire appeared everywhere. He said that the walls fell outward so completely that attackers could easily climb over their ruins into the city.[5] Garstang also claimed that all evidence pointed to a fall of the city to the Israelites about 1400 B.C.

Many questioned Garstang's claims, but after World War II, when he again had access to materials stored during the war, he reiterated his earlier contentions about the walls and the date they fell. This appeared in *The Story of Jericho* by John and J. B. E. Garstang. It should be noted that Garstang was not an evangelical trying to defend the biblical narrative. The fact is that he was somewhat surprised by what he found.

Kathleen Kenyon conducted the third major archaeological campaign at Jericho for the British School of Archaeology in

Jerusalem (1952-58). She demonstrated that the wall on top of the mound that Garstang dated to Joshua's day belonged to the period 3000-2000 B.C. and could have had no connection with Joshua, and she dated the fall of the city some fifty years later than did Garstang.[6] There the matter lay until after Kenyon's death in 1978.

Her excavation reports, published posthumously at the end of the last decade, have received careful analysis by Bryant Wood, an archaeologist at the University of Toronto and a specialist on Jericho. Based on Kenyon's reports, Wood observes that there was a stone revetment surrounding the mound on which the town was built. A mud-brick wall topped this revetment. The revetment held in place a flat rampart, above which (higher up the slope) stood a second mud-brick wall that constituted Jericho's city wall proper. So, there were two concentric walls with houses in between (was one of them Rahab's?).

Kenyon herself had discovered piles of bricks that had fallen down from the revetment wall surrounding the city and that would have enabled attackers to climb up into the city.[7] Moreover, in line with God's command not to take the city's goods, abundant and valuable supplies of grain turned up in the excavation.[8]

Evidently the city did not fall as a result of a starvation siege, as was common in the ancient Near East. Archaeologists found stones, bricks, and timbers blackened from a citywide fire, tallying with the biblical indication that the Israelites burned the city. On the basis of Kenyon's excavation reports, Wood also argued that all evidence pointed to an approximate 1400 B.C. date for the fall of the city.

To summarize, Wood concludes that the walls of Jericho did indeed fall so attackers could climb up over the debris to burn the city but not to plunder it. He, like many others, believes that an earthquake triggered the destruction.

Debate over the Date of the Conquest

The claim that Jericho fell about 1400 B.C. raises the whole question of the date of the

conquest. A 1400 date tallies with the biblical indication in 1 Kings 6:1. That verse talks about the dedication of the temple in the fourth year of Solomon's reign (967-66 B.C.). And it says that the Exodus took place 480 years earlier, about 1446 B.C. Allowing for the forty years of wandering in the wilderness, the conquest should have taken place about 1400.

A 1400 date also tallies with historical developments. By around 1400 Egypt had slipped into the Amarna Age, with the pharaohs neglecting to maintain the empire that the great conqueror Thutmose III had built there. They were much more interested in making religious reforms and expending the energies of the nation on gratifying their personal desires than they were on maintaining a powerful empire. The royal correspondence found at Amarna demonstrates that Egyptian puppet rulers of Palestine sent the pharaohs frequent calls for help in the decades after 1400, without response.

A problem confronting one who accepts the early date of the Exodus is the fact that the Israelites built Pithom and Ramses (Exodus 1:11). Ramses I did not rule until about 1300 B.C. Unger suggested the difficulty here may be removed by concluding

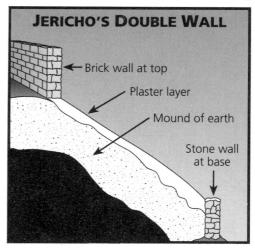

JERICHO'S DOUBLE WALL

← Brick wall at top

↙ Plaster layer

↙ Mound of earth

Stone wall at base

A stone wall surrounded the mound on which Jericho was built. This held in place a flat rampart, above which (higher up the slope) stood a second (mudbrick) wall that constituted Jericho's city wall proper. So there were two concentric walls. When the walls fell, the mudbrick wall collapsed and slid down the slope, creating a pile of rubble over which the attackers could climb.

that *Ramses* is a modernization of the ancient place-name *Zoan-Avaris*, the name by which it was known when the Hebrews built it. A similar situation occurs in Genesis 14:14, where *Dan* is substituted for the older city name of *Laish*.[9] It should be added that Avaris served as the old Hyksos capital in the Delta, and we now know that Ramses adjoined it on the north. That is, Ramses-Avaris had become almost a double city, with Ramses on the north and Avaris on the south.

But many Old Testament scholars, and certainly almost all Israelis, hold to a later date for the Exodus, during the reign of Ramses II, about 1290-1275 B.C., and thus for a later date for the conquest. In general they reach this conclusion on the assumption that Ramses II must have been the great pharaoh of the oppression and the Exodus, who put the Hebrews to hard labor.

Second, Yigael Yadin, eminent excavator of Hazor, claimed that Hazor did not fall to the Israelites until the second third of the thirteenth century B.C.[10] But Scripture indicates that Hazor fell to the Israelites twice: in the days of Joshua (Joshua 11:10-11), when Jabin I ruled; and in the days of Deborah and Barak (Judges 4:2, 23-24), when another Jabin ruled. Yadin assumed that Joshua's conquest was to be related to thirteenth-century destruction in the lower city of Hazor. He found, however, evidence of destruction at the site around 1400 B.C. or a little later in Areas H and K of the lower city.[11] What is more natural than to conclude that the 1400 B.C. destruction dates to Joshua's day and the thirteenth-century destruction dates to the period of the judges?

Third, it is argued that the palace's accessibility to Moses militates against the early date of the Exodus and thus of the conquest. The reasoning is that such accessibility indicates the palace was in the delta region, where the Israelites lived, and the periods when the palace was located in the delta were the days of Joseph and during the thirteenth century B.C. It may be pointed out, however, that the pharaoh of the Exodus could have met Moses at a secondary palace or administrative center. The argument is not conclusive proof for the late date of the Exodus. Moreover, both Thutmose III and Amenhotep II, who ruled 1482-1425, were active in building projects in the delta.

Fourth, archaeologists claim that the destruction of Bethel, Lachish, and Debir, presumably by the Israelites, occurred about 1230 B.C.[12] and therefore supports a late date for the Exodus and the conquest. Seemingly, this is strong evidence for the late date of these two events, but a second glance puts the matter in a different light. Those cities fell about the same time and near the beginning of the conquest, according to the Joshua narrative. But certainly the conquest did not occur as late as 1230 B.C., because the inscription on the Stele of Pharaoh Merneptah represents the Hebrews as settled in Canaan when Merneptah's armies attacked them about 1230 B.C. If adjustment in the dates assigned to the destruction of those sites needs to be made, how effective is the use of this evidence in establishing the date of the Exodus and conquest?

Additionally, while the Bible reports that Joshua captured Bethel, Lachish, and Debir, it says nothing about his men destroying them; they burned only Ai, Jericho, and Hazor (Joshua 6:24; 8:19; 11:13). Some of Joshua's conquests were not permanent

The mound of Old Testament Jericho as it appears today, after considerable archaeological work.

either. We know that Debir had to be recaptured later (Joshua 15:13-17), and possibly the others did also. If the 1230 date of destruction at Bethel, Lachish, and Debir is correct, it may well refer to attacks during the days of the judges instead of to Joshua's conquests.

Fifth, those who hold to the late date note that Ramses II made conquests in Canaan and restored the Egyptian Empire after the loss of power during the Amarna Age. They say that an early date for the conquest would require that the Hebrews already be in the land then, and Ramses does not mention them. Yet we know that Ramses moved through the coastal plain and Hebrews occupied the hill country and they need not have met. The Egyptian Merneptah did battle with the Hebrews somewhere in Canaan only about 1230 and claims to have destroyed them.

Last, Benno Rothenberg explored and excavated in the Timna Valley (15 miles north of the Gulf of Aqaba) between 1964 and 1970 and concluded that the Egyptian working of the copper mines in the area was especially extensive in the days of Ramses II. Therefore, hordes of Egyptian soldiers and workers would have been moving around the Sinai and the Arabah at the time when many scholars, including Israelis generally, believed the Exodus and wilderness wandering took place. No way would the Hebrews have been moving through the area then. So he believed his discoveries would require a "reconsideration" of the thirteenth-century date of the Exodus.[13]

Ai—Defeat and Victory

"Then the Lord said to Joshua: 'Do not be afraid, nor be dismayed; take all the people of war with you, and arise, go up to Ai. See, I have given into your hand the king of Ai, his people, his city, and his land.'" (Joshua 8:1 NKJV)

Having gained a foothold west of the Jordan with the destruction of Jericho, Joshua next turned his attention to the Judean highlands, a wise move. Canaanite chariotry and other heavy armed units could not so easily maneuver there and so lost some of their advantage over the Israelites. Moreover, as long as they stayed out of the

maritime plain, the Israelites had no worry about Egyptian interference, for the Egyptians were content just to maintain communications along that route to the north. Then, too, the sparsely populated highlands offered a region of settlement to the Hebrews.

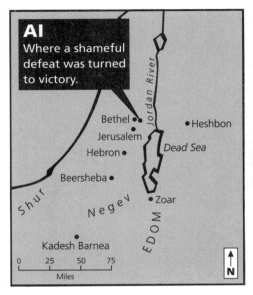

AI

Where a shameful defeat was turned to victory.

Joshua decided to move against Ai, located ten miles north of Jerusalem somewhere to the east of Bethel. Interestingly, God did not direct this foray. Joshua's scouts advised him to send only two or three thousand men against Ai because it was a small bastion. Joshua's men took casualties, met defeat, and their morale snapped. The problem was not faulty tactics or deployment of too few men, but disobedience at Jericho in taking some of the condemned booty and then lying about it. Joshua got the word: no more victories until the cancer had been removed (Joshua 7:12). After the execution of Achan God again blessed the Hebrews with victory (Joshua 7:18-26).

This time God called the shots: take the whole army, set up an ambush behind the city, destroy the city utterly, but its spoil you may claim for yourselves (Joshua 8:1-2). During the night, Joshua stationed 5,000 men at ambush on the west of Ai. He and another 25,000 camped in a valley on

The Canaanite high place or worship shrine at Et-Tell, identified by many archaeologists as Ai

the north. Presumably the Israelite battle ready force that possessed weapons at this time numbered 30,000 (Joshua 8:3. Note Joshua 8:1, "all the people of war").

Joshua and the men with him then prepared for battle. The men of Ai came out of the city and attacked Joshua, who pretended to retreat and thus drew the defenders farther out in the open. When Joshua felt he had pulled the army of Ai far enough away from the town, he gave the signal to the men at ambush to move in and set fire to the city. That done, they came out of Ai to attack the rear of the army of Ai and Joshua's men stopped their retreat. They closed the pincer movement and annihilated the population of Ai. The Hebrews could take spoil on this occasion, since as a have-not people, deprived of manna and other supplies from God, they had to start living off the land.

The Problem of Ai

Judith Marquet-Krause first excavated the site commonly identified as Ai (Et-Tell) in 1934–35. She found that apparently the mound had not been inhabited between 2400 and 1200 B.C.[14] Subsequently it became fashionable to claim that the Bible was in error because Ai was not inhabited at whatever date we assign to the conquest. This professedly became a good example of the historical undependability of the Old Testament. When Professor Joseph A. Callaway began a new series of excavations at Et-Tell in 1964, he concluded that the identification of Et-Tell with Ai was very much in doubt.[15] More recently, John Bimson and David Livingston have proposed Khirbet Nisya, eleven miles north of Jerusalem, as the site of Ai, and they have excavated there for six seasons (1979–1986).[16] The jury is still out on this proposal, however.

I am personally quite convinced that Et-Tell is not Ai and base my belief especially on the four objections of J. Simons.[17] (1) Et-Tell is not particularly near Beitin (Bethel), whereas Joshua 12:9 indicates that Ai is "beside Bethel." (2) Et-Tell is a large site, whereas Joshua 7:3 describes the people as "few. (3) Et-Tell was not a ruin in the post-conquest period, whereas Joshua indicates that Ai was destroyed (8:28). (4) There is no broad valley to the north of Et-Tell, whereas Joshua 8:11 indicates the existence of such a valley near Ai. If Et-Tell is not Ai, the assertion of biblical inaccuracy on this point disappears.

Khirbet Nisya, another candidate for biblical Ai

But soon it became evident that these people were Israelite neighbors. Gibeon is about eight miles northwest of Jerusalem, and its satellite towns of Chephirah, Beeroth, and Kirjath Jearim lay just to the south and west of Gibeon.

The Hebrews did not break the alliance, sworn by the name of God, but subjected them to perpetual slavery to provide wood and water for the Hebrew sacrificial system (Joshua 9:27). The Gibeonites answered, "We are in your hands, do with us as it seems good and right" (Joshua 9:25 NKJV).

It is beyond the scope of this book to go into great detail on all archaeological or historical problems of this sort, but it seemed necessary to mention this one because it calls into question this whole military action of Joshua at Ai and the trustworthiness of Scripture. The best approach to this problem is to accept the discussion of Joshua's military action there but leave the exact location of Ai open.

Campaign in the Judean Hills

"Therefore the five kings of the Amorites. . . went up, they and all their armies, and camped before Gibeon and made war against it. (Joshua 10:5 NKJV)

Israelite victories galvanized into action the tribal peoples living west of the Jordan. They knew they had to present a united front to survive ("with one accord," Joshua 9:2). A few of them apparently had the fighting spirit knocked out of them by reports of overwhelming Israelite success. In the spirit of recent times when some have said, "Better Red than dead," some of these people decided that "Better Israelite subjects than dead."

So a delegation from Gibeon went to the Hebrew camp at Gilgal and pretended to come from a distant country (Joshua 9). They sought an alliance with Israel and offered to become their servants. Joshua and the elders of Israel bought their deception, and, not seeking "counsel of the Lord" (Joshua 9:14), made the desired covenant.

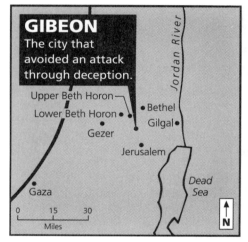

GIBEON
The city that avoided an attack through deception.

Upper Beth Horon
Lower Beth Horon
Bethel
Gilgal
Gezer
Jerusalem
Jordan River
Gaza
Dead Sea
0   15   30
Miles
N

When the nearby Amorite league heard that the Gibeonites had broken ranks with them, they decided to destroy the defectors before turning attention to the Israelites. That league consisted of the towns of Jerusalem, Hebron, Jarmuth, Lachish, and Eglon. Gibeon immediately sent an s.o.s. to Joshua, who in turn responded quickly. Of course the Hebrews did not act disinterestedly, for what had arisen was a divide and conquer situation: the Gibeonite league vs. the Amorite league. Joshua had subjugated the weaker one and could use it to help conquer the other.

As Joshua prepared to act, God promised total victory (Joshua 10:8). Joshua then led his men on a night march of some fifteen miles uphill from his camp at Gilgal to Gibeon. Men did make forced marches at night long before Julius Caesar

The mound of Gibeon

adopted this strategy. And like Julius Caesar, Joshua totally surprised the enemy in the morning. Evidently the Amorites had no scouting parties to warn of hostile movement in the area. Apparently, too, the Hebrews had the benefit of a moonlit night to make the march (Joshua 10:12-13). And the hilly, wooded terrain gave adequate cover.

Gibeon stood on a low hill. The Amorite camps lay in the valley before the city. From the hills to the east the Hebrew forces rushed down on the Amorites, completely surprising them. And no doubt the defenders rained missiles from the walls in a new show of defiance. Soon the Amorite lines broke and they fled in utter confusion westward along the Beth-horon pass and then southward toward Azekah. Joshua's men pursued their foe another eleven miles or so. What stamina! These men had marched all night from Gilgal, fought a battle in the morning (of uncertain length), and now chased the enemy another eleven miles!

In the midst of all this Joshua had begged God that the "Sun, stand still over Gibeon; And Moon, in the Valley of Aijalon. . . till the people had revenge upon their enemies" (Joshua 10:12-13

NKJV). That is, while the moon was still visible in the west and before the dawn had given way to full day, he wanted revenge on his enemies. Was Joshua asking for a quick victory for his exhausted men? Or did he want a long day with enough light to pursue the enemy? Or was he concerned that as the sun came up his nearly exhausted men would soon have to fight under a hot, cloudless sky and he sought relief for them? Perhaps the third alternative reflects Joshua's special desire.

The word translated "stand still" could also be translated "be dumb" or "desist," that is, "be darkened." And in this case we should talk about Joshua's long night instead of his long day. God could have provided local darkness, and apparently

The Valley of Aijalon

did in connection with the violent hail storm.

In any case, God added a totally devastating hail storm to the element of surprise and the bravery and physical prowess of Joshua's men. How much the Gibeonites may have harassed and killed the fleeing Amorites the Bible does not say. The armies of the five kings were totally devastated and a few stragglers reached safety (Joshua 10:20). The five kings, who had fled and hidden in a cave, were caught and executed (v. 26). Later, the Israelite forces fought against Makkedah, Libnah, Lachish, Gezer, Eglon, Hebron, and Debir, exterminating the armies and their populations (Joshua 10:28-39). As a result the Hebrews gained control of the Negev from Kadesh Barnea in the south to Gaza in the west and the Judean hills north to Gibeon (Joshua 10:40-41).

The Campaign in Galilee (Joshua 11:1-15)

But the struggle had not ended. Jabin king of Hazor pulled together an alliance of northern Canaanite kings with numerous soldiers and large auxiliary chariot units.

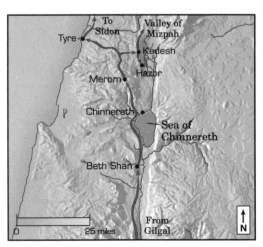

The Conquest of Canaan (Northern Campaign). A large coalition of kings gathered at the waters of Merom to fight against Joshua. In a surprise attack, Joshua's armies drove the forces back, some toward Tyre and Sidon, others toward Kedesh. Joshua divided his forces, destroying Hazor along the way.

The equivalent of an ancient Sherman tank, a chariot combined shock with fire power. Not only did chariots strike fear into the hearts of soldiers as they advanced across a field of battle, they also carried bowmen and javelin men with considerable firepower.

The allied forces of the Hebrews gathered at the Waters of Merom, a few miles west of Lake Huleh and just northwest of the Sea of Galilee, a good central location for the allies. Roads radiated from it in all directions. The Canaanites, on the other hand, camped in a narrow gorge with no space to deploy their chariots right there. Moreover, chariot units require time to get ready for battle. Horses need to be harnessed and hitched up to chariots. Joshua and his men came against the Canaanites "suddenly" (Joshua 11:7), evidently while the chariots were temporarily unprepared for battle. With surprise and speed he and his men came charging down the nearby slopes into the Canaanite camp. No doubt many horses bolted and added to the confusion. Joshua's pre-emptive strike proved completely successful. With no use for the chariots or the horses, the technically backward Hebrews destroyed both, as well as decimating the army and burning the city of Hazor. In fact, they liquidated the people of the allied towns and carried off their livestock and other possessions.

Summary on the Conquest

This successful campaign completed the basic elements of the conquest. The Hebrews had taken the highlands east of the Jordan and the highlands of Galilee, Samaria, and Judea west of the Jordan, in addition to the Jordan Valley. The whole coastal plain from Hazor in the south to Lebanon in the north remained unconquered, as well as the plain of Jezreel and chunks of land here and there and a number of towns or cities—notably Jerusalem.

By and large the Hebrews did not destroy cities (with the exception of such places as Jericho and Ai), nor livestock or vineyards in keeping with Deuteronomy 6:10-11: "And it shall be, when the Lord your God brings you into the land of which He swore to your fathers . . . to give you

The strategic mound of Hazor (center), a Canaanite city which Joshua took during the conquest of the Promised Land (Joshua 11:1–13)

large and beautiful cities which you did not build, houses full of all good things, which you did not fill, hewn-out wells which you did not dig, vineyards and olive trees which you did not plant" (NKJV). In other words, the Hebrews simply took over for themselves what was in the land when they arrived. And they were influenced in house construction, clothing, diet and much else by the ways of the Canaanites. We shall explore this further.

The Wars of the Judges

Deborah's War with Hazor (Judges 4)

"Has not the Lord God of Israel commanded, saying, 'Go and deploy troops at Mount Tabor; take with you ten thousand men of the sons of Naphtali and of the sons of Zebulun; and against you I will deploy Sisera, the commander of Jabin's army, with his chariots and his multitude at the River Kishon; and I will deliver him into your hand'?" (Judges 4:6-7 NKJV)

Deborah the judge gave General Barak a plan for throwing off the yoke of Canaanite oppression in the north. That oppression had lasted for twenty years (Judges 4:3) and especially came at the hands of the king of Hazor (Jabin), who headed a confederacy that dominated the region. Which towns were allied with Hazor can be surmised from the location of the recorded battle, which took place in the Valley of Jezreel and

on its fringe. Probably Taanach, Megiddo, and Jokneam were included. In developing a strategy, Deborah had to be especially concerned with neutralizing the Canaanite chariot corps, which numbered 900 (Judges 4:13). The Israelites had none.

From a careful reading of the passage quoted above and all of Judges 4 and 5, the strategy and action appears to have been as follows. Barak was to muster at least 10,000 men from the tribes of Naphtali and Zebulun and station them on Mount Tabor at the northeast of the Plain of Esdraelon (Jezreel). Heber the Kenite, related to the Hebrews, then reported to Sisera, captain of the forces of Hazor, that the Hebrews were gathering at Mount Tabor. Evidently the plan was to get them to concentrate on dealing with the threat.

Meanwhile Deborah was collecting an army in Ephraim, which entered the Jezreel Valley and engaged in conflict at Taanach by the waters of Megiddo (Judges 5:19). Sisera now turned his attention from the force at Mount Tabor to the one attacking his allies to the southwest. As he marched along the River Kishon to do so, the force on Mount Tabor charged the rear of Sisera, throwing his army into confusion. Then the Canaanite chariots became mired in the river or by a sudden rainstorm. In the midst of the confusion and carnage, Sisera, seeking to save his own skin, jumped off his chariot and fled on foot, soon to meet his end at the hands of Jael, wife of Heber the Kenite, who drove a tent peg into his temple while he was sleeping (Judges 4:17-22). So the Hebrews got relief from oppression.

Gideon's Campaign (Judges 6—8)

"And they cried, 'The sword of the Lord and of Gideon!'" (Judges 7:20 NKJV)

Midianites and Amalekites became a terror to the Israelites, especially to the tribes living in border regions. Hordes of them, like locusts, came upon the land with their camels and livestock and ravaged the territory, especially in the south of Judea, in the lands of Judah and Simeon. No border defense existed at the time, so when the nomads came in force, apparently when dry conditions in the Negev made them desperate, the Israelites fled to caves and refuges in the mountains.

Finally these marauders launched a wholesale invasion through Gilead and into the Jezreel Valley. Perhaps "invasion" is too strong a word, for their coming was probably not so much an organized raid of warring tribes as a movement of nomads looking for food and pasture. In any case the text says that 135,000 swarmed over Israel

Gideon's Campaign
The Angel of the Lord appeared to Gideon in Ophrah, instructing him to rally the Israelites against the Midianites. With only 300 men Gideon left Harod and descended upon the sleeping armies just north of Mount Moreh. He pursued the Midianites through Succoth and Penuel, finally capturing the Midianite kings in Karkor.

The Midianites—Friend and Foe

The Midianites sprang from Midian, a son of Abraham by Keturah, whom he married after the death of Sarah. But Abraham did not permit Midian's sons to inherit with Isaac. Instead he gave them gifts and sent them away "to the country of the east" (Genesis 2:6), which probably included the desert fringes of Moab, Edom, and parts of the Sinai Peninsula.

Midianites next appear as tribes who bought Joseph and sold him into slavery in Egypt (Genesis 37:25-36). Later as Moses fled from Egypt, he went to the land of Midian, where he married Zipporah, daughter of Jethro, a Midianite priest (Exodus 2:15-22; 3:1). Relations with the Midianites were therefore friendly, and Jethro helped Moses with certain organizational tasks (Exodus 18).

Midianites soon became enemies of Israel, however. Feeling threatened when Israel attempted to penetrate the Transjordan region at the end of the wilderness wanderings, they and the Moabites hired Baalam to curse Israel (Numbers 22:4-7). When the curse did not succeed, the Midianites involved their women in an attempt to lead Israel into apostasy and initially succeeded. The judgment fell on the Midianites, associated Moabites, and defecting Israelites (Numbers 25). Midianites were singled out for destruction (Numbers 25:16-18). And Israel enjoyed a great victory over them (Numbers 31).

Thereafter the Midianites remained adversaries of Israel, and during the period of the judges periodically harassed some of the Israelite tribes. During the days of Gideon they raided the stockpiles of new grain during harvest time, but Gideon dealt them an overwhelming defeat (Judges 7—8). Scripture later cited this defeat as an example of God's deliverance of His people from oppression (Psalm 83:9, 11; Isaiah 9:4; 10:26).

(Judges 8:10). Gideon rose to the occasion and succeeded in mobilizing men from Asher, Zebulun, Naphtali, and Manasseh to meet them (6:35).

He raised 32,000 recruits and encamped at Mount Gilboa. God made it clear that a large army that achieved a victory might believe it had done so by its own prowess instead of by divine intervention. Therefore God gave Gideon a strategy whereby 22,000 were permitted to go home because of fear (Judges 7:3). But He still wanted to reduce the size of the Israelite force—this time by a test at the spring of Harod, located on the northwest slope of Mount Gilboa, eight miles west northwest of Beth-Shan. Gideon knew that this was one of the most copious springs in Palestine, an important consideration for any military movements in the neighborhood. The test featured the way the men drank water. Evidently the ones who were kept (300) held their right hands on their swords while scooping up water in their left hands and lapping it.

God promised to save the Israelites by the 300 men. Clearly it would have to be by

The copious springs of Harod spilled water into several channels and provided room to test many soldiers at a time. Today the area is a public park.

a surprise night attack when the Midianites could not determine the size of the attacking force. Nor could they benefit from their swift dromedary contingents and their mobile archers and pikemen. To bolster Gideon's faith, God invited him to go down with his swordbearer into the Midianite

camp. At an outpost he came upon a man who had had a dream which his companion interpreted as an attack of Gideon that would result in total defeat of the invaders. This was evidently a message from God and all the confirmation Gideon needed.

Gideon planned an immediate attack. All three hundred hid burning torches in earthen jars in their left hands and held trumpets in their right hands. Then the men were divided into three groups and deployed to attack the Midianite camp from three different directions. As the three hundred ran down the slopes of the mount near the eastern end of the plain of Megiddo, they blew trumpets, smashed jars revealing torches, and shouted the battle cry, "The sword of the Lord and of Gideon." The enemy fled in panic, thinking they were pursued by a great host. Probably each of the three hundred was thought to be a platoon commander, who carried a torch and a trumpet to give direction and to provide a rallying point for them. The timing of the attack was significant, at the beginning of the middle watch of the night (10:00 p.m.), at the changing of the guard (Judges 7:19).

As the Midianites fled, some even attacked each other in the confusion. And men from Naphtali, Asher, and Manasseh pursued the Midianites toward the Jordan. Gideon belatedly alerted the clans of Ephraim living around the fords of the Jordan in the area of Adam to block passage of the routed nomads. The Midianites suffered heavy casualties as they fled. A total of 120,000 of them fell west of the Jordan and at the fords of the Jordan (Judges 8:10). Another 15,000 fled east of the Jordan and stopped to rest in the mountains on the Ammonite frontier, where they "felt secure" (Judges 8:11). Gideon surprised them there and "routed the whole army" (8:12). "Thus Midian was subdued before the children of Israel, so that they lifted their heads no more. And the country was quiet for forty years in the days of Gideon" (Judges 8:28).

Activities of Other Judges

Other judges carried on military actions. Ehud fought against Moab (Judges 3:12-30). And Jephthah battled the Ammonites (Judges 11:1—12:7), but we have no details of their conflicts. Moreover, Samson made sporadic attacks on the Philistines, but they did not really constitute warfare.

Cruelty of the Israelites?

The question is sometimes raised as to whether the Israelites were cruel in the treatment of the enemy during all this warfare in the days of the conquest and the judges. One account might be singled out as an example of cruelty. Early in the period of the judges Simeon and Judah had a great victory at Bezek, a town near Gezer (18 miles northwest of Jerusalem). They captured Adoni-Bezek, king of the town, and cut off his thumbs and big toes. This may be considered punishment for his conduct as king; he himself said that he had cut off the thumbs and big toes of seventy kings he had defeated in the past and recognized his punishment as an act of retributive justice (Judges 1:5-7). Such amputation incapacitated men for ancient warfare because they could no longer handle weapons or pursue an enemy. Other than this action, which may be interpreted in the light of the ancient Semitic law of retaliation (an eye for an eye and a tooth for a tooth), we do not have crass examples of cruelty.

Weapons of the Israelites

"Among all this people there were seven hundred select men who were left-handed; every one could sling a stone at a hair's breadth and not miss." (Judges 20:16 NKJV)

As noted earlier, the Israelites must have carried some swords with them out of Egypt. Then, as they conquered peoples east of the Jordan, they took their weapons. The same may be said for conquests west of the Jordan. No doubt they captured spears or javelins in limited numbers, along with swords. The metal in all these cases would have been bronze. Iron was not used extensively until well after 1200 B.C.

While the accounts of battles usually do not specify the kinds of weapons involved, occasionally it becomes clear that slingers using stones were important. For example, a contingent of left-handed slingers from

Gibeah became known for their deadly accuracy (Judges 20:15-16). And David effectively used his sling in killing Goliath. Slings must have been an important part of all Israelite arsenals because they are so easy and inexpensive to make. Anyone who has seen modern Arab boys demonstrate them is impressed with their capability.

Wooden clubs can also be formidable weapons, as can clubs with sharp stones attached to form battle axes. Bows and arrows were standard equipment. The Hebrews also employed unconventional weapons. For example, the judge Shamgar killed 600 Philistines with an ox goad (Judges 3:31). Samson killed a thousand men with a fresh (nonbrittle) jawbone of an ass (Judges 15:15).

As noted, Joshua burned the chariots of the northern Canaanites, partly because the Hebrews did not have the capability of maintaining or constructing them and partly because chariots had little value in most of the hill country where the Hebrews lived. The Hebrews had little access to metal and forgot what knowledge they had of how to work it during the wilderness wanderings. Moreover, in the latter days of the judges the Philistines denied them either access to metal or the ability to work it (1 Samuel 13:19).

(For more on this topic, go to p. 100 or p. 103.)

Housing and Furniture

"So Joshua blessed them and sent them away, and they went to their tents." (Joshua 22:6)

During the days of the conquest the Israelites continued to live in tents, as they had in the period of wilderness wandering. Evidently the two and one-half tribes east of the Jordan did it even after they had conquered substantial areas. Subsequently Joshua gave his blessing to them and sent them back to their "tents" (Joshua 22:4, 6, 7, 8). In such a mode of existence they had no more furniture now than when they were wandering.

But as the Israelites settled down in the land at the end of the conquest, and gradu-

The one-two room house style at Et-Tell, commonly identified as Ai. A row of stone pillars placed about five feet from one wall divided the interior into the main room (about ten feet wide) from a side area.

ally during the time of the judges, this changed. Excavations reveal two kinds of houses in the general period of the judges and early monarchy: the one-two room style and the typical four-room or courtyard style.

The former had a thick exterior wall consisting of two parallel courses of field stone with a core of rubble and earth providing stability. A row of stone pillars placed about five feet from one wall divided the interior into the main room (about ten feet wide) and a side area. Beams resting on the pillars supported the roof, which was composed of pieces of wood and brush and sealed with clay.

There was no furniture, only stone ledges along the wall for chairs, bedrolls that could be rolled out on the floor for sleeping, and a central fire pit for warmth. Cooking was done outside; since there were no bathrooms, people also had to go outside to find/make a toilet (cf. Deuteronomy 23:12-13). Cisterns in some of these houses collected rainwater and provided an adequate water supply.

A second style of house was the courtyard or four-room house. A door led into a courtyard of tamped earth, with a room on one side for storage, on the opposite side for a cow or mule, and a room on the end for living and sleeping. Pillars rather than walls often separated the rooms from the courtyard. The courtyard had a fire pit and commonly served as a kitchen, dining room, and workroom. Of course this basic four-room style might be modified, with more than one room for storage or animals or family rooms.

Rooms were small because long timbers were not available. Commonly the roof was strong enough to provide an additional work or sleeping area. A stairway led up to it. Along the courtyard might stand large jars for water, grain, or olive oil. The exterior wall consisted of stone, which is extremely plentiful in Palestine. In the Jordan Valley, where stone was not so easily available, the Hebrews tended to build house walls of sundried brick, perhaps on a stone foundation.

Eventually a wooden door that could be barred replaced the earlier skin coverings. No one used hinges in the biblical period, so doors were made similar to the arrangement in Mycenean structures in Greece. That is, a door was attached to a pole that was inserted into hollowed out stones above and below so the pole would pivot in these sockets. God asked devout householders to put Deuteronomy 6:4-5 on their doorposts as a sign of adherence to the Mosaic covenant (Deuteronomy 6:9; 11:20). But in the days of the judges, when "every man did that which was right in his own eyes," we cannot be sure how many did so. Whether houses were of the one-two room or the four-room variety, they were usually windowless. In the four-room style the courtyard provided light and ventilation.

In the four-room houses too there was essentially no furniture. Occasionally they built a stone bench on which to sit or on which to unroll a bedroll. One might sit on a stone in the courtyard to do some work or to eat. For real comfort an animal skin could be folded up to make a pillow, or they might make a pillow of a skin stuffed with goat hair. *(For more on this topic, go to p.101 or p. 204.)*

Diet and Foodstuffs

"For the Lord your God is bringing you into a good land . . . a land of wheat and barley, of vines and fig trees and pomegranates, a land of olive oil and honey." (Deuteronomy 8:7-8 NKJV)

Wheat

This passage lists seven crops and fruit trees most abundant in the land of Canaan: wheat, barley, grapes, figs, pomegranates, olive oil, and honey. But of course other crops could be and were grown. Let us combine this passage with 1 Samuel 25:18, where Abigail is described as sending a generous present to David's men. It included 200 loaves of bread, 2 skins of wine, 5 dressed sheep, 5 measures of roasted grain, 100 clusters of raisins, and 200 fig cakes. These two passages taken together give a fairly good idea of what was grown and what therefore provided a typical menu for the Hebrews during the conquest and the days of the judges. We'll comment on these foods first and then supplement with a note on other foods produced or available. Some of the techniques of agriculture appear in the last section of the chapter.

Wheat was a winter crop sown between the end of October and mid-December and harvested between the end of April and the end of May. In Canaan it grew best in the coastal valleys, the Valley of Jezreel, the upper Jordan Valley, the Beth-shan Valley, and in the northern Negev during the more rainy seasons. Therefore, because the Hebrews did not control much of this land during this period, they produced limited quantities of wheat. They ground wheat into flour for use in bread, but also ate it parched and raw.

Barley is a winter cereal sown about the same time as wheat but harvested between the end of March and the end of April. It tolerates saline and alkaline conditions and grows well on soils derived from limestone and located in high altitude and low rainfall regions. Popular in Canaan, barley was used in bread and other baked goods and eaten parched (2 Samuel 17:28) and raw (2 Kings 4:42).

Grapes. Red grapes seem to have been the dominant if not the exclusive variety grown in Canaan. Vineyards could be used for grapes alone or they could be grown among olive trees. The Hebrews had to protect their grapes from animals and people, so they erectedwalls, thorn hedges, and watch towers for the purpose. Grapevines might be allowed to spread on the ground, to grow on trees, or trained to grow on poles or trellises. There was an official arrangement for harvesting grapes. The fourth year the produce of the vines was brought to Yahweh. In the fifth and subsequent years the farmer could consume the crop himself (Leviticus 19:24-25).

The Hebrews used grapes to make wine or eat as fresh fruit. In addition, they used them to produce vinegar (a popular condiment) and raisins. They soaked grapes in oil and water or in a solution of potash and then spread them in the sun to dry as raisins. Persons on a journey took raisin cakes along as a favorite food. The time for grape harvesting varied from region to region.

Figs. Fig trees produce two crops a year, the first ripening in June and the second in August and September. The Hebrews ate the first fresh and dried the second for use as a food during the winter or on trips (see 1 Samuel 25:18). They also used them in making wine.

A fig tree loaded with its small green fruit

A pomegranate grove with fruit on the trees at Ashkelon

Pomegranates. The pomegranate ripens in the summer and its fruit contains compartments filled with juicy seeds, which can be eaten fresh or dried and stored. The juice of these seeds can be consumed fresh or fermented for wine.

Olives. The olive tree sometimes reaches a height of about twenty-five feet. It grows best in well-drained or rocky soils. Leaves stay on the tree all year round. It flowers at the beginning of summer and ripe olives are ready for picking in September and October. At harvest the branches are beaten with sticks (Deuteronomy 24:20). The fallen olives are then gathered into baskets and taken off to the press. Evidently the Hebrews did not eat olives in Old Testament times but used the oil in food preparation, for burning in lamps for light, for anointing the body, in the treatment of wounds, and for official anointing of kings, prophets, and priests.

Dates—Honey. Borowski believes that the honey of Palestine (Exodus 3:8; Deuteronomy 8:8) was a product of the date palm tree.[18] The juice extracted from the trunk could also be served as a drink, either fresh or fermented. The fronds of the date

palm can be woven into mats and baskets and its fibrous sheath used for making ropes, pillows, and mattresses.

Other produce of the land. In addition to the seven major commodities of Canaan noted above, numerous other products provided variety in the diet of the Israelites. Other fruit trees include the sycamore, which produces figs in the summer, eaten mostly by the poor; a tree hard to identify but possibly the apricot; and the black mulberry. Then

An ancient olive tree in the Garden of Gethsemane, Jerusalem, probably over one thousand years old

they had nut trees: almond, pistachio, and the common walnut. Known legumes included broad beans, lentils, chick-peas, and peas. Though difficult to identify, vegetables or fruits are referred to in the Bible by a whole collection of Hebrew words, which seem to indicate cucumbers, watermelon, leeks, onions, and garlic.[19]

Of course we know that the Israelites raised large numbers of sheep and goats and some cows. Therefore, they produced milk, butter, and cheese in quantity. But all three of these commodities came from goats more often than from cows. We should not assume, however, that just because the Israelites raised a lot of sheep, they ate a lot of meat. The poorer element of society could not afford to kill their livestock but lived on a diet of grain, fruit, and dairy products. The list of seven items in Deuteronomy 8:7-8 especially defines their basic diet.

(For more on this topic, go to p. 101 or p. 206.)

Dress

As we noted earlier, the Bible does not say very much about clothing. It certainly does not spell out differences in clothing styles in the subsequent periods of biblical history. So we are left with hints in Scripture and information from secular sources to help us discover anything about what the Hebrews wore.

The fabric of choice in Egypt, linen, was worn by the Hebrews as they came into Canaan. As noted earlier, the Hebrews' clothing did not wear out during the wilderness wandering; so the linen clothing they wore at the Exodus was the linen clothing they wore at the conquest. Moreover, as is evidenced from the construction of the tabernacle, they must have carried many yards of linen with them in the Exodus. Moreover, also as noted earlier, the priests' garments were to be made from linen, not only in the wilderness but in subsequent generations.

The question immediately arises as to whether or to what extent the Hebrews had access to linen in Canaan. Note that when the spies hid in Rahab's house she covered them with flax stalks—from which linen is made (Joshua 2:6). Later, during the days of the judges, Samson offered thirty linen garments to whoever could solve his riddle (Judges 14:12). Just after the end of the period of the judges the Gezer Calendar (see last section of this chapter) mentioned a month when flax was especially to be hoed. Evidently, then, flax was produced all during the long period covered in this chapter, and a fair amount of linen was available. Incidentally, for whatever reason, the law spelled out that linen and wool were not to be mixed in making clothing (Leviticus 19:19).

Of course when the Hebrews got into Canaan they began raising large numbers of sheep and wool became available in quantity for making clothing. Moreover, the colder climate would permit or demand the wearing of warmer clothing.

But all this says nothing about what the clothing looked like. To begin with, we know what the clothing of the priests looked like and we spelled that out in the last chapter. Second, as just noted, the climate was colder in Palestine than in Egypt. At least that was true in the hilly areas

Tribute bearers from Canaan, depicted in the tomb of Thutmose IV (c. 1400 B.C.), showing clothing of the time of the Hebrew conquest

A scene from ivory inlay, Megiddo, early twelfth century B.C., showing clothing of the period of the judges

where most Hebrews lived. Of course, the Jordan Valley was extremely hot. Thus the clothing of necessity was generally heavier. And even the poorer people had to wear outer cloaks in colder seasons and at night to keep warm rather than for adornment or show—as was the case with the aristocracy. Third, from early times in Canaan the clothing of most people was made from undyed cloth and thus tended to be white or off white. The more well-to-do wore dyed and/or embroidered clothing.

Fourth, we no doubt get some help from contemporary Canaanite styles. Some of the clothing the Hebrews wore was actually Canaanite—captured as spoils of war. Furthermore, as the Hebrews saw Canaanites on a daily basis, they must have been influenced by their styles. But here we have a problem, because most of the Canaanite pictorial representations we have in bronze, ivory, or some other medium are of kings or officials or wealthy aristocrats. They are pictured with long robes below the calf or to the ankle, dyed, and sometimes with fringes or embroidery and usually with sleeves. They might wear a poncho-like outer garment that extended to the waist or an outer robe extending to the knees.

The poor classes, as noted, wore undyed garments, and shorter loose-fitting robes, about knee length. A girdle secured the robes of men at the middle, but those of women hung loosely. Presumably the reason for this is that men often lifted their skirts and tucked them in their girdles while engaged in manual labor or walking in difficult terrain. The reason why both men and women of the lower classes wore shorter robes than the aristocracy was that the long clothing got

in the way while they were working. Soldiers generally, and many manual laborers, wore reasonably short kilts, which would have permitted greater freedom of movement. A primitive safety pin made of bronze came into use about the time of Joshua and helped hold clothing together. Shoes consisted of sandals made from animal skins or less durable material, but people went barefoot much of the time.

(For more on this topic, go to p.103 or p. 207.)

Family Life

Before the Israelites entered Canaan God instructed them to marry within their tribes and so to preserve their inheritances (Numbers 36). By and large they probably did, because the tribal units were allocated separate tracts of land. But pagan inhabitants remained and Israelites were attracted to them. For example, Samson insisted on marrying a Philistine woman, even though his parents tried to change his mind (Judges 14:3).

Though Samson took the initiative in this case, parents of the bride and groom usually arranged the marriage. Note that even in this case Samson expected his family to arrange for his marriage.

Apparently the payment of a bride price also continued in this period. And when the groom could not provide one, as in the case of Jacob long before, a deed or some service was accepted as a substitute. For example, Caleb promised his daughter Achsah to whoever could conquer Debir. When his nephew Othniel was successful, Achsah additionally, possibly as a dowry, asked for

Boaz Claims a Bride

The Bible contains a very beautiful example of levirate marriage, or the kinsman redeemer, in this period. As noted in the last chapter, this was called levirate marriage from the Latin levir, a husband's brother. That is, when a man died without leaving a son, a single brother or next of kin was expected to marry his widow and carry on his name and family.

Ruth the Moabitess had returned to Bethlehem with her mother-in-law Naomi after her husband Mahlon had died. In the course of events it turned out that Boaz was a near kinsman but was second in line to marry Ruth. He bargained with the next of kin at the city gate of Bethlehem and won the right to marry her. Subsequently their son Obed became the grandfather of David (see Ruth 3—4).

some land and water rights in the Negev (Joshua 15:15-19; Judges 1:11-15). Later Saul offered a daughter in marriage to the one who was able to slay Goliath and subsequently demanded one hundred Philistine foreskins from David as a further bride price for his daughter Michal (1 Samuel 17:25; 18:25).

We do not know how many Hebrews practiced polygamy. Possibly the practice depended on the economic or social status of the male. Gideon had many wives (Judges 8:30) and Samuel's father had two wives (1 Samuel 1:2). During the period of the judges the preservation of more than one family was at stake. A civil war broke out between the tribe of Benjamin and the other tribes, with the result that the strife virtually annihilated the tribe of Benjamin. Only 600 Benjamite males fled and survived. At that point the rest of the tribes became grief stricken over the loss of a whole tribe in Israel and provided wives for the Benjamites. Thus the tribe survived and in time was rebuilt (see Judges 19-21).

Inviolable Hospitality of the Home

The crime that led to the civil war concerned the inviolability of the hospitality of the home. From time immemorial in Semitic society the host was supposed to do whatever it took to protect one's guests. They considered hospitality inviolable. Remember how Lot had angels as guests and the men of the whole town of Sodom surrounded his house and sought to have sex with them. Lot was willing to give the men of Sodom even his daughters to spare his guests (see Genesis 19:1-14).

Shades of Sodom, the homosexuals of Gibeah of Benjamin surrounded the house of a man in a town where a Levite and his concubine were staying for the night. Considering the laws of hospitality more important than protecting the opposite sex, he like Lot offered them his daughter and the concubine. Either they did not hear him or refused his offer. But the Levite pushed his concubine out the door. They abused her all night and killed her (Judges 19:22-26).

Later the Levite dismembered the concubine's body and sent the parts to the twelve tribes of Israel to arouse the nation to action by calling for a national judicial hearing. It is hard for us to understand all this and to excuse the Levite, but the point here at the moment is to comment on the inviolability of hospitality and to explain how the civil war erupted in Israel when the people of Gibeah refused to surrender the murderers. The whole tribe of Benjamin actually went to war to defend the "sons of Belial" of Gibeah in a day when "every man did that which was right in his own eyes."

Education

During this period the focus in education was vocational and religious. From the time that children were old enough to take instruction, they were expected to participate in the family enterprises: to learn how to farm the land, to care for animals, to cook food properly, to grind grain, to weave cloth, and much more. The father of the family took the lead in religious instruction, rehearsing the history of Israel and teaching by rote such Scripture passages as he might happen to know.

But there must have been some formal education. The story is told how Gideon caught a young man of Succoth, who wrote down for Gideon the names of the leaders and elders of Succoth—a total of seventy-seven men (Judges 8:14). This implies a certain amount of literacy in that area of Transjordan. This young man and others could read and write at least minimally, and so could Gideon and some of the men in his immediate following. Of course the priests—at least the higher priesthood—had to be able to read and write in every period in order to carry on religious duties, but there is no hint that this man of Judges 8 was of the priestly class.

Earlier Joshua had written words of the Law (Joshua 8:32; 24:26) and presumably at least some of his inner circle knew how to read and write. As noted elsewhere, if householders were to write a bit of the Law on their doorposts or if people were to read what was written there, a certain amount of literacy was necessary. The same is true for writing on the village gates (Deuteronomy 6:9; 11:20).

Beyond this we cannot go in assessing the literacy of the period. Nor should we claim too much. Hebrew scrawled in public places does not guarantee that people could read it, any more than Arabic of the Koran scrawled in public places of the Middle East during the later Middle Ages could be widely read.

The gate was a place where business could be transacted in ancient Israel. Excavators at Dan uncovered an open square in front of the gate with a place for the king's throne if he chose to preside there, and benches built around the other sides.

Jael and the Hospitality of Her Tent

But what about Jael who welcomed Sisera, the commander of forces of Hazor, into her tent and then killed him? What happened on that occasion was that Sisera fled from the Israelite armies defeated by Deborah and Barak. Jael let him into her tent, gave him some milk, and made him comfortable. When he went to sleep she drove a tent peg through his temple and killed him (see Judges 4:18-23). Wasn't that betrayal of the principle of the inviolability of the hospitality of the home?

Matthews and Benjamin[20] argue that Jael was not a hostess who betrayed her guest. Dramatically they tell the story of how she stalked him as an enemy. They make the point that Sisera came to the tent of Jael (the wife), not Heber (her husband), not to enjoy the hospitality and protection of the head of the house. Sisera came on foot "secretly" to her tent, her private tent, having slipped past the guards in the camp. He sought to have sex with her and to take over Heber's household. Her word to him to "turn aside" is interpreted to mean to turn away from his plans. He asked for water; she served him milk, which is soporific and helped to put him to sleep. Then she drove a tent peg through his temple and killed him, in an act of self defense, thus delivering herself and her husband, as well as the hosts of Israel. This account in Matthews and Benjamin deserves a read as an outstanding piece of literature.

Care for the Poor

"Then she [Ruth] left, and went and gleaned in the field after the reapers." (Ruth 2:3)

Without a social security system or welfare checks, the resourceful poor were allowed to gather some food for themselves. The Law of Moses stipulated that

Places of Doing Business

Ruth first made her appeal to Boaz at his threshing floor (Ruth 3). Threshing floors in various towns seem to have served as a kind of "courtroom" where village elders could settle minor disputes of various sorts. Later we have a good example of their use when the kings of Israel and Judah sat on thrones at the threshing floor of Samaria for a significant hearing (1 Kings 22:10; 2 Chronicles 18:9).

Ruth's appeal was taken to the gate of Bethlehem, where Boaz met with the village elders to get a decision on his legal situation (Ruth 4:1). Business and legal deals were often settled at the city gate. For example, at Tell En-Nasbeh and Dan excavations show that there was an open square in front of the gate with benches built around it. David's rebellious son Absalom met at the gate of Jerusalem with the inhabitants to hear their complaints and win them to his cause (2 Samuel 15:2-4). Later, Amos condemned injustice "in the gates" (Amos 5:10, 12, 15).

landowners during grain harvest should not carefully harvest the corners of the field, glean the field clean, or go back at the end of the day to look for forgotten sheaves (Leviticus 19:1; 23:22; Deuteronomy 24:19). Evidently these injunctions were obeyed at least in part after the Israelites settled in the land because Ruth the Moabitess acted upon them (Ruth 2).

Likewise, during grape harvesting season, the vineyard was not to be picked clean; the smallest bunches of grapes had to be deliberately left for the poor. Also, anyone coming into the vineyard before harvest could eat the ripe fruit but could not collect any in a basket (Leviticus 19:10; Deuteronomy 23:25; 24:21). During olive harvest the workers beat the branches with sticks to cause the ripe olives to fall, but they were not to glean the trees clean. Especially they should leave those at the top of the tree for the poor. Incidentally, in none of these cases were conditions made easy for the poor. They would have to work for what they got.

(For more on this topic, go to p. 103 or p. 208.)

Work, Travel, and Commerce

During the days of Joshua and the judges the Hebrews did not produce commodities for export, so they did not travel or do commerce during these centuries. The work or livelihood of the populace consisted essentially of subsistence agriculture and the production of necessities. In fact, life generally revolved around the rhythm or activities of the seasons.

The Gezer Calendar, discovered by R. A. S. Macalister in his excavations at Gezer and dating about 925 B.C. confirms this. It begins with two months of olive harvest (mid-September to mid-November), continues with two months of planting grain, wheat, and barley (mid-November to mid-January), and follows with two months of late planting (January to March), involving chick-peas, melons, cucumbers, and the like. March-April was the month for "hoeing up flax," cut with the hoe near the ground for making cord, linen cloth, and the like. April or early May was the month of barley harvest. After that was the month of "wheat harvest and festivity," later known as Pentecost. Next came "two months of grape harvesting" (June and July), rather than two months to prune and clean the grape vines, as the translation used to be rendered. Finally, in August came "the month of summer fruit," when figs, grapes, pomegranates and other fruits could be picked.[21]

Grain Production

Hebrews made their plows entirely of wood, except for the bronze plow-point, the part that penetrated the soil. Iron plow-points began to come in at the end of the period. Normally a team of oxen pulled the plow with a wooden yoke that rested on the back of their necks. Young cows were also used (Judges 14:18). An ox and a donkey were not supposed to be yoked

Oxen drag a weighted sled over harvested grain at the threshing floor in Samaria, to separate the grain from the stalks.

together (Deuteronomy 22:10). Normally a farmer broadcast seed over the field first and then plowed the field to cover the seeds and protect them from birds and animals.

Reaping of a small area could be done without tools. The farmer simply pulled up the whole plant. In a larger operation, foreman led reapers (e.g., Ruth 2:3-6) as they held a sickle in one hand while grabbing a bunch of stalks with the other. Usually the sickles had flint blades; bronze was used to a limited extent.

Sometimes reapers cut off only the top of the stalk to reduce the amount of straw to contend with on the threshing floor. Harvested bundles of stalks were bound into sheaves and carted off to the threshing floor. Since harvesting occurred during a warm time of year the farmer provided water and

An ancient winepress near Shechem.

food for the work force. The workers ate bread dipped in vinegar, and parched grain. Though not part of the work force, Ruth was permitted to share both (Ruth 2:9, 14).

The Hebrews transported grain to the threshing floor by wagon, mule back, or people carrying large baskets. The threshing floor might be private or a community facility. Located outside of town, it could not easily be defended from attack. So Gideon resorted to threshing wheat in the winepress inside the city (Judges 6:11). Threshing might be done with a stick (beating out the grain), by means of animals treading over the stalks while they were tied next to each other to form a row, or a wooden sledge dragged across the grain by oxen or donkeys. The sledge was a wooden platform with stones on the underside to break the grain from the stalks.

During winnowing the farmer threw the grain into the air with a winnowing fork of five or seven tines on a windy day, so the wind could blow away the chaff (cf. Psalm 1:4). After that they used a wooden shovel to winnow the grain further and collect it into a heap. Finally, they took a sieve to sift out stones, small pieces of straw, and other undesirable matter.

Of course grain also had to be properly stored. It might be put in containers in a private or public storeroom, in a public building, or stored in bulk in a granary. Below ground it might be put in a cellar in containers or stored in bulk in a stone-lined or plastered pit.

In the winnowing process workers throw grain in the air on a windy day to let the wind blow away the chaff.

Grape and Olive Production

For the processing of grapes, the wine-press consisted of a flat surface for treading the grapes and a receptacle for the juice, located in or next to the vineyard. Sometimes a press might be built of stones and mortar inside a city. Workers collected the grape juice into large jars holding about ten gallons each. They then sealed the mouths with clay, leaving a small hole to permit the escape of gases produced through fermentation. The jars were then put in rock-cut cellars to ferment and were sealed completely when the fermentation process was complete. Smaller jars were used for transportation of the wine.

Olive processing required a different technique. In this case slow pressing of the olives was required to squeeze out the oil. The common press in use during the period of the judges was the beam-press.[22] This process involved piling baskets of olives on a collection basin. On top of these was placed a large stone and on top of that a beam with one end inserted in a large stone and the other end free. On the free end were hung stones that would continue to exert a crushing pressure. Alternatively, if one wanted a small amount of olive oil for immediate use, a few olives could be pounded in a stone mortar. The uses of olive oil have been noted above; they were too bitter for eating without pickling or salting, which came in the Hellenistic period. Evidently they were not eaten in Old Testament times.[23]

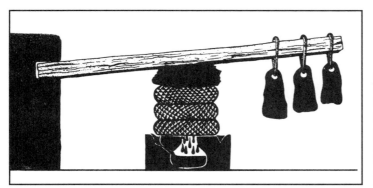

The beam-press for extracting olive oil. Baskets of olives were piled on a collection basin and then a large stone was placed on top of them. On top of the pile was a beam with one end inserted in a large stone and the other end free. On the free end were hung stones that would continue to exert a crushing pressure.

Animal Husbandry

The Hebrews raised sheep in substantial numbers throughout Israel's life in Palestine. They sheared the sheep twice a year: in the spring, after lambing time, and in the fall. Before shearing, sheep were put in a pool for washing their fleece and then dried out. After shearing the women washed the bulk wool again and combed it.

Thus sheep produced wool for clothing, as a "cash crop," as well as milk and thus butter and cheese. When killed they provided meat, and their skins were made into bags and coverings. The Hebrews used the male sheep, the ram, as the sacrificial animal at the central sanctuary.

Goats and sheep got along well and were raised together, with goats usually leading the way when on trek. Thus in Scripture they are sometimes compared to political leaders (e. g., Ezekiel 34:17; Daniel 8:5). A nanny goat provided a substantial supply of milk (up to three quarts a day). *Leben,* a favorite dish resembling yogurt, came from sour goat's milk. A young roasted kid was considered to be something of a delicacy. The goat was a sacrificial animal and it produced hair from which tent and garment cloth, tent curtains, and pillows could be made. And goatskins could be cleaned and turned into water or wine "bottles."

The Textile Industry

The textile industry during this period of time tended to be domestic. As least the professional shops discovered in the archaeological excavations or the biblical references to professional aspects of textile production date to the united monarchy or later. There were several steps in woolen textile production. First workers prepared the wool for spinning, which involved washing in hot water, drying, and carding. Next came spinning: the process of producing continuous threads by drawing out and twisting fibers. To do this they usually rotated a spindle in the hand while feeding the threads continuously. Last came weaving. First they stretched threads vertically on a loom (the warp), interweaving woof threads at right angles to the warp.

A type of loom mentioned in the story of Samson and Delilah (Judges 16:13-14) was a horizontal loom. This consisted of two beams secured to the ground by four pegs, with the warp stretched between the beams. The vertical loom consisted of two vertical beams with crossbars above and below. The warp was then stretched between the crossbars. A third type of loom, also vertical, had two vertical beams, slanted toward the rear, with a single crossbar at the top. The warp

threads were attached to the crossbar and weighted at the bottom by loom weights. These weights consisted of objects of stone or clay pierced with a hole through which warp threads were tied.

Pottery Production

The Hebrews fashioned everyday bowls, pots, and other vessels from clay. Fashioning these products required some time and skill. First the potter had to prepare the clay for use because few clays can be worked directly. They mixed the clay with water and worked it in settling tanks in an effort to make it more plastic. Sometimes a clay became too plastic and required the addition of a filler of fine sand or chopped straw. Then the potter had to beat and knead the clay by hand to remove pockets of air and mix it evenly.

When the clay was ready for working, vessels could be hand molded, built up on a slow wheel, pressed in molds from rolled-out sheets of clay, or thrown on a fast wheel. The latter involved putting a mass of clay on the throwing head and moving the clay up and down between the potter's wet hands as the wheel turned.

After partially drying the pot, they trimmed, sanded, or applied decoration. When the pot was carefully dried, it was put in a kiln and baked for at least three days, during which the temperature was gradually increased and then gradually reduced.

Meal Preparation

By and large farming, animal husbandry, and pottery production were men's work, though of course women did work in the fields seasonally. Men performed some aspects of textile production, but spinning and weaving were usually women's work. Women had the special responsibility of preparing meals and caring for the children. In a society without freezers or cans or pre-packaged foods or take out restaurants, women's work was hard and time consuming. It took most of the day to get the meals on.

Of special importance in the diet was bread, made of wheat or barley, but usually of barley for the poorer people. During the period covered in this chapter, the saddle-quern was the most commonly used means of grinding grain. This consisted of a stone that looked like a saddle, higher in the back and lower in the front. It measured 20-30 inches long and 10-15 inches wide. The grain was placed on this stone and ground with an upper stone that was flat on the bottom and rounded on top. The Hebrews pushed the upper stone backwards and forwards across the grain to grind it as one knelt behind the higher end of the saddle.

Occasionally they used a mortar and pestle for some grinding. This consisted of a hollowed out stone in which they ground grain with a pestle, a cylindrical stone with a rounded end.

The flour was usually mixed with olive oil and yeast to make it rise. The loaves looked much like pancakes and they were commonly baked on the outside of an oven. In the courtyard houses they had small ovens two to three feet in diameter, made of pottery or mudbrick or plastered stone. They kindled a fire on stones underneath it to heat the oven. Cooking was also done in pots on an open fire. For that they filled a hearth with stones, and several cooking pots could have simmered there at the same time, filled with vegetables and grains.

(For more on this topic, go to p. 106 or p. 212.)

NOTES:

[1]Keith N. Schoville, "Canaanites and Amorites," *Peoples of the Old Testament World,* edited by Alfred J. Hoerth and others (Grand Rapids: Baker, 1994), 167.

[2]Merrill F. Unger, *Archaeology and the Old Testament* (Grand Rapids: Zondervan, 1954), 182-87, has worked out a chronology for the judges on this basis; see also Leon Wood, *A Survey of Israel's History* (Grand Rapids: Zondervan, 1970), 212-29.

[3]Wood, 223-24.

[4]John Garstang, *Joshua and Judges* (London: Constable & Co., 1931), 137.

[5]Ibid., 145-146.

[6]Bryant G. Wood, "Did the Israelites Conquer Jericho?" *Biblical Archaeology Review* (March/April 1990), 50. Kathleen Kenyon, *Digging up Jericho* (New York: Praeger, 1957), 262.

[7]Bryant G. Wood, 54.

[8]Ibid., 56.

[9]Unger, 151.

[10]Yigael Yadin, "Hazor," in *Encyclopedia of Archaeological Excavations in the Holy Land,* vol. 2, edited by Michael Avi-Yonah (Englewood Cliffs, N.J.: Prentice-Hall, 1976), 494.

[11]Ibid., 481-2.

[12]J. L. Kelso, "Bethel," *Encyclopedia of Archaeological Excavations in the Holy Land,* 1, 192; Y. Aharoni, "Lachish," in ibid., 3, 743; W. F. Albright, "Tell Beit Mirsim," in ibid., 177.

[13]Benno Rothenberg, *Were These King Solomon's Mines?* (New York: Stein & Day, 1972), 184.

[14]*Encyclopedia of Archaeological Excavations in the Holy Land,* 1, 49.

[15]Joseph A. Callaway, "The 1964 'Ai (et Tell) Excavations," *Bulletin of the American Schools of Oriental Research* (April 1965), 27-28.

[16]John J. Bimson and David Livingston, "Redating the Exodus," *Biblical Archaeology Review* (September/October, 1987), 48.

[17]"Archaeological Digest" of *American Journal of Archaeology* (July-September 1947), 311.

[18]Oded Borowski, *Agriculture in Iron Age Israel* (Winona Lake, Ind.: Eisenbrauns, 1987), 127.

[19]Ibid., 137-139.

[20]Victor H. Matthews and Don C. Benjamin, *Social World of Ancient Israel 1250-587 BCE* (Peabody, Mass.: Hendrickson, 1993), 87-95.

[21]See James B. Pritchard, ed., *Ancient Near Eastern Texts* (Princeton: Princeton University Press, 1955), 320.

[22]Borowski, 122-123.

[23]Ibid., 123-125.

BIBLIOGRAPHY:

Albright, William F. *Yahweh and the Gods of Canaan.* New York: Doubleday, 1968.

Bierling, Neal. *Giving Goliath His Due.* Grand Rapids: Baker, 1992.

Garstang, John. *Joshua and Judges.* London: Constable & Co., 1931.

Garstang, John, and J. B. E. Garstang. *The Story of Jericho.* London: Marshall, Morgan and Scott, rev. ed., 1948.

Glueck, Nelson. *The Other Side of the Jordan.* Cambridge, Mass.: American Schools of Oriental Research, rev. ed., 1970

Herzog, Chaim, and Mordechai Gichon. *Battles of the Bible.* London: Greenhill Books, 1997.

Hoerth, Alfred J. and Others, eds. *Peoples of the Old Testament World.* Grand Rapids: Baker, 1994.

Kenyon, Kathleen. *Digging Up Jericho.* New York: Praeger, 1957.

Rothenberg, Benno. *Were These King Solomon's Mines?* New York: Stein & Day, 1972.

Smick, Elmer B. *Archaeology of the Jordan Valley.* Grand Rapids: Baker, 1973.

Tubb, Jonathan N. *Canaanites.* Norman, Okla.: University of Oklahoma Press, 1998.

LIFE DURING THE UNITED MONARCHY

Chapter 7

(1—2 Samuel; 1 Kings 1—11; 1 Chronicles; 2 Chronicles 1—9)

A child learns to creep, then to walk, and finally to run—and falls often in the process. Just so the infant Hebrew state crept along during the latter days of the judges, took its first tentative steps during the days of King Saul, and was off and running under the leadership of King David. But there were also plenty of tumbles along the way. When we read about this period of Israel's history, we can see a lot of ourselves in the actions taken—but we also can see the grace of God shining through again and again.

The Land

Canaan during the Days of Samuel and the Kings

"This shall be your land with its boundaries all around." (Numbers 37:12 NRSV)

The political geography of Canaan during the latter days of the judges and the kingship reflects the pattern of a child's growth. In the days of Samson and Samuel we see the Hebrews often very much on their knees and creeping along. Samson had his personal victories over the Philistines, and Samuel enjoyed a surprising military success over them that brought about tem-

Area conquered by Israel by the end of Joshua's life

porary relief from Philistine oppression. The tribal groups of Israelites had a certain

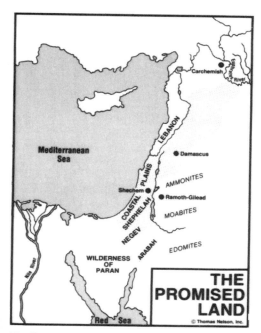

The Promised Land, as given to Abraham and his descendants, ultimately stretched from the eastern branch of the Nile River in the south to the Euphrates River in the north.

Galilee, and Gilead; the coastal plain; Edom, Moab, and Ammon in Transjordan; and Damascus and the rest of Syria all the way to the Euphrates. He had also taken Jerusalem from the Jebusites and established it as his capital. The story of his conquests appears later in the chapter. The concern here is to lay out the political geography.

The Promised Land

Casual observers sometimes say that David managed to control the whole of the Promised Land. But the Promised Land as spelled out to Abraham extended "from the river of Egypt unto. . . the river Euphrates" (Genesis 15:18). The "river of Egypt" must not be identified as the Wadi el-Arish, the traditional border of Egypt. The Hebrew word translated "river" in Genesis 15:18 refers to an ever-flowing river and apparently must be applied to the Nile; other streams of southern Palestine and the Sinai flow only during the rainy season. The easternmost branch of the Nile, the Pelusiac, flows out near modern Port Said and hence near the ancient line of fortifications which protected Egypt from marauding Asiatics. Thus the Pelusiac branch could properly be thought of as the border of Egypt.

The distance from Port Said (including the Sinai) to the Euphrates may be variously measured—in a straight line or in an arc. The former would be some 650 to 700 miles. Of course the Hebrews have never enjoyed possession of all this land; fulfillment of the prophecy must be reserved for a future day.

Possibility of a Large Hebrew Kingdom

People with a vague awareness of ancient history have a jumble in their heads of the empires of Egypt, Assyria, Babylon, Greece, and more. And they wonder how the Hebrews could have built a considerable empire at the eastern end of the Mediterranean when those great powers were on the scene. In fact, even some critics of a former era belittled the biblical claims.

The answer to our question is simple. The empire of David and Solomon was at its

amount of independence and control over the highlands of Galilee, Samaria, Judea, and Gilead east of the Jordan. But Philistines continued to hold the southern coastal plain and the Canaanites the northern coastal plain, the Valley of Jezreel, Jerusalem, and other enclaves.

In their areas the Hebrews did not enjoy political unity, however. Saul took care of that, unifying the lands held earlier by tribal groups. He gained some significant victories over the enemies of Israel, and Israel was now starting to walk. But Israel stumbled badly in Saul's latter days, and the Philistines once more advanced into Israelite territory and threatened their very existence.

Then came David, successful against everyone of Israel's enemies. The child was now maturing and running. "He [David] had dominion over all the region west of the Euphrates from Tiphsah [on the Euphrates] to Gaza, over all the kings west of the Euphrates. . ." (1 Kings 4:24 NRSV). This meant that David, and Solomon who followed him, had established an empire that included the core territory of Judea, Samaria,

greatest extent between about 1000 and 930 B.C. The other peoples of the Mediterranean world were not powerful at that time. By 1100 B.C. the Egyptian, Hittite and Mycenean Greek empires had come to an end. Assyrian power was quiescent; the Babylonian empire of Hammurabi was long gone (by 1500 B.C.), and the Neo-Babylonian power of Nebuchadnezzar (c. 660 B.C.) had not yet been heard of. Nor had the Medo-Persian Empire of Cyrus the Great (c. 550 B.C.). The Athenian Empire and Alexander the Great came later yet. There was a political vacuum in the area between 1100 and 900 B.C. So there is really no difficulty in finding a niche for David and Solomon and their empire.

(For more on this topic, go to p. 109 or 233..)

Government

The Transitional Leadership of Samuel—the Kingmaker

"Give us a king to judge us." (1 Samuel 8:6 NKJV)

What was it like to live at the end of some three centuries when people did according to what was right in their own eyes? A time when there was only an occasional touch of God's mercy through judges whom He used to remind the people what life could be like if they truly worshiped and served God? How was it possible to get them to think seriously about God again?

God prepared Samuel, a boy who grew up at Israel's religious center at a time when Eli, a weak priest, led worship. He lived during dark days politically, militarily, and religiously. While he was still young, the ark had been taken to battle, captured by the Philistines, returned to the Hebrews and finally brought to Kiriath Jearim, about ten miles west of Jerusalem. There it remained for twenty years (1 Samuel 7:2). Apparently it was not returned to Shiloh because the Philistines had destroyed the town.

Somehow the religious foundation his mother, and possibly father, had laid helped Samuel to doggedly persevere

during all those years, trying to get his people to turn to God. Finally his efforts began to pay off. After twenty years of treating God as irrelevant to life, "There was a movement throughout Israel to follow the Lord" (1 Samuel 7:2 REB). Samuel called on the people to turn their backs on their idols and commit themselves unreservedly to God. His exhortation was accompanied by a promise that after personal and national reformation God "will deliver you out of the hand of the Philistines" (1 Samuel 7:3).

Next Samuel called "all Israel," at least their official representatives, to gather at Mizpah, probably Tell en-Nasbeh, eight miles north of Jerusalem. There he promised to pray for them, to intercede for them. There he also "judged" them. That is, through his intercession for Israel he attained forgiveness and the renewal of God's favor. With His people in a right relationship to Him once more, God was free to vindicate their rights (another meaning of the verb "judge") or deliver them. Samuel won that vindication and deliverance for his people by his leadership role.

Apparently the Philistines sought to take advantage of Israel's preoccupation with a religious observance. Or they resolved to launch a preemptive strike because they interpreted the Hebrew gathering as preparation for war. So they gathered to attack the Hebrews. Fear gripped the Hebrews as reports of a Philistine advance reached the holy convocation. Unprepared for war, they begged Samuel not to stop crying out to God on their behalf. Though not a priest, Samuel offered a lamb as a whole burnt offering, thus representing the total consecration of the people to their God.

While Samuel offered the sacrifice and as the Philistines advanced against the Hebrews, Yahweh split the heavens with a terrorizing thunderstorm that threw the Philistine army into complete panic. Perhaps He struck down many of them with bolts of lightning. God defeated the Philistines before the Hebrews had a chance to strike a blow. All the Hebrews had to do was launch a mopping-up exercise.

Mizpah of Benjamin was important in the ministry of Samuel. Among other things, here he first presented Saul to Israel (1 Samuel 7:16–17).

Emboldened by the turn of events, they rushed to attack the confused and fleeing foe. They were so successful that the Philistines "no longer encroached on the territory of Israel" (7:13 REB). Evidently this does not mean the Philistines made no effort to recover lost territory or supremacy. The following clause indicates that such attacks did take place, but they were doomed to failure because of divine intervention.

The event at Mizpah, together with God's intervention against the Philistine army, so dramatically vindicated Samuel's ministry that the Hebrews accepted him as leader, permitting him to serve as the judge and exercise rule over the nation. He continued this leadership function for the rest of his life, alongside his prophetic office. To make it possible for more of the people to have direct access to his ministry, he established a judicial circuit, including Bethel, Gilgal, Mizpah, and Ramah. They were only a few miles apart in the hills of Ephraim in central Palestine. So, even though Samuel may have been respected at a greater distance, his itinerant ministry did not take him to Galilee, Trans-Jordan, or farther afield than the northern edge of Judah. That his authority was accepted widely is clear from the next chapter, in which his sons acted as his deputies at Beersheba in the south and "all the elders of Israel" (8:4) came to him with the request for a king.

So it is clear that Samuel became recognized as the government of Israel for some decades. This included a certain amount of executive activity; religious leadership in prayer, proclamation, and sacrifice; a military role in bringing about defeat of the Philistines; and a judicial function in holding court. Moreover, he served as kingmaker—as the one who introduced the monarchy. In all of this a theocratic form of government continued. God called the shots.

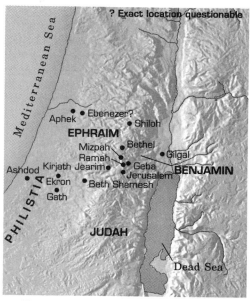

Towns important in the ministry of Samuel

Samuel's sons' behavior reveals that he possibly fell into the trap of many leaders— he was so busy leading others he did not provide adequate leadership at home. He delegated responsibilities in the judicial branch of government to his sons as he grew older. But they did not have the moral fiber of their father and were guilty of perversion of justice (1 Samuel 8:3). The people realized that when Samuel was gone they could not count on a continuation of his responsible ways and therefore on God's ongoing blessing. Furthermore, they looked over their shoulders at the Philistines and other enemies and wanted a vigorous commander to lead them into battle.

So "all the elders of Israel" went to Samuel and begged "make for us a king to judge us like all the nations" (1 Samuel 8:5). Samuel took this as a vote of no confidence in his leadership and a lack of appreciation for his many years of dedicated service. When he brought his heartache to God, He told Samuel that they were not really rejecting his leadership but divine control over them. And God told Samuel to grant their wish. As a kind of parting shot, Samuel warned the people that a king would draft their sons into his army, put the people to forced labor (corvée) on personal and government projects, and exact heavy taxes.

But they would not listen; they wanted a king "like all the nations" (1 Samuel 8:20). As a matter of fact, long before the Israelites had conquered Canaan, God had foreseen the day when Israel would have a king. But He did not want their king to be like those of all the other nations. Rather, God wanted His man to be "a man of the book," who read God's Word and lived by its principles, one who did not seek to hoard wealth for himself, or gather a harem, or build an excessive military establishment (Deuteronomy 17:14-20, see sidebar on p.151).

The concept of theocracy was not dead. When Samuel told the people God had honored their request and sent them home to await fulfillment of the promise, they dutifully obeyed. How long the Hebrews had to wait for the choice of a king is not clear. There was no emergency that required haste. The elders of Israel had the commitment of God's prophet, and thus of God Himself, that the monarchy would be established. Therefore they were content to allow events to unfold in due course. The patience of the Orient does not require immediate or rapid implementation of promises made.

But the sacred historian proceeds immediately to introduce the person who was to become Israel's first king. The rather elaborate genealogy indicates he was from a prominent family (1 Samuel 9:1). Saul was also from a family of "substance" or "property" (9:1). The KJV description of his father, Kish, as "a mighty man of power" (9:1) is misleading. It implies that he had great physical prowess, but the Hebrew original means that he had the power in his community that comes with extensive possessions.

As to his personal qualifications, Saul was a young man "in the prime of life" (9:2), but it is impossible to be more definite than that about his age. If one follows some later manuscripts of the Septuagint translation of 1 Samuel 13:1, he was thirty when he began to reign. And as to appearance, there was no one more handsome than he and he was a head taller than anyone else.

The Kingmaker in Action —Anointing of Saul

"And Samuel said to all the people, 'Do you see him whom the Lord has chosen. . . ?' So all the people shouted and said, 'Long live the king!'" (1 Samuel 10:24 NKJV)

The sacred historian also tells how God brought Samuel and Saul together as Saul was out looking for his father's donkeys (1 Samuel 9:3-27). Samuel privately anointed Saul (1 Samuel 10:1) and in a public ceremony at Mizpah Samuel presented him to the people (10:17-27). The anointing served as an investiture of office and a symbol of the endowment of the Spirit of God. Now the monarchy had taken its place alongside the priesthood as a divine institution. Through it would come the blessings of the sovereign God-king for civil government, as through the priesthood came the blessings of God for spiritual and ethical government.

The Law of the King
(Deuteronomy 17:14-20)

1. He shall be a native Israelite.
2. He shall not multiply horses for himself.
3. He shall not multiply wives for himself.
4. He shall not multiply silver and gold for himself.
5. He shall provide for himself a copy of the book of God.
6. He shall read it all the days of his life.
7. He shall observe the principles and statutes of God's Law.
8. He shall not be haughty.

The Government of Saul

"So all the people went to Gilgal, and there they made Saul king before the Lord in Gilgal." (1 Samuel 11:15)

After Samuel presented Saul to the people at Mizpah, he sent the people home. And Saul had nowhere to go either but home. What an incredible situation. The king had no capital! No government buildings! No treasury! No army! But as Saul walked the five miles back to Gibeah, God put it on the hearts of some to accompany him. Regarding allegiance to be their conscientious duty, they became a sort of bodyguard and the nucleus of a standing army and government. And no doubt the many gifts of fealty and good wishes helped to finance Saul's operations in the early days of the kingdom (v. 27).

In fact, when Saul returned home he went back to farming (1 Samuel 11:6-7). And it was from the farm that he sallied forth to battle against the Ammonites a short time later. Subsequently most of his administrative acts had to do with military affairs, as he sought to establish the power and viability of the Hebrew state. The story of those battles is told later.

Saul chose 3,000 stalwarts as a sort of "palace guard" or a nucleus of the standing army. Of these, one thousand were stationed with Saul at Micmash, about nine miles northeast of Jerusalem, and another thousand under his jurisdiction around Bethel, about ten miles north of Jerusalem. A third thousand served under the command of Jonathan at Gibeah, about three miles north of Jerusalem (1 Samuel 13:2). His cousin Abner served as the commander of his forces (1 Samuel 14:50).

Saul as King

As we look at Saul's administration we ask, "What sort of king was he?" From his earliest acts we might guess that he was basically wise and big-hearted. When some rebellious people had opposed his elevation to the kingship, he ignored them. That was not a time to insist on unanimity. He would prove himself (1 Samuel 10:27). Then after his early victory over the Ammonites, some of his supporters wanted to execute those rebellious individuals who had opposed his kingship. But he wisely refrained from a sour note of executions in the midst of a victory celebration (1 Samuel 11:12-15).

Possibly he would have continued on that high road if he had not run afoul of the specific dictates of God. Saul had two great failures that led to his rejection at God's hands and colored everything else he did. The first came near the beginning of his reign when he faced the overwhelming superiority of Philistine forces. Samuel told him to wait for him at Gilgal. And he did. But when his military situation rapidly deteriorated and Samuel did not come, Saul determined to offer sacrifices himself and prepare for battle. Thus he intruded on the office of priest, and he prepared to go into battle without divine directions.

No sooner had he completed the offering, however, than Samuel arrived and rebuked him for disobedience and lack of faith. For his lack of faith in an hour of crisis, Saul came under the condemnation of God and heard the sentence from Samuel that his dynasty would not endure-not beyond his own administration. God would choose a king "after his own heart" (13:14), and that man proved to be David. As subsequent events would demonstrate, however, that judgment did not mean God would fail to give Saul some great victories.

The mound of Gibeah, home of Saul and his "capital"

Saul's second test and failure occurred during his struggle with the Amalekites. God commanded total destruction of these people and all of their possessions. Saul waged war against them and destroyed them and part of their belongings, saving the best livestock and the king. For his partial obedience, God rejected Saul's kingship (1 Samuel 15). Thereafter he lost his grip on his kingdom and even on his sanity.

As the power of the Holy Spirit left Saul, the power that had enabled him to lead during the years of his kingship (1 Samuel 16:14), Saul no longer had the resources to enable him to run the kingdom—or even to maintain his mental health. In fact, as a pun-

Egyptian lyres from the Empire period are somewhat more sophisticated. They could be played with or without the plectrum. (From a tomb painting at Thebes)

David's lyre probably did not look much different from the lyre played by a Semitic visitor to Egypt about the time of Joseph. (From the tomb of Khnumhotep at Beni Hassan in Egypt)

ishment God sent on him a form of severe depression. As time went on his depression became more severe and perhaps was not far removed from a psychotic condition.

The only treatment Saul's attendants knew for such a malady was the soothing music of a harp. Or perhaps it is better to call it a lyre, for it was a small stringed instrument in the form of a flat sounding-box with two wooden arms joined by a crosspiece. The strings stretched from the box to the crosspiece. Saul listened to his advisers and instructed them to find an accomplished musician. David, next king of Israel, proved to be that musician.

It is not hard to imagine how Saul's depression developed. He lived under the

The mound of Ziklag, a base of operation for David's army during the
early years of fugitive life (1 Samuel 27:6)

(Levant Photo Service)

judgment of God. He was deprived of the support and counsel of Samuel, who left him to his own devices after the divine rejection (1 Samuel 15:10-35). And David increasingly won the accolades of the masses while Saul's reputation slipped: "Saul has slain his thousands, And David his ten thousands" (1 Samuel 18:7).

During subsequent years, as Saul fought his mental depression and had the services of David the musician, he established his house or palace at Gibeah. William F. Albright of Johns Hopkins University excavated Saul's administrative center there in 1922-23. Dating the structure to about 1020-1000 B.C.,

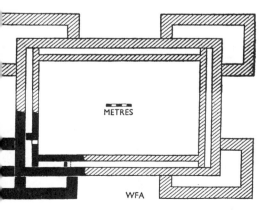

The floor plan of Saul's palace at Gibeah

he believed that Saul probably built it and David possibly repaired it. Later archaeologists have suggested that the Philistines built it to control the trade routes and that Saul later occupied it. In any case, it would have been Saul's palace. The structure measured some 169 feet long by 114 feet wide with towers extending from each of the four corners (see Albright's reconstructed floor plan accompanying).[1]

On the basis of Acts 13:21 and Josephus we conclude that Saul's reign lasted forty years. The first-century Jewish historian Josephus states that Saul reigned eighteen years before Samuel's death and twenty-two years afterward.[2]

Whatever Saul's failures, amassing a harem was not among them. His wife's name was Ahinoam, and she bore him four sons that we know of (Jonathan, Abinadab, Malchishua, and Ish-botheth) and two daughters (Merab and Michal). See 1 Samuel 14:49-50; 2 Samuel 2:8; 1 Chronicles 8:33.

Apparently, too, Saul did not fall to the temptation of hoarding great wealth. But there is no indication that he gave much thought to the Word of God or that he had any real fellowship with God. His fear over losing the opportunity of depending on Samuel showed that without Samuel he was nothing spiritually. (For specifics on the way a king should behave, see sidebar on "The Law of the King.")

Many people overlook Saul's military successes because so much emphasis is placed on Saul's personal failures in Scripture and in the minds of Bible students. His list of victories is almost as extensive as those of David, though his conquests were not so permanent as those of his successor. East of the Jordan he defeated the Edomites on the south, and then the Moabites and Ammonites, conquering all the way up to Zobah, north of Damascus (1 Samuel 14:47). But though he fought "bitter warfare" (14:52) with the Philistines on the west all during the rest of his reign, he never subdued them and finally met his end at their hands. God had told the Hebrews what kind of king their sovereign was to be and Saul did not meet the test. Now God would choose another.

The Government of David

"And the Spirit of the Lord came upon David from that day forward." (1 Samuel 16:13 NKJV)

This special empowerment for leadership and for life came upon David when Samuel anointed him. That anointing came soon after Saul's second great failure: his disobedience in exterminating the Amalekites (1 Samuel 15). What that anointing meant was not clear to David or his family at the time. And he had to wait many years for it to have any evident or official effect in his life. First he enjoyed the victory over Goliath (1 Samuel 17). Then came the years of sparring with Saul and flight in the wilderness (1 Samuel 18—30).

David's Rule at Ziklag

Finally, totally demoralized, David defected to Achish, Philistine king of Gath, who permitted him to settle in the village of Ziklag. This is now thought to have been at Tell esh-Shariah, about fifteen miles northwest of Beersheba and twenty-five miles south of Gath. During the year and four months there he was involved in raids against the Geshurites to the southwest (cf. Joshua 13:12); the Girzites, otherwise unknown; and the Amalekites, marauders along the southern border, after Saul's victories over them (1 Samuel 27:6-9). In the process he supported his own men (now 600 strong in addition to their families) and bought favor with the Israelites as he defended their southern border against marauders. Thus he built a base of acceptance in preparation for the day when he would be hailed king of Judah.

In the final Philistine battle against Saul's forces, the Philistines released David and his men from service in the Philistine army because of Philistine fear that he would defect at a strategic moment (1 Samuel 29:1-11). What happened next is important to the administration of David. While he and his men had gone to the front to join the Philistine forces, Amalekite raiders took Ziklag, burned it to the ground and carried off Hebrew goods and families, probably intending to sell them into the Egyptian slave market.

David and his men caught up with the Amalekites and destroyed most of them, recovering their families and goods and taking much additional spoil. Administratively the action became important for two reasons. First, David established the policy that in warfare those who fought and took spoil would share equally with those who stayed behind and guarded the baggage and equipment (1 Samuel 30:24-25). Second, from his part of the spoil David sent gifts to several towns in Judah. These gifts paid off in helping to bring recognition to David as king in Judah soon afterward when news of the death of Saul came ringing through the land.

A further administrative principle according to which David operated was to avoid taking vengeance against royal opponents, either against Saul (who had tried to kill him on numerous occasions) or against his house. After the death of Saul, an Amalekite came to David with the king's crown and gold armband and reported that he had killed the king. Presumably he hoped for an immediate reward and possibly for a position in the kingdom. Regicide certainly was a capital offense, and David himself did not want to let anyone think he had had a part, however indirect, in the death of Saul. David took the man's statement at face value and declared, "Your blood be on your own head" (v. 16). This

Modern Hebron, successor to the ancient city of the same name where David ruled for seven years over the tribe of Judah

meant the man's guilt rested on himself and he deserved to die; otherwise, it would rest on David and could be avenged. Then he ordered his execution.

About seven years later, when the continuing monarchy of Saul's son Ish-Bosheth came to an end with his assassination, his two assassins came to David with the head of the king to claim a reward from him. Contrary to their expectation, he ordered their execution. And as was common in the case of criminals guilty of treason, their hands and feet were cut off. Then David had their mutilated corpses hanged in a public place as a warning and deterrent to others. Finally, David accorded proper respect to the head of Ish-Bosheth by burying it in the tomb of Abner, his kinsman. Thus David not only showed his abhorrence for such a crime, but also demonstrated that he had had no part in this murder.

David's Elevation to the Kingship at Hebron

After the death of Saul, David knew he could safely return to Israelite territory and that the road to kingship had opened for him. He logically entertained thoughts of going into Judah, both because he and his wives had come from that area and because he had been careful to maintain good relations with various towns in Judah. But David wanted to be sure that he was in the will of God, so he sought God's direction

for his life. God responded positively, encouraging him to go to Judah and more specifically to the "cities of Hebron" (2 Samuel 2:3), referring no doubt, to the villages near Hebron and belonging to it. David's six hundred men and their families (probably at least fifteen hundred people) and livestock would have inundated the town of Hebron itself.

Then the "men of Judah" (2:4), representative elders, invited David to be king over their tribe, and he accepted. The actual anointing (2:4) probably would have been done by Abiathar the priest. We could consider this public ceremony natural because Samuel's earlier anointing had been private, and it was not clear how many had any knowledge or understanding of its significance.

Meanwhile, Abner, commander of Saul's forces, gradually pulled together the northern tribes of Israel and pushed back the Philistines. After five and one-half years of interregnum, Abner felt strong enough to install Saul's remaining son on the throne. He established the capital at Mahanaim, located east of the Jordan and south of the Jabbok River.

Negotiations with the Other Tribes

Eventually a rift occurred between Abner and Ish-Bosheth, and Abner decided to turn over the kingdom to David. He proposed an "agreement" (3:12) which undoubtedly would be mutually beneficial, bringing to

Anointing of Kings and Priests

Anointing with olive oil in Old Testament times invested individuals with power or consecrated them to service. The anointing set them apart for a holy purpose.

The kings of Israel were supposed to be God's servants, ruling His people in God-appointed ways. In the United Kingdom Saul (1 Samuel 10:1), David (1 Samuel 16:3), and Solomon (1 Kings 1:39) were all anointed. Presumably the kings of Judah were too, but we have only the mention of the anointing of Joash (2 Kings 11:12). The apostasy of the Northern Kingdom probably resulted in discontinuation of the ceremony there. We have mention only of Elisha's anointing of Jehu—to exterminate the house of Ahab (2 Kings 9:6-12).

Priests, especially the high priests, were anointed and consecrated for service as mediators between God and His people. This practice began with Aaron (Exodus 29:7).

Evidently prophets were also anointed for office (1 Kings 19:16), but we have only this single reference to Elijah's anointing Elisha.

Objects, too, could be anointed with oil and consecrated for the worship and service of God. The tabernacle and all its furniture was to be anointed (Exodus 40:9). Jacob anointed a pillar at Bethel, calling the place a house of God (Genesis 28:18).

son-in-law he was Saul's legitimate successor, (3) to win to himself by this means whatever lingering affection there was for Saul (a child born to the union would join the two rival lines), and (4) to enlist the support of the Benjamites.

Then before he even met David, Abner carried out negotiations with the elders of the various tribes of Israel in an effort to persuade them to declare for David. In addition, he had private conversations with the leaders of the tribe of Benjamin, which would lose some of its special advantages when the royal family no longer came from its midst.

After Abner had won over to David all the leaders of the tribes of Israel, he went to Hebron with twenty representatives of all Israel to confirm Abner's announcement of the intentions of all the tribes. David then hosted a banquet for his guests, after which Abner declared his resolve to call a solemn assembly of representatives of all the tribes. These were to enter into negotiations and a covenant with David to the end that he might "rule over all that [his] heart desires" (3:21), i.e., all Israel. Then Abner "went in peace"; he was no longer treated as an enemy, for he had ceased all animosity to David.

With the assassination of Ish-Bosheth, already referred to, the way was open for David's acceptance by all the tribes. Evidently in response to the efforts of Abner, representatives of all the tribes gathered at Hebron to make David king. They gave three reasons for offering him their allegiance: (1) They were his blood relatives; all were descendants of Jacob. Though for a while they may have had some fears of his being a naturalized Philistine because he was for a while subordinate to them, his years of rule in Hebron had erased their apprehensions. (2) They recognized his prowess as a victorious military leader (cf. 1 Samuel 18:5-7). (3) God had called him to be their shepherd and prince.

Probably after considerable negotiations between David and the elders, they made an "agreement" (5:3), or "compact" (NIV). This certainly involved a recognition of the general rights and duties of kingship (see 1 Samuel 10:25). But in addition it must have included an understanding that the other

David kingship over the north and to Abner personal advantages and immunities.

But before David was willing to receive Abner in person to negotiate with him, he demanded the return of Saul's daughter Michal, who had been given to Paltiel (3:13; cf. 1 Samuel 25:44). It may be argued that David's love for her had prompted the request, but far more was at stake. On political grounds she was important to him (1) to show that he harbored no ill will toward the fallen king, (2) to demonstrate that as

tribes would enjoy equal rights with the tribe of Judah in the new national monarchy. The conclave lasted three days (1 Chronicles 12:39) and involved the presence of numerous military personnel along with the clan leaders.

Despite the hard bargaining behind the scenes, a gala atmosphere prevailed, with much feasting and joy in the camp (1 Chronicles 12:39-40). A new day was dawning for Israel. Hopes ran high with the installation of a new divinely approved leader who had proven his prowess on the battlefield. Gone were ineffective leadership and division. The "compact" guaranteed a form of constitutional monarchy. The fact that David found it necessary to "consult" with every captain of a thousand or a hundred in the army (cf. 1 Chronicles 13:1) demonstrated the necessity of ruling by persuasion and personal prowess.

David as King over All Israel

Then "they anointed David king" (5:3). Abiathar probably administered the sacred rites. This was the third anointing of David, the first having been privately performed by Samuel and the second having occurred when he began to rule at Hebron. The chronological note is added that David was thirty when he began to reign and that he reigned a total of forty years: seven and one-half in Hebron and thirty-three in Jerusalem.

Hardly had David been elevated to the kingship over all the Hebrews when the Philistines realized the threat he was to them. They attacked before he could consolidate his power, but he defeated them (see later discussion under warfare).

Making Jerusalem the Capital

Soon after David's accession as king he began the consolidation of the kingdom. The strategically located citadel of Jerusalem remained as one of the important Canaanite strongholds in the south central part of the land. Much of the town had fallen to the Israelites during the period of the judges (Judges 1:8), but the stronghold remained in alien hands. The residents considered themselves especially impregnable because deep ravines surrounded it on three sides. In fact, it appeared so impregnable that the Jebusite defenders believed even the "blind and lame" could ward off attackers (2 Samuel 5:6). But David determined to take it (see discussion under warfare), and he did, making it his capital.

This was a stroke of brilliance because Hebron in the south would not have been an acceptable capital to the northern tribes. On the other hand, a northern capital would have been unacceptable to Judah. Moreover, Jerusalem was located between the two political units and was within the territory of none of the tribes. So it was an excellent compromise. Belonging to none of the tribes, it became known as the "city of David." The new capital tended to elevate the government above tribal jealousy.

Bringing in the Ark

Not long after he made Jerusalem his capital, David sought to bring the ark there. David's lifelong spiritual emphasis by itself would have led him to take such a step. But certainly his aim to make Jerusalem the religious as well as the political capital of the kingdom fueled that desire. The state now became the patron and protector of the sacred institutions. His actions must have done much to bind the feelings of the tribes to Jerusalem, and those feelings continue to the present. In fact, the city holds a special place in the hearts of Jews, Christians, and Muslims alike. The discussion of David's efforts to transport the ark appears in the section on religion following.

Building a Palace

Of course David had to have some kind of administrative center. Rulers of that part of the world used the palace as a government building. David was no exception. What his palace looked like or how large it was we do not know, but apparently it was built of cut stone with interior cedar paneling (2 Samuel 7:2). Phoenician craftsmen provided the construction skills (2 Samuel 5:11).

Seeking to Build the Temple

As David settled himself comfortably he became conscience smitten that he had not provided a house for God. But when he set out to do so, God stopped him through Nathan the prophet, telling David that his son would build the temple and that He (God) would honor David's desires by building a permanent house for him. That is, God made a covenant with David in which He promised: (1) David would have a son to succeed him and establish his kingdom (2 Samuel 7:12); (2) that this son (Solomon) would build the temple (v. 13a); (3) the throne of Solomon's kingdom would be established forever (v. 13b); (4) David's house, kingdom, and throne would be established forever (v. 16); (5) Israel would be planted in her own land forever—"not disturbed again" (v. 10 NASB).

These are unconditional, eternal, and literal promises that follow and enlarge on the unconditional Abrahamic Covenant (Genesis 12:1-3; 13:14-17; 15:1-21; cf. Galatians 3:8, 16). To be sure, the Abrahamic and Davidic covenants did not promise uninterrupted occupation of the land or enjoyment of the kingship, but they did pledge that the right to rule would always remain with David's dynasty and that his kingship ultimately would enter an eternal phase. Jesus Christ, in the line of David, was destined to fulfill these everlasting features of the covenants (cf. Luke 1:31-33). One day He will rule on the throne of David on Mount Zion in the messianic kingdom (Psalm 2).

David's Administrative Arrangements (2 Samuel 8:15—9:13)

During all of David's foreign wars, which receive attention in the section on warfare, he maintained an excellent system of government at home. In saying David ruled over "all Israel" (8:15), the historian puts emphasis on the united kingdom. As an ideal king David maintained "law and justice" (v. 15). In connection with what follows, with the naming of heads of departments of government, the conclusion must be reached that David himself acted as chief justice of the court system and was relatively accessible to the people. Joab served as commander of the army, having gained his position by heroism in the conquest of Jerusalem (5:8). He maintained this role throughout David's

Phoenicians and Hebrews Together

In the days of the great Hiram of Tyre, Hebrews and Tyrians worked closely together in several ventures. Hiram's thirty-four-year reign overlapped that of David and Solomon. Hiram sent cedar trees, carpenters, and masons to Jerusalem to build David's palace (2 Samuel 5:11; 7:2). Later David obtained cedar wood from Tyre for building the temple.

After David's death Hiram and Solomon continued the close relationship. Hiram provided cedar and cypress wood and skilled artisans for construction of the temple, Solomon's palace, and a palace for the daughter of Pharaoh. In return Solomon sent large quantities of agricultural goods which the limited lands of the Phoenicians could not provide for an industrial and commercial society. It is generally believed that all this Hebrew construction bore similarities to Phoenician architecture.

After Solomon conquered Edom, he had access to the Gulf of Aqaba, an arm of the Red Sea. After that Hiram worked with Solomon to develop a Hebrew merchant marine. And the two had a profitable commercial relationship. First Kings 10:22 refers to a fleet of ships of Tarshish which Solomon had at sea with the fleet of Hiram. Once every three years ships of Tarshish sailed off to bring back gold, silver, ivory, and rare animals. Obviously the commerce was good for Solomon. And Hiram, without a Suez Canal, was looking for a way to tap the markets of East Africa, Arabia, and the Persian Gulf. There is considerable debate over identification of "ships of Tarshish," but they were probably a type of strong ship capable of long distance travel.

Keeping a Promise to a Friend

A very human and tender aspect of David's administration concerned fulfillment of his covenant with Jonathan. Appropriately the sacred historian inserted this account in the midst of his description of David's government since Jonathan had said something about David's caring for his family when the earth should be rid of David's enemies (1 Samuel 20:15). David learned that Jonathan had a son named Mephibosheth, born during David's wanderings. Mephibosheth had been dropped by his nurse and crippled at age five during the flight after the disastrous battle of Mount Gilboa (2 Samuel 4:4). David had no knowledge of him, since Mephibosheth had been living in seclusion ever since. Now David summoned Mephibosheth to come to Jerusalem, gave him his personal assurances of kindness, and backed them up in a tangible way with the grant to him of all his grandfather's royal estates. Moreover, he welcomed him to the king's table to dine with his sons as a member of the family and provided him with an adequate servant staff to manage his estates.

reign until he supported Solomon's rival for the throne (1 Kings 1—2).

Jehoshaphat acted as "remembrancer" (8:16). As recorder or historian, Jehoshaphat would have kept the annals or registered the current events. Zadok and Ahimelech, the son of Abiathar, are listed as priests (8:17). In the latter case the names of father and son seem to have been reversed as the result of a copyist's error. Zadok had been priest under Saul and Abiathar under David; now both retained their dignity. Seraiah as scribe or secretary of state kept the records and carried out instructions. Benaiah commanded the royal bodyguard of Cherethites and Pelethites, mercenaries from Philistia. David followed the practice of many rulers to secure a bodyguard of mercenaries rather than home guards because they were more dependent on the ruler alone. There was less chance of a rival buying them off and penetrating the palace with murder in mind.

The bureaucracy also included David's sons, who in the Hebrew are called "priests" (8:18). But evidently they did not perform a priestly function. In the parallel passage in 1 Chronicles 18:17 they are called "the first at the hand of the king," which the NIV translates as "chief officials at the king's side." And in 1 Kings 4:5 the priest is called "the king's friend," or adviser. Justifiably the NIV translates 2 Samuel 8:18, "David's sons were royal advisers."

After Absalom's rebellion and defeat, David had to reestablish his government. As he did so, the sacred historian listed the members of David's cabinet once more (2 Samuel 20:23-26). Most names are the same in both lists. Sheva succeeded Seraiah as scribe. Ira the Jairite replaced the sons of the king as a confidential adviser. With a couple of sons now gone and shaken by a filial rebellion, David might be expected to choose a personal adviser. "Adoram" (20:24; Hebrew text) was put in charge of the corvée, or forced labor battalion. He is probably the same person as Adoniram of 1 Kings 4:6 (cf. 1 Kings 12:18). The practice of exacting forced labor on public works as a form of taxation evidently developed late in David's reign and continued throughout that of Solomon's. God had warned the Israelites, when they demanded a king in the days of Samuel, that the king would establish the corvée (1 Samuel 8:16). Now reality matched the prediction.

David's Harem

As with other Oriental monarchs, David assembled a harem in violation of God's express command in Deuteronomy 17:17, and numerous progeny followed. Six different wives bore David six sons in Hebron. The first two wives, Abigail and Michal, came to Hebron with David. He married the other four while there. The third was the daughter of the king of Geshur, a region of Syria northeast of Bashan. Evidently David entered this marriage for political reasons; it was designed to strengthen David's hand in the north against the kingdom of Ish-Bosheth. Absalom, born of that union, led the rebellion against his father that almost proved successful. Solomon expanded the practice of making marriage alliances with pagan rulers, resulting in considerable dilution of Yahweh worship at court and eventually among the populace. Of the last three of David's wives nothing is known. A similar list of David's sons appears in 1 Chronicles 3:1–4. There his second son is called Daniel and here Kileab; so he probably had two names.

When David moved to Jerusalem, he married additional wives, perhaps some for political reasons. These unnamed women bore him sons and daughters, of whom eleven sons are named. Solomon is the only one of the group who appears again in Scripture, except in parallel passages (2 Samuel 5:13-14).

David's Hoarding of Treasure

David collected tremendous amounts of booty from the various peoples he conquered. From Zobah he brought the shields of gold carried on ceremonial occasions by courtiers of Hadadezer, as well as a large quantity of bronze. From Hamath came silver, gold, and bronze. And from the other nations he collected silver and gold and other wealth. Down through the ages sovereigns of the East have hoarded quantities of treasure. David did, too, but with a difference. After meeting his expenses, he dedicated vast quantities of precious metals to God for construction of the temple (2 Samuel 8:11). The shields of gold taken from Hadadezer (8:7) found their way into the Temple treasuries and stayed there until carried off by Shishak I of Egypt during the days of King Rehoboam in 926 B.C. (1 Kings 14:26). So David obeyed God's command that the king shall not multiply silver and gold "for himself" (Deuteronomy 17:17).

David's Failures and Punishment

Coloring all of David's political administration and even the course of Hebrew history were David's failures and the resultant punishment. A remarkable feature of

Why David Stayed Home

Critics sometimes charge that David's remaining in Jerusalem during the Ammonite war constituted a dereliction of duty. And he got into trouble with Bathsheba for shirking that duty. But that is not necessarily true.

Kings did not always lead their forces into war. And, in fact, the time came when the people at large insisted that David stay home from the front for his personal safety and for their good. "You are more help to us in the city," they said (2 Samuel 18:3 NKJV). Moreover, the autocratic kings of the ancient Near East had so much administrative detail to attend to at home that they could not always handle both military and domestic affairs adequately.

Scripture, and certainly one of the indications of its inspiration, is the fact that it does not overlook the faults of the great leaders of biblical times. No doubt this reporting is intended as a warning to others (1 Corinthians 10:11-12).

One day during a war against the Ammonites, David walked about on the roof of his flat-topped house after his siesta. Looking down into a nearby open courtyard he saw a beautiful woman taking a bath. One cannot exactly accuse Bathsheba of inviting trouble, but she was not as modest as she might have been. She must have known that she could be seen from the rooftops of nearby houses. Her conduct gave rise to lustful desire in David, so he immediately inquired about her. Shortly he "took her" (2 Samuel 11:4) and had sexual relations with her. Oriental potentates reserved the right to add to their harems, but a man of God was supposed to conduct himself differently.

The Bible does not indicate that Bathsheba resisted David, and in fact she seems to have been a very ambitious woman. She came to dominate him to a degree and soon secured from him the promise that her son Solomon

DAVID'S ACCOMPLISHMENTS AND FAILURES

David's humility before the Lord (2 Samuel 7:18–22) recalled the Lord's initial assessment of him: David was a "man after [God's] own heart" (1 Samuel 13:14). David could be counted on to trust God and try to walk in His ways. But it did not mean that David would do that perfectly.

David as a Spiritual Leader

Incident	Results
Trusted God to help him kill Goliath (1 Samuel 17:37).	Killed Goliath and led Israel's army in victory (1 Samuel 17:48–54).
Twice spared Saul's life (1 Samuel 24:1–7; 26:7–12).	Showed himself to be more righteous than Saul (1 Samuel 24:16–21; 26:21).
Listened to Abigail and spared Nabal's life (1 Samuel 25:23–35).	Showed himself to be more compassionate and just than Saul (compare 1 Samuel 22:16–19).
Consulted the Lord before assuming the throne (2 Samuel 2:1).	Became king over Judah at Hebron (2 Samuel 2:2–4).
Relocated the ark of the covenant to Jerusalem (2 Samuel 6).	Consolidated worship at Jerusalem and established his kingdom there.
Desired to build a temple for the Lord (2 Samuel 7:1–2).	Learned that God would establish his kingdom forever (2 Samuel 7:12–16).
Honored his covenant with Jonathan by showing kindness to Mephibosheth (2 Samuel 9).	Increased the loyalty of his subjects.
Repented of his sins in regard to Bathsheba and Uriah (2 Samuel 12:13; Psalm 51).	Received the Lord's forgiveness (2 Samuel 12:13).

David's Spiritual Failures

Incident	Results
Took many wives for himself (2 Samuel 3:2–5; 5:13–16; compare Deuteronomy 17:17).	• Complicated his domestic life. • Set a bad precedent for Solomon (compare 1 Kings 11:1–4).
Allowed Joab to exterminate 18,000 Edomites (2 Samuel 8:13–14; 1 Kings 11:15–16).	• Raised up a permanent adversary against Solomon (1 Kings 11:14, 19–22).
Committed adultery with Bathsheba and had Bathsheba's husband Uriah murdered (2 Samuel 11).	• Fighting among his descendants (2 Samuel 12:10; 13:1–33). • Rebellion from within his own family (2 Samuel 12:11; 15:1–12; 1 Kings 1:5–10). • Public violation of his wives (2 Samuel 12:11–12; 16:21–22). • Death of Bathsheba's child (2 Samuel 12:14–19).
Took a census that God had not ordered (2 Samuel 24:1–9).	Caused the death of 70,000 Israelites. (2 Samuel 24:15–17)

would take precedence over the other children in the harem and would become the next king (cf. 1 Kings 1:13, 15, 17, 28). As soon as Bathsheba knew she was pregnant, she informed David so he could take steps to protect himself and her.

David took his first step to cover himself by bringing Uriah back from the front to spend time with his wife. The pregnancy could then be passed off as a normal one within the family. But Uriah did not do what David expected. Instead, he slept at the door of the king's house with the servants.

David decided he had to dispose of Uriah. In this case it was fairly simple; he could have him killed in battle. So the king sent Uriah's death warrant to Joab by his own hand! The instruction was simple: put Uriah in a dangerous spot on the battle line and retreat from him so he would be killed. Joab loyally followed orders without question, and this privileged information henceforth would give him an advantage in dealing with David.

God left David in his unrepentant state for almost a year. In the meantime Bathsheba's son had been born. He finally sent the prophet Nathan to pronounce a twofold judgment on the wayward king: (1) The sword would never depart from his house, and insurrection would rise against him in his own household. This prophecy was fulfilled in the murder of Amnon (2 Samuel 13:28), Absalom's revolt and death (2 Samuel 18:14), and Adonijah's execution (1 Kings 2:25). His sin certainly weakened his authority and respect with his own family. In addition, because his sins had done great injury to the cause of the true faith, Bathaheba's child would be struck down. (2) While his sin was committed in secret, his wives would be taken from him and another would violate them in broad daylight and in public. This was fulfilled by the action of Absalom (2 Samuel 16:22).

Nathan's words of judgment pierced the heart of David like an arrow. To his credit, he did not rationalize or offer excuses but bowed before God in true contrition. God graciously forgave his sin and spared his life; the record of David's spiritual experience during this crisis period appears most clearly in Psalms 32 and 51. But though David was pardoned and restored to divine favor, his reputation had been forever besmirched. The effects of his sin continued to plague his life and the history of his dynasty for a very long time to come. Soon after David's encounter with Nathan, Bathsheba's child fell ill and died.

A postscript to this judgment scene is a note about the second pregnancy of Bathsheba and her being comforted by a replacement for the son she had lost. The child was named Solomon, meaning "peaceable," or "a man of peace." David most likely had in mind a renewal of peace with God.

Near the end of David's reign he committed another sin. He took a complete census of his people (2 Samuel 24:1-25; cf. 1 Chronicles 21). Since a census was not wrong in itself, the sin that was judged in the present case must have been the attitude of the king's heart. And punishment for David's sin became an occasion for the chastisement of the nation for its waywardness.

In what sense David's taking of a census was sinful has to be deduced from the context in 1 Chronicles and 2 Samuel and especially from Joab's response. That David's attitude was sinful certainly is to be seen in his pride, or self-exaltation, as he sought to glory in the number of his fighting men and the strength of his military establishment. And perhaps, worse, he fell to the temptation of measuring his real strength in terms of human and material resources instead of the "Rock" and "Shield" of chapter 22. Joab responded, in effect, that if David had such great delight in numbers, he wished that God would greatly multiply the troops and that the king would live to see it.

Joab remonstrated with the king, evidently because he felt the king was on an "ego trip" (v. 3). He probably believed that any effort to take a census would unsettle the populace. It could raise fears of new taxes and military conscription. No amount of remonstrance on the part of Joab and the military council was of any avail, however; and the king had his way.

Evidently, soon after the census was completed, David realized he had done a very foolish thing. Conscience-smitten, he

The Temple Mount

Mount Moriah is the rocky hilltop of Jerusalem north of the old Jebusite city of Jerusalem where Solomon built the temple. Actually the place earlier had been called the "threshing floor of Araunah the Jebusite." David bought it so he could offer a substitutionary sacrifice for himself and his house after he met the angel of death there during the great plague (2 Samuel 24:17).

The writer of 2 Chronicles 3:1 calls the site Mount Moriah. Genesis 22:2 speaks of the "land of Moriah," where Abraham offered Isaac and where he received the divine visitor. Again a substitutionary sacrifice was offered. Josephus, the first century Jewish historian, linked the site of the offering of Isaac with the site of the temple (*Antiquities* I, xiii.2). Rabbinic literature follows this identification, and so does Muslim folklore concerning the Dome of the Rock, which stands there now. Substitutionary sacrifices of Abraham and David at the site and the whole sacrificial system of the temple point forward to the substitutionary work of Christ on the cross.

prayed to God for forgiveness. During the night God responded by delivering a message to the prophet Gad who was directed to communicate it to David. God gave the king a choice of seven years of famine, three months of pursuit before his enemies, or three days of pestilence. All would humble the pride and diminish the resources of the king. Knowing that God was merciful, David chose the last of the three alternatives.

So the virulent plague descended. "From the morning until the time designated" (24:15), commonly taken to mean until the time of evening sacrifice (about 3:00 p.m.), seventy thousand "men" (presumably of combat age) died. At that point, on the first day instead of the third, God "relented" 2 Samuel 24:16 NASB). The plague must have

been terrible to kill so many in such a short time; that very fact helped to establish it as a supernatural act.

As David saw the terrifying specter of the angel of death, he offered a substitutionary sacrifice: himself and his house "Let your hand fall upon me and my family" (2 Samuel 24:17 NIV). God responded with a command through the prophet Gad to build an altar on the threshing floor of Araunah, a descendant of one of the original Jebusite inhabitants of the city. David acted promptly and sought to buy the floor. Second Chronicles 3:1 makes it clear that the threshing floor of Araunah was on the northeast hill of Jerusalem, which was also Mount Moriah, the place where Abraham offered Isaac (Genesis 22:2). So this sin and its results were important in bringing under royal control the area where the Temple was later to be built.

David, a Man after God's Own Heart

With the rehearsal of David's sins and the terrible punishment of them, we wonder how Scripture could be so positive about him and could describe him as a man after God's own heart (Acts 13:22; cf. 1 Samuel 13:13-14). In fact, many sneer at the description and ask how that can be can be applied to David when he was guilty of adultery and murder. The answer must lie first in the evaluation of Saul's actions. He had been disobedient in carrying out God's direct commands. In his public policies he had failed God and later had even sought to kill God's anointed (David). Therefore, God had rejected him. And God sought out a man after His own heart to lead His people (1 Samuel 13:14).

David, on the other hand, remained faithful to God in his public pronouncements and actions. He respected the anointed of God (Saul) and refused to kill him even under the greatest duress. In his early warfare, which is all that is described in any detail, he sought God's instruction about going into battle. He made the sanctuary of God prominent in Jerusalem at the center of the affairs of state and sought to build a house for God. When denied the privilege, he amassed quantities of precious metals for the purpose instead of collecting them for himself as other Oriental potentates did. He organized the worship of Israel and honored God in prayer in the presence of the whole assembly (1 Chronicles 29:10-13). Moreover, he wrote many psalms, some of which were adapted for the ritual of public worship.

Second, David was a man after God's own heart even in his private or inner life. He meditated on the Word of God and generally had a beautiful devotional life, as the psalms he wrote indicate. To be sure he sinned and sinned grievously, and he paid dearly for his failures. But what matters especially is what he did about his sins. He had a heart tender toward God. When he realized his sins or was confronted with them, he demonstrated a broken and a contrite heart and sought God's forgiveness. It must be remembered that he lived before the cross, before there was a canon of Scripture, and before the permanent indwelling of the Holy Spirit in the believer. His was the faithful struggle of an earnest human soul to know God. Even though he suffered shipwreck as he sailed the seas of life, by the grace of God he never went down for the third time. Modern believers may identify with him as they struggle against heavy seas, and by grace they may experience the same rescuing and sustaining hand of God.

The Government of Solomon

Contested Accession to the Throne

Adonijah announced, "I will be king." (1 Kings 1:5)

King David was "old, advanced in years" (1 Kings 1:1) and obviously no longer capable of governing effectively. When an absolute monarch ceases to function, there is virtually no government at all and ambitious persons grow impatient to take power.

Adonijah clearly represents such an ambitious person. Evidently he was David's eldest living son now that Amnon, Absalom, and probably Chileab had died. Though primogeniture had not been established for succession to the throne in Israel, it was common elsewhere in the Near East and

in other aspects of Israelite society. Moreover, he is described as "very handsome" (v. 6) and presumably that made him somewhat popular. To bolster his image he procured chariots (state chariots, not war chariots) and horsemen and fifty runners (as a guard of honor), as Absalom had done before him (2 Samuel 15:1). Absalom also won the support of two of David's inner circle: Joab, who had served as his commander of the armed forces, and Abiathar, the high priest.

Adonijah began his usurpation, as Absalom had (2 Samuel 15:12), with a sacrifice and a common meal at which he was proclaimed king. Such a meal had the effect of uniting his followers in a joint venture. The feast took place at En-Rogel, the southern spring of the city, located where the valleys of the Kidron and Hinnom join, near the modern village of Silwan. Invited to the feast were all the king's sons except Solomon, the Judeans who were in the king's service, and Joab and Abiathar (v. 19). Specifically excluded was the Solomonic faction, including Nathan (the court prophet), Benaiah (captain of the king's bodyguard, 2 Samuel 8:18; 23:20-23), Zadok (the priest), and David's "mighty men." Either they were not invited or refused to participate in Adonijah's coronation.

Jerusalem was a small city of less than fifteen acres in David's day, and Adonijah's plans could not have been kept from the Solomonic faction for very long. Nathan swung into action and staged a carefully orchestrated drama involving the entrance of Bathsheba, his own precisely timed entrance, the manipulated response of David, and the coronation of Solomon (1 Kings 1:11-31).

Deeply stirred by these audiences and goaded by the urgency of a coronation ceremony in progress, David acted promptly. First he called Bathsheba and assured her that Solomon would succeed him on the throne. Then he laid careful plans to defuse the impact of Adonijah's actions. He called in Zadok, Nathan, and Benaiah, the ranking priest, prophet, and soldier loyal to him, and issued a series of commands.

(1) "Take the servants of your lord," the total party loyal to him, including the Cherethites and Pelethites, the palace

guards. (2) "Cause Solomon . . . to mount my own mule," evidence that David was turning authority over to Solomon. (3) "Take him to Gihon" (just outside the east wall of the city in the Kidron Valley) and let Zadok and Nathan anoint him there (Adonijah was not officially anointed). As there was no prophet in Adonijah's camp, Nathan's presence indicated divine choice of Solomon as king. (4) "Blow the ram's horn and cry, 'Long live king Solomon,'" as a solemn proclamation after the anointing. (5) Accompany Solomon back into the city and place him on my throne where he is to be king over Israel and Judah.

Immediately the three stalwart supporters of the king, the Cherethites and Pelethites, and others hurried to do exactly as David had ordered. Zadok "took the horn of oil" (evidently the animal's horn that held holy anointing oil used for anointing priests and vessels of the sanctuary) "from the tent" (the tent David had set up for the ark of the covenant on Mount Zion, 2 Samuel 6:17) "and anointed Solomon." "All the people," both the official group and the spontaneous gathering, made a tremendous racket as they celebrated. "Piping with pipes" is a better rendering than "playing on flutes." This was no gentle sweetness of orchestral flutes, but pipes used as noisemakers. The din was so great that the earth seemed almost "to burst in pieces" (v. 40).

The noise of Solomon's inaugural celebration reached the ears of Adonijah and his company just as their feast was coming to an end. They could hear but not see the inauguration for although less than seven hundred yards separated the two companies, there was a slight rise in the ground and a curve in the valley between. As the group stood there looking at each other and asking questions, Abiathar's son Jonathan came on the scene and reported exactly what had happened.

The news of the day's events spread terror among Adonijah's guests. They all fled, seeking to distance themselves from the traitor as fast as they could. Adonijah fled to the tabernacle and claimed refuge by grasping the horns of the bronze altar in the tabernacle courtyard. Someone brought a report of Adonijah's action to Solomon with the plea that Adonijah not be executed. Solomon agreed on the condition that Adonijah behave himself in the future. Then Adonijah came and did homage to the newly enthroned king and Solomon sent him home in peace, with the expectation that he retire to private life.

"Oriental Cruelty" or Administrative Justice?

Was David's advice to Solomon that he deal with Joab and Shimei just a "piece of oriental cruelty," as the critics often claim? Not necessarily. After all, both Joab and Shimei had committed acts worthy of the death penalty. Moreover, as both of them had been a problem or threat to David, they could also be a threat to Solomon. Then, too, modern Americans need to remember that ancient Semitic governance prescribed the death penalty for many crimes that would not warrant the same treatment today. In today's business world, people who were an irritant have sometimes been tolerated until a new executive or supervisor takes over—and then they are gone.

If David, in fact, erred in his judgment here, it should be noted that inspiration of Scripture does not necessarily involve approval of the conduct of an individual; it only guarantees accurate reporting of what the person thought or did.

His Father's Charge (1 Kings 2:1-12)

After Solomon had been anointed and installed into office, he probably assumed the day-to-day responsibilities of government. Some months later, as David grew weaker, he recognized that his death was near. So he issued a twofold deathbed charge to his son: a personal charge and an administrative charge. The personal charge is similar in some respects to the one Moses gave Joshua (Joshua 1:6-9) and to the farewell God gave to Joshua (Deuteronomy 31:23). Keeping the commandments of God would assure Solomon of personal success and dynastic perpetuity. Though God's covenant with David was perpetual, it did not necessarily promise that it would be visibly operative in every generation, regardless of the conduct of kings in the Davidic line.

David turned Solomon's attention first to Joab, commander of the armed forces, who had often served David well. He had captured Jerusalem (2 Samuel 5) and Rabbah, capital of Ammon (2 Samuel 12), and had protected David at the beginning of Absalom's revolt (2 Samuel 14). But Joab was guilty of a double murder: of Abner (2 Samuel 3:22-27) and Amasa (2 Samuel 20:4-10). In both cases Joab had caused David great administrative and personal hurt. At the time David was unable to deal forcefully with Joab because of the unstable political and military situation and Joab's great clout with the army. Joab had also killed Absalom and had just recently been involved in the Adonijah affair, but David passed over those and other failures of Joab. Do not let him die a natural death, he urged.

Shimei, a Benjamite, had cursed David and had threatened his life at the time of Absalom's rebellion, but David had spared his life (2 Samuel 16:5-14; 19:22-23). Why the king now felt that judgment had to be executed against Shimei is not clear. Possibly David felt that Shimei, as a Benjamite from the neighborhood of King Saul, might strike at David's son as he had struck at David.

But David was not all negative. He wanted Solomon to show kindness to the sons of Barzillai, an aged man who had provided for David during his flight from Absalom and perhaps had saved him from starvation (2 Samuel 17:27-29).

His Purge of Royal Enemies (1 Kings 2:13-46)

"Thus the kingdom was established in the hand of Solomon." (1 Kings 2:46 NKJV)

After the death of David, Solomon eliminated those who posed any threat to him or those his father had urged him to dispose of. Critics are often cynical about Solomon's actions in this passage, considering him to have engaged in a callous, systematic elimination of all threats to his rule. They have him looking for pretexts to destroy all who might be dangerous to him. At this distance and on the basis of the limited amount of biblical material available, we cannot possibly accurately assess his actions. He did have good reasons for most of his actions, and he was young and inexperienced— supposedly not much over twenty at the time. If he was too severe, perhaps his immaturity and insecurity led him to be more suspicious, condemnatory, and vengeful than he needed to be. After all, he had just survived his older brother's plot to take the throne. In addition, he may well have been aware of intrigues that are not recorded in Scripture.

First Solomon moved against Adonijah (1 Kings 2:13-25). Adonijah's undoing was his request to marry Abishag, David's nurse and constant companion during the last couple of years of his life. To help us understand Solomon's action we need to remember that custom dictated that the royal harem belonged to the new king (see 2 Samuel 3:6-16; 16:20–23). Solomon interpreted the request as a claim to the throne and retorted that his mother might as well have requested the kingdom for Adonijah, Abiathar, and Joab (v. 22). Keep in mind that the king was young and somewhat insecure. The entire Adonijah faction was also still alive and potentially threatening. Finally, a young adolescent coming of age had just entertained a request from a mother who may have been somewhat domineering. Evidently Bathsheba had touched a raw nerve. Under the circumstances, Solomon's reaction was predictable; he ordered Adonijah's execution.

Having disposed of Adonijah, Solomon next moved against Abiathar the priest. He removed Abiathar from office and sent him back to private life in his home village of Anathoth, about three miles northeast of Jerusalem. Solomon deemed him worthy of death for participation in Adonijah's revolt, but because of Abiathar's high-priestly dignity and his faithful service to David from the time of his persecution at the hand of Saul through Absalom's rebellion, he simply banished Abiathar (2:26-27).

When Joab heard what had happened to Adonijah and Abiathar, he evidently concluded that Solomon was now moving against all the principals in the abortive attempt to crown Adonijah. Joab, like Adonijah after the coup, fled to the "tent," probably the sanctuary at Gibeon, and grasped the horns of the bronze altar of sacrifice in the courtyard. God had declared this a place of refuge for those unjustly accused of a crime or those guilty of minor crimes or accidental manslaughter—but not for deliberate murder (Exodus 21:13-14). Therefore, Joab must have thought Solomon was after him for insurrection. But David in his charge to Solomon had mentioned only Joab's guilt for two deliberate murders, for which there was no protection. Solomon ordered his execution. Thus Solomon removed any blood guiltiness that remained on the king and his house—a guilt that existed because Joab had committed his crimes while dispensing official duties.

Then Solomon proceeded to deal with Shimei, the last person mentioned in David's charge (2:36-46). He put Shimei on a short tether. He had to live in Jerusalem and not cross the Kidron. After three years two of his servants ran away and Shimei violated the restrictions placed on him by going to search for them and paid with his life.

Solomon may have shared some of the superstition of Near Easterners that executing one who had levied a curse eliminated the curse on his house and himself. With the curse lifted, he could be more sure "King Solomon will be blessed" (v. 45). And with the elimination of all the known threats to the throne, the historian could confidently announce: "The kingdom was established in the hand of Solomon" (v. 46).

His Choice of Wisdom (1 Kings 3:2-28)

Solomon held a kind of inaugural religious ceremony at Gibeon near the beginning of his reign. A large number of officials and clan leaders of all Israel attended it (see 2 Chronicles 1:1-13). Zadok apparently served as the resident priest (1 Chronicles 16:39). On that occasion Solomon offered "a thousand burnt offerings," either to be taken literally or to indicate a very large number. At such sacrifices it was customary to burn only part of the animal as an offering to God; the worshipers ate the rest in a fellowship meal. The size of the crowd would have required a very large number of sacrifices. In the context of this moment of religious ecstasy and in response to this sacrifice to God for blessing on his reign, God appeared to Solomon and in effect said, "Ask for what you would like me to give you."

Was Solomon Uniformly Wise?

God gave Solomon judicial wisdom or discerning judgment, not necessarily wisdom for all of life. He was not uniformly wise. For example, his lack of fiscal judgment or fiscal restraint left the kingdom virtually bankrupt at his death. His lack of wisdom in marital matters resulted in the collection of a harem of seven hundred wives and three hundred concubines. This dramatically increased idolatry, the financial burden on the state, and created impossible conditions for the conduct of proper family life. Having said this, however, we have to infer that the book of Proverbs and other biblical and non-biblical references do indicate that Solomon's wisdom was far-reaching. But possession of wisdom of a certain sort does not necessarily mean that one will have the courage or restraint or perseverance to pursue a wise course of action.

The king responded first with thanksgiving, then with a sense of inadequacy, and finally with his request. Solomon thanked God for His great covenant love and favor to His faithful, covenant-keeping servant David and then for extending His kindness in putting Solomon on the throne.

Solomon's Cabinet

Whereas David established the Israelite kingdom as a viable, unified monarchy, his successor Solomon turned the nation into a world-class trading and military power. Twelve governors oversaw administrative districts (see 1 Kings 4:7–19), while a cabinet of senior officials served Solomon at Jerusalem.

Name	Position	Responsibilities
Azariah the son of Zadok	High priest	Oversaw worship and religious rituals, representing the people to God.
Elihoreph and Ahijah, the sons of Shisha	Scribes	Similar to secretaries of state or chancellors.
Jehoshaphat the son of Ahilud	Recorder	Maintained written historical records of the king's business and decisions.
Benaiah the son of Jehoiada (see 1 Kings 2:29)	Military commander	Oversaw the nation's defenses, including its storage and chariot cities; led the army in military engagements; handled royal police matters (for example, 1 Kings 2:28–35).
Zadok and Abiathar	Priests	Oversaw religious matters and served as custodians of the Law.
Azariah the son of Nathan	General	Carried out the military orders of Solomon and Benaiah.
Zabud the son of Nathan	Personal confidant	Consulted with the king on personal matters.
Ahishar	Manager of Solomon's household	Oversaw the palace complex and the needs of Solomon's extensive court (1 Kings 4:22–23; 11:3).
Adoniram the son of Abda	Manager of the labor force	Oversaw Solomon's numerous construction projects (1 Kings 5:13; 7:1–8; 9:15–19).

But he was overwhelmed with his youth and inexperience and the multitude of the people to be governed. "Little child" (v. 7) is an oriental figure of speech expressing humility; but he was young, as noted earlier. The statement should be taken in conjunction with what follows: "I do not know how to go out or come in," which is an idiom for "inexperienced in leadership."

Then Solomon made his request for a "discerning heart" or "judicial wisdom" to "judge" or "govern your people," to "judge between good and evil," or in equity and truth. God congratulated Solomon and said that since he had not asked for long life or wealth or victory in warfare but for "discerning judgment," He would grant his request. He would give him a "wise and discerning mind" such as never had been before nor ever will be in the future. Unfortunately, except for a hint or two, such as his actions when two women squabbling over possession of a baby appeared before him, the Bible gives us no report on Solomon's legal or juridical system or his social order.

Then the God of the "superabundantly above" granted Solomon what he did not ask for: riches and honor greater than that of all other contemporary kings. It is hard to evaluate verse 14: a promise of long life in return for obedience to God's statutes. Solomon was obedient during the early part of his reign and then became involved in idolatry. Though he ruled for forty years, life may have been cut short for disobedience. He must have died when not much older than sixty.

His Wisdom in Evidence in Administration (1 Kings 4:1-19)

His chief officials (4:1-6). Solomon appointed eleven men as a kind of cabinet for administration of the state. Though delegation of authority is a mark of wisdom, he was not the first ruler in Israel to do so. In fact, his father had appointed men with similar functions, and even some of the names are the same (2 Samuel 8:16-18; 20:23-26). We cannot give Solomon credit for something David inaugurated.

The list of officials seems simple enough, but identification of the individuals and their functions is another matter. Four of the eleven are called priests: Azariah, Zadok, Abiathar, and Zabud. But that does not necessarily mean that they functioned as such. Zadok clearly served as high priest. Abiathar had been demoted from the priesthood at the outset of Solomon's reign but presumably retained the title and honor even though Solomon did not permit him to function. Some scholars believe that Azariah served as administrator of the kingdom, a sort of prime minister. Zabud was "the king's friend," evidently a personal counselor. The NIV captures the intent: "personal advisor to the king."

The Bible lists Elihoreph and Ahijah as secretaries. Apparently they had responsibilities connected with writing, and one should not think of them as holding such posts as secretary of state or secretary of the interior. They probably took care of domestic and foreign correspondence, kept records and supervised the archives. Jehoshaphat is commonly identified as "recorder," as maintaining records of daily affairs in the kingdom. But secretaries do that. In recent years the idea of "herald" has been extracted from the Hebrew. So this person may have had the task of communicating between king and country and of taking charge of arranging royal ceremonies (including audiences).

Solomon appointed Benaiah commander-in-chief of the forces. He put Azariah (v. 5) in charge of the regional or district governors named in verses 7-19. This was a new office instituted by Solomon in his reorganization of the kingdom. Ahishar was "in charge of the palace"; the NEB has "comptroller of the household." Apparently he had charge of the household staff, functions of the household (preparation of meals, etc.), and the maintenance and cleaning of the palace structure. Adoniram supervised "forced labor," evidently for such purposes as fortification, building of

the seaport at Ezion-geber, or the construction of roads and bridges.

We have to assume that these eleven functioned as only a small part of the official family. Jones estimates that in the days of David and Solomon the public payroll in the Jerusalem area probably stood at upwards of 5,600 court officials and their dependents.[3]

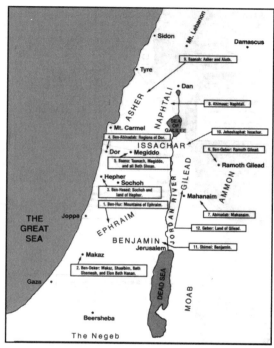

Solomon's Administrative Districts
The growth and extension of Israel's borders under Solomon's leadership resulted in a very large kingdom (1 Kings 4:20–21). Solomon faced an urgent need for ever increasing revenues to meet expenditures on building and commercial projects throughout his expanding kingdom. To address this need, the king divided Israel into twelve districts and appointed over each district a governor responsible for levying and collecting taxes.

His District Organization (4:7-19). As the bureaucracy grew, Solomon found it necessary to make provision for it. He divided the land into twelve districts, each under the supervision of a district governor. He ordered each district to provide food for the royal household for one month of the year—but there was a fatal flaw in the divisions. He exempted Judah. Yes, the twelve districts in number equaled the twelve tribes of Israel, but the districts were not coextensive with the old tribal regions. Since he exempted Judah from the obligation, the term "Israel" does not refer to all of Israel in this passage. Judah's favored status accentuated tribal rivalries and contributed to the split that occurred in Rehoboam's day.

The districts were as follows. (1) The hill country of Ephraim (including Samaria, Shiloh, Bethel, etc.). (2) A section of the Shephelah or foothills southeast of modern Tel Aviv. (3) The central Sharon plain and Mount Carmel. (4) The coastal region north of the third district. (5) The northern hill country, including Megiddo, Taanach, and Dothan. (6) The old territory of Bashan, northeast of the Sea of Galilee. (7) Gilead and western Ammon. (8) The land of Naphtali, west of the Sea of Galilee and north to Dan. (9) The land of Asher, to the west of Naphtali. (10) Land southwest of the Sea of Galilee, including Jezreel. (11) Benjamin, a narrow swath extending west from Jericho about two-thirds of the way across western Palestine. (12) The land of Gad, much of old Moab.

This organization and list must date to the latter half of Solomon's reign because two of the governors are clearly sons-in-law of Solomon (vv. 11, 15). The list also does not include the towns of the plain of Acco, which were transferred to Hiram of Tyre about the middle of his reign (1 Kings 9:10-14).

His Wisdom in Evidence in Intellectual Achievement (1 Kings 4:29-34)

Again the sacred historian emphasizes that "God gave Solomon wisdom." But the wisdom described here is of a more general sort than the judicial wisdom of 3:28. God's endowment of "wisdom," "discernment" or "insight," and "understanding" or "largeness of mind" was to be immeasurable "as sands on the seashore." This "wisdom" (hokmah) involves an understanding of the basic issues of life, a proper discernment between good and evil, and a skill in performing business affairs and the han-

dling of people.[4] "Discernment" or "insight" (bînah) concerns the ability to distinguish between truth and error, between the valid and invalid.[5] "Largenes of mind" probably refers to breadth of interests. Solomon's wisdom exceeded that of the "people" or "sons of the east" (usually a reference to the Arab tribes east of Israel and extending to the Euphrates) and of "Egypt" (known for its wisdom literature; e. g., of Ptah-hotep, ca. 2450 B.C.; and Amenemope, ca. 1000 B.C.).

Next, his wisdom is declared to be superior to that of several specific individuals who must have been highly regarded in Solomon's day. They are almost completely unknown now. Ethan the Ezrahite appears in the title of Psalm 89 and presumably he wrote that psalm; Ethan and Heman were musicians according to 1 Chronicles 15:19.

The biblical record credits Solomon with three thousand proverbs (short, pithy sayings setting forth truth in the form of simile or metaphor) and "a thousand and five" songs. Since canonical proverbs contain only eight hundred verses and the Song of Solomon a limited number of songs (in addition to Psalms 72 and 127), the great king must have been responsible for much that has not been preserved. The reference to his knowledge of botany and zoology may refer only to his insights in those fields as revealed in his proverbs, or to more scientific studies such as botanical or zoological classifications.

The fame of Solomon's wisdom attracted people who wanted to "hear" it from his own lips. The coming of the queen of Sheba (1 Kings 10), whose visit will be discussed later, is the only biblical example of such a visit. "All the kings of the earth" is hyperbole designed to describe a widespread practice.

His Palace Complex (1 Kings 7:1-12; 10:18-20)

Solomon spent thirteen years building his palace complex, which functioned as the administrative hub of his kingdom. The buildings or functional structures in the royal complex are five in number, apparently introduced from south to north as one moves from the City of David toward the

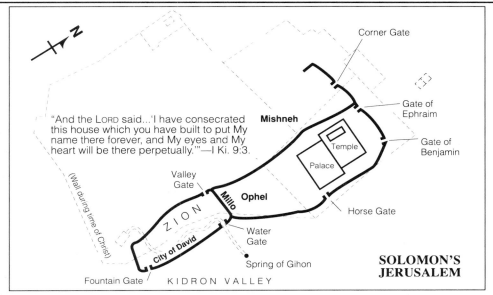

"And the LORD said...'I have consecrated this house which you have built to put My name there forever, and My eyes and My heart will be there perpetually.'"—I Ki. 9:3.

SOLOMON'S JERUSALEM

temple. They are: the House of the Forest of Lebanon, the hall of pillars, the throne room, a palace for Pharaoh's daughter, and a palace for Solomon. A courtyard enclosed by a stone wall surrounded the area. Unfortunately detail is so sketchy as to prevent a clear picture of size, nature, and function of the structures.

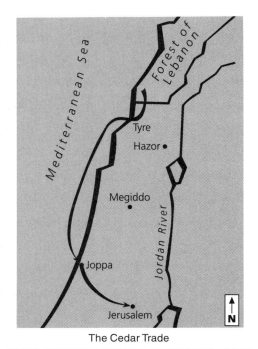

The Cedar Trade

The House of the Forest of Lebanon is so called because of the extensive use of cedar of Lebanon in the building. The exterior was built of stone, as was true of the rest of the constructions in the complex. The dimensions were about one hundred-fifty feet long, seventy-five feet wide and forty-five feet high. It functioned primarily as a storehouse, though Solomon also used it as an armory (1 Kings 10:17; Isaiah 22:8). Four rows of cedar pillars supported the upper part of the structure (so Hebrew text, preferable to the three rows of the Septuagint). Then, presumably, two rows stood against the side walls and two rows stood opposite them to form side aisles.

The four rows then supported cedar beams that, in turn, supported chambers above them. I infer from the Hebrew that verse 3 refers not to forty-five pillars but to forty-five chambers in three stories, fifteen to a story on each side of the building. Thus the rooms could be about ten feet wide and useful for storage of armaments.

Visualization of the interior of the building based on this interpretation is as follows. Two rows of pillars supported three stories of rooms on either of the long sides of the building. A large assembly hall with a high ceiling occupied the middle section, with the central aisle open to the roof beams. At either end of the hall were three rows of windows (v. 4) with latticework (see Hebrew; cf. 1 Kings 6:4). Three doors faced each other at either end of the structure (v. 5).

The hall of pillars (v. 6) may have been freestanding, though it was probably attached to one end of the House of the Forest of Lebanon. It measured fifty cubits (seventy-five feet) long, as long as the previously mentioned structure was wide. Apparently it was an open portico. The last part of verse 6 is difficult to translate, but very possibly it refers to a columned porch placed in the middle of the portico, much as a propylaeum or vestibule to some Greek temple or complex, such as the Acropolis at Athens.

Next, the writer mentions the throne hall or hall of judgment (v. 7), which probably was a separate freestanding structure, and may have been connected with the hall of pillars. The latter could provide plenty of space for persons to wait to see the king or to socialize after an audience with him. The building was paneled with cedar from floor to ceiling.

Solomon's throne was made of wood and inlaid with ivory. Apparently the wooden parts not inlaid were covered with gold. Though there is some controversy over the nature of the back of it, the Hebrew text indicates it was "rounded" (10:19), and there were arm rests. Six steps approached the throne, which apparently stood on a seventh level or dais. At either end of each of the six steps stood a lion, perhaps representing the twelve tribes of Israel. The lion seems to have been the symbol of the tribe of Judah and symbolized royal strength. We know nothing about the composition of the lions.

"Set farther back" (v. 8 NIV), or "in a court set back from the colonnade" (NEB), that is, in an inner courtyard, separated from the outer courtyard where the previously mentioned structures stood, Solomon had his private apartments and a house for Pharaoh's daughter (cf. 3:1; 9:24). We do not know what the chronicler means by the observation that these private dwellings were "similar in design." They were both built of limestone and paneled with cedar, as the following summary indicates.

"All these structures," all the ones described in verses 2-8, were made of "choice" or "costly" stone "cut to size" in the quarry and carefully dressed, "trimmed with a saw" on both the inside and outside. This was true of the foundations and the upper courses of the buildings all the way to the eaves, and of the wall surrounding the courtyard. Foundation stones were sometimes eight or ten cubits (twelve or fifteen feet) long.

Once plentiful in the mountains of Phoenicia, the cedars of Lebanon have suffered from centuries of reckless cutting. Only a few isolated groves remain today.

Carefully dressed cedar beams supported the roofs. The wall surrounding the royal complex was constructed like the temple courtyard wall with three courses of cut stone and one of cedar beams to give greater ability to absorb the shock of an earthquake. Perhaps it would be useful to note that Palestinian limestone is quite soft when first quarried, and hardens with exposure.

His Administrative Successes

"Judah and Israel. . . ate and drank and lived happily." (1 Kings 4:20, my translation)

His General Prosperity (4:20-28). This passage portrays Solomon's kingdom as secure and prosperous. Prosperity is defined first in terms of a large population: "as numerous as the sand by the sea" (v. 20; and secondly by the fact that these people generally enjoyed the basic comforts of life: "They ate, and drank, and lived happily" (v. 20; the last expression appears only here in the Old Testament).

Earthquake Proofing the Temple

The effort to make the temple more earthquake proof by using three courses of cut stone and one of cedar beams—enabling the building to absorb more shock—was a wise one. The whole Mediterranean region is earthquake prone, and Palestine is no exception. Serious earthquakes occur in Palestine about once every fifty years. A great geological fault extends from Mount Hermon through the Gulf of Aqaba down into East Africa.

The Bible frequently mentions earthquakes. For instance, a great earthquake in the days of King Uzziah was remembered long afterward (Amos 1:1; Zechariah 14:5). Matthew mentions an earthquake at the time of the Crucifixion when the curtain of the temple was ripped in two, the earth shook, and the rocks were split (Matthew 27:51).

Interestingly, the temple area is on a line of structural weakness. The El-Aqsa Mosque, which stands there today, has been damaged by earthquakes more than once in history. The last serious earthquake occurred in 1927. Some tremors have been strong enough to cause damage to the Church of the Holy Sepulcher and the buildings in the temple area.

Israel experienced a wonderful security, a kind of *Pax Hebraica* or Hebrew peace. Solomon's rule extended to all the lands from Tipsah (Greek, Thapsacus) at the bend of the Euphrates in the north to the land of Philistia in the west and the "border of Egypt" (the Wadi el-Arish at the northern edge of the Sinai) in the south. The various subject peoples of these lands brought tribute, and Solomon generally enjoyed peace. Presumably the unrest in Edom and Syria that arose at the beginning of his reign (1 Kings 11:14-25) was not a serious threat to the well-being of the empire. At least from Dan to Beersheba, the traditional borders of Hebrew Palestine, Judah and Israel "dwelt in safety" (v. 25).

This security pervaded not only because of the blessing of God but also because of Solomon's fortifications and military preparedness. He kept 12,000 horses (v. 26; cf. 2 Chronicles 1:14) in 4,000 "stalls" or "chariot parks," where three horses for each chariot were stabled together in pens. The figure of 40,000 stalls in the Hebrew of verse 26 must be a copyist's error and 4,000 has been adopted from the parallel passage in 2 Chronicles 9:25. Solomon maintained 1,400 chariots (2 Chronicles 1:14) in several locations called "chariot cities" (2 Chronicles 9:25; cf. 1 Kings 9:19).

The general peace and prosperity made it possible for the twelve district governors to maintain regular deliveries of barley (the ordinary food of horses in ancient Palestine) and straw for the horses and a large daily provision for the king's table (for the support of public officials). That provision included thirty kors of fine flour (if computed at the usual rate of 6.3 bushels to the kor, the total would be 189 bushels), sixty kors of ordinary flour (378 bushels), and a substantial list of domesticated and wild animals. Fruits and vegetables were not included in the tally.

The Elements of His Glory (1 Kings 9:10—10:29). Solomon's construction projects are almost too numerous to itemize. They include the temple, the palace complex, supporting terraces on which buildings could be erected, the extension of the wall of Jerusalem northward to enclose the palace complex and the temple (more than doubling the enclosed area of the city), a string of fortresses and store cities (for horses and chariots and supplies for the army), a seaport, and merchant marine.

Solomon's system of fortresses created a formidable barrier for would-be invaders. Hazor guarded a strategic point north of the Sea of Galilee; Megiddo stood at the base of the Plain of Esdraelon; Beth-horon blocked the pass to Jerusalem by way of Aijalon; Baalath stood on the highway from Jerusalem to the port of Joppa; Gezer protected the main road and entrance to the valley of Sorek; Tamar on the southern border could defend caravans from Ezion-geber. No

Remains of the massive gate complex at Gezer. Solomon rebuilt the city and its defenses (1 Kings 9:15–17).

fortress stood east of Jerusalem, the valley of the Jordan being considered a sufficient barrier. Excavations at Hazor, Megiddo and Gezer reveal significant Solomonic construction at each place.

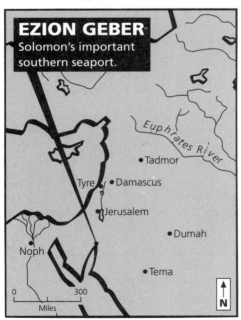

EZION GEBER
Solomon's important southern seaport.

Euphrates River
• Tadmor
Tyre • Damascus
• Jerusalem
• Dumah
Noph
• Tema
0   300
Miles
N

Though Joppa provided a port of sorts on the Mediterranean, Solomon established a much more effective port at Ezion-geber, near modern Eilat on the Red Sea. Hiram was happy to help build harbor facilities there, to help the Hebrews construct a mer-

chant marine, and then to provide sailors to operate the fleet.

The chronicler pegs Solomon's annual income in gold at 666 talents (1 Kings 10:14), computed to weigh twenty-five tons, according to the NIV margin. We need to remember, however, that this was not his personal income but revenues of the national treasury, to be used for national defense, the public payroll, capital improvements, ceremonial functions, sacrifices (e. g., 1 Kings 9:25), maintenance of the merchant marine, and much more. Of course, Solomon's income would not have been so substantial during the early part of his reign. We do not know when he reached this plateau or from what sources his income came.

(For more on this topic, go to p. 111 or p. 224.)

Religion

Institutional Religion

God's Dwelling Place— the Tabernacle

"Then the cloud covered the tabernacle of meeting, and the glory of the lord filled the tabernacle." (Exodus 40:34 NKJV)

From the time of its construction in the wilderness until Solomon built the temple the tabernacle or "tent of meeting" served as the place where God's people might meet Him. During and after the Conquest, the tabernacle was centrally located at Shiloh, about twenty miles north of Jerusalem. But choice of location may also have been partially dictated by the powerful tribe of Ephraim, in whose territory Shiloh lay. The tabernacle remained in Shiloh during the whole period of the judges and was there during the youth of Samuel, along with the Ark of the Covenant.

For many, confidence in the presence of the Ark had beccome a form of fetishism—the ultimate good luck charm. They believed magical potency dwelt in the object itself. When the Philistines pressed the Israelites virtually to the wall during the time of the judges, the Israelites took the Ark of the covenant into battle. But when the army of the people of God went into battle with greater trust in a piece of religious furniture than in the God whose presence it symbolized, they lost the battle and the Ark itself (see subsequent discussion on warfare). When the Philistines returned the Ark seven months later, they took it to Kiriath-jearim (c. 10 miles west of Jerusalem), where it remained until the time of David (1 Samuel 7:2).

What happened to the rest of the tabernacle is not clear. Evidently the Philistines leveled the site of Shiloh after capturing the Ark. Excavations there indicate Shiloh's destruction about 1050 B.C. Of course the tabernacle was portable, but we do not know whether the Israelites were able to flee with all of the furniture to another location. Later Samuel transferred worship to Mizpah, probably Tell en-Nasbeh, eight miles north of Jerusalem (1 Samuel 7:6). But nothing is said about the tabernacle's location there. In David's day at least the bread of the Presence was kept at Nob, on a hill near Jerusalem, location uncertain (1 Samuel 21:1-6).

Then as Solomon began his reign, he made a great sacrifice at Gibeon, about eight miles northwest of Jerusalem on the route to Joppa. Scripture says that the tabernacle which Moses had made in the wilderness was there, and before it was the bronze altar which Bezaleel had cast in the wilderness (see 1 Kings 3:4; 1 Chronicles 16:39; 21:29; 2 Chronicles 1:3-6). Very possibly the tabernacle had been transferred to Gibeon after the destruction of Nob at the hands of Saul (1 Samuel 22:17-19).

So then, the tabernacle may have been moved from Shiloh to Nob after the destruction of Shiloh and transferred from Nob to Gibeon after the destruction of Nob. But the comments dating to Solomon's reign say nothing about the table of the bread of the Presence, the altar of incense, or the seven-branched lampstand. The focus of attention centers on the tabernacle and the altar of burnt offering. We do not know whether the other pieces of furniture still existed.

David's Bringing the Ark to Jerusalem (2 Samuel 6:1-23). As David tried to establish his kingdom effectively, he thought it was high time to give the Ark a proper home. The Ark of the Covenant was so-called because it contained the two tablets of stone on which God had written the Ten Commandments, the terms of God's covenant with Israel. It was also called the "ark of God" (1 Samuel 3:3; 4:11) because it was the throne of divine presence.

To give the occasion proper grandeur, David assembled thirty thousand chosen representatives of the nation to accompany the Ark. On the appointed day the vast throng marched out of Jerusalem westward to Baale Judah (an alternate name for Kiriath Jearim), about ten miles away. There the Ark had rested in the house of Abinadab ever since it had returned from Philistine territory some seventy years before.

Evidently, during the Ark's long tenure in the household of Abinadab, little effort had been made to learn the sacred regulations concerning it. Thus neither Uzzah and Ahio nor David and his advisers paid attention to the Levitical laws governing its transportation. For example, it was to be properly covered and carried by Levites and was never to be touched except by staves on pain of death (cf. Numbers 4:5, 15, 19-20). So, contrary to divine instructions, they carried the ark on a new carriage. When Uzzah put his hand on it to steady it at the threshing floor of Nachon (place unknown, but certainly near Jerusalem), God struck him down "for his irreverence" (6:7 NASB).

Suddenly the great celebration of David and the other Israelites turned to stunned silence. The "anger" (6:7) that God had demonstrated over the act of Uzzah was reciprocated by the anger of David, but against whom is not clear. Some commentators feel that he was extremely displeased with himself for being a party to faulty arrangements. He could also have been very distraught because what had begun as such an auspicious occasion had turned into a fiasco, and the tragedy was a reflection on his own administration. Soon David's displeasure turned to the fear of God, the fear of further judgment of God against him and his people. To avoid that and to wait for further light and direction, he decided not to bring the ark into the citadel.

We are not told how the thirty thousand representatives of the nation responded as they witnessed this act of God, but His fear must have fallen on them also. And the lesson that God sought to teach Israel should not be lost on our generation with its tendency to ignore the majesty, sovereignty, and holiness of God and the resultant lack of connection between Christian profession and personal holiness.

Unwilling to take the ark into Jerusalem, David deposited it in the home of Obed-Edom the Gittite, evidently near the threshing floor where the death of Uzzah had occurred. Apparently Obed-Edom fulfilled the Levitical requirements for caring for the ark, and God blessed him and his household.

Weeks passed. David saw no evidence that Obed-Edom's household would suffer harm or inconvenience from the presence of the ark. In fact, the reason for God's judgment against Uzzah had been improper transportation of the ark (1 Chronicles 15:13). When these two facts converged in David's mind, he resolved to bring the ark into Jerusalem and install it in the tent he had prepared for it.

This time proper arrangements had been made for carrying the ark, with extensive preparations to ensure that everything would be just right. Then with solemn rejoicing the multitude brought the ark to Jerusalem (1 Chronicles 15). But when the bearers of the ark had carried it six paces and saw that God was pleased with their conduct, they stopped and David offered sacrifices. Then the procession continued to the place in the citadel of Jerusalem that David had prepared for the ark. Once the Ark of the Covenant had been properly installed, David sacrificed burnt offerings and peace offerings. A fellowship meal followed for the assembled throng, with David distributing food (2 Samuel 6:19).

God's Dwelling Place—the Temple

"And the glory of the LORD filled the temple" (2 Chronicles 7:1) *"Behold, heaven and the heaven of heavens cannot contain You. How much less this temple which I have built!"* (1 Kings 8:27 NKJV)

Solomon had established himself on his throne and had developed a certain amount of governmental machinery. Moreover, he had arranged a treaty with Hiram of Tyre that would assure him of the supplies and expertise required to build the temple. He began the project in the second month of his fourth year (967 or 966 B.C.) and completed it in the eighth month of his eleventh year (1 Kings 6:1, 38).

The General Plan (1 Kings 6:2-10). The temple measured sixty cubits long, twenty cubits wide, and thirty cubits high, double the dimensions of the tabernacle (Exodus 26:16,18). If the cubit is computed at its usual length of about eighteen inches, the measurements were ninety feet long, thirty feet wide, and forty-five feet high. Thus it was not a large structure; its expense in time and materials resulted not from size but care and exquisiteness of ornamentation.

The "portico" or "porch" in front of the temple extended across the entire structure (twenty cubits or thirty feet) and was ten cubits or fifteen feet deep. We do not know for sure what the windows were like (v. 4). The NIV considers them to be "clerestory windows," and they probably were, but that does not really describe them. The JPS and

NJB identify them as "latticed." Perhaps they were framed with immovable lattice-work that would permit circulation of air but would cut down the glare of bright light; small latticework would prevent the entrance of birds. "'Windows of narrow lights" (KJV) may indicate windows of close or small latticework.

According to verses 5, 6, 8, 10, rooms were built around three sides of the temple (excluding the entrance side). Constructed in three stories, they were entered on the "right" or "south" side of the temple. Rooms on the lower floor were five cubits broad on the inside; those on the middle level, six cubits; and those on the upper level, seven cubits. Thus the builders made the walls successively thinner on the two upper levels, creating ledges ("narrow ledges," NKJV) on which ceiling beams of cedar could be placed. This avoided cutting holes in the temple wall for ceiling beams (v. 6).

"Winding" stairs provided access to the upper floors, according to KJV, NASB, and JPS, but the nature of the stairs is not clear in the Hebrew. Evidently each of the three floors was five cubits high, giving a total of fifteen cubits. So the height of the roof of the temple proper was thirty cubits and the height of this service area fifteen cubits plus (if one adds ceilings), and windows on the side of the temple above the addition thus would be "clerestory" windows (v. 4 NIV).

There is a question whether the "cover-ing" with beams and planks of cedar (v. 9) refers to roofing (so NIV) or paneling on the inside of the stone work (so JPS). It seems that roofing ("beams and planks") is in view in this general descriptive; paneling of the interior is mentioned later (vv. 16-18). To maintain the dignity and sanctity of this holy place during construction, stone was so carefully prepared in the quarries that it was not necessary to use heavy tools to dress it on location (v. 7).

Completion and Ornamentation (1 Kings 6:14-38). When Solomon had completed the exterior stone work, he turned his attention to the interior of the temple. He lined the entire interior with boards of cedar from floor to ceiling, and covered the floor with planks of cypress. He left no stone exposed.

To form the Most Holy Place, Solomon instructed that a wooden screen be erected from floor to ceiling to partition off the rear twenty cubits of the interior. That left a Holy Place forty cubits long as a main hall.

He decorated the interior surface with "gourds" (oval ornaments) and "open flow-ers" (v. 18), with cherubim and palm trees (v. 29) carved into the wall. We do not know where all of this decoration was placed, but

Comparative Size of Temples

The temple of Solomon was not large, compared with other temples of antiquity. But to some degree it made up for lack of size with quality and expense of decoration. Its dimensions were 75 feet long, 30 feet wide, and 45 feet high. Its mea-surements were somewhat influ-enced by divine instructions, being double those of the tabernacle, which had been built according to God's specific direction.

By comparison, the well-known Parthenon in Athens was 238 feet long, 111 feet wide, and 65 feet high. The nearby temple of Jupiter was 354 feet long, 135 feet wide, and over 90 feet high.

At Baalbek in Lebanon the great temple of Jupiter measured 290 by 160 feet; its 65-foot columns were the tallest in the Greco-Roman world. Of course the top of the roof would have risen almost double that height. The adjacent temple of Bacchus was 87 feet long by 75 feet wide and had columns 57 feet high.

Babylon had many temples. Three of those excavated include the Ishtar (111 by 102 feet), Ninmah, goddess of the underworld (175 by 115 feet), and Marduk, patron deity of the city. The main building of this temple measured 281 by 262 feet. It was joined by a larger building (380 by 293 feet), of which only the outlines are known.

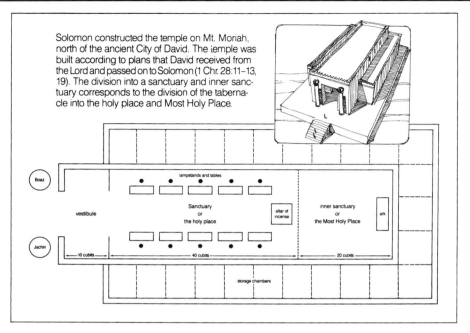

Solomon constructed the temple on Mt. Moriah, north of the ancient City of David. The temple was built according to plans that David received from the Lord and passed on to Solomon (1 Chr. 28:11-13, 19). The division into a sanctuary and inner sanctuary corresponds to the division of the tabernacle into the holy place and Most Holy Place.

on the basis of Ezekiel 41:17-18 and other Near Eastern decorative motifs, Keil suggests the alternation of cherubim and palm trees, with garlands of flowers above and a border of gourds below. A single band or row could have run around the wall, but he thinks a double or even triple band, located one above the other, was more likely.[6]

Then Solomon ordered preparation of an "inner sanctuary" or Most Holy Place. This was to be a cube: twenty cubits long, twenty cubits wide, and twenty cubits high that was placed behind the screen. That left ten cubits between it and the ceiling. Some suggest that it was elevated on a platform, but there is no evidence of that fact or of any steps needed to ascend to it. Probably there was simply a loft above it.

Within the Most Holy Place stood two immense cherubim (winged creatures with human faces), carved from olive wood and covered with gold. These were ten cubits high (half the height of the room) and each had a wingspan of ten cubits. When they were put in place against the west (back) wall, their combined wingspan extended across the entire wall, the wing of the one touching the north wall and the wing of the other touching the south wall. And their wings met in the center above the ark of the covenant. In front of the inner sanctuary

stood the altar of incense made of cedar wood and covered with gold. In fact, the entire inner surface of the temple is said to have been covered with gold (vv. 20-22, 30).

Verses 31-35 describe the doors, but the Hebrew is extremely difficult and unclear. At the entrance to the Most Holy Place there were doors of olive wood carved with cherubim, palm trees and flowers to match the inner walls and they were overlaid with gold, but the nature of the doors is uncertain. It seems that there was also a curtain (2 Chronicles 3:14) and a gold chain (v. 21) across this doorway. The doors of the Holy Place are likewise hard to visualize. But they were made of cypress wood and matched the doors of the Most Holy Place in carving and gold overlay.

The inner courtyard of the temple is described only in the most general terms (v. 36) as constructed of three rows of cut stone and a row of cedar beams. This would then be timbered masonry, with timber alternating with every three rows of masonry to provide flexibility in the walls in the event of an earthquake. We do not have the size of the courtyard, but if it was proportionate to the dimensions of the tabernacle courtyard, it must have been about one hundred-fifty feet wide by about four hundred feet long.

Furniture of the Temple (1 Kings 7:13–51). At Solomon's request (2 Chronicles 2:7), Hiram, king of Tyre, sent a craftsman to Solomon to direct the work of furnishing the temple. Though he had the same name as the king, he was unrelated to him. Perhaps it is important to note that he was half Israelite. His mother evidently was a Danite (2 Chronicles 2:13) who had married into the tribe of Naphtali. When her husband died, she married again as a widow of a Naphtalite, a Tyrian, and bore him Hiram. He was "endowed with wisdom, understanding, and knowledge" (v. 14) in craftsmanship in bronze; but according to 2 Chronicles 2:14, he could work effectively in gold, silver, iron, and other mediums as well. No doubt he brought with him additional skilled craftsmen.

Hiram's first task was to cast two great bronze pillars to flank the entrance to the temple. These freestanding columns rose twenty-seven feet into the air, and with their capitals reached to a total height of over thirty-four feet. They were eighteen feet in circumference and about six feet in diameter with a hollow center, the metal itself being three inches thick.

Freestanding pillars stood in front of some Phoenician temples and held a fire that glowed at night, but what function these pillars were supposed to serve is unclear. The pillar on the south (left) was called Jachin, "He [Yahweh] establishes," and the one on the north (right) Boaz, "In Him [Yahweh] is strength." At the minimum they were a witness to God's security and strength available to the Hebrews.

The next item to be described is the "sea of cast metal" (v. 23 NIV). According to 2 Chronicles 4:6 the sea was for priests to wash in. In view of the fact that it was seven and one-half feet high, either there had to be some means of siphoning off water or there was a means of ascent. Possibly this was also a source of water for lavers described later. This great bronze basin was fifteen feet from rim to rim. It rested on twelve bulls; their hindquarters toward the center and three of them facing each point of the compass. They may have represented the twelve tribes of Israel. The sea could hold two thousand baths. Computed at the usual rate of just under five gallons per bath, its capacity would have been a little less than ten thousand gallons.

Hiram also cast ten lavers for distribution of water for purification and for cleansing the altar and the court (1 Kings 7:27–39; 2 Chronicles 4:6). These consisted of two parts: the basins and the stands to put them on. The stands were about six feet square and four and one-half feet high and mounted on four wheels like chariot wheels. The stands consisted of four panels attached to uprights, and the whole of the exterior was decorated with lions, bulls, cherubim, and wreaths. In the top of the stand was a circular band on which the laver itself could rest. The bronze lavers measured six feet across and each held forty baths or just over 190 gallons. Hiram put five of these stands on the south side of the temple and five on the north.

The list of furniture also included the "golden altar" (table of incense made of cedar and overlaid with gold), the "table of the bread of the Presence" (likewise of cedar and overlaid with gold; there were ten of these), the "ten lampstands of pure gold," an assortment of gold dishes, wick trimmers and the like for use in the Holy Place (1 Kings 7:48–50).

All that Hiram made he cast from burnished bronze (polished to make it shine), and he cast his productions in clay molds in the "plains of the Jordan between Succoth and Zarethan." Succoth is usually identified with Deir Alla, on the east side of the Jordan Valley just north of the river Jabbok. Excavations there demonstrate that it was a center of metallurgy during the Hebrew monarchy. Deposits of metal slag and furnaces have been found. The clay in the region was of a superior kind for making molds, and a supply of charcoal was available nearby.

Dedication of the Temple (1 Kings 8:1–66). At last the great day of dedication had arrived. The completed temple stood there in all its splendor, the exterior white limestone reflecting the brilliant rays of the sun and the interior gold surfaces displaying their richness in the muted light that shone through the latticed windows. The marvelous burnished bronze creations of

The modern city of Jerusalem, showing the Dome of the Rock and the hill on which
Solomon's temple was built

(Photo by Ben Chapman)

Hiram of Tyre and his crew stood in place, as brightly polished as devoted priests could make them. The gold furniture reposed in all its pristine glory in the appropriate places. The treasury was filled with the precious service utensils that David and Solomon had collected. Only the ark of the covenant was lacking, and the Shekinah glory of God had not yet filled the place. Nor had the prayers and sacrifices of dedication been offered.

To proceed to the dedication, Solomon called together the "elders of Israel" (the community chiefs), the "heads of the tribes," and the "princes of the father's houses," as representatives of all Israel to bring up the ark from the "City of David," where it was located in a tent only a few hundred yards to the south (2 Chronicles 6:5-7). The time of this gala occasion was the month Ethanim (the earlier name for Tishri), the seventh month of the year (September-October), when the "Feast" (v. 2, of Tabernacles) was celebrated.

When the company arrived in the temple courtyard, they stopped and offered numerous sacrifices, no doubt as acts of thanksgiving and rejoicing; on this occasion the focus was not on penitence. After the sacrifices the priests carried the ark into the Most Holy Place and set it beneath the protective wings of the cherubim. "When the priests came out of the Most Holy Place, the cloud filled the temple" (v. 10), visible evidence that God Himself had taken up residence in the house. A similar phenomenon had occurred when the tabernacle was completed (Exodus 40: 34-35). The Shekinah glory was not removed until just before the Babylonians destroyed the temple (Ezekiel 9:3; 10:4; 11:23).

While still facing the Most Holy Place, Solomon responded to God Who had come to take up His abode: "I have built for you a stately house, a place for you to dwell forever" (1 Kings 8:13).

Then the king, who had been facing the Most Holy Place, turned around and addressed the assembled crowd in the court. First he praised God who had fulfilled His promise to his father David. Then he introduced a historical summary. God, who in the earlier centuries of Hebrew history had not chosen a place for His abode,

Solomon's Prayer Reveals Advanced Theology

An analysis of Solomon's prayer demonstrates the maturity of his theology and that of Israel at the time and argues against the critical view that Israel's theology was not highly developed until about 500 B.C. Critics are so obsessed with the evolutionary view of Israel's religion that they find it hard to take anything in the early history of Israel at face value, even though archaeological and historical evidence continues to mount in support of the authenticity of the Old Testament.

In this prayer Solomon includes all the usual items—thanksgiving to God, prayer for forgiveness from sin, for victory in battle, and more. But Solomon includes two other remarkable concepts. The first is that while he was building a house where God could especially dwell, He did not live in Jerusalem or the temple alone but was the omnipresent God of all the earth.

Second, God was not a sort of personal possession of the Hebrews but was a God for all peoples, and he asks that as Gentiles pray toward this house they may have their prayers answered too.

Pagan peoples generally believed that their gods dwelt in specific shrines and protected certain specific peoples and were related to a limited geographical turf. Hebrews often seem to have been afflicted with the same viewpoint to a degree. But in this prayer Solomon rises above all that.

had ultimately chosen Jerusalem (see 2 Chronicles 6:6) and David to rule there. David had had it in his heart to build the temple, and God had complimented him for it but had denied him the privilege, saying that his son would do it instead. God has kept His word. Solomon now sits on the throne of Israel and has built the temple "for the name of Yahweh."

Next Solomon made a prayer for the people, at first standing before the altar and then kneeling. Apparently he prayed from a bronze platform or pulpit that he ascended in the outer court (2 Chronicles 6:13).

As the king finished speaking, "fire came down from heaven and consumed the burnt offering and the sacrifices, and the glory of the Lord filled the temple" (2 Chronicles 7:1 NIV). Thus, God demonstrated His acceptance of the proceedings up to that point. Naturally, all the assembled throng were awestruck and they worshiped God. Yahweh's march from Sinai to the place of His earthly enthronement had reached a culmination.

Then began a round of sacrificial offerings in dedication of the temple; the sacred historian gives a total of 22,000 cattle and 120,000 sheep and goats. The number seems unbelievably large, but thousands of priests were involved and many auxiliary altars must have been used (see 1 Kings 8:64). In dealing with these large numbers of sacrifices, several factors need to be kept in mind. First, the parallel passage in 2 Chronicles 7 gives the same numbers, so a discrepancy in transcription of numbers does not cast doubt on the totals noted here. Second, the dedication of the temple coincided with the Feast of Tabernacles, and the usual one-week feast was extended to two weeks (v. 65). Third, substantial numbers of Israelites from Hamath in the far north to the border of Egypt in the south (v. 65) were present in Jerusalem for all or part of the two weeks. These people had to be fed and it was customary to have fellowship meals after the sacrifices; parts of the animals were offered to God and the worshipers ate the rest.

It can readily be seen, then, that the large number of sacrifices coincided with the need to feed crowds of pilgrims. At the end of the twofold celebration the people returned home thankful for all God had done and with a new sense of the divine destiny of king and country.

The two pillars, Jachin and Boaz, that flanked the main entrance of the temple, had counterparts in columns that frequently flanked the entrances of temples in Syria and Phoenicia during the first millennium B.C. Perhaps the biblical pillars should be interpreted as giant fire altars. Each of them was crowned with an oil basin or lampstand (1 Kings 7:4). They might have reminded worshipers of the fiery pillar that led Israel through the wilderness.

Phoenician-Canaanite Architectural Influence in the Temple

Solomon's construction was considerably influenced by Phoenician or Canaanite design, as would be expected when Hiram and other workers from Tyre were so heavily involved in his building program. Proto-Ionic capitals ("in the shape of lilies," 1 Kings 7:19) on columns used in the temple also appeared in Solomonic construction at Megiddo and Hazor and later at Samaria (see designs accompanying). Therefore, though the temple has completely disappeared, discoveries at these other sites help us to visualize capitals on the columns in the temple. Temple decorations such as lilies, palmettes, and cherubim were also characteristically Syro-Phoenician. Cherubim or winged sphinxes appear often in the religious motifs of western Asia in the second and first millennia B.C.

Popular Religion

It is always easier to assess official or public religion than to learn what people really believe or how they act. Straws in the wind do help us sketch out some generalizations about religious conditions in the transitional period when the monarchy was being established and during the days of Saul, David, and Solomon.

To begin with, God worried about what would happen to the Israelites when they entered Canaan. He said they would capitulate to the religious practices of the Canaanites if they did not destroy the Canaanite altars, images, and the people themselves (Deuteronomy 7:2-5). During

the conquest they, however, did not break down all the pagan altars, burn the wooden images, or eradicate the corrupt population. What they left became a snare to them.

The ways of the inhabitants became a snare to the Hebrews because these people were "greater and mightier" than they (Deuteronomy 7:1). Their fortifications and weapons commanded respect, humanly speaking. Moreover, as residents the Canaanites had agricultural techniques, building practices, and many other achievements that they could teach the nomadic invaders. Since their success in agriculture would appeal to the Hebrews, they could easily fall under the influence of Canaanite means of guaranteeing good crops: the fertility rites.

As the Israelites entered the land, they did establish the sanctuary at Shiloh. They also possessed the detailed commands of the law, including the annual festivals, observance of the Day of Atonement, and the weekly sabbath (see chapter 5). Yet no compelling force existed to make them toe the line. So for generations during the period of the judges "everyone did what was right in his own eyes" (Judges 21:25 NKJV). The tribal groups lived in their own territories and seem to have largely ignored the central sanctuary. We find no indications in the books of Judges, 1, 2 Samuel, or 1 Kings that people observed the great festivals or kept the Sabbath.

But that does not mean the Hebrews became irreligious. Most people do believe in a higher power and work out some means of getting what they want from it. The Hebrews set up idolatrous shrines in various places. Gideon's father, for example, maintained one (Judges 6:25ff.). We also read about the idol in the house of Micah that the Danites carried off and established at the town of Dan (Judges 18).

Numerous Canaanite high places flourished as well. These might be a shrine on a mountainside or a hill or simply on the highest point in a town. Usually these involved an altar for sacrifice, accompanied by a wooden pole representing the female fertility deity (Ashtoreth) and a stone pillar representing the Baal, the male Canaanite god. Moses in Deuteronomy 7:5 refers to altars, pillars and wooden poles (Asherim) as objects of destruction. The worship featured licentious rites, including male and female prostitution, which the people thought would bring fertility of crops, herds, and human beings by sympathetic magic. Whether Eli's sons practiced religious prostitution in imitation of Baal worship at the sanctuary at Shiloh, or were simply doing "what comes naturally," must be left open to question (1 Samuel 2:22). In any case, God considered them "scoundrels" who "had no regard for the Lord" (1 Samuel 2:2).

An idolatrous people who had largely turned their backs on God could easily demand that the ark of the covenant be brought from Shiloh to the front as the Hebrews fought the Philistines (1 Samuel 4:4). For many, confidence in the presence of the ark had become a form of fetishism, the ultimate good luck charm. They believed magical potency dwelled in the object itself.

But not everyone forsook God. The parents of Samuel went "year by year" to sacrifice at Shiloh (1 Samuel 1:3), presumably at Passover time. No doubt the sacred historian did not single out everyone who deserved commendation. And when Samuel became judge or leader of his people he called on them to put away their baals and ashtoreths and return to God. His call to reform implies a general involvement in Canaanite idolatry. The people responded to Samuel (1 Samuel 7:3-6). At least the leaders of Israel did, representing the people.

Samuel's action of sacrificing at Mizpah (1 Samuel 7:6-12) and his involvement in the sacrifice at an unnamed town when he was meeting Saul and choosing him as king (1 Samuel 9:10), indicate that God-honoring worship centers in addition to the tabernacle remained in Israel.

But idolatry had a tenacious hold on the people. The fact that Samuel secured the repentance of the representative leaders, does not mean that the masses who did not come to Mizpah fundamentally changed their ways. Even the household of Saul contained idols at a later time. When Saul's men came after David to kill him, his wife Michal, Saul's daughter, let him out the window and grabbed a household idol and put it in his bed, pretending that it was David (1 Samuel 19:12).

After David established the central shrine in Jerusalem and Solomon built the temple, there must have been a certain percentage of the population that worshiped God. As observed earlier, the dedication of the temple coincided with the Feast of Tabernacles, then being observed. The establishment of the temple must also have given rise to observance of the Day of Atonement and the Passover, and more, at least in the capital. But we still do not hear of any general observance of religious practices, including the Sabbath, during the period of the united monarchy. And after Solomon began to marry pagan women, idolatry increasingly invaded even official circles.

In the light of all that has been said, we wonder whether the establishment of the temple in Jerusalem eliminated competing shrines elsewhere. We cannot make a generalization, but apparently the shrine at Dan (Judges 18) continued until the captivity of the Northern Kingdom (723/22 B.C.). We also have an archaeological discovery that throws some light on the question.

At Arad, about eighteen miles east-north-east of Beersheba, an Israeli team excavated for eighteen seasons (1962-1984), under the leadership of Ruth Amiran. In a royal Israelite citadel they uncovered the first Israelite temple discovered in an archaeological excavation. The excavators concluded that this temple was actually built during Solomon's reign and that it was a temple to Yahweh. Other archaeologists have assigned its founding to a later date. The temple lay in the northwest part of the fortress and consisted of a hall, a sanctuary, and a Most Holy Place. In the latter, three steps led to a raised platform. Standing on the last step were two stone incense altars. The temple measured about 65 by 50 feet, and it was demolished in the seventh century, probably with the reform of King Josiah.[7] If one separate temple existed during the reign of Solomon, what is to prevent the discovery of others in the future?

(For more on this topic, go to p. 113 or p. 226.)

The temple at Arad

The raid in the days of Rameses III he claims was launched by some Philistines and Tjekker invaders who intended to settle in Egypt. The Philistines he asserts came from the coastlands (not islands) between Gaza and Joppa, and the Tjekker from the coastland south of Mt. Carmel. The Egyptians repulsed them and they returned to Canaan.[9] There they established a loose confederation of five city-states: Gaza, Ashkelon, Ashdod, Gath, and Ekron. Apparently they had occupied the region by the permission of the Egyptians and for at least part of the time recognized Egyptian overlordship.

As Iron Age people, the Philistines had superior weapons. They maintained control of the region through a monopoly on the

Warfare

Early Philistine Fiasco

"Israel has fled before the Philistines, and there has been a great slaughter among the people." (1 Samuel 4:17 NKJV)

The Philistines remained constant and fierce enemies of the Israelites all during the period of the judges and the early monarchy. Scripture represents them as coming originally from Caphtor (Amos 9:7; Jeremiah 47:4), usually identified with Crete. But questions of their origin and early history remain largely unanswered. Archaeological investigations are constantly throwing more light on them, however.[8]

Egyptian records tell of the attacks of Sea Peoples on the shores of Egypt during the reigns of Merneptah (c. 1215 B.C.) and Rameses III (c. 1190 B.C.). These usually have been interpreted as attacks of Philistines who were repulsed and went off to settle in Canaan. But Robert Drews has demonstrated that we have to rethink these records. He asserts that the king of Libya launched the first attack by sea on the western Delta, with the intent of occupying at least parts of it. To help him he hired mercenaries from many northern lands, such as Sandinia, Sicily, Italy, Greece, and Asia Minor, not a migration of Sea Peoples and certainly not Philistines.

Goliath's Weapons

The armor and weapons of a Philistine included greaves for the protection of the legs, plated armor or scale armor for the breastplate, a bronze helmut for the head with a horsehair crest, and a shield. For weapons he had a sword, a spear, and in the case of Goliath, not a javelin but a scimitar. Bierling argues that kidon, translated "javelin" in various versions in 1 Samuel 17:6, was a single-edged sword, with a curved cutting blade on its outer, curved side, i. e., a sicklesword, a sword for slashing.[10] And he tries to show that the armor and weapons of Goliath represented those of a typical Philistine and of a Greek of the Aegean world as well. He also observes that Aegean Philistines typically chose representatives from each army to fight, as reported in the David-Goliath narrative.[11]

THE PHILISTINE THREAT

The Philistines (1 Sam. 28:4–5) were a constant threat to the Israelites throughout the periods of the judges and the kings. God often used Israel's neighbors to the southwest to discipline His people. On the other hand, victory over the Philistines often confirmed spiritual revival among the Hebrews.

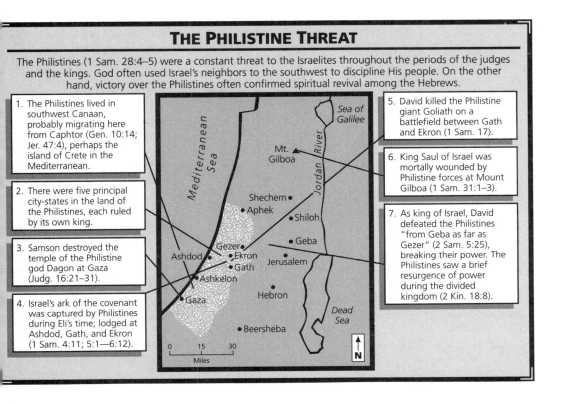

1. The Philistines lived in southwest Canaan, probably migrating here from Caphtor (Gen. 10:14; Jer. 47:4), perhaps the island of Crete in the Mediterranean.

2. There were five principal city-states in the land of the Philistines, each ruled by its own king.

3. Samson destroyed the temple of the Philistine god Dagon at Gaza (Judg. 16:21–31).

4. Israel's ark of the covenant was captured by Philistines during Eli's time; lodged at Ashdod, Gath, and Ekron (1 Sam. 4:11; 5:1—6:12).

5. David killed the Philistine giant Goliath on a battlefield between Gath and Ekron (1 Sam. 17).

6. King Saul of Israel was mortally wounded by Philistine forces at Mount Gilboa (1 Sam. 31:1–3).

7. As king of Israel, David defeated the Philistines "from Geba as far as Gezer" (2 Sam. 5:25), breaking their power. The Philistines saw a brief resurgence of power during the divided kingdom (2 Kin. 18:8).

iron industry. Not only did they attempt to subject the Hebrews by keeping iron weapons out of their hands, but they also profited economically by charging for sharpening plowshares, sickles, and other agricultural tools (1 Samuel 13:19-22).

The Philistines remained a trial for the Hebrews all the days of Samson. And they continued on the warpath in the latter days of Eli. Expanding from their base along the Mediterranean in southwest Palestine, they gradually moved up the valleys into the highlands. The Hebrews decided to challenge the Philistines near Aphek, a strategically located site at the headwaters of the Yarkon River, about ten miles northeast of modern Tel Aviv. While the Philistines camped at Aphek, the Hebrews camped at Ebenezer, now identified with Izbet Sartah, about two miles east of Aphek.

The initial encounter proved costly for the Hebrews—they suffered almost four thousand casualties. Accustomed to having

God fight for them, they anguished, "Why did God defeat us?" (1 Samuel 4:3). Apparently they failed to keep in mind that God did not bless people who turned from Him and entered into idolatrous practices (1 Samuel 7:3). If God had not been present with them in battle, then one way to guarantee His presence, they thought, might be to bring His ark into the camp. But the ark did not prove to be a good luck charm for a people who deserved judgment. The Hebrews suffered great casualties—as well as the loss of the ark. The chronicler reports a casualty figure of thirty thousand (1 Samuel 4:10).

Some doubt the large numbers given for the armies and casualties in the historical books of the Old Testament. But there is no need to be particularly skeptical when we understand the nature of the warfare described. Commonly all able-bodied men, including the older teenagers, turned out when enemies threatened a town or an area

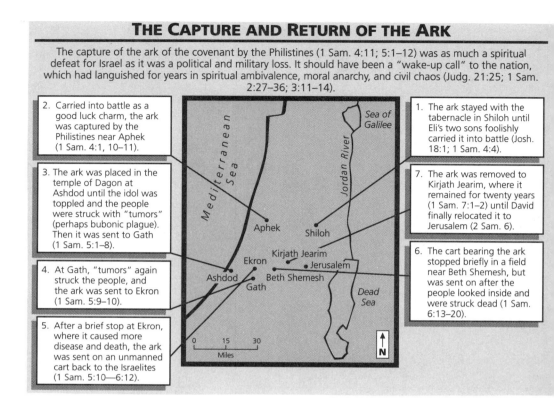

THE CAPTURE AND RETURN OF THE ARK

The capture of the ark of the covenant by the Philistines (1 Sam. 4:11; 5:1–12) was as much a spiritual defeat for Israel as it was a political and military loss. It should have been a "wake-up call" to the nation, which had languished for years in spiritual ambivalence, moral anarchy, and civil chaos (Judg. 21:25; 1 Sam. 2:27–36; 3:11–14).

2. Carried into battle as a good luck charm, the ark was captured by the Philistines near Aphek (1 Sam. 4:1, 10–11).

3. The ark was placed in the temple of Dagon at Ashdod until the idol was toppled and the people were struck with "tumors" (perhaps bubonic plague). Then it was sent to Gath (1 Sam. 5:1–8).

4. At Gath, "tumors" again struck the people, and the ark was sent to Ekron (1 Sam. 5:9–10).

5. After a brief stop at Ekron, where it caused more disease and death, the ark was sent on an unmanned cart back to the Israelites (1 Sam. 5:10—6:12).

1. The ark stayed with the tabernacle in Shiloh until Eli's two sons foolishly carried it into battle (Josh. 18:1; 1 Sam. 4:4).

7. The ark was removed to Kirjath Jearim, where it remained for twenty years (1 Sam. 7:1–2) until David finally relocated it to Jerusalem (2 Sam. 6).

6. The cart bearing the ark stopped briefly in a field near Beth Shemesh, but was sent on after the people looked inside and were struck dead (1 Sam. 6:13–20).

Sea of Galilee

Jordan River

Mediterranean Sea

Aphek Shiloh

Kirjath Jearim
Ekron • Jerusalem
Ashdod Beth Shemesh
Gath

Dead Sea

0   15   30
Miles

N

---

during the days of the conquest of Canaan, the period of the judges, or the monarchy. This resulted in considerably swollen numbers. Then precisely because most of those engaged in conflict were not disciplined soldiers, casualties frequently were excessive. When these troops put an enemy to flight, the confusion or the rout often was total.

Discussion of the fortunes of the ark in Philistine hands (seven months, 1 Samuel 6:1), its return to the Israelites, and treatment among the Israelites after its return (1 Samuel 5:1—7:2) may be traced out in the biblical narrative (see summary in sidebar, "Travels of the Ark of the Covenant"). Suffice it to say fighting renewed after twenty years (1 Samuel 7:2). On that occasion Samuel called representatives of the people together at Mizpah (identified by most scholars with Tell en-Nasbeh, eight miles north of Jerusalem) to engage in national repentance and abandonment of idolatry.

At that moment the Philistines decided to strike, either to launch a preemptive strike or to take advantage of Israel's preoccupation with a religious observance (as Arabs did in the Yom Kippur War of 1973). Fear gripped the Hebrews as reports of a Philistine advance reached the holy convocation. Unprepared for war, they begged Samuel not to stop crying out to God on their behalf. Though not a priest, Samuel offered a lamb as a whole burnt offering, thus representing the total consecration of the people to their God.

God responded dramatically. While Samuel offered the sacrifice, and as the Philistines advanced against the Hebrews, God split the heavens with a terrorizing thunderstorm that threw the Philistine army into complete panic. Perhaps He struck down many of them with bolts of lightning. God defeated the Philistines before the Hebrews had a chance to strike a blow. All the Hebrews had to do was launch

TRAVELS OF THE ARK OF THE

COVENANT

(1 SAMUEL 4:1—7:2)

The Philistines had pushed the Hebrews to the wall. And because of their waywardness God apparently was not fighting their battles for them. To force God's presence in the camp, they decided to bring the ark of the covenant, the ultimate good luck charm, to the battlefield (1 Samuel 4:4). But the presence of the ark did no good as the Philistines defeated the Hebrews and captured the ark. Perhaps the Philistines concluded that they and their gods were able to overcome Yahweh. Subsequent events proved just the opposite.

First they took the ark to Ashdod (33 miles west of Jerusalem and 3 miles from the Mediterranean). There they put it in the temple of Dagon. First the image of the god fell down before the ark and later fell down again, smashed to smithereens. "Tumors" and "plague-boils" afflicted the people in the groin (1 Samuel 5:6). God's judgment also affected their crops. So they decided to send the ark to Gath (21 miles due west of Bethlehem). Perhaps they were suffering some natural disaster, rather than the judgment of God, they thought. At Gath the disaster repeated itself. When the people of Gath sent the ark to Ekron (some 10 miles east of Ashdod), widespread death followed it (5:11-12). The whole account reads like a triumphal march of Yahweh. Before Him pagan gods proved powerless to protect either themselves or their worshipers.

Finally the Philistines had taken all they could bear. After seven months they decided to give up their rich prize of war and send it back home. The priests and diviners or soothsayers gave counsel about a test to prove whether Yahweh had been responsible for their woes: Provide a new cart for transportation of the ark. Hitch up to it two cows (rather than oxen) that had calved and never been yoked, with their calves remaining penned up at home. Then the cows were to be sent on their way to take the ark back into Israelite territory.

Instead of jumping around and breaking the cart or seeking out their calves, the cows headed straight for Israelite territory on their own, without a driver. The Philistines wanted the ark to go to Beth Shemesh, some ten miles east of Ekron and about fifteen miles west of Jerusalem, evidently the nearest Israelite town. The "lords of the Philistines" (6:12), the princes of the five Philistine towns, followed the cart, probably to prevent any manipulation of the venture and to gain firsthand evidence of what happened. They trooped behind the cart all the way to the edge of Beth Shemesh. When the people of Beth Shemesh saw the ark they rejoiced. They sacrificed the cows and used the cart as fuel for the fire. The power of Yahweh had been abundantly demonstrated.

a mopping-up exercise. Emboldened by the turn of events, they rushed against the confused and fleeing foe with such success that the Philistines "no longer encroached on the territory of Israel" (7:13 NEB). Evidently this does not mean the Philistines made no effort to recover lost territory or supremacy. The following clause indicates that such attacks did take place, but they were doomed to failure because of divine intervention.

Verse 14 probably does not imply that the important towns of Ekron and Gath fell to the Israelites, but only that borderlands adjacent to them did. Moreover, resurgent

Israelite power became so impressive that the Amorites, the most powerful of the Canaanite tribes, did not greatly trouble the Hebrews either during the rest of the days of Samuel's leadership.

Saul's Victories and Defeat

"Now there was fierce war with the Philistines all the days of Saul." (1 Samuel 14:52 NKJV)

Saul's first confrontation did not, however, involve the Philistines, though it was connected with their actions. By oppressing and/or threatening the Israelites west of the Jordan, the Philistines made it possible for peoples east of the Jordan, the Ammonites, to rise against them. They now threatened the Hebrew city of Jabesh Gilead, a site about ten miles southeast of Beth Shan and about two miles east of the Jordan River. The crisis provided an opportunity for Saul to act kingly, to demonstrate ability in warfare or public administration—and thus to gain greater acceptance in Israel.

With no hope of rescue by Hebrews west of the Jordan, the townsfolk of Jabesh Gilead believed they would have to surrender to the Ammonites, so they sought a "treaty" (1 Samuel: 11:1; "covenant") that would give them the best possible terms. But the Ammonites demanded a terrible price—the blinding of all the men in the right eye. The reason for this requirement was twofold: to bring disgrace on Israel in retaliation for their subjugation to them, and incapacitation of the men so they could not fight, i. e., rebel. The Israelites considered such a demand too high a price to pay, and they begged for seven days of grace to obtain help. We should not consider granting such a request unthinkable because the Ammonites probably did not believe help would be forthcoming—and they wanted to avoid a siege of a walled city if possible. They could easily wait seven days for the inevitable to occur. Messengers from Jabesh Gilead immediately began to scurry among the tribes of Israel looking for support, and soon they arrived in Gibeah.

There Saul performed the symbolic act of cutting up a yoke of oxen and sending the pieces throughout the tribes. He threatened that what he had done to the oxen would be done to anyone who failed to respond to the call for military action. This general summons to "come out after Saul and . . . Samuel" (1 Samuel 11:7) was an accepted way of issuing a call to arms, as the grisly act of Judges 19:29—20:1 indicates.

Bezek, a place in the hills on the western side of the Jordan opposite Jabesh Gilead, became the mustering point for Saul's forces. Presumably on the night of the sixth day, the people of Jabesh Gilead informed the Ammonites that on the following day they would "come out" (1 Samuel 11:10) to them. The Hebrew could mean to come out "against" or "in subjection to"—the ambiguity was convenient.

Apparently the Israelite relief forces marched all night from Bezek, fording the Jordan on the way. They formed three great divisions for the attack and fell on the Ammonites "during the last watch of the night" (11:11 NIV), i. e., between three and six in the morning. They completely surprised the Ammonites and routed them. Saul's kingship had been accredited by victory. Now the kingship could be renewed in a great convocation at Gilgal, just northeast of Old Testament Jericho. The lesson learned from this campaign was the importance of a standing army, ready for immediate action. This could be augmented by tribal recruits. Saul chose three thousand stalwarts. Of these one thousand were stationed with Saul at Micmash, about nine miles northeast of Jerusalem, and another thousand were under his jurisdiction around Bethel, about eleven miles north of Jerusalem. A third thousand were under the command of Jonathan at Gibeah, about three miles north of Jerusalem.

Apparently soon thereafter Saul began to deal with the Philistines. In a preliminary move, Jonathan took out a Philistine post at Geba (1 Samuel 13:3). This act led to a Philistine general mobilization, with a resultant Hebrew mobilization. The overwhelming military superiority of the Philistines scared the Hebrews to the point that many fled and hid in caves. Meanwhile, Saul had set up his camp at Gilgal and there waited for Samuel, who had promised to

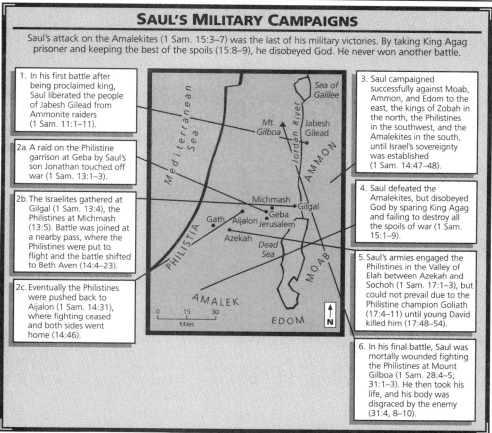

SAUL'S MILITARY CAMPAIGNS

Saul's attack on the Amalekites (1 Sam. 15:3–7) was the last of his military victories. By taking King Agag prisoner and keeping the best of the spoils (15:8–9), he disobeyed God. He never won another battle.

1. In his first battle after being proclaimed king, Saul liberated the people of Jabesh Gilead from Ammonite raiders (1 Sam. 11:1–11).

2a. A raid on the Philistine garrison at Geba by Saul's son Jonathan touched off war (1 Sam. 13:1–3).

2b. The Israelites gathered at Gilgal (1 Sam. 13:4), the Philistines at Michmash (13:5). Battle was joined at a nearby pass, where the Philistines were put to flight and the battle shifted to Beth Aven (14:4–23).

2c. Eventually the Philistines were pushed back to Aijalon (1 Sam. 14:31), where fighting ceased and both sides went home (14:46).

3. Saul campaigned successfully against Moab, Ammon, and Edom to the east, the kings of Zobah in the north, the Philistines in the southwest, and the Amalekites in the south, until Israel's sovereignty was established (1 Sam. 14:47–48).

4. Saul defeated the Amalekites, but disobeyed God by sparing King Agag and failing to destroy all the spoils of war (1 Sam. 15:1–9).

5. Saul's armies engaged the Philistines in the Valley of Elah between Azekah and Sochoh (1 Sam. 17:1–3), but could not prevail due to the Philistine champion Goliath (17:4–11) until young David killed him (17:48–54).

6. In his final battle, Saul was mortally wounded fighting the Philistines at Mount Gilboa (1 Sam. 28:4–5; 31:1–3). He then took his life, and his body was disgraced by the enemy (31:4, 8–10).

come within seven days. Saul grew desperate. No Samuel. No word from God. He decided to make a sacrifice to God and prepare for battle. No sooner had he done so when Samuel appeared, rebuked him for his lack of faith and for having invaded the office of priest, and told him that God would terminate his line and choose a king "after his own heart" (1 Samuel 13:14).

In preparation for the next major event, the sacred historian observes that only Saul and Jonathan had proper weapons and body armor. The Philistines had been so successful in keeping iron weapons out of the hands of the Hebrews. That does not mean the Israelites had to fight with their bare hands, however. Their weapons ranged from crude clubs to deadly slings to bows and arrows.

As the stalemate continued between the Philistine and Israelite forces, Jonathan had a sudden inspiration. He determined somehow that God would use him as His instrument and launched a surprise attack on a strategic Philistine outpost. Jonathan and his armor bearer overran the Philistine contingent, killing about twenty of them. Apparently supernatural power intervened, and the panic at the outpost rapidly gripped the entire army. A severe earthquake increased the panic. The sacred historian indicates: "It was a panic sent from God" (1 Samuel 14:15; literally, "a terror of God").

Saul's spies or scouts in the vicinity of Gibeah detected a great confusion in the Philistine camp: "The multitude was surging to and fro in all directions" (1 Samuel 14:16). Saul gave the order to advance. As the men did so they found the enemy camp in total confusion, with Philistine striking Philistine. When Saul and his men appeared, the Hebrews serving in the Philistine army, either as mercenaries or conscripts, now had a rallying point and turned against their masters. Ultimately, the bedlam reached such a pitch that terrified Israelites who had hidden from the Philistines emerged from their shelters and pursued the enemy. The rout was complete. The Hebrews gave God the primary credit: "God rescued Israel that day" (1 Samuel 14:23).

Apparently the Hebrews defeated the Philistines so completely that they had the freedom to turn their attention to enemies on the south and east for a while. We put so much emphasis on Saul's personal failures in Scripture that in the minds of many Bible students his military successes are often overlooked. Saul achieved victories almost as extensive as those of David, though his conquests did not prove as permanent as those of his successor. To the south he devastated the Amalekites. East of the Jordan he defeated the Edomites on the south, and then the Moabites and Ammonites, conquering all the way up to Zobah, north of Damascus (1 Samuel 14:47).

Saul's War Against the Amalekites (1 Samuel 15:1–9). Saul's first major test had come at Gilgal near the beginning of his reign. Failure, as demonstrated by lack of faith and intrusion into the priestly office, had brought the divine pronouncement that his dynasty would extend only through his own reign (1 Samuel 13:13–14). Now God came to Saul with a second test. Perhaps he received a hint that he was being given a second chance to make good, though that is not specifically stated. Unfortunately, he did not make good; his partial obedience resulted in God's rejection of his kingship. Thereafter he increasingly lost his grip on his kingdom and even on his sanity.

God's test of Saul involved a command to destroy the Amalekites utterly. There was a basis for such an order. The Amalekites had harassed Israel during the Exodus (Exodus 17:8–16; Deuteronomy 25:17–19). They had opposed Israel's entrance to Canaan (Numbers 14:25) and continued as implacable enemies during the period of the judges (Judges 3:13; 6:3).

Saul promptly mobilized the troops. The place of mustering the troops, Telaim, cannot be identified (15:4). The number of Israelites called up (210,000) is probably not unduly large, considering the nature of the operation. The Amalekites lived in a semi-

nomadic state, and it would have required numerous contingents of troops to chase them over the countryside. In fact, Saul attacked them "all the way from Havilah to Shur, to the east of Egypt" (15:7 NIV), from northwest Arabia to the eastern border of Egypt, i. e., the line of the Suez Canal. Saul himself concentrated on "the city of Amalek" (15:5), perhaps the only settled population center among them. What and where it was are unknown.

The Bible does not give us any details of Saul's campaign against the Amalekites, only the detail that Saul's obedience was incomplete. Saul and his army spared King Agag, the best of the livestock, and other attractive booty. Everyone else and everything else was destroyed. For this failure God pronounced the terrible sentence: "Because you have rejected the word of the Lord, he has also rejected you from being king" (15:26).

The David and Goliath Contest (1 Samuel 17). As noted above, "there was fierce war with the Philistines all the days of Saul." But the sacred historian does not provide us with all the specifics of that struggle. He describes only the contest between David and Goliath and Saul's last battle at Mount Gilboa. In neither case does he provide much detail.

First let's look at the battle between David and Goliath. The Philistines had moved up the Valley of Elah on one of their periodic incursions into the territory of Israel. They advanced as far as Socoh, about fourteen miles west of Bethlehem, and camped at Ephes Dammim, about a mile northwest of Socoh. Of course, the Israelites had mustered to meet the threat, and the two armies stood facing each other on the hills that rose on either side of the Valley of Elah.

At length a champion came down from the Philistine side of the valley and strode into the valley to taunt the Israelites. He proposed that single combat replace fighting between the two armies. We know about such a procedure from both Semitic and Greek sources (e.g., the combat between Achilles and Hector recorded in Book 7 of *The Iliad*). The fight between twelve men from each side in 2 Samuel 2:12–16 is only a variation of the principle.

The Valley of Elah, site of the battle between David and Goliath (1 Samuel 17; 21:9)

This champion could afford to make the offer that the people of whichever champion lost would be servants of the winning side (1 Samuel 17:9). He was reasonably confident no one in the Israelite camp could match him, since he probably was a member of the tall Anakim. Though no longer existing in Israel after Joshua's day, they continued to live in Gaza, Gath, and Ashdod (Joshua 11:22).

A Gath resident, Goliath certainly appeared fearsome to the Hebrews. He stood to a height of six cubits and a span. If the cubit is computed at the commonly accepted length of seventeen and one-half inches and the span of about nine inches, the height of the giant was about nine feet six inches. A coat of chain mail made of bronze (giving the appearance of overlapping scales of fish) and weighing about one hundred twenty-five pounds protected his body. He had a bronze helmet and bronze greaves or shin guards and had a scimitar slung across his back (see previous discussion). The wooden shaft of his spear was as big as a weaver's beam (a pole or a beam from a large loom), and it had an iron point weighing about fifteen pounds. Of course, he had a sword at his side; and before this formidable warrior, well protected by body armor, walked a shield bearer. Goliath ter-

rified the armies of Israel, not only with his appearance, but also with his braggadocio. They heard his taunts every morning and evening as he challenged the Israelites (17:16).

David's three oldest brothers had left for the front, and Jesse wanted to find out how they were doing and to send them a "care package." Actually, the Hebrews had no central commissariat, and the men in the army depended on supplies from home. Jesse sent an ephah (about a half bushel) of parched grain (wheat or barley roasted when it was ripe) and ten loaves or cakes (shaped like pancakes) of bread for his sons and ten small soft cheeses for their commander.

In talking with the men in their stations along the crest of the hill, David heard a report about a reward to be given to the one who killed Goliath: riches, the king's daughter in marriage, and freedom from various kinds of public obligations. David grew increasingly interested in this reward and evidently went to several to ask about it. At this distance in time and place from the event, and hampered by a very brief summary in Scripture, we are hard-pressed to know David's motives for wanting to get involved. We do know that David wanted to fight Goliath and that he did so. We shall return to this contest in the next section on David's conquests.

After trying on and rejecting Saul's armor, David decided to fight Goliath with his shepherd's staff and sling.

A Deadly Weapon

In the hands of a skilled slinger, the sling had proved to be a deadly weapon. Made of two ropes attached to a thong of leather or goat hair into which a stone could be fitted, it could hurl a stone a considerable distance with hair's breadth accuracy. Benjamites from the area of Gibeah were especially known for their prowess as slingers (Judges 20:14–16). Other Israelites used slings effectively as well, with slingers a regular part of the army. Monuments reveal Assyrians also had contingents of slingers.

As the two closed in on each other, David utilized speed and surprise. One well-aimed stone to the forehead of the Philistine downed him. Since the rest of his body was well protected with armor, why aim there? It is not clear whether the stone killed Goliath or merely knocked him out, with death coming by decapitation. David apparently used Goliath's own sword to behead him.

According to the terms of the challenge, the Philistines now should have submitted to the Israelites, but they fled in fear. The Israelites followed in hot pursuit all the way to the Philistine cities of Gath, about seven miles west, and Ekron, about the same distance to the northwest. Fleeing men are no match for attackers, and the carnage among the Philistines was heavy. The Israelites, having no resources for a siege of the Philistine cities, circled back to their own camp and plundered the Philistine camp on the way. Years later the story was different.

Saul's Last Battle on Mount Gilboa (1 Samuel 31:1–13). Since the Philistines had

not been successful in penetrating the central plateau of Palestine from the west, they decided on an encircling movement. Marching north along the coastal plain, they planned to move east through the Jezreel Valley and then south along the plateau. Their main camp was in the vicinity of Aphek. Saul mustered the Israelite army and prepared to engage the Philistines.

The Philistines mounted the attack against the Israelite lines in the Valley of Jezreel and cut them to ribbons with their superior chariotry and archery. Retreating up the slopes of Mount Gilboa, the Israelites tried to regroup and make a stand; but the cause seemed hopeless and the loss of people was great.

Apparently much of the Israelite army simply melted away, but the sector of the front held by Saul and his sons momentarily stood their ground and took heavy losses. Saul's three sons were all killed and finally Saul himself, according to the Septuagint, was wounded "under the ribs" by Philistine archers.

Unable to fight any longer, Saul commanded his armor bearer to kill him, lest the enemy find him alive and "abuse" (31:4 NIV) him—possibly torture him to death. The armor bearer refused, perhaps out of great respect for the Lord's anointed. So Saul felt he had no recourse but to commit suicide, not unfavorably commented on here because soon he would have died anyway. Then the armor bearer also committed suicide, since he was accountable for the life of the king. If he were found alive beside the dead king, he would likely have been executed for failure in the line of battle. So Saul, his armorbearer, three of his sons, and "all his men" (31:6) died on that day. The latter cannot refer to the whole army and so must apply to his servants or the bodyguard that stood with him in that sector of the front. Saul had one son, Ish-Bosheth, remaining. For some reason he must not have been at the front. Possibly he had been left at the head of the government in Gibeah. Abner, commander of the forces, escaped too and later was able to help reestablish the government east of the Jordan (2 Samuel 2:8–10).

Mount Gilboa, site of the battle in which King Saul and his three sons were killed (1 Samuel 31:8)

When the Israelites heard that Saul and his sons were dead and saw that the resistance had totally collapsed, they panicked. Refugees began to stream out of the villages all along the Valley of Jezreel and the Jordan Valley and fled to the east bank of the Jordan. The Philistines then occupied those towns and thus came to control the whole of northern Israel. Apparently the Israelites continued to maintain a shaky hold on the hill country of Samaria and Judea.

The day after the battle of Gilboa the Philistines plundered the battlefield, making off with jewelry, weapons, and anything else of value. As they did so they came on the bodies of Saul and his sons, evidently identified by clothing, insignia, and seals hung about their necks or in waist pouches. They cut off Saul's head and probably those of his sons and took off their body armor and deposited all of this as trophies in the temple of Ashtoreth, the female deity worshiped beside Dagon. Where that temple was is open to question. Some have concluded it was at Ashkelon, where the most ancient temple of Ashtoreth was supposed to have existed. But a temple of Ashtoreth has been excavated at Beth Shan, and it certainly would have been more convenient to have put the battle trophies there.

The people in the Near East often publicly displayed the bodies of their enemies.

Thus it is not surprising that the Philistines fastened the bodies of the four to the wall of Beth Shan, standing just east of the battlefield and four miles west of the Jordan River. Perched on a dominant hill overlooking the whole region, Beth Shan's walls could be seen from a considerable distance. Meanwhile, the Philistines sent messengers throughout Philistia with news of the victory, not only among the people but "in the temple" (31:10). Apparently they placed some sort of memorial in the temples of the five major Philistine cities as a votive offering of thanks to the gods.

As some of the refugees passed Beth Shan and saw the bodies of Saul and his sons, they were horrified but helpless. When the men in Jabesh Gilead on the east bank heard it, they felt duty-bound to do something for the benefactor who had rescued them from their plight (1 Samuel 11:1-11). They journeyed through the night and stole the bodies of Saul and his sons and brought them back to Jabesh Gilead. Verse 12 states that they "burned" the bodies, according to most translations; but Israelites did not practice cremation except for an occasional criminal. In this case the bodies may have been so mutilated and putrified that they were cremated. They may also have wanted to prevent further indignities. In any case, they provided a

The mound of Beth Shan, where the Philistines hung the bodies of Saul and his three sons after killing them on Mount Gilboa. From this picture it is clear that they could have been seen from a great distance.

memorial grave and held a seven-day fast in mourning for the honored dead.

So ended the pathetic life of one who repeatedly refused total obedience to God.

David's Conquests

"You have shed much blood and have made great wars; you shall not build a house for My name, because you have shed much blood on earth in My sight." (1 Chronicles 22:8 NKJV)

The Bible presents David as a real scrapper. From fighting lions and bears in defense of his sheep, to killing Goliath, to leading a band of outlaws, to commanding Saul's army, to building an empire, to putting down revolts against him, David remained almost constantly in conflict. And in every case the fight came to him—whether he defended his sheep against wild animals, himself and his compatriots against attacks of Saul, the Israelites against Philistines and others, or his administration against rebels. His prowess as a military man came not from any schooling in theory but from personal experience in the arena of conflict or from observation.

What are the natural endowments of this fighter and leader of men? The chronicler describes him as "ruddy" (probably with auburn hair and fair complexion instead of the usual black hair and dark complexion), "with beautiful eyes," and "handsome features" (NIV), i. e., graceful and well proportioned when Samuel anointed him king (1 Samuel 16:12),. When a little later Saul's men recommended him to play his lyre to restore Saul's mental health, they described him as "skillful in playing, a mighty man of valor, a man of war, prudent in speech, and a handsome person; and the Lord is with him" (1 Samuel 16:18 NKJV). They represent him as an excellent musician, a brave man, a fighter, skilled in the use of words, handsome, and blessed of God.

A little further information about David's capability for war comes in connection with his preparation to fight Goliath. When David volunteered to fight the Philistine, Saul argued that Goliath was a seasoned warrior, while David was a youth untrained in warfare. David responded with impressive credentials of his own. He had had extensive and successful combat experience with lions and bears while protecting his father's sheep. The tense in the original is imperfect and indicates repeated action. Thus one should not conclude that David tackled only one bear and one lion. First

The Oasis of En Gedi, where David hid from King Saul during his years as a fugitive
(1 Samuel 23:29; 24:1)

Samuel 17:34 might better be translated, "Whenever a lion or bear" (NJB). David's life reflected both combat experience and an abundance of courage.

Then as Saul proceeded to prepare David for the contest, he dressed him in his own tunic and coat of mail. That it was possible for David to wear Saul's clothes indicates both the loose-fitting nature of the garments and the substantial size of David. We remember that Saul was head and shoulders taller than other Israelites. And there is no reason to conclude that David was a stripling; he was merely the youngest son of his father. Goliath's ridicule of David's size was part of his psychological warfare, and anyone in the Israelite camp would have been small compared to him. So we conclude that David was well built and strong, handsome, brave, and had a way with words that would be valuable as a leader.

David's Contest with Goliath (1 Samuel 17)

What might have been David's motives for wanting to get involved? Could he have been looking for a road to riches and glory, or did the situation call forth his courageous spirit. Maybe he had sufficient understanding of his anointing to believe he would live through this challenge to become the king, or he may have wanted to vindicate the name and reputation of God before these pagans (see especially 1 Samuel 17:26). And who can prove that the Spirit of God may not have prompted David to take on this pagan, who not only threw taunts against the Israelites but also against their God?

As David fought Goliath, the spiritual dimension became paramount. Goliath cursed David "by his gods" (v. 43). David responded with a kind of manifesto on the power of God about to descend on anyone who dared to defy Him, on one who supposed he could stand against the devastating might of Israel's God. And "the whole world" (17:46; Gentiles present and many who will hear of this event) and "those gathered here" (17:47), or "this congregation" (a term for the assembly of Israel) will see an apologetic for the existence and power of God acted out before their eyes.

God does not depend on heavy armor for victory in battle. In this instance, as in so many others, David's spiritual perspective shines forth.

David's Flight and Wanderings (1 Samuel 21—26)

After David killed Goliath, he was received into the royal court and rose in standing in the army and in acceptance with the general populace. But it did not take long for Saul to become jealous of him and to believe that David might take over the throne. So he made attempts on David's life and David fled.

David's Conquest of Jerusalem (2 Samuel 5:6-9; 1 Chronicles 11:4-9)

After David became king of all Israel, he needed a capital that all the tribes could accept. Hebron was too far south and was a city of Judah. David chose Jerusalem—a stroke of genius politically because it did not belong to any tribe, militarily because it was easily defensible (on a ridge surrounded by valleys) and was controlled by the Jebusites (a small ethnic group with no real support from the Canaanites), geographically because it was fairly centrally located, economically because it stood on the north-south and east-west trade routes. Moreover, it had an adequate water supply.

But Jerusalem seemed virtually impregnable. The cocky defenders said the blind and lame could ward off the attacks of David. David offered the captaincy of the armed forces to the one who would lead a successful attack against the Jebusite defenders. And David said such a one should go up by means of the *tsinnor* (2 Samuel 5:8). Scholars generally have translated the word as some sort of water course or a grappling hook used in scaling a wall. In the last few years the preponderance of opinion has gravitated to the former, and the Bible versions have fallen in line; e.g., NKJV, "water shaft"; REB, "water-shaft"; NIV, "water shaft"; NASB, "water tunnel"; NRSV, "water shaft."

In this view, the Israelites had discovered the main water system of the city and scaled that to come up inside the walls and

---

David's Leadership Learning Process

We cannot dwell on David's exploits in the armies of Saul, as a leader of a band of outlaws, and as a vassal of the Philistines. But we should not ignore important developments in this period. First, as David commanded regular forces in Saul's army, as he engaged in guerrilla actions, and as he commanded a band of mercenaries, he learned the role of a first-rate military leader. Second, he built a power base by attracting to himself other men with a grievance—first a band of 400 (1 Samuel 22:2), later increased to 600 with their families (1 Samuel 27:2). Third, he bought favor with the people of Judah by destroying tribal groups that attacked their southern towns (1 Samuel 27:8-12). In this way he prepared for the day when he would be accepted as king in Hebron. Fourth, when he became king in Hebron, he settled many of his band of followers in the "cities of Hebron" (2 Samuel 2:3), villages nearby. There they would protect against nomadic incursions from the south. And David eliminated this dissatisfied element by making them landowners.

---

surprise the defenders. The means they used to enter the city is called "Warren's Shaft," after Charles Warren, who discovered it in 1867 while exploring underground Jerusalem. This ancient water channel consists of two parts: a tunnel (about 147 feet long) cut diagonally from inside the city wall, and a vertical shaft (52 feet) down which a bucket or jar could be lowered to obtain water from the gushing Gihon spring below.

A. Rendle Short observed that some British army officers scaled Warren's Shaft in 1910.[12] The water system was finally cleared in 1980, and two young Americans subsequently did manage to ascend the shaft.

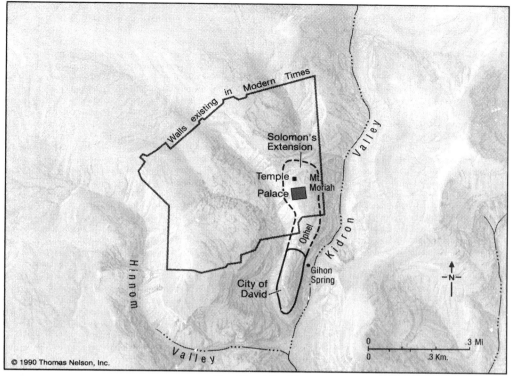

The City of David

Kathleen Kenyon, in her 1961–1967 excavations at Jebusite Jerusalem, concluded that David's men did indeed capture the city in this way when they made it the capital of Israel about 1000 B.C. And she computed the size of the city at the time at just under eleven acres.[13] Though Amihai Mazar of the Hebrew University in Jerusalem stated in his 1990 *Archaeology of the Land of the Bible* that Warren's Shaft dated after David's day,[14] subsequent geological investigation demonstrates that it was in existence in 1000 B.C.[15] I believe that Joab did indeed scale the water system called Warren's Shaft and led the successful attack on the Jebusite city, becoming David's commander-in-chief.

David's Contest with the Philistines (2 Samuel 5:17–25)

Soon after all of Israel anointed David king, the Philistines became alarmed at the threat a united Israel posed for them, especially when headed by a ruler with such prowess on the battlefield. As long as two quarrelsome Israelite states contended for the mastery, and as long as David appeared to be a Philistine vassal, the Philistines had nothing to fear. Now they decided to attack before David could consolidate his power and become a more formidable foe.

The Philistines camped in the Valley of Rephaim, the western approach to Jerusalem. David took up a position west of the Philistines and attacked them from the rear, demolishing their forces. When the Philistines fled from the battlefield, they left behind their idols. They evidently looked to these for support in the way the Israelites had sought the help of God when they took the ark into battle against the Philistines (1 Samuel 4). David and his men carried off the idols and burned them (1 Chronicles 14:12) as prescribed in the law (Deuteronomy 7:5, 25).

David probably did not have the resources to follow up his victory over the Philistines and reduce them to the point that they could not attack again. So, either later in the year or during the next fighting season, the Philistines again gathered in the Valley of Rephaim. This time when David waited on the Lord for instructions, God told him to circle around behind the enemy and attack them in front of a grove of trees that are variously described in the translations of the Old Testament. Then David was instructed to wait until he heard the sound of "marching" (5:24) in the tops of the trees as if an army of God was approaching to smite the Philistine camp. When this sound brought panic to the Philistines, David was to advance from the rear.

From a naturalistic standpoint, the sea breeze reached Jerusalem about noon, with the rustle of the leaves covering the sound of the movement of Israelite troops through the woods. Thus they completely surprised the Philistines. Following God's instructions, David attacked with tremendous success. He routed the enemy and destroyed their forces all the way from Gibeon, six miles northwest of Jerusalem, to Gezer, some fifteen miles farther to the northwest.

Subsequently David carried the struggle to Philistine territory, defeating them at Metheg Ammah in the plain of Philistia, breaking the back of Philistine power, and incorporating Gath and its dependencies into his kingdom (2 Samuel 8:1; 1 Chronicles 18:1). Evidently he brought the Philistines within the Israelite sphere of influence. But he merely contained the Philistines within their borders; he did not occupy their land nor utterly crush them the way he did other peoples surrounding Israel.

David later employed a bodyguard of Philistine mercenaries. These Cherethites, Pelethites, Gittites and Carites proved to be so loyal to him that when Absalom revolted against him, they stuck with him. They remained loyal even when he invited them to go home because of his uncertain future (2 Samuel 15:17–22).

After David neutralized the Philistines, it would have been logical for him to gain firm control of lands west of the Jordan before embarking on Trans-Jordanian conquests. Herzog and Gichon claim that he did just that. He conquered the Sharon Plain, the Valley of Jezreel, and remaining Canaanite holdouts, as is clear from numer-

ous archaeological excavations.[16] The Old Testament does not spell out these military ventures.

David's Conquests East and North (2 Samuel 8:1–14; 10:1–11:1; 12:26–31; 1 Chronicles 18:1—20:3)

Now free to move east of the Jordan, David first turned his attention southeastward to Moab (2 Samuel 8:2; 1 Chronicles 18:2). Whatever friendly relations had existed between David and the Moabites (1 Samuel 22:3–4), they had evaporated. After defeating them, David used a well-known tactic for dealing with enemies notorious for their atrocities. He made them all lie down on the ground and passed a measuring line over them, putting to death two-thirds of them (Hebrew text; the Septuagint and Vulgate say one-half). Ancient Jewish commentators state that David's actions reflect their massacre of his parents and family.

Next came the Ammonites. In good faith David had sent a delegation to their capital Rabbah (modern Amman) to express his sympathy for the death of their king and to extend good wishes to the new one (2 Samuel 10:1–5). The Ammonites interpreted this as a spying mission and deliberately humiliated the delegation. Then the Ammonites realized that in effect they had made a declaration of war. So they hired a substantial number of mercenary troops from Aramean states in the north, and that is how these far northern principalities became involved in hostilities with the Israelite state.

Then David mobilized the army and sent it out under the command of Joab. Apparently Joab walked into a trap that may not even have been planned. Evidently the Ammonites came out of the city and drew up in battle array and Joab deployed his forces before them. Meanwhile, the Aramean mercenary troops were still "in the open field" (10:8), out of sight at his rear. Soon Joab realized that he could easily be squashed in a pincers movement. He determined rightly that the Arameans should be defeated first and probably were more vulnerable because they were hired troops and were without a fortification to fall back on. The Ammonites, on the other hand, were fighting for their homes and had the walled city of Rabbah to protect them.

So Joab divided his forces and prepared to lead the attack against the Arameans, while his brother Abishai faced the Ammonites and held them in check. Joab's attack proved completely successful and the Arameans fled. When the Ammonites saw that their support forces had been scattered, they panicked and fled inside the city walls. Joab probably did not have the resources to lay siege to the city, and/or it may have been too late in the year to begin the siege; so Joab returned to Jerusalem with his army after a successful campaign.

After their defeat the Arameans apparently went back home. Realizing that they would be forced to fight on alone, they immediately pulled together all the troops they could muster from the small states of northern Syria. When David learned of this threatened invasion, he mobilized the armies of Israel and apparently moved with great energy against the Arameans under the leadership of Hadadezer of Zobah and routed them completely. The northern confederacy lost over 40,000 men in the battle. David so decisively squashed the Arameans that the vassals broke away from Hadadezer and became subject to Israel. Evidently Hadadezer also became tributary to Israel. David stationed troops in Damascus. Moreover, the Arameans no longer had the strength or the will to help the Ammonites, so the Israelites no longer had to fight on two fronts.

After this fall engagement in the north, the rainy season set in and warfare ceased. The end of the rains in the spring signaled the beginning of the campaign season once more, and David sent the armies against the Ammonites under the leadership of Joab (2 Samuel 11:1). After initial victories in the countryside, Joab began the siege of the capital city of Rabbah. It was during this siege that David's adultery, the murder of Uriah the Hittite, and the birth and death of Bathsheba's son took place. Thus the siege evidently lasted about a year and involved some fierce contests (e.g., 2 Samuel 11:15).

We do not need to conclude that Solomon was actually born before David joined the men at the front (12:24), thus requiring a two-year siege. It is enough that Bathsheba was "comforted" and had another child on the way before David went to Rabbah.

Joab finally succeeded in taking the lower city, the "city of waters" or "water fort," the area where the water supply was located (12:26–27). With the main source of water gone, the defenders could not hope to hold out much longer. As a loyal subordinate, Joab wanted David to have the honor of taking the citadel, so he urged the king to come with some reinforcements and complete the conquest. David complied and conquered the city, bringing Ammonite resistance to an end.

David subsequently engaged in a campaign against the Edomites, with Abishai as military commander (1 Chronicles 18:12). The scene of the action, the Valley of Salt, cannot be identified with certainty but likely was the Arabah south of the Dead Sea. Once Edom had been vanquished David stationed occupation forces in the key centers of the country.

The Extent of David's Empire

David's empire extended from the Gulf of Aqabah in the south, almost to the Euphrates in the north, and from the Mediterranean in the west to the desert in the east. It controlled the three main north-south communication or trade routes of the Palestinian land bridge between Asia and Africa: Via Maris or the Mediterranean coastal road, the central route (through Jerusalem and Hebron), and the King's Highway that ran along the edge of the desert in the east.

Now Israel had achieved reasonably secure borders. David had subdued the Edomites, Moabites, and Ammonites on the east of the Jordan. Thus the foes of Hebrew tribes settled there were dislodged and the

HAMATH

(ZOBAH)

Mediterranean
Sea

PHOENICIA

Damascus

Tyre   Dan

Megiddo
Beth Shan

Shechem

Joppa   ISRAEL

Bethel   Jericho   Rabbah
Ashdod   (AMMON)
Ashkelon   Gath Jerusalem
Gaza   Hebron   Dead
                  Sea
Raphia   Beersheba
                    (MOAB)

Zoar

Bozrah

Kadesh Barnea
        (EDOM)

–N–

0   60 Mi.
0   60 Km.

Elath

© 1990 Thomas Nelson, Inc.

David's Kingdom

gold carried on ceremonial occasions by courtiers of Hadadezer, as well as a large quantity of bronze. From Hamath came silver, gold, and bronze. And from the other nations he collected silver and gold and other wealth. Differing from other oriental sovereigns, David did not hoard this wealth for himself but dedicated vast quantities of precious metals to God for construction of the temple.

Absalom's Rebellion

David's last military conflict differed from all the rest. Absalom's increasing estrangement from David finally erupted in full rebellion. As Absalom collected his forces and prepared to take over the government, David decided to flee Jerusalem. Soon both David and Absalom with their respective armies moved east of the Jordan, David to the strong town of Mahanaim in Gilead and Absalom not far away.

David divided his army into three groups: one under the command of Joab, a second under his brother Abishai, and the third under Ittai of Gath—probably the Philistine mercenaries. David's men forced him to stay in town, fearing something would happen to him. Inspired by their capable leadership, his men fell on Absalom's forces in the forest south of Mahanaim.

tribes were secure. Likewise, the southern frontier was pacified with the defeat of the Amalekites, the western frontier with the subjugation of the Philistines, and the northern frontier with the vanquishing of Zobah and Damascus. The repetition of the statement "The Lord gave David victory wherever he went" (2 Samuel 8:6, 14) helps to underscore divine involvement in the cause of Israel.

David collected tremendous amounts of booty from the various peoples he subjugated. From Zobah he brought the shields of

"The people of Israel" (2 Samuel 18:7), the heterogeneous mass of men who followed Absalom, broke ranks before the highly disciplined veterans of David and suffered twenty thousand casualties. As

Absalom's men fled, the forest "devoured more people than the sword" (2 Samuel 18:8). That is, the thick forest, the underbrush, and the rocky terrain impeded flight; and more of them were killed in the aftermath of battle than in the battle itself. Evidently many fell to their death over precipices.

While he was fleeing, "Absalom happened to run into some of David's followers" (18:9 JB). As he was riding his mule (a mark of royalty), his "head" became wedged between two branches. When he raised his hands to try to dislodge himself, he let go of the bridle and the unrestrained mule kept on going. More than likely he was riding without a saddle and simply slipped off the beast's back and hung suspended in midair. The text does not say he was caught by his hair; the historian Josephus stated that. He probably had a helmet over his hair on this occasion; so his hair would not have caught in the branches.

One of the men in Joab's force promptly reported Absalom's plight to him, thinking that Joab should capture him and so end the conflict. Joab grabbed three darts and ran off to deal with Absalom. Once Joab had taken the lead in wounding Absalom, perhaps mortally, his bodyguard had no fear of finishing the deed. Perhaps Joab dared to disobey David because he believed Absalom had to die for David's own good and the peace of Israel. Once Absalom had died, there was no reason for continuing the carnage. Joab blew the ram's horn and signaled a cease-fire. They threw Absalom's body into a pit and heaped a huge pile of stones over it as an ignominious monument. Perhaps each of the men of the army threw a stone on the pile to curse Absalom's memory. They had no idea how deeply David would mourn the loss of his son.

David's Army and Its Weapons

Every able-bodied adult Israelite male had to serve in the military during the monarchy (see, e.g., 1 Samuel 8: 11–12). David organized this national army into units of thousands, hundreds, fifties, and tens. But whether those number designations indicated the exact size of a unit is open to question. Very possibly they were simply designations of units of relative size.

Just as, for example, the Roman century (or hundred) in actuality consisted of seventy or eighty men.

The tribes maintained military training programs and in many instances concentrated on certain specialties (see discussion below). Then from these tribal programs twenty-four thousand served in the active reserves for one month each year (1 Chronicles 27:1). In an emergency the other eleven divisions could be called up, providing an army of 280,000. Of course a citizen army consisted of men who needed to raise food and in other ways to support themselves and keep the war effort going. The tendency was to plan military actions in the spring or early summer when farmers were least inconvenienced: "in the spring of the year, at the time when kings go out to battle" (2 Samuel 11:1 NKJV).

Seasonal conscript armies could not meet all the needs of the Hebrew state. Therefore David established and maintained a standing army that consisted of three regiments. The first comprised the band of "mighty men" who gravitated to David while he was a fugitive and later was king in Hebron. The second contained the "mighty men" who came to him in Hebron from the northern tribes and east of the Jordan (for both, see 1 Chronicles 12). The third regiment consisted of foreign mercenaries—Cherethites and Pelethites, the Gittites under the command of Ittai, the Gittite from Gath, and more. Then David maintained a sort of home guard staffed by Levites in some of the militarily unstable districts. Herzog and Gichon conclude that the Israelite kingdom could not have kept more than 50,000 men in the field for any length of time.[17]

In David's day the Hebrew army was no longer without conventional weapons, as it had been during the days of the Conquest, the judges, and Saul. David had broken the Philistine monopoly on iron with the defeat of those people. Victories over various other kingdoms resulted in the acquisition of armor as booty. In that connection came the introduction of the chariot corps. With the defeat of Hadadezer, king of Zobah, David captured one thousand chariots (1 Chronicles 18:4). He hamstrung or lamed many of the horses but saved enough of them for one hundred chariots. He now had a small chariot corps, but they were of limited use in hilly Palestine. Solomon kept only fourteen hundred chariots in his army (1 Kings 10:26).

As to the variety of weapons available to David, we get some help from 1 Chronicles 12, which details weapons and military expertise of some of the Hebrew tribes. Men of Benjamin demonstrated special abilities as slingers and bowmen—and they were ambidextrous (v. 2). Gadites adeptly handled shields and spears and provided rapidly moving light infantry units ("swift as gazelles on the mountains," v. 8). Likewise, the tribes of Judah and Naphtali proved expert with shield and spear, giving David the closely arrayed heavy phalanx (vv. 24, 34).

The Zebulunites were more versatile ("expert in war with all weapons of war," v. 33); and the Zebulunites, Danites, and Asherites were known for standing their ground in battle formation, i. e., trained to fight in rank and file (vv. 33, 35, 36). The tribe of Issachar seems to have specialized in intelligence missions ("had understanding of the times, to know what Israel ought to do," v. 32 NKJV).

The tribes east of the Jordan—Reuben, Gad, half tribe of Manasseh—came equipped "for battle with every kind of weapon of war" (v. 37). Possibly their higher level of equipment meant that the Philistine effort to deprive the Hebrews of iron weapons did not so greatly affect peoples east of the Jordan. Though the chronicler does not mention swords specifically, men of the army generally must have had them by David's day.

Solomon's Fortifications

"And this is the reason for the labor force which King Solomon raised: to build. . . the wall of Jerusalem, Hazor, Megiddo, and Gezer. . . . Lower Beth Horon, Baalath and Tadmor in the wilderness." (1 Kings 9:15-18 NKJV) *"And Solomon gathered chariots and horsemen; for he had one thousand four hundred chariots and twelve thousand horsemen, whom he stationed in the chariot cities and with the king in Jerusalem."* (1 Kings 10:26 NKJV)

A power vacuum in the middle East, with the Egyptians, Hittites, Myceneans, Assyrians, Babylonians, and Medo-Persians all weak, gave David the opportunity to build his empire. Most of them were, however, down but not out, and new royal lines might spur them to aggressive action once more. Besides, smaller kingdoms, such as the Syrians of Damascus or the Moabites of Transjordan, did not like being dominated by a Hebrew superpower and looked for a chance to break free. Solomon had to run hard just to stand still—just to maintain what David had conquered. In fact, in his twenty-fourth year when he began his fortification efforts (1 Kings 9:10), the ambitious Shishak I or Sheshonk I of Egypt took the reins of government there. Not only did he make expansionist noises, but he also harbored and encouraged such political exiles as Jeroboam, who had presumably tried to mount a coup against Solomon and who later would rule the Northern Kingdom (1 Kings 11:26). And Damascus successfully revolted under the leadership of Rezon (1 Kings 11:23-25).

A quick look at the short list of Solomon's fortified cities noted above makes it clear that there were not enough of them to create a sort of "Maginot Line." In fact, it would have been virtually impossible for him to build such a line of defense. If he had tried, he would have been forced to construct a southern line in the Negev, an eastern line along the edge of the desert, and a northern line south of Mount Hermon. The result would have been "fortress Israel." Such an expenditure would have bankrupted the kingdom and the manpower requirement would have overtaxed the state's human resources.

Solomon's employed the only workable alternatives. He built and equipped several fortress centers or anchor points in the defense system Then he established a mobile force that could quickly meet offensive or defensive needs as they arose: a chariot corps.

He built a formidable system of fortresses. Hazor guarded a strategic point north of the Sea of Galilee; Megiddo stood at the base of the Plain of Esdraelon;

Beth-horon blocked the pass to Jerusalem by way of Aijalon; Baalath stood on the highway from Jerusalem to the port of Joppa; Gezer protected the main road and entrance to the valley of Sorek; Tamar on the southern border could defend caravans from Ezion-geber. No fortress stood east of Jerusalem, the valley of the Jordan being considered a sufficient barrier. Tadmor is usually identified with Palmyra in Syria, which provided a means of policing the desert and protecting the valuable trade route that passed through the Syrian desert from Damascus to Mesopotamia. The terrain in all of them permitted a swift deployment of chariots.

Excavations at Hazor, Megiddo, and Gezer reveal significant Solomonic construction at each place. All three have six-chambered gates, which seem to be an improvement on earlier four-chambered gates of Canaan and Syria. But the gates are not sufficiently identical to point to a single or centralized planning office.

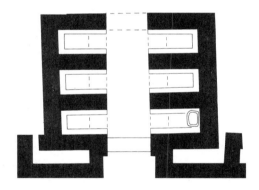

Plan of the six-chambered Solomonic gate at Gezer

At Hazor and Gezer the Solomonic gates are attached to casemate walls. These consist of two parallel walls with the space between them divided into small rooms by partition walls. Each room is called a casemate and has a door on the city side of the wall. The outer wall is about four and one-half feet thick and the inner one about three feet thick, with about eight feet between. The casemates could serve as storerooms, barracks, or the rear room of a house. Casemate construction has been

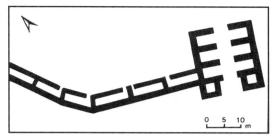

Plan of the six-chambered Solomonic gate at Hazor, attached to a casemate city wall

found at other places in Israel, and it has been found in later building activity. Solid walls were more common during later centuries, and sometimes casemates were filled in. The change reflects an effort to defend against Assyrian battering rams.

What Solomon's chariots looked like must be left open to question. Egyptian chariots tended to be fairly light and quite speedy in the field. The heavier chariots of Asia Minor (Hittite) and Mesopotamia possibly contained a crew of three and thus had greater attack power. Which style Solomon preferred we cannot tell, but the fact that David began Israel's chariot corps with one hundred chariots captured from Hadadezer of Zobah in the far north (1 Chronicles 18:4) may provide a hint. These heavier chariots may have provided the pattern for Israelite chariot builders to copy.

The fact that Solomon had 12,000 "horsemen" or charioteers for 1400 chariots allows for a double crew of trained men to spell each other, and at least some of the chariots

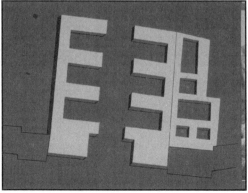

Plan of the six-chambered Solomonic gate at Megiddo

Solomon's Stables at Megiddo

When the University of Chicago team excavated Megiddo between 1925 and 1939, they identified Stratum IV as Solomonic, and they concluded that two groups of pillared buildings were stable compounds. Each stable consisted of three parts, a central passage flanked by two parallel aisles, and separated from the central passage by rows of square pillars. Between the pillars were troughs or mangers carved from single blocks of stone. The central passage was paved with crushed limestone and the side aisles with blocks of stone. The roof of the central passage evidently was higher than the side aisles and had windows for illumination of the structure. In the northern compound were twelve horse barns and in the southern compound five barns and a large parade ground. The excavators believed that the two compounds housed about 450 horses.

Similar pillared buildings have been found at Hazor, Beersheba, Tell el-Hesi and elsewhere. And the debate has raged for decades over whether they were stables, barracks, or storerooms. Gabriel Barkay has argued cogently that these buildings served the same function everywhere and that their identification as "stables is to be preferred over other views."[18] No strong evidence indicates anything else.

Housing and Furniture

As noted in the last chapter, the four room house persisted as the basic plan of most Israelite houses. This house plan seems to have originated before 1200 B.C. and continued through the united monarchy and the northern and southern kingdoms down to the destruction of Jerusalem at the hands of the Babylonians in 586 B.C. After that it passed out of fashion. How the Israelites came to adopt this house plan we do not know, but it seems that they developed it. In excavations it appeared everywhere—in town, on the farms, and in isolated houses.

What we are talking about was a fourfold division of space (not necessarily four rooms), with three parallel units closed on the end by a perpendicular unit. Normally the door led into an open court where cooking and other kinds of work took place,

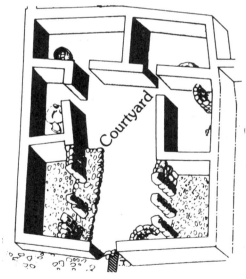

A four-room house at Tirzah, first capital of Omri before he built Samaria. The four-room house was the typical Israelite house for centuries. This was not literally four rooms but a fourfold division of space with three parallel units closed on the end by a perpendicular unit. The middle unit was an open court, with storage on the right, often animal pens on the left, and living quarters on the end. There could be a second story.

may have had a crew of three. In such a case, there would have been a driver, a bowman, and a third man with a shield and lance or spear. Lighter chariots had crews of two: the charioteer and a warrior—an archer or spearman. But if the second man was primarily a bowman, the chariot also commonly carried a warrior with a lance or spear.

(For more on this topic, go to p. 118 or p. 232.)

Megiddo was one of Solomon's great fortress cities. This is Stratum IV, identified as Solomonic, with its wall, impressive gate, and horse and chariot facilities. The southern compound, with its five barns and a large parade ground, is at the top of the picture. The northern compound, with its twelve horse barns, is at the bottom of the picture.

such as grinding of grain or weaving of cloth. On the right a storage area might be separated from the courtyard by a solid wall or square stone pillars. And of course it might be divided into two or more rooms. On the left were usually animal pens.

Israelites often subdivided this area. The perpendicular area in the rear served as living quarters and also could be subdivided. Sometimes this area was a casemate in the city wall. Often external stone stairways led to an upper floor or roof where additional living space was available. No doubt in some cases wooden stairs or ladders to a second floor have disappeared. The Israelites usually constructed roofs of houses with wooden beams covered with brush and finished off with tamped clay.

We find little furniture in these houses. People normally sat on the ground. Bedrolls might be laid on the ground or on a stone or brick bench which could serve as a place to sit during the day. While King Saul or King David or King Solomon may have sat at a low table to eat, probably most poor people spread their food on skins or some other covering on the ground.

Light reached the other rooms from the central courtyard. But additional illumina-

tion came from small oil lamps. These changed style frequently, but during the united and divided monarchies were open clay saucers that would fill an adult hand when held open. The lamp was pinched to hold a wick of flax; the fuel was olive oil. Normally there were no toilets in the houses; human excrement was disposed of in nearby waste ground. Sewage and animal manure commonly littered the streets of towns. Conditions in houses or in town usually were anything but sanitary.

Not only did houses not have sewage disposal, they also did not have a water supply piped in either. From time immemorial and on down into New Testament times women went with their water jars to the village well in the evening to get water for the next day. To protect themselves, people chose to live on hills and surrounded themselves with walls. Of course water does not flow uphill, so providing a water supply during a siege proved especially difficult.

During the monarchy, when forced labor could be commanded, the kings built great water systems at numerous places; e.g., Megiddo, Gezer, Hazor, and Gibeon, and about a dozen other places. In general, these systems involved a cut down inside the city wall, at the bottom of which a diagonal shaft ended in a spring fed pool where water could be collected for personal and family use. The pool or spring normally would have been outside the city wall but now was covered over and brought within the system. Archaeologists argue about whether these systems were created in Solomon's day or later, but the fine points of archaeological debate are beyond the scope of our present study.

With the greater degree of peace and security in Solomon's reign and following, there was a considerable amount of city planning reflected in newly-established or refurbished towns. The best example of a complete city plan is that of Beersheba. The town was oval-shaped. Inside the gate was a square that served as the central place of business. The street plan consisted of concentric ovals. At the southeast corner of town was the water system that descended to the water table. Similar city planning may be seen at Tell Beit Mirsim, Mizpah (Tell en-Nasbeh), Beth Shemesh, and elsewhere.

(For more on this topic, go to p. 132 or p. 243.)

Diet and Foodstuffs

Variety in the diet, means of production, and processing of food did not change appreciably during the monarchy from what it had been in the days of the judges (see chapter 6). But there were two developments in land ownership. They are important and relevant here because Hebrew society was essentially agricultural.

Before we look at these changes, we should understand basic attitudes toward land ownership and management. First, God had declared that He owned the land. "The land is Mine," says Leviticus 25:23. And He granted Canaan to Abraham and his descendants (Genesis 13:14–15). As Joshua and the Israelites entered Canaan, God renewed the promise of ownership of the land, which would now be theirs by conquest and settlement (Joshua 1:2; 24). That land was divided among the tribes by lot (Joshua 13—19). Then each tribe had the responsibility of allocating its land to clans and families.

Families guarded their inheritance carefully. The eldest son inherited the family possession (Deuteronomy 21:17). But if a man had no sons, the land passed to his brother. If that could not happen, the next of kin received it (Numbers 27:11). Daughters might inherit the land if there were no sons to inherit the land, provided they married within their father's clan (Numbers 27:1–8; 36:1–9).

A family could lose its inheritance through drought or economic hardship. In such an event a close relative could buy it back (the kinsman redeemer, Leviticus 25:25). Or the one selling the land could buy it back himself at a later time. The Mosaic law also provided that in the year of Jubilee, every fiftieth year, unredeemed lands had to be returned to their original owners (Leviticus 25:31).

Crown Lands

The first major development in land ownership during the monarchy was the introduction of crown lands. Evidently Saul accumulated substantial acreage by the time of his death, and David gave it all to Saul's son Mephibosheth (2 Samuel 9:9–10).

David must have amassed extensive royal estates. He conquered Jerusalem, which was in a neutral area belonging to no tribe of Israel. Thereafter it became royal property by right of conquest and was known as "the city of David" (2 Samuel 5:7, 9). As he conquered territories (1 Chronicles 18), he no doubt appropriated estates for the support of the palace. Other pieces he granted to friends and supporters to strengthen his political network (e.g., 2 Samuel 9:7; 14:30; 1 Kings 2:26). Also, he had received Ziklag from the Philistines, and there is no indication that he ever relinquished it (1 Samuel 27:5–10). Royal properties increased during the days of Solomon. As an example in point, he received Gezer as dowry from the Pharaoh of Egypt when he married his Egyptian wife (1 Kings 9:16).

G. I. Benefits?

A second development in land ownership may have been land grants to officers in the military in return for service. First

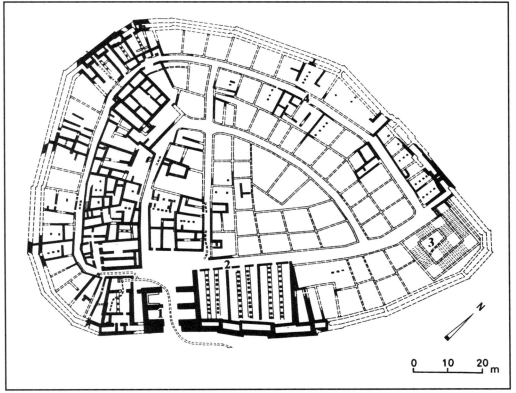

City plan of Beersheba: 1. City gate. 2. Storehouse. 3. Water system. 4. Peripheral street.
(After Z. Herzog)

Samuel 22:7 hints at this: "Then Saul said to his servants who stood about him, 'Hear now, you Benjamites! Will the son of Jesse give every one of you fields and vineyards and make you all captains of thousands and captains of hundreds?'" (NKJV). The question intimates that Saul made such grants. And there is no reason why David should not have given tracts of land to other veterans. Kings customarily shared booty with the troops after victory in battle. What would have been more natural than to bestow some conquered farmland·on victorious troops, especially the officers?

(For more on this topic, go to p. 133 or p. 245.)

Dress

Not much can be said about Israelite clothing during the united monarchy that differs from comments on clothing in the last chapter. As in the earlier period, wool and linen dominated as the two fabrics available. Linen seems to have been more expensive and thus appears to have been reserved for special occasions. For example, when David accompanied the ark as it was brought into Jerusalem, he wore "fine linen" (1 Chronicles 15:27).

With dyestuffs and the dyeing process so expensive, men and women of all classes tended to wear undyed fabrics a good part of the time. Tamar, King David's daughter, wore a "robe of many colors" (2 Samuel 13:18), fit for a princess, and signifying her virginity. Presumably this was a robe with broad colored stripes. The same Hebrew word used here appears in Genesis 37:3, to describe Joseph's special coat.

During the monarchy period both men and women of all classes wore loincloths and long robes or tunics—ankle or calf length—most of the time. Their cloak also doubled as a blanket at night. And though soldiers often wore shorter garments to facilitate movement and fighting, Saul as king and officer in the military wore a long robe or tunic (see 1 Samuel 24:4, 11). Presumably men engaged in such occupations as fishing or cutting and working stone or sailing ships along with the Phoenicians wore short kilts without shirts or short tunics.

(For more on this topic, go to p. 136 or p. 245.)

Family Life

Fathers

Hebrew society was a patriarchy. That is, the father ruled an extended family. In fact, he had the power of life and death over the household. The law charged him to protect and provide for his land and children, so he determined how the household would farm and herd.

The father negotiated marriages and covenants for his sons and daughters. Marriage was a negotiated covenant, often a drawn-out process, involving a political or economic contract. It brought together two households in a business arrangement. Betrothal involved a choice of partners, an agreement on a bride-price, and a dowry. The father of the household of the groom sent a gift, a bride-price, to the father of the household of the bride. If the father of the bride accepted the proposal, he provided a dowry for his daughter and allowed the groom to take the bride to his household. After the marriage, the couple usually lived with the father of the groom until he chose an heir. Society was "patrilinear," that is, the heir must be a natural or adopted son of the father.

Only fathers of households could extend invitations of hospitality. Wives and daughters could do so only with the permission of the father. Strangers could and usually did refuse the first invitation, probably as a matter of protocol. Commonly the host offered little to the guest—some water, a little food, and a night's lodging. This kept the guest from declining the invitation because the fear of accepting it would be a burden on the family. And it gave opportunity for the host to provide more later. The host was expected to supply the best available for his guests. Hosts washed the feet of strangers, indicating that they were under the care and protection of the household. The length of a visit was usually specified at the time of the invitation. A society without inns or hotels depended on family hospitality.

Mothers

Child-bearing remained the primary responsibility of the mother or wife, who had the authority to manage the household. She rationed and allocated food supplies, prepared food and processed and stored it. She served as administrator with economic responsibilities as she managed the "family budget," and judicial responsibilities as she adjudicated squabbles within the household. And while the father or patriarch designated an heir, the mother often exercised the power (note Bathsheba's role in the selection of Solomon to be king). The mother taught the children. This is an important point to keep in mind when we think of all the pagan women in Solomon's harem—incapable of bringing up children in the ways of God and thus contributing to the rise of idolatry. When boys became young men, fathers took over the responsibility for their education, but mothers continued the responsibility of teaching girls after they became young women. Although women often helped out with herding and farming, the primary responsibility for such activity rested with the men.

In modern feminist discussion the assumption is often made that women in ancient Israel had inferior roles. But the women in Hebrew households had a status equal to or greater than the status of many men. And the biblical pattern is to honor one's "father *and* mother" (e.g., Exodus 20:12; 2 Samuel 19:37; Proverbs 15:20). Honoring involved respect, deference to, obedience to, and caring for in old age or adverse circumstances in a society that had no social security provisions.

Midwives

In a society without physicians, midwives played an essential role. They provided women with prenatal education, aid in childbearing labor, assistance in the delivery of a baby, and postnatal care. Evidently they got their education through long periods of apprenticeship. They certified that a woman was pregnant and helped her through the stages of pregnancy. At the time of delivery they saw to the availability of a birthing stool, which supported the mother's weight and positioned her hips for delivery. Normally this birthing stool consisted simply of two stones arranged close enough together to support the mother's hips. After the mother had delivered the baby, the midwife cut its umbilical cord and tied off the stump. Then they washed the baby with a saltwater solution and rubbed its body with olive oil. Midwives provided the mother with postnatal advice. Female infants were normally weaned in eighteen months and male infants at thirty.

Slaves

War and debt reduced people to slavery in Israel. But in both cases their lot and numbers differed from that of their pagan neighbors. In warfare the Israelites commonly killed off defeated peoples who were under the curse of God, rather than taking large numbers of them captive. They did not sell captives on the open slave market but they became slaves of the state and worked for the temple, the palace, the farms of the king and other officials. A case in point is what happened to the Gibeonites in the days of Joshua. After their deception of Israel, Joshua permitted them to live but enslaved them as woodcutters and water carriers to help prepare the sacrifices of the tabernacle and later the temple (Joshua 9:27). Such slaves remained in perpetual bondage, and their servile status was more evident because they were racially different from the Hebrews.

Debt slaves were Hebrews and thus racially the same as their masters. They became temporary slaves who worked for the people to whom they owed goods and services, and they were set free after the debt was paid or after a maximum of six years of service. But Exodus 21:1–6 introduces contingencies. If a male became a slave, he could go out free. If he and his wife had become slaves together, they

could both go out free. But if the master had given a man a wife, he could go free but his wife and children could not. If the slave then declared that he would continue his servitude because of his love for his wife and children, he should be brought to the doorpost and his ear pierced with an awl and his servitude made perpetual. Also, if a woman was sold into servitude and her master or master's son married her, she could not go free at the end of six years (Exodus 21:7–8).

Education—Music Education

"David ordered the chiefs of the Levites to install as musicians those of their kinsmen who were players skilled in making joyful music on their instruments—lutes, lyres, and cymbals." (1 Chronicles 15:16 REB)

We have seen that society held mothers and fathers responsible for the education of their children during the united monarchy. We do not know whether that education included a knowledge of reading and writing. In the homes of Levites and priests it probably did, because of their obligations in tabernacle and temple worship.

The performance of vocal and instrumental music developed as an important dimension of Hebrew culture during the united monarchy, though largely on an informal basis. One person learned from another how to make a musical instrument and/or how to play it. We do not know how David got his lyre and how he learned to play it. But he came recommended to the court of Saul as an accomplished musician. And it is interesting to learn that Saul's courtiers knew the therapeutic value of playing the lyre to treat mental depression. Evidently they considered that an acceptable way of dealing with emotional distress (see 1 Samuel 16:16–23). Later David was called the "sweet singer of Israel" (2 Samuel 23:1).

In the days of Saul, David, and Solomon numerous musical instruments were made and played on a variety of occasions. Prophets played as Saul was entering on his office of kingship (1 Samuel 10:5). Court and temple musicians played at the procession of the ark into Jerusalem (2 Samuel

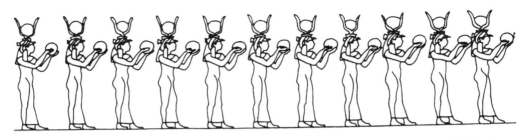

Tambourine players from the Temple of Dendera, Egypt. This procession is reminiscent of Miriam's celebration with the women with their tambourines and dancing after crossing the Red Sea (Exodus 15:20–21).

Harp, lute, and double pipe, from a tomb painting at Thebes, Egypt. Two harps, from a tomb painting at Thebes, Egypt. Sistrum in the Berlin Museum.

6:5); at Solomon's enthronement (1 Kings 1:39–40); and at the dedication of the temple (2 Chronicles 5:12–14).

David must be credited with the appearance of professional musicians in Israelite society—in temple and royal court (1 Chronicles 6:31–48; 15:16—16:6; 25:1–31). He probably paid them from either the royal or temple treasury. David appointed four thousand to praise the Lord with instruments (1 Chronicles 23:5), placing the musical program under the direction of Asaph, Heman, and Jeduthun and their sons and relatives (1 Chronicles 25:1). This group totaled 288 men (1 Chronicles 25:7) organized into twenty-four divisions of twelve each. The appointment to specific responsibilities was assigned by lot, assuring that there would be no favoritism in assigning their duties. Plenty of education in music and rehearsal must have been involved. The text talks about "teachers and students" and "instruction in the songs of the Lord" (1 Chronicles 25: 7, 8).

Interestingly, their work was called a "ministry of prophesying" (1 Chronicles 25:1), which must have meant a sort of musical proclamation of the Word of God and expressions of praise and worship. Moreover, David and the captains of the army took an active role in appointing the leaders and organizing the musical program. Was this shades of the West Point Band and Chorus serving God and country?

In the foregoing verses the chronicler refers to a substantial number of musical instruments. Now we make an effort to describe briefly the musical instruments known in Israel about 1000 B.C. Unfortunately the English versions do not

Some biblical instruments: left to right: flute, double flute or oboe, ram's horn or shophar, tambourine or hand drum, metal trumpet, rattle, sistrum, conical cymbals, flat cymbals (only about five inches in diameter; not large like modern counterparts).

translate the Hebrew names consistently, either within or between the versions, so it is necessary to resort to the Hebrew names here. For ease of discussion the various instruments are arranged in three classes: string, wind, and percussion. The KJV translations appear in parentheses.

Stringed Instruments

`Asor (translated three times as instrument of ten strings; ten, once; tenth, 12 times) was neither a lyre nor a harp but an instrument of ten strings of some other nature. Probably a zither.

Kinnor (harp, 42 times). This was the lyre, made of wood with gut or metal strings. Its sound box was below the strings. David did not play a harp at all but a lyre. And wherever the word "harp" appears in the KJV of the Old Testament it should be translated "lyre." A plectrum was generally used to play it; but in the case of David in Saul's court it is said that he played with his hand (e.g., 1 Samuel 16:23). The explanation of this may be that players did solo work with the hand and accompaniment with a plectrum. The body of the instrument is really a quadrangular-shaped board with the upper half cut out.

Nebel (psaltery, 23 times; viol, 4). This instrument had the sound box above and was the true harp. The harp is also different from the lyre in that it has a bridge about two-thirds of the way down the instrument, over which the strings pass. Harps known in Egypt at the time of David include one that was bow-shaped, sporting twenty strings, a triangular variety with nine strings, and one that looked like a flat boat with strings running from mast to deck.

Neginah (music, 1; song, 5; stringed instrument, 1). This term occurs in the titles of various Psalms (e.g., 4, 6) and was not an instrument but a word for string music in general.

Wind Instruments

Chalil (pipe, 6 times). This was a flute, made of box, lotus and laurel wood, reed, bone, ivory, and metal at a later date. It could be a single straight pipe or a double flute. It was the most ancient and the most widely popular of all musical instruments. Egypt knew two kinds of flutes, one that had a mouthpiece on the end and the other which resembled the embouchure of our modern instrument. The Egyptian flute was over two feet long and it touched the ground when the player was seated. Chalil may be a term for woodwinds generally, including the single and double flute, the single and double clarinet, and the single and double oboe. During the monarchy, pipers in countries surrounding Israel were using the double oboe and Hebrews must have been using it too.

Chatsotserah (trumpet, 28 times; trumpeter, 1). This is the silver trumpet that God commanded Moses to make (Numbers 10:1). Josephus describes it as nearly a yard long, a little wider than a flute, with a bell-like end, and a slight expansion at the mouthpiece to catch the breath.[19] Almost entirely a religious instrument, it was used to give signals during the years of wanderings, to proclaim the fiftieth year of Jubilee, and to sound a sabbatical year and Day of Atonement (Leviticus 25:8–11). The use of the instrument began with a pair of them (Numbers 10:2). And on the Arch of Titus at the Forum of Rome the two *chatsotserah* are shown being carried off with the table of shewbread and the seven-branched lampstand. This is the only Hebrew instrument of which we have an undoubtedly authentic representation.

Shophar (cornet, 4; trumpet, 68; taken to be synonymous with *qeren,* horn, 75 times). Originally a ram's horn in its natural form; the Hebrews heated, flattened and bent it to form a right angle. A skilled performer could play several tones on it, but many got only two tones—the tonic and fifth. In later times these horns were made of metal and straightened, leading to confusion with the *chatsotserah.* Its tone was loud and piercing and unsuited for concert music. It was blown at the proclamation of the law (Exodus 19:13); opening of the year of Jubilee (Leviticus 25:9); heralded the approach of the ark (2 Samuel 6:15); and announced a new king (2 Samuel 15:10).

Ugab (organ, 4). Some call this a pan's pipe, similar to a mouth organ. Others identify it as a flute. We can't identify it certainly.

Percussion Instruments

Menaanim (cornets, 1). The Hebrew word comes from the verb which means "to move to and fro unsteadily," "to vibrate," probably signifying that it was an instrument for shaking like the sistrum. This instrument has an oval frame, with iron rods having hooked ends lying loosely in holes in the sides. A handle was attached to this.

Metsiltayim (cymbals, 13 times). Probably they were cymbals clashed together horizontally. Josephus describes this type of cymbal as flat, probably like a plate, made of heavy bronze.

Toph (tabret, 8; timbrel, 9). Miriam and other women in Exodus 15:20 played this instrument. Scriptural references show that women usually played it, but men were not excluded (1 Samuel 10:5). Some equate this with the Arabic *duf,* which was a wooden hoop about eleven inches in diameter and about two inches deep. A skin was stretched over it and metal disks hung loosely in openings around the side. This, then, was held in one hand and beaten with the other, producing a jingling effect. Others believe it was a wooden hoop with two skins and without a

jingling contrivance. So it would be closer to a snare drum. The term may be an over-all classification for drums. If a single drum, it might sound something like a tom-tom when beaten by hand.

Shalishim (instrument of music, 1). This instrument is classified here because of the prevalent suggestion that it is a triangle and as such would belong to the percussion class. But scholars suggest various other identifications and no satisfactory conclusion seems available at the present time.

Tseltselim (cymbals, 3 times). These are probably the conical type of cymbals known in Egypt and Assyria which are struck together vertically.

Vocal Music

Very little light can be shed upon the vocal music of Israel, but from such passages as Exodus 20 it is clear that antiphonal singing remained the favorite style. Antiphonal singing could be done in three ways: with a leader and choir, a choir and the congregation, or two choirs (cf. Pss. 13, 20, 38). Musical instruments accompanied singers and commonly did not provide orchestral entertainment. The expression "instruments of song," which occurs in several passages of the Old Testament as a general term for all kinds of music instruments, shows plainly that the ancient Hebrews used instrumental music primarily to accompany singing.

Indications which may be gleaned from titles of the Psalms reflect something of the high development of Hebrew vocal music. Apparently many of them are instructions telling how the Psalms should be sung. A few examples follow: Psalm 9: To the tune of "Death of the Son"; Psalm 22: To the tune of "The Deer of the Dawn"; Psalm 45: To the tune of "The Lilies"; Psalm 53: To the tune of "Mahalath"; Psalms 54 and 55: With String Music.

(For more on this topic, go to p. 137 or p. 246.)

Work, Travel, and Commerce

In a sense Israel came out of her shell during the united monarchy. Instead of being concerned primarily or exclusively with survival and with local affairs and food production, she became aware of a wider world and came to dominate part of it. And though most of her people still engaged in subsistence agriculture, many of them began to take up other occupations because of the new international involvements and the building of a national infrastructure. Palestine served as the land bridge between Asia and Africa, and thus was naturally caught up in the cross currents of the eastern Mediterranean world and the movement of peoples and goods across the region. The establishment of peace and stability in the region brought an increase in the flow of goods and ideas and the stimulation that comes from international trade.

For the mass of population still engaged in subsistence agriculture, life remained much the same as it had been for generations. Military requirements, however, imposed new demands on the populace, as did the need to establish an infrastructure, and the commercial adventures of the monarchy.

Demands of War and Military Preparedness

A standing army served the needs of the monarchy, beginning with Saul and continuing on in the reigns of David and Solomon. In the initial stage, during Saul's reign, the force numbered 3,000; but it grew much larger during subsequent administrations. As noted earlier, every able-bodied male entered compulsory national military service. During David's administration a new group of 24,000 active reservists was called to duty each month (1 Chronicles 27:1). To the standing infantry units, Solomon added 12,000 charioteers on constant duty in the cities where his chariots were stationed (1 Kings 10:26). It is unnecessary to determine the exact number in the standing armies of Israel at any given time. The point to be made here is that alongside those engaged in agriculture a substantial number learned the art of war and made their living from that activity.

Tens of thousands engaged in actual warfare from time to time during the reigns of Saul and David in addition to the standing army. The demands of war and military preparedness siphoned off the wealth of the state and kept many busy in non-productive activity. Also, many made their living supplying the troops with foodstuffs and "uniforms," and making weapons.

Demands of the Infrastructure

Solomon as a man of peace with an empire to govern, had a lot of work to do to develop the infrastructure of the state. As noted in connection with his wisdom, he organized the administrative machinery to guarantee the functioning of the government and the collection of revenues. He employed many in the state bureaucracy.

He needed men to build government facilities. The palace served not only the vanity of the king. In an absolute monarchy, the king is the government, and his palace serves both as the White House and the Capitol building. Again, the satisfaction of vanity did not alone dictate the grandiosity of the structure. It had to be capable of expressing the power of the central government that could keep the people in line, as well as providing the grandness that could impress foreign dignitaries and command their respect. Comments have already been made about the construction of David's palace and Solomon's palace complex.

Furthermore, Solomon as head of the Israelite state had to build a house for God that would be sufficiently grand to impress citizens and foreigners alike with the magnificence of Israel's God. Something tacky wouldn't glorify God.

Construction of both government buildings and the temple required a work force and architectural skill, materials, and craftsmen Israel did not have. To provide the work force Solomon introduced the Corvée, or forced labor, into Israel. First Kings 5:13 mentions thirty thousand men conscripted from all Israel and divided into relays of ten thousand to help build the temple. Each man served one month in Lebanon and two months at home or "in his house," that is, in Solomon's temple; so the total service was three months a year. Apparently thirty thousand were called up at one time; on this relay plan a total of one hundred-twenty thousand would be needed in the course of a year.

This passage should not be thought to conflict with 1 Kings 9:20–22, which says that only non-Israelites were conscripted. The forced labor here is temporary and did not involve serfdom; the forced labor in 9:20–22 is forced labor on slaves or aliens and may be taken as more permanent.

In addition, Solomon had seventy thousand burden bearers or porters and eighty thousand stonecutters working in the hills north of Jerusalem under the supervision of 3,300 foremen. These were evidently all aliens, for 2 Chronicles 2:17 mentions a Solomonic census of aliens that turned up 153,600 of them, of which seventy thousand became burden bearers or carriers and eighty thousand stonecutters. Master carpenters and masons employed in Jerusalem came from Gebal (v. 18) or Byblos (about 25 miles north of Beirut).

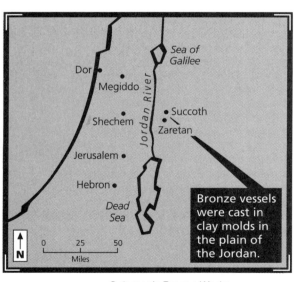

Solomon's Bronze Works

To fill his needs in producing quality construction, David had turned to Phoenicia and had established a virtual alliance with Hiram, king of Tyre (2 Samuel 5:11-12). With the death of David and the accession of Solomon to the throne, Hiram sent condolences to Solomon and best wishes for his administration; but especially he wanted to negotiate a treaty of alliance or trade with Solomon. Solomon jumped at the chance to meet his building needs (cf. 2 Chronicles

2:3-15). Solomon then made the proposal that Hiram provide him with cedar of Lebanon and that Hebrews work with Phoenicians to complete the temple.

Hiram's responded enthusiastically. He would provide the needed cedar and cypress logs. In return he requested wheat and olive oil for his royal court. So the two of them made a treaty (1 Kings 5:12; cf. 2 Chronicles 2:3-15).

We have already seen that a certain Hiram of Tyre (not the king), skilled in metal working, directed the making of bronze and gold furnishings for the temple. He cast his productions in clay molds in the "plains of the Jordan between Succoth and Zarethan" (1 Kings 7:46) on the east bank of the Jordan. In the process he would have employed many Israelites. Thus a metal-working industry developed in Israel at this time.

Solomon's developing of an infrastructure also involved building a string of fortresses and store cities (for horses and chariots and supplies for the army). We have already mentioned these briefly. Solomon needed a substantial number of non-agricultural workers to build the walls, gates, stables, storage buildings and more in these cities. And of course the public payroll expanded with all of this activity, requiring huge expenditures. Thus the tax burden weighed ever more heavily on the shoulders of the Israelites.

Commercial Ventures

Solomon, His Seaport, and the Queen of Sheba

"King Solomon also built a fleet of ships at Ezion Geber, which is near Elath on the shore of the Red Sea. . . Then Hiram sent his servants with the fleet, seamen who knew the sea, to work with the servants of Solomon. And they went to Ophir, and acquired four hundred and twenty talents of gold from there, and brought it to King Solomon." (1 Kings 9:26–28 NKJV)

The Phoenicians helped Solomon build a seaport on the Gulf of Aqaba branch of the Red Sea, near modern Eilat in Israel. Modern archaeologists have looked for the site and even thought they found it, but

The mound of Dothan (center), the Old Testament city where Joseph's brothers threw him into a pit and later sold him to slave traders (Genesis 37:17–28).

The traditional tomb of Joseph at Shechem. At the time of the Exodus, Moses took the bones of Joseph with him and they were finally buried at Shechem (see Exodus 13:19; Joshua 24:32).

The Wilderness of Sin, an uninhabited region through which the
Israelites passed between Elim and Mount Sinai during the
wilderness wanderings (Exodus 16:1).

The Valley of Aijalon, where the sun stood still during a battle
between Joshua and the Amorite kings (Joshua 10:1–15).

Hazor (center) was a strategic Canaanite city in northern Israel. Joshua defeated its king Jabin and a Canaanite coalition there at the time of the conquest (Joshua 11:1–13). Later, during the period of the judges, Deborah and Barak defeated another king Jabin there (Judges 4).

During the united monarchy Solomon fortified Hazor, and after the kingdom divided Ahab refortified the city. Most of the remains pictured here date to the days of Ahab.

The mound or tell of Mizpah, about eight miles north of Jerusalem. Here Samuel gathered the Israelites after the ark was returned from Philistine territory and here he first presented Saul to Israel as king (1 Samuel 10:17). It became the capital of the Babylonian province of Judah after the destruction of Jerusalem.

The pagan temple of Baal-Berith (meaning "lord of the covenant") at Shechem, where Israelites worshiped after the death of Gideon, when his restraining influence was lifted (Judges 8:33–34; 9:4).

The mound of Gibeah, the place from which King Saul came and where he later maintained his palace.

Mount Gilboa, on the slopes of which King Saul and his three sons were killed in battle (1 Samuel 31:8). (Willem A. VanGemeren)

The mound of Beth-Shean, where a city stood in Saul's day. On the walls of that city the Philistines hanged the bodies of Saul and his three sons after the battle of Gilboa (1 Samuel 31:10). In New Testament times the city came down off the hill. Ruins of a Roman theater appear in the foreground

Cedars of Lebanon still grow on the mountainsides of Lebanon, though only a few hundred are left. They were highly prized in the timber-starved ancient Near East. Solomon imported cedar wood for the temple and his palace. And the roof of the palace at Shushan (Susa) in Esther's day was made of cedar. (Gustav Jeeninga)

Oasis at En Gedi, where David hid from King Saul during his years as a fugitive
(1 Samuel 23:29; 24:1).

The mound of Ziklag, a base of operation for David's army during the early years of his reign
(1 Samuel 27:6). (Levant Photo Service)

The high place at Dan, where Jeroboam established calf worship after the division of the kingdom in 931 B.C. (1 Kings 12:29).

Remains of Ahab's palace at Samaria. At the far end of the picture stands part of the substructure of the temple to Augustus Caesar, which Herod the Great built there.

Entrance to the throne room of Ashurnasirpal II of
Assyria (883–859 **B.C.**) at his palace at Calah.
Huge human-headed winged bulls weighing some
thirty tons each flank the entrance.
(The Archaeological Museum, Berlin)

Archers and slingers on attack, a relief in stone from the palace of King Sennacherib of Assyria (704–681 B.C.). He was the king who attacked Hezekiah and Jerusalem (Isaiah 36–39). The large shields that stood on the ground to protect archers, knee-length tunics, short swords, and helmets are all clearly evident. (British Museum)

An Assyrian chariot in pursuit, from a relief in the north palace at Nineveh, about 640 B.C. Note the small round shields, the conical helmets, and the eight-spoked chariot wheel. (British Museum)

Above: King Ashurbanipal of Assyria (668–626 B.C.) is anointed by divine creatures. From his palace at Nineveh. He is the Osnapper of Ezra 4:10. (British Museum)

Left: A stone monument of King Ashurnasirpal II of Assyria, from his palace at Calah. Symbols of five Assyrian gods appear before him. An Assyrian altar from a temple in Calah is also pictured. (British Museum)

Procession Way leading to the Ishtar Gate in Babylon, as reconstructed with original materials in the Archaeological Museum in Berlin. Daniel and Ezekiel would actually have laid eyes on the scenes from Babylon pictured here and on the next pages.

The Ishtar Gate of Babylon as reconstructed in the Archaeological Museum in Berlin. The gate is about half the original size and contains original materials taken from Babylon by German excavators .

The actual facade of Nebuchadnezzar's throne room as it is preserved in the
Archaeological Museum in Berlin. Not having stone, the Babylonians made
enameled colored brick for decoration.

A lion from Procession Way in Babylon. The lion was the animal holy to Ishtar, goddess of love, fertility, and war. (Archaeological Museum, Berlin)

The tomb of Artaxerxes, cut into the cliffs above the ruins of Persepolis, one of Persia's ancient capitals. Artaxerxes was the king whom Nehemiah served (Nehemiah 2:1).

Cliffside tomb of the Persian king Xerxes I, the ruler generally identified as King Ahasuerus of the book of Esther (Esther 1:1).

The magnificent stairway leading up to the stately audience hall at the Persian palace complex at Persepolis—a structure begun by Darius I and completed by Xerxes.

Enameled, colored bricks used as tapestries on the palace walls
Shushan (Susa) in the days when Esther and Nehemiah were act
there. *Upper left:* a griffon; *lower left:* an archer; *lower right:* wing
sphinxes; *upper right:* detail of the stonework of the stairway lead
to the palace at Persepolis.

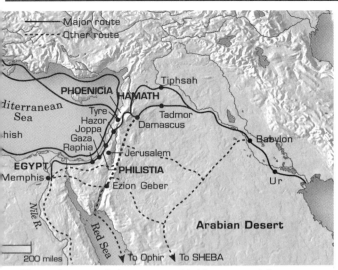

The trade routes Solomon tapped in his commercial ventures

According to 1 Kings 10:22, Solomon employed a "fleet of ships of Tarshish," large sea-going vessels that "once every three years" returned to port (Ezion-geber), probably moving very slowly from port to port and trading as they went. They brought back cargoes of gold, silver, ivory, apes, and another species that used to be identified as "peacocks" but now is thought to have been baboons. Where they went is not clear, certainly along the coasts of Arabia and Africa, and possibly into the Persian Gulf and as far as India. The Phoenicians had a reputation as intrepid sailors, the greatest in antiquity; and Israelites, though agriculturalists, could learn the ways of the sea.

earlier suppositions are no longer convincing. One suggestion is that it was on an island near the shore of the Gulf. In any case, Solomon had a port built on the Red Sea with the help of the Phoenicians, who also helped him develop a merchant marine. In those days there was no Suez Canal and the Phoenicians could not get luxury goods from East Africa and India for their Mediterranean trade. Luxury goods from the Orient would be brought to Ezion Geber and carried by caravan, especially on the King's Highway, to the ports of Tyre and Sidon and from there to other Mediterranean destinations.

It is in the context of Solomon's maritime activities that we must view the visit of the queen of Sheba. In the past, critics have tended to classify this narrative as legendary, but in recent years they have increasingly come to accept it as historical. Sheba was located in southwestern Arabia, in the region of modern Yemen. Former doubt that a queen could have ruled in Arabia has been severely blunted by discovery of Assyrian records referring to five queens of Arabia during the eighth and seventh centuries B.C. Though those inscriptions do not have direct bearing on events as early as Solomon's day, they do give greater plausibility to the account reported in Scripture.

The ostensible reason for the queen's visit was that she could test Solomon's wisdom and bask in his glory (1 Kings 10:1), but that tells only part of the story. Scripture is extremely selective in its political and biographical accounts and rarely delves into economic and social factors of a narrative. In this case we should note that Sheba controlled the ports of southwest Arabia and the trade routes between India and East Africa and the Mediterranean. One can argue on the one hand that Solomon's maritime and commercial activity in the Red Sea, along the east coast of Africa, and in the Indian Ocean threatened Sheba's economic well-being. On

How Solomon's ships may have appeared if built on the Egyptian pattern

(Haifa Maritime Museum)

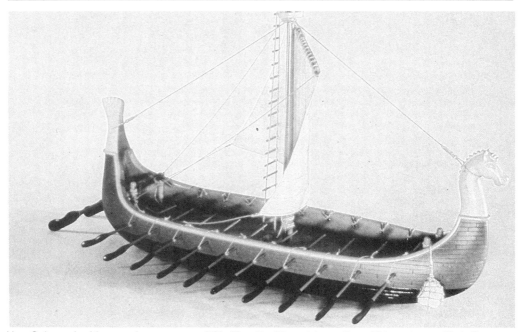

How Solomon's ships may have appeared if built on the Phoenician pattern. This was more likely the case because of Phoenician help in building the merchant marine.

(Haifa Maritime Museum)

the other hand, it can be just as cogently argued that Solomon's commercial successes and the validity of his commercial agreements with Hiram of Tyre depended on an effective working relationship with the Sabaeans.

In any case, commentators now often agree that the queen's visit really had the character of a trade mission. Nelson Glueck anticipated this point of view back in 1940 and commented, "When one realizes what a terrifically hard journey it must have been for the fair ruler of a rich part of southern Arabia, to come by camel a distance of some 1200 miles or more on her famous trip to Jerusalem to see Solomon, it is hard to believe that she undertook the long and arduous journey merely to bask in the brilliance of the king of Jerusalem."[20]

Solomon as Horse Trader

"*Solomon's import of horses was from Egypt and Kue, and the king's traders received them from Kue at a price. . . so through the king's traders they were exported to all the kings of the Hittites and the kings of Aram.*" (1 Kings 10:28-29 NRSV)

We have already seen that Solomon added a chariot corps and cavalry units to his army (1 Kings 10:19, 22) and that he had established chariot cities where chariots, horses, and charioteers could be stationed as rapid deployment strike forces to defend the kingdom. Now we discover that Solomon became a horse breeder and horse trader. Solomon imported his horses from Egypt and Kue or Cilicia (1 Kings 10:28), the plain in southeast Asia Minor where the metropolis of Tarsus (the apostle Paul's hometown) was to rise later. Probably the latter part of verse 28 should read, "the king's agents took delivery from them from Cilicia at a fixed rate." Verse 29 indicates that the price ratio of horses to chariots was 4 to 1 (chariots imported from Egypt for 600 shekels, and a horse for 150).

While Egypt bred horses and Solomon did too, the best horses came from Cilicia. Solomon stood in a good position to tranship Cilician horses to Egypt and to buy there chariots for his own chariot corps and to sell to the Hittites and Syrians (Aramaeans). Of course, the Hittite Empire had ceased to exist shortly after 1200 B.C. But Hittite city-states continued to exist in Syria and Solomon's trade mentioned here was with some of those city states. In passing, it may be noted that Uriah the Hittite, first husband of Bathsheba, Solomon's mother, had come from one of those city-states.

Note, too, that Solomon did not have to buy or breed all his horses. Some came as tribute. First Kings 10:25 states that "Each man brought his present [tribute]... horses, and mules, and a set rate year by year" (NKJV).

Horse trading and breeding required that Hebrew agents be stationed in Egypt and various places in Cilicia and Syria to engage in activities or employment not previously known to Hebrew nationals.

We have already seen that David established control over the three main trade routes through the land bridge of Palestine: the King's Highway along the edge of the desert in the east, the central route through Hebron and Jerusalem, and the Via Maris or the Way of the Sea. During Solomon's reign, horses and all sorts of other goods could flow with ease and safety across the land bridge between Asia and Africa to the enrichment of the Hebrew kingdom. And industry and commerce had come to take their place alongside agriculture as sources of employment for large numbers of people. So one might be a farmer, a government bureaucrat, a soldier, a carpenter, a mason, a manufacturer of weapons, a merchant or be employed in many other occupations. *(For more on this topic, go to p. 140 or p. 247.)*

Conclusion

When the Hebrews asked for a king they had no idea what truly cataclysmic changes their demand would bring. From a people basically living in the "back woods" of the region when Saul became king, they became the dominant force under David. From barely subsisting on agriculture when they crowned Saul king, they became a trading nation under Solomon with an economic impact well beyond their borders. Once oppressed by the Philistines, they now oppressed nation states in all directions. But religiously they went from a mobile tabernacle with its sacrifices to temple-centered worship with choirs and orchestras. In the process, however, Solomon introduced the seeds of religious decay. Their harvest was the disappearance of Israel and Judah as a social, economic and religious force in the region. This chapter ends with King Solomon the wonder of the then-known world, but the next chapter introduces the first steps in the deterioration of the nation and splintering of its religious life.

NOTES:

[1]William F. Albright, Rev. ed., *Archaeology of Palestine* (Baltimore: Penguin Books, 1960), 120-21.

[2]Josephus, *Antiquities* 6.14.9.

[3]Gwilym H. Jones, "1 and 2 Kings" in *New Century Bible Commentary* (Grand Rapids: Eerdmans, 1984), 1,133.

[4]Gleason L. Archer, *A Survey of Old Testament Introduction*, rev. ed. (Chicago: Moody, 1974), 467.

[5]Ibid.

[6]C. F. Keil, "The Books of the Kings" in *Biblical Commentary on the Old Testament*, ed. by C. F. Keil and F. Delitzsch, 2nd ed. (Edinburgh: T. & T. Clark, n. d.), 80.

[7]See "Arad," *New Encyclopedia of Archaeological Excavations in the Holy Land* (New York: Simon & Schuster, 1993), 1, 82-84; Amnon Ben-Tor, ed., *Archaeology of Ancient Israel* (New Haven: Yale, 1992), 325.

[8]See, e.g., Neal Bierling, *Giving Goliath His Due* (Grand Rapids: Baker Book House, 1992);. Alessandra Nibbi, *The Sea Peoples and Egypt* (Park Ridge, N.J.: Noyes Press, 1975); N. K. Sandars, *The Sea Peoples* (London: Thames & Hudson, 1978); Edward E. Hindson, *The Philistines and the Old Testament* (Grand Rapids: Baker, 1971); Trude Dothan, *The Philistines and Their Material Culture* (New Haven: Yale, 1982); Trude Dothan and Moshe Dothan, *People of the Sea* (New York: Macmillan, 1992); and Amihai Mazar, *Archaeology of the Land of the Bible* (New York: Doubleday, 1990), 300-328.

[9]Robert Drews, *The End of the Bronze Age* (Princeton, N.J.: Princeton University Press, 1993), see chapter 4, especially pp. 50, 52-53.

[10]Ibid., 148-49.

[11]Ibid., 150.

[12]A. Rendle Short, *Modern Discovery and the Bible*, 3rd ed. (London: InterVarsity, 1952), 182.

[13]Kathleen Kenyon, *Royal Cities of the Old Testament* (New York: Shocken, 1971), 24-27.

[14]Mazar, 480-81.

[15]Dan Gill, "Jerusalem's Underground Water Systems," *Biblical Archaeology Review,* July / August 1994, 30. This subject is completely reopened with the work of Ronny Reich and Eli Shukron. See their article, "Light at the End of the Tunnel," *Biblical Archeaology Review*, Jan.–Feb. 1999, 22–23, 72.

[16]Chaim Herzog and Mordechai Gichon, *Battles of the Bible* (Jerusalem: Steimatzky's Agency Ltd., 1978), 81-82.

[17]Ibid., 88.

[18]Gabriel Barkay, "The Iron Age II-III," in *The Archaeology of Ancient Israel*, ed. by Amnon Ben-Tor (New Haven: Yale, 1992), 315.

[19]*Antiquities* III.12.6.

[20]Nelson Glueck, *The Other Side of the Jordan* (New Haven, CT: American Schools of Oriental Research, 1940), 85.

BIBLIOGRAPHY:

Aharoni, Yahanan. *The Archaeology of the Land of Israel*. Philadelphia: Westminster, 1978.

Ben-Tor, Amnon, ed. *The Archaeology of Ancient Israel*. New Haven: Yale University Press, 1992.

Bierling, Neal. *Giving Goliath His Due*. Grand Rapids: Baker, 1992.

Borowski, Oded. *Agriculture in Iron Age Israel*. Winona Lake, Ind.: Eisenbrauns, 1987.

Dorsey, David A. *The Roads and Highways of Ancient Israel*. Baltimore: Johns Hopkins University Press, 1991.

Dothan, Trude. *The Philistines and Their Material Culture*. New Haven: Yale University Press, 1982.

Dothan, Trude and Moshe Dothan. *People of the Sea: The Search for the Philistines*. New York: Macmillan, 1992.

Gordon, Cyrus H. and Gary A. Rendsburg. *The Bible and the Ancient Near East*. New York: W. W. Norton, 4th ed., 1997.

Herzog, Chaim and Mordechai Gichon. *Battles of the Bible*. Jerusalem: Steimatzky's Agency, Ltd., 1978.

Hoerth, Alfred J. *Archaeology and the Old Testament.* Grand Rapids: Baker, 1998.

Kenyon, Kathleen M. *Digging Up Jerusalem.* New York: Praeger, 1974.

Kenyon, Kathleen. *Jerusalem, Excavating 3000 Years of History.* New York: McGraw Hill, 1967.

Kenyon, Kathleen. *Royal Cities of the Old Testament.* New York: Shocken, 1971.

Matthews, Victor H. and Don C. Benjamin. *Social World of Ancient Israel.* Peabody, Mass.: Hendrickson Publishers, 1993.

Mazar, Amihai. *Archaeology of the Land of the Bible.* New York: Doubleday, 1990.

Nibbi, Alessandra. *The Sea Peoples and Egypt.* Park Ridge, N.J.: Noyes Press, 1975.

Patai, Raphael. *The Children of Noah: Jewish Seafaring in Ancient Times.* Princeton: Princeton University Press, 1998.

Sandars, N. K. *The Sea Peoples.* London: Thames & Hudson, 1978.

Wood, Leon J. *Israel's United Monarchy.* Grand Rapids: Baker, 1979.

THE DIVIDED KINGDOM: LIFE IN ISRAEL

Chapter 8

(1 Kings 12—24; 2 Kings; the Prophets)

How quickly the glory can fade! Up until Solomon's death in 931 B.C. the Hebrew empire remained essentially intact and at least outwardly prosperous. Only Syria and Edom had gained their independence under Solomon. Yet within about a year a revolt in the north cut the kingdom in two, and most of the conquered territories shed the Israelite yoke. The empire David had created and Solomon had effectively organized collapsed like a house of cards.

Israel would never again command the respect it enjoyed during the reign of Solomon, when "all the earth sought the presence of Solomon" and "each man brought his present" (1 Kings 10:24, 25 NKJV). Though these words are an exaggeration, they may be interpreted to mean that his fame was so great that a steady flow of visitors came every year, some to bring presents, and others, from the subject states, to bring tribute. In fact, just the opposite now took place. Within six years (in 925 B.C.) Egyptian armies invaded Israel and carried off wagon loads of booty (1 Kings 14:25-27). And Assyrians would follow suit. Why the reversal?

Why the Kingdom Split

What caused a truly powerful kingdom to become fragmented remnants of what David and Solomon had once ruled effec-

tively? What contributed to the breakup into two entities, each sparring for mastery over the other? The decline in the nation's fortunes and the division of the kingdom may be explained from at least three points of view.

The Religionist's Perspective

The *religionist* will say categorically that Solomon's idolatry brought on the decay. After all, God appeared personally to Solomon after the completion of the temple with a specific promise and a warning: "Now if you walk before Me as your father David walked. . . and if you keep My statutes. . . then I will establish the throne of your kingdom over Israel forever. . . . But if you or your sons at all turn from following Me. . . but go and serve other gods and worship them, then I will cut off Israel from the land which I have given them" (1 Kings 9:4-7 NKJV). Unfortunately, the newness of the temple had hardly worn off when Solomon began to drift away from both a commitment to the central sanctuary and the God who had manifested His presence there.

The religionist insists that Solomon's loss of focus on the God of Israel resulted largely from his marriage to idolatrous women from other nations. Yet from Solomon's perspective, he did only what he needed to do to be perceived as a powerful king. He knew that the leaders of nations and commerce evaluated greatness by the size of the harem. Solomon, supposed to be the most well-to-do ruler of his generation, therefore might be expected to have the largest harem.

Moreover, marriage alliances commonly served the cause of peace with one's neighbors. Solomon seems to have employed this approach as well to maintain a *Pax Hebraica* (Hebrew peace). And he did enjoy peace with all his neighbors. Solomon's marriage to princesses from Egypt, Moab, Ammon, Edom, Phoenicia, and the Hittite states (1 Kings 11:1) went a long way toward establishing his borders. Egypt was located on the far south; Edom, Moab, and Ammon on the east; the Phoenician city-states on the northwest; and the Hittite city-states on the far north. If other princesses were daughters of Arab sheiks and tribal chiefs located south of Judah and of the city-states of inner Syria, then his marriages would ring Israel proper with friendly border states and would help to cement the subject states of some of them as part of the Hebrew Empire.

As plausible and defensible as all this might sound, God condemned both the king's multiplication of wives and especially his marriage alliances with pagan peoples, since such practices would lead to idolatry (Deuteronomy 7:3–4; 17:17).

"When Solomon was old, . . . his wives turned his heart after other gods" (1 Kings 11:4). The process of apostasy must have set in as his harem grew ever larger during the last half of his reign. Actually he had married Naamah the Ammonitess and had fathered by her Rehoboam the crown prince by about the age of twenty (1 Kings 14:21). Possibly she had never really converted to the religion of Yahweh. Solomon's heart "was not wholly true" to Yahweh. Along with the worship in the temple, he "followed after" (v. 5) the worship of foreign deities. The text does not say he actually sacrificed to those gods, but he did build high places to them to accommodate his wives and other foreigners in the vicinity and thus involved himself in their worship—and influenced his son Rehoboam to do so later (2 Chronicles 12:1).

Foreign Religious Practices Brought in with Idols

When Solomon accepted the religious practices of his foreign wives, he tolerated some of the worst examples of heathen idolatry. Solomon accepted the worship of Ashtoreth, Chemosh, and Molech. Ashtoreth, variously known as Ishtar, Astarte, and Venus, was principally the goddess of sex and war. Her name was altered from Astarte to Ashtoreth by vocalizing with the vowels of the Hebrew word *bosheth*, meaning "shame." Chemosh was the national god of Moab, and was sometimes worshiped with child sacrifices; Molech or Moloch, an Ammonite deity, also could be worshiped with human sacrifice. Solomon built high places for Chemosh and Molech on "a height east of Jerusalem" (1 Kings 11: 7), the Mount of Olives.

It is interesting that Scripture does not mention any prophet's stepping out to warn Solomon of the danger of his ways as he slid into apostasy. Perhaps God considered it sufficient to have made the point so specifically in a revelation to him after the completion of the temple (cf. 1 Kings 9:6–7).

God's patience with the waywardness of Solomon finally wore out and He sent His sentence of judgment to the king, probably through a prophet (1 Kings 11:9–13). Again the Davidic covenant is introduced. Solomon's failure to keep God's commandments and His covenant will now result in the kingdom's being torn away from him, but not in his lifetime (v. 12) nor in its entirety (v. 13). Solomon's unfaithfulness will not lead God to cancel His promise to David nor His choice of Jerusalem as His special abode. The Davidic dynasty and the city will continue. God's promise will be fulfilled through the tribe of Judah and ultimately through the Messiah, David's greater Son.

Anath, Astarte, and Asherah were three Canaanite goddesses of sex and war that are not always distinguishable. These fertility goddesses appear in the role of sacred prostitutes and are frequently pictured on plaques, pendants, or amulets. Here the fertility goddess is engraved on a gold pendant from Ras Shamra in Syria. The rams portray sexual vigor. The Canaanite deities had "no moral character whatever." The crass immorality of Canaanite religion, with its male and female prostitution, was far worse than elsewhere in the Near East of the time. (C. F. A. Schaeffer)

The chronicler gives us an account of a later encounter between Jeroboam (one of the officers in Solomon's government) and the prophet Ahijah of Shiloh on the open road outside Jerusalem (1 Kings 11:29-39). As an act of prophetic symbolism Ahijah took off his outer cloak and tore it into twelve pieces, giving ten to Jeroboam and indicating that the kingdom would be split. He would rule the ten tribes and Solomon's son would rule one. Of course, ten plus one equals eleven. Perhaps Levi was omitted because it was without a territory of its own. As an alternate way of computing, some think that by this time the territory of Simeon, south of Judah, had been absorbed into Judah and virtually ceased to exist. Judah also evidently had absorbed part of the tribe of Benjamin. In any case, Ahijah

gave the same reason for the rupture that the Lord had (earlier) given to Solomon (11:9-13).

Moreover, the prophet asserted that God would honor the Davidic covenant in a continuation of the kingdom of Judah and He would continue in a special sense to dwell in Jerusalem. Jeroboam would be king only over "Israel," evidently referring to the northern state. Then Ahijah made a promise to Jeroboam similar to that made to David and Solomon (v. 38), to build "a sure house" in return for faithfulness to God. Especially, Israel would serve as an irritant to the house of David (v. 39). "But not forever" makes it clear that the house of Jeroboam would not be permanent, as David's was to be.

The Economist's Perspective

The *economist* will say the split occurred for financial reasons—an inflated bureaucracy and extensive construction resulted in a too-burdensome level of taxation. Solomon had lived "high on the hog." He built the temple, his palace complex, a well-equipped army, a seaport, and more. And he maintained an expensive lifestyle. The queen of Sheba was impressed with "food on his table," both the variety and the elegance of the table settings, the touch of class evident in the "seating of his courtiers," the quality of the attention and attire (livery) of the servants, and "his wine service" (in solid gold). "All King Solomon's drinking vessels were of gold, and all the vessels [plate] of the House of the Forest of Lebanon were of pure gold" (1 Kings 10:5, 21). Both the building of the infrastructure and the constant "show" in the court cost money and lots of it. Apparently the people felt the tax bite was too big. Perhaps, as some have asserted, Solomon left Israel in a near state of bankruptcy.

In any case, as the negotiations took place between Rehoboam, Solomon's successor, and the northern tribes after the death of Solomon, their representatives begged Rehoboam to lighten the "hard" or "harsh labor" and "heavy yoke" (as that worn by working beasts), that Solomon had imposed on them (1 Kings 12:4). The forced

Mediterranean Sea

PHOENICIA

Damascus

Tyre

Dan

ARAM

Megiddo

Beth Shan

Shechem

Joppa

ISRAEL

Bethel

Rabbah

Gezer

Jericho

AMMON

Ashdod

Jerusalem

Ashkelon

Gath

Dead
Sea

Gaza

Hebron

PHILISTIA

JUDAH

Beersheba

MOAB

Bozrah

Kadesh Barnea

EDOM

N

0   60 Mi.
0   60 Km.

Thomas Nelson, Inc.

favored Saul as king when he was chosen (1 Samuel 10:27; 11:12–13). And there seemed to be tribal overtones in Saul's appeal to Benjamites for their support against David, who was of the tribe of Judah (1 Samuel 22:7).

There had also been an earlier division of the kingdom. After Saul's death, David ruled over only the tribe of Judah for seven years from Hebron (2 Samuel 5:5). Meanwhile, Saul's son Ishbosheth reigned over the rest of the tribes from Mahanaim (2 Samuel 2:8-11). Only after the murder of Ishbosheth did the rest of the tribes send their representatives to Hebron to negotiate with David for his kingship over all the tribes (2 Samuel 5:1–5).

Solomon in his administrative policies had treated the northern tribes differently and apparently more harshly than he treated Judah. In fact, in Solomon's district organization (1 Kings 4:7–19) he exempted Judah from the obligation to pay taxes for the support of the national bureaucracy. Judah's favored status accentuated tribal rivalries and contributed to the split that occurred in Rehoboam's day. The sacred historian, commenting on the population and security of the Hebrews in Solomon's day, specified or singled out "Judah and Israel" (1 Kings 4:20, 25). Clearly the people already perceived a fairly clear-cut distinction between the two parts of the kingdom.

The Land

Israel, the Northern Kingdom

Even when controlled by a single government Palestine has to be considered a small nation. But when divided into two states, each of them was small indeed. At its height, the Kingdom of Israel could have

labor and heavy taxation had been almost more than they could bear or were willing to bear. When he, taking the bad advice of young and restless advisors, threatened an even heavier burden (vv. 10, 11), the northern tribes decided to bolt and form a separate state with Jeroboam as king.

The Sociologists' and Political Scientists' Perspective

Sociologists and *political scientists* contend that a key reason for the breakup of the kingdom lay in the old tribal divisions, which had always lain under the surface, but now exploded. True, not all Israel

The Kings of Israel

Name	Length of Reign	Reference
Jeroboam I	22 years	1 Kings 11:26—14:20
Nadab	2 years	1 Kings 15:25-28
Baasha	24 years	1 Kings 15:27—16:7
Elah	2 years	1 Kings 16:6-14
Zimri	7 days	1 Kings 16:9-20
Omri	12 years	1 Kings 16:15-28
Ahab	21 years	1 Kings 16:28—22:40
Ahaziah	2 years	1 Kings 22:40—2 Kings 1:18
Jehoram (Joram)	11 years	2 Kings 3:1—9:25
Jehu	28 years	2 Kings 9:1—10:36
Jehoahaz	16 years	2 Kings 13:1-9
Jehoash (Joash)	16 years	2 Kings 13:10—14:16
Jeroboam II	40 years	2 Kings 14:23-29
Zechariah	6 months	2 Kings 14:29—15:12
Shallum	1 month	2 Kings 15:10-15
Menahem	10 years	2 Kings 15:14-22
Pekahiah	2 years	2 Kings 15:22-26
Pekah	20 years	2 Kings 15:27-31
Hoshea	9 years	2 Kings 15:30—17:6

fitted into the state of Delaware. The land mass extended from Bethel in the south (about ten miles north of Jerusalem) to a few miles north of Dan in the north, a distance of just over a hundred miles. The width of the country around Dan measured approximately twenty miles. In the central region, from the Mediterranean to the desert east of the Jordan, the kingdom extended eighty miles.

The topography of this small area varied greatly. Along the Mediterranean lay the virtually sea level Plain of Sharon. Inland rose the hills of Samaria (about 2,000–4,000 feet in altitude). Farther east lay the Jordan Valley, which Israel controlled from the Sea of Galilee approximately to the northern shore of the Dead Sea. The valley gradually sloped downward from about 700 feet below sea level at the Sea of Galilee to about 1,300 feet below sea level at the northern end of the Dead Sea. East of the Jordan, Israel's domain included the hills of Gilead (c. 2,000–4,000 feet in altitude) and the northern part of Moab, to the edge of the eastern desert. The whole of the Plain of Jezreel lay within her territory.

(For more on this topic, go to p. 146 or p. 252.)

Government

"There was none who followed the house of David, but the tribe of Judah only." (1 Kings 12:20)

When the rupture between Rehoboam in Judah and the northern tribes of Israel was complete, the northern rebels cried, "To your tents, O Israel" (1 Kings 12:16), the equivalent of "Let's go home." But before they went, they had to establish a government, and they called Jeroboam to be their king. Jeroboam, an official in Solomon's administration, had fled to Egypt after apparently intending rebellion against Solomon. On the death of Solomon he returned from Egypt and now took the reins of the kingdom.

The rocky history of the kingship in Israel brought to the throne a total of nineteen kings in nine dynasties or family lines (twenty kings in ten dynasties if we include Tibni's rule over only part of the kingdom for about five years, 885-880). From a biblical standpoint the turnover in royal lines came largely because of God's judgment on moral or spiritual waywardness. From a human standpoint, or that of a political scientist, the turmoil arose from the competing interests of the numerous northern tribes with their individual agendas and their jealousies. These fueled the political and social factions and constant rivalry for the throne.

The Search for a Capital

Jeroboam really had to start from scratch in 930 B.C. He didn't have a government, a bureaucracy, or a capital. For a capital it seems that he first chose Shechem, then Penuel, and finally Tirzah (1 Kings 12:25; 14:17). We do not know the degree to which each served as a capital or merely as an administrative center. In building Penuel (1 Kings 12:25), he may have been merely trying to make it part of his outer line of defense for Shechem. It has also been suggested that in moving the capital he was trying to elude or avoid Shishak of Egypt.

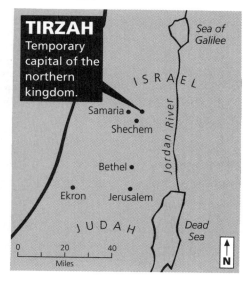

The point is this. King Shishak of Egypt invaded the southern kingdom in the days of Rehoboam of the Kingdom of Judah, in 925 B.C. (1 Kings 14:25). But Scripture says nothing about his movement into the Northern Kingdom. However, we know from one of Shishak's inscriptions in Luxor,

Egypt, that he claimed to have ranged across both the southern and the northern kingdoms. Some scholars now identify town #53 on his list of towns taken as Penuel and town #59 as Tirzah. Tirzah is modern Tell el-Far'ah, about seven miles northeast of Nablus and Shechem. More on Shishak's invasion appears in the next chapter.

In any case, Tirzah remained the capital until Omri, father of Ahab, moved the capital to Samaria (about forty-two miles north of Jerusalem and twenty-three miles east of the Mediterranean) about 880 B.C. Samaria was a good choice. Situated on an easily defensible hill three to four hundred feet above a fruitful plain and surrounded by rich farmland, Samaria controlled the whole surrounding area of central Palestine, including the main caravan roads to the north, south, and west. According to 1 Kings 16:24, Omri bought the hill, and it thus became the private property of the royal family, as Jerusalem belonged to David and his descendants.

Institution of a New Religion

Jeroboam worried aloud that the central sanctuary in Jerusalem and the religious ties that bound the Twelve Tribes together would eventually heal the split. In fact, he believed that some day the people would kill him and accept the rule of Rehoboam.

The hill on which King Omri of the Northern Kingdom built the city of Samaria. It remained the capital of Israel until the fall of the nation in 723 B.C.

To save his skin he decided to set up a new national religion with important cult centers at Dan and Bethel (1 Kings 12:26-33). Discussion of this cult appears in the next section of this chapter.

Lack of Stability and Continuity in Governmental Policy

The frequent turmoil in the administration of the Kingdom of Israel makes it remarkable that the state survived some two hundred years. Six of the twenty kings died by assassination and a seventh probably did. An eighth died by suicide during a rebellion. A ninth died in battle, and the last was taken prisoner at the fall of Samaria to the Assyrians. So only ten or half of them died a natural death while in power.

Further, Baasha killed "all the house of Jeroboam" when he took power (1 Kings 15:29). Zimri massacred all Elah's relatives and friends (his official circle, 1 Kings 16:11), and Jehu exterminated the princes of Ahab's family (2 Kings 10:1–11) when he revolted and took the throne. These three revolutionaries liquidated nearly all who had been involved in the government and knew how to make it run. Certainly their actions must have severely affected the efficiency of the bureaucracy.

(For more on this topic, go to p. 148 or p. 253.)

Religion

"The king. . . made two calves of gold, and said to the people, 'It is too much for you to go up to Jerusalem. Here are your gods, O Israel, which brought you up from the land of Egypt!'" (1 Kings 12:28)

As we have seen, Jeroboam believed that if he did not take drastic steps, many of the people of Israel would make pilgrimages to the temple in Jerusalem and eventually would decide to liquidate him and rejoin the south. So he instituted the new religion as a result of political expediency.

Calf Worship

We can guess that Jeroboam may have decided on a form of calf worship as a result of Egyptian influence. He had been living in exile there for most of two decades. The Egyptians worshiped the whole bovine family in the cow, the calf, and the bull. They worshiped Hathor as the cow-goddess, daughter of the sun-god Re and symbolic mother of pharaoh. They worshiped the bull as Apis (the Ptah of Memphis); Mnevis (the sun-god of Heliopolis); and Ptah, the creator god. A calf was simply on the way to becoming a cow or bull. Many years earlier Israelites had succumbed to calf worship at Mount Sinai (Exodus 32).

Possibly, too, Jeroboam sought to establish a bridge between Yahweh worship and the Canaanite population. Bulls served as symbols of fertility gods among the Canaanites.

In any case, he had two calves or young bulls made (probably of wood and covered with gold) and installed in sanctuaries at the southern border town of Bethel (about ten miles north of Jerusalem) and the northern border town of Dan (in the foothills of Mount Hermon), and declared them to be their gods. At these worship centers he installed priests chosen from the non-Levitical elements in the population. Then he established a new religious festival on the fifteenth day of the eighth month. In addition, he built other shrines on high places. He himself offered sacrifices at Bethel (e.g., 1 Kings 13:1–10).

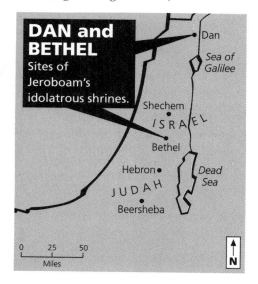

To answer the question of how he could expect his subjects to shift from the traditional Yahweh worship without images, to sanctuaries with calves, we need to look at Near Eastern practices. Various peoples of the ancient Near East portrayed their gods as sitting or standing enthroned on the back of an animal (usually a calf or a lion). In this case, Yahweh might be represented as invisibly enthroned on the back of the calf. Israel was never able to extricate itself from Jeroboam's false worship, and history

records that all the subsequent kings of Israel walked in the "ways of Jeroboam."

At a Hittite sanctuary near the capital of Boghazköi (in central Turkey) two gods stand on the backs of lions. In the ancient Near East, gods are often shown on the backs of lions or bulls. The Israelites at Sinai may have thought of Yahweh as enthroned invisibly on the golden calf. And at Dan and Bethel they may have had the same idea.

Baal Worship

"And he [Ahab] went and served Baal and worshiped him. Then he set up an altar for Baal in the temple of Baal, which he had built in Samaria. And Ahab made a wooden image. Ahab did more to provoke the LORD God of Israel to anger than all the kings of Israel who were before him." (1 Kings 16:31-33 NKJV)

Because Jezebel, daughter of Ethbaal of Tyre, married Ahab and introduced Baal worship to Israel, and because Athaliah, Ahab and Jezebel's daughter, married Jehoram of Judah and introduced Baal worship there, Phoenician religion holds considerable interest for most Bible students.

As a matter of fact, Baal worship had invaded Israel during the days of the judges. But Samuel made war on it (1 Samuel 7:3-4) and seems to have emerged victorious. Now, however, when Jezebel came to Samaria, Ahab, like Solomon before him, made religious provision for his foreign wife. He built a temple for Baal in Samaria and an altar in the temple for sacrifice to the god, the Baal-Melqart of Tyre. Though Ahab may have originally built this temple for the use of Jezebel and any servants she may have brought with her from Phoenicia, it seems to have become the center of the state cult.

Now let's try to understand Baal worship as practiced in Phoenicia and imported into Israel. El ruled as father of the gods and head of the Phoenician pantheon or family of gods. Baal, his son, ruled as one of the chief male deities and served as god of agriculture. As such he was responsible for fertility of the field and was associated with human and animal reproduction. Baalath, who seems to have been the consort of Baal, represented the principle of fertility and generation. Actually, Baal simply means "lord" and Baalath, "lady."

The worship centers of Baal were often merely high places in the hills, consisting of an altar, a sacred tree or pole, and a sacred stone pillar. The pillar represented the Baal, and the tree or pole symbolized the Baalath. But commonly the Phoenicians, an urban people, worshiped in temples consisting of a court or enclosure and a roofed shrine at the entrance of which was a porch or pillared hall. The altar, conical stone pillar, and pole or tree stood in the court. A statue of the deity was housed in the shrine. In one of the temples excavated at Gebal or Byblos about twenty stone pillars came to light. Cut in the general form of obelisks, the highest was ten feet high.

Dan's High Place Excavated

Avraham Biran in his excavations at Tel Dan has uncovered the high place of the town (an almost square platform about fifty-nine by sixty feet), which he believes Jeroboam erected and which was later enlarged during the reigns of Ahab and Jeroboam II. The high place consisted of a podium for a temple structure, a square where the sacrificial altar was located, and side chambers used for ritual or administration. Under this high place they found cultic remains that may have been part of the Danite shrine erected there during the days of the Judges (Judges 18).

As to the worship connected with Baalism, it will be recognized immediately that one important feature was the sacrifice of animals, food, and drink.

Religious festivals, associated with the rhythm of the seasons, also focused on Baal worship. That is to say, the people viewed the god as dying in the fall and arising in

The high place of Dan built by Jeroboam I and enlarged by Ahab

The Baals as City-state Idols

Every Phoenician community worshiped its own Baal and Baalath. Melkart (Melqarth) reigned as the supreme deity or Baal of Tyre and was styled "lord of the sun, supreme ruler, giver of life, embodiment of the male principle, god of productivity." The Greeks identified him with Heracles or Hercules. At Sidon they worshiped Eshmun, god of vital force and healing. The Greeks identified him with Asclepius. Reshef, the lightning god, was especially popular in Cyprus and identified with Apollo by the Greeks. The Baalath of Gebal, Ashtaroth (or Astarte), a fertility goddess, was the most popular Baalath of Phoenicia.

the spring. (Perhaps Elijah was referring to these festivals in 1 Kings 18:27.) In the fall festival the people engaged in great mourning, funeral rites, and perhaps self-torture or mutilation. The spring festival featured sacramental sexual indulgence. All of the temples had prostitutes, both men and women, attached to them, with chambers for sexual intercourse readily available. Women frequently sacrificed their virginity at the shrines of Astarte in the hope of winning the favor of the goddess.

The festival of Adonis was regularly held at Byblos or Gebal, and the festival of Melkart at Tyre. The debased and debasing worship of Phoenicia deserved the total condemnation meted out to it in the Old Testament.

Counterattack Against Baal Worship

"Thus Jehu destroyed Baal from Israel." (2 Kings 10:28)

Two dramatic events fueled the counterattack against Baal worship in Israel. Elijah dealt a telling blow in his public contest with the prophets of Baal and his execution of them. Jehu eradicated Baal worship in the kingdom—lock, stock, and barrel—by killing the priests, other leaders in the cult,

the patroness (Jezebel), and by the destruction of his temple.

Elijah's tussle with King Ahab. As Ahab's apostasy bit ever deeper into the very fabric of Israelite life and threatened to extinguish the flickering light of Yahwism, stalwart Elijah appeared on the scene. Coming from backward Gilead across the Jordan and dressed only in camel's hair clothing (2 Kings 1:8), he joined battle with the king and queen and the sophisticated religionists at the court. Elijah means "Yahweh is God" and that fact exemplified his mission, which was to show that Yahweh is indeed God (1 Kings 18:39) and He alone.

Whether Elijah burst in on Ahab at the palace or met him on the way is not clear, but he did have a personal encounter with the king, during which he made his dire prediction that "there will neither be dew nor rain these years, except at my order." The duration of the drought is not specified; Luke 4:25 and James 5:17 give the figure of three and one-half years. The

Baal, the god of fertility, was also portrayed as the storm god. Here he brandishes a club and wields a stylized thunderbolt. From Ras Shamra in Syria.

(C. F. A. Schaeffer)

THE LIFE OF ELIJAH

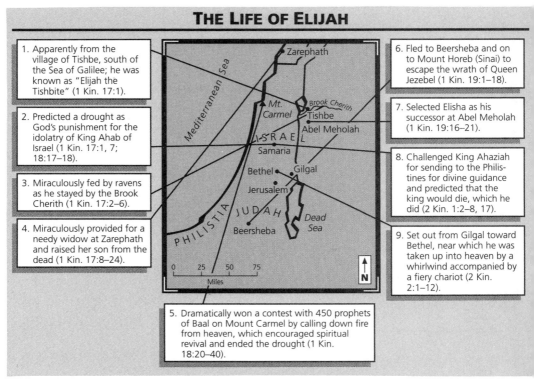

1. Apparently from the village of Tishbe, south of the Sea of Galilee; he was known as "Elijah the Tishbite" (1 Kin. 17:1).

2. Predicted a drought as God's punishment for the idolatry of King Ahab of Israel (1 Kin. 17:1, 7; 18:17–18).

3. Miraculously fed by ravens as he stayed by the Brook Cherith (1 Kin. 17:2–6).

4. Miraculously provided for a needy widow at Zarephath and raised her son from the dead (1 Kin. 17:8–24).

5. Dramatically won a contest with 450 prophets of Baal on Mount Carmel by calling down fire from heaven, which encouraged spiritual revival and ended the drought (1 Kin. 18:20–40).

6. Fled to Beersheba and on to Mount Horeb (Sinai) to escape the wrath of Queen Jezebel (1 Kin. 19:1–18).

7. Selected Elisha as his successor at Abel Meholah (1 Kin. 19:16–21).

8. Challenged King Ahaziah for sending to the Philistines for divine guidance and predicted that the king would die, which he did (2 Kin. 1:2–8, 17).

9. Set out from Gilgal toward Bethel, near which he was taken up into heaven by a whirlwind accompanied by a fiery chariot (2 Kin. 2:1–12).

inclusion of dew along with the rain is very important, because in the hills of Palestine the dew falls between 100 and 180 nights per year and is a significant supplement to the rain. Elijah's pronouncement served as a slap in the face of Baal, who was supposed to be a rain god and god of fertility.

At length God announced that the drought would come to an end and directed Elijah to return to Ahab. The Bible does not tell us where the two met, nor is there a record of any polite court protocol. Probably there wasn't any. Ahab blurted out, "You troubler of Israel" (1 Kings 18:17). A "troubler" or "scourge" was one who brought a certain ritual disability. In this case Ahab charged that Elijah had brought the wrath of Baal on Israel in withholding rain, the giving of which was Baal's province (as rain god and god of fertility) according to Canaanite belief. Then Elijah threw the charge back in the teeth of the king. It was, after all, Baal worship, apostasy from Yahweh worship, that had brought the punishment of Yahweh upon them. "Baals" (v. 18) in the plural refers to the various shrines or manifestations of Baal (meaning "lord").

The conversation launched a debate over which was the true god, Baal or Yahweh, so Elijah proposed a test. Call representatives from among the people of Israel to meet on Mount Carmel, a mountain ridge rising just south of Haifa Bay and standing close to Phoenician territory. A pagan worship center stood there—it was not really Yahweh territory. Elijah also invited the 450 prophets of Baal (the male deity) and the 400 prophets of Asherah (Baal's female consort), Jezebel's subsidized religious establishment.

Apparently Ahab liked the idea and probably was so naive as to think his side would win any contest. The fact that the four hundred prophets of Asherah were not heard from again has led some to conclude that this detail is not a genuine part of the text, but one answer might be that they found a way to evade Ahab's command and did not participate.

The day agreed upon arrived and the group assembled, probably at the traditional site of the contest, the Muhraka, in the south-east part of the mountain. From there one can descend to the Brook Kishon. Near there, water was available on the mountain itself to meet the requirements of the sacrifice. Elijah proposed a test. Get two bulls for sacrifice; prepare one for Baal and the other for Yahweh. Then prepare the sacrifices, but do not light the sacrificial fires. The devotees of each god were to call on their deity and the one who answered by kindling the fire was to be recognized as God. All agreed to the contest.

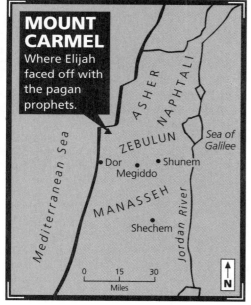

MOUNT CARMEL
Where Elijah faced off with the pagan prophets.

ASHER
NAPHTALI
ZEBULUN
Sea of Galilee
Dor • Shunem
Megiddo
MANASSEH
Shechem
Mediterranean Sea
Jordan River

0   15   30
Miles

N

Elijah let the prophets of Baal make their sacrifice first. Then they could not claim he had left them with an inferior bull or that he had in any other way put them at a disadvantage. Moreover, he believed they would not be able to get their sacrificial fire lit and that he could achieve a dramatic effect with Yahweh's intervention. Nothing happened and Elijah began to taunt them sarcastically. They shouted louder and slashed themselves in a more intense attempt to draw their god's attention to gain his favor. They "raved on" until time for the evening sacrifice (about 3:00 p.m.) but there was no response.

Finally Elijah took his turn and called for the attention of the people. On the ruins of an old Israelite altar he placed twelve stones—one for each of the twelve

tribes—symbolizing the continuing unity of Israel under the covenant in the mind of God. Then he dug a trench around the altar and had water poured over the sacrifice and the wood three times until everything was thoroughly soaked and the trench itself was filled with water. By this means he sought to demonstrate that no trickery was possible—a real miracle would have to take place. Then instead of all the frenzied calling, ritual dance, and laceration, Elijah prayed a simple prayer that Yahweh would prove that He was God and that He would accredit His messenger. The fire fell and consumed the sacrifice, the wood, and even the water in the trench. The effect on the people was the desired one: "They fell on their faces and cried, 'Yahweh is God'" (1 Kings 18:39).

With the people on his side, Elijah commanded that they seize the prophets of Baal, take them down to the Kishon Valley, and kill them there. This command fulfilled the law that condemned false prophets to death (Deuteronomy 13:5), and was retribution for Jezebel's killing of the prophets

Statue of the prophet Elijah at the Muhraqah on Mount Carmel, commemorating his victory over the pagan worshipers of Baal
(Levant Photo Service)

of Yahweh. There is no record of Ahab's opposition to the execution, nor is there any indication of how he really felt about Yahweh's miraculous demonstration of Himself. After the sacrifice, Elijah now appropriately prayed that God would send rain. And He did.

Jehu's destruction of the Baal cult in Israel. After the death of Ahab and Jehu's massacre of Ahab's family (2 Kings 10:1–11), Jehu proceeded to root out Baalism in the kingdom (2 Kings 10:18–28). Upon his arrival in Samaria Jehu "outwitted" (v. 19, REB) the prophets of Baal or acted "deceptively" (NIV) in trapping them. He set up the equivalent of a sting operation. He pretended that his zeal for Baal would be much greater than that of Ahab, who had served Baal only "a little" (v. 18) by comparison. He planned a great "sacrifice" (v. 19) for Baal, which may be a play on words because the word is also used for the "slaughter" of apostates (1 Kings 13:2; 2 Kings 23:20).

He made sure that all the prophets or priests of Baal and all other leaders of the Baal cult came to the sacrifice and then made certain they would be clearly identified by dressing them in festal robes or vestments. Next he posted eighty "guards and officers" (evidently members of an elite infantry unit that constituted the palace bodyguard) at all the entrances to the temple. Jehu himself officiated at the offering to Baal; and "just as" he finished, he gave the signal to the guards to attack. From the way Jehu planned the grisly event, one gets a chilling view of his character.

Then they brought out the sacred pillars, the pole representing the Baalath and the stone representing Baal, and "burned it" (v. 26) and "demolished" it (v. 27). The pole they could burn; a stone cannot be burned. Evidently they heated it red hot and then threw cold water on it and smashed it into fragments. Finally they tore down the temple and used the location for a latrine (literally, "the place of dung"), parallel to the allusion to the remains of Jezebel in 9:37. People without toilets in their houses could go there or could bury their excrement there. They thus heaped a final indignity on the Baal!

But the extermination of the Baal cult did not mean that Israel returned to God. The king and people were irrevocably set in their idolatrous ways. "Jehu did not turn away from the sins of Jeroboam. . . from the golden calves that were at Bethel and Dan" (2 Kings 10:29 NKJV). So God let foreign powers start chipping away at Israel's territory during Jehu's reign. Jehu himself lost all lands east of the Jordan River to Syria (2 Kings 10:32–33). Eventually God sent the whole nation into captivity in Assyria. *(For more on this topic, go to p. 174 or p. 257.)*

Warfare

Jeroboam's "Almost War"

Jeroboam had an "almost war" on his hands as soon as he became king. Rehoboam, king of Judah, intended to quash the rebellion of the northern tribes and actually mustered the troops. But before the army could march, the prophet Shemaiah received word from God to stop Rehoboam, and he persuaded the king to disband his forces. Shemaiah argued against going to war with blood brothers and made the point that God was in the rupture (1 Kings 12:21-24).

We should note that if there had been war, it would have been a bloody one. Judah had the advantage of the machinery of government and control of the general staff and organization of the army. Israel had the greater population resources and much of the chariotry and equipment Solomon had stored in his fortress cities. The fact that God stopped a major pitched battle between the two kingdoms on this occasion does not indicate He would likewise intervene to prevent all the border skirmishes between the two kingdoms later on. The "continual warfare" mentioned in such passages as 1 Kings 15:6, 7, 16, 32 must refer to such skirmishes.

Jeroboam's Tangle with Shishak

Egypt ate "humble pie" all during the days of Solomon, when he enjoyed a commercial alliance with Phoenicia and the Sabeans (Sheba) and challenged Egyptian commercial dominion in the Red Sea. As the fortunes of Israel sagged in the latter days of Solomon, and as a new and vigorous dynasty came to power in Egypt under Sheshonk I (biblical Shishak, 945–924 B.C.), Egypt had her chance at a comeback. Evidently Shishak had befriended Jeroboam in Egypt and sent him back to Palestine with his blessing, since Jeroboam returned to split the Hebrew monarchy and thus reduce its danger to Egypt.

Shishak had at his disposal some 1,200 chariots and regiments of Libyan and Nubian infantry. As he invaded Judah in the fifth year of King Rehoboam (1 Kings 14:28), the Judeans were no match for him. But, at the same time the Judean highlands proved to be a difficult challenge for Shishak's chariot corps. So the Egyptian contented himself with a heavy tribute—and Rehoboam paid it rather than lose everything.

Scripture doesn't say what happened next. But evidently Shishak turned on his former protégé and had great military success all over the Kingdom of Israel, even crossing the Jordan and taking the old Israelite center of Mahanaim. Our primary source of information about the invasion is an inscription that Shishak had carved on a wall of the Temple of Karnak at modern Luxor, Egypt. The inscription pictures Amon, god of empire, with ropes in his hand leading to the necks of captives, on the bodies of which are carved names of towns. A total of 120 town names are legible, but only a minority can be identified with known places. A few examples of towns in the northern kingdom are Beth-Shan, Shunem, Megiddo, Magdala, and Mahanaim.

Shishak achieved his goal of greatly weakening the Hebrew states and rendering them incapable of interfering with the Egyptian sphere of influence. So he packed up his immense booty and went home.[1]

Asa, Baasha, Syria, and a Significant Archaeological Discovery

After the great victory of Asa of Judah over the Egyptians (discussed in the next chapter), people began streaming south from Israel because they saw God was with Asa. Baasha, who was now king of Israel (ruled 908-886 B.C.), decided to build his own "Berlin Wall" to keep his people from going to Judah. He decided to fortify Ramah, only about five miles north of Jerusalem (2 Chronicles 16:1; 1 Kings 15:17). At that point, only approximately a year after his great victory over the Egyptians and in the midst of his reform moves, Asa had a strange lapse of faith. Instead of depending on God to see him through the new emergency, he stripped the treasuries of the temple and palace and sent a large gift to Ben-hadad, king of Aram in Damascus, requesting a renewal of a treaty that their fathers had had and a breaking of the non-aggression pact Aram now had with Israel (1 Kings 15:19).

Asa's diplomatic initiatives proved successful and Ben-hadad prepared to attack Israel's north. When Baasha heard about this threat (v. 21) to his northern border, he naturally stopped work on fortifying Ramah and rushed back to his capital at Tirzah (7 miles northeast of Nablus) to prepare to meet Ben-hadad in the field. Ben-hadad conquered several towns in the far north around Dan and in the Galilee region.

Now with a contemporary record we may be able to breathe down the necks of Baasha and Ben-hadad. As Israeli excavators continued their work at Dan in 1993,

Shishak, in his inscription on the wall of the Temple of Karnak at Luxor, Egypt, personalized the towns he captured in Israel in his invasion of 925 B.C., putting the names of the towns on the bodies of captives.

they came upon an inscription in Aramaic which has been interpreted as part of Ben-hadad's victory stele erected at Dan on this occasion, around 890 B.C. After the Israelites reconquered the town, they broke up the stele and reused it in a wall which the Assyrians knocked down when they took Dan in 732.

There is some uncertainty about whether this is Ben-hadad's inscription, erected on the occasion of his victory over Baasha. But there is no debate over a couple of major points in the inscription itself. (1) It mentions "the king of Israel" and "the House of David" (the dynastic name of the Kingdom of Judah), thus confirming the existence of the two separate kingdoms in the ninth century B.C. (2) More importantly, for the first time we have a mention of King David outside the Bible, in an ancient Palestinian inscription, dating probably within a hundred years of David's reign (1010-970 B.C.)![2]

Philistine Resurgence

Israel was forced to deal with enemies in all directions: with Judah to the south, with Syria to the north and east, with Philistia to the west, with Edom to the southeast, and later with Assyria as she moved west against several states of greater Syria. Both Nadab (909–908), son of Jeroboam, and Elah (886–885) found it necessary to deal with the Philistines, who had benefited from the humiliation of the Hebrew states at the hands of Shishak. They were especially concerned with elimination of the Gibbethon bulge, which jutted out into Israel's territory and commanded routes into the Samarian hills from the Philistine plain and protected the rear of Jaffa. Both efforts ended in fiasco. Nadab was killed in action while besieging Gibbethon, and assassins killed Elah while his commander, Omri, led the unsuccessful attack. But failure against Ben-hadad and the Philistines does not mean that Israel survived as fundamentally weak and about to expire, as further discussion will show.

Army and Fortifications of Israel

It appears that the military continued to operate much the same under the Israelite kings as it had during the reign of Solomon. Both the regulars of the standing army and the general levy of trained reservists and raw recruits could be called up in the event of war. The chariot corps became more significant with the passage of time. Zimri as captain of half of King Elah's chariots (1 Kings 16:9), commanded the strategic reserve close to the king at the capital (Tirzah). The other half were no doubt dispersed in other chariot towns throughout the kingdom. Thus Zimri had a power base from which to launch a successful revolution.

The role of permanent fortifications in the national defense changed fundamentally, however. Instead of a few major defense bastions with a highly mobile chariot corps that could easily and quickly be deployed (as in Solomon's day), there was now a line of closely placed fortresses spread out across the country, especially across the northern and central parts of it. One scholar has called this the "Naphtali Line" (see 1 Kings 15:20). Beginning in the north with Ijon at the foot of the valley between the Lebanon and Anti-Lebanon Mountains, the line continued south to Dan, Abel-beth-maachah, Kedesh, Hazor, Chinnereth (on the Sea of Galilee), Megiddo, Beth-Shan, Tirzah, Samaria and points south. The list identifies a fortified city every ten miles or less, giving the northern kingdom a defense against the Syrians and others that might attack from the east and the north.

Though earlier kings of Israel tried to do their part in arming the state, Omri (885–874) and Ahab (874–853) launched major new efforts. They recognized their major exterior challenge in the rapid expansion of Assyria. As we have already seen, Omri established a new, more strategically-located and better-defended capital at Samaria. Ahab continued to build there and rebuilt the fortifications at such important centers as Hazor and Megiddo, as excavations at those sites have shown.

In fact, archaeologists argue over whether Solomon or Ahab built the horse barns and other installations at Megiddo. It seems reasonable to conclude that Ahab repaired and rebuilt Solomon's earlier construction. The house of Omri became so powerful and respected by the Assyrians that in their

Ahab's fortifications at Hazor

(Willem A. VanGemeren)

inscriptions they called Israel "Bit Humria" ("the house of Omri"). As Ahab and his successors had to fight Syrians and Assyrians with their formidable chariot corps, it became necessary to increase the size of the Israelite chariot forces. We saw in the last chapter that Solomon had a total of 1,400 chariots. Ahab sent off 2,000 chariots to fight the Assyrian Shalmaneser III at the Battle of Qarqar (853 B.C.; see following discussion). How many additional chariots he had in the armory we have no way of knowing.

The Assyrian threat changed the approach in construction of city walls. Previously the Hebrews had frequently built casemate walls. Now, with Assyrian battering rams as a standard part of siege equipment, the thinner casemate walls proved inadequate, and the Hebrews commonly built solid city walls.

Ahab's Early Wars with Syria (1 Kings 20:1-43)

"Ben-Hadad the king of Syria gathered all his forces together; thirty-two were kings with him, with horses and chariots. And he went up and besieged Samaria, and made war against it." (1 Kings 20:1 NKJV)

As Omri and then Ahab built up the internal political structure and the military capability of Israel, Ben-hadad II of Syria worried that his neighbor to the west would grow too powerful to handle. In fact, Israel not only increased in strength but became expansionistic. Omri had reconquered Moab, and possibly Ammon en route, as the Moabite Stone indicates (see following discussion). A further cause for Ben-hadad's worry was an apparent alliance between Omri and Tyre, which was cemented by the marriage of his son Ahab to Jezebel, daughter of the king of Tyre. That alliance presumably gave Tyre access to the food supply and raw material needed for her people and her commerce.

Ben-hadad decided to launch a preemptive strike before he was gobbled up. As allies he gained thirty-two kings of city-states of Syria. Apparently the Syrians moved with speed and stealth and appeared before the walls of Samaria before Israel's reserves could be called up. Ahab was in conference with his chief advisors and the 232 district governors as the Syrians arrived. Very quickly the plight of the Hebrews became desperate, and the Syrians demanded what amounted to complete surrender: the right to sack the city (v. 6).

At Israel's darkest moment a prophet appeared—with the promise that God would deliver the Syrians into Ahab's hand. Not because of a spiritual about face in Israel but so Ahab and Israel would "know that I am the LORD" (v. 13).

God directed Israel to attack at siesta time, when the thirty-two kings were drinking themselves drunk at the command post (v. 16) and the Syrian troops were "at ease." The 232 provincial governors created quite a spectacle as they charged out of the gates of Samaria toward the massed Syrian forces. But they were only a decoy as some 7,000 Israelite troops and the chariot corps overran some of the Aramean contingents. Without their commanders, those regiments broke ranks and fled, setting off a general stampede. To escape, Ben-hadad himself had to jump on an unfamiliar horse and flee; his chariot was not ready for action. As the Syrian stragglers fled eastward, they undoubtedly passed Israelite army contingents and armed civilians who inflicted heavy casualties. The rout was total.

That does not end the story. The Syrians may have been down but were not out. They engaged in an agonizing reappraisal and came up with three ingredients in a recipe for victory. (1) The Hebrew god was a god of the hills. The next battle should take place in the plain where Syrian armament (chariots and cavalry) was superior and where the Hebrew god would be at a disadvantage. (2) Since the generalship of numerous kings leading their ethnic bands into battle had created a disunified military posture, Ben-hadad's advisors recommended a reorganized army with a centralized command and regional contingents led by professional military men. (3) Rebuild the cavalry and chariot corps and restore them to the level they had achieved before the last battle (vv. 23-25). Ben-hadad adopted these recommendations. Whether

the spring (v. 22) when the battle took place was in the next year or later is immaterial.

The Aphek where the battle took place was probably the one east of the Sea of Galilee commanding the road to Damascus (there were five Apheks). As Ahab divided his troops into two companies, the Israelite army looked like "two herds of goats" compared to the Syrian troops (v. 27). Into this hopeless situation walked a "man of God" or a prophet who said in effect that because the Syrians thought Yahweh was powerful in the hills only, He was bound to give the Israelites victory to prove His omnipotence to the Syrians. And the Israelites who had been so idolatrous would know that Yahweh truly was God.

If we have identified the right Aphek, the valley leading to the town was less than 350 feet wide for a considerable stretch and virtually unconquerable by frontal attack. A flanking attack was possible, however, and apparently that was successfully tried. But we are not told the logistics of the situation. For seven days the two armies took each other's measure and worked on battle strategies. Finally on the day of battle Israel inflicted heavy losses on the Syrians, and a collapsing wall of Aphek killed an additional number.

Ben-hadad fled and later begged for mercy at Ahab's hands. The treaty they arranged called for return of the cities in the Golan that Ben-hadad's father had taken from Ahab's predecessor (Baasha, 1 Kings 15:20), Israelite trade privileges in Damascus, and Syrian trade privileges in Samaria. Some of Ahab's contemporaries opposed the lenient terms. And a prophet judged Ahab severely for his actions, telling him he would forfeit his own life in exchange for Ben-hadad's (v. 42).

And we wonder what was going on and how Ahab could have been so generous when his victory was so complete. The explanation is simple: Assyrian power loomed on the eastern horizon, and Ahab believed he needed Syrian power as a buffer against the Assyrians and as an ally if open warfare should erupt. Within a very few years, perhaps only two or three, the two kings fought side by side against the Assyrians.

Shalmaneser's Invasion

Hardly had the opponents caught their breath when the Assyrians under Shalmaneser III (858–824 B.C.) launched a major offensive into Syria. The powers of the West met him in his sixth year (853) at the great battle of Qarqar on the Orontes River. Syrian states, Israel, Egypt, and others contributed to the force that opposed Shalmaneser.

The Assyrian spelled out in great detail on his Monolith Inscription (now in the British Museum) the forces opposing him. Ahab contributed 10,000 men and 2,000 chariots to the venture. The figures that Shalmaneser reports are usually taken fairly much at face value; he is so precise that some combatants are said to have contributed as few as 200 soldiers or 10 chariots. The total is striking, however: 52,900 foot soldiers; 3,940 chariots; 1,900 in the cavalry units.[3]

On his Monolith Inscription (now in the British Museum), Shalmaneser III tells of his battle with a great coalition of forces, including Ahab of Israel. The cuneiform text runs all across the face of the monument, so it appears indistinct.

While Shalmaneser claimed a great victory, he must have overstated the case considerably, since Ahab felt free to take on Ben-hadad in another war later in the year 853 and met his death in the process. The Bible makes no reference to the titanic struggle at Qarqar. We'll look at it in connection with Assyrian warfare in the next chapter.

Ahab, Jehoshaphat, and Benhadad (1 Kings 22:1-38)

"Now a certain man drew a bow at random, and struck the king of Israel [Ahab] between the joints of his armor . . . and [he] died at evening." (1 Kings 22:34-35)

The kingdoms of Israel and Judah didn't fight all the time. In fact, periodically they enjoyed good relations and even had periods when they were allied. Such a time came in the year 853. This alliance was cemented by the marriage of Ahab's daughter Athaliah to Jehoshaphat's son Jehoram.

At this point Ahab's concern was that Ben-hadad had not returned Ramoth Gilead, an important city on the eastern caravan route, when he restored the northern towns to Israel. So Ahab persuaded Jehoshaphat to join him in getting it back. Presumably Jehoshaphat saw something in a victory that would benefit Judah: the value of regaining the Yarmuk River as a border for the security of both kingdoms, and the importance of Hebrew control of the strategic town of Ramoth Gilead on the King's Highway.

Ben-hadad approached the battle with great trepidation. Ahab had beaten him twice. Therefore he ordered his men to search out Ahab and fight only this dangerous enemy. Certainly he recognized that if the king died or were captured, the army would cease to fight. It is also possible that Ben-hadad wanted to kill Ahab only so the army might remain intact to join him in future warfare against Assyria. Because the prophet Micaiah predicted that Ahab would be slain in battle, the king went into battle disguised, but Jehoshaphat did not.

During the conflict a bowman shooting at random hit Ahab in the joints of his armor (perhaps between the breastplate and abdomen and thigh armor) and mortally wounded him; thus the prophecy was "accidentally" fulfilled. He died at sunset and the news spread through the army. The siege of Ramoth Gilead ended and the army disbanded. The Syrians did not press their advantage because the limited objective of successfully defending the city had been achieved. Moreover, as noted, they may have wanted Israel as an ally against Assyria.

The Moabite War

Moab, which had slipped out of Hebrew control about the time of the division of the kingdom, found itself subjugated again in the days of Omri. Apparently during the latter part of the reign of Ahab's son

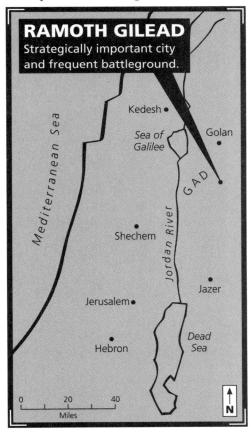

RAMOTH GILEAD
Strategically important city and frequent battleground.

Kedesh

Sea of Galilee

Golan

Mediterranean Sea

Jordan River

GAD

Shechem

Jazer

Jerusalem

Hebron

Dead Sea

0   20   40
Miles

N

Ahab died in battle at Ramoth Gilead.

Ahaziah, while he lay ill and incapacitated, the Moabites took advantage of the situation and rebelled. Mesha, king of Moab, led the revolt (see 2 Kings 1:1).

After Ahaziah's death, his brother Joram inherited the revolt and proceeded to squelch it (2 Kings 3:6–27. The Moabite Stone, inscribed by Mesha, and found in 1868 and now housed in the Louvre Museum in Paris, supplements the biblical account.[4] These accounts do not really contradict but supplement each other.

Joram mobilized his forces (c. 852 B.C.) and then sought to utilize the alliance with Judah to give him success. One reason for Joram's desire to have Judah's help in the fight is that Moab had highly fortified its northern frontier and it would therefore be advantageous to attack from the south. Joram and the Judean king Jehoshaphat agreed to attack through the "wilderness of Edom," to the southeast of the most heavily fortified areas of Moab. It was possible to march through Edom at the time because Judah controlled it. The "king of Edom" (v. 9) was not a sovereign ruler of the state but some kind of puppet under the domination of Jehoshaphat. The line of march ran south from Samaria through Jerusalem, Hebron, and Arad, and then south around the southern end of the Dead Sea and eastward in a circuitous route through the wilderness of Edom.

This "circuitous march of seven days" exhausted the water supply of the combined armies and reduced them to desperate straits. An attendant of the king of Israel informed the kings that Elisha lived nearby and might help them. The three kings "went down" to see him, evidently descending from the headquarters on a height to the wadi where he was located and where the men and the animals probably were bivouacked.

He told them that in the wadi or dry streambed they would find an abundance of water for the army and all their animals. They would see "neither wind nor rain," so evidently a flash flood was involved—rain in the west with water flowing eastward down the wadi, a common occurrence in the region. The miracle in this case was the timing, not the means of supplying the water.

The famous Moabite Stone (now in the Louvre in Paris) celebrates the revolt of King Mesha of Moab against the rule of Israel.

(Gustav Jeeninga)

does not mean that powerless Chemosh had the capacity to bring down punishment on the kings. Nor does it appear that Yahweh had any special reason to discipline the army. The most natural explanation is that the tide of battle turned at that point. Such a change of events could have occurred because the sacrifice so inspired the Moabites with a conviction that they would win that they fought with an indescribable fury. This infusion of spirit may have been coupled with the belief of Edomites, pagan Israelites, and even many from Judah, that Chemosh should be effective in his own land, especially after a sacrifice like that; and their morale snapped. In any case, the Hebrew expeditionary force withdrew after their earlier victories.

Jehu, Shalmaneser, and Hazael

Jehu won God's commendation for destroying Baal worship and the house of Ahab, but he, like all the other kings of Israel, followed in the steps of Jeroboam in maintaining calf worship at Dan and Bethel. So for his degree of faithfulness to God's instructions he had a promise of a dynasty lasting four generations. For his degree of unfaithfulness, God began to "whittle Israel down" (2 Kings 10:32).

What happened historically was this. Shalmaneser III tells how in the eighteenth year of his reign (841 B.C., the first year of Jehu) he crossed the Euphrates River for the sixteenth time and on this occasion received tribute from King Jehu of Israel (841–814). The event is actually pictured on the Black Obelisk of Shalmaneser, now in the British Museum. Jehu presented the Assyrian with various gold and silver objects.[5] After that Jehu had relative peace during the years 841 to 838 B.C. while Shalmaneser was harassing Damascus. After 838 Assyria quit pressuring Syria, and its king, Hazael, was free to move against Israel in order to strengthen his rear. Eventually he took

According to Elisha, providing water was an "easy thing" for God to do; He would also give the allied forces victory over the Moabites, and they would engage in a scorched-earth policy. When the Moabites attacked, they were completely surprised and put to rout. Subsequently the allied forces ranged over the countryside engaging in a scorched-earth policy. Finally only one major city, Kir Hareseth, the capital, was left.

As the three kings besieged the Moabite capital, King Mesha tried to break through "to the king of Edom," apparently believing that if he could breach the Edomite section of the line he might win a victory. That effort failed; and finally in desperation he sacrificed his son, the crown prince, to his god Chemosh, on the city wall in an effort to appease his anger and win his favor.

That "a great wrath came upon Israel" is hard to explain or interpret. It certainly

The Black Obelisk of Shalmaneser III of Assyria (now in the British Museum) commemorates the achievements of the first thirty-one years of his reign. Jehu of Israel pays tribute to the Assyrian in the second register from the top.

(Gustav Jeeninga)

nearly all of Israel's holdings in Transjordan and held them until Jeroboam II managed to regain them (2 Kings 14:25).

Jeroboam II, Uzziah, and Hebrew Resurgence

During the days of Uzziah of Judah (792–740) and Jeroboam II (793–753) the two Hebrew kingdoms regained power once more. Together they controlled most

of the territory David had ruled at the height of the united Hebrew kingdom. This resurgence of power must be attributed in large measure to the weakness of Assyrian monarchs during the first half of the eighth century B.C.

Jeroboam expanded the borders of Israel in the north to the "entrance to Hamath" or "Lebo-Hamath" and in the south to the "Sea of the Arabah" (2 Kings 14:25). The "entrance to Hamath" may refer to a general area south of Hamath that would give access to the Euphrates; it was the northern border of the kingdom of Solomon (1 Kings 8:65). Some identify it as a city, Lebo-Hamath, about fifty miles north of Damascus. The "Sea of the Arabah" must be the Dead Sea (cf. Deuteronomy 3:17) and indicates establishment of the border at the north end of the Dead Sea (the old Moabite-Israelite frontier) or farther south toward the Arnon.

This expansion under Jeroboam II must have taken place during the latter half of his reign; Assyrian weakness of activity elsewhere would have permitted it then. Moreover, it would have taken an extended period of time for Jeroboam to build up his military establishment and infrastructure to permit expansionist moves. Israel enjoyed control of both Hamath and Damascus during Jeroboam's reign (2 Kings 14:28).

Tiglath-Pileser III to the Rescue

Tiglath-Pileser III (744–727) in a sense may be thought of as rescuing Assyria, Menahem of Israel, and Ahaz of Judah. He rescued Assyria by bringing it back from the deadly decline of the previous half century. Assyrian developments appear in the next chapter.

Menahem sought "his support in strengthening his hold on the kingdom" (2 Kings 15:19). At that time (probably 738) Pekah was actually ruling the part of Israel east of the Jordan and Menahem wanted Assyrian help in consolidating his hold on the kingdom. So he made a payment for help—not tribute in the usual sense of the term.

The Assyrians did withdraw from the area and let him alone, but they didn't put any pressure on Pekah to recognize Menahem's sovereignty. So it does not seem that Menahem got much for his money.

Incidentally, scholars used to claim that the Bible was wrong in using the name "Pul" to refer to Tiglath-Pileser (2 Kings 15:19; 1 Chronicles 5:26), but we now know that he was so addressed in Babylonian circles. Tiglath-Pileser did claim that Menahem paid tribute.[6]

Six years later King Ahaz of Judah also sought Tiglath-Pileser's help. As Assyria threatened the Westland, Syria and Israel sought to persuade Judah to join them in a coalition against Assyria. Ahaz refused to cooperate and Rezin of Syria and Pekah of Israel attacked in an effort to force Ahaz to do so. The allies decimated Judah's army and even killed the king's son and some of his chief officers. Then they virtually depopulated a whole section of Judah and carried the inhabitants into slavery. But as a result of the intercession of a prophet named Oded, the Israelites returned all the captives (see 2 Chronicles 28:5-15 for an account of the war).

In his desperation Ahaz stripped the treasury of the temple and palace and sent the silver and gold to Tiglath-Pileser. In doing so he pled with the Assyrians to rescue him from Syria and Israel. Tiglath-Pileser was happy to oblige. In 732 he obliterated the kingdom of Syria and reduced it to provincial status within the Assyrian Empire. In the same campaign he also defeated Israel, annexed her northern districts, and carried off numerous captives (2 Kings 15:29). The number he deported must have been substantial. He took away over 30,000 from the northern districts of Syria at this time.[7] By deporting the best educated and most prosperous people he doubtless hoped to prevent future rebellions. All he left of the northern kingdom was the tiny province of Samaria, and that was a vassal state to the Assyrians.

The Flickering Light Goes Out; End of the Northern Kingdom

Hoshea had become king of Israel in 732, either as a result of Assyrian intervention or a popular uprising, but he did become tributary to the Assyrian king. When the son of Tiglath-Pileser III, Shalmaneser V, came to the Assyrian throne in 727 B.C., at first

Tiglath-Pileser III conquered the nothern part of Israel and destroyed the kingdom of Damascus in 732 B.C. (A relief from his palace at Nimrud now in the British Museum)

Hoshea apparently paid him tribute. The NIV translation of 2 Kings 17:3 is preferable, with its rendering in the English past perfect: "had been Shalmaneser's vassal" and "had paid him tribute." The verse should be treated as a kind of topic sentence with development following. There is no evidence for two invasions of Shalmaneser (vv. 3-5). After initial subservience Hoshea developed a false hope that he could rebel successfully against Assyria with Egyptian help, and stopped the annual tribute payments.

We may easily conclude from reading verse 4 that Shalmaneser caught Hoshea and imprisoned him before the siege of Samaria. But the verse is probably only a summary statement about the king: he had been a vassal, he rebelled, and was finally seized and imprisoned. If he had been taken before the siege, the people probably would have chosen a new ruler.

In any case, Shalmaneser invaded Israel, subdued the countryside, and launched a three-year siege of Samaria (2 Kings 17:5; 18:9–10). Apparently the siege took place during 725, 724, and 723, with the fall occurring in 723. Since parts of years counted as years, the siege needed to last only one full year and parts of two others, or less than a total of two years.

Scripture leaves the harrowing tale of the long siege to the imagination. It never seeks to tell tearjerker stories about the suffering of either the Hebrews or their enemies. There is

Assyrian Campaign (734–732 B.C.)
In 734 B.C. Tiglath-pileser III moved along the coast all the way to the Egyptian border. In 733 and 732 he made two invasions into Israel, taking control of the northern part of the kingdom and bringing to an end the kingdom of Damascus.

deported from the city—almost certainly this was a number taken from the region. The areas in which Shalmaneser or Sargon settled the deported Israelites were in northern Mesopotamia east of Haran; in Gozan (modern Tell Halaf) on the Khabur River, an important tributary of the Euphrates; in Halah (possibly an alternate spelling of Calah or Nimrud, about 24 miles south of Nineveh); and in Media, east of Mesopotamia (2 Kings 17:6). These people became the ancestors of the Jews who lived in Media in Esther's day. And when we evaluate the account of Esther, it may be useful to keep in mind the idolatrous people of this community probably came from the Kingdom of Israel.

After Sargon removed the flower of Samaria's population, he brought in people from "Babylon, Cuthah [east of Babylon], Ava [in Syria], Hamath [in Syria], and Sepharvaim [probably in Syria], and placed them in the cities of Samaria instead of the children of Israel" (2 Kings 17:24 NKJV). The descendants of these foreigners intermingled

nothing here about the desperate lack of food and water among the besieged, about any reports of cannibalism, or about the spread of disease among resistance-weakened defenders. Nor are there any accounts of Assyrian cruelty to those who finally surrendered—of rape, of torture, or massacre. Apparently the Jewish historian Josephus had no information about the fall of Samaria either, as he did about the fall of Jerusalem, because he said nothing on the subject.

Increasingly, scholars are attributing the fall of Samaria to Shalmaneser, who died in 722. Samaria fell in the ninth year of Hoshea (2 Kings 17:6). If he took the throne in 732, his ninth year was 723. Note, too, that Josephus seemed to believe that Shalmaneser was still in command when the Assyrians took the city.[8]

Sargon II (721–705) used to be given credit for the victory—and still often is—because he took the credit, claiming to have taken the city and deported 27,290 people.[9] At most, he probably engaged in some mopping-up activity later on. And 27,290 is a very large number for him to have

Assyrian Campaign Against Israel (725–723 B.C.)
In 725 B.C. Shalmaneser V invaded Israel and marched on Samaria. After a three-year siege Samaria finally fell in 723 B.C., apparently during Shalmaneser's reign. But Sargon II, his successor, claimed credit for the Assyrian victory.

with the descendants of the remaining Hebrews and a half-breed race, ethnically and religiously, known as the Samaritans, arose there.

The Jews returning from the Exile treated these people as "different" (not fully orthodox), and they did not include them in the rebuilding of the temple in Jerusalem (see Ezra and discussion in chapter 12, Persia and the restoration). The Samaritans continued as a separate sect in Jesus' day and down to the present. They maintain their synagogue in Nablus, and currently there are several hundred of them on the West Bank and in Israel.

(For more on this topic, go to p. 184 or p. 259.)

Housing and Furniture

"But Elisha was sitting in his house [in Samaria], and the elders were sitting with him." (2 Kings 6:32 NKJV)

What sort of house would Elisha the prophet have been living in at the time he met with the elders? Let's go visit. The exterior is of stone. As we walk through the door, we find ourselves in an open courtyard. This is where the elders are gathered because there is no other place big enough for the meeting. To our right is a little pillared room (open to the courtyard) that serves as a kitchen. Across from it to our left is another small pillared room that is used as a workshop. Both are paved with fieldstones. Then in a horseshoe arrangement around the rest of the courtyard are closed rooms that are either storerooms or family rooms. Above them is a second story.

Of course Elisha did not stay in one place all the time. Periodically he ministered in the area of Shunem (some seven miles east of Megiddo). Here a "wealthy" or "prominent" woman showed him hospitality. And she and her husband decided to build him a "prophet's chamber" that would be available to him whenever he came (2 Kings 4:8–10). This house in a village no doubt had a floor plan like the Samaria house, without a second story. But the roof could be used for sleeping in hot weather by erecting an open booth of branches on it. This is what is

Were the Ten Tribes "Lost"?

Many teach that the "Ten Tribes" were "lost" or deported. Yet most of them continued to live where they had for hundreds of years. Sargon exiled only some of the people from right around Samaria. And when the return from the Babylonian captivity occurred, there was a great sacrifice to Yahweh: "The children of those who had been carried away captive, who had come from the captivity, offered burnt offerings to the God of Israel." Note, the children or descendants of the captives offered burnt offerings. Note further, they offered "twelve bulls for all Israel" and "twelve male goats" (Ezra 8:35 NKJV).

Moreover, at the dedication of the rebuilt temple in 515 B.C. "the descendants of the captivity" offered "for all Israel twelve male goats" (Ezra 7:16–17). Furthermore, in Ezekiel's prophecy of the Millennium, he details the boundaries of the land of Israel and marks out a specific territory for each of the twelve tribes (Ezekiel 47—48).

described when the Bible says the host built for Elisha "a small walled upper room."

The simple furniture provided for Elisha gives us some idea of furniture now being used. We need to remember that this was a wealthy home. In his room they put a bed, a chair, a table and a lamp on a lampstand. The bed could have been a bedroll that the prophet could unroll on the floor at night. But the bed seemed to be open and ready for occupancy because the hostess later laid her son in it (v. 21). Therefore it was probably a bedroll placed on a wooden frame. The chair was likely a stool without a back. The table was probably a small, low wood table. The lampstand could have been made of wood, stone, or brick and the lamp that sat on it was an open clay saucer with a pinched lip in which a wick was placed and in which olive oil was burned. For the well-to-do, furniture had become more

"Beds of Ivory"

What about "beds of ivory" or "beds inlaid with ivory" (reb) and "couches"? And "houses of ivory" or "houses adorned with ivory" (reb, Amos 3:15)? Or what about Ahab's "ivory house" (1 Kings 22:39)?

Couches must refer to dining couches, on which one could recline while eating. We'll think about them and see pictures of contemporary Assyrian dining couches in the next chapter. Beds or houses of ivory must, of course, refer to beds or houses decorated with ivory inlay, as some of the newer versions indicate. Never were beds or houses made of ivory. The use of ivory inlay on chairs, tables, and beds and for wall decorations in houses must have been a way of "putting on the dog." Excavators at Samaria found hundreds of ivory plaques and ivory fragments in the royal quarters. The largest number turned up in the so-called "Ivory House" near the inner wall in the north. Some of these definitely dated to the time of Ahab (874-853 B.C.) and some dated later.

Though many of these pieces are very fragmentary, a substantial number are in fairly good condition. There are plaques in high relief with the background commonly being pierced or open work. Syrian and Egyptian themes and styles can be recognized. There are winged sphinxes (cherubim), fighting lions, human figures, and scenes from Egyptian mythology. Ivory plaques in low relief often have insets of precious stones and gold. Some have been incised with Hebrew letters. Phoenician workshops produced most of these ivories, with Hebrews importing them.

Ahab's "ivory house" apparently had plenty of ivory plaques or panels decorating the walls and furniture. Also, when the walls were faced with high quality white limestone they would give the appearance of an "ivory" palace as it stood there gleaming in the bright Palestinian sun. Citizens of western industrial countries plagued by soot-belching smokestacks can't appreciate the beauty of white limestone structures standing in relatively clean air in many places in Israel and Jordan today. Some of them look as if they were built yesterday.

elaborate than in previous periods, but the poor still commonly sat and slept on the floor.

The house plans described here basically remain the same as the "four-room" houses of the earlier period, with some modifications (see the last chapter). And while the individual houses tended to be much the same during the United Monarchy, there is now evidence of class distinction in such places as Hazor and Tirzah. Some occupied houses built fairly large and well-planned; others lived in less elaborate dwellings. At Tirzah, for example, the king had located his palace near the city gate and adjacent to a plaza. To the south of that stood the more elaborate houses of the wealthy. A wall separated the "better sort" from the houses of the poor.

Apparently, too, the very wealthy tended to oppress the poor, or at least to show an unconcern for them that deserved a severe reprimand. The prophet Amos, writing about 755, really took the upper classes to task. He pronounced doom on those "Who lie on beds of ivory," "Stretch out on your couches," "Who drink wine from bowls, and anoint yourselves with the best ointments" (Amos 6:4, 6). Yet they "trample on the needy" (8:4), "falsify the balances" (8:5), force the poor into debt slavery and "sell bad wheat" (8:6). The list of their faults goes on and on. But here we are especially interested in the furniture.

Ahab's Palace

Omri and Ahab developed a royal acropolis on the crest of Samaria covering an area of four acres, the size of many country towns. It measured some 275 by 600 feet. Retaining walls had to be massive to create and maintain the rectangular area on the top of the hill. We don't know anything about Omri's construction inside this wall. Apparently what little we can know dates to Ahab's day. He replaced the northern and western walls with a casemate wall that provided storage for weapons, food, and supplies.

Unfortunately we can't find out as much as we would like from the excavations because of massive destruction over the centuries and incomplete excavations. For

Remains of Ahab's palace at Samaria.

example, remains of Herod's temple to Augustus Caesar cover the northwest corner of the acropolis. We do know that there was a large rectangular courtyard surrounded by several wings. The one remaining wing stands against the south wall to the west and consists of an inner courtyard surrounded by rooms and measures some 90 by 75 feet.

An administrative complex stood between this wing and the western wall of the acropolis. Archaeologists found sixty-three ostraca (broken pieces of pottery inscribed in ink) in this building. These are records of oil and wine deliveries, possibly received from the royal estates. They give the year of one of the kings of Israel (but do not name the king), the name of the place sending the goods, and the name of the person receiving them. They are interesting in that they show us how people wrote then, while the personal names that are compounds of Baal demonstrate the inroads of Baal worship. We can identify many of the places from which the commodities came. The debate over the date of these records need not detain us here.

As already noted, excavators found a large collection of ivories in a building inside the north wall of the acropolis. As already noted, too, the expertise needed to dress the cut stone of the acropolis wall exceeded that of Solomon's construction. Several proto-Aeolic capitals (decorative tops of columns) have been found that may have graced the entrance to the royal quarter on the east.

(For more on this topic, go to p. 204 or p. 266.)

Diet and Foodstuffs

The growing, preparation, and variety of foods enjoyed during this period, is roughly the same as during the United Monarchy and may be reviewed from the last chapter.

(For more on this topic, go to p. 206 or p. 268.)

Dress

Ancient Hebrews tended to be traditionalists in matters of dress. We cannot add much for the northern kingdom to what was said in the last chapter. But we do have a pictorial representation that gives us some contemporary information. We already saw that Jehu had paid tribute to Shalmaneser III of Assyria after Ahab's struggle with the Assyrian at the Battle of Qarqar in 853 B.C. Shalmaneser pictures Jehu's appearance before him on what is known as the Black Obelisk, now in the British Museum

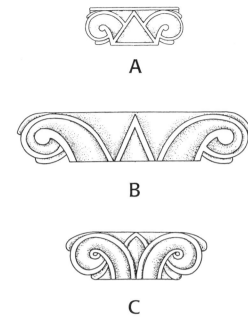

Proto-Ionic capitals from Israel. After Gabriel Barkay. Samaria (A), Megiddo (B), Hazor (C).

Development of Capitals

In Samaria, as well as elsewhere in Israel and Judah during the divided kingdom, proto-Ionic capitals remained a standard feature of architecture (note comments in the last chapter). This type of capital developed in Egypt before 1200 B.C. Then in Palestine, and probably also in Phoenicia, it appeared between 1000 and 900 and continued to be used there for several centuries. From Palestine and Phoenicia it spread to Cyprus and the Greek world, where it developed into the Ionic capital of the classical period. Hence the term "proto-Ionic."

The Black Obelisk shows the king with a short rounded beard and a soft cap on his head. He wears a long sleeveless tunic with a girdle and fringed at the bottom. Behind him a row of Israelites (also bearded) bear tribute. They wear long tunics (extending almost to the ankles) with fringed bottoms. Over these they have sleeved robes open at the sides and fringed down the edges of the split (see accompanying picture). At least this picture tells something about the formal dress of royalty and the upper classes.

(For more on this topic, go to p. 207 or p. 269.)

Family Life

Changes did occur in the daily lives of the people of Israel because they were cut off from the national religious life. No attention would have been paid to such events as Passover, the day of Atonement,

the Feast of Tabernacles, and the like under calf or Baal worship. Possibly observance of the Sabbath as a religious event largely ceased too, but a day of rest may have been given to workers. It is interesting to note, however, that Amos 8:4 shows that at least some of the wealthy kept the Sabbath.

But other aspects of social life continued in customary fashion. Parents still arranged marriages for their children. Bride prices continued to be paid and dowries given. Midwives continued their work. And while we have no solid information, it is likely that circumcision was still practiced, both as a matter of custom and an indication that the people belonged to "some deity out there." Children continued to be weaned at age two or three. And mothers continued to be responsible for much of the education of children.

Mothers probably did not bear responsibility for teaching reading and writing, however. We do not know who taught these arts. But something amazing was happening in all of Israel and Judah. Present evidence

indicates that "by the end of the eighth century Israelite society as a whole was literate."[10] The spread of the Hebrew alphabet, which reduced the number of signs to twenty-two, made this possible. Meanwhile Egypt, with its hieroglyphic (picture) writing, and Mesopotamia, with its cuneiform (wedge-shaped signs) script, both demanded the learning of hundreds of signs and symbols. Hence only professional scribes mastered the task of reading and writing in those lands.

Excavators found considerable evidence for widespread literacy among the Hebrews. For example, many pieces of clay pottery have ownership inscriptions. Commonly these were incised before firing, indicating that the potter put them there. And on the backs of decorated ivories from Samaria appear inscriptions intended as instruction for furniture makers, showing where they were to be placed on furniture. Words appear on stone weights used in commerce. Then there are the Samaria Ostraca that record receipts of oil and wine received at the palace. Evidence for widespread literacy can be even more extensively documented for Judah and appear in the chapter on the southern kingdom.

(For more on this topic, go to p. 208 or p. 271.)

Work, Travel, and Commerce

The Kingdom of Israel enjoyed a strategic geographical position. During most of

From the Black Obelisk of Shalmaneser III of Assyria we get some idea of Israelite clothing. There King Jehu and some of his attendants are pictured. In one panel Jehu bows before the Assyrian king. In a second panel (below) Israelite porters bear tribute. They are wearing fringed robes, floppy caps, and boots that turn up at the toes. (British Museum)

her history she held the plains of Sharon and Jezreel and northern Transjordan. Thus she had access to the Mediterranean Sea and close contact with Phoenicia and Damascus, control of the north-south trade route through Transjordan, and of the major coastal road, "the Way of the Sea."

Therefore Israel could benefit from international trade. Goods from far and wide could reach her territory in Phoenician ships. Mesopotamian products and ideas made their way to Israel through Damascus. And Egyptian products and influences came north along the coastal road. Hence a degree of cosmopolitanism

THE RICH GOT RICHER

AND THE

POOR GOT POORER

A new class distinction, apparently not common in the earlier periods, appeared during the divided monarchy, and especially in the northern kingdom. The upper classes enjoyed more elegant houses and more elegant furniture. But, unfortunately, they often gained their wealth by fraudulent or oppressive means. Apparently much of the rise of the upper class and their oppressiveness occurred during the half century between about 800 and 750 B.C. Assyria's weakness permitted Israel and Judah to gain control of most of what David and Solomon had once ruled during the long and prosperous reigns of Jeroboam II in the north and Uzziah in the south.

The unscrupulous rich felt no need to pay attention to divine commandments about honesty and concern for the poor. As they went their merry way, Amos came along about 755, preaching repentance and judgment on their sins. Ten years later Tiglath-Pileser III rose to power in Assyria, restored the nation's military might, and soon began to move against both kingdoms, as is indicated elsewhere in this chapter.

An example of the social oppression of the wealthy occurred during the ministry of Elisha. A widow came to Elisha for relief (2 Kings 4:1–7). Her creditors were about to foreclose and even to seize her two children and reduce them to debt slavery. The prophet heard her plea and met her immediate need by providing her with a large supply of olive oil that she could convert to cash.

that we would hardly expect existed in this small Hebrew kingdom.

Moreover, as Solomon's alliance with Hiram of Tyre brought him Phoenician skills and techniques, so the alliance of Omri and Ahab with Ethbaal of Tyre (1 Kings 16:31) brought Phoenician skills in their day. In fact, archaeologists were impressed that the dressing of stone in the royal complex at Samaria was done with greater skill and finesse than in Solomon's construction. Chariot builders and arms makers also had success at a fairly high level in the Kingdom of Israel. And producers of wool and wool fabrics, olive oil, and wine enjoyed good profits.

All this sounds positive and indicates that the northern kingdom should have been prosperous and successful. But Israel did not always enjoy access to Phoenician know-how. And gradually they lost control of or access to trade routes and foreign markets. Political instability and frequent civil wars periodically destroyed prosperity. The numerous foreign wars described earlier in this chapter took their toll in lives lost, man hours consumed in non-productive activity, destruction, and a drain on the economy. The cost of maintaining the standing army and building and maintaining military installations must have been almost prohibitive.

We almost smile when we hear Jeroboam and his friends complaining about high taxes under Solomon and bolting from the kingdom because they did not win a promise of relief (1 Kings 12:1-16). Could they possibly have been any better off on a wartime economy under many of the kings of the northern kingdom than under Solomon? And of course they could not in their weakened condition stand up to the Assyrian juggernaut as it marched triumphantly into the Westland.

We have now had an opportunity to look at the formidable Assyrian enemy that Israel faced on the battlefield and what life was like for the scores of thousands of Hebrews, from both Israel and Judah, who were carried into captivity in the Assyrian Empire. In the next chapter we will examine what life was like under Assyrian domination.

(For more on this topic, go to p. 212 or p. 272.)

NOTES:

[1]See especially Jack Finegan, *Light from the Ancient Past*, 2nd ed. (Princeton: Princeton University Press, 1959), 126; George A. Barton, *Archaeoloqy and the Bible*, 7th ed. (Philadelphia: American Sunday-School Union, 1937), 456; James H. Breasted, *Ancient Records of Egypt* (New York: Russell & Russell, 1962), IV, 348–356.

[2]See "'David' Found at Dan," *Biblical Archaeology Review*, March/April, 1994, 26–39.

[3]James B. Pritchard, ed., *Ancient Near Eastern Texts Relating to the Old Testament* (Princeton: Princeton University Press, 1955), 276–282.

[4]See Barton, 460-62; Pritchard, 320–21.

[5]Pritchard, 280–281.

[6]Pritchard, 283.

[7]Ibid.

[8]Josephus, *Antiquities of the Jews*, 9.14.1.

[9]Pritchard, 285.

[10]Amnon Ben-Tor, ed., *The Archaeology of Ancient Israel* (New Haven: Yale University Press, 1992), 349.

BIBLIOGRAPHY:

Albright, William F. *Archaeology and the Religion* of Israel. Baltimore: Johns Hopkins Press, 1942.

Albright, William F. *Yahweh and the Gods of Canaan*. Garden City, N.Y.: Doubleday & Company, 1968.

Borowski, Oded. *Agriculture in Iron Age Israel*. Winona Lake, Ind.: Eisenbrauns, 1987.

Finegan, Jack. *Light from the Ancient Past*. Princeton: Princeton University Press, 2nd ed., 1959.

Fleming, Wallace B. *The History of Tyre*. New York: AMS Press, reprint, 1966.

Fleming, Wallace B. Sidon, *A Study in Oriental History*. New York: AMS Press, reprint, 1966.

Herm, Gerhard. *The Phoenicians*. New York: Frederick A. Praeger, 1962.

Hitti, Philip K. *History of Syria*. New York: The Macmillan Company, 1951.

Jidejian, Nina. *Sidon Through the Ages*. Beirut: Dar El-Machreq Publishers, 1971.

Jidejian, Nina. *Tyre Through the Ages*. Beirut: Dar El-Machreq Publishers, 1969.

Kraeling, E. G. H. *Aram and Israel*. New York: Columbia University Press, 1918.

Mazar, Amihai. *Archaeology of the Land of the Bible*. New York: Doubleday, 1990.

Moscati, Sabatino. *The World of the Phoenicians*. New York: Frederick A. Praeger, 1965.

Pitard, Wayne T. *Ancient Damascus*. Winona Lake, Ind: Eisenbrauns, 1987.

Thiele, E. R. *The Mysterious Numbers of the Hebrew Kings*. Grand Rapids: Zondervan, rev. ed., 1983.

Unger, Merrill F. *Israel and the Aramaeans of Damascus*. Grand Rapids: Zondervan, 1957.

LIFE IN ASSYRIAN CAPTIVITY

Chapter 9

(2 Kings 15—19; Isaiah 36—37; Nahum)

"Assyria, rod of My anger, in whose hand, as a staff, is My fury! I send him against an ungodly nation." (Isaiah 10:5, 6 JPS) *"Like a tempest of hail and a destroying storm, like a flood of mighty waters overflowing."* (Isaiah 28:2 NKJV)

The "floods" mentioned by Isaiah surely did come, engulfing the Kingdom of Israel and nearly swamping the Kingdom of Judah, as God's judgment began to play out on a nation that had largely abandoned Yahweh. Storm clouds appeared on the horizon as Shalmaneser III led his armies into the Westland and Ahab and his allies tried to stop the Assyrians at Qarqar in 853 B.C. The waters rose as Tiglath-pileser III annexed Galilee and other northern districts in 732 B.C. and carried off thousands of Israelites into Assyria (2 Kings 15:29). The whole Northern Kingdom was submerged in 722 as Sargon II annexed what was left of the Hebrew state as an Assyrian province and deported 27,290 captives (2 Kings 18:9–12).

Flood waters lapped at the Southern Kingdom in 701 B.C. as Sennacherib moved against Hezekiah and failed to take Jerusalem (2 Kings 18:17—19:37). But Sennacherib's destruction was great, and he claimed to deport 200,150 people from Judah.[1]

The reason why God commissioned Assyria as the "rod of My anger" appears in the last chapter. In brief, Rehoboam had installed idolatrous calf worship as the official religion of the state, and all of the kings subscribed to it. Worse, the Ahab dynasty instituted Baal worship as the state religion. As noted in the next chapter, the Kingdom of Judah also had its share of idolatry, and Baal worship made its inroads there too, especially in the days of Queen Athaliah, daughter of Ahab and Jezebel, and wife of King Jehoram. She spread the infection into the southern kingdom!

The Lot of the Captives

No doubt many Bible students think that Assyrian deportation of Hebrews from Palestine was much like Nazi deportations of Jews and political prisoners during World War II, where the goal was to inflict suffering and to exterminate. But that is not how the Assyrians treated their prisoners of war. In the first place, the Assyrians maintained no death camps or concentration camps. In the second place, the Assyrians wanted the labor of captive peoples; they did not seek to destroy them. They settled some deportees in cities to carry out building projects or provide skilled craftsmen. Others they sent to rural areas to maintain or expand the region of cultivation. Yet others peopled regions depopulated by punitive action after a rebellion (e.g., 2 Kings 17:24).

Deported people going into exile, in a relief of Ashurbanipal at Nineveh. (From the Louvre Museum in Paris) In the upper register women are shown riding in a cart. In the lower register captives are being fed.

Professor Saggs has shown that the Assyrians took care that their deportees arrived in good condition. They fed them adequately on the way, provided footwear to protect their feet on the march, and made carts or donkeys available for the transport of women and children. Moreover, they did not break up families, but commonly deported families and whole communities as a group.[2]

The Land

"Until I come and take you away to a land like your own land, a land of grain and new wine, a land of bread and vineyards." (Isaiah 36:17)

The Assyrian army laid siege to Jerusalem during the reign of Hezekiah. Sennacherib, the Assyrian king, taunted the defenders of Jerusalem, threatening to deport them. But he also promised them that he would settle them in a new land similar to their own. And he could do that, for Assyria had a lot of similarities to Palestine. Moreover, Assyrians found it advantageous to settle deported

peoples in lands similar to the ones they came from, since then they could immediately adapt to the agricultural possibilities of their new homes and quickly achieve maximum production.

Though Assyria was originally quite small, it was expansionistic. As noted in the last chapter, in 732 B.C. Assyrians defeated Syria and deported the population of its capital, Damascus (2 Kings 16:9). In the same year Assyria annexed the northern part of Israel. About the same time she engaged in a running struggle with Babylon and established her mastery there with the destruction of Babylon in 689. Then she turned her attention to Egypt and subsequently to Elam (Persia) and for some decades controlled both kingdoms. So at Assyria's height as a nation during the seventh century, its control stretched from Iran or Persia on the east to Egypt on the west.

Assyria Very Similar to Palestine

Consider some of the similarities between Assyria and Palestine. Assyria proper was about the size of Palestine, or a little larger than the state of Connecticut. The Tigris cut down the middle, as did the Jordan in Palestine. Furthermore, it rained enough in Assyria to permit dry farming in most areas, differing from Babylonia to the south, where irrigation was absolutely essential.

Moreover, its plains and hill country permitted good to excellent grain yields, olive and grape production, the growth of vegetables, and nomadic pastoralism. Then, too, like Palestine, it was predominantly a land of country towns. There were only four major cities (Arrapkha and Erbil in the eastern hills, and Nineveh and Ashur on the Tigris). And by the time Sennacherib addressed these Judeans, Assyria had come to control stretches of Syria to the west that were similar in many ways to Judea.

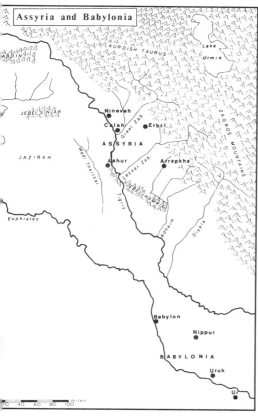

Assyria and Babylonia

The Assyrian heartland was located along the Tigris River, between Nineveh in the north and Ashur in the south, and stretched eastward toward the Zagros Mountains. Eastern cities were Erbil and Arrapkha.

To be more specific about Assyria itself, it extended some one hundred miles along the middle Tigris, from a little north of the present city of Mosul southward. Nineveh once stood across the river from Mosul (a modern city of over a half million people) on the east bank of the Tigris; Calah (Nimrud) was twenty miles south of Nineveh; and Ashur, sixty miles south of Nineveh.

To the west of the Tigris sprawled an extensive plain or limestone plateau that Assyria usually managed to control. East of the Tigris the Great or Upper Zab river flows into the Tigris about twenty-five miles south of Mosul and the Lesser Zab about fifty miles farther south. Assyria included the territory between the Tigris and the Zagros Mountains to the east. The land of Assyria is largely rolling plains cut by streambeds (wadis), aflow after spring rains but dry in the summer.

(For more on this topic, go to p. 223 or p. 275.)

Government

"The kings of Assyria have laid waste the nations and their lands." (2 Kings 19:17 NKJV)

What contributed to the seeming invincibility of the Assyrians? What made them so effective?

King Ashurbanipal of Assyria (the Osnapper of Ezra 4:10) being anointed by divine creatures
(From a relief in the British Museum)

Multi-lingual Scribes Kept the Records

Assyrian scribes functioned in numerous languages, as did administrators and formal interpreters, since Assyria controlled a considerable variety of subject states and was usually involved in the conquest of others. In the Assyrian inscriptions and in the pictorial representations scribes are everywhere, recording numbers of prisoners and booty, tax receipts, battle accounts, and all sorts of other information.

The reference above to Assyrian command of languages introduces the fact that they had quite an intelligence system. This is reflected in the account of Sennacherib's attack on Jerusalem in 701, where Assyrian officials gave evidence of knowing about internal affairs in Judah—and spoke in Hebrew (see 2 Kings 18:26-35).

Assyrian soldiers pile up booty. Scribes make a record while soldiers of the royal bodyguard look on. From the southwest palace at Nineveh.

(British Museum)

All during the New Assyrian Empire (c. 934–612 B.C.) autocratic warlords maintained Assyria as a completely militarized state. Year after year they attacked and destroyed until they beat down their opposition and brought into existence the largest empire the Middle East had seen since the heyday of Egyptian imperial power (c. 1400 B.C.). In fact, they built the largest empire the region had seen up to that time.

At the head of the state stood the king, whom the people viewed as holding his position by divine appointment and as the chosen representative of the god Ashur on earth. He managed or at least served as the final authority in every facet of the life of the state—international, political, military, and religious. When possible, the king designated the crown prince early and educated him thoroughly for the task of

A sculptured stone slab from Sennacherib's palace at Nineveh, showing heads of defeated enemy piled up while scribes make a record. Scribes kept detailed records of all sorts of things.

(From the British Museum)

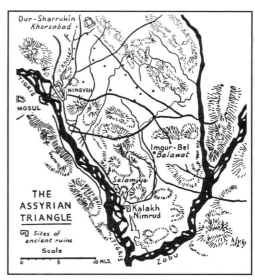

In the Assyrian Triangle, the area where the Zab and Tigris rivers joined, three capitals were located: Khorsabad in the north, Nineveh in the center, and Nimrud or Calah in the south.

government. That education included, among other things, mathematics, astronomy, cuneiform scripts, the art of decision-making and management, and learning to use different types of weapons.

High officials in the government included the prime minister, the commander-in-chief of the army, the city governors and provincial governors. At the court were a master of ceremonies, cupbearers, stewards, and others. Though the king served as the national high priest, each temple had its

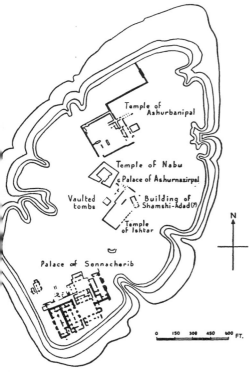

The Monuments of Nineveh, with the great palace of Sennacherib at the south edge of the mound of Kouyunjik

(After A. Parrot)

own priesthood. Scribes were important and necessary to the function of the government, so training schools prepared them for that service. We do not know about schools for other kinds of education.

The *ekallu* or "big house," which we would call a palace, functioned as the center of government, for the king and his family lived there. But it was also the Capitol

building, the White House, the State Department, and the Treasury. State dinners for foreign dignitaries were staged there. Guest rooms had to be available for them too. Military officers, the king's bodyguard, cooks, scribes, interpreters, musicians and other entertainers were housed there or nearby as well.

To provide for all these, substantial structures had to be built, providing an outlet for royal ostentation or braggadocio. But even such impressive display was politically important, for it impressed the citizenry and foreign dignitaries with the power and wealth of the state. Sennacherib (705-682) called his new palace at Nineveh "Palace without a Rival." His claim may well have been valid. The more than seventy rooms spread over two and one-half acres and were decorated with sculptured stone slabs for a total of almost two miles of reliefs.

As part of their governance, Assyrian kings periodically moved the capital. Ashur served as the early capital in the south. Ashurnasirpal II (883–859) created a new capital at Calah, about twenty miles south of Nineveh. Sargon II (722–705) decided to move the capital to Khorsabad (twelve miles

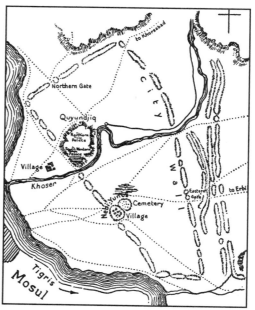

The site of Nineveh today. The remains of the eight-mile-long brick wall still stand to a height of ten to twenty feet.

northeast of Nineveh). Then Sennacherib transferred the capital to Nineveh, where it remained until the fall of Assyria.

In each case there was apparently an underlying reason. With the passage of time, entrenched interests dug in deep at each place. In Ashur, a religious center, the inhabitants had obtained and continued to hold numerous special privileges, such as exemption from taxation. Feeling very much fenced in, Ashurnasirpal developed his new capital at Calah. Also, battling the entrenched interests at Ashur and Calah, Sargon II decided to build a new capital at Khorsabad, but did not live to complete it.

Sennacherib had some of the same concerns in mind when he decided to locate his capital at Nineveh. It would have been very difficult to overcome the entrenched interests elsewhere to reorder a city for the building of his new palace. The palace itself covered two and one-half acres. Another administrative building housed horses and war equipment, with a parade ground for training cavalry and chariotry horses. Sennacherib widened

Huge winged, man-headed bulls, weighing some thirty to forty tons, commonly stood at the gates of the king's palace or the door of the throne room as silent sentinels. The long plaited beard and hair is typical of the king.

Governors of Provinces Gained Power

Though the Assyrian king reigned as absolute ruler during much of the nation's history, that was not true at all periods of Assyrian history. The king set up a provincial system with provincial governors strong enough and free enough to protect Assyrian interests in some of the border areas. This meant that forceful governors might gain a considerable amount of independence and be able to virtually flout the will of the king. This was especially true if kings were fairly weak.

As a matter of fact, Assyrian kings were weak during the whole first half of the eighth century B.C. and governors did much as they pleased. During that period of time Jeroboam II ruled in Israel and Uzziah in Judah and during their long reigns brought Israelite territorial holdings to virtually the borders of Solomon's kingdom. With the threat of Assyria temporarily removed, the Hebrews tended to ignore prophetic warnings against idolatry and oppression of the poor. But then came the reign of Tiglath-pileser III (745–727) and the resurgence of Assyrian royal and imperial power—and the virtual extermination of the Kingdom of Israel.

the streets to create a royal road over ninety feet wide. He created a great park where varieties of trees and plants were brought from various places. No doubt a great many people would have been uprooted to build all this, and the king would certainly have had to exercise his right of eminent domain to achieve all his goals. He couldn't have gotten his way at Ashur or Calah.

There were also strategic concerns in the move of the capital. Ashur was too far south to manage effectively the expanding territory of Assyria. So Ashurnasirpal decided to establish the capital in a more central location (Calah). Sargon II wanted a capital (Khorsabad) closer to the theater of military operations in Urartu (Ararat) to the north.

(For more on this topic, go to p. 224 or p. 276.)

The Sword, a Symbol of Power

The eminent Thorkild Jacobsen of Harvard paints a pitiful picture of Iraq with its foreign wars, civil wars, and other troubles during the tenth and ninth centuries b.c. The world had "become rank jungle." People in their despair tended to "turn to force for salvation, to the warlike hero," to a "trust in human prowess." Moreover, the climate of constant wars and disorders brutalized people; it hardened them to the sufferings of others. And worse, the gods are pictured as ruthless killers and the religious ritual of the millennium "had become remarkably lacking in sensitivity."[3] The sword had even become a symbol of the god Ashur. An Assyrian sculpture shows a worshiper kneeling before an altar on which stands an upright sword, and oaths were often taken "before the dagger of the god Ashur."[4]

Left: The god Ashur, from a glazed brick panel found in Ashur. Right: King Ashurnasirpal II of Assyria in ceremonial religious dress. Although Assyrian kings were not deified, they were the chief priests of the god Ashur. (From an ivory panel at Nimrud [Calah])

Religion

"Has any of the gods of the nations at all delivered its land from the hand of the king of Assyria?" (2 Kings 18:33 NKJV)

Confidence. That's what characterized Sennacherib of Assyria as he stood before the defenders on the walls of Jerusalem. He assumed his god Ashur superior to the God of Israel and the gods of all the peoples against whom he had to fight. And perhaps he had some sense of religious superiority because of military superiority—in the spirit of "might makes right."

Polytheism

The Assyrians had gods for all the supernatural forces and phenomena, as well as the variety of human activities. Thus, they worshiped a moon god, a sun god, a weather god, a god of brewers, a god of carpenters, and on and on—thousands of them.

The average person was concerned with very few of them. First, the king honored Ashur, the national god, at every state occasion and involved him with everything he did. Ashur's consort was Ishtar, goddess of love (associated with sexual activities, procreation) and war. The people also worshiped

Musicians Aid Chanter in Temple

Temples of any size had considerable staffs, including the chief administrator (steward); his deputy, who looked after the temple's financial affairs; and the kalu or chanter, who presented requests or songs to the god. The chanter usually accompanied himself with a drum or harp, and he might also be accompanied by other vocalists. The kings tended to use these musicians for palace entertainment too, sometimes even bringing them along on military campaigns. The royal Assyrian interest in such musicians occasionally led them to conquer them as part of their booty.

Assyrian musicians available for use in temples and the palace. A chanter might be accompanied by harp or drum or both. The drum pictured here is a tambourine or hoop with a skin stretched across it. The musician beat it with his hand.

the gods of natural phenomena (the sun, moon, weather), as well as the god of the underworld and death. And of course there were personal gods that varied from person to person.

Houses for the God

Each god had his dwelling and his household staff, just like a human ruler. Though the temples could be wealthy, in Assyria they did not have the vast holdings that might enable them to call the shots in the local economy or in the state. The kings kept the temples under wraps. In the temples, statues of wood or stone overlaid with precious metals represented the gods.

The household staffs (the priests) fed and clothed the god. We do not have information about processions and ceremonies connected with clothing the Assyrian gods as we do for Athena in Athens (see chapter 19). The Assyrians served the gods morning and evening meals at Nineveh and presumably elsewhere. There were numerous special ceremonies connected with the worship of the god or the state's honoring of the god.

Other Religious Practitioners

Ashipus, or magicians, served on the staffs of temples or of the king, or even other officials. They recited incantations,

expelled evil demons from the presence of the king or from being involved in (hindering) public projects (e.g., an aqueduct) or military expeditions. So an incantation might be recited at the dedication of an aqueduct.

Barus or diviners practiced divination by examining the organs of a sacrificial animal. The procedure was to write a question on a clay tablet and lay it before a god. A sheep (normally) was then sacrificed and its organs examined. The belief was that the god had put the answer on the organs of the animal in the form of a variety of abnormalities. The diviners had clay models of organs which supposedly indicated which features were positive or negative. The *baru* then added up the positive and negative features to see which was in the majority. If the positive features were, the answer was yes; if the negative, the answer was no. A typical kind of question a king might ask was whether a certain enemy would attack within the next three months. The chief *baru* had an office in the royal palace. Some *barus* marched with the royal army. Others were available to private persons.

Sennacherib storming the city of Lachish, southwest of Jerusalem

(British Museum)

Sha'ilus were interpreters of dreams.

Astrologers predicted affairs of state, not of private individuals, by movements of the moon and the planets and sometimes by thunder and earthquakes. They were believed capable of giving warning of forthcoming events of importance for the

Hebrew Faith in a Strange Land

What happened religiously and ethnically to the people of the Northern Kingdom who were carried off into captivity? We can only speculate, but we have a few clues to go on. In the first place, these Hebrews were scattered in at least four regions of the Assyrian Empire, as is clear from 2 Kings 17:6 and 18:11. And some of them were drafted into the Assyrian armed forces. So it was difficult for them to continue as cohesive units religiously or ethnically. Moreover, few of them had any belief in Yahweh when they were carried off, so there was not much faith to be preserved. Apparently in time they were assimilated into the local population and disappeared from the pages of history. Religiously, in time they probably subscribed to or participated in the religious beliefs and practices of the Assyrians described above.

But there does seem to have been at least one exception to this generalization. Some of these people were taken to the land of the Medes (2 Kings 17:6). Hundreds of years later Esther, Mordecai, and other Jews living there in Susa (Shushan) apparently had considerable faith. Thus exiles somehow must have stood against the prevailing polytheism there and maintained their faith when carried off. That lamp of faith was still burning when Esther took her stand in 479 B.C.

Of course what happened to the Judean exiles in Babylonia was quite different. They lived in more cohesive Jewish communities. Moreover, a considerable amount of faith remained among them. And there were priests and Levites among their number to teach and encourage devotion to God.

Assyrian Campaign Against Judah
In 701 B.C. Sennacherib of Assyria moved southward along the coastal plains, defeated an Egyptian army, and then turned his attention toward Judah. From his camp at Lachish he moved against Jerusalem, but did not capture the city. For maps of earlier Assyrian attacks on Israel, see last chapter.

Ashipus were supposed to use their magic to protect individuals against the forces of evil everywhere present.

(For more on this topic, go to p. 226 or p. 279.)

Warfare

"And in the fourteenth year of king Hezekiah, Sennacherib king of Assyria came up against all the fortified cities of Judah and took them." (2 Kings 18:13 NKJV)

"As to Hezekiah, the Jew, he did not submit to my yoke, I laid siege to 46 of his strong cities, walled forts and to the countless small villages in their vicinity, and conquered (them) by means of well-stamped (earth-) ramps, and battering-rams brought

state and giving opportunity for *ashinus* to perform rituals to avert evil occurrences.

Mesopotamians believed generally that wizards and witches could send evil spirits against them and bring on misfortunes.

(thus) near (to the walls) (combined with) the attack by foot soldiers, (using) mines, breeches as well as sapper work. I drove out (of them) 200,150 people, young and old, male and female, horses, mules donkeys, camels, big and small cattle beyond counting, and considered (them) booty. Himself I made a prisoner in Jerusalem, his royal residence, like a bird in a cage. I surrounded him with earthwork in order to molest those who were leaving his city's gate." (Sennacherib's records)[5]

Officials regarded as responsible for rebellion against Assyria were treated more severely than other prisoners. Here two officials at Lachish in Hezekiah's day are being skinned alive.

(British Museum)

That the Assyrians were warlike and cruel, even sadistic at times, is the belief of most Bible students and even students of ancient history. In addition to biblical statements of Assyrian warfare, there are numerous inscriptions detailing Assyrian wars, victories and horrible, even sickening, treatment of defeated enemies. On top of that, there are lots of pictorial representations from the walls of Assyrian palaces showing battles and Assyrian treatment of the vanquished. The 2 Kings reference above tells of Sennacherib's invasion of Judah (701 B.C.), and his own records describe the thoroughness and effectiveness of Assyrian blitzkrieg tactics.

Responses to Stereotypes of Assyrians

What is our response to the stereotypes of Assyrians? To begin with, some ancient

Cyrus the Persian also Cruel

The Assyrians were not the only ancient people to terrorize their opponents into submission. Cyrus the Great of Persia often comes down to us as a magnanimous man, in part because he reversed the deportation policies of the Assyrians and Babylonians and let the Jews go back home. Yet he was capable of terrible cruelty—for effect. Olmstead makes the point: "Near the beginning of October, Cyrus fought another battle at Opis on the Tigris and burned the people of Akkad with fire. After this example of frightfulness, his opponents lost courage and on October 11 Sippar was taken without a battle."[6] Two days later his troops entered Babylon without a fight.

historians suggest that the Assyrians may not have been more cruel than other Near Eastern peoples; they just kept better records of their actions. For example, Egyptian temple walls of the Empire period (c. 1570–1085 B.C.) show pictures of dismemberment of defeated enemies. And even the Hebrews dismembered vanquished enemies. Note the actions of David as he brought to Saul two hundred genitals of the Philistines (1 Samuel 18:27) and Jehu as he demanded and got and then piled up at the gate of Jezreel the heads of Ahab's seventy sons and relatives (2 Kings 10:1–8).

Then, too, life was cheap in the ancient Near East, as it seems to be in the modern Near East, with the terrorist acts of Israelis before independence in 1948, of Arabs against Israelis and Israeli retaliation, and of Islamic fundamentalists against their various opponents. A Western or Christian mentality of the sanctity of life should not be imposed on the ancient Near East.

Further, as we try to evaluate Assyrian actions, we observe that they were not unduly severe with defeated peoples who were for the first time coming under Assyrian control. They vented their full fury against the rebellious, however, with punishments so severe that they would not dare to rebel again—and that others who entertained thoughts of rebellion would immediately dismiss them from their minds. Those who dared to rebel might have their hands chopped off or be skinned alive and have their skins publicly displayed on a pole.

The Assyrians often used their actions as propaganda or psychological warfare. If they could sufficiently impress their enemies with the terror of their might, possibly they would not have to fight. The opponents would just wilt before their awesome terror. That was, of course, the approach of Sennacherib's men before the walls of Jerusalem in Hezekiah's day (see 2 Kings 18 and Isaiah 36). Why not so intimidate the enemy that a terrible siege or the prospect of a fierce battle with hand-to-hand combat could be avoided?

The propaganda value of Assyrian display of fierceness is abundantly clear in the palace of Ashurnasirpal at Calah. There scenes of war and Assyrian prowess appeared in the audience chamber where visiting rulers and ambassadors might see them. Elsewhere in the palace the artistic representations were mostly of a religious or ceremonial nature.[7]

As noted elsewhere, when Assyrians conquered a territory they were normally not too severe on the populace. They didn't want to maim them but to use them in productive ways. Thus, when Sennacherib's men stood before the walls of Jerusalem, they promised the people a new life in a pleasant land (2 Kings 18:32). In captivity they would not be thrown in jail or killed but would contribute to the Assyrian economy and to Assyrian power.

By force or enticement—perhaps both—Assyrians established military contingents of Philistines, Aramaeans, Elamites, and other conquered peoples, including the Hebrews, and had them fight as units in the Assyrian army. As Sargon II mopped up in Samaria in 722-21 after the fall of the Northern Kingdom, he did not want to waste the expertise of the captives. Among the 27,290 that he carried off, he took trained warriors and formed them into a contingent of fifty Israelite chariot teams.[8]

Why the Assyrians Fought

Assyrians had no easily defensible natural boundary that would help secure their farmlands. They had to be ever on the watch against threats of occupation by fierce hill peoples to the north, northeast, and northwest. When they brought one area under control and so eliminated a threat, just beyond was another threat to security. So they kept going ever farther afield in quest of stability.

Linked to the desire for security was the economic benefit that came from warfare. With victory came booty in the form of valuable metals (especially iron), wood, livestock, horses, captive populations, and control of trade routes. In time security needs became enmeshed with material prosperity. That is, it was necessary for security and the way of life to which they had become accustomed to have, for example, supplies of iron and horses. They also needed to control the trade routes over which came their supply of strategic materials of various sorts.

Some have also suggested a kind of manifest destiny as a reason for military expansion: "The will of the god Ashur that the king should expand his domains."[9]

And so for a variety of reasons the Assyrians fought. The Shalmaneser, who met Ahab at the battle of Qarqar in 853 B.C. and forced Jehu to pay tribute (see last chapter), for example, tells us that he was at war for thirty-one of his thirty-five years as king.

Organization of the Assyrian Army

The Assyrian army was a disciplined, well-organized force with specialist units of many types. In the early days of the empire (tenth–ninth century B.C.) it consisted of the king's bodyguard and a conscripted native levy that usually campaigned during the summer months after the crops were harvested. Then the Assyrian farmers would be free to fight. Even back then kings could command armies of 100,000–200,000. For example, Shalmaneser III in 845 (after the great battle of Qarqar) said that he had mustered a force of 120,000.[10]

Assyrian soldiers crossing a river, with horses swimming, led by a groom. A bed and a jar are carried on a coracle (boat). Some men swim supported by inflated goatskins under the left arm. From Nimrud (Calah), northwest palace.

(British Museum)

With Tiglath-Pileser (745–727 B.C.) came a fundamental reform of the army. The dates of this king's reign are important because he destroyed the independent kingdom of Damascus and conquered and annexed the northern part of the Kingdom of Israel (732 B.C.). After Tiglath-Pileser's death, his new "model army" went on to destroy the northern kingdom (722) and to attack Judah in the days of King Hezekiah and his prophet Isaiah (701). After 745 the army was largely a standing army available for service throughout the empire at any time of the year.

The standing army consisted first of the king's personal bodyguard composed of cavalry, chariotry, and infantry. This corps of several thousand did more than protect the king. Its members fulfilled whatever tasks the king assigned to it, such as delivering messages or providing safe conduct to members of his staff. Perhaps it compared a little to the Praetorian Guard of the Caesars in Rome during the first century A.D. This body of troops might also engage in limited military action on its own.

The bulk of the standing army came from the provinces and were native professional Assyrians augmented by units of foreigners, such as Aramaeans, Philistines, Greeks, or Hebrews. These were levies raised by provincial governors on orders of the king. In addition, there were troops provided by vassals, whose service was specified as part of the tribute levied. So non-Assyrian units were mixed in with Assyrians on a regular basis and were issued Assyrian uniforms. Non-Assyrians tended to be more numerous in the infantry while the cavalry and chariot arms tended to be more strictly Assyrian. In addition to the standing army, there could be a seasonal call-up of Assyrian reserves or raw recruits.

The king often led the army in person. There were also two field marshals or commanders (*tartanu*), the Tartans of 2 Kings 18:17 and Isaiah 20:1. Below them were commanders of 1,000, 500, and 100. Chariots were formed into squadrons of 50.

The Army on the March

Almost always the mustering point for a military campaign would be a place where there were barracks and an armory. A capital—Calah or Nineveh—or some other barracks center was designated and a date given by which men were to arrive. The local governor was ordered to prepare for the campaign by collecting masses of food and equipment. Other governors would also

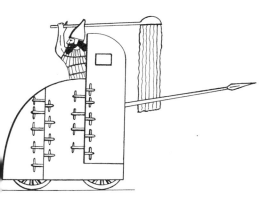

One of Sennacherib's siege engines. Made up of assembled parts, it was transportable. The wooden frame is covered with sheets of leather held together by toggles. To prevent it from being burned, a soldier uses a ladle to pour water. The ram ends in a heavy iron spearhead.

(Courtesy of Osprey Publishing, Ltd., London)

have responsibilities to send supplies and to call up their provincial levies. Vassal states in that general area were also ordered to send their contingents of troops. Then, at the appropriate time, the king, his bodyguard, and the standing army would arrive and the total body of troops was ready to march.

As the army set out from its base inside Assyrian territory, local governors provided supplies. In the territory of vassals, the native ruler was expected to do the same. As the army advanced into enemy territory it looted provisions whenever possible and especially sought to capture cities with their granaries. But the men did carry some food and water, and the "quartermaster corps" accompanied the forces with supplies carried by wagons or pack animals. Obtaining adequate water supplies was often more of a problem than procuring food.

Leading the line of march came the standards of the gods and their religious functionaries. Next came the king in his chariot accompanied by his bodyguard and the army chariotry and cavalry—ready for action if the need should arise. Following them marched the infantry of the regular army, behind which came the provincial and then the vassal levies. Bringing up the rear were the equipment and supply wagons drawn by oxen or mules. This vast assemblage could move up to thirty miles a day.

The army "corps of engineers" sometimes had to fell trees, widen paths in the mountains, or facilitate the crossing of a river. Occasionally a river was shallow enough to be forded. Or it might be crossed on rafts. Or it could be crossed by means of a bridge using boats as pontoons. Small contingents of soldiers engaged in attack might cross a stream with the help of inflated goatskins. Reliefs on palace walls show soldiers with inflated goatskins under the left arm and holding some war equipment in the right hand.

An effective military intelligence system was also part of the Assyrian military establishment. Spies entered enemy territory. Sometimes they took prisoners and extracted information from them. Or they bought informants. They found out about enemy troop movements, battle plans, and anything that might affect enemy or Assyrian morale. Many languages were understood at the Assyrian court and in the Assyrian intelligence system at the front. Generals always had staff personnel who could communicate with the enemy. Communication was by messengers, runners, and fire or smoke signals.

The Army in Actual Conflict

The army always preferred to be in the offensive mode—to attack rather than to be

Another kind of battering ram appears in this Assyrian relief from the British Museum. Bowmen behind large shields of reeds support a four-wheeled battering ram in an attack against the walls of an enemy city. The bodies of three townsmen are impaled on stakes outside the city.

Remains of the Assyrian siege ramp at Lachish

attacked. As the forces drew up on the battlefield, usually the infantry took the center, with archers and slingers. Chariots and cavalry composed the wings. The battle would begin with long-range arrows that would sling fire to cause casualties and demoralize the enemy. Then chariots, the ancient equivalent of the Sherman Tank, might create a breach in the enemy lines, through which the infantry would pour. Or possibly the infantry would advance against the center while the chariots and cavalry attacked the wings and engaged in an encircling movement.

Of course the battle didn't always turn out that way, and the Assyrian army showed great flexibility in adapting its tactics. It also became adept at fighting guerrilla warfare in such widely diverse ways and places as the mountains of Urartu (Armenia) and the swamps of Sumer.

The Assyrians knew as well as we do that the best way to take a city was to approach it with such overwhelming force that no other military action was necessary. But sometimes the gates clanged shut and the defenders were determined to hold out. Occasionally the Assyrians simply settled down for a siege and sought to starve the inhabitants into submission. On other occasions they chose to storm a city.

As the Assyrians besieged a city, they were prepared to go through the walls with battering rams or over the walls with scaling ladders or by building earthen ramps. As the archaeologists began their work at Lachish, the Assyrian ramp there was still almost intact (from 701 B.C. when Sennacherib attacked), as was the counter

ramp of the desperate Judean defenders. It's an eerie feeling to stand on the counter ramp today and imagine the brave determination of the Judean defenders as they scrambled to build their ramp and then to hurl down stones or burning objects at the Assyrian attackers. If Assyrians did not succeed in going over walls or through them, they tried to go under them or cause their collapse by tunneling. Probably they used all three methods simultaneously.

Ramps were made of piled up earth or rubble. Battering rams were brought up by animal and human effort and put in position. A ram of metal-tipped wood was housed in a wooden framework shielded by a covering. If a town was located by a river, a siege tower was constructed upstream and floated into position.

As the Assyrians fought, they inflicted heavy casualties and often made claims of rather astronomical proportions. They also recorded large quantities of booty and large numbers of prisoners taken and carried off into captivity. Assyrian scribes were busy men, and apparently their records were quite accurate. We wonder about Assyrian casualties though. Typical of military commanders, the Assyrians did not release lists of their own casualties. There are hints here and there that they knew who had been killed and would not be returning to their villages,

King Ashurbanipal in his chariot, from his palace at Nineveh.
(British Museum)

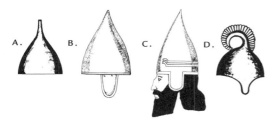

Assyrian Helmets
A. Assyrian iron conical helmet, eighth century B.C.
B. Assyrian iron conical helmet with hinged
earpieces, seventh century B.C.
C. Assyrian conical helmet with integrated
earpieces, seventh century;
bronze bands indicate rank.
D. Helmet with a crest, late eighth century B.C.

set on a metal undercarriage with the wheel axis moved from the center to the rear. The wheel had up to eight spokes and was fitted with a metal rim to increase wear. In the earlier period two-horse chariots had a crew of two, a driver and archer or lancer. After the ninth century a third man was added to strengthen the rear defense with one or two shields. In the eighth–seventh century two shield bearers were common. So at that point chariots had a crew of four and were pulled by four horses hitched in a row in front of the chariot. It was now a mobile weapons platform.

but we do not have the records. Once in a while we get an inkling of what happened. For example, after the fierce contest at Lachish and the fall of that Judean city, the Assyrians buried about 1,500 of their dead in a mass grave on the side of the hill. It is sobering to stand there and imagine the ferocity of the conflict and the terrible carnage.

Weapons and Weapons Systems

Chariots were employed in shock action in the center of the attack line or on the wings in an encircling movement in concert with the cavalry. The chariots that the Assyrians designed and used from the ninth century on consisted of a wood frame

Sling stones with a modern sling, found near the
main gate at Lachish
(British Museum)

Horses (cavalry) were used instead of chariots on rough terrain and in concert with chariots on level ground. Cavalrymen rode bareback or on "saddles" consisting of animal skins; the stirrup was not invented until the sixth century A.D. By Sargon's time (c. 700 B.C.) cavalry units of 1,000 at a time were deployed. The archers who rode these horses commonly carried shields on their backs.

Bowmen. The bow was the chief offensive weapon of the Assyrian infantry. Several types of bows were used, capable of shooting an arrow between about 250 and 700 yards. Arrowheads were made of iron. Some arrows were set with flaming tow (a loose tuft of wool). A quiver could hold up to fifty arrows, so a body of archers had a tremendous amount of fire power. Some of their shields were small and round, protecting the upper and middle part of the body, but the Assyrians often used very

Assyrian archers and slingers in a battle scene,
from the palace of King Sennacherib at Nineveh
(British Museum)

large shields that stood on the ground and were managed by a shield bearer. These shields were greater than the height of a man and curved inward at the top to ward off missiles. Shields were made of metal or oiled skins over matted reeds. Special areas in the rivers were set aside for growing reeds for shield use.

Slingers and lancers were also important to the Assyrian war effort. The latter were sometimes chariot-borne and sometimes marched on foot. Lances were iron-tipped.

Swords. Long swords were very uncommon. The short dagger, carried singly or in pairs, was the standard weapon for close-quarter fighting.

Armor consisted of metal strips sewn on leather and worn down to below the waist or even to the knee level by cavalry men, some charioteers, and some infantrymen. Helmets of the ninth or eighth century were pointed or conical. During the seventh century they were replaced by a crested helmet curving forward from the top. Many warriors wore high laced boots but some, especially cavalrymen, fought barefoot. Horses were often protected by partial coverings of skins.

(For more on this topic, go to p. 232 or p. 283.)

buildings than to private houses. This is true in part because such structures are better preserved and easier to work with, in part because they make more dramatic reporting for their constituencies, and in part because they usually house more museum pieces that can help to drum up popular and institutional support for archaeological ventures.

In recent years technical advances and a shift of focus in excavation work have led to greater interest in private houses and ability to evaluate their remains. In the case of

Ivory inlay from a chair back or bed head. Six carved panels reconstructed in original positions, with plain ivory framework. Eighth century B.C.

(British Museum)

Assyria we now have material remains of some private homes, as well as written accounts dealing with house sales.

But unfortunately we still don't have enough solid information to generalize about Assyrian home building. Whole residential districts have not been uncovered so we can compare the houses of various social and economic classes. Written materials primarily cover houses of the middle and upper classes.

What we can say is that walls tended to be of mudbrick covered with mud plaster. Beaten mud covered most floors, though the Assyrians paved some rooms with burnt brick. Houses in town had several rooms (up to a dozen) on the ground floor; and from the thickness of the walls and presence of stairs it appears that they had

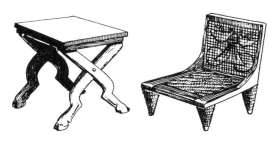

One style of Assyrian table. A chair with a rush seat.

Housing and Furniture

When archaeologists work through ancient sites, they tend to give more attention to palaces, temples, and larger public

King Ashurbanipal on a banqueting couch with his queen, about 645 B.C.

(British Museum)

a second story. Residents entered through an outer courtyard and then proceeded to one of several rooms off an inner courtyard. These included a reception room, a kitchen with its conical bread oven, a lavatory (usually with terracotta drainage pipes), storage rooms, servants' quarters, and a family burial vault. Some walls had niches that could serve as cupboards. Apparently family rooms were upstairs.

Furniture

The poor normally had no furnishings in their houses beyond a few reed mats, on which they might sit, or eat, or sleep. And they probably did not have the many rooms indicated above.

The middle or upper classes used furniture of varying sophistication and value. Basic stools with a solid wood frame, or wooden frames with a reed seat, served as chairs or footstools. The more well-to-do owned stools of more expensive hardwoods, decorated with inlays of ivory or gold.

Chairs with backs were made of various hardwoods and inlaid with copper, bronze, silver, gold, or ivory. The seat could be covered with leather, palm fiber, or rushes, and padded with felt. A chair could be an armchair or outfitted with poles to become a sedan chair and carried about by servants.

The most wealthy or the king used banqueting couches. They consisted of a wooden frame with cushions. While eating, one supported himself on his left elbow and ate with his right hand. Servants placed food

on a fairly high square table alongside the couch (see picture of King Ashurbanipal).

Wood tables might have metal decorations added. Some tables cast in bronze have been found. During the first millennium B.C. the main type of table seems to have been a fairly small square table on four ornamented legs that might terminate in feet of an ox-hoof design.

As with other furniture, beds varied with social or economic classes. The poor slept on straw or reed mats on the floor. Others slept on a wooden frame that might support slats, rope, reeds, or a criss-cross of metal strips on which mattresses were placed. The bed might be supported on legs with feet that terminated in the shape of a claw or an ox-hoof. The bed frame could be decorated with gold, silver, or carved ivory. Mattresses were stuffed with wool, goats' hair, or palm fiber. Bed covers were made of linen or wool. Possibly there was a pillow. We do not know about that. Alongside the beds, mats were used as floor coverings. At least in palaces there must have been carpets; floors at doorways

Agricultural Workers Belonged to the Land

During the New Assyrian Empire (beginning with the rule of Ashur-dan in 934 B.C.) officials in the royal administration often bought out the old peasant landholders. By the eighth century, when the Hebrews entered Assyrian captivity, the peasants who actually worked the land were no longer fully free citizens. They were viewed as belonging to the land they worked and were sold or transferred with it, like serfs in western Europe during the Middle Ages. Serfs worked the land and shared in the community. They also had obligations for community service, such as road building or military service. Deported persons, including the Hebrews, took their places alongside free Assyrians as agricultural serfs, working the soil, and hence in time achieving a quasi-citizenship.[11]

have limestone slabs carved to simulate carpeting.

Storage was arranged in various ways. As with us, the Assyrians made wooden crates for storing vegetables. They shaped reeds waterproofed with bitumen into forms for keeping clothing dry and holding liquid. Containers for food or liquids included copper or wood bowls, earthenware jugs or pots, and earthenware or metal drinking flasks. The Assyrians also used glass, especially for bottles. They stored wine in special jars holding several gallons each. For eating, the Assyrians employed spoons made of wood or metal and sometimes of ivory. Knives had blades of bronze, iron, or flint. They honed metal cutting implements on small flat whetstones.

Lamps made of containers holding linseed oil provided light, with wicks made from a reed or wool. In early times shells were used as containers; in the first millennium B.C. the shell form was imitated by clay or metal. Apparently at some palace ceremonies blazing torches were made by bundles of reeds dipped in oil and held up by servants.

(For more on this topic, go to p. 243 or p. 293.)

Supplies for a banquet in Sennacherib's palace, including fruits and locusts on a spit
(From A. H. Layard, *Nineveh and Babylon*)

Diet and Foodstuffs

The agricultural season in Assyria ran from plowing and sowing time in October or November to harvesting in May or June.

Men carrying hares, locusts, and fruit in preparation for a royal dinner. Note the tunics with short sleeves, belted at the waist.

The plow could be either the conventional one for breaking up the soil or the seeder plow, which cut a furrow and planted the seed at the same time. The seeder was essentially the same implement as had been used in Mesopotamia since the third millennium B.C. (see chapter 2 for description and picture). Normally oxen and sometimes donkeys drew the plow.

For harvesting, farmers increasingly used sickles with an iron blade during the first millenium B.C. But copper or bronze sickles had not completely gone out of fashion. Harvesters tied the grain in sheaves and took it to a threshing floor—a smooth outcrop of rock—where oxen dragged a threshing sledge over the grain to separate the grain from the ear. The threshing sledge resembled what has been used in many places in the Middle East down to the present—a wooden board or platform with sharp stones on the underside. After threshing, farmers used wooden shovels to toss the grain into the air to allow the breeze to blow away the chaff. Finally, the grain was carried away and stored.

The main cereal crops enjoyed were first barley, then wheat, emmer (a variety of wheat), and millet. Vegetables included lentils (a kind of bean), chick-peas, cucumbers, onions, garlic, lettuce, dill, radishes, turnips, and several others that are named in Assyrian records but cannot be identified. The main fruits cultivated were grapes, figs, olives, and pomegranates. Coriander, cumin, and saffron were among the herbs they produced, and many of the words we still use for herbs are Assyrian terms that have come to us through Greek or Arabic. Flax was grown for the production of linen, with linseed oil pressed from it for illumination. About 700 B.C. Sennacherib introduced cotton woven into cloth.[12]

Though locusts in large numbers were a threat to a farmer's crops, the Assyrians caught and ate them as a luxury. A scene from King Sennacherib's palace in Nineveh shows supplies for one of his banquets that included locusts on a spit (see illustration).

Animal Husbandry

Assyrians raised various breeds of sheep for their meat, their milk, their wool, and sacrificed them to their gods. Goats too were important for their meat, for their milk, and for their hair, which the Assyrians probably used for making tents and rugs, and certainly as filling for mattresses for beds. Goatskins served as water "bottles" and were inflated to give buoyancy to rafts, and soldiers tucked them under their arms to help them cross rivers (see illustration).

The rich ate beef cattle and oxen, with cows' milk an important addition to their diet. As noted, oxen served as draft animals, pulling plows, carts, and threshing sledges. Donkeys were used as pack and riding animals. Horses primarily served in the cavalry and the chariot corps of the fearsome Assyrian military establishment. Assyrians did breed horses, but most of them came from lands to the north and east. Assyrians hunted wild ducks and geese and also raised domesticated varieties.

(For more on this topic, go to p. 245 or p. 294.)

Dress

Fortunately we don't have to guess as much about Assyrian clothing as we do about what the Hebrews wore at various periods of time. Not only do we have literary references but also many pictorial representations. Apparently everyone wore clothes except a few prisoners of war at the point when they were first taken into captivity. It isn't necessary to comment on Assyrian clothing for all periods. The following applies especially to the first millennium B.C.

Women wore an undergarment around the hips very much like a baby's diaper, though it was tied instead of pinned. There may also have been an undergarment for the upper body, though slave girls are sometimes shown topless. Whatever Assyrian women wore in the house, they usually wore a loose gown extending from shoulder to ankle, with half-sleeves and held by a belt, when they went out. Married women were veiled in public.

King Ashurnasirpal enthroned. Note the full beard, long hair, and bracelets.

(British Museum)

Men wore a sort of tunic with short sleeves, which extended from the neck to the knees and was belted at the waist. Sometimes the upper part seems to have been a sort of shirt and the lower part a kilt. Occasionally the kilt appears to have been supported by straps that ran diagonally from the shoulders and crossed on the chest. Common soldiers and lower class civilians wore this garment by itself. But military officers, government officials, and

A eunuch, a servant of Tiglath-Pileser.
(British Museum)

sometimes wore leather slippers that covered only the front half of the foot.

Hair and Beards

Assyrian men wore full beards, heavy moustaches, and long hair, arranged to leave the ears exposed. Those without facial hair were probably eunuchs or very young. Both head hair and beards are usually shown waved and curled at the ends. They must have needed the services of hairdressers to keep themselves looking presentable. Women also wore their hair long (sometimes supplemented with partial wigs) and elaborately braided. Men and women used headbands to keep their hair in place. Kings and high officials sometimes sported turbans; soldiers wore helmets. Religious personnel occasionally had professional headdresses.

Jewelry

Both men and women of Assyria wore jewelry. Women often sported gold or silver anklets. Usually Assyrian men of rank, and sometimes women, wore bracelets on the wrists and armlets on the upper arms. Rosettes on these bracelets sometimes make them look like wrist watches in the pictorial representations. Both men and women wore

upper class civilians also wore a cloak over it. For official occasions a king had a richly decorated ankle-length garment. When the Assyrians portrayed a king as hunting or fighting, he wore a simple tunic like that of a common soldier, but of ankle length.

Most clothing was of wool, though linen was often used for better quality garments. Cotton came into Assyria about 700 B.C.—shortly after the fall of Samaria. Leather and papyrus were occasionally used in place of fabric.

Assyrians often went barefoot, especially when indoors (including women of the royal family). But even when outdoors many, including soldiers, went barefoot a good part of the time. When they wore something on their feet, they commonly had sandals with a wedge heel. But Assyrians did have shoes covering the whole foot, with the top usually made of wool cloth stitched into the leather of the sole. Hunters and soldiers engaged in battle often wore boots over long stockings. As with shoes, the front of the boot seems to have been of cloth. Women

King Ashurbanipal sought to preserve the literature and history of Assyria in his library. Tens of thousands of texts have been recovered from it. One important find is an account of a great flood (the Flood?). Here is a flood tablet from his library.
(British Museum)

Even the Greeks Benefited from Assyrian Trade

There was no love lost between the subject peoples and their Assyrian overlords. Yet the subject peoples benefited economically from the existence of the empire. Trade flowed along the Tigris and Euphrates arteries between the Mediterranean and the Persian Gulf. Though, for instance, the Phoenician city-states chafed under Assyrian control, their commercial ventures prospered greatly. Those far-flung ventures, especially in search of metals, took them as far west as Spain and as far north as the British Isles. And as they established trading posts prosperous colonies grew in Carthage, Spain, and elsewhere. The new prosperity created by a politically unified Near East even contributed to the revival of Greece and laid the foundations for classical Greek civilization.[13]

pendants of semi-precious stones on gold chains. Earrings were usually crescents of gold or silver, with pendants of various shapes attached to them. Women used eye shadow of antimony paste, applied with a carved ivory pin, as well as rouge.

(For more on this topic, go to p. 245 or p. 295.)

Family Life

Marriage

The senior male controlled the family in Assyria. Upon marriage a woman left the jurisdiction of her father for that of her father-in-law. Marriage contracts sometimes spelled out that if the wife did not bear children, the husband might take a slave girl as a concubine, the children then being counted as the wife's.

It seems that part of the marriage ceremony involved veiling the wife, who thereafter had to be veiled in public. Infant or under-age marriage did occur when children were linked by a marriage contract, though they continued to live in their parents' homes until the physical consummation of marriage. The couple celebrated with a wedding feast between the contract and the consummation in such a marriage.

By contract, a bride-price passed from the husband's family to the bride's father, but it had to be returned if the woman died without giving birth to a male child. A wife also brought a dowry with her. This eventually went to her children, not to her husband's heirs, who might be his brothers. At marriage the husband gave jewelry to the bride, but this remained in the family estate and on his death passed to his heirs. If there were sons, the wife was not her husband's heir. If there were no sons, she was his heir. A man might divorce his wife by cutting off the hem of her dress before official witnesses.

High Infant Mortality

High infant mortality plagued ancient Mesopotamia, with the angel of death no respecter of classes. The royal family was no more immune than the lowliest subject. The practice of magic, the use of amulets, and rituals did not seem to promote healthy births. Mothers often died in childbirth. Even when the birth was healthy and normal, the mother might fail to lactate, and the infant would starve to death—unless, of course, the family was rich enough to afford a wet-nurse.

Not all babies were wanted. Some were born to temple prostitutes. If a baby was unwanted, it might simply be thrown out into the street, where it might be rescued. Some infants were born deformed. We know this because Assyrians thought such births to be omens and reported them.

Mothers kept newborns in a basket. When carried around by the mother, babies might be in a baby sling.

Sexual Matters

Ancient Assyria recognized homosexuality among men, with those guilty of homosexual rape castrated. But we cannot be sure whether homosexuality in general was proscribed. Babylonians tended to be more permissive toward homosexuals than Assyrians. Lesbianism was almost totally unknown, but that is not surprising in a male-dominated society where women were expected to bear children and provide heirs.

Assyrian craftsmen

Eunuchs were quite common, but were usually boys castrated to serve at court, not individuals punished for a crime. Many of them became high officials. This practice continued among the Persians and Turks up to the last century. Not all courtiers in Assyria were eunuchs, however.

Education

We have little information about education in first millennium Assyria. We know that there were schools for the training of scribes, but we know nothing about schools for other areas of education. Almost universally a son was expected to follow his father's trade or profession and began learning it at a very young age. Apprenticeship to a craftsman was possible and contracts exist spelling out the obligations on the two sides.

(For more on this topic, go to p. 246 or p. 296.)

Work, Travel, and Commerce

Highways and Waterways

Highways provided an efficient communication system. A rapid postal system transported mail across the empire with relays of horses (or mules). Any provincial governor or other official of the empire could send a message to the capital and get an answer back within about a week.[14] Thus the Assyrian road system anticipated the famous and better known Persian road system of a later period.

The ass served as the primary pack animal, and caravans of them made possible the shipment of large quantities of goods over long distances and difficult terrain. Quantities of goods also moved on the Tigris through the central part of the empire, and substantial quays have been excavated at Nineveh and Calah. The vessel used for shipment consisted of a large raft buoyed up by inflated skins of sheep and goats. Boats also traveled on the irrigation canals and provided ferry service there and on the river. Several boats could be tied together to create a bridge across a river or a major canal.

Money, Weights, and Measures

A quasi-money economy facilitated commerce. This did not involve the true coinage of money (which first occurred in Lydia in western Asia Minor near the end of the Assyrian Empire) but metal weighed out. Thus gold, silver, tin, copper, and bronze achieved a certain standard of value. One could then sell a sheep or a quantity of grain or a chair for a certain amount of metal. A system of weights and measures also developed. Merchants used balances made of stone or bronze. They also had a system of measuring by value. For example, the *qu* was just over three pints. We know the volume measures from the fact that storage jars have been found marked with their capacity.

Broadening of Horizons

Assyrians themselves never seem to have entered into trade and industry extensively, remaining farmers. So their subjects carried on trade and industry—and there was plenty of both to go around. We have already noted that Phoenicians conducted much of the trade in the West. Aramaeans and others were also involved. Phoenicians and other Canaanites made furniture, carved ivory, and cast metals for the Assyrians.

Recurring warfare created a constant need to make arrowheads, swords, chariots, and other war materiel. The demand for armor, boots, and the treatment of large numbers of animal skins for military and civilian use remained strong. We are not sure of the nationalities of the artists who carved miles of bas reliefs in the palaces of Nineveh, Khorsabad, and Calah. The various kinds of production required skills that were passed on from father to son, as noted above.

With large numbers of men marching across the empire to engage in military action, and with others crisscrossing the Near East to engage in commerce, the Assyrians had a frequency of contact with people of other nationalities and cultures to a degree previously unknown in the region.

Mixing of Peoples and Cultures

This movement and exposure to other cultures was enhanced by the Assyrians' uprooting of some four or five million people and settling them elsewhere among other ethnic groups. This mixing of peoples led to the introduction of new craftsmen, new ideas, new processes, new products—a kind of new internationalism. This resulted in a considerable amount of cultural and intellectual cross-pollination. Some idea of what happened appears in the array of texts collected in the great library of King Ashurbanipal (669–627 B.C.)—the Osnapper of Ezra 4:10. Jones comments, "The extent of scientific and technological knowledge revealed by texts from this library is astonishing. The medical and chemical texts, for example, have shown how much the Assyrians knew about drugs, minerals, and glassmaking."[15]

The Assyrian cultural and ethnic mixing "prepared the way for the growing cultural unification of the whole area" and prepared the way for "the hellenization of the Near East after Alexander," as Saggs has observed.[16]

What the Assyrians began with their deportation of peoples, the Babylonians continued. We shall now look at developments in the Kingdom of Judah and its ultimate capitulation to Babylon. Following that we shall see what life was like in the Babylonian Empire.

(For more on this topic, go to p. 247 or p. 298.)

NOTES:

[1] Daniel D. Luckenbill, Ancient Records of Assyria and Babylonia (Chicago: University of Chicago Press, 1927), II, 120; James B. Pritchard, ed., Ancient Near Eastern Texts Relating to the Old Testament, 2nd ed. (Princeton: Princeton University Press, 1955), 288.

[2] H. W. F. Saggs, *The Might That Was Assyria* (London: Sidgwick & Jackson, 1984), 263.

[3] Thorkild Jacobsen, *The Treasures of Darkness* (New Haven: Yale University Press, 1976), 226-231.

[4] Saggs, 201.

[5] Pritchard, 288.

[6] A. T. Olmstead, *History of the Persian Empire* (Chicago: University of Chicago Press, 1948), 50.

[7] Saggs, 249.

[8] Pritchard, 285.

[9] Saggs, 246.

[10] Ibid., 253.

[11] Ibid., 133-34.

[12] Ibid., 165.

[13] Tom B. Jones, *Ancient Civilization,* Rev. ed. (Chicago: Rand Mc-Nally & Co., 1964), 135.

[14] Saggs, 196-97.

[15] Jones, 134.

[16] Saggs, 268.

BIBLIOGRAPHY:

Curtis, J. E., and J. E. Reade, eds. *Art and Empire.* New York: Metropolitan Museum of Art, 1995.

Healy, Mark, and Angus McBride. *The Ancient Assyrians.* London: Osprey Publishing Ltd., 1991.

Luckenbill, Daniel D. *Ancient Records of Assyria and Babylonia.* Chicago: University of Chicago Press, 2 vols., 1926.

Olmstead, A. T. *History of Assyria.* Chicago: University of Chicago Press, 1951.

Parrot, André. *The Arts of Assyria.* New York: Golden Press, 1961.

Parrot, André. *Nineveh and the Old Testament.* New York: Philosophical Library, 1955.

Reade, Julian. *Assyrian Sculpture.* London: British Museum Press, 1983

Roux, Georges. *Ancient Iraq.* London: Penguin Books, 3rd ed., 1992.

Russell, John M. *Sennacherib's Palace without Rival at Nineveh.* Chicago: University of Chicago Press, 1991.

Saggs, H. W. F. *The Might That Was Assyria.* London: Sidgwick & Jackson, 1984.

THE DIVIDED KINGDOM: LIFE IN JUDAH

Chapter 10

(1 Kings 12—22; 2 Kings; 2 Chronicles 10—36; the Prophets)

What was life like in the Kingdom of Judah after the Kingdom of Israel had been established in the north? Why were there more godly kings in the Kingdom of Judah than in the northern kingdom? Why did it last longer than the northern kingdom? Let's look at what was left after Rehoboam led the ten tribes to break away and go it alone.

If you mounted your bicycle and rode the length and breadth of what was the Kingdom of Judah after the breakup of Solomon's empire, you could cover its territory north and south in a good day's ride and east and west in much less time than that. The total population could have fit into a smallish North American city, despite the glory that remained in the Solomonic temple and the palaces of Solomon. Because Judah controlled much less territory than the northern kingdom, Israel, it had smaller population resources. You would wonder why anyone would want to attack it, except for what the temple represented in terms of its gold inlay and special golden utensils!

Let's get some understanding of who constituted the two kingdoms first. Usually we think of Israel as the ten tribes and Judah as one tribe, but that is not quite accurate. Judah had more or less absorbed Simeon to the south and at least the part of Benjamin that lay in the vicinity of

Jerusalem. Moreover, a great many of the Levites, who led the worship in the temple and carried on the religious traditions, also eventually came to live in the southern kingdom, the Kingdom of Judah.

The Land

A Mere Slice of Territory

Though for part of its history Judah controlled Edom and the land far south to the Gulf of Aqaba branch of the Red Sea, most of the time its territory consisted of a slice of territory wedged between the Dead Sea and the coastal plain or the land of the Philistines. So the Judean heartland stretched some forty to fifty miles east and west. Extending from a little north of Jerusalem in the north to Kadesh-barnea in the south, the kingdom stretched only about 110 miles north and south. You might say that it was a little larger than Delaware or about twice the size of Rhode Island. During those periods when Judah controlled the Negev from Beersheba to the Gulf of Aqaba, she had an additional area of about 4,700 square miles, roughly equal to the land area of Connecticut.

Economically, the southern kingdom was no powerhouse either. Water resources were always at a premium. Since the watershed ran through Jerusalem, much of the eastern part of the country received little rainfall. The Negev, the region south of Beersheba, enjoyed only about six inches per year. And the little valleys, nestled among the hills of Judea (rising some 2,000–4,000 feet in altitude), did not provide a lot of good farmland—and very little in the way of timber resources.

The Divided Kingdom

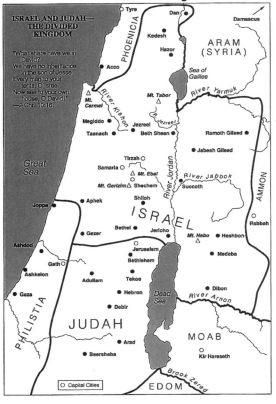

The Kingdoms of Judah and Israel

Nor did the kingdom control any great trade arteries such as the Mediterranean coastal road, the King's Highway in Transjordan, or the major east-west route through Damascus, though a trade route ran north and south through Beersheba, Hebron, and Jerusalem. This meant that the Kingdom of Judah had little access to the important road systems of the eastern Mediterranean world. Only periodically as she ruled the Negev could she dominate the trade between the Gulf of Aqaba and the

Philistine plain on the north, just south of the Plain of Sharon.

(For more on this topic, go to p. 252 or p. 303.)

Government

"He [Asa] commanded Judah to seek the Lord God of their fathers, and to observe the law and the commandment." (2 Chronicles 14:4 NKJV) *"He also removed the high places"* (v. 5). *"And he [Asa] built fortified cities in Judah."* (2 Chron-icles 14:6 NKJV) *"Then he [Jehoshaphat] set judges in the land throughout all the fortified cities of Judah."* (2 Chronicles 19:5 NKJV)

The King as the Government

When you read these historical books of the Bible it becomes obvious that the religious commitment of the king determined the religious commitment of the people. For those of us living in a democracy, that does not make sense. When, however, we realize the power of the king, as indicated in the verses at the head of this section, we begin to understand.

The verses quoted underscore the fact that the king was the government. He supervised the religious, military, and judicial aspects of public life—and served as the final court of appeals in judicial matters. If we read further into the chapter we could show that he controlled all other affairs of state. He regulated the economy. He stood at the head of the administrative organization and appointed officials at all levels. If you did not salute him or crossed him in any way, you were gone.

The king ruled as the wealthiest person in the kingdom. For starters, he owned vast royal estates. We know this to be true generally, but occasionally the sacred historian gets specific. For example, we read that Jehoshaphat "had much property in the cities of Judah" (2 Chronicles 17:13 NKJV). The king's monopoly of the international trade is indicated in Jehoshaphat's attempt to restore the seaborne trade to Ophir, though he proved unsuccessful (1

Kings 22:48; 2 Chronicles 20:35–37). The king undertook major building programs, as seen in the efforts of Rehoboam (2 Chronicles 11:5) and Asa to build fortified cities (2 Chronicles 14:6). The king served as commander-in-chief of the military forces. He might appoint a field commander, but the Judean kings seem generally to have commanded the troops in person. And the king had carefully chosen bodyguards for his protection (2 Kings 11:4–12).

Judah's Kings' Sacred Destiny

The Judean people treated their king almost like a sacred person. All the kings of Judah were in the line of David, and God had promised rulership and continuity to his line. When Abijam's waywardness tempted God to turn his back on David's line, God stuck by His promise to David (1 Kings 15:3–5). The king had the responsibility to maintain Israel's religious heritage and to root out idolatry. He had control of the temple treasuries and on occasion raided them to pay tribute to some invading power (e.g., 1 Kings 14:26; 2 Kings 12:18).

The king lived in his palace with his wives as a mark of wealth and power. Though none of the kings of Judah tried to beat Solomon's record (with 700 wives and 300 concubines), some of them did have large households. For example, the Chronicler tells us that Rehoboam had eighteen wives, sixty concubines, twenty-eight sons, and sixty daughters (2 Chronicles 11:21) and Abijah had fourteen wives, twenty-two sons, and sixteen daughters (2 Chronicles 13:21).

When the children grew up, the king selected one as the prince and gave the rest money and land and allowed them to live independent lives. Second Chronicles 21:3 is especially specific on this point: "Their father [Jehoshaphat] gave them great gifts of silver and gold and precious things, with fortified cities in Judah; but he gave the

kingdom to Jehoram, because he was the firstborn" (NKJV; cf. 2 Chronicles 11:23).

The King's Enthronement

So how did this power to rule get passed on? Judah had no CNN to broadcast a ceremony to the whole nation. So they developed a special ceremony to pass the power and authority on to the new ruler, the king's enthronement.

The king's enthronement gave him the power to run the government and gain title to the royal properties, and it set him apart as God's elected choice. In the Kingdom of Judah enthronement also represented a renewal of the Davidic Covenant (cf. 1 Chronicles 28:4–8). The enthronement of Jehoash or Joash provides us with details of the enthronement or coronation process there (see 2 Kings 11:12–20). Of the five specific acts, three took place in the temple and two in the palace.

First they crowned the king with the royal crown and presented him with the "testimony," variously interpreted as regulations governing the conduct of kingship in Judah, the covenant between God and the Davidic king and the obligations associated with it, a copy of the Law, and the demands made upon him in his new office. Second, he received the anointing of the priest, indicating that God had chosen him. Third came the proclamation of the anointed as king and his acclamation by the people, with the shout of "Long live the king." Fourth, the whole gathered throng proceeded to the palace, where they seated the king on the throne, an act that marked his assumption of power. Last, the king then received the highest officials of the state, who declared their loyalty.

The Royal (State) Officials

The Minister of the Palace

The Minister of the Palace (literally "he who is over the house") appears to have held a position second only to that of the king. Solomon had such an officer (1 Kings 4:6) and kings of both Israel (1 Kings 16:9; 2 Kings 10:5) and Judah (2 Kings 18:18) did

The Kings of Judah		
Name	Length of Reign	Reference
Rehoboam	17 years	1 Kings 11:42–14:31
Abijam	3 years	1 Kings 14:31–15:8
Asa	41 years	1 Kings 15:8–24
Jehoshaphat	25 years	1 Kings 22:41–50
Jehoram	8 years	2 Kings 8:16–24
Ahaziah	1 year	2 Kings 8:24–9:29
Athaliah (queen)	6 years	2 Kings 11:1–20
Joash	40 years	2 Kings 11:1–12:21
Amaziah	29 years	2 Kings 14:1–20
Azariah (Uzziah)	52 years	2 Kings 15:1–7
Jotham	18 years	2 Kings 15:32–38
Ahaz	19 years	2 Kings 16:1–20
Hezekiah	29 years	2 Kings 18:1–20:21
Manasseh	55 years	2 Kings 21:1–18
Amon	2 years	2 Kings 21:19–26
Josiah	31 years	2 Kings 22:1–23:30
Jehoahaz	3 months	2 Kings 23:31–31
Jehoiakim	11 years	2 Kings 23:34–24:5
Jehoiachin	3 months	2 Kings 24:6–16
Zedekiah	11 years	2 Kings 24:17–25:30

also. Jotham, son and successor of King Uzziah, occupied this position and governed the "people of the land" (2 Kings 15:5) after Uzziah contracted leprosy. Shebna held this office early in Hezekiah's reign (Isaiah 22:15–25) but was replaced by Eliakim, who led the three-man delegation that sought to come to terms with Sennacherib when the Assyrian invaded the land (2 Kings 18:18ff.).

The Minister of the Palace wore a distinctive robe and belt (Isaiah 22:21), and he had the "key of the house of David" so he could open and shut the gates (Isaiah 22:22). We gather this meant that he could open and close the gates of the king's house and so control the official court day and appointments on the king's calendar.

A certain Gedaliah had been appointed "over the house," or governor of Judea, during Babylonian occupation of the kingdom after the destruction of Jerusalem (2 Kings 25:22–26; Jeremiah 40—41). Excavators found a clay seal at Lachish inscribed with the words "[belonging] to Gedaliah, who is over the house." The style of the writing helps to date it about 600 B.C. This may well have been the personal seal of the last Minister of the Palace of the Kingdom of Judah.

The Royal Secretary

The Royal Secretary apparently ranked just below the Minister of the Palace. Functioning as the king's private secretary, he carried on both foreign and domestic correspondence and served as head of the royal archives, located in the king's palace. The archives room is called "the scribe's chamber" in Jeremiah 36:12. The first draft of the book of Jeremiah—the scroll written by Baruch the scribe under Jeremiah's dictation—was deposited here before King Jehoiakim destroyed it (Jeremiah 36:20–23).

Presumably secretaries kept such annals as the "Book of the Chronicles of the Kings of Judah" (e.g., 1 Kings 14:29; 15:7, 23; 22:45) there as well. Probably written on papyrus, they would have decayed in time. Also, the destructiveness of war would have caused their dispersal or destruction. So we should not expect to find them. Shaphan, the royal secretary, was involved with the discovery of the book of the Law in King Josiah's day (2 Kings 22:8–10). The Royal Secretary, Shebna, also acted as something of a Secretary of State, who engaged in negotiations between King Hezekiah and King Sennacherib of Assyria (2 Kings 18:17–37).

The Royal Herald

King Hezekiah sent the Royal Herald as one of the three delegates that negotiated with Sennacherib's officials during the siege of Jerusalem in 701 B.C. (2 Kings 18:18). He did not serve as an archivist or recorder (so KJV and RSV) but as "herald," as the New Jerusalem Bible properly translates. The Royal Herald directed communications between the king and the nation. He announced visitors to the king and proclaimed the king's orders to the people.

Supervisor of District Governors

Solomon had divided the kingdom into twelve tax districts, placing an officer in charge of each (1 Kings 4:7–19). Over all of them he appointed a supervisor of the administrative districts (1 Kings 4:5). He administered the entire bureaucratic system and saw to it that it functioned effectively. Taxes for each of Solomon's twelve districts furnished the royal court with supplies for one month each year. City dwellers paid taxes in money and rural people paid their taxes in produce, which was stored in royal storehouses (1 Kings 9:19; 2 Chronicles 32:28). Evidently both Israel and Judah used a system similar to that of Solomon. A hint of Jehoshaphat's arrangement appears in 2 Chronicles 17:5, 12 and of Hezekiah's in 2 Chronicles 32:27–29.

Supervisor of the Corvée or Forced Levy

Solomon had instituted the system of corvée or forced labor, first of Canaanites (1 Kings 9:20–21) and then of Israelites also (1 Kings 5:13–14). Solomon's supervisor, Adoram (Adoniram) continued on into the reign of Rehoboam and the rebels stoned

him at Shechem (1 Kings 12:18). After that the office does not again appear in either the northern or southern kingdom. But the practice of requiring the corvée reappeared briefly during at least the reign of King Asa of Judah in a military emergency (1 Kings 15:22).

(For more on this topic, go to p. 253 or p. 304.)

Religion

"Now it came to pass, when Rehoboam had established the kingdom and had strengthened himself, that he forsook the law of the LORD, and all Israel [southern kingdom] along with him." (2 Chronicles 12:1 NKJV).

"So they resolved to make a proclamation throughout all Israel . . . that they should come to keep the Passover to the LORD God of Israel at Jerusalem, since they had not done it for a long time in the prescribed manner" (2 Chronicles 30:5 NKJV)

We might think that because Judah had the temple and the priesthood—and because many of the most devout had migrated there from the north—her religious history would have been exemplary. Not so. As noted above, idolatry plagued the kingdom from its earliest days, but as 2 Chronicles 30:5 indicates, there were periodic revivals. Eight of the twenty kings of the south sparked revivals and called the people back to God.

A quick thumbnail sketch of Judah's religious history, administration by administration, will paint a picture of what was going on. The situation was quite different from the Kingdom of Israel, where all the kings were guilty of idolatry and we can generalize about them.

Rehoboam (931–913; 1 Kings 14:21–31; 2 Chronicles 10—12) started well. During the first three years of his rule, he led the kingdom in ways of righteousness. But then a rapid decline set in, and high places and groves began to appear everywhere. In punishment, God sent a massive Egyptian invasion under the leadership of Shishak (Sheshonk I, 945–924 B.C.), probably in the spring of the year 925 B.C. When God made it clear to Rehoboam that this punishment had come because of idolatry (2 Chronicles 12:5), the king and many of the leaders of the country confessed their sins and God moderated the attack.

Abijam (913–910; 1 Kings 15:1–8; 2 Chron-icles 13) fell into idolatry, as his father had done. In fact, conditions got so bad that God would have brought an end to Abijam's line if it had not been for His covenant with David.

Asa (910–869; 1 Kings 15:9–24; 2 Chron-icles 14—16) began his forty-one-year reign well. He launched a reform program and destroyed many of the foreign altars and idols that had infested the land during the days of his father. When the Ethiopian Zerah, apparently commander under Osorkon I (924–889), invaded the land (probably in 896 B.C.), his force appeared so overwhelming that Asa ran to God for help. God gave Asa a great victory. He then listened to the appeals of the prophet Azariah and launched a major religious reform throughout Judah.

But strangely, he soon suffered a spiritual relapse. In the face of an attack by Baasha of the northern kingdom, he robbed the temple treasury and sent a gift to Benhadad in Syria, with a plea for an attack on the northern kingdom. Though this move proved very successful, the prophet Hanani criticized the king for failure to depend on God and for making an unholy alliance. Angered, the king threw Hanani into prison and from then on does not appear to have been gen-uinely faithful to God.

Jehoshaphat (873–848; 1 Kings 22:41–50; 2 Chronicles 17—20) is described as a good king. Like his father before him, he insti-tuted reforms near the beginning of his reign and gave orders to the Levites to teach the Law (2 Chronicles 17:7–9), an indication that they had become lax in their duties. When Jehoshaphat faced a combined attack of Moab, Ammon, and Edom (2 Chronicles 20:1–30), he called for a time of fasting and prayer. God rewarded him with a great vic-tory. He also improved and expanded legal services in the kingdom.

In spite of his good points, Jehoshaphat failed miserably when he made an alliance with the house of Omri. This involved mar-riage of the crown prince, Jehoram, to Ahab's daughter Athaliah, who introduced Baal worship in Judah. (For discussion of Baal worship, see chapter 8 on life in Israel.)

Jehoram (853–841; 2 Kings 8:16–24; 2 Chronicles 21). His reign contrasted markedly with his father's. No doubt under the influence of his wife Athaliah, daughter of Ahab and Jezebel, he restored the idola-try that Jehoshaphat had destroyed. He also murdered his six brothers, endured two successful revolts by Edom and Libnah, and experienced a humiliating invasion by Philistines and Arabians.

Ahaziah (841; 2 Kings 8:24–29; 9:27–29; 2 Chronicles 22:1–9) ruled Judah for less than a year. Under the domination of his mother (Athaliah) and influenced by the example of his father, he promoted Baal worship and allied himself with his uncle Jehoram of Israel in a war against Syria.

Athaliah (841–835; 2 Kings 11:1–16; 2 Chronicles 22:10—23:15) was cruel and ambitious like Jezebel, her mother. After the death of her son, she decided to seize the throne for herself, and killed her grandchil-dren so there would be no pretenders to the throne. But she was not completely success-ful. Loyal people hid one of Ahaziah's sons, the infant Joash, for six years. Then Jehoiada, the high priest, laid careful plans to crown Joash. When he did so, Athaliah fled. Soldiers caught her and executed her.

Joash (835–796; 2 Kings 12; 2 Chronicles 23:16—24:27) had a good record in his early years, thanks largely to the counsel of Jehoiada, the high priest. He destroyed the temple of Baal in Jerusalem and fully re-instituted Mosaic offerings in the tem-ple. A religious revival broke out in the land, and he made needed repairs to the temple. But after the death of Jehoiada, Joash lapsed into idolatry. He slipped so far that he even had Jehoiada's own son, Zechariah, stoned to death for rebuking his sinful actions (2 Chronicles 24:20–22).

Amaziah (796–767; 2 Kings 14:1–20; 2 Chronicles 25) ruled for twenty-nine years, only about five as sole ruler and the rest as co-regent with his son Uzziah. Like Joash, his father, Amaziah started well and enjoyed the blessing of God. Greatly inter-ested in regaining use of the port of Ezion-geber, he launched a very successful war against Edom. But he made the great mistake of bringing back Edom's false gods and worshiping them. For this a prophet of God forecast the king's destruction.

The Prophets of Judah

Prophet	During the Reign of ...
Shemaiah (2 Chronicles 11:2–4; 12:5–7, 15)	Rehoboam (931–913 B.C.)
Iddo the Seer (2 Chronicles 12:15; 13:22)	Rehoboam (931–913 B.C.) Abijam (913–911 B.C.)
Azariah, the son of Oded (2 Chronicles 15:1, 8)	Asa (911–870 B.C.)
Hanani (2 Chronicles 16:7–10)	Asa (911–870 B.C.)
Jehu, the son of Hanani (2 Chronicles 19:2–3)	Jehoshaphat (870–848 B.C.)
Jahaziel (2 Chronicles 20:14–17)	Jehoshaphat (870–848 B.C.)
Eliezer (2 Chronicles 20:37)	Jehoshaphat (870–848 B.C.)
Obadiah	Jehoram (Joram; 848–841 B.C.)
Elijah (2 Chronicles 21:12–15)	Jehoram (Joram; 848–841 B.C.)
Joel	Joash (Jehoash; 835–796 B.C.)
Unnamed prophets 2 Chronicles 25:7–9, 15–16)	Amaziah (796–767 B.C.)
Isaiah	Uzziah (767–740 B.C.) Jotham (740–731 B.C.) Ahaz (731–715 B.C.) Hezekiah (715–686 B.C.)
Zechariah (2 Chronicles 26:5)	Uzziah (767–740 B.C.)
Micah	Jotham (740–731 B.C.) Ahaz (731–715 B.C.) Hezekiah (715–686 B.C.)
Nahum	Manasseh (686–642 B.C.)
Unnamed prophets (2 Kings 21:10; 2 Chronicles 33:18)	Manasseh (686–642 B.C.)
Jeremiah	Josiah (640–609 B.C.) Jehoahaz (609 B.C.) Jehoiakim (609–598 B.C.) Jehoiachin (598–597 B.C.) Zedekiah (597–586 B.C.)
Zephaniah	Josiah (640–609 B.C.)
Huldah the prophetess (2 Kings 22:14–20; 2 Chr. 34:22–28)	Josiah (640–609 B.C.)
Habakkuk	Jehoiakim (609–598 B.C.)
Daniel	Jehoiakim (609–598 B.C.) Jehoiachin (598–597 B.C.) Zedekiah (597–586 B.C.)
Urijah, the son of Shemaiah (Jeremiah 26:20)	Jehoiakim (609–598 B.C.)
Ezekiel	Zedekiah (597–586 B.C.)

Uzziah (792–740; 2 Kings 14:21–22; 15:1–7; 2 Chronicles 26), also known as Azariah, ruled as a very good king, and his success is directly related to his dependence on God (2 Chronicles 26:5, 7). He ruled as sole ruler for only seventeen years, serving as co-regent with Amaziah at the beginning and with Jotham at the end of his reign. Unfortunately, at the height of his power, Uzziah forgot the real source of his strength, and in the face of opposition by eighty priests insisted on going into the holy place and burning incense. For this act of sacrilege God smote Uzziah with leprosy, and he could no longer go into the temple at all and could not even enjoy ordinary social privileges.

Jotham (750–732; 2 Kings 15:32–38; 2 Chronicles 27) merely carried out the policies of Uzziah during much of his reign. He is classed as a good king, and enjoyed the favor of God. Isaiah and Micah prophesied in Judah during this time, and as is evidenced by their words, continuing prosperity had made its inroads. Judah had settled into a complacent type of secularism; sacrifices continued at the temple, but there was no real religious vitality.

Ahaz (735–713; 2 Kings 16; 2 Chronicles 28) drifted into religious apostasy: he made images to Baal and worshiped in the high places. For his sins he began to experience military reverses at the hand of the Edomites and Philistines. Meanwhile, Tiglath-Pileser of Assyria was successful against Judah's enemies; he destroyed the kingdom of Syria and annexed it along with part of the kingdom of Israel (732 B.C.).

Hezekiah (715–686; 2 Kings 18—20; 2 Chronicles 29—32; Isaiah 36—39) ruled as one of Judah's very best kings. He worked hard to destroy idols, high places, altars, and other trappings of idolatry, and is said to have conducted himself as David his father (2 Chronicles 29:2). There was plenty of need for reform after the evil influence of Ahaz. He suffered a major invasion by the Assyrian Sennacherib.

Manasseh (696–642; 2 Kings 21:1–18; 2 Chronicles 33:1–20) did not follow in the steps of his father, but became one of the very worst kings of Judah. During the first eleven of his fifty-five years of reign (longest of any king of Israel or Judah) he was co-regent with Hezekiah and must have been kept on a tight leash. But after Hezekiah's death, Manasseh established altars of Baal throughout the land and even set up an image of a Canaanite deity in the temple. He killed many who opposed his idolatry, perhaps even the prophet Isaiah, as tradition indicates.

The prophets warned Manasseh about his evil ways, but he paid no attention. Finally, the Assyrians invaded Judah and carried Manasseh captive to Babylon. There the Judean had a real change of heart and subsequently the Babylonians allowed him to return to Jerusalem. On return home, Manasseh attempted to abolish the idolatry for which he had earlier been responsible, but he does not seem to have been extremely successful.

Amon (642–640; 2 Kings 21:19–26; 2 Chronicles 33:21–25) ruled only two years and reverted to the idolatry of his father's earlier years. Some of his servants banded together and assassinated him.

Josiah (640–608; 2 Kings 22:1—23:30; 2 Chronicles 34—35), the eight-year-old son of Amon, next became king. He must have had excellent advisors from the onset. By his sixteenth year, he began of his own accord "to seek the God of his father David" (2 Chronicles 34:3). Subsequently, he launched a major program to cleanse the entire kingdom of idolatry and even extended his efforts to the northern kingdom, now only loosely under Assyrian control. Assyria was rapidly declining and about to fall, so Judah had nothing to fear from that quarter.

Jehoahaz, Jehoiakim, Jehoiachin, Zedekiah (609–586; 2 Kings 23:31—25:21; 2 Chronicles 36:1–21) ruled in the final days of the Kingdom of Judah, while Assyria was passing off the scene and Babylon was rising. What they did could not rescue the state, nor did it hasten its demise. They ruled as pathetic caretakers after the prophets had pronounced doom for royal and popular spiritual waywardness.

Some Conclusions on Religion in Judah

What does all this detail from the reigns of Judean kings add up to? First, it appears that the kings and people did not regularly keep up the national observances and festivals commanded in the Law, such as the Passover. In fact, two special Passovers are singled out: in the days of Hezekiah (2 Chronicles 30) and Josiah (2 Chronicles 35). The regular observance of the Sabbath is not mentioned either.

Second, the Law does not seem to have been regularly taught. It apparently even disappeared for a while, being rediscovered during the reign of Josiah (621 B.C.; 2 Kings 22:8).

Third, they did not maintain the temple. Periodically the kings stripped away its revenues and gold decor to pay tribute to foreign invaders (see section on Warfare).

Fourth, during much of the history of the Kingdom of Judah rampant idolatry angered God. Prophets especially inveighed against Baal worship, present in force during the reign of many kings, as noted in Scripture and archaeological discoveries. Figurines of the fertility goddess Ashtoreth have been found in large numbers in Judean sites, dating mostly to the eighth and seventh centuries B.C.[1]

High places dotted the landscape. One at Beersheba seems to have been destroyed in the reform of Hezekiah (2 Kings 18:3–4, 22).[2] Excavators unearthed an altar of ashlar (carefully cut) stone construction with horn-shaped cornerstones there. Such construction contravened biblical law, which required that altars be made of uncut stones (Exodus 20:25–26; Deuteronomy 27:5–6). Another competitor of the temple in Jerusalem stood at Arad (c. 18 miles northeast of Beersheba). Excavations show that the temple there operated during the United Monarchy and early Judean Monarchy. Its use terminated probably in the reform of Josiah (2 Kings 23).[3]

(For more on this topic, go to p. 257 or p. 309.)

Warfare

"It happened in the fifth year of King Rehoboam that Shishak king of Egypt came up against Jerusalem." (1 Kings 14:25 NKJV) *"It came to pass in the ninth year of his [Zedekiah's] reign . . . that Nebuchadnezzar king of Babylon and all his army came against Jerusalem and encamped against it."* (2 Kings 25:1 NKJV)

From the beginning of the separate Kingdom of Judah in the days of Rehoboam to the end of the kingdom in the days of Zedekiah, Judah engaged in frequent warfare. In fact, three quarters of her twenty kings called out the troops and either defended against attacks or launched them. It would be tedious to look at all this military action. We shall pick only a few of the most important developments for consideration.

Rehoboam, Defenses, and Egyptian Invasion

After the death of Solomon, his son Rehoboam failed in his negotiations with the northern tribes. They had asked for tax relief, but he threatened them with even higher taxes. From the biblical record he appears tactless and severe, and he may have been. But perhaps what really went on was a realistic facing up to fiscal realities. Solomon's excesses appear to have brought the nation into serious financial trouble, so there was no way to cut taxes.

In any event, Rehoboam tried to solve his problem of breakaway provinces as rulers often have from his day to Abraham Lincoln's in the American South to Boris Yeltsin's in Chechnya. He called out the troops (1 Kings 12:21–24). But before the army could march, the prophet Shemaiah received a word from God that he was to stop Rehoboam, and he persuaded the king to disband his forces. Rehoboam had sufficient fear of God to know that if he disobeyed, God could strike him down in defeat.

Then Rehoboam sought to build up his defenses by especially fortifying fifteen cities of Judah. There he collected supplies of food and stores of weapons (2 Chronicles 11:5–12). The way the biblical account reads,

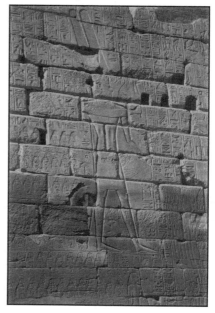

Shishak recorded his invasion of Palestine during Rehoboam's reign (925 B.C.) on a wall at the Temple of Karnak at Luxor, Egypt. He pictured his god Amen as holding ropes tied to the necks of personified captive towns and claimed to have conquered 156 towns.

it appears that Rehoboam fortified these cities before the invasion of the Egyptian Shishak. Many commentators put his rearmament after the Egyptian invasion. Probably the activity continued over a period of years before and after Shishak came. Certainly he would not have had fifteen adult sons to put in privileged positions in these fortified centers at the beginning of his reign (cf. 2 Chronicles 11:23).

In any case, he must receive credit as the architect of a defense system that continued to protect the kingdom during the rest of its history. With it he attempted to protect the Judean heartland, to block invasion of that area. Without a listing of which forts blocked which valleys, the generalization can be made that they stood at strategic points where roads led from the foothills into the mountains of Judea.

Rehoboam's approach was defensive rather than offensive. His strategy was the opposite of Solomon's, who maintained a few main centers from which troops could be deployed in all directions. Rehoboam built forts to protect specific, limited areas. Moreover, since the Kingdom of Judah was more mountainous than Solomon's kingdom as a whole, Rehoboam de-emphasized chariots and cavalry and concentrated on the infantry. Of special importance to the maintenance of this defense system was the watershed road that ran from Jerusalem through Bethlehem, Hebron, and beyond. Along this road threatened fortresses could be reinforced.

The fact that Rehoboam chose existing towns as national fortresses may lead to the conclusion that he really didn't do very much that was new. More of that in a moment. He naturally chose these towns because towns had been built on their locations for their defensive capabilities. Moreover, they had good water supplies and were on good communication routes. Finally, when it comes to defense, townsfolk could be expected to fight fiercely alongside the royal garrisons because they were defending their homes and families.

Of course Rehoboam didn't just declare existing towns to be royal fortresses. In each case he stationed a garrison there and provided barracks for them. He laid in stores of food and weapons, making efforts to protect

the town's water supply. He strengthened the walls and constructed headquarters for the garrison commander. To link these fortresses he erected many observation posts, small forts, and signal stations, as archaeological exploration of recent years has revealed.

A Judean fort at Arad, eighteen miles northeast of Beersheba.

Egyptian Invasion

Regardless of when Rehoboam began his fortification of the kingdom, during his fifth year, probably in the spring of 925 B.C., Shishak of Egypt invaded Judah (1 Kings 14:25). He wrought havoc not only in Judah, but also in the northern kingdom and even in Transjordan, as Shishak's inscription at Luxor, Egypt, shows, and as we have noted in chapter 8.

Interestingly, Shishak did not include Jerusalem in the list of towns he took or sacked; so the impression one gets is that Shishak's high price for sparing Jerusalem required that all the treasures of temple and palace be plundered to pay the ransom. Especially, all the gold ceremonial shields that Solomon had commissioned were surrendered and replaced with burnished bronze shields. After Shishak's invasion of the north, he campaigned in the Negev and probably moved south against the port of Ezion-geber in an effort to stop Judah's trade with Arabia. When God made it clear to Rehoboam that this punishment had come because of idolatry (2 Chronicles 12:5), the king and many of the leaders of the nation confessed their sins and God spared them.

Additions to Rehoboam's Defense System

Rehoboam did not seal off his northern border. Perhaps he hoped for reunification with Israel. But developments in the north changed that. During the reign of Baasha of Israel (908–886), probably about 895 B.C., northerners streamed south to live in Judah under the rule of King Asa (910–869). Baasha decided to build his own "Berlin Wall" to keep his people at home and began to fortify the border town of Ramah, about five miles north of Jerusalem (2 Chronicles 16:1; 1 Kings 15:17). To deal with the emergency, Asa removed more of the treasures from the temple and palace and sent a large gift to Benhadad, king of Aram in Damascus. Benhadad responded and attacked Baasha, who left off building Ramah.

The gate area at Lachish

Now Asa moved to fortify the northern border, taking materials Baasha had gathered at Ramah to build his own defenses at Mizpah (some eight miles north of Jerusalem) and Geba (about six miles northeast of Jerusalem). And he or one of his successors built new fortifications at Saul's old home of Gibeah. Asa also supplemented Rehoboam's defense system elsewhere, but Scripture doesn't say where (2 Chronicles 14:6–7). Asa's son Jehoshaphat (873–848) also supplemented Rehoboam's defense system by building forts and storage cities (2 Chronicles 17:2), plugging up gaps between main defenses. Perhaps both he and Asa were responsible for some of the defenses in the northern Negev, such as at Arad, with

which we are now familiar as a result of exploration and excavation.

With all this construction, Judah had become "like a large porcupine that could turn its bristles in all directions."[4] Hence the Assyrians generally, down to the attack of Sennacherib in 701, chose to avoid campaigning in the Judean mountains. Ditto the Egyptians. And when Pharaoh Necho came north in 609 to aid the Assyrians, he marched along the coastal route (the Via Maris or Way of the Sea) and begged King Josiah of Judah to let him alone because he had no quarrel with Judah (2 Chronicles 35:21).

Judean Fortifications and Siegecraft

As noted earlier, Hebrews commonly built casemate walls. That is, they built a double wall with space between the two walls divided into square compartments or casemates. Also, as noted earlier, they sometimes built solid walls to protect more effectively against Assyrian battering rams. But they did not always do so because a casemate wall could stand effectively against attack. Defenders might fill casemates with rubble or earth, providing a fairly wide wall. And when battering rams went to work they might batter the fill into an even more solid mass. Furthermore, the wide top of the wall gave a larger platform on which defenders could operate, and the greater width of the wall made it harder to tunnel under or to breach.

They built solid walls (and sometimes casemate walls) in segments that protruded or recessed while following the contours of the land. Thus, if an enemy breached a segment, this affected only a small part of the wall. More importantly, this protruding and recessing arrangement provided an opportunity for flanking or enfilading fire. That is, defenders would stand in towers on a protruding segment and rake broadside with devastating fire power a recessed segment that was under attack. Defenders also added moats outside the walls or embankments (glacis) at their feet to make scaling or tunneling more difficult.

In addition, they often built double gates, as at Lachish. If attackers broke through the outer gate, they found themselves in a small enclosure where they were attacked on all sides from above as they attempted a further breakthrough.

That the Hebrew kingdoms knew how to lay siege to a fortified center and did on occasion is clear from Scripture. Way back in Moses' day there is reference to siege warfare (Deuteronomy 20:19). This is not surprising because the Egyptians used rams to batter down walls as early as about 2000 B.C. Joab cast an embankment and used a battering ram at Abel Beth-Maachah in David's day (c. 1000 B.C., 2 Samuel 20:15). It may have been swung in a harness attached to a wooden framework or held by men charging a wall. Laying siege, building embankments, and using battering rams are referred to in Jeremiah 6:6 and Ezekiel 4:2; 26:8–9 in the latter days of the Kingdom of Judah.

The Judean Army

The Judean army, like in the United Monarchy and the northern kingdom, consisted of the regulars and the national levy. The regulars included the royal guard, the "runners" (picked infantry) that fought in conjunction with the chariot corps, and the chariot corps. Foreign mercenaries included Cherethites and Pelethites (Sea Peoples, Philistines) and apparently some Greeks. These formed divisions of thousands, hundreds, fifties, and tens.

The difficulty of using chariots in the hilly terrain of Judah led to a greater emphasis on infantry than in the north. But when Judah controlled Philistia and the Negev it became necessary to increase the chariot corps.

Judah organized the national levy or the people's army into five divisions, three from Judah that carried shields and spears and provided a phalanx of pikemen, and two from Benjamin who fought as archers and carried shields and bows (2 Chronicles 14:8). These reservists apparently saw active duty only for a fixed period every year (2 Chronicles 17:14–19).

It is interesting to discover that Judah set the age of compulsory military service at twenty. This was true of Amaziah's levy (2 Chronicles 25:5), as it had been from the days of Moses. Then God Himself had established the age limit in the taking of

military censuses (see Numbers 1:1–3; 26:2, 4). The wisdom of such a policy is immediately evident. The sixteen to twenty-year-olds could man the farms and fill other adult jobs left vacant. They also proved capable of providing a home guard to protect homes and families when the occasion demanded.

The chief officers of the national levy appear to be the 2,600 mighty men of valor. These probably descended from David's elite guard of mighty men or heroes who still retained special status in the social and military structure of Judah (2 Chronicles 26:12; cf. 2 Samuel 20:7; 23:8–39; 1 Chronicles 11:10–47).

The ordnance or military supplies provided for the army in Uzziah's day (792–740) and probably generally in Judah, is spelled out in 2 Chronicles 26:14: "Then Uzziah prepared for them, for the entire army, shields, spears, helmets, body armor, bows, and slings to cast stones" (NKJV). The men did not pay for their own equipment.

Significant Royal Judean Military Action

Amaziah

Edom had been lost to Judah from the days of Joram (2 Kings 8:20–22) and Amaziah sought to recover it and the route through it to the Gulf of Aqaba and Judah's seaport at Ezion-geber (2 Kings 14:7–14). To ensure success he had hired one hundred thousand mercenaries from Israel (2 Chronicles 25:6), but a prophet of God warned against employment of these men and Amaziah sent them home. The Israelites were furious, probably at the loss of a chance to get booty; on the way home they plundered and destroyed some cities of Judah (2 Chronicles 25:10–13).

Amaziah pursued his Edomite campaign, leaving the squaring of accounts with Israel until later. He had a great victory over Edom in the "Valley of Salt." Though there are differences of opinion on the matter, the valley must be the Arabah south of the Dead Sea, and Sela is to be located there. This conclusion seems to fit conditions better than the identification of Sela with Petra in the mountain vastnesses southeast of the Dead Sea. After his signal victory over the Edomites, giving him all of northern Edom, Amaziah carried Edomite gods back to Jerusalem and worshiped them (2 Chronicles 25:14). For his idolatrous breach God determined to destroy Amaziah (2 Chronicles 25:15–16). This sets the stage for the war with Israel.

With the Edomite conflict behind him, Amaziah sent a delegation to Jehoash, proposing that they "arrange a meeting" or "meet face to face" (2 Kings 14:9). This could have been an invitation to a discussion of matters of mutual concern or a polite invitation to battle. However the invitation may have been intended, Jehoash made conflict inevitable by his haughty reply (vv. 9–10). Probably neither king was in a mood to lie down and play dead. Jehoash had been enjoying victories over Syria, and Amaziah had just trounced Edom.

The two kings prepared for war. Instead of descending on Jerusalem from the north where defense was easier, Jehoash moved along the valley of Sorek into the central highlands of Judah. The two armies met at Beth Shemesh, about fifteen miles west of Jerusalem. There is no hint as to why the Israelites were so successful, but apparently Judean morale snapped completely and the army fled the field, deserting even the king himself, who was captured by the enemy. As noted above, there was a theological reason for Judean defeat.

Then the Israelites advanced on Jerusalem and broke down a six-hundred-foot segment of the wall, from the Ephraim Gate (thought to be about where the present Damascus Gate is located) westward to the corner gate. Probably they only broke through the wall here but did not demolish it, because Uzziah later had only to repair the wall (2 Chronicles 26:9). Then from this high ground to the north of the city Jehoash was in a good position to plunder the temple and palace treasuries, taking what he possibly felt was justly his for payment of his one hundred thousand troops hired by Amaziah. He also took "hostages," possibly as a pledge of further payment in the future. The temple treasury must not have offered him all he expected at this time, because Hazael of Syria had so recently plundered it (2 Kings 12:18).

Uzziah

During the days of Uzziah of Judah (792–740) and Jeroboam II of Israel (793–753) the two Hebrew kingdoms were powerful once more. Together they controlled most of the territory David had ruled at the height of the united Hebrew kingdom, due in part to the weakness of Assyrian monarchs during the first half of the eighth century B.C.

Like his contemporary in the north, Uzziah enjoyed great success during his reign. As noted, his father Amaziah had regained Judean control over Edom; that made possible Uzziah's restoration of Eloth (Elath) on the Gulf of Aqaba (2 Kings 14:22) and hence the redevelopment of Judean maritime activity there. Uzziah also had great military success against the Philistines in the west. There he tore down the defenses of some of their main towns and put Judean garrisons on Philistine territory. As a result Uzziah could dominate

A section of Hezekiah's "Broad Wall" in Jerusalem. It stood twenty-three feet wide and probably twenty-seven feet high.

the trade outlets of the Arabian tribes in the Negev. As a kind of domino effect, when the Hebrews controlled Philistia, Edom, and the Negev, the Ammonites farther east found it necessary, for economic reasons, to accept Uzziah's rule and become tributary to him. He now extended the Judean defense system into the Negev and built up the border militia there.

Internally, he repaired the walls of Jerusalem and fortified other centers, enjoyed economic prosperity, and increased the size of the army and outfitted it with conventional and sophisticated weaponry (for elaboration see 2 Chronicles 26 and 2 Kings 15:1–7).

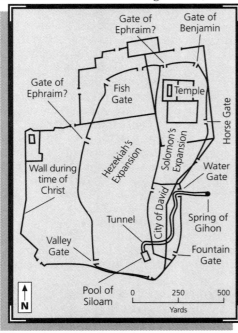

Hezekiah's Waterworks

In his efforts to fortify Jerusalem against Sennacherib and the Assyrians, King Hezekiah ordered the construction of a tunnel to bring water from the spring of Gihon to inside the city walls (2 Chronicles 32:30). The tunnel was excavated through solid rock sixty feet underground for a distance of almost six hundred yards. Workers started at opposite ends and dug with hand tools until they met in the middle of the shaft. When it was completed, Hezekiah's tunnel emerged at a spot that later came to be known as the Pool of Siloam.

Hezekiah

Hezekiah (715–686) must be considered the very best king in the history of Judah,

Dramatic Moment Described in Inscription

In 1880, boys swimming in the Pool of Siloam found an inscription carved into the wall of the tunnel near its exit into the Pool of Siloam. It describes the dramatic moment when the two crews of tunnelers met. Subsequently antiquities hunters cut the inscription from the wall, and it ultimately found its way to the Archaeological Museum in Istanbul. There are various translations of this inscription. The following is by George A. Barton:

"The boring through [is completed]. And this is the story of the boring through: while yet [they plied] the drill, each toward his fellow, and while yet there were three cubits to be bored through, there was heard the voice of one calling unto another, for there was a crevice in the rock on the right hand. And on the day of the boring through the stone-cutters struck, each to meet his fellow, drill upon drill; and the water flowed from the source to the pool for a thousand and two hundred cubits, and a hundred cubits was the height of the rock above the heads of the stone-cutters."[5]

from the standpoint of his trust in God and faithfulness to His commandments (2 Kings 18:5). And God blessed Hezekiah for his faithfulness (2 Kings 18:7–8), including the reconquest of territory lost to the Philistines during the days of Ahaz. As noted earlier, control over Philistia was related to Judah's domination of the Negev and Edom, where he effectively reestablished his sway. Then he brought Egypt into an alliance with Judah and may have opened negotiations with Babylonian rebels even before the attack of Sennacherib.

At home he strengthened the fortifications of Jerusalem, repairing the walls and building "another wall outside" (2 Chronicles 32:5). This wall is apparently the same as the "Broad Wall" referred to in Nehemiah 3:8. It evidently brought the southwestern hill of the city (currently called Zion) within adquate defenses. Professor Nahman Avigad of the Hebrew University in Jerusalem uncovered part of this wall in his excavations in the Jewish Quarter of Jerusalem. The wall stood twenty-three feet wide and probably twenty-seven feet high.[6]

This clay prism of Sennacherib (now in the British Museum) gives an account of his invasion of Judah and his siege of Jerusalem (Isaiah 36; 37).

He also "made weapons and shields in abundance" (2 Chronicles 32:28). And he made sure that the fortress towns had well stocked storehouses, full of grain, wine, and oil and equipped with "stalls for all kinds of livestock" (2 Chronicles 32:28). In a day when stored meat would quickly spoil, it was important to have livestock that could be butchered and eaten.

The major accomplishment of Hezekiah's rule must be considered his provision of a permanent supply of water for Jerusalem in the event of siege. Scripture speaks of his feat: he "stopped the water outlet of Upper Gihon, and brought the water by tunnel to the west side of the City of David" (2 Chronicles 32:30 NKJV). In other words, Hezekiah's engineers closed the upper outlet of the Gihon Spring outside the city on the east and caused the water to flow through a new tunnel under the City of David to the Pool of Siloam inside the walls at the southwest edge of the city. The tunnel, still to be seen in Jerusalem, was dug from both ends and is a remarkable feat of engineering for that period of time. Some seventeen hundred feet long, it varies from three to eleven feet in diameter.

The most trying event of Hezekiah's reign had to be the invasion of the Assyrian, Sennacherib, in 701 B.C. Scripture devotes considerable space to it, and Sennacherib records his victories and the taking of many cities and captives. We looked at this campaign in the last chapter and there is no need to repeat the discussion here. Suffice it to say that Scripture declares

Drawing of Lachish, a walled city of Judah which Sennacherib of Assyria took before his siege of Jerusalem

that Sennacherib did not succeed in taking Jerusalem because of divine intervention and Sennacherib did not claim to have done so. Hezekiah was left to restore his battered kingdom. Subsequent Assyrian rulers did not invade the fortified centers of Judea, and the Hebrews did not try to prevent Assyrian movement along the coastal road to invade and conquer Egypt.

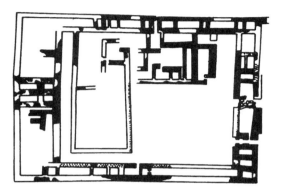

Ruins of a late seventh century B.C. palace at Ramat Rahel (between Jerusalem and Bethlehem) built during the reign of one of the later kings of Judah. The dark walls are original; the rest is reconstructed. The structure measured about 160 by 245 feet.

Josiah

"In his days Pharaoh Necho king of Egypt went to the aid of the king of Assyria, to the River Euphrates; and King Josiah went against him. And Pharaoh Necho killed him at Megiddo when he confronted him." (2 Kings 23:29 NKJV)

After the religious reforms of Josiah (2 Kings 22:1—23:30), this good king faced the ambitions of Necho, Pharaoh of Egypt. The political situation was this: Nineveh had fallen in 612, and Assyrian forces held out precariously in the western part of the country. Pharaoh Necho, son of Psammetichus I (Psamtik), founder of the Twenty-sixth Dynasty, moved north along the coastal plain to link up with the remnants of the Assyrian army in 609 B.C.

The key players in the power struggle of the day were Babylon, Assyria, and Egypt. Necho (like his father, who died in 610) wanted to help Assyria, with the

hope that he could help prevent Babylon from becoming the successor to Assyria as the main power. And he wanted to secure this position for Egypt. Josiah had some hope for his kingdom as long as the three major powers seemed to cancel each other out.

Attacking along a coastal route, Sennacherib took Lachish and established his military headquarters there. King Hezekiah of Judah paid him tribute to ward off an attack on Jerusalem, but Sennacherib attacked it anyway. His general Rabshakeh besieged the city, but withdrew suddenly through the miraculous intervention of the Lord. Judah lived in relative security for nearly a century thereafter.

Necho tried to assure Josiah that he had no quarrel with him and that he merely wanted to move northward along the coastal plain (2 Chronicles 35:20–21). But Josiah would not listen to this Egyptian offer of neutrality and met Necho in battle near Megiddo, where the Iyron Pass opened out into the Jezreel Valley. Hopefully he could overcome the Egyptians as they moved out of the narrow pass into the valley. Necho seems to have sized up the situation and apparently launched a withering barrage of arrows. When one of them mortally wounded the charismatic Judean king, his military effort collapsed.

Egypt, Nebuchadnezzar, and the Last Days of Judah

After the death of his father Josiah, Jehoahaz ascended the throne of Judah. Three months later Necho came back south, dethroned Jehoahaz, made Josiah's son, Eliakim, king and changed his name to Jehoiakim. If Necho had no previous plan to control all of Syria, he certainly did after Josiah's death and after the demise of Assyrian power. He enjoyed some domination of the area until his forces met Nebuchadnezzar at Carchemish in May or June of 605 and suffered defeat. Then Necho's Syrian empire crumpled like a house of cards, and Babylon established control over the region. Jehoiakim, a vassal of Necho, submitted voluntarily to Nebuchadnezzar, who took some Jews (including Daniel the prophet) as captives or hostages to Babylon.[7]

In the midst of this campaign, on August 15/16, 605 B.C., Nebuchadnezzar's father, Nabopolassar, died in Babylon. Following a speedy notification sent to Nebuchadnezzar and his equally speedy return to Babylon, the new king arrived in the city September 6/7 and immediately took the throne.

After some successful campaigns in Syria and Palestine in subsequent years, Nebuchadnezzar in 601 attacked Egypt and sustained such heavy losses that his imperialistic designs received a severe setback. Jehoiakim seems to have interpreted the situation as an opportunity to strike for independence, for he "rebelled" against Nebuchadnezzar (2 Kings 24:1). Again Judah entertained the elusive hope that she could count on Egyptian help against a powerful force from the north.

Unable to come in person with a Babylonian army, Nebuchadnezzar evidently sent "raiding bands," lightly armed mercenaries, from east of the Jordan (Syrians, Moabites, and Ammonites) to engage in guerrilla activities and weaken the state (2 Kings 24:2). Jehoiakim ruled for eleven years (609–598) and apparently died in December, 598, about the time Nebuchadnezzar finally sent an army to deal with rebellious Judah.

Jehoiachin's Reign and Captivity (2 Kings 24:8–16)

When Jehoiakim died, his eighteen-year-old son Jehoiachin came to the throne and continued the evil policies of his father. After Josiah, nothing good could be said for the kings of Judah. While Jehoiachin was trying to consolidate his power in Jerusalem, Babylonian forces were on the way. They must have begun the siege of the city in January of 597, and apparently it did not last much over two months. Jerusalem fell to the Babylonians on the second of Adar, March 15/16, 597 B.C.[8] Evidently the siege began at the hands of the advance guard and concluded after Nebuchadnezzar himself arrived (v. 11).

Assyrian and Babylonian sieges were slow torture for an invested city. Since this was the winter season there would have

Nebuchadnezzar's Campaigns

Nebuchadnezzar became king of Babylon in 605 B.C. and conducted several campaigns in Palestine. He squelched Jehoikim's rebellion in about 602 B.C., deported Jehoiachin in 597 B.C., and destroyed Jerusalem in 586 B.C.

been enough water, but food would have grown increasingly scarce—especially for a population greatly swollen by refugees from the surrounding countryside. Some have attributed the remarkably lenient treatment of the king and his officials to the quick surrender.

Then the Babylonians helped themselves to the spoils of war, thoroughly looting the treasuries of temple and palace, in fulfillment of the prophecy of 2 Kings 20:16. Probably not everything was taken, because Nebuchadnezzar provided for continuation of the religious, economic, and political life of Judah after the first deportation. Therefore Jeremiah 27:19–22 need not be thought of as contradictory when it speaks of furnishings still remaining in the temple during the reign of Zedekiah. Of course, what Jeremiah referred to was largely made of bronze rather than of gold or silver.

The captives deported included the king, his mother, wives, officials, the notables of the land, craftsmen and metalworkers, the 7,000 in the standing army left within the city, and Ezekiel (Ezekiel 1:1–3)—a total of some 10,000. Nebuchadnezzar left only the poorest of the land (v. 14); he carried off all those capable of mounting an effective rebellion and running a viable war effort.

Zedekiah and the Destruction of Jerusalem (2 Kings 24:17—25:21)

Nebuchadnezzar made Mattaniah (subsequently known as Zedekiah), the full brother of Jehoahaz and uncle of Jehoiachin, king on the condition that he would keep the kingdom for him and make no alliance with the Egyptians.[9] Zedekiah, the last king of Judah, reigned for eleven years (597–586) and was classified as an evil king, like Jehoiakim, probably denoting that he also refused to heed the prophetic word.

The reason for Judah's troubles in the days of Zedekiah was "God's anger" with the nation for her apostasy. Therefore he "cast them out of his presence," i.e., out of the land and from the vicinity of the temple, where He especially chose to dwell. From what little there is about Zedekiah in Scripture, he appears to have been a weak and vacillating figure, easily swayed by circumstances (see, e.g., Jeremiah 27—30).

The sacred historian skipped over the events of Zedekiah's reign down to his ninth year and the rebellion against Nebuchadnezzar. All during his reign the pro-Egyptian faction pressured him to rebel against Babylon, and Jeremiah repeatedly urged him to knuckle under to Babylon (Jeremiah 21:1–10; 34:1–3; 36:6–10; 38:17–23).

Finally, in his ninth year, Zedekiah decided to rebel, and the inevitable happened. Nebuchadnezzar prepared to attack. The assertion that "Nebuchadnezzar. . . advanced against Jerusalem" (2 Kings 25:1) when he remained at his headquarters at Riblah (v. 6), and his officers conducted the siege (Jeremiah 38:17), is not a mistake. He masterminded the campaign and his army represented his power and will, and he was therefore present in a very real sense in the persons of his deputies. The beginning of the siege in the ninth year and tenth day of the tenth month of Zedekiah's reign is to be equated with January 15, 588 B.C., according to Thiele.[10] And it continued until the eleventh year, the fourth month, and the ninth day, or July 18, 586. The destruction of the city began a month later, on August 14 (the seventh day of the fifth month, v. 8). Nebuchadnezzar temporarily lifted the siege, probably at about the halfway point, when Pharaoh Hophra of Egypt (588–570) invaded Palestine with his army and sent his fleet against Phoenicia (cf. Jeremiah 37:5–11; Ezekiel 17:15–17).

Assyrian and Babylonian sieges of ancient cities were terrifying experiences. They did not merely surround a city and cut off its supplies, but they built siege ramps around it (2 Kings 25:1). On these they deployed battering rams for breaching the walls and constructed platforms higher than the city walls in order to rain down arrows and other missiles on the defenders. In the case of Judah, they also reduced all the fortified towns (e. g., Lachish and Azekah), as archaeological discoveries indicate, and engaged in psychological warfare to encourage defections. That the latter effort was successful is clear from Jeremiah 38:19, where Zedekiah expressed a fear to surrender because he thought the Babylonians might turn him over to these defectors to make sport of him as they wished. Of course, "famine" (v. 2) always became the real horror of the siege. The lengths to which people went to get food are unimaginable. As a result of Hezekiah's efforts, the city had an adequate supply of water.

Finally on July 18, 586 B.C. the food supplies gave out completely and about the same time the Babylonians breached the wall (39:3). Probably they broke through the wall on the north of the city where access was easiest. The king and a body of troops fled at night through a narrow passage at the southeast end of the city into the Hinnom Valley and out to Jericho. Presumably this was possible because the Babylonians were concentrated at the north and west of the city. The precipitous slopes on the east and south would have been hard to attack, and scaling the walls there would have resulted in unnecessary loss of life. Perhaps the Judeans hoped to get across the Jordan to Moab and Ammon, who had also been involved in the revolt against Babylon (Jeremiah 27:3). The Babylonians caught up with the refugees on the "plains of Jericho," probably the next day. This area, east of Jericho, offered little or no cover to troops trying to cross it. The Judeans deserted their king in panic and scattered to the winds.

Nothing is said about whether the Babylonians tried to round them up. The Babylonians were after Zedekiah, and they hauled him off to Riblah in northern Syria to face Nebuchadnezzar. The Babylonian king "pronounced judgment on him" (39:5), presumably for breaking his covenant of vassalage or treaty obligations and meted out harsh punishment. Nebuchadnezzar's men "butchered" Zedekiah's sons before his eyes and then blinded him to render him powerless and sent him off to Babylon in chains. At thirty-two he had nothing to look forward to but a dark and lonely life in exile.

About a month after the fall of Jerusalem, on August 14, "Nebuzaradan, commander of the guard," came to take charge of liquidating the Judean state and reorganizing government there. The intent of 2 Kings 25:9 is clear: destruction of every important structure in the city—the temple, palace, and houses of the well-to-do. But the Hebrew is unclear in the latter part of the verse and may

mean either important or "notable buildings" or "houses of the notables."

Verse 10 concerns the destruction of protective walls so the inhabitants could not again stage an effective rebellion against Babylon. Apparently the destruction was most complete on the east where stones could be thrown down the slope toward the Kidron Valley. When Nehemiah rebuilt the walls in 444 B.C., he constructed a whole new section on the east but had only to repair the walls elsewhere.

Verse 11 alludes to the depopulation of the city and deportation of its inhabitants, of the defectors to the enemy, and the upper classes (craftsmen and managerial types) from the countryside. Nebuzaradan left some of the lower classes, including farmers and vinedressers, behind to continue some form of agricultural life in the land.

Most of the really valuable possessions of the temple had probably been carted off to Babylon when Nebuchadnezzar took the city in 597. At this stage the Babylonians focused on the bronze—tons of it—breaking it up into manageable pieces to take it to Babylon.

Finally Nebuzaradan dealt with a group of people who did not fit into any of his other categories of deportees or people to be left behind: leaders of state and ringleaders of the rebellion against Babylon (2 Kings 25:18–21). A total of seventy-two, believed to be expendable, were paraded before Nebuchadnezzar at Riblah and executed. "Judah was carried away captive" declared the sacred historian (v. 21). The temple had been destroyed and the ruling elite removed by execution or deportation.

(For more on this topic, go to p. 259 or p. 311.)

Housing and Furniture

As we have seen, houses of the United Monarchy and of the Kingdom of Israel tended to follow the four-room style. In Judah such houses do appear but seem to have belonged to high officials or landlords.

The middle and lower classes generally lived in smaller, less imposing structures. They retained the rectangular shape, but the house itself frequently consisted of a courtyard open to the sky and divided by stone

Terracing on hillside farmland outside Bethlehem

pillars, with one or two rooms at the rear. In some instances, as at Beersheba, the back room became part of the casemate wall surrounding the town. A variation on this arrangement is a small room in the front off the street, that may have served as a shop or workshop. Behind this lay an open courtyard, with a family room or two adjacent.

The courtyard contained a clay baking oven, grinding stones for producing flour, wooden weaving looms, and sometimes a very small olive or grape press. Rarely do we find cisterns or lavatories. The water supply usually came from nearby springs or wells. A man and woman and three or more children crowded into such small quarters.

Furniture

Families had little furniture. A great many of the poorest classes simply sat on the floor on mats of reeds or skins to do their work or to eat, or they slept on the floor on bedrolls. Those who could afford them had stools or simple chairs with a back, small tables, and wooden bed frames with mattresses supported by wooden slats or ropes.

(For more on this topic, go to p. 266 or p. 314.)

Diet and Foodstuffs

As we observed in commenting on life in the northern kingdom, the growing, preparation, and variety of foods eaten during this period was roughly the same as during the United Monarchy. Yet because most of the good farmland in the plains of Palestine belonged to the northern kingdom, Judean farmers greatly increased the terracing of hillsides so they could provide the food necessary for the populace. Any modern tourist may see that these practices continue to the present.

To be sure, terracing the hillsides did not begin at this time. When the Israelites arrived in Canaan, they began terracing the hillsides of Judea and Galilee because the Canaanites controlled the best lands. Farming the hillsides involved clearing the forest first and then terracing the cleared land. Joshua had said to the children of Joseph, "Go up to the forest country and clear a place for yourself" (Joshua 16:15 nkjv). Now because their fellow Israelites controlled the best lands, terraced lands became "the cornerstone of the Judean agricultural economy."[11]

Terracing involved clearing stones from the land and using them to form an embankment. The resultant arrangement gave the appearance of a series of horizontal ridges made in the hillside. And these were subdivided into family plots. Terracing increased cultivable land, conserved moisture, and minimized erosion. Because they had so little soil on the hillsides, farmers sometimes brought in additional deposits from wherever they could get them.

(For more on this topic, go to p. 268 or p. 315.)

The people of Lachish, prisoners brought before Sennacherib, illustrate the clothing of the period.
(British Museum)

Dress

Definitely a conservative society, the Hebrews resisted change in clothing styles—at least among the lower classes. They chose wool as their fabric, which they could produce from the backs of the sheep that they raised. And for centuries they seem to have worn fairly standard garments. These are shown in the reliefs from Sennacherib's palace. This Assyrian king pictured in some detail his attack on the Judean city of Lachish and the captives taken after the surrender of the city (c. 701 B.C.). Men, women and children wore long tunics, extending from the neck almost to the ankles. Women and older girls also had long capes that covered their heads and reached to the bottom of their tunics.

Though Sennacherib did not show these Judeans with girdles or belts, we know they often wore them—if for no other reason than to provide a place to tuck the bottom of their tunics when working, or to keep their clothing from billowing in a breeze. Sennacherib shows these Judeans barefoot, and much of the time they were—both inside and out of their houses. Sometimes they did wear sandals.

About the same time as Sennacherib's invasion, Isaiah severely criticized the well-to-do women of Jerusalem for their ostentation. In the following passage he provides an extended catalog of their attire. Translations of these verses differ consider-

ably. The NRSV rendering is probably as good as any.

"In that day the Lord will take away the finery of the anklets, the headbands, and the crescents; the pendants, the bracelets, and the scarfs; the headdresses, the armlets, the sashes, the perfume boxes, the amulets; the signet rings and nose rings; the festal robes, the mantles, the cloaks, and the handbags; the garments of gauze, the linen garments, the turbans, and the veils. Instead of perfume there will be a stench; and instead of a sash, a rope; and instead of well-set hair, baldness; and instead of a rich robe, a binding of sackcloth; instead of beauty, shame" (Isaiah 3:18–24).

Here we see, among other things, that like the Assyrians the Judeans wore gold or silver bands around their ankles, bracelets for the wrist, armlets for the upper arm, earrings (crescents), turbans or head bands, veils, fabric of linen, pendants of precious or semi-precious stones, amulets (to ward off evil or as good luck charms), and had their hair elaborately dressed. In addition, they even wore nose rings.

About seventy-five years later in 630–625 B.C. Zephaniah criticized the officials and king's sons who dressed themselves in "foreign apparel" (1:8). Probably they attired themselves in the latest styles from Assyria or Babylonia (see chapters 9 and 11). Foreign styles in and of themselves would not have been either wrong or sinful. More than likely adopting foreign dress outwardly implied absorbing foreign (pagan) values and practices inwardly. *(For more on this topic, go to p. 269 or p 316.)*

The Bubonic Plague

The plague that attacked the Philistines after they captured the ark of the covenant and brought it to Ashdod (1 Samuel 5:6) was apparently bubonic plague, spread by rats. It is interesting that when the Philistines returned the ark, they sent along five golden tumors and five gold rats (1 Samuel 5), a hint that they understood their problem to be bubonic plague. Bubonic plague may also have decimated Sennacherib's Assyrian army in the days of Hezekiah (2 Kings 19:35).

Family Life

What I wrote about the arrangement of marriages, the payment of the bride-price, dowries, the activities of midwives, circumcision, and the like in the chapters on the United Monarchy and the northern kingdom also applies to life in Judah. Additional comments appear here on medicine and disease, death and burial, and literacy.

Medicine and Disease in Israel

"His [Asa's] malady was very severe; yet in his disease he did not seek the LORD, but the physicians." (2 Chronicles 16:12 NKJV)

Israelites commonly looked on disease or ill health as punishment for sin. The chronicler recording King Uzziah's affliction with leprosy clearly states that (2 Chronicles 26:20), and he implies it in the experience of King Asa, noted above. If illness came as the result of God's judgment, then the treatment should involve squaring accounts with God. Thus a priest or a prophet rather than a doctor should be consulted. Presumably Asa's fault was not in consulting a doctor, and doctors are not being condemned here, but Asa

needed to address his primarily spiritual problem. Similarly, David recognized the affliction of his son as God's judgment on his adultery and murder, so he sought healing by fasting and prayer (2 Samuel 12:16–23).

The connection made between good health and upright living tended to minimize the role of the physician in ancient Israel. The development of medicine appears to have been further impeded by the teaching that contact with a corpse resulted in "uncleanness" that had to be removed by ritual purification (Numbers 5:2–3; 6:7; 19:1–22). Hence they did no autopsies or postmortem examination of corpses. Furthermore, the Hebrews' aversion to shedding of blood prevented the development of surgical methods. On top of all that, both Canaanites and Hebrews strongly believed in the existence of demons who could afflict and cause disease.

The diagnosis of disease in the Old Testament is much too technical to deal with here. Apparently at the minimum, malaria, typhoid fever, dysentery, leprosy, boils, eye diseases, dropsy, gout, and palsy should be included in a list of diseases indicated. Doctors now generally believe that biblical and modern leprosy are not the same, and the biblical term includes various fungus conditions and psoriasis.

Of special importance in medical practice were midwives, who aided in childbirth and pre- and postnatal care. Leviticus 11—15 contains regulations concerning sanitation and infectious diseases. Israelites used olive oil as the common home remedy for burns and wounds of various sorts.

Death and Burial

"They buried him [Asa] in his own tomb, which he had made for himself in the City of David; and they laid him in the bed which was filled with spices and various ingredients prepared in a mixture of ointments. They made a very great burning for him." (2 Chronicles 16:14 NKJV)

Well-planned and even monumental tomb architecture appeared in Israel in the tenth to the seventh centuries B.C. Normally burial took place in the family plot, in rural areas located on the land of the deceased; in town it was nearby. Burial had to be outside town walls; only the king could be buried inside the City of David. Sometimes they erected monuments over the tombs of dignitaries. The tomb-cave plan achieved its regular form in the eighth and seventh centuries B.C. and so is found in Judah after the fall of the northern kingdom. Judean-type tombs do not appear in the northern kingdom.

During this period Israelites cut tombs in caves, with stone benches for the deceased. There they laid out the dead without covering of earth or a coffin (see the treatment of Asa above: "they laid him in the bed"). Funeral gifts often accompanied the dead—including lamps, personal seals, jewelry, weapons, and bottles or juglets that probably contained perfumes. In these family tombs secondary burials required the gathering of bones to make room for later burials. They cut hollows under the benches or in the rear of the tombs as bone repositories. So one was literally "gathered to his fathers" (2 Kings 22:20). About 250 of these rock-cut tombs have been discovered in Judea.[12]

With bodies not embalmed, burial took place on the day of death, and the corpse was buried in the clothes worn in life. The "very great burning" made in honor of Asa (see 2 Chronicles 16:14 reference above) are believed to refer to the burning of much incense in his tomb. Presumably families with the means to afford the incense commonly did this. Also, as noted in the reference cited above, they used various spices and ointments to anoint the body.

When a person died, those affected by the death were expected to express their grief. This might involve some tearing of clothing and wailing (2 Samuel 1:11–12). Sometimes the mourner composed a personal lament honoring the deceased, such as David's laments over Saul and Jonathan (2 Samuel 1:17–27) and Abner (2 Samuel 3:33–34). In time professional mourners became available to those who could afford to hire them. They called them "singing women" (2 Chronicles 35:25) or "mourning women" (Jeremiah 9:17) who would wail, beat their breasts, tear their hair, and sing dirges, while wearing sackcloth (a mourning garment of goat or camel hair, Jeremiah 6:26; Isaiah 32:11). Canaanites also made use of professional mourners.

Literacy

Literacy was evidently widespread in the Kingdom of Judah, though archaeologists cannot confirm the existence of formal schools. Presumably the extensive activity of the priests and Levites in the religious affairs of the state contributed to the greater literacy in Judah over the northern kingdom. Additionally, many priests migrated south to Judah (2 Chronicles 11:14–17). Knowledge of the Law, maintenance of the temple, and administration of the official religion of the state required a literate priesthood.

But the large number of inscriptions recovered from Palestinian sites show that "by the end of the eighth century Israelite society as a whole was literate."[13] A great many of the pottery vessels bear ownership inscriptions written in clumsy script before firing, showing that the potter himself wrote it. And there would be no use in inscribing the pot if purchasers could not read the inscription.

Curses directed against tomb robbers carved on the outside of tombs presupposes that persons tempted to break in could read the messages. Numbers and words on stone weights, building stones, and clay vessels show that traders, potters, builders, and others and their customers knew how to read and write.

The Siloam inscription, written by Hezekiah's engineers or workers, previously noted, is another example of literacy. Then there are ostraca, pieces of pottery written on with ink. Two especially important Judean collections are the Lachish and Arad Ostraca.

Jeremiah said at one point, "I signed the deed and sealed it" (Jeremiah 32:10 NKJV). What he referred to was one of the bullae (singular bulla). That is, they rolled up documents written on papyrus and tied them with a string to which a lump of clay had been attached and to which was applied a seal. They called the clay lump with the applied seal a bulla. Many of these seals have writing on them. Over time the papyrus (or parchment) documents disintegrated and only the bulla remains.

The large number of bullae in existence also help to underscore the literacy of the period. Two of the important bullae connected with the biblical narrative belonged to Baruch, Jeremiah's scribe or secretary (Jeremiah 36) and Gedaliah, whom the Babylonians appointed governor of Judah after the destruction of Jerusalem (Jeremiah 39:14).[14] Incidentally, we sometimes hear about a papal bull—an official pronouncement of the pope with his seal attached.

Other examples of literacy could be given, but the point has been made. By the time the Babylonians destroyed Jerusalem (586 B.C.) most people in Judah could read and write.

(For more on this topic, go to p. 271 or p. 316.)

Judean pottery of the period 700–650 B.C.

Wine Production and Storage

Israelites crushed the grapes by foot in these wine presses. Then they separated the juice from the skins and pulp and allowed it to ferment. After that they filtered it and poured it into large storage jars, covered with a thin layer of olive oil to hold the flavor, sealed the containers, and deposited them in the underground wine cellars, where the temperature held at a constant 65 degrees.

Work, Travel, and Commerce

The economy of Judah remained essentially dependent upon subsistence agriculture. Industrial installations tended to be small and to be household workshops for processing agricultural products. The same was true of oil and winepresses, looms for weaving, and installations for making leather. Pottery and metal products tended to be mass-produced in workshops.

Families generally manufactured olive oil in their homes. The process of extracting the oil and the kind of presses used were much the same as in the United Monarchy (see chapter 7). But the number of presses in existence in the western region at least exceeded local demands, so they had plenty for export from the region.

Wine production could be domestic, but archaeologists have found evidence of larger industrial operations. They excavated an especially successful installation at Gibeon, eight miles northwest of Jerusalem. There James B. Pritchard uncovered sixty-three bell-shaped cisterns or wine cellars hewed out of the rock and capable of holding twenty-five thousand gallons of wine. Excavators also found rock-cut winepresses, fermenting tanks, and settling basins.

Gibeon's industry flourished in the seventh century B.C. Producers sold the wine and oil of the area in Jerusalem, but they also sold some in foreign markets, presumably shipped there in Philistine vessels.[15]

We see little evidence of change in styles in pottery production during the history of the kingdom. Most of the pottery is of quite good quality and appears to have been mass-produced in specialized workshops. Characteristic of the period was exterior burnishing with an orange-red slip while the vessels were turned on the potter's wheel.

No remains of iron workshops have been discovered in the Kingdom of Judah, but they produced numerous iron objects, including knives, shovels, plows, and weapons such as arrows and spearheads. Efforts to harden iron into steel became increasingly widespread during the history of the kingdom.

Since Sennacherib reported receiving couches and chairs inlaid with ivory from Hezekiah as tribute,[16] they probably produced ivory objects in Judah, though no ivory has yet been found in the excavations.

Possibly they purchased these objects abroad. Only the king and some of the wealthy could have afforded them.

These Israelite stone weights were used to determine the value of gold and silver. The smaller stone equals the weight of one shekel; the larger equals four shekels.

Children probably learned craft and industrial production in Judah as they grew up in the family. Boys were expected to learn the trades or skills of their fathers and to practice them on growing to maturity. We do not know of an apprentice system that prepared boys to work in the trades. Girls grew up learning how to work, spin, and weave and to do other things that a subsistence economy demanded.

Commerce

A class of merchants that dealt with domestic commerce does not seem to have existed in ancient Judah. A few sold wares in a little shop in the front room of their houses. Commonly people sold goods in an open area just outside the city gate or in the town square inside it.

Often the sale involved simple barter—the exchange of one commodity for another. But a primitive form of a money economy did exist. Silver and sometimes copper was weighed out as a means of payment. Collections of silver ingots have been found at Eshtemoa in the southern Hebron hills and at En Gedi on the western shore of the Dead Sea. Judeans used marked stone weights for weighing silver on bronze scales. The basic unit of weight was the shekel (weighing 11.4 grams), and there were stone weights marked with 1, 2, 4, 8 shekels and fractions of a shekel. Philistia also used Judean weights.[17] Yigal Ronen has recently addressed many technical questions about this system of weights.[18]

As noted in the earlier section on warfare, Judah was at least periodically in control of the southern Negev and thus involved in international trade. Especially in the days of Jehoshaphat, Ahaziah, and Uzziah they made an effort to conduct trade with Arabia and points east and south. Edomites and Ammonites traded across the Negev with Philistia. The sea-going Philistines bought and sold in Cyprus and the Aegean world. Judah tapped this trade and also practiced greater direct commercial relations with the Philistines than previously recognized. Excavations in Jerusalem have confirmed commercial relations between Judah and South Arabia during the eighth and seventh centuries, while discoveries in the Arad-Beersheba region indicate trade with Cyprus and the Aegean.[19]

The Babylonians became dominant during the last years of the Kingdom of Judah, so we will focus on them in the next chapter.

(For more on this topic, go to p. 272 or p. 317.)

NOTES:

[1] Amihai Mazar, *Archaeology of the Land of the Bible* (New York: Doubleday, 1990), 502.

[2] Ibid., 495.

[3] Ibid., 498.

[4] Chaim Herzag and Mordechai Gichon, *Battles of the Bible* (Jerusalem: Steimatzky's Agency Ltd., 1978), 145.

[5] Hershel Shanks, *Jerusalem An Archaeological Biography* (New York: Random House, 1995), 80–81.

[6] George A. Barton, *Archaeology and the Bible*, 7th ed. (Philadelphia: American Sunday-School Union, 1937), 476.

[7] D. J. Wiseman, *Chronicles of the Chaldaean Kings* (London: British Museum, 1961), 26.

[8] Ibid., 33.

[9] Josephus, *Antiquities of the Jews*, X.7.1.

[10] Edwin R. Thiele, *The Mysterious Numbers of the Hebrew Kings*, rev. ed. (Grand Rapids: Zondervan, 1983), 190.

[11] Oded Borowski, *Agriculture in Iron Age Israel* (Winona Lake, Ind.: Eisenbrauns, 1987), 17.

[12] Amnon Ben-Tor, ed., *The Archaeology of Ancient Israel* (New Haven: Yale University Press, 1992), 359.

[13] Ibid., 349.

[14] Mazar, 519-20.

[15] James B. Pritchard, *Gibeon, Where the Sun Stood Still* (Princeton: Princeton University Press, 1962), see especially 93–99.

[16] James B. Pritchard, *Ancient Near Eastern Texts*, 2nd ed. (Princeton: Princeton University Press, 1955), 288.

[17] Mazar, Ibid.; Ben-Tor, 360–61.

[18] For discussion, see Yigal Ronen, "The Enigma of the Shekel Weights of the Judean Kingdom," *Biblical Archaeologist*, June 1996, 122–25.

[19] Mazar, 514.

BIBLIOGRAPHY:

Ben-Tor, Amnon, ed. *The Archaeology of Ancient Israel*. New Haven: Yale University Press, 1992.

Borowski, Óded. *Agriculture in Iron Age Israel*. Winona Lake, Ind.: Eisenbrauns, 1987.

Davis, John J., and John C. Whitcomb. *A History of Israel*. Grand Rapids: Baker Book House, 1980.

Free, Joseph P. *Archaeology and Bible History*. Revised by Howard F. Vos. Grand Rapids: Zondervan, 1992.

Hoerth, Alfred J. *Archaeology and the Old Testament*. Grand Rapids: Baker, 1998.

Kaiser, Waiter C., Jr. *A History of Israel*. Nashville: Broadman & Holman, 1998.

Mazar, Amihai. *Archaeology of the Land of the Bible*. New York: Doubleday, 1990.

Shanks, Hershel. *Jerusalem An Archaeological Biography*. New York: Random House, 1995.

Vos, Howard F. *Bible Study Commentary: 1, 2 Kings*. Grand Rapids: Zondervan, 1989.

Wiseman, D. J. *Chronicles of the Chaldaean Kings*. London: British Museum, 1961.

Wood, Leon J. *A Survey of Israel's History*. Revised by David O'Brien. Grand Rapids: Zondervan, 1986.

LIFE IN BABYLONIAN CAPTIVITY

Chapter 11

(2 Kings 24—25; Daniel; Ezekiel; Jeremiah)

If you've ever felt your world has crashed around you and nothing seems to go your way anymore, you know a little of how the exiles from Judah felt in Babylonia. The Babylonian steamroller had flattened the land of Judah. Scripture indicates and archaeological discoveries confirm that Nebuchadnezzar's army had not only sacked the fortified towns of Judah, but also had broken down their walls and buildings and burned them. According to Scripture, Nebuchadnezzar then pulled up around Jerusalem and settled in for a multiyear siege, eventually breaking through its wall in 586 B.C. He removed everything valuable and leveled the city in a burst of savage destruction. As Nebuchadnezzar's army retreated, it took with it the remnants of Judah's army and anyone who might lead another uprising.

God's Sovereign Watchcare

When we think of exiles, we usually think of groups like the Kurds on the border between Iraq and Turkey, living in poverty in makeshift tent cities and surviving on relief aid by the United Nations. That's not how Judah's exiles lived in Babylon.

Consider the remarkable story of Daniel. Within about three years, as a reward for interpreting a dream for Nebuchadnezzar, the king raised him to the important position of chief of the "wise men," on whom

the king depended for advice. Then Nebuchadnezzar appointed Daniel ruler over the province of Babylon (Daniel 2:48), clearly a position of luxury and power that in most countries would have gone to a local politician.

Evidently Daniel continued in this leadership role for a number of years. Thus he could ease the lot of Ezekiel and the other captives who were brought to Babylon in 597, and probably again in 586, when Jerusalem was destroyed and thousands of additional Hebrews were brought to Babylonia. Daniel's intervention would help to explain why Ezekiel had his own house (Ezekiel 8:1) and freely interacted with his people and counseled them. Moreover, the elders, acting as representatives of the Jews, could visit him and seek counsel (Ezekiel 8:1; 14:1; 20:1). Evidently they also maintained some of Judah's institutions and retained a certain amount of local autonomy.

Daniel may also have been influential in the release of King Jehoiachin from imprisonment during the days of Evil-Merodach (Amel-Marduk, 561–559), Nebuchadnezzar's successor (2 Kings 25:27–30). At any rate, the king released Jehoiachin from prison. He and his five sons received food and other provisions at the Babylonian court for the rest of their lives. Cuneiform tablets found in Babylon support the biblical statement.[1] Second Kings 25:28 may indicate that

Nebuchadnezzar's Policy of Selective Depopulation

The process of depopulation had been going on for some time. Nebuchadnezzar had initially carried off a few promising young men in 605 so he could train them for positions in his kingdom. That included the prophet Daniel (Daniel 1:4). Then in 597 the Babylonians deported about 10,000 (2 Kings 24:14). This apparently included the 7,000 of the standing army left within Jerusalem, 1,000 craftsmen, and 2,000 other notables of the land, including Ezekiel (Ezekiel 1:1–3). Jeremiah's reference to 3,023 taken in this captivity probably includes all the non-military personnel from the highest classes of Jerusalem (Jeremiah 52:28).

How many thousands Nebuchadnezzar deported when he leveled Jerusalem in 586 we do not know, but his policy was to remove the enterprising elements of society that might organize a rebellion in the future. He executed those judged guilty of rebellion or leading the opposition to his invasion in 588–86. Of course other thousands died in battle or fled to Egypt, Moab, Ammon, and elsewhere. The result was that only the poorest of the land remained (2 Kings 25:12). Usually we talk about these three deportations (605, 597, 586). But Jeremiah mentions a fourth in the twenty-third year of Nebuchadnezzar, about 582 (Jeremiah 52:30), and there may have been others.

Some idea of the total number of captives may be guessed from the fact that 42,360 returned in the restoration of 538–6 (Ezra 2:64; Nehemiah 7:66), and only a fraction of the deportees decided to return. Of course by that time the exile population had increased for close to seventy years.

Jehoiachin even enjoyed some limited authority after his release. The king's experience further illustrates the favor shown the Hebrews while in captivity.

Apparently the lines of communication were open too. Jeremiah wrote letters to the captives in Babylonia (Jeremiah 29:1). The captives in Babylon also wrote letters to friends in Judah (Jeremiah 29:25).

Though Daniel seems to have lost his high office under a couple of successive kings, Belshazzar, the last Babylonian king, recalled him to service (Daniel 5:29). He lived a long life, for he stuck around until at least the first year of King Cyrus of Persia (Daniel 1:21). Thus he was in a position to be involved with Cyrus' decree permitting the Jews to return to Jerusalem. Moreover, he may well have been able to facilitate the Hebrew return to Palestine approximately seventy years after the final assault on Jerusalem because he was still around during the third year of King Cyrus (Daniel 10:1).

Economic Opportunities Abounded

Economic opportunities evidently abounded. Nebuchadnezzar imported craftsmen and artisans in the captivity of 597 B.C. (2 Kings 24:14–16), ostensibly to remove those who might stir up revolt against him. But he probably also intended for them to contribute to the Babylonian economy—and these progressive people might do well under adverse conditions. Jeremiah urged them to "build houses and dwell in them; plant gardens and eat their fruit" (Jeremiah 29:5 NKJV).

Note that the exiles lived in various places with "tel" in the name (e.g., Tel-Melah, Tel-Harsha, Tel-Abib). "Tel" may mean "mound" or "ruin"; so the Jews may have been settled on abandoned sites where they became tenants to the king and where they could provide labor, pay taxes, and serve in the military.[2] Many lived near the river Chebar (Ezekiel 1:1, 3; 3:15, 23, etc.), probably the large irrigation canal *nar kabari* (meaning "the great canal"), which flowed out of the Euphrates north of Babylon, past Nippur, and then reentered the Euphrates.

In time many of the Jews became quite wealthy (see Ezra 1:6; 2:68–69) and even had slaves (Ezra 2:65). Scripture indicates that 7,337 slaves were counted among the 42,360 Jews in the first stage of the return to

Jerusalem, revealing how well the Jews did while in captivity. Another hint of their success appears in the archives of the great Babylonian firm Murashu Sons, bankers and brokers at Nippur in the last half of the fifth century B.C. In these records Hebrew members of the firm appear—renting, buying, and selling.[3] Though these texts date after the period of the Exile, they do mention Jews who were prominent in the economic life of the community.

The Land

"Thus Judah was carried away captive from its own land." (2 Kings 25:21 NKJV)

The Hebrew exiles found their new home in Babylonia very different from what they had left in Palestine. Instead of a land of hills and valleys, they now lived in a flat land—no hills as far as the eye could see. Instead of dry farming made possible in most places in Judah by a minimally adequate rainfall, they were forced to irrigate crops in soil that received only about five or six inches of rainfall per year. Instead of a land with lots of stone and some timber and other resources, they now found themselves in a region of alluvial soil left by overflowing rivers with no stone or good timber or metal. Instead of reasonably comfortable temperatures in the hills of Judea, they faced unrelieved summer heat of 108° in the shade and 120 to 140° in the sun in the vicinity of Babylon. And there is no evidence of any climatic change in the region from that day to this.

Southern Mesopotamia was then called Babylonia, a territory that stretched from the vicinity of modern Baghdad to the Persian Gulf. In earlier days residents there had called it Sumer and Akkad—Sumer in the area north of the Persian Gulf and Akkad around Baghdad. But after the rise of the city of Babylon, the whole region came to be known as Babylonia.

Of course the Tigris and Euphrates rivers, which provided water for irrigation, made life in that area possible. The two rivers flowed only about twenty-five miles apart in the region of Baghdad, then diverged to flow as much as 150 miles apart. Finally they joined as a single stream one hundred miles north of the Persian Gulf. So Babylonian territory extended only about 150 miles from border to border at its widest part. As to length, the distance from Baghdad to Ur is about 220 miles and from Ur to the Persian Gulf about 150; hence the total length was about 375 miles.

North of the Persian Gulf lay extensive marshes, inhabited in ancient and modern times by the marsh Arabs. While they could not farm, the waters around them contained an abundance of fish, marsh birds, and numerous kinds of reeds, which they used to build their houses, their furniture, and their containers. A high level of decay in this region of Mesopotamia makes it difficult for scholars to investigate carefully the region's civilization. Hebrews did not move there.

The exiles settled in the alluvial plain to the north, where they found an irrigation culture and a civilization based on sun and soil and water. People there formed clay into bricks for houses, into clay pots for utensils, and into tablets for writing material. The rich soil yielded abundant food crops and produced cotton and flax (linen) for clothing,

The Babylonian Empire in the days of Nebuchadnezzar

with sheep providing the wool. The abundance of production provided a surplus for export to exchange for metal, stone, and wood. Asphalt in the valley of the Euphrates, especially near Hit, northwest of Babylon, served as a bonding agent to join bricks together and make floors and walls watertight.

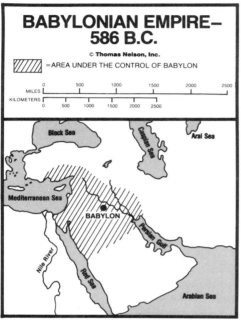

BABYLONIAN EMPIRE— 586 B.C.

© Thomas Nelson, Inc.

////// = AREA UNDER THE CONTROL OF BABYLON

The Babylonian Empire in Middle East perspective

In this irrigation culture the increase of salt content in the soil (salinization) was always a problem, largely because of the high temperature and high evaporation rate of water used for irrigation. As the water evaporated it left behind a residue of salts. Salinization also occurred because there were no scouring rains to wash the soil. Low, flat lands had poor drainage. Moreover, with continued irrigation the water table rose, bringing increasingly saline waters closer to the roots of growing plants. Increasing salinization made it difficult to grow wheat and emmer; farmers were forced to restrict grain production to barley, which was more salt tolerant. Ultimately many had to leave their land and go somewhere else. But the problem of salinization did not become really acute in the

Location of the Gulf Coastline

Debate continues about where the coastline of the Persian Gulf lay in ancient times. Of course we know that the Tigris and Euphrates carried large quantities of silt and dumped it as they flowed to the sea. The old generalization is that as the rivers deposited this silt they advanced the seacoast and that in Abraham's day (c. 2000 B.C.) the shoreline was near Ur. Then scholars discovered that the rivers dropped nearly all their silt on the land before reaching the coast and that the river valley was a slowly subsiding basin. For example, the water table in Babylon has been gradually rising, so that now most of the city of Hammurabi's day (c. 1800 B.C.) is under water and cannot be excavated. Thus it seems reasonable to believe that the coastline has remained about the same as in ancient times.

Studies conducted in the last couple of decades indicate that there has been a fluctuation in the level of Gulf waters, which of course affects the position of the shoreline. Though the shore may have been much farther north in Abraham's day, by Nebuchadnezzar's reign and Hebrew settlement there it was probably about where it is now.

south until the days of Alexander the Great (fourth century B.C.).
(For more on this topic, go to p. 275 or p. 321.)

(For more on this topic, go to p. 275 or p. 321.)

Government

"You, O king, are a king of kings. For the God of heaven has given you a kingdom, power, strength, and glory." (Daniel 2:37 NKJV)

When we think of the Hebrew exiles in Babylonia we imagine their being captive under a despotic and all-powerful king—an image created by Daniel's address to King Nebuchadnezzar of Babylon and his destruction of Jerusalem. Because Scripture and poets and artists in the West have so played up his deeds, Nebuchadnezzar and the Babylonian Empire have enjoyed a reputation for power and glory far beyond what they deserve. As a matter of fact, after the promise shown by Nebuchadnezzar, he was followed by weak and irresponsible kings. The Persian colossus in the East overmatched them and Babylon fell to Cyrus without a fight in 539 B.C. In reality God, who called Nebuchadnezzar "My servant" (Jeremiah 25:9), primarily used him to carry out God's judgment against Judah and the surrounding states.

To understand how Nebuchadnezzar got his power, we need to backtrack a little. After the Assyrian king Ashurbanipal died in 627 B.C., the Assyrian Empire fell apart. With the breakdown of the central government, provincial governors enjoyed greater freedom. One of these, Nabopolassar, father of Nebuchadnezzar, established himself as king of Babylonia within about a year. By and large, the political structures established under the Assyrians continued—with a twist. The temples, and the priests who controlled them, gained greater power.

The fact is that during the political uncertainties of the late second millennium and early first millennium B.C., Babylonians had tended to gravitate to the temples for protection and livelihood, much as many people in Western Europe turned to the monastic communities during the Middle Ages. The Assyrians had kept the temples from gaining too much power, but when the overwhelming power of the Assyrians was lifted, Babylonian political figures found themselves in a different position.

Throughout the Neo-Babylonian Empire (625–539), the king reigned as a kind of tenant of the god. Evidence of this fact is especially clear in what happened during the New Year Festival or *akitu,* celebrated for eleven or twelve days every spring in

A brick from ancient Babylon impressed with the name of King Nebuchadnezzar

(Gustav Jeeninga)

March–April. On the fifth day the king went to the great temple of Esagila in Babylon (sacred to Marduk). There he surrendered his insignia of rule—scepter, mace, and crown—to the priest, who put them on a chair in front of the god Marduk. Then the priest struck the king on the cheek, after which the king made a ritual confession in which he asserted that he had not neglected the sovereignty of the god, had not oppressed subordinates, and watched out for the city of Babylon, among other things.

After this the priest assured the king of the god's acceptance of his prayer and his blessing upon the king. Then the priest struck the king on the cheek once more and returned his insignia of office. The ceremony made it clear that the king atoned for the sins of the community and that he owed his powers to the gods.

The king appointed royal revenue officers in the temples to serve alongside the priests to collect taxes, since temples owned much of the land in Babylonia. And gradually they managed to gain greater authority for the king, but there was always a tug-of-war between temple and state. Of course the situation was different outside the power base in Babylonia. In places such as Judah or Phoenicia, where the king had military success and took control of new territories, he appointed officials at will, ruled without religious restraints, and retained all the revenues.

After Nebuchadnezzar took the reins of government, he evidently did not either occupy the Assyrian Empire or try to rebuild it. Instead he concentrated on subjection of Syria-Palestine in order to maintain a gateway to the Mediterranean. Almost all Babylonian trade was with the West. Internally he devoted his efforts to the religious and cultural revival of southern Mesopotamia, combined with extensive architectural activity. Nebuchadnezzar and his successors launched reconstruction programs in all the main cities of Sumer and Akkad. Babylon became one of the great cities of the world. And Hebrew artisans undoubtedly made significant contributions during the building programs when they were exiles in Babylonia.

If you had been publishing a Hebrew newspaper for the exiles in Babylon, you would have read a lot about Nebuchadnezzar as a builder. But you would have seen a lot more about his military campaigns. He found it much easier to win battles and declare control in the Westland than to maintain effective control there. He was compelled to make an almost annual show of force somewhere in Palestine, Syria, or Phoenicia. His frequent military actions led to a substantial standing army. Of course at the court his word was law, and he was the "supreme court" of the state. Though the power of the crown was checked by the temple, the king had control of the political, military, and legal machinery of the state.

Nebuchadnezzar and His Successors

Imagine being a political figure like Daniel in Babylonia during the Exile, experiencing constant government upheaval after the reign of Nebuchadnezzar. After Nebuchadnezzar died of an illness late in 562 B.C. (total reign 605–562), his son Amel-Marduk (Evil-Merodach of 2 Kings 25:27; Jeremiah 32:31) ruled for two years.

He so badly managed the affairs of state that his sister's husband Neriglisaros (Neriglissar, Nergal-Sharezer, Jeremiah 39:3, 13) rebelled against him and killed him. Nergal-Sharezer then ruled for four years (559–556), carrying out some public works and winning a short war in southeast Asia Minor. His young son and successor, Labashi-Marduk, was so totally inept that a group of conspirators killed him after a nine-month rule (556) and installed one of their number, Nabunaid (Nabonidus), as king.

Now imagine the rumors circulating in Hebrew communities during the rule of Nabonidus (556–539), described as "enigmatic" and "fascinating." At this distance we find it hard to know exactly what he was trying to do, especially because his enemies worked hard to stain his reputation. We do know, however, that he favored the moon god Sin and sought to restore his temples at Ur and Haran. Moreover, he tried to expand the power of the monarchy at the expense of the priestly power in the temples. In the process he probably alienated the Marduk priesthood. He also weakened his position in the state by spending almost a decade in Arabia. It now appears that he was trying to gain control of trade routes with south Arabia to compensate for those lost to the Medo-Persians farther north. During those years he made his son Belshazzar the ruler in Babylon. Belshazzar is remembered as the king who saw the handwriting on the wall and had Daniel provide the explanation for it.

Meanwhile, Cyrus the Great of Persia grew stronger, establishing his rule in Persia and building his empire. When he came banging on the gates of the Babylonian Empire, the empire proved to be a hollow shell and fell without much Persian effort. But that is a story for the next chapter.

Babylon

"Is not this great Babylon, that I have built for a royal dwelling by my mighty power and for the honor of my majesty?" (Daniel 4:30 NKJV)

Nebuchadnezzar's question as he talked with Daniel reveals how his perceived his

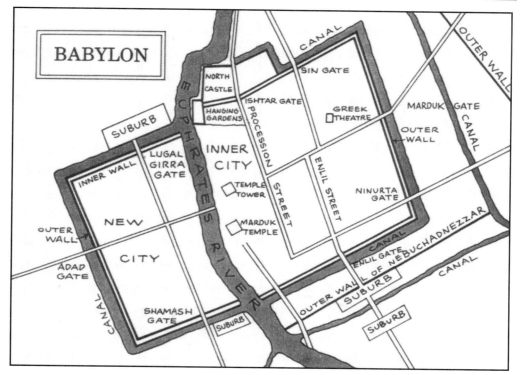

reign. It reveals his pride in building his magnificent capital, which he developed into one of the greatest cities of the ancient world. Supplementing this question is a long inscription in the British Museum that describes his building activities in Babylon. Confirming indicators are the archaeological discoveries by Robert Koldewey for the German Oriental Society (1899–1917). The subsequent description of the city is based on Koldewey's work. In recent decades the Iraqi government has spent millions of dollars in further archaeological investigation and in refurbishing the site. And Saddam Hussein conducted what were to be annual festivals there in 1987 and 1988. But of course the Gulf War of 1991 interrupted his plans.

The exiles like Daniel saw a new city in Babylon, rebuilt like Berlin after the bombing of the war years. In punishment for Babylonian rebellion, the Assyrian Sennacherib had virtually destroyed the venerable city of Hammurabi in 689 B.C. Sennacherib's son and successor Esarhaddon did some rebuilding there to placate the Babylonians. But the city remained in bad shape until Nebuchad-

nezzar took the throne, so he had an opportunity to build the city of Babylon largely from scratch.

Much larger than Nineveh, Ur, or other ancient Mesopotamian cities, Greater Babylon covered an area of some 2,100 acres; the area within the inner walls (roughly rectangular) was about half that. Up to 200,000 people could have lived in the more heavily fortified inner area and probably twice that in the larger complex. The circuit of the fortifications was just under ten miles.

Babylon sat astride the Euphrates, with the older part to the east of the river and a new section west of it, linked by a bridge. Iron gratings closed the entrance to the river between the two sectors.

Running north-south through the eastern part of the city lay Procession Street, the main thoroughfare, probably frequently traveled by Daniel, Ezekiel, and other Hebrew exiles who had gained prominence. Built by Nebuchadnezzar in honor of Marduk, this roadway was paved with imported white limestone and sometimes reached a width of sixty-five feet. Sidewalks of red breccia bordered it. The city's major

Babylon's Defenses

A double mudbrick wall surrounded the two parts of the inner city of Babylon. The inner of these walls was twenty-one feet thick, with towers every fifty-nine feet. After an intervening space of twenty-four feet, filled with rubble and supporting a military road, Nebuchadnezzar had constructed an outer wall twelve feet thick, with towers every sixty-seven feet. Eight gates with doors covered in bronze led into the city. Surrounding this heavily fortified area, waters from the Euphrates filled a moat about 150 feet across.

If these defenses were not enough, about a mile and a half beyond this wall an outer triple wall surrounded the part of the city of Babylon that lay east of the Euphrates. This outer defense system had an inner mudbrick wall about twenty-four feet thick. About thirty-five feet beyond it stood a slightly thicker wall of baked brick, against which lay a ten-foot scarp of baked brick that faced another moat filled with Euphrates water.

rounded by a casing of burnt brick about fifty feet thick. A thirty-foot wide staircase led up to the first and second stages.

The Esagila temple, south of the ziggurat, served as the great temple to Marduk. Its main chapel measured about 66 by 132 feet. Nebuchadnezzar said that he covered the whole of the interior, including the rafters, with gold. On a pedestal inside the chapel stood a golden image of Marduk. Dozens of other temples were scattered throughout the city. In addition to these, cuneiform texts of the period indicate the presence of almost four hundred altars at gates and crossroads and nearly a thousand shrines scattered throughout the city.[4]

This drawing of Babylon shows Procession Street (the main avenue of the city) as it passes through the Ishtar Gate. (For scenes of Babylon as Daniel and Ezekiel might have known it, see color section in the front half of this book.)

structures opened on this roadway. These included the palaces of Nebuchadnezzar, the ziggurat, and the great temple of Marduk, the latter two representing the idolatry of the Babylonians—and probably a constant reminder to Hebrew exiles that their temple had been destroyed.

About midway along the street stood the great ziggurat or staged tower, often called the Tower of Babel. In its earliest stages it went back to the days of Hammurabi (c. 1800 B.C.). But the Assyrian Esarhaddon began the rebuilding, which was completed by Nebuchadnezzar. He built the shrine on its uppermost level. Through the centuries robbers removed the brick, leaving only its foundation and the outline of its monumental stairs to the south by the time the archaeologist Koldewey began his work there. The dimensions of the first level of the ziggurat were about 300 feet on a side. The number of stages and the arrangement of the staircases remain in dispute. The main mass of the ziggurat was of clay, sur-

Nebuchadnezzar chose the Southern Palace as his principal palace. This had rooms grouped around five courtyards. The third or middle section was the most important. Here at the south end of the courtyard stood the great white plastered throne room of Nebuchadnezzar (56 by 170 feet), probably the scene of Belshazzar's feast and Alexander's death. Nebuchadnezzar's artisans decorated the facade of the throne room (now in Berlin, Germany) with richly ornamented glazed bricks and portrayed animals, pseudo-columns, and floral designs in yellow, white, red, and blue on panels of glazed bricks.

The great Ishtar Gate, probably over seventy feet high, led into Procession Way on the north. In Nebuchadnezzar's latest rebuilding of the gate he decorated it with bulls and dragons in glazed brick, the former symbols of the god Adad and the latter of Marduk. The animals appeared alternately in yellow and white on a dark blue background. The double gate pierced the two main defense walls of the city.

This reconstruction of Babylon from the time of King Nebuchadnezzar shows the huge ziggurat or stepped tower on the left and the temple of the chief god Marduk on the right. In the foreground a bridge connects the two parts of the city of Babylon.

In the original arrangement, a section of paved road over two hundred yards long led into the Ishtar Gate. On either side of the roadway lions (sixty on each side), symbols of Ishtar, in molded glazed brick, in red, white, and yellow, lined the walls. The roadway still contains the paving stones inscribed with Nebuchadnezzar's dedication.

The excavator Koldewey carried off to Berlin many bricks from the Ishtar Gate and the approach to it, and a diminutive gate with

its approach has been recreated in the archaeological museum in Berlin. Anyone who walks through this part of the museum can imagine himself as Daniel or Ezekiel walking into Babylon to meet Nebuchadnezzar. Panels of these sacred animals are also on display in the archaeological museums in Baghdad and Istanbul and the Metropolitan Museum in New York. A half-sized reconstruction of the gate has been erected at the entrance to the Babylon excavations.

There are educated guesses, but where and what the famous hanging gardens were cannot now be determined. *(For more on this topic, go to p. 276 or p. 325.)*

Religion

"But. . . let it be known to you, O king, that we do not serve your gods." (Daniel 3:18 NKJV)

When the chips were down, Daniel made it clear to King Nebuchadnezzar that he and his friends would not serve the gods of Babylon. Instead they would hold true to the worship of the God of heaven. Immediately we are curious about the religion on which they were turning their backs.

The Official Religion of Babylon

Daniel and his friends opposed the official polytheistic religion of king and state and temple. They thus had a fairly large family of gods to talk about, but a few were especially important. The view of their functions changed slightly over time, and there tended to be a fusion of one divine figure into another. We shall try to look at the situation as the Hebrew exiles arrived.

Anu, the sky god, from whom the institution of kingship originally descended, stood at the head of the family of gods. In time his consort became Ishtar, goddess of love (fertility) and war. Anu's son Enlil gradually replaced Anu as king of the gods. The national god of Sumer, he was considered the possessor of the Tablet of Destiny, which decreed the fates of men and gods. Babylonians worshiped Ea, another of the major gods, as lord of the deep on which the world rested. They regarded him as the instructor of men in arts and crafts. At least one early myth makes Marduk the son of Ea, but his origins are obscure.

In any case, Marduk came to assume the central place in the Babylonian pantheon long before Nebuchadnezzar's day. He had been enthroned as the patron god of the city of Babylon and gradually assimilated the functions of other gods: for example, of Shamash as god of justice, of Adad as god of rains, and of Sin as the moon god and illuminator of the night.

The astral deities—the sun, moon, and Venus—served as a second group of gods. The populace regarded Sin or Nanna, whose main centers of worship were Ur and Haran, as the greatest. Because he served as controller of the night and of the lunar calendar, with the crescent moon as his symbol, they considered his activities important to mankind. Nabonidus, last king of Babylon, spent much time refurbishing Sin's worship centers. And apparently his efforts to make Sin the head of the Babylonian pantheon and his ineptness in running the government led to his undoing. The leading priests bitterly opposed his

efforts on behalf of Sin. The struggle weakened the state and helped to pave the way for Cyrus' takeover of the empire.

The Babylonians worshiped Ishtar as goddess of war and goddess of sexual love and procreation. She revealed herself to human beings as the morning star and evening star, that is, as the planet Venus. They often associated Adad, the weather god, with Shamash (sun god) and Ishtar. They described him as the lord of abundance, the controller of the floodgates of heaven and earth, with lightning and thunder as his representations. They worshiped Nergal, a much feared god, as the god of pestilence and the underworld. By Nebuchadnezzar's day Marduk, who received the title Bel, "Lord," and Ishtar, often called Belit, "Lady" stood out above the others.

Service to the Gods

The genuine worshipers of the Hebrew God found themselves in a religious environment that had often been denounced by their prophets. Daniel and his three friends considered Yahweh the only god worth worshiping. Now imagine what it must have meant for them to live in Babylon.

Marduk, the chief god of Babylon, with his snake-dragon

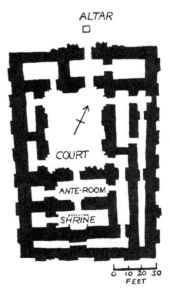

Floor plan of the temple of the goddess Ninmah, located just inside the Ishtar Gate. This has now been fully rebuilt on its original foundations.

Babylonian religion considered the god or goddess present in its image, the idol. Worshipers constructed most of these images of precious wood, dressed with expensive garments, and crowned with tiaras. The image stood on a pedestal in the holy of holies of the temple. There the god lived and was served like the king. Lesser gods paid visits, and the god was fed and entertained with music and dancing. When the god had eaten, the dishes from his meal were sent to the king; dishes from meals of lesser gods were sent to temple administrators and their craftsmen.

A variety of priests and religious functionaries arose to care for the gods and to determine the affairs of the state. Discussion of the classes and duties of these individuals is quite beyond our present interests. But diviners who practiced various kinds of divination became increasingly important at court for the purpose of discovering the will of the gods and prediction of future events. The variety of techniques used in divination included observation of animals' entrails, behavior of birds and other animals, astronomical omens, and the interpretation of dreams. This subject has been introduced briefly in the preceding chapter but needs a Babylonian twist here.

Though the prophetic aspect of astronomy (astrology) appeared in primitive form in Babylonia as early as Hammurabi's day, it reached a high point of development in the first millennium B.C., especially at such centers as Babylon, Nippur, and Uruk (biblical Erech). Babylonian "astrologers" (Daniel 2:10 NKJV, NIV) were active at Nebuchadnezzar's court in Daniel's day and sought to interpret all sorts of meteorological phenomena: thunder, hail, earthquakes, eclipses, positions of planets, and more. The astrologers at a network of observatories throughout the country had the responsibility of making regular reports to the capital. Some of these merely made astronomical observations; others added interpretations based on their fund of astrological texts.

The Babylonians thought that the stars indicated the will of the gods, and by studying their movements it was possible to predict events on earth. They believed that the five planets—Mercury, Venus, Mars, Jupiter, Saturn—along with the sun and moon, represented special manifestations or interpreters of the gods. They represented the gods as follows: Mercury (Nebo), Venus (Ishtar), Mars (Nergal), Jupiter (Marduk), Saturn (Ninib), moon (Sin), and the sun (Shamash).

Personal Religion

The official religion probably did not significantly affect the general public—and that may explain why the Hebrews were able to maintain their religion. To be sure, Babylonians watched the great public processions of the gods and participated in the religious festivals, but they do not seem to have had access to the temples. Individual Babylonians had their own personal gods or goddesses, to whom they offered prayers and sacrifices. They considered it the duty of such deities to protect their worshipers against evil spirits and to intercede on their behalf with the other gods.

Babylonians wore amulets to ward off evil spirits, and they had access to various "priests" or "exorcists" (Daniel 2:10 REB), who could recite incantations and perform rituals to ward off evil powers. Evidently they consulted various types of exorcists and offered prayers and sacrifices at home to their personal gods, but we do not have a lot of light on personal religion. In the nature of the case it was "personal" and therefore largely remains a private affair and unknown to us. In sharp contrast, prophets like Ezekiel and Jeremiah constantly exhorted the Hebrew exiles to worship God on a personal basis.

(For more on this topic, go to p. 279 or p. 333.)

Warfare

A review of the warfare of the period might explain why the Hebrew exiles were so well employed and successful as artisans. Demands of the war effort were great.

Nabopolassar of Babylon won independence from Assyria in 626 B.C. While he consolidated his power, the Medes reorganized their army and strengthened their position on Assyria's northern border. Then in 615 the Medes invaded Assyria, enjoying initial

Hebrew Religious Experience While in Captivity

The story is quite incredible—how the faith of one man, Daniel, influenced and helped preserve the faith of a nation. We are tempted to think of others who influenced a whole nation in their own time—of John Wycliffe, John Hus, Martin Luther, and others. But this is not a book on the heroes of the Christian church. And any such listing of names is dangerous because it is doomed to leave out important figures, especially the unsung heroes.

So what happened to the faith of the Hebrews during Babylonian captivity? What can we know for sure and what can we legitimately surmise? Of course our story begins with Daniel, who was carried off to Babylon in 605 B.C. He took his stand for God and was rewarded for his faith (Daniel 1). He became, in effect, the prime minister (Daniel 2:48). And he continued in some sort of leadership role until the first year of Cyrus (Daniel 1:21, 539 B.C.) and even into his third year (10:1). By that time he would have been at least eighty-five (assumuing that he was fifteen or sixteen when taken to Babylon).

It is tempting to tell the story of Daniel's experience in the Babylonian and Persian courts, but there is not room to do so here (see Daniel 1, 2, 5, 9, and 10 especially). The important point to make is that he served in a high administrative post when the second contingent of exiles (including Ezekiel) arrived in Babylon in 597, when the city of Jerusalem and the temple were destroyed in 586 and more captives were brought to Babylon, and in 539–536, when the restoration of Jews to Palestine took place. While we do not know exactly what he did in each case, he occupied a position in which he could do a great deal.

Daniel's three friends stood with him in his initial test (Daniel 1) and served as his prayer partners as they all dealt with the issue of Nebuchadnezzar's dream (Daniel 2:17, 18). Nebuchadnezzar appointed them to administrative posts in Babylon at the same time (Daniel 2:48, 49). Subsequently Nebuchadnezzar had these men thrown into the fiery furnace for refusing to worship the image of the king. And when God delivered them, they were once again promoted to responsible positions where they could encourage and protect the faith. Their deliverance became the occasion for a royal decree in favor of the worship of God in the king-

dom (Daniel 3). (Daniel may have been away on some administrative business at the time and thus did not become involved in the charge against his three friends.)

From all this we can conclude that God protected the Hebrew exiles in the exercise of their religion. He kept that faith alive during the whole Babylonian exile, for when the restoration took place, those who remained behind made offerings for the rebuilding of the temple in Jerusalem (Ezra 1:4–6). And when the whole company of 42,360 (including a large number of priests and Levites, Ezra 2:36–42) arrived in the Jerusalem area, they reinstituted the sacrificial system and the Feast of Tabernacles and proceeded to lay the foundation for the temple (Ezra 3). The enthusiastic response demonstrates the vitality of the Hebrew faith during captivity.

We therefore surmise that in the various Jewish communities by the River Chebar and elsewhere they kept the Sabbath. Moreover, in Jewish communities they presumably practiced the rite of circumcision as a sign of the covenant with Yahweh. Private prayers, other than by Daniel and his friends, must have been practiced by devout individuals. Note that Daniel prayed three times a day toward Jerusalem (Daniel 6:10, 11). Certainly few of the Jews had access to parts of the Bible, but it seems that Daniel did (see Daniel 9:2, 11).

The synagogue probably originated during the Exile in Babylonia. It may have begun as a gathering for communal worship and mutual support and perhaps for observance of the Sabbath and Hebrew religious festivals. We get some idea of what happened behind the scenes from Ezekiel 8:1, when Ezekiel was with the elders of Judah in his house, or when Ezekiel was "among the captive by the River Chebar" (Ezekiel 1:1).

To what degree they preserved the true faith among the Jews in captivity must be left open to question, but they do not seem to have succumbed in any substantial numbers to the idolatry of the Babylonians. At the end of the captivity large numbers were ready to endure the hardships of reestablishing a community dedicated to the worship of Yahweh, and those who stayed behind gave substantial sums to finance the venture.

successes. At this point the Babylonians and Medes joined hands and cooperated in a three-month siege of Nineveh in 612 and turned the city into heaps of debris. By the end of the year all the main Assyrian towns lay in ruins.

For their part the Medes do not appear to have laid claim to Assyria proper, south and west of the Tigris. They expanded to the east, north, and west. The Babylonians controlled Assyria south of the Tigris but did not occupy it or rebuild damaged towns. Instead they concentrated on the religious and cultural advance of southern Mesopotamia and on the conquest of Syria and Palestine.

Pharaoh Necho II of Egypt went north in 609 to help the remnants of the Assyrian Empire to stand against the Babylonians. Killing King Josiah of Judah, who tried to stop him, he saw an opportunity to expand his holdings and took control of Judah, Philistia, and Phoenicia and held the crossing of the Euphrates. Since nearly all Babylonian trade was with the West, the Babylonians could not tolerate Egyptian control of their gateway to the Mediterranean.

Therefore, after the Babylonians polished off the remnants of the Assyrian Empire in 606, they prepared to move against the Egyptians. Early in the summer of 605 they annihilated the Egyptian garrison at Carchemish. The whole newly-established Egyptian Empire in Palestine-Syria fell like a house of cards. As the crown prince, Nebuchadnezzar took Daniel and other hostages from Judah and moved against Egypt. In August word came that his father had died and he rushed back to Babylon to take the throne.

Almost annually thereafter Nebuchadnezzar found it necessary to lead his troops into the rebellious Westland. Sometimes Egypt stirred up trouble there; sometimes inhabitants of the region rebelled with the hope that Egypt would come to their aid. In 601 Nebuchadnezzar fought a fierce battle with the Egyptians that nearly exhausted both sides and required major rebuilding of their military establishments. The inconclusive nature of the Babylonian attack encouraged the Judeans and others to seek independence from Babylon, resulting in Babylonian determination to crush Judean

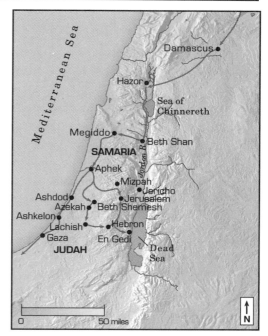

Nebuchadnezzar's Campaigns Against Judah
From 605 to 586 B.C. Nebuchadnezzar conducted several campaigns in Judah. King Jehoiachin was forced to surrender to Nebuchadnezzar in 597 B.C. Jerusalem's destruction came in 586 B.C. as the Babylonians approached from the south.

resistance. They first besieged Jerusalem in 598–97 and deported some of the Jews. The second siege in 588–86 resulted in the destruction of Jerusalem and the temple. Egyptians again came to Judean aid during the final siege, forcing the Babylonians to lift the siege temporarily. After destroying Jerusalem, Nebuchadnezzar laid siege to mainland Tyre; it took him thirteen years to take the city (585–572), which he left in ruins.

After the death of Nebuchadnezzar (562), not only was Babylon internally weak but a new threat arose on the northern and eastern border. Cyrus the Persian rebelled against his Median overlord, took control of the Median Empire, and proceeded to expand it. He defeated Lydia and moved all the way through Asia Minor to the Aegean. Then he circled back to deal with Babylon. Nabonidus (556–539) left the capital for extended periods to refurbish the temples of the moon god Sin in Ur and Haran and establish trade connections in Arabia. His son Belshazzar ran the government in Babylon.

Cyrus had to do little fighting to overwhelm the Babylonians. His propaganda machine served him well, and the inhabitants of Babylon looked on him as a deliverer. The Persian army marched into Babylon on October 12, 539, and Cyrus himself arrived on October 29. The Persians used the strategy of diverting the course of the Euphrates, making the water defenses of the city useless. True to his word, Cyrus kept his army in check, forestalling the usual plunder and destruction. Unlike Nineveh, which had been totally destroyed, Babylon continued prosperous.

The Babylonian army was largely mercenary from Nebuchadnezzar's day on, and it included Greek mercenaries. Thus he could keep the army in the field for extended periods of time and could easily call them up on an annual basis. The Babylonians knew all the tactics of the Assyrians well, as well as the kinds of equipment they used, but they do not seem to have fought as fiercely. Nor do they appear to have used so extensively the tactics of terror for which the Assyrians are known. And of course it is not possible to get the same success from a mercenary army as from a citizen army.

(For more on this topic, go to p. 283 or p. 334.)

Housing and Furniture

To date archaeologists have paid little attention to the private houses of the Neo-Babylonian period (625–539). And were they to do so, they would have problems in reconstructing an understanding of them because construction materials were extremely pulverable. The information we have comes largely from the city of Babylon, where few Hebrews seem to have lived, but the basic style of architecture probably was similar elsewhere. A further limitation on our knowledge is that the houses of the poor and lower middle class were not so well built and have not survived as well as those of the more affluent.

Babylonians built houses of unbaked brick (usually a foot long and four inches thick), which, though it could easily crumble, would not be destroyed by the extremely low rainfall of the region. Roofs and ceilings consisted of mud and tree branches supported by palm poles. From such a ceiling snakes or scorpions might and did fall on people and their beds below. The Babylonians used various magical and practical treatments for scorpion stings.

Presence of Greek Words in the Book of Daniel

Some have contended that the appearance of Greek words in the book of Daniel indicates that the book was written centuries later, after the days of Alexander the Great. The fact that Greek mercenaries served in the Babylonian army, however, implies that the Greek language must have been known to some degree in Babylonia—even by Daniel. Hence the argument for a later date does not seem to carry any weight. The Greek words in question are names of musical instruments appearing in Daniel 3:5, 7.

As in the days of Abraham, houses consisted of rooms surrounding courtyards that were open to the sky. Light and air entered rooms only from the courtyard. Houses were whitewashed inside and outside. One entrance led from the street and there were no windows in the outer walls. Houses frequently had an upper story, especially in town. The thick mud brick walls did help to insulate against the intense heat of the region. Most streets were quite narrow, not much over five or six feet wide, and unpaved.

A moderate-sized house in the city of Babylon might measure some 40 by 60 feet and consist of a living room (30 by 10 feet), a courtyard (c. 20 feet square), and smaller rooms. The wealthy or administrators erected much larger houses. The largest room in the house served as the living room and, with a table and chairs, doubled as a dining room. Located to the south of the courtyard, its entrance faced north, away from the sun. Kitchens and slave quarters lay to the north of the courtyard, with family bedrooms opening off the living room. A doorkeeper had a room inside the entrance to the house. Larger houses with more than one courtyard probably accommodated an extended family, such as a married son and his family.[5]

Floors of the houses of the poor were normally of packed earth covered with reed matting. Floors in the houses of the wealthy usually consisted of burnt brick set in bitumen and might be covered with wool rugs.

Furniture and Equipment

What might the homes of the Hebrew exiles have been like—especially those who were successful artisans or merchants? Furniture for people of at least moderate means included tables for eating, wooden chairs (often with a back and arms and rush seats), stools, wooden beds, and wooden storage chests. Built-in mud brick benches have also been found in excavations. Poorer people might sit on low pottery stools.

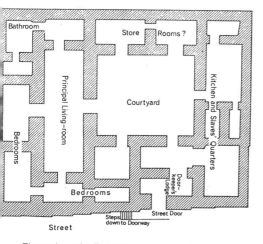

Floor plan of a Babylonian house of the more wealthy. The principal living room ranged from about eighteen by eight feet in the smallest house to forty-five by seventeen feet in the largest.

Eating utensils included spoons normally made of bone or wood, knives of iron or bronze or copper, and single-pronged bone forks. Plates, bowls, and cups were made of pottery, wood, stone, or metal.

Mortars and pestles for the preparation of grains and legumes appear frequently in the excavations. Women usually prepared food on a pottery oven located in the courtyard of the house, but indoor hearths have

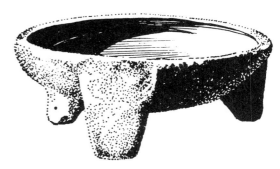

A basalt bowl for crushing grain, from a house in Babylon

been found. And they used copper and bronze kettles and pans for cooking or frying foods during this period.

Torches or lamps provided artificial lighting. Torches consisted of bundles of reeds dipped in oil or bitumen. Lamps were small shoe-shaped pots of oil with a wick sticking out of a hole in the top. The oil burned in them usually came from sesame seed, but olive oil was also used. Babylonians had a kind of soap made of ashes of certain plants mixed with fats.

For more on this topic, go to p. 293 or p. 340.)

Diet and Foodstuffs

Babylonians of the days of Hebrew captivity enjoyed a rich and varied diet. Grain and dates formed the staple food of the period. Among the grains, barley was the main cereal because it tolerated a slightly saline soil, but they also grew wheat, emmer (a variety of wheat), and millet. Fruits and vegetables included dates, pomegranates, grapes, figs, lentils, chickpeas, beans, turnips, leeks, cucumbers, watercress, lettuce, onions, and garlic. Farmers grew these in the shade of the date palms that stood along the canals and rivers, since such crops had to be watered frequently. Dates and date syrup provided a sweetener. Cattle, sheep, and goats provided meat, milk, cheese, hides, and fabrics. The rivers, canals, and the sea furnished fish in abundance. The poor rarely ate meat or fish but lived on a diet of bread and vegetables.

A kitchen hearth, from a house in Babylon

Because rainfall was so sparse in Babylonia, at planting time crops were first watered with moderation. Farmers plowed and seeded at the same time with the seeder (see chapter 2), in furrows approximately two feet apart. Then while barley and other grains grew, the fields were inundated three or four times. They carried on harvesting, threshing, and winnowing about the same as in Assyria (see chapter 9).

For more on this topic, go to p. 294 or p. 341.)

Dress

Though cotton had come in during the Assyrian Empire period, nearly all clothing in Babylonia was made of wool or linen. The poorer people wore a single wool tunic, with short sleeves, that extended to the feet, and they normally went barefoot.

Wealthier individuals wore linen tunics with short sleeves, also extending to the feet, with woolen tunics over them. They topped these with white cloaks that were often beautifully embroidered with animals or plants. Men and women let their hair grow long and kept it in place with a headband or turban. Women often wound their hair around their heads, but both men and women might let it hang to shoulder length. Men wore long wavy beards, frequently extending down on the chest. Both sexes sported necklaces, bracelets, and earrings and used a lot of perfumes and body oils, no doubt to counter some of the stench around them. Men carried hand-carved walking sticks with the top shaped like an apple, a flower, an eagle, or some other figure. Sometimes these fancy walking sticks

were buried with their owners. Both men and women wore sandals.

For more on this topic, go to p. 295 or p. 341.)

Family Life

Two great social divisions dominated Babylonian society and in the country at large during the Neo-Babylonian Empire. One division was between free persons and slaves, and the other between temple personnel and lay persons. To a degree they cut across each other. As large-scale businesses, the temples of Babylonia probably owned about half of the total land of the country in Nebuchadnezzar's day and so were very important to the national economy. Farmers rented some temple farms, while temple slaves worked others. The temple social structure ranged from the lowest grade of slaves to the highest ranking priests, who could influence governmental policy at the highest level.

In secular society, slaves occupied the lowest category. Often slaves in private households had better lives than temple slaves, or even poor freemen, if they enjoyed good relationships with their masters. Male private slaves usually performed manual labor in keeping with the craft of the owner. A young female slave served as a maid in the household and possibly also as a concubine for the master of the house or his teenage son. Soldiers might bring home a captive girl as a concubine. Children born to slaves continued in slavery unless adopted by the family, which commonly did not occur unless the head of the house had no children. The more affluent in Nebuchadnezzar's day might have two or three or more household slaves, the poor none. Some of the wealthy might own a hundred or more slaves if they had large farms or industrial or business establishments.

Though free men might engage in a wide variety of crafts and professions, the individual did not usually have much choice. A son generally followed in his father's footsteps, and he learned the trade from his father, or possibly by an apprenticeship arrangement with another. Formal education seems to have been available largely or almost exclusively at the temples for those who entered some of the religious professions. But we know almost nothing about that. There must have been some educational opportunity for those who went into business, especially in international trade, where knowledge of other languages and cultures was important.

The king and the royal officials stood at the apex of society. The royal officials included provincial governors, army commanders (including the commander-in-chief), the Lord Chamberlain or supervisor of the palace, the Chief Baker or the head cook of the palace, Secretary of the Crown Prince, and Supervisor of the Harem, among others.

Marriage arrangements were made between parents of the groom and parents of the bride. The girl would probably live in the groom's father's household until he set up a household of his own or his father died and he inherited the property. There is no evidence that married women had to be veiled in public.

Houses, furniture, and diet have already been discussed, but a word is in order about the eating of meals. Babylonians who could afford it ate four meals a day: a good breakfast, a light lunch, a heavy meal, and a light supper late in the day. The average worker got up by 5:00 a.m., had breakfast and was at work before 8:00, took a light lunch around noon and then had a siesta during the impossibly hot part of the day. Following additional hours of work, he returned home at dark for the main evening meal. After that they might enjoy short entertainment somewhere nearby (perhaps at a temple). Or members of the family might play one of the board games known in the region. Before retiring, the family had a light supper.

Meals began with a slave pouring water over the hands of the diners into a basin beneath. The family then sat around the table and the head of the family said a prayer, calling on one of the gods. The food was brought in, usually in one large vessel, from which all helped themselves, generally with their fingers.

Most of the time the meal consisted largely of vegetable products, but the more well-to-do might have beef, mutton, goat meat, poultry, or fish. Barley bread, which looked like a pancake, served as the main source of carbohydrates for all classes. They also frequently ate barley meal cooked with water to make a kind of porridge. Beer made from barley served as the main drink, but cold water was also widely consumed. After a meal the diners wiped their mouths on table napkins and slaves again poured water over their hands.

Babylonian Medicine

What kind of medical service was available in Babylon during the Hebrew exile? Much of our knowledge of Babylonian medicine comes from texts discovered in the library of King Ashurbanipal in Nineveh (7th century B.C.), but other materials exist. These texts contain a tangle of crude superstition and practical observation. There were two main classes of medical texts: accounts of symptoms and prescriptions for various complaints. Illness was usually thought to be due either to possession by a devil or the action of a deity. For example, a text on symptoms says, "If he grinds his teeth, and his hands and feet shake, it is the hand of the god Sin [the moon god]; he will die." So sometimes an exorcist made an attempt to effect a cure through magic. At other times a physician administered a variety of curative potions, enemas, purgatives, lotions, and poultices. For diseases considered incurable, no medical or magical treatment was suggested.

Our knowledge of Babylonian healing potential is limited by the fact that we cannot identify hundreds of names of plants they used in medical prescriptions. Their ability to treat disease was hindered by their ignorance of the functions of most internal organs. And they did not advance their knowledge of anatomy and physiology because of a religious taboo on dissection of the human body. Surgical methods appear to have been virtually unknown.

For more on this topic, go to p. 296 or p. 341.)

Work, Travel, and Commerce

We have already seen that the temples controlled up to half of the land of Babylonia. The temples owned boats and sailed them on the canals of Babylonia to pick up produce from various agricultural units and bring it into central warehouses. Much of the goods collected in this way went out again to other parts of the country and even abroad. In the existing commercial records of the time we find the temples exchanging agricultural goods for metal, timber, cloth, and other commodities from as far away as Asia Minor. We also discover that the temples leased boats from private concerns to carry on their business. And there are indications that secular establishments, private or government, also en-gaged in extensive commercial activities.

As the sixth century wore on, the economic strains became increasingly evident in Babylonia. Government expenditures to build Babylon and other cities in Nebuchadnezzar's day and to refurbish religious centers during Nabonidus' reign put the pressure of high taxes on the economy. So did the cost of supporting a large standing army. Meanwhile Phoenician centers (part of the Babylonian Empire) lost much of their former wealth and commercial prowess as Greek commercial centers came into their own. Between 600 and 550 B.C. there was an inflationary spiral while wages remained depressed.

Weights and Measures

The Hebrews encountered a more sophisticated system of weights and measures than they had access to in Judah. The Babylonians developed a system of weights and measures that was essentially sexages-imal (based on the number 60). These measures varied somewhat from period to period and town to town. In the Neo-Babylonian period a talent or load was the weight that a man theoretically could carry (67 pounds). They divided this into 60 minas. The mina as 1/60 of a talent was 18 ounces. The shekel was 1/60 of a mina. Measures of length were based on the cubit (about a half meter). The Babylonian mile was some ten kilometers in length or about six of our miles.

The Trades

Nebuchadnezzar's Babylonians experienced a great deal of division of labor in a wide range of crafts or professions. They had boatmen, fishermen, leatherworkers and shoemakers, matmakers and weavers, confectioners and bakers, brewers, oil-pressers, coppersmiths, silversmiths, goldsmiths, ironsmiths, jewelers, millers, fowlers, carpenters, stonemasons, brickmakers, canal diggers, and scribes, to name a few. As we have noted, one usually learned how to follow these trades from his father or in an apprenticeship arrangement.

God graciously cared for His people during the decades of Babylonian captivity, while preparing them for the day when the Persians would restore them to the land of Palestine. That is the story of the next chapter.
For more on this topic, go to p. 298 or p. 342.)

NOTES:

[1]W. F. Albright, "King Joiachin in Exile," *Biblical Archaeologist* (1942), 49–55.

[2]J. Maxwell Miller and John H. Hayes, *A History of Ancient Israel and Judah* (Philadelphia: Westminster Press, 1986), 433.

[3]H. V. Hilprecht, *Explorations in Bible Lands* (Philadelphia: A. J. Holman, 1903), 409–15.

[4]H. W. F. Saggs, *Everyday Life in Babylonia and Assyria* (London: B. T. Batsford, 1965), 158.

[5]See James G. Macqueen, *Babylon* (London: Robert Hale, 1964), 181.

BIBLIOGRAPHY:

Black, Jeremy and Anthony Green. *Gods, Demons and Symbols of Ancient Mesopotamia.* London: British Museum Press, 1992.

Beaulieu, Paul-Alain. *The Reign of Nabonidus King of Babylon 556–539 B.C.* New Haven: Yale University Press, 1989.

Larue, Gerald A. *Babylon and the Bible.* Grand Rapids: Baker, 1969.

Macqueen, James G. *Babylon.* London: Robert Hale, 1964.

Oates, Joan. *Babylon.* London: Thames & Hudson, rev. ed., 1986.

Parker, Richard A., and Waldo H. Dubberstein. *Babylonian Chronology 626 B.C.–A.D. 45.* Chicago: The Oriental Institute, rev. ed., 1946.

Saggs, H. W. F. *Babylonians.* Norman, Okla.: University of Oklahoma Press, 1995.

Saggs, H. W. F. *Everyday Life in Babylonia and Assyria.* New York: G. P. Putnam's Sons, 1965.

Saggs, H. W. F. *The Greatness That Was Babylon.* London: Sidwick & Jackson, 2nd ed., 1988.

Wellard, James. *Babylon.* New York: Saturday Review Press, 1972.

Wiseman, D. J. *Chronicles of Chaldaean Kings.* London: British Museum Press, 1961.

LIFE UNDER PERSIAN PATRONAGE

(2 Chronicles 36; Ezra; Nehemiah; Esther; Daniel 6; Haggai; Zechariah; Malachi)

I magine the Cubans of Miami and many other American cities suddenly being granted the opportunity to return to Cuba to a dilapidated Havana, a wasted-away infrastructure, a poverty-stricken countryside. How many would return? Would they have the patience to rebuild their beloved country if they did return? How would they react if pockets of communists waged guerrilla warfare? In many ways that would be a picture of what happened to the Hebrews who had been resettled in Babylon and Assyria in what was called a captivity—but for seventy years had been a growing adaptation to the economic and social realities that existed in their communities. The one thing this captivity had seemingly done for them is healed them of idol worship and generated a new devotion to Yahweh.

In God's providence, and in answer to the prophecy given by Isaiah (Isaiah 44:28), the Jewish state was reborn in a Persian cradle. From the devastation wrought in Israel and Judah by Assyrians and Babylonians under the judgment of God, Israel was revived as a political unit within the new Persian Empire. Her people, scattered to the winds, responded in substantial numbers to the Persian invitation

to return to their homeland of Palestine. There in the province of Judah they built new homes, a social structure, a house for God, and ultimately the walls of Jerusalem. The condemnation for national and personal sins had brought divine justice. Now God in His wrath remembered mercy (Habakkuk 3:2). Cyrus, God's "anointed" (Isaiah 45:1), issued a decree permitting the Jews to return to their land (Ezra 1:1–4). Many of those who had wept by the waters of Babylon could rejoice once more on Mount Zion.

The Story of Hebrew Restoration

Details of Hebrew restoration appear in the discussion of the reigns of the Persian

The Cyrus Cylinder (now in the British Museum) records Cyrus's permission for captive peoples to return to their homes and rebuild their temples. This was a broad decree that included more than the Hebrews.

Shifts on the International Stage

The return of the Hebrews from captivity became possible because of a major change of the actors and props on the international stage. Nineveh, capital of powerful Assyria, destroyer of the northern kingdom of Israel, fell to the combined armies of the Medes from the East and rebellious Babylonians in 612 B.C. In the division of the Assyrian Empire that followed, the Medes took the eastern part (east and north of the Tigris); the Babylonians took the western part, but could not retain a hold on Egypt. In 586 B.C., under the leadership of Nebuchadnezzar (605–561), Babylon brought to an end the Kingdom of Judah, utterly destroying her cities (including Jerusalem and the temple) and deporting a large segment of her population. Later, Cyrus the Persian successfully took control of the Median Empire and began to chip away at Babylonian power in the East. Finally he took Babylon in 539 B.C. and promptly set the stage for Jewish repatriation and state building.

kings. But the story is clearer if it is first told in summary. Cyrus the Great in 539–38 B.C. issued a decree permitting the exiles to return to the Jerusalem area and rebuild their homes and the temple (Ezra 1). A large contingent did return within a year or two under the leadership of Zerubbabel and laid the foundations of the temple but did not complete it.

Beginning in the second year of Darius (520 B.C.; Haggai 1:1; Zechariah 1:1), the prophets Haggai and Zechariah sought to remedy that situation by exhorting the people to complete the temple. This was completed in the sixth year of Darius (515; Ezra 6:15). Ezra himself returned with another contingent of Jews in the seventh year of Artaxerxes (458 B.C.; Ezra 7:1, 8).

Meanwhile, the story of Esther took place, beginning in the third year of the reign of Ahasuerus or Xerxes in 484–3 (Esther 1:3). Thus this event occurred during the chronological gap between Ezra 6 and 7.

Nehemiah became greatly disturbed over run-down conditions in Jerusalem in the twentieth year of King Artaxerxes (Nehemiah 2:1) and won permission to return and rebuild the walls of the city (444). Malachi did his preaching about 435 B.C. and closed out the Old Testament history of the Jews and the Old Testament canon of Scripture as well.

The Land

Hebrews in the Land

When we say Jews lived in Persia and under Persian auspices, they lived in both Persia proper and the Persian Empire at large. In Persia proper they are especially connected with Shushan (Susa), the winter capital or residence of the royal court. Nehemiah's conversation with King Artaxerxes about rebuilding the walls of Jerusalem took place there (Nehemiah 1:1), as did Esther's appeal to Xerxes (Esther 1:2). Therefore we know that both accounts took place during the winter. Susa stood in the lowlands at the foot of the Zagros

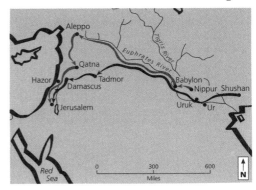

When Cyrus the Persian captured Babylon in 539 B.C., government controls on captive peoples began to loosen. That made it possible for Jews to gradually return to Palestine. Repatriation occurred in three major waves.

Zerubbabel's return (538-537 B.C.; Ezra 2:2)
Ezra's return (458 B.C.; Ezra 7:1–9)
Nehemiah's return (444 B.C.; Neh. 2:1–9)

The Jews return from Exile

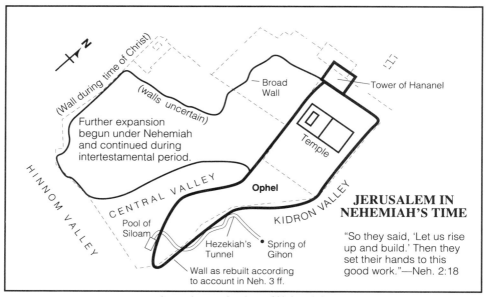

Jerusalem at the time of Nehemiah

Mountains, some 150 miles north of the head of the Persian Gulf. The pleasant winter climate there provided the Persian kings with the equivalent of going to Florida for the winter.

How Jews got to Susa we do not really know. After destroying the northern kingdom, Sargon II of Assyria settled some of the captives from Samaria in the "cities of the Medes" (2 Kings 17:6). Presumably Susa was one of those cities. But the Jews of Susa in Esther's day seem to have been more devout than the inhabitants of the northern kingdom in general. So possibly some or most of those people spilled over into Persia from the later Babylonian captivity.

All Jews lived in the Persian Empire at large during the great days of that empire. Persia came to control Babylonia, where other exiles lived. And the homeland of Palestine as well as the land of Egypt, where many Jews had fled, fell under Persian control.

The territory of Judah in the days of the Restoration, as indicated in the books of Ezra and Nehemiah, extended from just north of Bethel almost to Hebron in the south, and from the Jordan River to Gezer in the west. This was an area about twenty-five miles north and south and

slightly more than that east and west. In size the district was about eight hundred square miles, or four-fifths as large as Rhode Island.

Time Capsule

539–38	Cyrus's decree permitting the Jews to return to Palestine
538–36	First group of exiles returns to Jerusalem. Work on reconstruction of the temple began and was soon stopped.
520	Work on the temple was resumed
515	Temple completed and rededicated
484	Story of Esther began
479	Esther became queen
458	Ezra's return
444	Nehemiah returned and rebuilt the walls of Jerusalem
435	Malachi's preaching and the end of the Old Testament

The Extent of Empire

When we first come upon the Medes (and the Persian lands within their realm), we find them controlling an area in the western part of modern Iran. Subsequently they cooperated with the Babylonians in destroying the Assyrian Empire in 612 B.C. Then in 559 B.C., Cyrus, a Persian, later called the Great, rebelled against his Median overlord and established control of the Achaemenid (Persian) dynasty over the Median Empire. He went on to add Asia Minor and Mesopotamia to Medo-Persian holdings and died fighting to extend his borders in the east. His successor, Cambyses (530-522 B.C.), added Egypt to the empire, and Darius I (521-486 B.C.) expanded holdings in the east and moved across the Hellespont into Greece.

Although the Greeks were able to repel the Persians, Darius with his conquests had created the greatest empire of Western Asia up to that time. More than 3,000 miles in extent from east to west, the empire stretched from the Indus River in India to the Mediterranean and also included Asia Minor and part of Greece. To give some idea of size, Darius built a great postal road to connect the biblical cities of Susa in west-

The Country of the Aryans

Persia is the anglicized form of Persis (Parse or Fars), the section of Iran adjacent to the Persian Gulf. Native Persians have always used the term Iran to designate their indefinitely bounded country. And this has been the official name of the country since 1935. The modern name Iran is derived from the ancient Ariana, meaning "the country of the Aryans." The Aryans were various Indo-European peoples who settled during prehistoric times in areas north and east of the Persian Gulf.

ern Iran and Sardis in western Asia Minor, a span of 1,600 miles. The empire included three great river valleys: the Indus, the Tigris-Euphrates, and the Nile.

The Persian Homeland

Geographically, Iran is an inclusive term referring to the large plateau between the plain of the Tigris on the west and the Indus River valley to the east. On the south it is bounded by the Persian Gulf and the Indian

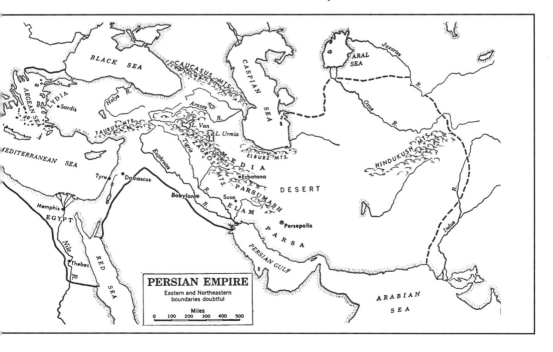

PERSIAN EMPIRE
Eastern and Northeastern
boundaries doubtful

Miles
0   100   200   300   400   500

Ocean, and on the north by the Caspian Sea and chains of mountains that extend eastward and westward from the south end of the Caspian.

The Plateau

The plateau of Iran, the homeland of the ancient Persians, averages 3,000 to 5,000 feet in altitude. Over half of the drainage of the plateau flows inward to form inland lakes and sterile swamps. In its central region lie great sand and salt deserts. This continuous desert region stretches northwest to southeast about 800 miles in length and varies from 100 to 200 miles in width.

At the western edge of the plateau rise the Zagros Mountains, with several peaks over 10,000 feet. This range is about 600 miles in length and 120 miles in width. It consists of numerous parallel folds enclosing fruitful valleys where wheat, barley, and other grains and fruits grow. South of the Caspian Sea stand the Elburz Mountains, the highest peak of which is Mount Damavand (or Demavand), about 60 miles northeast of modern Tehran. Once volcanic, it is a conical peak 18,934 feet high.

To the northwest, the highlands of Armenia and the mountains of Asia Minor unite the Iranian Plateau. To the northeast, the mountains of Khurasan (or Khorasan) and the Hindu Kush Range link the plateau to the Himalayas. The total area of the plateau is over one million square miles, more than one-third the size of the forty-eight contiguous United States.

Rainfall

As a whole, Iran suffers low rainfall totals. Abundant rainfall falls only on the plain south of the Caspian Sea and on the Elburz and Zagros Mountains. For example, at Resht, near the Caspian, precipitation totals over fifty-six inches per year, but south of the Elburz Mountains at the national capital of Tehran the figure drops to nine inches. Farther south in the interior rainfall comes to only two inches per year. At the head of the Persian Gulf it annually measures about ten inches.

Resources

Iran is primarily an agricultural and stockbreeding country. The northwestern part of the country, Azerbaijan, contains fertile valleys with sufficient rainfall for growing various kinds of grain and fruits and vegetables. Agriculture prospers on the plain between the Caspian Sea and the Elburz Mountains, as it does in the fertile valleys of the mountains of Khurasan. The latter constitute the granary of Iran.

But Iran also possessed rich mineral resources. Its quarries provided marble, and its mountain slopes yielded building woods for the Sumerian princes as early as the third millennium B.C. The Persians exploited gold, iron, copper, tin, and lead mines early and especially attracted the attention of the Assyrians. Sargon of Akkad had already been interested in the wealth of the region 1,500 years earlier.

Some Great Imperial Cities

The modern city of Hamadan occupies the site of ancient Ecbatana, about 180 miles southwest of Tehran, high in the Zagros Mountains of western Iran. Cyrus the Great made it his summer capital and apparently from this site issued the decree allowing the Jews to return to Jerusalem and build the temple. We conclude this from the fact that in the palace there Darius I later found the scrolls of Cyrus containing this authorization. Ezra 6:2 gives the name of the place as Achmetha, the Aramaic form of Ecbatana. The city had been the capital of the Medes before Cyrus' revolt. A magnificent palace and fortress once stood there, remains of which archaeologists have discovered in the northeastern part of the modern city.

Cyrus, however, established his main capital at Pasargadae, thirty miles northeast of the later royal center at Persepolis. Indica-tions are that he founded it on the site of his victory over Astyages the Mede. The royal complex seems to have consisted of several pavilions set among gardens and surrounded by a masonry wall. The tomb of Cyrus still stands there.

Darius I constructed the great center of Persepolis soon after his accession in 521

B.C. There he built a large stone platform forty feet high, covering thirty-three acres. On this he erected several impressive structures, some of which scholars have not yet been able to interpret. Discussion appears in the next section.

We've already discussed Susa, at the foot of the Zagros Mountains, and it will receive further attention in the next section on government.

(For more on this topic, go to p. 303 or p. 346.)

(For more on this topic, go to p. 303 or p. 346.)

Government

The Administration of Cryus

"Thus says Cyrus king of Persia: All the kingdoms of the earth the LORD God of heaven has given me. And He has commanded me to build Him a house at Jerusalem which is in Judah. Who is there among you of all His people? May the LORD his God be with him, and let him go up!" (2 Chronicles 36:23 NKJV)

As Cyrus conquered territories he emphasized winning the favor of the gods, the priesthoods, and their followers in those lands. According to the Cyrus Cylinder (found by H. Rassam at Babylon late in the nineteenth century; see chapter 1), dating almost certainly to 538 B.C., Cyrus reversed the deportation policies of the Assyrians and Babylonians. He permitted deported peoples to return to their ancestral lands to rebuild their homes and the temples of their gods.[1] In the process he removed sources of irritation among captive peoples.

Presumably he implemented this general policy by specific decrees to individual subject peoples. Ezra 1 and the 2 Chronicles 36 quotation noted above detail the pronouncement given to the Jews. Hence, while the Bible clearly says that Cyrus served as God's "anointed" in restoring the Jews to their homeland, it becomes clear that this was not an isolated policy aimed at Jews only.

As to other aspects of Cyrus' administration, we discover that he apparently chose to rule the provinces of the empire through his own appointees instead of vassal kings, but he did not insist that they all be Persians. A case in point is the Jewish Sheshbazzar (Ezra 1:8, 11), whom he sent as governor to Jerusalem, but other examples could be given. Likewise, Cyrus and his son Cambyses appointed non-Persians as army commanders. Of the three known generals of Cyrus, two were Medes and one a former Babylonian governor. He seems to have been generous toward his nobles and apparently had a certain charisma, or at least an effective propaganda machine, that led Medes, Babylonians, Elamites, Jews, and others to accept him as their legitimate ruler.

Generally Cyrus seems to have been humane. For example, when he took over the Babylonian Empire, he permitted Nabonidus (Nabunaid), the last king, to live in peace. When Nabonidus died a year later, Cyrus ordered a

Tomb of Cyrus
Isaiah prophesied the coming of Cyrus, first king of the Persian Empire, to deliver the Jews from their Babylonian Exile (Isaiah 44:28; 45:1). A powerful ruler, Cyrus united the Medes and the Persians to conquer Babylon, Assyria, and Lydia. He then permitted the exiles within these conquered lands to return to their homes. It was Cyrus who ordered the rebuilding of the temple at Jerusalem. He died in 530 B.C. and was entombed at Pasargadae, Persia, in this vault built in limestone blocks tied together by iron clamps.

period of national mourning for him. Though Cyrus may have been a worshiper of Ahuramazda, he followed a policy of religious tolerance that portrayed himself as a ruler chosen by Marduk among the Babylonians, Yahweh among the Jews, and by other deities as it served his purpose.

Cyrus' Sons

Cyrus left behind two sons: Cambyses and Bardiya or Smerdis. Cambyses held the kingship from 529 to 522. While he was leading a military campaign in Egypt, his brother organized a revolt in Persis. When Cambyses got wind of it, he jumped on his horse in a great hurry and apparently wounded himself with his own sword. He died from the wound. I conclude that he did not commit suicide, as is often charged.

Meanwhile Darius, an Achaemenid prince of a collateral line, was rising to power in the military and got control of the disciplined Persian infantry and cavalry. He put forth the story that Cambyses had murdered Smerdis earlier in his reign to eliminate a threat to his rule. And he claimed that a certain Gaumata had impersonated Smerdis and seized the throne in 522. Then Darius declared that he and six others slew the imposter and took the throne. I believe that there was no imposter; Darius killed the real Smerdis and was therefore guilty of regicide.

Darius' Administration

In any event, Darius did take the throne and spent all of 521 putting down revolts and consolidating his hold on the empire, which had dissolved into virtual chaos after the death of Cambyses. Then he launched major conquests (to be discussed later) and built an empire that extended from the Indus River in the East to the Aegean Sea and on into Greece in the West, and through Syria, Palestine, and Egypt to Libya in the southwest. From east to west, it was as wide as the continental United States, and was the largest empire of western Asia in ancient times. After he took this vast territory, Darius proceeded to organize his empire as Cyrus had never done—and became a key figure in the rebuilding of Jerusalem.

To begin with, Darius evidently divided his empire into twenty provinces or satrapies, ruled by governors or satraps. Many of these satrapies encompassed several peoples, with one of them serving as a nucleus. He initiated land surveys and assessed annual taxes/tribute. He placed Palestine in the fifth satrapy, along with Phoenicia, Syria, and Cyprus. He installed strong garrisons, partly Persian in composition, in great cities and at important frontier posts. Satraps normally shouldered both civil and military responsibilities. They collected tribute, raised military levies, and provided for justice and security. They modeled their courts and their protocol after that of the king.

Sculptured head of Darius I
(From the rock relief of Behistun)

For purposes of commerce and communication, Darius reopened the canal between the Pelusiac branch of the Nile near Bubastis and the Red Sea near Suez. About eighty feet wide, it was broad enough for two ships to pass. The last Egyptian pharaoh to concern himself with this canal had been Necho (c. 600 B.C.). Thus Darius united by water the three heavily populated river valleys of the ancient world (Indus, Tigris-Euphrates, Nile). On land, he built some important roads, queen of which was the great royal road extending 1,600 miles from Susa to Sardis.

Darius also sought to provide a standard currency and a system of weights and measures. He tried to ensure that the laws of the land were known to those who administered them, but he does not seem to deserve

Tombs of Darius I (left) and Artaxerxes I near the royal city of Persepolis

his reputation as a lawgiver claimed for him in modern times.

Darius transformed a feudal kingship into an oriental despotism with an elaborate court ceremony, and thus he greatly increased the distance between himself and his subjects. He enjoyed building palaces and constructed several, but the two greatest were at Susa and Persepolis. A faithful Zoroastrian, Darius viewed himself as the representative on earth of Ahuramazda.

During his reign the second stage of the Jewish restoration in Palestine took place: the completion of the temple. Though the foundations of the second temple had been laid in the second year after the return from Babylon, fierce opposition to the work had forced its stoppage. Finally during the second year of Darius (520), the preaching of the prophets Haggai and Zechariah stirred up the people to resume construction (see Haggai 1:1; Zechariah 1:1; Ezra 5:1–2).

When the local enemies of the Jews tried to stop the work again, the leaders of the Jews asked that a check of the archives be made to see if Cyrus' decree permitting reconstruction of the temple could be found. As previously mentioned, they located the decree. They did not find the decree in Babylon, where Jewish leaders thought it would be. Instead, they found it at Ecbatana in Media. Hence the decree must have been issued when the court was there during the summer of the year 539–538. Darius fully honored the decree and ordered that the costs of construction should be paid out of the royal treasury (Ezra 6:1–15). The temple was completed in the sixth year of Darius (Ezra 6:15), on the third day of the month Adar, which would have been March 12, 515 B.C.

The governmental procedures and practices that Darius I initiated continued more or less intact through the two centuries of Persian history down to the days of Alexander the Great. But of course there were variations. For one thing, the number of provinces apparently varied slightly from time to time. And within the provinces there were dozens of ethnic groups or "nations," frequently mentioned in Greek or Persian sources. The 127 provinces of Esther 1:1 and the 120 of Daniel 6:1 are to be understood as groups of peoples or ethnic districts within the satrapies, and should not be thought to

The royal titles of King Xerxes (the biblical Ahasuerus of Esther 1:1) found at his palace at Persepolis

conflict with official numbers of 20 or 23 satrapies. Though the Hebrews spoke of provinces of Judah and Samaria, they were only sub-districts in the fifth Persian satrapy.

Rule of Xerxes

Darius died near the end of November 486 B.C. and his son Xerxes (485–465) ascended the throne. Xerxes was the king's Greek name; in the Old Testament he is known as Ahasuerus (Ezra 4:6; Esther 1:1; etc.), a rough equivalent of his Persian name. As Ahasuerus he appears as the husband of Esther. Xerxes inherited his major tasks. First he had to suppress a revolt in Egypt, which had flared just before his father's death, and then he had to deal with the Greek problem. Within about a year he thoroughly squelched the Egyptian rebellion. The Greek challenge was quite another matter and is described in the section on warfare. Comments on the Esther story appear there too.

Reign of Artaxerxes

After Xerxes, Artaxerxes I ruled Persia (464–424). Records of his reign are sparse, so it is not as well documented as other Persian administrations. During the first twenty years of his reign he was involved in considerable warfare, but a treaty with Athens in 445 brought an end to that. Thereafter the reign of Artaxerxes seems to have been peaceful, and the king enjoyed a reputation for mildness and magnanimity.

Evidently Artaxerxes I figures in the narrative of Ezra and Nehemiah, rather than Artaxerxes II (404–359 B.C.). This is the general (but not universal) conclusion of scholarship today.[2] Ezra led a second contingent of Jews to Jerusalem in the seventh year of Artaxerxes I or 458 (Ezra 7:1, 8). It is clear, then, that the narrative of Ezra has a gap of over fifty-seven years between chapters 6 and 7. Chapter 6 ends with the dedication of the temple in 515, in the sixth year of Darius. Chapter 7 picks up the account in the seventh year of Artaxerxes (458).

Between the two chapters occurred the reign of Xerxes. Since Esther was married to Xerxes, the story of Esther must be placed between Ezra 6 and 7. The events of the book of Nehemiah occurred later in the reign of Artaxerxes. Nehemiah returned to Jerusalem in the twentieth year of Artaxerxes or 444 B.C. to rebuild the walls

This relief from Persepolis shows King Darius I on the throne and the crown prince Xerxes behind him.

Cliffside tomb of Xerxes (Gustav Jeeninga)

(Nehemiah 2:1) and made a second visit to Jerusalem in the thirty-second year of Artaxerxes or 433 B.C. (Nehemiah 13:6).

Comments on the government during the last days of the empire appear in the next chapter in connection with Alexander's successes.

The King and His Court

"So it was, when the king saw Queen Esther standing in the court, that she found favor in his sight, and the king held out to Esther the golden scepter that was in his hand. Then Esther went near and touched the top of the scepter." (Esther 5:2 NKJV)

The Persians did not consider their king divine while alive, nor was he deified after death. But he was considered to be the elect of the god Ahuramazda, whose regent he was on earth. From the reign of Darius I on, the king became increasingly inaccessible, even unapproachable (note the Esther reference above). In fact, he lived largely in seclusion and was viewed as being above his subjects: in physical prowess, judgment, and control of property. He could do anything he pleased—and he could do no wrong.

The king was, in fact, supposed to keep his promises perfectly. Once he gave an order, he could not revoke it. This is reflected in the story of Esther, when Xerxes could not simply negate the order engineered by Haman to annihilate the Jews, but had to issue a counter order permitting the Jews to defend themselves (see Esther 8:8). The king's counselors did not really advise him but told him what they thought he wanted to hear. So he had little opportunity to benefit from their individual and collective wisdom, growing out of honest debate.

Persians expected their king to be brave in battle, and he received extensive training in archery, throwing the spear, horseback riding, and hunting. They also expected him to be the father of many children. To that end Darius I had six known wives, but subsequent kings normally had only one. They did have many concubines in their harems, however. They also expected the eldest son of his wife to succeed the king on the throne, but other sons or sons-in-law could be appointed to positions in government, business, and the army to extend his power base. Persian kings did not fill their harems with non-Persian women, however, as did Solomon, for political reasons. They came from the leading Persian families.

What the king ate and the way he dressed appear later in connection with diet and clothing in general. But comments on his regal aspects are in order here. He sat on

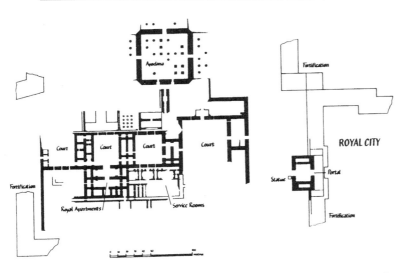

Plan of the palace of Darius I at Susa. The Apadana is the audience hall.

(After J. Perrot)

courts) and the audience hall were decorated with glazed brick panels of lions, winged bulls and griffons, and the famous spearmen of the guard. Many of these the French excavators carted off to the Louvre in Paris, where they are now on display. There we can look at the very scenes Esther saw when she walked the palace in 479 B.C.

A monumental gatehouse stood to the east of the palace. This measured 131 by 92 feet and had a central room 69 feet square. It was in this area that Mordecai sat (e.g., Esther 2:19, 21; 5:9, 13).[3] The Persians commonly used Susa as a capital during the winter months from October to May, and Xerxes held court there. In the summer temperatures grow intolerable—as high as 140° in August, and the king and his court moved to the mountains. Susa (biblical Shushan) was located about 150 miles from the head of the Persian Gulf.

Ecbatana (Achmetha)

Ecbatana, where Cyrus in the summer of 538 B.C. issued the decree permitting the

a high throne with a footstool and normally wore a crown in public. A purple canopy resting on columns covered the throne. In his hand he held a golden scepter, and he was decked out with an abundance of jewelry: necklaces, bracelets, and earrings. Individuals prostrated themselves before the king with the chin or forehead touching the ground or floor, a posture that the Greeks called "proskynesis." Attendants held fly whisks and scent bottles, and incense burners stood in the court. Greek and Egyptian doctors cared for the king's physical needs. An umbrella protected him when out in the sun.

The Capitals and Palaces of Persia

Susa

Darius I made Susa the administrative capital of the Persian Empire. There, north of the acropolis of Susa, he built a great terrace almost fifty feet high and covering about thirty-five acres. He surrounded the entire city of some 175 acres with a defensive wall and perhaps a moat. North of the palace he erected a great audience hall with columns presumably about 65 feet high and topped with capitals in the form of bulls' heads. The palace (arranged around three

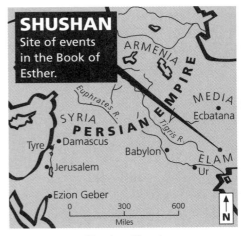

Shushan (Susa)

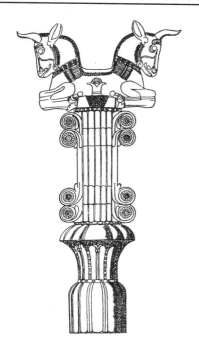

On the top of the sixty-five-foot columns of the audience hall at Susa were capitals of white marble, fifteen feet high. These capitals were composed of four elements, as pictured, topped with bulls' heads, as shown above. Examples may be seen in the Louvre Museum in Paris.

feet high and eight feet square. The other may have had a black limestone cap and was almost seven feet high and nine feet square. While we cannot be dogmatic about the identification of these structures, some believe that they were twin altars to Ahura-mazda and Anahita (see next section on Religion).

The citadel stood on a hill that rose over 160 feet above the plain. A terrace constructed on the hill was 48 feet high and consisted of well-formed limestone blocks fitted together with metal clamps. On this stood a columned hall 82 by 23 feet. Many believe the citadel to have been one of the Persian treasuries.

The palace complex had, first, the residential palace, measuring 250 by 138 feet. This had a brilliantly decorated central hall with five rows of six columns. Side rooms probably served domestic purposes. South

Jews to return to Palestine and rebuild the temple (see Ezra 6:2), was located at an altitude of 5,500 feet about 230 miles southwest of Tehran. This former Median capital often served as the summer residence of the Persian kings. The palace there had been built of cedar and cypress, with exposed parts plated with silver or gold.[4]

Pasargadae[5]

Cyrus the Great chose Pasargadae (about fifty miles north of Persepolis) as his capital in 550, and most of the buildings there date from 546 to 530. In later years it served as a religious center where they crowned Persian kings. The site today consists of four areas: at the north, a sacred precinct; south of that, the citadel; farther south, the palace area; and southwest of the palace, the tomb of Cyrus.

In the sacred area are two blocks of limestone. The one consists of an eight-step staircase and a white limestone block seven

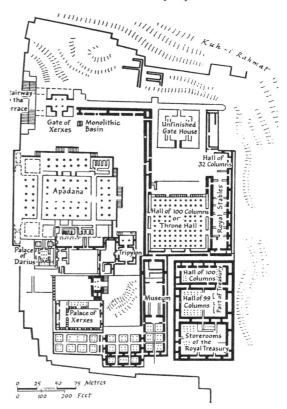

Plan of the terrace at Persepolis

(After Hauser, Courtesy of Chicago Press)

A reconstruction of the complex at Persepolis. At the left is the Apadana, a great reception hall. At the left corner of the Apadana stands the gate of Xerxes. (After J. A. Gobineau, Geneva)

of the residential palace stood the audience palace with its central columned hall measuring 106 by 72 feet. One of these columns still stands to a height of 43 feet. The gatehouse was a monumental entrance to the palace area measuring 93 by 83 feet. Between the audience palace and the residential palace stood two pavilions in a park-like setting.

About a mile southwest of the palace area Cyrus erected his tomb, where his gold coffin was originally placed. Built of white limestone, this consists of a base of six steps, eighteen feet high, on which stands a rectangular gabled mausoleum (now empty) also eighteen feet high.

Persepolis

Persepolis (meaning Persian city) is forty-eight miles south of Pasargadae and thirty-five miles northeast of modern Shiraz. The altitude of almost 6,000 feet gives it a comfortable climate in the summer months. Darius I began construction there shortly after 520, and for all practical purposes Artaxerxes I completed it about sixty years later. Because Persepolis is so far off the beaten track, it did not serve very well as an administrative center, so many scholars earlier in this century thought of it primarily as a religious shrine—for the celebration of the new year. But for various reasons (beyond the scope of our present purposes) there is currently a tendency to back off that view and simply to treat this great center as a pompous statement of Persian power and wealth.

Darius designed the structures of Persepolis to stand on a great terrace. Not quite rectangular, this terrace was over 1,400 feet long, about 1,000 feet wide, and 40 feet high, built of stone blocks bound together by iron bands. A double stairway 24 feet wide with steps only four inches high and easily ascended by mounted horsemen gave access to the platform. At the top of the stairs Xerxes built the Gate of All Nations, 118 feet square, which housed a throne room. At the eastern and western entrances stood pairs of guardian bulls, winged and human-headed.

The audience hall or Apadana was the largest building on the terrace, almost 400 feet square. It consisted of a main hall almost 200 feet on a side, surrounded on three sides by porticoes. A total of 72 columns 62 feet high supported the roof of the structure. The columns were capped by the heads and shoulders of bulls. The walls were of sundried bricks.

At the southwest corner of the audience hall Darius built a palace measuring 95 by 131 feet. South of that Xerxes outdid Darius by constructing a palace twice that in size (135 by 187 feet). At the southern edge of the terrace stood the harem and next to it at the southeast corner, the treasury. Three other palaces and the throne hall completed the group of structures at the site.

Darius the Great (521–486 B.C.) and his successors created a magnificent group of buildings at Persepolis. Here at the northwest corner of the complex (see Plan), stairs led up to the great platform. Columns of the Apadana or audience hall stand on the right.

A close-up of part of the stairway up to the Apadana

North of Persepolis three and a half miles rises a rock cliff (Naqsh-i Rustam). Four tombs of Persian kings were cut into the side of the cliff. Inscriptions identify one of them as the tomb of Darius I. The others are thought to belong to Xerxes, Artaxerxes I, and Darius II.

(For more on this topic, go to p. 304 or p. 347.)

Religion

Persian Zoroastrianism

Any discussion of Persian religion during the period of the Jewish restoration to Palestine must center on the development of Zoroastrianism. The evolution of Zoroastrianism, the degree to which Persian kings or others in Persian society subscribed to its beliefs in the days of Zerubbabel or Ezra or Nehemiah, and the possible influence of Zoroastrianism on Judaism are very controversial and involved subjects.[6] Certainly we should not base our conclusions about this religion on its later fully developed stage or on current practices. Some popular books simply assert that the Persian kings of the Restoration period were Zoroastrians and then proceed to discuss some of the beliefs of that faith. But the matter is not so simple as that.

To begin with, scholars do not agree on when the prophet Zoroaster lived (the Greek spelling of his name is *Zoroaster,* the Avestan, *Zarathushtra*). Some place him as late as Cyrus or Darius I in the fifth century B.C., others centuries earlier. Second, there is no agreement as to his home—perhaps in the east near the Indus valley or in northwest Iran. Third, scholars debate whether Zoroaster preached monotheism, a dualism, or the superiority of one god over others. Fourth, scholars disagree over whether the Persian kings (of the Achaemenid line) embraced Zoroastrianism.

To be sure, Darius and Xerxes exalted Ahuramazda, the god Zoroaster preached, but they do not mention Zoroaster. Cyrus comes across as very tolerant of various religions, making him simply an Iranian polytheist. Though some argue that he embraced Zoroastrianism, we really cannot be certain of his religious belief.

In his inscriptions Darius mentions Ahuramazda dozens of times and claims to be under that god's protection. Though Darius calls him the "greatest of gods," he does not describe Ahuramazda as the only god. In Darius' tomb the king is pictured as facing a fire altar—a Zoroastrian symbol. It appears, then, that Darius may have been a Zoroastrian, but he was not an intolerant worshiper of the god. Likewise Xerxes in his inscriptions claimed to be under the favor of Ahuramazda and in opposition to the demons. Presumably Zoroaster's preaching about the god influenced the worship of Ahuramazda in the days of Darius and Xerxes.

A fire-altar with the relief of a Magus, a member of the Zoroastrian priestly tribe—the Magi (From Kayseri, Turkey)

Zoroastrianism

Zoroastrianism contains a dualism, a contradiction of good and evil, a Good Spirit and an Evil Spirit with his demon henchmen. The Good Spirit represents light, fire, summer, fertile land, and health. The Evil Spirit represents darkness, winter, drought, sickness, and death. At least in the later development of Zoroastrianism, individuals would be judged by whether their good deeds outweighed their evil deeds. And they considered fire a symbol of the god Ahuramazda, as an indication that the god himself was there when they performed a religious ceremony.

Some have claimed that Zoroastrianism influenced Judaism. They see this connection in judgments by fire found in numerous Old Testament passages. But this assertion is founded on extremely late Persian texts, and if there was any Zoroastrian influence on Judaism, it came during the late intertestamental period, not at this time.[7]

Judaism during the Restoration

The Jews tried to "do it right" as they returned to Palestine. In the first place, those who went back were the ones God had "stirred up" (Ezra 1:5) to do so. Second, those who remained generously helped finance the venture (Ezra 1:6). King Cyrus for his part sent along 5,400 gold and silver articles that Nebuchadnezzar had confiscated from the temple of Solomon (Ezra 1:11). Third, when the exiles reached Jerusalem, they gathered with great unity (as "one man," Ezra 3:1) to rebuild the altar of sacrifice and correctly offer on it the sacrifices prescribed in the Law and to keep the Feast of Tabernacles. Then they laid the foundation for the rebuilt temple (Ezra 3:6–13).

To be sure opposition arose and the work that had begun with great fanfare came to an abrupt halt, but later under the urging of the prophets Haggai and Zechariah (Ezra 5:1) work began again. And they completed the temple in the sixth year of Darius, 515 B.C. (Ezra 6:15).

Though slippage occurred in the conduct of the Jews from time to time, they remained responsive to calls of renewal on the part of their leaders. For example, under Nehemiah's leadership they renewed the covenant to keep the Law of Moses and adequately support the cost of maintaining the temple and the whole worship system of Israel (Nehemiah 9:38).

The renewal of the covenant also involved a pledge not to marry into pagan families of the land. The prohibition against mixed marriages had nothing to do with racial purity or racial snobbery. Its intent was to prevent the true faith from being submerged in a sea of idolatry, as Exodus 34:12–16 clearly demonstrates. We find that the problem continued in Ezra 9—10; Nehemiah 10:30; 13:23–28. But it is noteworthy that the people responded to Ezra and Nehemiah, and the practice seems to have been greatly reduced from time to time.

(For more on this topic, go to p. 309 or p. 350.)

Warfare

The Army on the March

When the Persian army marched by on its way to war civilians experienced it as high entertainment. First came the empty chariot of the invisible god Ahuramazda drawn by eight white horses, with the charioteer trotting alongside on foot. He could not ride in the chariot with the god. Then the king himself rode in a chariot. But he also had a covered carriage in which he could relax when he grew tired. Next came the carriages containing his wives, concubines, and children and their governesses. Some of the ladies-in-waiting were mounted. The size and nature of this group varied from king to king and battle to battle.

Mess tents and luxurious furnishings—gilded and silver tables and chairs carried on camels—accompanied the king and army. Valets came along to see to the king's wardrobe. Dozens of cooks and bakers also rode by. And though they requisitioned foodstuffs from subject peoples en route,

Worship during the Restoration

We find no reference to synagogues in Ezra or Nehemiah or the post-exilic prophets. But even if they existed, that silence should not be surprising. The emphasis in those books is on restoration of the temple; it would not have been appropriate to mention a rival institution. Yet because the synagogue arose not as a rival but a place for coming together for prayer, Scripture reading or exhortation, and socializing (rather than sacrifice), it may well have been in existence. The usual view is that it must have been around at least fairly early in the Restoration period, because it was so well established in later centuries.

We know little about the religious expression of the people in the early Restoration period. We do know that they had revived the sacrificial system, and individuals would have made periodic sin and trespass offerings. Presumably they observed the Sabbath fairly regularly (see Nehemiah 13:15–33) and practiced circumcision as a sign of the covenant. And they celebrated the Passover (Ezra 6:19) and "the appointed feasts" (Ezra 3:5; Nehemiah 8:14) at least periodically. The people seem to have responded to the teaching and the leadership of Ezra and Nehemiah. That is, they proved to be teachable and respected God's authority over them in the person of divinely appointed administrators. It seems the residents of Jerusalem wholeheartedly engaged in rebuilding the wall of the city. This effort did not merely protect the temple but also the whole covenant-relationship way of life.

large it had to be carried by hundreds of mules and camels. It does not take much imagination to see how the troops of Alexander the Great, who carried much of their supply on their backs and rarely used supply wagons, could out-maneuver the lumbering Persian armies.

But what about the soldiers? This was, after all, a war effort. First came the Ten Thousand Immortals—the elite corps. If one of them fell in battle, another superbly trained soldier took his place. So there were always 10,000 of them—an immortal unit. A thousand of them served as the king's bodyguard. Each of them carried a spear with a glittering silver blade. A bow and quiver of arrows hung from every man's left shoulder. And they were decked out in brightly-colored robes that extended to their wrists and ankles and in earrings and bracelets. Their full beards were curled, as were the buns of long hair at the neck. This pampered unit also had concubines and attendants who traveled in carriages, with their food transported on camels and other baggage animals. Apparently they drew this unit from the Persian nobility and other regiments from Persian commoners.

Behind the Immortals came the crack cavalry units. And after them came Persian

Guardsmen from glazed brick reliefs at Susa, probably the Immortals.

they herded flocks of animals along to provide the king and the top brass with fresh meat. Because the king could not drink ordinary local water, mule-drawn four-wheeled carts carried silver urns filled with boiled water from the Choaspes River, near Susa. The king also traveled with a war chest of gold and silver, both in coin and bullion so

How Many Soldiers?

How big was Persia's army and its retinue when they went off to war? Some competent scholars conclude that some 300,000 soldiers marched under the banner of Xerxes as he started for Greece in 480 B.C. If all the support personnel are counted, as many as 750,000 people may have been on the move with the king. Some today suggest smaller numbers for the Persian military, but we know that it contained at least three corps of 60,000 each under Xerxes' command when he marched into Europe.

infantrymen with loose felt caps and varicolored sleeved tunics over iron-scaled armor and trousers. They carried wicker shields, long bows with quivers filled with reed arrows, short spears, and a short sword in a belt on the right hip. Parenthetically, we should note that military service was compulsory for all Persians.

Finally the masses of mercenaries marched by in their national dress, a sort of "walking encyclopedia of the empire." It would not have been possible to outfit all of them in standard uniforms, and it was probably unwise to try to do so. Since they fought in units with national dress they reflected a certain pride and camaraderie.

Organization of the Military and Its Weapons

Persians organized the army in divisions of 10,000, subdivided to regiments of a thousand, which were in turn subdivided into 10 units of 100 and again into 10 units of 10. In the early days, under Cyrus the Great and following, the "archer pair" dominated—an archer firing from behind the cover of a large body-shield managed by a shield bearer. In time the shield bearer also became a spearman, carrying a fighting spear six feet long. The infantry were also armed with swords, which were broad and curved, with the edge on the convex side. As noted earlier, the Immortals carried a spear and a bow.

By the end of Cyrus' reign Persian nobility formed the cavalry, supplemented by units of eastern tribesmen. At first the cavalry did not carry shields, but after about 450 B.C. they not only had shields but a certain amount of armor for the horses. Probably from the days of Cyrus the Great, the Persians also had chariots with scythes attached. These served as real weapons of terror as they charged enemy infantry units.

In the early days the Persians had no navy, but when Cambyses invaded Egypt (525) he found it necessary to build one. He recruited boats and oarsmen from the Phoenician coastal cities, and Persians served as marines on board ship, ready to fight when two ships locked into each other. The usual practice in naval warfare of the time was for one ship to try to ram another with its metal "beak" on the prow or to shower burning material on enemy ships. It appears that at the Battle of Salamis in 480 the Greeks defeated the Persians mainly by the use of the ram to cripple and wreck ships. And the Phoenician ships appeared to be more fragile than Greek ships.

Greek style triremes (110–120 feet long) normally had a crew of about 200, of which 170 were oarsmen and the rest deck hands and marines. Though ships might sail

Guardsmen in Persian dress from the Apadana at Persepolis, with spears and shields. The fluted cap may mean that they were Persian nobles.

Use of Military Intelligence

Though Persians could and did fight bravely, they counted heavily on the use of espionage for military intelligence and bribery of defectors in the camp of the enemy. They had plenty of money to buy off anyone who might be for sale. They tampered with the loyalty of leaders of mercenary forces. Xerxes, for example, bribed a Greek to show the Persians a way to surround the Greeks at Thermopylae in 480. And during the winter of 481–480 Persian agents secured the cooperation of nearly all Greeks of Thessaly and central Greece. Athens and Sparta and her southern allies had to fight on alone during the following year. Scholars claim that victory over the Lydians was the only major Persian conquest achieved without fifth column activity.[8]

Persian Warfare in Biblical Context

It is quite unnecessary to our present study to comment on all the battles the Persian kings fought. But it is of some interest to look at Cyrus' conquest of Babylon in the days of Daniel and the Restoration and Darius' and Xerxes' contest with the Greeks as background for the Esther narrative.

Defeat of Babylon

"God has numbered your kingdom, and finished it. . . Your kingdom has been. . . given to the Medes and Persians." (Daniel 5:26, 28 NKJV)

Under the weak rule of Nabonidus and Belshazzar the Babylonian Empire fell apart because of rampant graft, and oppressed peasants. Nabonidus successfully alienated the powerful priesthoods of the state. Now enter Cyrus on the Babylonian stage. He propagandized the people that he was their deliverer. On the other hand, near the beginning of October 539 at the battle of

Opis on the Tigris, he so cruelly destroyed the people and the city that the Babylonian army had no heart to continue the war.

Then, near Opis, he diverted the Euphrates so the water defenses of Babylon were useless and his troops marched down the dried-up riverbed into the city. With the defenses gone, the army demoralized, the government in disarray, and the people propagandized into acceptance of the Persians, Cyrus did not have to fight to take control of Babylon. Belshazzar's kingdom was indeed given to the Medes and Persians, as Daniel had predicted. Subsequently Cyrus continued to propagandize his way into the hearts of the people. He was their liberator from a corrupt regime and the appointee of the Babylonian god Marduk for the blessing of the people. He was also Yahweh's "anointed" (Isaiah 45:1).

Defeat at the Hands of the Greeks

While the Hebrews completed the temple, King Darius busily expanded the borders of his empire. In 512 B.C. he crossed the Hellespont and invaded Thrace. But when he moved north of the Danube and sought to defeat the Scythians, they simply migrated farther north, engaged in scorched-earth tactics along the way, and refused to fight him. Subsequently his

before the wind on the open sea, in battle they stowed masts, sails, and rigging and movement depended on oarsmen.

Guardsmen in Median and Persian dress from Persepolis, with spears and bows

armies established his control in Thrace and secured a pledge of allegiance from Macedonia.

The next chapter in the Greco-Persian saga came in 499. Greeks living under Persian rule in Asia Minor grew increasingly restless and under the lead of Miletus openly rebelled. The Greeks initially had great success and even burned the city of Sardis. Athens and Eretria sent token forces and withdrew them when Persia began to get the upper hand. By 494 Persia had put out all the fires of revolt and punished Miletus with complete destruction.

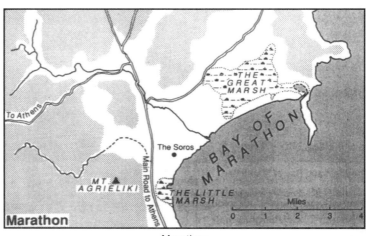

Marathon

Darius could have ignored the participation of Eretria and Athens but decided to bring them to heel. If he threw his might against them, perhaps he could keep the mainland Greeks from further meddling in Greek affairs in Asia Minor. Darius sent two expeditions against Greece—the first in 492 and the second in 490. The first had to turn back when its fleet was destroyed by a storm off Mount Athos in northern Greece.

The second struck directly across the Aegean with a force of some 25,000 and besieged Eretria, while part of the Persian force landed on the Plain of Marathon. The Athenians were hardly in a position to help the Eretrians, whose town fell after a siege of six days. Surviving inhabitants were shipped off to Susa. Athens sent for help to Plataea and Sparta. The Plataean army of 1,000 arrived soon. Sparta's involvement in some religious observances prevented them from sending a force until after the Battle of Marathon.

The Athenian army, some 10,000 strong, camped in the hills overlooking the Persian camp. They waited for some days, not knowing whether to attack. The Persian army was an unknown quantity, as far as battle tactics and fighting skill were concerned. When the Athenians finally decided to attack, they looked for an opportune time. Lengthening the line to equal the length of the Persian line, they thinned the center. But the wings remained deep. They attacked when the Persian cavalry was unprepared. Moving toward the enemy lines with great speed, they did not give the Persian archers time to do their softening up routine. But the thin Greek middle did buckle, while the Greek wings held and even pushed the Persian wings back. The result was that the Greeks soon surrounded the Persian forces and cut them up. Scholars differ on whether the Greeks planned the strategy or just happened to be fortunate with the outcome. In any case, the casualty figures usually given are 6,400 Persians lost to 192 Greeks.

A runner lasted through the 26-mile race to Athens to gasp out news of the victory and to give rise to numberless 26-mile marathon runs in modern times. As the Persian troops boarded ship and prepared to sail around the southern tip of Attica to attack Athens, the Athenian army marched home through the night. When they drew up in battle array at the harbor the next morning, the arriving Persians decided they had had enough and sailed away. For the next ten years Greece had a reprieve while the Persians fought an Egyptian uprising, buried King Darius, and prepared for another Greek war under the leadership of Xerxes.

Xerxes (485–465) wanted to make sure he was ready to deal effectively with the

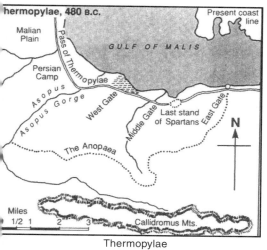

Thermopylae

Greeks. He sent his agents to buy off the city-states of northern Greece, which left Athens and Sparta and her allies in southern Greece to stand alone. Extensive military preparations took place in 483–81 for the great march into Greece. Esther 1:4 speaks of a planning session lasting 180 days in Xerxes' third year (483 B.C.). Months before the Persians marched into Greece, Persian advance men had moved ahead to prepare grain, cattle, and poultry supplies for the king and his men. Some put the size of Xerxes' army at 300,000 or more. Even conservatively it consisted of three corps of 60,000 men each.

In the spring of 480 the Persian army broke camp at Sardis and marched north to the Hellespont and across boat bridges into Europe. As they came through Thrace and Macedonia a huge fleet supported them. Though the Greek allies wanted primarily to make their stand at the Isthmus of Corinth, they consented to try to hold some of the narrow passes of central Greece against the Persians. As the Spartans entrenched themselves in the pass at Thermopylae, a traitor showed the Persians a means of encirclement. The Spartans stood to a man, even in their defeat, inflicting heavy losses on the Persians.

With the pass of Thermopylae open, the Persians poured into central Greece. Athenians evacuated their city, which the advancing army promptly burned. The future looked very bleak for the allies. But then Themistocles, admiral of the allied

fleet, got the Persian fleet bottled up in the Bay of Salamis (near Athens) and persuaded Xerxes to attack them. Attack was stupid and unnecessary because all the king had to do was wait for the Greeks to run out of supplies and be forced to surrender. But Xerxes wanted a spectacular victory. What he got was a loss of 200 ships and multitudes of Persian sailors as they advanced into the narrow channel and were destroyed. Then he lost his head and executed the Phoenician captains for alleged cowardice. As a result the Phoenician and Egyptian squadrons deserted, which freed the allied ships to sail the Aegean at will.

Without naval cover and supply ships, Xerxes hurried off by land to Sardis, where he kept watch over the Greek cities of Asia Minor to prevent their rebellion. The Persian commander Mardonius wintered at Plataea, northwest of Athens in central Greece, with a crack Persian army corps. In the spring of 479 the Persians and the Greek allies joined battle. As at Salamis, the Persians at Plataea had the Greeks in a box and with patience would have won. But then Mardonius assumed that the retreat in progress was a rout and led his troops to battle on the run, hoping for a spectacular victory. When he entered the battle in person he was slain. Leaderless, the Persians panicked and fled. The Greeks and their allies slaughtered almost the entire army of the 10,000 Immortals and the other crack troops.

While this was going on, another great battle was in progress at Mycale on the Asia Minor coast. There the Persians, distrusting the loyalty of Ionians who sailed most of what was left of the great Persian fleet, beached the ships and built a stockade of stones and tree trunks. When the Athenian navy attacked on August 27, 479, Ionians and other Persian subjects turned against the Persians, and the combined force killed the Persian marines almost to the last man.

The Greeks destroyed two of the six Persian armies that had gone off to war. A third had to be pulled out of Europe to hold restless western Asia Minor, which soon rebelled and joined the Delian League, which became the Athenian Empire. Greece was now free and entered her period of classical glory. Xerxes went back to Susa (Shushan) to drown his sorrows in his harem. As Xerxes licked his wounds after the catastrophe in Greece he completed his search for a new queen. He chose Esther in the seventh year of his reign(Esther 2:16) in 479. At this point the Bible begins the story of Esther.

(For more on this topic, go to p. 311 or p. 352.)

Housing and Furniture

Jews living in Babylonia under Persian control had houses and furniture much the same as during the days of the Babylonian Empire (see last chapter). Those who settled in Judah once more tended to pattern their houses after those of the people they found living in the land. What we said about houses of the people of the Kingdom of Judah before the captivity roughly still applies at this time.

It does not appear that the Babylon-ian practice of building houses with rooms arranged around an open court caught on with those returning to Palestine. Open courtyards in the middle of a house don't work very well in the colder and wetter climate of Judah. Moreover, the abundance of stone in Palestine and the greater amount of rainfall led to stone being substituted for mudbrick in construction.

In the Susa area Persians or Jews living among them in the days of Esther or Mordecai lived in houses that differed greatly, according to social and economic classes. Most of the people, the poor, had houses of sun-dried mudbrick, many of which contained only one room with a mud floor. Commonly these had a vestibule built around the open door to provide a little privacy. Such people slept on pallets on the floor and had little if any other furniture.

Middle-class families might have houses of several rooms grouped around an open courtyard. They owned little furniture and slept on beds of cushions. They cooked in kettles over an open fire, in brick ovens, or on the surface of pottery jars tipped on their sides, with fires burning inside. Most of these houses were constructed of sun-dried brick too, but some were of baked brick

Map of Greece

The route of the Persian army in 480 B.C. After the victory at Thermopylae, they went on to suffer a naval defeat in the Bay of Salamis. Then Xerxes left Greece, but part of his army wintered around Plataea, where they were cut to pieces in 479, probably in mid-August.

held together with bitumen (tar) that came from the middle Euphrates region.

Homes of the wealthy and temples and palaces may also have been built of baked brick, but contained touches of cut stone and wood, such as cypress or cedar. Usually constructed around open courts, these houses had beds, chairs, tables, and wool carpets. The most wealthy reclined on banquet couches while eating, as noted in connection with Xerxes' feast prior to the invasion of Greece (see Esther 1:6).

But very few of any class owned their houses, at least in town. Real estate values skyrocketed under the Achaemenids, and most had to rent. Tenants paid rent twice a year, in the first and seventh months, in advance. And renters could not expect landlords to make repairs; they had to make do on their own.

(For more on this topic, go to p. 314 or p. 359.)

Royalty and the nobility used gold and silver utensils and goblets at their banquets. A good example is this golden drinking horn from Susa in the Louvre in Paris. It features the head and forebody of a griffon at its base. This horn is probably similar to vessels carried by Nehemiah when he was cupbearer to the king of Persia (Nehemiah 2:11).

Diet and Foodstuffs

Jews returning to Judah during the Restoration farmed and ate much as their ancestors had in the days of the southern kingdom before the Exile (see chapter 10). Terracing the hills of Judea continued to be important agriculturally. For Jews still living in Babylonia life continued on much the same as in previous decades there (see last chapter).

But there were important changes under Persian administration. Darius, especially, and other Persian kings as well, took interest in the introduction of new species of plants and trees into various parts of the empire. Some of this took place as a result of the Greco-Persian wars. They introduced alfalfa, or lucerne, from Media, an ideal fodder for horses, to Europe and points west, as well as domestic fowl and the white dove. The fisheries of the Persian Gulf and Tigris and Euphrates region exported salted and dried fish in jars to fairly great distances. Beekeeping was widely practiced and honey was used for sugar. A great many of the people, rich and poor, lived on staples of bread, fish, oil, and wine.

Serfs worked large estates attached to the land in the empire at large, but in Persia free peasants worked the land. Wheat, barley, grapes, and olives comprised the chief crops, and donkeys, mules, and horses were bred. *(For more on this topic, go to p. 315 or p. 360.)*

Dress

The common Persians wore plain tunics of wool or goat hair all seasons of the year. These normally had short sleeves and extended to the ankle. Dyed fabric was too expensive for them. The wealthy could afford linen tunics and slippers, and in cool weather they added a woolen cloak, perhaps brightly colored. Both men and women wore earrings and bracelets. Wealthy women sported eye shadow, glass beads, and rings. Men engaged in various kinds of physical labor are pictured in short-sleeved tunics that extend to the knees and are belted at the waist.

Artists portray the king on his throne with purple-edged trousers under a purple robe, with his outer robe weighted down with gold embroidery and extending to the ankles. His beard is cut square and curled, as is his long hair. His gold earrings have inset jewels. On his head is a tiara. Gold bracelets and a gold collar add to the effect, and a short Persian sword is inserted into his golden girdle. His pointed shoes are yellow. *(For more on this topic, go to p. 316 or p. 362.)*

Family Life

"You shall not give your daughters as wives to their sons, nor take their daughters for your sons or yourselves." (Nehemiah 13:25 NKJV)

Meat Largely for the Rich

The working classes rarely ate meat. They might enjoy a goose or a duck on a special occasion. And if they lived near a river or the gulf or the Mediterranean they might have an occasional fresh or dried fish. Their staples were barley bread and cheap beer made from dates. Garlic was inexpensive and plentiful and consumed in quantity. Sesame seed oil was a substitute for fat.

The Persian king, the top government officials, and the army brass consumed large quantities of meat (much more than during earlier periods of history and for other places) and good imported grape wines, along with local grains and vegetables.

During the Persian period, as before and afterward, Hebrew families, especially fathers, customarily arranged for the marriage of their sons and daughters. Of course, then as at other times, there was the "way of a man with a maid," and the prospective brides or grooms sometimes pressured their parents to work out a marriage with some desirable person. Samson, for example, demanded that his father negotiate a marriage agreement for him with a Philistine woman (Judges 14:1–10).

At the time of the Restoration, apparently a number of the young men did not have families to arrange marriages for them, so they took matters into their own hands. Then either they or their families contracted many marriages with non-Hebrew inhabitants of the land. Such marriages were attractive for reasons of personal preference or economic or social advantage. Propertyless returning exiles could gain estates in Judah by marrying into established families of the region. And they could blunt the antagonism against them by establishing marriage bonds with the people then living there. Scripture clearly implies that the people who had been living in Palestine during the Exile had very strong feelings of antagonism against those who now came in to settle there. We can better appreciate the situation when we look at how Arabs living on the West Bank in Palestine today feel about Jewish immigrants to their region.

In any case, whether young single men or their families made the arrangements, and for whatever reasons, numerous marriages of Jews to inhabitants of the land took place. This was in clear violation of the Mosaic covenant. Ezra dealt with this problem of marriage to heathen women when he returned to Jerusalem in 458 B.C. (Ezra 9—10) and Nehemiah faced it some thirteen years later (Nehemiah 10) and again about fifteen years after that (Nehemiah 13: 23–28). Worse, apparently what was going on in Judah at the time was that some Jewish men divorced their Jewish wives and took heathen women instead. We gather this from the condemnation of the contemporary prophet Malachi (Malachi 2:10–17).

Nehemiah indicates some of the results of mixed marriages. Jews married women of Ashdod, Ammon, and Moab, and many of their children grew up speaking "the language of one of the other people" (Nehemiah 13:24). Evidently most of the pagans marrying into Israel were women (as here, cf. Ezra 10:2, 14, 17).

Judah experienced serious economic distress in the days of Nehemiah. Heavy Persian taxes and poor crops had forced many of the poor into bankruptcy, and together with their children they had been reduced to slavery. Some of the wealthy had taken advantage of the situation (see Nehemiah 5:1–5). Nehemiah demanded that the wealthy forgive the debts and restore what they had taken. This they agreed to do.

(For more on this topic, go to p. 316 or p. 362.)

Work, Travel, and Commerce

The Persian crown engineered a tremendous economic advance and awareness of a wider world. The whole vast area from the Indus to the Aegean and the Mediterranean and across a chunk of North Africa became a single political and economic unit under central control. Sea routes linked the Indus, Tigris-Euphrates, and the Nile river valleys

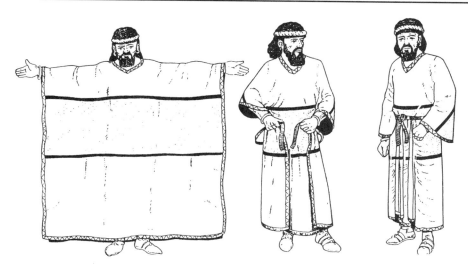

Persian nobles wore a robe, as seen in this illustration. It was a rectangular sheet with a hole in the middle for the head and reaching to the ankles and wrists. The rear half of the robe was drawn forward and tied with a sash around the waist. Then the robe was pulled up slightly through the sash at the front, creating curving folds at the sides.

Land routes also linked the different parts of the empire. A system of weights and measures, and for the first time in history, coinage, stimulated domestic and foreign commerce.

A bimetallic monetary system, in gold and silver, came into existence in the seventh century in Lydia, and Darius adopted this for his empire. Gradually money replaced goods as wages and payment for other commodities. As noted, the kings introduced useful plants and trees to ever-increasing areas of the Near East. Exploiting deposits of gold, silver, copper, and iron across the empire made it self-sufficient in metals and timber for military, luxury, and industrial purposes. Likewise, timber was used extensively for war chariots and weapons, and also for houses, boats, carts, and furniture.

Industry expanded rapidly—on the large estates under the creative stimulus of artisan-serfs and in the towns. Among the leading industries were manufacture of clothing, shoes, furniture, metal objects, jewelry, and boatbuilding. They designed ships larger and faster than ever before. Voyages of exploration took place. Countries and regions that had not traded with each other before now established contacts.

India, Ceylon, the Danube and the Rhine regions, to name a few, now sent goods to Babylonia, Persia or Egypt.

Interestingly, instead of this commerce involving luxury goods alone, it centered primarily on household articles, cheap clothing, and ordinary everyday commodities, thus serving all classes. Private individuals established banks, and checks came into use.[9] In the interest of the working classes, the state sought to regulate both work and wages.[10]

With all this activity, an increasing percentage of the population went to faraway places—as sailors, businessmen, government officials, or military personnel. And even if they didn't go to some of these exotic or not-so-exotic places, they became aware of them as they learned that the chair, or shoe, or bracelet they were making was destined for Ceylon, or Sparta, or Memphis in Egypt.

But let's not get carried away with a glorified statement about the economy. The province of Babylonia as a whole, where many Jews lived, was oppressed and impoverished by the time Alexander the Great came through in 331 B.C. A double standard of living existed between the wealthy and the masses. High inflation persisted and wages

The Raising of Children

The pagan women in post-exilic Judah brought up the children, who not only did not have facility in the language of the Jews but also did not know their religious traditions. While women continued to educate girls in the conduct of household tasks, including weaving, spinning and the like, at some point fathers stepped in to train boys to follow their trades. We know nothing of formal schooling during this period. Presumably those who learned how to read and write were largely of the priestly class who learned from their fathers how to do so as part of their preparation to follow their fathers' trade.

Among the Persians of the time boys lived entirely with their mothers until age five. Fathers then assumed responsibility for them and taught them to use the bow and ride horses and to learn whatever occupation the father followed. At age twenty young men began their active military service. This they continued until they were twenty-four years old—and then they were in the reserves until age fifty.

The Persians were fine craftsmen. In this drawing of one of a pair of gold armbands, the two carefully detailed creatures represent griffons, mythological beasts that were part eagle and part lion. Persian artists often pictured griffons with rams' horns. Both men and women wore a profusion of jewelry, especially earrings, bracelets, and armbands. This armband is 4 ¾ inches in diameter. (See the color section in the first half of this book.)

remained quite depressed. The interest rate for a loan from a temple or private bank was 20 percent. There were taxes or service dues on just about everything. Those who couldn't pay their taxes became forced laborers on public projects.

The laborer commonly had his wage entered in his employer's books. Then he took goods against his balance, but he was generally overdrawn and forever in debt. Temples lent money and goods to their peasants, who then were expected to pay up at harvest time. But at that point they rarely could pay the whole bill. So they lived from debt to debt, year after year.

Life in the military provided a way out of such an economic plight. The empire supported the army, and a large percentage of the tax levy went for the upkeep of the troops. For a Mede or Persian, leadership in the army was a noble career with a comfortable life by the standards of the day. Persians manned the garrisons in the cities and the strategic points throughout the empire. Ordinary subjects of other lands also had a good enough life while in the army. Veterans who settled in places important for defense and keeping the peace received parcels of land. The army provided much of the glue that held the empire together. And even in the final years when Persian foundations were crumbling, it kept the facade of empire intact.

But a day would come when the facade could no longer be maintained. And when Alexander the Great came charging across the landscape, the whole glorious structure collapsed like a house of cards.

(For more on this topic, go to p. 317 or p. 363.)

This stone relief from Susa depicts a woman holding a spindle in her left hand, and a fibrous material, perhaps wool, in her right. Behind her stands a servant with a large fan.

NOTES:

[1] James B. Pritchard, ed., *Ancient Near Eastern Texts Relating to the Old Testament*, 2nd ed. (Princeton: Princeton University Press, 1955), 316.

[2] See, e. g., A. T. Olmstead, *History of the Persian Empire* (Chicago: University of Chicago Press, 1948), 304–7, 313–17; Gleason Archer, *A Survey of Old Testament Introduction*, 3rd ed. (Chicago: Moody Press, 1994), 457–62; Jack Finegan, *Light from the Ancient Past*, 2nd ed. (Princeton: Princeton University Press, 1959), 238.

[3] For a discussion of excavations at Susa, see Edwin M. Yamauchi, *Persia and the Bible* (Grand Rapids: Baker, 1990), 293–301. See also Prudence O. Harper and others (eds.) *The Royal City of Susa* (New York: Metropolitan Museum of Art, 1992).

[4] Finegan, 243.

[5] David Stronach of the British Institute of Persian Studies led the definitive excavations at Pasargadae. See his *Pasargadae* (Oxford: Oxford University Press, 1978).

[6] For extended discussion, see J. M. Cook, *The Persian Empire* (New York: Schocken Books, 1983), 147–57; Yamauchi, 395-466.

[7] See Yamauchi, 463-66.

[8] Cook, 106.

[9] R. Chirshman, *Iran* (Baltimore: Penguin Books, 1954), 186.

[10] Ibid., 187.

BIBLIOGRAPHY:

Cook, John M. *The Persian Empire*. New York: Schocken Books, 1983.

Culican, William. *The Medes and Persians*. New York: Frederick A. Praeger, 1965.

Ghirshman, R. *Iran*. Baltimore: Penguin Books, 1954.

Gobineau, J. A. de. *The World of the Persians*. Geneva: Minerva, 1971.

Green, Peter. *The Greco-Persian Wars*. Berkeley: University of California Press, 1996.

Harper, Prudence O., and Others, eds. *The Royal City of Susa*. New York: The Metropolitan Museum of Art, 1992.

Head, Duncan. *The Achaemenid Persian Army*. Stockport, England: Montvert Publications, 1992.

Hole, Frank, ed. *The Archaeology of Western Iran*. Washington, D.C.: Smithsonian Institution Press, 1987.

Marsden, E. W. *The Campaign of Gaugamela*. Liverpool: Liverpool University Press, 1964.

Matheson, Sylvia. *Persia: An Archaeological Guide*. London: Faber and Faber, 2nd ed., 1976.

Olmstead, A. T. *History of the Persian Empire*. Chicago: University of Chicago Press, 1948.

Rolle, Renate. *The World of the Scythians*. London: B. T. Batsford, 1980.

Sekunda, Nick. *The Persian Army 560–330 B.C.* London: Osprey Publishing Ltd., 1992.

Whitcomb, John C. Jr. *Darius the Mede*. Grand Rapids: Baker, dist., 1963.

Wilber, Donald N. *Persepolis*. New York: Thomas Y. Crowell, 1969.

Yamauchi, Edwin M. *Persia and the Bible*. Grand Rapids: Baker, 1990.

THE INFLUENCE OF ALEXANDER THE GREAT AND HIS SUCCESSORS

Chapter 13

Great generals stir our admiration and imagination as we read accounts of their exploits. Unfortunately we often think of them only as military men, when usually they were more important off the battlefield than on it. The classic example is Alexander the Great of Macedonia. He launched developments that were to change the whole character of Western civilization. After Alexander, the world—including Judea—could never be the same again.

Alexander the Great. This youthful king of Macedonia (ca. 356–323 B.C.) changed the world militarily and culturally. He destroyed the Persian Empire and spread Hellenistic culture from the eastern Mediterranean to the Indus River.

Alexander and his successors spread Greek culture across the vast area between the Aegean Sea and India and to North Africa. As they did, various peoples modified it and thus it developed into what we call Hellenistic culture. The Romans fell under the spell of that culture and adopted it as their own. Then in modified form the Hellenistic-Roman way of life was passed on through the Middle Ages and in time became the basis of modern Western civilization.

For our present purposes we need to note that in Judea, upper-class Jews, forgetting much of their heritage, built Greek theaters and gymnasiums, spoke Greek, adopted Greek dress and names and even thought patterns. Jewish circles in Egypt and Syria and points east felt the same impact. Some description of that development appears in the following pages of this chapter.

The Land

When Alexander's father Philip died in 336 B.C., he left his son the kingdom of Macedonia and a cause: destruction of the Persian threat to Greece. We cannot describe the exact size of Macedonia because its boundaries varied over the centuries and because the exact boundaries during much of the country's history are not known. The kingdom was, however, always located at the northeast corner of the Aegean, with Pella (24 miles northwest of Thessalonica) the capital during much of its history. Under Philip II (359–336 B.C.), Macedonia came to include Thrace and eventually dominated all of Greece.

Macedonia's fertile plains along the northern rim of the Aegean gave way to a mountainous interior. Four substantial rivers—west to east, the Haliacmon (Vistritsa), Anios (Vardar), Strymon, and Nestos—of the European type (which flow all year instead of drying up in the summer) break through the coastal ridges to the sea and deposit around their mouths rich alluvial plains. In the west, the Haliacmon and Vardar plains have been joined at least since the fifth century B.C. Moving east, we come to the Strymonic Plain, which is the most fertile plain of the north Aegean area. Next comes the Philippian Plain, and finally, the Nestos Plain.

Under Alexander the Great, Macedonia conquered the entire Persian Empire (for a description see the previous chapter). So Alexander's empire extended from the Indus River in the east to the Mediterranean in the west and included Macedonia and Greece, Asia Minor, and Egypt. The distance across it was more than 3,000 miles, equivalent to the distance across the continental United States.

(For more on this topic, go to p. 321 or p. 367.)

Government

Alexander, Macedonia, and the Empire

Macedonia was a hereditary monarchy in which the king had virtually absolute power. As intermediary between the Macedonian people and the gods, the king sacrificed to the gods on behalf of the state. He commanded the military forces in person and led them in battle. In foreign affairs he initiated diplomatic relations. Scholars differ in their conclusions about the assembly and its powers, but it seems that in the days of Philip and Alexander it elected the king, acted on treaties, decided on disbursement of certain major sums, and passed judgment in cases of treason for which the sentence was normally death. There is also uncertainty as to whether the assembly consisted

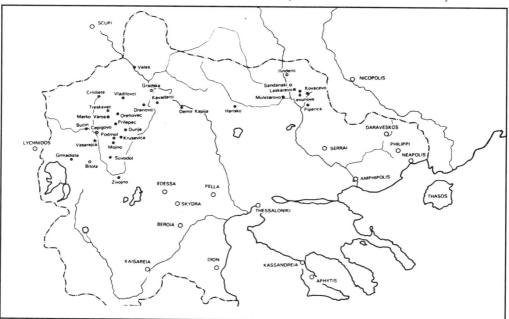

The borders of ancient Macedonia, with its four rivers, west to east: the Haliacmon, Anios, Strymon, and Nestos, all of which flowed into the northern Aegean.

of the standing army or only a kind of council of commanding officers and leading members of the state—close associates of the king. After the military campaigns against Persia were over, the kingships of the various conquered territories were united in the single person of Alexander.

To placate the Persians and to obtain the necessary personnel to run the empire, Alexander declared that Persians were to have a place in administration along with Greeks, under his rule. As he organized conquered territories, he carefully kept a line of communication open with Macedonia. In effect, he simply took over the Persian satrapy system. But to make sure that the satraps did not become so powerful that they might set themselves up as independent kings, Alexander divided their authority. That is, he put them in charge of civil administration in the provinces, while military and financial officers reported directly to Alexander.

An important aspect of Alexander's organization of the empire was his urban strategy. He founded a number of cities that at first served as garrison towns but later became urban centers for their districts—places where Greek culture could be maintained and disseminated. These centers grew to be important economically, politically, and militarily—and as centers for the maintenance of imperial power. But they also contributed to the development and spread of Hellenic culture.

We cannot be sure what Alexander had in mind for his cities, nor can we be sure how many cities he intended to found. The old generalization that he founded seventy cities must be discarded. As a matter of fact, he established only a dozen or so, of which Alexandria in Egypt is the best known and the most significant. Nor could he have imagined how important these cities would become in the creation of a Hellenistic culture. His successors—and later the Romans—continued the practice of urbanizing the Mediterranean world. And the apostle Paul, as a Roman citizen, followed an urban strategy for his conquest of his world for Christ. But that is a subject for a later chapter.

A year before the end of his short life, Alexander tried a new tactic for the management of the empire. He issued an order

Alexander the god. A generation after his death, Alexander is shown with the ram's horns of the Greek-Egyptian deity Zeus-Ammon, on this silver four-drachma coin, minted about 300 B.C. in Thrace, where one of his followers, Lysimachus, ruled.

for his deification in the Greek centers. This introduced the concept of loyalty on religious grounds rather than on political grounds alone.

The older history books find an oriental basis for the origin of the ruler cult—in Persia, Egypt, and Babylonia. But the newer books root this demand in Greek soil. The Greeks always had an unclear distinction between what was human and what was divine. Their gods were always human—they were simply more powerful human beings and had immortality. Did Alexander believe himself to be a god? We don't and can't know. This order for establishment of a ruler cult was never carried out in Macedonia, but rulers in the Hellenistic monarchies of the East did establish it there (see below).

The Successors of Alexander

After the death of Alexander in 323 B.C., his ambitious generals all tried to take over the empire. Failing to do that, each of them tried to get as much of it as he could. As they tried to justify their rule, they thought that claim to divinity gave them the best qualification for royal rule.

Ptolemy first established his throne—in Egypt (323 B.C.). There the pharaohs had always been considered divine. And there it is commonly believed that Alexander the Great managed to get himself declared divine by the priests at the Oasis of Siwah when he conquered the land in 331 B.C. His general Ptolemy succeeded in getting hold of the conqueror's body and enshrined it in a great tomb in Alexandria, where it remained on display, like Lenin's. He did this to set himself up as a legitimate successor to Alexander.

The religious trappings of the Ptolemies remained Greek, however, rather than Egyptian. And they imported their own deities and built temples for them—for Zeus, Hera, Apollo, Artemis, and others. Dionysius was Ptolemy's supposed ancestor. Ptolemy II reclaimed the marshy Arsinoite area, south of Memphis. This region, about thirty by forty miles, was thoroughly Hellenized and colonized by veteran Greek soldiers and retired officials, to whom Ptolemy gave tracts of land.

As in other Hellenistic monarchies of the East, large numbers of Macedonians and Greeks settled in Egypt, where they became the ruling class and provided the basis of Ptolemaic power. For obvious reasons, the Ptolemies could always count on the loyalty of this community. So they ruled in absolute power and with great splendor until Cleopatra, the last of the line, committed suicide in 30 B.C. and the Romans took over.

Seleucus as a young man accompanied Alexander to Asia in 333. In 321 he won control of Babylonia and between 311 and 302 by force of arms conquered the eastern part of Alexander's empire all the way to the Indus. Thus by that time he ruled most of Alexander's empire—from the Aegean to the Indus. He founded his new capital at Antioch-on-the Orontes in Syria, the place where believers were first called Christians and from which Paul launched his missionary journeys.

As with the other successors of Alexander, Seleucus developed the ruler cult, which could help to bring political unity to a widely diverse population. Some of the Seleucid military contests come up later in this chapter. Like the Ptolemies, the Seleucids tried to exercise absolute rule, and they depended on an army that consisted of Greek mercenaries recruited from Greek cities that the rulers established across their empire. And as with the Ptolemies, they were a minority ruling caste in their empire.

Ptolemy I. A general of Alexander the Great, Ptolemy received Egypt as his share of the Greek empire after Alexander's death. His descendants ruled Egypt until 30 B.C. (when Cleopatra died), infusing the land of the pharaohs with Hellenistic culture and running the state on a business basis, with profits payable to the crown. The Ptolemies also controlled Palestine until the Seleucids of Syria took it in 198 B.C.

In Macedonia confusion reigned after the death of Alexander the Great. Finally Antigonus II Gonatas, grandson of Antigonus, one of Alexander's generals, established the Antigonid Dynasty as ruler of Macedonia in 279 B.C. The monarchy dominated all aspects of state affairs, though the king maintained close contact with his people. The external trappings of monarchy were modest, and there was no worship of the king, nor was he part of an ancestor cult. He paid attention to public opinion and individual petitioners had access to him.

Power in the state lay in the hands of the king and the upper level of the aristocracy. Though the king led the state, he was also viewed as a servant of the state. He made treaties, served as chief judge in the judicial system, and controlled the economy. That included managing the mines producing gold and silver and the levy of customs duties. The monarchy served as a patron of the arts and appreciated good architecture and painting. We need to remember that Aristotle's father was on the staff of the king of Macedonia, and he himself spent several years as tutor to the young Alexander. The cities of Macedonia had little individual power, in contrast to the city-states of central and southern Greece. The state depended on a citizen army, rather than a mercenary force, as was the case among the Ptolemies and Seleucids.

(For more on this topic, go to p. 325 or p. 367.)

Religion

Ruler cults dominated much of the Near East in the general period from about 350 B.C. to the time of Christ, including in the Kingdom of Pergamum in western Asia Minor, which broke away from the Seleucid Empire in the second century B.C. In this kingdom they deified their kings and made them part of the ruler cult after death. Ruler cults helped leaders maintain loyalty; they didn't really satisfy the heart needs of people.

In many places, as in Egypt for instance, the masses of common people continued to follow the paths they had trod for millennia. All they needed were the gods of their ancestors.

This general period saw a whole new development—the rise of science and philosophy. Beginning with Thales of Miletus in Asia Minor about 600 B.C., the Greeks started to divorce the explanations of things from religion. They linked science and philosophy in the work of Thales, his associates, and successors. They studied and thought about the original form of matter and even came up with elementary explanations of human evolution.

In time science and philosophy separated. Hellenistic scientists developed some revolutionary conclusions. Among these were some who computed the circumference of the earth, taught that the solar system revolved around the sun, believed that it was possible to reach the Far East by sailing west from Spain, and more.

Among the philosophers arose the schools of Plato, Aristotle, the Stoics, the Epicureans, the Cynics, and others. Together they brought about a growing belief that reason or intellect rather than revelation or the gods should serve as a guide to living.

H. A. Frankfort in *The Intellectual Adventure of Ancient Man* has shown perceptively

Both the Ptolemies and Seleucids set up the ruler cult in their respective domains. Here Antiochus IV Epiphanes (meaning "God Manifest") is pictured on a second century B.C. coin. He is one of the most famous rulers of the Seleucid line because his religious demands set off the Maccabean revolt in 167 B.C. (Gleason Archer)

that the ancient Near Eastern way was the belief that there was a live relationship between mankind and the phenomenal world. That is, they believed that the divine was present in nature and nature was connected with society. So they had an "I-Thou" relationship with everything around them. For example, there was generative life, divine force, in the sun and soil which should be worshiped as gods, representing a kind of animistic approach. The Greek way by contrast now reflected an "I-It" way of thinking; nature was inanimate or impersonal.

The naturalistic thought patterns of the Greeks eventually impacted Jewish thought. Hellenistic ways as they developed in Ptolemaic Egypt affected Jews living in Egypt and those in Palestine during the long period when the Ptolemies ruled Palestine. The non-supernaturalistic or materialistic views of New Testament Sadducees and those they succeeded are a case in point. We shall discuss these developments in later chapters.

Mystery Religions

The ruler cults and the philosophical systems touched only a minority of the

THE RULER CULT AND THE HELLENISTIC KINGDOMS

The Ptolemies and Seleucids ruled over a very diverse assortment of peoples. In these large Hellenistic kingdoms there was no longer loyalty to a small city-state with its deity and its particular way of life. As the corporate orientation of the city-state declined, individualism took its place.

And yet, as people were thrown together in larger political units, a kind of universalism also developed—a cultural interplay previously unknown. Life was similar in Alexandria, Pergamum, Ephesus, Antioch-on-the-Orontes, Salamis, Thessalonica, and many other places—just as it is in many of the world's great cities today.

As thinking people among Greeks, Egyptians, Syrians, and others were exposed to each other, they sought to combine or reconcile certain ideas and materials. One approach was eclecticism—picking and choosing elements from separate systems and combining them into new belief systems. And they looked for common denominators for seemingly diverse things. Thus, in the field of religion, they equated the Greek Zeus with the Roman Jupiter, the Persian Ahuramazda, and the Egyptian Ammon. To the Egyptian, Horus became Apollo; Thoth, Hermes; Hathor, Aphrodite.

This development of a new individualism alongside a new universalism provides some background for the ruler cult. In the large, diverse empire there had to be a means of achieving unity. For starters, the ruler governed as an autocrat through an efficient bureaucracy. But individuals had to be bound to the ruler and to the central government in some effective manner. Alexander himself apparently decided to go the way of the Near East, ruling as a god or at least holding his position by divine right. He became a god-king in Egypt and a divine-right ruler in Persia. The apotheosis (making man god) was only a political device which both the Ptolemies and Seleucids followed. As a god, the king held himself above the laws of men and felt free to make demands on his subjects. Later the Romans developed the ruler cult in connection with worship of the goddess Roma, the personification of the Roman state. Again, they used it as a device to promote political unity in a diverse empire.

Of course the ruler cult presented horrendous problems for believers in all ages—for Daniel's friends in Nebuchadnezzar's day (Daniel 3); for the Maccabeans who finally revolted against Syrian rule and established an independent Jewish state; and for Christians who suffered great persecution and martyrdom at the hands of the Romans.

To those who ask how a political system could develop and maintain such a fiction, we reply that it is still possible. The Shinto faith of Japan venerated the emperor as a descendant of the sun goddess. The Japanese worshiped their emperor as divine until Japan's defeat in World War II, when he gave up his claims to divinity.

---

population. Oriental religions had a much wider appeal. We know these religions as mystery religions because they had secret initiatory rituals into the cults (*mysterion* comes from a root meaning "initiate"). Through that, in some mysterious way, the initiate established communion with a god or goddess and obtained a promise of living in bliss with the deity beyond the grave. The special appeal of the mystery religions lay in their threefold provision: a personal involvement with a god, an emotional stimulation,

Hebrew Religious Thought

Hebrew religious thought patterns were fundamentally different from those of the ancient Near East and Greece. They did not see generative life or divine force in the sun, soil, a great river, or a storm in some animistic sense, as Egyptians and Babylonians and others did. God created all matter and existed above and before all matter. To the Hebrew, matter remained impersonal, inanimate.

Philosophically-oriented Greeks also might consider nature to be inanimate or impersonal. But their gods and goddesses served only as supermen or superwomen—just one level above the great heroes of human society.

Greeks and Near Easterners needed a whole family of gods to bring the world and the social order into being and maintain it. They recognized no single all-powerful God who could make things happen and control events.

Moreover, among all other peoples, only the Jews held to moral absolutes—commands to observe a code of conduct, with details to be followed or avoided. They alone had a concept of a totally holy or righteous God, who exemplified the standard of conduct He expected human beings to attain.

with the god or goddess was established in an emotional and sometimes orgiastic way; this assured the initiate of eternal bliss in companionship with the deity. Initiates commonly grouped themselves together into local organizations or fellowships, which had great social and psychological value for the individual in an increasingly uncertain world.

Because Christianity shares some of these elements, at least to one viewing it superficially, many have classified Christianity as a mystery religion. But the differences greatly exceed the similarities. Christianity is based on a historical rather than a mythological person, on a being who died and rose once purposefully in a substitutionary atonement for mankind, rather than repeatedly in some rhythm of the seasons. Normally the mystery religions did not put specific demands on an individual to live a new lifestyle. Nor did they offer a supernatural enablement for living, as Christianity did. While the rites of initiation in the mystery religions were secret and were never fully revealed even by initiates who defected, the means of becoming a Christian have been almost literally shouted from the housetops and have been published in detail in the Scriptures—available in more than two thousand languages.

(For more on this topic, go to p. 333 or p. 372.)

Warfare

There is no question about the military genius, administrative ability, and personal drive and bravery of Alexander the Great. But he, like many others in history, was able to accomplish what he did in part because of the weakness of his enemy.

In the earlier history of the Persian Empire, the Persian royal family had generally pulled together and maintained effective control of the empire. The fourth century saw an increasing amount of squabbling in the extended ruling family. The young king Darius III had taken the throne only two years before Alexander's attack. And he did so after a series of murders that left bitter competing factions among the high nobles of the court. While

and a promise of a future life—none of which the official cults could offer.

The major mystery religions dominating that period were the Cybele-Attis of Phrygia in central Asia Minor, Isis-Osiris of Egypt, Eleusinian of Athens, Cabeiri or Cabiri of several Greek centers, Aphrodite-Adonis of Alexandria and Asia Minor, and Mithraism of Persia.

The mystery religions all had at their base a divinity whose annual death and resurrection corresponded to the rhythm of the seasons. As plants died in the fall and were reborn in the spring, the vegetation spirits were thought to have gone to the underworld and to have returned from it. Raised from death, they could bestow immortality on mankind. The initiate believed that communion or even union

the royal family was at odds with itself, powerful satraps shook the control of the central authority during the century in a series of revolts. Some ruled their provinces almost as private kingdoms.

Further, in an effort to bring tighter integration of the populace, Darius' predecessors had discarded the traditional policy of religious tolerance for subject peoples and began to put pressure on all to become Zoroastrians. The resulting revolts illustrated the declining loyalty to the Persian government. Jews, Egyptians, and Babylonians especially objected to this loss of religious freedom and welcomed Alexander as a liberator.

We need to remember too that the Persians were a small minority in their empire, ruling a wide variety of peoples. Historian Tom B. Jones estimates that they constituted only one-sixtieth of the total population of the empire.[1] Hence their armies remained largely mercenary and might even take service with the enemy if it was to their advantage to do so. By contrast Macedonia reflects a tightly-knit unitary state with a patriotic citizen army.

Furthermore, the Persian monarchy of the fourth century did not pay the kind of attention to the economic health of the empire that Darius I and his immediate successors had. So inflation, depressed wages, and a heavy tax burden made the populace increasingly less enthusiastic about the maintenance of the empire.

Macedonian Attack

Philip II and his son Alexander sought to launch an all-Greek war of revenge against the Persians for all their interference in Greek affairs. To that end, Philip had built an effective war machine and systematically worked the gold mines near Philippi to help finance the effort. When Philip's advance guard was already in Asia Minor to begin the attack, he was assassinated (336), and his mantle fell on his son Alexander, then only twenty. Two years later, in 334, Alexander began to realize his father's dream and marched across the Hellespont into the Persian Empire to do battle with the colossus of the East. Certainly his original intention was not to conquer the whole

Isis wearing a cow-horn crown, holding a ritual rattle and necklace. The Isis cult was immensely popular throughout the Mediterranean world and northern Europe. Her sanctuaries could be found on the Acropolis at Athens, at Pompeii, and elsewhere. Christianity had an uphill struggle in defeating her worship.

empire but to free the coast of Asia Minor. One success led to another, however, and he ultimately did lead his troops all the way to the Indus River.

To get the job done, Alexander marshaled an army of only about 35,000 men, but they were well trained and well coordinated. At the core were 12,000 in the phalanxes of Macedonian foot soldiers and 2,000 in the heavily-armed Macedonian cavalry. Then there were 3,000 excellently trained cavalry from Thessaly and 5,000 light-armed troops from the tribal peoples on the Macedonian frontiers. Finally, the Greek city-states sent 7,000 foot soldiers, and Alexander hired 5,000 Greek mercenaries. His nearly empty treasury wouldn't allow him to employ more, but he also had the Macedonian and

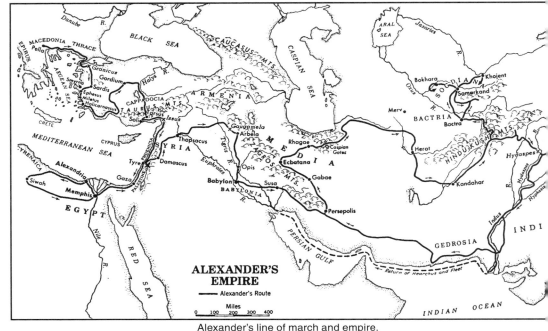

Alexander's line of march and empire.

allied Greek navies of some 180 ships manned by crews of about 38,000. And as he moved east he added recruits and mercenaries. Several years later he began to integrate some thousands of Persians into his army. From the beginning the campaign had the character of an exploratory expedition, with Alexander taking along scientists, geographers, and historians.

Unfortunately for Alexander, he always had to be looking over his shoulder. The Greek city-states were restless under Macedonian control and could break into revolt at any time. Therefore he had to leave important contingents of his army in Macedonia to keep the lid on. Worse, he was not sure how dependable some of his Greek allied and mercenary troops might be on the battlefield. That fact sometimes hampered his battle plans.

Logistics

Alexander faced a staggering task provisioning his troops, his cavalry, and pack animals as they moved through the vast stretches of the Middle East. An older view is that as he conquered an area he collected supplies there for the next campaign. But Engels has shown that in advance of his arrival he arranged for the collection of supplies. The local officials "regularly surrendered to him before the army marched into their territory."[2]

Engels goes into great detail about the provisioning of Alexander's army (including how many pounds of food his men and animals needed daily) and concludes that his success was due in large part to "his meticulous attention to the provisioning of his army."[3] Engels' study is invaluable in showing the needs of Alexander's army, the speed with which it moved, the length of time it took them to get from point A to B, and much more. All of us who think about Alexander and his conquests so quickly go over the top of the story that we do not even think about how such a great conqueror made it happen.

Organization, Armor, and Weapons

The core of the Macedonian army consisted of the phalanx. The basic unit was the *dekad,* which in 334 B.C. consisted of sixteen men—a double file in eight-deep battle order. Their characteristic weapon was the *sarissa,* a long shaft made from corner wood (a hard and lightweight wood of the cherry or dogwood family), some eighteen to nineteen feet long in Alexander's day. They attached an iron point to the upper end and a butt-spike on the lower end. If the forward point broke off in battle, the butt-spike could be used for fighting. It also permitted the sarissa to be planted in the ground so a charging horseman or horse could be impaled on it. The sarissa actually consisted of two parts joined by an iron coupling sleeve so it could be dismantled and carried during the march.

The phalangite carried or thrust his sarissa with both hands, using one-third of its length to balance and hold the weapon and keeping it aligned with the weapons of the other members of the *dekad.* The sarissas of the first five ranks would extend beyond the file, while the last three ranks held them above the heads of their comrades. The result was a towering hedge and a solid mass of sarissas, impenetrable to the enemy. Phalangists carried small bronze shields suspended from the left shoulder by a neck strap. They wore leather corslets rather than heavy metal breastplates, helmets (usually conical), greaves, and used knives as additional weapons.

Other infantry units carried thrusting spears about twelve feet long, shields, and swords. With their longer spears, they had the edge on the ordinary Greek soldier of the day (fighting as Persian mercenaries) whose spears were only about eight feet long. They also had corslets and greaves. In addition, Alexander's army included contingents of bowmen and slingers.

The Macedonian cavalry fought alongside the phalanx under the king's personal leadership. They charged in delta-shaped wedge formation. Like the phalangite, the cavalryman carried a sarissa at least fifteen feet in length but having iron weapon heads on each end. This he held underarm for an upward stroke, aiming at the enemy horseman's face or his horse's head. Without stirrups or saddles, these cavalrymen did not have the thrust to unhorse opponents that medieval knights did. Cavalrymen normally wore bronze corslets with strap-on greaves, bronze helmets, and carried straight or curved swords.

Increasingly powerful and sophisticated weapons had become available by Alexander's day. For example, he had stone throwers or catapults to use in attacking Tyre and Gaza. These machines could throw stones weighing 10 to 180 pounds, depending on their size and construction. Their range was about 150 to 200 yards.

Alexander's Battles

The Granicus River

As Alexander crossed the Hellespont into Asia Minor in the spring of 334, he faced a Persian force of 10,000 cavalry and 4–5,000 Greek mercenary infantry. Alexander advanced with about 18,000 (13,000 infantry and 5,000 cavalry) to meet them at the Granicus River. He left behind his allied and mercenary infantry because of their doubtful reliability.

His tactic here was to send some of his crack cavalry units against the left of the Persian line, giving the impression of a full-scale attack. Then the Macedonians retreated, drawing the Persian left-wing cavalry down into the Granicus riverbed in disorderly pursuit. At that point Alexander took his main force against the Persians in an oblique or sideways motion, breaking through the disorganized Persian cavalry and cutting them up.

The Persian Greek mercenaries remained in position, at first apparently not sensing their danger. Then presumably they hoped to transfer to a new employer. When they requested terms they were refused, and a massacre of some 2–3,000 followed. The rest (c. 2,000) surrendered unconditionally. So Alexander had destroyed the only Persian army in Asia Minor. He now moved down the coast of the Aegean, freeing the Greek cities there.

The Battle of Issus

Then Alexander subjugated central Asia Minor and in October of 333 met Darius III

The Macedonian Phalanx

The Macedonian Phalanx was a fearsome unit. In Alexander's expeditionary force there were six or seven such units, each fifteen hundred men strong. They were drawn up for battle eight deep, each man with a sarissa or pike some eighteen to twenty feet long. The first five lines extended their pikes beyond the bodies of the men in the front line, raising their weapons progressively higher in each line. The last three lines held their pikes above their heads. Further, the men attacked in close formation, each occupying only about a yard of space. Thus, there was a solid wall of pikes facing the enemy, who rarely would close with the phalanx in hand-to-hand fighting.

at the east end of the peninsula, at Issus. The Persians had something over 100,000 cavalry and foot soldiers, while Alexander had less than half as many. As the combatants prepared for battle, they were spread from the shore of the Gulf of Issus to the hills along the River Pinarus. Initially Darius stationed his army behind a screen of cavalry and light troops. But just before the battle began, he pulled his cavalry off to his right near the shore, where the land was flatter and he could use them to better advantage. To counter, Alexander sent most of his cavalry off to his left.

As the battle began, Alexander's light troops were able to push back the Persians on the hills, and he outflanked the Persian left and routed it. Fierce fighting raged in the center as the Macedonians tried to cross the river and push back the Persian Asiatic corps and their Greek mercenaries. Finally Alexander was able to swing around to the left and move toward Darius' chariot, about which there was bitter fighting. Alexander was wounded in the thigh, but Darius, believing that the Macedonians had turned the tide of battle, fled.

The Persian right flank, seeing Darius run, panicked. The Greek mercenaries in Darius' army took heavy losses. As the battle scene degenerated, Alexander's men fell to plundering the Persian camp. They took Darius' wife and family as prisoners, and Alexander got his hands on the tremendous supply of cash that the Persians always carried when going to war. He finally could pay his men, whose salary was badly in arrears. This made the victory important to Alexander financially, militarily, and politically.

Tyre, Gaza, and the Mediterranean Coast

During 332 Alexander proceeded down the Mediterranean coast. As along the Aegean, here one of his goals was to take the ports of the Persian navy and so to neutralize the fleet without having to build one of his own. Most towns capitulated, including Jerusalem, which threw open her gates to the conqueror. But Tyre did not.

Back in the fifth century B.C., the prophet Ezekiel had predicted that Nebuchadnezzar would capture and destroy the city, and that the place would be scraped bare as the

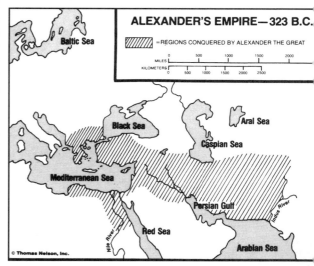

Alexander's empire in regional perspective

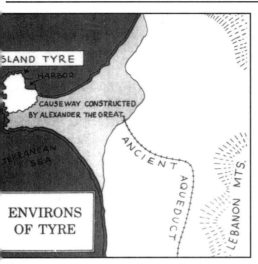

ENVIRONS OF TYRE

Because Tyre was one-half mile offshore and he was without a navy, Alexander decided to build a road out to the island. In time sand drifted against the road, and both the island and the road became encased in a peninsula. The approximate shoreline is indicated above, adjacent to the peninsula.

top of a rock when its stones and timbers would be dumped in the water (Ezekiel 26:3–12, 14, 19). Tyre had once been a two-part city: one on land and the other on an island a half-mile offshore. Nebuchadnezzar did destroy the city on land and it remained in ruins.

When Alexander came along without a navy, he decided to build a road out to the island city. To get the material he used the debris of the mainland city and literally threw it into the water. After a seven-month siege he managed to take the island city, slaughtering 8,000 in the process, later executing another 2,000 and selling the remaining women and children into slavery. The dramatic story of Alexander's siege and the determination and bravery of the defenders would fill a book.

For our present purposes it is enough to make two comments. (1) Alexander's destruction of Tyre specifically fulfilled prophecy. (2) And while Alexander was trying to reduce Tyre, Darius III sent him a message offering him the empire west of the Euphrates, a huge sum of gold, and his daughter in marriage. In return he asked for

the restoration of his family and a treaty of friendship. Alexander rejected the offer. He was about to take all the territory anyway and he had Darius' daughter as a prisoner and could marry her if he wished.

Alexander continued on down the coast to Gaza, which also resisted. Taking the city, he killed all the males and sold the women and children into slavery. After Tyre and Gaza, Egypt had no will to resist. Unhappy with Persian rule anyway, the Egyptians treated Alexander as a liberator. At the oasis of Siwa (west of the Nile) he reportedly was declared to be divine, the son of Ammon. He founded the city of Alexandria, which became so important in the history of culture.

Gaugamela

Alexander next led his troops eastward to confront Darius (331 B.C.). This battle took place east of the Tigris on the plain of Gaugamela, near the town of Arbela. Both sides prepared intensively for the conflict. Darius leveled the ground so his 200 scythed chariots could easily maneuver there. Alexander questioned prisoners to discover Darius' order of battle and led in person a cavalry reconnaissance of the area where he intended to fight, to make sure there were no cavalry traps confronting him (e.g., pits). Because Darius had suffered so many casualties among his Greek mercenaries, he depended more on Asiatic infantry here. Darius amassed an army of some 100,000, about 35,000 of which were cavalry. Alexander did not have half that many, with about 6,000 in the cavalry.

As the battle got underway, the Persian left wing pushed back the Macedonian right wing, but the Macedonians were able to stabilize the situation. When the scythed chariot charge sought to cut up the center of their line, the Macedonians simply opened their ranks and let them pass through, while the troops hurled missiles at them and managed to cut them down. Next the Macedonians routed the Persian left wing.

At this point a gap appeared between two divisions of the Macedonian phalanx, and Persian troops broke through to the Macedonian baggage train. Eventually, however, Macedonian reserves drove the Persians from the baggage. Next Alexander's left wing came under strong pressure and he raced to support them. Persian retreat in that theater freed Alexander to pursue Darius, who had started to flee when his left wing crumbled. Soon the whole army followed the king's example. If Darius had been more steadfast here or at Issus, he might have saved the day.

The Aftermath

Darius became a refugee in the northeastern provinces, where one of his officers eventually murdered him. Meanwhile, Alexander took possession of the capitals of the Persian Empire—Babylon, Susa, and Persepolis, burning the latter. After the death of Darius he took the title of King of Persia.

Alexander's guerrilla wars in the northeast and his great battle of the Hydaspes (326) in India need not detain us here. By the time he had defeated the Persian armies, taken the Persian capitals, and become King of Persia, he had reached his goal of Greek revenge against the Persians and the destruction of the empire.

Ptolemies and Seleucids

It would be tedious and time-consuming to tell the whole story of the successors of Alexander and their military conflicts. From the standpoint of the involvement of the Jews it is necessary to make a few comments on the Ptolemies and Seleucids, however. Nearly all Jews lived under their administration during the fourth to the second centuries B.C.

Ptolemy became satrap of Egypt in 323, after the death of Alexander. He sought in addition to control Cyprus, Cyrenaica (modern Libya), and Palestine. In fact, he invaded Palestine four times between 318 and 301, holding it briefly during the first three occupations. His dynasty controlled it for the next hundred years, from 301 until 198. The victory of the Seleucids at the battle of Panium (198) resulted in the transfer of Palestine to the Seleucids.

The hundred years of Ptolemaic control of Palestine are important to the history of

This inscription, found at the city of Tyre, lists the names of nine Greek generals who accompanied Alexander the Great when he destroyed the city in 332 B.C.

Judaism. Jews were at first forcibly taken to Egypt, to Alexandria especially, and later were welcomed there. Many settled in Alexandria. Gradually they forgot their Hebrew and between 250 and 150 B.C. they translated their Bible into Greek (the Septuagint). In time some Jews of Palestine and Egypt also modified their thought patterns, accepting aspects of non-supernaturalistic Hellenism and the pagan lifestyle that went with it. Hellenistic ways caught on more readily under the Ptolemies and the early

Seleucids because at that time they were not forced on the populace.

Seleucus received the Babylonian satrapy in the second partition of Alexander's empire (321). A successful warrior, he eventually managed to bring almost the whole of Alexander's empire except Egypt under his control. After he took Syria, he founded his new capital there, Antioch-on-the-Orontes. The fortunes of the Seleucid dynasty fluctuated greatly over the years but reached a high point during the reign of Antiochus III, the Great (223–187). He conquered Palestine in 198, taking advantage of the weakness of Egypt while the infant Ptolemy V had come to the throne. But at the end of his reign he suffered defeat at the hands of the Romans and lost all of Asia Minor.

Antiochus IV Epiphanes (176–164) remains especially important to the history of the Jews because the Maccabean revolt took place during his reign (see next chapter). The Seleucid effort to force the Jews to accept Hellenistic religious practices precipitated that revolution. The reason Antiochus did so was the need to unify his people for the defense of his realm.

The impact of Hellenism in Palestine during the Ptolemaic and Seleucid periods resulted in part from the founding of Greek colonies there since Alexander's conquests—of Sebaste (Samaria), Philadelphia (Amman), Ptolemais (Acre), Philoteria (south of the Sea of Galilee), Scythopolis (Beth-Shan), and Marisa (Mareshah) in the Judean foothills.

(For more on this topic, go to p. 334 or p. 374.)

Housing and Furniture

When we ask what houses were like in the days of Alexander and his successors, the answer has to be, "Where?" And of course we are really asking about houses in places where Jews lived. In Susa and elsewhere in Persia, as well as Judah itself, they remained essentially the same as during the period of the Persian Empire (see last chapter). Jews remaining in Babylonia lived much as in the days of Babylonian captivity (see chapter 11).

A large percentage of Jews residing in Egypt lived in Alexandria. And we can't know much about houses there because changes in the shoreline have submerged a good part of the ancient city. But in the villages of Egypt the common arrangement was of three rooms on the main floor, one of which provided an entrance from the street. The second was a courtyard of about a quarter of the total floor area. There we might find animal pens and feeding troughs for livestock (pigs, goats, chickens, geese), storage jars for water and grain, clay ovens for baking bread, and millstones for grinding grain. Houses commonly consisted of two stories, sometimes three, and occasionally had a basement area divided into storage

Alexander's death resulted in the division of his empire into smaller kingdoms ruled by his generals. Two of those generals, Ptolemy and Seleucus, took control of large chunks of the Middle East and fought for possession of Palestine. By 275 the Ptolemies controlled Egypt, Palestine, Cyrene, Phoenicia, Cyprus, and the coast of Asia Minor.

bins. The floor space on the ground floor commonly was about sixty square meters.

They built their structures with mud-brick—clay mixed with straw. Wooden rafters, floor supports, and doorways created a fire hazard in the crowded residential areas where streets were very narrow. Such wood gets very dry in a land with almost no rainfall.

The wooden household furniture consisted of tables and writing desks, chairs, bedsteads, and chests. They also had cooking pots, bronze cauldrons, and oil-burning clay lamps.

Houses in Macedonia and the Greek cities of Asia Minor generally differed greatly from Egypt and Mesopota-mia. We don't yet have information about the houses of the middle and lower classes of Pella, the capital of Macedonia (24 miles northwest of Thessalonica) in the days of Philip and Alexander. The villas excavated there had open courtyards surrounded by colonnades, with Doric capitals and floors of mosaics of small pebbles, instead of the cut stone tesserae with which they were usually made.

Excavated houses of the Greek islands and the Asia Minor coast (where Jews began to filter in) were also of the peristyle type (arranged around square courtyards and surrounded by Doric or sometimes Ionic columns). A narrow entrance passage led to one large room, with smaller rooms and offices around the court and lighted from it. This Greek influence spread into Mesopotamia, and during the second century B.C. houses of the peristyle type were built even south of Babylon.

(For more on this topic, go to p. 340 or p. 377.)

Diet and Foodstuffs

Egypt

Jews living in Egypt generally had plenty of food. Until the 1990s Egypt has always been a food-exporting country. The ancient pharaohs had engineered an irrigation system, which the early Ptolemies expanded—especially in the Arsinoite region south of Memphis. But the last Ptolemies, feeble and financially strapped, let the system fall into disrepair.

For the very poor the staple foods were wheat and barley, made into flat loaves that resembled pancakes. This they supplemented with boiled vegetables that were plentiful and inexpensive. Papyrus stalks and other stems of marsh plants could be boiled and roasted. Beans and lentils grew in great quantities all over the country. The more affluent ate meat, fish, cheese, and a greater range of vegetables, as well as having milk, wine, and beer to drink.

Mesopotamia

Jews who did not return to Palestine in the Restoration, remaining in Mesopotamia instead, enjoyed a diet much the same as during the Persian period (see last chapter). There were minor differences, however. As noted earlier, the Persians had

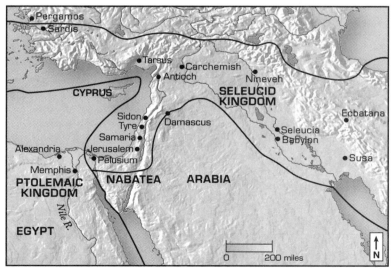

Originally the Seleucids controlled Mesopotamia, Syria, most of Asia Minor and Iran. But after 198 B.C. they also controlled Phoenicia and Palestine.

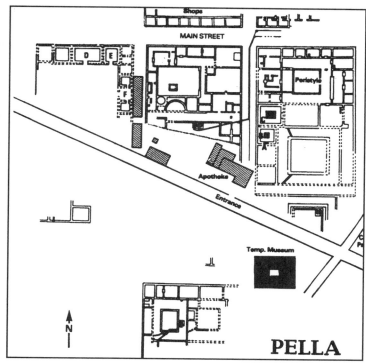

Floor plans of the large houses of Pella, birthplace of Alexander the Great, show colonnaded peristyle courtyards surrounded by reception rooms, dining rooms, and family rooms.

Asia Minor

As Jews went to Asia Minor under the invitation of the Seleucids and the blessing of the Kingdom of Pergamum, they went to an area that was agriculturally prosperous. Wheat and barley were grown there but not enough for local needs; some was imported from Egypt. Grapes for wine grew all over the peninsula and wine was extensively exported. In fact, Asia Minor was probably the original home of the grape. Olives were cultivated extensively, especially along the coast in the west and south and on the offshore islands. Fruits and nuts grew in most regions: e. g., apples, pears, cherries, almonds, hazelnuts, chestnuts, and more. The fig was the most important fruit commercially. Onions, radishes, and cucumbers were among the numerous vegetables grown.

With sheep raised extensively throughout the peninsula, both coarser and finer varieties of wool were available in quantity. Fine breeds of horses raised there were much sought after by Persians, Seleucids, Romans, and others. Oxen were the chief draft animals for plowing and drawing oxcarts, and their hides were also valued. Mules and cows (for their meat, milk, and cheese) abounded in the region. And we must not neglect to mention ducks and barnyard fowl.

The diet of people of the area was probably as varied and abundant as anywhere in the eastern Mediterranean lands and the Near East. Modern Turkey is still a garden land in many of its regions.

(For more on this topic, go to p. 341 or p. 377.)

brought in rice and it was grown more extensively now. Also, the salination of the soil continued to get worse. Therefore wheat cultivation declined in favor of barley because barley can tolerate greater salt content in the soil. So when commentators talk about Babylonian cereal consumption at this time, they commonly have barley in mind.

Persia and Judah

The Jews who were still living in the area of biblical Shushan (Persian Susa) consumed a diet that was much the same as in the days of Esther and Ezra (see last chapter). Jews now living in Judah ate much as did their ancestors in the Kingdom of Judah (see chapter 10). But when they were part of the Ptolemaic and then the Seleucid empires, they had slightly more variety, resulting from being part of a larger political unit and from the international trade that took place then.

Dress

It is difficult to discover specific information about the kind of clothing Jews might have worn wherever they lived during the third and second centuries B.C. To narrow the subject to manageable proportions, let's look at the situation in Egypt and Palestine during the period.

In Egypt almost all clothing was made of linen. And in general it was very simple. Men engaged in agriculture, carpentry, and other crafts or construction wore little more than a loincloth or short kilt. Even the king is shown in a short kilt during the Ptolemaic period. Men also wore knee-length tunics or shirts, lightweight ones in summer and heavier ones in winter. In addition, their wardrobes included lightweight summer cloaks and heavier winter cloaks. These could be worn over the shoulders with kilts or tunics. Girdles or belts served more as pockets to carry things than as a means of keeping clothing in place or for decoration.

Sheath-like dresses extending to the ankles and held up by one or two straps over the shoulders remained the garment of choice for women. They wore cloaks over their shoulders for warmth or for show. Among the more well-to-do, both sexes simply had more clothing and better quality fabrics. Men and women either went barefoot or wore sandals, often of papyrus. Unfortunately, modern studies of ancient Egyptian clothing are based too much on wall paintings, reliefs, and sculptures. Textiles have not been studied in sufficient detail.

In Palestine during this period the upper classes increasingly preferred linen, though most clothing still was of wool. In the event that they owned tunics of linen, outer cloaks normally consisted of wool. Both men and women wore long garments, extending from the neck to the ankles. Sashes or belts or girdles served as substitutes for pockets; expensive colored ones were for show. Much of the time they went barefoot, but they did own sandals that might be made of sheepskin or cowhide.

(For more on this topic, go to p. 341 or p. 378.)

Family Life

In Palestine families continued to arrange marriages for their sons and daughters. These were almost always monogamous. And they generally avoided intermarriage with non-Jews. Midwives continued to assist in the birthing process, and male infants were circumcised as sons of the covenant.

They kept the Sabbath quite rigorously, attending synagogue services on that day. They offered sacrifices regularly in the temple, and regularly observed the great national feasts (e. g., Passover, Pentecost). We know all this because when the Seleucids ordered Sabbath observance, circumcision, and the sacrificial system stopped, they brought on the Maccabean revolt (for discussion see next chapter). Moreover, the Gospels clearly show that the Sabbath, circumcision, regular observance of feasts and festivals, and the offering of temple sacrifices remained important facets of Jewish life and had been for a long time.

Boys usually grew up learning the trade of their fathers. Women ran the affairs of the household and men had great power over the family. Eldest sons had superior inheritance rights but younger sons also expected to inherit property. We know nothing of formal education or organized schools, but apparently at least the priestly element in society learned how to read and write. Jews did not embalm and it was customary to bury the dead on the day they died.

Jews of the dispersion, living in such places as Alexandria and Babylon, considered themselves to belong to the Palestinian community. They gave an annual contribution to the temple and made pilgrimages to Jerusalem when possible. And they maintained their own synagogues for instruction and fellowship. While individually they tried to keep the Sabbath and observe other Jewish rituals, they had to figure out how to do so in a society that did not. They tended not to intermarry with the people of the lands where they lived, and they also lived in their own sections of the city in places like Alexandria in Egypt and Antioch of Syria.

(For more on this topic, go to p. 341 or p. 379.)

Work, Travel and Commerce

If Alexander had lived, the roadways and sea lanes would have remained open across greater distances. And the arteries of trade would have been less clogged by political roadblocks. But as it was, political units remained fairly large, and cultural ties leapfrogged political boundaries. To get some idea of the work and commerce of the time, we shall look first at the Ptolemies, then the Seleucids, then at some social and economic trends, and finally at a few cultural developments.

The Ptolemies

Under the Ptolemies part of the land of Egypt was cultivated directly as crown land. The native temples held another segment. Greeks and others who were reservists in Ptolemy's army farmed yet other land. The Ptolemies taxed this class and workers on crown lands to help provide royal revenues. In addition to levying taxes, the Ptolemies imposed many monopolies, such as on oil-producing crops (sesame, castor oil, linseed, safflower), the mines, quarries, and salt production. Over many other branches of the economy they exercised strict control, e. g., over the production of linen, papyrus, and beer. In the case of the oil monopoly, for example, they controlled sowing of the seed, manufacture in state factories, and retailing of oil at fixed prices. The primary goal was always government revenues rather than the well-being of native Egyptians.

We do not know whether the Ptolemies tried to exercise the same controls outside Egypt proper as inside it. For instance, there was a rather large olive oil industry in Palestine at Mareshah (Marisa), about eighteen miles southeast of Ashkelon, during the third and second centuries B.C. Excavators found about twenty olive presses there, with an estimated annual output of some 270 tons.[4]

A Greek and Macedonian ruling class ran Egypt, primarily from the capital at Alexandria. They scattered reservist Greek soldiers over the countryside because the Ptolemies did not encourage city-founding, as did the Seleucids. Greeks, Macedonians, Jews, and Egyptians mixed together in Alexandria. But unfortunately we cannot know the city as we would like. With the change in sea level, much of the old city now lies under water. By and large the Greeks kept themselves separate from the Egyptians. Though slavery existed in Alexandria, there was no real place for slaves in the countryside, where free men did all types of manual labor.

An antipathy developed between the native Egyptians and the Ptolemies. This even led to civil war and the breakaway of southern Egypt for a couple of decades around 200 B.C. Eventually non-Greeks found their way into the bureaucracy and even into the army when Greek immigration dried up.

Whether native Egyptian or Greek, people were essentially frozen in their occupations, boys learning their trades from their fathers and following in their footsteps. Excessive taxes in Egypt kept the lower classes quite impoverished.

The Seleucids

The Seleucids, like the Ptolemies, ruled with the help of a Greco-Macedonian elite, separate from the native populations that they governed. Unlike Alexander, they had no place in their government for the Iranians. To encourage Greek and Macedonian immigration, they granted land and planted cities across the country. They were even able to produce a phalanx of Macedonians 16,000 strong at the Battle of Magnesia against Rome in 189. These military settlements of active soldiers furnished a military reserve, acted as garrisons to hold down the countryside, and provided a class of people with a certain productive expertise.

The Seleucids founded cities all the way from the Mediterranean to Bactria in the Far East. To name a few, there was Antioch-on-the-Orontes, Apamea, Seleucia-on-the-Tigris, Europus in Media, Tanagra in Persis, and Thera in Bactria. Excavators have found dozens of new foundations or renamed or refounded ancient cities. These cities helped spread Greek culture all the way to India. They were especially successful in hellenizing the Syrian coastline and much of Asia Minor.

Social and Economic Trends

Cities became centers of Greek culture and were organized like Greek city-states, with a closely-defined citizen body which owned land and worked it with the help of slaves. Resident aliens shared in the cultural and economic life but not in the government. The forces of production changed little from earlier days.

Ptolemies, Seleucids, and Pergamenes introduced new fruits and crops and some improvements in farm equipment, such as increased use of plows with iron tips. Most of the new commodities merely provided luxury products for a small minority without causing a drain of specie outside the country.

The money economy spread to the cities of Asia and North Africa, with virtually an international coinage. But natives living in their villages still functioned with a barter economy. Excavators find no evidence of a fundamental increase in the level of agricultural production or the development of industry. There is no sign of anything like mass production. Much economic distress, and great extremes of poverty and wealth, are evident everywhere. Some Egyptian peasants simply abandoned over-taxed farms.

The Economy and Cultural Developments

During this period Greek creative energy spread widely. There tended to be a concentration of cultural activity in great royal cities, such as Pergamum and Alexandria. Alexandria, for example, dominated the intellectual life of the Greek world. Contributing to that was its great library of some 500,000 scrolls, as well as its museum, really a research institute.

Ptolemaic patronage brought many poets to Alexandria. In Pergamum the Attalid kings exercised a similar patronage. Rhodes, Cos, and Tarsus became other important centers of culture. Athens became the home of philosophy. Epicurus (founder of Epicure-

anism) of Samos settled there, as did Zeno (founder of Stoicism) of Cyprus. New Comedy also developed in Athens.

The gymnasium arose as an important institution during this period. Participants combined physical exercise with studies in literature and music. Gymnasia became popular and significant in Athens, Pergamum, and the Seleucid cities. With the flowering of Greek culture there developed a belief in the superiority of Greeks over other races.

Greek scientists also made their contributions. Heracleides of Pontus (4th century) is famous for being the first to maintain that the apparent daily rotation of the heavens is accounted for not by the circling of stars around the earth but by the rotation of the earth on its own axis. Aristarchus of Samos (3rd century) produced a treatise on the size of the sun and the moon and the distance of the sun and moon from the earth. He also taught that the sun was the center of the universe, which revolved around it. Copernicus was aware of the achievement of Aristarchus. Eratosthenes (3rd century), librarian at Alexandria, in his *Geographica* computed the measurement of the earth's circumference, coming within 200 miles of the correct figure. Euclid of Alexandria (c. 300 B.C.) produced his *Elements of Geometry*, which have remained almost unchanged from his day until now, as modern high school students work through them. Herophilus of Alexandria (c. 300 B.C.) advanced the knowledge of the brain, liver, and more, through dissection.

Invention generally lagged behind because of classical contempt for manual labor. Of course people who work with processes learn how to improve them—to invent new ones. But those capable of such invention were divorced from the processes. Moreover, with the existence of slavery and cheap labor, no one needed to find labor-saving devices. Rulers, however, patronized military technicians in a search for more powerful weapons—and they got results. But there was no drive by society as a whole to spur investigation and invention.

(For more on this topic, go to p. 342 or p. 379.)

Notes:

[1]Tom B. Jones, *Ancient Civilization* (Chicago: Rand McNally, 1960), 155.

[2]Donald W. Engels, *Alexander the Great and the Logistics of the Macedonian Army* (Berkeley: University of California Press, 1978), 1.

[3]Ibid., 3.

[4]*New Encyclopedia of Archaeological Excavations in the Holy Land* (New York: Simon & Schuster, 1993), 3, 951.

Bibliography:

Adams, W. Lindsay and Eugene N. Borza, eds. *Philip II, Alexander the Great and the Macedonian Heritage.* Washington, D. C.: University Press of America, 1982.

Borza, Eugene N. *In the Shadow of Olympus: The Emergence of Macedon.* Princeton: Princeton University Press, 1990.

Bosworth, A. B. *Conquest and Empire: The Reign of Alexander the Great.* Cambridge: Cambridge University Press, 1988.

Ellis, J. R. *Philip II and Macedonian Imperialism.* Princeton: Princeton University Press, 1976.

Engels, Donald W. *Alexander the Great and the Logistics of the Macedonian Army.* Berkeley: University of California Press, 1978.

Errington, R. Malcolm. *A History of Macedonia.* Berkeley: University of California Press, 1990.

Fox, Robin Lane. *The Search for Alexander.* Boston: Little, Brown, 1980.

Fraser, P. M. *Cities of Alexaznder the Great.* Oxford: Clarendon Press, 1996.

Grant, Michael. *From Alexander to Cleopatra: The Hellenistic World.* New York: Charles Scribner's Sons, 1982.

Green, Peter. *Alexander of Macedon, 356–323 B.C.* Berkeley; University of California Press, 1991.

Green, Peter. *Alexander to Actium.* Berkeley: University of California Press, 1990.

Gruen, Erich S. *The Hellenistic World and the Coming of Rome.* Berkeley: University of California Press, 2 vols., 1984.

Hammond, N. G. L. *The Genius of Alexander the Great.* Chapel Hill, N.C.: University of North Carolina Press, 1997.

Hammond, N. G. L. *The Macedonian State.* Oxford: The Clarendon Press, 1989.

Martis, Nicholaos. *The Falsification of Macedonian History.* Athens: Euroekdotiki, 1984.

O'Brien, John M. *Alexander the Great.* New York: Routledge, 1992.

Sherwin-White, Susan and Amelie Kuhrt. *From Samarkhand to Sardis: A New Approach to the Seleucid Empire.* Berkeley: University of California Press, 1993.

Walbank, F. W. *The Hellenistic World.* Cambridge, Mass.: Harvard University Press, rev. ed., 1993.

Wood, Michael. *In the Footsteps of Alexander the Great.* Berkeley: University of California Press, 1997.

Chapter 14

LIFE DURING THE MACCABEAN AGE

(1, 2 Maccabees; Josephus)

If you are like most Americans, you thrilled to the stories of the patriots who rebelled against the British: the Boston Tea Party; Paul Revere's ride, the heroism of the Minutemen at Lexington and Concord. They inspired courage, poems, songs, great statements about the role of freedom. Now if you are Jewish, there is another period that inspired the same kind of heroism, stories of courage, poetry and songs, and even an annual celebration: Hannukah.

For American readers the American Revolution has the same kind of significance as the time of the Maccabees to Hebrews of Jesus' day and Jews around the world today. And just as we must study the history of revolutionary America to understand the role of freedom today, so we must study the Maccabean period to understand the days in which Jesus Christ lived and the apostle Paul ministered.

The two centuries before Christ was born was a period filled with tumult. First the Seleucids of Syria successfully invaded Palestine as they wrenched control of the region from the Egyptian Ptolemies (198 B.C.). Then the Seleucids moved in with new religious dictates designed to bring about greater political and social unity, moves that only fractured the social and religious fabric. When they forced pagan religious views on the populace, the results were predictable—some capitulated and some did not. Thus they pitted Jew against Jew and/or Jew against Syrian Seleucids and their Jewish supporters, very much like the division between the British loyalists and the American patriots.

This friction between those who found it politically and economically expedient to side with the dominant political and social force and those who resisted resulted in open revolution, the successful Maccabean

Antiochus III. This Seleucid king took Palestine from the Egyptians (Ptolemies).

Expansion of the Jewish State
under the Maccabees

Joppa and its surroundings, gaining a seaport.

His successor, John Hyrcanus (135–104) conquered east of the Dead Sea, then Samaria (destroying the Samaritan temple on Mount Gerizim) and the Idumeans (Edomites) south to Beersheba. He forced the Idumeans to accept Judaism and be circumcised. This is the only known instance in all of history that Jews were responsible for forced conversion of another people to Judaism.

Aristobulus (104–103) conquered Galilee, and Alexander Janneus (103–76 B.C.) completed the conquest of almost the whole of Palestine. Thus by the end of his reign the Maccabean kingdom included Galilee, Samaria, Judea, and Idumea west of the Jordan River; and the Golan, Perea, Moab, and part of Edom east of the Jordan.

(For more on this topic, go to p. 346 or p. 389.)

revolt. After Jewish independence became a fact, the Maccabeans or Hasmoneans continued to fight to take chunks of territory from Syria and add them to the Jewish state. But then there arose new dimensions to the tumult as hellenized Jews contested with traditional or conservative Jews and as ambitious personalities tried to build their constituencies and advance their causes. Finally, Roman imperial designs resulted in Roman conquest in 63 B.C.

The Land

Of course the physical geography of Palestine remained as it had been for thousands of years. But the political geography changed greatly with succeeding Maccabean rulers. Under Simon in 142 the Maccabean or Hasmonean state gained independence. At that time Simon controlled Judea from a little north of Hebron to a point north of Bethel and from the Jordan River to the modern airport at Lod. He also ruled the southern part of Perea east of the Jordan. Expansionistic, Simon later took

Government

Seleucid Rule

The Seleucid kings ruled as autocrats; their word was law. They had gained their position by conquest and they chose helpers, with little regard for class or wealth, to run the state. In occupied Norway during the Second World War similar sympathizers of the Nazis were called Quislings. These Seleucid "friends" constituted something of a governing council in Palestine. With their friends the Seleucid kings filled army positions, officers of state, and ambassadorships. And from them they expected and received a high degree of loyalty. But their councils were not merely a group of military and political experts. The Seleucids also kept scholars—artists, writers, philosophers, and others—at their courts.

The Seleucid kings also ruled with the help of a Greco-Macedonian elite in the cities that they founded. In such cities Syrians, Jews, Persians and others were welcomed for their contributions to the

Citizen Privileges

In passing, it is interesting to note that Seleucus Nicator (306–280 B.C.) made the Jews citizens of the cities he built in Asia and Syria and in Antioch itself, and gave them privileges equal to those of the Macedonians and Greeks. These privileges they continued to enjoy down through the first Christian century.[1] As citizens they would have had the protection of local laws and access to the courts, the right to establish businesses and to trade freely, and the opportunity to serve in local government agencies.

economy and society, but the Seleucids generally excluded them from rule, and they never constituted more than a tiny percent of the ruling group. With a collection of Greeks and Macedonians planted in cities across their kingdom on land granted by the crown, and subscribing to a Hellenistic culture, the Seleucids sought to bring cohesion to their greatly varied subjects.

The ruler cult and the state religion provided a unifying feature of Greco-Macedonian ways. Though they did not at first impose this state religion on the non-Greco-Macedonian elements of the population, the religious climate changed after Roman defeat of the Seleucids in 189 B.C. More and more the worship of the king as the Seleucid state religion impacted heavily on the monotheistic faith of the Jews and sparked a revolution among them (see subsequent discussion under Religion and War).

Maccabean/Hasmonean Rule

After the successful Jewish revolt and the establishment of their independent state, the victorious Jews of course had to set up a government of their own. In the early years—under Judas Maccabeus (167–161) and Jonathan (161–143)—whatever territory the Maccabeans ruled, they did so as generals of an army. As they shouted orders to their troops, they also controlled whatever civilians depended on them for their livelihood and safety.

Simon

The situation changed somewhat in 142 B.C. when Simon won independence of Judea from Syrian control. The next year the Jews conferred on him and his descendants permanent authority as ruling high priests (1 Maccabees 14:25–49), and the Roman Senate recognized him as a friendly independent ruler (1 Maccabees 14:16–19, 24; 15:15–24). In international affairs, for the next eighty years the Romans valued the Hasmonean dynasty as a counterbalance to the Seleucid state.

With Simon, the Hasmonean line took over rule of the Jews and held sway until the Roman conquest in 63 B.C. Incidentally, the name *Hasmonean* is thought to be derived from an ancestor of the Maccabeans named Asmoneus.

Domestically, the Hasmoneans depended on the aristocratic Sadducean party with its power base in the temple. Partially hellenized, this sect usually contested with the Pharisees—with their power base primarily in the synagogue—for control of the public at large.

Not only did Simon win permanent authority as ruling high priest for himself and his posterity, but he secured Joppa as a Jewish harbor and conquered Gazara (Gezer), Beth-zur, and the Acra or citadel in Jerusalem where Seleucids had continued to hold out. Though he was successful against the Syrians, he met a violent death

Coins of the cities of Antioch (above, the capital) and Seleucia (below, its port) of the Seleucid Kingdom.

at the hands of the governor of Jericho, who assassinated him and two of his sons in 135 B.C. But John Hyrcanus, a third son, escaped to become the next high priest (1 Maccabees 16:18).

John Hyrcanus

John Hyrcanus (135–104 B.C.) began his reign fighting for his life and his kingdom but ended it with the Jewish state at the height of its power. Internally the Jewish state changed significantly too. It transformed itself from a religious community into a secular state. Though the Hellenistic party as a separate group disappeared, as did Syrian interference in Jewish affairs, its views were perpetuated by the Sadducees, as the views of the Hasidim were perpetuated by the Pharisees. Those two parties, so prominent in the New Testament, first surfaced during Hyrcanus' reign. Hyrcanus publicly aligned himself with the Sad-

Greek Education

What kind of education would Hyracanus' sons have received in the Greek schools, in the gymnasiums? Greek education was humanistic—man-centered instead of God-centered, relativistic instead of based on absolutes. The subject matter would have included literature: the *Iliad* and *Odyssey* and various tragedies and comedies with their polytheistic thrust, instead of the Bible and Hebrew history. Further, Plato and Aristotle and their philosophies and scientific observations, Stoic and Epicurean teachings, and the new Hellenistic scholars of Alexandria would have been included in the curriculum.

ducees, but he was safely Jewish, having brought both the Samaritans and Edomites to heel. Thus he did not unduly upset the more conservative elements of the realm. But his sons received an education in Greek culture and tended to repudiate the Pharisees.

Aristobulus

Aristobulus (104–103 B.C.), the eldest of those sons, emerged as victor in the dynastic struggle that erupted after the death of Hyrcanus. Then he proceeded to imprison his brothers and his mother to guarantee his position as chief of state. It is said that his mother starved to death in prison, and he unjustly executed his brother Antigonus for supposed involvement in a plot against him. Aside from these family tragedies, he apparently ruled well. He continued the expansionist policies of his father and extended Jewish rule into Galilee. He also continued the Hasmonean tendency to transform the religious community into a secular state, adopting the title *Philhellene* ("love of things Greek") and taking the title of king.

It is easy to understand why the Hasmoneans decided to assume the title of king. The Jewish state was no longer confined to Jerusalem and its environs. It now

The monumental tomb of Alexander Jannaeus. (From the Jerusalem model at the Holyland Hotel in west Jerusalem)

ROMAN TAKEOVER OF PALESTINE

I n 66 B.C., while the Roman general Pompey was involved in conquests in the East, one of his lieutenants visited Judea, where he heard appeals from representatives of Hyrcanus and Aristobulus. He made tentative decisions. And when Pompey came to Damascus in 63 B.C., he heard appeals from the two brothers and the Jewish people, who wanted abolition of the monarchy and a return to priestly government.

After that the political situation gradually unraveled, and a Roman army marched in and took over in 63. The Romans detached all non-Jewish areas (the Mediterranean coastlands, Transjordan, and Samaria) from the Jewish state. They placed what remained under the rule of Hyrcanus II as high priest. Thus they abolished the kingship, as the representatives of the Jews had asked, and Hyrcanus (with Antipater, father of Herod the Great, at his elbow) controlled the state, at the pleasure of the Romans.

After Palestine passed under Roman rule, it inevitably became embroiled in Roman politics. Over the following decades Jews formed factions loyal to Hyrcanus, Aristobulus, Pompey, Julius Caesar, Mark Antony, Augustus, Herod the Great, and others. Even the best informed scholar finds it difficult to follow accurately the history of the period, but some details are clear.

First, Hyrcanus II continued as high priest and ruler of the Jews during the confused period from 63 to 40 B.C. During almost all those years, Antipater faithfully carried out Roman policies as the real power in the state. Second, after Pompey's defeat at the hands of Julius Caesar in 48 B.C., Hyrcanus and Antipater became loyal supporters of Caesar. In appreciation, Caesar confirmed their position in Judah and showed numerous favors to Jews of the Dispersion, many of which were continued under subsequent rulers during the New Testament period. Third, the Romans appointed Herod king of the Jews in 40 B.C. After a confused political and military situation, he became king in fact in 37 B.C. and ruled until his death in 4 B.C. Thus we have made the political transition from the Maccabeans to the Romans and to the situation that existed as the New Testament period begins.

included a much larger territory and almost thirty hellenized cities. Gentiles in this larger territory, and especially the inhabitants of the hellenized cities, would consider the high-priestly authority to be confined to the temple-state in Judea, or at most to Jews in the territories. A king could claim authority over all kinds of people— Greeks, Samaritans, Idumeans, and others—throughout his kingdom.

Alexander Jannaeus

When Aristobulus died from drink and disease, his widow, Salome Alexandra, released his brothers from prison and married the eldest, Alexander Jannaeus (103–76 B.C.). Jannaeus continued the expansionistic policies of his predecessors. By the time he died he had extended the borders of the Jewish state to include almost all the territory that Solomon had ruled. Jannaeus was almost constantly at war, however, and more than once suffered nearly total disaster (see later discussion on Warfare).

One of these conflicts involved an internal rebellion, which came in part because of his violation of temple ritual at the Feast of Tabernacles. At that time the crowd had assaulted him for his impiety and he had

Tomb complex of Bene Hezir overlooking the Kidron Valley in Jerusalem—the burial site of a priestly family of the Maccabean period. The pyramid-topped tomb is mistakenly known as Zechariah's tomb. (Ben Chapman)

called in troops to restore order, with the resultant death of a large number (Josephus said 6,000) of defenseless people. In the following conflict Jannaeus almost lost his kingdom. And when he reestablished his control, he hunted down his enemies and crucified about eight hundred of them.[2]

Salome Alexandra

When Jannaeus died, his widow Salome Alexandra (76–67 B.C.) succeeded him on the throne, as she had when Aristobulus, her first husband, died. Because she was a woman she could not exercise the high priesthood. Her eldest son, Hyrcanus II, filled that position. Her more able second son, Aristobulus II, received command of the army. The Pharisees, who had enjoyed little influence under earlier Hasmonean rulers, now played an important role in the government and for the first time were admitted to the Sanhedrin or council. This change in their fortunes seems due in part to the fact that Alexandra's brother was the famous Pharisee, Simon ben Shetach. In general, Alexandra's reign was peaceful and prosperous. When she died at the

age of seventy-three, the days of Jewish independence were nearing an end. As a matter of fact, the sparring between Alexandra's two sons gave the Romans the chance to add Palestine to their empire (63 B.C.).

Operation of the Government

During the whole Maccabean/Hasmonean period the government could not operate effectively and efficiently. At first the Jews fought to establish their independence. Having done so, they still faced occasional intrusions of either Syrian or Egyptian forces—sometimes invited in by a faction in Israel. Then they experienced the occasional revolution, as in the days of Alexander Jannaeus. And strife persisted between Pharisees and Sadducees. Under these chaotic circumstances, it became difficult to establish government agencies and make them operate efficiently. It also proved difficult to put in place a workable taxing system for the support of the government.

The rulers, as kings and high priests, exercised great power, and there was little check on them. The Sanhedrin or Council always operated under the leadership (or dominance) of the high priest and did not enjoy the power it had earlier under the Seleucids or later under the Romans. Both of them permitted a degree of internal autonomy in which the Sanhedrin could flourish.

(For more on this topic, go to p. 347 or p. 390.)

Religion

"In those days certain renegades came out from Israel and misled many, saying, 'Let us go and make a covenant with the Gentiles around us' . . . and some of the people eagerly went to the king, who authorized them to observe the ordinances of the Gentiles. So they built a gymnasium in Jerusalem, according to Gentile custom, and removed the marks of circumcision, and abandoned the holy covenant. They joined with the Gentiles and sold themselves to do evil." (1 Maccabees 1:11–15 NRSV).

Growing Hellenistic Influence

Hellenism had been growing in influence in Palestine all during the years when the Ptolemies ruled there and increasingly after the Seleucids took over in 198 B.C. The upper classes in Jerusalem bowed and scraped to things Greek and seemed increasingly embarrassed by things Jewish. As noted in the passage quoted above, they campaigned for many elements of pagan culture and even sought to turn Jerusalem into a Greek *polis* or city, complete with a Greek-style gymnasium.

During the century of Egyptian occupation and the early decades of Syrian or Seleucid rule, Jews enjoyed the freedom to worship as they chose, but that situation changed in the days of Antiochus IV (175–163 B.C.). In an effort to bring greater unity to his kingdom, Antiochus IV tried to force Greek religion on the Jews, along with all the other subject peoples—and there were plenty of Jews willing and eager to go along with him. The Seleucid kings assumed the right to appoint the Jewish high priests, and ambitious Hellenists vied for the position.

Jason's Actions

When Antiochus IV came to the throne in 175, Onias III, an orthodox Jew, was serving as high priest. But many Jews had become so hellenized that they were ready for a change in the religious system. At that point apparently some accused Onias of pro-Ptolemaic leanings, and his brother Joshua paid a huge bribe for appointment as high priest and the right to build a gymnasium in Jerusalem (2 Maccabees 4:8–10). Taking the Greek name Jason, Joshua proceeded to build the gymnasium, to introduce athletic competition in the nude, and to encourage other actions totally repugnant to orthodox Jews. The orthodox organized under the name *Hasidim* (pious), a movement from which the Pharisees eventually arose.

Menelaus' Excesses

After Jason had been in office three years (175–172 B.C.), Menelaus, a close associate, deposed him by outbidding him in the bribery game (2 Maccabees 4:23–26), and Jason fled to Transjordan. Menelaus proved

A bronze head of Zeus with plaited hair and beard

to be an even more thoroughgoing Hellenist than Jason, and more unscrupulous as well. He helped himself to temple assets to pay off his debt to Antiochus. Jason waited impatiently in Transjordan for a chance to regain his lost position. Finally, in 168 B.C., when Antiochus was busy with a military campaign in Egypt, Jason raised a force and attacked Jerusalem. The disorders that followed evidently were clashes primarily between those loyal to Jason and Menelaus and between the pro-Egyptian and pro-Syrian factions. Antiochus, however, chose to regard them as open rebellion against his rule. He sent a force to Jerusalem that broke down the walls, destroyed many houses, slaughtered countless inhabitants, and built a fortified citadel for a Syrian garrison.

Antiochus' Proscription of Judaism

Then in 167 B.C., realizing that Jewish opposition to him rose ultimately from their religion, Antiochus decided to destroy Judaism, much as Communists in Russia and China more recently tried to destroy Christianity. He made such religious observances as circumcision and Sabbath-keeping and the possession of a copy of the Law punishable by death. He dedicated the temple to the Olympian Zeus, and desecrated it with a sacrifice of swine on the altar. Worship of heathen gods became compulsory.

Maccabean Rebellion

Response to these severe measures was predictable. Some capitulated, some offered passive resistance, and some decided to fight for their faith. The spark that ignited open revolt was struck at the mountain village of Modin, west of Jerusalem. There a priest named Mattathias lived with his five sons. When a royal officer came to town to enforce the decree requiring the Jews to perform pagan sacrifice, Mattathias killed a Jew who was about to offer sacrifice, as well as the officer. Then he fled to the hills with his sons, there to conduct guerrilla warfare. A few months after the beginning of the struggle Mattathias died, but before he did he saw to it that the mantle of leadership fell on his third son Judas, "the Maccabee" (interpreted to mean "the hammer").

Ultimately Judas entered Jerusalem and cleansed the temple (where for three years sacrifices had been offered to the Olympian Zeus) on the twenty-fifth of Chislev (December), 165 B.C. The day has been celebrated ever since as the feast of Hanukkah or Rededication or Lights. The story of the Maccabean wars or the military struggles of the Hasmonean dynasty will be featured in the next section.

After the death of Judah, his younger brother Jonathan took up the fight and maintained the religious goals of the Maccabean struggle (161–142). The same was true of Jonathan's son Simon, who led the movement 142–135 B.C. As noted, he won for his family permanent authority as ruling high priests, along with independence of the Hasmonean state.

Hasmonean Slippage

Erosion of Maccabean goals began to occur during the reign of Simon's son, John Hyrcanus (135–104),. He publicly aligned himself with the Sadducees and gave his sons an education in Greek culture.

The eldest of those sons, Aristobulus (104–103 B.C.), continued the religious slide. He adopted the title of *Philhellene* ("love of things Greek") and took the title of king.

Coin of Antiochus IV, a Seleucid king of Syria who desecrated the temple in Jerusalem and precipitated the Maccabean revolt

The Faith of the Masses

The faith of the masses at the close of the Maccabean period demonstrated various levels of commitment. A great many believed themselves acceptable to God because they practiced circumcision (as sons of the covenant) and kept the Sabbath. Some were faithful to the temple and corporate worship, keeping the feasts, especially the Passover, and being careful to make proper sacrifices required by the Law. A substantial percentage, following the Pharisees, concerned themselves with law-keeping as a way of life, and they were faithful in synagogue attendance.

During the long period of Ptolemaic and Seleucid occupation and Maccabean Hellenistic orientation, many, especially among the upper classes, tended to drift away from a supernatural approach to religion. They did not believe in a life after death, a resurrection, or a coming Messiah who would establish a spiritual kingdom. Most of those who still thought about a Messiah centered on a prince who would establish a political kingdom. We have no opinion polls to indicate the percentage of the population that fell into each camp. The spiritual condition of the masses must have been much the same as during New Testament times.

His brother Alexander Janneus (103–76 B.C.) was notorious for his power and cruelty. Favoring the party of the Sadducees, he alienated the people and thus the Pharisees. When they revolted against him he killed thousands in battle and hundreds more subsequently in executions.

In their alliance with the Sadducees, the temple leadership, and the Hellenistically oriented aristocracy, the Hasmonean kings betrayed the ideals that had inspired the Maccabean revolt. By the time Rome took over Palestine in 63 B.C., the political leadership had moved dangerously close to the position held by the Syrians before 168 B.C. And by New Testament times the Sadducees were denying the supernatural.

Pharisees and Sadducees

To better understand the religious landscape in the second century B.C., we need to examine the positions of the Pharisees and Sadducees. The Sadducees belonged to the wealthy priestly aristocracy and were primarily concerned with temple administration and ritual. They recognized only the written law of the Pentateuch as binding on them and tended to ignore the development of the oral law. Generally they subscribed to Hellenistic beliefs and practices and, as noted, at many points turned their backs on supernatural points of view. Though they were always a minority in Judaism, their political power at times was great. Because their sphere of activity was the temple, they died out after the temple was destroyed in A.D. 70.

The Pharisees did not reject the temple and the privileges of the priestly class. But as trustees of the nation's culture, they enjoyed greater support among the masses. Sticklers for observance of the Law, they paid great attention to ceremonial purity, fasting, and Sabbath observance. Concerned with both the written and oral law, they subscribed to the canonicity of the entire Old Testament and continued to refine and add to the interpretation of Scripture. Thus they were progressive in their constant reinterpretation of the Law and in their seeking proselytes to Judaism. They were more inclined to impose duties than to grant rights to their followers. Their sphere of influence centered especially in the synagogue. And they tended to separate themselves from the influences of Hellenism and to hold to a supernatural faith.
(For more on this topic, go to p. 350 or p. 405.)

Warfare

"But Judas said to those who were with him, 'Do not fear their numbers or be afraid when they charge. Remember how our ancestors were saved at the Red Sea, when Pharaoh with his forces pursued them. And now, let us cry to Heaven, to see whether he will favor us and remember his covenant with our ancestors and crush this army before us today. Then all the Gentiles will know

that there is one who redeems and saves Israel.'"
(1 Maccabees 4:8–11)

The Maccabean Hope of Victory

Mattathias and his sons fled into the hills after killing the government agent who had commanded sacrifice at Modin. How could they hope to survive when they were hunted like animals in the wilderness? How could they expect to take on the military might of the Seleucids? How could they outfit an army with no resources or a dependable source of supply? How could they hope to win?

1. To begin with, they were a guerrilla force that moved about in hills and caves and woods that were familiar to them. In all periods of history a few guerrillas have been able to operate effectively in rugged terrain with minimal equipment.

2. With a fierce dedication to a cause, they had the edge on mercenary armies. Witness the success of American patriot armies during the Revolution when fighting German mercenaries.

3. They fought in defense of their faith, homes, and freedoms, and the Seleucid forces were merely trying to maintain the power of the central government. Judas told his men, "We fight for our lives [our wives and our children] and our laws" (1 Maccabees 3:20, 21).

4. As the Maccabean conflict progressed, the need to fight the Parthians on the eastern frontier sometimes distracted the Seleucids. And Rome sometimes reined them in as well. Moreover, the Seleucid royal family engaged in factional infighting. For example, when Demetrius I and Alexander Balas were slugging it out for control of the Seleucid kingdom in the 150s B.C., Alexander granted Jonathan the privileges of a royally appointed commander and permitted him to recruit an army and forge weapons.

5. The Maccabeans captured many weapons that they turned back against the Seleucids. Judas himself captured the sword of the Seleucid general Apollonius "and used it in battle the rest of his life" (1 Maccabees 3:12). Often the Jews seized weapons (e. g., 1 Maccabees 3:12; 4:23; 5:3). The statement in 1 Maccabees 6:6 is quite specific in this connection: "The Jews had grown strong from the arms, supplies, and abundant spoils that they had taken from the armies they had cut down."

6. The Jews sometimes made their own weapons. In one battle the Seleucids "set up siege towers, engines of war to throw fire and stones, machines to shoot arrows, and catapults" (1 Maccabees 6:51). In response, "The Jews also made engines of war to match theirs" (1 Maccabees 6:52).

7. Judas, especially, encouraged his men to have faith in God, and God evidently intervened on their behalf. The speech recorded above is an especially eloquent exhortation. God responded by evidently causing confusion in the enemy ranks and giving the Jews the victory. Clearly, the Jews could not have won on their own on this occasion because they "did not have armor and swords such as they desired" (1 Maccabees 4:6).

Jewish Equipment of War

We know the Jews had swords because the Books of Maccabees say so. And if they captured a lot of military equipment, many of them must have had Greek body armor, which would have consisted of a corslet to cover the torso, made of leather or iron, and greaves to protect the lower legs. The Maccabeans also would have captured spears or lances and the round shields Macedonians and Greeks carried. Presumably some contingents became proficient slingers, as Jews had been from time immemorial. Then, as noted above, they sometimes built engines of war, such as catapults.

It does not appear that the Maccabeans had whole cavalry units (though they did have a few mounted soldiers), but that was not a great disadvantage in the hilly regions where most of their battles took place. Nor did they have war elephants, as did the Seleucids. From the little information we have, it is not clear how much difference elephants made in battle. Elephants could be almost as much of a problem to the forces that had them as to their enemies. If they were wounded they might become somewhat crazed. If the enemy killed their riders/trainers, they were left without adequate control and might run amuck among friendly forces.

The Size of the Maccabean Army

The Maccabeans organized their army into divisions of a thousand, which were subdivided into hundreds, fifties, and tens, with appropriate officers for each (1 Maccabees 3:54). We do not have information about training camps or about how they deployed fighting units on the battlefield (such as, for instance, the Macedonian phalanx). In a few instances we do have some idea of relative strength of forces. For instance, at Emmaus (165 B.C.) Judas had 3,000 infantry to face Gorgias with 5,000 infantry and 1,000 cavalry. Judas and Jonathan (in 163 B.C.) led 8,000 men into Gilead to relieve Jews being persecuted there; we do not know the strength of Seleucid garrisons in the several fortified cities. Jonathan marched at the head of 10,000 men and Simon commanded a further battalion in the battle in the Plain of Philistia in 147 B.C. Ten years later at the Battle of Kidron (southwest of the modern airport at Lod), John Hyrcanus and his brother Judas commanded 20,000 infantry.

Major Battles

1. The Battle of Emmaus (northwest of Jerusalem) in 165 was significant because against great odds Judas won an overwhelming victory. Evidently God intervened, showing that He was on the side of the rebels and giving them courage to continue the struggle. Judas' ragtag army of 3,000, without

adequate weapons, was pitted against 6,000 crack Seleucid troops (1 Maccabees 4:1–25).

2. At the Battle of Elesa (some 10 miles north of Jerusalem) in 161 B.C. the Seleucid forces under Bacchides trounced the Maccabean forces. Judas lost his life on the battlefield and his army scattered. Simon and Jonathan were able to carry away his body and bury it in the family tomb at Modin (see 1 Maccabees 9:5–19).

3. In 147 B.C. the Seleucid king Demetrius II commanded his general to take strong measures against Judea. This backfired, resulting in the first Jewish conquest of Joppa. Jonathan, leading 10,000 men, was joined by Simon and another battalion in that battle. Initially hardpressed, the Jews gained the upper hand and then took control of the whole southern coastal plain (the Plain of Philistia). The Jewish army emerged from that battle as the "strongest military power in the land of Israel" (See 1 Maccabees 10:69–87).

4. Tryphon, leader of one Seleucid faction, launched an attack on Jonathan (143–2 B.C.). By a ruse he captured Jonathan at Ptolemais (modern Acre) and killed the thousand men who were with him. Later Tryphon killed Jonathan, and the rest of Jonathan's troops chose Simon to lead the people in his brother's stead (see 1 Maccabees 12:39–54). Simon now threw in his lot with the Seleucid faction led by Demetrius II, who granted Simon independence in 142 B.C.

5. The conquests of John Hyrcanus (135–104). Though John Hyrcanus began his reign in a weak position, the situation changed after 129 B.C. when Antiochus VII was killed fighting against the Parthians. That greatly reduced the power of the Seleucid dynasty and Hyrcanus did not have to fear further interference. He proceeded expand his kingdom, first taking a chunk of territory east of the north end of the Dead Sea. This gave him control of a stretch of the King's Highway that ran from the Red Sea to Damascus. He already controlled a section of the Via

Maris (Way of the Sea) in the coastal plain. Then he conquered the Idumeans to the south and the Samaritans to the north. Following that he took the Greek cities on his northern border: Strato's Tower (later Caesarea), Samaria, and Scythopolis (earlier Beth Shan).

6. In the year that Aristobulus I reigned (104–103), he managed to conquer Galilee.

(For more on this topic, go to p. 352 or p. 429.)

Housing and Furniture

Houses in the nearly thirty Greek cities of Palestine, as well as those of the upper classes in Jerusalem during this period, imitated the Greek style. That is, they were of the peristyle type (arranged around square courtyards that were surrounded by columns, often with Ionic capitals). A narrow passageway gave entrance into one large room, with smaller rooms opening around the court and lighted from it. Depending on the affluence of the owners, some floors might have mosaics.

Houses of the middle and lower classes were small. Excavations have not revealed rooms arranged according to a clear plan. Remains of hearths and steps leading to a roof or a cellar are frequently found. Houses of the very poor might be of one or two rooms.

The kind and amount of furniture depended on one's economic condition. The upper and middle classes had wooden bed frames with mattresses filled with a variety of materials, chairs (with or without backs and arms), and tables. The very poor had almost no furniture, perhaps bedrolls that could be put on the floor at night, and a few stools.

(For more on this topic, go to p. 359 or p. 443.)

Diet and Foodstuffs

In normal times Palestine could provide enough wheat and barley (the staple diet of the poor) for its own population, but not enough for export. The good wheat and barley producing districts were located in Judea, Benjamin, Galilee, and the Decapolis, with the best wheat believed to grow near Michmash, about seven miles north of Jerusalem. Oats and rye were in plentiful supply.

Vegetables and Fruits

They had many vegetables. Cabbage and onions (especially those from Ascalon) abounded, with adequate supplies of mushrooms (especially from Jerusalem), lentils, kidney beans, and chickpeas. Among the many other vegetables raised and consumed were radishes, turnips, cucumbers, artichokes, asparagus, and pumpkins. Seasonings included coriander, mustard, anise, cumin, ginger, mint, and rue.

Increased commerce introduced many fruits into Palestine during the Hellenistic age. In the Maccabean period pears, apples, peaches, plums, cherries, dates, pomegranates, and figs flourished, with excellent fruit farms around Samaria, Ascalon, Scythopolis, and around the Sea of Galilee. The date-palms of Judea (especially Jericho) and Galilee became famous throughout the whole ancient world, especially after Palestine became part of the Roman Empire. Fig culture of the region of Lydda (modern Lod) was especially extensive. Likewise the cultivation of the grape was extensive. The wines of Ascalon and Gaza were popular. But the wines of Galilee were considered the best quality. Fruit and date plantations were even more profitable than vineyards. Numerous fruit wines and fruit-beers were produced.

Olive oil had a multi-purpose use—for cooking, medicinal purposes, and lighting. As in other periods of history, residents burned it in small clay lamps to provide illumination. The province of Galilee as a whole had become the most important center for the production of oil, with olive trees grown widely. Palestine could not grow enough olives for its population. Therefore olive oil, like wheat and wine, generally was not exported. Dates and bee honey provided sweetening for meals.

Though dry farming was the rule in Palestine, artificial irrigation was practiced

During the Maccabean period, oil lamps looked like a slipper. Instead of being an open saucer, the two sides were pinched together.

in many districts, including Sepphoris in Galilee, Jericho, Gezer, and around the shores of the Sea of Galilee.

Animal Consumption

Though the poor could not afford to eat the meat , the Hebrews raised beef cattle widely. Milk, butter, and cheese were products they would more likely have consumed. The breeding of sheep and goats was extensive and highly profitable. Again the poor normally could not afford to eat the meat but did consume the milk, butter, and cheese. And of course wool and goat hair met many needs in society.

Poultry (geese, ducks, doves, pheasants, quails, ravens, sparrows) were eaten by rich and poor alike. Fishing went on everywhere—in rivers, lakes, and the sea. The Jordan River was very popular for its fish, and those of the Sea of Galilee were widely known. Dried fish from the Sea of Galilee were sold throughout Palestine.

(For more on this topic, go to p. 360 or 447.)

Dress

Three developments characterize the clothing of the period in Palestine. (1) Greek styles in the almost thirty Hellenistic cities influenced many among the upper-class Jews. (2) Instead of an almost universal preference for wool fabrics in earlier periods, many now chose linen. (3) With more dyes available and more dye works in operation, people increasingly wore more gaily colored clothing than in previous periods.

As to choice of fabric, the women of Judea still normally used wool for weaving, while the women of Galilee commonly used flax to produce linen fabric. Palestinian flax was now highly esteemed and was exported.

Dyes available included saffron, which produced a yellow orange; henna, a reddish dye; madder, red; and woad, blue. The women of the day highly valued the henna of Ascalon. Of course, they still produced the purple of Tyre, but it now was so expensive that only the most wealthy could afford to use it.

The literary and archaeological information available to us concerns the clothing of Judea more than that of the rest of Palestine. The basic garment consisted of a tunic made of two pieces of woolen material, joined at the top with a hole for the head to pass through. The usual length of these pieces was about three and one-half feet, so the tunic must have extended roughly to the knee or mid-calf. Tunics were normally decorated with two vertical stripes. The tunics themselves usually were red, yellow, or black, with contrasting stripes, or they were multicolored.

The mantle served as the Hebrews' other main garment (*talith* in Hebrew, *himation* in Greek). Also of wool, this consisted of one piece of cloth and was worn over the tunic. The mantles were yellow or brown and often decorated with checkerboard patterns. There were also woolen kerchiefs decorated with fringes and made of many colors. In addition, garments made of linen and of leather are known, but we cannot be sure of their exact shape and use. Apparently the Mosaic Law that forbade the mixing of linen and wool in the same garment (e. g., Deuteronomy 22:11) was obeyed. Sandals consisted of several pieces of leather stitched together.

We do not know as much about the clothing of Samaria or Galilee. From the fact that linen cloth was produced extensively in Galilee, we may guess that the tunics there commonly may have been made of linen, with the warmer mantles being made of wool. Also, possibly people in the other provinces were not so careful to avoid mixing wool and linen. It should be noted, however, that the basic garments of Judeans were similar to those worn by people all along the Mediterranean coast at that time. So the clothing of Judea, Samaria, and Galilee must have been similar.

(For more on this topic, go to p. 362 or p. 447.)

Family Life

At this time marriage continued to be largely by arrangement between parents of the bride and groom. Jewish bridegrooms continued to pay a bride-price and the father of the bride provided a dowry for his daughter. We have some knowledge of prices expected or paid, but they don't mean much when converted into contemporary coinage. Perhaps it is useful to note that by the end of the Hasmonean period a Jewish groom was expected to pay a minimum of one hundred denarii, equal to one hundred days of the daily wage of a day laborer. A dowry should be at least half as much. Sums in either case fluctuated according to one's social and economic standing.

Upper and middle classes usually ratified marriage and divorce by a written document, but legal marriage was possible without such documents. And generally the poor did not have them.

Even fairly small towns had midwives to assist in births. Mothers normally nursed for two years. Mothers ran the household, but in this patriarchal society fathers had considerable power over the family. Children commonly began to help in the fields or with the crafts as soon as they were able. Boys usually were brought up to follow in their fathers' occupations, though an apprenticeship to another craftsman could be arranged. By the end of the Hasmonean period, rudimentary education of boys included at least training in reading, writing, and arithmetic.

Sons were especially prized, since they carried on the family name. The eldest son received a double portion of the inheritance. Often younger sons received so little inheritance that they were forced to work as day laborers.

On death, burial took place on the same day because bodies were not embalmed. The wealthy and many of the middle class were laid out on stone slabs in caves or free-standing family mausoleums.

(For more on this topic, go to p. 362 or p. 448.)

Work, Travel and Commerce

Craftsmen

Hebrews practiced many crafts in Palestine during this period: tailors, masons, stonecutters, woodworkers, bakers, perfumers, smiths (goldsmiths, silversmiths, blacksmiths), dyers and tanners, carpet weavers, ceramic workers, glass smelters, washer-women, midwives (for women), to note a few.

The Phoenicians probably invented the art of glassblowing in the first century B.C. In the region near Acre they found sand that proved especially suitable for glassmaking. The industry quickly spread elsewhere. There were apparently no sculptors because the Second Commandment forbade the

Though this ostracon dates to the eighth century B.C., its use is similar to those of the Hasmonean period. Ostraca were pieces of pottery inscribed in ink or engraved with a stylus. It was found at Tell Qasile on the northern outskirts of Tel Aviv and is inscribed with the words "Gold from Ophir to Beth-horon—30 shekels."

making of graven images. Painters did produce art scenes.

The Hebrews employed professional scribes in writing documents or copying books. At this time imported papyrus from Egypt became too expensive to serve as a writing material, though they grew some papyrus in Palestine. The most important Hellenistic writing material was parchment, but it was also expensive to produce. Ostraca (pieces of pottery), wax tablets, and linen were substitutes. Ink was commonly made from gallnut resin.

They organized some crafts as home industries, such as families of linen weavers. And sometimes whole towns were connected with a certain trade or industry. Bethsaida apparently concentrated on its fishing industry. Nazareth is thought to have been a town of carpenters. Other towns were centers of pottery production.

Agricultural Workers

Though craftsmen were important and numerous, most people engaged in agricultural activity—largely subsistence agriculture. That is, they used much of what they produced to feed the farmer and his family. What little was left over was bartered or sold to supply necessities they could not produce themselves. Since farming provided a marginal existence, in the event of extensive drought or warfare farmers often lost their land and became day laborers. Or worse, if their debt was large enough, the whole family might become Hebrew slaves until their debt was paid.

In addition to the large class of small landholders, there were numerous peasants. These might work as day laborers or tenants who had rented the land on one basis or another.

Two other classes of workers were servants and slaves. The wealthy employed servants on a more or less permanent basis as personal attendants or assistants of one kind or another. Hebrew slaves were never very numerous and could be sold by a Jew only to a fellow Jew and only to his creditor in payment for a debt. While the servant could change masters, the slave could not. The advantage for the slave was that he could never become unemployed or die of

hunger. Nor was he a slave forever, for according to Mosaic Law he had to be released after six years of service, unless he declared that he loved his master and elected not to go free.

The Hebrews had some non-Jewish slaves, and some Jews were captured in battle and sold to non-Jewish owners. The non-Jews, known as "Canaanite slaves," were probably sold in the markets of Tyre and Sidon. They worked as tailors, bakers and cooks, tutors, nursemaids, entertainers, and in other ways. They were traded by bill of sale and marked, in case they should escape.

A few great landowners stood at the top of the social and economic scale. These commonly included the king, high officials, members of high priestly houses, and some of the wealthy merchants. Much of the time these could not, because of the pressure of other duties, live on the land and work it themselves. So they employed stewards to work it for them. Or they leased out their land.

Merchants

By the time the Hasmoneans conquered the Mediterranean coastal towns they had become completely hellenized. After the conquest, Jews began to move there and to engage in trade as merchants. Greeks carried on the overseas trade. By the end of the Hasmonean period, Palestinian production and commerce were poised to take advantage of the expanded economic opportunities that came with being part of the Roman Empire. Then new markets and more settled conditions especially contributed to a higher level of prosperity. Wine and olive oil were two of the main products exported. As noted earlier, Hasmonean control of sections of the Via Maris and The King's Highway enabled the Jews to tap into Mediterranean coastal trade and commerce on the Damascus route. Rule over the Idumeans enabled the Jews to dominate commercial arteries across the Negev.

Domestically, Friday, the day before the Sabbath, was market day in every town, when food, clothing, and other goods could be bought and sold. Because it was a "Day of Assembly," it was also a day for weddings, court sessions, and other events.

The coming Roman control of Palestine would prove to be a mixed blessing. On the one hand, a stronger control administratively brought a certain stability to the region and permitted or promoted greater prosperity. On the other, heavy Roman taxation and the inability of her governors to understand Jewish ways ultimately led to Jewish revolt and terrible destruction—of Jerusalem and the temple.

(For more on this topic, go to p. 363 or p. 456.)

NOTES:

[1]Josephus, *Antiquities of the Jews,* 14.3.1.
[2]Josephus, *Antiquities of the Jews,*
    13.13.5–14.2; *Wars of the Jews,* 1.4.6.

BIBLIOGRAPHY:

Fairweather, William. *The Background of the
    Gospels.* Edinburgh: T. & T. Clark, 4th
    ed., 1926.

Feldman, Louis H., and Gohei Hata. *Jose-
    phus, the Bible and History.* Detroit:
    Wayne State University Press, 1989.

Hitti, Philip K. *History of Syria.* New York:
    Macmillan, 1951.

Josephus, Flavius. *Antiquities of the Jews,*
    Books XII–XV.

Maccabees, First and Second. Contemporary
    English translations are available in
    the New Revised Standard Version
    and the Revised English Bible.

Pfeiffer, Robert H. *History of New Testament
    Times, with an Introduction to the
    Apocrypha.* New York: Harper &
    Brothers, 1949.

Sherwin-White, Susan, and Amelie Kuhrt.
    *From Samarkhand to Sardis: A New
    Approach to the Seleucid Empire.*
    Berkeley: University of California
    Press, 1993.

PALESTINE UNDER ROMAN RULE

Chapter 15

(The Gospels and Acts)

"When the fullness of the time had come" (NKJV) or "When the right time finally came" (Today's English Version), "God sent forth His Son, born of a woman." (Galatians 4:4 NKJV)

If you think America has been sinking into the "dark ages" morally and religiously, consider what it must have been like to live during the 400 years between the Old Testament prophet Malachi and the birth of Jesus. The public sector in our country may not be hearing the voice of the Lord as it once used to—but in Palestine God had not spoken a fresh word to the His own people for 400-plus years (Malachi prophesied about 435 B.C.). Finally He was beginning to speak again—to Zacharias (the father of John the Baptist, Luke 1:11–20), to the Virgin Mary (Luke 1:26–37), and to John the Baptist (Luke 3:4–6). Then He sent His Son as a communication of Himself in human form (Hebrews 1:2).

But God did not speak suddenly out of the blue without some preparation. Christ was able to make the impact He did because God had prepared the world for Him and what He had to offer.

Preparation of the World for Christ and the Church

Greek Cultural Contribution

The Greeks' cultural impact helped prepare the environment for Christ's coming.

As early as the Formative Age of Greece (c. 800–500 B.C.), colonies of Greeks had established themselves in Spain, southern France, southern Italy, Egypt, Cyrenaica (modern Libya), Cyprus, Asia Minor, and all around the Black Sea. Of course they brought with them their political, social, and economic institutions, and the religion, language, and other elements of Greek culture.

When Alexander the Great and his successors, the Seleucids of Syria and the Ptolemies of Egypt, arose in the fourth century B.C., they built on that foundation and extended the hold of Greek culture over the entire area from the Eastern Mediterranean to the Indus River.

When Rome completed her conquest of the Italian peninsula in the third century B.C., she fell under the spell of the Greek culture of southern Italy and adopted it as her own. Thus the Romans never did develop a distinctive culture of their own but rather a Greco-Roman culture, which spread throughout the whole Mediterranean world.

As Christianity came on the scene and heralds of the gospel made their way across the Roman Empire, they did not suffer the kind of culture shock modern missionaries do—there was only one basic culture for the

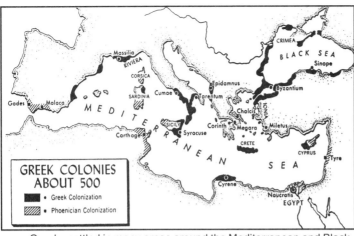

Greeks settled in many areas around the Mediterranean and Black Sea by 500 B.C., laying down a deposit of Greek culture wherever they went.

Greek, they were immediately understandable to the whole Mediterranean world.

The city building of the Greeks also helped prepare the world for the spread of Christianity. Alexander the Great had built cities as bastions for securing the countryside militarily, politically, and economically. And from the cities the superior culture (from the Greek standpoint) of Hellenism could be spread. Alexander's successors also built cities—and the Romans, seeing the advantages, established cities until the entire Mediterranean world had been urbanized.

entire empire. Moreover, this Greco-Roman culture had a single language: Greek. To be sure, the Roman government issued official documents and decrees in Latin. And regional languages, such as the Aramaic of Palestine and Syria, continued to be spoken at home. But everywhere they used Greek as the language of business and ordinary communication. When the books of the New Testament began to be distributed in

What had been used for the spread of the "gospel" (or good news of a supposedly superior culture) of Hellenism, Paul took up as a means to spread the gospel of the grace of God. Paul embarked on an urban strategy for reaching the Roman world with the gospel. He spent varying amounts of time in many cities, the longest being Corinth (eighteen months) and Ephesus (two–three years).

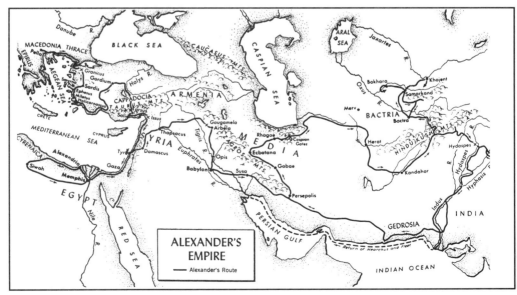

Alexander the Great built on the earlier Greek foundation when he conquered the whole area from the Mediterranean to the Indus. He and his successors strengthened the widespread hold of Greek culture.

Rome brought a political unity to the whole Mediterranean world by the time of Christ.

Roman Political Contribution

The Romans made the political contribution needed to prepare the world for the coming of Christ and the church. They united the Mediterranean world, permitting an easy flow of people across the entire region possible. The large number of places from which Jews gathered in Jerusalem for the feast of Pentecost illustrates the significance of this (Acts 2:5–11). The lack of boundaries made the movement of the apostles from province to province much easier. Today, however, a host of sovereign nations constitute the Mediterranean world, each requiring passports and most of them visas. In fact, when you leave Jerusalem today there are numerous counties you cannot travel to, such as Syria or Libya and other countries of North Africa.

Not only did Rome permit a free flow of people around the Mediterranean area, but she encouraged or facilitated that movement with her own version of interstate highways. That famous highway system got its start nearly 300 years before Christ

was born. The Romans continued its rapid expansion well into the first Christian century after Christ commissioned His disciples to go into all the world. By around A.D. 100, this universal road system comprised some 250,000 miles of paved or improved roads, a distance ten times around the earth at the equator. The familiar saying that "all roads lead to Rome" rose from the fact that a milestone stood in the Forum at Rome with a record of distances, by road, from Rome to the chief cities of the empire.

Roman citizenship and Roman law contributed greatly to the political climate favorable to the spread of the gospel. The first large-scale extension of Roman citizenship in provincial areas began under Julius and Augustus Caesar. The expansion continued throughout the first Christian century and finally, under Caracalla in 212, Roman citizenship became available to all free persons in the empire. Citizenship conferred special rights and privileges, as well as duties. What this status meant is well illustrated in the experience of the apostle Paul at Philippi (Acts 16:35–40) and later in

Roman roads stretched across the entire Roman Empire, facilitating political administration, commercial ventures, military action, and the spread of the gospel. Major roads, as this stretch between Aleppo and Antioch in Syria, were paved with stone. Secondary roads were covered with gravel. Comments on the Roman road system and the building of a Roman road appear in the last chapter. (Ben Chapman)

Jerusalem (Acts 22:22–29). Subsequently it gave him the right to appeal to Caesar as to the supreme court of the empire (Acts 25:11–12).

The *Pax Romana* or "Roman Peace" served as another Roman political contribution. This did not mean elimination of war, for there were several armed conflicts during the period (27 B.C.–A.D. 180). Rather, the *Pax* involved the exercise of sufficient military power to keep that world in some semblance of order and tranquillity, to keep the lid on the political and social cauldron of the Mediterranean world. And there was also the *Pax Augusta* (the peace of Augustus), the peace, prosperity and stability that his imperial administration was able to confer on that world.

Religious Contribution—Jews, Romans, Greeks

The Jews made an important religious contribution to preparing the world for Christ by establishing synagogues throughout the Mediterranean area. Usually considered to have originated among Jewish exiles in Babylonia during the Exile, synagogues later proliferated wherever Jews lived in substantial numbers. Jewish districts existed in all the major cities of the Roman Empire at the time of Christ, with possibly 150 synagogues scattered across the empire early in the first century. Whatever the number, these institutions served as lighthouses of monotheism in a polytheistic world. Moreover, they stood for high ethical standards in a world without moral absolutes. And they usually possessed the Scriptures in Greek rather than Hebrew, in a translation known as the Septuagint, produced in Alexandria, Egypt, between 250 and 150 B.C.

As a result, many Gentile seekers after truth became "God-fearers" or "proselytes" to the Hebrew faith and later to Christianity. Hints of their number and their receptivity to the Gospel appear in the New Testament. Some came to Jerusalem for the great feast of Pentecost (Acts 2:10). One rose to a position of leadership in the church at Antioch of Syria (Acts 6:5). An Ethiopian eunuch, highly placed in the court of his land, had also heard about the Hebrews' God and eagerly responded to the gospel (Acts 8:26–39). Numerous proselytes seem to have embraced the gospel at Antioch of Pisidia (Acts 13:43), and a "great multitude" of proselytes or "God-fearing Greeks"

Augustus brought peace and order to the Roman Empire and launched the *Pax Romana* (the Roman Peace).

deliver God's people Israel. The Scriptures present Him as Moses' Prophet "like unto me," Isaiah's "suffering Servant," Jeremiah's "Branch," Daniel's "Son of Man," and as the coming of God Himself to deliver His people.

During the later intertestamental period, after Israel fell under the domination of Rome, the Jewish community interpreted the setting up of Messiah's kingdom in largely political terms. Even Christ's disciples had a hard time conceiving of Jesus' kingdom as a spiritual one. James and John and their mother thought of it as a literal or political entity soon to occur and one in which they might sit on His right hand and His left (Matthew 20:20–22; Mark 10:35–39).

Yet one more way in which Judaism prepared for the coming of Christ involved a concern for salvation. The Law of Moses was doing its work. All the Law could really do was condemn. More and more it became evident that men and women could not live up to the standards of God. They became increasingly impressed with their own sinfulness. The Law had indeed become a tutor or pedagogue to lead them to Christ (Galatians 3:24–25). As is clear

A Roman milestone that stood along a major Roman highway at Iconium in Asia Minor. The marker told the traveler the distance to various cities along the highway. (Gustav Jeeninga)

at Thessalonica believed in Christ and became members of the church there (Acts 17:4).

The Jewish expectation of a Messiah also prepared the way for the coming of Christ. The Old Testament is shot through with the anticipation of a Messiah who would

How Many Jews in Jesus' Day?

Abba Eban concludes that during the first century some three million Jews lived in Palestine, four million in the Roman Empire outside Palestine, and one million in Babylonia, for a total of possibly eight million. In the eastern part of the empire Jews constituted about twenty percent of the population, and in the west about ten percent. All major cities contained a significant number of them. In Alexandria, for example, at least 40 percent of the population was Jewish.[1] Eban makes the claim that "at no time in history, before or since, have Jews formed so large a part of the known population of the civilized Occidental world."[2]

from the New Testament, nothing in official Judaism—that of the Sadducees, Pharisees, or scribes—brought heart satisfaction. That created an openness to a new way, the way of God's grace through faith in Christ.

Although God primarily used the Jews in religious preparation for the coming of Christ, and though the Son of God became incarnate as a Jew, the Romans and Greeks also made religious preparations for His coming. The Romans did this by their conquests. In defeating various peoples they contributed to a loss of faith in their gods, who were perceived as unable to protect them. Thus the Romans, unwittingly, helped to create a spiritual vacuum.

The Greeks contributed the speculations of their philosophers. These philosophers generally undermined the older polytheistic reli-

gions by their skepticism, but failed to provide a satisfactory alternative. Positively, Plato and his followers taught that reality existed not in this present temporal world of the senses but in the world of the spirit, where the highest ideals of the good, the beautiful and the true exist. Some philosophers concluded that behind all the multiplicity of gods there must be a monotheistic being. Zeno and the Stoics developed a high ethic that in many ways approached the New Testament ethic.

So philosophers generally repudiated the old polytheistic cults. Some were discovering a monotheistic being behind the welter of gods that people worshiped. Others taught the immortality of the soul. Yet others were developing elevated ethical systems. And some, such as Epicurus and Zeno (the Stoics), sought a more personal relationship to God, or Being, in the universe. Each in their way both reflected and helped to create a hunger for a personal relationship with a God who could provide eternal life and inner strength to live out an ethic that would embrace all human relationships.

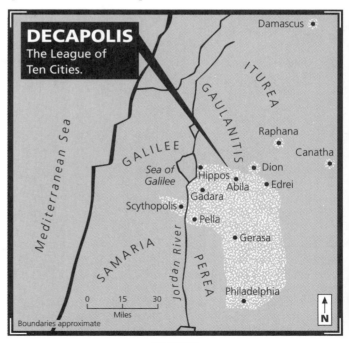

Decapolis

? Exact location questionable

Herod's kingdom at Jesus' birth

All this preparation came together in a meaningful way at the birth of Christ. History, it seems, was ripe for the coming of Christ and His birth in Bethlehem. The apostle Paul declared, "When the fullness of the time had come," or, "When the right time finally came," "God sent forth His Son, born of a woman" (Galatians 4:4). Not only did Paul speak by inspiration, but, living in that time, he understood from experience, as we cannot fully, how everything fit together to provide a proper context, or "right time," or "fullness of time," for Christ to be born. Jesus Christ made the impact He did because to some degree the world was ready for Him and what He had to offer.

The Land

Of course the physical landscape of Palestine during the Roman period remained essentially as it had been for millennia. Yet the climate had changed because of the cutting down of forests and of olive trees, especially around Jerusalem, during

the First and Second Jewish Revolts. And new studies have shown that the climate of the whole Mediterranean basin was colder and more humid during the Roman period (beginning about 300 B.C.) than today. The level of the Dead Sea was many feet higher then, and southern Judea and the Negev produced myrrh, frankincense, and quality wines under Nabatean cultivation. In fact, the whole eastern end of the Mediterranean and North Africa were much more agriculturally productive during the height of the Roman Empire than before that time and currently.[3] The political landscape changed considerably under the Romans as well.

Under Pompey

With Pompey's conquest (63 B.C.), completed by Gabinius, who was proconsul of Syria 57–55 B.C., Rome divided Palestine into numerous units. Pompey freed the Greek cities (e.g., Gaza, Joppa) that had been controlled by Jews since the days of John Hyrcanus (135–104) and made them autonomous enclaves under the supervision of the Roman proconsul in Syria. Most of those east of the Jordan he joined in a new "League of Ten Cities" or the Decapolis (Matthew 4:25; Mark 5:20; 7:31). Some of the better known cities of this group were Philadelphia (Amman), Gerasa (Jerash), Pella, Scythopolis (Beth Shan), and Gadara. Samaria became independent, while Judea, Perea, and Galilee were ruled by the Jews (also under the supervision of the Roman proconsul in Syria). The government of the Jewish territories is described in the next section.

Under Herod the Great

During the Roman civil wars Antipater, father of Herod the Great, won the favor of Julius Caesar and became the actual ruler of Palestine. He appointed his young son Herod to be governor of Galilee. When Antipater was murdered in 43 B.C., Herod and his brother Phasael were appointed rulers over all Judea. The subsequent invasion of the Parthians (40 B.C.) is a subject of later discussion. Herod fled to Rome, where Octavian and Mark Antony persuaded the Senate to appoint him king of

Palestine in the Time of Christ

0   20   40
Scale of Miles

Mediterranean, and nearly all the east bank of the Jordan as well.

Under Herod's Sons

After Herod died (4 B.C.), Augustus divided his kingdom among his three living sons, as the dead king had wished. Archelaus received Judea, Idumea, and Samaria. Herod Antipas got Galilee and Perea. Philip, the area east and northeast of the Sea of Galilee. Herod's sister, Salome, won the cities of Azotus and Jamnia on the Mediterranean and Pasaelis in the Jordan Valley.

Under Kings and Procurators

Archelaus proved to be a dismal failure in his rule. The Romans banished him in A.D. 6 and handed his lands over to a Roman procurator. Herod Antipas continued to rule until A.D. 39, when he fell out of favor with the emperor Caligula. Philip died a natural death in A.D. 34.

Caligula granted the lands of Philip to Agrippa I in 37, and of Antipas in A.D. 39. Then in A.D. 41 the emperor Claudius gave Agrippa the territory that Archelaus had ruled. Thus, from A.D. 41 to 44 he controlled almost all of the kingdom of Herod the Great. When Agrippa died in A.D.44 (Acts 12), the Romans decided to return to the procurators lands they had controlled earlier (Idumea, Judea, Perea, Samaria), plus Galilee. Agrippa II ruled the tetrarchy of Philip, A.D. 50–c. 100 (cf. Acts 25—26).
(For more on this topic, go to p. 367 or p. 470.)

Government

End of the Hasmoneans

The reign of Queen Salome Alexandra (76–67 B.C.) was a time of quiet before the storm. As a woman she could not serve as high priest and so appointed her son Hyrcanus to that post. In that position he

the Jews, giving him Judea, Idumea, Perea, and Samaria. But when Herod went to Palestine, he had to fight to take the granted territory. By 37 B.C. he was successful in conquering Judea, Idumea, Perea, Samaria, Galilee, and the port of Joppa.

After Augustus became master of the Roman world (31 B.C.), he confirmed Herod in his rule of the territories he now controlled and gave him several cities in the coastal plain. Later he added the Golan (Gaulanitis) and Panias (the area of Caesarea Philippi) and gave him the task of pacifying the region to the east of Gaulanitis. So Herod's kingdom at its height included almost all the territory between the Dead Sea and the Jordan rift and the

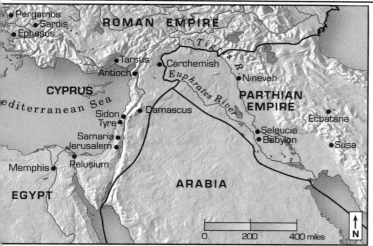

The Parthian Kingdom, controlling the area of Persia in the east, posed a threat to the Romans in the days of Herod and greatly complicated Roman affairs.

When Julius Caesar defeated Pompey at Pharsalus in 48 B.C., he had to reorder affairs in the East. The following year he went to Syria, where he confirmed Hyrcanus as high priest and appointed him Ethnarch ("ruler of the nation"), with the right to try capital cases. This right continued in Jewish hands until the appointment of the procurators in A.D. 6. Thus it was no longer in force when Jesus was put to death. Caesar also confirmed the special privileges of the Jews of the Diaspora or Dispersion in Asia Minor and Alexandria—the right to live according to their ancestral laws. Importantly, later Roman rules confirmed those privileges. Antipater was granted Roman citizenship and the office of "Custodian of Judea" (with vague duties). Antipater made his elder son Phasael governor of Jerusalem and his younger son Herod ruler of Galilee.

With the assassination of Julius Caesar (44 B.C.) a new instability occurred in Judea. Caesar's murderers, Brutus and Cassius, ransacked the treasuries of eastern lands to finance their war effort against Caesar's heirs. Antipater and his sons did their best to please the new Roman administration and ignored Hyrcanus and the Jewish aristocracy. A plot started to form to assassinate Antipater and he was poisoned at a banquet.

While Hyrcanus and the Jewish aristocracy contested with Herod and the Idumeans for the mastery in Palestine, news came of Mark Antony's victory over Caesar's assassins at Philippi (42 B.C.). Herod headed a delegation that went to Bithynia (in Asia Minor) to meet Antony. After Herod had generously greased Antony's palms, and after Antony on his own decided that the Idumeans would be more loyal to Rome than Hyrcanus and his allies, he confirmed Herod and Phasael in their official posts. But Hyrcanus remained

supervised the Sanhedrin and controlled the domestic policy of the kingdom. She kept her hand on foreign affairs and put her younger son Aristobulus in charge of the army. She sent him off to take Damascus, but he failed to add that region to the Hasmonean state.

After Salome's death, her two sons engaged in a fratricidal conflict for control of the kingdom. Finally, both appealed to the Roman general Pompey, who was then fighting in the East, for his support. This appeal gave Rome an excuse to interfere in Palestine, though it was just a matter of time before she would have done so anyway.

The complicated story of what happened with Pompey's involvement is beyond our present purposes. It is enough to say that Pompey confirmed Hyrcanus as high priest, defeated Aristobulus by force of arms in the Temple Mount and carried him in chains to Rome, and added Palestine to the Roman domains in 63 B.C. Ominously, the Idumean Antipater, father of Herod the Great, now held the real power in the Jewish state.

As high priest, Hyrcanus had the right to administer the Jewish nation's internal affairs according to the laws of Israel. Of course the government in Palestine was affected by events of the Roman civil wars.

as Ethnarch and high priest, with diminished powers.

While Mark Antony and Octavian (later Augustus) were slugging it out for control of the Roman Empire, the Parthians took advantage of Roman weakness in the East. And Antigonus, the youngest son of Hyrcanus' brother Aristobulus, saw a chance to take over in Palestine. Antigonus joined with the Parthians, and enemies of the Romans everywhere received both with open arms (40 B.C.). When Phasael and Hyrcanus went off to negotiate with the Parthians, they killed Phasael and disfigured Hyrcanus so he would be ineligible to continue as High Priest. Herod stashed his family at Masada, and he fled to Rome for support.

There Herod convinced the Senate to make him king over Judea as a tributary of Rome. But when he returned to Palestine to claim his kingdom, initially he had to depend on his own efforts to raise an army and gain control of the countryside. Eventually, however, Rome did put troops in the field. The Roman legions under the command of the Roman governor of Syria took Jerusalem, executing Antigonus at Antioch of Syria on the command of Mark Antony. Hasmonean rule had come to an end. The Parthians lost any enthusiasm for continuing the struggle. Beginning in 37 B.C., Herod was in a position to establish his rule in Judea.

The Reign of Herod the Great

In his early years as king (37–30 B.C.), Herod allied himself to Rome, and his rule was maintained by Mark Antony. Like the kings of Pontus, Cappadocia, and Galatia, Herod was important for his support of Roman policy—and as a ruler who knew how to maintain order in his domain. As a result Rome did not need to annex those states. Herod, however, could not keep the lid on by himself, so the Romans stationed a legion in Judea to maintain the stability of his rule.

One of Herod's greatest problems was that Cleopatra, now married to Mark Antony, wanted to bring Palestine back under the control of Egypt. Fortunately for Herod, Antony was neither willing nor able

to agree to such a course of action. But he did give some chunks of Herod's domain to Cleopatra. Cleopatra continued to give Herod grief by friendly contacts with the Hasmonean faction in Judea.

The Hasmonean faction continued to be a problem for Herod. First he negotiated with the Parthians for the return of Hyrcanus, the former high priest still held there. If he remained at the Parthian court, he could stir them up to attack Judea. But when Hyrcanus returned to Jerusalem, the question of the high priesthood became acute. Hyrcanus could not serve because he had been mutilated (Leviticus 21:17–20). Alexandra, daughter of Hyrcanus and mother-in-law of Herod (he had married Alexandra's daughter Mariamne), demanded that Herod appoint her young son Aristobulus III (brother of Mariamne) as high priest.

Herod feared that as high priest the young man would ultimately unseat him. His fears turned out to be justified, for when Aristobulus began to officiate he became immensely popular with the masses. Herod then decided to do away with Aristobulus. He had his servants drown Aristobulus while swimming in a pool in Jericho (35 B.C.). At the time Herod was a guest of Alexandra in the Hasmonean palace at Jericho; the pool was one of the palace's swimming pools. This pool has now been excavated and any tourist to Jericho may see it there (see accompanying picture). The uproar after this murder cost Herod dearly, but he was able to defend himself with Antony, who had no one to replace Herod in Judea. Presumably a good part of Herod's defense was that a popular Hasmonean threatened Roman power in the region.

After Octavian's defeat of Antony at Actium in 31 B.C., Herod, like other kings of the East (of Judea, Galatia, Cappadocia, Paphlagonia, and Bosphorus), found himself in a new world. Herod went to Rhodes to meet Octavian. He made no secret of his support for Antony but frankly stated that as he had been loyal to Antony, he would be faithful to Octavian if he would let him. Octavian had the good sense to know that these kings had no choice but to support

Antony and believed they would be loyal to him too. Herod welcomed Octavian as he marched along the Palestinian coast on his way to Egypt and presented him with a very large gift and supplies of water and wine for the journey. Octavian later reciprocated with considerable gifts of land (see previous discussion).

While Herod ruled, his subjects understood his dependence on Octavian (now Augustus) and the emperor's ultimate authority over them. Octavian expected Herod to send troops when Rome needed them, and pay annual taxes to Rome out of his revenues, as well as making special gifts. Because Rome did not collect those taxes directly, there was less friction between the people and Rome. In matters of major importance Herod was expected to

Pools at the Hasmonean palace at New Testament Jericho, where Herod drowned the high priest, Aristobulus III

seek the advice of the Roman governor of Syria, but Herod had a free hand in the internal affairs of his kingdom. The main check on his power lay in a fear of driving his subjects into rebellion and thereby destroying Rome's confidence in his ability to keep order and to pacify the region. He even had the right to nominate his successor, though such action was subject to the emperor's confirmation.

Herod had great influence within the Roman Empire because of his personal relationship with Augustus and other heads of the Roman government. He built cities and named them for the emperor. The

two outstanding examples were Caesarea and Sebaste (Samaria)—*Sebastos* is the Greek equivalent of Augustus. In both cities he erected statues and temples in the emperor's honor. At Caesarea, the Roman capital of Palestine, games were held in honor of the emperor every fourth year. In the province of Syria he built temples to Augustus in several cities.

Herod developed a friendship with Marcus Agrippa, Augustus' right hand man who was married to Augustus' daughter Julia. A significant result of that friendship was Agrippa's impressive visit to Judea in 15 B.C., when he received a warm welcome from king and people. He made a large number of sacrifices at the temple in Jerusalem. Herod also secured a reaffirmation of the rights of Jews in many cities of Asia Minor.

Herod sought to make a name for himself all over the empire. He made gifts to several Greek cities for the construction of buildings and the development of their institutions. Just outside his borders at Ascalon he built a colonnaded street, fountains and public baths. At Acre-Ptolemais he built a gymnasium, at Sidon a theater, at Damascus a gymnasium and theater. At Antioch he paved the main street with marble along its entire length and lined it with colonnades.

In Greece he made generous contributions to the Olympic games. In Rhodes he rebuilt the temple to Apollo which had been destroyed by fire. He gave gifts to Pergamon, Samos, and the towns of Cilicia, Pamphylia, and Lycia. And this is only a partial list of his benefactions. It would be tedious to note them all.

Herod's Building Activities

Caesarea[4]

Along with the rebuilding of the temple in Jerusalem (see next section on Religion), Caesarea ranks as Herod's most spectacular building project. He constructed it on the site of Straton's Tower, a small town twenty-five miles north of Tel Aviv (22–9 B.C.) and named it for Augustus Caesar. When the Romans removed

Herod Archelaus in A.D. 6 and appointed procurators to rule Palestine, they made Caesarea the capital of the province. Caesarea became a prosperous city, half the size of Manhattan Island.

Herod's theater at Caesarea, in the process of restoration.

Herod laid out the streets of his city in a checkerboard pattern. At least the main north-south street was paved with limestone blocks. He had the sewer system constructed in such a way that it would be constantly flushed by action of the sea— unique for a Mediterranean city. At the south end of the main street stood a theater that could probably hold about 4,000 spectators. In the theater excavators found a block with an inscription mentioning Pontius Pilate as the prefect of Judea in the reign of Tiberius, providing extra-biblical evidence of his existence. Just west of the theater on a little promontory stood a sumptuous building which excavators increasingly believe was Herod's palace. We can still see fine mosaic floors there.

Herod provided an adequate water supply by means of a high-level aqueduct that brought good fresh water from springs on Mount Carmel, some six miles to the north. There was also a low-level aqueduct that brought water from the Zarqa River, about three miles away. Its date is uncertain, but it may have functioned as early as Herod's day to provide water for irrigation.

For his port Herod constructed a breakwater made of huge blocks of concrete and enclosing a harbor area of forty acres.[5] Caesarea had the first protected harbor along the Palestinian coast. And the object of all of Herod's efforts here was to provide a safe harbor along this stretch of the Mediterranean coast. Overlooking the harbor to the east he erected a huge platform on which he built a temple to Augustus and the goddess Roma. South of the temple stood warehouses. Judging from objects found in them, trade was carried on with North Africa, Spain, Italy, and the

This inscription from the theater at Caesarea mentions Pontius Pilate, prefect of Judea, who ruled at the time of Jesus' death. (Gustav Jeeninga)

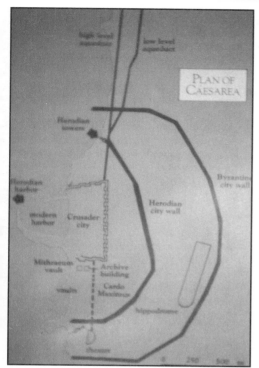

A plan of Caesarea, showing the location of the hippodrome, theater, harbor, and the route of the two aqueducts.

The high-level aqueduct

Aegean. Herod also built an amphitheater northeast of the city. Its arena measured some 290 by 190 feet and compared favorably with the arena of the Colosseum in Rome (281 by 177 feet).

The Herodium

Herod built the Herodium on a spot (7.5 miles south of Jerusalem) where he enjoyed one of his most important victories over the Parthians and Hasmoneans in 40 B.C. Near the end of his life he gave orders that he be buried there. Josephus' account in the accompanying sidebar describes Herod's funeral procession.

The Herodium was a hill some two hundred feet high, on which a round building was erected. This consisted of two parallel circular walls (diameter of the outer one 200 feet) with four towers extending from the outer wall at the points of the compass. Herod built three of them semicircular and the fourth round. Then he surrounded the walls with earth and stone, so the com-

pleted structure looks like a truncated cone.

He divided the inside of the palace-fortress into two parts, the eastern half occupied by a garden surrounded by columns and the western half by a bathhouse and various rooms. This eastern sector may have had three upper stories. The bath was a typical Roman bath with a dressing room and warm, hot, and cold rooms. It had mosaic floors and wall frescoes similar to some of those found in Pompeii. The hot bath had the usual form, with hot air passing under the floor and through pipes in the walls. A network of huge cisterns provided water for the site. A rectangular room about 35 by 50 feet was slightly remodeled for use as a synagogue during the first or second Jewish revolt (A.D. 67–70 or A.D. 132–135).

The platform on which the temple to Augustus Caesar stood at Caesarea

Herod's Burial

"Archelaus omitted nothing of magnificence. . . but brought out all the royal ornaments to augment the pomp of the deceased. There was a bier all of gold, embroidered with precious stones, and a purple bed of various contexture, with the dead body upon it, covered with purple; and a diadem was put upon his head, and a crown of gold above it, and a sceptre in his right hand; and near to the bier were Herod's sons, and a multitude of his kindred; next to which came his guards, and the regiment of Thracians, the Germans also and Gauls, all accoutred as if they were going to war; but the rest of the army went. . . armed, and following their captains and officers in a regular manner; after whom five hundred of his domestic servants and freed-men followed, with sweet spices in their hands: and the body was carried. . . to Herodium, where he had given order to be buried." —Josephus, *Wars of the Jews*, 1.23.9

Thus it ranks with the synagogue at Masada as among the earliest known.

The Lower Herodium sprawled at the foot of, and to the north of, the palace-fortress. There can be seen a large pool—a kind of artificial lake, possibly for swimming or sailing small boats. Adjacent to the pool lay an ornamental garden, and several buildings stood nearby. One of these was a bathhouse, but the use of most of them has yet to be decided. To date Herod's tomb has not been found.

Herodian Jericho

The Hasmoneans built the first aqueducts in the western Jordan Valley. And later, after date palm and other cultivation prospered, they and King Herod built winter palaces there. The Hasmoneans constructed a winter palace (probably two stories high) about 165 by 165 feet and dug two small swimming pools adjacent to it. As noted earlier, Herod had the young Aristobulus III drowned in one of them.

Early in his reign (c. 35–30 B.C.) Herod built a rectangular winter palace nearby, just south of the Wadi Qelt. This had a central peristyle or colonnaded court, a bath-house, and a pair of small pools. Later Herod created an enlarged winter palace on both sides of the Wadi Qelt and connected the two units with a bridge. On the north side of the Wadi stood a five-room bathhouse, two peristyle courts and several other rooms.

On the south side lay a sunken garden with an impressive facade holding statuary niches. At the end of the facade he had built a pool for swimming and water games. Behind the facade stood an artificial mound with a building on it. Herod also built a hippodrome and a theater south of ancient Jericho.

Jerusalem

Of course pride of place among Herod's building activities in Jerusalem goes to the temple (discussed in the next section on religion). But while Herod may have sought to win favor with the Jews by rebuilding the temple, he alienated many of them by erecting structures that offended their religious sensitivities. Some of his construction also served merely to assure his hold on the city or to provide for his creature comforts.

Chief among the latter were his barracks and palace. He located these on the west of the city in an area enclosed by its own separate wall, just south of where the Jaffa Gate

The Herodium

The eastern half of the Herodium consisted of a garden surrounded by columns.

now stands. At the north of the compound he built three great towers to protect the palace. The biggest of the three was called Phasael after his brother. Its base still stands inside the Old City and is commonly called "David's Tower." The lower part of it was a fortification, and the upper part was outfitted like a palace. It was 148 feet high. The second tower (named Hippicus for a friend of the king) was 132 feet high. The third was called Mariamne after his queen. A total of 74 feet high, it had luxurious residential quarters.

Part of the elaborate bath complex in Herod's palace on the north side of the Wadi Qelt at New Testament Jericho

The pillared reception room next to the bath complex of Herod's palace at New Testament Jericho. (1–2 miles northwest of the mound of Old Testament Jericho)

A reconstruction of Herod's palace in Jerusalem. (From the Holyland Hotel in West Jerusalem)

Between these towers and the palace stood barracks for Herod's soldiers. The palace itself consisted of two great buildings, each with banquet halls, baths, and bedrooms for hundreds of guests. Around the palace were groves of trees and ponds and bronze figures discharging water.

Offensive to the Jews were Herod's theater and hippodrome. The theater stood on the eastern edge of the hill of the upper city on what is now Mount Zion. Like all ancient Greco-Roman theaters, it was open to the sky and had seats arranged in step-like fashion in a semicircle and facing the stage. Players performed Greek and Roman plays there.

South of the Temple Mount in the Tyropoeon Valley Herod built a hippodrome or stadium. This served primarily as a place for chariot races. Shaped like a giant hairpin, it had a rounded end and a straight end. Spectators sat on stair-like seats, and chariots raced around a spina or divider that ran down the middle of the structure.

Machaerus

Herod Antipas imprisoned and then executed John the Baptist on the demands of Herodias (Matthew 14:3–10; cf. Josephus, *Antiquities* XVIII.5.2) at Machaerus (about 38 miles south of Amman). Initially the Hasmoneans had erected the fortress there on the southern border of Perea to

defend against the Nabateans. The site consists of ruins of the fortress and of the adjacent Roman-Byzantine village.

Alexander Jannaeus (103–76 B.C.) built the fortress, and the Roman Gabinius destroyed it in 57 B.C. Herod the Great rebuilt it after he consolidated his hold on Palestine (37 B.C. ff.), and it served the Jewish rebels as an important bastion during

The "Tower of David" in Jerusalem, which Herod the Great built and named for his brother Phasael. (Willem A. VanGemeren)

A reproduction of Herod's hippodrome. (From the model at the Holyland Hotel in West Jerusalem)

Mamre and Hebron

The walled enclosure at Mamre (2 miles north of Hebron), sacred to the memory of Abraham (see Genesis 13:18; 23:19; 35:27), seems to date to the reign of Herod the Great.

The monumental structure at Hebron (now a mosque), covering what is commonly identified as the Cave of Machpelah (where some of the Patriarchs were buried, beginning with Abraham's wife Sarah, Genesis 23:19), is commonly attributed to Herod the Great.

Masada

"Herod . . . built a wall around the entire top of the hill. . . there were also erected upon that wall thirty-eight towers. . . . Moreover, he built a palace therein at the western ascent. . . . He also had cut many and great pits, as reservoirs for water, out of the rocks." (Josephus, Wars of the Jews, VIII.3)

the war that resulted in the destruction of Jerusalem in A.D. 70.

The most important excavations at the site took place in 1978–1981 under the direction of Virgilio Corbo of the Franciscan order. The Herodian palace-fortress measured about 360 feet east-west and 195 feet north-south. A north-south corridor divided the palace into two blocks. The eastern section had a paved courtyard in the center flanked by baths on the south. The western part had a small court surrounded by columns. Several of the rooms showed traces of mosaic floors. The lower city, that provided housing for the palace personnel, has yet to be excavated.[6]

Herod the Great fortified Masada, a wonderful, almost impregnable bastion, as a defense against internal Jewish opposition and the Romans—especially Cleopatra and her designs on him. It rose some 1,500 feet above the sea on an isolated mesa about two-thirds of the way down the western shore of the Dead Sea. Its summit of twenty-three acres gave space for palaces, barracks for soldiers, and storerooms for

Remains of Machaerus, fortress of King Herod, where John the Baptist was beheaded, according to the Jewish historian Josephus

The monumental structure at Hebron (now a mosque) is commonly attributed to Herod the Great.

Masada, with the Roman ramp built up during the siege

military equipment and supplies of food. Yigael Yadin of the Hebrew University in Jerusalem led an excavation team of professionals and thousands of volunteers there for two years, in 1963 to 1965. They accomplished an almost total excavation of the site. The exciting account appears in Yadin's *Masada* (1966).

Though the Hasmoneans had built some fortifications at Masada, and Herod had left his future wife Mariamne and members of her family there when he fled to Rome, Herod must have dismantled the earlier construction. Yadin found that almost everything on the site dated to Herod's day or later.

A casemate wall about 4,250 feet long surrounded the boat-shaped rock, and had an abundance of defense towers. A casemate wall is a double wall with the area between divided into rooms or compartments. The excavators found about 110 rooms or casemates inside the wall and towers. The enclosed area provided space for four palaces—three small ones and a large one next to the western gate. The large western palace had four blocks of rooms: royal apartments, workshops, storerooms and an administrative section with what the excavators identified as a throne room with a colored mosaic.

At the northernmost point of Masada, at the cliff's edge, stood a palace-villa built in three tiers. On the top level Herod built living quarters with a semicircular porch. The middle terrace, about 65 feet below the

upper terrace, contained a circular building and was connected with the upper terrace by a staircase. The lower terrace lies some fifty feet below the middle terrace, and contains a small bathhouse with a mosaic floor and plastered walls.

Samaria

Herod renamed Samaria (thirty-five miles north of Jerusalem) Sebaste, the Greek equivalent of the Latin Augustus (meaning "the revered one") and built extensively there. But we need to be careful not to give him credit for the work of others during the Roman period. The provincial

The hot bath room or sauna in the bath complex at Masada had a hollow floor supported by stone pillars; hot air could pass under the floor and through flues in the wall.

Herodian tower at the gate of Samaria

governor Gabinius (57–55 B.C.) seems to have rebuilt the walls, almost two miles long, which surrounded an irregular area of some 160 acres. He also appears to have been largely responsible for the Roman Forum and the adjacent basilica. However, Josephus gives Herod credit for the city wall (*Wars*, I.21–2). Perhaps the truth is that those projects were too ambitious for Gabinius' brief tenure and Herod finished what Gabinius had started.

But Herod does deserve credit for the round towers of the west gate of the city and the stadium (some 750 by 195 feet). He definitely built the great temple to Augustus on a height overlooking the city. The complex included the temple building proper (114 by 78 feet) and a large forecourt (on a platform 270 by 234 feet). A wide staircase led from the forecourt to the temple. The emperor Septim-

Steps up to Herod's temple to Augustus at Samaria

ius Severus (193–211) rebuilt the temple complex, according to its original plan, and the stairs and other remains the modern tourist can see there today date from this later period.

Remains of the theater to be seen there today date to about A.D. 225. And the colonnaded covered bazaar street that seems to have run the length of the city evidently dates to about the same time. So the New Testament student should not include either in an imaginary recreation of the city in the days of the apostles.[7]

Summary of Herod's Building Activities

Through Herod the Great's constant construction in Palestine and all over the eastern part of the Roman Empire he sought to play up to the emperor or the official family (e.g., Caesarea, Samaria). He also sought to improve his standing with the governments and peoples of the East, in part so they would not hinder Jews from sending the annual temple tax to Jerusalem. Some of his building was done to placate the Jews (e.g., the temple in Jerusalem); some to provide his defense needs (e.g., Herodium, Masada); and some to indulge his own vanity and to impress observers with the splendor of his kingdom (e.g., his palace in Jerusalem).

Richardson in his new 1996 biography of Herod lists eighteen building projects in Jerusalem, twenty-seven outside Jerusalem but within his territories, ten in Phoenicia and Syria, and fifteen in Asia Minor and Greece.[8]

Succession to the Throne

After Herod's murder of the young Aristobulus III, it became increasingly easy for him to destroy others of whom he was jealous and whom he suspected of plotting against him. Ultimately he disposed of his wife Mariamne and her mother; her two sons Alexander and Aristobulus; Antipater, his firstborn; many of his loyal courtiers; army officers; three hundred soldiers suspected of supporting Alexander and Aristobulus; and others. Ultimately he suspected treachery in every corner, and a poisoned

Tiberias was once the capital of Herod Antipas.

atmosphere invaded the court that reflected Herod's declining powers and judgment and made it increasingly hard for him to govern. Herod's execution of Mariamne and subsequent grief temporarily cost him his sanity. Eventually he remarried and finally had a total of nine wives.

When we look at the state of Herod's mind and the atmosphere at his court in his last years, it is easy to imagine him looking over his shoulder at the birth of a Jewish child in Bethlehem who was supposed to become king of the Jews. And when we see how many had become expendable during the previous few years, we can understand why he could give the order for the mass murder of infants in Bethlehem to be sure he had disposed of Jesus (Matthew 2:16–18).

With all of these executions and Herod's suspicions, he changed his will several times. Five days before his death he changed his will for a final time, appointing Archelaus king of Judea, leaving Galilee and Perea to Herod Antipas, and the territories northeast of the Sea of Galilee to Philip (son of Cleopatra of Jerusalem). Archelaus and Herod Antipas were sons of Malthace, a Samaritan. Of course Augustus had to approve these arrangements.

Government Under the Herodian Family

With Herod's body entombed at the Herodium (southeast of Bethlehem), his sons or their representatives went off to

Rome to make their case before Augustus. Meanwhile, revolts flared in all the Jewish sections of Palestine. Evidently these were spontaneous, independent of each other, and had no concerted plan. Varus, governor of Syria, required large forces of legionnaires and auxiliaries to put them down. When the smoke blew away, Augustus essentially approved Herod's will but made Archelaus the ethnarch instead of king of Judea. Some of the Hellenistic towns he made directly subject to the governor of Syria.

Archelaus

Archelaus proved to be totally incompetent and aroused the anger of both Jews and Samaritans. When the Samaritans sent a delegation to Augustus in A.D. 6 to accuse Archelaus of cruelty to their people against the specific orders of Augustus, the emperor removed Archelaus and banished him to Vienne in Gaul (France). We shall return to Augustus' arrangements for Archelaus' lands after a quick look at the administration of the rest of Palestine.

Herod Antipas

Herod Antipas appears more often in the New Testament than the other Herods because he ruled Galilee and Perea when Jesus and John the Baptist spent much of their time in those territories. A builder like his father, he rebuilt Sepphoris (about four miles northwest of Nazareth), which served as his capital until he transferred it to the newly-constructed Tiberias on the

Sea of Galilee. He named Tiberias for the reigning emperor and completed construction there about A.D. 25. He had great difficulty populating Tiberias because during construction the workmen uncovered a cemetery, so Jews considered the site to be ritually unclean. He also rebuilt Livias and named it in honor of Augustus' wife Livia.

The execution of John the Baptist marred Antipas' rule. John's denunciation of Antipas for his marriage to his brother's wife Herodias precipitated this murderous act. Antipas' first wife was the daughter of the Nabatean king Aretas IV, whom he divorced to marry Herodias, wife of his brother Herod Philip. The reason for John's opposition to Antipas' second marriage was that Mosaic law forbade marriage to a brother's wife except to raise up an heir for a childless brother who died prematurely (levirate marriage, Leviticus 18:16; 20:21; Deuteronomy 25:5). Antipas' brother was still alive and had an adult daughter. John's condemnation won Herodias' undying hatred, and she saw her chance to do away with John at Antipas' birthday party, when her daughter Salome's dance won Antipas' approval (see Matthew 14:1–12; Mark 6:14–29).

Antipas also had a brush with Jesus. While Jesus was beginning his final journey to Jerusalem but was still in Galilee, some Pharisees told him that he ought to leave because Antipas wanted to kill him (Luke 13:31–33). Jesus declared that this threat would not stop him. Later, as part of Jesus' trial, Pilate sent Jesus to Herod Antipas because he had come from Herod's province of Galilee (Luke 23:6–12). But Antipas refused to take action and left Pilate to stew in his own juice as he sought to get out of the responsibility of deciding Jesus' fate.

Later Antipas suffered military defeat at the hands of king Aretas of the Nabateans for the treatment of his daughter. In A.D. 39 accusations against Antipas resulted in his exile to southern France and Augustus gave his lands to Agrippa I.

Herod Philip

Augustus appointed Herod's son Philip tetrarch over the northern part of Herod's domain—the region northeast of the Sea of Galilee. Because the population was largely non-Jewish, he was the only Herodian to mint coins with the emperor's image on them. He rebuilt two cities: Paneas which he renamed Caesarea Philippi (joining the emperor's name with his) and Bethsaida as Julias, in honor of Augustus' daughter Julia. Near the first, Peter made his great confession of Jesus' messiahship (Matthew 16:13–20) and near the second the feeding of the 5,000 and the 4,000 took place. A generally successful ruler, Philip was well liked by his subjects. When he died in A.D. 34 Tiberius annexed his territory to Syria and in 37 gave it to Agrippa I.

Herod Agrippa I (A.D. 37–44)

"So on a set day Herod, arrayed in royal apparel, sat on his throne and gave an oration to them. And the people kept shouting, 'The voice of a god and not of a man!' Then immediately an angel of the Lord struck him, because he did not give glory to God. And he was eaten by worms and died." (Acts 12:21–23 NKJV)

Herod Agrippa I was the son of Aristobulus, who was the son of Herod the Great and Mariamne I. Though rather incompetent and inept, especially in handling finances, Agrippa happened to be in the right place at the right time. Thus, because he had sufficiently flattered Caligula before he became emperor, Caligula gave him the territory of Philip and bestowed on him the title of king. When Caligula was murdered in 41, Agrippa helped Claudius ascend the throne. Claudius not only confirmed him in his rule but added Judea and Samaria to his domain. Thus he gained control of all the land Herod the Great had ruled.

To gain favor with the Jews Agrippa persecuted the early Christians (Acts 12:1–19), killing James the son of Zebedee and jailing Peter. After Peter's release by divine intervention, Agrippa ordered the death of the guards.

Ultimately Agrippa's sins caught up with him. As Acts 12:20–23 states, he was struck down with a fatal and loathsome disease while he was playing god at Caesarea. Josephus (*Antiquities* XIX.8.2) gives a roughly similar account.

Herod Agrippa II (A.D. 50–100)

"Therefore, King Agrippa, I was not disobedient to the heavenly vision." (Acts 26:19 NKJV)

When Agrippa I died in A.D. 44, he left behind a seventeen-year-old son also named Agrippa. He was judged to be too young to take over the reins of his father. But in 50, after the death of Agrippa's uncle, the emperor Claudius gave him his uncle's territory of Chalcis in northern Syria and three years later the emperor exchanged that for the tetrarchy of Philip (northeast of the Sea of Galilee). To that holding Nero later added some towns in Galilee and Perea. Agrippa also had control over the vestments of the high priest and the right to appoint the high priests (Josephus, *Antiquities* XV.11.4; XX.1.1–3), so the Romans tended to consult him on religious matters. Probably for this reason the procurator Festus asked him to hear Paul's case at Caesarea (Acts 25—26).

Agrippa evidently had an incestuous relationship with his sister Bernice, which was the subject of gossip in Rome. She appeared with Agrippa during the interview with Paul (Acts 25:23; see also Josephus *Antiquities* XX.7.3). When the Jewish revolt broke out in A.D. 66, Agrippa sided with the Romans, and the emperor Vespasian confirmed him in his kingship. As for Bernice, she became for a time Titus' mistress during the Jewish revolt (66–70) and again in Rome after 75. But Roman revulsion against the idea of an Oriental queen (as with Mark Antony and Cleopatra) led Titus to send her away. With Agrippa's death about A.D. 100, the Herodian family came to an end.

Rule of the Procurators

"And when they had bound Him [Jesus], they led Him away and delivered Him to Pontius Pilate the governor." (Matthew 27:2 NKJV)

When the New Testament speaks of a Roman ruler of Judea in Jesus' day, it calls that official a *hegemon* (Greek) or chief man (e.g., Matthew 27:2). Officially he bore the title of Prefect. Later the Roman historian Tacitus and others called him a procurator. Modern students of the New Testament commonly follow that practice. Actually procurators in the empire during the first century dealt primarily with imperial finances in their districts or ran departments of the government, such as the mint or the mines. A few of them ruled minor provinces such as Thrace or Judea. And they had the power of life and death in their jurisdictions. The taxes and tolls or customs duties they collected flowed directly into the imperial treasury, not that under senatorial control. Thus when Jesus said to "render . . . to Caesar" (Matthew 22:21) it had a literal meaning in Judea.

Procurators (prefects) ruled Judea from the deposition of Archelaus until the kingship of Agrippa I (6–37) and from the death of Agrippa (44) until the Jewish revolt in 66. A listing of all of them would be tedious and they have no direct bearing on Scripture. But the New Testament mentions three: Pontius Pilate (26–36), Felix (52–58; Acts 23:24–26, etc.), and Festus (58–62; Acts 24:27; 25:1–12).

The primary responsibility of procurators in Judea was to maintain public order, but they normally did not manage the government on a day-to-day basis. In Jerusalem the high priest and the council or Sanhedrin did that. In legal or criminal cases the governor heard accusations leveled by provincial individuals and had the power to impose any form of punishment: death, hard labor, exile, etc., as in the case of

A tribute denarius of the emperor Tiberius

The western wall or the Wailing Wall is part of the remains of Herod's temple complex.

Pilate's trial of Jesus. A Roman citizen, such as the apostle Paul, could demand a trial at Rome by using the formula "I appeal to Caesar" (see Acts 25:11f., 25).

The Roman prefects generally proved quite inept in handling the Jews. Pilate, for example, came across as harsh, stubborn, and insensitive. He smuggled military insignia bearing the emperor's image into Jerusalem by night, but when Jews declared themselves ready to die rather than tolerate this violation of the Ten Commandments, he removed them. On another occasion he attacked and dispersed a crowd protesting the use of temple moneys to pay costs of an aqueduct in Jerusalem. Scripture mentions other instances of his ruthless massacres. When he fell on crowds of Samaritans gathered to witness the discovery of sacred objects allegedly hidden by Moses on Mount Gerizim, the governor of Syria (Vitellius) sent him to Rome to justify himself. The emperor ordered his removal in A.D. 36.

From the time of Felix constant tension and open hostility increasingly strained the relationship between Jews and Romans, leading to the first Jewish revolt in A.D. 66. The spark that lit this fire rose from friction between Jews and Gentiles in Caesarea. Subsequently the Roman prefect took sev-enteen talents from the temple treasury. The Jewish war party stopped sacrifices in behalf of Nero in 66. Meanwhile Masada fell into the hands of the rebels, who butchered its Roman garrison. Shortly thereafter in Jerusalem zealots took Herod's palace and massacred the Roman troops there. Riots spread to other cities and full-scale conflict was under way.

(For more on this topic, go to p. 367 or p. 474.)

Religion

The Temple

"His disciples came up to show Him the buildings of the temple. And Jesus said to them, '. . . not one stone shall be left here upon another, that shall not be thrown down.'" Matthew 24:1–2 NKJV).

For the loyal Jew, Jesus' statement came as a terrible shock. They were tremendously impressed with the magnificence of the temple as Herod had rebuilt it. In fact, ever since Solomon built the temple it has held a special place in the minds and hearts of Jews. How special became dramatically evident during the Six-Day War in 1967,

Jerusalem's Population During Festivals

Meir Ben-Dov has argued that Herod tried to relieve the city of Jerusalem of a "monstrous traffic jam" by building the temple. The masses of pilgrims crowding into Jerusalem during some of the festivals might number as many as 80,000 to 100,000 people. When you add these to a population of some 150,000–200,000, there could be 200,000 or more massed to witness the ceremonies performed in the temple courts.[9]

Parenthetically, if there were up to 100,000 pilgrims in Jerusalem at Pentecost, the conversion of 3,000 (Acts 2:41) is not as large a percentage as is often assumed. And while Peter's sermon is singled out in Acts 2, the preaching of the other apostles was necessary to reach such masses of people (see v. 7).

when deliriously happy Israeli soldiers reached the "Wailing Wall" or the western wall of the temple, long off limits to them. Or on a given Sabbath when Israelis go there to offer their prayers. And of course that western wall is only a fragment of the temple as it existed in Jesus' day. That temple may be called the "third temple," following the second temple of Ezra's day (dedicated in 515 B.C.) and the first temple of Solomon, dedicated in 967 B.C.

Jews in Palestine and scattered abroad (Diaspora Jews) paid an annual temple tax of a half shekel in New Testament times—and Jesus did too (Matthew 17:24–27). Diaspora Jews made pilgrimages to the temple from abroad, coming at festival times such as Passover and Pentecost. Pilgrims "from every nation under heaven" (Acts 2:5) crowded into Jerusalem and heard Peter and the other disciples preach on that special Pentecost when God birthed the church.

That a common piety toward the temple existed is clear from such passages as Luke 1—2. Zecharias, father of John the Baptist, served as a pious priest in the temple. Mary and Joseph made the required offering

there after Jesus' birth. Anna and Simeon frequented the temple for the purpose of worship.

Herod's Rebuilding of the Temple

Herod's motivation in rebuilding the temple is commonly assumed to be the glorification of his reign. Through it he also attempted to win the loyalty of his often restless Jewish subjects. And some Jewish writers of the past believed it represents an act of contrition for his sins.

In any case, Herod did rebuild the temple. He doubled the temple area with the construction of great supporting walls and the leveling of the surface inside. The western wall is the longest (1,590 feet) and the eastern wall somewhat shorter (1,536 feet). The southern wall is the shortest (912 feet) and the northern wall a little longer than that (1,035 feet). So the trapezoidal area covers the equivalent of twelve soccer fields, including the stands, and was almost a mile in circumference.

The retaining walls of the Temple Mount rose 98 feet above the paved area at the foot of the mount. And in some places the lower courses of these walls, always planted on bedrock, go as far down as 65 feet below the street, making walls at such a point more than 165 feet high. Most of the stones in these walls weighed two to five tons. But in the southwest corner of the Temple Mount are stones that weigh about 50 tons apiece. And in the western wall may be seen stones unequaled in size anywhere in the ancient

Herod's temple (From the model at the Holyland Hotel in West Jerusalem)

A reconstruction of the Temple Mount viewed from the southwest. (After Benjamin Mazar)

1. Antonia fortress
2. Retaining wall
3. Street
4. Wilson's Arch, spanning Tyropoeon Valley
5. Robinson's Arch, leading to street below
6. Shops
7. Porticoes/stoas
8. Royal Stoa

9. Exit gate
10. Entrance gate
11. Solomon's Portico (pre-Herodian)
12. Mount of Olives
13. Court of Gentiles
14. Entrance to platform
15. Exit from platform
16. Steps and railing prohibiting Gentiles.

world, according to Ben-Dov. One of these is 40 feet long, 10 feet high, and 13 feet thick and weighs some 400 tons.[10]

Ben-Dov's enthusiasm must be tempered by discoveries at Baalbek in Lebanon, where larger cut stones appear in the temple complex. At Baalbek the three largest stones measure about 64 feet long, 14 feet high, and 11 feet thick, and each weighs some 1,000 tons.

Working with large stones avoided the necessity of using cement (which would have required huge quantities of fuel to manufacture), speeded construction, and assured permanence. A chiseled frame around the edge of each stone characterizes Herodian stone masonry, with each course of masonry set an inch or so further in than the one below it, for aesthetic reasons. That way the wall would not appear to lean but to stand up straight.

Herod began construction of the temple in his eighteenth year (20–19 B.C.). He respected the sacredness of the site by having most of the stonecutting and shaping

done before he brought the blocks to the temple area. In that way he reduced the noise and clamor of hordes of workers in the temple. Moreover, 1,000 priests were trained to work in the religiously sensitive areas of the sanctuary itself.

Herod's men built the temple building in a year and a half, while the courts and porticoes required eight years. Josephus said that construction and repairs continued into the reign of Nero (54–68; *Antiquities*, XX.9.7). Moreover, John 2:20 says that it took forty-six years to build the temple. Scholars argue over whether the Greek indicates that it was complete then (when Jesus was about 30) or was still in the process of construction. Probably the latter is true.

Description of the Temple Area

Watchtowers stood at the corners of the temple wall. And the Antonia Fortress abutted against the northwest corner of the enclosure. Much wealth needed to be pro-

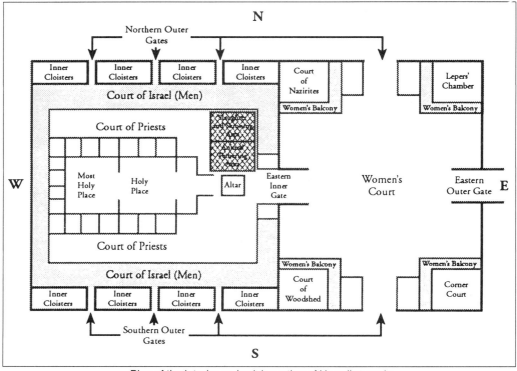

Plan of the interior or Jewish section of Herod's temple

tected in the form of expensive decoration and utensils. And the temple and state treasuries were kept there, as was true of temples elsewhere in Mediterranean lands (for example, the Parthenon in Athens or the Temple of Saturn in the Forum at Rome).

Along the southern side of the temple area broad stairways led through a triple gate at the southeast and a double gate at the southwest. These steps, as excavated, have special significance for modern Bible students. Jesus must have walked there and Paul probably sat there at the feet of the learned rabbi Gamaliel (Acts 22:3), as other students sat at the feet of their rabbis there. Also, the apostles must have preached on these stairways on the Day of Pentecost and subsequently.

Interestingly, some thirty mikves or ritual immersion baths (pools and plastered cisterns hewn out of bedrock), where worshipers purified themselves before entering the sanctuary, came to light in the vicinity of these stairs during the excavations. These answer the question of where the

large numbers converted on the day of Pentecost might have been baptized. Another stairway at the southwest corner (at what is called Robinson's Arch) descended to the street below. A bridge on the west side (at what is called Wilson's Arch) crossed over the Tyropoeon Valley and gave access to the Upper City.

Along the southern edge of the Temple Mount extended the Royal Stoa—a Roman basilica with a higher central aisle (nave) and two lower side aisles. Four rows of forty Corinthian columns each supported the roof. At the eastern end of the nave the Sanhedrin (the supreme Jewish legislative, religious, and judicial body) met in a semicircular apse. The northern colonnade was open and provided access to the temple court—the Court of the Gentiles.

Business could be conducted in the Stoa and the adjacent court. Pilgrims from abroad could change money into the sacred shekels there so they could pay their temple tax and buy sacrificial animals. When the Gospels talk about Jesus' kicking out of the temple those who did business there, they refer to this structure (Matthew 21:12; Mark 11:15–16; Luke 19:45; John 2:14–16).

Some scholars believe that Jesus scourged the sons of Annas, including Caiaphas, the reigning high priest, who manned booths there and charged exorbitant rates for the sacrifices and their services. In effect, he broke up the religious mafia that controlled business transactions in the temple and enjoyed a handsome take. Others do not believe that there is enough evidence to make such a claim. They think that the temple licensed men to carry on trade in sacrifices there; the sons of Annas did not control the booths. They also suggest that Jesus opposed the noise and confusion caused by carrying on business in the temple.

At the minimum, entrepreneurs carried sacrificial birds into the temple in cages (see Matthew 21:12; Mark 11:15–16; John 2:16). If instead of selling larger animals outside they actually stabled them in the temple and offered them for sale there, the activity was quite repulsive. Driving sheep and oxen up the temple steps, bedding them down, feeding them, and cleaning their stalls in the area of the Royal Stoa no doubt was totally out of character with what the

A mikve or ritual immersion bath, next to the temple steps

temple complex ought to be. It is not clear from John 2:14–16 what Jesus saw for sale in the temple on this occasion. Clearly he found doves there, and He may have seen sheep and oxen, but we do know that he drove out sellers of sheep and oxen.

While there may have been no religious mafia involved in the sale of sacrifices, no doubt some crafty individuals took advantage of the opportunity to make an extra shekel. In any event, Jesus overturned the low tables of the moneychangers, behind

On these steps of the temple, now excavated, learned rabbis taught. Among them was Gamaliel, under whom Paul studied (Acts 5:33–40; 22:3).

The synagogue at the Herodion

Excavators found one of these inscriptions in 1871 and it may now be seen in the Archaeological Museum in Istanbul. Translated from the Greek it reads, "Let no foreigner enter within the screen and enclosure surrounding the sanctuary. Whosoever is taken so doing will be the cause that death overtaketh him."[11] That this prohibition had real force is clear from Acts 21:28, where a mob scene erupted when a rumor spread that the apostle Paul had taken Trophimus, a Gentile, into the inner precincts. This fracas led to Paul's arrest and ultimately to his trial before Nero's court in Rome.

When Jewish worshipers moved on to the temple itself, they had to walk to the center of the temple area and turn left because the temple proper faced east. They passed the railing with its warning notices, climbed fourteen steps, crossed a terrace fifteen feet deep, and went up another five steps to the inner wall with its ten gates. Inside this wall lay first the Court of the Women. Apparently a gallery enabled women to see over the heads of the men into the Court of the Priests.

Men climbed fifteen more steps and went through a gate into the Court of the Israelites—for Jewish males who were not priests or Levites. There they could watch the priests at work from behind a low stone fence

which they sat on the ground, and the benches of those who sold doves and other animals, and expelled all those engaged in commercial dealings.

A tunnel ran under the Royal Stoa and led to the Court of the Gentiles, where anyone could go. This court was separated from the area reserved for Jews by a railing about 4.5 feet high. On this railing warning notices forbade Gentiles further access.

The synagogue at Masada (Gustav Jeeninga)

some eighteen inches high. In the court of the priests they saw the altar, the laver where priests washed their hands and feet, and the place where priests butchered animals.

From the Court of the Priests twelve steps led up to the temple, the front part of which (the Holy Place) contained a lampstand, a table for the showbread or the Bread of the Presence, and an altar for burning incense. A curtain separated the Holy Place from the Most Holy Place, which in Herod's day stood completely empty. It was appropriate that it should be, for God was invisible. Even the ark had become something of a fetish in Old Testament times and had been treated almost as the God who could help them in their war against the Philistines (1 Samuel 4:3). Apparently the Babylonians destroyed the original ark when they demolished Jerusalem and the temple in 586, and it had not been replaced in the second temple. Only the high priest could enter the Most Holy Place—and that only on the Day of Atonement.

The facade of the temple was 150 feet across and 150 feet high. But behind this the building narrowed to 90 feet in width, though the ceiling was almost as high as the top of the facade. Entrance to the Holy Place was through two doors covered in gold. On either side of the Holy Place were three stories containing rooms.

Sacrificial System in the Temple

"Without shedding of blood there is no remission [of sin]." (Hebrews 9:22 NKJV) *"For it is not possible that the blood of bulls and goats could take away sins."* (Hebrews 10:4 NKJV)

The sacrificial system carried out in the temple involved much shedding of blood, which looked forward to the once for all sacrifice of Jesus Christ. And it is quite remarkable how much animal sacrifice continued at the temple after the finished sacrifice of Christ, who "offered one sacrifice for sins forever" (Hebrews 10:12). Of course the destruction of the temple in A.D. 70 ended the whole system.

The daily sacrifices consisted of two whole lambs, one offered in the morning

The Synagogue in Israel

The only structure found to be originally built as a synagogue was at Gamla, in the Golan Heights, northeast of the Sea of Galilee. Constructed by the Hasmoneans, perhaps about 100 B.C., it measured some 80 by 55 feet and had stone seats arranged in stepwise fashion around the walls. It could accommodate about 300 people.[12] Two other first century synagogues that tourists to Palestine may see have been excavated at the Herodium and Masada. In both cases Jews of the First Revolt (that resulted in the destruction of Jerusalem in A.D. 70) converted existing structures to synagogue use while they lived there. Though they are smaller than at Gamla, their construction is the same: step-like seats of stone arranged around the walls. Such an arrangement would allow and even encourage congregational participation. Presumably this reflects the standard form of construction in New Testament times, as in later centuries.

This kind of arrangement provides easy visualization of Jesus' healing of the man with a withered hand in the synagogue (Mark 3:1–5). The crowd "watched him closely" (v. 2), which they could do if all of them faced each other (modern seating would arrange people in rows, some with their backs to him). He ordered the man to "step forward" or to step out in the middle of the floor where all could see. Jesus "looked around at them" (v. 5), which again he could easily do if all were seated roughly in a circle or an open square.

and one in the afternoon. On the Sabbath, priests sacrificed two additional lambs. On other holidays they added the sin offering of one goat. On the New Moon the daily sacrifice included two bulls, one ram, and seven male lambs. A listing of requirements for Pentecost, Passover, Rosh ha-Shanah (New Year), Yom Kippur, and the Feast of Tabernacles would be tedious and need not be given here.

The sin offering was proportionate to the rank and wealth of the offender: the high priest, a young bull; a ruler, a male goat; an ordinary man, a female goat or lamb, etc., down to the poorest who offered a pair of doves or pigeons. The person offering the sacrifice laid one hand on the head of the sacrifice to identify it with himself. A guilt offering consisted of a fine imposed on someone guilty of fraud or material damage.

Thanksgiving offerings expressed gratitude for a favor received and consisted of cakes and bread offered along with sacrificial animals. Peace offerings were partly burned on the altar, with a portion given to the priests and the rest eaten by the offerer and his family. The Jews made these sacrifices on a variety of occasions, for example, a military victory (1 Samuel 11:15), or the end of a famine or plague (2 Samuel 24:25). They also made freewill and miscellaneous offerings.

Such large numbers of animals were involved in the various sacrifices that we wonder whether the sacrifices in reality were made as the texts describe them. But at least it is clear that Jews understood the necessity of shedding of blood for remission of sin and the need to make one's peace with God.

Popular Religious Gathering Places: The Synagogue

We do not know exactly where or why the *synagogue* or *house of prayer* originated. Nor do we know the details of its administration or service at any given time. Possibly it arose in Mesopotamia during the Exile when the temple lay in ruins and when many Jews were cut off from their religious center in Jerusalem. Also, after the rebuilding of the temple, the synagogue served a need in the lives of people of Palestine not of the priestly class and who could not meaningfully participate in temple services. Then, too, it provided a religious outlet for those who lived at a distance from Jerusalem and could not frequently have access to the temple.

Whatever our uncertainties, synagogues were important in Jewish life during the first Christian century. Josephus, the Jewish historian who lived in Palestine and Rome; Philo, the Jewish philosopher and theologian of Alexandria in Egypt; and the New Testament all take them for granted. To date we have found remains of only three synagogues in Palestine dating before A.D. 70, when the Romans destroyed Jerusalem and the temple.

Presumably administration of the synagogue and conduct of the synagogue service were not very formalized in New Testament times. It appears that the head or ruler of the synagogue presided over the synagogue service, maintained order (Luke 13:14), and invited visitors to address the congregation (Acts 13:15). Mark 5:22 and Acts 13:15 speak of "rulers" of the synagogue in the plural, so perhaps there was a sort of board of elders, as in modern Presbyterian or Reformed churches, with their chairman, who ran the show. There was also an "attendant" (Luke 4:20 NKJV, NRSV) or "man in charge" (Luke 4:20 CEV), a person who had charge of the synagogue, presumably a sort of trustee who looked after the building and especially its valuable or priceless copies of Scripture.

At this point we need to ask what really went on in the synagogue. What was the service like? The Greek-speaking Jews of the dispersion (those living outside Palestine) used a Greek word meaning "prayer" to describe a synagogue, indicating they considered them "prayer houses." Jews of Palestine used the term "synagogue" to refer to a place that had a communal purpose and served a variety of needs. Often, though, the prayer houses resembled schools because their purpose was to teach the words or truths of God. Ultimately three functions came to be served by the synagogue: prayer, teaching, and social activity or bonding. During New Testament times these three elements had not yet combined to form a single, consistent entity.

There were many kinds of synagogues, the earliest two of which are attested by inscriptions in Egypt dating to the reign of Ptolemy III (242–221 B.C.).[13] Those were especially houses of prayer. The earliest

Palestinian synagogue, of the first century A.D., was built especially for the reading of the Law and teaching the word of God.[14] Some of them were under the control of local communities and some of private individuals and located in their houses. The priests (Sadducees) dominated some and the Pharisees others.

The New Testament indicates that anyone with something important to say would be permitted to speak. The activities of Paul and Jesus are cases in point. The reference in Acts 13:15–16 (NKJV) is very specific: "And after the reading of the Law and the Prophets, the rulers of the synagogue [in Antioch of Pisidia] sent to them [Paul and Barnabas], saying, 'Men and brethren, if you have any word of exhortation for the people, say on.' Then Paul stood up, and motioning with his hand said, 'Men of Israel, and you who fear God, listen.'" Jesus also spoke in the synagogue on occasion (see, e.g., Mark 6:2–3; Luke 4:16–28). So the opportunity for private individuals to speak in the synagogue was available both in Palestine and the dispersion.

As noted above, synagogues also served as places of gathering. For example, at the time of the First Jewish Revolt (66–70), the people of Tiberias met in the synagogue to hold a town meeting about the war.[15]

From what we can learn from the New Testament and other sources, the synagogue service included reading from the Law and the Prophets and time for a comment on the passage (Scripture reading and a sermon). There were also prayers, sometimes a benediction at the end, and the singing of one or more hymns (perhaps the chanting of a Psalm). The New Testament indicates that Jews sang hymns when they came together. After the Passover in the Upper Room, the disciples "sang a hymn" and went out to the Mount of Olives (Matthew 26:30; Mark 14:26). No doubt early Christian congregations were influenced in their form of worship by the synagogue services with which they were familiar, involving the reading of Scripture and the comment on it, the singing of hymns, and prayers.

The Theology of the Sadducees

Sadducees shared the main points of common Jewish theology and practice. God had chosen Israel, and Jews were in a covenant relationship with God. Israelites were to obey theLaw. They kept the Sabbath, ate kosher food and practiced circumcision as a sign of the covenant. All Jews were concerned about pollution (e.g., after funerals, childbirth) and washed frequently to remove its effects. Pollution was a force that attacked the physical and spiritual well-being of people. In mourning customs Sadducees, like others, engaged in extravagant weeping, hired professional wailers and flute players. The concern was not what happened to the soul of the dead (e.g., whether there was life after death) but the comfort of the bereaved. Public banquets held to mark the end of the mourning were as lavish as the social and economic stature of the family permitted.

Among the populace at large there was a general expectation of a messianic age, of a process of destruction and renewal for the world. In it some looked forward only to a return to kingship by the house of David. Others anticipated the supreme kingship of God in a new order of things, with the cessation of strife and a time of prosperity.

But the Sadducees, though good Jews, differed from others at significant points. They accepted only the written Law and rejected the oral law and the massive amount of interpretation of theLaw that the Pharisees spun out. Second, they denied a belief in the afterlife and with it the resurrection (e.g., Mark 12:18). Third, they believed in free will, that God exercised no influence on human activities. A person could choose to do good or evil, being entirely responsible for one's own fortune or misfortune. They denied that God always controlled what happened. Fourth, they denied the belief of most Jews of the period in angelic intermediaries between men and God, which gave comfort to the many who needed it.

Parties in Judaism

As early as the middle of the second century B.C. there were three distinct parties in the religious structure of Judaism: Sadducees, Pharisees, and Essenes. And these continued on into the New Testament period.

Sadducees

"Then some of the Sadducees, who deny that there is a resurrection, came to Him." (Luke 20:27 NKJV)

Nearly all the Sadducees were aristocrats, but not all aristocrats were Sadducees. Certainly the high priest and the aristocratic priests were Sadducees. With the destruction of Jerusalem in A.D. 70, the priestly aristocracy passed out of existence and the Sadducees dropped from sight.

The high priest, with the assistance of the council or Sanhedrin, took care of those aspects of local government not in the hands of the Romans. During the New Testament period Herod the Great appointed the high priests. In later years they were appointed by his son Archelaus, by Roman prefects (6–41), by Herod Agrippa I (41–44), by Herod of Chalcis (44–48), and by Agrippa II (48 until the outbreak of the revolt in 66). The "chief priests" (see, for example Matthew 2:4; 16:21; 20:18) presumably belonged to the most powerful families of priests, from whom the high priests were drawn.

In short, it appears that the Sadducees, as wealthy aristocracy, tended to be self sufficient, living in the present and not much concerned about life in the hereafter. They had the same general attitude as the wealthy in other ages: they enjoyed the "good life" here and now and were not concerned about whether you could take it with you or whether you needed to prepare for a life beyond the grave.

The Pharisees

"For the Pharisees and all the Jews do not eat unless they wash their hands in a special way, holding the tradition of the elders." (Mark 7:3 NKJV).

This verse points up the fact that the Pharisees, like the rest of the Jews ("and all the Jews"), including the Sadducees, were concerned with ceremonial purity. And we could repeat the other ways in which they were like the rest of the Jews (including the Sadducees), as we did for the Sadducees in the last section. How, then, did they differ from the Sadducees and from other Jews in general?

The apostle Paul when on trial before the Sanhedrin gave part of the answer: "Brothers, I am a Pharisee, a son of Pharisees. I am on trial concerning the hope of the resurrection of the dead" (Acts 23:6, NRSV). This points up a major difference from the Sadducees, who did not believe in life after death or in the resurrection of the dead. The next verse in Acts goes on to say, "The Sadducees say that there is no resurrection, or angel, or spirit; but the Pharisees acknowledge all three" (NRSV). In other words, the Pharisees differed from the Sadducees in believing in the resurrection and in angels, but they were like the rest of the Jews in believing in angels. Galatians 1:14 implies that they were zealous for the Law. Various sources indicate that they were strict or precise with regard to the Law, including Acts 22:3, where Paul said that under Gamaliel he "was taught the exact observance of the Law of our ancestors" (NJB). Pharisees committed themselves to "the traditions of the elders" as supplementing biblical law. They focused on interpreting the Law accurately and obeying it precisely.

Though from lower social ranks than the priests, the Pharisees were educated. They really did not control anyone. The chief priests and the powerful ran things as they wished and as the Romans permitted. They could harass Jesus and the apostles, but it was the chief priest and his associates who instituted the persecutions of the early church (see, e.g., Acts 4:1—7:1). And only once that we know of did a Pharisee (Gamaliel) have the power to persuade the Sanhedrin to modify their behavior (Acts 5:33–42).

According to Josephus' often quoted figures, some 20,000 priests, 6,000 Pharisees, and 4,000 Essenes lived and ministered in the days of Herod. The priests served as the official teachers of the Jewish people, though Pharisees and Essenes also taught.

Apparently Pharisees controlled some synagogues, but not all of them. Note that they gathered at synagogues with others (see Mark 3:1–6). The ruler of the synagogue in Luke 13:14 is not called a Pharisee, nor is Jairus (Mark 5:21–24). It is therefore not accurate to claim, as some do, that the Pharisees controlled the synagogues.

If we try to find out whether the Pharisees, the Sadducees, or the Essenes were the most popular, the Pharisees win hands down. The Sadducees as wealthy aristocrats did not receive popular acclaim, nor did the exclusivistic, retiring Essenes. But the people usually did not find it necessary to line up behind one group or another.

The Pharisees were laymen, either farmers or small merchants. People of modest but sufficient income, they had time to study and teach the Law. We do not find them agitating for the causes of the working class, however.

The Essenes

Josephus tells us that about 4,000 Essenes can be identified during the days of Herod the Great (*Antiquities* XVIII.1.5). Most worked the land, but some lived in various cities and villages. In the past there was debate over whether they avoided Jerusalem, but new excavations on Mount Zion in the area of the Jerusalem University College (formerly American Institute of

Air view of the Qumran excavations. Qumran is commonly thought to have been an Essene community.

Holy Land Studies) have found Josephus' "Gate of the Essenes" and remains of the Essene quarter. There some fifty Essenes lived in Jesus' day.[16] Most scholars believe that the Qumran community that produced or possessed the Dead Sea Scrolls were Essenes, but some are not yet convinced of that.

In any case, we know a fair amount about the Essenes in New Testament times. Though Essenes who married are known, most of them were celibate and lived in monastic type communities, holding property in common and engaging in normal occupations. They did not keep servants. Monastic type communities practiced complete community of goods, while those living in town made monthly contributions to a central treasury that provided charity.

As deeply dedicated people they lived an extraordinarily strict way of life and subjected themselves to a strict hierarchy. A prospective member did not join easily. He went through a two-stage novitiate and probation that lasted about four years. The oath they took was to obey the Law of Moses as the group interpreted it.

Their daily routine consisted of work, a meal at approximately noon, more work, and an evening meal. Before meals they took a purification bath and put on special clothing. After the meal they put on their work clothes again. Essenes rigorously maintained ceremonial purity.

Essenes believed in immortality of the soul and, along with other Jews, in angels. These served as mediators, and the existence of evil angels explained to some degree how evil could occur in a world that a good God controlled. They believed in God's sovereign determination of all things. Their theology combined a feeling of worthlessness and total reliance on God's grace with the belief that members could lead virtually spotless lives. The "rewards of righteousness were to be earnestly striven for" (Josephus, *Antiquities* XVIII.1.5).

The Essenes must be considered the most pious of the various Jewish groups, the most rigorous and legalistic, the most exclusive, and the most reliant on the grace of God.

Scribes

"The scribes and the Pharisees sit in Moses' seat. Therefore whatever they tell you to observe, that observe and do." (Matthew 23:2, 3 NKJV)

The scribes occupied Moses' position among the Jews as expounders of the Law. Because they taught the injunctions of God as recorded in inspired Scripture, they were to be obeyed—at least as far as their teachings tallied with the clear intent of Scripture. But how do the scribes relate to the parties we have identified in Judaism?

The New Testament also referred to scribes as "lawyers," individuals trained in the interpretation and application of the Torah or Law, and as "teachers of the law" (Luke 5:17). Their function was to copy Scripture, to interpret and teach the Law, and to guard the orthodoxy of the faith. As interpreters of the Law they developed the oral tradition that was such an important part of Pharisaism. Of the fifty-seven times that the scribes appear in the Gospels, more than a third link them with the Pharisees, concerned with the interpretation and teaching of the Law. But several connect them with the Sadducees or priests, especially responsible for teaching the Law.

As the Pharisees interpreted the Law, occasionally their traditions actually canceled out the clear teachings of the Law (see, for example, Matthew 15:3–9). In their quest for righteousness, they came across as hypocritical, and Jesus scorched them for that: "Woe to you, scribes and Pharisees, hypocrites!"

It is understandable that these scribes, trained in the Law, and respected in the community as authoritative interpreters of Scripture, should cross swords with Jesus. Here was one not formally trained as they were, yet he spoke with a unique authority. Sometimes he castigated them for their teachings, at other times he announced the dawning of the awaited kingdom—for which Israel in general longed. They lined up against him and became heavily involved in the plot to destroy him. Jesus predicted that Christians, whom he would send out as missionaries, as Christian scribes, interpreting the Scriptures and preaching true righteousness, would

suffer a like fate: "Therefore, indeed, I send you prophets, wise men, and scribes: some of them you will kill and crucify, and some of them you will scourge in your synagogues and persecute from city to city" (Matthew 23:34 NKJV).

Other Groups

Herodians seem to have been religiously the same as the Sadducees, but politically they were more in favor of the house of Herod than the Sadducees, who supported the rule of the Hasmoneans.

Zealot is a broad term that includes those interested in national liberation, brigands, and economic and social opponents of the existing order. They opposed the ruling Jewish aristocracy as much as they did Roman rule. In general they showed concern for the temple and the Law and sought to defend both from contamination. They seem to have expected a war of rebellion that would bring in the kingdom.

Popular Observance of the Law of God

"Hear, O Israel: The LORD our God, the LORD is one! You shall love the LORD your God with all your heart, with all your soul, and with all your strength. And these words which I command you today shall be in your heart. You shall teach them diligently to your children, and shall talk of them when you sit in your house, when you walk by the way, when you lie down, and when you rise up. You shall bind them as a sign on your hand, and they shall be as frontlets between your eyes. You shall write them on the doorposts of your house and on your gates." (Deuteronomy 6: 4–9 NKJV).

God had set the Israelites apart as the people of God. Theirs was a religion of things to be done more than of doctrine. But it did involve the extension of divine law to all areas of life—and God's law was to be internalized and individualized.

In time religious practice came to be to pray in the morning and at night, to recite the Shema of Deuteronomy 6:4, 5, and to put biblical passages in little containers and wear them on the arms and the forehead (phylacteries), as well as to attach them to the doorways of their houses. They also studied Scripture at the synagogue. And all this was certainly going on during the New Testament period.

But a fuller survey of popular observance of the Law of God in Judaism during New Testament (Roman) times is in order. Numerous statements by Josephus in his *Antiquities of the Jews*, of Philo of Alexandria (contemporary with Christ) in his writings, of the New Testament, and other sources all help to create a rather consistent view of Jewish conduct.

Most of them worshiped God daily in prayer and repeated the Shema.

Most attended synagogue on the Sabbath.

The vast majority kept the Sabbath, both in Palestine and in other provinces of the Roman Empire. Outside of Palestine many decrees exempted them from military service because such would require their training and/or fighting on the Sabbath.

Almost all Jews circumcised their sons as a sign of the divine election of Israel.

Some purity observations were general (see, e.g., Mary's purification 40 days after the birth of Jesus, Luke 2:22–24).

Jews in Palestine and abroad commonly brought the temple tax and made other gifts to the temple. They also brought numberless sacrifices of birds and animals.

Of course this does not mean to say that all who brought sacrifices to the temple, or attended synagogue service, or kept the Sabbath did so with a sense of true worship. But unbelief pure and simple was rare in any ancient religious context. Certainly, most Jews believed in God and his word and served him to some degree.[17]

Jewish and Pagan Response to Early Christians

Jewish Response

"Then Saul [later called Paul], still breathing threats and murder against the disciples of the Lord, went to the high priest and asked letters from him to the synagogues of Damascus, so that if he found any who were of the Way,

---

The Shema

"Hear, O Israel; The LORD our God, the LORD is one!" (Deuteronomy 6:4 NKJV).

The Shema, originally introduced in Deuteronomy 6:4, became the "watchword of Israel's faith." It was not a prayer but a confession of faith, which expressed the oneness and uniqueness of God. And linked to verse 5, it required devotion to God of one's entire being—with heart, soul, and might. Boys were taught the first verse of the Shema as soon as they could speak. And Jewish males, as their minimum religious requirement, were expected to recite it in the morning and evening. The priests recited it in the temple.

The Shema originally contained only Deuteronomy 6:4, but it was later expanded to include verses 5–9, with their requirement of total devotion to God. They also attached Deuteronomy 11:13–21, with the emphasis on blessing for its fulfillment and curse for its neglect. When Jesus was asked to identify the greatest commandment, he answered with the Shema and combined it with Leviticus 19:18, "You shall love your neighbor as yourself" (Mark 12:28–34; Matthew 22:34–40).

---

whether men or women, he might bring them bound to Jerusalem." (Acts 9:1–2 NKJV)

In an established community those who have been living there all along are always wary of new kids on the block and sometimes are downright hostile to them. Jewish responses to the early Christians are no exception to the rule. No doubt some Jewish leaders feared a rapidly rising movement that would pull away their supporters and so reduce their political, economic, and social power in the community. Thus some Jews in Thessalonica attacked "these who have turned the world upside down" (Acts 17:6 NKJV).

Others worried that Jews would lose their privileged position in the empire if society became infected with individuals who spoke of a kingdom ruled by a king other than Caesar. Those same Jews in Thessalonica charged, "These are all acting contrary to the decrees of Caesar, saying there is another king—Jesus" (Acts 17:7).

Evidently many Jews, like Saul of Tarsus, honestly believed that Christianity represented a perversion of true Judaism and that they were doing God a favor by snuffing out this heresy. The quote above shows Saul in action against Christians. Galatians 1:14 notes the motivation: "zealous for the traditions of my fathers."

Jews in considerable numbers in Jerusalem and in other cities of the eastern Mediterranean came to recognize Jesus as their Messiah and to place their faith in Him. This conversion rate stirred opposition to the early Christians. But not all leaders in Judaism were quick to jump on these Jewish "renegades." The great Rabbi Gamaliel, for instance, counseled the Sanhedrin in Jerusalem, "And now I say to you, keep away from these men and let them alone; for if this plan or this work is of men, it will come to nothing; but if it is of God, you cannot overthrow it—lest you even be found to fight against God" (Acts 5:38–39 NKJV). Such Jews wanted to give Christians a fair hearing. A more extensive review of Jewish response appears in Claudia Setzer's *Jewish Responses to Early Christians* (Augsburg, 1994).

Pagan Responses

Reasons for Roman persecution were much more complex. Christians spoke of a kingdom with Christ as its ruler, making them politically suspect. Materialistically minded Romans took statements concerning such a kingdom to imply a plan for overthrow of the government. Moreover, there was in ancient Rome a union of religion and state. So refusal to worship the goddess Roma or the divine emperor constituted treason. And no government has ever dealt lightly with treason.

Christians suffered social ostracism because as good Christians they could not participate in much of the public life of their time. For example, as civil servants they might be required to join in ceremonies in honor of the divine Caesar. Because sacrifice to a pagan deity normally occurred before a drama or an athletic festival, they could not engage in sporting or theatrical events. The Olympic Games were held in honor of Zeus and the Isthmian Games at Corinth in honor of Poseidon (see 1 Corinthians 9:24–27). Christians also condemned public games in which gladiators fought in mortal combat to entertain spectators and in which prisoners were thrown to wild beasts for entertainment of the crowds. And the fact that Christians proclaimed the equality of all people before God put them in direct opposition to the generally accepted institution of slavery. They do not seem to have launched campaigns for its abolition, however.

The persecution of Christians also persisted for economic reasons. Priests, idol makers, and other vested religious interests could hardly look on disinterestedly while their incomes dwindled and their very livelihoods stood in jeopardy. Since leaders of the old religions held important positions in society, they could easily stir up mob opposition to Christianity. The success of Demetrius and the other idol makers of Ephesus is a good example of what could happen (see Acts 19). Christians were also made scapegoats for great calamities such as famine, earthquakes, and pestilence—which were sometimes thought to be divine punishment because people had forsaken the Greco-Roman gods.

Religiously, Christianity suffered because of its exclusivity, its intolerance of other faiths of the empire. They recognized only one way of salvation and aggressively tried to win followers from other faiths. Because Christianity declared the views of all other faiths wrong and incapable of bringing their followers salvation, they naturally made enemies. Often the fur really began to fly.

With persecution, Christians had to hold religious observances in secret, making it easy for all sorts of rumors to circulate about them. Some saw in their love for each other an evidence of sexual orgies. Others interpreted their statements used in connection with Communion to refer to cannibalism.

With all that has been written about the horrors of Roman persecution and the

Nero was the first Roman emperor to persecute Christians.

James the brother of John and arrested Peter (Acts 12:1–3).

The years 62 and 63 brought a turning point in the relations between Christianity and the Roman authorities. The great Stoic Seneca retired from public life and Nero broke with the Stoic members of the Senate. The emperor then moved in the direction of an oriental and theocratic form of rule. That is, he sought a form of government in which the ruler ruled as absolute and asked to be virtually worshiped as a god. He began to persecute Christians as adherents of a "new religion," or a "superstition," an "illicit superstition," and objects of mass hatred. Then, after the fire of Rome in 64, he evidently accused Christians of arson in order to turn aside the accusation that he had started the fire.[18] Nero's general change in policy also resulted in condemnation of Stoic members of the ruling classes in 65 and 66.

The second persecution broke out under the emperor Domitian in A.D. 93, first against Stoics and then against Jews who refused to pay a tax designed to help fund construction of the magnificent new temple to Jupiter on the Capitoline Hill in Rome.

large number of martyrdoms between the time of Christ and the Edict of Toleration under Constantine (A.D. 313), three important points need to be made. (1) Ruling powers rarely organized general persecutions. (2) A mob or a political faction stirred up most small, localized persecutions. (3) There were long periods of toleration or even friendship between authorities and Christians.

In fact, between the death of Christ and the persecution of Nero (after A.D. 64), Romans generally followed a hands-off policy. At least they did not want to get involved in the conflict between Jews and Christians. For example, note what happened when leaders of the local synagogue brought Paul before the Roman governor Gallio in Corinth (Acts 18:12) and when Jewish authorities in Jerusalem hurled accusations against Paul before Felix and Festus (see Acts 21; 23:28–29; 25:19). Roman authorities treated these issues as matters of Jewish law, refused to get involved, and dismissed the accusations. It is interesting to note that the only official persecution suffered by the church in Judea between about A.D. 30 and 60 came when Roman prefects were off the scene, during the reign of king Herod Agrippa I (41–44). He killed

The Great Fire of Rome

The great fire of Rome began on July 19 of A.D. 64 and lasted for nine days. Gutting ten of the fourteen districts of the city, it brought untold suffering to a population of about one million. Some of Nero's enemies circulated a report that he had started the fire. The charge was probably untrue, but Nero apparently diverted attention from himself by making scapegoats out of the Christian community in Rome. The penalty suffered by many of the supposed incendiaries was burning at the stake at night to light the gardens near Nero's circus in the Vaticanus section of Rome (now the Vatican). He crucified some and had others thrown to wild beasts or mad dogs. Paul suffered martyrdom at the hands of Nero; Peter is said to have suffered the same fate.

Under the emperor Domitian, a persecution sent the apostle John into exile on the Isle of Patmos. (The Capitoline Museum, Rome)

Since Christians were still associated with Judaism, they also suffered during this persecution. Like Nero, Domitian promoted a theocratic and autocratic form of government. As he sought to enforce emperor worship, Christians who refused to participate were charged with treason. Some were martyred, some dispossessed of property, and others banished.

At this time the Romans exiled the apostle John to the Isle of Patmos, where he received the vision of the Revelation. It is not clear that John's exile was instigated by the emperor, however. Probably local opposition in the province of Asia was responsible for that. The modern tourist visiting Ephesus can see ruins of the great temple to the divine Domitian, which reminds us of the power of the emperor cult and provides background for the New Testament narrative. Marta Sordi in *The Christians and the Roman Empire* (1986) has provided us with an excellent discussion of the beginnings of Roman persecution of Christians.

We are also curious about the spread of Christianity—about the response to the gospel. The usual view is that Christianity spread rapidly among the lower classes and that it was essentially a lower-class movement. Those who have taken such a position point to verses like 1 Corinthians 1:26, which says that not many "wise," "mighty," or "noble" are called. But of course some of them were—and the percentage of those who are members of the upper class in any society is always small.

What does the Scripture itself indicate? Look at the Twelve. Peter and Andrew seem to have been business partners with Zebedee and his sons, James and John. When James and John accepted the call of Jesus, they left their boats and the business in the hands of their father and the hired help (Mark 1:20). Peter continued to maintain a house in Capernaum big enough for his family and to provide a headquarters for the Twelve. This indicates that they were from the upper class of their area.

Other followers included Joseph of Arimathea, a rich man and a member of the Sanhedrin, and Nicodemus, a ruler of the Jews and a member of the Sanhedrin. Then there was Joanna, the wife of Chuza, one of Herod Antipas' stewards. And don't forget

The Church of the Annunciation in Nazareth

the Ethiopian eunuch, a man "of great authority under Candace the queen of the Ethiopians, who had charge of all her treasury" (Acts 8:27). Or Sergius Paulus, the governor of Cyprus (Acts 13:7–12); the Philippian jailer (Acts 16); many of the "leading women" of Thessalonica (Acts 17:4); Dionysius of the prestigious Areopagus Council in Athens (Acts 17:34); and Crispus, the ruler of the Corinth synagogue (Acts 18:8).

Sociologist Rodney Stark has made a case for the view that "Christians were not a mass of degraded outsiders but from early days had members, friends, and relatives in high places."[19] And these people were in a position to protect their friends and others from persecution. Also he shows that conversions among Jews and Gentiles were extensive.

Sites Sacred to the Beginning of Christianity

Houses of Mary and Joseph in Nazareth

"And behold, you will conceive in your womb and bring forth a Son, and shall call His name JESUS" (Luke 1:31 NKJV), the angel Gabriel announced to Mary.

The house where the angel met Mary of Nazareth is today, on the basis of tradition, marked by the Church of the Annunciation. The Franciscans built the present church between 1955 and 1959 where they had previously built one in 1730. The 1730 church stood on the spot where the Crusaders erected their sanctuary in the twelfth century (destroyed by the Mamelukes in 1263). The Crusaders had put up a cathedral over the spot where the Persian conquest of 614 had destroyed a Byzantine church (the first on the site), built around A.D. 427. The cave house under the present church may be the one that the pilgrim Egeria visited in 384 and identified as the house of Mary. Beyond this we cannot go in locating the traditional house of Mary.

Next to the Church of the Annunciation stands the Church of St. Joseph (completed

in 1914), which according to tradition was built over the cave where the Holy Family lived and where Joseph had his carpentry shop. In its crypt are remnants of Byzantine and Crusader churches and below them a cave where Joseph supposedly worked. This has been identified as Joseph's workshop only since the seventeenth century and there is no real basis for the tradition.

The Place of Jesus' Birth

"Joseph also went up from Galilee. . . into Judea, to the city of David, which is called Bethlehem. . . to be registered with Mary, his betrothed wife, who was with child. So it was, that while they were there, the days were completed for her to be delivered. And she brought forth her firstborn Son." (Luke 2:4–7 NKJV)

Bethlehem was indeed a "little town" on the caravan route between Jerusalem and Egypt by way of Hebron. That fact would later facilitate Joseph's flight with the infant Jesus. The place, some five miles south of Jerusalem, gained new importance when Herod built fortresses at Herodium and Masada because Bethlehem overlooked the roads to those fortresses.

In the second century a tradition existed that Jesus' birth had occurred in a certain cave that had been behind the inn. Apparently many people lived in caves in the area or used them for stables. If Mary had lived in a cave in Nazareth (see previous discussion), it would not have been extremely unusual for Mary and Joseph to stay in one now. The argument that the traditional cave was too small to be used as a stable is not very strong because its present division into sections is misleading. This cave is presumably the same one that the Emperor Hadrian (A.D. 117–138) desecrated by including it in a grove dedicated to Tammuz-Adonis. At that time both Bethlehem and Jerusalem were declared off limits to Jews.

Bethlehem's status changed dramatically, however, under Constantine. After a pilgrimage to Palestine by his mother, Queen Helena, he ordered construction (in 326) of a church over the revered cave. This structure

The Church of the Nativity in Bethlehem

were crowned there: Baldwin I (1101) and Baldwin II (1109). Not only did the Crusaders repair the structure, but they also covered much of the interior with paintings and mosaics, very little of which survives to the present. Over the years the main door has been gradually reduced in size to its present small opening.

The present Church of the Nativity in Bethlehem stands over a cave which has been revered since the second century as the birthplace of Jesus. It may indeed be the place where Jesus was born.

Archaeological work at the site of the church was conducted in 1934 under the leadership of W. Harvey for the Department of Antiquities of the British Mandate and by the Franciscans from 1948 to 1951.[20]

was roughly square, with an octagonal apse over the traditional grotto. The church was about eighty-six feet on a side and was divided internally by four rows of nine columns each into a nave and four aisles, two on each side. He paved the entire floor with mosaics, some of which a modern tourist can see under the floor of the present church. At the end of the fourth century Jerome lived in the cave and translated the Hebrew Bible into Latin (the Vulgate) there.

After Constantine's church was destroyed by a Samaritan revolt in 529, the emperor Justinian (527–565) rebuilt the church, essentially in its present form. He reconstructed the side walls of the church on Constantinian foundations, but lengthened the structure to about 107 feet, making it a rectangle instead of a square. He widened the nave and narrowed the side aisles. Only minor changes have been made in the church since Justinian's day.

The church escaped destruction during the Persian conquest in 614 because, according to the oft-repeated tradition, the Magi portrayed in the scene of the birth of Christ on the facade were shown in Persian dress. The church also escaped destruction during the Muslim conquest and subsequent occupation, but it fell into decay from neglect. When the Crusaders took the area they launched a program of restoration. The first two kings of Crusader Jerusalem

Sychar, Jacob's Well, and Samaritan Conversion

"So He came to a city of Samaria which is called Sychar, near the plot of ground that Jacob gave to his son Joseph. Now Jacob's well was there." (John 4:5, 6 NKJV)

The familiar story of Jesus' meeting with the woman at the well marked the beginning of the conversion of the Samaritans.

Mosaic in the floor of Constantine's church (A.D. 315)

The village of Sychar

The approximate location of the village from which the woman came is clear: the vicinity of Jacob's well in the narrow valley between Mounts Ebal and Gerizim on the direct route between Galilee and Jerusalem. The site of Jacob's well is acknowledged by Jews, Muslims, and Christians alike. Over the well stands an unfinished Greek Orthodox Church, begun during the Czarist regime and abandoned when the Communists took over in Russia.

But the identification of Sychar is less clear. Some ancient manuscripts read "Shechem" for "Sychar" in John 4:5. If this is the correct reading, the woman would have come from a small village located on the site of ancient Shechem, which was destroyed by the Hasmonean John Hyrcanus in 108/107 B.C. The edge of Shechem (Tell Balatah) was about 1,000 feet west of Jacob's well.

Many Greek manuscripts, however, read "Sychar," and the Madeba Map (6th century map discovered in 1884) identifies a Sychar on the slope of Mt. Ebal distinct from Shechem. Apparently this is to be located at the present site of Askar, about 3,000 feet north of Jacob's well. It seems to me that Askar is the likely place from which the woman came to converse with Jesus at Jacob's well. But the precise location of the town remains debatable.

Pool of Bethesda

"Now there is in Jerusalem by the Sheep Gate a pool. . . . Bethesda, having five porches. In these lay a great multitude of sick people." (John 5:2, 3 NKJV)

One of the men at the pool had been paralyzed for thirty-eight years, and Jesus healed him—on the Sabbath. The controversy that arose led many Jews to try to kill Jesus. This was one of the more dramatic of Jesus' miracles, and there has been considerable interest in finding the Pool of Bethesda.

The Pool of Bethesda as now identified lies inside the modern St. Stephens Gate in the eastern wall of Jerusalem. It is part of a compound owned by the French Government since 1865 and run by the White Fathers. The pool itself is adjacent to the Crusader Church of St. Anne. Identified by the White Fathers at the turn of the century, the pool has been exposed by extensive excavations carried out there since 1956.

Actually the pool was double and separated by a twenty-foot-wide pathway. The two pools together form a trapezoid about 165 feet across the north and over 215 feet on its southern side. They have a long side measuring over 300 feet. The John 5 reference mentions five porches or porticoes or

The Pool of Bethesda

colonnaded walkways. There were colonnades around the four sides of the two pools and in between them, making a total of five.

Pilate's Judgment Hall—the Pavement

"Pilate. . . brought Jesus out and sat down in the judgment seat in a place that is called The Pavement, but in Hebrew, Gabbatha." (John 19:13 NKJV)

Christians have been eager to locate The Pavement, made sacred by the sufferings of Christ. No doubt it would have been connected with the palace that Pilate used in Jerusalem, which stood in the Upper City, just inside the present Jaffa Gate—not in the Antonia Fortress, just to the north of the temple area, as is often assumed.

During much of this century the Pavement has been identified with a wonderful Roman pavement (believed to have been part of the Antonia Fortress) in the basement of the Sisters of Zion Convent, located at the Second Station of the Cross on the Via Dolorosa. Outside the convent an arch crosses the Via Dolorosa and was presumed to be the arch under which Pilate proclaimed,

"Behold the Man" (John 19:5). Hence the name the *Ecce Homo* Arch, Latin for "Behold the Man." Part of the triple Roman arch may still be seen inside the convent.

I have often sat on a bench by this wonderful pavement with other visitors listening to one of the sisters telling about the passion of our Lord. We looked at the large beautifully-cut flagstones made smooth by the feet of people and horses, and grooved to prevent their feet from slipping. We were sobered by discussion of the dice game cut in the pavement where bored guards probably gambled for Jesus' cloak (John 19:24).

But no more. The sisters have bowed to research, which demonstrates that the pavement dates to the second century. The emperor Hadrian laid it as part of the city forum after putting down the second Jewish revolt in A.D. 135. And the arch was a triple victory arch celebrating Hadrian's victory over the Jews. Neither the pavement, nor the arch, nor the Via Dolorosa existed in Jesus' day.

Now we look for the Pavement in the area of the palace in the Upper City. But though the foundations of that palace have been excavated, the Pavement has not yet been found.[21]

Caiaphas' House

"Then Annas sent Him bound to Caiaphas the high priest." (John 18:24 NKJV)

The sacred steps leading up to St. Peter's in Gallicantu (of the Cockcrowing), which some believe to be the site of Caiaphas' palace

Gordon's Calvary

As with other places sacred to the life and death of Jesus, the location of his trial before Caiaphas and Peter's denial has been the subject of much investigation. Apparently Caiaphas' palace was located on the summit of the Upper City in Jerusalem, not far from the modern St. Mary Church (Dormition Church).

A few hundred yards east of the St. Mary Church, on the lower slope of Mount Zion, stands the Church of St. Peter of the Cockcrowing, built in 1931. Beneath it are ruins of another church dating back to the fifth century.

Below the earlier church were rooms cut out of the rock that had iron rings on the wall and other means for restraining or whipping prisoners. Some believe this to be the prison where Jesus was kept until Caiaphas could see him.

Unfortunately, there is no clear evidence to identify the Church of St. Peter of the Cockcrowing as the site of Caiaphas' palace,

though some feel that it was the place. However, the stone steps up the side of the hill to the church may date to the time of Jesus, and he may have walked on them.[22]

While we must be very tentative in identifying the site of Caiaphas' palace, we can be fairly certain about finding his name and perhaps his bones. In 1990 Zvi Greenhut, with the Israel Antiquities Authority, unearthed a tomb from the New Testament period in the Jerusalem Peace Forest. In it were twelve ossuaries or bone boxes, one of them (elegantly decorated) with the name "Caiaphas" scratched on it. In fact, the inscription reads "Joseph son of Caiaphas." The first century Jewish historian Josephus said that the high priest in the days when Pontius Pilate governed Judea was "Joseph who was called Caiaphas" (*Antiquities* XVIII. 2.2). The limestone ossuary contained the bones of a 60-year-old man. So we may have the name and the bones of the man who presided at Jesus' trial.[23]

The Garden Tomb

Church of the Holy Sepulcher

Calvary and the Tomb

"And He, bearing His cross, went out to a place called the Place of a Skull, which is called in Hebrew, Golgotha, where they crucified Him." (John 19:17–18 NKJV)

"Now in the place where He was crucified there was a garden, and in the garden a new tomb in which no one had yet been laid. So there they laid Jesus." (John 19:41–42 NKJV)

Some have opted for Gordon's Calvary and the nearby Garden Tomb as the place of the crucifixion and burial of Jesus. Though with a degree of imagination Gordon's Calvary may look a little like a skull today, it has assumed its present form since New Testament times as a result of quarrying or soil use over the centuries.

As for the Garden Tomb, there always remained some doubt as to whether the site had any validity. A few years ago, Gabriel Barkay, who teaches at Tel Aviv University and the Jerusalem University College (formerly American Institute of Holy Land Studies), made a new study of the case for the Garden Tomb. And he concluded that it was first hewn in the Iron Age II period, during the eighth to the sixth centuries B.C., and was not used again for burial purposes until the Byzantine period. So it could not have been the tomb in which Jesus was buried.[24]

The traditional site of Calvary and the tomb of Jesus is in the Church of the Holy

Sepulcher, now located deep inside the old city of Jerusalem. But was it outside the city in New Testament times? As a result of various discoveries in recent decades, the line of the wall has now been established. There was a jog in the wall in Jesus' day. The wall lay about 500 feet to the south and 350 feet to the east of where the church now stands.[25] If the church was outside the wall, the next issue is the legitimacy of the claim that Jesus was buried there.

The Church of the Holy Sepulcher as it now stands is essentially a Crusader structure, begun after the Crusaders captured

The tomb of Jesus in the Church of the Holy Sepulcher

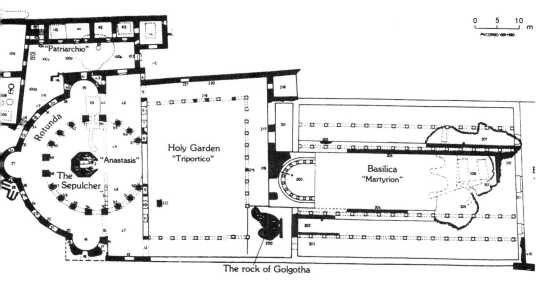

Plan of Constantine's Church of the Holy Sepulcher. (After Corbo)

Jerusalem in 1099. The prior history of the site requires a considerable amount of space to describe in full,[26] but we can describe the main outline. When Hadrian rebuilt Jerusalem early in the second century, he desecrated the site of Jesus' burial by constructing a temple to Venus/Aphrodite upon it.

Later, when Constantine prepared to build his memorial there, he totally destroyed Hadrian's temple and then constructed a complex adjacent to the north-south main street of Jerusalem (dedicated A.D. 335). Laid out in an east-west direction, the complex involved first (on the east and next to the street) an atrium open to the sky, then a basilica type church with a nave and a double colonnade on each side, next a holy garden open to the sky and surrounded on three sides by columns—at the southeast of which rose the rock of Calvary– and finally (on the other side of a wall with eight gates) a rotunda covering the tomb of Jesus (which had been under Hadrian's temple).

Fire damaged this complex by the time of the Persian invasion of 614 and it was repaired. Then El Khakin, Caliph of Cairo almost completely destroyed the entire church complex in 1009. The basilica was never rebuilt, but the Byzantine emperor

Constantine IX restored the rotunda and the holy garden fairly successfully between 1042 and 1048. Finally the Crusaders rebuilt the church essentially in the form we know it today. The entrance is now from the south. Inside and to the right rises the rock of Calvary. Straight ahead is the nave, which lies across the old holy garden. At the western end of the nave (to the left) is the rotunda with the tomb of Jesus. Thus both Calvary and the tomb are now within the church and covered.

Over the centuries the Crusader church became quite decrepit. The religious bodies having access to the church finally agreed on a restoration plan in 1959. The following year Virgilio Corbo of the Franciscan School in Jerusalem was appointed archaeologist for the project. The restoration involved a considerable amount of excavation under the church. The Franciscan Printing Press published the three-volume report, *The Holy Sepulcher of Jerusalem*, in 1981–1982.

After completing his study on the Church of the Holy Sepulcher, Finegan concluded, "We may with confidence seek beneath the roof of this structure the true place of Golgotha and the sepulcher of Christ."[27] More specifically, in response to the question of

The Upper Room as it appears today

whether the Constantinian rotunda was built over the true site of Jesus' burial, Bahat responds, "It seems very likely that it was,"[28] "and we really have no reason to reject the authenticity of the site."[29]

The Upper Room

On the southwestern hill of Jerusalem, now called Mount Zion, next to the Dormition Abbey stand the remains of the first century Church of the Apostles. This church was built to mark the place where the apostles prayed after they returned from witnessing the Ascension. All that remains of that church is a small chamber now venerated as the tomb of King David. Of course it is impossible that David was buried here because the early kings of Israel were entombed at the southeast edge of the City of David.

In the twelfth century the Crusaders incorporated the remains of the first century church into the Church of St. Mary. Above it they built a room to commemorate the spot where Jesus and the disciples celebrated the Last Supper and where the Spirit descended on the day of Pentecost (Matthew 26:17–30; Acts 1:12–14; 2:1–13). In the sixteenth century Muslims turned the Upper Room into a mosque by adding a prayer niche in its southern wall. An Arabic inscription on the wall dating to 1524 commemorates this event. The Upper Room was restored in the mid-1980s. Obviously this chamber cannot be the Upper Room of New Testament times. About the best that can be said for this traditional Upper Room is that somewhere near here the Last Supper and the Pentecostal drama took place.

Site of the Ascension

"Then he took them out as far as the outskirts of Bethany, and raising his hands he blessed them. Now as he blessed them, he withdrew from them and was carried up into heaven." (Luke 24:50 NJB)

In an alternative translation, Jesus led the disciples "to the vicinity of Bethany" (NIV). There he ascended to heaven. Bethany remains a small village about a mile and a half east of Jerusalem on the eastern slope of the Mount of Olives. On the face of it, Jesus seems to have ascended to heaven near the spot where he began the Triumphal Entry into Jerusalem, the place where he raised Lazarus from the dead, and the home of Mary, Martha, and Lazarus.

The Acts account of the Ascension (1:12) indicates that the apostles returned to Jerusalem from the Mount of Olives after Jesus' departure. And it says that the Mount of Olives lay a "Sabbath day's journey" from Jerusalem. As a matter of fact, the distance from the top of the Mount of Olives to the wall of the city is about 3,000 feet—the extent of a Sabbath day's journey. The common assumption is that Jesus ascended from the top of the Mount of Olives. But the Luke reference seems to locate the event on the east slope of the Mount near Bethany.

The Chapel of the Ascension

Gospel Spreads through Trade

At the same time as *Pax Romana* brought peace to Europe and Asia Minor, a contemporary Chinese Peace under the Han Dynasty had the same effect in Asia—except that it lasted longer than *Pax Romana* (from about 200 B.C. to A.D. 220). Between them the Romans and Chinese were able to enforce a certain degree of order across Asia, the Near East, North Africa, and Europe. This era of peace facilitated the spread of the message of the Prince of Peace. And by the end of the first century the gospel had reached almost the entire known world—the Mediterranean lands, Western Europe, Africa, and even faraway Britain, India, and China. While some of this spread of the gospel came through deliberate missionary activity, more than we will ever know came through the arteries of trade, especially to India and China.

Scripture does not say he ascended from the highest point. It is possible that reference to the Sabbath day's journey indicates only the last and more organized part of their walk—the descent after they had wandered up from Bethany.

At least by the late fourth century the site of the Ascension had been localized on the summit of the Mount of Olives, and about 378 the faithful built the Church of the Holy Ascension there.[30] This seems to have consisted of an inner circular colonnade of sixteen columns that supported a dome. Surrounding this they built an octagonal outer wall. When the Persians destroyed this building in 614, the patriarch of Jerusalem rebuilt it. In their turn the Crusaders rebuilt that decaying structure early in the twelfth century.

When the great Muslim conqueror Saladin took Palestine in 1187, he converted the Church of the Ascension into a mosque, which it remains to the present. It consists of an octagonal wall enclosing a courtyard about 100 feet in diameter. Near the center of this stands an octagonal building (the old Crusader chapel), 21 feet in diameter topped by a dome. The arches on the eight sides have now been walled in. It is appropriate for Muslims to use this as a place of prayer because Sura IV of the Koran says of Jesus (a great prophet) that "God raised him up unto himself." In this chapel a modern tourist may see what is supposed to be the footprint of Jesus as he ascended. But this print likely marks the extent of the Sabbath day's journey from Jerusalem (Acts 1:12).

From my perspective, it seems unnecessary to conclude that Jesus rose from the top of the Mount of Olives. It is enough to say that he rose from somewhere on the Mount. And what would have been more beautiful than his Ascension from near Bethany, where the resurrection of Lazarus anticipated his own resurrection and a household of faith (especially Mary) symbolized complete faith in him?

(For more on this topic, go to p. 372 or p. 475.)

Warfare

Dawn of the Roman Peace

It was September 2, 31 B.C., showdown time between the forces of Mark Antony and Octavian. With some 500 ships, Octavian had bottled up the navy of Antony in the Bay of Actium on the western side of Greece. Antony's army was drawn up on nearby land. The great battle concocted by later historians never took place. At an untimely moment Cleopatra panicked and broke through the blockade with a squadron of sixty ships and the treasure. Antony slipped away in her wake with a smaller squadron. Only a few skirmishes actually took place. Antony's fleet, believing that their commander had deliberately deserted them, went over to Octavian immediately. The army defected soon afterward.

Octavian pursued Antony and Cleopatra to Egypt, where he defeated their forces and they committed suicide. He annexed the wealthy province to the Roman Empire. During the next year or two Octavian restored order in the Mediterranean world. Then he was ready to tidy up things politically. Early in January of 27 B.C. he suddenly announced in the Senate that he was giving up all his powers and the provinces under his control and putting them at the disposal of the Senate and the Roman people. There must have been considerable work behind the scenes to bring about the carefully orchestrated political settlement that evolved.

What evolved was a partnership of rule between Octavian and the Senate. The political forms of the republic continued, but in effect a monarchy had been established—the rule of one. On January 16 the Senate conferred on him the title of "Augustus," the Revered One (from the Latin *augere*, meaning "to increase"), equally applied to gods and men. The second title they bestowed was that of "Imperator," earlier a title of honor assumed upon victories won and now the title or prerogative of the Roman commander in chief.

Augustus retained command of the army and rule over provinces that required military action to maintain order (e.g., Spain, Gaul, and Syria), and the Senate ruled Italy, Sicily, Sardinia, Macedonia, Achaea, and other provinces where no army was required. As a matter of fact, Augustus would not have been willing to give up control of the army—his power base. Nor would anyone have wanted him to do so. It was unthinkable that control of the military should be lifted and ambitious generals should be free to launch a new era of civil war. The form of government as established is often called a dyarchy—a rule of two, Augustus and the Senate. It is also called the Principate: Augustus as first or principal citizen ruled not as a military dictator but a civilian figure in cooperation with the Senate and with the support of the Roman people.

Augustus had launched the *Pax Romana* or the Roman Peace. That did not mean there were no local bonfires in subsequent decades or generations. It only meant that Rome's terrifying might kept the lid on the cauldron of local strife, always about to boil over. And if an open rebellion broke out in the Mediterranean world, Rome would quickly and forcefully deal with it. An example of the fury and determination of Rome's military efforts appears in her squelching of the First Jewish Revolt and the destruction of Jerusalem and the temple (66–70/72). That fire would have been put out sooner but for the bloodshed connected with the death of Nero, complicating Roman efforts to settle local problems. The *Pax Romana* also meant that Rome's power maintained a certain order among the tribal peoples all along her borders and beyond them. The *Pax Romana* was destined to last for some 200 years, until about A.D. 180.

Augustus' Management of the Military

When Augustus won the Battle of Actium, he found himself at the head of an army of some 250,000 citizens—larger than he needed and more than he could finance. Of these he released more than 140,000 and sent them to their home communities or settled them on lands confiscated from supporters of Antony. Henceforth most recruits came by voluntary enlistment; he tried to avoid the draft.

During the civil war that brought Augustus to power, men from low social background tended to rise through the ranks and to form a professional officer class. He worked to restore such posts to men from the middle and the senatorial classes. In that way Augustus restored the prestige of the office and avoided development of a possibly dangerous military vested interest. He recruited legionnaires from Roman citizens living in Italy or the provinces. Legions nominally consisted of 6,000 men—infantry with a cavalry unit of 120. But they were usually maintained at about 5,500. The length of service was at first sixteen years; later he increased it to twenty, with a substantial discharge payment and/or land grant. He settled discharged legionnaires in colonies throughout the empire. This practice helped to Romanize the empire.

Model of a Roman warship. (Haifa Maritime Museum)

In the early empire stationed twenty-five legions, some 150,000 men along the Rhine, the Danube, and in Syria. Clearly their job was to protect the borders and not to police the empire internally or to maintain the power of the emperor. As a matter of fact, in most areas Roman power was so well established that the legions were not needed.

The emporers supplemented the legionnaires with auxiliary forces, also about 150,000 in number. Recruited from the provinces, these were organized into infantry and cavalry corps, each 480 or 960 men, under Roman officers. Enlisted for twenty-five years of service, they commonly received Roman citizenship at the end of their terms when they were mustered out.

The Praetorian Guard

"Now when we came to Rome, the centurion delivered the prisoners to the captain of the guard." (Acts 28:16 NKJV)

The "guard," the Praetorian Guard, served as a very special unit in the Roman military establishment. Before Augustus, Roman generals commonly chose a private contingent of soldiers from the ranks to act as a bodyguard. Augustus formed an official body of troops known as the Praetorian Guard. These could act as his private guard, keep order in Rome and elsewhere in Italy, carry out special assignments, and serve as an elite corps of warriors in battle. Augustus' guard had nine cohorts, each of 500 to 1,000 men. He stationed only three of these cohorts in Rome so they could be no threat to the civilian nature of the state. Men enlisted in the Praetorian Guard for sixteen years.

After the death of Augustus the place of the Guard in Roman politics changed radically. During the reign of Tiberius (14–37), who ruled while Pilate served as prefect or procurator in Judea, the powerful Praetorian prefect Sejanus virtually ran the government in Rome. Tiberius spent much of his time on the Isle of Capri. Sejanus built the Praetorian Camp just outside of Rome on the northeast.

From this time on the Guard proved to be quite political. Out of ambition, or for the right amount of money, they assassinated emperors or made other bids for power. In A.D. 41, along with conspirators from the Senate, they killed Caligula and put Claudius on the throne. In 68 they deserted

Nero and within a year killed the emperors Galba and Vitellius. In 96 they were involved in the murder of Domitian, who had exiled the apostle John to the island of Patmos. Their place in later Roman history is beyond the scope of this book. We shall return to comments on the Guard in the last chapter of this book.

The Roman Navy

The Roman navy was at the height of its power during the first century. With fleets based in Italy, Syria, Egypt, Mauretania (northwest Africa), the Black Sea, English Channel, and on the Rhine and Danube, it could meet both local and imperial needs.

Ships were narrow and long (proportion of one to seven, usually less than 200 feet in length) and propelled by oars arranged in one, two, or three banks, with the trireme the main warship in the Roman fleet during the first century. This term could apply to a ship with three banks of oars (one above the other) or three men to an oar. Fours, fives, and more are known. What these terms mean has been long debated, but it seems that there could not be five, six, or more banks of oars. There must have been a way of having several men pull a single oar. Of course, a ship had sails for movement on the open sea. The crew of a trireme is estimated at 200, including 150 oarsmen.

The two fleets based in Italy may have had crews totaling 15,000. How large the other fleets were we do not know. Men enlisted in the navy for twenty-six years. A great many were non-Romans who won citizenship when they left the service.

Roman Garrisons in the Provinces—Palestine

"The centurion sent friends to Him, saying to Him, 'Lord do not trouble Yourself, for I am not worthy that You should enter under my roof.'"
(Luke 7:6 NKJV)

"And the soldiers twisted a crown of thorns and put it on His head, and they put on Him a purple robe. Then they said, 'Hail King of the Jews!' And they struck Him with their hands."
(John 19:2–3 NKJV)

In noting two different military responses to Jesus, we are almost certainly dealing with two different peoples. The soldiers of the army of occupation were presumably auxiliaries recruited from the cities of Sebaste (Samaria) and Caesarea—non-Jewish people almost violently anti-Semitic in sentiment. The army consisted of five infantry regiments or cohorts of about 500 each and one cavalry regiment of about the same number, all drawn from the non-Jewish element of the population. These were officered by Romans (who might be less antagonistic to the Jews—or Jesus), and there would have been five centurions (commanders of about 100 or slightly less) to each cohort. In addition, during Jesus' day another cohort of Roman citizens had been drafted in Judea. The centurion who made an appeal to Jesus (Luke 7:6 above) and the centurion present at the Crucifixion (Luke 23:47), both Romans, were positive toward Jesus, while the rank and file non-Romans in the occupation army were not.

The behavior of these soldiers from Sebaste and Caesarea became so scandalous that Claudius (emperor A.D.41–54) planned to transfer them to Asia Minor and bring in fresh troops not infected with the violent anti-Semitic bias of these Gentiles. But the two cities set up such a howl that Claudius gave up the plan. Unfortunately the actions of these troops against the Jews helped goad them to rebellion against Rome later on.

The military arrangement in Judea was similar to that of other provinces. Generally the Roman legions were not stationed in the provinces to maintain order or Roman authority. Any auxiliary troops under arms were recruited from local sources.

Organization and Training of the Legions

The Romans divided their legions into ten units called cohorts, and each of these they divided into six contingents called centuries. At the beginning of the New Testament period the legion theoretically had 6,000 men. Thus the cohorts stood at 600 and the centuries at 100. As the first century wore on, legions were seldom maintained at full strength. By the second century they usually had only about 5,300 men, so the century numbered 80 and the cohort 480.

The Romans attached several hundred clerks and specialists to the first cohort, which was smaller than the others. Clerks kept accounts, maintained supplies and personnel records, and acted as paymasters. Specialists included engineers, surveyors, and the like, who could build roads, select campsites and fulfill other special tasks. The cohort also contained musicians, trumpet players, who could play a salute to senior officers, but their main job was to signal orders. There were medics too, often Greeks, and standard-bearers. The main standard-bearer, the Aquilifer, carried the gold or silver eagle, the badge of Rome. The eagle standard was sacred and to lose it was a terrible disgrace. Legionnaires fought fiercely to protect it.

The commander of a century was called a centurion, of the cohort a tribune. Five tribunes came from the equestrian or middle class and the sixth from the senatorial class. All tribunes served in the army as a step to advancing in the government bureaucracy. The senior tribune served as the commanding general of the legion. Overseeing all centurions (career soldiers) in the legion was the *primus pilus*, head of the first century of the first cohort. He served as the prefect of the camp and headed the entire legion in the absence of the senior tribune.

The centurions served as the backbone of the legion. As drill sergeants, they trained the men in their own century and led them into battle. They had to account for the equipment that belonged to the century. For this they had the help of two clerks. They also posted guards and made inspections.

How did they train the legions to be the model or standard of excellence? Their training included running and jumping exercises and running obstacle courses. Every month they had to make three eighteen-mile marches. These had to be covered in a day while carrying sixty pounds of equipment, plus armor and weapons. They had to learn drill, which was both practice for movements used in battle and ceremonial performance. And of course they learned how to handle

weapons. They copied training in fighting with a sword from techniques or exercises used in schools for gladiators, where every man had to fight for his life. A recruit might fight a dummy with his sword in his earlier training. But in the more advanced drill adversaries sparred together.

Discipline of Roman soldiers was severe, and they learned how to be rough, tough warriors. A centurion carried a staff made of hard vine wood, with which he might whack a soldier to keep him in line—while in training or in battle. If he found a soldier guilty of a minor fault, such as being late on parade, he might make him stand outside headquarters all day without weapons or armor to show he was not worthy to be a soldier.

If he committed a more serious infraction such as sleeping while on guard duty or deserting, he would be flogged or reduced in rank. In time of war the penalty would be death. To sleep while on duty was such a serious offense and so unworthy of a soldier that it leaves us speechless to hear that soldiers of the guard claimed to have been sleeping while Jesus' disciples came and stole his body after his burial (see Matthew 28:11–15). The seriousness of the offense gives a character of unreality to the stolen body theory of the resurrection of Jesus.

Iron cavalry helmet (upper left), legionary helmet (upper right), iron body armor, front view, laced up (lower left), and iron body armor, rear view, showing hinges (lower right)

A Roman stone-throwing machine (Gustav Jeeninga)

Clothing, Armor, and Weapons of the Legionnaires

Unlike poorly equipped ancient armies in other times and places, Roman legionnaires served standardly dressed in uniforms and were provided with uniform equipment.

On their heads they wore helmets, while their enemies often fought bareheaded. Helmets normally were of bronze with an iron inner plate over a leather skullcap that protected the head from the shock of blows and the rough edges of metal. The helmet had a neck protector extending in the back, a small peak jutting out at the front, and commonly hinged cheek pieces on the sides.

On the body soldiers wore first a linen undercloth, then a linen or wool tunic with short sleeves, that extended to mid-calf or possibly to just above the knees. If they were fighting or stationed in a cold climate, they wore short leather pants that extended to just below the knee. Styles of body armor changed from time to time, but during much of the first century it apparently consisted of strips of metal secured by leather

cords at the front and back. They buckled shoulder pieces of metal together in such a way that shoulders and arms could move freely. The common soldier had no leg armor so he could move faster, but centurions wore greaves.

On their feet the legionnaires wore sandals, reinforced with three-quarter inch thick leather soles and hobnails. For cold winter weather the sandals were lined with fur.

Soldiers carried swords, two feet long, with bone grips on the handles. Though they were two-edged, they were usually used for stabbing rather than cut and thrust. Soldiers also had a dagger and two throwing spears. Spears had wooden shafts seven feet long attached to spear points with thin, soft pieces of iron. When a soldier thrust a spear into an enemy shield, the spear point stuck into the shield while the weight of the wooden pole bent the thin iron shaft. The result was that the enemy had a spear sticking into his shield with the long shaft dragging on the ground. He had no choice but to throw away his shield and face the Roman legionnaire unprotected, with whatever weapons he had.

Roman shields changed considerably over time. During the early days of the empire they were oval in shape with a boss or protuberance that extended out from the center. They could be used to ward off an enemy spear or deflect sword blows. The curve of the shield could also deflect blows. As the first century wore on, the shield was

Roman catapult stones found at Masada

redesigned to be rectangular, with curved edges and of course retaining the boss. Archaeological discoveries indicate that shields were made of laminated plywood bound with iron or bronze rims and covered with tough leather.

Rugged, well-equipped, and highly trained legionnaires represented a fearsome foe at close range or in hand-to-hand combat. But they did not always choose to fight that way—at least not at the beginning of a battle. They themselves made good use of their lances or spears, thrown at substantial distance. Then the Romans themselves, or auxiliary forces, especially Syrian archers, might lay down a barrage of arrows.

They also had artillery. Romans used both bolt-shooting machines and stone throwers. There were normally ten of the latter to a legion and fifty to sixty of the former. Stone-throwing machines used in the siege of Jerusalem in A.D. 70 could hurl fifty-pound stones a distance of 1,300 feet or more. We know some could hurl stones a distance of over 2,000 feet.[31] Such missiles could terrify or at least disorder either cavalry or infantry in the field and destroy enemy machines. But they were more frequently used in sieges to break walls of brick or wood and to smash gates. They proved less effective against walls of stone.

Portable bolt-shooting machines could fire iron bolts or arrows as much as a thousand feet. A trigger released an arrow, or a bolt shot along a trough through an aperture in the front. Thus bolt-shooting machines differed from stone-throwing machines, which were larger and catapulted stones by a single wooden arm. The more powerful "bows" could lay down a barrage of arrows at a distance in advance of the legions. And arrows smeared with flaming pitch could set wooden defenses or camps on fire. Both of these kinds of artillery used twisted ropes for torsion and worked on the principles of the later crossbow.

Roman siege equipment also included battering rams, mobile towers (sometimes with bridges or drawbridges), iron pointed wall borers and hooks for dislodging masonry. The Romans had chariots, but did not use them in battle, only in triumphal or ceremonial processions.

The First Jewish Revolt and Roman Military Tactics

"His disciples came up to show Him the buildings of the temple. And Jesus said to them. . . 'Not one stone shall be left here upon another, that shall not be thrown down.'. . . The disciples came to Him privately saying, 'Tell us, when will these things be?'" (Matthew 24:1–3 NKJV)

The answer to the question was, of course, near the end of the First Jewish Revolt, in A.D. 70. At that time the Romans demolished the temple completely. The fact that the exterior western wall or Wailing Wall still stands to a considerable height does not prove the prediction false. As a matter of fact, the temple itself completely disappeared.

Causes of the Revolt

Religious nationalism—their view of a religious community—stood at the root of Jewish opposition to Rome. That is, they considered national loyalty and devotion to their religion identical. The Jews hated Romans not just as foreign occupation forces but as Gentiles whose rule over the people of God was a sacrilege. Compounding the problem was the fact that Roman procurators or prefects (governors) of the first century were generally inept or tactless and/or offended Jewish sensitivities.

The emperors also sometimes brought on Jewish hatred or resistance. A particularly galling imperial action was Caligula's order in A.D. 40 that a statue of the divine Caligula be set up in the temple in Jerusalem. Roman officials in Palestine and Syria knew that such an action would bring on armed conflict and tried to delay or block the action. When Caligula was murdered on January 24, A.D. 41 the order became a dead issue, but the animosity lingered.

Then there was an economic issue. The severe pressure of taxation made agriculture unprofitable and drove many farmers to the hills, where they became brigands. Unfortunately, many of the peasants fell into the hands of moneylenders and were squeezed out of their holdings. Severe famines in the decades before the revolt compounded the situation. An indication of the frustration and suffering of the lower classes is the fact that one of the first actions of the revolutionaries was to burn down the record office where mortgages and deeds were kept.[32]

It is not crystal clear from Josephus (*Wars of the Jews*) or other sources exactly what touched off open warfare. But one of the sparks was a Roman decision that Jews were not entitled to citizenship in Caesarea, the capital of the province, and a subsequent riot there in 66 between Jews and their neighbors over the synagogue and Jewish efforts to buy adjacent property. About the same time the Roman prefect or procurator Florus stole seventeen talents from the temple treasury, for what reason is not clear, possibly to make up arrears in tribute. In any case, his action stirred up violent demonstrations against the procurator.

Course of the Conflict

As violence broke out, the Sanhedrin and then Agrippa II, king of Chalcis, made efforts to calm the storm. They were only temporarily successful. Soon, by a ruse, the rebels took Masada and massacred the Roman garrison there. Likewise, they overwhelmed Roman forces in Jerusalem and slaughtered them. Meanwhile, disorders spread to other cities of Palestine, with Jews or Romans and their supporters gaining the upper hand here or there. Whichever side had temporary supremacy was guilty of massacre, destruction, and plunder.

The Romans had to bring order out of chaos. Cestius Gallus, the legate of Syria, collected a force at Antioch. His legionnaires, forces sent by small allied kingdoms of Syria, and volunteers from many of the cities the army passed through, totaled 33,000. He quickly restored order in Galilee, marched along the coast through Caesarea, seized Joppa, and advanced on Jerusalem. He hoped that a show of force would bring a quick surrender. The rebels abandoned the Upper City without a fight and hunkered down in the Lower City and the temple area. The Roman army launched an attack on the Lower City for five days, without success. An attack on the north

wall of the temple also proved unsuccessful.

At this point Gallus decided to retreat. He was not in a position to launch a regular siege. He had not pacified the countryside but depended on a show of strength with the hope of demoralizing the Jewish rebels. Thus during the coming winter (it was now November) he ran the risk of being cut off without adequate provisions. There are also indications that some of his legionary forces were not completely reliable. Fully half of his army consisted of inadequately trained or disciplined troops.

As Gallus retreated in orderly fashion, the Jewish rebels with their guerrilla tactics turned it into a rout. They were able to take vast amounts of plunder, including equipment that they later turned against the Romans to kill 5,780 men, to vastly improve their morale by a significant victory over Roman forces, and to improve greatly their recruitment capability. This is the only example we have of a defeat of Roman regular forces by the population of an established province. So great was the Roman defeat that when the next Roman army advanced into Judea, it had to recapture the province city by city.

In A.D. 67 Nero appointed Flavius Vespasianus (Vespasian) commander of forces to subdue the Jews. He had three legions under his command, as well as a force of some 15,000 auxiliaries recruited largely from Syria, and about 18,000 archers and cavalry units contributed by four dependent kings of the general area of Palestine and Syria, for a total army of some 50,000.

In the course of A.D. 67 Vespasian reconquered Galilee. One of the towns taken was Jotapata, after a siege of forty-seven days. This town (located midway between the Sea of Galilee and the Mediterranean) is interesting because the Jewish commander there was Josephus. When Josephus was taken prisoner he predicted Vespasian's elevation to the imperial office.[33] From this event he ultimately enjoyed imperial patronage and became the great Jewish historian. His *Wars of the Jews* provides us with the primary source for events of the period. Josephus tells us that the Romans surrounded the city with 160 engines for

The Arch of Titus in Rome, memorializing the victory of Titus over the Jewish rebellion in A.D. 70.

In A.D. 68 Roman forces reconquered Perea and all Judea, except Jerusalem. Then came news that Nero had committed suicide on June 9. Vespasian, unsure of his orders, suspended operations to engage in imperial politics. He watched and waited as Galba succeeded Nero, then Otho replaced Galba, and Vitellius took the throne in 69. The Jews had respite for about a year. When Vespasian took the field again in 69, he soon halted attacks for a second year. This time he was busy trying to secure the imperial office. Army after army in various provinces hailed him as emperor.

Jewish respite, as before, did not result in effective preparation for Roman attack but in struggle between factions in Jerusalem. The upper class of wealthy landowners and Sadducees did well with the system and were generally loyal to Rome. Another class in society consisted of impoverished peasants ground down by the system. Pharisees were strongly nationalistic and anti-Roman, while Zealots wanted to liberate Judea by force.

Finally in A.D. 70, Vespasian's son Titus took his father's command and reduced the city of Jerusalem to rubble in a five-month siege, from April to September. It took

throwing stones and darts, including flaming missiles. The catapults lobbed stones weighing 100 pounds on the defenders of the city.[34]

Panel on the Arch of Titus, showing Romans carrying the lampstand and the silver trumpets from the temple in Jerusalem after the destruction of the city

The mountaintop fortress of Masada

(Werner Braun)

roughly one-seventh of the whole imperial army to accomplish the task. Jerusalem's population, greatly increased through the influx of refugees, suffered terribly but resisted bravely, fighting for every inch. And when Titus finally defeated the Jews, he occupied only a field of ruins.

The Roman army completely surrounded Jerusalem and cut off the city from all supplies of food and armament. They built great towers seventy-five feet high to stand higher than the walls and knock defenders off them. With catapults and battering rams they breached the three walls, one by one. With flaming projectiles they set fires within the city. The temple was burnt down in the siege, probably not by accident but on orders of Titus.

In the summer of 71 Vespasian and Titus celebrated a great triumph in Rome (Rome's version of a ticker tape parade), the only triumph ever to celebrate the subjugation of an existing province. Vespasian, Titus, the victorious army, plunder from Judea, and thousands of Jewish captives paraded through the city. The Arch of Titus was erected at the east end of the Forum in Rome to commemorate the victory. A badly eroding panel still portrays the silver trumpets, the seven-branched lampstand, and

Remains of a Roman camp at Masada (one of eight)

(William White, Jr.)

The Sea, or Lake of Galilee, at the point where the Jordan River flows into the northern end of the lake. It is not more than three or four miles across at the point shown in this photograph.
(Willem A. Van Gemeren)

The plains of Jericho and the lush oasis in the region north of the Dead Sea.

The Jordan River. The Jordan is neither large nor impressive, but it has become the most famous river in the world because of scriptural events associated with it. This is one of the myriad of bends in the Jordan's path from the Sea of Galilee to the Dead Sea. Though the distance between the two seas is only about sixty miles, the streambed is about two hundred miles. (Willem Van Gemeren)

Papyrus plant. The ancient Egyptians and other peoples used papyrus reeds to make a smooth writing material resembling paper. The pith of the plant was sliced into thin strips, which were crisscrossed and pressed into sheets. Our English word paper is derived from the Greek word for the papyrus plant—papyros. This papyrus is growing in front of the Cairo Museum.
(Willem Van Genteren)

Roman milestone. This stone marker stood along a major Roman highway in Iconium in Asia Minor. The marker told the distance to various cities along the highway. The emperors put their names on these posts as public officials put their pictures or names in public buildings today. Notice the title of Caesar in the first line and Divi in the third line. The emperors claimed divinity and were worshiped along with the goddess Roma. (Gustav Jeeninga)

A model of Jerusalem as it might have looked in the time of Jesus. The city was protected by massive walls, fortified gates, and defense towers built into the wall system. Prominent in the picture is the Antonia Fortress, behind which is the temple. (E. B. Trovillion)

This cave at Qumran, designated as Cave 4 by archaeologists, contained thousands of manuscript fragments, including parts of all the Old Testament books except Esther.

The Golden Gate in the eastern wall of Jerusalem in the temple area, as seen from the Garden of Gethsemane.

Modern Nazareth, successor to the town in Galilee where Jesus grew up (Luke 4:14–16, 33, 34). Dominant in the right center of the picture is the tower of the Church of the Annunciation. (E. B. Trovillion)

Mount Gerizim in the district of Samaria, site of the Samaritan temple in Jesus' time (John 4:20–21). The woman at the well asked Jesus if it was proper to worship on Mount Gerizim or in Jerusalem.

Remains of a church at ancient Gergesa which memorialized Jesus' healing of the demoniac (Matthew 8:28–34). This region east of the Sea of Galilee was also known as Gadara and Gerasa.

The fig is still a popular food in Palestine. Notice the small green fruit on this healthy fig tree. Jesus used the fig to illustrate His teachings about the last days. Just as the Jews could observe the sprouting fig leaves and know that summer was approaching, they could observe the signs He described and know that He was about to return (Matthew 24: 32–33). (Gustav Jeeninga)

A tourist examines a mustard bush in Palestine. Unlike our mustard, this plant has a small black seed like petunia seed. The tourist is over six feet tall, and the bush over fourteen feet. The ability of the small seed to grow into such a large bush provided a good object lesson for Jesus' teaching about the kingdom of God (Matthew 13:31–32).

A head of Zeus in the Ephesus Museum. Zeus was the chief god of the ancient Greeks, and he was widely worshiped in the Mediterranean world in Jesus' day.

The Taurus Mountains north of Tarsus in Cilicia. This would have been a sight familiar to Paul as he was growing up.

The lion of Amphipolis still stands guard along the highway near the ancient town as it did when Paul and Silas went by on the journey between Philippi and Thessalonica (Acts 17:1).

Starting blocks for runners at the stadium of Delphi in Greece; they were the same for other games. Runners started from a standing position, with their toes in the grooves. Iron posts were placed in the holes between lanes so runners could swing themselves around them when the races called for more than one lap. The apostle Paul used imagery from these races in his writings (2 Timothy 4:7).

The Parthenon in Athens dedicated to the Greek goddess Athena, would have been at the height of its glory when Paul ministered in the city (Acts 17).

The temple of Hephaestus (Vulcan) in Athens is one of the best-preserved Greek temples. It towered over the Agora or marketplace when Paul ministered there (Acts 17:17).

The Temple of Apollo at Corinth and the acropolis of the city in the background. Though these columns were only twenty-seven feet high, they were more impressive than those of other temples because they were composed of solid blocks of marble instead of being built up with drums of marble.

Ruins of the civil law court in Corinth, known as the Julian Basilica. Some of the charges Corinthian Christians brought against one another may have been reviewed here (1 Corinthians 6:1–11).

The great theater at Ephesus, where Paul was almost mobbed by the worshipers of the pagan goddess Diana (Acts 19:21–41).

At the end of Paul's third missionary journey, he spent seven days at Tyre (Acts 21:4). Here is an excavated street of Roman Tyre.

Ruins of the theater at Myra, a city in Asia Minor where Paul and his centurion escort boarded a ship bound for Italy (Acts 27:5-6).

St. Paul's Bay at Malta. The beach where Paul's ship was thought to have run aground (far center of the picture) has eroded across the centuries, leaving a rocky shore. A statue of Paul stands on the small island at the entrance to the bay. The position taken in this book is that Paul's ship probably ran aground in the next bay, Salina Bay, instead (see chapter 20; Acts 27:39–28:10).

The modern Appian Way near Rome has blacktop over the roadbed that Paul would have walked (Acts 28:14–15)

The restored Senate building in Rome. The Senate lost its power during the Empire, when the Caesars took control.

The Roman Forum looking toward the east with the Colosseum in the distance. At the right in the distance is the fairly well-preserved Arch of Titus, built to commemorate Titus's destruction of Jerusalem and the temple in A.D. 70.

The mound of ancient Colosse, a city in western Asia Minor where a church was established during the days of the apostle Paul and to which he wrote an epistle.

Roman ruins at Hierapolis, a city in the province of Asia mentioned by the apostle Paul in Colossians 4:13. This was a Roman bath that was later turned into a Christian church .

Ruins of the palace of Domitian stand silent and alone on the Palatine Hill above the racetrack of the Circus Maximus. The divine Domitian demanded that people worship him as "Lord and God" in the days when the apostle John ministered in Ephesus. This scene speaks eloquently of the transitory nature of the emperor and by comparison indicates the everlasting power of the Lord of heaven.

Reconstruction of the entrance to the Roman gymnasium at Sardis, one of the seven churches that John addressed in Revelation 2–3. Both the Greeks and the Romans built gymnasiums throughout the Mediterranean world.

THE HISTORY OF CRUCIFIXION

"So the soldiers, out of the wrath and hatred they bore the Jews, nailed those they caught. . . to the crosses. . . when their multitude was so great, that room was wanting for the crosses" (Josephus, *Wars of the Jews* V.II.I).

In the midst of the siege of Jerusalem the Romans caught large numbers of Jews who tried to escape and crucified them, both as an act of vengeance against the defenders and as a means of terrorizing those who continued to resist. Bible students are, of course, familiar with the crucifixion of Jesus, but they are unaware of the origins or the extent of the practice.

As we follow the historical trail backward we cannot discover its use before the Persian period. To be sure, the Assyrians practiced impalement (mounting a living body on a pointed stake), and the Persians did too. But the Persians also crucified as punishment, as the fifth century B.C. historian Herodotus tells us. The earliest example we are aware of occurred in 522 B.C. when a Persian official killed an opponent and then crucified him. A few years later Darius the Great crucified one of the royal judges but then relented and restored the man to a position of leadership.[37] In neither case do we know what the cross looked like. Presumably the offenders were only tied to a cross.

A few examples of the mass use of crucifixion will show something of its extent. After the fall of Tyre to Alexander the Great in 332 following a seven-month siege, the infuriated conqueror crucified 2,000 men of military age and sold some 30,000 others into slavery.[38] The Hasmonean (Maccabean) Alexander Jannaeus (103–76 B.C.) near the end of his reign crucified 800 Pharisees after he put down a revolt in the rebellious town of Bemeselis, north of the city of Samaria.[39] A few years later, in 71 B.C., at the end of the Roman slave revolt led by Spartacus, 6,000 recaptured slaves were crucified on crosses set up along the Appian Way.[40] Then, as is often observed, many Christians were crucified in Rome during the persecution of Nero, following the great fire of Rome.[41]

We know that at the least Persians, Greeks, Phoenicians, Carthaginians, Jews, and Romans practiced crucifixion. They used crucifixion as a punishment or deterrent for crime and rebellion. It was especially a punishment for runaway slaves and robbers; slaves often became brigands. Jesus himself was crucified between two robbers (Mark 15:27). Crucifixion was employed especially in the provinces and it was usually reserved for those who did not possess Roman citizenship. In time, however, some lower-class Romans suffered crucifixtion. Constantine finally abolished the practice.

the table of Shewbread (or the Presence), taken as spoil from the temple.

Josephus tells us that 1,100,000 perished during the siege, and 97,000 captives were carried off to work in mines, to engage in wild beast hunts and gladiatorial contests for the entertainment of the populace in numerous provinces of the empire, and to

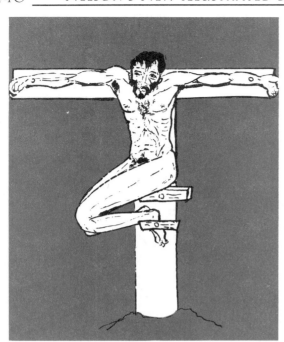

This drawing of a crucifixion is based on the remains of a crucified man from the first century A.D. discovered in a cave in Jerusalem. Both of his feet had been pierced with a spike just below the heel. (Drawing by Gaalyah Cornfeld)

perform a variety of tasks.[35] The Romans permanently stationed the Tenth Legion on the site of Jerusalem. They abolished the Sanhedrin and banned Jewish proselytism. The half shekel tax previously paid to the temple in Jerusalem was now to be given to the temple of Jupiter Capitolinus in Rome. On the plus side, those born in Judaism were still exempted from Caesar worship throughout the empire.

After the fall of Jerusalem, fortresses at Herodion and Machaerus were soon taken. But Masada held out until 73. There, in the wilderness, because of the preservative nature of the climate, one can still see remains of the encircling wall that the Roman army built to cut off the defenders from all outside contact, the eight army camps the Romans established there, and the high ramp on which the Romans mounted their artillery to breach the walls and to lob projectiles into the fortifications of the defenders. Masada withstood a final

siege of six months, though surrounded by a Roman wall and attacked by 7,000 legionnaires and auxiliaries under the command of Flavius Silva. The valor of the defenders and their ultimate decision to burn their houses and commit suicide is a story well told by Josephus and confirmed and elaborated by the excavations of Yigael Yadin.[36] Two women and five children survived the holocaust.

Crucifixion in Jesus' Day

"And when they had come to the place called Calvary, there they crucified Him, and the criminals, one on the right hand and the other on the left." (Luke 23:33 NKJV)

Ancient secular writers commonly felt that crucifixion was a totally revolting, sickening experience and do not provide us with detailed accounts of the crucifixion and suffering of crucified persons. Nor does the Scripture, which consistently avoids tearjerker accounts of the life of Jesus or of other biblical personalities.

Crucifixion persisted as an example of class justice (especially a punishment for slaves) and a political-military punishment. It certainly was political in the case of Jesus, who was accused of sedition, of trying to establish another kingship. The charge read, "Jesus the king of the Jews" (Matthew 27:37). We do not know the procedure of crucifixion in the mass executions noted

Masada, overlooking the Dead Sea

Excavated remains at Capernaum, showing the early church over the supposed house of Peter (closest to the Sea of Galilee), houses of fishermen, and the synagogue

(Werner Braun)

above, but in the case of individuals or two or three we have adequate information.

After they condemned an individual to crucifixion, they customarily tortured them. Among the Romans this normally took the form of flogging. Jesus was "flogged" or "scourged." And because he was accused of sedition, it would have been especially severe. The Greek of Matthew 27:26 indicates that Jesus was scourged with the *flagellum,* a whip of leather straps, often weighted with pieces of metal or bone at the ends, which tore the flesh as it struck. So the accused would have been beaten to a bloody pulp. Also, in Jesus' case the torture included a crown of thorns. As the soldiers made sport of this one who claimed to be king of the Jews, they wove a crown of thorns and struck him on the head to drive the thorns into his skull (Matthew 27:29–30).

Next they marched or paraded the accused past crowds of onlookers to the place of execution. As part of his shame he was forced to carry his cross—not the whole cross, only the crossbeam. The upright part was permanently installed at the place of execution and had a groove into which the crossbeam could be inserted. Pictures showing Jesus carrying the whole cross and commemorative marches at Easter time using a whole cross are erroneous. Evidently Jesus had been beaten within an inch of his life and he simply could not carry the crossbeam the entire distance, so Simon of Cyrene (modern Libya), probably a Jew in Jerusalem for Passover, was commandeered to do so (Matthew 27:32). Also, they forced the criminal to wear around his neck a sign indicating the crime of which he was guilty. Alternatively, someone would precede him carrying the sign. All along the way bystanders could ridicule him.

They stripped the prisoner of his clothing on reaching the place of crucifixion. This was part of his shame, and there was no consideration of niceties. Modern pictures that appear in our Sunday schools and

The model of first-century Jerusalem (at the Holyland Hotel in West Jerusalem) showing the upper city with some public buildings, but especially houses of the wealthy with their open courtyards

(Ben Chapman)

churches showing Jesus draped are erroneous and simply cater to contemporary sensitivities. Then his arms were attached to the crossbeam. They could be tied but were often nailed—through the hands or wrists. Scripture indicates that Jesus was nailed to the cross (John 20:25).

Now they inserted the crossbeam into the upright post. A peg or ledge halfway up the upright helped to support the body. The

A one-room house of the very poor, with holes in the walls for light and to allow smoke to escape

(Gustav Jeeninga)

During the first century, most Jewish families slept on mats on the floor, the children in the middle and a parent at either end. The wealthy had more elaborate beds.

legs could be tied to the upright pole or nailed to it. If nailed, a nail might be driven through each foot or ankle as the legs were extended down the sides of the pole. Alternatively the body might be turned sideways, the knees bent, and the one foot put on top of the other so a single nail could be driven through both feet. They tied a rope around the upper body to hold it in place. And if there was an accusation they nailed that above the head of the victim.

Because the accusation that Jesus was "King of the Jews" was placed above his head, we assume that there was room for it. Thus his cross appeared as we see it in our churches and on jewelry: the upright extended above the crossbar. Crosses without such an extension looked like a T and other crosses looked like an X (St. Andrew's Cross).

So they left the crucified one to die, the feet of the victim only a few inches from the ground, not high in the air, as is often portrayed in artwork. He suffered greatly, including the taunts and indignities of passersby, the exposure to heat and cold and insects (sometimes animals). He suf-

fered the pain of wounds, often infected, and the intense thirst. Depending on the strength of one's constitution, death might be prolonged but usually took at least thirty-six hours. And then the body hung there to decay and to be devoured by scavenger birds. Mercifully, Jesus died in just a few hours, presumably in part because of the severity of his beating. They took his body away and buried it before nightfall because the next day was the Sabbath (John 19:31).

(For more on this topic, go to p. 374 or p. 482.)

Housing and Furniture

Houses at Capernaum

Houses of the New Testament period in Palestine varied considerably. The private houses excavated at Capernaum (a village of some ten acres) tended to belong to extended families. They were built with drystone walls of black basalt. Small dwelling chambers surrounded a court, commonly paved. The courts contained ovens, staircases to the roof, and an exit to the street. Stone pillars helped to hold up flat roofs, The main street ran north-south from the shore of the Sea of Galilee. Lanes oriented east-west led to the main street and divided the village into quarters or *insulae.*

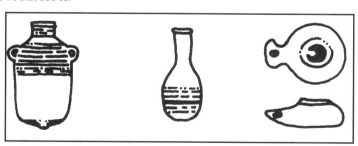

Some pottery types characteristic of Palestine in the New Testament period. On the left appears the large two-handled water pot. Women used such pots to carry drinking water from the town well. These pots could also be used to store water, wine, or other liquids. In the middle is a simple clay pitcher, used for household meals and other purposes. On the right appears the oil lamp small enough to hold in the palm of the hand. At the beginning of the first century the spout was shaped as pictured. By the middle of the century it had a pointed spout for the wick.

A first century house, widely believed to be that of Peter, stood near the shore and later had an octagonal church built over it. The later construction on the site so changed the character of it that an idea of how Peter's house may have looked is impossible.[42] But if Peter's mother-in-law and others lived with him (see Mark 1:29–31), probably his house was also of the extended family type. Moreover, if Peter's house was a place where Jesus often ministered, it must have had a large living room where gatherings could take place. See, for example, Mark 2:1–12, where men lowered a paralytic through a roof into the midst of a crowd where Jesus taught and healed. Furthermore, if Jesus made Peter's house in Capernaum his headquarters, it had to be big enough for several disciples to sleep there.

Houses in Jerusalem

Houses in the Upper City of Jerusalem on the Western Hill belonged to the wealthy. They were constructed in stone in Hellenistic style with rooms grouped around central courtyards surrounded by stone columns. That these upper-class people did not turn their backs on Judaism is clear from the number of *mikvehs* excavated, at least one for each house. These stepped pools were used for ritual purification. Clearly their use was not for bathing, since bathrooms with their bathtubs adjoined them. Bathrooms and some of the other rooms were paved with colored mosaics. Again in conformity to Jewish law, they avoided figural art, decorating with geometric and floral motifs instead. They also decorated their plastered walls with frescoes, some similar to the decor of Pompeii. These would have been the sort of houses in which a chief priest, a Zacchaeus, or a Nicodemus might have lived.

Stone tables found in these houses are of two types: a circular slab on three wooden legs and a rectangular slab on a central stone leg shaped like a column. Residents used stone vessels made from local limestone, but also pottery made from clay.[43]

Houses of the Poorer Classes

Houses of the poorer classes often had only one or two rooms. The result of such cramped quarters appears in Jesus' Parable of the Persistent Friend. A neighbor calls to a friend at midnight asking to borrow bread to meet the needs of unexpected guests. The reply is, "Do not trouble me; the door is now shut, and my children are with me in bed" (Luke 11:7 NKJV). It is late, the whole family has gone to bed with their clothes on, on mats unrolled side by side on the clay floor. Their cloaks are their blankets. The door is bolted. The father would find it difficult to go to the door because he would probably step on a child in the dark as he did so.

During the day they rolled up the bedrolls and stacked them in a corner or in an alcove. Then the family spent much of the day out of doors and sat on the floor around a cloth or skin to eat meals. Preparation of meals might take place outside

Clothing of women and men as described in the text. The man is shown as bearded because during the second century, when these clothes actually date, beards had become fashionable again.

Julius Caesar, pictured here with no beard and short-cropped hair, and other rulers who followed him during the first century set the pattern for men of the Roman Empire.

When we read in the New Testament that Joseph and Jesus were carpenters, we must not conclude that they built houses with wooden boards or baked brick as modern carpenters in North America do. The house itself normally consisted of stone—fieldstone for the poorer classes, bonded with clay or a sort of plaster, and cut stones for the wealthy. A thief might then break through the walls of most people by dislodging some stones, instead of trying to crash a bolted door, and steal (note Matthew 6:19, 20 KJV and the original Greek, "break through"). Roofs were flat and made of poles and branches, as noted. Carpenters made doors, window frames, and the like, and furniture. Doors could be barred from within with a timber.

Furniture

Furniture of all classes was rather minimal by our standards. As we have seen, the very poor often slept on bedrolls (commonly of straw) on the floor and sat on the floor to eat. But in the New Testament

or around a hearth in the corner. They kept their clothes or other possessions in wooden storage chests.

The house itself was commonly built of fieldstone with a floor of tamped earth or stone. The flat roof consisted of wooden beams resting on the walls. Across these they laid smaller poles or branches and then layers of reeds or brush covered with grass and clay and pressed down with a roller.

In an effort to gain more space, householders commonly used the roof for a variety of purposes. Ascending by an outside stairway or even a ladder, they might sleep there in hot summer months and live there in booths during the week-long Feast of Tabernacles. It was a convenient place to dry dates, figs, or flax. One might also escape the crowded conditions of the house and get alone there to pray. Peter was praying on the housetop in Joppa when he received a vision from God (Acts 10:9–17). Apparently it was also a place to make public announcements (Matthew 10:27).

The emperor Hadrian (A.D. 117–138) made beards fashionable again. He wore a full beard to cover the natural blemishes on his face.

Paul's Comments on Men's Hair Length

The apostle Paul condemned long hair on men (1 Corinthians 11:14), so he must not have worn it himself. Moreover, he probably would not have been so adamant on the subject if other members of the apostolic company were wearing long hair. Above all, if Jesus had worn long hair, Paul would not have dared to make an issue of hair length.

Sunday school materials that picture Jesus with long hair and a long beard are very misleading. He, his disciples, and the apostle Paul probably looked more like the emperor Hadrian most of the time. Some American and British Christian young people of an earlier decade tried to look like something that never was. And people in the settled areas of New Testament Palestine did not dress like Bedouin, with their longer hair and longer beards. It is interesting that Jesus as the Good Shepherd is pictured in one of the catacombs of Rome with short hair, no beard, and a tunic extending only to mid-thigh.

period all classes tried to have some furniture. When they could afford it and when they had space for it, they had stools (three and four-legged), chairs with backs, low tables around which they sat to eat (often sitting on the floor), and beds with slats or ropes to support a mattress. They also might have lampstands on which to place the small clay lamps of the period, but frequently lamps were simply put in niches in the wall. Wooden storage chests served as wardrobes. They did not have closets in their bedrooms as we do.

The more well-to-do reclined on couches at dinner. As diners reclined on couches, with their heads at the table, they supported themselves on their left elbow and ate with their right hand. At least two passages indicate that Jesus traveled in this sophisticated company, as well as among the poor. When he ate in the home of Mary, Martha, and Lazarus, while the guests were reclining at dinner, Mary came in with an alabaster flask of pure nard (ointment from India), poured the contents on his head and his feet, and then wiped his feet with her hair. She could easily wipe his feet, which were pointed away from the table and up off the ground (Matthew 26:6–13).

This fresco from a catacomb in Rome portrays Jesus as the Good Shepherd, with short hair and no beard

At the Last Supper, "As they were reclining and eating" (Mark 14:18 BERKELEY VERSION) one of the disciples (John) "was reclining close beside Jesus" (John 13:23 REB) or "leaning on Jesus' bosom" (John 13:23 NKJV). As John reclined next to Jesus, he simply leaned back against Jesus' chest and whispered in his ear to inquire who would betray the Master. We do not properly grasp the situation if we allow ourselves to be influenced by current Western practices or by Leonardo da Vinci's famous painting of the Last Supper, where the Twelve are seated upright around a table.

I mentioned lampstands earlier. Lamps of the period were small clay vessels that would fit in the palm of the hand. Olive oil could be poured in through a hole in the top. A small spout held a wick of flax or wool that could be ignited to give light (see accompanying picture).

(For more on this topic, go to p. 377 or p. 483.)

Diet and Foodstuffs

"Or what man is there among you who, if his son asks for bread, will give him a stone? Or if he asks for a fish, will he give him a serpent?" (Matthew 7:9–10 NKJV)

What kind of food did the people of Palestine put on their tables in Jesus' day—or serve to their guests? There was little change from what they ate during the Maccabean period or the early years of Roman control. The last chapter gives the contents of the grocery bag. But a summary statement is in order. Basically the diet consisted of wheat (some 50 percent), legumes, olive oil, and fruit (especially dried figs, but also grapes—eaten fresh, dried as raisins, and pressed as wine). The "land flowing with milk and honey" enjoyed a good supply of butter and cheese made from the milk of sheep and goats. Honey from bees seems to have been plentiful. Dates provided a sweetener that was a substitute for bees' honey. Eggs and fowl, and fish around the Sea of Galilee, supplied additional protein. People could rarely afford red meat, eating it as a special treat during the shared sacri-

fice made during a festival (Passover, Weeks, Booths).

As far as agriculture is concerned, we need to underscore the effects of Roman warfare around Jerusalem at the time of the First Revolt (66–72). The Romans cut down trees for about eleven miles all around Jerusalem to get wood for war purposes and to deny sustenance to the populace. This resulted in soil erosion and contributed to the thinness of soil on the hillsides of Judea down to the present time. We cannot know the extent of change brought on by the effects of warfare then and in subsequent centuries. But all indications point to fairly prosperous agricultural conditions in the region before the devastation of the First Revolt.

The sowing, harvesting, threshing, and winnowing processes farmers engaged in had not basically changed for centuries. Most Jews outside the cities engaged in agriculture.

(For more on this topic, go to p.377 or p. 484.)

Dress

How did Jesus or his disciples dress—or anyone else in society for that matter? Clothing that Jews wore in Palestine in New Testament times was essentially the same as that worn by other peoples of the Mediterranean world. The tunic served as the basic garment (generally of wool, but linen in the Jordan Valley and other warmer places). Wearers made it by sewing two pieces of cloth together, leaving a hole for the head and neck. It had sleeves, normally extending at least to the elbow, and it was belted and bloused a bit above the belt. We are not sure about the length of the tunic, but it apparently extended to just below the knees. In Greece they wore it shorter, even as short as mid-thigh. In Palestine and elsewhere in the Mediterranean world men had a vertical stripe on their tunics, over each shoulder and running its full length. Commonly the width of the stripe indicated age or prestige (see accompanying illustration).

Over the tunic men and women wore a mantle (Greek, *chiton, himation*) which was a large square or rectangle of cloth

If Jesus was properly swaddled and did indeed look like a little mummy, he might easily have been placed in a manger like this one in the Good Samaritan Inn on the road to Jericho. There is no reason why he had to be put in a long trough on the ground as usually portrayed in Christmas manger scenes.

wrapped around the body and supported on the left arm. This might be draped in such a way as to expose one or both shoulders or pulled up around the neck or over the head to act as a cloak. Mantles of women had an L-shaped strip at the corner, and men a stripe with a notch cut out. In addition, women had hair coverings that reached approximately to the waist. Men's mantles were usually yellow or yellow-brown. Women's often were too, but sometimes were red or blue or purple. Professionals probably did the dyeing, but housewives did most of the spinning and weaving.

The cloak or mantle of a great many, especially of the middle and lower classes, served as a blanket at night. The Old Testament Law had specified, "If you ever take your neighbor's garment as a pledge, you shall return it to him before the sun goes down" (Exodus 22:26 NKJV). Such a cloak might be his only bed covering in Old or New Testament times.

Women wore their hair to the nape of the neck or shoulder length and covered it with a net or a cloth. Wealthy women piled their hair high on their heads and sometimes dressed it elaborately. Men wore their hair short, about the length shown on the familiar statues of Roman rulers, such as Julius Caesar or Augustus. They were either clean shaven or had short beards, trimmed close to the face. Soldiers or Palestinian farmers were not always neatly trimmed, but most men shaved or trimmed their beards close every few days. Probably the most Hellenized element of the population, those who had most to do with the government and the business community wore the shortest beards or none at all. While this was the situation in the first Christian century, the emperor Hadrian (117–138) made beards fashionable again during the second century. He wore a full beard to cover the natural blemishes on his face. The accompanying illustrations of dress, hair treatment and beards date after the time of Hadrian.[44] The use of the iron razors of the New Testament period provided something of a challenge and required fairly good barbers.

(For more on this topic, go to p. 378 or p. 485.)

Family Life

Betrothal

"The angel Gabriel was sent by God to a city of Galilee named Nazareth, to a virgin betrothed to a man whose name was Joseph, of the house of David. The virgin's name was Mary." (Luke 1:26–27 NKJV)

Our story of family affairs in Jesus' day logically begins with the betrothal of the prospective bride and groom. The usual age for a girl's betrothal was between twelve and twelve and a half,[45] but it could come earlier. Among all classes of people betrothal was commonly to a relative. In part this occurred because they kept daughters secluded from the world, making it difficult for young people to meet. In addition, they considered marriage within the tribe and the family normal and desirable. Also, they were concerned to keep inheritances and dowries within an extended family. The marriage of first or second cousins was common, and the marriage of a man with his niece was frequent. In such a case the man might be considerably older than his bride, but not necessarily so. There are plenty of examples in our society of uncles and nieces that are about the same age. We have no evidence of whether this degree of inbreeding in all classes of society affected the physical or mental health and well-being of the populace at large.

The age of boys at betrothal and/or marriage is hard to determine, but it would have been older than that for girls. It was generally expected that they would be capable of supporting a wife, so they needed to be established in some sort of trade. Of course the fact that the young couple was for some time part of an extended family (see below) meant that boys need not be entirely self-sufficient. Much of the time they must have married while still in their teens or about age twenty.

We do not know how old Mary and Joseph were when we first meet them in Scripture. Mary may not have been much more than thirteen or fourteen and Joseph probably not yet twenty. If Matthew 1 provides us with the genealogy of Joseph and Luke 3 the genealogy of Mary, as I conclude, they were both descended from David and related.

Families of the bride and groom arranged the betrothal, but not necessarily without the involvement or even urging of the young people. They held the betrothal ceremony in the presence of witnesses, concluded by a benediction, perhaps over a cup of wine tasted in turn by the betrothed. The marriage contract accompanying the betrothal specified what the bride's father was to pay, what part of that became the property of the husband, and what reverted to the wife in case of divorce or the death of her husband. The groom presented a gift to the bride. In much of Palestine, the ceremony was followed by a festive meal.

After the betrothal ceremony the woman was called a wife, could become a widow if her husband died, could be divorced, or put to death for adultery. The marriage itself might take place up to a year after betrothal.

Marriage

"On the third day there was a wedding in Cana of Galilee, and the mother of Jesus was there. Now both Jesus and His disciples were invited to the wedding. And. . . they ran out of wine." (John 2:1–3 NKJV)

On the eve of the wedding the bride was led from her family home to that of her husband. First there was music, then a distribution of wine and oil among the people and nuts among the children. Next came the bride, covered by the bridal veil and surrounded by her companions. Some carried torches or lamps or flowers. Everyone along the way applauded the procession or joined it. When the bride arrived at the home of the bridegroom, she was led to her husband, and the bride and groom were crowned with garlands. A formal legal instrument was signed, in which the groom promised to care for and keep his wife in the manner of the men of Israel. There were benedictions and the prescribed washing of hands, followed by the marriage feast, at which the guests contributed to the general enjoyment.

Finally "friends of the bridegroom" led the bridal pair to the bridal chamber and bed. This last act took place in Judea but not in Galilee. Because "friends of the bridegroom" often said and did some rather raunchy things (then as now), the simpler people of Galilee did not have these "friends of the bridegroom" as part of the wedding celebration. It is interesting that John 2, with its Galilean setting (Cana) does not mention "friends of the bridegroom," while John 3 with its Jerusalem setting does. The marriage feast could last for a day or several days. Evidently the wedding feast at Cana lasted longer than originally anticipated, and the supplies of wine ran out (see John 2:1–3 above).

After the wedding, the couple as a rule lived with the husband's family. The bride often found this very difficult for she had to adapt herself to a family circle strange and even hostile to her. The obligations of the husband involved especially the support of his wife, including provision of food, clothing, shelter, fulfillment of conjugal duty, and even to provide a funeral for her if she died. In that case, even the poorest man had to hire two flute players and one woman mourner.[46] The wife's duties were first household duties: to grind meal, bake, wash, cook, bear and care for the children, and spin and weave. And she was obliged to obey her husband as she would a master.

Incidentally, they washed clothes much like they do in some places in the Near East today. Women went to a riverside where a current could pass through the dirty clothes or where they could lay clothes on flat stones and pound out the dirt. There was a crude soap, however, known from Old Testament times, made from vegetable alkali (ashes of certain plants) and olive oil. Palestine had few flowing streams, however, so most women had to agitate clothing in a container of water.

Childbearing

"Now Elizabeth's full time came for her to be delivered, and she brought forth a son [John the Baptist]. When her neighbors and relatives heard how the Lord had shown great mercy to her, they rejoiced with her." (Luke 1:57–58 NKJV)

The chief function of women was to bear children, especially sons. In a society that had no social security benefits they sons carried on the family line and name, cared for and occupied the family inheritance, and provided for the parents in old age. Daughters were considered less valuable because their lives became involved in the affairs of their husbands' families, and they would not inherit and care for the family estate. A girl's responsibility to her own family and that of her husband

limited her ability to meet the needs of aged parents.

Midwives served in the birthing process. At birth the infant's umbilical cord was cut and tied, the baby washed, rubbed with salt and oil, and wrapped with swaddling clothes (Luke 2:7). These were strips of cloth four or five inches wide and several yards long that were wrapped around an infant to keep it warm and to help guarantee that its limbs would grow straight. When swaddled an infant looked a little like a mummy.

Circumcision

"He who is eight days old among you shall be circumcised, every male child in your generations. . . . My covenant shall be in your flesh for an everlasting covenant." (Genesis 17:12–13 NKJV)

Circumcision, practiced among various Near Eastern peoples (especially the Egyptians), assumed special significance when God commanded Abraham to circumcise all the males in his family and extended company (slave or free) as an outward sign of God's covenant with Israel. This rite continued through the Old Testament period and on into New Testament times. All the Jews of Palestine, whether hellenized or not, observed this practice. The element of the dedication of the son to service of God was present. And the shedding of the infant's blood represented some indication of his consecration or devotion to God. Of course it symbolized separation from heathen neighbors and dedication to the true God. Heads of families, priests, or physicians might perform the act.

A happy occasion for parents, relatives, and friends, the day probably called for some celebration. It meant that the son had become specially related to God, that there was continuation of the family line, and that the boy had some reasonable hope of growing up healthy. Childbirth and the days immediately following marked a period of high mortality. If a child and his mother got through the birthing process and the child began to eat on his own, the family could hope that all would be well.

Purification

"Now when the days of her purification according to the law of Moses were completed, they brought Him to Jerusalem to present Him to the Lord." (Luke 2:22 NKJV)

At the end of forty days it was time for Mary's defilement to be removed, since a woman was considered unclean for forty days after the birth of a son (eighty days after the birth of a daughter). Then she was expected to come to the temple, to make an offering, and to be purified in the prescribed way. "Their purification" (as it appears in the best texts), rather than "her purification," indicates that Joseph was a party to the act and had to see to it that the necessary sacrifices were provided.

The sacrifice appears in v. 24: "A pair of turtledoves," a requirement for poor people, instead of the usual expectation of the sacrifice of a lamb. Mary and Joseph didn't actually bring a pair of turtledoves. They went to the court of the women where there were thirteen trumpet-shaped chests for offerings. Into one of these they were to drop the price of the sacrifice needed for

their purification. No doubt a superintending priest was stationed there to tell them the price of the doves at that time. The temple leaders fixed the price of offerings once a month.

Mary and Joseph presented their son to God. The law required that every firstborn male (human and animal) be considered "holy" or separated unto God. Human males were then redeemed or bought back from the Lord. Verse 22 implies that Joseph paid the redemption price; though poor, he was not penniless.

Weaning

In subsequent weeks and months the mother breast-fed her child, or a wet nurse might be employed to do so. The weaning of the child did not occur, in some cases, for two to three years. When the child was weaned, the mother was free to bear another.

Development of Children

The mother shouldered the responsibility for training the children in their earlier years and, no doubt, for daughters until their marriage. They learned to grind grain, cook, care for the other children, to spin, to help in the fields or care for the sheep, and more.

At some point, probably about age five or six, fathers assumed responsibility for educating their sons. This included apprenticeship in the father's occupation and learning the Law and the history and traditions of Israel. Though fathers themselves shouldered this obligation, they were helped by the synagogue services held every Saturday.

Some formal schools existed by the time of Jesus. Primarily they seem to have been extensions of the synagogue, and they

This clay statuette from eighth century Cyprus depicts a woman giving birth.

An example of a stone that was rolled across the entrance of a tomb to seal it (see Mark 15:46)
(Ben Chapman)

stressed rote memorization of the Torah and related matters. Evidently some instruction in reading and writing accompanied the oral exercises. A very few schools of a more secular variety existed; for example, the gymnasium in Jerusalem taught physical education and Greek. We know little about formal education in the first century; our more solid information dates after 200. Though parents saddled children with adult tasks at an early age, children did play, as the New Testament indicates (Matthew 11:16–17).

A Jewish boy entered manhood at thirteen years of age, when he became a "son of the Law." This fact is interesting in connection with Jesus' being left behind at the temple at twelve (Luke 2:41–49). This was the last time he would attend Passover as a child.

Some rabbis believed girls should not be educated, but certainly not all families felt that way. Though girls were not permitted to attend synagogue schools, mothers could pass on religious education to their daughters, as could fathers, and girls could learn from their brothers. The fact that girls did get religious instruction is underscored by Mary's repeated allusions to the Old Testament in her Magnificat (Luke 1:46–55).

The Work Force in the Family— Jewish and Gentile Slaves

Normally members of the family provided the work force for family industries and activities, though there were some hired servants, as well as Jewish and Gentile slaves. A Jew might become a slave when convicted of theft and unable to make restitution for stolen goods. Second, one might voluntarily sell himself in an act of despair because he was hopelessly in debt. Third, a Jewish father might sell an underage daughter to another Jew. This usually meant that she would later marry her owner or his son.

The longest a Jew could serve as a slave was six years (Exodus 21:2), except in the case of marriage. He could acquire possessions and could shorten his term of service by payment. He was to be treated as a hired servant (Leviticus 25:40). But if his master gave him a wife and she bore sons and daughters, they belonged to his master. If at the end of his period of servitude the slave did not want to be separated from them, he

If a body was buried in a cave, it might be laid in a leveled-out spot, as here in the Garden Tomb. Or it might be laid on a slab, as pictured earlier in the Church of the Holy Sepulcher.

was to be taken to the doorpost and his ear pierced with an awl. He was then to remain in perpetual servitude (Exodus 21:4). Indications are that the number of Jewish slaves in Palestine in New Testament times was small.[47]

There were Gentile domestic slaves in considerable numbers in the important households in Jerusalem and in the houses of the priestly nobility. They surface in the biblical narrative too. Rhoda served as a slave in the house of John Mark's mother (Acts 12:13). Malchus was a slave of the high priest (John 18:10). He apparently was an Arab from Nabatea, as was Corinthus, Herod's bodyguard. Arabia is thought to have supplied the majority of Gentile slaves owned by Jews of Palestine in the time of Christ. A large number of Arabian prisoners of war taken by Jews in the Herodian wars became slaves.[48] They cost more than Jewish slaves because they were bought for a lifetime of service, not for only six years.

Jews forced Gentile slaves to accept baptism, which signified conversion to Judaism, and males had to submit to circumcision. In fact, this had been true since Abraham's day (see Genesis 17:12–13). Such slaves could not then be sold to Gentiles. As subjects of the covenant they had the right toSabbath rest and to take part in the feast of Passover, including the Passover meal. This was true from the days of the Exodus (Exo-

dus 12:44). But Gentile slaves were still slaves. Males had no protection against harsh treatment or violent abuse and females had to submit themselves to their masters' sexual advances. But indications are that their treatment in Israel was more humane than elsewhere in the ancient world.[49]

Divorce

Marriages did break up, and when they did the man had an almost exclusive right to initiate proceedings. Among the few bases that a woman had for divorcing her husband was his occupation as a dung-collector, a copper-smelter, or a tanner. In each case the constant foul smell was so repugnant as to make life almost unbearable. A woman could even divorce when she knew at marriage that this would be a problem but thought she could endure it.[50]

In Jesus' day the Jews divided into two schools of thought as to the basis for a man's divorcing his wife. Those who followed Rabbi Shammai in his interpretation of Deuteronomy 24:1 granted divorce only on the basis of something shameful, immodest, unclean or some indiscretion in his wife. It is not quite clear what this might have been. Certainly not known adultery, as some claim, because that was punishable by death. Nor suspected adultery, because there

Romans normally cremated their dead. Here is a columbarium at Masada. Jars containing ashes could be put in the niches. Perhaps soldiers were buried here. The wealthy built impressive tombs (e.g., along the Appian Way in Rome).

An ossuary of Nicanor of Alexandria, found on the summit of the Mount of Olives and dating to the first century A.D.

were procedures for dealing with that. Rabbi Hillel's interpretation of Deuteronomy 24:1 was quite broad, including childlessness, the spoiling of food, or even finding another woman more attractive.

When a man divorced his wife he had to give her a bill or writ of divorcement, which allowed her to take her dowry with her and to remarry. This financial hook gave many men pause and no doubt prevented or delayed divorce. We have no idea how common divorce was in New Testament times. God made it clear in various Old Testament passages that He was opposed to it (e.g., Malachi 2:16, "He hates divorce"). And Jesus declared, "So then, they are no longer two but one flesh. Therefore what God has joined together, let not man separate" (Matthew 19:6 NKJV).

Death and Mourning

"The days of our lives are seventy years; And if by reason of strength they are eighty years, Yet their boast is only labor and sorrow; For it is soon cut off, and we fly away." (Psalm 90:10 NKJV)

As Moses wrote this he was commenting only on the transitory nature of life, not on its length. Perhaps one might hope to live as much as seventy or eighty years, but was soon cut off. This is no hint as to how long people lived in his day, nor is it a clue to longevity in biblical times in general. As a matter of fact, Moses lived to the age of 120, but his whole generation died off in the wilderness at fairly early ages under God's judgment. Only now, with all our modern medical miracles, has life expectancy in the United States reached 76; in 1900 it was 47. Israel's and Jordan's today roughly equals that of the United States. But in underdeveloped countries such as Haiti, it hovers around 50 and in Malawi at just over 35.

A high infant mortality rate, death in childbirth, a high mortality rate in accidents, and much else kept life expectancy short in Jesus' day. If it was only about 35 in the United States at the time of the Civil War or during the Golden Age of Athens in the fifth century B.C. (as is sometimes stated)—perhaps it was not much different in the Roman world during New Testament times.

Death brought great lamentation, not only in ancient Israel but in New Testament times and in the Semitic world in general. In fact, in many places in the modern Near East death and other calamities bring great public demonstration. In New Testament times individuals or groups of mourners commonly tore their clothes and/or wore sackcloth and tore at their hair in public demonstration of grief. Mourners might raise their hands over their heads and wail "Alas, Alas" or "Alas my brother," or some other united cry.

Early in Hebrew history it seems that people decided they were not good enough at mourning on their own. At least by Amos' day (c. 750 B.C.) professional mourners, "those skilled in lamentation" (Amos 5:16) were hired to wail, play dirges, and the like. Flutes were especially adaptable to creating mournful sounds. The practice of using professional mourners was common in Jesus' day and is reflected in the death of Jairus' daughter (Matthew 9:23; Mark 5:38). In fact, the number of such professional mourners at a funeral indicated the wealth and social position of the family.

The use of professional mourners occurs very early among the Canaanites and Egyptians also. For example, in the Beirut Museum is the famous Ahiram sarcophagus (dating to c. 1000 B.C.), on which are pictured four Canaanite professional mourners.

Burial

After death burial normally took place the same day, since the hot climate brought quick decomposition and offensive odors. (The corpse was considered ritually unclean, a belief that ran through the Law and the prophets.) They put the body on a litter or bier and carried in a procession of members of the family, sympathizers, and professional mourners to the place of burial (see, e.g., Luke 7:12–14).

Burial usually occurred in the cemetery outside of town in fairly shallow unmarked or temporarily marked graves, with the dead buried in their own clothes, as excavations indicate. We know this because with human remains are found rings or pins which may have been in their clothing.

Though Israelites had never practiced embalming, the more affluent made greater preparations for burial. They wrapped the body in long strips of linen and treated it with a mixture of spices. When attendants finished, the body looked somewhat like a mummy. This is how Nicodemus and Joseph of Arimathea prepared the body of Jesus (John 19:39–40).

It is important to keep this treatment in mind because when the apostle John came to the tomb on Resurrection morning, he saw the linen cloths lying there—still in the form of a mummy. And the cloth that had been wrapped around his head was "folded" and lying by itself (John 20:6–7). Jesus simply passed through the wrappings, as his resurrection body could pass through doors and other objects (e.g., John 20:19), and He went on his way. If the disciples or anyone else had stolen his body, as some claim, in their haste they would not have taken the time to remove the grave wrappings.

Moreover, if Jesus had merely swooned, as others assert, he would have required medical attention. Certainly attendants would have taken him somewhere for recuperation and have unwrapped him in that place.

The body of Lazarus, from an upper-class family, was prepared in the same way.

When Jesus raised him from the dead, He commanded that these wrappings be removed so Lazarus could function normally (John 11:44).

In saying above that Jews did not embalm, we immediately raise a question about the embalming of Jacob and Joseph. Joseph as vizier or prime minister of Egypt was in the top class of Egyptian society and would have been treated like other Egyptian aristocracy. And Jacob was his father. Moreover, Jacob had charged his sons to bury him in the Cave of Machpelah at Hebron where Abraham and Sarah were buried. The only way that could be accomplished very well was to embalm the body (Genesis 49:29). The trip was long and the climate hot. Moreover, Joseph, in faith, had ordered that his remains be taken back to Palestine when the children of Israel left Egypt (Genesis 50:25–26). To keep them from being a mere bag of bones, he had to be embalmed.

While Hebrews did not embalm, neither did they cremate. Some remains of the individual continued on, looking forward to the day of resurrection, in which there was evidently a general belief in Jesus' day. For example, after Lazarus died, Jesus told Martha, "Your brother will rise again." And Martha responded, "I know that he will rise again in the resurrection at the last day" (John 11:23–24 NKJV).

The more well-to-do buried their dead in caves, either natural or man-made. There were numerous caves in the hillsides of Palestine that had been used for burial sites from time immemorial. Many of these were located on the estates of the wealthy. The affluent also made a practice of cutting cave tombs in the hillsides of their property. Joseph of Arimathea had cut the tomb in which Jesus was put (Matthew 27:60), no doubt planning it for himself or his family.

These rock-cut tombs might be closed by using a stone as a sort of plug or by a rolling stone. In the latter case a large flat, circular stone stood in a trough in front of a tomb. Then at burial they rolled the stone in the trough and allowed it to drop into a declivity at the tomb entrance, making it very difficult to move. The guards used this type of closure for Jesus' tomb (Mark

A threshing floor at Samaria. Here farmers are winnowing or separating the grain from the chaff.

An oil press at Capernaum

(Gustav Jeeninga)

15:46). And at the Resurrection the angel not only rolled the great circular stone from its groove in front of the tomb entrance but also had tipped it back flat, away from the entrance, and sat on it (Greek of Matthew 28:2). There was a practice of whitewashing outsides of tombs to prevent ritual uncleanness through accidental contact at night (Matthew 23:27). In New Testament times Greco-Roman architectural influences appear on the exteriors of tombs, with pediments, pillars, and the like used for decoration.

Whether cave tombs were natural or man-made, the interiors permitted a number of bodies to be laid out on stone beds or slabs. Sometimes they cut a kind of shelf or niche into the side of a tomb where a body could be inserted. Alternatively, they cut a small indentation in the side of the tomb, large enough and long enough to insert a body perpendicular to the main burial chamber.

Burial space was always at a premium in these tombs. So by the third century B.C. ossuaries were used. These were stone bone chests about three feet long and having a cover. After bodies decayed, the bones might be gathered from the stone beds, preparing them for reuse, and put in these boxes. The bones of more than one person might be deposited in an ossuary (e.g., a man and his wife, a woman and her child), and the ossuary might be decorated and/or incised with names.

(For more on this topic, go to p. 379 or p. 485.)

Work, Travel, and Commerce

Work

"A sower went out to sow" (Matthew 13:2). *"If a man has a hundred sheep, and one of them goes astray. . ."* (Matthew 18:12).

FISHING ON THE SEA OF GALILEE

Numerous scenes in the Gospels took place on or near the Sea of Galilee. Actually the sea was only a good-sized, pear-shaped lake 13 miles long and 7 miles wide (64 square miles). Therefore it was smaller than many American lakes, especially some of those in New York and Minnesota. Fishing was extremely profitable on the lake, and formed the basis of the economy of towns such as Capernaum, Bethsaida, and Magdala or Taricheae.

But the fishing business there was different from what most modern Bible students imagine. Individuals didn't just go out fishing and sell their catch to some processor. The local ruler (during Jesus' ministry, Herod Antipas) controlled the sea, the harbors, fishing rights, and roads and bridges over which the catch traveled. They sold those rights to brokers, the New Testament "tax collectors" or "publicans," who contracted with the fishermen. Matthew (Levi) evidently was one of those publicans or contractors, and Zebedee was a fisher with two working sons (James and John) and hired laborers. Fishing families sometimes formed collectives or cooperatives to bid for fishing contracts or leases. Peter, Andrew, James, and John with their fathers seem to have formed such a cooperative (Matthew 4:21; Luke 5:10).

The common mode of fishing appears to have been with nets made of flax. The fishermen made them, mended, washed, and dried them. The casting net was cast from a boat or along the shoreline (Matthew 4:18); the larger dragnet was also cast from a boat (Matthew 13:47).

As noted and pictured in chapter 1, an ancient fishing boat, dating to the New Testament period, was found in the mud just north of Magdala in 1986. It was 26.5 feet long, 7.5 feet wide, and 4.5 feet deep, and was made of cedar and oak. Clearly Peter, Andrew, James, and John used this type of boat. It could hold a crew of five (four oarsmen and a tillerman) and a substantial catch.[51]

"Is this not the carpenter's son?" (Matthew 13:55).

"He saw Simon and Andrew his brother casting a net into the sea, for they were fishermen" (Mark 1:16).

"It has taken forty-six years to build this temple" (John 2:20).

As Scripture indicates, workers engaged in agriculture, sheep-herding, carpentry, stone masonry, fishing, and much more to support themselves in New Testament times.

The majority of the Jewish population lived off the land. Some owned their own plots and some were tenant farmers of the larger estates (Mark 12:1ff.). Others were landless peasants, day laborers, employed to meet specific needs for a day or more at a time (Matthew 20:1–16). The agricultural workers faced a great tax burden, a dual tax burden: the tithing laws of Judaism and the

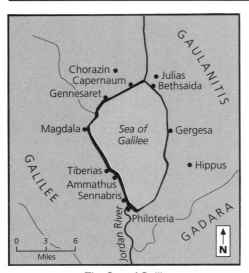

The Sea of Galilee

Fishermen cast their nets while moored on the Sea of Galilee.

secular tax system. The ordinary people found themselves at the mercy of the financial needs of rulers, native and foreign alike.

Increasingly this lower class slipped into tenancy or even slavery as the result of drought or other emergencies. And increasingly, as the social gulf widened, the country peasant developed a hatred toward the city aristocrat, whether in Sepphoris or Tiberias or Jerusalem. There is no middle class in the Gospels' background. The country peasant had less to lose than most city

dwellers from questioning Roman rule or even open rebellion at the time of the First Revolt.

Farm Work

In a good year rains begin to fall in October ("early" or "former") and continue intermittently until April. March and April

Fishermen with their catch in the Sea of Galilee

Jerusalem—Glory of the Herods

The Herodian family had reason to be proud of their massive construction projects in Jerusalem. Herod the Great had rebuilt the temple and had built a grandiose palace with the adjacent towers of Hippicus, Phasael, and Mariamne. Then at the northwest corner of the temple area he erected the huge fortress of Antonia. His entertainment structures included a Greek-style theater and a hippodrome. And he apparently erected the 27-foot-high porticoes around the Pool of Bethesda (see John 5). Then Agrippa I (41–44) enlarged the city and built the north wall (two miles long). And Agrippa II (king of an area of northeast Palestine, 53–100) finished the temple and paved the streets of Jerusalem with white stone (probably limestone).

The city had a total circumference of 3.4 miles within its three walls when Titus besieged it and then destroyed it in a.d. 70. The circumference of walls one and two had been 2.67 miles. The temple area occupied about one-tenth of the total.[52] Because the Kidron (east) and Hinnom (south) valleys were so precipitous, only a single wall was necessary there.

The Lower City extended south of the Temple Mount and included the old original City of David and the Tyropoeon Valley. Densely populated, its inhabitants were mostly poor. In the valley sprawled Herod's hippodrome, where he held horse and chariot races. At the northern end lay the commercial center of Jerusalem. Especially the wool market, the clothing market, and shops of the coppersmiths were located here. Even today this is the market quarter of the Old City.

North of the Lower City along the Kidron stood the Temple Mount. Just north of that was the sheep market and the Pool of Bethesda. And at the northwest corner of the Temple Mount rose the Antonia Fortress.

The Upper City was the southwest hill, modern Zion. It extended north from the Hinnom and west from the Tyropoeon. A Hellenistic style market surrounded by colonnades dominated this area—and here the aristocracy lived, including the high priests. Their expensive houses in Mediterranean style surrounded open courtyards and had numerous beautiful mosaic floors. On the eastern slope, overlooking the Tyropoeon, rose the Greek-style theater. And at the west, near the present Jaffa Gate, lay the great palace complex of Herod the Great with its three towers, and in the northeast corner, the Hasmonean palace.

North of the second wall, Herod Agrippa enclosed the New Quarter or Bezetha with his third wall. Here was the wood market, and here was room for expansion. The quarter was never fully built up.

JERUZALEM
BEGIN 1ᵉ EEUW

An artist's sketch of what Jerusalem might have looked like in New Testament times. The temple appears within the square wall in the foreground. Herod's palace appears within the walled rectangle in the left background. (Amsterdam Bible Museum)

rains are usually lighter and known as "latter" or "spring" rains. Sometimes the rainy season does not start until January but continues adequately until April. On the average, annual rainfall on the seacoast at Mount Carmel is 26 inches and at Gaza 16 inches. In the hills at Nazareth it is 26 inches, in Jerusalem 22 inches, and at Hebron 19 inches. In the Jordan Valley it is only 12 inches at Beth-Shean and 5 inches at Jericho.

The two most important grains were wheat and barley. Wheat grew best in the coastal plain, the Jezreel Valley, around Samaria, on the western side of the Sea of Galilee, and in the Jordan Valley. Barley, the common food of the poor, was normally grown on poorer soil. It was also fed to horses, asses, and cattle. Jesus fed the 5,000 with barley bread (John 6:9ff.) .

Unfortunately Bible versions and commentators often speak of the growing of corn in Palestine. "Corn" is an old English generic term for grain and should not be confused with the maize of the New World, which Europeans only began using after the Spanish discovery of America.

Wheat sowing took place in November and December and harvest between April and June. Barley sowing occurred about the same time as wheat, but it ripened about a month earlier, in March or April. In New Testament times farmers commonly sowed and plowed at the same time. Seed was plowed into the soil. Oxen or donkeys pulled the plow that covered seed scattered on the ground. Alternatively, the ground was plowed first and then sown.

At harvest time farmers cut the grain with a sickle. During the Roman period the sickle was a hand-held crescent-shaped tool made of iron that had a sharp inner cutting edge. Today we use sickles very similar to it for a number of yard chores. They then tied the grain into bundles and loaded them onto donkeys or carts and took them to a threshing floor—a hard surface of soil or stone.

There they might beat the grain to separate it from the straw, or they drove oxen round and round to do the same thing. Often they used threshing sleds for large quantities of grain. These were wooden platforms with stones attached underneath that were dragged over the grain by oxen or donkeys.

Last came the winnowing process. On a breezy day farmers used five-pronged winnowing forks to throw the grain and straw into the air. The wind blew away the chaff (Psalm 1:4) or straw, and the grain fell back on the ground. As the last part of this process the harvesters used wooden shovels to toss up the remaining grain. Finally they used a sieve to sift impurities from the grain.

Then it was ready to be stored. The reference to barns in several versions of the New Testament (e.g., Matthew 6:26; 13:30; Luke 12:18, 24) is misleading. Thus probably the average Bible reader thinks of a large red barn on a farm in rural America. But what is in view here is simply a place for storing grain. From archaeological excavations we know that granaries may have been clay jars, pits lined with plaster or brick, or brick silos (beehive shaped with vents at the top).

In addition to wheat and barley, Palestinian farmers in New Testament times grew millet, spelt, oats, and rye. Generally Palestine had enough grain for its own needs, and even some to export. For example, during the days of Herod Agrippa I (41–44), Tyre and Sidon depended on "the

A first-century anchor from the Sea of Galilee.

king's country" (Judea) for foodstuffs (Acts 12:20). Though most agriculture was dry farming, during New Testament times they also practiced irrigation, especially in the Jordan Valley around Jericho. They tapped the water of rivers, springs and wells and sent it by means of pipes, aqueducts and man-made channels to the thirsty fields.

Of course Jewish farmers grew more than grain. In fact, diversification kept some of them from going under financially in a bad year. Farmers provided a wide variety of vegetables and fruits in season on the local market day. The housewife could buy cabbage, turnips, lettuce, lentils, beans, chickpeas, cucumbers, asparagus, Egyptian beans, Egyptian pumpkins, and more. They also grew pomegranates, figs, grapes, and olives, as well as plenty of plums, cherries, dates, apples, pears, and peaches.

They sold dates at home and abroad, along with the products of date wine and date honey. Judean dates were famous all over the Mediterranean world. They usually marketed figs as dried fruit, both at home and abroad. Palestinian grape wine was also known and marketed abroad—especially the wines of Carmel, Ascalon, and Gaza. Viticulture also produced dried grapes (raisins) and vinegar.

Any reader of the New Testament knows how important olives and their oil were to the economy of Israel and the life of the people. They ate its fruit raw, but olive oil was more important for cooking, treating wounds, as a fuel (especially in lamps for illumination), and as a cosmetic. And of course they used it in worship, in the sacrificial offerings and the anointing of rulers and priests. It was also extensively exported. While the finest wines came from Judea, the best oils were produced in Galilee. But olives were important in Judea too, as such names as the Mount of Olives and Gethsemane (meaning "oil press") attest. Olive growing was more extensive in Palestine in New Testament times than at present.

The olive tree is slow growing and requires years of patient work before production of fruit. At maturity the tree rises to about twenty feet. The tree flowers about May and the fruit matures between September and December, varying with locality. When ripe, the olives are beaten or shaken from the trees. Then normally they are crushed in a mill, which is a circular stone basin about eight feet in diameter. Into this they put a millstone that was stood up vertically and revolved around a central pivot by either human or animal (donkey) energy. They collected the oil squeezed out in this way in jars. The rest of the pulp was put in baskets and taken to an oil press. The most common of these was a pole with the lower end inserted into a hole in the rock and the upper end weighted down with stones. The baskets of olive pulp were placed on a rock under the pole and the oil allowed to drip into a stone container.

Balsam trees were cultivated in Gilead and Jericho, as well as along the northern and western shores of the Dead Sea. Extract from them served as a spice and medicine and was an expensive luxury product.

Land that would not support grain production could provide small patches for growing vegetables. Terrain not feasible for

Major Roads of Palestine

Major roads crisscrossed Palestine. The Romans built a coastal road from Pelusium in Egypt through Gaza, Ascalon, Caesarea and Tyre. Then it continued north to the Syrian capital of Antioch and east to the Tigris. This route had been used from antiquity.

Other ancient roads were busy with commerce. One led from Babylon across the central Euphrates and the desert to the Jordan River, crossed it north of the Sea of Galilee, descended into the Jordan Valley to Beth Shean, where it turned into the Jezreel Valley and finally joined the coastal road at Mount Carmel. Another ran from southwest Arabia north parallel to the Red Sea, carrying luxury goods of Arabia and Africa. At Petra (about 50 miles south of the Dead Sea) it branched to Egypt, Gaza, and Damascus. A road also ran north-south along the watershed, through Hebron, Jerusalem, Samaria, and points north.

Model of a grain ship, used by the Romans in commercial trading. (Haifa Maritime Museum)

producing either usually could grow grapes or fruit trees. Rocky hillsides not useful for any type of agriculture provided pasturage for sheep, goats, and cattle.

Jews in New Testament Palestine raised sheep and goats in large numbers. Both were needed for temple sacrifices. Beyond that they were extremely useful in daily life. Goats provided milk (about six pints per goat per day), a type of yogurt and cheese, hair for coarse clothing (sackcloth) and tent covering (for Bedouins), skin for leather, and a skin that was often sewn up and used as a bottle—for either wine (e.g., Matthew 9:16–17) or water.

Goatskins are still used as water containers in various places in the Near East. I have seen Egyptians walking along the Nile with their goatskin water bottles at Luxor. Sheep also gave milk and especially provided wool for clothing. Though women wove wool for clothing all over Palestine, they especially preferred it in Judea, while the women of Galilee and the Jordan valley commonly used flax. Shearing time came after the summer grazing and often gave rise to a time of celebration.

Shepherding and the Great Shepherd

Any family in Palestine might keep a few sheep, but large flocks required full-time shepherds and probably some hired hands. Shepherds often cared for the sheep of a whole village. After spring rains there was plenty of pasturage, while after the harvest sheep could eat remains of wheat, oats and rye in the fields. Thereafter shepherds had to take their flocks in search of dried grass or remaining patches of green grass.

The shepherd had to care for his sheep at all times, providing them with food, water, and protection. Jesus called himself the "good shepherd" (John 10:11). In protecting the sheep he gave his life for the sheep, as shepherds might have to do in battling wild animals (John 10:11, 15). He as the true shepherd did not, as the "hired man," flee when the sheep were attacked by wild animals (John 10:12)

In the words of Psalm 23:4: "Your rod and Your staff, they comfort me" (NKJV). The rod or club (and the sling) protected the sheep from harm. And the shepherd used

TELLING TIME

"Now from the sixth hour until the ninth hour there was darkness over all the land." (Matthew 27:45 NKJV)

"Are there not twelve hours in the day?" (John 11:9 NKJV)

Telling time was a little different and a little more sophisticated in New Testament times than it had been in the Old Testament. The day as a period of time was divided into day and night. Day extended roughly from 6:00 a.m. to 6:00 p.m. and night from 6:00 p.m. to 6:00 a.m. Each was divided into twelve hours (John 11:9; Matthew 20:1–12). "Dawn" and "midday" were common designations and easy to determine.

Jesus was crucified at the third hour, 9:00 a.m. (Mark 15:25), and darkness descended on the land from the sixth to the ninth hour, from noon to 3:00 p.m. (Matthew 27:45; Mark 15:33). Also the morning sacrifice took place at the third hour, and the afternoon sacrifice at the ninth hour (cf. Acts 2:15; 3:1; 10:30).

In New Testament times, Jews followed the Roman custom of dividing the night into four watches: evening, midnight, cockcrowing, and morning (Mark 13:35; Luke 12:38; cf. Matthew 14:25; Mark 6:48). Jesus walked on the water in the fourth watch of the night (Matthew 14:25). Sundials and water clocks served as a means of telling time.

The Jewish month began with the renewal of the moon; therefore they had a lunar calendar of just over twenty-nine days in each month. There were twelve months in each solar year. Jews saw the discrepancy between the lunar and solar year and added extra days in the lunar year to bring the two into conformity.

Julius Caesar instituted a calendar reform late in his administration, in 46 B.C. Based on the Egyptian calendar, it was only a few hours in error. Of course this calendar was followed throughout the Roman Empire in Jesus' day. The Venerable Bede, an Anglo-Saxon monk, discovered in 730 that Caesar's calendar was eleven minutes and some seconds too long each year, making an error of a day every 128 years. But nothing was done about this until 1582, when Pope Gregory XIII produced a calendar that dropped ten days. Various countries of the world gradually adopted the Gregorian calendar. Britain and her colonies did so in 1752. The Soviet Union finally made the change in 1918 and Turkey in 1925. Now the whole world is on one calendar.

his staff or walking stick to control sheep and to count them as they entered the sheepfold at night.

When a sheep was lost the shepherd went out to search for it (Luke 15:3–6). And when he found a lost or sick sheep, he sometimes tenderly carried it on his shoulders (Luke 15:5). At night a shepherd kept watch over the sheep in the fields, as the shepherds did on that first Christmas Eve near Bethlehem (Luke 2:8). A sheepfold was preferable to the open fields, however. A fold could be a cave or a stone enclosure, and the shepherd would lie down across the opening ("the door of the sheep," John 10:7). In fact, the shepherd had such an intimate relationship with his sheep that they knew him, followed him, and responded to his voice. And they *would not follow strangers* (John 10:4, 5, 14).

Other Animals

Farmers also raised other animals for food and for sacrifices during the New Testament period. Cattle had been raised in significant numbers from antiquity, as had turtle doves and pigeons. Hens and roosters were introduced from abroad (from the East) about the time of Christ. Hunting of wild animals for food assumed less and less significance during the first century.

Fishing around the Sea of Galilee provided the basic economy for several towns, including Bethsaida in the north, Capernaum in the northwest, and Magdala (Taricheae) in the west. Those who profited from the industry included the fishermen who caught the fish, those who processed the fish, and those who marketed the fish (three separate groups). The fish had to be pickled, salted, or dried in order to be preserved and transported. Processed fish were distributed to merchants throughout Palestine and shipped through Cana and Acre to various Mediterranean ports. The shipping containers were large clay jars (amphorae).

Town Industry

The Jewish culture expected every father to teach his son a craft, whether in Jerusalem or elsewhere in Judaism. The list of crafts practiced in the cities is long indeed and included tailors, cobblers, masons, stonecutters, woodworkers or carpenters, bakers, tanners, perfumers, butchers, cooks, cheesemakers, barbers, launderers (men and women), smiths (in gold, silver, copper, iron), dyers, linen weavers, carpet weavers, embroiderers, potters, glassmakers, doctors, scribes, and more. Sometimes a whole town concentrated on one industry. Apparently Nazareth contained a lot of carpenters. In the cities, shops and stalls where bakers, dyers, linen and wool merchants, smiths, clothiers, and others sold their goods provided a livelihood for many. Workers engaged in the same crafts tended to live together in one section of the city. And there is some evidence that they also developed rudimentary guild organizations.

The masons, stonecutters, and woodworkers had plenty to do in Jerusalem during the days of the Herods. Herod the Great rebuilt the temple (20 B.C.–A.D. 64); his palace with the three adjacent towers of Hippicus, Phasael, and Mariamne; the fortress of Antonia north of the temple, a theater, and a hippodrome, among other things. Herod Agrippa I (41–44) built the northernmost wall of the city, two miles long. After completion of the temple, some 18,000 workers were unemployed and conditions in and around Jerusalem grew a little tense. In order to relieve the situation, Herod Agrippa II had Jerusalem paved with white stone (probably limestone). But this was only a temporary solution, so Agrippa, in cooperation with the high priests, began new construction at the site of the temple about 66. This, too, was only partly successful in reducing unemployment.

Increasingly unemployment, a generally worsening economy, heavy taxes, and unwise administrative acts of the prefects (procurators) tended to radicalize the lower classes of the Jerusalem area and to make them supportive of revolt against Rome when it came in 66 and following.

Commerce

"Today or tomorrow we will go to such and such a city, spend a year there, buy and sell, and make a profit." (James 4:13 NKJV)

"Beware of the scribes, who. . . love greetings in the marketplaces." (Mark 12:38 NKJV)

"A certain man went down from Jerusalem to Jericho, and fell among thieves." (Luke 10:30 NKJV)

By New Testament times Palestine had experienced extensive urbanization. In addition to Jerusalem and the cities of Decapolis, other towns with large populations included Caesarea, Sebaste (Samaria), Hebron, Bethlehem, Lydda, Jamnia, Tiberias, Sepphoris, and Taricheae. This is significant because they provided a market for agricultural goods from their hinterlands, developed town industries, and had aristocratic classes that wanted luxury goods from home and abroad. A large part of the foreign trade of the Jews passed through Greek hands.

From time immemorial, market day had been on Friday in the towns. On this day before the Sabbath, rural people came to sell their produce (food, clothing, etc.) at the town market. In the large towns, where there was a non-Jewish majority (such as Caesarea, Ascalon, or Gaza) fairs were held (connected with pagan religious festivals). At these one could buy all kinds of foreign goods from itinerant salesmen.

Of course pilgrims spent large sums of money in Jerusalem and along the way as they passed through the land on the way to participate in one of the great festivals. Commercial contacts continued at other times of the year between the Jews of Palestine and the Diaspora. Jewish exports were primarily agricultural. From the Sharon plain went wine and cattle; from Jericho and the plain around the Sea of Galilee, fruit; from Judea, wine and oil; from Galilee, oil and vegetables. Chief destinations of these exports were Egypt, Syria, and Rome. It would be tedious to list all the imports (some 250 different items), but asses from Libya, jewelry and papyrus from Egypt, and a variety of wines and beer from Egypt, Babylonia, and Greece were the chief products brought in.

Goods traveled by donkey caravan through the length and breadth of Palestine. This was necessary for protection against ever-present highwaymen who might be lurking around the next bend in the road, as was the case with the Samaritan who fell among thieves (see above, Luke 10:30–37).

Jewish mariners learned the ways of the sea and Jewish boats sailed from Jaffa, Ascalon, Acre, and especially Caesarea, for Spain, Italy, Gaul, Cilicia (especially Tarsus), Greece, Antioch, and elsewhere. And foreign vessels in considerable numbers put in at Israelite ports.

Travel

"His [Jesus] parents went to Jerusalem every year at the Feast of Passover." (Luke 2:41)

"Now there were dwelling in Jerusalem Jews, devout men, from every nation under heaven." (Acts 2:5 NKJV)

Jews traveled more than almost any other people of the Mediterranean world during the first century, with the exception of navy men, merchant marines, and a few others. Jews were supposed to go to Jerusalem for Passover, Pentecost, and the Feast of Weeks. And they were supposed to contribute their half shekel annually for the support of the temple.

Since it was not safe for a single family to travel alone, nor a few to transport the temple tax over a great distance, people joined "festival caravans" headed for Jerusalem. Evidently Jesus' parents joined such a group at the time Jesus was twelve (Luke 2:44), and Jesus and his disciples later attached themselves to a similar group around Jericho (Mark 10:46).

The account of the Pentecost just after the Resurrection (Acts 2:9–11) gives a formidable list of pilgrims from Roman provinces and even territories beyond the borders of empire: Parthians, Medes, Elamites, dwellers in Mesopotamia, Judea, Cappadocia, Pontus, Asia, Phrygia, Pamphylia, Egypt, Libya around Cyrene, Rome, Crete, Arabia. Put in modern terms, they came from Iran, Iraq, Turkey, Egypt, Libya, Italy, Crete, and Arabia. Then Barnabas and certainly others had come from Cyprus, and the treasurer of the Ethiopian queen Candace made a journey to Jerusalem for some religious purpose (Acts 8:27–39). Proselytes or God-fearers also went to the festivals: "Now there were certain Greeks among those who came up to worship at the feast" (John 12:20 NKJV).

There was constant movement between Syria and Palestine, and within Palestine people who were closer to Jerusalem could come more often. Palestinian residents might hope to go to Jerusalem for one of the three festivals annually. Those living abroad did well to make a pilgrimage to the Holy City once in a lifetime. As we have noted earlier, more than 100,000 might attend one of the festivals.

In addition to all this travel to Jerusalem, religious leaders occasionally came to the city from Jewish communities abroad to confer with members of the establishment. And think of the comings and goings of apostles and other missionary teams as they sought to spread the gospel. That story is told in subsequent chapters.

Of course there were also members of the official circle who moved between Palestine and Rome and members of the commercial community, referred to in the last section, who transported imports and exports.

(For more on this topic, go to p. 379 or p. 486.)

NOTES:

[1]Abba Eban, *My People* (New York: Random House, 1968), 100, 104. Eban's estimate roughly agrees with that of J. Juster, who concluded that there were six to seven million in the Mediterranean world alone. See J. Juster, *Les Juifs dans l'Empire Romain* (Paris: P. Geuthner, 1914), 1, 209–12.

[2]Ibid., 104.

[3]Arie S. Issar and Dan Yakir, "The Roman Period's Colder Climate," Biblical Archaeologist, June 1997, 101–106.

[4]See Kenneth Holum, and others, *King Herod's Dream: Caesarea on the Sea* (New York: W. W. Norton, 1988); Josephus, *Wars of the Jews*, I. 21.5–8.

[5]For discussion see NEAEHL, I, 270–291.

[6]*Oxford Encyclopedia of Archaeology in the Near East* (Oxford: Oxford University Press, l997), 3, 391–92.

[7]For dating of the various structures at Samaria, see NEAEHL, 4, 1307–1308.

[8]Peter Richardson, *Herod* (Columbia, S.C.: University of South Carolina Press, 1996), 197–202.

[9]Meir Ben-Dov, "Herod's Mighty Temple Mount," in *Archaeology and the Bible*, edited by Hershel Shanks (Washington, D.C.: Biblical Archaeology Society, 1990), 22–23.

[10]Ibid., 27.

[11]Adolf Deissmann, *Light from the Ancient East*, 4th ed. (New York: Harper & Brothers, 1922), 80.

[12]See NEAEHL, 2, 460.

[13]Shaye Cohen, *From the Maccabees to the Mishnah* (Philadelphia: Westminster Press, 1987), 111.

[14]Ibid., 112–113.

[15]Ibid., 113.

[16]See Bargil Pixner, "Jerusalem's Essene Gateway," *Biblical Archaeology Review* (May/June 1997), 22–31, 64–66.

[17]For extended discussion, see E. P. Sanders, *Judaism, Practice and Belief 63 BCE–66 CE* (Philadelphia: Trinity Press International, 1992), 190–278.

[18]This is the view of the early Roman historian Tacitus. See Tacitus, *Annales*, XV.44.

[19]Rodney Stark, *The Rise of Christianity* (Princeton: Princeton University Press, 1996), 46.

[20]See Michael Avi-Yonah and Vassilios Tzaferis, "Bethlehem," NEAEHL, 1, 204–209.

[21]For discussion, see Hershel Shanks, *Jerusalem, An Archaeological Biography* (New York: Random House, 1995), 189–196.

[22]For discussion of the problem of identifying the site of Caiaphas' palace, see John McRay, *Archaeology and the New Testament* (Grand Rapids: Baker, 1991), 199–202.

[23]Shanks, 189.

[24]Gabriel Barkay, "The Garden Tomb—Was Jesus Buried Here?" *Biblical Archaeology Review* (March/April 1986), 57.

[25]Dan Bahat, "Does the Holy Sepulcher Church Mark the Burial of Jesus?" *Biblical Archaeology Review* (May/June 1986), 38.

[26]Jack Finegan, *Light from the Ancient Past*, 2nd ed. (Princeton: Princeton University Press, 1959), 527–32; Bahat, 26–45.

[27]Finegan, 531–32.

[28]Bahat, 37.

[29]Ibid., 38.

[30]Jack Finegan, *The Archeology of the New Testament*, Rev. Ed. (Princeton: Princeton University Press, 1992), 167–70.

[31]Michael Grant, *The Army of the Caesars* (New York: M. Evans & Company, 1974), 301.

[32]A. H. M. Jones, *The Herods of Judaea* (Oxford: Oxford University Press, 1967), 223.

[33]Josephus, *Wars of the Jews* III.8.9.

[34]Ibid., III.7.9.

[35]Ibid., VI.9.3.

[36]See Yigael Yadin, *Masada* (New York: Random House, 1966).

[37]Herodotus, *Histories*, 3.125; 7.194.

[38]Peter Green, *Alexander of Macedon, 356–323 B.C.* (Berkeley: University of California Press, 1992), 262.

[39]Josephus, *Wars* I.4.6.

[40]Jo-Ann Shelton, *As the Romans Did* (New York: Oxford University Press, 1988), 182–3.

[41]See Tacitus, *Annals*, 15.44.

[42]NEAEHL, 1, 291–296.

[43]NEAEHL, 2, 729–735.

[44]E. P. Sanders, *Judaism Practice and Belief, 63 BCE–66 CE* (London: SCM Press,

1992), 122–24; Cynthia L. Thompson, "Hairstyles, Head-coverings, and St. Paul," *Biblical Archaeologist*, June 1988, 99–115; Albert A. Bell, Jr. *Exploring the New Testament World* (Nashville: Thomas Nelson, 1998), 246–47.

[45]Joachim Jeremias, *Jerusalem in the Time of Jesus* (London: SCM Press, 1967), 365.

[46]Ibid., 368–369.

[47]Ibid., 312.

[48]Ibid., 346.

[49]Ibid., 348.

[50]Ibid., 308.

[51] K. C. Hanson and Douglas E. Oakman, *Palestine in the Time of Jesus*. (Minneapolis: Fortress Press, 1988), 6–10.

[52]Sanders, 125.

BIBLIOGRAPHY:

Applebaum, Shimon. *Judaea in Hellenistic and Roman Times*. Leiden: E. J Brill, 1989.

Avi-Yonah, Michael, ed. *The World History of the Jewish People: The Herodian Period*. New Brunswick, N.J.: Rutgers University Press, 1975.

Batey, Richard A. *Jesus and the Forgotten City*. Grand Rapids: Baker, 1991.

Bell, Albert A. Jr. *Exploring the New Testament World*. Nashville: Thomas Nelson Publishers, 1998.

Bouquet, A. C. *Everyday Life in New Testament Times*. London: B. T. Batsford, 1953.

Bruce, F. F. *Jesus and Paul, Places They Knew*. Nashville: Thomas Nelson, 1983.

Cohen, Shaye. *From the Maccabees to the Mishnah*. Philadelphia: Westminster Press, 1987.

Connolly, Peter. *The Jews in the Time of Jesus*. Oxford: Oxford University Press, 1994.

Couasnon, Charles. *The Church of the Holy Sepulchre, Jerusalem*. London: Oxford University Press, 1974.

Dalman, Gustaf. *Sacred Sites and Ways*. London: SPCK, 1935.

Fairweather, W. *The Background of the Epistles*. Edinburgh: T. & T. Clark, 1935.

Finegan, Jack. *The Archeology of the New Testament*. Princeton: Princeton University Press, rev. ed., 1992.

Finegan, Jack. *Handbook of Biblical Chronology*. Peabody, Mass.: Hendrickson, 2nd ed., 1998.

Finegan, Jack. *Light From the Ancient Past*. Princeton: Princeton University Press, 2nd ed., 1959.

Freyne, Sean. *Galilee from Alexander the Great to Hadrian, 323 B.C.E. to 135 C.E.* Notre Dame, Ind.: Notre Dame Press, 1980.

Gonen, Rivka. *Biblical Holy Places*. London: A. & C. Black, 1987.

Goodman, Martin. *The Ruling Class of Judaea*. Cambridge: Cambridge University Press, 1987.

Grant, Michael. *The Army of the Caesars*. New York: M. Evans & Company, 1974.

Hanson, K. C., and Douglas E. Oakman. *Palestine in the Time of Jesus.* Minneapolis: Fortress Press, 1988.

Hoehner, Harold W. *Chronological Aspects of the Life of Christ.* Grand Rapids: Zondervan, 1977.

Hoehner, Harold. *Herod Antipas.* Grand Rapids: Zondervan, 1972.

Holum, Kenneth G., and Others. *King Herod's Dream: Caesarea on the Sea.* New York: W. W. Norton, 1988.

Jeremiah, Joachim. *Jerusalem in the Time of Jesus.* London: SCM Press, 1967.

Johnson, Sherman E. *Jesus and His Towns.* Wilmington, Del.: Michael Glazier, 1989.

Jones, A. H. M. *The Herods of Judaea.* Oxford: Oxford University Press, 1967.

Mazar, Benjamin. *The Mountain of the Lord.* Garden City, N.Y.: Doubleday, 1975.

McNamara, Martin. *Palestinian Judaism and the New Testament.* Wilmington, Del.: Michael Glazier, 1983.

McRay, John. *Archaeology and the New Testament.* Grand Rapids: Baker, 1991.

Murphy-O'Connor, Jerome. *The Holy Land.* New York: Oxford University Press, 1998.

Parrot, Andre. *Land of Christ.* Philadelphia: Fortress Press, 1968.

Pax, W. E. *In the Footsteps of Jesus.* Jerusalem: Steimatzky's Agency, 1970.

Perowne, Stewart. *The Life and Times of Herod the Great.* London: Arrow Books, 1960.

Richardson, Peter. *Herod.* Columbia, S.C.: University of South Carolina Press, 1996.

Rousseau, John J., and Rami Arav. *Jesus and His World.* Minneapolis: Fortress, 1995.

Sanders, E. P. *Jesus and Judaism.* Philadelphia: Fortress, 1985.

Sanders, E. P. *Judaism, Practice and Belief 63 BCE–66 CE.* Philadelphia: Trinity Press International, 1992.

Shanks, Hershel, ed. *Archaeology and the Bible.* Washington, D.C.: Biblical Archaeology Society, 1990.

Shanks, Hershel. *Jerusalem, an Archaeological Biography.* New York: Random House, 1995.

Sperber, Daniel. *The City in Roman Palestine.* New York: Oxford, 1998.

Strickert, Fred. *Bethsaida, Home of the Apostles.* Collegeville, Minn.: The Liturgical Press, 1998.

Thompson, J. A. *The Bible and Archaeology.* Grand Rapids: Eerdmans, 1962.

Wilkinson, John. *Jerusalem As Jesus Knew It.* Jerusalem: Steimatzky's Agency, 1978.

Yadin, Yigael. *Masada.* New York: Random House, 1966.

SYRIA AS A CRADLE FOR THE CHURCH

Chapter 16

(Acts)

"And the disciples were first called Christians in Antioch." (Acts 11:26 NKJV)
"Now separate to Me Barnabas and Saul for the work to which I have called them." (Acts 13:2 NKJV)

In a day when we have been taught to believe that the Syria of recent decades contains one of the most dangerous training centers for Islamic terrorists, it is hard to imagine that Syria was once the cradle for the church of Jesus Christ. Yet at Antioch, her capital, believers were first called by the name they are known to the present time: Christians. And there as the Christian community grew, God moved the church to send out missionaries. They commissioned Paul and Barnabas, and from Antioch Paul launched all three of his missionary journeys—to Cyprus, Asia Minor, and Europe.

"Christian" (*Christianos*) was a coined word, thrown at believers by their enemies in Antioch, or at least by people outside the Christian movement there. So we have to ask what they had in mind when they used the term. Obviously they saw believers as followers of Christ or as partisans of Christ.

But can we discover any deeper meaning from some parallel Greek term or concept? I think we can. A *Caesarianos* was an imperial slave or soldier belonging to Caesar. The comparable Greek form *Christianos* implies

a slave or soldier belonging to Christ. The apostle Paul made the point that we are not our own because we have been bought with a price (1 Corinthians 5:19–20), the shed blood of Christ. He also spoke of being a bondslave of Christ (Romans 1:1; Philippians 1:1; Titus 1:1). And he called on us to "fight the good fight of faith" (1 Timothy 6:12), and as we do so to "put on the whole armor of God" (Ephesians 6:11).

The Land

Political Boundaries

The boundaries of Syria have shifted over the centuries, depending on political arrangements in the area. Before the New Testament opened, the Roman general Pompey conquered the Seleucid kingdom in 64 B.C. and made it the province of Syria. Actually, the Seleucids had once managed to control most of the old Persian Empire and to extend their sway to the Indus River. But gradually they lost their grip on this

Syria

vegetation, and stony or sandy tracts in the east which are either desert or largely unproductive.

The Mediterranean coast of Syria is quite straight, with no deep estuary or gulf and no protecting island of any size. But Latakia (ancient Laodicea) had a small harbor in New Testament times. Seleucia (the port for Antioch) was hardly more than a roadstead. The coastal plain, never more than a few miles wide, was largely inconsequential in Syrian history. Much of it remains merely a broad strip of sand dunes covered by short grass and low bushes.

Overlooking the coastal plain is a line of mountains that begins with the Amanus Mountains in the north and extends all the way to the towering massif of Sinai in the south. The Amanus (rising to a height of some 5,000 feet) are a southward offshoot of the Taurus system. Separating Syria from Asia Minor, the Amanus is cut on its southern fringe by the Orontes gorge and is crossed by roads to Antioch and Aleppo.

The chief pass over the mountains is at Beilan, the Syrian Gates, at an altitude of 2,400 feet. South of the Orontes the range continues until eventually it is broken by the Kebeer River, which today forms the border between Syria and Lebanon. To the south of the Kebeer extend for 105 miles the Lebanon Mountains (with peaks over 10,000 feet).

Behind the western mountain range is a deep valley, a great fault extending from

vast territory. And when Pompey took over, they controlled only a fairly small kingdom at the eastern end of the Mediterranean.

The boundaries of the province of Syria extended from the Mediterranean south of Tyre inland to a point east of Damascus, then north in an arc along the edge of the desert to the border of Cilicia. So the northern boundary lay at the bend of the Mediterranean. Antioch on the Orontes River was the great capital, and Damascus the venerable old city lay almost due east of Sidon. Thus the province of Syria included much of what is now Syria, plus Lebanon (ancient Phoenicia), and a small chunk of southern Turkey.

Physical Features

Syria consists of a series of strongly marked zones, west to east—coastal plain, mountain ranges, valleys with luxuriant

The Syrian Gates

The Bika is one of the richest agricultural regions of the Near East.

Armenia to the Gulf of Aqaba, the eastern arm of the Red Sea, and containing the deepest ditch on the earth's surface. We may start along this third topographical region of Syria in the neighborhood of Antioch, where the Orontes River turns westward to cut through the mountains to the sea. Here the plain is broad and extremely rich, none of it more than 600 feet above sea level. From Antioch the valley of the Orontes ascends slowly between the western range and the high plateau of north Syria. At Hama (Hamath) the altitude is 1,015 feet, and at Homs (ancient Emesa) it rises to 1,660 feet.

After Homs the valley becomes El Bika ("the cleft") between the Lebanon and Anti-Liban Mountains. Varying in breadth from six to ten miles, El Bika rises around Baalbek (ancient Heliopolis) to over 3,770 feet. Here is the watershed; to the north flows the Orontes (246 miles long and largely unnavigable), to the south flows the Litani (90 miles long). Both rivers eventually turn westward and flow into the Mediterranean.

El Bika is some 75 miles long and has always been a rich agricultural and pastoral region. Its grazing land supports large flocks of sheep and goats. Its vines and other fruits flourish, and there is good wheat land. Here, as well as along the lower course of the Orontes, there are abundant ruins of ancient towns, testifying to the fact that this whole area was prosperous in ancient times—much more so than at present.

The eastern mountain range (Anti-Liban) constitutes the fourth topographical region of Syria. But it has no counterpart to the northernmost sections of the western mountain range. Rising from the Syrian plateau south of Homs, it opposed the Lebanons in almost equal length and height. This mountain complex is divided into two parts by the broad plateau and gorge of the Barada (biblical Abana, 2 Kings 5:12) River. To the north is the Jebel esh Sherqi ("Eastern Mountain"), the uppermost ledge of which is a high plateau some twenty miles broad and about 7,500 feet high. It is a stony desert resting on a foundation of chalky limestone. Its western flank falls steeply to El Bika and is virtually uninhabited; the eastern side is more accessible.

The southern part of the eastern range, Jebel esh Sheikh, or Mount Hermon, rises to a height of 9,232 feet and is one of the highest and most majestic peaks of Syria. Here snow settles deep in winter and hardly disappears from the summit in summer. In contrast with the northern part of the Anti-Libans, Mount Hermon has more villages on its western slopes and fewer on its eastern.

Mount Hermon stands on the border between Israel and Syria.

The Barada (biblical Abana, 2 Kings 5:12) as it flows through downtown Damascus.

On the south and east, the slopes of Hermon fall swiftly to the vast plateau of Hauran, the treeless surface of which is volcanic and its soil a rich, red loam. This lava field covers an area almost sixty miles long by as many wide. On the east the Hauran is bounded by the mountain of Hauran, or the "Mountain of the Druzes." This bulwark is about thirty-five miles north and south and twenty east and west, with a summit that rises to 6,000 feet. In the north the Hauran is two to three thousand feet above sea level, but on the south it shelves off to its limit in the deep valley of the Yarmuk. Known in New Testament times as "Auranitis" and in Old Testament times as "Bashan," the Hauran has some of the best wheat land in the Near East. During the Roman period it served as one of the granaries of the empire.

The Anti-Libans collect their waters and send them southward into the Jordan system and eastward far into the desert (Damascus is about thirty miles east of Hermon) in the channel of the Barada River. On a lofty and drainable plateau some 2,200 feet in altitude, the Barada has created 150 square miles of fertility, the Ghutah, from which rises the city of Damascus, civilization's outpost in the desert. Though defenseless and on no natural line of commerce, Damascus has learned to exploit the fertility of her hinterland and to bend to herself much of the traffic between Egypt and Mesopotamia, as well as points west. In this way she has retained her prosperity over the centuries

and today has a population in excess of 1.6 million.

The Barada River (c. 45 miles long) divides into five branches in the Damascus oasis and finally loses itself in the desert. Another river which rises in the Anti-Libans is the biblical Pharpar, identified with the Awaj, which flows some distance south of Damascus and disappears in swamps east of the city. Naaman was immensely proud of both of these life-giving rivers of his homeland (2 Kings 5:12).

East of the Hauran Plateau and its boundary of Jebel ed Druz lies the Syrian Desert, which is a continuation of the great Arabian Desert. This Syro-Iraqi Desert forms a huge triangle whose base rests on the Gulf of Aqaba on the west and the Gulf of Kuwait on the east and whose apex reaches toward Aleppo on the north. At its widest this desert stretches about 800 miles.

The climate of Syria has changed since New Testament times. Syrians of Jesus' day cultivated large areas now mere desert. East

Damascus as a Commercial Hub

Damascus sat astride several caravan routes over which people moved to all areas of the ancient Near East. From Mari on the middle Euphrates came a route over which traveled products from the entire Mesopotamian valley. To the west, goods from all over the Mediterranean world landed at ports in Beirut, Tyre, Sidon, and Accho. Especially from Accho they came across northern Galilee to Damascus.

From this north Galilee road merchants also could journey south through the Plain of Esdraelon and along the coastal road to Egypt. Or one could take another branch of that road through the hills of Samaria to Jerusalem or the Jordan Valley.

And it was possible to go south from Damascus through the highlands east of the Jordan on the Kings Highway to the Gulf of Aqaba and Arabia.

The street called Straight, where Saul (Paul) met
Ananias (Acts 9:10–18)

(Matson Photo Collection)

of Homs, where there is now not a green
leaf nor a drop of water, archaeologists
have found the heavy basalt slabs of former
oil presses in large quantities. And as
pointed out in the last chapter, new
research demonstrates that the whole
Mediterranean basin was cooler and wetter
at the height of the Roman Empire.

The Syrian summer is hot and long (May
to September), its winter being short and
mild. But there is considerable regional
variation. Rainfall on the western mountain
slopes and in the north of Syria is adequate.
The eastern slopes have less precipitation.
While Latakia on the coast enjoys over
thirty inches of rainfall per year, the average
at Damascus is about nine inches and at
Aleppo approximately eighteen inches.
(For more on this topic, go to p. 389 or p. 493.)

Government

When the Roman general Pompey converted
the kingdom of Syria into the
province of Syria in 64 B.C., he was working
with a land that had fallen into virtual
chaos under late Seleucid kings. Arab
chiefs, Nabateans, Jews, pirate chiefs, and
others had virtually established their independence in various nooks and crannies of
the land.

At first Pompey allowed several client
principalities or political entities to subsist
on the outskirts of the province or within its
general framework. Arab dynasts paid
annual tribute. The Nabatean king kept
Damascus for a lump sum of money. Judea
was a subject state within the province. He
granted Greek cities internal freedom; he
formed ten of them into a league known as
Decapolis. The provincial government
ruled from the capital at Antioch.

Because this was a frontier province that
faced on the powerful Parthian kingdom,
Rome placed Syria under the rule of a proconsul with the power to raise troops and
wage war. Gabinius, Pompey's legate, was
in charge 57–55 B.C. He rebuilt a number of
cities destroyed by the Maccabees, such as
Samaria and Gaza. Gabinius was succeeded
by Crassus, associate of Pompey and Julius
Caesar in the First Triumvirate. He died in
battle with the Parthians in 53 B.C.

The subsequent civil war in Rome,
involving forces of Pompey and Julius Caesar and then Augustus Caesar (Octavian)
and Mark Antony, threw Syria once more
into confusion, with Parthians temporarily
taking over the province (40–38). The victory of Octavian at Actium in 31 B.C.
brought welcome relief to the Syrians, who
longed for a restoration of stable government.

St. Paul's Window, the traditional spot where Paul
was lowered from the wall of Damascus to escape
his pursuers (Acts 9:25).

St. Peter's Church, a Crusader facade of a cave where early Christians were supposed to have met

Meanwhile Herod the Great had won control of Jerusalem (37 B.C.) and kingship of the Jews. He had some success where Antiochus Epiphanes had failed in making Judea an imitation of a Hellenistic kingdom. His great new city of Caesarea became the capital of Roman Judea. Other construction was noted in the last chapter. Actually Judea was associated with Syria at times and at others was under one or more native rulers. After Titus' destruction of Jerusalem in A.D. 70, Judea became a separate imperial province under a legate, with a legion stationed at Caesarea.

A certain cultural cohesiveness developed in Syria with the onward march of Hellenism. Greek was the lingua franca, and Greeks were strong in the artistic and philosophical fields. Though Rome permitted the native communities a great deal of local autonomy, there was ethnic and cultural similarity and unity. All Syrians became Semitized, speaking Aramaic at home and on the informal level, and Greek in business and other dealings. They used Latin for official communications. Hence the inscription over Jesus' head on the cross was written in Greek, Latin, and Hebrew (the Aramaic vernacular) according to John 19:20. The Phoenicians were even more hellenized than their neighbors in the province, and in the first century lost their old Canaanite speech.

Rome worked at urbanization, as the Seleucids had, and eventually organized almost the entire province into urban units. Romans assumed responsibility for Syrian defense with Italian troops, financed by tribute from the local population.

Under the Roman emperors Syria was a bastion of imperial power. They stationed four legions there to protect the frontier. A province directly under the supervision of the emperor, it had imperial legates as governors, whose term of office lasted three to five years. The legate was responsible for security of Roman holdings throughout Western Asia. They established security from brigands and piracy. General prosperity and security led to an increase in population, which by the beginning of the second century reached 7,000,000, according to one estimate.[1]

(For more on this topic, go to p. 390 or p. 494.)

(For more on this topic, go to p. 390 or p. 494.)

Religion

Antioch—The Cradle of Christianity

When I first visited Antioch in 1960 it betrayed little of the greatness it had known when it was the cradle of Christianity in the first Christian century. The city was hard to get to. We negotiated with a driver and his car in Adana to take us through the pass known as the Syrian Gates into Turkish Antakya (ancient Syrian Antioch). The city of some 50,000 (now about 125,000) was economically depressed. The hotel with its twenty-eight rooms was just "adequate," but the manager was friendly and helpful.

We found and walked the Kurtulus (Caddesi, the main street when Paul and Barnabas were there), walked across the Roman bridge over the Orontes River. The excellent museum had a wonderful display of mosaics taken from houses of the Roman period during the Princeton excavations there (1932–39). We could see firsthand some of the elegance and affluence of early Antioch. The memory of the Christian church had been preserved as well in what they called St. Peter's Church, a cave in which Christians supposedly met, and in front of which the Crusaders erected a facade.

Antioch, the main street in Paul's day

As the third most important city of the Roman Empire in the first century, and with a population commonly put at about 500,000, Antioch stood only behind Rome and Alexandria in Egypt. A crossroads of the world, it had business connections in all parts of the Roman Empire. And the cosmopolitan nature of its population contributed to the success of the gospel there.

A large Jewish community helped greatly with the development of Christianity in Antioch. Metzger estimates that they comprised one-seventh of the population. These people lived in three separate settlements: one west of the city near Daphne, a second east of the city in the plain, and a third in the city proper.[2] As everywhere else, the Jewish faith attracted Gentiles who found in Judaism an ethical doctrine superior to what they knew in their pagan teaching.

The Entrance of Christianity

When persecution broke out in Jerusalem, many of Jesus' followers fled, and some came to Antioch, preaching to Jews (Acts 11:19). But some began to preach to Greek-speaking pagans as well (Acts 11:20). Parenthetically, it is interesting to see that a Gentile from Antioch (Nicolas) became one of the seven first deacons in Jerusalem (Acts 6:5). Evidently most of the early converts in Antioch came from the Gentile community. In that large cosmopolitan city traditional barriers of race and religion meant less than in Palestine and elsewhere, and the church grew rapidly.

When reports of the success of the gospel in Antioch reached Jerusalem (300 miles to the south), the elders sent Barnabas, from Cyprus, to check out what was going on (Acts 11:22). With a wider exposure to the Gentile world himself, Barnabas felt at home there. And as he sought to find leadership for the new movement, he thought of Paul (Saul) of Tarsus, who might help in the venture (Acts 11:25). He brought Saul to the city, and they worked together for a whole year to advance the cause of the gospel (Acts 11:26).

The movement evidently grew rapidly, and people of some means were converted to the faith. The church contributed funds for the relief of poor saints in the Jerusalem church (Acts 11:29) and later for the missionary journeys of Paul, Barnabas, and others (Acts 13:3). Paul launched all three missionary journeys from Antioch. As previously noted, believers were first called Christians in Antioch. Downey believes that Roman authorities in the city coined the term to have an official designation for the new sect, already becoming distinct from Judaism.[3]

As Christianity grew in Antioch and among Gentiles in Cyprus and Asia Minor, the question arose as to whether Gentiles had to keep the Law. The Council of Jerusalem (Acts 15) determined that it was not necessary for them to do so. Especially important was that they would not have to submit to circumcision, which to a convert probably would mean that he became a member of the Jewish race and gave up his Greco-Roman heritage. Having said all this, we need to discover what Antioch was like when the gospel invaded it.

Richly Endowed by the Romans

The fully-developed city of Antioch during the New Testament period lay along the east bank of the Orontes River as a walled enclave. Nestled between the river and 1,500-foot high Mount Silpius, the city enjoyed major structures bestowed on it by a succession of Roman emperors and others. Julius Caesar had shown the way by building a theater, amphitheater, aqueduct, and public bath. Claudius (41–54) reorganized the great games begun by Augustus

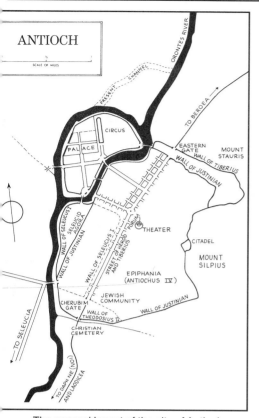

ANTIOCH

SCALE OF MILES

ORONTES RIVER

PRESENT CHANNEL

TO BEROEA

CIRCUS

PALACE

EASTERN GATE

MOUNT STAURIS

WALL OF TIBERIUS

WALL OF JUSTINIAN

WALL OF JUSTINIAN

WALL OF SELEUCUS I

SELEUCID AGORA

THEATER

STREET OF HEROD AND TIBERIUS

WALL OF SELEUCUS I

FORUM

CITADEL

MOUNT SILPIUS

EPIPHANIA
(ANTIOCHUS IV)

CHERUBIM GATE

JEWISH COMMUNITY

WALL OF JUSTINIAN

WALL OF THEODOSIUS II

CHRISTIAN CEMETERY

TO SELEUCIA

TO DAPHNE (NO!) AND LAODICEA

The general layout of the city of Antioch

is enough to say that the walls enclosing the city measured close to ten miles. A great amphitheater stood inside the southwest gate of the city. About midway along the main street sprawled the forum and just above that on the slope of Mount Silpius stood the theater. On the crown of Mount Silpius towered the citadel for the city's defense. The great circus or hippodrome stood in the northwest of the city. Great temples to various gods functioned here and there.

From the southwest gate the road ascended to Daphne, five miles away to the southwest. The walk was a beautiful one. A constant succession of orchards and gardens filled with roses and other flowers scented the air. Here gardeners grew the roses to make the perfume for which Antioch was famous. Beautiful country houses and villas stood among these gardens. One could pause at inns along the way where, in the shade of vine-covered arbors, a visitor could sip wine or fruit juices cooled in underground cellars.

The pleasure garden of Daphne, ten miles in circumference, was famous for its laurel

and named "Olympic Games" to include theatrical, dramatic, and musical events, as well as athletic contests and races in the hippodrome.

Herod the Great paved the main street with marble. Over two miles long, it measured thirty-one feet in width. Tiberius (14–37) built roofed colonnades thirty-two feet wide along each side of the street. And at each intersection he erected tetrapylons–vaulted stone roofs supported on four columns. Over 3,200 columns (many of pink and grey granite) composed the colonnade, and bronze decorations were attached to many of them. Through the columns one could enter public buildings, shops, and villas. Thus one could walk the entire length of the city (northeast to southwest) under cover—possibly the world's first enclosed shopping mall.

It is not necessary to list all the benefactors of Antioch and to tell what they built. It

The City of Antioch

Seleucus I founded the city of Antioch in May of 300 B.C. in the valley of the Orontes River, about sixteen miles from the Mediterranean. He brought in retired Macedonian soldiers, Athenian colonists, and Jews. And he laid out the city on a grid plan with streets intersecting at right angles. City planners also sought to make the best use of the sun in both summer and winter and to take advantage of the sea breezes that blew up the Orontes Valley. To the original quarter Seleucus later added a second quarter with its own separate wall. Seleucus II (247–226 B.C.) and Antiochus III (223–187 B.C.) built a third quarter on an island in the Orontes, with its palace and circus or hippodrome–with an arena over 1600 feet long. Antiochus IV Epiphanes (175–163 B.C.) added a fourth and final quarter.

The Tragedies of Antioch

Antioch had its share of woes. Located in an earthquake-prone area, it suffered a severe quake in A.D. 37. The emperor Caligula provided help in rebuilding. Another earthquake occurred during Claudius' reign (41–54) and an even more severe one came in 115 when the emperor Trajan happened to be in the city. He was injured in the disaster. But the worst earthquake struck in 526, leveling almost the entire city and reportedly killing 250,000 people. Hardly had the survivors been able to catch their breath when an earthquake in 528 killed another 5,000.

Though the emperor Justinian helped to rebuild the city, within a few years afterward Antioch suffered a military disaster. In 540 the Sassanian king Chosroes I captured the city, burned it, and carried off a large percentage of the inhabitants to Mesopotamia. Though Justinian soon recaptured it and rebuilt it, the new Antioch was much smaller and never regained its ancient glory.

The Tyche of Antioch. Early in the history of Antioch, Seleucus Nicator erected the famous statue of Tyche, goddess of good fortune, cast by Eutychides of Sicyon. A symbol of prosperity and good luck, the bronze goddess was draped in a long robe and was seated on a rock representing Mount Silpius. On her head she wore a turreted crown representing the walls of the city. Beneath her feet a figure of a nude youth lay in a swimming position, symbolizing the Orontes. In her right hand she held a sheaf of wheat, signifying the material prosperity of the city.

trees, old cypresses, flowing and gushing waters, its shining temple of Apollo, and its magnificent festival of the tenth of August. At the center of Daphne stood an agora with baths and temples. Spacious houses lined the streets, which were laid out on a regular grid plan. At the south edge of the suburb gushed ever-flowing springs. The temple of Apollo (built by Seleucus Nicator) stood at the foot of the springs. Nearby lay the Olympic stadium. Daphne was dedicated to Apollo as Antioch was to Zeus.

In a westerly direction from Antioch a road led to the port of Seleucia, which could also be reached by boat in New Testament times, since the Orontes was navigable up into the center of Antioch. Through the port flowed local products and goods from afar. Seleucia especially offered an outlet on the Mediterranean to the silk route that came from the heart of Asia through Iran and the Fertile Crescent or by way of the Persian Gulf and the Euphrates.

The Old Paganism

The polytheistic era preceding and contemporary with Christianity was one of great and sustained piety. Paganism and pagan institutions did not lie down and play dead just because Christianity was rising. Great temples to the ancient gods of Syria and to Greco-Roman deities thrived all over the land.

For example, Tiberius Caesar (14–37) restored, rebuilt, or built the great temples to Jupiter Capitolinus, Dionysus, and Pan in the capital of Antioch during the days of Jesus' earthly ministry. The temple of Apollo was going strong in the sacred groves of Daphne near Antioch during the time that Paul launched the apostolic missionary ventures from the capital. The great days of the Baal of Apamea were to come only during the latter part of the second century. And the great temples at Baalbek just began to take shape during the first Christian century.

Baalbek—Heliopolis

Modern Christians are probably much more impressed with the greatness of Baal-

The Orontes River still flows through the center of Antioch. The river was a greater stream in New Testament times, when less of its waters were used for irrigation. And in flood stage it can still become a considerable torrent.

A huge substructure (24–42 feet above the ground) was built for the temples to fulfill a psychological function–to render them more imposing by lifting them high above the neighboring landscape. A worshiper would enter the temple complex through a tower-flanked propylaea 165 feet wide and

bek than first-century Christians would have been, for the magnificent complex of temples there was not completed until sometime during the third century.

Baalbek is located on a superb site fifty-one miles east of Beirut at an altitude of 3,850 feet above sea level. On the caravan route linking Damascus, Emesa, and Tyre, it had a fertile hinterland as well as commercial advantages. The beautiful site is nestled between the Lebanon and Anti-Liban ranges.

Baalbek means "town of Baal" and seems to have been of Phoenician origin. Because it was considered to be the birthplace of the worship of the sun or of Baal, the site was held in special veneration. The Seleucids called the city "Heliopolis" ("the City of the Sun"), and the Romans identified the Baal of this city with Jupiter and called him "Jupiter Heliopolitanus." When the Romans took over, Augustus planted a Roman colony there.

Probably as early as the reign of Augustus, the massive temple complex at Heliopolis was begun. Inscriptions show that the work on the temple of Jupiter was well underway during Nero's reign. And construction on the temple of Bacchus apparently began about the middle of the first century A.D. For three centuries construction went on at the site to produce a magnificent complex exhibiting a sense of power, size, and glorious magnificence.

The Power of Pagan Religions

Pagan religion exerts great spiritual power. This is true first because of satanic energy or strength. Those who minister in animistic communities often speak of the spiritual force that seems to pervade the air when a witch doctor works a crowd. But even in the most sophisticated western society we need to remember that the "prince of the power of the air, the spirit who now works in the sons of disobedience" (Ephesians 2:2 NKJV) everywhere seeks to hold unbelievers in his grip. The Greek is chilling: Satan is energizing (English, "works in") unbelievers and seeks to keep them from faith in Christ.

Second, there is the eremonial-social aspect. Religion persisted as a community affair. A whole community periodically swept along its members in great public demonstrations. For example, during the annual Panathenaic procession in Athens the whole citizenry wound its way through the agora and up the Acropolis to bring the new robe to Athena. Great public demonstrations at Ephesus during the month-long Artemision (March–April) included athletic, dramatic, and musical contests. The world that now participates in and celebrates the Olympics so enthusiastically and so intensely needs to remember that they used to be held in honor of Zeus. Also, dramas began with sacrifice to the god Dionysus. In short, almost all public life was wrapped up in the worship of pagan deities. So anyone who became a Christian bucked the social current and came to be classified as anti-social—actually opposed to or harmful to the existing social order.

The temple of Bacchus at Baalbek is one of the best preserved Greco-Roman temples.

38 feet deep. He would then pass through a hexagonal court into a great altar court about 350 feet square. On either side of the altar he found large stone basins (actually tanks) 68 feet long by 23 feet broad and 2 feet 7 inches high for ritual washing.

From this court a magnificent stairway led to the temple of Jupiter. Surrounded by a colonnade of fifty-four columns, the cella, or holy of holies, was 290 by 160 feet, over five times as large as that of the Parthenon in Athens. Six of the great 100-ton Corinthian columns of the peristyle (colonnade) remain standing. Sixty-five feet high, they are the tallest in the Greco-Roman world. Atop the columns is a sixteen-foot entablature ornately decorated with lions' and bulls' heads showing oriental influence.

Adjoining the temple of Jupiter on the south is the temple of Bacchus with a cella 87 by 75 feet, originally surrounded by a peristyle of 46 columns 57 feet high. It has been beautifully preserved, leaving us no better example of a Roman temple interior. East of the acropolis was a round temple, rare in Syria, that was probably a temple of Venus, constructed about A.D. 250.

The walls of the temple complex were two miles in circumference. Huge stones appear in this wall, the three largest being about 64 feet long, 14 feet high, and 11 feet thick and each weighing some 1,000 tons. The largest stone of all never made it out of the quarry and may be seen about a mile south of the modern town. It measures 70

by 14 by 13 feet. The busy town that once surrounded the temples at Baalbek has vanished. No attempt to excavate its remains has yet been made. One estimate puts the population of ancient Baalbek at more than 200,000.

The Ruler Cult

Near the beginning of the Seleucid or Syrian kingdom, Antiochus I (280–261 B.C.) deified his father, Seleucus the Conqueror, after

Six columns of the temple to Jupiter still stand at Baalbek to a height of sixty-five feet, the tallest in the Greco-Roman world.

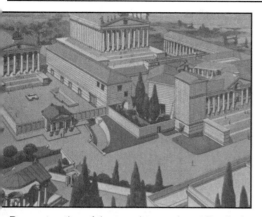

Reconstruction of the temple complex at Baalbek. The Temple of Jupiter towers above the rest and is entered through a magnificent gateway and a courtyard. To the left, foreground, is the round Temple of Venus. Behind that, below the Temple of Jupiter, stands the Temple of Bacchus.

his death. His successors developed an official dynastic cult, which served as a kind of cement to provide a central focus for the state. The worship paid the king was really an expression of political loyalty rather than real religious experience. With this Hellenistic ruler cult as a background, Augustus could easily introduce the cult of the personification of Rome (the worship of the goddess Roma) and to associate with it the worship of the Caesars. This was an important element on the religious scene in New Testament times.

The Mystery Religions

While most people still worshiped the old gods, a large number turned to the mystery religions during the Hellenistic Age. In the mysteries they sought a more personal faith that would bring them into immediate contact with deity and a faith that would offer a more emotional experience than the worship of the old gods or involvement in the newer philosophies.

Each of the mystery religions was centered about a god who died and was resurrected. Each had a ritual through which the initiate participated in the experience of the god and was rendered a candidate for immortality. Each guaranteed its devotees an ultimate escape from the miserable world about them into an immortal after-life. They were called "mysteries" because

they aimed by secret and mysterious ritual to achieve the fusion of the worshiper and a divine savior. The chief mysteries holding popular sway were the Eleusinian of Greece, Cybele of Asia Minor, Isis and Osiris of Egypt, Mithraism of Persia, and AphroditeAdonis of Syria and Asia Minor.

The mystery religions all had at their base a divinity whose annual death and resurrection corresponded to the rhythm of the seasons. As plants died in the fall and were reborn in the spring, the vegetation spirits were thought to have gone to the underworld and to have returned from it. Raised from death, they could bestow immortality on mankind.

Because Christianity has some similarity to the mystery religions, it is sometimes classified as a mystery religion. But the differences greatly exceed the similarities. Christianity is based on a historical rather

The Baalbek Temples

The great temples at Baalbek, built in the second and third centuries A.D., speak of the vitality of paganism during the centuries that Christianity was beginning to make its impact in Syria. They clearly demonstrate that paganism did not roll over and play dead when Christianity invaded. They also show the energy that pagans will exert to glorify their gods and raise the question of whether Christians will do as much.

Eventually the temples ceased to function, and at the end of the fourth century a Christian church was built in the middle of the complex. During the sixth century the emperor Justinian carried some materials from Baalbek for use in his great church in Constantinople (now Istanbul), which we call Hagia Sophia. But as late as the end of the sixth century the ruling class in Baalbek was still heathen. The ruin of the Baalbek temples came partly as a result of deliberate destruction of pagan worship centers, but a series of earthquakes over the centuries also had a great impact.

A coin of Antiochus IV (king 175–163 B.C.), once worshiped as a divine king of Syria.

than a mythological person, on a being who died and rose once purposefully in a substitutionary atonement for mankind, rather than repeatedly in some rhythm of the seasons. Normally the mystery religions did not put specific demands on an individual to live a new lifestyle; nor did they offer a supernatural enablement for living, as Christianity did. While the rites of initiation in the mystery religions were secret and were never fully revealed even by initiates who defected, the means of becoming a Christian have been almost literally shouted from the housetops and have been published in detail in the Scriptures.

(For more on this topic, go to p. 405 or p. 496.)

Warfare

As a frontier province, Syria had an important part to play in the defense of the Roman Empire. Rome stationed nearly all the standing army in Syria, along the Danube, along the Rhine, and in North Africa. Within the pacified provinces a few squadrons of police or local militia maintained order. The emperor did not need to rely on the army everywhere to keep himself in power. He had other props to maintain his authority. Chief among them were the ruler cult (see under Religion above) and the vast and growing bureaucracy.

Rome had a neat little arrangement by which the emperor could keep control of

the military power of the state and still ensure its essential civilian character. Augustus divided rule in the empire between the emperor and the Senate, both in Rome and abroad. He divided the provinces into imperial and senatorial provinces, the former either needed pacification or border defenses. In these, Rome maintained troops and the emperor appointed the governors. In the senatorial provinces the Senate appointed governors and managed provincial affairs. Naturally the military and political situation remained somewhat fluid, and provinces might be moved from one category to the other.

Another way of gaining some support for Rome and some Romanization in the provinces was to plant colonies of veterans there. Augustus made Berytus (Beirut) a veteran colony. Claudius and Vespasian established other Roman colonies in Syria later in the first century.

Four Roman legions were regularly stationed in Syria. Early in the first Christian century, between Augustus and Caligula, about 65 percent of these came from Italy. But that percentage was hard to maintain, and between about A.D. 50 and the outbreak of the First Jewish Revolt (66) that percentage dropped to just under 50, with the rest coming from the provinces.

The boundaries of Syria that the army had to defend were in the northeast, along the upper Euphrates, and in the south, what is now desert. But the modern observer should not conjure up a scene of trackless or uncharted desert with fluid conditions as they appear today. In Roman times much of this land was under prosperous cultivation. As noted in the last chapter, there has been a climate change. The area was cooler and wetter during the early Christian centuries than is now the case. Moreover, soil exhaustion, deforestation, and especially the breakdown of the elaborate system of irrigation have left the area desert today. There is plenty of evidence of prosperous towns along the Syrian frontier in New Testament times.

Sometimes the Romans billeted soldiers in towns in the populated areas. They built structures for them alongside private buildings: barracks, administrative headquar-

A floor mosaic from a second-century house at Antioch. The various rooms of the upper classes also often had busts or full-sized statues. (Antakya Museum)

ters, and storage depots. At other times the military camp gave rise to a town. Merchants and camp followers gathered around the camps. So legions gave birth to towns and some of them never had any name but that of the legion stationed there. Incidentally, pairs of platforms for sending fire signals have been discovered in Syria along the Roman roads.[4]

Military Action

The enemy beyond the Syrian border remained the powerful Parthian Kingdom. Twice since the Romans had taken over Syria the Parthians had scored big against the Romans. In 53 B.C. at Carrhae (Old Testament Harran or Haran) they killed Crassus and 30,000 of his men. And during the Roman civil wars they took advantage of Roman weakness and occupied Syria and Palestine from 40 to 38 B.C.

During the New Testament era, however, Rome did not have to fight a major war with the Parthians. She stabilized the situation in part by depending on client kings to keep things under control. Especially useful proved to be the kingdom of Armenia and the Judean kingdom of Herod the Great. And, fortunately for Rome, when conditions deteriorated seriously, Parthia was distracted by problems on her other borders. Roman diplomatic ventures in the East also proved to be moderately successful.

Rome's scuffles with Parthia do not really concern the biblical narrative. And Rome's troops in Syria do not really get involved in Palestine until the time of the First Jewish Revolt (66–72) and the Roman

civil war after the death of Nero in 68. So an account of their military action is unnecessary here.

(For more on this topic, go to p. 443 or p. 500.)

Housing and Furniture

The more durable houses of the wealthy have left fairly substantial remains for the excavator to investigate. There are similarities in style of upper-class houses all over the Mediterranean world during this period. Whether in Pompeii or Jerusalem or Antioch-on-the-Orontes, owners beautified their floors with mosaics. Even individuals of moderate means tried to have a little mosaic in at least one room. The top classes might have them everywhere. During the first century, decor might be in black and white or preferably in color. But color productions usually had geometric designs. The intricate floor tapestries that appear in many of the art books date from later centuries, at least in Syria and North Africa (Pompeii is an exception). So the fact that Hellenistic houses excavated near the temple in Jerusalem have geometric designs in their floors is not necessarily a result of Jewish adherence to the First or Second Commandments.

Mediterranean and Near Eastern house construction going all the way back to Abraham featured a central open courtyard with rooms built around it. Hellenistic and Roman-style houses also had these open courtyards but surrounded them with stone pillars.

The well-to-do in Antioch in the early Christian centuries built rectangular houses with a colonnade on the entrance side. Through the colonnade one entered a large square dining room (with floor mosaics, of course), surrounded by rooms on the other three sides, also with mosaic floors.

Another increasingly common feature of houses of the wealthy during the first century and following was spaciousness. People seemingly spent more time indoors and entertained friends or business or government associates more often. They especially had ever-larger household staffs, usually composed of slaves. Thus in Apamea, on the Orontes south of Antioch, a city of 400,000 or more with an aristocracy of rich landowners, houses might be as large as 5,000 to 15,000 square feet.[5]

People lower on the economic and social scale still frequently lived in houses of several rooms arranged around an open central court. If they could not afford that, they might live in a rectangular house of three or four rooms or even in a single room.

Furniture

The poorest, as in earlier periods, might still sleep on the floor on bedrolls and sit on the floor around a mat or cloth to eat, but all classes tried to have some furniture. So, according to their means, householders had three- or four-legged stools, chairs with backs and arms, beds with mattresses supported on a wooden frame with slats or ropes, wood or reed clothes storage boxes, low wooden tables for dining, or even couches on which to recline while eating. An alternative to a freestanding bed was a brick bench with a bedroll on it. A brick bench with a cushion could also serve as a "sofa." The more affluent might have wood furniture with inlay or tables or chairs made largely of bronze or iron.

(For more on this topic, go to p. 443 or p. 500.)

Diet and Foodstuffs

Abundance and variety of food and improved methods of production characterize Syrian agriculture in the first Christian century. The Roman Peace and scientific methods of Hellenistic agriculture especially contributed to increased production. Stable political conditions and the protection of production and the arteries of supply are essential to prosperous agriculture.

But advances in technique are necessary if improvement is to do more than merely enhance the *status quo*. As a result of Hellenistic studies of agriculture, rotation of crops and the practice of leaving some land fallow became more common. Other improvements included soil fertilization, some production of quality seed in special plantations, as well as attention to irrigation where that was practicable.

Wheat, oats, barley, and rye constituted the principal nourishment of all classes. Rice, which requires irrigation, grew along the coast. Popular vegetables included lentils, beans, kidney beans, chickpeas, cabbage and radishes. Antioch was famous for its cucumbers. The poor especially relished onions, leeks, and garlic, with the garlic of Heliopolis valued highly. Spices produced in Syria included coriander, mustard, anise, cumin, ginger, and mint. Only the rich ate meat regularly, enjoying fowl, fish, beef, ham, and mutton, seemingly consuming fairly large quantities by the second century, when prosperity reached its peak.

Among the fruitbearing trees of Syria the olive, date, fig, and pistachio were especially important. The Nicolaän dates of Damascus were large and as sweet as honey. The Damascus plum was also much enjoyed.

The culture of the vine was generally conducted on large estates. Syrian wines were popular throughout the ancient world. Antioch, Byblos, Tripoli, Berytus, and Tyre were among the wine-producing centers. The wines of the Antioch area were especially prized.

Of course agriculture involves more than the production of foodstuffs. Syrian farmers also raised quantities of papyrus, flax, hemp, and cotton. Papyrus especially provided writing material, but also rope, baskets, mats, and more. Flax furnished linen for clothing. Hemp supplied rope and strong fabrics. And of course cotton provided clothing.

(For more on this topic, go to p. 447 or p. 501.)

Dress

As we think about those early believers and the beginning of the church in Antioch, we wonder how they dressed. Much of what was said in the last chapter applies to contemporary Syria. But some additional comments may be helpful.

First, fabrics might be made of wool, linen, or cotton. Probably most were made of wool because it was more readily available and probably cheaper. Also the mountainous and hilly areas of Syria called for clothing providing greater warmth than in Palestine farther south. How much fabric was made of cotton this early in history we cannot say, though we know that farmers over the border in Assyria produced it by 700 B.C.

Second, the price of dyeing depended on the color and the dye used, so the poorest tended to wear white clothing. But all classes liked to have some color in their wardrobes. Several dyestuffs were available: woad (producing blue), saffron (orange, orange yellow), henna (reddish brown), madder (moderate to strong red), and the murex shells (rose to dark violet), to name the most important. Most of the production of dyes occurred in the vicinity of the textile manufacturing district of Tyre, but there were other places.

Third, for Syria we have a substantial number of mosaics from houses of the Antioch area that portray both men and women. Admittedly they date after the New Testament period, but they confirm what we know or surmise from other information. We have to be careful in our use of these mosaics, however, because they usually feature the upper classes and probably people living in towns.

Women have hair of shoulder length or shorter or have it dressed and piled high on the head. Men standardly wear short hair and rarely have beards. Poorer people in towns and in the rural areas may not have had sufficient access to barbers. While sandals were still the footwear of choice, many men are shown wearing boots laced up to the calf. This may be due to the kind of activity in which they are engaged (e.g., hunting boots) or the terrain of Syrian mountains.

As to clothing styles, the tunic was still the basic garment, made by sewing two pieces of cloth together, leaving a hole for the head and neck. Belted, it usually had sleeves to the elbow or wrist, but some were sleeveless. Upper-class men usually wore a robe over the tunic, extending to the ankle. But lower-class men engaged in some kind of activity were ready for action, wearing only a tunic extending to the knees. This is consonant with what we know of Roman society. Upper-class men were not supposed to engage in physical labor. Nearly all the mosaic representations we have date after A.D. 212, when all free men in the empire had Roman citizenship. So lower-class men would frequently be slaves and therefore not portrayed as "gentlemen."

In all of these pictures women are shown with long robes over their tunics, extending to the floor. Some of these seem to be held together at the shoulders by elaborate pins or brooches. Sometimes women also wear shawls over their hair.

(For more on this topic, go to p. 447 or p. 501.)

Family Life

"We have heard that some who went out from us have troubled you with words, unsettling your souls, saying 'You must be circumcised and keep the law'—to whom we gave no such commandment." (Acts 15:24 NKJV)

As the apostles went out to Syria and elsewhere they had not preached the necessity of keeping the Law–apparently to either Jews or Gentiles. And the Council of Jerusalem (Acts 15) made it clear that believers henceforth would not be expected to keep the Law. Moreover, for the people of Syria it was physically or geographically impossible for them to keep the Law as Jews of the Jerusalem area could. They did not live close to the temple. And the day was coming (A.D. 70) when the temple would be destroyed and no devout person could go there to keep aspects of the Law.

The new freedom meant that male infants would not need to be circumcised, though Jews all over the empire generally continued the practice. We have no way of knowing what percentage of converted Jews continued to circumcise their infant males. Moreover, the new freedom meant that purification of the mother in the prescribed way after childbirth would not occur because of the distance to the temple. Furthermore, it meant less frequent family pilgrimages to Jerusalem for the feasts (Passover, etc.) for Jews and probably none for Christians.

Then while dietary laws might still control the eating habits of Jews of the Dispersion, they would have no effect on Christians–Jews or Gentiles. In the weekly round of activities, Sabbath observance had less of a grip on believers. It appears that from the very beginning of the church the first day of the week, as a recognition of the resurrection of Christ, began to take the place of the Sabbath (e.g., Acts 20:7; 1 Corinthians 16:2). And with the passage of time holding services on Sunday became the almost universal practice. The claim of some that Constantine (erroneously) changed the day of worship from Saturday to Sunday in the fourth century simply does not hold water. Ritual uncleanness as a result of touching dead bodies and for other reasons also tended to disappear.

Now we need to ask how other first-century family relationships and daily life in Palestine (last chapter) compared to those of Syria in the first century. First, families of the bride and groom commonly arranged marriage, though not necessarily ignoring the wishes of the young couple. Second, the bride's family provided her with a dowry; and the bridegroom, especially a Jew, was required to give his bride a substantial gift. Marriage and divorce contracts were commonly drawn up. Those involving land and other monetary settlements were usually kept in public archives. Third, among the upper and middle classes marriage was usually ratified by a legal document; among the poor it commonly was not. The wealthy, as part of their social standing, spent huge sums on weddings, funerals, and tombs. Fourth, funerals with professional mourners were expected in Syria, as well as elsewhere in the Near East.

Fifth, the development of children continued the same as in first-century Palestine. Mothers trained young children; fathers trained boys in the trade or craft that they pursued. The family work force included many more slaves in Syria than in Palestine. Primarily slaves were domestic, but some were employed in industry and agriculture.

As to education, there was some study connected with the synagogues. And in Syria important educational centers began to develop in major cities. A school of rhetoric and philosophy existed in Sidon as early as the time of Augustus. In the first century, a school of law, rhetoric, and medicine operated in Berytus (Beirut); a school of literature in Antioch; of philosophy in Apamea; history in Damascus; and medicine in Laodicea and Sidon. Most of what we can effectively document concerning the flowering of Syrian education dates to the second or third century. But important beginnings occurred in the first century.

Entertainment

Entertainment abounded in pagan, secular Syria during the first century. Antioch had its theater, amphitheater, hippodrome, stadiums, and baths. So did Laodicea, Berytus, Tyre, and other cities. Horse races, musical and dancing displays, theatrical plays, and arena shows of gladiators and wild beast hunts, especially put on by convicts and prisoners of war, abounded. Large numbers of Jews taken prisoner at the fall of Jerusalem (A.D. 70) were condemned to put on gladiatorial combats and wild beast hunts, fighting to the death in the arenas of Syria. The wealthy of Syria especially enjoyed hunting and fowling.

(For more on this topic, go to p. 448 or p. 502.)

Work, Travel, and Commerce

Perhaps the average Bible student thinks of Syria as a rather sleepy, backward agricultural province with its one city of Antioch in New Testament times. Nothing

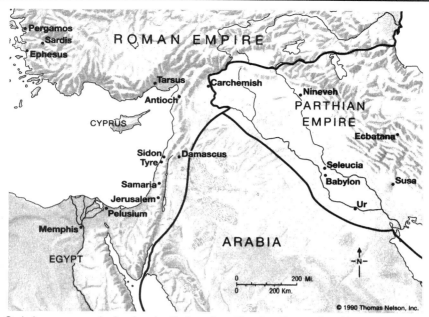

Syria lay across major land routes that ran from Egypt on the south to Mesopotamia on the east and Asia Minor to the north and northwest. Tyre, Sidon, and Seleucia-Antioch, among others, maintained ports for overseas trade.

could be further from the truth. If we accept the population figure of 7,000,000 proposed in this chapter, over a quarter of the people must have lived in cities. If we go with the view of some that the population was about 5,000,000, some 40 percent of them lived in bustling centers of industry and commerce. The list of great cities was long: Tyre, Sidon, Berytus, Byblos, Tripoli, Laodicea, Seleucia, Antioch, Apamea, Emesa, Heliopolis, Damascus, and others. Moreover, Syria was a crossroads of the world, as will shortly become clear.

Work, Employment

Agriculture was the basis of the Syrian economy. Many were subsistence farmers who produced nearly all their food and had enough left over to provide for the other necessities of life. Large landholders worked land on shares with contract labor or directly with the use of slaves. Substantial quantities of grain and olive oil and grapes supplied domestic consumption and export markets. And we must not forget the production of wool and flax (linen).

But town industry especially thrived during the first Christian century. The art of glassblowing was probably invented on the Phoenician coast in the first century B.C. and quickly spread to all Asiatic provinces and Egypt.[6] The best workers in bronze in the Near East lived in Sidon in the mid-first century, but Syria as a whole had a good reputation for such work. The Hellenistic invention of the waterwheel made the art of milling a professional occupation.[7] The presence of four legions in the province and the need to supply them also spurred industry. The producers of armaments and military machines, leather shields, and army boots had a ready market.

The production of writing material also occupied many. Quantities of papyrus plants were grown in Syria and then processed into sheets of "paper." Others turned animal skins (sheep or goat) into parchment. Wax tablets, sheets of linen, and best (the inner bark of Linden or other trees) provided additional writing material.

Though a lot of weaving and cloth production occurred domestically, increasingly it was taken over by shops in the cities. The

Seleucia, Antioch's seaport, was hardly more than a roadstead, but it handled a huge amount of trade. And Paul and his companions were among the large numbers of people who took passage or landed there. The present deserted beach area, with no remains of warehouses, gives no hint of the ancient bustling port.

finishing of imported silk yarn was especially important in the shops of Berytus and Tyre. Laodicea, Byblos, Berytus, and Tyre became important producers and distributors of linen and woolen goods.

Dressmaking, fulling, dyeing, carpentry, metal work, stone work, and architecture supported thousands of others.

Many crafts, in fact most occupations, were hereditary. Fathers taught their sons, but boys also might be apprenticed to a master craftsman, such as a scribe, carpet weaver, smith, carpenter, tanner, confectioner, or doctor. Apprenticeship contracts might extend to as much as ten years in Syria.[8] Workers in the same craft might inhabit the same streets and sometimes whole villages.

Commerce

From Augustus on, Syria was important not only as a frontier but a thoroughfare of some of the most important trade routes in the Roman Empire. Antioch and its port, Seleucia, connected Syria with all the ports along the coast of the Mediterranean from Asia Minor and Egypt to Spain and Morocco. Tyre, Sidon, Berytus, Byblos, Tripoli, and Laodicea had similar connections in the West.

Numerous trade routes crossed the sands of Syria. A Transjordanic route led from the Gulf of Aqaba to Petra and from there to Damascus. A coastal route ran from Gaza to Carmel, across Esdraelon, and in Galilee divided into two branches, one to Damascus and the other north along the Orontes. The northern road to Mesopotamia led from Damascus north and passed through Homs (ancient Emesa), Arabian Haleb (Aleppo, ancient Beroea) and then east down the Euphrates River. Another link between Syria and Mesopotamia by a more southerly track took off from Damascus or Homs and proceeded by way of Palmyra to ancient Dura-Europos or elsewhere in Mesopotamia and thence through Iran to India and China. In the days of the Sino-Roman world peace (1st and 2nd centuries A.D.), the Aleppo Road formed the last stage of the "silk route" from the Yellow Sea to the Mediterranean.

Syria served as such an important transit center that a permanent colony of Roman businessmen settled in Antioch as early as Caesar's time.[9] For their part, Syrian businessmen settled as far away as Britain and Central Asia, India, and even China to the east.[10] Wealthy traders in Syria usually owned shops, but temples and public baths were popular meeting places for transaction of business. Often traders in the same product lived together in the same section of town.

Through Syria the West especially sent textiles, wines, copper, tin, lead, and vessels of bronze, silver, and glass to Iran, India, and even Thailand.[11] In return the West imported textiles, carpets, embroidery, furs, and hides from Mesopotamia, Iran, India, and East Asia; pottery and carved ivory from Iran and Mesopotamia; silk from China; and perfumes and drugs from Arabia, Iran, and India.

Syria herself imported pottery from Italy, Greece, and Asia Minor; dried fish from Egypt and Spain; cheap cloth, gold, silver, jewels, and valuable woods from various places; Negro slaves from Egypt; horses from Spain for the races in Antioch; Indian fabrics; and Chinese silks. The list of what Syria sent in return was long indeed and included textiles, glass, jewels, embroidered cloths, carpets, wine, olive oil, wheat, hides, furs, drugs, figs and other fruits, metal goods, slaves, and more. Her export destinations were especially Italy, Egypt, East Africa, and India.

Travel

The imports into Syria, exports from it, trans-shipment of goods through it, and the movement of merchants to faraway places to look after commercial interests, caused large numbers of people constantly to be on the go into, out of, and across Syria. That number grew as thousands of troops came from Italy and elsewhere and bureaucrats came from Rome and reported back to headquarters.

In addition to that travel, large number of Jews in the province went to Jerusalem on pilgrimage. For that reason, Jews probably traveled more than Gentiles did. Or Christians who began to take an increasingly active role in spreading the gospel. Persecution drove some there from Jerusalem (Acts 11:19). Barnabas came to Antioch to check on the church there (Acts 11:22). He brought Saul (Paul) to Antioch to minister (11:25). And the Antioch church sent Paul on three missionary journeys across the eastern Mediterranean.

Travel to and from Syria and across the province remained constant and relatively expeditious. It had to be fairly fast if Rome was to maintain the border defenses and effective communications. The road system was kept in good repair and expanded during the first century.

Merchant ships on the Mediterranean did not run on a regular schedule though they traveled constantly. Generally they "tramped" from port to port. Heichelheim concludes that it would have taken about 200 days to travel from Berytus to Brundisium on the east side of Italy and back, about 137 days from Tyre to the west coast of Italy, 70 days from Antioch to Babylon, and less than a day from Antioch to its port at Seleucia.[12] I estimate that with a favorable wind, sailing time from Seleucia to Salamis on Cyprus would have been about 24 hours.

With that kind of world trade it is not surprising that God established the first Gentile church in Antioch. Christians engaged in trade were undoubtedly key conduits of the gospel wherever they went.

In the next chapter we look at life in Cyprus during the New Testament period. *(For more on this topic, go to p. 456 or p. 503.)*

NOTES:

[1] Philip K. Hitti, *History of Syria* (New York: Macmillan, 1951), 292.

[2] Bruce M. Metzger, "Antioch-on-the-Orontes," *The Biblical Archaeologist*, December 1948, 81.

[3] Glanville Downey, *Ancient Antioch* (Princeton: Princeton University Press, 1963), 123.

[4] Graham Webster, *The Roman Imperial Army*, 3d ed. (Totowa, N.J.: Barnes & Noble, 1985), 255.

[5] *Oxford Encyclopedia of Archaeology in the Near East*, I, 146.

[6] F. M. Heichelheim, "Roman Syria," *An Economic survey of Ancient Rome*, ed. Tenney Frank (Baltimore: Johns Hopkins Press, 1938), IV, 189.

[7] Ibid., 197.

[8] Ibid., 198.

[9] Ibid., 201.

[10] Ibid., 204.

[11] Ibid., 200.

[12] Ibid,. 210.

BIBLIOGRAPHY:

Boulanger, Robert. *Hachette World Guides: Lebanon*. Paris: Librairie Hachette, 1965.

Downey, Glanville. *Ancient Antioch*. Princeton: Princeton University Press, 1963.

Downey, Glanville. *A History of Antioch in Syria from Seleucus to the Arab Conquest*. Princeton: Princeton University Press, 1961.

Finegan, Jack. *The Archeology of the New Testament: The Mediterranean World of the Early Christian Apostles*. Boulder, Colo.: Westview Press, 1981.

Hitti, Philip K. *History of Syria*. New York: Macmillan, 1951.

Hopkins, Clark. *The Discovery of Dura-Europos*. New Haven: Yale University Press, 1979.

McRay, John. *Archaeology and the New Testament*. Grand Rapids: Baker, 1991.

Ragette, Friedrich. *Baalbek*. Park Ridge, N.J.: Noyes Press, 1980.

Rostovtzeff, Mikhail. *Social and Economic History of the Hellenistic World*. Oxford: Clarendon Press, Vol. 2, 1953.

Sherwin-White, Susan, and Amelie Kuhrt. *From Samarkhand to Sardis*. Berkeley: University of California Press, 1993.

CYPRUS AND THE BEGINNING OF "FOREIGN" MISSIONS

Chapter 17

(Acts)

"So . . . they went down to Seleucia, and from there they sailed to Cyprus."
(Acts 13:4)

an you picture the scene in the church at Antioch of Syria? Every week new Jewish and Gentile believers joined the fellowship, and the church was really thriving. A year of concentrated effort on the part of Barnabas and Saul had paid off (Acts 11:26). Yet a certain unease began to come over the church. This unease gave way to a conviction that they should be doing more than evangelizing the Antioch area or contributing to famine relief in Jerusalem (Acts 11:29-30). They should be reaching the larger world with the gospel.

As they became convinced of their larger mission, they concluded that Barnabas and Saul, who had represented them in delivering relief money to Jerusalem,

should now be their representatives in taking the gospel abroad. So under the direction of the Holy Spirit, this church sent off what appear to have been their first designated missionaries—on the first of the most remarkable series of evangelistic and church planting journeys on record. John

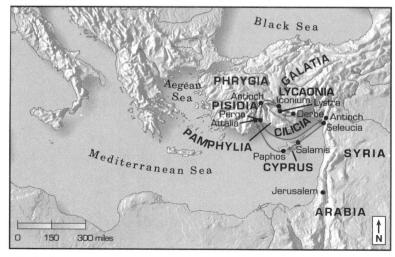

On his first missionary journey, Paul struck out from Syria for Cyprus. The distance from the port of Seleucia to the eastern tip of the island was about sixty miles, to Salamis about one hundred miles.

Mark, the nephew of Barnabas, accompanied them (Acts 13:5). The year was probably A.D. 45.

Reason for Missionary Work

Why Barnabas, Saul, and John Mark went to Cyprus is not hard to discover. Barnabas himself was a native of Cyprus (Acts 4:36) and could be expected to have an interest in the evangelization of his Jewish kinsmen there. Moreover, Jews of Cyprus had been partially responsible for sparking a revival at Antioch (Acts 11:20–21). No doubt the Antiochian church, which had now become quite large, felt an obligation to send Christian workers to Cyprus. Since Barnabas and Saul had accomplished such a remarkable ministry in Antioch (where Barnabas had been sent by the Jerusalem church), it seemed only logical that these men would be entrusted with further evangelistic and supervisory work. Who better to send to Cyprus than these experienced leaders—one of whom was a native of the island?

That the gospel message preceded Barnabas and Saul to Cyprus by some years is evident from such a passage as Acts 11:19, which declares that the persecution arising at the time of the martyrdom of Stephen scattered a number of converts to Cyprus. Stephen's martyrdom occurred shortly after the Pentecost of Acts 2. Perhaps these early Christians on Cyprus appealed to Antioch for help—with the result that Barnabas and Saul went to them.

Magnitude of the Task

The task of evangelizing the Jews on Cyprus was a substantial one, as is shown by the evidence of a large numbers of Jews on the island. Apparently Ptolemy Soter brought the first Jews to Cyprus after the capture of Jerusalem in 320 B.C., when he reportedly transported large numbers of Jews to Egypt and other parts of his dominions.[1] Many more came to the island just before the birth of Christ with the hope of employment in the copper mines, which at one time were put under the supervision of Herod the Great.[2]

That the number of Jews on Cyprus was large in the first century A.D. is indicated by events of the early second century. In A.D. 116 a Jewish revolt spread over the eastern Mediterranean world. And according to Dio Cassius, Jews killed 240,000 of their fellow citizens on Cyprus alone.[3] Even if this figure is exaggerated, as is very likely the case, atrocities of such approximate magnitude would require a considerable Jewish population. In retaliation, imperial forces killed thousands of Jews, and banished the rest from the island. For centuries thereafter no Jew was allowed on Cyprus.

So it is easy to see why Paul and Barnabas went to Cyprus. But whether Cyprus was their ultimate goal is another question. According to Acts 13:13, after fruitful ministry in Cyprus, and after reaching the western shore of Cyprus at Paphos, Paul and his party set sail for Asia Minor. Did they plan to do that when they left Antioch? Or did it occur to them to do so after success at Paphos? We can't fully answer that question. But it is useful to note that the usual Mediterranean trade route from Antioch/Seleucia Pieria was by way of Cyprus to Asia Minor, and from there to Italy, if that was in the commercial person's travel plans. Possibly success of the Cyprus venture indicated the next step.

CYPRUS

The Land

Location and Size

Cyprus is the third largest island of the Mediterranean Sea. Exceeded in size only by Sicily and Sardinia, it has an area of 3,572 square miles. Located in the extreme northeast corner of the Mediterranean, Cyprus can be seen from both Asia Minor and Syria on a clear day. The former distance is about 43 miles and the latter about 60. Between Egypt and Cyprus the distance is about 250 miles. It is therefore easy to see why cultural influences from Asia Minor and Syria were felt on Cyprus long before those of Egypt.

As to shape, Cyprus is sometimes likened to a silhouetted wheelbarrow being pushed along. The long Karpas Peninsula represents the handles, and the Akrotiri Peninsula to the south, the wheels. In ancient times it was compared to a deerskin or bullock's hide spread out on the ground. The tail is represented by the Karpas Peninsula and the legs by four large promontories. The greatest length of the island is 138 miles and the greatest width 60 miles. Subtracting the approximately 40-mile-long Karpas Peninsula, Cyprus averages some 90–100 miles in length. The total coastline is 486 miles.

Mountains

The surface of Cyprus divides almost evenly between mountain and plain. The mountains divide into two ranges: the Kyrenia, or Northern, Range and the Troodos Range. The gray-pink limestone Kyrenia Range extends along the whole of the northern coast some three miles from the coast and rises from two to three thousand feet. Highest of the several peaks of this range is Akromandra, 3,433 feet in altitude. Conveniently, three gaps pierce this range: Panagra in the west, Kyrenia in the center, and Akanthou in the east. The Kyrenia Range tends to force the moisture from the vapor-laden winds from the north, providing sufficient moisture for the fertile coastal plain. Trees cover the

The Kyrenia Range. The southern slopes (here) are often bare.

seaward slopes of the Kyrenia Mountains (especially olive in modern times), as well as shrubs, and flowers; the southern slopes are often bare.

Most of the southern half of Cyprus consists of a confusion of steep-sided mountain ridges, arrayed in such tangled profusion that it is almost impossible to discover any backbone or watershed. Several of the peaks of these Troodos Mountains rise more than 4,500 feet. The highest is Chionistra, or Olympus (6,404 feet). White limestone plateaus occupy the area south of the Troodos massif. These fall in step-like fashion as they approach the coast. In places they become sea cliffs, but occasionally they recede to allow coastal plains with quite rich alluvial soil.

The Central Plain

Between the two mountain ranges lies the broad plain of Mesaria, or Mesaoria, some 60 miles long by 30 miles broad. Nicosia, the modern capital of Cyprus, is located in the center of this plain. The granary of the island, this plain also produces substantial quantities of vegetables and fruit. Though now treeless except for a few recently planted trees, Mesaria was in ancient times heavily forested. Through this plain flow the two chief rivers of Cyprus—the Pedias (anc. Pediaeus) and Yalias (anc. Idalia)—which dump their waters into the Mediterranean near ancient Salamis on the east coast. During the rainy season these are fairly substantial streams,

The known copper veins of Cyprus are almost completely worked out now. Here is a mine that was in operation a couple of decades ago.

but they are not navigable during the dry season. Reservoirs now tap most of their water before it reaches the Mediterranean, and stream beds are dry part of the time.

Rainfall and Climate

Rainfall occurs mainly during the months of December to February, but the amount is not large. The main agricultural areas receive only twelve to sixteen inches per year. Even this amount comes irregularly, and serious droughts occur on the average of every ten years. And since high evaporation involves considerable loss, the supply of water constitutes a serious problem.

It is easy to guess from what has been said about rainfall that prolonged drizzling from gray skies is rare in Cyprus even during the rainy season—when the sun usually shines for at least some part of every day. The mean temperature of the lowland areas in the coldest months is about 50–54 degrees; for the hottest months it ranges from 80 to 84 degrees. The climate is very healthful, and the death rate is one of the lowest in the world. The growing season roughly corresponds with the rainy season, and crops are harvested by March or April. During the summer and early fall, when there is rarely any rainfall, the fields look very dry.

Forests

Forests once constituted one of the main resources of Cyprus. Her timber, so impor-

tant for shipbuilding, was much sought after by the ancient imperial powers of the Mediterranean area. Actually, however, they felled more trees for copper and silver smelting than for shipbuilding. The famous cedars have almost disappeared, but there are considerable stands of Aleppo pine and black pine. Forests now cover about twenty percent of the land area.

Mineral Deposits

Copper proved to be more important than timber to the economy of Cyprus in antiquity. In fact, so extensive was the island's export of this mineral that copper obtained its name from the name of Cyprus. The English word *copper* is derived from the Greek name of the island, Kypros, through the Latin *cuprum*. Produced as early as the third millennium B.C., copper continued to be mined extensively throughout antiquity and into modern times. Gold, silver, and iron were also mined on Cyprus in ancient times. But the known mines have been almost entirely worked out, and not more than a thousand men are employed in mining on Cyprus today.

(For more on this topic, go to p. 470 or p. 507.)

Government

"... the proconsul, Sergius Paulus, an intelligent man. This man called for Barnabas and Saul and sought to hear the word of God." (Acts 13:7 NKJV)

The Romans took over Cyprus in 67 B.C., claiming a right to the island as heirs named in the last legitimate Ptolemy's will (Ptolemy Alexander II, 105–80 B.C.). Moreover, they claimed that the king of Cyprus had given aid to pirates in their raids along the Cilician coast and that the annexation of Cyprus was necessary to future security of the seas. The Romans looted the island on a grand scale. They auctioned off the king's treasures and sent the money to Rome. A brilliant chapter in Cypriot history had come to an end.

Cyprus became part of the province of Cilicia in 58 B.C., being ruled from Tarsus. The self-aggrandizing thievery of the early

Site of the port of Salamis in New Testament times. Though the capital had been moved to Paphos, Salamis was still the largest city and had the busiest port.

Roman governors was indescribable. And when Cicero, an honest man, became governor in 51 B.C. he could hardly find words strong enough to expose the injustices of his predecessor. He withdrew troops from the island and reduced interest payments with which the island had been saddled.

In 47 B.C. Julius Caesar restored Cyprus to the Ptolemies. But with the victory of Augustus over the forces of Antony at Actium in 31 and the subsequent suicide of Antony and Cleopatra, the Romans took command once more. Now Cyprus became a province separate from Cilicia. From 27 to 22 B.C. the Romans administered it as an imperial province and ruled it through the personal appointee of Augustus. In 22 Augustus turned it over to the Senate. Thereafter an ex-praetor with the title of proconsul governed it. Luke refers to him accurately in the Greek of Acts 13:7, and most English versions now properly translate "proconsul."

The victory of Augustus led to administrative reorganization and the reintroduction of stable conditions in the eastern Mediterranean. Economic prosperity resulted and continued on Cyprus for a couple of centuries. The emperor took over the mines of Cyprus, and laborers in the mines tended to be convicts.[4]

Apparently Rome did not markedly disturb the pattern of social and political life as it existed under the Ptolemies. Municipalities possessed self-government in varying degrees, as was true of cities elsewhere in the empire. For instance, Salamis had a popular assembly, senate, and a council of elders. Probably the Romans officials appointed the officials in the cities.

The *Koinon Ton Kyprion*, a sort of representative body acting on behalf of the Greek inhabitants of the island, a carryover from Ptolemaic days, exercised a degree of power. It issued coins, organized festivals and games, and seems to have served as a bulwark of national existence in opposition to Roman encroachment.

The Romans transferred the capital of Cyprus from Salamis to Paphos, perhaps because it was the port closest to Rome, or because they wished to honor Aphrodite, whose temple was located at Paphos, or because the port at Salamis was beginning to silt up.

Sergius Paulus (see Acts 13:7 above) served as proconsul of Cyprus about 46 to 48. The fact that he held this position is confirmed by an inscription from Paphos, dating to the middle of the first century, which mentions the proconsul Paulus.[5] Other inscriptions have been found which speak of "Lucius Sergius Paullus the Younger" and "Sergia Paulla, daughter of Lucius Sergius Paullus." Ramsay thought these individuals were the son and daughter of the proconsul. Ramsay also advanced an argument to demonstrate that Sergius Paulus and his family became Christians.[6] In passing, it should be noted that the Latin spelling of the governor's name would have been rendered with one l while the Greek rendering would have required two.

The People of the Province of Cyprus

The potential audience to whom Barnabas and Saul might have ministered on the island of Cyprus is usually estimated at about 500,000. But some argue that it was not over 300,000. It seems to me that the smaller figure is too low, however, because Salamis alone seems to have had a population in excess of 100,000. That the Jewish population was large is evident from what was said earlier.

But the dominant element was Greek. According to Homer's *Odyssey* and other Greek writers, some of the Greek heroes returning from the Battle of Troy settled on Cyprus and established towns there— including such sites as Salamis, Curium, and Nea Paphos. Archaeological evidence confirms the arrival of Greeks on the island around 1230 B.C.[7] Greeks secured cultural dominance on Cyprus by the sixth century B.C.

(For more on this topic, go to p. 474 or p. 512.)

Religion

The General Situation

When the group from Antioch came to Cyprus, they certainly did not face a religious void. As we saw earlier, Jews had settled in large numbers on the island. These of course maintained their synagogues, and the indication in Acts 13:5 is that there was more than one of them in Salamis alone. The mystery religions had also made their impact there, as had the emperor cult. But since the Senate ruled Cyprus, people prob-

ably paid less attention to the emperor cult than was true of Syria, since that was governed directly by the emperor and had many soldiers to pledge allegiance. We do know that a cult image of Tiberius stood in the gymnasium at Lapithos on the north coast. The old paganism was alive and well on Cyprus, however. And while they worshiped all the Greek gods, Aphrodite received special attention on the island, with important sanctuaries for Apollo and Zeus.

The Worship of Aphrodite

Because Cyprus was the meeting place of so many peoples, there occurred a fusion of the worship of Aphrodite as practiced among various peoples. The rites included Oriental, Greek, and Roman practices. Aphrodite ruled as the Greek goddess of love, beauty, and fertility and was akin to the Phoenician Astarte, the Babylonian Ishtar, the Anatolian Cybele, and the Roman Venus. Extensive religious prostitution accompanied her rites at Paphos.

During the last century De Cesnola investigated what was believed to be the great temple of Aphrodite at Old Paphos. He traced the wall of the sanctuary itself and found that it measured 221 feet on the east and west sides and 167 feet on the north and south sides. It was surrounded

Greek mythology held that Venus or Aphrodite was born at sea (on the Mediterranean) and was blown ashore on a shell on Cyprus. Here Botticelli (sixteenth century) portrays the birth of Venus. (Uffizi Gallery, Florence)

by an outer wall, which he was not able to trace completely. But on the basis of his discoveries, he concluded that the east and west sides of this enclosure measured 690 feet and the north and south sides 539 feet. The entire structure was built of a kind of blue granite which must have come from Cilicia or Egypt.

Between this large structure on the heights (probably visible for many miles at sea) and the shoreline stood a smaller temple. De Cesnola suggested that this temple had been built to commemorate the spot on which the goddess was said to have appeared to the Cyprians for the first time. Here the annual procession stopped to sacrifice before ascending the hill to the sanctuary.[8] Paul probably passed this temple while on Cyprus with Barnabas.

Combining evidence from archaeological investigation on the site, coins, a reference to this temple in Tacitus, and a comparison of this temple with what is known of Phoenician temples, Perrot and Chipiez put together a description of the worship center.[9] Surrounding the complex was a wall, against the inside of which abutted a covered colonnade designed to protect worshipers or pilgrims from the heat. Within this was an inner court, to which the faithful gained entrance after accomplishing certain rites and paying certain fees. This "holy of holies" was roofless and the deity stood in the center of it, perhaps raised on a pedestal and covered with some sort of canopy. The goddess herself

The traditional spot near Paphos where Venus is supposed to have come ashore. A temple was built nearby.

The Legends about the Goddess Aphrodite

The most commonly accepted legend concerning the birth of Aphrodite indicated that she was born of the foam of the sea, floated in a shell on the waves, and later landed on Cyprus near Paphos. The greatest festival in Cyprus in honor of Aphrodite was the Aphrodisia, held for three days each spring. Each year great crowds attended it, not only from all parts of Cyprus but also from surrounding countries. During the Aphrodisia a religious procession started at New Paphos and wound its way to Old Paphos, some ten miles away, passing through the gardens and sanctuaries of the goddess there.

was represented by a conical stone (a symbol of fertility) to which a head and arms may have been attached. In its entirety the structure reflects Phoenician influence. The Phoenicians seem to have been the original builders of Old Paphos.

Sanctuaries of Apollo and Zeus

Old Paphos also contained a sanctuary to Apollo. Dating to the end of the fourth century B.C., it was cut as a cave in the solid rock just to the east of the ancient city. It consists of two underground chambers entered by a flight of steps. The front chamber is rectangular and the back one circular with a dome-shaped roof. Another temple of Apollo stood about a mile west of Kourion. Worshipers approached that temple by a paved street that led into a walled enclosure. The temple itself was a small structure with a four-columned porch in front of it, reached by a broad flight of steps. The enclosure included dormitories for pilgrims, store-rooms for their offerings, a treasury, baths, and a priest's house. According to the apocryphal *Acts of Barnabas* (44), Paul and Barnabas visited Kourion on their first missionary journey.

The known temple of Zeus stood on the south side of the agora at Salamis. Originally built in Hellenistic times, it stood on a

Not Many Noble?

Saul is first called Paul in connection with the interview with the governor of Cypros. This was his first significant Gentile contact and the first use of his Greek name. It is also noteworthy that Sergius Paulus as governor believed. Later the ruler of the synagogue in Corinth did also (Acts 18:8), as did a member of the prestigious Areopagus Council in Athens (Acts 17:34). Other examples of outstanding or upper-class individuals coming to faith in Christ could be given. We should not fall into the mistaken view that only the poorest or most insignificant members of society constituted the church in the early days. Christians often quote 1 Corinthians 1:26 to prove that not many wise, mighty, or noble are called to faith, and that the church therefore consisted mostly of the poor, slaves, and others of the lower classes of society.

high platform and had a square holy place at the rear. The column drums and Corinthian capitals at the site suggest an impressive building.

The Apostolic Ministry

Judging from the usual practice of Paul to preach in the synagogues of the Jews and from the specific reference of Acts 13:5, it seems that missionaries came to Cyprus to reach only the Jewish element of the population. Of course they attracted some God-fearers (sympathetic Gentiles) who would form part of the audience. Since Christian witnesses preceded Barnabas and Saul to Cyprus, it may be assumed that at least a few were ready to listen to them (Acts 11:19).

After ministry in Salamis, Barnabas and Saul went through the island to Paphos (Acts 13:6). The passage is better rendered "through the whole island" (so NRSV and other versions). Probably this means a relatively complete tour of the Jewish communities on Cyprus, involving preaching in

the synagogues. How long this mission took is open to conjecture. Estimates range between two and four months.

We can only speculate about the route of the apostolic itinerary. The Romans built a road around the main part of the island. It ran from Salamis diagonally to Kyrenia in the north, and from there roughly followed the west and south coasts and then back to Salamis. They constructed other roads in the interior. Probably Saul and his companions went to Paphos by the southern road through Kition. If so, they passed the temple of Apollo at Kourion and the temple of Aphrodite at Old Paphos.

When Saul and Barnabas reached the capital of Paphos, Saul successfully led Sergius Paulus, the proconsul, to faith in Christ. Thus a great victory was won for Christianity (Acts 13:6–12).

The Great Cities of Ministry

Two great Cypriote cities figure in the biblical account. And it will give a little more realism to the biblical narrative to note briefly what they were like.

Salamis

Founded on the east coast of Cyprus about 1100 B.C., Salamis seems always to have been a Greek city with a predominately Greek population. Because of several destructions and rebuildings since New Testament times, and because of partial

Remains of the Temple of Zeus on the south side of the agora at Salamis.

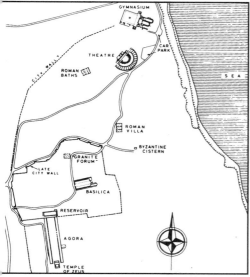

Plan of Salamis

South of the baths stand ruins of the great theater of Salamis, evidently built in Augustus' day (27 B.C.–A.D. 14). Its semi-circular orchestra measured about thirty yards in diameter, and originally it had over fifty rows of seats with a capacity of some 15,000. It was considerably larger than the famous theater at Epidaurus, the best preserved in Greece, which might have held 14,000. In the southern section of the city, near the harbor, stood a complete system of defenses with many parallel walls. In the second century B.C. Salamis ceded its place to Paphos as the leading city of the island. It is usually concluded that Salamis had a population of about 100,000 during the New Testament period. The town may have covered an area in excess of 5,000 acres.[10]

excavation of the site, it is hard to picture exactly what it was like when Paul and Barnabas came through. But at the center of community life stood the forum or agora about 675 feet long by almost 200 feet wide. It was lined on the two long sides by stone colonnades about 27 feet high and carrying Corinthian capitals. These stood about 15 feet apart and between them access could be gained to the shops. On the south side on a high platform stood the temple of Zeus, already noted.

Excavators found the remains of a complex of baths and a gymnasium north of the forum. In New Testament times Hellenistic baths and a gymnasium did occupy the site.

The theater of Salamis originally could seat some fifteen thousand people.

Paphos

Founded during the fourth century B.C., Nea (New) Paphos became the capital of Cyprus in the second century B.C. Largely destroyed by an earthquake in 15 B.C., the city was rebuilt primarily with funds received from Augustus. During the following decades the city was adorned with magnificent temples and public buildings. It became important not only as the capital but as the port for Old Paphos (Kouklia) and the shrine of Venus, or Aphrodite. Here countless pilgrims landed to visit and worship. Paphos became a great center for the worship of Aphrodite, just as Ephesus was for the worship of Diana.

Archaeologists have traced the city wall for most of its course, and the breakwaters of the ancient harbor are still in place. They

The forum or agora of Salamis, about 675 feet long by 200 feet wide, and lined on the long sides by stone colonnades

The palestra or exercise ground of the gymnasium at Salamis

have found the site of the gymnasium, as well as that of the Hellenistic theater, a garrison camp, and the temple of Apollo (see above). Ruins of the city remain unexcavated. The excavated House of Dionysos (third century A.D.) occupies an area of over 6,000 square feet, of which about a fourth is paved with mosaics. It had painted stucco walls.

(For more on this topic, go to p. 475 or 514.)

Warfare

As a senatorial province Cyprus had no Roman troops stationed there. We know of a garrison camp located in the capital of Paphos, but undoubtedly, local Cypriot militia served there. Roman naval contingents in the eastern Mediterranean kept down piracy on the high seas. And no doubt the heavy Roman military presence in nearby Syria (about 64 miles away) helped to intimidate any Cypriots that were tempted to get out of line. There was no military action on Cyprus during the New Testament period, in fact none until the

Jewish conflicts of the early second century, noted earlier in this chapter.

(For more on this topic, go to p. 482 or p. 526.)

Housing and Furniture

Our knowledge of the houses of Cyprus in the New Testament period is quite limited. But some useful generalizations can be made. When Paul and Barnabas came through, in such towns as Salamis, Paphos, and Kourion (Curium) they found houses of the Greek style. That is, houses had an unroofed court with rooms on two or three sides. A colonnade might run all the way around the court or face only a couple of the sides. Since property was more expensive in town than in the countryside, these courts were kept fairly small. And the builders then took advantage of upper space and went to two or possibly more stories. Most if not all bedrooms were on the second floor.

A plain black and white chessboard mosaic usually decorated the floor of the court. Underneath this homeowners

There was an element of modernity in the houses and public facilities of Cyprus. Here in a public latrine is a spigot in the wall that could be turned on to flush the facility.

commonly built a cistern where rainwater was carefully collected for household use. A porch often opened to the street outside the front door. The exterior was normally made of brick. Small and high first floor windows protected privacy, while second floor windows were larger and more varied.

In the rural areas, where land was a little cheaper, courtyards tended to be larger and completely surrounded by a colonnade. Houses spread out a little more and might be only one story. Comments on furniture appearing in the last chapter on Syria are appropriate here.

(For more on this topic, go to p. 483 or p. 526.)

Diet and Foodstuffs

Strabo, writing at the time of Christ, said that Cyprus grew "enough grain for its own use."[11] That included wheat and barley. In fact, at times the island also exported grain to Palestine, Athens, and Cilicia. The Cypriots raised a superior quality of olives and plenty of them. They shipped abroad quality wines from their extensive grape and wine production. The plain provided wine and grain products. Bees produced excellent honey for an otherwise almost sugarless world, with beeswax a valuable byproduct. The salt pans of Salamis and Citium produced the most famous brand of salt in the east.

Only the wealthy could afford to eat much meat. Cattle, sheep, and goats pro-

vided that meat, as well as milk, cheese, and butter. The average person lived on a diet of grain, vegetables, olive oil, and dairy products, with radishes, cabbage, and various kinds of beans adding variety, but at the present time information is not available to provide a comprehensive list of vegetables grown.

(For more on this topic, go to p. 484 or p. 527.)

Dress

As we come to this discussion, it is far more interesting to ask how Barnabas, Saul, and John Mark looked as they walked along the road from Salamis to Paphos than to ask about clothing in general. What the three wore is, of course, what they brought with them and what they would have worn in Jerusalem, or Antioch of Syria. And as we have already seen, men would have worn much the same clothing all over the eastern end of the Mediterranean in those days.

A tunic with sleeves and extending to about knee length served as the garment of choice. Though it may have been of linen, most tunics were made of wool. Whether in Palestine, Syria, or Cyprus, plenty of hilly or mountainous terrain provided pasture for sheep, making wool readily available. Lest we think that wool was too warm for the climate (it was probably summer in Cyprus when Paul and Barnabas and Mark arrived) we need to remember that wool breathes and that it can be woven with a tight or a coarse weave. Furthermore, air circulates around the body when one wears a loose-fitting tunic.

They belted their tunics at the waist, and not just for appearance or convention. The belt consisted not just of a cord or thin strip of material but a folded sash in which they could carry coins or other valuables. Then the men carried cloth or leather traveling bags (see Matthew 10:10), in which they could put their outer cloaks, additional sandals, or other personal effects.

As a Roman citizen Saul could have worn a toga. But evidently he did not. In that case he would have upstaged Barnabas and John Mark, who presumably were not citizens. And as they began their journey, the pecking order was "Barnabas and Saul" (Acts 13:2). Moreover, as a Jew Saul would not have cared to emphasize Roman domination. And as he ministered to Jews in the synagogues, he would not have erected a barrier between himself and them. Furthermore, as he traveled there was no hint that he was a Roman citizen. As a case in point, at Philippi the magistrates commanded that Paul and Silas be beaten, not knowing that Paul was a citizen and not subject to such treatment (Acts 16:22, 38).

We should make the point too that a majority of Roman citizens did not normally wear a toga on the street. As they carried on various manual tasks it would have gotten in the way. But certainly Sergius Paulus, the governor, and his associates would have worn togas as they carried on official duties.

All three of these men were city dwellers. Therefore they would have been more careful of their appearances than if they had come from the rural areas. Barnabas apparently came from Salamis originally and served in Jerusalem and Antioch. Saul came from the proud city of Tarsus, lived in Jerusalem, and ministered in Antioch. John Mark was evidently of the upper class in Jerusalem. He came from a substantial house and his mother had at least one slave, Rhoda (Acts 12:13). And Paul's ministry followed an urban strategy on Cyprus and everywhere else. They moved from city to city, preaching in the synagogues. The whole route from Salamis to Paphos was only about 100 miles, and the several cities along the way permitted them to walk from one to the next during the course of a day.

Being in the cities meant they needed to attend to their personal appearance and have constant access to barbers. As noted earlier, men in the provinces followed the Roman practice of keeping their hair short during New Testament times. And I have made the point that Paul condemned long hair on men in 1 Corinthians (11:14). Cyprus, like Corinth, was inhabited primarily by Greeks. Further, men in the city tended to be clean shaven or at least to have beards regularly trimmed.

Some elements of Cypriot society would not have been so careful of their appear-

ance. Men (often slaves or convicts) working in the mines, woodsmen felling timber, and shipbuilders were a more scruffy lot. They did not keep their hair as short or their beards as regularly trimmed. And instead of wearing only sandals on their feet, safety called for boots laced up to the calf a good part of the time. Conditions under which they worked would have injured their feet or at least have kept them from working effectively when they wore sandals. If the cold of the winter season or the dampness of the mine required an outer cloak, they simply picked it up and tucked it in their belts to keep it out of the way.

Comments already made about the dress of women in Palestine and Syria during the first century apply here. They also wore tunics extending to the knees, covered by longer robes, possibly a shawl over the head, and sandals.

(For more on this topic, go to p. 485 or p. 528.)

Family Life

Families in Cyprus lived basically the same as in Syria and Palestine, at least among the Jews. Families arranged marriages. The bride's family provided a dowry and the groom made a gift to the bride. Midwives commonly assisted in the birthing process. Male Jews were circumcised as sons of the covenant. Purification and dietary laws were at least partially followed. Because of the proximity to Palestine and the relative ease of travel, many went to Jerusalem for Passover from time to time and sent their annual half shekel tax for the support of the temple.

They weaned infants at about two years of age and mothers saw to the early care and upbringing of the children. Fathers took over the training of boys later on and prepared them to become adult sons of the Law and to follow in their occupations. There was little consideration, as with us, of the various employment options available. The synagogues provided some educational opportunities, at least in a Sabbath school for learning the Law. By the end of the century this began to include more formal and more extensive education. By New Testament times everyone on the island spoke Greek, though at home families often spoke Aramaic.

The Jews buried their dead, rather than cremating them, as Romans commonly did. The wealthy might afford mausoleums or family tombs in caves, but the majority buried their dead in the town cemetery. *(For more on this topic, go to p. 485 or p. 529.)*

Work, Travel, and Commerce

Work

During the New Testament period Cyprus thrived as a prosperous province, with plenty of employment opportunities. As already indicated in connection with agriculture, the farms produced adequate supplies of wheat and oats, and an abundance of high quality olives, grapes (wine), and honey.

But more important to the Cyprus economy were her mining and related industries. Western Asia and Egypt depended on Cyprus' extensive copper resources. In fact, the copper of Cyprus had become the predominant metal for the eastern Mediterranean bronze industries (Syria to Sardinia) from about 1300 B.C. on.[12] The implication is that Cypriots shipped only refined copper—in the form of ingots.

An extensive iron industry thrived on the island. Few iron products were shipped in finished form but were made to order by local smiths. Cypriot smiths produced weapons of special renown in the Hellenistic period.[13] Miners also exploited lead, gold, silver, and gypsum resources during New Testament times.

Shipbuilding served as another important industry on Cyprus. An early Roman historian commented that Cyprus was capable of "producing everything required to build and equip a ship,"[14] even though forests were being depleted during the first century. Depletion resulted from extensive use of wood for smelting and clearing of land for cultivation.

Commerce

Commerce flowed on the routes between Cyprus, Syria, Asia Minor, and points west.

Where Did Paul and Barnabas Find Accommodations?

Where did Barnabas and company find accommodations, food and laundry facilities as they traveled? The physician Luke reports on their going about from place to place, but he writes nothing about where they stayed and how they met their personal needs. In the first place, they were sent by the Antioch church and evidently carried funds for their support. Second, there were inns or places where businessmen and government agents could stay. Third, Oriental or Mediterranean hospitality was practiced from earliest times to the present. The Old Testament has accounts of perfect strangers being entertained in the home—from Abraham's day onward. Fourth, Barnabas had owned property on Cyprus and presumably still had relatives and possibly even property on the island. Fifth, by the time the trio landed there were converts of the persecuted preachers (Acts 11:19) who would probably receive them. Sixth, there were their own converts or others who might receive them into their homes. Jesus himself had given instruction to itinerant evangelists about staying in private homes (see, e.g., Matthew 10:11–13).

The freighters that carried official government cargoes during the first century A.D. were commonly 340 tons; those of Rome's grain fleet ran to 1,200 tons and were sometimes almost 200 feet long. Generally ships of the period carried a square sail, above which was a topsail, and at least a few oars for emergency or auxiliary work. Some freighters were designed to be driven by sail and rowers together. Merchantmen were fairly beamy: a length to beam ratio of four to one was common. Freighters generally had a cabin aft and above deck—big enough for the captain and his mates. Passengers, such as the missionary trio, lived and slept on deck. If they wanted some privacy, they might erect a tent-like shelter. Behind the cabin rose the sternpost, generally carried high and finished off in the shape of a goose head.

Depending on what was available, shipbuilders used pine, fir, or cedar for the planks of the hull. Inside, they used any kind of wood, preferring fir for oars because of its light weight. They made sails chiefly of linen, with ropes made of flax, hemp, papyrus, or sometimes leather. They often sheathed the underwater surface of the hull with sheet lead, placing a layer of tarred fabric between the hull and the lead. They painted ships in bright fashion with purple, blue, white, yellow, or green— unless they were pirate or reconnaissance vessels, in which case they might use a shade that matched sea water and served as a camouflage.

As to speed, merchantmen averaged four to six knots.[15] So the journey of the missionary trio between Seleucia and Salamis on Cyprus would have taken about twenty-four hours, with a favorable wind. It is about 80 miles from Seleucia to the eastern tip of Cyprus and another 50 along the southern shore of the Karpas Peninsula to Salamis.[16]

Ships of the early Roman Empire were well built and equipped with charts to plot courses, a lead line to test depths, semaphore flags to send messages, a ship's boat (usually pulled behind) for emergencies, an anchor, but not a compass. The lack of a compass—along with the fear of winter storms—dictated a sailing season of March to November in the Mediterranean. The point is that in the Mediterranean the skies are clear enough in the summer to permit mariners to sail by sun, stars, and landmarks.

Goods carried on these ships from Syria to Cyprus to points west almost defy tabulation. Luxury goods came from the east— the silk route from China terminated in Syria just across the water from Cyprus. And as noted, the dyes and finished goods of Syria moved west in quantity, often in Cypriot bottoms. The copper, iron, olive oil, wines, and more from Cyprus flowed west in ever-increasing quantity to satisfy the markets of Asia Minor and Italy.

Travel

The people of Cyprus traveled. Business people journeyed to points east and west, while the Jews of Cyprus sailed to Palestine on pilgrimage. Barnabas was one of those (Acts 4:36), but there were others (Acts 11:20).

In reverse, missionaries also traveled to Cyprus to convert the inhabitants to Christianity. Persecuted Christians, for example, journeyed to Cyprus after persecution broke out in Jerusalem (Acts 11:19). Then came Barnabas and Saul and John Mark.

After traveling about on Cyprus for some months, Paul and his party embarked at Paphos and headed for the Asia Minor coast about 180 miles away (Acts 13:13) from that point. With a favorable wind they could have made the journey in a little more than a day. What they found we'll see in the next chapter.

(For more on this topic, go to p. 486 or p. 533.)

NOTES:

[1] J. Hackett, *A History of the Orthodox Church of Cyprus* (London: Methuen & Co., 1901), 3.

[2] Josephus, *Antiquities of the Jews*, XVI.4.5.

[3] Hackett, Ibid.

[4] W. T. Arnold, *Roman Provincial Administration* (Chicago: Ares, 1974), 207.

[5] Camden M. Cobern, *New Archeological Discoveries*, 9th ed. (New York: Funk & Wagnalls Co., 1929), 552.

[6] William M. Ramsay, *The Bearing of Recent Discoveries on the Trustworthiness of the New Testament* (London: Hodder and Stoughton, 1915), 150–72.

[7] Prophyrios Dikaios, former director of the Department of Antiquities, Cyprus, lecture at the Oriental Institute of the University of Chicago, March 18, 1964.

[8] Louis P. De Cesnola, *Cyprus: Its Ancient Cities, Tombs, and Temples* (London: John Murray, 1877), 210–13.

[9] Georges Perrot and Charles Chipiez, *History of Art in Phoenicia and Its Dependencies* (London: Chapman and Hall, Ltd., 1885), I, 274–80.

[10] *Oxford Encyclopedia of Archeology in the Near East*, 4, 456.

[11] T. R. S. Broughton, "Roman Asia," *An Economic Survey of Ancient Rome*, Tenney Frank, ed. (Baltimore: Johns Hopkins Press, 1938), IV, 608.

[12] Jack M. Sasson, ed., *Civilizations of the Ancient Near East* (New York: Scribner, 1995), III, 1513.

[13] Broughton, 827.

[14] Ibid., 616.

[15] A knot is a unit of speed equivalent to one nautical mile, or about 6,080 feet, per hour.

[16] One of the finest introductions to a study of seafaring in the Mediterranean in ancient times is Lionel Casson, *The Ancient Mariners* (New York: Macmillan, 1959). See especially pages 215–227 for documentation on the preceding.

BIBLIOGRAPHY:

Antiquities Department of Cyprus. *A Brief History and Description of New Paphos.* n.d.

Cobern, Camden M. *New Archaeological Discoveries.* New York: Funk & Wagnalls, 9th ed, 1929.

Herscher, Ellen. "Archaeology in Cyprus," *American Journal of Archaeology,* April 1998, 309-54.

Karageorghis, Vassos. *The Ancient Civilization of Cyprus.* New York: Cowles Education Corporation, 1969.

Karageorghis, Vassos. *Cyprus: From the Stone Age to the Romans.* London: Thames & Hudson, 1982.

Karageorghis, Vassos. *Salamis in Cyprus.* London: Thames & Hudson, 1969.

Keshishian, Kevork K. *Everybody's Guide to Romantic Cyprus.* Nicosia: Government Tourist Office, 1966.

Mitford, T. B. *The Inscriptions of Kourion.* Philadelphia: American Philosophical Society, 1971.

Robertson, Noel, ed. *The Archaeology of Cyprus.* Park Ridge, N.J.: Noyes Press, 1975.

Soren, David, and Jamie James. *Kourion: The Search for a Lost Roman City.* New York: Doubleday, 1988.

Asia Minor and the Expansion of the Church

Chapter 18

(Acts; Ephesians; Revelation)

"Now when Paul and his party set sail from Paphos, they came to Perga in Pamphylia. . . . When they departed from Perga, they came to Antioch in Pisidia, and went into the synagogue on the Sabbath day and sat down." (Acts 13:13, 14 NKJV)

It was a beautiful sight. The arms of the breakwater of the Attalia (modern Antalya) port stretched wide to welcome Paul and his party as they sailed slowly toward the dock for the invasion of Asia Minor with the gospel. Along the coast on both sides of the town the mountains soared up in tier after amber-colored tier, clothed in a forest of leaves, woods-green and olive-green, the sea sweeping their feet.

We don't know what the trio expected as they approached the shore. Paul had spent his early years in Tarsus in southeast Asia Minor, but he had not been to this region. In fact, Paul and his companions were not really interested in Attalia. Nor in Perga, about twelve miles northwest of Attalia. Instead they traveled some one hundred miles north of Perga to Antioch of Pisidia.

Why Paul would have gone there seems fairly obvious when we look at his strategy of missions and the position of Antioch. He worked longest in fairly large and strategic centers with a mobile population, in centers that could act as springboards for the rapid spread of the gospel. Corinth and Ephesus illustrate this strategy.

Antioch was a main stop on the great eastern trade route from Ephesus to the Euphrates. The Seleucids had established the city in the third century B.C. to strengthen their hold on native tribes and to spread Hellenistic culture in this Phrygian area. More recently the Romans had used it

The port of Antalya

From Cyprus, Paul and Barnabas moved into the interior of Asia Minor.

York, New Jersey, Pennsylvania, Delaware, Maryland, and West Virginia—approximately the entire Northeastern United States.

The Land

Asia Minor is the general geographical term for the peninsula that forms the bulk of modern Turkey. Not in use in New Testament times, the descriptive seems to have arisen in the fifth century A.D. Anatolia commonly applies to that part of the peninsula west of the Halys River but is frequently used virtually as a synonym for Asia Minor.

Asia Minor is bounded on the north by the Black Sea, on the west by the Aegean and the straits of the Bosphorus and Dardanelles, on the south by the Mediterranean Sea, and on the east by a line running northeastward from below the Gulf of Iskenderun to the Euphrates and up that river to the Coruh (Chorokh) River and then to the Black Sea.

The Central Plateau

The mass of Asia Minor is a plateau 3,000 to 5,000 feet above sea level, tilted down toward the north and west. Extensive and irregular, this plateau is fringed on all sides by higher mountain ranges, but on the west

as a chief center for the pacification of southern Galatia. Moreover, it was located in a fertile valley at the natural center of its district.

Dangers still lurked in the area of Pisidia between Perga and Antioch when Paul came through on this first missionary journey. Some think that Paul had the trek through Pisidia in mind when he made his autobiographical comment about "perils of robbers" in 2 Corinthians 11:26. Scholars also suggest that the dangers in further missionary activity to the north of Perga caused John Mark to leave the other two and return to Jerusalem. And for that reason Paul refused to take the young man with him on his second missionary journey (Acts 13:13; 15:37–39). Of course there is no way of knowing whether either supposition is correct.

In any case, when Paul and Barnabas entered the region they had launched the message of the gospel into an area that dwarfed Cyprus, Palestine, Syria, or even the Nile Valley. Asia Minor had an area of approximately 200,000 square miles. It was equal to that of New England, New

GENERAL MAP OF ASIA MINOR

The Taurus Mountains

the hills are fewer and less imposing. While the plateau consists largely of rolling upland, highland massifs and numerous sunken basins occupied by lakes and marshes add variety. Today rivers entering the interior plains from the adjoining mountains flow into salt lakes and swamps. In New Testament times, however, farmers used the waters for irrigation and city dwellers of numerous large cities depended on them for water. Erosion has cut deeply into the surface of the northern part of the plateau—in many places there are steep valley walls and rugged hillsides.

As a whole, the central plateau has slender resources. Because of its enclosed nature, much of the plateau is arid. It supports little plant or animal life and is used for grazing of sheep. Not until the Hellenistic and Roman periods did town life develop there, and even then the larger towns were strung out along the edge rather than across the heart of the tableland. The middle part of the plateau has never produced an important coordinating center.

The Mountain Ranges

As already noted, the central plateau is surrounded by mountain ranges. The Armenian mountains extend westward and fork near the eastern boundary of the peninsula into two ranges—the Taurus on the south and the mountains of Pontus on the north. The northern rim of mountains rises to about 8,000 feet and the southern to 10,000 feet. Both consist of a series of overlapping ridges which permit only a few narrow and tortuous passages between the coast and the interior. East and northeast of the main Taurus system and parallel to it lies the Anti-Taurus Range.

Along the southeast edge of the plateau groups of volcanic peaks rise for a distance of about 150 miles. At the northeast end of this range stands Mount Erciyas Dagi (ancient Argaeus) at a height of 13,100 feet, the highest point in Asia Minor. Here in western Cappadocia, fertilized by lava dust and supplied with snow waters in summer, were fine orchards and the best horse pastures of the Near East. On them grazed a strain of race horses bred for the Roman circus.

From the Phrygian mountains on the west of the central plateau extend three mountain ranges, which delimit the valleys of the Caicus, Gediz (ancient Hermus), and Menderes (ancient Maeander). Since these valleys run east and west, they naturally conduct traffic in those directions. Thus the only open face of Asia Minor is toward the west and northwest, where the plateau ends in a staircase down to a piedmont country. Since the western shore is easily accessible, most invasions of Asia Minor that have had lasting results have been launched from Europe: e.g., Phrygians, Greeks, and Galatians (Gauls).

As intimated, the mountains of Asia Minor constitute formidable barriers, but there are strategic passes. The most important was, of course, the Cilician Gates north of Tarsus. Two passes made possible routes from Antalya (biblical Attalia) to Laodicea and to Pisidian Antioch or Apamea. Another gave passage between Seleucia in western Cilicia to Karaman (ancient Laranda) in the interior. One other gave access between central Cappadocia and eastern Cilicia.

While the mountains might and did constitute hindrances to communication and transportation, they provided sources of mineral wealth. Since Asia Minor is significant in the biblical narrative during Roman times, only a statement of minerals known and mined then is provided here. By Roman times the gold of Asia Minor had been depleted. Miners still dug a little silver in Pontus and some in central Cappadocia, and they produced some copper at Chalcedon and in Pontus and Cilicia. How many of the abandoned copper pits all over the country were worked in Roman times is not known. Iron came chiefly from Pontus, Cappadocia, Bithynia, and some from the Troad and possibly Caria. Lead was mined in western Mysia. Zinc seems to have been produced in the Troad and on Mount Tmolus. While various marbles of local importance were quarried, the variegated marble of Docimium was exported widely, as well as the white marble of the territory of Cyzicus (modern Kapidagi). Forests of pine, oak, and fir abounded in the mountains of both the north and the south.

The Black Sea Coastlands

The Black Sea coast is generally steep and rocky, with an irregular line of highlands rising 6,000 to 7,000 feet within fifteen to twenty miles from the sea and almost no coastal plain. Rivers of the region generally are short torrents which do not provide access to the interior, and good harbers are few. All of these drawbacks, plus the liability to earthquakes, tended to hold back the progress of the area.

The northern seaboard of Asia Minor may be divided into two sections. The eastern section consists of the biblical Pontus and Paphlagonia. A persistent northerly wind keeps the area cool and moderately rainy throughout the entire year. But Trapezus (modern Trabzon or Trebizond), the capital of ancient Pontus, enjoys the weather of a Mediterranean Riviera, screened as it is by the Caucasus Range.

The Cilician Gates

The straits of the Bosphorus

The mountains of the region provide ship and carpenter's timber and deposits of silver and iron, which probably gave rise in Hittite days to the earliest iron industry of Nearer Asia. The inner side of the mountains opened to fertile valleys, and the broad valley of the Lycus River served as a main artery for the Pontic area. Though poor harbors always were a drawback, Sinope (modern Sinop), at the most northerly point on the Black Sea coastline, did become a great maritime center.

The western section of the northern seaboard of Asia Minor consists of ancient Bithynia and Mysia. Here the climate is similar to that of the eastern region. The mountains stand farther back from the coast, leaving room for good grain and orchard country, though they provide little mineral wealth. And there are better harbors, an especially good one being located at Kapidagi (ancient Cyzicus).

Western Asia Minor

The western fringe of Asia Minor contributed most to the country's history in Greek and Roman days, with weather milder than the Greek homeland and soil that is more fertile. The coastline is highly intricate and broken, with many irregularly shaped islands.

Beginning in the north, the Bosphorus is sixteen miles long and on the average one mile wide, though it narrows in places to less than 700 yards. Both banks rise steeply from the waters. The Sea of Marmara is a natural creel for trapping shoals of fish on their annual migration from the Mediterranean to the Black Sea. The Dardanelles is twenty-five miles long and increases in width toward the south, from two-fifths of a mile in the north to four and one-half miles in the south. Because of evaporation in the Mediterranean, a continuous flow of water south from the Black Sea produces a strong current in the Bosphorus and Dardanelles. The current is three miles an hour at Istanbul.

Moving farther south along the Aegean coast one encounters a series of broad and flat-bottomed east-west valleys, well furnished with rich alluvial deposits laid by the rivers. But while this deposit makes for very productive valleys when drained and cultivated, it also contributed to the silting up of river mouths and harbors. For instance, the mouth of the Menderes is now several miles west of Roman times. The site of Miletus, once a focus of naval communication, is entirely cut off from the sea, while the harbor of Ephesus is completely filled in. This silting has also created marshes with their malarial threat.

In biblical times there were four broad river valleys in western Asia Minor: Caicus, Hermus, Cayster, and Maeander. Each provided access to an important hinterland. Pergamum was located in the Caicus. Smyrna, Sardis, and Philadelphia had access to the Hermus. The Cayster flowed north of Ephesus, and that great city of Diana also tapped the trade of the Maeander, as did Laodicea. In Roman times Miletus also lay on the Maeander.

The towns of western Asia Minor drew material for their textile industries from the sheep downs of the Phrygian tableland, with Laodicea known for its black wool and Pergamum for brocades and sheep hides. These were made into parchment, which displaced papyrus as a writing material.

The accidents of geography led to the development of two largely distinct cultures in Asia Minor. While the culture of the coastal cities became largely Greek or Greco-Roman, the culture of the plateau in the interior stayed essentially Oriental.

The Mediterranean Coastlands

Along the entire length of the southern seaboard of Asia Minor, the mountains descend steeply to the sea, except in the regions of Pamphylia and eastern Cilicia. Thus the Mediterranean coastlands entered little into ancient history. The southerly winds of the winter season brought sufficient rainfall for a rich forest growth which the Egyptians and many after them coveted for timber resources. Western Cilicia was the most trackless part of the coast and became known as a pirate hideout.

The mountains of southern Asia Minor are fold ranges, not rift valleys. In the north the western Taurus folds are so closely packed against the plateau of Anatolia that hardly any streams cut their way through the mountains to the sea. Here the mountains have long been a serious barrier to contact with the interior, with few roads accessing the region. The main Taurus, reaching 12,000 feet, are much higher than the western Taurus. Because they are not as wide as the western Taurus, erosion has cut a number of narrow and steep river valleys through the mountain chain. One of these gorges has been cut by the Yeziloluk, a tributary of the Cydnus, and forms the famous Cilician Gates.

Eastern Asia Minor

Eastern Asia Minor consists of a series of mountain ranges in the north, falling away into broken plateaus and finally into an undulating plain which continues into north Syria and Iraq.

Climate

Extremes characterize the climate of Asia Minor. While parts of the Aegean coastlands never experience frost, snow remains in the valleys for a third of the year in the east. The Black Sea coastal lands have a rainfall ranging from 25 inches in the west to 100 inches in the east and a mean temperature of 45 degrees for January and 70 degrees for August. The Aegean coastlands have a rainfall of 25 to 30 inches and a mean temperature of 45 degrees for January and 75 degrees in July and August. The Mediterranean coastlands have a rainfall of about 30 inches and a mean temperature of 50 degrees in January and 83 degrees in the summer. The central plateau has about 10 to 17 inches of rainfall; all districts have more than 100 days of frost during the year. The January temperature mean is 30 degrees and the summer mean about 70. In the east the climate is one of the most difficult and inhospitable in the world, with hot and dry summers and bitterly cold winters. Rainfall averages 17 to 24 inches, and temperatures of 40 degrees below zero have been recorded in January.

Rivers and Lakes

Several rivers have already been mentioned. Others should be noted. The most important river of the peninsula is the Kizil Irmak (ancient Halys), 600 miles long, which originates in eastern Asia Minor and flows in a great bend to the southwest and finally into the Black Sea through what was Pontus. Unfortunately its gorge is often too narrow to permit it to be an important means of communication into the interior. The Sakarya (ancient Sangarius), 300 miles long, originates in what was ancient Phrygia and makes a great bend to the east and flows into the Black Sea through biblical Bithynia. The Cestrus (c. 80 miles long) was the chief river of Pamphylia. The Calycadnus (c. 150 miles long) drained western Cilicia. And the Cydnus (c. 40 miles long), the

The Halys River

Sarus (780 miles long), and the Pyramus (230 miles long) flowed through eastern Cilicia, the latter two originating in the mountains of Cappadocia.

Numerous lakes might be mentioned. The greatest is Tatta, a salt lake in the central plain, some sixty by ten to thirty miles in winter and a mere marsh in the summer drought. A fine freshwater lake is Karalis, southeast of Pisidian Antioch on the road to Lystra. About thirty-five miles long, it lies at 3,770 feet in altitude. Southwest of Pisidian Antioch is Limnai, thirty miles long, at 2,850 feet in altitude.

(For more on this topic, go to p. 493 or p. 541.)

Government

When Paul and Barnabas ranged across Asia Minor in their missionary ventures, the Romans controlled the entire peninsula. This they had divided into six provinces, five of which the Senate governed and one (Cappadocia) the emperor.

Asia

Asia came into the Roman Empire by the will of the last king of Pergamum, who died in 133 B.C. The Romans organized the province in 129 and by the middle of the first century A.D. had included the territories of Phrygia and Pisidia; the total then approximated the western third of Asia Minor. A proconsul, assisted by three legates, acted as governor. He made his headquarters at Ephesus rather than at the old capital of the city of Pergamum. There were several free towns (such as Ephesus and Aphrodisias) that ran their own municipal governments and a few Roman colonies (e.g., Alexandria Troas, where Paul received his Macedonian call, Acts 16:8–10).

All inhabitants considered free city status very important. Any threat to that status struck fear into the hearts of even the unruly. Look at what happened when Demetrius the silversmith stirred up a mob against Paul in Ephesus. Some 25,000 rushed into the theater and yelled and demonstrated for two hours in support of their goddess Diana (Acts 19:34). Finally the city clerk was able to quiet them and to point the way of law and order: "Therefore, if Demetrius and his fellow craftsmen have a case against anyone, the courts are open and there are proconsuls. Let them bring charges against one another" (Acts 12:38 NKJV). Then he added the chilling warning: "For we are in danger of being charged

A Roman gate at Tarsus, commonly called St. Paul's Gate. It was there in Paul's day. Tarsus was the chief city in the province of Cilicia and the birthplace of the apostle Paul (Acts 21:39).

(Gustav Jeeninga)

The Seven Cities or Churches of the Revelation

chief town of the region Tarsus played some part in the civil wars of the latter part of the first century B.C. Apparently Pompey, Mark Antony, and Augustus all showed some favor toward the city and the region. Tarsus became a seat of learning in the east, with Athenodorus, Augustus' teacher and friend living there. The granting of Roman citizenship to some Jews of Tarsus (including Paul's family) is thought to date back to Pompey's actions (in the 60s).

There were six free towns in the province and some areas were governed by native kings until the emperor Vespasian reconstituted the province in A.D. 72. The governor, appointed by the Senate, resided in Tarsus. The eastern part had fertile farmlands that produced flax, fruit, olives, wine, and wheat in abundance. The western part of the province was still rather wild in New Testament times but was valued for its timber resources. The population of the province during the days of Paul's activity there has been estimated at about 900,000.

with rebellion [riot] for today's uproar, there being no reason which we may give to account for this disorderly gathering" (Acts 19:40 NKJV, alt.). With that he was able to persuade the crowd to go home. A city could remain free and have the right to run its own affairs only as long as it maintained law and order. If it did not, Rome had a heavy hand when it came to serious disturbances of the peace.

Asia was the jewel in the crown of empire, and this proconsulate was the most honorable post the Senate could confer—and no wonder. Its population conservatively stood in excess of 4,600,000.[1] There were the seven cities of Revelation 2—3. Among them Ephesus had perhaps 225,000 and Smyrna and Pergamum each 200,000. In addition to the seven, there were other large population centers; e.g., Miletus (100,000) and Aphrodisias (whose stadium alone could seat 30,000). The province's plentiful agricultural production and thriving commerce gave the region importance.

Cilicia

After a war with pirates, Rome pursued them to their bases in Cilicia and established a province there in 103 B.C. Gradually Rome extended the province to include much of the southeastern corner of Asia Minor. As the

Pamphylia

Pamphylia, in southwest Asia Minor, had also been established as a province in 103 B.C. It had been linked to Cilicia in pirate activities, with pirates disposing of their loot in her ports. At first the Romans joined Pamphylia to Cilicia in a single Roman province, but they separated it in 25 B.C. Lycia, on its north in the interior, was joined to Pamphylia in A.D. 43 just before Paul's first missionary journey. Lycia and Pamphylia each had a national assembly. The principal towns of Pamphylia were Side, Attalia, Perga, and Aspendos; of Lycia, Myra, Patara, and Xanthos. Excellent harbors played an important role in the province's prosperity. Quite a rural province, Lycia and Pamphylia together had a population of some one million in the first century.

A coin of Augustus declares his deity ("Divus") and that he was "Father of the Fatherland" (Patria). (Gleason Archer, Jr.)

Bithynia

Bithynia (in northwest Asia Minor) came into the Roman Empire in 74 B.C., when its ruler Nicomedes IV bequeathed his kingdom to the Roman people. A few years later Rome added Pontus to the province. Like all the other provinces of Asia Minor, except Cappadocia, Bithynia was ruled by a senatorial proconsul during the first century. But because of its strategic importance at the mouth of the Black Sea, the Romans converted it to an imperial province in the second century. There were several Greek towns on the Black Sea coast, some of which were free. A few Roman colonies were founded there early in the first century. Pontus had a separate provincial assembly. The municipal system was not well developed, but Bithynia probably had a population of a million during the first century. Most of its wealth came from agricultural production, but it also provided high quality marble and timber. Two of the chief cities were Nicomedia (the capital) and Nicaea (later site of the Nicene Council).

Galatia

The Romans annexed Galatia (interior Asia Minor) to the Roman Empire after the death of its king Amyntas in 25 B.C. The province included Galatia with its capital Ancyra (modern Ankara) and eastern Phrygia, Pisidia, and Lycaonia. A few towns such as Antioch of Pisidia and Iconium had colonial rights. Urbanization was slight and the population was small—perhaps a half million when Paul came through. Celts, who crossed over from Europe in the third century B.C., provided its population nucleus.

Cappadocia

Cappadocia sprawled along the eastern frontier of Asia Minor and the eastern frontier of the empire. After the death of its king Archelaus in A.D. 17, Tiberius made it an imperial province. Much of the land became imperial property. There were few towns, with the population just under a million in the New Testament period. The Romans took over government bureaucracy from the native kings. The governor (procurator), appointed by the emperor, had no troops but he could be supported by Syrian legions if necessary. Vespasian (69–79) stationed troops there by the end of the New Testament period as a guard against the Parthians.

(For more on this topic, go to p. 494 or p. 546.)

Religion

"Then Paul and Barnabas grew bold and said, 'It was necessary that the word of God should be spoken to you first; but since you reject it, and judge yourselves unworthy of everlasting life, behold, we turn to the Gentiles.'" (Acts 13:46 NKJV)

When Paul and Barnabas moved into Asia Minor, they went first to the Jews with the gospel. And as Bible students look at the narrative of Acts, they probably think especially about the reception the missionaries experienced at the hands of the Jews. But the major contest was with the ruler cult and the other pagan religions that had such a strong grip on the population at large.

Worship of Rome and the Emperor

Beginnings

The ruler cult in the Roman Empire began during the struggle of the Kingdom

Temple to the divine Domitian (81–96) at Ephesus. His persecution sent the apostle John into exile on the Isle of Patmos. The temple stood on a height opposite the city council chambers. Here in the foreground is the altar to the state cult, with the foundation of Domitian's temple behind it.

In this context Pergamenes easily switched their allegiance and deified the Roman state. What began there spread elsewhere in the eastern Mediterranean and in Rome itself. Then it was a short step from worshiping the personification or spirit of the Roman state to worshiping her rulers. The cult of Augustus and other emperors spread rapidly, beginning with the establishment of the empire. In 29 B.C. Augustus permitted the inhabitants of Asia and Bithynia to set up sanctuaries in their leading cities, dedicated to the cult of Roma and of Julius Caesar. There resident Roman citizens could worship. At the same time he let the Greeks of Asia set up a worship center for himself at Pergamum.[6] Romans were not yet ready to worship the living emperor, but Greeks of the east were prepared to do so.

By 26 B.C. shrines for Roma and Augustus had been established at Ephesus and at Philadelphia. By 9 B.C. apparently every major city in the province had an imperial sanctuary. Inscriptions have surfaced attesting the existence of priests of Augustus in thirty-four cities of Asia.[7]

Other regions quickly followed the example of Asia, with the ruler cult expanding to other places in Asia Minor, Macedonia, and as far away as Britain only six years after the conquest of the island in A.D. 43. It would be tedious to detail further the advance of the imperial cult, but something must be said about its significance.

of Pergamum to stand up to the Seleucids of Syria. When Antiochus III of Syria threatened Smyrna, it appealed to Rome, and in the year 195 B.C. "formally placed itself under Rome's protection by consecrating a temple to the deified *Urbs Roma* [city of Rome], a *new cult, hitherto unknown either in Italy or in Greece"* [italics mine].[2] Soon other principalities followed suit. Alabanda in Caria founded a temple to the Goddess Roma and established a festival in her honor.[3] Magnesia celebrated a festival in honor of the Goddess Roma, with tragedies, comedies, and farces.[4] Pergamum and Ephesus also established temples to Roma early on.

Parenthetically, we need to ask why the cities of Asia could declare for a Goddess Roma as the personification of the Roman state and then accept the divinity of Roman emperors. The answer lies in what was happening in the Kingdom of Pergamum. Just before 200 B.C. Attalos I of Pergamum had been honored with annual sacrifices at Sicyon and a great statue of him was placed beside that of Apollo in the agora there. At the same time a priesthood of Attalos was established at Athens. Then shortly after 188 regular deification of the Pergamene kings took place at their death, and at Pergamum they established the worship of the living king.[5]

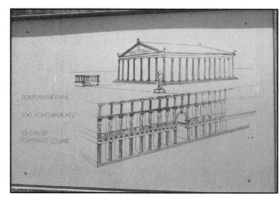

A reconstruction of the temple with a statue of the emperor and an altar in front of it

Cybele

Significance of the Emperor Cult

First, emperor worship dominated local public life. The calendar of the cult tended to bring an order to public affairs with the special observances of days, months, and seasons. The chief citizens filled the priesthoods of the imperial cult. As priests they sought to gain social and political prestige by means of service to the emperor. So they wound up building temples and other buildings, staging games and festivals and gladiatorial shows for public entertainment in his name. Commonly the games and festivals held in a community were jointly sponsored by the imperial cult and one of the other deities (e.g., Diana). The cult priests also made numerous benefactions in terms of distribution of grain and oil and feasts and banquets for the less fortunate.

What cities could offer their inhabitants commonly came as a result of the imperial cult. The wealthy and ambitious could find through the imperial cult a means of impressing their communities and achieving power and authority. (They were not really interested in public welfare.) And in this way the emperor could gain and maintain the loyalty of his subjects and guarantee the stability of the government and society.

Second, emperor worship erected one of the chief deterrents to the advance of Christianity. As noted, the calendar revolved around the worship of the emperor and the promotion of his affairs. The birthday of Augustus was a holiday. All festivals and games were held in honor of Roma, the divine emperor and/or one of the pagan gods. The sacrifices in honor of the emperor or one of the other gods provided the chief source of meat which the Council of Jerusalem forbade Christians to eat ("abstain from things offered to idols," Acts 15:29). The feasts held in the dining rooms located in temple gardens (see discussion of Diana following) had as a main feature the serving of meat and other foods offered to idols.

The whole of society was wrapped up in the ruler cult. Those who tried to live as consistent Christians stayed away from festivals, games, dramas, and other social events with religious connections. They came to be known as antisocial and even against the good of society as a whole. As they withdrew from a wide variety of social interaction, Christians could not conceal their beliefs and practices from other citizens of the country. They could not hide, and periodically mob action targeted them. The mob Demetrius the silversmith incited in Ephesus is a case in point (Acts 19:23–41).

A large part of the persecution of early Christians had nothing to do with the actions or wishes of the ruling emperor but arose from local conditions. And when the day came that the emperor tried to pressure everyone in the empire to engage in worship of the Goddess Roma and the emperor or suffer the consequences, local antipathy to Christians was already strong. Public pressure proved to be a real deterrent to acceptance of the gospel.

Other Pagan Religions

Men

"They came to Antioch in Pisidia, and went into the synagogue on the Sabbath day and sat down." (Acts 13:14 NKJV)

When Paul and Barnabas arrived in Antioch, they invaded a stronghold of the god Men, one of the chief gods of western Anatolia. From Men's home territory of Mysia (northwest corner of the province of Asia), his worship had spread throughout

Professional Dancers Honor Gods

These festivals honoring Cybele involved dances and dramatic presentations by dancers and actors who were more or less interchangeable. As itinerant professional dancers and instrumentalists, they put on performances appropriate to or peculiar to a given cult. Thus they changed their act to fit each worship center they visited and made their living as professional religious actors. They were not local villagers or cottagers.

Asia Minor and abroad. One of his chief worship centers stood high on a hill about fifteen miles south of Antioch at the modern village of Sagir. From the time when the temple was built there in the second century B.C., it had accumulated extensive lands cultivated by temple slaves, as had the centers of other ancient Asian deities. However, some of its estates were taken to provide land for Roman veterans of Legions V and VII when the city was refounded as Colonia Caesareia in 25 B.C. after the creation of the province of Galatia. Presumably Amyntas, the last Galatian king, had claimed temple lands which Augustus used for his Galatian colony, because the Romans were slow to violate existing sacred rights. But the temple was still wealthy and powerful. A second temple to Men stood on a hill called Kara Kuyu, an hour's climb above the city to the southeast.

Worshipers invoked Men to obtain healing, safety, prosperity, agricultural fertility, and the protection of tombs. As the moon god he was linked with the underworld. His most characteristic sign was the crescent moon, which might appear by itself or behind the god's shoulders. He was pictured as riding a horse or carrying a spear or scepter. He was regularly regarded as a "despot" or king of the gods.

At Antioch, Men and the cult of the Roman emperor and his family dominated the public religious life, particularly as the Roman military colonists gradually assimilated into local religious life. Leading citizens held the priesthood of Men. The temple to Roma and the imperial cult was begun soon after the accession of Tiberius to the throne (A.D. 14) and was hardly complete when Paul arrived. A triumphal arch celebrating Augustus' Pisidian victories was erected in A.D. 50, between Paul's first and second visits.

To attract crowds and to whip up enthusiasm for the god and for the imperial cult, the priests periodically put on athletic contests and theatrical or festival celebrations. They hired professional actors and dancers for these events, and plenty of money could be made from merchant activities connected with them.

Cybele

The name of the great mother-goddess of Anatolia was Cybele, considered the earth mother, the goddess of nature, of the mountains, of fertility. Attendant lions symbolized her role as goddess of the mountains, mistress of wild nature. People believed she could cure diseases, give oracles, and protect her people in war. Wherever one turned in the highlands of Phrygia there stood shrines and holy places dedicated to the worship of Cybele, Lady of the Wild Beasts, the great Phrygian goddess.

Religious Centers Were Cultural Centers

Religious centers also served as cultural centers, with public lectures, zoological parks, museums, concerts, art galleries, and botanical gardens. Cybele shrines in every province of Asia Minor established and maintained arboretums. And we should note that at Ephesus the shrine of Diana had woods that contained rare trees, and provided the usual lectures and concerts.

Diana or Artemis of the Greeks was portrayed as a beautiful woman. (The Louvre Museum)

Worship of the mother goddess goes back to the early Phrygians. Her statue stood in the door niche of the Midas Monument, sixth century B.C., near Eskisehir some 130 miles west of Ankara. Earlier yet, her worship goes back to the Hittites (1500 B.C.) and before. In fact, the prototype of Phrygian Cybele was found at Çatal Hüyük in south central Turkey, dating to perhaps 6000 B.C.[8]

A black stone, supposedly a meteorite, represented Cybele's throne and was brought from Asia Minor to Rome in 204 B.C. In 191 she got her own temple on the Palatine Hill. The cult spread from Rome to the provinces and took root in Greece, Africa, Spain, Gaul, and elsewhere in Italy. Her worship was associated with forms of Artemis and Venus worship. The agrarian character of the cult made it more popular with fixed populations than with soldiers. Women especially favored it. Her legendary lover was the youth Attis. She generally represented as enthroned in a shrine, wearing either a mural crown or a basket, carrying a libation bowl and either flanked by lions or bearing one in her lap.

Or she might be shown in a chariot drawn by lions.

The annual rites for Cybele began on March 15 with a procession of reed-bearers and a sacrifice for the crops. Worshipers celebrated at a spring festival in her honor.

The worshipers of Cybele typically played pipes made of reeds like oboes or bagpipes—with a shrill and carrying note. To the sound of rattles, drums, and shrill pipes accompanied by their own howls and yells, the dancers wheeled about and worked themselves into a state of frenzy.

The various cults, whether of Cybele or Diana at Ephesus or another cult somewhere else, found cult festivals to be good business. They drummed up support for the cults, and there was always something for sale. The festivals did what lectures on philosophy or beliefs could not in building interest in them.

Diana—Artemis

"So not only is this trade of ours in danger of falling into disrepute, but also the temple of the great goddess Diana may be despised and her magnificence destroyed, whom all Asia and the world worship." (Acts 19:27 NKJV)

Diana of the Ephesians was a fertility goddess. Here is one of her statues excavated at Ephesus— a many-breasted figure. (The Ephesus Museum)

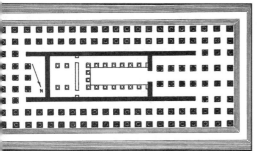

The Temple of Artemis or Diana at Ephesus was one of the seven wonders of the ancient world. A flight of ten steps led up to the pavement of the platform on which it sat, and three more to the pavement of the peristyle (colonnade around the temple). The temple was 180 feet wide and 377 feet long, and the roof was supported by 117 sixty-foot columns. These columns were six feet in diameter and thirty-six of them were sculptured at the base with life-size figures.

In front of the temple stood an altar. A floor plan and reconstruction of it appear here. (The Ephesus Museum, Vienna)

A Circuit of Games and Festivals

A circuit of games or festivals annually entertained worshipers at Ephesus, Smyrna, Pergamum, and a few other places. These were associated with the celebration of both Artemis (Diana) and emperor cults. A time of carnival included athletic games at the stadium, plays at the theater, concerts at the Odeum or Odeion. Of course enterprising individuals have always taken advantage of an opportunity to make a buck or a drachma or a sesterce from the milling crowds. Demetrius was one of the silversmiths who crafted small silver models of the temple of Diana or statues of the goddess as souvenirs for sale to the crowds who came to the festivals (Acts 19:24–27). The inroads of the gospel endangered their business.

So whimpered Demetrius the silversmith in Ephesus as he watched the missionary efforts of the apostle Paul and the success of the gospel. "Whom all Asia and the world worship" was not an idle claim. Diana's worship was practiced in nearly all the cities of Asia, and extensively on the Greek mainland, in Syria, Gaul, and Rome.

But Diana of the Ephesians had little in common with the classical Roman Diana or the Greek equivalent of Artemis. Yes, she was known as the daughter of Zeus and Leto and sister of Apollo—and the moon goddess and goddess of forests and groves and of hunting. But as worshiped in Ephesus and elsewhere in Asia Minor and in many other places all over the Roman Empire, she represented a form of the Asian mother goddess, the embodiment of the female principle, the goddess of fertility in man, beast, and vegetation. As the mother-goddess figure she represented more than fertility—also resurrection, the eternal return of life to the earth. She had become the patroness of maidens of marriageable age, the helper of women in childbirth. She was also the moon goddess, the goddess of wild nature and of the hunter and fisher-

The main temple at Sardis (another of the seven cities of Revelation 2 and 3) was also dedicated to Artemis. It measured 160 by 300 feet and was never finished. Most of its 75 Ionic columns are unfluted.

The altar of Zeus at Pergamum, sometimes called "Satan's Seat" (Revelation 2:13). The rectangular foundations of the altar were 125 by 115 feet. The altar itself rested on a great horeshoe-shaped plinth, thirty feet high. The arms of the horeshoe flanked twenty-eight sixty-foot steps which approached the altar on the western side. These steps led through a colonnade into a square court where the altar proper stood. The three outer sides of the monument were sculptured with scenes of struggle between gods and giants. The gods were victorious in this symbolic struggle between civilization and barbarism. The frieze, about four hundred feet long, is exceeded only by that of the Parthenon. The altar was carted off to Berlin, where it has been reconstructed.

man. In the peasant's mind such a divinity would ensure that his beasts and land were fruitful. To the intellectual, she presented the idea of an all-creating mother who sustained the universe. We need to remember that Artemis worship in Asia Minor also became intertwined with the veneration of Cybele (see discussion preceding).

The claim that Diana's image "fell down from Zeus" (Acts 19:35) helps to confirm the belief of many that initially her image or part of it was a meteorite. But as commonly represented in her statues that have been unearthed in Ephesus, she was a female figure with multiple breasts, with lions, bulls, and rams worked in relief on her shoulders

Gold offerings to Artemis found in the excavations at the temple (The Ephesus Museum)

and around her legs. A turret-crown appeared on her head.

The fame of Diana of the Ephesians had spread so widely that Ephesus became a kind of Lourdes of the ancient world. It was the "foremost cult center of all."[9] The city was "temple keeper of the great Artemis" (Acts 19:35 NRSV), a title granted by the Romans usually in connection with the imperial cult. But apparently Ephesus was temple keeper of both the emperor and Artemis. Temple properties of Diana at Ephesus included quarries, pastures, salt-pans, fisheries, and extensive estates.

Eunuch priests and large numbers of female slaves served in the temple of Diana. They do not appear to have been prostitutes, as was true of nearly all other cults of the Great Mother in Anatolia. Woods surrounded the area around the temple. In these woods and gardens there were stoas, off which dining rooms opened. These could hold three to twenty-five or more individuals, with lavish entertainments staged there by those who could afford them. Sacrifices offered to the deity could then be shared in a common meal, in a joining of religious and social life on a single occasion.[10] Places under the trees accommodated those who wanted to have a sort of "picnic."

Even in the homes of the wealthy, dining rooms usually could not accommodate more than nine persons. Frequently the upper classes staged dinner parties in the lovely temple gardens and sometimes served meat and other foods that had been offered to idols. Often wedding celebrations and dinners were held in these surroundings. It is against this background that we

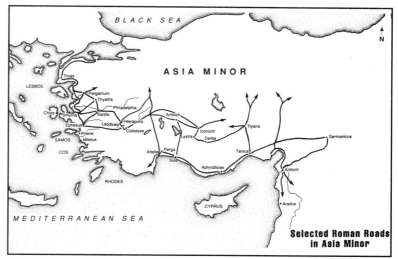

ASIA MINOR

Selected Roman Roads in Asia Minor

The route Paul and Barnabas took through Asia Minor, along the southern edge of the plateau, was on the Roman roads of the area. These were also the main roads that government officials and merchants traveled.

should read 1 Corinthians 8:10, "For if anyone sees you . . . eating in an idol's temple," or 1 Corinthians 8:4, "concerning the eating of things offered to idols."

The temple of Diana at Ephesus became fabulously wealthy, and unscrupulous persons tried to dip their hands into the till. City officials commonly sold priesthoods at what might be termed a public auction on terms by which the buyer obtained the benefits of office and the right to draw large sums from the temple revenues. In Paul's day the emperor Claudius (41–54) made an effort to curb

Close-up of the left corner of the altar

this corruption in Ephesus. He also tried to restrict excessive expenditures on hospitality for victors in the contests and for other aspects of the festivals. He discharged from office priests who had obtained priesthoods at public auctions. In the future, he prohibited priests and city councilors from giving or receiving money in connection with these sales.[11]

Notes on Paul's Missionary Activities in Asia Minor

The Route Taken

"But when they departed from Perga, they came to Antioch in Pisidia." (Acts 13:14 NKJV)

The question needs to be asked why Paul went to Antioch—and then on to Iconium and Lystra and Derbe. Antioch was the most important Roman colony in Asia Minor and the home of several senators and other high class Romans in the first century. These included Sergius Paullus, the proconsul of Cyprus. He may have urged Paul to pick Antioch as the main target of his first missionary journey in Asia Minor.

Paul's urban strategy may also have led him to focus on Antioch. That is, he used

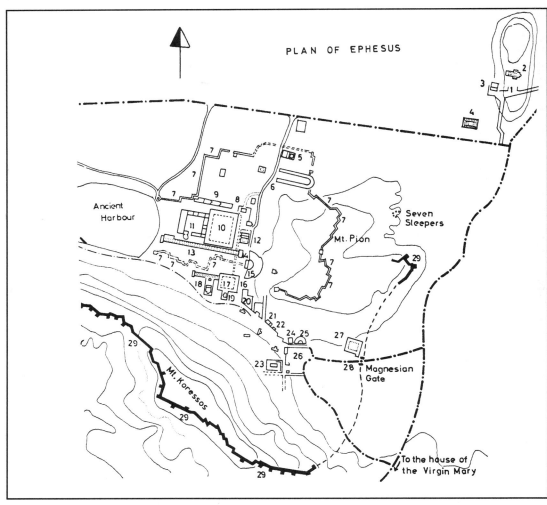

PLAN OF EPHESUS

1. Gate to Church of St. John
2. St. John's Church
3. Isa Bey Mosque, A.D. 1375
4. Temple of Diana or Artemis
5. Vedius Gymnasium
6. Stadium
7. City wall of Byzantine period
8. Byzantine baths, sixth century
9. Church of the Virgin Mary, a building used for commercial purposes in John's day
10. & 11. Harbor gymnasium and baths
12. Theater gymnasium
13. Arkadiane or harbor street
14. Hellenistic fountain
15. Theater
16. Marble street
17. Hellenistic agora, shops of silversmiths
18. Temple of Serapis
19. Library of Celsus.
20. Baths of Scholastika
21. Fountain of Trajan
22. Memmius monument
23. Temple of Domitian
24. Town Hall
25. Odeion or music hall
26. Roman agora
27. East Gymnasium
28. Magnesian Gate
29. City wall, built by Lysimachus, founder of the Hellenistic city

The great theater of Ephesus, capacity twenty-five thousand, where the mob scene of Acts 19 took place.

ministry in the cities to reach the surrounding countryside with the gospel. As one of the cities founded along the southern edge of the central plateau of Asia Minor, Antioch served as a center of civilization and foreign domination of the region. Like Attaleia (Attalia) on the coast and Iconium and Lystra, Antioch was a military colony—a colony of Roman veterans. A military road, the via Sebaste, linked all these cities, having been completed in 6 B.C. by the governor of Galatia. The road was 20–26 feet broad and could carry wheeled traffic along its entire length. Also, substantial numbers of Jews

Shops of silversmiths were found here in the Hellenistic Agora of Ephesus.

had settled in all these towns, as the Acts narrative indicates.

If Paul sought to minister to the Jews first, and if he followed an urban strategy, he would go where there were Jews and to towns that were strategically located. Moreover, he would be expected to stop at towns on the main road that were located at convenient distances from one another. Certainly the Roman road system was one of the important preparations for the coming of Christ and the spread of the gospel.

Antioch of Pisidia

By the time Paul arrived in Antioch, a large building program—decades in extent—had been essentially completed. An enormous imperial sanctuary comprising a temple to Augustus, porticos, and squares dominated the city center. By the time of Paul's second visit, it included a triumphal arch celebrating Augustus' victories over the Pisidians. The whole complex could be seen for miles across the plain of Antioch.

Ephesus

[While Paul preached in Ephesus] "all who dwelt in Asia heard the word of the Lord Jesus, both Jesus and Greeks." (Acts 19:10 NKJV)

Reconstruction of the Arkadiane or Harbor Street
that led from the theater to the harbor

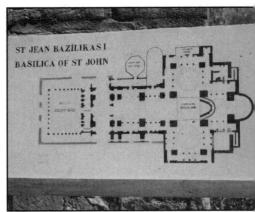

Plan of the Church of St. John, built by Justinian
(527–565)

Paul's urban strategy is abundantly clear from his ministry in Ephesus. This had become in effect the capital of the great province of Asia as the Roman governor made this his headquarters. Ephesus sat astride the main north-south road of the province and the important route into the interior, making it economically or commercially important. As the great center of Diana or Artemis worship and of the cult of Roma and emperor worship it had become religiously significant.

We don't know exactly how long Paul preached in Ephesus. Acts 19:8 and 10 mention two years and three months and Acts 20:31 gives a summary statement of three years. If we need to reconcile the two figures, it is easy to do so. Romans counted part of a year as a year. So a few months in year one, followed by the entire year of year two, followed by a few months of year three would equal three years in round numbers. But Paul may have preached somewhere else after the two years at the school of Tyrannus (Acts 19:9).

In any case, the gospel made a significant impact in the entire province. Paul later wrote a letter to the Colossians, though there is no record that he went there to establish a church. Also, the other six of the seven churches that John addressed in the Revelation (2—3) probably got a real shot in the arm from Paul's preaching in Ephesus.

In Paul's day Ephesus had a population of some 225,000. And archaeologists have

The place under the altar of the Church of St. John where, according to tradition, the apostle is buried

been working there ever since 1863 to discover what it was like. This is not a book on archaeology, but we do want to know about the great temple of Diana and the theater, because they figure in the Acts narrative.

Though there were earlier phases of the temple of Diana, the temple as Paul would have known it was begun before about 350 B.C. and completed in the middle of the third century B.C. The temple platform was 239 feet wide and 418 feet long. A flight of ten steps led up to the pavement of the platform and three more to the pavement of the peristyle (colonnade around the temple). The temple itself was 180 feet wide and 377 feet long, and the roof was supported by 117 sixty-foot columns. These columns were six feet in diameter and thirty-six of

The island of Patmos (thirteen square miles) off the coast of Asia Minor where the apostle John was exiled

The Monastery of St. John on the crest of Patmos

them were sculptured at the base with life-size figures. Praxiteles and Scopas are believed to have done some of the sculpture of the columns. White, blue, red, and yellow marble, as well as gold, decorated the structure.

Apparently open to the sky, the cella or holy of holies was seventy feet wide. In it stood the statue of Diana. The temple treasury acted as a bank in which cities, kings, and private persons made deposits. As noted earlier, sacred gardens and woods surrounded the temple, with facilities for dining. The sacred month especially devoted to the worship of the goddess was the Artemision (March–April).

A general view of the island and town of Patmos

The great theater, measuring some 495 feet in diameter, could seat about 25,000 persons. The cavea or auditorium of the theater was divided into three bands of twenty-two rows of seats each, and twelve stairways divided the cavea into huge wedge-shaped sections. The orchestra, the semicircular area between the stage and the seats, measured eighty by thirty-seven feet. Behind the orchestra stood a stage eighty feet long and twenty feet deep, supported by twenty-six round pillars and ten square ones. While it predated Paul's time, the theater was rebuilt between the reigns of Claudius (41–54) and Trajan (98–117).

The temple to the emperor Domitian, who ruled 81–96 is another great structure important to the New Testament narrative. Domitian demanded to be addressed as *"dominus et deus,"* lord and god. The persecution that he launched against Christians sent John to the Isle of Patmos, where he received the message of the revelation. Domitian's temple towered over the Roman State Agora on its high podium, approached from an open square. It had eight columns across the front and thirteen along the sides. Not much of it now remains.

The "school of Tyrannus" (Acts 19:9), where Paul ministered after minimal response in the Jewish synagogue, evidently served as a private school. Possibly it was one of the lower schools maintained for training children 7–14. If it were one of the gymnasiums, for 15 to 17-year olds, it probably would have been a public institu-

Clay pipes used in the plumbing of Ephesus

tion and not so readily available to Paul (see later discussion on education).

(For more on this topic, go to p. 496 or p. 548.)

Warfare

The New Testament period in Asia Minor was the time of the *Pax Romana,* the Roman Peace. The entire area had been pacified and it did not need more than local police, though the emperor stationed Roman troops on the eastern frontier in Cappadocia to protect against the Parthians. Cities did not need walls as they had in the past. And they did not have to perch on hills for protection, as was previously the case. The New Testament city of Pergamum came down off the acropolis and sprawled in the valley below, though the earlier city continued to function. The same was true of Sardis. Anyone visiting the sites of the seven cities of the Revelation (see Revelation 2—3) today can drive around in roughly flat territory and will not have to climb over piles of rubble left from defense walls of New Testament times.

While all this is true, small detachments of troops were stationed along roads that ran through some mountain areas to control banditry. The Romans also posted substantial military detachments on the military highways of eastern Anatolia, especially on the route that ran from the Black Sea to the upper Euphrates. Soldiers and officers of the Roman army were also used for super-

vising the building of the Roman road system.

(For more on this topic, go to p. 500 or p. 568.)

Housing and Furniture

Unfortunately solid archaeological investigation of houses in Asia Minor of the New Testament period is very limited. This is true because in places like Pergamum the modern city covers the New Testament site. In other places, such as Antioch of Pisidia and Miletus, archaeologists have concentrated on theaters, temples, baths, and forums/agoras. To most, it is much more exciting to work on a temple or a city theater than a house or two—and much more gratifying to their financial supporters. Then, too, public buildings made of stone are far more durable than private houses made of cheaper materials.

But we do have a collection of houses unearthed at Ephesus that provide some basis for discussion. Two blocks of houses on the hillsides across the main street from the Temple of Hadrian have been fully excavated and evaluated. Since they were lived in for hundreds of years and were extensively remodeled, archaeologists had considerable difficulty determining how they looked in the first century. They were all arranged around open courtyards, often surrounded by a colonnade or peristyle. The walls were decorated with paintings as at Pompeii and Herculaneum, but we can-

An upper courtyard in one of the houses on "villa hill, Ephesus"

Wall frescoes with protective covers in a lower courtyard of one of the houses on "villa hill," across from the Baths of Scholastika, Ephesus.

or at some other shrine in another city (see under Religion).

Furniture in Asia Minor was similar to that of Syria (which see). Remains of bronze furniture and fragments of ivory inlay have been found in the excavations of Ephesus. *(For more on this topic, go to p. 500 or p. 569.)*

Diet and Foodstuffs

As I have traveled around in Cilicia and Western Turkey, I have been impressed that people in the days of Paul and John must have eaten well. At least that is the case in Tarsus and the river valleys of the province of Asia, if the lush fields and beautiful peaches, apples, cherries, and other fruits are any indication.

Almost everywhere on the peninsula they cultivated various kinds of wheat and barley, though some areas could not produce enough and had to import grains, especially from Egypt. The province of Asia produced an unusually large quantity of wheat and barley, while a high quality of barley grew in Galatia. The wheat of Assos was highly regarded. And we have good reports of wheat production in Pontus, Cappadocia, Bithynia, Phrygia, and Pamphylia.

Asia Minor may well have been the original home of the grape.[13] Ancient commentators had good things to say about the wine production and exports of Phrygia, Galatia, Pamphylia, Cappadocia, and the Ephesus area. Cappadocian wines were especially highly regarded, along with those of some of the islands—e.g., Chios, Lesbos, and Rhodes. Several varieties of raisins were produced.

The raising of olives was restricted to the valleys and the coast, especially the coastal plains of the west. Olives do not flourish much above about 2,000 feet in altitude.

Fruits and nuts grew in abundance in most regions of Asia Minor, as did apples, pears, peaches, cherries, and figs. The most important fruit economically was the fig, produced primarily in the west and southwest, which was dried and then distributed widely. The dried figs of Caria and Antioch were especially important. Among the nuts,

not be sure of the subject matter in the first century. The floors were covered with mosaics.

In the eastern block of houses there was a two-story house of a wealthy family. That consisted of a courtyard surrounded by an Ionic colonnade, next to which was a kind of reception hall or living room with a roof supported by four columns. Off that opened a dining room and a large assembly hall. A stairway led from the reception hall to the second floor. There were also several middle class houses in this block.

In the western block of houses there were five luxurious peristyle houses. All of these had running water. The walls were painted with frescoes and the floors decorated with mosaics. One two-story house had twelve rooms and a living space of about 3,000 square feet. It had three rooms covered by barrel vaulting, one room that was discernibly a kitchen and another that was a bathroom with a bath tub. It would be tedious to describe the other four in detail because they were so similar. One of them had a wall fresco representing Socrates seated that can be dated to the first century.[12]

Dining rooms did not seat over nine even in the wealthy homes, and many houses of the lower classes had no dining rooms. So if someone wished to throw a special party, he could do so in the dining rooms in the gardens of Diana at Ephesus

almonds, hazelnuts, and chestnuts were the most popular. Pontus and Sardis were chief nut producers.

Most holdings, small and large, were self-supporting in raising vegetables and seasonings. Farmers grew pulse, varieties of beans, chickpeas, lettuce, onions, radishes, cucumbers, and more. And then there were licorice, mastic, mustard, caraway, rue, and sage—to note some of the herbs and seasonings.

Of course agriculture involves more than the production of grains, fruits, and vegetables. Perfumes manufactured from flowers helped offset odors in a society without deodorants and overwhelmed by stenches of various kinds. Perfume production centered in Smyrna, Pontus, Cilicia, Lycia, Phrygia, and Tarsus. Cilicia was the chief producer of flax (hence linen), with Sardis, Ephesus, and Smyrna important competitors. Alabanda in Caria was the chief producer of hemp—for making rope and strong fabrics. Ephesus was one of her competitors.

Animal Husbandry

Agriculture also involves animal husbandry. And that in turn helped to round out the diet of the region. The mountainous zones in Asia Minor, as well as the plateau, provided abundant grazing areas, with goats and sheep raised in large numbers all over the peninsula. Especially good grazing lands were to be found in Pontus, Phrygia, Galatia, Cappadocia, Lycia, and Pisidia. While the whole of Asia Minor was known for its wool, Phrygia with its centers of Laodicea, Hierapolis, and Colosse produced the famous black wool. And along with Miletus they marketed their products far and wide. In fact, Miletus furnished breeding stock for Italy and elsewhere. The long-haired goats of Phrygia and Cilicia provided hair for military cloaks, sacks, and horse blankets.

Goats were important for their milk and cheese as well. Bithynian cheeses surpassed all others outside Italy. Cheeses of Mysia, Pergamum, and Phrygia also commanded a good price. Cattle raising was especially important in Pontus, Bithynia, Mysia, and Pergamum. With cattle came the produc-

We know that there were numerous synagogues in Asia Minor, but so far two early ones have been excavated, one at Miletus near the harbor and one at Sardis. The Sardis synagogue was located in the center of town next to the gymnasium. Here it is under reconstruction.

tion of milk and cheese, though they took second place to goats for that. As generally true in ancient society, the lower and middle classes rarely ate meat—only the wealthy could afford it.

Oxen did most of the plowing, pulled oxcarts, and were important for their hides and cheeses. The best horses in the empire came from near the Taurus Mountains, from Cilicia and Cappadocia. The Romans maintained imperial horse ranches in Phrygia. Bees provided honey for an otherwise almost sugarless world, and their wax was a valuable by-product. Though barnyard fowl are mentioned, they seem to have been unimportant. Mountainous regions afforded natural hunting grounds. In Pontus some people made a living from hunting.

(For more on this topic, go to p. 501 or p. 570.)

Dress

When Paul and Barnabas walked into Antioch of Pisidia, they were wearing the kind of clothes they had been wearing for years—in Palestine, Syria, Tarsus, and Cyprus. And they were not out of place here or wherever else they went, because clothes were basically the same in all these places. They had on wool tunics with long sleeves, extending to the knees, and sandals. If it was toward dusk, they probably had thrown their cloaks over their shoulders because it was now likely late summer or early fall. And there was a nip in the air in the highlands. It had not been necessary for them to put on boots to hike over the mountains from Perga because the Roman road, the via Sebaste, was well surfaced for foot or wheeled traffic.

When they traveled from Lystra and Derbe and went back over the mountains to Perga and Attalia to return to Antioch of Syria, it may have been late enough in the fall for them to wear short, knee-length pants under their tunics in order to keep warm. Women they met in their travels would also have worn tunics—knee-length or angle-length—and sandals, and perhaps shawls over their heads. And they would have worn cloaks, depending on the weather.

Men had short hair and women hair of shoulder length. Since Antioch, Iconium, and Lystra were colonies of Roman veterans, there would have been a tendency for men to follow the prevailing Roman practice of the day to go clean shaven or have their beards trimmed close.

(For more on this topic, go to p. 501 or 571.)

Family Life

Jews

If we accept a commonly suggested population figure for Asia Minor in New Testament times, there were some thirteen million living on the peninsula.[14] And if we accept the figure of over a million Jews living there,[15] we have some idea of how at least a significant portion of the population carried on. In the days of Augustus Caesar the Roman government had granted the Jews of the empire the right to live as they had been accustomed.[16] That meant he had exempted them from emperor worship, military service, and some civic duties on the Sabbath and holy days, and that they could send the annual temple tax to Jerusalem and practice their faith as the Mosaic Law and custom prescribed. They could circumcise their infant males as sons of the covenant and follow purification rites and dietary laws as

What Can We Know about Jews in Asia Minor?

Current research on the Jews of Asia Minor leaves us with many unanswered questions, but permits some generalizations that can be made with reasonable certainty.

It seems that as early as the third century B.C. Seleucids permitted them to "follow their own laws."

During the first century B.C. the Romans confirmed numerous special rights to the Jews (e.g., to hold Jewish festivals, feasts, and gatherings; to send the annual temple tax to Jerusalem; exemption from enrollment in the legions and taking part in public events on the Sabbath).

Jews were so numerous that their special privileges created considerable problems for society at large.

Cities or provincial governments periodically attempted to abridge Jewish rights. As a result, friction arose.

Difficulties occurred especially when Jewish citizens demanded exemption from civic religious practices (e.g., emperor worship or worship of local deities). They wounded civic pride by abstention from idolatry and limited participation in the main currents of civic life.

Evidently Jews generally kept the Sabbath, sent the annual temple tax to Jerusalem, practiced circumcision as sons of the covenant, went to synagogue worship, kept the Mosiac Law, and many traveled to Jerusalem for Passover.

Apparently the Jews of Asia Minor did not give support to the Jewish revolt that resulted in the destruction of Jerusalem in A.D. 70 or in the revolt of 116–117.

It seems that Jews developed a sense of belonging in their communities and made significant social contributions without compromising their Jewish identity.[18]

Illegitimate Children of Roman Soldiers

Roman soldiers were not supposed to marry while in service, but they often had de facto wives and thus illegitimate children. Presumably this prohibition existed to avoid encumbrance and distraction, but evidence suggests that families of soldiers did accompany them at least part of the time. Though Septimus Severus lifted the ban in A.D. 197, individual emperors granted special privileges before that from time to time. Claudius (emperor 41–54), contemporary with Paul's missionary work in Asia Minor, permitted soldiers to name wives and children as beneficiaries in their wills. Soldiers who were not citizens became citizens on discharge.

Judaism prescribed. Moreover, they could go on pilgrimages to Jerusalem at Passover time and for other feasts. As a manner of fact, Jews of Cappadocia, Pontus, Asia, Phrygia, and Pamphylia were present in Jerusalem on the day of Pentecost—from five of the six provinces of Asia Minor (Acts 2:9–10).

It is unnecessary to repeat what it was like to live as Jews of the Dispersion during New Testament times. Reference to the chapter on Syria will be enough. We need to be aware that Jews had become fully integrated into their communities in Asia Minor economically and in other ways, however. They were as prosperous as other members of the community and were engaged in virtually all occupations. As in other families, Jewish boys were expected to follow in their fathers' occupations, but we do not have evidence of whether an apprentice system existed.[18] Boys attended synagogue schools, but they had other opportunities for education (see subsequent discussion).

Other Members of the Community

But what about the rest of society? It resembled the Jewish experience. The families arranged marriages, and the father of the groom's family, the *paterfamilias*, had to give his consent. The mother of the bride was also actively involved in the process, and presumably the bride and groom agreed. The arrangement was usually celebrated by an engagement party, during which agreements and gifts were exchanged. Since all

Reconstructed entrance to the Roman gymnasium at Sardis

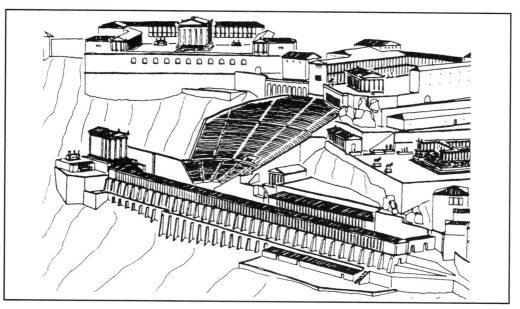

An artist's sketch of the west side of the acropolis at Pergamum. In the side of the hill is the great theater. Above that on the right stands the temple of Athena, goddess of wisdom. Appropriately, next to her temple was the great library of Pergamum, second only to the library of Alexandria. The Pergamum library of perhaps two hundred thousand volumes gave great stature to the educational program of the city. Pergamum also gets credit for the invention of parchment, which provided writing material for the city's many academic pursuits. Note that to the right of the theater on the middle level is the altar of Zeus, discussed earlier under religion. On the crown of the hill is the Temple of Trajan, built after the close of the New Testament period.

this negotiation and agreement was to enhance or preserve the economic and social position of the families involved, and perhaps to advance the career of the groom, presumably there was more maneuvering among the upper classes than among those lower on the social scale. Possibly the bride and groom had more to say about arrangements among the poorer classes. Marriages were arranged within class everywhere in the empire.

Wedding rites probably began at the home of the bride, and she and her friends then processed to the home of the groom. When the bride arrived there, a religious ritual occurred to mark her entry to her new home. And the bride and groom grasped their right hands symbolically. Dowry agreements or contracts were signed, which provided for the husband's return of the dowry in the event that the marriage was dissolved by divorce or death. Evidently

children were entitled to part of the mother's dowry for their maintenance if there were children at the time of divorce or estate settlement. If neither bride nor groom had a living father, the couple would arrange their own marriage and their own contracts.

When a baby was born to a Roman citizen, it would be placed on the ground for the father to raise up ritually to indicate that he accepted its paternity and wished to raise it. The doorway of the house would then be decorated with flowers and a sacrifice made to the family gods. On the eighth day after the birth of a girl and the ninth for a boy, a party was held for family and friends, who came with presents—a kind of baby shower. The child received a name and a special necklace to indicate that it was freeborn. At the age of fifteen a boy went through a ceremony during which he put aside his childhood dress and the necklace and donned his adult *toga virilis*. At puberty girls participated in a ceremony in which they sacrificed their girlish toys and were given a special bridal headdress.

Education

As boys and girls grew up, their mothers especially saw to their education and development. And fathers coached their sons in pursuit of a career. Of course it was expected that a son would follow in his father's footsteps. But there were more options available in the first century than there had been in the past. And an educational system had been developed to help them to be more effective in their chosen pursuit. We must not get the idea that education would necessarily broaden the range of career options, however, or present an array of options from which to choose, as is true with us today. Education especially helped the upper classes maintain their superior place in society and to do better what the family had always done.

Asia Minor emphasized education, with scores of gymnasiums in the larger cities and in the small urban centers as well. The gymnasiums included rectangular open spaces, exercise grounds, surrounded by colonnaded porticos, off which opened instructional rooms. Here boys fifteen to seventeen learned physical training, music, some mathematics and science, but especially literature and speech and social behavior. Thus what they got there became a sort of preparation for citizenship. As it provided companionship and fostered common ideas and interests, it became the principal training ground of the young and tended to replace family life to an important degree.

Directors of the gymnasiums were called *gymnasiarchs*, and they were chosen from among the most influential and most affluent of the citizens. The position was one of the highest municipal honors. His was an administrative position; he did not actually teach. Sometimes a city might maintain a gymnasium, but frequently wealthy private citizens endowed them or otherwise provided financial backing. To win the title of "Benefactor" was much coveted.

Of course the youth could not enroll in what amounted to high school without preparation. Lower schools for children seven to fourteen were private and were maintained by tuition fees. But there was a magistrate, a "pedonomos," who supervised the programs of the lower schools. A child learned reading, writing, gymnastics, music, and sometimes painting there. The degree of opportunity that girls enjoyed in attending lower school is not known, but supervisors of girls' education are known in several places, including Pergamum and Smyrna.[19]

Education beyond the gymnasium was available for the *neoi,* aged eighteen to twenty. Sometimes they shared facilities with the gymnasium group; sometimes they had facilities of their own. Coming only from the most wealthy families, the *neoi* studied athletics, music, literature, philosophy, and civic affairs. For more serious study they could go on to one of the universities—Pergamum or Rhodes for philosophy and rhetoric, Cos or Pergamum or Ephesus for medicine. Hellenistic education showed little concern for science and technology. More information on education for a specific career appears in the next section of this chapter.

Before the time of Christ, the Greeks of the eastern Mediterranean, perhaps at the University of Pergamum, had codified or canonized the classics and listed what should be studied in the schools: ten Attic orators, ten historians, ten painters, philosophers, poets, and more. Then they went on to select lists of plays to be studied in school classes—from Aeschylus, Sophocles, and others.[20] This effort tended to influence the classical literature that was to survive. For example, dramas not studied in school existed in fewer copies, and some of them finally disappeared.

Social Conduct in Village Life

Extensive studies of funerary monuments and temple records of rural Anatolia throw interesting light on pagan society during the New Testament period. The tomb inscriptions call down divine punishment for violation of the tombs, and confession inscriptions record the admission of guilt in crimes against society and the gods.

What they reveal is a strict morality and respect for divine authority. Offenses confessed included such things as theft of clothes from a bathhouse and money from a granary, cheating orphans out of their inheritance, perjury, deception, offenses against the gods and their sanctuaries, and much more. No malefactor could escape the glare of the gods of justice and of their punishment when wrongdoing occurred.[21]

(For more on this topic, go to p. 502 or p. 572.)

Work, Travel, and Commerce

Work

Almost everyone in Asia Minor had plenty of work during the first century. The Roman Peace, good communications, and abundant resources all contributed to a general prosperity that continued throughout the century and reached a peak early in the second. And in most areas there was enough diversity in the economic base to prevent a complete catastrophe if some calamity struck.

Textile Production

"A certain woman named Lydia heard us. She was a seller of purple from the city of Thyatira, who worshiped God." (Acts 16:14 NKJV)

Textile production persisted as the most important industry in Asia Minor. In fact, they produced woolens almost everywhere grazing was possible. Coarse woolen goods were worked into cloth by women of individual households for their families and for local use. Professionals prepared goods for general sale and for export. Long before the Roman period, Miletus had become a predominant center for the processing of fine wools for commercial purposes. By Roman times several other cities of the Ionian coast competed effectively with her and used the purple dyes from nearby murex beds to good advantage. And Sardis had learned to use the madder root to produce "Sardis red" blankets, tapestries, and curtains for the luxury trade.

Primacy had, however, passed from Miletus to the district of Laodicea with the adjacent cities of Hieropolis and Colosse. Laodicea had a glossy black wool and alongside it dyed cloth with madder that rivaled wool dyed with murex purple. The area of Laodicea produced a wide variety of goods, but especially fine cloaks that were fairly rain repellent and plain tunics trimmed with purple borders. The woolen industry of Hierapolis had been organized into groups of skilled workers who were wool washers, fullers, dyers, and workers.[22]

We have made no effort to note all the cities of Asia Minor where the woolen industry was well established. The reference above to Lydia of Thyatira calls attention to another town (between Pergamum and Sardis) where the cloth industry prospered. The dye used there was probably madder root. In all the centers where woolen fabrics were produced for export it appears that basic spinning and weaving were done at home by women and slaves. Skilled workmen produced specialty items and worked the cloth into finished products.

Cilicia was probably the most important region for the production of linen, and by the end of New Testament times Cilicia and Judea seem to have captured the linen market from Egypt. Sardis, Thyatira, Ephesus, and Miletus also manufactured quantities of linen goods. Cos, especially, was known for its silks, and apparently cotton was produced in Pamphylia.

Other Industries

The invention and production of parchment as a writing material had made Pergamum famous. Tanners and leather workers appeared at Mitylene, Ephesus, Philadelphia, and elsewhere. Guilds of bakers were fairly strong at Ephesus, Thyatira, Sardis, and elsewhere.

Builders rated Pontic iron highly for building purposes, while Lydian iron became famous for swords, razors, graving tools, and other specialty items. We do not know whether the superiority of Lydian iron was due to its chemical composition or the method of tempering. While Asia Minor as a whole was not known for its production of gold and silver, there was a guild of silversmiths and goldsmiths at Smyrna. And evidently,

Medical Education

Medical education involved, first and foremost, the writings attributed to Hippocrates, though much of this body of material was written later. Instruction even included how to behave in the sickroom. There were groups of physicians offering instruction in some of the major cities, but essentially the trainee did his apprenticeship under a practicing physician. Students went with the physician as he made his rounds and examined his patients. This was not a "quick fix." One might study this way in several cities over a period of time. The famous Galen of Pergamum studied in this manner for eleven years.[25]

from the reference beginning in Acts 19:24, there was a guild of silversmiths at Ephesus that made shrines or statuettes of Diana for the tourist trade. There was also a luxury trade in silver plate for wealthy households. The Romans commercialized glassblowing in the empire and it became quite inexpensive. How many production centers there were in western Asia Minor we do not know, but apparently Pergamum was one of them.

Potters were probably the most common of all artisans. The three kinds of commercial production included: (1) large jars to hold wine, oil, or grain; (2) table ware; (3) works of art in terra-cotta. The more important centers of pottery production in the first century included at Samos, Pergamum, and Tralles (east of Ephesus).

The greatest shipbuilding activity took place in the ports around the Sea of Marmara and along the Black Sea in Bithynia, Paphlagonia, and Pontus—where there were marvelous stands of timber and iron mines. But we must not ignore the dockyards of Caria (southwest Asia Minor) and Cilicia, and the fact that most ports had one or more shipbuilders. We could highlight further centers of industry in Asia Minor. But the truth is that apart from great centers of textile production or shipbuilding, or manufacture of certain luxury goods, most industrial

production was intended to supply local needs and involved individual workers in small shops.

Labor in Asia Minor

Labor on the farms and in the commercial and industrial activity of Asia Minor in the first century was essentially free labor. Slavery is thought to have been restricted largely to household service.[23] Presumably slave labor did not then compete with free labor to keep wages artificially low. We need to remember, however, that women, assisted by slaves, produced a lot of the wool thread and did some weaving at home. Commercial textile producers do not seem to have done much spinning or weaving.

Industrial and commercial guilds existed in most of the important industrial and commercial centers, but most of the information available to us dates from the second century and following. We have no evidence covering the training of workmen, nor whether there was a formal apprentice system, nor whether there were grades or levels of status within the guilds (e.g., apprentice, journeyman, master craftsman).

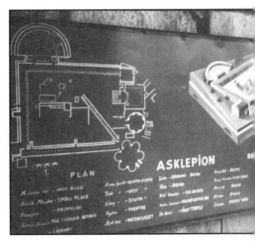

A reconstruction of the famous medical center of Pergamum, which reached a height of recognition in the second century under the leadership of the great Galen. This Asklepion, or center of the god Asklepios, god of healing, had a temple to the god dormitories, a theater for lectures and recreation, and more.

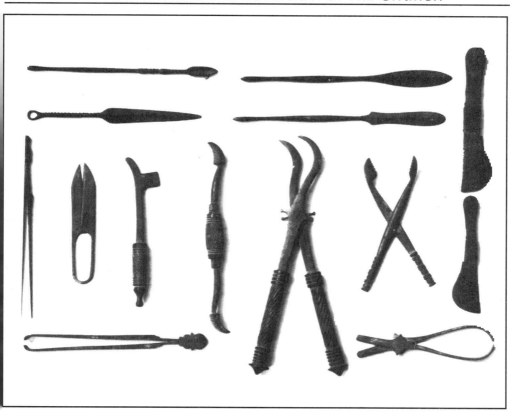

Certainly the surgeons at Pergamum were familiar with the knives, scalpels, tweezers, and clamps used by the doctors of Pompeii in Italy during the first century. Surgical arts were becoming quite sophisticated by the first century A.D.

The Professions

Men engaged in the professions in Asia Minor, including architects, physicians, teachers, lawyers, and actors and performers in the games were held in high regard and often gained wealth and political prominence. Apparently cities employed architects on a permanent basis; some were hired to build individual structures.

Some Asia Minor men went to Alexandria to study medicine, but there were distinguished schools on the peninsula: the Asclepium of Cos, the Herophileian school of Men Carou near Laodicea, the Asclepium of Pergamum, a school at Smyrna, and one at Ephesus. These schools contributed much to the development of medicine in Asia Minor. There were private physicians, but some cities also maintained public physi-

cians—which formed a real "health service" directed by master physicians.[24]

A regular budget item for all cities imitating the Greek tradition was public education. Teachers might gain great wealth from private lessons to wealthy pupils. Sophists served as itinerant professors of higher education who traveled extensively through the Greek world. They were not a school or a movement and had no set of common instruction. Their curriculum included mathematics, history, geography, anthropology, techniques of persuasion and argument, grammar, literary criticism, speculative philosophy, and more. Smyrna, Ephesus, and Pergamum especially enjoyed enhanced reputations from sophists of note who came to teach there. When the great Scopelian taught at Smyrna, students flocked from all over Asia Minor and elsewhere in the eastern Mediterranean to attend his lectures.

Information about lawyers and their increase in number occurs rather late because of the gradualness in the rise of Roman citizenship and the lateness of acceptance of Orientals in any considerable number into administrative positions.

Commerce

Asia Minor stood in the path of almost all commerce of the eastern Mediterranean and Black Sea. The common route by sea from Egypt and Syria skirted the coast of Cilicia or passed Cyprus to Pamphylia or Lycia before turning west or north. Of course, bulky and heavy goods moved by sea, since transporting them any distance by land was difficult. But weather controled maritime shipments, since for all practical purposes the Mediterranean was closed from about November 10 to March 10. The captain of the ship carrying the apostle Paul to Rome took a chance on the weather and suffered shipwreck (Acts 27:9–44). As an alternative to transporting goods, cities or provinces would import trained workmen rather than their products. A good example of this practice was the Roman government's taking glassblowers from the Phoenician coast to Italy and elsewhere in the first century.

Much of the trade remained local, and cities had long provided for such commerce with their agoras—open spaces surrounded by porticos with shops selling a vast array of goods. Some shops were open every day, but most towns had special market days. In addition, festivals and fairs brought numbers of peddlers who could pitch their tents and sell their specialty wares. They offered good textiles, precious metals, fine industrial products, ointments, and other luxury items. These fairs were often held during a festival sacred to one of the goddesses or gods—including the emperor. And they were commonly held near some spot of special sanctity.

Asia Minor required little in imports for its existence or moderate well-being. And from its production and a favorable trade balance it achieved a measure of affluence.

Its chief agricultural exports consisted of wine, oil, dried or preserved fruits, fish, timber, and marble. Textiles led among manufactured products, but goods in bronze, iron, precious metals, and stone were also in demand abroad. Some cities had to import grain but imports primarily consisted of luxury goods.

Travel

Economic historians and others often speak of the relative ease with which the apostle Paul moved through Asia Minor as an example of the ease and security of travel in Asia Minor in the first century. The Romans built and maintained roads all over the peninsula. It would be tedious to describe them and to tell the details of their routes. It is enough to say that there was a road that ran north and south close to the western seaboard. A second extended east and west from Antioch of Syria through the Cilician Gates and along the southern edge of the plateau to the Aegean Sea. A third system of roads connected Attalia with interior towns. Roads along the eastern frontier facilitated defense there. Among others, roads connected the major cities of the peninsula—for example, the seven cities of the Revelation (chapters 2—3).

Rome built and maintained these roads, imposing considerable taxes and labor requirements on local communities for roads in their areas. These served official purposes—to move couriers and whole armies and administrative personnel. They also served unofficial purposes—to accommodate the commerce between countryside and city and the interior and overseas connections. And of course they facilitated travel of early evangelists and missionaries who preached the gospel.

Commercial ships sailed in considerable numbers all around the coasts of Asia Minor—not on regular schedules, but as "tramps," moving from port to port with a cargo when they had a ship full and could sail with profit. Paul traveled on such a ship from Cyprus to Asia Minor and from Troas across the north Aegean to invade fortress Europe with the gospel.

In retrospect, Asia Minor became a relatively productive area spiritually for the apostle Paul, despite the stoning he received at Lystra. We do not know how many of the beatings he describes in 2 Corinthians came at the hands of brigands in Asia Minor, but because he traveled through that territory several times he may have run into them. And the persecution he experienced there (Acts 14:19) compared to the vicious beating he got at Philippi when he invaded Europe. The next chapter covers that period.

(For more on this topic, go to p. 503 or p. 573.)

NOTES:

[1] T. R. S. Broughton, "Roman Asia," *An Economic Survey of Ancient Rome*, Tenney Frank, ed. (Baltimore: Johns Hopkins Press, 1938), IV, 815.

[2] David Magie, *Roman Rule in Asia Minor* (Salem, N.H.: Ayer Co., Reprint, 1988), I, 106.

[3] Ibid., I, 106.

[4] Ibid., I, 167.

[5] R. E. Allen, *The Attalid Kingdom* (Oxford: Clarendon Press, 1983), 147–152.

[6] Stephen Mitchell, *Anatolia* (Oxford: Clarendon Press, 1993), I, 100.

[7] Mitchell, 100.

[8] Caroline H. E. Haspels, *The Highlands of Phrygia* (Princeton, N.J.: Princeton University Press, 1971), I, 110.

[9] Ramsay MacMullen, *Paganism in the Roman Empire* (New Haven, Conn.: Yale University Press, 1981), 37.

[10] Ibid.

[11] Magie, I, 545–46.

[12] Ekrem Akurgal, *Ancient Civilizations and Ruins of Turkey*, 7th ed. (Istanbul: Net Turistik Yayinlar, 1990), 354–58.

[13] Broughton, 609.

[14] Ibid., 815.

[15] Abba Eban, *My People* (New York: Random House, 1968), 104.

[16] Peter Richardson, *Herod* (Columbia, S.C.: University of South Carolina Press, 1996), 271.

[17] See John M.G. Barclay, *Jews in the Mediterranean Diaspora* (Edinburgh: T & T Clark, 1996), chapter 9.

[18] Broughton, 846.

[19] H. I. Marrou, *A History of Education in Antiquity* (New York: New American Library, 1964), 159.

[20] Ibid., 225.

[21] Mitchell, I, 187–195.

[22] Broughton, 821.

[23] Ibid., 839–40.

[24] Marrou, 263.

[25] Ibid., 265.

BIBLIOGRAPHY:

Akurgal, Ekrem. *Ancient Civilizations and Ruins of Turkey*. Istanbul: Net Turistik Yayinlar, 7th ed., 1990.

Allen, R. E. *The Attalid Kingdom*. Oxford: Clarendon Press, 1983.

Bean, George E. *Aegean Turkey*. New York: Frederick A. Praeger, 1966.

Bean, George E. *Lycian Turkey*. London: John Murray, 1989.

Bean, George E. *Turkey's Southern Shore*. New York: Frederick A. Praeger, 1968.

Blake, Everett, and Anna G. Edmonds. *Biblical Sites in Turkey*. Istanbul: Redhouse Press, 2nd ed., 1982.

Broughton, T. R. S. "Roman Asia," *An Economic Survey of Ancient Rome*, Tenney Frank, ed. Baltimore: Johns Hopkins Press, IV, 1938.

Darke, Diana. *Guide to Aegean and Mediterranean Turkey*. London: Michael Haag, 3rd ed., 1989.

Erdemgil, Selahattin. *Ephesus*. Istanbul: Turistik Yayinlar, 1992.

Freely, John. *The Western Shores of Turkey*. London: John Murray, 1988.

Hanfmann, George M. A. *Sardis from Prehistoric to Roman Times*. Cambridge, Mass.: Harvard University Press, 1983.

Haspels, Caroline H. W. *The Highlands of Phrygia*. Princeton: Princeton University Press, Vol. 1, 1971.

MacMullen, Ramsay. *Paganism in the Roman Empire*. New Haven: Yale University Press, 1981.

Magie, David. *Roman Rule in Asia Minor*. Salem, N.H.: Ayer Company, 2 vols., Reprint Edition, 1988.

Marrou, H. I. *A History of Education in Antiquity*. New York: New American Library, 1964.

Meinardus, Otto. *St. Paul in Ephesus*. New Rochelle, N.Y.: Caratzas, 1979.

Mitchell, Stephen. *Anatolia*. Oxford: Clarendon Press, 2 vols., 1993.

Onen, U. *Lycia*. Istanbul: Net Turistik Yayinlar, 2nd ed., 1990.

Radt, Wolfgang. *Pergamon*. Istanbul: Turkiye Turing ve Otomibil Kurumu, 1984.

Ramsay, William M. *The Cities of St. Paul*. Grand Rapids: Baker, reprint, 1979.

Ramsay, William M. *St. Paul the Traveller and the Roman Citizen.* Grand Rapids: Baker, reprint, 1979.

Steele, James. *Hellenistic Architecture in Asia Minor.* New York: St. Martin's Press, 1992.

Syme, Ronald. *Anatolia.* Oxford: The Clarendon Press, 1995.

Toksoz, Cemil. *Ancient Cities of Western Anatolia.* Istanbul: Zafer Ofset, 1974.

Vos, Howard F. *Archaeology in Bible Lands.* Chicago: Moody Press, 1977.

Yamauchi, Edwin. *The Archaeology of New Testament Cities in Western Asia Minor.* Grand Rapids: Baker, 1980.

GREECE AND THE INVASION OF FORTRESS EUROPE

(Acts; 1—2 Corinthians; 1—2 Thessalonians; Philippians)

"And a vision appeared to Paul in the night. A man of Macedonia stood and pleaded with him, saying, 'Come over to Macedonia and help us.' Now after he had seen the vision, immediately we sought to go to Macedonia, concluding that the Lord had called us to preach the gospel to them." (Acts 16:9, 10 NKJV)

How would you react if an evangelist friend told you, "Last night in a vision I saw and heard a man from Bucharest, Romania, asking me to come there and help him evangelize the city. I'm leaving for Romania as soon as I can get a visa"? You might wonder what he had for dinner the night before. You most certainly would encourage him to "Think this thing through." Yet the Bible reports that something very similar happened to the apostle Paul—and he and his companions, Silas and Luke and Timothy, left promptly on their mission without seeking any other confirmation that this was really God's call. So began the invasion of fortress Europe.

Since the call came from Macedonia, they sailed across the northern Aegean instead of to Athens or Corinth in the south. They embarked from Troas, about ten miles south of the western end of the Dardanelles (ancient Hellespont) and thus about ten miles south of the site of ancient Troy. Troas and Troy are not to be confused. As the group sailed for Europe, they were never out of sight of land. On the first day they passed the little islands of Tenedos (modern Bozcaada) and Imroz (Imbros). In keeping with the custom of small Aegean sailing ships, they anchored for the night off the island of Samothrace, and on the second day docked at the port of Neapolis (modern Kavalla, Acts 16:11).

The port of Troas from which Paul sailed has now silted in and looks like a salt pan

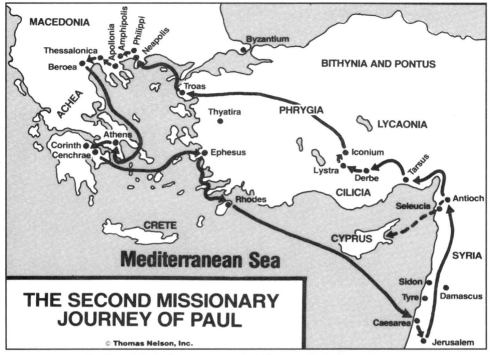

MACEDONIA
Thessalonica
Beroea
Apollonia
Amphipolis
Philippi
Neapolis
Byzantium
ACHEA
Troas
Thyatira
PHRYGIA
LYCAONIA
Athens
Corinth
Cenchrae
Ephesus
Iconium
Lystra
Derbe
Tarsus
CILICIA
Antioch
Seleucia
Rhodes
CRETE
CYPRUS
SYRIA
Mediterranean Sea
Sidon
Tyre
Damascus
THE SECOND MISSIONARY
JOURNEY OF PAUL
Caesarea
Jerusalem
© Thomas Nelson, Inc.

Paul's activity in Greece was part of his second missionary journey.

The Land

Political Geography

The political organization of Greece in New Testament times differed from what it had been in the classical period, and it varied from time to time during the first century. When Augustus became emperor in 27 B.C. he constituted Macedonia and Achaea as separate senatorial provinces. Achaea encompassed all of Greece proper and most of Epirus in the west. Macedonia, to the north, included Thrace on the east and land in the west all the way to the Adriatic Sea. In A.D. 15 Tiberius again made them imperial provinces and combined them into one large province, along with Moesia (area south of the Danube).

In A.D. 44 Claudius established the arrangement that existed in Paul's day. Achaea and Macedonia became senatorial provinces once more, the former with the

capital at Corinth and the latter with the capital at Thessalonica. The eastern part of Macedonia became the province of Thrace. Luke (in Acts 19:21) and Paul (in Romans 15:26; 1 Timothy 1:7, 8) referred to Macedonia and Achaia (Achaea). But Luke also spoke of Macedonia and Achaea as Macedonia and Greece (Acts 20:1–2), perhaps a carryover of the old

The port of Neapolis where Paul landed for his invasion of Greece

A Divine Appointment

Paul went to Greece by divine appointment. He received a vision in the night of a man of Macedonia begging him to come over into Macedonia and "help us." Presumably this person was a pagan crying out for some spiritual good news. Luke does not call him a brother, and the Greek word translated "help" is not used anywhere in the New Testament to mean or involve collaboration in God's work.[1] Moreover, Paul customarily did not build on someone else's foundation but preferred pioneer ministry (Romans 15:20). Nor does the Acts report indicate that any Jews or believers from Greece were present in Jerusalem on the day of Pentecost (Acts 2:9–11). Also, the call for "us" to "preach the gospel to them" fits with the idea that the call for help did not come from a Christian who wanted help. I believe, then, that the man from Macedonia was not Luke, as is sometimes suggested, or some other Greek believer seeking help in the ministry.

idea that Macedonians were not really Greeks. The further rearrangement of political boundaries in Greece late in the first century and the second does not concern us now.

Physical Geography

Mountains

The mountains and the sea dominated Greek life. Mountains covered two-thirds to three-fourths of the land surface, leaving not more than 25 percent as cultivable soil. No other country of the Mediterranean area presents a more tumbled surface than Greece, so while the mountains of Greece are not especially high, one is seldom out of sight of them.

Mount Olympus, the highest (located in the northeastern corner of the peninsula), is only about 9,600 feet, and few of the others are over 8,000 feet. Thus it is obvious that the capacity of Greek mountains for holding snow is limited, and the constancy of the water supply is thus unreliable.

Although the placement of mountains in Greece is chaotic, there is a degree of symmetry. The Magnesian Range extended south from Olympus in eastern Greece; the Pindus Range lay between Thessaly and Epirus in central Greece; and the Epirus Range stretched along the western coast. Ridges that crossed these ranges divided the country into a vast checkerboard of tiny valleys, few of which were more than a dozen miles long and more than half as

Rome's provincial arrangement in Greece during Paul's missionary work

The top of Mount Olympus with the traditional throne of Zeus in center foreground

GREECE

some of the rivers formed stagnant pools, breeding mosquitoes. Therefore the rivers remained a hindrance to Greek development, eroding the land, forming breeding places for malarial mosquitoes, silting the mouths of rivers so their harbors became unusable, and impeding travel. During floods these rivers were difficult to cross for either human beings or animals. Building bridges was almost an impossibility over streams that varied from a few feet in width to more than five hundred feet with the seasons. Moreover, these streams were too muddy to serve as a water supply for humans or animals.

The Sea

While the mountains dominated the landscape of Greece and also affected her politics, economy, and climate, the sea also remained a major factor in Greek life. Although the mountains almost closed Greece to the European continent, she was accessible on her sea fronts. The deeply indented coastline gives Greece the longest coastline in proportion to enclosed area of all important historical regions. With a coast of 2,600 miles, it exceeds Italy's (2,150 miles) and that of the Iberian Peninsula (2,300), though its land area is only one-third of the former and one-sixth of the latter. As a result,

wide. Often the mountain passes between these valleys were 3,000 feet or more in altitude and buried in snow at least part of the winter.

With communications so hampered, Greece developed a provincialism that has probably not existed in any other historically important area of the world. The mountain barriers contributed much to the city-state development of ancient Greece. Though periodic efforts were made to overcome this suicidal division, none was really successful until Macedonia, Rome, and other powers exerted an external pressure for unity.

Rivers

Down from the mountainsides coursed the rivers of Greece. They were mostly non-navigable winter and spring torrents whose floods overflowed onto the arable land. These raging torrents washed soil away from the hillsides during the rainy season. In summer their dry beds served as highways for travelers. During the dry season

Greece and Europe, a Stronghold of Satan

Greece and the rest of Europe may properly be spoken of as a stronghold—in the grip of Satan, the "ruler of this world" (John 12:31; 14:30). This prince resisted the invasion of his territory and fought Paul wherever he went. As an added thought, when Satan offered Jesus all the kingdoms of this world in the great temptation (Matthew 4:8–9), he was making a legitimate offer. He actually does control them now. Worse, this "spirit" "energizes" ("works in") unbelievers (Ephesians 2:2, Greek), keeping them from exercising faith in Christ.

nowhere in central or southern Greece can a person travel more than forty miles from the sea.

The many indentations made numerous harbors possible. And because of the many offshore islands, men who sailed the Aegean, were constantly in sight of land on a clear day until they moved south of Crete into the eastern Mediterranean.

So the Greeks, unable to wrest a living from the rocky farms, became a seafaring people. Learning from all the peoples with whom they came in contact, they cross-fertilized the whole Mediterranean area. Significantly, Greece's best ports and many of her valleys lay on the east coast. Therefore her eastern areas received civilizing influences from the Orient first. In contrast, Italy faced west and was slow to receive eastern culture.

It is easy, however, to overemphasize the place of the sea in Greek economic life. The mountains adjacent to many of the city states did not produce good ship timber and sometimes were literally a barrier between the inhabitants and the sea. Moreover, the Aegean waters are too clear and too devoid of plant life to support large schools of fish. Nor was overseas trade vital in the early days when most of the communities of Greece were self-sufficient.

Then, too, the seas around Greece are typically Mediterranean. In winter the Adriatic Sea is a storm center, with gusty north winds plaguing the northern Aegean. The surrounding seas remained closed to all Greeks in winter and to some Greeks most of the time. Sheer cliffs line a good part of the Greek coast. The Thessalians and Boeotians always remained landsmen. Only the inhabitants of Corinth and Megara among the peoples of the Peloponnesus or of the area around the Corinthian Gulf had much of an overseas trade. Sparta only broke out of her land-locked condition for a period during and after her great war with Athens (during the late fifth century B.C.), when she built a navy with the help of Persia. Even the peoples of the Aegean Islands were not continually seafarers.

The Greeks have always been primarily rural and agricultural. As late as the end of the nineteenth century, 70 percent of them still lived in rural areas. The lack of soil forced them to terrace the hillsides and plant grapevines, olive trees, and whatever else they could produce on some very unpromising land. The stony nature of the soil also often forced them to raise barley and millet rather than wheat. Sheep and goats fared better on the pasture lands than cattle. They imported most of their wheat.

Climate

The climate of Greece is generally quite mild. Northern Greece has a climate similar to that of the Continent with a fair amount of snow, while southern Greece has a climate more Mediterranean in nature. Cold winds, however, bring snow even to Athens in winter. There are two seasons: rainy or winter (October to April) and dry or summer (May to September). The winters are rather boisterous but not devoid of sunshine. Rainfall is fairly heavy, measuring forty inches in the west and slightly less in the east, though there is little precipitation in the summer. This period of drought lasts for two months in the North and four months in the Peloponnesus. Sea breezes temper the hot summer sun in most places, but some of the cup-shaped valleys are effectively isolated from this relief by the surrounding mountains. In such places summer weather equals that of the tropics.

Natural Resources

"To Hellas [Greece] poverty has always been a foster sister," the great ancient Greek historian Herodotus well observed. It is remarkable indeed that this minor, poverty-stricken people soared above its environment and produced great cultural achievements.

While in most ancient times Greece had a considerable amount of timber, by the fifth century B.C. she no longer could supply her needs and had to import.

Neither did she have much in the way of minerals. Silver and lead were mined in Attica, iron and copper in Euboea and Laconia, and a little gold on the islands of Siphnos and Thasos. Most of the ancient mine fields are now exhausted. Some mines that do exist were never exploited in antiquity. Athens and Corinth in particular had considerable supplies of potters' clay.

Greece also had plenty of good building stone and was famous for her marble.

The finest of the white marbles (especially used for temples, e.g., the Parthenon) came from the islands of the Aegean and on Mount Pentelicus near Athens. While Pentelic marble had a smooth grain, the ancient Greeks preferred the marble of Paros, which was more translucent, for sculpture. The only colored marbles of Greece quarried extensively in ancient times were the white and green *cipollino* of Euboea, much desired by the Roman emperors, and the *verde antico* (old green) of northern Thessaly.

Significant Areas of Greece

Macedonia

In northern Greece lay Macedonia. Since its boundaries varied over the centuries and since during much of the country's history the exact boundaries are not known, it is hard to describe its exact size. The kingdom was, however, always located at the northeast corner of the Aegean; and Pella (twenty-four miles northwest of Thessalonica) was the capital during its later history (from about 410 B.C. on). Under Philip II (359–336 B.C.) Macedonia came to include Thrace and to dominate all of Greece. Under Alexander the Great it conquered the entire Persian Empire.

The boundaries of the Roman province of Macedonia in which Paul ministered had been quite well fixed. They stretched from a point near the Nestos River in eastern Greece to the Adriatic at approximately the latitude of Tiranë (Tirana), modern capital of Albania, then south to the northern border of Epirus, which it skirted to its southern end and turned eastward to the Gulf of Volos (ancient Pagasaeus). Therefore it may be seen that the province included not only most of the northern part of modern Greece but also parts of Bulgaria and Yugoslavia and about half of Albania.

While Macedonia was very mountainous, it also had some fertile plains along the northern rim of the Aegean. Four great rivers (west to east, the Haliacmon [Vistritsa], Vardar, Strymon, and Nestos) of the "European" type (which flow all year instead of drying up in the summer) break through the coastal ridges to the sea and deposit around their mouths rich alluvial plains. The fertility of these plains has enabled the Greeks to export wheat during recent years—a considerable achievement for such a rocky country.

Attica

Extending into the Aegean from Boeotia is the peninsula of Attica. Though very significant for the history of civilization, this small territory comprises only about 1,000 square miles and is approximately the size of Rhode Island. The peninsula is roughly triangular in shape and measures some forty miles east and west and a like distance north and south. No spot in Attica is more than twenty-five miles in a straight line from Athens.

Those who are enamored with the greatness of this area often are unaware of its drawbacks. The driest region of Greece, it has an annual rainfall of only sixteen inches. Only about one-fourth of its soil is arable, and part of that will raise nothing but olives. On the credit side of the ledger are a coast where the mountains leave room for easy landing places, excellent clay beds for pottery manufacture, the famous marble of Mount Pentelicus, and the lead and silver mines of Laurium in the south of the peninsula (largely exhausted by the New Testament period).

Athens gradually became the true center of all of life in Attica. At the center of Athens stood her citadel on the Acropolis, an isolated hill about five miles from the coast and three to four hundred feet above the town. It has an almost vertical drop on all sides but the west. After about 500 B.C. the great port of Athens was developed at Piraeus. Another important town of Attica was Eleusis, a religious center fourteen miles northwest of Athens (see subsequent discussion).

The Peloponnesus

Moving southwest of Athens, we cross the Isthmus of Corinth and enter the Peloponnesus. This peninsula, shaped like a mulberry leaf, has actually been an island since the Corinth Canal was finished in A.D. 1893. Slightly smaller than

New Hampshire, the Peloponnesus had several important districts, six of which are noted here. The Peloponnesus formed the larger part of the Roman province of Achaea.

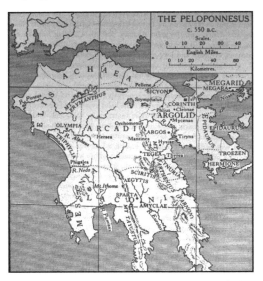

Occupying the northeast corner of the Peloponnesus was the city state of Corinth, which controlled only about 330 square miles, a third of the size of Rhode Island. Blessed with considerable deposits of white and cream-colored clay, Corinth developed the most prolific ceramic industry of early Greece, but after about 550–525 B.C. lost out to Athenian competition.

More important to the development of Corinth, however, was her geographical position. Located a mile and a half south of the Isthmus of Corinth, she commanded this four-mile-wide neck of land, as well as its eastern port of Cenchreae (Cenchrea, Acts 18:18) and its western port of Lechaeum. In New Testament as well as classical times, a large amount of shipping passed through Greek waters, and the trip around the southern tip of Greece was not only long but extremely dangerous. Therefore it became customary to transport goods across the Isthmus of Corinth, a saving of more than 150 miles. Teams pulled smaller ships across the isthmus on a tramway; they unloaded larger ones and reloaded their cargoes on the other side. Short stretches of this tramway can still be seen. Corinth served as the capital of the Roman province of Achaea.

South of Corinth lay Argolis with its important site of Mycenae, famous in classical times for launching the attack against Troy. Across the top of the Peloponnesus stretched Achaea. To its southwest lay Elis. That area had the best cattle pastures of the Peloponnesus and produced flax as well. Its significance in Greek history arose from the fact that the great sanctuary of Olympia was located there. The local population was entrusted with the stewardship of the Olympic Games.

The two southern districts of the Peloponnesus were Laconia and Messenia. Each consisted of a fertile plain framed in a horseshoe of mountains fronting on a sea gulf. The more significant of these plains historically was the Laconian, where Sparta was located.

(For more on this topic, go to p. 507 or p. 583.)

Government

"Now when Gallio was proconsul of Achaia, the Jews with one accord rose up against Paul and brought him to the judgment seat, saying, 'This fellow persuades men to worship God contrary to the law.'" (Acts 18:12–13 NKJV)

The *diolkos* or tramway on which ships and goods were moved across the Isthmus of Corinth in ancient times.

Paul appeared before Gallio, the governor of Achaea, at this rostrum in the market place or agora of Corinth (Acts 18:12–17). Paul would have stood before it on the lower level.

We have already learned that in Paul's day Greece was divided into two senatorial provinces: Macedonia in the north with its capital at Thessalonica and Achaea (Achaia) in the south, with its capital at Corinth. This meant that the Senate appointed the governors (proconsuls).

We must not get the idea, however, that these two provinces had been neatly divided into a number of city units under the close and efficient supervision of the governors. There is evidence that several leagues with their assemblies continued to exist. These exercised considerable power over their respective districts. For example, we know of an Achaean League that functioned in the northern part of the Peloponnesus, a Thessalian League in eastern Greece south of Mount Olympus, and a Phocian League in central Greece in the area of Delphi, and there were others. Sometimes the leagues dealt with disputes between communities; sometimes towns went directly to the governor with their concerns. Priests of these leagues often sponsored or supervised events connected with emperor worship or veneration of the goddess Roma.

To complicate matters further, some cities enjoyed a variety of freedoms or exemptions or privileged status, granted by the Senate or leading generals or emperors. They might enjoy virtual autonomy, the right to manage their own affairs as long as they conducted themselves responsibly. And some of them were Roman colonies, such as Philippi and Pella, where Roman veterans had been settled. Exemptions often included freedom from paying certain taxes. Some cities, such as Athens and Sparta, were free cities. It is not surprising then that the provincial governments could not always operate smoothly and efficiently.

The Proconsul Gallio

One of the governors of Achaea (Achaia), Gallio, holds special interest for us because of his contact with the apostle Paul. He came from a distinguished family and was a brother of the philosopher Seneca. After he was adopted by the orator and senator L. Junius Gallio, he was known by the name Gallio.

The date of his governorship in Corinth is of special interest in fixing the chronology of Paul's missionary activity. An inscription found at Delphi indicates that Gallio probably took office about the beginning of July of 51. Presumably Paul arrived in Corinth before the procurator took office, perhaps in 50.[2] The hearing before Gallio probably took place near the beginning of the governor's term of office, after Paul had been there for a year. The edict of Claudius, which expelled the Jews from Rome and sent Aquila and Priscilla to Corinth (Acts 18:2), may be dated in 49. The Council of Jerusalem (Acts 15) must have taken place in 48. The first missionary journey, then, probably occurred in 46–47.

Paul appeared publicly before Gallio—before the judgment seat or bema or rostrum in the agora in Corinth. Any tourist may see the excavated remains of it there today. What the Jews meant to say in their charge ("This fellow persuades men to worship God contrary to the law," Acts 18:13) is not clear. Perhaps they were deliberately ambiguous. Did they mean contrary to Jewish law or to Roman law, which forbade proselytizing of Roman citizens? But there is no evidence here that he had been involved in converting Roman citizens. Judaism was a legally recognized religion in the Roman Empire. Perhaps these Jews were trying to get Gallio to distinguish between Jews and Christians and to declare that Christians were operating outside the Roman law. That would have embroiled Christians in real trouble.

Gallio concluded that he was dealing with a prejudiced group and that the issue

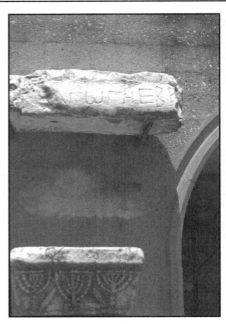

There is abundant evidence of Jews in ancient Greece. Here is a block (in the Corinth Museum) with an inscription "Synagogue of the Hebrews" and the lampstand below. It is thought to be a lintel of the synagogue of Corinth in New Testament times.

was an internal Jewish dispute, a quibbling with "words and names." So he ruled that it was beyond his legal jurisdiction to try the matter and dismissed the hearing—even before Paul had a chance to defend himself. Gallio's action should not be taken to mean that he was indifferent to religion, as Bible expositors often claim, but rather that he refused to be involved in a case over which he had no rightful or clear jurisdiction.

(For more on this topic, go to p. 512 or p. 584.)

Religion

Probably the most interesting way to discover the religious situation in Greece in New Testament times is to follow the apostle Paul around the countryside. Before we set out, let's take another quick look at the ruler cult and the Jewish population, both of which were important to what happened.

The temple to the goddess Roma and the imperial cult was a round temple built at the eastern entrance to the Parthenon. It appears at the far end of this reconstruction of the Acropolis of Athens.

The traditional spot by the Gangites River where the prayer meeting of Acts 16 is supposed to have taken place.

The Ruler Cult

The ruler cult had become well established all over the eastern Mediterranean world before the birth of Christ, and examples of the ruler cult in Greece abound. After Julius Caesar refounded Corinth in 44 B.C., following its destruction a century earlier, a grateful populace introduced veneration of the deified Caesar there. Subsequently they built a temple of Octavia, sister of Augustus, in Corinth and it became the center of the imperial cult in the city. Evidently this is to be identified with the ruins of the rather imposing temple that stood just west of the agora of Corinth. By the beginning of the first century a Roman official was seeking to promote the imperial cult in Messene (in the southwest of the Peloponnesus) and other cities of Achaia. A little later they established a provincial imperial cult for cities of the Achaean League in Corinth.

The Panachaean assembly staged an imperial festival on the accession of Caligula in A.D. 37 and Claudius in A.D. 41. They established a cult in honor of Antonia, grandmother of Caligula (died A.D. 37), during her lifetime, at Ilium (Troy) and at Athens. Athenians built a temple to the goddess Roma and the imperial cult on the acropolis at Athens opposite the eastern entrance to the Parthenon during Augustus' day, and its ruins may be seen there today.

The ruler cult was not just a way for the government to gain the loyalty of its people. By participation in the cult, Romans and provincials demonstrated their own relationship to the emperor, whose powers were so great that he seemed to be both man and god. They were buttering up the boss, so to speak. Moreover, by participation in the cult they advanced their own social standing and political position in the community. This came as people at all levels of society sacrificed animals to the divine spirit of the emperor, animals that could be eaten in community feasts. Or as they provided wine on the same occasion for supplication to his spirit. Or as they made other offerings for the benefit of the community (for example, oil for the baths). And they gained the same kind of self-fulfillment that contributors to local symphonies and museums, disaster relief drives, and a Christmas dinner for the homeless get today.[3]

The Jewish Population

As previously noted, the Jewish population of the eastern Mediterranean world had grown considerably. If we follow the calculations of Abba Eban, every fifth person in Macedonia and Achaia was a Jew.[4] This is extremely important because it meant that Paul and his associates, as Jews who sought to preach to the Jews first (Acts 13:46), had an audience and point of contact in preaching the gospel. They received protection under Roman law as a movement within Judaism that sought to present Jesus as the fulfillment of the Mosaic Law and the Messiah promised by Jewish prophets.

As long as they were nurtured in the cradle of Judaism, early Christians were safe from official persecution. When the day came that the populace viewed Christians as a separate movement, persecution really started. The whole ruler cult establishment and the populace that supported it could bear down on them. That is why the ruling of Gallio, previously noted, was so important. If Gallio had viewed Paul's ministry as something other than a debate within Judaism, Paul's Jewish opponents would have had the club of state to hold over his head.

Paul in Philippi

"... to Philippi, which is the foremost city of that part of Macedonia, a colony.... And on the Sabbath day we went out of the city to the riverside, where prayer was customarily made; and we sat down and spoke to the women who met there. Now a certain woman named Lydia heard us." (Acts 16:12–14 NKJV)

After the great battle fought on the plain of Philippi in 42 B.C., in which Octavian and Antony defeated Brutus and Cassius, Octavian made Philippi a Roman colony and many veterans settled there. Then after Octavian defeated Antony at Actium in 31 B.C., additional veterans settled in Philippi. A few years later Augustus granted the town the *ius Italicum* or Law of Italy, which gave them immunity from imperial taxation. Thereafter the people of the place became conscious of and proud of their Roman heritage (see Acts 16:20-22).

Near the traditional spot of the prayer meeting at Philippi a "Baptistry of Lydia" has now been constructed.

Paul and his associates (Silas, Timothy, and Luke) probably came to Philippi before the end of A.D. 50. How long they stayed is open to question, but it has been suggested that they ministered there for as long as two months. Perhaps on the first Sabbath the apostolic company went out by a riverside to attend a prayer meeting held by Jews of the place (Acts 16:13). Apparently there were very few Jews living in Philippi, because if there had been ten heads of families there they would have been obligated

The agora of Philippi where the mob scene of Acts 16 took place.

to build a synagogue. The fact that the group met outside the city probably indicates that they were well beyond the pomerium, or sacred boundary, within which worship of foreign deities was not permitted. If Jews had been organized in a synagogue, they would have attained a status recognized by the Roman state, and they could have worshiped in town.

As they met by the riverside, probably the Krenides, or possibly the Gangites, Paul's ministry seems to have been almost immediately successful, for a certain businesswoman by the name of Lydia, a seller of purple cloth, accepted the message of Paul and turned to faith in Christ, along with her whole household (Acts 16:14–15). The evangelization of Europe had begun.

Subsequently a slave girl possessed by a strange spirit or a "spirit of divination" (Greek *pythōna*) pestered them. Evidently she brought her masters much profit by her "fortune-telling" (Acts 16:16). The Greek *pythōna* has led commentators to conclude that the Greeks believed she was inspired by Apollo. A pythoness was a prophetic priestess of Apollo; oracular power was thought to be a gift bestowed by that god. After the girl had been a repeated irritant to the apostolic team, Paul practiced exorcism on her and her fortune-telling gift was gone.

Her masters, seeing that their source of gain had vanished, stirred up a riot against Paul, falsely charging that he was spreading social teachings that would destroy the citizens' Roman way of life. They dragged

Paul and Silas into the agora or marketplace and accused the missionaries before the magistrates. Luke called these officials *stratēgoi* (Acts 16:20), a Hellenistic title to render the untranslatable *duovir*—the two chief officials of a Roman municipality that corresponded to the consuls of the period of the Republic.

The ruins of the rostrum at the north side of the agora of Philippi, where Paul and Silas would have been dragged before the local magistrates.

The agora, where the judgment scene took place, has been completely excavated by the French School at Athens (1914–38) and by Greek archaeologists since World War II. A rectangular area about 300 feet long and 150 feet wide, it was bounded by porticoes, temple facades, and other public buildings. On the north side stood the rostrum or judgment seat where the magistrates rendered their judgment. They commanded that Paul and Silas be beaten and cast into prison, ordering the jailer to keep them securely (Acts 16:22–24).

Paul's Roman Citizenship

"But Paul said to them, 'They have beaten us openly, uncondemned Romans, and have thrown us into prison. And now do they put us out secretly? No indeed! Let them come themselves and get us out.'" (Acts 16:37 NKJV)

The story of the earthquake which opened the prison doors, the conversion of the jailer and his family, and the decision of the magistrates to let Paul and Silas go is familiar to most Sunday school students. What is probably not so familiar is the dis-

The Purpose of Paul's Letter to Philippians

It is my view that Philippians was especially an appeal to Christian unity.[9] To those proud of their Roman citizenship, he spoke of a superior citizenship in a spiritual commonwealth (Philippians 3:20; conversation in AV). To those accustomed to marching in step he addressed an appeal that they should walk in step (literal Greek of Philippians 3:16) and in unity of purpose instead of allowing the ranks of the church to be rent with dissension. Those walking out of step (literal Greek of 3:18) and living in a confused way religiously were compared by Paul to enemies of Christ.

To those proud of their military connections he commented that through his imprisonment in Rome the gospel had been preached to the whole Praetorian Guard, the elite guard of the empire (literal Greek of 1:13). Again, he appealed to the military-minded by calling one of the faithful members of their church a fellow soldier (2:25). To those interested in feats of bodily prowess and success in war, he made a number of appeals in the choice of verbs and figures of speech (e.g., "stand fast" and "striving," 1:27; the figure of the race in 3:14).

tinctly Roman element in the Acts account and in the later epistle to the Philippians.

Roman citizens were a special breed in the early first century. They could not be abused or manhandled the way the non-citizen masses might be treated. Roman law protected against punishment, execution, or torture without trial. Moreover, they were protected throughout the Roman Empire from the capital crimes jurisdiction and violent coercion of provincial governors. A citizen in the provinces had the right of appeal to higher courts in Rome for adjudication in capital cases.[5]

The apostle Paul's stern objection to his treatment in Philippi (see Acts 16:37 above) is parallel to expressions of wronged secular citizens in the late republic and early empire.[6] Sherwin-White observes that, "The force of this feeling ultimately petered out with the large extension of the citizenship through the provinces, just as the privileges of the Romans came to be whittled down at a similar rate."[7]

Fifty years later than the episode at Philippi, the position of citizens in the empire had changed. Their rights were less distinctive. Sherwin-White concludes, "The dramatic date of Acts belongs to the period when the spread of Roman status in the provinces was still on a small scale."[8] Interestingly, while the date of the composition of Acts is not under discussion here, Paul's approach and handling of his citizenship (here and in the subsequent appeal to Rome) fit the period of about 50–60 rather than a half century later. So we have here another detail that argues for an early date of the writing of the New Testament.

Of course we wonder about the recording of citizenship. During the Republic censors took the census of citizens every five years and drew up lists of those on the citizen rolls. In 44 B.C. a law transferred census taking to the magistrates of the Roman municipalities. The law required them to register the citizens with their full names, parentage, and record a statement about their property, making the document the basis for taxation and military service.

In A.D. 4 Augustus established a system of compulsory birth registration. As part of this a citizen had to register the birth of his children within thirty days before a Roman official. And he received a wooden diptych recording the registration, which served as a kind of certificate of citizenship for the child for the rest of his life. The diptych was a two-leaved hinged tablet folding together to protect writing on its waxed surfaces. This contained the names of seven witnesses and provided proof of citizen status.[10] Presumably Paul's citizenship was recorded in Tarsus. But how he satisfied people in Philippi and Jerusalem and Caesarea of his citizenship status we do not know. Nor do we know how his father managed to get his citizenship. Paul was "born a citizen" (Acts 22:28).

Why the Philippian magistrates did not recognize Paul's Roman citizenship before his beating and imprisonment is not clear. Perhaps he had tried to make it clear that he was a Roman citizen during the mob scene of the previous day, but no one paid any attention to him or, possibly, did not hear him in the din and confusion.

Because Philippi was a Roman colony with many veterans of the Roman army, elements of interest to Romans are numerous in the epistle to the Philippians. Paul wrote this during his Roman imprisonment to thank them for a gift and to stop some sort of quarrel among them.

Soon after Paul's release from prison, he left Philippi, but he left Luke behind. This is

The Egnatian Way near Philippi

clear from the fact that the "we" phraseology, always used when Luke accompanied Paul, abruptly ceased. The narrative is described in the third person until Paul left Philippi on his last journey to Jerusalem, some five years later (Acts 20:6). If Luke remained at Philippi during the entire interim, there would be some explanation for the solid establishment of the church there and its special interest in helping Paul over the years.

Paul in Thessalonica

When Paul left Philippi by the Krenides (or west) Gate, he struck out on the

Part of the Roman agora of Thessalonica

Egnatian Way for Thessalonica. Comments on the Egnatian Way appear in the last section of this chapter.

Thessalonica or Thessaloniki lay on the Gulf of Thessalonica, the largest gulf indenting the Balkan Peninsula, and rose at the end of the bay in amphitheater form, on the slopes of the foothill of the Cortiates Mountains. On the east and west sides of the city, ravines ascend from the shore and converge toward the highest point, on which the citadel stood. The port, an open roadstead (anchorage) sheltered by Chalcidice, was and still is convenient for large ships. In the fifth century B.C., the Gulf of Thessalonica was perhaps twice as large as at present. As a result of the silting action of the Vardar (or Axios) River, the western portion of the gulf was gradually filled in. By Paul's day silting action had enclosed the western area so that it was a large lake, which has since silted up. This silting action created marshy areas which have bred malarial mosquitoes, plaguing the city until very recent times.

Mount Olympus stands in clear view from the upper streets of the city, rising 9,600 feet above the sea. In ancient times its glittering snow-covered dome was thought to be the throne before which Zeus gathered in council the deities of Greece. Dense forests at the mountain's base concealed the Pierian spring, beside which the Muses were reputedly born and Orpheus first saw the light.

When Macedonia capitulated to Rome in 168 B.C., its affairs became entangled with those of Rome. During the civil wars of the first century B.C., it was the headquarters of the Pompeian party and the Senate and later took the side of Antony and Octavian against Brutus and Cassius. As a free city it had its own city council and was ruled by politarchs, according to the New Testament narrative (Acts 17:6). This fact used to be doubted because such a name was unknown from other sources. But numerous inscriptions have turned up in the area confirming the accuracy of the New Testament.

An important city in Paul's day, Thessalonica served as the capital of the province of Macedonia and was the main stop on the Egnatian Way, provided a naval base, and had an important commercial port. With overland caravans thronging its hostelries, with its harbor filled with ships' bottoms from overseas, with old salts, Roman officials, and thousands of Jewish merchants rubbing shoulders in its streets, Thessalonica presented a very cosmopolitan picture. It is very suggestive that the Jewish opponents of Paul should have called Paul and his co-workers "world-topplers" (Acts 17:6).

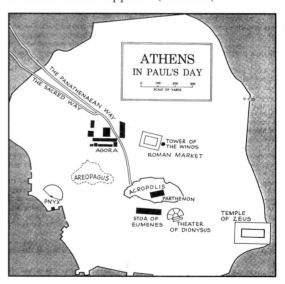

This cosmopolitanism apparently appealed to Paul. Judging from the fact that he spent so long a time at great centers like Corinth and Ephesus and sought to minister at other large centers with great moving populations, it would seem that Paul's strategy was to use these cities as springboards

Altar to an unknown god (see Acts 17:23), now in Istanbul Museum

for the propagation of the gospel. Individuals converted in them would move all over the Roman world and would rapidly spread the Christian message. It should be remembered, however, that in general Paul also ministered in cities that had fairly large Jewish populations and that he preached first to the Jews wherever he went. When they rejected his message, he then turned to Gentiles.

That Thessalonica contained a fairly large Jewish population may be seen from the fact that so great a number of Greeks had become "God seekers" or converts to Judaism. Of these a "great multitude" (Acts 17:4) were won over to Christianity. Moreover, the ease with which the Jews of Thessalonica marshaled the city crowd against Paul and Silas (Acts 17:5) indicates that their numbers were either large or at least influential.

As usual, Paul began his ministry among the Jews of Thessalonica, preaching to them in their synagogue for three Sabbaths (Acts 17:2). It need not be concluded, however, that Paul remained in the city for so short a time. The success of Paul's labor among Gentiles indicates an extended ministry

outside the synagogue. A stay of longer than three weeks would certainly have been required for the Philippians to collect and send two gifts to the apostle while he was in Thessalonica (Philippians 4:16).

Paul's ministry in Thessalonica proved to be so successful that many of the Jews, taking exception to his message, stirred up a

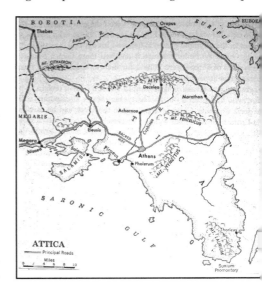

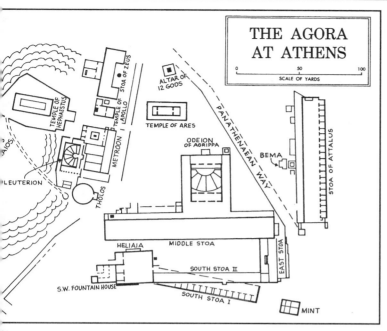

THE AGORA
AT ATHENS

0   50   100

SCALE OF YARDS

grounds. The beautiful old furniture is still in place; the coat of arms still hangs over the mantel. But the rugs are threadbare. Few servants circulate about the place. It grows increasingly hard to keep up appearances. And the conversation often turns to a better day long since gone.

Athenian silver mines had been largely worked out by the beginning of the Roman Imperial Period. Athens no longer controlled an empire. And great rival centers such as Corinth, Ephesus, Antioch, and Alexandria had cut into the Athenian share of the economic and cultural pie of the Mediterranean world.

In spite of the decline of the imperial city, it remained outwardly beautiful. Her acropolis, agora, and other public centers remained intact. The city was still respected for its learning, its arts, and its past prestige. The young Roman elite especially appreciated the city's beautiful monuments and the brilliance of her schools of rhetoricians.

riot against him. The mob attacked the house of Jason, Paul's host, but the apostle was away at the time. So they dragged Jason and some fellow Christians to the politarchs, with the accusation of sedition: "These all do contrary to the decrees of Caesar, saying that there is another king, one Jesus" (Acts 17:7). The politarchs required the suspects to post bond for good behavior, and then they freed the Christians. Though greatly disturbed because of the tumult, the rulers were apparently bent on justice and legal protection of Paul and his companions. The inability of free cities to keep order raised a threat of Roman interference.

Paul and Silas now seemed to be a liability to the young church; besides, their lives were in danger. So the Thessalonian believers decided to send the pair to Berea (modern Veroia). When opponents from Thessalonica followed them there, Paul decided to go to Athens to wait out the storm, hoping to go back north when things quieted down.

Paul in Athens

As Paul walked in Athens, he must have had much the same feelings as a postwar guest of an impoverished London gentleman. The great house is still intact, though there is some destruction around the

The Stoa of Attalus stretched across almost the entire east side of the Agora

The Roman Agora

"Therefore he reasoned in the synagogue with the Jews and with the Gentile worshipers, and in the marketplace daily with those who happened to be there" (Acts 17:17 NKJV).

Though Paul may have been waiting for the storm to subside in the north, he immediately resumed his ministry in Athens. Of course he went to the Jews first. But he also reasoned daily with chance comers to the Agora or marketplace. Ramsay believed that this "reasoning" was according to the Socratic style of discussion characteristic of the city and cites this as an example of Paul's ability to be "all things to all men"[11] (1 Corinthians 9:22).

Thanks particularly to the excavations of the American School of Classical Studies at Athens during the years 1931–40 and since 1946, it is now possible to see quite clearly what the Agora was like in Paul's day. Along the south and east sides and across the center stood stoas or colonnaded structures housing shops. The magnificence of these structures is not left to the imagination because the east stoa has been entirely rebuilt by the excavators and serves as the Agora Museum. It is 385 feet long and 64 feet wide and faced by a two-story colonnade of 45 columns, Doric at the base and Ionic at the top. The second story is reached by stairs at either end. Shops lined the back wall of the structure. In front of it stood the Bema, or public rostrum, where officials could address citizens gathered in the square. The largest of the law courts of Athens had been set up at the west end of the south stoa.

The Role of the Areopagus Council

In Roman times the Areopagus Council was charged mainly with religious and educational affairs. Ramsay concluded that the Areopagus had power to appoint or invite lecturers at Athens and to exercise some general control over the lecturers in the interests of public order and morality. The scene described in Acts 17:18 seems to indicate that recognized lecturers had power to take a strange lecturer before the council. This authority of appointing lecturers existed at least as early as about 50 B.C. What such a privilege entailed is not known.[13]

The west side of the Agora was the political center of Athens. Here stood the Bouleuterion, where the Council of Five Hundred met, the state archives, and the Stoa of Zeus, which housed various administrative offices. Again our imagination is helped by the fact that on the hill behind these structures stands the Temple of Hephaestus (god of the forge), one of the best preserved of all Greek temples, constructed entirely of Pentelic marble. It is 104 feet long, 45 feet wide, and 34 feet high. The Doric colonnade consists of six columns at the ends and thirteen on the sides.

Mars Hill or Areopagus, with Paul's Areopagus speech in Greek on a bronze plaque at the right (see Acts 17).

Paul's Religious Tourism

"As I was passing through and considering the objects of your worship" (Acts 17:23 NKJV).

Oscar Broneer is quite convinced that Paul spent part of his time in Athens engaged in religious sightseeing. He feels that the full force of the Greek of Acts 17: 23a demands "going about and examining objects of religious devotion."[14] Ramsay translates the passage, "As I went through the city surveying the monuments of your religion."[15] If Paul engaged in religious tourism in Athens, among the more significant structures he visited would have been the Temple of the Olympian Zeus, the Theater of Dionysus, and the Acropolis with the Parthenon and the worship of Athena.

Across the north of the Agora stood the Painted Stoa, so-called for a series of battle scenes painted on its walls (including Troy, Athenians vs. Amazons, Marathon, etc.). Here philosophers hung out in the fourth and third centuries B.C. And here Zeno, founder of the Stoic school, held academic court. In front of this lay the Altar of the Twelve Gods, considered to be the very center of Athens, to which distances to outside points were measured. In the center of the Agora stood the Odeion or music hall of Agrippa, with a seating capacity of about 1,000. The Agora was over 500 feet on a side.

At the east of the old Athenian Agora sprawled the newer Roman Agora, a rectangular area 367 by 315 feet and lined with shops, where especially wine and olive oil were sold.

Areopagus—Mars Hill

"Then certain Epicurean and Stoic philosophers encountered him. And some said, 'What does this babbler want to say?' Others said, 'He seems to be a proclaimer of foreign gods,' because he preached to them Jesus and the resurrection. And they took him and brought him to the Areopagus, saying, 'May we know what this new doctrine is of which you speak?'" (Acts 17:18–19 NKJV)

These philosophers laid hands on Paul and brought him "unto Areopagus." This could mean either to the council meeting (wherever it met) or to the hill of Areopagus. Oscar Broneer argues that in Acts 17:19 the Greek (*epi* with the accusative) means "up to" Areopagus and therefore indicates that Paul was taken to Areopagus or Mars Hill.[12]

The council said that they wanted to hear what this "babbler" had to say. The Greek term means "seedpicker" and implies one who picked up refuse and scraps of literature without the ability to use them correctly. At any rate, the appearance before the Areopagus does not seem to have been a formal trial, because it did not conclude with any sort of verdict. Some mocked, and others expressed interest in hearing him again (Acts 17:31)

In his appearance on Mars Hill, Paul showed an acquaintance with Greco-Roman culture, which he tried to use to make contact with his hearers. It has also been suggested that the speech indicates that he may have addressed the group in the flowery New Alexandrian Rhetoric, which was a favorite among the educated classes of the day. He showed, too, that he had been greatly impressed by the religiosity of the Athenians, as reflected by the multitude of altars and other religious monuments he had seen all over the city. He observed that they even had an altar to an "unknown god," erected just to make sure they had not omitted any possible gods from their worship. This was the god that Paul claimed to be

Temple of Zeus, Athens

The Theater of Dionysus in Athens

inches in diameter at the base. These were arranged in two rows on the sides and three rows at the ends and rested on a foundation 354 feet long and 135 feet broad. The height was over 90 feet. The image of Zeus was made of gold and ivory. This temple was one of the four largest in the Roman world. Of its three rivals, the best known to Bible students is the Temple of Diana at Ephesus.

The Theater of Dionysus

Nestled in the southeast corner of the Acropolis hill lay the semi-circular Theater of Dionysus. To us a theater is not a religious structure. But drama in ancient Athens rose from presentations in honor of Dionysus, god of wine.

preaching to them. At least one such altar has been found and now is on display in the Archaeological Museum in Istanbul.

The Temple of Zeus

One of the most colossal religious structures of this city of idol worship was the Temple of Olympian Zeus or Jupiter Olympus, located not far to the southeast of the Acropolis. Unfinished and roofless in Paul's day, Hadrian completed it in the second century. Fifteen of its gigantic columns are still standing.

The structure had 104 Corinthian columns of Pentelic marble 56 feet high and 5 feet 7

The fully developed dramas presented in New Testament times somewhat resembled our musicals. Three actors interspersed acting with music performed by a chorus of fifteen. Each spring (at the end of March) at a festival honoring Dionysus they awarded prizes to playwrights and actors. The festival began with a procession in the god's honor, during which an image of the god was brought to the theater and sacrifices made to him.

Though people could become frenzied with drink and commit terrible acts, the Greeks, and other peoples of the Mediterranean, chose to emphasize the benefits of drink: to make people merry, banish fear, to give them the sense that they could do what they thought they could not. The effect of drink was to give a feeling of being possessed by a power greater than themselves. Dionysus was not only outside of them but within them too, they thought. The power of wine drinking was to show them that they had an untapped power within; "they could themselves become divine."

The Theater of Dionysus, originally in wood, was seated in stone about 330 B.C. It is estimated that the 78 rows of seats could hold between 14,000 and 17,000 spectators. Originally action took place in the orchestra area, but in the Roman period it occurred on a rather elaborate stage.

A sculpted figure of the god Dionysus. (From the stage area of the Theater of Dionysus)

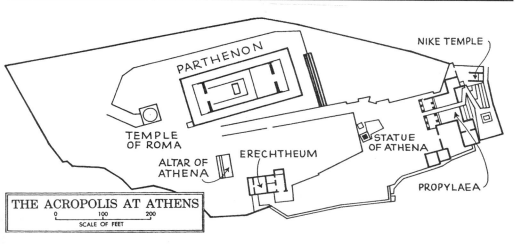

NIKE TEMPLE

PARTHENON

TEMPLE
OF ROMA

STATUE
OF ATHENA

ALTAR OF
ATHENA

ERECHTHEUM

PROPYLAEA

THE ACROPOLIS AT ATHENS

0   100   200
SCALE OF FEET

Plan or diagram of the Acropolis

The Acropolis

Like the modern tourist, Paul eventually must have gone to the Acropolis of Athens. As he walked up the hill and was about to enter the sacred complex, he would have passed below the exquisite little Ionic Temple of Athena Nike (victory). The parapet around it was sculptured with figures of victories in a variety of poses. Passing next through the impressive ornamental gateway or the Propylaea, Paul gazed on the colossal bronze figure of Athena Promachos (the goddess who fights in front), made by Phidias from spoils taken from the Persians at Marathon.

He could now see the Parthenon. But the main entrance was on the east, so the apostle continued on the sacred way. He would have noticed, however, that on the west pediment the statuary portrayed the quar-

rel between Athena and Poseidon for possession of Attica, while the other gods and heroes looked on.

On Paul's left he would have seen the Erechtheum, temple of Athena Polias (of the city) and Erechtheus (son of Athena) with its beautiful porch of the maidens (caryatids). The main part of this structure is a rectangle 78 feet long by 42 feet wide with an Ionic colonnade at either end standing 25 feet in height. The porch, with its six maidens whose heads support the roof, extends from the southwest corner of the temple.

Next on the left he would have seen the great Altar of Athena. As the sacred way turned toward the eastern entrance of the Parthenon, the apostle would have seen on his left a circular structure surrounded by nine Ionic columns housing the altar of Roma and Augustus. This was built between 27 and 14 B.C.

At last the apostle would have reached the main entrance of the magnificent Parthenon. Begun in 447, it was dedicated to the goddess Athena in 438, when Athens stood at the height of her glory. With Pericles as the political chief, the supervision of the work had been entrusted to the great sculptor Phidias. What an impressive sight it must have been for the apostle, who lamented that so much effort and expense had been devoted to the worship of a deity that did not exist.

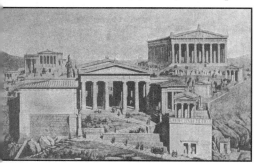

Reconstruction of the Acropolis as it appeared in Paul's day

The statue of Athena as it stood in the Parthenon

The great marble structure measured at its base 238 feet in length and 111 feet in width. Its encircling row of 46 fluted Doric columns (17 on each side and 8 on each end) stood to a height of 34 feet, each column having a diameter of six feet at the base. The top of the pediment rose to a height of 65 feet. And the east pediment was filled with sculptures of the important gods of Greece. In the center of the group was Zeus, from whose head, according to Greek mythology, Athena (goddess of wisdom) sprang fully armed. Encircling the entire structure above the colonnade was the Doric frieze. Divided into 92 panels, this frieze consisted of groups of sculptures depicting legendary and mythological stories dear to the hearts of the Greeks. On the east end Paul must have found himself looking up at scenes from the struggle between the gods and the giants.

Looking between the columns of the peristyle, the apostle surely saw another frieze near the roof, known as the Ionic frieze, 524 feet in length. A continuous series of sculptures completely encircled the building. The approximately 600 figures of this frieze included men, women, and animals that participated in the Panathenaic Procession, formed every year to carry a new robe to Athena in proper state.

If he peered through the tremendous bronze doors into the sanctuary, Paul would have seen the great gold and ivory image of Athena, one of the greatest works of Phidias. The fleshy parts were carved ivory and the rest consisted of plates of gold suspended on a framework of cedar wood. The room was surrounded by a two-story Doric colonnade and measured 98 feet long, 63 feet wide, and 43 feet high. The west room, or treasury of the city, Paul would not have seen, but he would have been told that in the center of it were four great Ionic columns arranged in a rectangle and extending from the floor to the ceiling. The room was 44 feet long and 63 feet wide.

Walking around the outside of the temple, the apostle surely noticed the perfect form of the structure. He would have been told that there was not a straight line in the building and that the columns bowed slightly inward at the top to avoid optical illusions of sagging lines or crooked columns. Moreover, the upper part of the friezes was cut deeper than the lower to cause optical equalization.

As Paul turned to leave the Acropolis, he would have noticed that numerous statues of gods and famous men bordered the walk, many of which were votive offerings to the gods. In fact, wherever he went in Athens he was impressed with the

A scene from the Parthenon frieze showing the new garment for Athena (woven annually).

many altars to the gods, statues of them, and other evidences of the religiosity of the people.

Worship of Athena

The whole of Athens focused on the worship of Athena, especially during the Panathenaia. This festival, celebrated annually during the first month of the year, which approximated our month of July, lasted for eight days. It touched the lives of all Athenians, rich and poor, male and female, young and old. Though male citizens participated in team sports, and individual athletic events and equestrian events were dominated by the more well-to-do, the whole city got involved in the procession up to the Parthenon to bring the new robe to Athena and in the public revelry. This can be clearly seen from the pictorial representation of the procession on the Ionian frieze on the Parthenon and from literary representations, as well as the public feasting. While they celebrated the Panathenaia every year, the Great Panathenaia occurred every fourth year (in the third year of each Olympiad).

During the Great Panathenaia they sacrificed one hundred cows to Athena, and during the annual Lesser Panathenaia over a hundred sheep and cows. The bones and fat went to the gods and the people feasted on the roasted flesh. Athenians had a chance to dine on meat chiefly during this and other sacrifices to the gods.

The schedule of the Panathenaia seems to have been as follows: musical and recitation contests (recitations from the *Iliad* and *Odyssey*), day 1; athletic contests for boys and youths, day 2; athletic contests for men, day 3; horse and chariot races, day 4; contests between the Ten Tribes of Athens, day 5; torch race and an all-night revel, day 6; followed by the procession to the Acropolis at the dawn of day 7. The animal sacrifice took place as the procession reached the altar of Athena. Boat races occupied day 7. On day 8 they awarded prizes, accompanied by feasting and celebrations.

The Panathenaia had become all things to all people: an athletic event, a cultural event (music and poetry), a religious exercise, a great show, a great party, and a great

Demeter was honored in the mysteries at Eleusis.

feast. Those who became Christians and could no longer honor the goddess dropped out of the celebration and became social misfits. It is easy to see how Christians could be considered anti-social in Athens and other places where comparable festivals in honor of the gods occurred (e. g., Ephesus).[16] It is also easy to see how the whole of society could be emotionally swept up in the worship of a deity of wood or stone that really did not exist. The social dimension of pagan religion had a strong hold on the people.

En Route to Corinth—Eleusis

In a sense Paul had been marking time in Athens until conditions in Macedonia quieted enough for him to return there. When that did not seem to be happening, he decided to go to Corinth, about sixty miles to the west. In so doing he left the intellectual center of Greece for the commercial center. And fourteen miles down the road he would pass Eleusis, cult center of the Eleusinian Mysteries, the most famous of the Greek mysteries.

Since Paul was not an initiate, he would have had a difficult time learning anything about this religion. He would have found the sanctuary on the east slope of the acropolis at Eleusis. It was surrounded by a wall about twenty-five feet high. A temple of Artemis stood outside the entrance. There was a double wall on the entrance side, between which was a long inner courtyard. The entrance through the second wall into

The Telesterion or initiation room of the mysteries at Eleusis

the inner enclosure was an elaborate monumental gateway donated by a friend of Cicero, Appius Claudius Pulcher, about 50 B.C. If Paul could have passed through this monumental gate and ascended the Sacred Way, paved with white marble, he would have seen two caves on his right. Before the larger stood a sanctuary of Pluto. The cave represented the entrance into Hades. Farther on he would have passed a megaron-type temple of Demeter.

And finally the Sacred Way led to the northeast entrance of the Telesterion (sanctuary or initiation room) of the Mysteries. This was a large covered building 168 by 177 feet backed against the rock. Each of the three free sides had two doors. The timber roof was carried by six rows of six columns each at a height of twenty feet. These must have greatly impeded the vision of spectators who sat on banks of stone seats around the four sides.

If the apostle could not have found out much about the sanctuary at Eleusis, he would have found out less about the religious practices connected with it. Initiates would not, of course, divulge the secrets of the cult. Paul knew that the Mysteries involved worship of Demeter and her daughter Kore. According to legend, Hades, god of the underworld, had

snatched away Kore (Persephone); and in her great sorrow and searching for her daughter, Demeter had come to Eleusis. After having received hospitality, she revealed her secret rites to the people of the place. Paul also knew that Demeter was considered a sister of Zeus and goddess of agriculture.

While in Athens he had learned that on the thirteenth of Boedromion (parts of our September and October) some of the socially elite young men marched out to Eleusis and returned to Athens the next day with some religious objects. On the fifteenth there was a gathering of the catechumens to hear an address by the current cult leader. On the following day the candidates for initiation went to the seashore for ceremonial purification rites and returned to offer sacrifices to the goddess. On the seventeenth of Boedromion there was a great sacrifice with prayers for Athens and the cities of the other delegates participating. The next day was a day of rest for most, and there was opportunity for latecomers to be prepared for initiation.

On the nineteenth of Boedromion a great religious procession started along the sacred way bearing the "fair young god" Iacchus, probably the youthful Dionysus. Arriving at Eleusis, they held a midnight celebration under the stars. The twentieth of the month was spent in resting, fasting, purification, and sacrifice. As to what went on inside of the sanctuary, Paul could not have found out. The whole ceremony lasted for nine days.

From various bits of information, it now appears that initiation included a kind of passion play, probably centering about the sufferings of the goddess. Then there seems to have been a revelation of sacred cult objects and, among other things, the celebration of a sort of holy communion involving a barley drink and certain foods. In this initiation service (little is known of the details) the initiate supposedly established mystic contact with the mother and daughter. And by an act of faith he regarded himself certain of blessing at the hands of Demeter and Kore in the next life because he had established friendship with the pair in this life. Both the sacred pageant and the viewing of sacred objects presumably took place in the Telesterion.[17] As with the other mystery religions, the Eleusinian Mysteries involved a dying and resurrecting god and the rhythm of the seasons. (See discussion of Mystery Religions in chapter 16.)

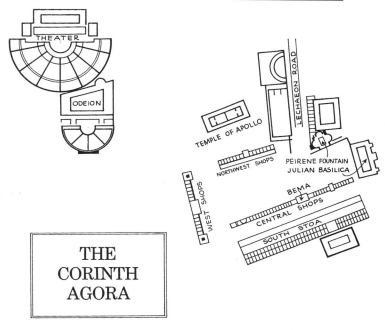

THE
CORINTH
AGORA

Paul in Corinth

"After these things Paul departed from Athens and went to Corinth. . . . . And he continued there a year and six months, teaching the word of God among them." (Acts 18:1, 11 NKJV)

To subdue the rebellious Corinthians, Rome in 146 B.C. destroyed the ancient city of Corinth, killing the adult male population and sending the women and children into slavery. It is generally believed that the city was virtually uninhabited for a century, but there are indications that there was at least a small settlement there. At any rate, Julius Caesar refounded the city in 44 B.C., largely with freedmen, per-

haps many of them descended from slaves taken at the second century destruction. Corinth grew rapidly, and by the time Paul arrived it had become the largest and most flourishing center in southern Greece. Perhaps the most definitive assessment of the population at that time is that about 80,000 lived in the urban area, with another 20,000 in the countryside nearby.[18]

Of course we are curious to know what sort of place Corinth was when Paul arrived and what sort of ministry he had in it. As to the city's physical situation, it has already been noted that Corinth controlled the trade routes between the Peloponnesus and central Greece and across the Isthmus of Corinth. In this connection, she had built a tramway across the Isthmus and was served by ports on the Saronic and Corinthian gulfs. She administered the Isthmian Games, thereby serving as a religious, athletic, and cohesive center in Greece. The city itself lay about a mile and one-half south of the Corinthian Gulf on the north side of its acropolis at an altitude of about 400 feet. The acropolis towered about 1,500 feet over the city to an altitude of 1,886 feet. From its peak on a clear day the Acropolis at Athens can be plainly seen.

A wall over six miles in circumference enclosed the city and its acropolis. Numerous large towers were spaced along this wall. In the north central part of town, about equidistant from the east and west walls (about a mile from each) stood the Agora, nerve center of the metropolis. Outside the walls in the surrounding plain stretched grain fields, olive groves, vineyards, and other agricultural holdings of the city.

As to the nonphysical aspects of Corinth, several generalizations need to be made. As a new city—less than 100 years old when Paul visited it—it had not had time to develop a social structure with an aristocracy possessing illustrious genealogies. Probably the social and economic structure was more fluid than at most other centers in Greece. Many of those possessing wealth were the *nouveaux riches*, with all of the attendant inadequacies of that class. Since Corinth had not had time to develop a native culture, the culture it had was imitative and, as a result of the overweening economic interests of the community, was only a shallow veneer.

The Temple of Apollo and the Acropolis of Corinth, with its Temple to Aphrodite and its one thousand priestesses given to religious prostitution.

Since much of the population was mobile (sailors, businessmen, government officials, *et al.*), it was cut off from the inhibitions of a settled society. To make matters worse, the Corinthians commonly practiced religious prostitution in connection with the temples of the city. For instance, religious prostitution employed 1,000 priestesses of the Temple of Aphrodite on the Acropolis.[19] The social mobility and the evils of religious practices produced a general corruption of society. "Corinthian morals" became a byword even in the pagan Roman world.

It is no wonder that Paul had so much to say about the sacredness of the body in his first Corinthian letter. And if he wrote the epistle to the Romans from Corinth (as is commonly believed), he had plenty of reason for condemning the unmentionable practices alluded to in Romans 1. The conditions which Paul and the Christian gospel faced in Corinth should give pause to the modern preacher who laments the moral corruption of his own day and feels that his task is almost impossible in such a context. Conditions in Corinth were far worse. The message and power of the gospel are the same in the twentieth century as they were in the first.

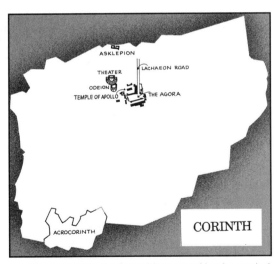

The road from the Corinthian port of Lechaeon led into the north side of the Agora. On this road near the foot of the marble steps leading into the Agora excavators in 1898 found a large block of stone bearing the words "Synagogue of the Hebrews." This has been identified as the lintel of the synagogue, believed to have stood nearby. Archaeologists differ as to whether this dates to Paul's time or later. In any case, Paul began his ministry in Corinth by preaching to the Jews (Acts 18:4).

The Agora Area and the New Testament

The Agora served as the center of Corinthian life. Located in the north central

Ruins of the civil law court known as the Julian Basilica in ancient Corinth. Some of the charges of the Corinthian Christians against one another (1 Corinthians 6:1–11) may have been reviewed on this very site.

part of town, it measured about 700 feet east and west and 300 feet north and south. Following the natural configuration of the land, the southern section was about thirteen feet higher than the northern part. At the dividing line of the two levels a row of low buildings flanked the rostrum, which served as a speaker's stand for public addresses and a judgment seat for magistrates. Here Gallio heard the case that the Jews presented against Paul, as we have

The South Stoa had shops for the sale of wine and meats. In the back room of each was a well (covered, in foreground) supplied with cool water from the Peirene Spring.

seen earlier. Gallio could walk out from the higher southern level onto the rostrum, and he would stand above the heads of those who addressed him.

On the east side of the Agora stood a large basilica of the Augustan period. In this court building many of the cases must have been tried in which believers were going to law before unbelievers (1 Corinthians 6:1–8). Alternatively, another court building stood at the south of the Agora, south of the south stoa.

The south stoa stretched across almost the entire south side of the Agora. About 500 feet long, it was probably the largest secular structure in Greece proper and consisted of a double colonnade behind which were thirty-three small shops. All of these except two had a well in them, connected with a water channel, which in turn was connected to the Peirene Fountain. These were apparently wine shops, each with its private cooler. Other perishables were sold there as well.

The stoa also contained shops for the sale of meat. In one of them an inscription "Lucius the butcher" was found. In another an inscription appeared which called the shop a *macellum*, the Latin equivalent of the Greek *makellon*, used in 1 Corinthians 10:25 and commonly translated "meat market."

Erastus is memoralized in the theater of Corinth. Some scholars think he was the New Testament Erastus (2 Timothy 4:20; Acts 19:22).

Paul dealt with the question of meats offered to idols here and in effect tells his readers that they need not be concerned about the source of meats displayed in public markets. If the meats retailed there had been sold by the temples to legitimate businessmen, housewives were not responsible for that fact.

Eating meat or other foods offered to idols involved more than what one bought in the market, however. In the last chapter and in the last section on Athens we saw that it was common practice for people who were or were not devotees of a pagan deity to share in the eating of sacrificial meat in the deity's temple grounds. That such a practice existed in Corinth is evident from the fact that numerous dining rooms have been found on a terrace of the acropolis of Corinth in the sacred grounds of Demeter and Kore. They have appeared elsewhere in Greece as well.[20]

As a matter of fact, Paul specifically referred to eating in a dining room of a temple in Corinth food offered to idols (1 Corinthians 8:10). He observed that such an act might not negatively affect the one who did so because he had in his own mind dismissed the reality of the god. But the act of eating might serve as a stumbling block to brothers who were weaker (1 Corinthians 8:11–13) or had not yet fully turned to God from idols (1 Thessalonians 1:9).

This knowing participation in religious feasting is what the Council of Jerusalem must have had primarily in mind when it commanded that Gentiles "abstain from things offered to idols, from blood, from things strangled and from sexual immorality" (Acts 15:29 NKJV). The "sexual immorality" in this context certainly involved abstaining from patronizing the religious prostitutes connected with pagan temples all over the Mediterranean world.

Of course Corinth, like all other Greco-Roman cities, was given over to idolatry. Towering above the Agora on the northwest, on a rocky terrace of its own, stood the Temple of Apollo. In the terror of 146 B.C. the Romans did not destroy the temple built during the sixth century B.C. The temple measured 174 feet long by 69 feet wide, and the 38 columns of its peristyle stood almost 24 feet in height. These fluted Doric columns were more impressive than many in Greece because they were made of single blocks of stone instead of being built up with drums of stone.

Cut into the hill just to the northwest of the Agora rose the great theater of Corinth. Its seating capacity was probably over 18,000, but it is impossible to give an accurate estimate for Paul's day. Our interest in the theater centers in the fact that near the stage building is an inscription that concerns Erastus, an aedile (a

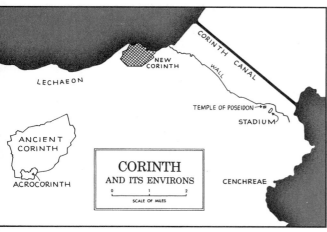

Corinth and its surrounding area, showing the location of the Isthmian Games (Stadium, Temple of Poseidon).

was probably alluding to this important event in the life of the people in 1 Corinthians 9:24–27.

The competitors came chiefly from Corinth, Aegina, Thebes, Athens, and some of the islands of the Aegean, but crowds at the Isthmian Games probably exceeded those at the Olympics. Corinth administered the games. Held in honor of Poseidon, god of the sea, and beginning with a sacrifice to the god, the games included athletic, equestrian, and musical competitions, and perhaps also a regatta. They held separate competitions for men, youths, and boys.

The athletic events included footraces of 200 and 800 yards, races in armor, throwing the discus and javelin, two-horse chariot racing, the Pentathlon (running, jumping, discus and javelin throwing, and wrestling), and the Pankration (a combination of boxing and wrestling). It is difficult to determine exactly what events occurred during the first century A.D. when the great athletic festivals of Greece were in a state of decline.

Ministers who paint glowing pictures of the Isthmian Games in their sermons on Paul or 1 Corinthians often do not realize how corrupt and degraded Greek athletics were during Paul's lifetime—and they were nowhere more degraded than at the Isthmia.[21] Professionalism had taken over, with plenty of quackery in training and dieting. "The gymnasia, instead of producing healthy, useful citizens, had become schools of idleness and immorality; from a physical and military point of view the whole nation had degenerated."[22] The victor's crown seems to have been withered wild celery during the first century A.D., a corruptible crown indeed (1 Corinthians 9:25).

Judging from the available accounts of what went on at the Isthmian Games, one gets the impression that they were more like "old home week" than a serious religious

Roman municipal official) of the city who laid a pavement at his own expense. Paul in writing to the Romans from Corinth sent greetings from a "chamberlain" (Greek, *oikonomos*) or steward by this name (Romans 16:23). Erastus is also referred to in 2 Timothy 4:20 and Acts 19:22. A Roman aedile and a Greek *oikonomos* would both have been commissioners of streets and public buildings. Perhaps the Erastus of this inscription may be equated with the person of the same name mentioned in the New Testament. Some scholars think so.

The Race and the Isthmian Games

"Do you not know that those who run in a race all run, but one receives the prize? Run in such a way that you may obtain it. And everyone who competes for the prize is temperate in all things. Now they do it to obtain a perishable crown, but we for an imperishable crown." (1 Corinthians 9:24–25 NKJV)

When Paul came across the isthmus to Corinth, he passed the location of the Isthmian Games. The following year, in April and May of A.D. 51, while he was still in Corinth, the biennial games would have been held. Paul probably saw these. And perhaps the opportunity of preaching to the large crowds gathering for the event had led Paul to go to Corinth in the first place. Some scholars think so. In any case, Paul

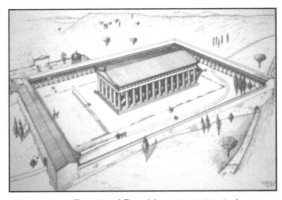

Temple of Poseidon reconstructed

Starting blocks at the Isthmian race track

and athletic event. Philosophers parried intellectual blows; their students wrangled. Magicians showed off their stunts. Fortune-tellers preyed on a gullible and superstitious public. Hucksters hawked their wares among the assembled throngs.

The area given over to the Isthmian Games was about six miles from Corinth, just south of the east end of the present Corinth Canal. In recent years the area has been quite thoroughly investigated and largely excavated. The three main structures at the site are the Temple of Poseidon, the stadium, and the theater. Originally constructed in the seventh century, the temple was ravaged by fire and was rebuilt about 470 B.C. Heavily damaged by fire in 390 B.C., it was restored and stood until the mid-sixth century A.D. Inside stood colossal statues of Poseidon, lord of the sea, and the goddess Amphitrite, joint ruler of the sea. Near the temple stood an impressive altar to Poseidon.

The great altar of the Temple of Poseidon

From the temple to the stadium, located to the southeast of the sanctuary, stretched an avenue lined with pine trees and statues of victorious athletes. About fifty yards northeast of the sanctuary of Poseidon stood the theater, where musical and dramatic events could be staged.[23] Very likely the Isthmian Games occurred prior to Paul's arraignment before Gallio. After his acquittal he remained in Corinth a little longer.

(For more on this topic, go to p. 514 or p. 584.)

Warfare

The New Testament period coincided with *Pax Romana* or the Roman peace. Though Rome had fought fiercely to subdue both Macedonia and Achaia in the second century B.C., that era was now long gone. Romans were generally philhellenes, admirers of Greek culture, and sought to imitate it. Especially did they esteem the Spartans for their military qualities and the Athenians for their literary, philosophical and architectural achievements.

The provinces of Macedonia and Achaia had been thoroughly pacified and were therefore administered by the Senate rather than the emperor. In the New Testament period Rome stationed no troops in Greece and it was not normally even necessary to move troops through Greece to guard the Danubian frontier. Legions could be sent by land through Illyricum (modern Yugoslavia) to the province of Moesia (areas of Bulgaria and Romania), where they were encamped

The Theater

south of the Danube. Very occasionally a legion might be funneled through Thessalonica to the northern frontier. *(For more on this topic, go to p. 526 or p. 585.)*

Housing and Furniture

"Likewise greet the church that is in their house." (Romans 16:5 NKJV)

So said Paul as he wrote to the Romans from Corinth.

In what sort of house would the house churches have met in Rome or in the Corinth of the period? Two styles of house construction could be found in Greece at that time: the traditional Greek or Mediterranean and the Roman. The tradi-

tional Greek, as we have seen, had an open courtyard in the center or on the side, with or without a surrounding colonnade. Family rooms opened off that. The Roman-style house had an entryway that led into an atrium or courtyard containing a room with an opening in the roof called a compluvium, through which light and rain might enter. Residents collected water in a pool in the middle of the floor called an impluvium. Adjacent to the atrium was the triclinium or dining room, with its standard number of couches for nine to recline. These two units comprised the public part of the house. In addition, there were of course bedrooms, a kitchen, servants' quarters, and storage.

Upper-class houses of Corinth tended to be of the atrium style. One has been excavated dating to the first half or middle of the first century and thus contemporary with Paul's ministry there. This had an atrium measuring about sixteen by nineteen feet and a dining room eighteen by twenty-four feet. Murphy-O'Connor compares this house with another upper-class house in Corinth dating to the early second century, a house near Thessalonica, and one in Rome and finds the size of the atrium and dining rooms to be similar in size in all four. The atrium might hold as many as thirty people on average and the dining room nine. And he observes that probably the host would bring the upper-class members of the church into the dining room and seat the rest in the atrium. Thus he sees factions or resentments

Upper-class houses of the New Testament period were of the atrium or courtyard style. Here is a typical house with its atrium on the island of Delos.

Houses commonly had mosaic floors, as here in the House of the Trident on Delos.

Houses also frequently had painted walls, as in this house at Amphipolis (Acts 17:1).

developing within the church, and church groups meeting in different houses and establishing variant views that created the problems Paul addressed in the Corinthian epistles.[24]

A further word on dining rooms is in order. In late Hellenistic times the *triclinium* arrangement was developed. That is, three large couches were installed in a *pi* arrangement (π), each with three diners, with head to center and feet to the outside. The Romans adopted this system to facilitate conversation. Dining rooms for ritual feasting in the sanctuaries of the pagan gods were larger. Some large halls had as many as one hundred couches. In such places the wealthy could throw large parties, and especially, could hold wedding feasts.

Houses of the period had mosaic floors and plastered walls painted to look like marble or with mythological scenes. Light and air reached the dining and sitting rooms and bedrooms from the inner court (not from windows). Rooms were not very well stocked with furniture by our standards. They contained a few chairs, tables, chests of various shapes (especially for storage of clothes), couches, and portable ovens.

In the homes of the wealthy, couches might be real works of art, adorned with bronze sculptures on the legs, backs, or side supports; inlaid with ivory and colored glass; and covered with mattresses and pillows. Tables and chairs, too, might be elegantly carved and decorated with inlay. Sometimes exquisite statuettes in bronze or terra cotta decorated the atriums or other rooms. The subject of house construction is more fully developed in the last chapter, as is the topic of house furnishings.
(For more on this topic, go to p. 526 or p. 585.)

Diet and Foodstuffs

In New Testament times large parts of Greece were devoted exclusively to agriculture and herding. There was little mining or manufacturing for export. Low-growing plants and shrubs that covered the lower slopes of the mountains almost everywhere provided pasturage for sheep, goats, and pigs. Cattle do not seem to have been raised in any quantity. So of course there was plenty of wool and goat hair for clothing and other fabrics and goat milk and cheese for food. Many places produced woolen goods for local use.

Grain, olives, and wine served as dietary staples. The stony nature of the soil often forced the Greeks to raise barley rather than wheat. But the deep alluvial loam of Thessaly (south of Mount Olympus in eastern Greece) was ideally suited for wheat production. And Boetia (north of Attica) also yielded wheat of high grade. Messenia and Laconia (plain of Sparta) in the southern Peloponnesus contained good crop and pasture land. Most parts of Greece produced the wine used locally by the average person. Mainland Greece exported very little.

Olives flourished all over the country, and they exported quantities of olive oil from Attica. As a matter of fact, only about one-fourth of the soil of Attica was cultivable, and it was ill-suited for growing anything but the drought-resistant olives. Attica has the lowest amount of rainfall of any region of the country. The olive provided food, cooking oil, a lubricant, a wound dressing, and oil for lamps. Even today the olive is important. On my first trip to Athens in 1960 a guide commented that the lowly olive saved them during the Nazi occupation of World War II.

Important to the diet of the lower classes was a porridge of mixed pulse (peas, lentils, lupine). Sesame flavored bread. Lettuce and cucumbers were common. Fishing helped to supplement the diet in many places. Domesticated fowl provided meat and eggs. The flanks of the mountains of Thessaly were well-clad with fruit trees. Arcadia in the central Peloponnesus produced quantities of nuts. And Attica produced honey for a diet lacking in sugar.

Flax, especially for the manufacture of linen cloth, grew in Achaea in the northern Peloponnesus, in Elis in the western Peloponnesus, and apparently near Corinth. Hemp was also raised in Elis.

Elis had the best cattle pastures in the Peloponnesus. Thessaly produced a large breed of horse which furnished the best cavalry of all Greece. Corinth was always a breeder of horses, and the majority of the known equestrian victories in the Isthmian Games in Roman times were Corinthian.[25] Aetolia was also well adapted to horse raising. Elis raised horses for the Roman hippodromes and the army. Arcadia in the central Peloponnesus had good breeding grounds for mules.

In the Greek world of Paul's day a few wealthy men controlled large tracts of land with its produce, the breeding of finer stock (e. g., race horses for the circus), as well as asses and mules, and perhaps goats and sheep. Larsen makes the point, however, that they did not manage all this with slave labor, as is sometimes thought, but with employed free men as farmers, goatherds, swineherds, shepherds, and drivers for oxen or horses.[26]

(For more on this topic, go to p. 527 or p. 586.)

Dress

From the golden age of Athens in the fifth century B.C., both men and women of Greece had worn the wool (sometimes linen) *chiton* (Roman tunic) as the basic item in their wardrobe. This consisted of two strips of cloth sewed along the sides with a hole in the top for the head to pass through. This could be knee-length but sometimes went only to mid-thigh. Normally it had sleeves extending to the elbow but might be sleeveless. The feminine variety was fuller than the masculine. Both men and women sometimes wore a loincloth under the chiton and women also might wear a breastband.

Women typically had a short tunic under a longer one. In such a case the outer one commonly would be sleeveless and held together at the shoulders by pins or brooches. These "dresses" could be of a variety of colors and often had some embroidery or designs around the hem or the neck. In cold weather people might put on two, three, or four chitons in a layered effect. Belts were normally long strips of cloth into the folds of which one could put money or other objects. There was no set length to these belts. Paul's belt, for example, was so long that the prophet Agabus could tie his own hands and feet with it to symbolize Paul's coming imprisonment in Jerusalem (Acts 21:11).

Over the tunic both men and women wore cloaks when necessary. Men doing active work wore the *chlamys,* a square of cloth fastened with a clasp over the shoulder, leaving both arms free. But the cloak (*himation*) was normally a large square of cloth wrapped around the body. The way this was done was to throw one corner over the left shoulder and, held tightly with the left arm, it was then pulled across the back towards the right side, over or under the right arm, and then again thrown over the left shoulder. They sometimes bleached cloaks white but they normally left them in their natural color. They usually turned out to be about knee length. Except when traveling neither sex wore a head covering, though a woman might pull the corner of her cloak over her head in bad weather.

Sandals almost universally served as the standard footwear, but shoes or boots were worn by soldiers, hunters, and workmen. Because the streets were so dirty, it was common to leave foot coverings at the door when entering a house. The poor probably went barefoot nearly all of the time.

From the time of Pericles during the golden age of Athens (c. 450 B.C.) it became customary for men to wear their hair cut short and their beards trimmed. Certainly this was the practice in places like Athens, Philippi, Thessalonica, Corinth, and elsewhere in the first century. In fact, many men were clean-shaven in the first century. But we wonder whether men in rural Greece were so meticulous about their appearance. The apostle Paul mirrored current practice in his condemnation of long hair on men in Corinth (1 Corinthians 11:14). Barber shops were numerous and well patronized and a place of public gathering and gossip mongering.

Women might sport elaborate coiffures and hold their hair in nets, probably usually made of linen. Greeks and Romans bathed frequently and used cosmetics and ointments. So did Jews, who dressed like the rest of the Hellenistic world.

(For more on this topic, go to p. 528 or p. 587.)

Family Life

A girl's father had the right and responsibility to arrange for her marriage. The goal was not to find a rich young groom, because that might make the bride's family subject to that of the groom. Rather, the desire normally was to bring about a marriage between those roughly equal in economic status. Negotiations led to betrothal, at which time a dowry was usually agreed upon. This might include money, linens, clothing, furniture and other household goods, and even slaves. When the legal formalities were settled, a family feast took place in the father-in-law's house in many places in Greece. Before the act of marriage they made proper sacrifices to the divinities who protected marriage—especially to Hera and Zeus, but also to Athena and Artemis.

The wedding banquet was generally given in the house of the bride's father. This was one of the few times that men and women ate together in public, though they ate at separate tables. The richness or elegance of this meal and the entertainment depended on the financial resources of the bride's family. At the meal toasts were drunk to the couple. After the meal the bride was driven in a carriage drawn by oxen, mules, or horses to the house of the bridegroom. She sat in the middle between the groom and his best friend or nearest relative. The rest of the people in the procession moved on foot, carrying torches lighted by the mothers of the bride and bridegroom and accompanied by flutes and lyres. Normally the bride wore a multicol-

ored dress with a flaming veil and the groom wore white. Both of them were crowned with multicolored headbands.

At the home of the groom the young men and young women arranged themselves into two separate choirs and engaged in a contest of song about marriage, the single state and more. There was more feasting, an invocation to Aphrodite, and a toast for blessing on the bride and bridegroom. Finally the groom took the bride to the nuptial chamber and bolted the door. The relatives serenaded and showered the couple with all kinds of gifts the next morning.

Thereafter only the bedroom and eating room were common to husband and wife. In the event that the husband had guests for dinner, women did not participate in the meal. The duties of the wife involved the supervision of the movable and unmovable property of the house, male and female slaves, the kitchen, the nursing of the sick and more. She had to know how to make clothes and prepare wool. The two basic tasks assigned to her were the management of domestic affairs and the bringing up of her children, of girls until they were married and boys until they were taken over by adult male training in the gymnasium or elsewhere. The wife controlled all domestic affairs.

The goal of marriage was to acquire a legitimate generation to follow—to guarantee the continued existence of the community by the procreation of descendants—and an organized and trustworthy management of household affairs. In fact, the official formula of betrothal included the statement "for the procreation of legitimate offspring."[27] Nevertheless, the number of unmarried men in Greece appears to have been fairly large. Unmarried women also were no rarity.[28]

Women spent their time in the seclusion of the house. They normally did not show themselves in public unless accompanied by some older trusted male person of the household and generally followed by a female slave. Unmarried girls likewise lived rather secluded lives. Their mothers taught them spinning and weaving, cooking, management of the household, and possibly elementary knowledge of reading

Gymnasia were places where boys studied reading, writing, arithmetic, and music, along with physical education. Here is an image from an Athenian cup of a boy's sports instructor. His power to punish is embodied in the stick he carries. Since this instructor dates before the New Testament period, he wears a longer beard. In the New Testament period, he probably would have had a short beard or have been clean shaven. He is wearing a cloak or a *himation*.

and writing. The women and girls of Sparta tended to lead a more public life, however.

"Exposure" of Infants

We often hear of the "exposure" of infants in ancient Greece, especially in Sparta, but it was not unknown in Athens or elsewhere. The impression we get is that these children were simply thrown out on a hillside to die with a heartlessness that is foreign to us. The reason for exposure is that they were identified as feeble or deformed, or were simply unwanted for some reason. But the facts are quite different from the perception. They placed unwanted infants in large clay vessels in such a manner that they would be found by other people—either childless or those with humanitarian concerns. Often neck-chains, rings, or other distinctive identification accompanied the infants so their paternity could later be traced.[29] Sometimes people also sold their children to childless women who did not want to lose their husbands.

Education of Youth

We have looked at the subject of the education of youth, primarily Greek youth, in the last chapter (especially as it took place at the gymnasia and the lower schools). It is unnecessary to repeat that here. Some further generalizations need to be made, however:

First, Greece was less prosperous than most Greek (Hellenistic) communities in Asia Minor and there was less money in the community treasuries or in the hands of the wealthy for maintenance of the school system.

Second, commercial activity in mainland Greece was weaker than in Asia Minor, so there was not so much necessity to read and write.

Third, the amount of education is always related to the perceived need for it. Some people in the religious, academic, administrative, and commercial communities would provide it for their children so they could follow in family activities (or their fathers' footsteps). Many in the rural areas, or in the agricultural community, did not have the same interest in education.

Fourth, the learning of reading and writing was always a problem because books (scrolls) and writing materials were scarce and expensive.

Fifth, assumptions about the percentage of ancient population that was literate are probably too high, and reasonably reliable estimates of literacy are very difficult to produce.[30]

(For more on this topic, go to p. 529 or p. 587.)

Work, Travel, and Commerce

Work

Greece suffered terribly during the Roman civil wars of the first century B.C. For example, at Pharsalus in 48 B.C. Julius Caesar worsted Pompey. At Philippi in 42, Octavian (later Augustus) and Mark Antony overcame Julius Caesar's assassins Brutus and Cassius.

At Actium in 31, Octavian defeated Mark Antony and for all practical purposes gained the empire. During these and earlier conflicts the treasuries of the Greek cities were ransacked, the economy was bled white, great destruction took place, and many men were impressed into one army or another. Athens had suffered great destruction at the hands of the Roman general Sulla in 86 B.C., and Corinth was wiped out in 146 B.C.

As a result of all this, economic historians often give very pessimistic accounts of Greece in the first Christian century. We need to be careful about accepting these jeremiads at face value, however. It is easy to compare the disadvantages of the first century A.D. with the golden age of Athens of the fifth century B.C. or the relative poverty of Greece with the wealth of the more richly endowed provinces of the empire at that time. As a matter of fact, there was rising prosperity during the first century as Greece benefited from the *Pax Romana* (Roman peace). And it would achieve a new height of prosperity during the second century. Fine new public buildings in various cities and records of wealthy men in numerous cities of the two provinces show that there was a higher level of prosperity and money to be made in the New Testament period.

Generally speaking, the export industry was not important during the period, but there was a great increase in the production of livestock: of sheep, goats, and horses especially. As a result, many were employed in herding. And there was industry of local importance—to produce clothing, foodstuffs, and other necessities for popular consumption. The majority of the populace worked in agriculture. Though the mines seem to have produced little, the quarries were exploited as never before. In several places about half the population engaged in "purple fishing," fishing for mollusks from which purple die was extracted. This was true of Laconia, Thessaly, and Euboea especially. Work opportunities are further indicated in the earlier discussion of diet and agriculture.

Commerce

The commerce of Greece moved largely on the sea. Greeks rarely transported bulky goods on the highways. The Egnatian Way was designed for maintaining communication and movement of troops. The more local roads were not well maintained, so the ports of Thessalonica and Athens and especially Corinth handled most of the commerce. Among other things, Thessalonica exported grain from the northern plains to Athens and elsewhere. Athens exported huge quantities of olive oil to various places in the Mediterranean world. Corinth was the commercial center of Greece. As noted in the discussion of geography, she sat astride the isthmus and commanded the east-west commerce that rolled across the isthmus instead of going around the southern part of Greece. Horses and mules bred in the Peloponnesus also left her ports.

Travel

"Now when they had passed through Amphipolis and Apollonia, they came to Thessalonica." (Acts 17:1 NKJV)

As Paul and Silas traveled from Philippi to Thessalonica (a distance of about ninety miles), they walked the Egnatian Way, the main highway across Macedonia. The road got its name from its builder, Gnaeus Egnatius, who was Roman governor in the 140s B.C. This paved road some fifteen feet wide served as the great military highway that connected Illyria (modern Yugoslavia), Macedonia, and Thrace. The road started at two points on the Adriatic coast—Dyrrachium (Albanian Durrës) and Aulon (modern Vlona). These two branches merged inland and continued as a single road all the way to Byzantium (Istanbul), a distance of 535 Roman miles (a Roman mile is 1,614.6 yards). On such a road one would probably travel about seventeen to twenty Roman miles per day on foot and would probably drive a vehicle about four Roman miles per hour for an average of twenty-five Roman miles per day.

Later Paul would travel from Athens to Corinth, a distance of some fifty miles. On the way, west of Megara, he would have passed under the dangerous precipices of the famous Scironian rocks. Here travelers had to pick their way on a track along the face of the cliff for six miles at a height of 600 to 700 feet. At points the road was perilously poised on the edge of a cliff. Later, in the second century, Hadrian provided a safer road. Gliding along in comfort in a car or bus on the highway between Athens and Corinth, today's tourist little suspects the difficulties of travel experienced by the ancients in this area.

These two comments illustrate the more easy and difficult stretches of travel on Paul's itinerary and in travel through Macedonia and Achaia in general. Movement between other cities and villages of Greece remained fairly difficult. Between the middle of November and the middle of March little moved by land. The sailing season on the Aegean and the Mediterranean also virtually closed from November to March. But the captain of the ship carrying Paul from Palestine to Rome decided to venture out on the sea during the closed season anyway and the ship wound up on the bottom of the Mediterranean at Malta.

In keeping with God's promise to Paul, everyone on board the ship made it safely to land. Yet what was that island like and what was Paul's witness there? The next chapter delves into the answers to those questions.

(For more on this topic, go to p.533 or p. 587.)

NOTES:

[1] Everett F. Harrison, *Acts: The Expanding Church* (Chicago: Moody, 1975), 248.

[2] Merrill C. Tenney, *New Testament Times* (Grand Rapids: Eerdmans, 1965), 276. See also D. A. Carson and others, *An Introduction to the New Testament* (Grand Rapids: Zondervan, 1992), 228–31.

[3] For documentation and further discussion, see David W. J. Gill and Conrad Gempf, *The Book of Acts in Its First Century Setting* (Grand Rapids: Eerdmans, 1994), 2, 93–98.

[4] Abba Eban, *My People* (New York: Random House, 1968), 104.

[5] A. N. Sherwin-White, *Roman Law and Roman Society in the New Testament* (Grand Rapids: Baker Book House, reprinted 1992 by permission of Oxford University Press), 58–60.

[6] Ibid., 172–73.

[7] Ibid. , 173.

[8] Ibid.

[9] See Howard F. Vos, *Philippians* (Grand Rapids: Zondervan, 1975).

[10] A. N. Sherwin-White, *The Roman Citizenship*, 2nd ed. (Oxford: Clarendon Press, 1973), 314–16.

[11] William M. Ramsay, *St. Paul the Traveller and the Roman Citizen* (Grand Rapids: Baker Book House, reprinted 1979), 237.

[12] Oscar Broneer, "Athens, 'City of Idol Worship,'" *The Biblical Archaeologist*, XXI (Feb., 1958), 27.

[13] Ramsay, 246–47.

[14] Broneer, 3.

[15] Ramsay, 237.

[16] For documentation and elaboration on the Panathenaia see Jenifer Neils, *Goddess and Polis* (Princeton, N.J.: Princeton University Press, 1992), 13–15, 23–24.

[17] Both the ritual and the structures at Eleusis are discussed authoritatively and thoroughly by George E. Mylonas, *Eleusis and the Eleusinian Mysteries* (Princeton, N.J.: Princeton University Press, 1961).

[18] Donald Engels, *Roman Corinth* (Chicago: University of Chicago Press, 1990), 33.

[19] Oscar Broneer, "Corinth, Center of St. Paul's missionary Work in Greece," *The Biblical Archaeologist*, XIV (Dec., 1951), 87. These priestesses were slaves who were bought and dedicated to the goddess and thereafter served her. See Mario A. Del Chiaro, ed., *Corinthiaca* (Columbia, Mo.: University of Missouri Press, 1986), 20.

[20] Ramsay MacMullen, *Paganism in the Roman Empire* (New Haven, Conn.: Yale University Press, 1981), 161–2.

[21] E. Norman Gardiner, *Greek Athletic Sports and Festivals* (London: Macmillan and Co., 1910), 218.

[22] Ibid., 164.

[23] Elizabeth R. Bethard, *The Theater at Isthmia* (Chicago: University of Chicago Press, 1973); David G. Romano, *The Origins of the Greek Stadion* (Philadelphia: American Philosophical Society, 1993).

[24] Jerome Murphy-O'Connor, *St. Paul's Corinth* (Collegeville, Minn.: The Liturgical Press, 1983), 153–59. For the whole subject of house churches, see Vincent Branick, *The House Church in the Writings of Paul* (Collegeville, Minn.: The Liturgical Press, 1989); and Robert Banks, *Paul's Idea of Community* (Peabody, MA; Hendrickson, 1994).

[25] Engels, 32.

[26] J. A. O. Larsen, "Roman Greece," *An Economic Survey of Ancient Rome*, ed. by Tenney Frank (New York: Octagon Books, 1975), IV, 474.

[27] Hans Lecht, *Sexual Life in Ancient Greece* (New York: Dorset, 1993), 33.

[28] Ibid., 35–36.

[29] Ibid., 37.

[30] See William V. Harris, *Ancient Literacy* (Cambridge, Mass.: Harvard University Press, 1989).

BIBLIOGRAPHY:

Angus, S. *The Mystery Religions*. New York: Dover Publications, 1975.

Banks, Robert. *Paul's Idea of Community*. Peabody, Mass.: Hendrickson, 1994.

Biers, William R. *The Archaeology of Greece*. Ithaca, N.Y.: Cornell University Press, rev. ed., 1987.

Branick, Vincent. *The House Church in the Writings of Paul*. Collegeville, Minn.: The Liturgical Press, 1989.

Broneer, Oscar. "Athens, 'City of Idol Worship.' " *The Biblical Archaeologist*, Feb. 1958.

Broneer, Oscar. "Corinth, Center of St. Paul's Missionary Work in Greece." *Biblical Archaeologist*, Dec. 1951.

Burkert, Walter. *Greek Religion*. Cambridge, Mass.: Harvard University Press, 1985.

Camp, John M. *The Athenian Agora*. London: Thames & Hudson, 1986.

Carson, D. A. and Others. *An Introduction to the New Testament*. Grand Rapids: Zondervan, 1992.

Del Chiaro, Mario A., ed. *Corinthiaca*. Columbia, Mo.: University of Missouri Press, 1986.

Drees, Ludwig. *Olympia*. New York: Frederick A. Praeger, 1968.

Engels, Donald. *Roman Corinth*. Chicago: University of Chicago Press, 1990.

Finegan, Jack. *The Archeology of the New Testament: The Mediterranean World of the Early Christian Apostles*. Boulder, Colo: Westview Press, 1981.

Gardiner, E. Norman. *Greek Athletic Sports and Festivals*. London: Macmillan & Co., 1910.

Gebhard, Elizabeth R. *The Theater at Isthmia*. Chicago: University of Chicago Press, 1973.

Gill, David, and Conrad Gempf. *The Book of Acts in Its First Century Setting*. Grand Rapids: Eerdmans, 1994.

Habicht, Christian. *Athens from Alexander to Antony*. Cambridge, Mass.: Harvard University Press, 1997.

Harris, William V. *Ancient Literacy*. Cambridge, Mass.: Harvard University Press, 1989.

Kerényi, C. *Eleusis*. New York: Pantheon Books, 1967.

Larsen, J. A. O. "Roman Greece." *An Economic Survey of Ancient Rome*, Vol. IV. Tenney Frank, ed. New York: Octagon Books, 1975.

Lecht, Hans. *Sexual Life in Ancient Greece*. New York: Dorset, 1993.

Leekley, Dorothy, and Robert Noyes. *Archaeological Excavations in Southern Greece*. Park Ridge, N.J.: Noyes Press, 1976.

MacKendrick, Paul. *The Greek Stones Speak*. New York: W. W. Norton, 2nd ed., 1981.

MacMullen, Ramsay. *Paganism in the Roman Empire*. New Haven, Conn.: Yale University Press, 1981.

McRay, John. *Archaeology and the New Testament*. Grand Rapids: Baker, 1991.

Meinardus, Otto F. A. *St. Paul in Greece*. New Rochelle, N.Y.: Caratzas Brothers, 1979.

Metzger, Henri. *St. Paul's Journeys in the Greek Orient*. New York: Philosophical Library, 1955.

Murphy-O'Connor, Jerome. *St. Paul's Corinth*. Collegeville, Minn.: The Liturgical Press, 1983.

Mylonas, George E. *Eleusis and the Eleusinian Mysteries*. Princeton, N.J.: Princeton University Press, 1961.

Neils, Jenifer. *Goddess and Polis*. Princeton, N.J.: Princeton University Press, 1992.

Ramsay, William M. *St. Paul the Traveller and the Roman Citizen*. Grand Rapids: Baker, reprinted 1979.

Raschke, Wendy J., ed. *The Archaeology of the Olympics: The Olympics and Other Festivals in Antiquity*. Madison, Wisc.: University of Wisconsin Press, 1988.

Robertson, Martin, and Alison Frantz. *The Parthenon Frieze*. Oxford: Phaidon, 1975.

Romano, David G. *The Origins of the Greek Stadion*. Philadelphia: American Philosophical Society, 1993.

Sherwin-White, A. N. *The Roman Citizenship*. Oxford: The Clarendon Press, 2nd ed., 1973.

Sherwin-White, A. N. *Roman Law and Roman Society in the New Testament.* Grand Rapids: Baker, reprinted 1992 by permission of Oxford University Press.

Swaddling, Judith. *The Ancient Olympic Games.* Austin: University of Texas Press, 1984.

Tenney, Merrill C. *New Testament Times.* Grand Rapids: Eerdmans, 1965.

Wycherley, R. E. *The Stones of Athens.* Princeton, N.J.: Princeton University Press, 1978.

MALTESE INTERLUDE

(Acts 27—28)

"Now when neither sun nor stars appeared for many days, and no small tempest beat on us, all hope that we would be saved was finally given up." (Acts 27:20 NKJV) *"Once safely on shore, we found out that the island was called Malta. The islanders showed us unusual kindness."* (Acts 28:1–2 NIV)

Storms have a way of defining who is the leader in the group caught in the storm. Often the most undervalued person in the group turns out to be the leader. The ship that was supposed to carry Paul to Rome carried at least two official leaders: the ship's captain and the Roman military officer in charge of prisoners being taken to Rome. Yet when life was on the line, it was the prisoner, Paul, who stood tall with a faith that demanded attention. He literally took over at the height of the storm and delivered the instructions that saved the lives of those on board. But his greatest triumph lay ahead—on the island of Malta after the last straggler had staggered ashore. With the survivors grouped around a fire, the apostle Paul demonstrated why he had such great leadership qualities.

The storm that blew the ship on shore at Malta had the power and fury of one of the great hurricanes that hit the Caribbean, the Southeastern United States, or the Gulf Coast. It blew the ship uncontrollably for fourteen days (Acts 27:27). The sailors had a name for it: *Eurakylōn* (preferred reading of Greek, v. 14, see KJV *Euroclydon*), an "East-

Northeaster." They were "exceedingly tempest-tossed" (v. 18). Squalls strengthened the unabated fury of the gale.

The squalls interrupted the long breaking action of the waves and turned the ship, plunging it heavily into the trough of the sea. Then it took unusually long to recover. The battering of the waves strained the hull severely. The voyage of terror did not seem to have an end.

After two weeks the crew sensed they were nearing land and took soundings at twenty fathoms (120 feet) and fifteen fathoms (90 feet). At daybreak they decided to beach the ship to avoid being dashed against rocks somewhere. First, they threw out the cargo of wheat to lighten the ship and make it float higher in the water, and then they cut the ropes to the anchors. Hoisting the mainsail they made full tilt for shore.

As they ran aground, the ship broke up, but the entire crew and the prisoners and other passengers (276 in all, Acts 27:37) made it safely to shore, as God and Paul had promised (Acts 27:24–25). Luke describes it as an Alexandrian ship (27:6), one of the ships of the fleet that carried wheat from

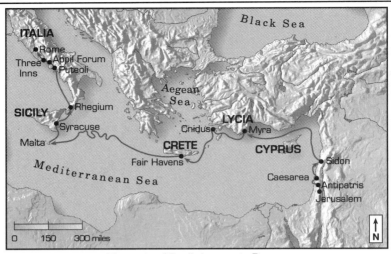

The route of Paul's journey to Rome

Egypt to Italy (27:38). Such ships commonly were about 180 feet long, 45 feet wide, and about 40 feet deep, with an estimated cargo of 1,200 tons.

The Place of Landing

The crew did not recognize the land, perhaps partly because of weather conditions, and partly from the fact that ships putting in at Malta normally docked at the southeast end of the island in Marsascirocco (Marsaxlokk) Bay. Evidently they had landed in the northwest part of the island. The person who, more than any other, described and popularized the apostle Paul's shipwreck on Malta was James Smith, who wrote *The Voyage and Shipwreck of St. Paul* in 1848 (currently published by

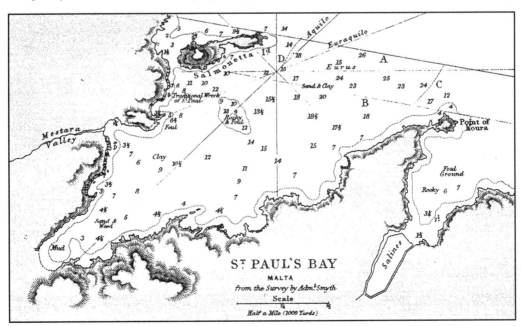

Smith's map of St. Paul's Bay, with adjacent Salina Bay and the reef of Koura, on which the ship may have broken up. Numbers on the map are fathom depths.

St. Paul's Bay. St. Paul's Island or Selmunett, with its statue of Paul, lies in the right background. The beach where the ship ran aground and broke up is supposed to be in the left background.

Baker Book House). Smith concluded that the shipwreck occurred in what is now called St. Paul's Bay. A town by that name presently stands at the foot of the bay.

At the entrance of the bay lie some tiny rocky islands. On the largest, Selmunett, stands a statue of Paul, erected in 1845 to mark the spot where Paul and the others supposedly landed. Smith argued, among other things, that "the place where two seas met" (Acts 27:41 KJV) and where the ship broke up, was a beach between two creeks on the west side of the bay.

Nearby the natives of the island built a fire and tried to meet the needs of the shipwrecked company. Publius, the "chief man" or magistrate of the island, lived on an estate in the vicinity (Acts 28:7) and extended further courtesies. In part he probably did so because of his inclination to show kindness, and in part because he was dealing with a Roman centurion and his guard (and his prisoners) who were on official business. Today a church stands on the supposed site of Publius' house, called San Pawl Milqi (meaning "St. Paul Welcomed").

Before we look further at the church and the supposed authenticity of the site, let's think about the shipwreck site itself. Over time, some have questioned Smith's conclusions (though they are generally accepted today). The questioning does not concern whether Malta is the place where the ship ran aground but whether Smith had found the exact spot. As a matter of fact, for centuries people have associated the shipwreck with the bay that now bears Paul's name, but not the western part of the bay where Smith thought it occurred.

George H. Musgrave is one of those who questioned Smith's conclusions. To begin with, he raised a point about the real meaning of Acts 27:41. He observed that Smith himself had said the Greek is "generally supposed to mean an isthmus," rather than "a place where two seas met."[1] The newer

Selmunett Island with the statue of Paul

San Pawl Milqi

translations take a different tack from Smith's: "striking a reef" (NRSV); "ran aground on a sandbank" (CEV); "struck a sandbar" (NIV). Second, he argued that the area around St. Paul's islands in the western part of the bay was not a place to expect exhausted people to get ashore. Third, exhausted personnel of the ship could hardly walk from the site on the west of St. Paul's Bay around the end of the bay to the traditional site of Publius' entertainment of them (St. Pawl Milqi), some four or five miles away.

Fourth, the sailors "noticed a bay with a beach" (Acts 27:39 NRSV) at fifteen fathoms. They could not have seen a beach in St. Paul's Bay unless they were already in the bay at a depth well under fifteen fathoms. Fifth, the sailors saw no sign of human habitation, but on the eastern side of St. Paul's Bay at that time stood a neolithic temple that had been there for a very long time.

Musgrave argued that the shipwreck actually took place in Salina Bay, just to the east of St. Paul's Bay. There sailors on the ship, while still outside the entrance of the bay, could have looked down the bay to see a sandy shore on which to land. When the ship beached, the passengers could fairly easily have gotten to shore. Further they would not have had to go more than a mile or so to Publius' estate, assuming San Pawl Milqi is built on the site.[2] If we want to stick with the translation of a "place where two seas met" (Acts 27:41), or even the "reef" or "sandbar," that could be the peninsula or reef which divides St. Paul's Bay and Salina

Bay. After walking all over the area on a couple of different trips and looking at all the pros and cons, I am inclined to agree with Musgrave and to conclude that Paul's ship was perhaps wrecked on the reef separating Salina Bay and St. Paul's Bay and that the men made it ashore in Salina Bay, walking to San Pawl Milqi.

Publius' Estate?

What can we say about San Pawl Milqi? The Italian Archaeological Mission in Malta excavated at the site of the church in the 1960s, finding a villa dating to the New Testament period. It involved a substantial residential and agricultural complex laid out around a peristyle courtyard. They found olive oil presses, remains of a flour mill, and possibly some form of a ceramics industry. Living quarters, extending to the west, were decorated with painted wall plaster. One room was given a special treatment and a series of chapels was later built on the spot. The church that stands there today dates between 1620 and 1622, and there is a documentary record of a building there in 1488. Excavations turned up evidence of three previous churches at the site. The place was a pilgrimage center by at least the seventh century.

Salina Bay with a reef at the end of the peninsula in the center background

Excavators found numerous indications that the spot was venerated as connected with Paul and Christianity. A block of a wellhead with the name "Paulus" on it dated between the fourth and seventh centuries. A stone with a fish (symbol of Christ) and a stone with a cross on it dated to the fourth or

Publius was one of his converts, and that he became the first Christian bishop of Malta. Interestingly, catacombs on Salina Bay have burials dating to the early Christian centuries. Musgrave notes the claim of Harrison Lewis that pottery sherds found in the catacombs date as early as the second to the fourth centuries A.D.[4]

The Land

The Geography of Malta

Malta is an arid, rocky island 58 miles south of Sicily, 149 miles south of the European mainland, and 180 miles north of Cape Bon in Tunisia. A little over 17 miles long, 9 miles wide, and 60 miles in circumference, it is the chief island of the Maltese group—which also includes Gozo and Comino Islands. The three islands together total 122 square miles, approximately one-tenth the size of Rhode Island.

Thin but fertile soil covers the limestone formations on the island of Malta. Agriculture has always been its chief occupation, but uncertain rainfall makes farming a rather risky business. With an average rainfall of twenty-one inches per year, it actually has a rainfall that varies from ten to forty inches; and periods of drought have extended over three years. There are no rivers or rivulets on the island. Springs flow, but the largest part of the water supply is pumped from strata just above sea level. Today tourism, commerce, and even industry provide jobs for an increasing percentage of the population.

The climate is temperate and healthful for the greater part of the year, with a mean annual temperature of about 65 degrees. There are no high mountains on the island. The hills are nowhere higher than 850 feet; the Bingemma Range in the west rises to

fifth century. A stone with the figure of Paul went back to the seventh century, a grafitto of a boat to the seventh or eighth century, and bricks with a cross and a fish to the fourth or fifth century.[3]

Evangelization of Malta

Tradition has it that the island was evangelized at the time of Paul's visit, that

786 feet. Sheer cliffs 400 feet in height stand along the southwest coast.

(For more on this topic, go to p. 541 or p. 592.)

Government

"And the natives [barbaroi=barbarians] showed us unusual kindness; for they kindled a fire and made us all welcome." "In that region there was an estate of the leading citizen of the island whose name was Publius, who received us and entertained us courteously for three days." (Acts 28:2, 7 NKJV)

The Phoenicians established trading contacts with Malta in the late eighth century B.C. Carthage, a Phoenician colony, took control of Phoenician commercial activity in the west in the mid-sixth century and gradually established control over Malta. Thus, when Carthage fought Rome in a series of conflicts known as the Punic Wars, their colony of Malta was a target of Roman expansion. Rome sacked the islands in the 250s B.C., during the First Punic War, and annexed them in 218 B.C., during the Second Punic War.

An early shrine at Hagar Qim in the southwest of Malta

Rome later joined Malta to the province of Sicily, which was governed by a propraetor from 122 B.C. Sicily became a senatorial province in 27 B.C., which means that the Senate rather than the emperor appointed the governors. Syracuse, in eastern Sicily, was the seat of government. Melite (modern Rabat-Mdina), in the center of Malta, was the Roman capital of the islands and the headquarters of Publius, the "chief man" or "leading citizen" or Roman administrator. The modern town of Valletta was not founded until 1566. Gaudos (modern Victoria) was the chief town of Gozo.

As a result of continued contacts with the Greek city of Syracuse and other Greek cities of Sicily, Greek culture and language became widespread on Malta. Latin also made inroads, but a great many of the people were still Semitic in culture and spoke a dialect of Phoenician when Paul landed there. This fact is clearly indicated in Luke's observation that the natives or barbarians (non-Greek or Latin-speaking people) had shown them kindness. In this context, barbarian must mean non-Greco-Roman and has nothing to do with their being uncivilized. No doubt the Phoenician dialect of Malta was close enough to the Aramaic Paul spoke that he could converse with them. There was also a small Jewish community on Malta. Some believe that the Maltese obtained Roman citizenship after the assassination of Julius Caesar (44 B.C.), when the Sicilians did. Others put that grant later.

(For more on this topic, go to p.546 or p. 594.)

Religion

Though Malta is something of an archaeological paradise, with ruins of several shrines or temples going all the way back to about 5000 B.C., these contribute nothing to the present discussion. During the New Testament period the Maltese practiced Carthaginian (Phoenician) religion alongside the Greco-Roman cults. They had a celebrated temple of Juno, queen of the gods, as well as of Apollo, and Persephone (Kore), daughter of Demeter, the protector of marriage. A temple to Hercules seems also to have involved worship of the Phoenician deity Melkart. It was located near the old harbor of Marasascirocco, as many chance finds attest.

The sanctuary of Tas-Silg in the southeast part of the island is believed almost certainly to be that of Juno, praised as world-famous by the orator Cicero. Here the Maltese extended the old Carthaginian temple of Astarte (identified with Juno) on a lavish scale. The new complex had a monumental portico and a fine mosaic pavement. It seems

In Rabat, adjacent to St. Paul's Church, is St. Paul's grotto, where Paul is reputed to have lived during his three-month stay on the island. The site is marked by a statue of the apostle.

to have been abandoned in the second century A.D., and a Christian monastery was later built on the site.

(For more on this topic, go to p. 548 or p. 610.)

Warfare

The New Testament period was the time of the *Pax Romana*, the Roman peace. Roman power not only protected the empire but also kept it in line. There were no troops stationed in Malta, and a few police maintained order.

The Roman navy helped to guarantee the peace and security of Malta. To hold what he had won, Augustus had created a superbly organized and equipped navy. On Misenum, the cape that stands at the northern arc of the Bay of Naples, he established the headquarters for his main fleet. Here was a force of 10,000 men and over fifty large ships, plus a variety of smaller ones. Substations were built north on the Italian coast and on the islands of Corsica and Sardinia. A second major fleet made up of large ships of the line was stationed at Ravenna on the Adriatic.

Augustus and his successors also built up small provincial squadrons at Alexandria in Egypt and Seleucia in Syria and wherever else Rome had shipping to protect: in the Black Sea, on the Danube, the Rhine, and the English Channel. These ships helped Rome not only to dominate the Mediterranean but also to guarantee an adequate flow of grain from Egypt to the capital. Malta, located on the strategic shipping lanes, enjoyed a wonderful security.

(For more on this topic, go to p. 568 or p. 612.)

Housing and Furniture

In what sort of house might Governor Publius have lived when Paul came to Malta during the first century? Fortunately our answer does not need to be a product of our imagination. Remains of a Roman town house of a wealthy citizen, probably a dignitary, came to light in Rabat in 1881 and have received considerable attention since. Today they are incorporated in the Museum

The mosaic in the central courtyard of the first-century house. Three columns of the peristyle are visible.

of Roman Antiquities. The house dates to early in the first century B.C. and was at the height of its glory during the first century A.D. At that time the owner installed several marble statues in the house, some carrying portraits of members of the imperial family. One represents the emperor Claudius (A.D. 41–54) and another his mother Antonia.

Hellenistic in style, the house had a central courtyard surrounded by sixteen columns in the Doric order. The floors of the courtyard (peristyle) and the surrounding rooms, one of which must have been a triclinium or dining room, were decorated with magnificent mosaics. Generally these consisted of geometric designs with centrally placed *emblemata* (small square scenes). The *emblema* in the peristyle shows two doves perched on the rim of a bowl. One in another room is an allegorical representation of autumn. In it a boy holds a duck while a flying dove hovers overhead.

The walls of the house were plastered and painted. Measurements of the peristyle were about 22 by 21 feet. One of the rooms next to it was about 11 by 11. Another, a "reception" room off the peristyle, was somewhat larger than the peristyle itself. It is not possible to determine the size of the house because all of the rooms have not been uncovered (about ten have been).[5]

About twenty-five first-century villas scattered on the islands' countryside have come to light. These tend to be farmsteads attached to large country estates, not designed as residences only. Part of the building—usually much of the first floor—was clearly intended for agricultural activities, such as the processing of olive oil, or for the production of cloth. Rooms opened off open courtyards. A stairway led to the second floor, where most of the family rooms were located. The house connected with the church of San Pawl Milqi is of this type. These houses have cisterns for the collection of water (usually under the central courtyard) in this land with slim water resources.

The houses of the poor town dwellers or farmers have not been well preserved and we cannot say much about them specifically. The very poor lived in houses of a couple of rooms and the middle class tried

Excavations in the house adjacent to San Pawl Milqi with an olive oil press in the center

to have an inner courtyard surrounded by a few rooms.

The furniture found in all these houses was sparse by our standards, with a few tables, chairs, beds, and chests for storage. The level of elegance of materials and design varied according to family wealth. Those who could afford them had dining couches in the dining room. Since most of these houses were of the typical Roman variety, comments on Roman houses and furniture in the next chapter will apply to the Maltese situation.

(For more on this topic, go to p. 569 or p. 617.)

Diet and Foodstuffs

The agricultural system of Malta during the Roman period focused mainly on the production of wheat and barley, olives, and grapes. The soil was stony and precipitation minimal. So all through history terracing, with the building of stone fences (stone gathered from the fields), has been common to prevent erosion. A view across the countryside of Malta today probably is much the same as in New Testament times: patches of land worked fairly intensively and surrounded by stone fences. Conditions favored the raising of olives and grapes and were more conducive to growing barley than wheat. Gardens yielded lettuce, onions, and other vegetables, along with various fruits.

The diet was supplemented with poultry and fish. Sheep and goats thrived on the geographical conditions of the islands and provided milk and butter for food and wool and goat hair for clothing and industry. Cattle were not so plentiful as sheep and goats. The third island of the Maltese group, Cuminum (modern Comino) takes its name from the cumin (seasoning) grown there. Quantities of honey were also produced on Malta. The name Malta may come from the Phoenician *malat*, meaning port or refuge, or the Greek *meli* (Melita), meaning honey.

(For more on this topic, go to p. 570 or p. 621.)

Dress

The people of Malta had perhaps been Roman citizens for a hundred years by the time Paul arrived. At least many of them enjoyed that privilege, if it was not universal. That meant that men could wear the toga and women the stola whenever they went out in public. But as previously noted, the average citizen, engaged in daily tasks, normally did not wear clothing that was a badge of citizenship.

Certainly the farmers, stonecutters, and manual laborers did not. As they went about their daily work, they appeared in the rather universal garb of the Mediterranean world—in the tunic, a long shirt that extended to the knees and usually had sleeves extending to the elbows or wrists. We have described this garb several times already, and we shall return to the subject of Roman clothing in the next chapter.

(For more on this topic, go to p. 571 or p. 624.)

Family Life

If the Maltese received Roman citizenship in April of 44 B.C., when the province of Sicily as a whole did,[6] Malta must have become quite Romanized by about A.D. 60, when Paul arrived. Romanization no doubt occurred even if Roman citizenship was not granted to the islands so early. Though the Phoenician-Carthaginian ways of doing things continued to a degree, as indicated by the reference to "barbarians" in Acts 28:2, Roman ways no doubt predominated. Since that is probably the case, it seems unnecessary to anticipate here what is spelled out in some detail under "Family Life" in the next chapter.

(For more on this topic, go to p. 572 or p. 626.)

Work, Travel, and Commerce

The Maltese islands were populous, flourishing and well cultivated in New Testament times. They had become famous for the production of fine textiles and excellent sailcloth. In fact, Malta had empire-wide fame for skill in manufacturing women's dresses and soft cushions made of Maltese fabrics. These were especially in demand in Rome. Of course some of this fabric was made of wool. But sources speak of a kind of Maltese linen, widely believed to have actually been cotton. It appears that not much linen could have been produced because processing linen requires more water than Malta has available.

The textile industry of Sicily centered in Syracuse. Through this market passed most of the delicate fabrics of adjacent Malta, only fifty miles south of Sicily. In fact, production houses of Syracuse sometimes had Maltese weavers working for them.[7]

Some people worked as stone cutters and in the building trades. Geologically Malta consists of Upper Coralline limestone and Lower Coralline limestone with Globigerina limestone and clay in between. The Globigerina is soft and easily quarried and hardens on exposure to the atmosphere. The beautiful buildings of Malta are generally built of this limestone.

Most of the Maltese worked in agriculture in New Testament times. Outside the two Roman towns at Melita (Rabat-Medina) on Malta and Gaudos on Gozo, the population was largely spread over the countryside, raising sheep and cattle, wheat and barley, and olives, and producing honey. Shipping interests in Syracuse were probably largely responsible for transporting goods into and out of Malta.

On to Rome

After Paul had stayed for three months in Malta, the weather improved enough to sail again. Paul and his companions boarded ship for Italy (Acts 28:11) on another "ship of Alexandria." This one, likely part of the grain fleet supplying Rome, had spent the winter in the island (Acts 28:11), probably at the southern port of Marsascirocco. Where the company of 276 had spent the winter is not stated. Probably they had found quarters in Melite (Rabat-Medina) and now went south to the port.

For the apostle Paul this leg of his trip landed him in Italy. He was soon in Rome, where he was to write some of his most cherished epistles. But Italy and its culture will be treated in the next chapter.

(For more on this topic, go to p. 573 or p. 635.)

NOTES:

[1] James Smith, *The Voyage and Shipwreck of St. Paul*, 4th ed. (Grand Rapids, Baker Book House, reprinted, 1978), 142.

[2] George H. Musgrave, *Friendly Refuge*. Privately published in Malta (ISBN 09506480 00)

[3] Michelangelo Cagiano de Azevedo, *Testimonianze Archeologiche Della Tradizione Paolina A Malta* (Rome: University of Rome, 1966), 55.

[4] Musgrave, 94, 100, noting Harrison Lewis, *Ancient Malta*, published by Colin Smythe (Bucks, England, 1977). See also, Jack Finegan, *The Archeology of the New Testament* (Boulder, Colo.: Westview Press, 1981), 103.

[5] Tancred C. Gouder, *The Mosaic Pavements in the Museum of Roman Antiquities* (Malta: Department of Museums, 1983).

[6] A. N. Sherwin-White, *The Roman Citizenship* (Oxford: Clarendon Press, 2nd ed., 1973), 365.

[7] V. M. Scramuzza, "Roman Sicily," *An Economic Survey of Ancient Rome*, ed. by Tenney Frank (New York: Octagon Books, 1975), III, 290.

BIBLIOGRAPHY:

Blouet, Brian. *The Story of Malta*. London: Faber and Faber, 1967.

De Azevedo, Michelangelo. *Testimonianze Archeologiche Della Tradizione Paolina A Malta*. Rome: University of Rome, 1966.

Ellul, Joseph S. *Malta's Prediluvian Culture at the Stone Age Temples*. Malta: Printwell Ltd., 1988.

Finegan, Jack. *The Archeology of the New Testament: The Mediterranean World of the Early Christian Apostles*. Boulder, Colo.: Westview Press, 1981.

Gouder, Tancred C. *The Mosaic Pavements in the Museum of Roman Antiquities*. Malta: Department of Museums, 1983.

Musgrave, George H. *Friendly Refuge*. Privately published in Malta, n. d. (after 1977).

Rossiter, Stuart. *The Blue Guides: Malta*. London: Ernest Benn Ltd., 1968.

Smith, James. *The Voyage and Shipwreck of St. Paul*. Grand Rapids: Baker Book House reprint, 1978 (originally published in 1880).

ROME AND ITALY IN THE CAREER OF PAUL

Chapter 21

(Acts 28; Romans 16; Ephesians; Philippians; Colossians; 2 Timothy; Philemon)

"The next day we came to Puteoli, where we found brethren, and were invited to stay with them seven days. And so we went toward Rome." (Acts 28:13–14 NKJV)

On the Way to Rome

For Paul, going to Rome was the fulfillment of a dream—only to some of us it might seem more like a nightmare. He had written Roman believers that he wanted to come and "impart. . . some spiritual gift" (Romans 1:11) and be "encouraged together with you" (v. 12). However, when he wrote that from Corinth he had no idea he would be arriving as a prisoner with a Roman escort. Yet the reception he received from the "brethren" as soon as he landed at Puteoli tells us that word of his arrival had preceded him. While "the brethren" royally welcomed him, the Romans still considered him a prisoner about to go on trial before the emperor.

The grain ship on which Paul and his companions sailed from Malta to Italy docked over 150 miles from Rome at Puteoli (modern Pozzuoli). Puteoli had an excellent harbor, well sheltered by the natural configuration of the Bay of Naples. A substantial mole or pier extended out into the bay at least 418 yards. And a far-flung dock system cared for the city's widespread maritime interests. Some of the remains of the pier of New Testament times have been built into the modern facility.

Rome used a port so far from the capital because the coast of Italy near Rome did not provide favorable landing spots for ancient ships. Though the emperor Claudius had started to create the port of Ostia at the mouth of the Tiber River during the earlier years of Paul's ministry, it was still quite inadequate when Paul landed, and would continue to be until early in the second century. So travelers regularly walked or rode the 150 miles from Puteoli amid carts carrying the bulky grain supplies that had come from faraway Egypt. The Appian Way became the superhighway of its day, and traffic on it probably resembled rush hour in one of our cities, though at a slower pace.

The route followed the tomb-lined Via Consularis to Capua (twenty miles from Puteoli), where it joined the main line of the Appian Way. From Capua to Rome was considered to be a journey of five days for an active traveler, but Paul evidently took longer. Wagons moved at the rate of about twenty-five miles a day. (A discussion of the Roman road system and of Roman road construction appears near the end of this chapter.)

Believers at Puteoli wanted Paul to stay with them for a week (Acts 28:14). Exactly

The modern Pozzuoli wharf incorporates stones of the wharf that existed when Paul landed at the port.

how this was possible when the apostle was a prisoner is not quite clear, but comments on Paul's imprisonment and treatment appear under "Government." When Christians in Rome received word that Paul was coming, they went as far south as Appii Forum and Three Taverns (Inns) to meet him (Acts 28:15). Appii Forum was located 43 Roman miles from Rome and Three Taverns ten miles closer to the capital. From Three Taverns the apostolic party traveled the seventeen miles to Aricia and then moved along the last 16 miles between Aricia and Rome.

Paul now headed for the city that had for decades dominated the Mediterranean world. To say, as some carelessly do, that Rome dominated the then-known world during New Testament times is quite erroneous. The Romans knew of many lands beyond their borders in Europe, Africa, and Asia which they either did not choose to conquer or were not able to subdue. And the empire did not grow to its maximum size until A.D. 117.

In fact, Rome not only knew about faraway China but had extensive commerce with that empire along the famous silk route through central Asia. Interestingly, China dominated much of East Asia between about 200 B.C. and A.D. 200 in what we call the Chinese peace, while Rome dominated much of the west during the *Pax Romana* or Roman peace. So between them they controlled the most populous regions of the world—the vast territory from the Pacific Ocean across the Middle East and the Mediterranean to the Atlantic Ocean.

The statement in Luke 2:1 that Augustus had issued a decree for all the *world* to be taxed or registered (the decree that sent Joseph and Mary to Bethlehem) of course meant the Roman world. Though the NIV reads "Roman world," that is not in the Greek text. The Romans were under no illusion about world control. However, they did sufficiently

The last part of Paul's journey to Rome

control the Mediterranean and its environs to call it *mare nostrum* (our sea).

(For more on this topic, go to p. 32.)

The Land

Geography of Italy

Slashing diagonally across the center of the Mediterranean, Italy is strategically located for control of that sea. When the Romans had annexed Sicily, they were in a position to dominate the east-west sea lanes. Not only is it significant that the peninsula is centrally located in the Mediterranean basin, but it was important for the development of the Roman Empire that nature had brought certain forces to bear to constitute that basin as a unified area. The homogeneous character of the basin is manifested in a similar climate, a likeness of geological structure, and a similarly distinctive type of vegetation.

Moreover, the Mediterranean lands, while sharing a common sea front, are rather clearly separated from their hinterlands by an almost unbroken ring of mountains and deserts. The modern student, influenced by the differing religious and political ideologies in conflict there and the impact of the world power struggle in the area, loses sight of the factors that were so significant in unifying the Mediterranean world in antiquity. Roman arms made the Mediterranean a Roman lake, surrounded on all sides by Roman territory. The sea (some 2,300 miles from east to west), not the lands around it, was the center of the empire. The sea routes were the arteries through which the trade of the empire flowed. Not surprisingly, Mediterranean ports became the chief cities of the Roman world.

While Italy was strategically located for controlling the Mediterranean, Rome was strategically located for controlling the peninsula of Italy. Situated in the center of the peninsula, she could meet her enemies one by one and could prevent them from effectively uniting against her. If such a combination should be formed, she could move against it with the advantage of a central base and short lines of communication.

Early in her career of expansion, Rome developed the practice of building military roads to all parts of her domain. Moreover, Rome was located at the lowest point of the Tiber River, where firm abutments for a bridge could be found. So Rome controlled the main line of communication along the western and more populous side of the peninsula.

As is well known, Rome was originally built on seven hills. None of these exceeded two hundred feet above sea level, but they rose for the most part in steep slopes above the surrounding valleys and at some points formed sheer cliffs towering over these valleys. The Tiber flowed past, and later through, the city and was navigable for the fifteen-mile distance between the coast and the capital. Ships docked at the foot of the Aventine Hill. Her days as a leading center of trade did not come until the reign of Claudius, however, when her port of Ostia was developed. Even then, most of the trade consisted of imports.

Geographically, Italy comprises some 90,000 square miles, a little less than that of Oregon. It divides into two regions: the continental on the north and the peninsular on the south. The northern region is some 320 miles east and west and about 70 north and south. The boot-shaped peninsula stretches some 700 miles toward the continent of Africa and is never more than 125 miles wide. In the toe and the heel of the "boot," the peninsula is only about 25 miles wide.

Mountains

Mountains dominate much of the landscape of Italy. The Alps form an irregular 1,200-mile arc across the north. While they arise rather abruptly on the Italian side and impede expansion, they slope more gently on the European side and did not prevent migration into Italy.

The Apennines extend the full length of the peninsula in a bow-shaped range about 800 miles long and 25 to 85 miles wide. Since the average height of these mountains is only about 4,000 feet and since the passes through them are not generally difficult, they did not pose the problem to the unification of the country that the mountains of Greece did.

The Apennines approach closely to the Adriatic Sea, permitting little more than a coastal road in many places along the eastern coast, while on the west they leave room for arable lands which are carved up into plains by spurs extending from the main Apennine range. Therefore, Italy faced west. Because she did, the flow of culture from the more highly developed civi-

The Tiber River at Ostia near its exit to the sea

lizations of the east was slowed in its journey to her shores. Along the west coast of the peninsula, both north and south of the Tiber and on adjacent islands, are extinct volcanoes. Active since ancient times have been Vesuvius, Stromboli, and Etna.

Rivers

Several rivers originate in the mountains of Italy. Longest of these is the Po, which rises in the western Alps and flows eastward for 360 miles to the Adriatic Sea. This alone of the Italian rivers can be classified as navigable. Along the Adriatic, rushing mountain torrents punctuate the rocky coastline. Flowing into the Tyrrhenian Sea and navigable by small craft are the Volturno, the Liri (Liris), the Tiber, and the Arno rivers. Not only did the rivers of Italy fail to give the desired highway to much of the land but they also presented a special health problem. The sill at the Straits of Gibraltar breaks the force of the ocean tides flowing into the Mediterranean; and this lack of brisk tidal movement prevents a daily scouring of the coasts. Consequently, the accumulation of silt at the river mouths creates marshy areas that serve as breeding spots for malaria-carrying mosquitoes. Both in ancient and modern times Italy has suffered much from this dread disease.

Harbors

As should be obvious, the silting up of the river mouths prevented Italian rivers

The Apennine Mountains

from providing much in the way of harbor facilities. So extensive was this silting that in the days of the emperor Claudius (A.D. 41–54) it was necessary to make a new cut for the discharge of the Tiber into the sea. Moreover, throughout a coastal length of over 2,000 miles, Italy has few deep bays or good harbors. Almost all of those that do exist are located on the southern and western shores. The chief harbor on the Adriatic was Brundisium, far down on the heel of Italy; to the south was Tarentum (Taranto) on the gulf of that name; on the west was Puteoli (Pozzuoli) on the Bay of Naples. Genoa and Lunae Portus (La Spezia) became important only in late Roman times. Ostia, which assumed importance as the port of Rome during the first century A.D., was a man-made harbor.

Climate

The climate of Italy in the northern region differs from that of the southern regions. The Po Valley climate is similar to

Augustus commonly dressed in a toga as a civilian, rather than in a military uniform as commander of the troops. (Louvre Museum)

the continental climate of central Europe, with marked differences between summer and winter temperatures and clearly defined periods of spring and fall. The region experiences frequent winter snows, copious spring and fall rains, and moderate rains in the summer.

The climate of peninsular Italy conforms more closely to the Mediterranean type, with boisterous rain-washed winters during which the Apennines lie heavily mantled with snow, and summers of deficient rain. On most of the peninsula the drought extends over three or four months; at Rome it is of two months' duration. Land and sea breezes temper the heat. In general, the climate of the west and south coasts is subtropical. It is now generally believed that the climate of Italy has not changed since classical times.

Plains

A further word must be said about the plains of Italy. The large, level, and fertile Po Valley was the best grain land, but it never became an important source of supply for Rome. Since bulky goods had to be transported by water, Romans found it cheaper to obtain their food supply from a closer source. The distance from the mouth of the Po to Rome is longer than that from Sicily or North Africa and very little shorter than that from Egypt. Etruria is rough and broken by stone and better suited for pasture than for cultivation. Latium and Campania are small; their rich but shallow surface soil was soon exhausted, leaving a volcanic subsoil better for orchards and vineyards than for grain. But Campania was long the chief granary of peninsular Italy and produced large amounts of fruits and vegetables.

(For more on this topic, go to p. 583.)

Government

When the assassins of Julius Caesar struck him down on the Ides of March (March 15), 44 B.C., they were not trying to keep him from taking the crown and becoming king, as is sometimes stated.

The Senate building in Rome

Rather, some of them opposed the dictatorship that he had already established. Caesar had been named dictator for ten years in 46 and the following year dictator for life. Those fiercely opposed to Caesar's destruction of the Republic joined with jealous members of his own camp and supporters of Pompey to do in the conqueror. Caesar's death ushered in a whole new round of civil war from which Octavian or Augustus Caesar emerged victorious.

As he stood there triumphant in 27 B.C., Augustus faced the daunting task of restructuring the government and bringing order to a disheveled empire. The Republic was dead. Evidently he had no desire to resurrect it. Nor did he want to be a dictator as Julius had been. He chose a sort of middle way, which historians often call a dyarchy—that is, a rule of two, Augustus and the Senate. He shared with them the rule of the empire, dividing the provinces into senatorial and imperial provinces. The Senate governed those that were pacified and needed no troops to maintain order; the emperor supervised those requiring troops to keep them under wraps or to protect the frontiers. The Senate and the emperor appointed the governors in their respective provinces.

Augustus increasingly came to dominate the machinery of government of Rome. For instance, he was the Princeps (first man, or president) of the Senate. As such he could introduce legislation and thus control its agenda. Also, from time to time, the Senate bestowed on him powers or responsibilities it did not know how to handle or with which it did not want to be bothered. As a case in point, they gave him the responsibility of providing grain for the grain dole in the city

The Public Record Office in Rome on the Capitoline Hill has stood there since the first century B.C. and is still in use.

Remains of the Temple to Augustus that Herod the Great built in his honor at Samaria (Sebastos).

of Rome. At the time some 200,000 were on welfare and received "food stamps" from the government. Soon he also provided entertainment for the poor to keep them occupied. Hence arose the idea of government provision of "bread and circuses" for the public. In this way he and his successors could endear themselves to the masses.

Augustus liked the idea of being "first man" or Princeps in the government—first in honor and responsibility, rather than a dictator. Thus the idea of a principate developed—which was maintained more or less during the first two centuries.

At the beginning of his reign the Senate conferred on Octavian the name or title "Augustus," a word meaning sacred or revered. This was a title used by all later emperors. It was translated in the Greek half of the empire as "Sebastos." Hence, when Herod the Great refounded Samaria he called it Sebaste in honor of the emperor.

Augustus retained his position as commander-in-chief of the armed forces—of the army and navy. It was unthinkable that he not do so. The army, led by one ambitious person or another for most of a hundred years, needed to be kept in check to protect the public at large. And for his part, Augustus would not have trusted the army in the hands of anyone else. Another of his means of maintaining power was through the ruler cult, which he encouraged throughout his reign. This topic is developed in the next part of this chapter.

The cities of Italy continued to maintain their civilian or more democratic character and thus to hold elections for all local offices. The truth is that many ambitious men were quite content to remain in their hometowns, where they could be a big frog in a little puddle instead of moving to the capital and living in the shadow of an all-powerful emperor.

Augustus faced the very real problem of how to arrange for his successor. He decided to follow the plan of Julius Caesar. Julius had adopted Augustus and was planning to go off to war with him when he was assassinated. The wisdom of this arrangement was that the one adopted would be associated with his predecessor and gain experience in running the government. Moreover, he would become so entrenched in office that a peaceful transition would occur. The ideal was for the emperor to adopt his son, or at least a relative. The system worked reasonably well under the Julio-Claudians (27 B.C.–A.D. 68). When Nero committed suicide in 68, a brief civil war brought Vespasian and his Flavian line (Vespasian, Titus, Domitian) to power (69–96). The fate of the adoption procedure later in the empire is beyond our present concerns.

Tiberius

Before his death, Augustus adopted Tiberius (a stepson by his third wife) as his

Agrippa was Augustus' right-hand man and responsible for doling out funds for projects that won the emperor's favor.

son and associated Tiberius with himself in ruling the state. Upon his death in A.D. 14, the Senate and assembly voted Augustus' powers and prerogatives upon his successor. The new emperor was by birth a member of the Claudian family, by adoption a member of the Julian family. Therefore, in him these two great houses were united and from this Julio-Claudian line came the first four successors of Augustus in the principate.

Tiberius (who ruled A.D. 14–37) had become embittered and suspicious during the years of mistreatment at the hands of Augustus (Tiberius had not been Augustus' first choice as his successor), and his personality caused him much trouble with the Senate and the people of Rome. Finally, Tiberius grew tired of this friction and retired to Capri in A.D. 26 (the year he appointed Pilate procurator of Judea), leaving the rule of Rome to Sejanus, the commander of the Praetorian Guard. While Tiberius did not get along well with the Senate and while his economy in expenditures of the public funds won him unpopularity with the city mob, he was a blessing to the provincials, to whose welfare he directed particular attention.

Tiberius' reign is significant for several reasons. First, he allowed the Praetorian Guard to gain greater power. Subsequently they would have a lot to do with making

and unmaking emperors. Second, his foreign policy followed the advice of Augustus: to hold rather than expand the empire. Third, his wise administration provided a period of peace and stability that allowed the principate to take deeper root. Fourth, of special significance for the Christian movement is the fact that during his reign Christ was crucified and Christianity was launched. The growth of treason trials and the liquidation of his enemies because of his increasing fears for his personal safety proved to be his undoing.

Caligula

Tiberius' choice of a successor was even worse than Augustus'. But that fact could not have been apparent to Tiberius. Caligula (37–41), grandson of Augustus' daughter Julia, started with promise. After the stern and efficient rule of Tiberius, the lavishness of Caligula's public entertainments, his donations, his reduction of taxes, and his pardoning of political offenders imprisoned by Tiberius brought him great popularity.

But as a result of a serious illness, he seems to have become mentally deranged. Because so many of the literary sources were unfriendly to him, it is difficult to discover either the cause of his actions (mental condition) or the true nature of his conduct on various occasions. It seems clear, however, that he sought worship as a living god and that he wanted to be called *dominus* or "lord." He forcibly installed his statues in some Jewish synagogues and gave orders for one to be set up in the temple in Jerusalem. The legate of Syria, anticipating a revolt, delayed the order; and the news of the death of the emperor solved the problem.

Despotic in his rule, Caligula disregarded the Senate and engaged in tyrannical measures, judicial murders, and confiscations to get the money for his lavish entertainments and personal spending binges. His capricious violence also extended to his foreign policy. He contemplated invasions of Germany and Britain, but in both cases braggadocio ended in a whimper: the former with a military parade across the Rhine and the latter with a march to the Strait of Dover. Many feared they might fall victim to his

Tiberius

Caligula

caprice. At length a member of the Praetorian Guard struck him down on January 24, A.D. 41. His wife and infant daughter shared his fate. He had not designated a successor.

Claudius

In the Senate's enthusiasm over the death of the tyrant, it began to entertain heady ideas of restoring the Republic. However, the senators failed to realize how completely the reins of government had been removed from their hands. Some soldiers of the Praetorian Guard, while they were plundering the palace after the murder of Caligula, saw two feet sticking out from under a curtain. They belonged to Claudius, Caligula's uncle. The frightened captive evidently feared that the governmental purge would include him too. But the soldiers took him to the Praetorian camp, where he was hailed as emperor. The transaction involved a handsome bribe for each member of the Guard. This set a terrible precedent for future rulers, who were forced to buy off the military. The Senate had no choice but to confer the imperial powers upon Claudius.

Claudius was plagued all his life by a deformed and somewhat incapacitated body—some say as a result of a birth injury; others, as a result of poliomyelitis. This incapacity had turned him into a student and something of a recluse. His enemies have presented him as a much more grotesque figure than he probably was. They have also seen him as under the domination of members of his household rather than the real leader of the state. Whatever the real situation, it seems that the emperor Claudius provided a high quality of administration for the empire. He adjusted tax burdens and inaugurated an extensive program of public works. This involved building new aqueducts, roads, and canals; swamp drainage; and especially the development of Ostia as a harbor for Rome.

In foreign policy, Claudius followed more in the train of Julius than Augustus. He annexed Thrace and spread Roman influence around much of the Black Sea. In the Near East he reestablished the Roman protectorate over Armenia and restored Judea to its position as an imperial province after its brief experience as a client kingdom under Herod Agrippa I (41–44).

Claudius' forces invaded Britain and conquered it in the years 43 and following. Claudius personally accompanied the troops. Though Julius Caesar had invaded the island long before, he had never added it to the empire. Exactly why Claudius determined to undertake this conquest is uncertain. There were appeals to Rome by British tribes for help against other tribes of the island. British tribes posed a threat to the peace and security of Gaul. But probably of most importance was an exaggerated

Claudius

estimate of the resources of the island. Claudius extended Roman citizenship in the provinces and advanced the process of urbanization there.

At home Claudius, like Augustus, tried to give a large share of the responsibility of the state to the Senate and returned to that body some powers it had lost under Tiberius and Caligula. And he introduced Gallic members into the Senate. On the other hand, he dealt the Senate a mortal blow in his effective organization of the departments of government (treasury department, justice department, records department, etc.), each with a head who was a member of the imperial cabinet—an organization composed largely of freedmen loyal to the emperor.

Whether or not Claudius was dominated by his freedmen and adulterous women in his governmental policies, he was dominated by his second wife, Agrippina, to the point that he adopted Nero, her son by a previous marriage, as his son and successor, in preference to his own natural son. Subsequently Nero married Claudius' daughter Octavia and succeeded to the imperial chair when Claudius died in 54. Agrippina had had him poisoned.

Apparently Claudius had some trouble with the Jews in Rome. Suetonius (c. A.D. 75–160), made this statement in his *Life of Claudius*: "Since the Jews were continually making disturbances at the instigation of Chrestus, he [Claudius] expelled them from Rome."[1] This is a corroboration of Luke's statement in Acts 18:2: "Claudius had commanded all the Jews to depart from Rome." Many believe that the reference to Chrestus here is a Latin form of Christ and that the disturbance involved controversy between Jews converted to Christianity and those opposed to it.

Nero

Nero was the last of the Julio-Claudians. Coming to the imperial chair at sixteen, he was during the first five years of his rule largely dominated by his mother, Agrippina, and the very capable heads of the executive departments of government which Claudius had instituted. Chief of this circle of leaders was Nero's tutor, the Stoic philosopher Seneca—greatest of the literary figures of the Julio-Claudian period. During these early years, administration of the empire was generally efficient and peaceful, and prosperity continued. In fact, the empire as a whole was not seriously affected by Nero's inadequacies until the rebellion at the end of his life.

As Nero grew into manhood, he attempted to assert his independence. In so doing he clashed with his domineering mother. This conflict, involving as it did the threats of his mother, led Nero to fear plots against the throne. This fear, coupled with the ambitions of his mistress, Poppaea Sabina, proved to be his undoing. Ultimately his mother, his wife, and his stepbrother Germanicus (son of Claudius) were all disposed of. Increasingly Nero's rule became a reign of terror as plots against the throne were ruthlessly tracked down.

One hot July night in 64, fire broke out in Rome in the slums east of the Circus Maximus and burned with unabated force for nine days, gutting more than half of the city. No effort to check it succeeded. Even Nero's palace lay a charred mass, with all of its priceless art treasures forever lost to posterity. In spite of the emperor's measures to alleviate the sufferings of the homeless, he could not allay the people's suspicion that he started the fire in order to have the glory of rebuilding Rome along grander lines. Rebuild it he did, and he spared no expense in the process. In the middle of the new capital he built his great Golden House, which with its gardens and lakes covered 120 acres.

According to Tacitus,[2] Nero tried to lay the blame for this holocaust on Christians in order to divert suspicion from himself. This view has been generally accepted. Moreover, it has been frequently asserted that Nero was actually to blame for the fire. On the other hand, some have doubted that Nero persecuted Christians or that he blamed the fire on them.

What is the modern student to think of all this? To begin with, no one will probably ever know whether or not Nero had anything to do with starting the fire; very likely he did not. Second, apparently by Nero's day Christians were considered to be enemies of society. Increasingly numerous, they strongly opposed many social and religious practices (e. g., emperor worship) that acted as something of a cement for the pagan society of which they were a part. Therefore, they could be regarded as enemies of that society. In such a hostile atmosphere it was possible to charge them with incendiarism. Third, it seems that the testimonies of Tacitus and others are reliable and that a very severe persecution of Christians did occur in Rome, instigated by Nero and related to the charge of incendiarism, and that it began in the latter part of 64 and lasted until 66 when Nero went abroad. Ramsay has given a helpful and detailed discussion of the issue.[3]

Nero at age sixteen, when he was under the supervision of Seneca and others (The Capitoline Museum, Rome)

In 66 Nero embarked on a grand concert tour of Greece. Having pursued his musical interests for many years, he now invaded the land of the muses, accompanied by numerous musicians, actors, and soldiers. He won hundreds of prizes for his singing and acting. Whether or not he had much real ability modern students will probably never know. The judges at any contest awarded first prize to another at the peril of their lives.

While Nero "fiddled," or rather sang and played his cithara, Rome not only burned but plots against his rule thickened—in back rooms at the Senate, in barrooms around the city, and especially in barracks on the frontiers. Nero made the fatal mistake of not paying enough attention to the troops which were, after all, the basis of the emperor's power. Not only did he finally allow their pay to fall in arrears because of worsening financial conditions, but he had not even bothered to become acquainted with the commanders. Worse, the full effects of long-term service of men at one location on the frontier were now being felt. Men in the ranks became more attached to their commander than to the emperor or the state. They were willing to fight to raise their officers to the imperial chair.

Civil War

Not long after Nero's return from Greece, a rebellion broke out in Gaul and spread to Rome, where it was supported by the Praetorian Guard and the Senate. Nero fled from the capital and committed suicide. Whether or not he was really insane, as some writers have implied or charged, is open to question. His intense interest in music and drama need not be considered as evidence of his madness. His suspicious nature may in part be attributed to his conflicts with his mother and the resultant insecurity of his office. Some of his executions or exiles were more for the purpose of obtaining funds for such projects as the rebuilding of Rome than for the thwarting of plots. A few of the contemporary writers who endeavored to discredit him did so because of Hellenistic or Oriental or other non-Roman tendencies in his political and cultural pursuits.

With Nero, the last of the Julio-Claudians, removed from the scene, with armies on the frontiers determined to advance their particular candidates for the imperial chair, and with the Praetorian Guard interfering in affairs closer home, Rome was in for trouble. The year 68/69 is sometimes known as the year of the four emperors. The first, Galba, who had been governor of Hither Spain, bought the support of the Praetorian Guard, and the Senate followed their lead.

Galba ruled during the latter part of 68, but the lukewarm support of the Praetorians and his failure to win support of the Rhine legions were his undoing. Otho (a former husband of Nero's wife Poppaea) next bought the support of the Guard, which slew Galba. Otho ruled from January to April 69, then was defeated by the legions from the Rhine and committed suicide. The victorious army set up their commander, Vitellius, who lasted from April to December.

At that point the army of the east went into action under Vespasian. The Danubian legions soon declared for him too. Next the fleet sided with Vespasian. But hard battles were fought in Italy before the incumbent, Vitellius, was slain and Vespasian recognized as emperor. This inaugurated a dynasty which lasted through three imperial administrations.

Vespasian

Vespasian's rule (69–79) faced numerous problems. The entire empire was in a disheveled state after the civil wars. Rebellions continued in Germany, Gaul, and Judea. Finances were in disarray; his political position was not effectively established. However, the new emperor met the challenges. He had served in eight different provinces in various capacities and knew the empire better than most of those who occupied its highest office.

Vespasian suppressed all the rebellions in 70. Perhaps the most fiercely fought was the insurrection in Judea, which had begun in 66. Friction existed between the Jews and Hellenized inhabitants of the cities of Palestine. The Jews also opposed the pressure of Roman taxation. But the greatest cause of the rebellion lay in the monotheistic religion of the Jews, which would naturally be opposed to Greco-Roman polytheism and which identified national loyalty and uncompromising devotion to religion.

Vespasian was battering the Jewish rebels when he made his bid for power in 69. He had conquered the countryside and was ready to begin the siege of Jerusalem when he left for Rome. The conquest of the capital he left to his son Titus. After a protracted siege, Titus destroyed the city and temple, slaughtered many thousands, and sold many more into slavery. To commemorate this victory, Titus erected a triumphal arch adjacent to the Forum in Rome. One of the reliefs of this arch shows plunder from the temple, including the golden lampstand and the silver trumpets.

Next Vespasian reformed the army by developing legions and auxiliary troops of men of mixed nationalities, instead of recruiting them from the frontier regions in which they served. In this way their loyalty would not likely be accorded a given area in its struggle against the state. He also sought legionary enlistment in the provinces, thereby contributing to the broader policy of Romanizing the provinces. He effectively promoted the process of Romanization and urbanization, extending the benefits of citizenship to many communities and enrolling senatorial members from Spain and Gaul.

Vespasian (The Capitoline Museum, Rome)

To insure greater stability of the frontiers, he established extensive fortifications, strengthened defense lines, extended conquests in Britain, and came to terms with the Parthians in the east.

At home, Vespasian treated the Senate with respect but not in any sense as an equal partner. They obviously had less power now than earlier in the principate. Part of this decline resulted from an expansion of the civil service, which now was largely managed by equestrians (the wealthy business or capitalist class) rather than freedmen.

Vespasian showed tremendous ability in the fiscal affairs of the empire. Frugality, good business procedures, and sufficient control over the bureaucracy to prevent embezzlement—all contributed to his success. Especially he even had such firm control over the military that he did not have to bribe them to do what he wanted.

Though thrifty, Vespasian managed to find large sums for construction of defenses in the provinces and for public buildings and education in the capital. His most famous structure, which he was not able to finish, was the great Colosseum, built on the site of one of the lakes on the grounds of Nero's palace. On the whole he used much restraint in the treatment of his opposition in the Senate and the city of Rome. For some time he even permitted the Cynics and Stoics to continue their open-air tirades against him, but he finally banished them from the city.

When Vespasian marched into Rome at the head of an army and with the government in disarray, he could have set himself up as a military dictator, but he chose not to. Instead he became something of a second Augustus, restoring some of the power of the Senate, reactivating civilian agencies and processes, and reining in the army.

Titus

Before he died in A.D. 79, Vespasian had so effectively linked his son Titus with him in the government that there was a smooth transition to the new administration. Titus lasted only twenty-six months and died with the goodwill of the populace and the Senate. He showed great moderation in the treatment of political enemies and promoted the general welfare. He delighted the public with his splendid games and shows, and on the occasion of the dedication of the Colosseum held a festival that lasted 100 days.

Three major catastrophes marred his reign. In August of 79 Mount Vesuvius erupted, burying Pompeii, Herculaneum, and Stabiae. Then a plague descended on Campania. And in Rome another great fire burned for three days, destroying thousands of homes and several important public structures, including the Pantheon.

Domitian

Domitian (81–96), Titus's younger brother, succeeded him. The Praetorian Guard and the Senate received Domitian without opposition. Yet very soon he won the undying hostility of the Senate by his autocratic ways, which indicated his intention to achieve absolute dictatorship.

After A.D. 86 he seems to have required officials of his household to address him as "Lord and God." After the rebellion of Saturninus, legate of Upper Germany, during the winter of 88/89, Domitian grew increasingly suspicious, inaugurating something of a reign of terror in Rome. He executed many prominent persons on trumped-up charges of treason, others on the ground of "atheism."

Titus (The British Museum)

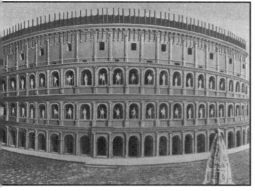

A reconstruction of the Colosseum

These included some notable converts to Judaism or Christianity. A persecution of Christians broke out in the empire about 90. Actually, it was originally directed against Jews who refused to pay a tax to Jupiter Capitolinus. Being associated with Judaism in the minds of many, Christians also suffered during this persecution.

Domitian generally enforced emperor worship. Upon their refusal to participate, he accused Christians of treason. He martyred some, dispossessed others of their property, and banished others. During this persecution he exiled the apostle John to the Isle of Patmos, where John received the vision of the Revelation. We should remember that John was living in Ephesus before he was exiled. In an earlier chapter we saw that a great temple to Domitian was built there.

But Domitian cannot be dismissed as a mere tyrant. In Rome he served as an able administrator and rebuilt the city extensively in an effort to erase the scars left by the great fire of 80. His finest public structure was the Temple of Jupiter on the Capitoline Hill, with columns of Greek marble, gold-plated doors, and a roof overlaid with gold leaf. He kept the populace happy with bread and games and the soldiers content with higher pay.

Domitian pushed Romanization in the provinces and saw to it that they were governed by men of ability, with the result that they flourished under his rule. Along the frontiers he built numerous fortresses and garrison camps. After costly battles in Dacia, he managed to stabilize the situation there. He increased Roman territory in Britain.

While Domitian had his abilities and demonstrated them, he is more often remembered for his tyranny and his reign of terror. Ultimately it seemed that no one was safe. His wife Domitia, believing she was to be the next victim, conspired with two members of the Praetorian Guard and others. When the emperor fell a victim to the assassin's dagger on September 16, 96, an exultant Senate cursed his memory. Nerva, who followed him, became the first of the group known as the five good emperors.

Rome of the Caesars and of St. Paul

It is hard to imagine what the apostle Paul's thoughts may have been as he stood at the Porta Capena, gate into the city of Rome from the Appian Way. If he had been a poor provincial from rural Palestine, he might have been overawed with the great metropolis. But

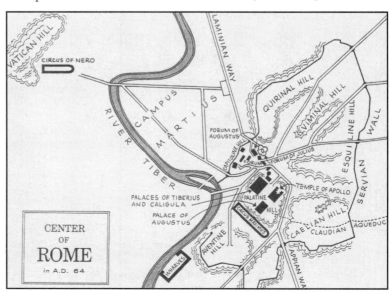

CENTER OF ROME in A.D. 64

The Circus: Entertainment Complex Deluxe

In Paul's day the total length of the circus was about 600 yards and the total width not over 200 yards. They achieved the width by building out over the streets on the north and south sides. The arena itself was about 570 yards long by about 85 yards wide. In the middle of it stood the spina (the central barrier around which chariots raced), 345 yards in length. On the spina were fountains, statues of dignitaries, an obelisk from Egypt, and bronze dolphins and large egg-shaped blocks of wood to help spectators keep track of the number of laps run in a given race.

At the west end were the twelve *carceres* or starting places for chariots. These were set on a curve so the distance was the same from each to the starting line, and they were closed by rope barriers which were dropped simultaneously at the start. The east end of the circus was curved, with a gate in the center. A raised platform surrounded the arena, on which chairs of high officials were placed. From this platform rose three tiers of seats, the lower of stone and the upper and perhaps the middle of wood. Estimates of seating capacity vary greatly, but perhaps 200,000 is not far off. The exterior consisted of a three-story arcade with engaged columns, like the Colosseum.

this strategic center to faith in the Lord Jesus. Finally he may have been energized by the fact that God had already established a beachhead in Rome through the brothers and sisters who had been accompanying him for many miles.

The Circus Maximus

As the apostolic company passed through the gate, before them stood the great Circus Maximus, and overhanging it on the right stood the palaces of the Caesars on the Palatine Hill.

Between the parallel slopes of the Aventine and Palatine lay a valley some 600 yards long and 150 yards broad. Here the great circus (arena) had evolved through a process of repeated destruction and rebuilding. And it was destined to be almost completely rebuilt by Nero after the fire of 64.

Romans had more options than the circus for entertainment in Paul's day. They could also visit amphitheaters, theaters, and baths. The emperor typically took the lead in building most of the structures for public entertainment, and he usually paid for the entertainment provided in these structures once they were finished.

Palaces of the Caesars

As already noted, the palaces of the emperors stood on the Palatine Hill overlooking the Circus Maximus. Today virtually all one can see on the Palatine are great masses of brickwork with arched roofs. In Paul's day these structures were all encased in marble. On the Palatine Hill Augustus, Tiberius, and Claudius had all built their palaces, which eventually covered the hill.

Connected with the palace of Augustus (more modest than the rest) was a beautiful temple of Apollo built of white marble and surrounded by porticoes with columns of yellow marble. Of the images within, of Apollo, Latona, and Artemis, the first was sculpted by Scopas. This temple lasted throughout the imperial period.

The location of neither the temple nor Augustus' palace can be identified with certainty today. But one can still see part of the house of Livia, Augustus' wife, with its wall paintings that are reminiscent of those to be seen at Pompeii. On the northwest part of

such was not the case. Paul had been born in the proud city of Tarsus. His missionary activities had taken him to most of the important cities of the east—to Antioch, Ephesus, Corinth, Athens, Thessalonica, and Jerusalem. Certainly he did not come with the curiosity of a tourist or the acquisitiveness of a businessman. No doubt he experienced some trepidation as he realized that the moment when he would stand trial for his life was drawing closer. Probably he also experienced the enthusiasm of an evangelist who longed for a means of winning many in

The center of Rome reconstructed. The Circus Maximus dominates the model.

the hill, Tiberius built his palace, an area today almost covered by the Farnese Gardens. Only a little of the southern and western sides of the palace can be seen, and little is known of it. Caligula extended the palace of Tiberius toward the Forum, and it seems that there were stairs leading from the palace down into the Forum in Paul's day. At that time, too, there were temples to Jupiter and Magna Mater (Cybele) on the Palatine.

Although Nero is probably responsible for some of the construction on the Palatine, he built his palace on the Esquiline, northeast of where the Colosseum now stands. The palace was destroyed by the great fire of 64. Paul probably appeared before Nero in one of the public buildings in the Forum, not in the palace itself.

Delay in Paul's Hearing

But Paul was not destined to be granted a hearing for a long time. After a stay of two whole years in the capital, his case still had not been adjudicated (Acts 28:30). Reasons for the delay can only be conjectured. Perhaps there was a large backlog of cases; perhaps the court did not meet often to deal with cases of this type; conceivably the prosecution failed to present its case; possibly the settlement of such cases depended on the whim of the emperor. At any rate, Paul experienced a significant delay.

When the emperor did act as judge, he called a council of about a half dozen of his advisers to consult with him on how to deal with the case at hand. Usually the commander of the Praetorian Guard, who might be almost a second ruler, as was Sejanus during Tiberius' reign, judged *vice principis*. And probably in the case of lesser individuals like Paul, the Praetorian commander handled the entire case as president of the emperor's court, without consulting his superior. Certainly the emperor could not handle all of the maze of detail which called for his attention. And during periods when the chief executive was out of the city, much work had to be deputized. Nero seemingly delegated the trial of capital cases on appeal to other persons and confirmed the sentences afterward.[4] Thus it is entirely possible that Paul never appeared before Nero.

Paul evidently had a considerable amount of freedom as he waited under a sort of "house arrest." I assume that he may well have walked in Rome on one or more occasions. If so, he would not have found it to be very impressive. True, the city had its palaces, some fine temples, recreational establishments, and the like. And there were parks (perhaps as much as one-eighth of the city was reserved for this purpose) and homes of the wealthy.

But in much of the old city the streets were narrow, steep, and crooked—often not more than ten feet wide. They were frequently littered with garbage and were unlighted at night. In the poorer sections of the city, wooden tenement houses (*insulae*) rose to a height of as many as six stories,

The Circus Maximus today, with the spina in the middle

The palaces of the Caesars overlooked the Circus Maximus. The ruins visible here are remains of Domitian's great palace.

flushed it. The sewer odors, mingling with the odor of decaying garbage, would have offended modern sensitivities.

Paul's Trial and the Forum Area

At last the day for Paul's trial came; exactly when it was we do not know. I am of the opinion that it may have occurred in the Basilica Julia at the southwest end of the Forum. To orient ourselves, if when he had entered the city Paul had turned right as he faced the Circus Maximus he would have followed the road around the foot of the Palatine Hill, on which the emperors had built their palaces. Shortly that road would have entered the Roman Forum, nestled between the Palatine, Capitoline, and Quirinal Hills.

Now for present purposes, let us suppose Paul came in from the east. And let us remind ourselves that the Roman Forum no longer served as the scene of as much business as it had in the days of the Republic. To the northwest Julius had begun a new forum of his own. Augustus had finished it and added one of his own alongside that of Julius'. After Paul's day other emperors would continue the expansion.

As Paul came into the Forum area down the Sacred Way from the east, the first building he would have passed was the house of the vestal virgins. He might have observed that the house was rather large for a sisterhood of only six priestesses. But such an objection is erased with the observation that the vestals were held in high esteem and that their house was chosen by private citizens and by the state as a safe deposit for documents.

Adjacent to this house was the Temple of Vesta, considered the goddess of the hearth and the patron of the fire that symbolized the perpetuity of the state. It was the responsibility of the priestesses to maintain this sacred fire and to renew it each year on March 1, the first day of the Roman year.

each one covering a block. Often poorly constructed, they sometimes collapsed. Running water from the aqueducts was available only on the first floors. Light and heat were inadequate. These huge tinderboxes provided abundant fuel when fire roared through the city in 64.

The wider streets, the great baths, and many of the finest buildings of Rome were to come during the rebuilding after the fire. Rome's imperial income increased enough to finance more beautiful and imposing structures in later centuries. Though reportedly Augustus had bragged that he had found Rome a city of brick and left it a city of marble, there was much lacking when Paul arrived close to a half century later.

A walk through the streets of Rome in the best of times must have been a challenge. Porters and pack animals with their burdens jostled pedestrians in the narrow thoroughfares. In fact, wheeled vehicles were prohibited on most of them except at night. Residents threw garbage in the streets and left it there to rot. The high stepping-stones still visible at the crosswalks in Pompeii suggest the probable condition of the roadway itself. Without them it may have been difficult, even impossible, to cross.

Rome had a fine supply of water,[5] and her sewers were as good as those of contemporary cities and of most modern cities until the nineteenth or twentieth centuries. But the same system served for surface drainage and sanitation, and only heavy rains effectively

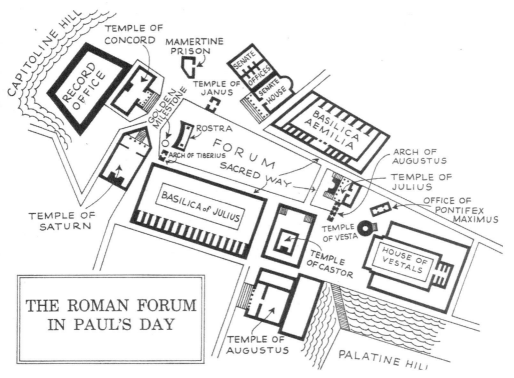

THE ROMAN FORUM IN PAUL'S DAY

Just in front of the Temple of Vesta stood the Regia, official residence of the Pontifex Maximus, head of the religion of the state and repository of the acts of the college of pontiffs concerning the religious life of Rome and the sacred law. As Paul continued westward, he passed the Temple of Caesar, or the Temple of the Divine Julius. This is supposed to have stood on the very site where the dictator's body was cremated on the pyre improvised by the crowds after Mark Antony's famous speech.

When the apostle came to the corner of the Temple of Caesar, the Sacred Way turned left and passed in front of the temple and led straight to the steps of the Temple of Castor and Pollux, which became the sanctuary of travelers (see Acts 28:11, the "Twin Brothers"). As Paul faced this temple with its eleven Corinthian columns about thirty-eight feet high (three of which may be seen today), to his left was the Arch of Augustus.

Now the Sacred Way turned right, and Paul found himself alongside the Basilica Julia at last. Straight before him in the cen-

ter of the Forum stood the Rostrum, where orators made public speeches. At one corner of the Rostrum stood the *miliarum aureum*, or golden milestone, a marble column covered with gilt bronze, on which the distances from Rome to the principal towns

A reconstruction of the west end of the Forum. High on the left stands the Temple of Jupiter on the Capitoline Hill. Just below it is the Temple of Saturn. Next to that in the middle background rises the Public Record Office. The arch—of Septimius Severus—dates to the second century.

A reconstruction of the Basilica Julia

of Italy and the empire were marked (hence the statement, "All roads lead to Rome"). Behind that the Temple of Saturn was visible; and beyond, at the edge of the Capitoline Hill, stood the Temple of Concord, behind which rose the Public Record Office. Incidentally, before we move on, the Temple of Saturn was connected with the celebration of the Saturnalia. As I note in the section on religion, aspects of the Saturnalia were later partially incorporated into the celebration of Christmas.

If Paul had made a half-turn to the right and looked across the Forum, he would have faced the Basilica Aemilia, a great commercial center about 300 by 80 feet, especially used for money changing. Next to that stood the Senate House and the Senate Office Building.

But Paul's concern must have been the Basilica Julia, the seat of the tribunal of the *Centumviri*, who judged civil cases. The structure was 312 feet long by 156 feet wide with a great center hall measuring 234 by 85 feet. The latter was surrounded on all sides by a double row of brick pillars, faced with marble, which formed aisles that were vaulted and stuccoed. Above the aisles were galleries.

A wooden roof covered the central hall. This rose above the roof of the side aisles on a clerestory. Through this light was admitted into the great hall. The floor had been paved with slabs of marble, colored in the central court and white in the aisles. Sculpture, mostly in the form of freestanding statues, abundantly beautified the structure.

Outcome of the Trial

The conviction that Paul left the emperor's court a free man has found growing support among Bible students. I hold to that view. To begin with, the charges of infraction of Jewish law brought against Paul would not have been serious in the eyes of a Roman. Apparently the case against him was not strong anyway. In this connection Acts 26:32 is quite revealing: "Then Agrippa said to Festus, 'This man might have been set free if he had not appealed to Caesar.'" Moreover, when the apostle arrived in Rome, he learned from Jews there that no documents from his opposition had reached the Jews of Rome (Acts 28:21). If his prosecutors did not carry the case to Rome, Paul might have won by default.

Second, even while in prison the apostle seems confident of his release (cf. Philemon 22; Philippians 1:25–26; 2:23–24). He had also planned to go to Spain, where he had not gone before his imprisonment (Romans 15:24, 28). Early church writers indicate that Paul did go to Spain, that his ministry there came after his first Roman imprisonment, and that he was imprisoned a second time in Rome and martyred.[6]

Third, there are several other biblical references that may indicate a fourth missionary journey. For example, in 2 Timothy 4:20, Paul mentions that he left Trophimus sick at Miletus. This could not have been on Paul's last journey to Jerusalem, because Trophimus was not left behind (Acts 20:4; 21:29), nor of the journey to Rome, because he did not touch at Miletus then. This seems to presuppose another voyage.

If Paul made a fourth missionary journey, he probably went first to Spain and then to the east once more. Very likely he spent some time in Crete winning converts—therefore the need for sending Titus there to organize the church on the island and for penning an epistle to him there later.

Probably he was arrested in Asia, possibly at Ephesus. He had left books, parchments, and clothes at Troas expecting to return for them. The particular wrong which Phygellus, Hermogenes, and Alexander had done him in Asia may have been misrepresenting him to the authorities and securing his arrest (2 Timothy 1:15; 4:14).

Rome Again

This second arrest would have occurred after the fire of Rome, when Christians could no longer enjoy the freedom they once had. It is not necessary to hold, however, that Paul was arrested because of his faith. Some of his enemies may have hauled him into the courts on false charges—perhaps devised by the men he berated in the references just noted.

When Paul arrived in Rome the second time, perhaps about 66, the city had a very different appearance from his earlier visit. The fire had made possible some extensive changes. Many streets had been widened and straightened, the Circus Maximus had been rebuilt and embellished, and many other public structures had been built or rebuilt. Much still lay in ruins. Nero had reserved the entire center of the city for his grand new palace, which justly deserved the name *Domus Aurea*, or "Golden House."

Tradition has it that during his second imprisonment Paul was detained in the Mamertine Prison in Rome. This was the ancient state prison of the city, at the foot of the Capitoline Hill. It was used as a place of detention, not of penal servitude, although some executions occurred there. We could spend time talking about how the prison now appears and looking at references in ancient writers to the horrors of imprisonment there. But the present condition of the prison does not seem to help much in visualizing Paul's last days. As I have stood there on several occasions, I could not imagine Paul's writing Second Timothy or anything else under such conditions. Apparently what now exists is only a small part of the first-century prison, only one of a number of cells, and Paul may have had somewhat better conditions in another part of the facility.[7] Visitors to the Mamertine today should be careful not to assume that it looked the same in the days of Peter and Paul.

In any case, Paul knew he could not expect release this time. "The time of my

---

Money for Imperial Construction

Of course Rome was not built in a day. Thus construction of important and expensive structures was always going on somewhere—much of it at the initiation of the emperor. And periodically an emperor sent aid to a city stricken by an earthquake or some other catastrophe to enable massive reconstruction. Where did he get all that money?

From the time that Augustus took Egypt in 30 B.C. and added it to the Roman Empire, that province became the personal possession of the emperor. He kept control of it so he would have adequate grain supplies for the troops and the city of Rome. Whatever taxes he levied there he could spend as he wished. Then in several provinces around the empire the emperor controlled mines, forests, and other wealth that had belonged to the rulers there before Rome took over.

Of course individuals, cities, and provinces that wanted something from the emperor were always making gifts to influence him. All this was in addition to taxes and tribute levied on the provinces. So there was always cash for a pet project. Then of course cities and provinces sometimes launched building projects on their own.

---

departure is at hand" (2 Timothy 4:6), he said. The English is so bland. The Greek for "departure" here is both a military and a nautical term. As a military expression it referred to taking down a tent and departing. As a nautical term it referred to the hoisting of an anchor and sailing a ship. The Greek may be literally translated "loosing away upward" and has a wonderful connotation for us. As a dirigible or balloon strains at its holding cables waiting to be released, so Paul's soul strained to be loosed away upward to join his Maker and Redeemer.

(For more on this topic, go to p. 584.)

Religion

The Old Roman Pantheon

The old Roman Pantheon consisted of twelve great gods worshiped to a greater or lesser degree in the various cities of Italy and the empire. Any one of them might become the chief patron of a city. A listing of the festivals and days sacred to them would try the patience of any reader.

Romans made sacrifices to these deities, especially during their festival times. And in connection with the worship of many of them devotees might share in a sacrificial meal and eat "meat [or other food] offered to idols," as we have seen in Asia Minor and Greece.

The Emperor Cult

We have discovered that the cult of the goddess Roma, the divine spirit of Rome, arose in the east. Likewise the worship of the emperor arose there. Augustus took a different approach in the west. He encouraged worship of the genius or spiritual power embodied in the emperor, not the emperor himself, and encouraged veneration of Julius Caesar. A temple to Julius was built in the Forum at Rome, on the supposed site of his funeral pyre. In spite of his wishes, however, altars to Augustus were established in the west. After Augustus died in A.D. 14 he was deified by an act of the Senate. And as other emperors died it was common for them to be deified too. But those who did not get on well with the Senate were not so honored. For example, neither Tiberius nor Caligula was granted deification. Members of the imperial family (e.g., Augustus' wife Livia) were also added to the cult.

In the west deified emperors were closely associated with the cult of Roma after death, but in the east living emperors were worshiped. Only Caligula and Domitian demanded worship of all subjects while still alive. Worship of the emperor became a test of loyalty to Rome, as Japanese used to worship their emperor in the state cult. In addition to the worship of Rome and the emperor, Romans could worship

The Gods of the Pantheon

Jupiter (Zeus was his Greek name), king of the gods, was the supreme ruler, lord of the sky and rain god. Neptune (Poseidon) governed the sea and Pluto (Hades) the underworld.

Vesta (Hestia) was goddess of the hearth, and the eternal flame of the state constantly burned in her temple in the Roman Forum. Juno (Hera), queen of the gods, might be worshiped as a fertility goddess, the special patron of the bride and the bringer of light.

Mars (Ares) was, of course, the god of war, and Minerva (Athena), goddess of crafts and trade guilds. Apollo, a healing god, a god of oracles and prophesies, history, music, and poetry, as well as the sun god, was a Greek god that was never properly identified with a Roman deity but was widely worshiped by the Romans nonetheless.

Venus (Aphrodite), the goddess of love and beauty, also presided over the fertility of vegetable gardens, fruits, and flowers. Mercury (Hermes), messenger of the gods, served as a god of trade and commercial success. Diana (Artemis) was a mother goddess of fertility and of the wilderness and a huntress. Vulcan (Hephaestus) was a god of fire and of the smithy. Our word vulcanize comes from his name.

whatever gods they chose. From the state calendars of the first century it appears that festivals or celebrations or sacrifices devoted to the emperor took place about twice a month.

State Religious Festivals

Romans celebrated a host of religious festivals. Only three are chosen for comment here, one with a purely secular Roman connection and two with contemporary American religious significance. The festival of Mars, which lasted most of the month of March, celebrated Mars as both a war god and an agricultural god. On March 1, they offered prayers to Juno and her son

In addition to being the object of worship, the emperor was also the head of the state religion, or Pontifex Maximus. Here Augustus is dressed as Pontifex Maximus. (National Museum, Rome)

honor Saturn, the god of seed sowing. The celebration featured a time of festivity, lighting of candles, and the giving of gifts. The festival began with a sacrifice at the temple of Saturn in the Forum, followed by a public feast open to everyone. There was also a sort of mock king in each household, who presided over the festivities, and slaves were allowed temporary liberty to do as they liked. Most of the items of this event were later absorbed into the celebration of Christmas.

Foreign Cults Imported to Italy and the West

The Romans imported Cybele worship, or worship of the Great Mother, from Pergamum at the end of the third century B.C., when Rome was allied with Pergamum against Hannibal and Carthage. They brought the sacred black stone of the goddess (probably meteoric rock) to Rome from Pergamum in 204 B.C. and installed it in its own temple on the Palatine Hill in 191 B.C. They worshiped Cybele as the goddess of nature, the mountains, and fertility. The worship of Cybele involved some rather wild parades of adherents through the streets of Rome and the castration of its priests, both of which tended to turn off native Italians. This religion did not gain respectability in Italy until the reign of Claudius.

Bacchic or Dionysian rites invaded Rome about 200 B.C. But in the early days they became immoral drunken orgies involving massive heterosexual and homosexual activity. In 186 B.C. the Senate moved to stamp out Bacchic rites and destroyed their sanctuaries. Later on, Bacchic rites resurfaced in a milder form in which initiation ended in a ceremony of drunkenness accompanied by frenzied dance given rhythm by the music of flutes, castanets, timbrels, and more. We need to separate these initiations from the earlier orgies and the later debauched dinner parties (often called Bacchanalian orgies), sometimes thrown by the wealthy.

Egyptian merchants and sailors introduced the cult of Isis to Puteoli in the first century B.C. and later to Rome. The worship

Mars, husbands gave their wives presents, and female slaves were feasted by their mistresses.

The Lupercalia, on February 15, involved purification and fertility rites. Priests called *luperci* sacrificed goats and a dog on the Palatine Hill. Two aristocratic youths were smeared with sacrificial blood, and with strips of skin of the goats they ran with some of the magistrates of Rome through the streets of the city. They struck everyone they met with the strips to make them fertile. Much revelry accompanied this festival. Because of this festival's popularity, the church absorbed it instead of abolishing it. Pope Gelasius V in 494 made it the Festival of the Purification of the Virgin Mary.

The Romans celebrated the Saturnalia, December 17–23, as the merriest festival of the year. It was a winter solstice festival to

of Cybele, Bacchus, and Isis all centered around a dying and resurrected god, usually following the rhythm of the seasons (dying in the winter, resurrecting in the spring). By identifying with the resurrected deity through an initiation ceremony, the initiates believed they had obtained a hope of life after death. And there was an emotional content to their faith that was lacking in emperor worship or the worship of the gods. The impact of the gods of Baalbek and Mithraism came after the New Testament period. A good survey of all the eastern religions appears in Robert Turcan, *The Cults of the Roman Empire* (Blackwell, 1996).

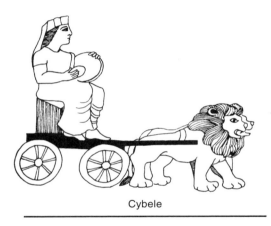

Cybele

Personal or Family Gods

As modern Bible students think about emperor worship or the gods of the Greco-Roman pantheon, they wonder how the ancients could find any personal satisfaction or involvement in such religion. The Lares met the need. They were originally gods of agriculture, supposedly sons of Mercury by Lara, and came to symbolize a protective force of nature. So at an early time people set up shrines to the Lares at crossroads, and travelers on land (and sea) believed them to be their patrons. Long before the New Testament period there developed the worship of Public Lares and Domestic Lares. Public Lares protected crossroads, cities, and even the whole Roman Empire. There was a temple to the *lares* at the head of the Sacra Via in Rome and one to the *lares* of the city next to the forum in Pompeii.

But we are more interested in the Domestic Lares here. They represented the spirits of the dead within the family and were viewed as protectors of the family. It was the responsibility of the *paterfamilias* (father or head of the family) to guarantee the continued protection of the *lar*. This was done through the maintenance of a *lararium* or private household shrine. It consisted of a gabled niche in the wall, a freestanding shrine, or even a niche painted on the wall, usually in a corner of the atrium. If a family moved, the *lararium*, if transportable, was taken to the new house. Food might be offered at the lararium in the morning and prayers for blessing and protection might then be said there as well. There was a *lararium* in every Roman household, and the absence of one in a Christian household represented a marked break with tradition and the old life. The Christian emperor Theodosius I banned the household cult and *lararia* in 392.

(For more on this topic, go to p. 584.)

(For more on this topic, go to p. 584.)

Warfare

Maintaining the Status Quo

The New Testament era was of course the time of the *Pax Romana*. Though it was not a period of total peace, at no time was Rome called on to fight a war that required all her resources. It was enough for the provincials to know that the power was there to keep them in line. The Romans kept about twenty-eight legions under arms on the frontiers throughout the century. Although in earlier times a legion at full strength numbered 6,000, by about A.D. 100 it regularly numbered 5,200. So about 145,000 served in the legions at any given time, with perhaps an equal number of auxiliaries, which included the cavalry.

As time went on, the Romans tended to erect a static defensive system on the major frontiers. Camps started to assume a more permanent appearance. Some camps had stone construction and traders began to settle outside the camps in small towns. And as more and more of the soldiers were recruited and served in the provinces, over 50 percent of the legionnaires came to be non-Italian.[8] When such men completed their twenty-five years of service, they and their wives and sons were granted Roman citizenship. Another long-term trend in the stationing of the legions was to reduce the size of the armies in Spain and Germany and increase those in the Balkans and the east.

The Temple of the Public Lares next to the Forum of Pompeii with its marble altar

Training for military service remained rigorous during the first century. It included marching in step, route marching (20 miles in five hours), running, charging, and jumping obstacles. In addition, there was swimming and arms drill with wooden swords, which weighed twice as much as the regulation sword. Finally the recruit was introduced to fighting drill in full armor and basic battle tactics. But all that said, some legions grew rather soft with inactivity in the camps on the frontier.

Warlike Actions of the Century

Conquest of Britain

For reasons already noted, in addition to Claudius' desire to obtain a military reputation for himself and strengthen his hold on the frontier garrisons, he set about to conquer Britain. He put Aulus Plautius in command of the operation. In 43 he ferried an army of four legions totaling between forty and fifty thousand men plus auxiliaries across the Channel.[9] The expeditionary force landed unopposed at Rutupiae (Richborough) in Kent in southeastern

England. After winning victories over the armies of the Belgic kingdom that ruled southeast England, the Romans stood before the royal capital of Camulodunum (Colchester), northeast of London. Plautius then restrained his forces until Claudius arrived. Upon his arrival the emperor rode as conqueror into the city amid the cheers of his troops. Vespasian, the future emperor, surfaced at this point as an important general. He won several engagements in his march westward along the Channel coast.

In 47, the centennial year of Caesar's second visit to Britain, Rome annexed southern England as the province of Britannia. Governors developed Camulodunum as the provincial capital and built a temple to Claudius and the imperial cult there. A colony of Roman veterans settled in the city as well. The details of a fierce revolt in 61, with destructive consequences and the savage repression of it, are beyond the scope of our present study. It is enough to say that in the last years of Nero's reign Britannia settled down under Roman rule.

The Subjugation of Palestine

The story of the First Jewish Revolt, beginning in 66, has already been briefly told, and it is not necessary to repeat it here. Suffice it to say that there was fierce fighting on both sides, and Rome found it necessary to concentrate seven legions, a quarter

A domestic Lares shelf in the House of the Faun in Pompeii.

A catapult like those used to besiege Jerusalem
(Now located at the tomb of Hadrian, Rome)

of the entire Roman army, in Syria temporarily to deal with the emergency.

The Year of the Four Emperors

By and large, the events of 68–69 did not involve military action. The commander of the Praetorian Guard withdrew his support of Nero in June of 68 and threw it to Galba, governor of one of the Spanish provinces. He lasted only six months, especially because he failed to make the expected payments to the army and the Praetorian Guard, and thus did not gain their support. Otho then won over the Praetorian Guard and governed with some ability during his brief reign.

Though most of the provinces swore allegiance to Otho, the provinces of Germany, and later Gaul and Spain, declared for Vitellius. Otho led his forces north to meet Vitellius but sought to wait to do battle until the legions of the Danube could arrive to help him. Vitellius forced the issue, however, and decisively defeated the Othonians in the Po Valley. Otho committed suicide on April 16, after only three months in office. Vitellius now became emperor.

What actually happened was this. The Rhine armies were not really for Vitellius (with no distinguishing qualities) but supported him in opposition to Galba, who had shunned them. By the time they got down into Italy, however, they found themselves opposing Otho instead of Galba. The transition to the new regime was generally smooth and peaceful. Vitellius, however, was forced to break up the old Praetorian Guard and substitute his own men.

But Vitellius hardly had time to catch his breath when news reached him about the middle of July that the army of the eastern provinces had set up Vespasian as a rival emperor. A distinguished general, he commanded widespread support. Before Vespasian could lead his forces from the Syrian frontier, however, the legions of the Danube declared for him and swung into action. Moving into Italy with only five legions and some auxiliaries, possibly as many as 30,000 men, they met the larger forces of Vitellius in the Po Valley before they were ready to do battle. On October 24 they thoroughly trounced Vitellius' army, pursuing them to the city of Cremona. There for four days they killed and looted in an orgy of destruction that horrified all who heard of it. The result was that Vitellius' army had no heart to oppose the Flavian advance, and the Danubian army marched toward Rome unopposed. On December 20 they fought their way into Rome, located Vitellius, killed him, and threw his body into the Tiber.

A biography of Vespasian is not necessary at this point. We need only report that he had first-hand experience in almost every corner of the empire, both in military and civilian capacities, under several emperors. For example, he had commanded the Second Legion in the conquest of Britain in 43–47 and was appointed governor of Judea in 67 with a military force of three legions. He was bringing the suppression of the Jewish Revolt to a successful conclusion when the events of 69 occurred. As emperor he was sufficiently in control of the military that he did not have to bribe them to do his will. He gave the empire a period of stable and efficient government. Though he could have become a military dictator, he chose not to do so and became something of a "second Augustus," governing with the cooperation of the Senate and maintaining civilian institutions.

A Soldier's Armor and Ephesians 6

"Therefore put on the full armor of God, so that when the day of evil comes, you may be

able to stand your ground, and after you have done everything, to stand. Stand firm then, with the belt of truth buckled around your waist, with the breastplate of righteousness in place, and with your feet fitted with the readiness that comes from the gospel of peace. In addition to all this, take up the shield of faith, with which you can extinguish all the flaming arrows of the evil one. Take the helmet of salvation and the sword of the Spirit, which is the word of God." (Ephesians 6:13–17 NIV)

There is Paul, a prisoner in Rome. He is constantly accompanied by a Roman soldier. As the Praetorian stands there, he makes an excellent object lesson for the Christian. Paul did not dream up all this imagery on the spot, however. A thorough student of the Old Testament, he could picture God as going forth as a warrior to deliver His people (Isaiah 59:15ff.) and as wearing a breastplate of righteousness and the helmet of salvation (Isaiah 59:17). Paul's special concern in verse 13 is that the Christian warrior will be able to stand his ground, to "stand at attention," ready for offense or defense. Having "done everything, to stand," must mean "after each fresh assault has been successfully repulsed," when one is most likely to be caught off guard, "stand at attention."

The belt of truth (v. 14)

The belt was a wide leather belt, studded with decorated metal plates, which carried a dagger and an apron. The apron consisted of a number of wide leather strips with bronze terminals. These swung between the legs on the march and gave protection to the stomach and private parts in battle. Much of the time the apron was tucked into the belt. This is truth in the sense of "truthfulness" or "faithfulness to His promises."

The breastplate of righteousness (v. 14)

The breastplate varied in construction from time to time. When Paul was in Rome it consisted of six or seven overlapping strips of bronze or iron that passed around the upper body. These were held together by leather strips or cords on the inside and by strips and buckles or hooks on the exterior. The shoulders were covered with

A soldier fully armed

curved strips of metal. Around the neck a scarf was worn to protect against chafing of the skin. The whole assembly weighed about twenty pounds and was constructed to provide great flexibility of movement. It was the safety provided by armor, combined with aggressive sword-thrusting, that made Roman soldiers so formidable. "Righteousness" involves a right relationship to God, and a sense of that makes us fearless: "The righteous are bold as a lion" (Proverbs 28:1).

Feet shod (v. 15)

The legionary wore heavy sandals specially reinforced with three-fourths-inch-thick leather soles and hobnails. The leather thongs that held them on continued halfway up the shin and were tied there. In cold

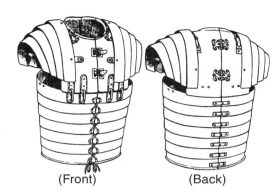

(Front)   (Back)

The breastplate

weather they could be stuffed with fur or wool and were probably as comfortable as anything worn today.

The shield of faith (v. 16)

The shield of faith makes it possible to extinguish the flaming arrows of the evil one. The shield of about A.D. 50 was rectangular and curved around the body. It was made of a kind of plywood, thin sheets of wood, glued so the grain of each piece was at right angles to the next. It was covered with tough leather and bound around the edge with an iron or bronze rim. An iron boss on the exterior made it possible with a shift of the shield to ward off an enemy spear or sword blow. And the construction tended to put out a flaming arrow.

The helmet of salvation (v. 17)

Like some other pieces of armor, helmet design changed from time to time. In Paul's day the Romans wore a bronze helmet with an inner iron skull-plate and a leather skull-cap to take the shock of blows. At the back a projection shielded the neck, and a ridge in the front gave protection to the face. Hinged bronze cheek-pieces protected the face and ears.

Sword of the Spirit (v. 17)

The sword commonly was two feet long, often with a corrugated bone grip for a handle. It was two-edged, but legionnaries were taught to stab rather than cut and thrust. They were known for their deadly

accurate thrust. Constant weapon drill made them experts at their trade. We also have the weapon of the sword of the Spirit, the Word of God, and constant weapon drill may make us experts in our trade.

As for the rest of their uniform, the soldiers wore a linen undergarment next to the skin and over it a short-sleeved woolen tunic that came down almost to the knees. Legionaries in cold climates could wear tight leather breeches that came just below the knees.

The Praetorian Guard and Paul's Imprisonment

"Now when we came to Rome, the centurion delivered the prisoners to the captain of the guard; but Paul was permitted to dwell by himself with the soldier who guarded him." (Acts 28:16 NKJV) *"Then Paul dwelt two whole years in his own rented house, and received all who came to him."* (v. 30 NIV). *"So that it has become known throughout the whole imperial guard [the "Praetorian camp"] and to everyone else that my imprisonment is for Christ."* (Philippians 1:13 NRSV)

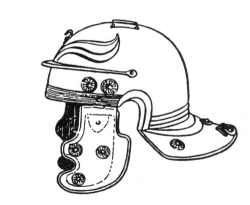

A legionary helmet

The Romans didn't have a prison system like ours where individuals were locked away for a period of time to pay their debt to society. Rather, someone sat in jail awaiting trial or execution, or sentence. They commonly exiled upper-class individuals to some faraway place, as the apostle John was sent to the Isle of Patmos. Paul was taken into protective custody in the military barracks in Jerusalem (Acts 21:37). When he was moved to Caesarea for his protection, he was kept in Herod's palace (Acts 23:35), now thought to be the recently excavated palace by the Mediterranean in Caesarea.

Individuals were rarely chained, except when they were moved, to keep them from escaping.[10] Yet Paul was not chained on the voyage from Caesarea to Rome. Paul talks about being chained while in Rome (Acts 28:20; Ephesians 6:20; Philippians 1:7, 13, 14; Colossians 4:3, 18; Philemon 10, 13), but that could be a figure of speech to describe his confinement. Or he, like others, may have been chained temporarily to prevent his escape when receiving visitors.

In any case, Paul had a considerable amount of freedom during his first Roman imprisonment, receiving numerous visitors (e.g., Acts 28:30). And he wrote the prison epistles and sent them to the respective churches (Ephesians 3:1; 4:1; Philippians 1:7; Colossians 4:3, 10; Philemon 9, et al.). Evidently he had to pay for his keep during the two years in Rome (Acts 28:30), so he would have been delighted with gifts from the church at Philippi (Philippians 4:10, 16, 17) and any other church that was moved to send one.

It seems clear from reference to the "captain of the guard" (Acts 28:16) and the conversions among the "palace guard" (Philippians 1:13) that the Praetorian Guard especially had supervision of his imprisonment and court appearance in Rome.

The Praetorian Guard was the imperial guard of the Roman Empire. Augustus created it as an elite force for his protection and to carry out numerous tasks he assigned to it. He organized it in 27 B.C. and stationed six of its nine cohorts of 500 men each in barracks outside Rome, keeping only three cohorts in Rome to patrol the palace and other major buildings. In this way he preserved the civilian veneer of his regime.

During Augustus' regime the Guard was properly subservient. But in the days of Tiberius conditions changed dramatically. The ambitious commander, Sejanus, persuaded the emperor to bring the Guard from the Italian barracks and install it in the new Praetorian camp at the edge of Rome. He also increased the size of the guard to 6,000. Closer at hand it could be at the disposal of the emperors, but rulers could be at its mercy as well. Henceforth the Praetorians became increasingly involved in Roman politics. At will, or for the right amount of money, they might assassinate emperors or turn on the people of Rome. For example, we have already seen that they killed Caligula and put Claudius on the throne and were heavily involved in the events of 68–69.

Evidently members of the Guard were assigned to deal with numerous court cases. Especially they were delegated the task of watching over prisoners (citizens) who appealed to Caesar. That is how Paul got involved with the Praetorian Guard. Perhaps we should note that when Vespasian sought to shore up the civilian character of the empire in 69, he reduced the guard to Augustus' level of 4,500.

(For more on this topic, go to p. 585.)

Housing and Furniture

"Greet Priscilla and Aquila, my fellow workers in Christ Jesus." "Likewise greet the church that is in their house." (Romans 16:3, 5 NKJV)

Members of the Praetorian Guard in full regalia

As Paul sent greetings to the church that met in the house of Priscilla and Aquila and to the many other groups in Rome identified in Romans 16, we wonder how some of those houses may have looked.

When the apostle traveled along the Appian Way toward Rome, he passed many houses of farmers. Some were subsistence farmers, eking out a living from a few acres of land. These lived in one or two-room huts of mudbrick or fieldstone. Smoke from open fires rose through a hole in the roof, and stalls for animals immediately adjoined the houses.

Then there were working farms run by slave managers. These might have storage rooms, slave quarters, a stairway, and a tool shed on the lower floor and family rooms above. An arrangement for some middle-class working farmers put a kitchen and small rooms for the family and slaves on one side of an enclosed court and on the other sides of the court facilities for livestock and the processing and storing of the produce of the farm.

A few working farmhouses were really quite luxurious. These had open courts, to the north of which was a dining room, bakery, kitchen, a bath complex (hot and cold baths, dressing room, latrine); and to the

A Roman soldier pictured on a stone monument in Ephesus

south of which were grape and olive presses, wine vats, slave quarters, a threshing floor, and cisterns. Stairs led from the kitchen and courtyard to family rooms above. In houses the toilets were frequently put beneath stairs when there was an upper floor. A few great houses in the country were truly luxurious villas instead of working farms. They had beautiful gardens, a luxurious layout, and magnificent furniture.

Builders gave a great deal of attention to the provision of a water supply for these houses. Architects, builders, and others urged construction close to rivers or permanent springs. Failing that, care was taken to obtain pure water from a well. In constructing these, the usual practice was to build a quadrangular well in stone with steps inside for reaching the bottom. Various methods were recommended for keeping the water clean and some suggested boiling the drinking water when in doubt. In some of the more luxurious houses pipes conducted water from cisterns and wells to need areas (e.g., baths, kitchens).

During the time when Paul came to Rome, huge blocks of wood houses (insulae) with tenements for the poor occupied major sections of the city. Landlords wanted the largest return possible on their investment, so apartments were small and sometimes only one room. In the larger apartments there was usually one larger room that served as a living room and smaller rooms of a standard size that could be used interchangeably for a variety of purposes. These apartment buildings rose to a height of six or seven stories in Rome, four in Ostia. Facades were of three types: one had apartments flush with the street on the first floor, a second had shops on the first floor with apartments above, and a third had covered arcades with shops opening under them and apartments above. Buildings for private use had a brick curtain; all evidence indicates that buildings were not finished with a coating of plaster on the outside.

An interior courtyard provided light and air and access to individual apartments.

A typical working farm, built of stuccoed wood or brick with a tile roof and arranged around central courts. Sleeping rooms for the owner or manager and his family opened on the far court; next to them were a dining room and kitchen, which had a high roof and vents for smoke to escape. Around the middle court were stables and sleeping rooms for slaves. In the front wing were storerooms, workrooms, and wine and olive presses. The enclosure at the left was a threshing floor.

Access to apartments on upper floors was, of course, by stairs, the steps of which were made of stone or brick with a wooden tread. Sometimes stairs reached individual apartments, sometimes landings or balconies on which the doors of several apartments opened. Living units were designated by numbers over the entrances and on the stairs leading to them. Window frames were rectangular and might be single or double or even triple. Panes were of selemite (a form of transparent gypsum) or mica but not glass. A few were open and shuttered or louvred.

The church that met in the house of Priscilla and Aquila (see Romans 16:5 above) or with the families of other believers in Rome (see Romans 16:10, 11, 14, 15) may have assembled in one of these larger apartments. But more likely they gathered in a larger home.[11] The houses of the more affluent are well illustrated by excavations in Pompeii, Herculaneum, and Ostia. Normally they were of single stories and windowless on the street. Commonly, small shops were built into the faces of them along the streets; such shops usually had minimal living quarters above them.

Entrances to the houses looked much the same, with attached half columns or pilasters surmounted by a triangular pediment. The houses themselves tended to combine the basic elements of the older Roman or Italic house and the Greek or Hellenistic house. A narrow entrance corridor led into an atrium covered by a roof with an inward tilt on all four sides. This had an opening in the center (compluvium) through which the rainwater ran down into a tank beneath (impluvium), from which it drained into a cistern. Around the atrium were grouped bedrooms and at the end a family or living room, beside which was the dining room.

This much of the house constituted any earlier Italic house. The floor plan was axial and, laid out on a piece of paper, the one side was identical to the other.

Then through a small hallway one passed into a Hellenistic style unit, with an open courtyard surrounded by a colonnade, bedrooms for summer sleeping, and other rooms. Light and ventilation came from the courtyard and the atrium. The whole house served as a windowless, self-contained unit for a single family or an extended family.

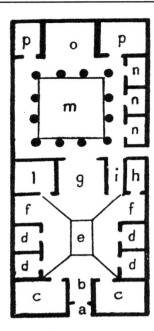

Floor plan of a typical town house of the more affluent in Pompeii or some other Italian town. Room identifications: (a) vestibule; (b) entrance passage; (c) perhaps a worship center, sometimes a shop open to the street; (d) bedrooms; (e) atrium, central hall; (f) "wing" rooms, flanking the dining room; (g) reception area; (h) storeroom; (i) corridor; (l) dining room; (m) peristyle courtyard, surrounded by columns; (n) summer sleeping rooms; (o) an alcove; (p) reception rooms. The kitchen and bathroom were commonly located in rooms adjacent to the peristyle.

Interior Decoration and Arrangements

During New Testament times wall painting in fresco or tempera on carefully prepared stucco became the rule in the better homes. Though various styles had been used in earlier periods of time, during the first century it was common to produce on the walls the appearance of framed panels like tapestries, filled with paintings of landscapes, figures, or still life, and especially scenes from mythology. Store rooms and slave quarters were commonly finished in rough plaster.

Builders used wood for floors in upper stories, but normally used concrete on the ground floor, sometimes with colored marble laid in geometric designs, but usually

with mosaics forming pictures or conventional patterns or pictures in color. Rugs do not seem to have been used, but there were hangings in doorways and sometimes against walls.

Aqueducts leading into Rome provided running water to most of the better houses and on the first floor of tenement houses. The lead and clay pipes of the period could not stand the pressure to bring water to the upper floors. They also piped running

Aqueducts provided water for Rome and other Italian cities. The Claudian Aqueduct provided water for Rome on a channel forty feet above the ground.

water into the better homes of the other cities of Italy. The modern tourist in Pompeii is amazed when the guard turns on the water fountains in the peristyle courtyard of the House of the Vettii. They still work.

Artificial heat came primarily from braziers burning charcoal. Freestanding iron stoves of the type found at Pompeii apparently were rarely used. In some private homes where baths were installed, there was a system of central heating in which smoke and hot air were led beneath the floor and up flues built in the walls of a room to be heated. The chief source of artificial light was the olive oil lamp of metal or clay. In its basic form it was a flat, covered vessel with a handle or with rings for suspension. Wicks were made of hemp, linen, or wool. There were lamps with more than one wick, and there were lampstands for

Peristyle of the House of the Vettii in Pompeii, with stone benches and tables, and fountains that still work

one or more lamps. Some lamps and their stands were very elaborate. Torches were used chiefly for ceremonial occasions.

Furniture

Furniture varied according to status and wealth. Some furniture was made of bronze, iron, or stone, but most was made of wood. Of course wood could be decorated with

Charcoal braziers usually provided heat but the affluent might afford an iron stove like this one excavated in Pompeii.

inlay and fittings of a wide variety. Couches of various types were used for sleeping, eating, or reading. These consisted of oblong wooden frames supported by four or six legs. The open top was filled with interwoven cords, upon which a mattress rested—stuffed with straw, feathers, or wool clippings. Some couches had backs or raised ends. One might sit on a couch, a bench, a backless stool, or chair with a back or arms or both. Some fine chairs were made of a kind of wickerwork or basket weave materials. All these might have movable cushions but there is no evidence of upholstered furniture. The love of display found greatest expression in the tables of many shapes and sizes—of wood, bronze, iron, stone, or a combination of these. Tables for the dining room were small and low. Clothing and household goods were stored in wardrobes and chests. Fountains, statuary, and concrete benches beautified the peristyle gardens.

(For more on this topic, go to p. 585.)

Diet and Foodstuffs

Diet

As with us, income determined what the Romans served at mealtime. The poor lived chiefly on cereals and vegetables and rarely ate meat. Wheat was crushed for porridge and ground into flour for many kinds of bread. All classes ate most of the commoner vegetables that we know. Those especially popular were cabbage, parsnips, lettuce, asparagus, onions, garlic, lentils, beans, and beets. Most of the fruits except citrus fruits were consumed daily. However, it is historically inaccurate for someone to be standing on the deck of a Roman ship eating an orange, as in Lloyd Douglas' novel *The Robe.*

Olive oil took the place of butter, as honey did of sugar. Cheese of many kinds was common food. Although some people drank milk, they mainly used it for making cheeses. Boiled must (unfermented grape juice concentrate), when diluted, was a common drink. The chief drink other than water was wine, and wines spiced with myrrh or flower essences were served at banquets. Honeyed wine was used both as a drink and a medicine. Wine was almost always diluted. The poorer classes commonly drank a watered-down, low quality wine similar to vinegar. Beer and mead (a fermented drink made of honey, water, malt, and yeast) were common in northern Italy. A special delicacy was *garum*, a sauce made by fermenting the intestines and other waste parts of fish. Processors strained the fish sauce after several months of fermentation.

Kitchen utensils excavated at Pompeii

The favorite meat was pork. Lamb, mutton, and goat meat came next in order of preference, with beef least popular. Hens, doves, geese, ducks, and guinea hens were raised for market and wild birds caught and sold. The many kinds of fish and shellfish now caught in the Mediterranean were caught and sold. The oyster was the most desired shellfish. For the most part, mer-

chants transported fish and shellfish live to their destination. Foods could be preserved by pickling—fish by drying, salting, and smoking. But contaminated food must often have caused sickness.

Eating

Probably most Romans sat upright to eat their meals, but the wealthy reclined on couches, especially at dinner parties. Tableware ranged from coarse pottery for the poor to fine pottery, glass, bronze, silver, gold, and pewter for upper classes. Bronze, silver, and bone spoons were used for eating liquids and eggs, and their pointed handles for digging shellfish from their shells. Diners used knives with iron blades and handles of bone, wood, or bronze to cut up food, which was then generally eaten with the fingers.

It almost stretches a point to say that Romans (Italians) ate three meals a day during the first century. Many, as is true in contemporary America, skipped breakfast altogether. All ate light in the morning, perhaps having only a piece of bread and something to drink (milk or wine), sometimes with the addition of eggs or cheese. Breakfast came about sunrise; the Romans began their day early. Lunch, at eleven or twelve, might consist of fruit, salad, and cold meat or a small hot meal of fish (meat) and vegetables. For a large percentage of the population a siesta and a trip to the baths followed the meal. Dinner then began about four or five and often lasted for some hours. In the absence of evening entertainment it became a social event. For the middle class and above it consisted of three courses. The first was an appetizer of perhaps eggs, raw vegetables, or fish; the second, cooked vegetables and meats; the third, fruit or pastries.

Food Preparation

Cooking was generally done over a charcoal brazier, but also over an open hearth with kettles suspended from a chain or in cooking vessels set on gridirons. Smoke escaped through the roof or a vent in the wall. Cooking was usually done outside (perhaps in a courtyard). Many people, especially tenement dwellers, had no cooking facilities, but communal ovens may have been available to them. Bread, cakes, and pastries were produced commercially and at home. Domed ovens were used mainly for baking bread; a fire was lit inside the oven to heat it and raked out before the food was put in.

For grinding grain in a commercial establishment, large rotary mills powered by donkeys and mules were common. These mills consisted of a bell-shaped lower stone and an hourglass-shaped upper stone. Industrial establishments occasionally used watermills for industrial purposes. In the household, grain might be placed on a flat stone and crushed by rubbing another stone backward and forward over it. Rotary hand grinders consisted of a lower convex stone with an upper concave stone. Grain was dropped through an opening in the upper stone which was simultaneously rotated.

Agriculture

Romans understood the importance or necessity of leaving land to lie fallow, crop rotation, manuring and other fertilization, and supplying the soil with lime. Literary figures addressed these subjects at least briefly on occasion.[14] During the first century Italian agriculture, horticulture, and cattle raising were all in fairly good condition. The wheat lands failed to meet expectations, however, and vineyards were overexpanded.

Grapes were widely grown—in the Po Valley, in Etruria in the northwest, in the northeast, in the south central and southeast parts of the peninsula, and around the Bay of Naples. During the early empire Italians imported relatively little wine from abroad, but probably did not export much either. In the vineyards farmers often used trees to support vines (especially elm, ash, and poplar), although they frequently supported them on wooden poles with crosspieces as well.

In general, olive culture used the limestone ridges too rough for cereals and small crops. The highest quality oil in Italy came from Campania around the Bay of Naples. But olives also grew in profusion in the northeast and southeast of the peninsula. Combination cropping, where farmers grew

Roman Recipes

One cookbook, attributed to Apicius, about the time of Tiberius Caesar (14–37) has survived. Evidently it was added to late in the first century. Here is a recipe for preparing cucumbers. "Stew the peeled cucumbers either in broth or in a wine sauce. You will find them to be tender and not causing indigestion. Usually cucumbers are parboiled in water and then finished in broth; most often after being parboiled they are stuffed with forcemeat and then finished in broth. Cucumbers another way: Peeled cucumbers are stewed with boiled brains, cumin and a little honey. Add some celery seed, stock and oil, bind the gravy with eggs. Sprinkle with pepper and serve."[12]

Here is one for cooking mushrooms. "Slice the mushroom stems; stew them in broth and finish by covering them with eggs, adding pepper, lovage, a little honey, broth and oil to taste."[13]

A cookbook that gathers a collection from the entire ancient world, from both Greek and Roman writings, and shows how they may be recreated in the modern kitchen is Andrew Dalby and Sally Grainger's *The Classical Cookbook*, published by the J. Paul Getty Museum in Malibu, California.

other crops, such as wheat, between the olive trees and grapevines persisted throughout the regions.

Legumes and vegetables were raised on practically all farms, especially near the cities. The list goes on and on and included beans, kidney beans, chickpeas, cucumbers, radishes, lettuce, cabbages, parsnips, and artichokes. The poor lived on vegetables and grains and rarely ate meat except when communal sacrifice made it available.

The richest fruit land lay around Capua on the Bay of Naples. There and in a few other areas (e.g., Umbria in the northeast, Apulia in the southeast) apples, peaches, plums, pears, apricots, cherries, quinces, and figs grew in abundance. Figs provided a cheap food for the poor and were also used as food for poultry. Nuts—especially walnuts, chestnuts, and almonds—were plentiful.

The wheat lands of the Po Valley were especially prolific, but wheat is bulky and must be transported by water. It was just as cheap or cheaper to ship grain from Egypt and North Africa as from the Po Valley all the way around the peninsula to Rome. There were also excellent wheat fields in Etruria in the northwest, Apulia in the southeast and in Campania on the Bay of Naples. But Italy could not produce enough wheat for all her needs and imported heavily from Egypt, as noted.

Agricultural tools from first century Italy (British Museum)

Flax was widely cultivated during the first century and increasingly so. Gradually linen took the place of wool in clothing. The best Italian grades of linen came from the Po Valley, and the second best from Retovium south of the Po. The flax of Campania was especially used for nets for fishing and fowling. Hemp was also grown.

Animal Husbandry

The farmers of Italy raised more sheep and goats than any other animals. They valued their milk and cheese as well as their wool. Sheep ranching took place especially in the south of Italy on the slopes of the Apennines. Apulia and Tarentum were celebrated for their wool. But Etruria and the

Alpine region also produced large numbers of sheep. Italians also raised extensive herds of pigs, primarily in forests that supplied acorns or nuts—forests of oak and hazel especially. Apicius had thirty-two recipes for the preparation of pork, revealing widespread interest in the consumption of pork

It appears that every farm had a poultry yard. Romans consumed chickens, geese, ducks, pigeons, pheasants, peacocks, and guinea hens in great quantity. Every farm probably also kept bees to produce honey for sweetening and the preservation of fruits and vegetables. Beehives were especially numerous in southern Italy where much thyme grew wild and the pastureland had an array of wild flowers.

The pastures of northern Apulia were famous for their fine quality horses, widely sought after for cavalry units of the army, rapid travel, and circus racers. Romans did not use horses as draught animals, however. They bred oxen for that purpose and for plowing.

Italians had always raised substantial numbers of cattle. In fact, the name Italy (Italia) derives from the ancient Italic word *Vitelia*, meaning "calf-land." Farmers valued cows for their milk, which they generally turned into cheese, rather than for butter or as a beverage. Of course they used the hides for a wide variety of civilian and military purposes.

(For more on this topic, go to p. 586.)

Dress

Men's Clothing

When Paul came to Rome, he could not tell exactly who was a Roman citizen. A male citizen was supposed to wear a toga, but most of the men he saw were carrying loads or doing work that made wearing a toga impossible. Most of them could have been slaves for all he knew. Some did wear white togas. Occasionally he saw a toga with a wide purple stripe running from the shoulder to the hem (belonging to a senator) or a narrow purple stripe (on an equestrian, or member of the wealthy capitalist class). When he saw a group of men in black togas, he knew they had just been to a funeral. Young lads also had togas with purple stripes, but when they reached adulthood they would revert to white. If Paul could have seen Nero, his toga would have been entirely purple.

The toga was a large oval of wool cloth about eighteen feet wide and seven feet deep, draped in such a complicated manner that it usually required a slave to help put it in place properly. Indoors men usually discarded the toga unless they were attending an official function. Without a toga a man appeared in a tunic, a shirt-like garment, sleeveless or usually with short sleeves, reaching to the knees when belted at the waist. In cold weather extra tunics might be worn; Romans like moderns engaged in layering. Under the tunic a man would have a kind of pair of shorts. Soldiers, especially cavalrymen, sometimes wore short leather trousers extending to the knees.

Proper dress of the Roman upper class is well illustrated by these scenes from the Altar of Peace of Augustus Caesar in Rome, dating to the time of Christ.

In cold weather, capes or cloaks of wool or leather (some with hoods) might cover or replace a toga. A fold of the toga could be pulled over the head, but normally Romans went with their heads uncovered. Travelers and farmers, exposed to a hot Italian sun or cold wind or snow for long periods of time, wore a *petasus*, a wide-brimmed hat. Various kinds of leather shoes and boots protected the feet: simple sandals or slippers in the house or for most street wear, or heavy hobnailed boots for farmers or soldiers. They fastened boots to the feet by leather bands that started at the instep and were wound around the leg.

As Paul walked along, he would have noticed that many men had blond hair. A few of them could have been slaves from Germany, but Italian Roman citizens should have had dark hair. Puzzled, on inquiry he might have found out that a considerable number of men dyed their hair because blond hair was fashionable. He would have seen some brown tints too. As we have seen previously, men were clean-shaven (with razors of bronze or iron) and wore short hair in the first century, especially in Italy, but commonly elsewhere. So Paul would not have been

surprised by what he saw. There were many barbershops.

The practice of wearing beards (well trimmed) came back in the second century. Then the emperor Hadrian (117–138), who had a facial blemish, grew a beard to hide it. So men in Italy and all over the empire began to follow the lead of the emperor.

Women's Clothing

Though in earlier periods the dress of women differed according to whether one was a matron, an unmarried woman, or slave, in New Testament times those distinctions had largely disappeared. Now a woman's basic garment was a tunic, sleeveless or short-sleeved. Over this she wore a *stola*, a long, belted dress with half-sleeves, gathered up by a girdle. It usually had a colored border around the neck. Her outer garment, the *palla*, was a four-cornered shawl draped over the left shoulder and either under or over the right. Out-of-doors she regularly covered her head with a corner of the *palla*. For underclothes she often wore a breastband and bikini-type panties. Female sandals and shoes tended to be a little lighter weight and more elegant than those for men.

Hairstyles changed considerably over time. During the New Testament period a mass of curls or plaits was piled high on the head. Usually slaves dressed the hair at home. The mirrors they used were of highly polished bronze or silver and sometimes of silvered glass. The King James translation of 1 Corinthians 13:12, "we see through a glass darkly," is properly rendered in the NKJV as "see in a mirror, dimly," or indistinctly. One cannot get a very clear image on highly polished metal. Women, like men, dyed their hair and sometimes wore wigs: of blond hair from Germans or black hair imported from India.

Women used perfumes and facial cosmetics and wore a considerable amount of jewelry, including brooches to fasten clothes, finger rings, necklaces, earrings, bracelets, armlets, anklets, and hairpins. Men also wore finger rings.

Fabrics and Dyes

The Romans used sheep's wool as the chief material for clothing, but linen (now produced in Italy) was frequently used in the men's garments that took the place of the toga in informal wear. Women did wear some silk, imported as cloth from China, or cotton, imported as cloth from India. In addition, they had a kind of "wild silk," produced in the Greek islands. In this process cocoons were not unwound but scraped and the resulting short fibers spun into thread.

While the toga was always white or black, other garments for common wear—by both men and women—were brown, russet, and several brighter colors. Weavers usually dyed the thread before they wove it, using several vegetable dyes. The permanent dyes came from shellfish. These colors ranged from scarlet to shades of red and purple to violet and black. A variation in fabric might be achieved by weaving with the warp of one color and the woof of another. More complicated patterns were tried, especially for hangings. Garments might also be embroidered in colors or decorations of one color sewed to cloth of another.

(For more on this topic, go to p. 587.)

Family Life

Marriage

Much that is written about Roman marriage applies to an earlier period in the history of the Republic. Conditions were freer in New Testament times. The older generation arranged marriages, and the *paterfamilias* or the head of the families of the bride and groom had to give their consent. Often a young upper-class girl had little to say in the matter because the families had arranged the marriage for the purpose of forging an alliance. Among middle and lower-class families, where social and political concerns meant less, presumably the young people had more to say about the choice of a mate. The minimum legal age of marriage was twelve for females and fourteen for males, but usually the actual ages of the bride and groom were much higher.

The marriage pact customarily involved a dowry provided by the bride's father. This would be returned to the widow in the event of the husband's death. And if a divorce occurred, part of the dowry might be retained for the maintenance of children. Various prenuptial agreements were arranged. Families usually celebrated the marriage accord with an engagement party at which they exchanged agreements and gifts.

A couple needed neither a dowry nor a marriage ceremony for a valid and legal marriage. If two Roman citizens who had the consent of the *paterfamilia* lived together with the intent of being married, that was viewed as a valid marriage and children born were accepted as Roman citizens. But this generalization was tempered by the economic and social status of the families involved—families who had the means made more of a wedding.

Families avoided the first half of June for marriages because they considered those days a period of ill omen; they favored the last half of June. Commonly the bride wore a flame-colored mantle over her tunic, and her hair was covered with a flame-colored veil. The groom dressed in his regular white tunic and toga.

The ceremonies began at the house of the bride, where, among other things, the couple gave their formal consent. Joining their right hands and repeating the formula, "Where you are, I shall be," they went on to participate in prayers, sacrifices, and a banquet. After that, wedding guests made a torchlight parade (even in the daytime) through the streets to the house of the groom, singing wedding songs as they went. The groom hurried on alone, and when his bride arrived he carried her over the threshold and presented her with fire and water as symbols of her new position. Often the guests returned the next day for another banquet, over which the bride presided.

Augustus decreed that soldiers must not marry during their term of service. And subsequently soldiers and sailors were forbidden to contract legal marriages during their terms of service. But many had common-law wives and children on retirement. The marriage prohibition on soldiers was lifted by Septimius Severus in 197. From the time of Claudius (41–54), auxiliaries serving twenty-five years were granted citizenship on mustering out, with the recognition of existing or future marriages, so their children gained citizenship.

Children

The Romans knew some methods of contraception and practiced abortion for undesired pregnancies. The birth of a child took place at home with the help of a midwife and with several female relatives present. The father determined whether the child was to be reared. After nine days a ceremony was held during which a child was given a name. Wet nurses were commonly employed in all social classes.

Newborn children could be killed, sold, or exposed. Deformed children were commonly killed (drowned) or exposed. What percentage of children were sold or exposed and so adopted by childless couples or brought up as slaves is not known. Some of the urban poor were simply incapable of feeding another mouth or finding a place to put another child in their cramped quarters. In the event of a divorce, children remained by law in the household of the father. At least part of the mother's dowry could be retained for their support.

Divorce

Divorce was quite easy during the New Testament period. No grounds need be given. Divorce could be by mutual consent or either party might divorce the other. It required no legal formalities, but the division of joint property and disposition of the dowry might require court action. It is estimated that one in six upper-class marriages ended in divorce during the first ten years. On divorce, a woman usually had the right to get her dowry back. Remarriage was fairly frequent and was easier for a man than a woman.

Childhood

Romans educated upper-class boys and groomed them to take their eventual place among the ranks of their social peers in the public life of the community. Parents met their son's material needs so they did not know economic hardship. The same held true for girls, though their roles as adults were to marry men of appropriate standing and bear children.

Sons of other classes of society tended to pursue their fathers' occupations. Though fathers might train their sons, frequently they apprenticed them to another in the same trade. Such apprenticeships generally began at age twelve or thirteen and lasted for terms of various lengths—from about six months to six years. The range of occupation in which boys were apprenticed was fairly extensive but especially involved weaving and related jobs. Smithing and stone masonry were also frequently pursued. Bakers, accountants, ornamental gardeners, and entertainers, less so. The life of the apprentice and of the craftsman later on was hard.

Child labor, whether as an apprentice in town, or on the farm, was extensive and expected among the lower classes. Families had to gain supplemental income through their children as quickly as possible. They put young children to work tending animals, supervising poultry, trimming the vineyard, weeding gardens, gathering fruit, and more. If the child was a slave, the owner wanted income from his "property" as quickly as possible. All classes considered childhood preparatory for adulthood, to be traversed as rapidly as possible.

Education

The Pedagogue

"Wherefore the law was our schoolmaster to bring us unto Christ," says the KJV rendering of Galatians 3:24. The NKJV calls the law a "tutor" in this reference, and the NJB translates, "the Law was serving as a slave to look after us, to lead us to Christ, so that we could be justified by faith." These and other translations are trying to put into English a Greco-Roman educational practice.

The Greek word used in Galatians 3:24 is *pedagogue,* and he was a family slave whose duty it was to take a boy to school (to the schoolmaster) and bring him home again each day. He carried the child's belongings or a lantern to light his path and protected him against danger in the streets. Positively he was to train the child in good manners and help to mold his character and morals. In short, he was entrusted with the moral education of the child as distinct from the technical instruction imparted by his various teachers.[15] Of course the Mosaic Law as a pedagogue did lead people to Christ; it did prepare them in a variety of ways for the superior ministry of Christ.

The School System

Then what about the school to which the pedagogue brought his master—and was there a more advanced training in later years? These were elementary schools, public (open to all) but private (in that they charged tuition). There children from seven to eleven (both boys and girls) studied reading, writing, and arithmetic. Equipment was simple: benches for the students, a chair for the master, and wax tablets for writing exercises. Tablets were often a triptych (three boards covered with wax and hinged) so there would be five sides to write on. They wrote with a stylus, sharp on one end for writing and flattened on the other to smooth the wax and prepare for a new lesson. Teachers were often slaves or freedmen, who were poorly paid and the social inferiors of their pupils. The school year began in March and extended through the year, but evidently there was a summer vacation of some sort.

Secondary schools for boys twelve to fifteen came into being by the middle of the second century B.C. The aim of these schools was oral and written expression in Latin and Greek and especially training in rhetoric. Girls rarely attended these schools because they had to be trained in household matters to prepare them for an early marriage. Physical education was less important than in Greece, but dancing was sometimes taught.

A small percentage of Roman youth went beyond secondary or grammar schools to rhetorical schools. During the Republic these schools prepared a lad for the kind of debate that took place in public office. As political debate declined under the empire, when political decisions were made by the emperor, these schools turned to preparing boys for careers in law. As a rule, formal education ended with the seventeenth year, after which the young man assumed the white toga of manhood.

Slavery and Roman Society

"That you [Philemon] might receive him [Onesimus] forever, no longer as a slave but more than a slave—a beloved brother, especially to me but how much more to you, both in the flesh and in the Lord." (Philemon 15, 16 NKJV)

As Paul wrote Philemon, a Christian leader in Colosse, from prison in Rome, he interceded for Philemon's runaway slave Onesimus, who had now become a Christian. In trying to bring together these two brothers in the faith, he effectively nullified the institution of slavery. In another book written from his Roman prison, Ephesians, he urged Christian slaves to be obedient to their masters and Christian masters to be kind to their slaves (Ephesians 6:5–9). In 1 Timothy 6:1 he also pled with slaves to honor their masters and be good witnesses to them. Thus the apostle Paul dealt with the universal institution of slavery—but he left the question of abolition to a later generation.

It should be pointed out that slavery pervaded every corner of the Roman Empire and in every household that could afford slaves and had room for them. It was not a regional or class or ethnic institution as in early America. Moreover, there was not a considerable Christian sentiment against the institution as in some colonies (later states) of America. Therefore any battle against slavery would have been titanic indeed. It was a war that fledgling Christianity was not prepared to take on.

Extent of Slavery and the Source of Slaves

During the New Testament period the Roman Empire needed over 500,000 new slaves annually. This compares with an annual average of 28,000 Africans brought to America during the centuries of New World slavery.[16]

Where did these slaves come from? In earlier years large numbers became available as captives of war. But during the first century warfare was not as extensive as during the previous two hundred years. Claudius did conquer Britain, however; in Nero's reign large numbers of Armenian captives were sold into slavery; and Vespasian sold over 100,000 Jews into slavery during the First Jewish Revolt. Second, large numbers of slaves were born to the existing slave population.

Third, trade with peoples beyond the frontiers of empire brought many to the slave markets of Rome. Especially the Black Sea and Caucasus regions, as well as what is now Somalia, sent captives from their border wars. And they sold weaker members of their own communities, including individuals accused of crime. Fourth, exposed or unwanted infants were often brought up as slaves. Indigent parents sometimes sold their children into slavery. Last, kidnapping and piracy netted many slaves, with children and sometimes even adults in remote areas carried off. Pirates on the high seas made limited raids even during the height of Roman naval power. Pliny (contemporary with the apostle Paul) tells of two men who vanished without a trace while traveling in Italy, one not far from Rome.[17]

Large numbers of slaves belonged to the households of wealthy town dwellers, often for show more than for needed services. Rural slaves on the large farms of southern Italy not only worked the land but also watched the flocks and herds. These had to be armed to protect themselves and their charges against robbers or wild animals. They often took advantage of the situation to become robbers and highwaymen themselves.

Condition of Slaves

The lot of slaves in the empire was not as bad as often has been the case in slave-holding societies. Slaves had no identifying mark and were the same color as freemen. Though they could not wear the toga, any citizen engaged in a variety of tasks didn't either. So slaves couldn't be differentiated from freemen on the streets. Further, though the law did not recognize marriage between slaves, such unions were permitted or even encouraged. And public opinion did not tolerate the breaking up of slave families. Although slaves and all their possessions presumably belonged to their masters, owners generally allowed slaves to keep any tips or other funds they could accumulate. Sometimes they could even buy their freedom. Finally, slaves were generally regarded as human beings, who might even become citizens.

Economic Results of Slavery

The existence of slaves tended to reduce the wages free laborers could expect, since wages were determined by the cost of buying and maintaining slaves. Slavery on the large farms tended to drive the small free farmer out of agriculture. Then, when such dispossessed farmers moved to town, they could not find employment because of the competition of slave labor. Moreover, it is often argued that both the ancient Greeks and Romans were industrially backward because of the cheapness of slave labor, with no incentive to find ways of improving labor efficiency. Finally, the fact that slaves performed most labor tended to cause upper classes to look on all labor as servile and beneath the dignity of a free person.

Moral Results of Slavery

The fact that upper-class people had at their command individuals over which they had absolute control and could order them around as they wished had terrible effects on them. It tended to make the upper classes immune to any consideration of the rights of lower-class citizens or of human rights in general. Slavery also had terrible effects on the slaves themselves. Torn from the inhibitions of their settled societies (family bonds, laws, public opinion, etc.), and made to live under conditions where they were not supposed to have any moral judgments of their own, they tended to lose all sense of right and wrong. The only control was force or fear of force. Worse, hundreds of these slaves were freed every year. What had made them good slaves made them terrible citizens.

Freeing of Slaves

Slaves could be freed fairly easily in Rome. Loyal service sometimes brought the reward of freedom. Likewise it might come through the provisions of the last will of their masters. Again, slaves occasionally bought their freedom. In any case, there were plenty of freedmen around. In fact, in Rome itself freedmen and their descendants outnumbered citizens of Roman and Italian stock four to one early in the first century.[19] So it became increasingly difficult for Rome to manage its affairs with the dilution of Roman stock by people unaccustomed to self-government or feelings of loyalty to Rome.

Public Entertainments— Recreation

Organized athletic contests, so popular in Greece, never caught on in Rome. But the Romans had plenty of public festivals. Originally these were religious in origin but they became thoroughly secular. By the beginning of the New Testament period they celebrated seven annual festivals, lasting a total of sixty-five days. But these were added to in number and length. Admission to the public games was free. Some seats were reserved for senators or other officials. Women sat with men at the circus but had special seats in the theater and amphitheater.

Horse racing headed the list as the most popular entertainment in the Roman world. Horse and chariot racing took place especially in the Circus Maximus between the Aventine and Palatine Hills. Some 200,000 could watch the competition of eight or twelve chariots as they raced around the spina or divider with a turning post on each end. The race was of seven laps, for a total distance of about three miles. Speed on the straightaways, combined with the skill of horses and drivers in keeping close to the pole and yet avoiding mishaps on the thirteen 180-degree turns, brought victory. Frequent accidents furnished part of the entertainment.

Chariot racing operated as a highly organized profit-driven business. Four corporations furnished horses, chariots, and drivers and were known for their racing colors as the Red, the Green, the White, and the Blue. Spectators bet large sums on the horses, and feelings often ran high between supporters of the different corporations, sometimes leading to violence among their supporters. Successful charioteers became rich and famous.

Jews in Rome

When Jews first came to Rome is not known, but a significant number arrived as slaves after Pompey's conquest of Judea in 63 B.C. In fact, when Philo of Alexandria wrote during Caligula's reign (A.D. 37–41), he stated that the majority of Jews in the capital then were freedmen or descendants of them. By Augustus' time as many as 30,000 Jews may have lived in Rome, primarily in the Trastevere section on the right bank of the Tiber. And there, on the Via Portuensis, may be seen the earliest Jewish catacomb (of a total of six in the city), with use dating to the first century B.C.

Julius Caesar granted the Jews of Rome the right to meet, to hold common meals, and collect monetary contributions and send them to Jerusalem. Augustus preserved those rights and, in recognition of Jewish observance of the Sabbath, even permitted those eligible to collect their grain dole (ancient equivalent of food stamps) the following day. Nero's persecution of Christians following the great fire of Rome in A.D. 64 did not extend to Jews; the distinction between the two groups evidently was clear by that time.

The Jews of Rome do not seem to have demonstrated against the Romans during the Jewish revolt resulting in the destruction of Jerusalem, and they seem to have been permitted to carry on their lives and their religion without disturbance then and afterward. They did not get involved in the Jewish revolt of 116–117 either, and therefore did not suffer persecution. Many of the approximately 100,000 Jews taken prisoner after the fall of Jerusalem in A.D. 70 found their way to the slave markets of Rome. We do not know the extent that Jews of Rome may have been affected by the conflict in Judea.[18]

Three great stone theaters existed in Rome during the first century. These were semicircular like Greek theaters, but differed from Greek theaters in that the audience sat in the orchestra as well as on the raised seats. The action took place on a high stage. Dramas, mimes, and dances were performed there. Mimes or pantomimes consisted of a dramatic solo dance accompanied by the songs of a chorus. The Pyrrhic dance was presented by a troop of dancers.

The games presented in the Circus Maximus later moved to the Colosseum when that was built in A.D. 80. Gladiatorial combats and wild beast hunts provided the main attractions. Gladiators were criminals, prisoners of war, slaves, or free persons who turned to this trade as a last resort. They were trained in gladiatorial schools to fight in various styles with various kinds of equipment. One style of gladiator wore some body armor, carried a large shield, and fought with a short sword. Another had a smaller shield, more armor, and a curved saber. A third fought without armor and was equipped only with a net in which to entangle his opponent, and a trident with which to attack him. Other variations occurred. Women sometimes entered the arena.

Sometimes pairs of gladiators fought, sometimes troops battled each other, or criminals or slaves fought wild beasts of all kinds. Naval battles between fleets of warships took place on artificial lakes where gladiators and slaves slugged it out. Vanquished gladiators might be spared or killed by their conquerors, the decision usually resting with the will of the crowd. Romans became very bloodthirsty and cruel, and the bloodletting went on for centuries until Christian influence put an end to it near the close of the fourth century.

Baths

The baths also provided recreation. Initially built for cleanliness only, their number in Rome had increased to 170 by the beginning of the empire period. A visit to the bath had become a part of the daily routine of respectable Romans—in fact, of nearly all Romans. Baths usually included a dressing room, a cold room with a small pool, the warm room (a waiting room between hot and cold rooms), and the hot room (sometimes a sauna) with a small pool. Usually there were separate sets of rooms for men and women; otherwise certain hours were set aside for women. In addition to these basic arrangements there might be open courts for exercise, an open-air swimming pool, lounges, lecture rooms, libraries, and more. In fact, they became a cross between a fitness club and a community center.

The most ostentatious of the baths were built by emperors who ruled after the New Testament period. The modern tourist to Rome might see an opera or some other entertainment in the ruins of the Baths of Caracalla, built at the beginning of the third century.

In New Testament times baths were smaller but adequate. For example, at Pompeii there were three public baths: the Stabian, dating back to the second century B.C.; the Forum Baths, to about 80 B.C.; and the Central Baths, still under construction when Vesuvius erupted in A.D. 79. Houses of the wealthy in the city and the suburbs had their own baths.

The modern tourist can see baths all over the eastern part of the empire—for example, next to the main street in Ephesus, at Tyre, or at the palaces of Herod the Great at New Testament Jericho or the Herodion (four miles southeast of Bethlehem). Always the hot bath or sauna is easily identified. The walls are hollow and the floor is supported on stacks of brick, so hot air can pass freely around the entire structure and create a sauna.

Medicine

The tourist who visits the Asclepion (hospital) at Pergamum (Pergamos, one of the seven cities of the Revelation, Revelation 2:12–17) or Corinth will probably come away with the idea that the medical profession did not have much to offer the New Testament world. The guide will talk about the healing powers sought by prayer to the gods, the wearing of amulets, the use of magical incantations, the taking of various herbs and drugs, and rest and relaxation. But

Pergamum was the center where the great medic Galen was to practice during the second century.

You get an entirely different view of medical practice in the Roman world from studying the first-century military hospital at Xanten on the left bank of the Rhine, seven miles west of Wesel in Germany. Built of stone, it had an entrance wing with a reception ward, at one end of which was a suite of baths with attached latrine and at the other end a kitchen. The reception ward opened into the operating area. This wing along with three other wings surrounded an open courtyard. There were numerous small wards, a doctor's surgery, a dispensary, isolation wards, and two lavatories.[20]

Medical Performance

Doctors performed surgery of various sorts with surgical instruments found widely throughout the Roman Empire. Surgeons' equipment included scalpels, forceps, hooks, and probes. Precision tools were sometimes made of iron, but more commonly of bronze and brass. Roman blacksmiths could produce steeled tools.

Doctors apparently did quite well in treating fractures. They also achieved considerable success in dentistry—in extracting teeth, in capping teeth, and doing bridgework. Eye operations, especially for the removal of cataracts, were carried out

The great Roman baths described in art history and architecture books date to the second century and following. A good example are the Baths of Trajan, built just after A.D. 100.

quite routinely. They treated urinary disorders and their catheters differed little from modern catheters.[21] They patched mutilations of ears, lips, nose, and more in "the earliest instances of plastic surgery."[22] They also practiced brain surgery. The treating and removal of hemorrhoids, a common ailment, was quite routine.

We need to be careful, however, not to become too enthusiastic. Doctors had a very imperfect knowledge of anatomy and were hindered by a lack of anesthetics. Primarily extracts obtained from the opium poppy and henbane were used as sedatives and painkillers. Doctors had to work fast and to have a steady hand. Good antiseptics were also not available; wine, vinegar, pitch, and turpentine were used. Blood poisoning often occurred with surgery and necessitated amputation of limbs.

Army doctors, especially, developed skill in treating wounds, even abdominal wounds, with abdominal surgery, which civilian doctors avoided whenever possible.

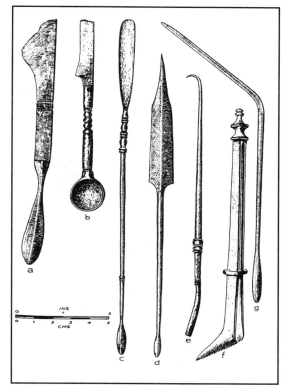

Bronze or iron surgical instruments available in Roman hospitals or doctors' offices: (a) scalpel; (b) scalpel with spoon; (c) spatula with probe; (d) flat-bladed spatula; (e) hook; (f) probably artery forceps; (g) tongue depressor.

Beginning with Augustus, medical provision was made for every branch of the armed forces, and every legion had a hospital. We have information about numerous army hospitals. Because army doctors traveled and worked on the frontiers, they came in contact with drugs and practices of other peoples. Thus they became the most important means for the improvement of Roman medicine and "the single most powerful agency in the spread of Greco-Roman medicine."[23]

Of course surgery or radical treatment was attempted only when exercise, diet, and other prescription did not restore health. The Roman army expended considerable effort to keep the troops from getting sick. For example, in army camps they paid considerable attention to the siting of forts: on well-drained ground, with a safe water supply, and good sewage disposal. They preferred stone-built flushing latrines.

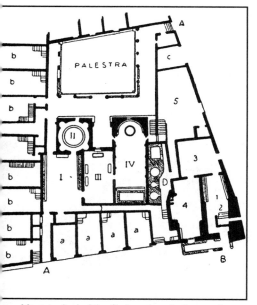

More typical of the first century baths are the Forum Baths of Pompeii. Key to the diagram above: *A* and *A 1* are entrances to the men's baths; *I* the men's dressing room; *II* the cold bath; *III* the warm bath; *IV* the steam bath. *B* is the entrance to the women's bath; *1* the dressing room, *2* the cold bath, *3* the warm bath, and *4* the steam bath. *a-a-a*, *b-b-b* identify small shops selling refreshments.

Though several military hospitals are known, civilians were apparently normally treated at home or at the home of the doctor or rooms he had rented. Without doubt the masses had little opportunity to benefit from what medical expertise the doctors did possess. We need to keep in mind that the well-appointed doctor's office in Pompeii was located in an affluent community. The tenement dwellers of Rome must have had little access to doctors. There was little medical care available in rural areas. Midwives often provided help in dealing with women's diseases and disorders, and some of them must have become quite proficient.

Funeral Customs and Burials

Funerals

Professional undertakers normally organized funerals, providing mourning women, musicians, and sometimes dancers and mimers. For an upper-class man a funeral might be quite elaborate. It included lying in state in the atrium of his house clad in the insignia of highest office held in life, followed by a procession through some of the main streets of the city, stopping in the Forum for a funeral oration. After that the procession moved outside the city to a place of burial or cremation. In the case of cremation, a near relative lit the funeral pyre. The funeral procession was led by musicians and singers of dirges. Then came actors wearing masks and imitating any of the family ancestors who had won high public office. Next the body was carried on a litter by near relatives. Friends, relatives, and freedmen followed.

Lower-class people had no waiting period for funerals. Corpses were taken from the city by a short route with a less elaborate procession of mourners. If the poor belonged to burial or funeral clubs, the club paid funeral expenses.

In the case of all classes of people, rites at the grave or cremation site were similar. These might include a meal for the mourners and offerings of food and drink to the deceased. A period of nine days of mourning was followed by another feast for the

mourners. Subsequently, during the Festival of Parentalia (February 13–21) people commemorated the dead—a kind of Memorial Day. During these days the temples were closed and marriages forbidden.

Burial

In the New Testament period generally the poorest were buried and all others cremated. There were a few among the wealthy who preferred burial, however. Though the bodies of paupers were commonly thrown into pits in the city dump, most of the poor joined burial societies that secured for their members a decent funeral for a small monthly payment. The associations built large tombs called *columbaria* (dovecotes), from the niches that lined the walls, and provided space for large numbers of cinerary urns. Wealthy men also built columbaria for the ashes of their slaves, freedmen, and clients. Columbaria for Roman soldiers may be seen on Masada.

Romans often built family tombs in the form of an altar or small temple and large enough to hold the ashes of several generations. They placed these cemeteries on streets leading from the city, where they may be seen surrounded by gardens and shrines for the convenience of mourners—and where they may be constructed to impress others with the family's wealth and social position. For the biblically-oriented, ruins of some of these tombs may be seen

Reconstruction of Augustus' tomb in northern Rome

along the Appian Way outside of Rome or outside the gate of Philippi near the Gangites River. Of course they appear in numerous other places throughout the Roman Empire.

Ashes from cremations were buried in containers of cloth, pottery, glass, or metal, gold caskets, and marble chests. In inhumations the body might be buried in a sack or shroud. Wooden coffins were common, but undertakers sometimes used lead and stone coffins. Graves might also be lined with stone or wood. Some regions practiced embalming, and bodies might be encased in gypsum plaster inside a coffin. Jews and Christians objected to cremation. Many graves were marked with tombstones (whether inhumations or cremations) that might bear sculpted representations of the dead and a dedicatory inscription. Obviously the wooden markers have not survived.

Views on the afterlife varied widely. The increased numbers initiated into the mystery religions and Neoplatonism in the first century brought a general increase in the hope of an afterlife. In addition, many believed that the spirits of the dead lived on in their tombs and could influence the fortunes of the living. So gifts were brought to the tombs and libations poured for the dead. And many burials were furnished with grave goods for use of the dead in the afterlife. These might include vessels full of food and drink and possibly boots or shoes and lamps for the dead person's journey through the underworld.

(For more on this topic, go to p. 587.)

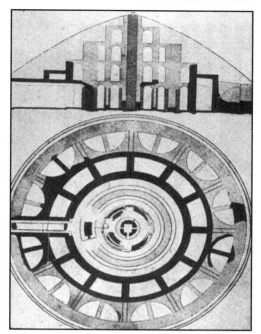

Tomb of Augustus, interior plan and elevation

The Romans produced iron on the island of Elba and partially processed it there. Then they took it to Puteoli, where smiths made garden tools (knives, sickles), butcher knives, and an array of instruments for various occupations.

Arretium (Arezzo) in Tuscany reigned as the great pottery manufacturing center, with Puteoli its chief rival. Greek workmen

Work, Travel, and Commerce

Work

What about the economy of Italy and the sort of work her people did during the first Christian century? To begin with, we are thinking about a free population of some ten million, plus about four million slaves.[24] Approximately one million lived in the capital. To a large degree articles were made and sold in small shops. Factories existed in only a few places.

In ancient times tombs lined major highways outside of town. Here are tombs still visible on the Appian Way.

produced much of the pottery, but owners of the shops were usually Roman citizens. They employed substantial numbers of slaves in this industry, with the largest number in a single shop at fifty-eight.[25] At first foreign markets provided extensive opportunities, but by the end of the first century many producers had migrated to Gaul and elsewhere. Thus the industry lost most of its worldwide export business.

Glass blowing apparently originated in Sidon and spread rapidly to Egypt and Italy. Oriental artisans soon set up their main factories in Italy, partly on their own initiative and partly on the urging of the emperors. Campania became an important center of production.

Campania also became the most important center for the processing of copper and the manufacture of bronze. At least in Capua a real factory system developed, apparently large enough to employ thousands of workmen.[26] The large number of statues, busts, and items of metal furniture (tables, lampstands, braziers, and more) found at Pompeii and Herculaneum probably originated in the factories of Capua. Petty artisans in small shops presumably made the bowls, ladles, pots and pans, and other kitchen utensils, as well as numerous farm implements. Another center of copper production was Milan, where it is believed the labor force consisted of free labor.

In cloth manufacture, homespun continued to flourish, with labor on the farms producing the fabrics worn in the rural areas. But a substantial percentage of woolen cloth was produced in "factories" run by slave labor, and about half the towns (especially in northern Italy) had them. Though these establishments made some fabrics of the better sort, they also produced cheap felt blankets for the poor. Silks, linen, and cotton fabrics worn by the wealthy were largely imported from the east.

Oil processing might take place on small farms. Villas that produced oil in quantity had the necessary equipment for processing it. But during the first century there were contractors who bought olives on the trees, harvested them, and pressed and marketed the oil of several farms.

Brickmaking received a great shot in the arm from the fire of Rome (A.D. 64). Previously concrete buildings had been faced with travertine (limestone), but it crumbled badly with intense heat. So brick came into favor. Actually brick facing began before the fire—in the days of Claudius. Now they brought in thousands of slaves for this work and a few large brickyards cashed in on the profits. Because bricks were too heavy and cumbersome to be transported very far, factories had to be established near where they would be used. On the average, a worker could produce two hundred bricks per day.[27]

Many jewelry shops had the raw materials and made pieces to order, though some remade pieces owned by their clients. Signet rings for use in signing documents were in special demand. Factories seem to have monopolized the production of silverplate and utensils, but we cannot be sure.

It is thought that the fine furniture of the period was probably produced in factories, especially in Capua or elsewhere around the Bay of Naples. Individual small shops would not have had the imported woods, inlay, iron, and copper pieces, and the expertise to produce the elegant tables, couches, and chairs manufactured during the period. Simpler, cheaper pieces could

The grain measurers' mosaic. (From the seat of the grain measurers, in the Forum of the Corporations of Ostia)

have been made in the smaller shops.

Because senators restricted themselves to agriculture or civil or military office, the lucrative business in shipping, industry, and banking rested almost entirely in the hands of foreigners and freedmen.

Commerce/Transport

Rome with its million inhabitants acted like a giant sponge, absorbing wealth from the empire and exporting little in return. Most of its food, clothing, furniture, and building material was brought in from elsewhere in Italy and from abroad. In respect to grain alone, Egypt sent five million bushels annually, North Africa twice as much, and Sicily two million. So oxen would draw six thousand barges, each carrying 2,500 bushels, up the river from Ostia (15 miles away) annually, or twenty-five barges each working day.[28] This provided for the grain dole to some 200,000 of the city's poor and kept prices low for the rest of the population. Free grain along with free entertainment at the games ("bread and circuses") helped to pacify the people of Rome and to retain their goodwill toward the emperor.

Moreover, Rome consumed some twenty-five million gallons of wine annually, nearly all of which came from Italian vineyards, and 1.5 million gallons of olive oil for cooking, table use, and illumination.[29] Large quantities of cloth and tanned leather were also brought into the city, where it was made into clothing and shoes in small shops. Small bakeries were established all over the city. A factory in the city processed Egyptian papyrus for a writing material. About twenty great warehouses of first-century Rome are known; there must have been more.

Claudius' policies greatly increased the number of freedmen in commerce and the volume of commerce itself. Around the middle of the century Roman trade with India showed a sudden increase. Independent shipowners "tramped" from port to port with any cargo that seemed to promise good

All along the streets in cities like Rome, Pompeii, and Ostia merchants offered their wares. Here is a wine shop in Ostia where the owner had a counter by an opening on the street.

The Business Network that Supplied Rome

The organization responsible for supplying Rome with food was headquartered at the port of Ostia. Called the *annona*, it superintended the shipping and distribution of merchandise, maintained quantity and quality control, attended to payments, and made contacts with private and government commercial agencies.

To maintain this commercial life they organized numerous associations—of laborers, owners of private shops, merchants in grain, oil, wine, etc., business representatives of producing countries, workers employed in shipbuilding and repair, maintenance of warehouses and docks, and loading and unloading of ships.

In the Forum of the Corporations behind the theater, any tourist may see mosaic pavements of seventy offices of these commercial associations that made up a kind of chamber of commerce of the Roman world. Groups of workers applied to the Roman Senate for the right to federate and then organized and elected presidents, who held office for five years. As modern unions or chambers of commerce build and maintain headquarters, so did their counterparts in ancient Ostia.

There were also large markets, as the Market of Trajan here, and forums or agoras in the cities of Italy and the empire.

profits. Some of these traders grew rich enough to own several vessels, placing each in charge of a trusted agent. Or members of a family might enter into a partnership.

How long it took a commercial fleet to go to India we do not know, but for Mediterranean waters we have better information. The grain fleet was able to make it from Puteoli to Alexandria (about one thousand nautical miles) in nine days in order to take on a fresh load of Egyptian wheat. But the return voyage required one to two months because the prevailing winds forced the loaded ships to bear north toward Cyprus and then west along the coasts of Turkey and Greece. The run from Ostia to Gibraltar took seven days.

On land some men traveled from place to place selling a particular product and employing wagons and pack animals similar to the sailors who "tramped" from port to port. Pack asses were extensively bred. Merchants used them to transport oil, wine, grain, and other produce from various large farms to the sea. The ass could carry a load of 200–300 pounds.

Locally in Rome or some other city, bakers, the sausage man or vendors of food sold their wares on street corners or from house to house, or hawked their wares from the front doors of their shops.

Romans became addicted to imports from foreign markets—especially the east. Tapestries, clothing, furniture, jewelry, and more came from Asia, Syria, and Egypt. The large quantities of grain from Egypt actually came as tribute. Egypt was the personal province of the emperor and could be counted on to provide grain for Rome. Egypt also sent linen, glassware, ointments and perfumes, quantities of granite and marble for Roman buildings, and papyrus—which provided all of Rome's supply of paper.

From India, Italy got pepper, spikenard, bdellium, indigo, cotton cloth, pearls, ivory, silks; from Abyssinia, myrrh, frankincense, ginger, cinnamon, and ivory; from Arabia, myrrh, ginger, and cinnamon. Syria was a vital transit center for the west, sending to Italy carpets, textiles, and embroideries of Babylonia and Iran, and goods from India, China, and Arabia, as noted. Asia Minor sent the woolens of Laodicea, Cilician linen, and wood from Pontus.

Italy did not have much to send in exchange. Early in the century pottery exports were considerable. Campania sent quantities of glass overseas. The iron smithies of Puteoli and the famous copper-ware of Capua did well. Campanian wine and oil also sold extensively abroad, as did the perfumes and ointments of the region. But increasingly imperial salaries, tribute from the provinces, and profits from for-eign and Italian investments paid for what Italy imported.

Travel—Roman Roads

When Paul traveled from Puteoli to Rome (Acts 28:13–16), he did so on the Appian Way, a distance of 155 Roman miles or 142 English miles (a Roman mile was 1,614.6 yards). Travelers seem to have accomplished sixteen to twenty miles a day on an average Roman road. Travelers driving wagons or other vehicles moved at the rate of about twenty-five Roman miles a day. The imper-ial post could travel as fast as fifty miles a day. We have no way of knowing whether Paul and his companions walked or rode.

In the days of the Roman Empire all roads did lead to Rome. To help insure that fact, Augustus Caesar set up a golden milestone in the Forum in 20 B.C. and recorded on it dis-tances to principal towns of Italy and the empire. Then each mile along a highway was marked by a circular stone pillar that had inscribed on it the distance from the golden milestone in Rome—and usually the name of the emperor who reigned at the time that section of road was built.

The Romans were prodigious road-builders. They spent five centuries com-pleting a road system that extended to every corner of their empire and eventually covered a distance equal to ten times the circumference of the earth at the equator. This total included over fifty thousand miles of first-class highways and about two hundred thousand miles of lesser roads.

Preliminary Survey

Before the Romans built a road they con-ducted a survey. Though they have not left much information about how they ran the survey or what instruments they used, they were evidently very competent. They could calculate distances to inaccessible points, run levels with accuracy, measure angles, and lay out tunnels and dig them from both ends. Surveyors preferred straight lines, plotted from ridge to ridge, but they took into consideration the slope of the land and questions of defense. Across a plain they tried to take a straight course, constructing bridges and paved fords to cross rivers and viaducts to span marshes.

Where necessary, as in regions such as Cumae and Naples, they cut tunnels through mountains with a skill that aroused admiration for centuries. In moun-tainous districts they laid out a zigzag course. Because Romans tried to build straight roads, often over hills rather than around them, slopes frequently were steep; 10 percent grades were common.

Construction

After the survey was complete, con-struction could begin. When building an important road, Roman engineers dug a trench the full width of the road and four or five feet deep. The roadbed was then built up with successive layers of large and small stone and rammed gravel; sometimes there was a layer of concrete. Normally roads were surfaced with gravel, which might rest on a bed of mortar. In the neighborhood of cities, in places where traffic was heavy, or in the construction of a very important road, engineers paved the surface with large carefully fitted stone (without the use of mortar or metal), about a foot thick and a foot and a half across.

Naturally the type of construction varied with expected traffic, terrain, and available materials. Mountain roads might be only five to six feet wide (with wider places for passing) and surfaced with gravel, while the main roads could be fifteen to twenty feet wide and sometimes paved with stone. The Appian Way was about eighteen feet wide, wide enough for two wagons to pass abreast, and it was paved with basaltic lava.

Where roads crossed streams, the Romans usually built stone bridges, resting on a series of arches based on piers of

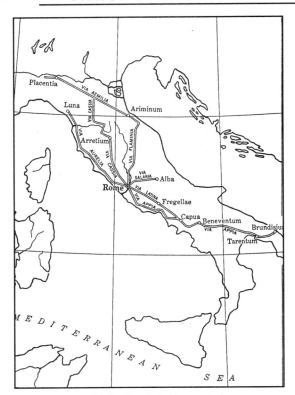

Major Roads in Roman Italy

Remains of the Golden Milestone in the Forum of Rome, on which was recorded distances to major cities of the Roman Empire, giving rise to the saying that "all roads lead to Rome."

masonry. Such construction was possible because the Romans had concrete almost equivalent in quality to that in use today. In order for lime mortar to set under water or to resist water action, it requires the addition of silica as in modern Portland cement. The Romans had large quantities of volcanic sand, *pozzolana,* which had a mixture of silica in proper proportions. This they discovered and used without a knowledge of the chemical properties of this cement. Some of the Roman bridges still exist. The best preserved is the Fabrician Bridge across the Tiber in Rome. It is about 190 feet long and consists of two main arches, each with a span of seventy-five feet.

Unfortunately we do not possess records that tell how long it took to build the Roman roads or the size of road gangs. The Appian Way, "Queen of Roads" and forerunner of so many other Roman roads on three continents, was begun in 312 B.C. as a military road for use in the Samnite Wars. The 132 miles to Capua must have been completed within about a decade. Though

originally paved with gravel, its surfacing with stone began in 295 B.C. and certainly was finished by 135 at the latest. Ultimately the Appian Way reached southward 360 miles from Rome to Brundisium on the Adriatic. The Appian Way had eight main stations between Capua and Rome, two of which are mentioned in the Acts narrative—Appii Forum and Tres Tabernae (Three Taverns).

Extension of the road system was gradual and involved the efforts of numerous Roman emperors. Augustus, Tiberius, Claudius, and Vespasian were among those who launched especially great road-building projects.

Some modern highways in the Mediterranean world are black-topped Roman roads. That is true of the Appian Way, here south of Rome.

Continuing Use

Some Roman roads served a continuing use throughout the Middle Ages and into modern times. The queen of them all, the Appian Way on which Paul traveled from Puteoli to Rome is, after blacktopping, still an important artery of Western Italy. The highway on which Paul traveled across Macedonia, the Egnatian Way, still serves as a main street in modern Thessalonica. Pieces of it may be seen in the agora of Philippi and elsewhere in the vicinity of Philippi. Sections of Roman highway may be seen in many other places of the Mediterranean world too, mute reminders of the glory of the empire when all roads led to Rome.

(For more on this topic, go to p. 587.)

Conclusion

The world in which Paul moved about was in many ways remarkably progressive and advanced. And Paul communicated effectively with Jews, Greeks, and Romans of that world at all levels. The gospel caught hold at the top level, with the Praetorian Guard and its power base providing legitimacy. Among political leaders, governors Publius in Malta and Sergius Paulus in Cyprus placed their faith in Christ.

At another level, the Philippian jailer and Dionysus, a member of the erudite Areopagus Council in Athens, responded to the apostle's evangelistic efforts. The merchant class also appears to have been penetrated with the gospel, spreading it as they traveled about. Whole households, like Lydia's at Philippi, turned to Christ. Presumably some of those Paul addressed in Romans 16 were business people whom he had met in the east and were now living in the capital.

The apostle reached numerous people in all walks of life—in the synagogues, in prisons, the agoras of Athens and Ephesus, at the Isthmian Games at Corinth, on board ship on the way to Rome, and more. With his letters to young churches he taught and strengthened groups of believers who needed his encouragement and instruction.

Though Paul died a martyr, the influence of his life, his ministry, and his writing rippled throughout Roman society. Ultimately the power of Jesus Christ, bringing new life to a people living without real hope, won out, despite repeated efforts of Roman emperors and entrenched religious, political, and economic interests to suppress it.

Milestones with various kinds of inscriptions appeared along all important highways. Here is one from the Via Maris in Palestine.

NOTES:

[1]Suetonius, "Life of Claudius," *The Twelve Caesars*, Chap. XXV, Section 4.

[2]Tacitus, *The Annals*, Chap. XV, Section 44.

[3]William M. Ramsay, *The Church in the Roman Empire Before A.D. 170* (5th, ed.; London: Hodder and Stoughton, 1897; Baker Book House reprint, 1979), 226–51.

[4]A. N. Sherwin-White, *Roman Law and Roman Society in the New Testament* (Grand Rapids: Baker Book House, 1992), 110.

[5]See Harry B. Evans, *Water Distribution in Ancient Rome* (Ann Arbor, MI: University of Michigan Press, 1994).

[6]Clement, *Epistle to the Corinthians*, chap. v; Eusebius, *Ecclesiastical History*, ii, 22; and the Muratori Canon.

[7]See Brian Rapske, *The Book of Acts and Paul in Roman Custody* (Grand Rapids: Eerdmans, 1994), 3, 20–22.

[8]Michael Grant, *The Army of the Caesars* (New York: M. Evans & Company, 1974), 155.

[9]M. Cary and H. H. Scullard, *A History of Rome*, 3rd ed. (New York: St. Martin's, 1975), 373.

[10]Albert A. Bell, *A Guide to the New Testament World* (Scottsdale, PA: Herald Press, 1993), 29.

[11]For an interesting and useful book on the house church, see Vincent Branick, *The House Church in the Writings of Paul* (Collegeville, Minn.: The Liturgical Press, 1989).

[12]Joseph Dommers Vehling, ed. and trans., *Apicius: Cookery and Dining in Imperial Rome* (New York: Dover Publications, 1977, 79.

[13]Ibid., 176.

[14]See K. D. White, *Roman Farming* (Ithaca, N.Y.: Cornell University Press, 1970), Chapter IV, V. This is a definitive study on Roman farming.

[15]A useful article on the subject is Norman H. Young, "The Figure of the Paidagogos in Art and Literature," BA, June, 1990, 80–88.

[16]Keith Bradley, *Slavery and Society at Rome* (Cambridge: Cambridge University Press, 1994), 32.

[17]Ibid., 38.

[18]John M. G. Barclay, *Jews in the Mediterranean Diaspora* (Edinburgh: T & T Clark, 1996), chapter 10.

[19]Herbert N. Couch and R. M. Geer, *Classical Civilization: Rome* (New York: Prentice-Hall, 1950), 183.

[20]Ralph Jackson, *Doctors and Diseases in the Roman Empire* (London: The British Museum, 1988), 134–35.

[21]Ibid., 125.

[22]Ibid., 124.

[23]Ibid., 137.

[24]Tenney Frank, *An Economic Survey of Ancient Rome* (New York: Octagon Books, 1975), V. 1.

[25]Ibid., 189.

[26]Ibid., 198.

[27]Ibid., 209.

[28]Ibid., 220.

[29]Ibid., 221.

BIBLIOGRAPHY:

Adkins, Lesley, and Roy A. Adkins. *Dictionary of Roman Religion.* New York: Facts on File, 1996.

Adkins, Lesley, and R. A. Adkins. *Handbook to Life in Ancient Rome.* New York: Facts on File, 1994.

Arnold, W. T. *Roman Provincial Administration,* rev. by E. S. Bouchier. Chicago: Ares, 3rd ed., 1974.

Auguet, Roland. *Cruelty and Civilization: The Roman Games.* London: George Allen & Unwin, 1972.

Austin, N. J. E., and N. B. Rankov. *Exploratio: Military and Political Intelligence in the Roman World.* New York: Routledge, 1995.

Barrett, Anthony A. *Caligula, The Corruption of Power.* New Haven: Yale University Press, 1989.

Barrow, R. H. *Slavery in the Roman Empire.* New York: Barnes & Noble, 1996.

Bell, Albert A. *A Guide to the New Testament World.* Scottsdale, Penn.: Herald Press, 1993.

Benko, Stephen. *Pagan Rome and the Early Christians.* Bloomington, Ind.: Indiana University Press, 1986.

Bowersock, G. W. *Martyrdom and Rome.* Cambridge: Cambridge University Press, 1995.

Bradley, Keith R. *Discovering the Roman Family.* New York: Oxford University Press, 1991.

Bradley, Keith R. *Slavery and Society at Rome.* Cambridge: Cambridge University Press, 1994.

Bradley, Keith R. *Slaves and Masters in the Roman Empire.* New York: Oxford University Press, 1987.

Branick, Vincent. *The House Church in the Writings of Paul.* Collegeville, Minn.: The Liturgical Press, 1989.

Bunson, Matthew. *Encyclopedia of the Roman Empire.* New York: Facts on File, 1994.

Campbell, Brian. *The Roman Army 31 B.C.–A D. 337.* New York: Routledge, 1994.

Carcopino, Jerome. *Daily Life in Ancient Rome.* New Haven: Yale University Press, 1940.

Cary. M. *The Geographic Background of Greek and Roman History.* Oxford: Clarendon Press, 1949.

Cary, M., and H. H. Scullard. *A History of Rome.* New York: St. Martin's, 1975.

Deiss, Joseph Jay. *Herculaneum, Italy's Buried Treasure.* New York: Thomas Y. Crowell, 1966.

Dersin, Denise, ed. *When Rome Ruled the World.* New York: Time-Life, 1997.

Dixon, Suzanne. *The Roman Family.* Baltimore: Johns Hopkins University Press, 1992.

Duncan-Jones, Richard. *The Economy of the Roman Empire.* Cambridge: Cambridge University Press, 2nd ed., 1982.

Earl, Donald. *The Age of Augustus.* New York: Exeter Books, 1968.

Edelstein, Ludwig. *Ancient Medicine.* Baltimore: Johns Hopkins University, Press, 1967.

Evans, Harry B. *Water Distribution in Ancient Rome.* Ann Arbor, Mich.: University of Michigan Press, 1994.

Fasola, Umberto M. *Peter and Paul in Rome.* Rome: Vision Editrice, 1980.

Frank, Tenney. *An Economic Survey of Ancient Rome.* New York: Octagon Books, Vol. 1.

Galinsky, Karl. *Augustan Culture.* Princeton: Princeton University Press, 1996.

Goldsworthy, Adrian K. *The Roman Army at War 100 B.C.–A.D. 200.* Oxford: Clarendon Press, 1996.

Grant, Michael. *The Army of the Caesars.* New York: M. Evans & Company, 1974.

Grant, Michael. *Augustus to Constantine: The Rise and Triumph of Christianity.* San Francisco: Harper & Row, 1990.

Grant, Michael. *Cities of Vesuvius.* New York: Penguin Books, 1976.

Grant, Michael. *Gladiators.* New York: Barnes & Noble, 1967.

Grant, Michael. *The Jews in the Roman World.* New York: Dorset Press, 1970.

Grant, Michael. *Nero.* New York: Dorset Press, 1970.

Grant, Michael. *The Roman Emperors.* New York: Charles Scribner's Sons, 1985.

Grant, Michael. *The Twelve Caesars.* New York: Charles Scribner's Sons, 1975.

Greene, Kevin. *The Archaeology of the Roman Economy.* Berkeley: University of California Press, 1986.

Griffin, Miriam T. Nero, *The End of a Dynasty.* New Haven: Yale University Press, 1985.

Gurval, Robert A. *Actium and Augustus.* Ann Arbor, Mich.: University of Michigan Press, 1995.

Gwynn, Aubrey. *Roman Education.* New York: Russell & Russell, 1964.

Hacket, John. *Warfare in the Ancient World.* New York: Facts on File, 1989.

Hamey, L. A. and J. A. *The Roman Engineers.* Cambridge: Cambridge University Press, 1981.

Jackson, Ralph. *Doctors and Diseases in the Roman Empire.* London: British Museum, 1988.

Jones, Brian W. *The Emperor Domitian.* New York: Routledge, 1992.

Keppie, Lawrence. *The Making of the Roman Army.* New York: Barnes & Noble, 1994.

Kiefer, Otto. *Sexual Life in Ancient Rome.* New York: Dorset Press, 1993.

Kirschenbaum. A. *Sons, Slaves and Freedmen in Roman Commerce.* Jerusalem: The Hebrew University, 1987.

Landels, J. G. *Engineering in the Ancient World.* Berkeley: University of California Press, 1978.

Levick, Barbara. *Claudius.* New Haven: Yale University Press, 1990.

Lieu, Judith and Others, eds. *The Jews Among Pagans and Christians in the Roman Empire.* London: Routledge, 1992.

Luttwak, Edward N. *The Grand Strategy of the Roman Empire.* Baltimore: Johns Hopkins University Press, 1976.

Laurence, Ray. *Roman Pompeii.* New York: Routledge, 1994.

MacKendrick, Paul. *The Mute Stones Speak.* New York: W. W. Norton, 2nd ed., 1960.

MacMullen, Ramsay. *Christianizing the Roman Empire.* New Haven: Yale University Press, 1984.

MacMullen, Ramsay. *Roman Social Relations.* New Haven: Yale University Press, 1974.

Martin, Ronald. *Tacitus.* London: B. T. Batsford, 1981.

McKay, Alexander G. *Houses, Villas, and Palaces in the Roman World.* Baltimore: Johns Hopkins University Press, 1975.

Meeks, Wayne A. *The First Urban Christians: The Social World of the Apostle Paul.* New Haven: Yale University Press, 1983.

Meeks, Wayne A. *The Moral World of the First Christians.* Philadelphia: Westminster, 1986.

Meier, Christian. *Caesar.* New York: Basic Books, 1995.

Meiggs, Russell. *Roman Ostia.* New York: Oxford University Press, 2nd ed., 1997.

Meinardus, Otto F. A. *St. Paul's Last Journey.* New Rochelle, N.Y.: Caratzas Brothers, 1979.

Mellor, Ronald, ed. *The Historians of Ancient Rome.* New York: Routledge, 1998.

Mellor, Ronald. *Tacitus.* New York: Routledge, 1993.

Millar, Fergus. *The Emperor in the Roman World.* Ithaca, N.Y.: Cornell University Press, 1977.

Millar, Fergus. *The Roman Near East.* Cambridge, Mass.: Harvard University Press, 1993.

Mommsen, Theodor. *The Provinces of the Roman Empire.* Chicago: University of Chicago Press, 1968.

Paget, Robert F. *Central Italy: An Archaeological Guide.* Park Ridge, N.J.: Noyes Press, 1973.

Parker, Geoffrey, ed. *Cambridge Illustrated History of Warfare.* Cambridge: Cambridge University Press, 1995.

Ramsay, William M. *The Church in the Roman Empire Before A.D. 170.* London: Hodder and Stoughton, 5th ed., 1897; Baker Book House, reprint, 1979.

Rapske, Brian. *The Book of Acts and Paul in Roman Custody.* Grand Rapids: Eerdmans, vol. 3, 1994.

Rawson, Beryl, ed. *Marriage, Divorce, and Children in Ancient Rome.* Oxford: Clarendon Press, 1996.

Richardson, L. *Pompeii: An Architectural History.* Baltimore: Johns Hopkins University Press, 1988.

Robertson, D. S. *Greek and Roman Architecture*. Cambridge: Cambridge University Press, 2nd ed., 1943.

Robinson, O. F. *Ancient Rome: City Planning and Administration*. New York: Routledge, 1992.

Robinson, O. F. *The Criminal Law of Ancient Rome*. Baltimore: Johns Hopkins University Press, 1995.

Scarre, Chris. *Chronicle of the Roman Emperors*. London: Thames & Hudson, 1995.

Scullard, H. H. *From the Gracchi to Nero*. London: Methuen & Co., 1959.

Setzer, Claudia. *Jewish Responses to Early Christians*. Minneapolis: Fortress, 1994.

Shelton, Jo-Ann. *As the Romans Did*. New York: Oxford University Press, 1988.

Sherwin-White, A. N. *The Roman Citizenship*. Oxford: The Clarendon Press, 2nd ed., 1973.

Sherwin-White, A. N. *Roman Law and Roman Society in the New Testament*. Grand Rapids: Baker, reprint 1992.

Shotter, David. *Nero*. New York: Routledge, 1997.

Shuckburgh, E. S. *Augustus Caesar*. New York: Barnes & Noble, 1995.

Sinnigen, William G., and Arthur E. R. Boak, *A History of Rome to A.D 565*. New York: Macmillan, 6th ed., 1977.

Sordi, Marta. *The Christians and the Roman Empire*. Norman. Okla.: University of Oklahoma Press, 1986.

Southern, Pat. *Augustus*. New York: Routledge, 1998.

Southern, Pat. *Domitian, Tragic Tyrant*. Bloomington, Ind.: Indiana University Press, 1997.

Stark, Rodney. *The Rise of Christianity*. Princeton: Princeton University Press, 1996.

Stowers, Stanley K. *Letter Writing in Greco-Roman Antiquity*. Philadelphia: Westminster Press, 1986.

Syme, Ronald. *The Augustan Aristocracy*. Oxford: The Clarendon Press, 1986.

Toynbee, J. M. C. *Death and Burial in the Roman World*. Baltimore: Johns Hopkins University Press, 1996.

Treggiari, Susan. *Roman Marriage*. New York: Oxford University Press, 1991.

Turcan, Robert. *The Cults of the Roman Empire*. Oxford: Blackwell, 1996.

Vehling, Joseph D., ed. and trans. *Apicus: Cookery and Dining in Imperial Rome*. New York: Dover, 1977.

Wallace-Handrill, Andrew. *Houses and Society in Pompeii and Herculaneum*. Princeton: Princeton University Press, 1994.

Ward-Perkins, J. B. *Roman Imperial Architecture*. New Haven: Yale University Press, 2nd ed., 1981.

Warmington, B. H. *Nero: Reality and Legend*. New York: W. W. Norton, 1969.

Watson, G. R. *The Roman Soldier*. Ithaca, N.Y.: Cornell University Press, 1969.

Webster, Graham. *The Roman Imperial Army*. Totowa, N.J.,: Barnes & Noble, 3rd ed., 1985.

Wedeck, Harry E. *Roman Morals*. Lawrence, Kans.: Coronado Press, 1980

White, K. G. *Roman Farming*. Ithaca, N.Y.: Cornell University Press, 1970

Wiedemann, Thomas. *The Roman Household, A Sourcebook*. London: Routledge, 1991.

Wilken, Robert L. *The Christians as the Romans Saw Them*. New Haven: Yale University Press, 1984.

Williams, Margaret H. *The Jews Among the Greeks and Romans*. Baltimore: Johns Hopkins University Press, 1998.

GENERAL
BIBLIOGRAPHY

The literature on the Bible lands is now incredibly vast. And it grows every day. How is it possible to construct a meaningful general bibliography for this book?

In the first place, we may eliminate the older books that are now somewhat dated in their conclusions. Then we may leave out the more technical materials for the advanced student, such as the *Journal of Cuneiform Studies*, or *Hesperia*, or Oriental Institute publications of the University of Chicago. Publications in foreign languages have not been included, in part because they are not usually readily available to the general reader, in part because of the language barrier, and in part because so many of the best ones have been translated into English. Further, it is not necessary to repeat the books and articles appearing in the footnotes and bibliographies of individual chapters of this book. What remains, then, is a limited number of periodicals, atlases, encyclopedias, and dictionaries, and various background study books.

PERIODICALS:

American Journal of Archaeology (almost every issue has a summary of recent work in one of the major Bible lands)
Archaeology
Archaeology Odyssey
Bible Review
Biblical Archaeology Review
Bulletin of the American Schools of Oriental Research
Expedition (published by the University of Pennsylvania Museum)
Journal of Biblical Literature
Near Eastern Archaeology (formerly *Biblical Archaeologist*)

ATLASES:

Aharoni, Yohanan, and Michael Avi-Yonah. *The Macmillan Bible Atlas.* New York: Macmillan, 1968.

Atlas of Israel. New York: Free Press, 3rd ed., 1985.
Baines, John, and Jaromir Malek. *Atlas of Ancient Egypt.* New York: Facts on File, 1980.
Beek, Martin A. *Atlas of Mesopotamia.* London: Thomas Nelson, 1962.
Beitzel, Barry J. *The Moody Atlas of Bible Lands.* Chicago: Moody Press, 1985.
Cornell, Tim, and John Matthews. *Atlas of the Roman World.* New York: Facts on File, 1982.
Levi, Peter. *Atlas of the Greek World.* New York: Facts on File, 1980.
May, Herbert G. *Oxford Bible Atlas.* Revised by John Day. New York: Oxford University Press, 1985.
Oliphant, Margaret. *The Atlas of the Ancient World.* New York: Simon & Schuster, 1992.
Pritchard, James B., ed. *The Harper Atlas of the Bible.* New York: Harper & Brothers, 1987.

Rasmussen, Carl G. *The Zondervan NIV Atlas of the Bible.* Grand Rapids: Zondervan, 1989.

Roaf, Michael. *Cultural Atlas of Mesopotamia.* New York: Facts on File, 1990.

Wiseman, Donald J., and Others. *New Bible Atlas.* Downers Grove, Ill.: InterVarsity Press, 1994.

Wright, George Ernest, and Floyd V. Filson. *The Westminster Historical Atlas.* Philadelphia: Westminster Press, rev. ed., 1956.

DICTIONARIES AND ENCYCLOPEDIAS:

Avi-Yonah, Michael, ed. *Encyclopedia of Archaeological Excavations in the Holy Land.* Englewood Cliffs, N.J.,: Prentice-Hall. Vol. 1, 1975; vol. 2, 1976; vol. 3, 1977, vol. 4, 1978.

Bromiley, Geoffrey, rev. ed. *International Standard Bible Encyclopedia.* Grand Rapids: Eerdmans. Vol. 1, 1979; Vol. 2, 1982; Vol. 3, 1986; Vol. 4, 1988.

Butler, Trent C., ed. *Holman Bible Dictionary.* Nashville: Broadman & Holman, 1991.

Buttrick, George A., and Keith R. Crim, eds. *Interpreter's Dictionary of the Bible.* Nashville: Abingdon, 5 vols., 1976.

Elwell, Walter A. *Baker Encyclopedia of the Bible.* Grand Rapids: Baker, 2 vols, 1988.

Harrison, R. K., ed. *The New Unger's Bible Dictionary.* Chicago: Moody Press, 1988.

Hillyer, N. *The Illustrated Bible Dictionary.* Wheaton, Ill.: Tyndale House, 3 vols., rev. ed., 1980.

Hillyer, N. *New Bible Dictionary.* Wheaton, Ill.: Tyndale House, rev. ed., 1982.

Hopkins, Daniel J., ed. *Merriam Webster's Geographical Dictionary.* Springfield, Mass.: Merriam-Webster, Inc., 3rd ed., 1997.

Hornblower, Simon, and Anthony Spawforth, eds. *The Oxford Classical Dictionary.* New York: Oxford University Press, 3rd ed., 1996.

Meyers, Eric M., ed. *Oxford Encyclopedia of Archaeology in the Near East.* New York: Oxford University Press, 5 vols., 1997.

Miller, Madeleine S., and J. Lane. *Harper's Encyclopedia of Bible Life.* Revised by Boyce M. Bennett, Jr., and Daniel H. Scott. New York: Harper & Row, 1978.

Neilson, William A., ed. *Webster's Biographical Dictionary.* Springfield, Mass.: Merriam-Webster, Inc., 1980.

Packer, J. I., ed. *Nelson's Illustrated Encyclopedia of Bible Facts.* Nashville: Thomas Nelson, 1995.

Pfeiffer, Charles F., and Others, eds. *The Wycliffe Bible Encyclopedia.* Chicago: Moody Press, 2 vols., 1975; reissued by Hendrickson Publishers, Peabody, Mass., as the *Wycliffe Bible Dictionary,* one vol., 1998.

Richards, Lawrence O., ed. *Revell Bible Dictionary.* 2nd deluxe ed., 1994. Revell is now a division of Baker Book House, Grand Rapids, Michigan.

Sasson, Jack M., ed. *Civilizations of the Ancient Near East.* New York: Charles Scribner's Sons, 4 vols., 1995.

Stern, Ephraim, ed. *The New Encyclopedia of Archaeological Excavations in the Holy Land.* New York: Simon & Schuster, 4 vols., 1993.

Stillwell, Richard, ed. *The Princeton Encyclopedia of Classical Sites.* Princeton: Princeton University Press, 1976.

Tenney, Merrill C., ed. *The Zondervan Pictorial Bible Dictionary.* Grand Rapids: Zondervan, 1988.

Tenney, Merrill C., ed. *The Zondervan Pictorial Encyclopedia of the Bible,* 5 vols., 1975.

Youngblood, Ronald F., ed. *Nelson's New Illustrated Bible Dictionary.* Nashville: Thomas Nelson, rev. ed., 1986.

BACKGROUND STUDY BOOKS:

Angus, S. *The Mystery Religions.* New York: Dover, 1975.

Archer, Gleason, L. *A Survey of Old Testament Introduction*. Chicago: Moody Press, 3rd. ed., 1994.

Aylen, Leo. *The Greek Theater*. Cranbury, N.J.: Associated University Presses, 1985.

Baigent. Michael, and Richard Leigh. *The Dead Sea Scrolls Deception*. New York: Summit Books, 1991.

Barber. Elizabeth W. *Women's Work, The First 20,000 Years*. New York: W. W. Norton, 1994.

Beacham, Richard C. *The Roman Theatre and Its Audience*. Cambridge, Mass.: Harvard University Press, 1991.

Becker, Jurgen. *Paul, Apostle to the Gentiles*. Louisville: Westminster John Knox Press, 1993.

Bimson, John J., ed. *Baker Encyclopedia of Bible Places*. Grand Rapids: Baker, 1995.

Boardman, John, and Others, eds. *The Oxford History of the Classical World*. New York: Oxford University Press, 1986.

Borowski, Oded. *Agriculture in Iron Age Israel*. Winona Lake, Ind.: Eisenbrauns, 1987.

Bremer, J. M, and Others, eds. *Hidden Futures, Death and Immortality in the . . . Biblical World*. Amsterdam: Amsterdam University Press, 1994.

Brothwell, Don, and Patricia Brothwell. *Food in Antiquity*. Baltimore: Johns Hopkins University Press, expanded ed., 1998.

Bruce, F. F. *Second Thoughts on the Dead Sea Scrolls*. Grand Rapids: Eerdmans, rev. ed., 1961.

Burkert, Walter. *Ancient Mystery Cults*. Cambridge, Mass.: Harvard University Press, 1987.

Burrows, Millar. *The Dead Sea Scrolls*. New York: Viking, 1955.

Burrows, Millar. *More Light on the Dead Sea Scrolls*. New York: Viking, 1958.

Casson, Lionel. *The Ancient Mariners*. Princeton: Princeton University Press, 2nd ed., 1991.

Casson, Lionel. *Ships and Seamanship in the Ancient World*. Princeton: Princeton University Press, 1971.

Casson, Lionel. *Travel in the Ancient World*. Toronto: Hakkert, 1974.

Clements, R. A., ed. *The World of Ancient Israel*. Cambridge: Cambridge University Press, 1989.

Coogan, Michael D. *Oxford History of the Biblical World*. New York: Oxford University Press, 1988.

Cross, Frank Moore, Jr. *The Ancient Library of Qumran and Modern Biblical Studies*. Grand Rapids: Baker, 1961, reprinted 1980.

Culican, William. *The First Merchant Venturers*. London: Thames & Hudson, 1966.

de Camp, L. Sprague. *Great Cities of the Ancient World*. New York: Dorset, 1972.

De Vaux, Roland. *The Bible and the Ancient Near East*. Garden City, N.Y.: Doubleday & Co., 1971.

Drinkwater, J. F. and Andrew Drummond, eds. *The World of the Romans*. Oxford: Oxford University Press, 1993.

Engberg-Pedersen, Troels. *Paul in His Hellenistic Context*. Minneapolis: Fortress, 1995.

Feldman, Louis H. *Jew and Gentile in the Ancient World*. Princeton: Princeton University Press, 1993.

Freeman, Charles. *Egypt, Greece and Rome*. New York: Oxford University Press, 1996.

Gordon, Cyrus H., and Gary A. Rendsburg. *The Bible and the Ancient Near East*. New York: W. W. Norton, 4th ed., 1997.

Gower, Ralph, and Fred H. Wight. *The New Manners and Customs of Bible Times*. Chicago: Moody Press, 1987.

Grant, Michael. *A Guide to the Ancient World*. New York: Barnes & Noble, 1986.

Harris, H. A. *Sport in Greece and Rome*. Ithaca, N.Y.: Cornell University Press, 1972.

Harris, Roberta L. *The World of the Bible*. London: Thames & Hudson, 1995.

Harrison, R. K., ed. *Major Cities of the Biblical World*. Nashville: Thomas Nelson, 1985.

Hoerth, Alfred J., and Others, eds. *Peoples of the Old Testament World*. Grand Rapids: Baker, 1994.

Humphrey, John H. *Roman Circus*. Berkeley: University of California Press, 1986.

Keener, Craig S. *The IVP Bible Background Commentary: New Testament.* Downers Grove, Ill.: InterVarsity Press, 1993.

Lamsa, George M. *Old Testament Light.* New York: Harper & Row, 1964.

LaSor, William S. *The Dead Sea Scrolls and the Christian Faith.* Chicago: Moody, rev. ed., 1960.

LaSor, William S. *The Dead Sea Scrolls and the New Testament.* Grand Rapids: Eerdmans, 1972.

Malamat, Abraham. *Mari and the Early Israelite Experience.* Oxford: Oxford University Press, 1989.

Marclay, John M. *Jews in the Mediterranean Diaspora: From Alexander to Trajan.* Edinburgh: T & T Clark, 1996.

Matthews, Victor H. *Manners and Customs in the Bible.* Peabody, Mass.: Hendrickson Publishers, 1988.

Matthews, Victor H. and Don C. Benjamin. *Social World of Ancient Israel 1250–587 BCE.* Peabody, Mass.: Hendrickson Publishers, 1993.

Meiggs, Russell. *Trees and Timber in the Ancient Mediterranean World.* Oxford: The Clarendon Press, 1998.

Meijer, Fik. *A History of Seafaring in the Classical World.* New York: St. Martin's Press, 1986.

Meijer, Fik, and Onno van Nijf. *Trade, Transport, and Society in the Ancient World.* London: Routledge, 1992.

Millard, Alan. *Discoveries from the Time of Jesus.* Batavia Ill.: Lion Publishers, 1990.

Millard, Alan. *Treasures from Bible Times.* Batavia, Ill.: Lion Publishersr 1985.

Modrzejewski, Joseph M. *The Jews of Egypt from Rameses II to Emperor Hadrian.* Princeton: Princeton University Press, 1995.

Murphy-O'Connor, Jerome. *Paul the Letter Writer; His World, His Options, His Skills.* Collegeville, Minn.: The Liturgical Press, 1995.

Niditch, Susan. *Ancient Israelite Religion.* New York: Oxford University Press, 1997.

Niswonger, Richard L. *New Testament History.* Grand Rapids: Zondervan, 1988.

Owens, E. J. *The City in the Greek and Roman World.* London: Routledge, 1991.

Patai, Raphael. *The Children of Noah, Jewish Seafaring in Ancient Times.* Princeton: Princeton University Press, 1998.

Peters, F. E. *The Harvest of Hellenism: A History of the Near East from Alexander the Great to the Triumph of Christianity.* New York: Barnes & Noble, 1970.

Pritchard, James B., ed. *Ancient Near Eastern Texts.* Princeton: Princeton University Press, 2nd ed., 1955.

Pfeiffer, Charles F., and Howard F.Vos. *Wycliffe Historical Geography of Bible Lands.* Chicago: Moody Press, 1967. New Edition by Howard F. Vos, Hendrickson Publishers, Peabody, Mass., 2000.

Rainey, Anson F., ed. *Egypt, Israel, Sinai.* Tel Aviv: Tel Aviv University, 1987.

Redford, Donald B. *Egypt, Canaan, and Israel in Ancient Times.* Princeton: Princeton University Press, 1992.

Reicke, Bo. *The New Testament Era.* Philadelphia: Fortress Press, 1968.

Richards, Lawrence O. *The Victor Bible Background Commentary: New Testament.* Colorado Springs, Colo.: Victor Books/SP Publications, 1994.

Romer, John. *Testament: The Bible and History.* New York: Henry Holt & Co., 1988.

Schiffman, Lawrence H. *Reclaiming the Dead Sea Scrolls.* New York: Doubleday, 1994.

Seltzer, Robert M., ed. *Religions of Antiquity.* New York: Macmillan, 1987.

Shanks, Hershel. *The Mystery and Meaning of the Dead Sea Scrolls.* New York: Random House, 1998.

Shanks, Hershel, ed. *Understanding the Dead Sea Scrolls.* New York: Random House, 1992.

Sussmann, Ayala, ed. *Excavations and Surveys in Israel.* Published almost annually by the Israel Antiquities Authority, Vol. 17, 1998. Distributed in the United States by Eisenbrauns, Winona Lake, Indiana.

Thompson, J. A. *Handbook of Life in Bible Times.* Downers Grove, Ill.: InterVarsity Press, 1986.

Torr, Cecil. *Ancient Ships.* Chicago: Argonaut, Inc., 1964.

VanderKam, James C. *The Dead Sea Scrolls Today.* Grand Rapids: Eerdmans, 1994.

Van Der Woude, A. S., ed. *The World of the Bible.* Grand Rapids: Eerdmans, 1986.

Van Der Woude, A. S., ed. *The World of the Old Testament.* Grand Rapids: Eerdmans, 1989.

Vermes, Geza. *The Complete Dead Sea Scrolls in English.* New York: Penguin Press, 1997.

Von Rad, Gerhard. *Holy War in Ancient Israel.* Grand Rapids: Eerdmans, 1991.

Von Soden, Wolfram. *The Ancient Orient.* Grand Rapids: Eerdmans, 1994.

Watts, John H, and Victor H. Matthews. *The IVP Bible Background Commentary: Genesis-Deuteronomy.* Downers Grove, Ill.: InterVarsity Press, 1997.

Young, Gordon D., ed. *Mari in Retrospect.* Winona Lake, Ind.: Eisenrauns, 1992.

Young, Gordon D., ed. *Ugarit in Retrospect.* Winona Lake, Ind.: Eisenbrauns, 1981.

SUBJECT INDEX

(The larger topics that form the basic structure of this book (e.g., geography, government, warfare, religion, clothing, etc. are listed in the table of contents and are not included here.)

SCRIPTURE INDEX